ISBN 978-0-265-06005-6
PIBN 10952452

FB &c Ltd, Dalton House, 60 Windsor Avenue, London, SW19 2RR.
Company number 08720141. Registered in England and Wales.

For support please visit www.forgottenbooks.com

THE
ENCYCLOPEDIC DIGEST
OF
ALABAMA REPORTS

BEING A COMPLETE

Encyclopedia and Digest of All the Alabama Case Law up to and Including Volume 175, Alabama Reports, Volume 6, Alabama Appellate Court Reports, and Volume 62, Southern Reporter

UNDER THE EDITORIAL SUPERVISION OF

THOMAS JOHNSON MICHIE

Volume II

THE MICHIE COMPANY, LAW PUBLISHERS
CHARLOTTESVILLE, VA.
1914

Table of Titles

Italics indicate cross references.

Encyclopedic Digest of Alabama Reports.

ATTACHMENT.

I. Nature and Grounds.

(A) Nature of Remedy, Causes of Action, and Parties.

§ 1. Nature and Purpose of Remedy.
§ 2. Constitutional and Statutory Provisions.
§ 3. Actions in Which Attachment Is Authorized.
§ 4. —— In General.
§ 5. —— On Express Contracts.
§ 6. —— For Torts.
§ 7. —— On Demands Not Liquidated.
§ 8. —— On Demands Not Matured.
§ 9. —— On Contingent Liabilities.
§ 10. —— In Suits in Equity or Actions on Equitable Grounds.
§ 11. Persons Entitled.
§ 12. Persons Liable.
§ 13. —— In General.
§ 14. —— Several Defendants.
§ 15. Simultaneous and Successive Attachments.

(B) Grounds of Attachment.

§ 16. Insolvency or Inability to Satisfy Demand.
§ 17. Nonresidence.
§ 18. Absconding, Absence, or Concealment.
§ 19. —— In General.
§ 20. —— Departure and Absence.
§ 21. —— Concealment and Avoidance of Process.
§ 22. —— Intended Departure.
§ 23. Removal or Concealment of Property.
§ 24. —— Removal from Jurisdiction.
§ 25. Fraudulent Transfer or Other Disposition of Property.
§ 26. —— In General.
§ 27. —— Transfers as Security.
§ 28. —— Intended Removal or Disposition.
§ 29. Evidence as to Grounds.
§ 29 (1) Admissibility.
§ 29 (2) Weight and Sufficiency.
§ 30. Waiver or Loss of Right.

II. Property Subject to Attachment.

§ 31. Personal Property in General.
§ 32. Real Property in General.
§ 33. Property Mortgaged or Otherwise Incumbered.
§ 34. —— Personal Property.

Cross References.

See the titles ASSIGNMENTS FOR BENEFIT OF CREDITORS; EXECUTION; EXEMPTIONS; FRAUDULENT CONVEYANCES; GARNISHMENT; HOMESTEAD; JUDGMENT; JUDICIAL SALES; LANDLORD AND TENANT; LIENS; LIMITATION OF ACTIONS; PROCESS; SEQUESTRATION; SHERIFFS AND CONSTABLES; TRIAL.

As to agricultural liens, see the title AGRICULTURE. As to review of cases involving attachment, see the title APPEAL AND ERROR. As to appearance in attachment, see the title APPEARANCE. As to assignments for benefit of creditors, see the title ASSIGNMENTS FOR BENEFIT OF CREDITORS. As to the authority of an attorney to sue out process of attachment, see the title ATTORNEY AND CLIENT. As to dissolution of attachment by adjudication in bankruptcy, see the title BANKRUPTCY. As to attachment by and against banks, see the title BANKS AND BANKING. As to certiorari as proper remedy to quash summary execution issued on forthcoming bond, see the title CERTIORARI. As to property of corporations in general, see the title CORPORATIONS. As to security for costs in actions by attachment, see the title COSTS. As to power of courts, see the title COURTS. As to creditors' suits, see the title CREDITORS' SUIT. As to attachment of witnesses, see the title CRIMINAL LAW. As to depositions and interrogatories, see the title DEPOSITIONS. As to obligors of forthcoming or replevy bond being estopped from denying defendant's title to property, or showing it was not subject to attachment, see the title ESTOPPEL. As to declarations as to ownership of property, see the title EVIDENCE. As to admissibility of parol evidence, see the title EVIDENCE. As to exemptions, see the title EXEMPTIONS. As to fraudulent conveyances, see the title FRAUDULENT CONVEYANCES. As to pleadings to set aside fraudulent attachments, see the title FRAUDULENT CONVEYANCES. As to collusive attachments, see the title FRAUDULENT CONVEYANCES. As to homestead exemptions, see the title HOMESTEAD. As to property of wife, see the title HUSBAND AND WIFE. As to injunction when parties claim under a void attachment sale, see the title INJUNCTION. As to judgments in attachment suits, see the title JUDGMENT. As to conclusiveness of judgment, see the title JUDGMENT. As to res adjudicata, see the title JUDGMENT. As to judgments by default, see the title JUDGMENT. As to attachments in justices' courts, see the title JUSTICES OF THE PEACE. As to attachment for rent, see the title LANDLORD AND TENANT. As to enforcement of landlord's lien, see the title LANDLORD AND TENANT. As to malicious attachment, see the title MALICIOUS PROSECUTION. As to mandamus to dismiss attachment, see the title MANDAMUS. As to priorities between attachments and mechanics' liens, see the title MECHANICS' LIENS. As to priorities between attachments and mortgages, see the title MORTGAGES. As to attachment against firm or partners, see the title PARTNERSHIP, § 208. As to variance in allegations in pleadings, see the title PLEADING. As to appointment of receivers to preserve attached property, see the title RECEIVERS. As to actions by or against receivers, see the title RECEIVERS. As to rights, duties and liabilities of sheriffs and constables, see the title SHERIFFS AND CONSTABLES. As to right of sheriffs and constables to demand indemnity, and matters relating to indemnity given to them, see the title SHERIFFS AND CONSTABLES. As to suits by attachment on Sundays, see the title SUNDAY. As to priorities between attachments and taxes, see the title TAXATION. As to trover and conversion, see the title TROVER AND CONVERSION. As to competency of parties as witnesses, see the title WITNESSES. As to competency of sureties on attachment bond, as witnesses, see the title WITNESSES.

I. NATURE AND GROUNDS.

(A) NATURE OF REMEDY, CAUSES OF ACTION, AND PARTIES.

§ 1. Nature and Purpose of Remedy.

Statutory Origin.—Attachments were unknown at common law, and are the creation wholly of statute. Kress *v.* Porter, 132 Ala. 577, 31 So. 377, 379; Henderson *v.* Alabama Gold Life Ins. Co., 72 Ala. 32.

Attachments are extraordinary process, unknown to the common law, not issuing out of a court, nor pertaining to the exercise of the ordinary powers and jurisdiction of a court; and no one has the power to issue them, unless he is thereunto specially authorized. Vann *v.* Adams, etc., Co., 71 Ala. 475.

Nature and Object.—"An attachment is an extraordinary proceeding, and, in some of its operations and effects, may prove to be a harsh and injurious one." Ex parte Damon, 103 Ala. 477, 15 So. 862, 863; Tucker *v.* Adams, 52 Ala. 254, 256. See Johnson *v.* Hale, 3 Stew. & P. 331, 336.

"The levy of an attachment on property is, by our attachment law, a substitute for, and is precisely equivalent to, service of personal process, and such levy creates a lien on the property attached, whether it be a chattel seized by the sheriff, or a debt attached in the hands of the garnishee. Cary *v.* Gregg, 3 Stew. 433; Thompson *v.* Allen, 4 Stew. & P. 184." Tillinghast *v.* Johnson, 5 Ala. 514, 515.

"An attachment, as the leading process in the commencement of an action at law, which is executed by a levy upon the estate, real or personal, of the debtor, is unknown to the common law, derived here wholly from statutes. Its purpose is, that the jurisdiction of the court, in ulterior proceedings, may be more effectual, and to afford the plaintiff security for the satisfaction of the judgment which he may obtain. The levy, from its date, creates a lien—a right to charge the property levied upon, with the payment of the judgment rendered, in priority of any subsequent alienations the defendant may make, or of any subsequent incumbrances he may create, or of subsequent liens arising by operation of law, in favor of other creditors. The lien differs from the lien of an execution, as it now exists, or the lien of a judgment on lands, as it formerly existed. It operates only on the particular property which is the subject of the levy, and is incipient, inchoate, and conditional. It begins with the levy, and depends upon the condition, that the plaintiff in the suit obtains judgment, upon which process may issue authorizing a sale of the property attached. The lien terminates, if such judgment is not obtained. In its very nature, the lien is, consequently, less stringent, frailer, and more uncertain, than the lien of an execution." Phillips *v.* Ash, 63 Ala. 414, 415. See Fitzpatrick *v.* Edgar, 5 Ala. 499; Hale *v.* Cummings, 3 Ala. 398; Lamar *v.* Gunter, 39 Ala. 324; McEachin *v.* Reid, 40 Ala. 410.

Proceedings by attachment in courts of law are purely of statutory origin, and can operate only on the legal rights of the defendant in attachment, that is, such rights, as he could enforce by action at law in his own name. Henderson *v.* Alabama Gold Life Ins. Co., 72 Ala. 32.

A suit commenced by attachment is not a proceeding in rem, but is personal against the defendant; and the judgment therein authorized is not merely one of condemnation of the property attached, but is personal and general, as in a suit commenced by summons and complaint. Betancourt *v.* Eberlin, 71 Ala. 461.

The theory of an attachment, whether it be process against or to subject the property or effects of a resident or nonresident of the state, as the remedy has been administered in this state, is that it partakes essentially of the nature and character of a proceeding in personam, and not of a proceeding in rem. Exchange Nat. Bank *v.* Clement, 109 Ala. 270, 19 So. 814, 817; Betancourt *v.* Eberlin, 71 Ala. 461.

In attachment, plaintiff seeks to subject the chattels to a satisfaction of his demand, and invokes judicial power to convert the chattels into a means of satisfaction thereof. Johnson *v.* New Enterprise Co., 50 So. 911, 163 Ala. 463. See M'Rae *v.* M'Lean, 3 Port. 138, 153.

The whole purpose of a writ of attachment is to fasten a lien upon specific property before the determination of the main suit; the attachment resting on its own facts, and not on the facts of the main action. Oliver *v.* Kinney, 173 Ala. 593, 56 So. 203; Rivernac Const. Co. *v.* Kinney, 173 Ala. 721, 56 So. 206.

Construction and Pursuance of Statutes.—Prior to the enactment of the statute, declaring that the attachment law should not be rigidly and strictly construed, great strictness was required in this state in the proceeding of attachment, and cases were frequently disposed of in mere technical objection. The rule for the construction of penal statutes was uniformly applied to the attachment laws. The rule has been changed by legislative enactment. The code now provides that "the attachment law must be liberally construed to advance the manifest intent of the law. Jackson *v.* Stanley, 2 Ala. 326, 328; Johnson *v.* Hale, 3 Stew. & P. 331, 336; Richards *v.* Bestor, 90 Ala. 352, 8 So. 30; Burt *v.* Parish & Co., 9 Ala. 211, 214; Bank *v.* St. John Powers & Co., 25 Ala. 566, 613; Ware *v.* Seasongood, 92 Ala. 152, 9 So. 138; Pearsoll *v.* Middlebrook, 2 Stew. & P. 406; Ex parte Damon, 103 Ala. 477, 15 So. 862; Flake *v.* Day & Co., 22 Ala. 132.

"Under the Code, where the rule was more stringent as to forms, and the intent of the legislature less evident, the attachment laws were required to 'be liberally construed to advance the manifest intention of the law.' Revised Code, §§ 2990, 2930." Watts *v.* Womack, 44 Ala. 605, 606.

Act Feb. 5, 1846, extending the remedy by attachment in chancery against nonresident absconding or fraudulent debtors to simple contract creditors, is remedial, and to be given a liberal construction in accordance with the general statutory declaration (Clay's Dig., p. 59, § 17) that "the attachment laws of this state, shall not be rigidly construed." Flake *v.* Day, 22 Ala. 132.

In suing out a writ of attachment either at law or in equity, there must be a substantial conformity to what the statute prescribes. This results from the nature of this statutory remedy. Ware *v.* Seasongood, 92 Ala. 152, 9 So. 138, 139.

A writ of attachment under the statute is a summary and extraordinary remedy in derogation of the common law, and the statutes authorizing the writ must be strictly followed. Earp *v.* Stephens, 55 So. 266, 1 Ala. App. 447; Woodley *v.* Shirley, Minor 14. See Exchange Nat. Bank *v.* Clement, 109 Ala. 270, 19 So. 814.

"The proceeding by attachment is strictly statutory, and the writ can only be issued in such cases as are clearly authorized by the law creating and allowing it. The courts are not permitted, in such cases, to extend the provisions of the law by construction, so as to make them include cases and persons which are not clearly within their meaning. If, upon an examination of the condition of the parties, all the rights and remedies secured to suitors, under the law authorizing the writ, do not or can not attach to them, it would seem to be evident that they are not included in the act, and consequently, the officers who are allowed to issue the writ in proper cases, would be without authority to issue it in those not named." Taliaferro *v.* Lane, 23 Ala. 369, 371.

Existence or Resort to Other Remedy.—An attachment may be sued out although the party has been previously arrested on bail process issued in the same cause. Massey *v.* Walker, 8 Ala. 167.

The Alabama statutes which authorize attachments, as ancillary to causes already depending, make no distinction between suits commenced by bailable process, and suits commenced in the ordinary mode. In either class the attachment is proper, if the statutory course for suing it out is shown. Massey *v.* Walker, 8 Ala. 167, 169.

§ 2. Constitutional and Statutory Provisions.

As to construction of statutes, see ante, "Nature and Purpose of Remedy," § 1.

Early Enactments.—The remedy by attachment seems to have been given as early as 1799, and was fully established and regulated by an act of the territorial legislature passed in 1807. In 1833, the attachment law was revised. McKellar *v.* Couch, 34 Ala. 336, 342.

Operation and Effect.—An ancillary attachment, sued out after the Code went into operation, in a suit commenced by ordinary process under the old law, is a part of the original suit, and must conform to the provisions of the old law. Frankenheimer *v.* Slocum, 24 Ala. 373.

An attachment lies against a foreign corporation, under the act of 1854, on a cause of action which arose prior to the passage of the statute. Coosa River Steamboat Co. *v.* Barclay, 30 Ala. 120.

§ 3. Actions in Which Attachment Is Authorized.

As to averments in affidavit as to cause of action, see post, "Averments as to Cause of Action," § 56. As to actions between partners, see the title PARTNERSHIP. As to actions to enforce liens, see the titles LANDLORD AND TENANT; LIENS; MECHANICS' LIENS. As to averments in affidavit as to nature of demand, see post, "Averments as to Nature of Demand," § 57.

§ 4. —— In General.

Civil Actions Generally.—Under Rev. Code, § 2927, any civil action founded on contract or in tort may be commenced by attachment. Hadley *v.* Bryars, 58 Ala. 139.

Statutory Penalties.—Under Code 1896, § 524, subd. 2, providing that "any money demand" may be enforced by attachment, that remedy will lie on a statutory penalty, where the amount is fixed or can be certainly ascertained. George F. Dittman Boot & Shoe Co. *v.* Mixon, 24 So. 847, 120 Ala. 206.

§ 5. —— On Express Contracts.

As to contingent liabilities arising out of contract, see post, "On Contingent Liabilities," § 9. As to unliquidated damages arising out of contract, see post, "On Demands Not Liquidated," § 7.

Ancillary Attachments.—The 8th section of the attachment act of 1837, does not warrant the suing out of an ancillary attachment in an action of detinue. This process is authorized in such actions only as can be commenced by original attachment. LeBaron *v.* James, 4 Ala. 687.

Contracts to Sell Lands.—When a purchaser of land or interests therein makes his contract orally only, but "the purchase money, or a portion thereof, is paid, and the purchaser put in possession of the land" (Code, § 1732, subd. 5), the contract is not void; hence an action by the vendor for the price is an action on contract, not in equity, and an attachment may issue for nonresidence. Steadham *v.* Parrish, 93 Ala. 465, 9 So. 358.

Contracts of Warranty.—An action may be commenced by attachment to recover for a breach of warranty of the soundness of a slave. Weaver *v.* Puryear, 11 Ala. 941.

§ 6. —— For Torts.

Trover and Conversion.—Where an attachment issues on affidavit of a money demand, a declaration subsequently filed in trover, against a defendant who does not appear, can not be allowed. But, if defendant appear, and plead to the merits—he will be too late to review the irregularity, after judgment. Marshall *v.* White, 8 Port. 551.

§ 7. —— On Demands Not Liquidated.

"Debt" or "Moneyed Demand."—Defendant hired a barge from plaintiffs for a certain per diem, with an agreement that, if it were not returned in as good condition as when hired, defendant was to pay the agreed value of the barge as upon a sale. The barge was returned in a worthless state. Held, that plaintiffs' claim is a "debt" or "a moneyed demand, the amount of which can be certainly ascertained," within the meaning of Code, §§ 2929, 2931, and will support an attachment. Tennessee River Transp. Co. *v.* Kavanaugh, 93 Ala. 324, 9 So. 395.

§ 8. —— On Demands Not Matured.

As to nonresidence as ground of attachment on a debt not due, see post, "Nonresidence," § 17.

In General.—An attachment may be authorized, when the claim forming the cause of action is not yet due. Ware *v.* Todd, 1 Ala. 199; Allen *v.* Claunch, 7 Ala. 788; Jones *v.* Holland, 47 Ala. 732.

Code 1886, § 3498, provides that a court of equity may issue an attachment on equitable demands in any case in which an attachment at law is authorized. Section 2929 allows the issuance of an attachment on a debt not due. Held, that an equitable attachment might be properly issued on an unmatured debt. Ware *v.* Seasongood, 92 Ala. 152, 9 So. 138.

If a vendor who contracts to deliver cotton at a future day certain receives payment of the price, and before the day appointed disables himself from complying with his contract, the purchaser may treat the contract as rescinded, and sue presently for the money paid out; and an attachment on such a debt would not be premature, though commenced before the time fixed for the delivery of the cotton; otherwise, where there is no proof of a breach of the contract, other than the failure to deliver on the appointed day. Russell *v.* Gregory, 62 Ala. 454

Rights of Nonresidents.—Act Dec. 1814, § 5, authorizes a resident of the state to issue an attachment against a nonresident debtor for a debt not due, and by Act 1824 the same benefits of the attachment laws of the state were given, to nonresidents as were secured to residents. Held, that a nonresident was entitled to maintain an attachment against a nonresident defendant on a debt not due. Pearsoll *v.* Middlebrook, 2 Stew. & P. 406.

Demand Not Constituting a Debt.—An attachment issued on the 9th of November, against one who had agreed to deliver cotton that fall, is void, the obligor not being in default until the expiration of the fall, and the demand not being a debt. Moore *v.* Dickerson, 44 Ala. 485. See Bozeman *v.* Rose, 40 Ala. 212.

§ 9. —— On Contingent Liabilities.

In General.—An attachment can not be sued out where the indebtedness of the defendant depends upon a contingency which may never happen; aliter, where the indebtedness is absolute, though the day of payment has not arrived. Miller *v.* McMillan, 4 Ala. 527; Planters', etc., Bank *v.* Andrews, 8 Port. 404.

Where neither the writ, affidavit or bond, allege that defendant's estate was attached to satisfy a contingent liability, it will be presumed that the undertaking for which plaintiff seeks redress is absolute. Planters', etc., Bank *v.* Andrews, 8 Port. 404.

Attachment by Surety.—Under the attachment laws, a plaintiff must show that the defendant is indebted to him in a sum of money past due, or else in a sum of money to be paid at a future time. Aik. Dig. 37, 38, 39. Therefore, where a writ of attachment states that plaintiff is security to a draft drawn on T. and L. for defendant, which he will probably have to pay, or on which suit will have to be brought in another state, it can not be sustained. Benson *v.* Campbell, 6 Port. 455.

The liability of the person primarily liable on a draft to a surety thereon is purely contingent until the maturity and dishonor of the draft; hence the surety can not sue the principal thereon by attachment before maturity. Benson *v.* Campbell, 6 Port. 455; Planters' & Merchants' Bank *v.* Andrews, 8 Port. 404.

§ 10. —— In Suits in Equity or Actions on Equitable Grounds.

Claims of an Equitable Nature.—The remedy by attachment for the recovery of a legal demand being given by statute to one nonresident against another, courts of equity by analogy must afford the same facility of collection to a creditor whose claim is of an equitable nature. Kirkman *v.* Vanlier, 7 Ala. 217.

§ 11. Persons Entitled.

Nonresidents.—Process of attachment by one nonresident against another will lie only for causes of action on which debt or indebitatus assumpsit could be brought. Hazard *v.* Jordan, 12 Ala. 180.

It has been stated broadly that none but a resident of this government was entitled to an attachment against one who is a nonresident, but the statute allows attachments by nonresidents in certain instances. Ala. Code, § 2930. Peters *v.* Bower, Minor 69. See Hazard *v.* Jordan, 12 Ala. 180.

"It is not required by the statute that the plaintiff in an attachment against an absconding debtor should be a resident of the state." Woodley *v.* Shirley, Minor 14.

A nonresident can not sue out an attachment against the property of a deceased nonresident debtor. Hemingway *v.* Moore, 11 Ala. 645.

§ 12. Persons Liable.

As to averments in affidavit as to parties, see post, "Averments as to Parties," § 55.

§ 13. —— In General.

Judicial Attachments.—To sustain a judicial attachment, it must appear in the record that the defendant is an inhabitant of the state. Wyatt *v.* Campbell, Minor 390; Evans *v.* Saltmarsh, 1 Stew. 43; Blair *v.* Cleveland, 1 Stew. 421.

Executors and Administrators.—An attachment lies under the statute (Clay's Digest, p. 58, § 14), in favor of a resident creditor, against the foreign executor or administrator of his deceased nonresident debtor. Branch Bank *v.* McDonald, 22

Ala. 474, cited on this point in note in 47 L. R. A. 353.

To authorize an attachment against the foreign executor or administrator of a deceased nonresident debtor, it must appear that he was a nonresident at the time of his death; and, when the attachment is sued out against the nonresident debtor himself while living, the suit can not be revived by sci. fa. against his foreign executor or administrator, because non constat that he was a nonresident at the time of his death. Branch Bank at Mobile *v.* McDonald, 22 Ala. 474.

Under the statutes, an attachment does not lie against a domestic executor or administrator whose testator or intestate resided in the state at the time of his death. Taliaferro *v.* Lane, 23 Ala. 369.

§ 14. —— Several Defendants.

Attachment for Tort.—In an action commenced by attachment against several persons for tort, where the affidavit discloses a ground of attachment as to all of them, a writ against all is proper. Hadley *v.* Bryars, 58 Ala. 139.

§ 15. Simultaneous and Successive Attachments.

As to alias writs, see post, "Alias Writs," § 90.

Permissibility.—Under the act of 1837, the plaintiff may sue out an ancillary attachment, not only where the suit is commenced by summons or capias ad respondendum, but where an original attachment is the leading process in the cause; yet it would perhaps be proper to quash the ancillary attachment, or the levy thereof, where the estate of the defendant levied on under the original was unquestionably ample to satisfy the plaintiff's demand. Brown *v.* Isbell, 11 Ala. 1009.

(B) GROUNDS OF ATTACHMENT.

As to averments in affidavit, see post, "Averments as to Grounds of Attachment," § 61. As to insufficiency or want of grounds as ground for quashing writ, see post, "Insufficiency or Want of Grounds of Attachment," § 136. As to action for rent, see the title LANDLORD AND TENANT. As to ground of attachment in justice's court, see the title JUSTICES OF THE PEACE.

§ 16. Insolvency or Inability to Satisfy Demand.

Mere Indebtedness or Insolvency Insufficient.—"Indebtedness alone will not justify a resort to the remedy by attachment, not even when coupled with pecuniary embarrassment, or actual insolvency. Floyd *v.* Hamilton, 33 Ala. 235; Lockhart *v.* Woods, 38 Ala. 631." Durr *v.* Jackson, 59 Ala. 203, 206.

The mere refusal of a debtor to pay a debt, to which he honestly believes he has a valid defense, will not warrant an attachment based on the ground that he has money or property liable to satisfy his debts, which he fraudulently withholds. Durr *v.* Jackson, 59 Ala. 203, cited on the point in note in 30 L. R. A. 488.

"A resident creditor can not sue out an attachment against a resident debtor, simply because the latter is insolvent; and no good reason can be assigned, why one nonresident should be allowed to attach the property of another, on grounds which would not justify such a proceeding on the part of one resident of the state against another. If any difference should be made, it should be rather in favor of the resident, than of the nonresident creditor. The remedy by attachment is a harsh one, at best; and this is especially the case, where both parties are nonresidents." Jones *v.* Lawrence, 36 Ala. 618, 620.

§ 17. Nonresidence.

Statutory Provisions.—The nonresidence of the defendant is one of the grounds given by statute for an attachment. Johnson *v.* Hale, 3 Stew. & P. 331, 336.

§ 18. Absconding, Absence, or Concealment.

§ 19. —— In General.

Statutory Provision.—Where the defendant "absconds," or "secretes," or "is about to remove out of the state," under the statute, these are a ground for attachment. Johnson *v.* Hale, 3 Stew. & P. 331, 336.

§ 20. —— Departure and Absence.

Absence Indicated by Return "Not Found."—On a capias the sheriff made return, "Not in time to execute." Defendants were residents of the county, and a judicial attachment was allowed, defendants suffering a judgment by default. As a mode of service, the judicial attachment is allowed whenever defendant is a resident of the county and the return is, "Not found." On appeal defendants assigned as error that the attachment was irregularly sued out. Held, that in support of the judgment the return on the writ would be read as "Not found," because the writ was received at too late a period to be executed. Thompson *v.* Hair, 7 Ala. 313.

After judgment by default, where the process is a judicial attachment, a return of "not in time to execute," to the Ca. Ad. Res., will be considered as a general return of not found. Quære—Whether in any case where the process is by attachment, advantage of defects in the process are available, where no plea in abatement has been interposed? Thompson *v.* Hair, 7 Ala. 313.

Temporary Absence.—A mere temporary absence of a person from the state, on business or pleasure, without informing his creditor of his intended absence, does not of itself authorize an attachment against his estate. Pitts *v.* Burroughs, 6 Ala. 733; Vandiver & Co. *v.* Waller, 39 So. 136, 143 Ala. 411.

The absence of a debtor from the state does not subject his property to attachment upon the allegation, that he absconds or secretes himself; and his neglect to inform a creditor of his intended absence, does not, per se, authorize the latter to resort to that extraordinary remedy. Pitts *v.* Burroughs, 6 Ala. 733.

§ 21. —— Concealment and Avoidance of Process.

Avoidance of Criminal Process.—Under Code, § 3253, subd. 3, providing for an attachment against any one who "secretes himself so that the ordinary process of law can not be served on him," an attachment may issue against one who so secretes himself, though solely to avoid a criminal prosecution. Malone *v.* Handley, 81 Ala. 117, 8 So. 189.

"The provision of the statute under which the attachment in this case was issued contains no word or phrase which indicates that the act of secretion or concealment shall be influenced by the motive or intent to avoid service of process. 'Secretes himself so that the ordinary process of law can not be served on him,' is the language of our statute. Code Ala., § 3253, subd. 3. That is, the secretion must be such, or so complete, as that process can not be served on him. Not being able to serve him personally, the law has furnished the creditor with another means of perfecting service; namely, by attachment of his goods. And this rule applies equally to the second and third grounds for attachment; for if the debtor absconds, he places it as effectually out of the power of his creditor to serve him with process, as if he secreted himself, or resided without the state. And fraudulent or other intent is not made one of the conditions on which this statutory remedy can be resorted to. * * * Inability to effect service of ordinary process in the ordinary way was the evil or inconvenience the statute was designed to remedy. It is the fact of absconding or secreting one's self—not the purpose of it—which interposes the obstacle. To hold otherwise, would be to declare that no matter how long the absence or secretion might continue, the creditor would be without remedy unless the debtor had absconded or secreted himself with the intent to avoid the service of civil process." Malone *v.* Handley, 81 Ala. 117, 8 So. 189.

A person who has been but transiently within the state, and never has permanently resided therein, will nevertheless be liable to attachment as an absconding debtor if he has absconded to avoid service of process. Under the attachment laws of this state, absconding within the state is alone a sufficient ground for an attachment, whether the plaintiff or defendant, or both, be resident or nonresident within the state. Middlebrook *v.* Ames, 5 Stew. & P. 158.

§ 22. —— Intended Departure.

In General.—That the defendant "is about to remove out the state," is a statutory ground for attachment. Johnson *v.* Hale, 3 Stew. & P. 331, 336.

Sufficiency of Intent.—A charge that,

to justify the suing out of attachment on the ground that defendant therein was about to remove from the state, it was necessary not only that such defendant had an intent, about to be carried into effect, to remove out of the state, but also an existing intent to acquire a residence or home in some other state, was properly refused. Troy *v.* Rogers, 20 So. 999, 113 Ala. 131.

Removal from County.—An affidavit that a party is about to remove from the county, so that ordinary process can not be served on him, is not sufficient to authorize an attachment to issue. Wallis *v.* Murphy, 2 Stew. 15.

§ 23. Removal or Concealment of Property.

§ 24. —— Removal from Jurisdiction.

Statutory Provisions.—Where the defendant is about to remove his property out of the state, under the statute, it is a ground for attachment. Johnson *v.* Hale, 3 Stew. & P. 331, 336.

Purpose of Removal.—A shipment of cotton from Alabama by the usual route, for the honest purposes of trade, by a citizen who has means in the state sufficient to pay all his debts, will not justify the issuance of an attachment against his estate, on the ground that he is about to remove his property out of the state, so that the plaintiff will probably lose his debt, or have to sue for it in another state. Stewart *v.* Cole, 46 Ala. 646.

§ 25. Fraudulent Transfer or Other Disposition of Property.

§ 26. —— In General.

Ground for Attachment.—"The fraudulent disposition, or attempt fraudulently to dispose of a part, of a failing debtor's effects is sufficient ground for attachment." Campbell *v.* Hopkins, 87 Ala. 170, 6 So. 76, 78.

Previous to the Act of 1850 (Pamphlet Acts, 45), an attachment could not be sued out on account of a fraudulent disposition of his property by the defendant, consummated prior to the issuance of the attachment. Yarbrough *v.* Hudson, 19 Ala. 653.

"The term 'goods' has as extensive a legal signification as 'effects,' and has even been applied in the civil law to real estate, though it has no such application in our law. The statute does not mean that the defendant must have disposed of, or be about to dispose of, all of his property. He may dispose of it all without giving ground for an attachment, if he does so honestly, and in good faith to all who are interested. But he can not dispose of any of it fraudulently without subjecting his property to this process." Hafley & Son *v.* Patterson, 47 Ala. 271, 272.

Disposition to Relatives.—The mere fact that plaintiffs, while largely indebted to defendants, sold certain goods to their brother, doing business in another state, does not raise a presumption of fraud. Marx *v.* Strauss, 93 Ala. 453, 9 So. 818.

§ 27. —— Transfers as Security.

Mortgage on Stock of Goods.—In the absence of a showing that plaintiff was insolvent, the mere fact that she had executed a mortgage on the stock of goods in her store, in which it was provided that goods subsequently purchased by her to replenish the stock should also be subject to the mortgage, and that she had used the money from current sales for the support and sustenance of herself and family, and in payment of the expense of conducting a farm, did not show a fraudulent disposition of her property, such as would permit defendant to attach the same to secure payment of his debt. Cox *v.* Birmingham Dry-Goods Co., 28 So. 456, 125 Ala. 320, 82 Am. St. Rep. 238.

Pledge of Wife's Property to Secure Bail for Husband.—In the absence of fraud, the mere fact that a wife offered to pledge her property to secure bail for her husband is no ground for an attachment against her. Schloss *v.* Rovelsky, 107 Ala. 596, 18 So. 71, cited on this point in note in 30 L. R. A. 479.

§ 28. —— Intended Removal or Disposition.

In General.—That a debtor was about to dispose of his property fraudulently, to avoid the payment of the debt, does not authorize the creditor to sue out an original attachment commanding its seizure. Reynolds *v.* Culbreath, 14 Ala. 581.

Acts Prior to Attachments.—Under the

statute authorizing attachment on the ground that defendant is "about to dispose of his property fraudulently," it is no ground for attachment that defendant had issued a deed of trust prior to the issue of the attachment. Yarbrough *v.* Hudson, 19 Ala. 653.

Acts after Attachment.—It is no justification for an attachment that the defendant made a fraudulent assignment three days after the attachment issued, unless the fraudulent intent of debtor existed at the time of the attachment. Donnell *v.* Jones, 17 Ala. 689, 52 Am. Dec. 194.

§ 29. Evidence as to Grounds.

As to evidence and effect of affidavits on motion to quash in general, see post, "Evidence and Effect of Affidavits," § 145.

§ 29 (1) Admissibility.

Fraud.—Whatever facts tend to show the good or bad faith of a party against whom an attachment is issued upon the ground of fraud are properly admissible in evidence. Marx *v.* Strauss, 93 Ala. 453, 9 So. 818, cited on this point in note in 30 L. R. A. 473.

Insolvency.—Upon an issue as to the insolvency of an attachment debtor, facts testified to by the creditor as of his own knowledge, tending to show insolvency, were admissible in evidence. Martin *v.* Mayer, 20 So. 963, 112 Ala. 620.

§ 29 (2) Weight and Sufficiency.

Insufficiency of Evidence to Show Bona Fides of Transaction.—In a suit to set aside an attachment by one H. on all the property belonging to his brother-in-law, on the ground that the debt was simulated and fraudulent, the only evidence of bona fides consisted of the testimony of H. himself. He testified that the debt consisted of a note given by the debtor to him as an indemnity for certain acceptances, and of several sums borrowed by him and loaned to the debtor, and also of other sums of his own loaned directly to the debtor. Held, that this evidence, considered in the light of H.'s failure to call the debtor as a witness, and of the intimate relations between them, is not sufficient to discharge the burden of proof resting upon H. to show his bona fides in the transaction. Henderson *v.* J. B. Brown Co., 28 So. 79, 125 Ala. 566.

§ 30. Waiver or Loss of Right.

Creditor Accepting Terms of Composition of Debtor.—If a debtor, assuming to make a composition with his creditors on equal terms, obtains from two of his creditors money to enable him to make the composition, and secretly secures them, by deed of trust on property subject to the payment of his debts, the full amount of their demands, this would be a fraudulent disposition of property, authorizing an attachment at the suit of any creditor thereby attempted to be defrauded; but if the nonpreferred creditor had knowledge of the source from which the money came, and the terms on which it was obtained, before he accepted the terms offered by the debtor, he can not be heard to claim that he was defrauded, or be justified in suing out an attachment on that ground. City Nat. Bank *v.* Jeffries, 73 Ala. 183.

Where a debtor in failing circumstances offered to make a composition with his creditors on equal terms, and, to enable him, with money he then had on hand, to make the composition, entered into an agreement with two of his largest creditors for a loan of money, he to secure them their debts and the contemplated loan by mortgage on property subject to sale under execution, but soon afterwards, the money not having been loaned, or the composition made, the creditors making the agreement, and another creditor who had agreed to compound on the terms proposed, but had no knowledge or information of said agreement, and acting by attorney, sued out attachments against the debtor; and, at the time the agreement was made, and the attachments were issued, the three attaching creditors were represented by the same attorney, who had full knowledge of the agreement at the time it was made, he then endeavoring to collect the claims of his several clients, and who, in fact, sued out the attachment in favor of the creditor agreeing to compound, and on whose advice that a ground of attachment existed, it was ordered to be issued—held, in an action by the debtor against the sureties of such creditor on his attachment bond, that the knowledge of said agreement by the attorney was constructive knowledge to the creditor. City Nat. Bank *v.* Jeffries, 73 Ala. 183.

II. PROPERTY SUBJECT TO ATTACHMENT.

As to property affected by lien or levy, see post, "Property or Interests Affected, and Extent of Lien, § 106. As to exemptions in General, see the titles EXEMPTIONS; HOMESTEAD. As to property subject to attachment in justice's court, see the title JUSTICES OF THE PEACE. As to particular property and property of particular corporations, see the titles BANKS AND BANKING; BUILDING AND LOAN ASSOCIATIONS; CORPORATIONS; COUNTIES; LOGS AND LOGGING; MUNICIPAL CORPORATIONS; RAILROADS. As to property fraudulently transferred by debtor, see the title FRAUDULENT CONVEYANCES. As to remedy of creditor of cestui que trust, see the title TRUSTS. As to liability of separate estate of married woman for debts of husband, see the title HUSBAND AND WIFE. As to what constitutes fixtures, see the title FIXTURES. As to mode of levying, see post, "Personal Property in General," § 96.

§ 31. Personal Property in General.

In General.—"Personal property, subject to execution, may be attached." Phillips *v.* Ash, 63 Ala. 414, 416.

Mere Right to Personal Property in Hands of Third Persons.—The mere right to personal property in the possession of a third person, which possession originated, and is continued, in good faith, is not subject to seizure under an attachment or execution; and where there is no evidence tending to prove mala fides, a charge to the jury, laying down the law as above stated, is not erroneous, because it omits to refer to them the bona fides of the adverse possession. Horton *v.* Smith, 8 Ala. 73.

§ 32. Real Property in General.

As to equitable estates or interests, see post, "Equitable Estates or Interests in General," § 38.

In General.—A levy may be made on real estate, whether the same be a fee-simple, or any less legal estate. Code of 1876, § 3268. The effect of a levy on real estate differs materially from a levy on personal property. No estate, or interest, passes to the officer, or to the plaintiff; no right to the possession, or to take the rents, issues, or profits. The possession, and right of possession, remain in the defendant, undisturbed. A lien in created by the levy, superior to subsequent liens, alienations, or incumbrances, which will be available to the creditor, if he obtains judgment, to which the real estate can be made subject by process issuing upon it. Phillips *v.* Ash, 63 Ala. 414, 416.

"Until the year 1837, lands were not subject to be levied upon by an attachment. By an act of that year (Clay's Dig., p. 60, § 29), it is provided that 'whether an original attachment shall be issued for, or upon any of the causes now provided by law, it shall be lawful to levy the same upon any land belonging to the defendant in such attachment, by the officer whose duty it may be to levy or execute the same, in the same manner that attachments are, or may be by law authorized to be levied on goods, chattels, or effects.'" Autry *v.* Walters, 46 Ala. 476, 478.

Levy on Both Land and Personalty.—An attachment sued out previous to the act of 1837, ought not to be quashed because levied on land, as well as personal estate. It may be doubtful whether the levy on the land would have any effect, but it is certain that the levy on the personal estate, is a good execution of the process. Green *v.* Pyne, 1 Ala. 235.

Equitable Interests.—Code 1886, § 3500, authorizes courts of equity to issue attachments on legal demands as attachments may issue from courts of law, which attachments operate only against property held by equitable title. Section 3498 provides that such attachments may issue on equitable demands in any case in which an attachment at law may issue. Held, that the jurisdiction of equity was coextensive with that of courts of law, and that an equitable attachment might issue against a debtor's equitable interest in a building on land owned by his wife. Ware *v.* Seasongood, 92 Ala. 152, 9 So. 138.

It seems that the lease-hold interest of the lessee of realty is held to be subject to attachment. McCreery *v.* Berney Nat. Bank, 116 Ala. 224, 22 So. 577, cited on this point in note in 17 L. R. A., N. S., 842.

§ 33. Property Mortgaged or Otherwise Incumbered.

As to equitable estates or interests in general, see post, "Equitable Estates or Interests in General," § 38.

§ 34. —— Personal Property.

Liability to Attachment as Dependent on Possession or Right of Possession. —The grantor in a deed of trust, who remains in possession of the personal property conveyed by it after default made, has not such an interest as is subject to be levied on by attachment, when the deed gives the trustee power to sell so much of the property as will pay the demands then due; and this, although only a portion of the demands secured is due and unpaid at the time of the levy of the attachment, and the property conveyed greatly exceeds in value the sum due. Thompson *v.* Thornton, 21 Ala. 808.

"It is well settled by the decisions of this court, that the grantor in a deed of trust, or the mortgagor, before the law day or default of payment, in cases where such grantor or mortgagor retains the possession of the property, has such an interest as may be levied on and sold. McGregor *v.* Hall, 3 Stew. & P. 397; Purnell *v.* Hogan, 5 Stew. & P. 192; Perkins *v.* Mayfield, 5 Port. 182; Williams *v.* Jones, 2 Ala. 314; Gardner *v.* Morrison, 12 Ala. 547. But it is equally well settled, that, after the law day or default, such property is not subject to be levied on; for then the mortgagee has the right to enter, or in case of a trust deed, the trustee has the right to the possession of the property, and the right of the grantor or mortgagor is purely the right to redeem; an equitable right, which, being disconnected from the legal right of possession, is not subject to be levied on by legal process. See the cases of Magee *v.* Carpenter, 4 Ala. 469; Planters', etc., Bank *v.* Willis & Co., 5 Ala. 770, 771; Marriott *v.* Givens, 8 Ala. 694; Fontaine *v.* Beers, 19 Ala. 722, 723. These cases are entirely reconcilable with the decisions previously referred to." Thompson *v.* Thornton, 21 Ala. 808, 812.

§ 35. —— Real Property.

Equity of Redemption.—An attachment is leviable on an equity of redemption in lands. British & American Mortg. Co. *v.* Norton, 28 So. 31, 125 Ala. 522. See Norton *v.* Mortgage Co., 113 Ala. 110, 20 So. 968; Central Min., etc., Co. *v.* Stoven, 45 Ala. 594; Goode *v.* Longmire, 35 Ala. 668.

§ 36. Corporate Stock.

As to mode of levying, see post, "Shares of Stock," § 97.

Stock a Chose in Action.—Stock in a plank-road company is a chose in action, which may be subjected in equity, under the attachment law of 1846. Bank of St. Marys *v.* St. John, 25 Ala. 566.

§ 37. Interests under Contracts.

Lease.—The interest of the landlord in the crops grown on the rented premises, by reason of his lien for rent and advances, is not such a title or interest as can be levied upon under attachment. Starnes *v.* Allen, 58 Ala. 316.

§ 38. Equitable Estates or Interests in General.

As to interests of devisees or legatees, see post, "Interests of Devisees or Legatees," § 39. As to property mortgaged or otherwise incumbered, see ante, "Property Mortgaged or Otherwise Incumbered," § 33. As to real property in general, see ante, "Real Property in General," § 32.

Operation and Effect of Equitable Attachment.—"An equitable attachment can 'operate only on the effects of the defendant held by an equitable title,' etc." Ware *v.* Seasongood, 92 Ala. 152, 9 So. 138, 139.

"When one person has the title or control of property which, in good conscience, should be applied to the debts of another, and that property is in such condition as that it can not be made available without the intervention of chancery powers, then the case is brought within § 3500 of the Code of 1886." Ware *v.* Seasongood, 92 Ala. 152, 9 So. 138, 139.

Devise in Trust.—Where a testator bequeathed a sum of money to a trustee, in trust for a debtor, "not subject to any debt or debts he may have contracted, but for his comfort and support," held that, under the statute, the money might be subjected to the payment of his existing debts, by equitable attachment. Smith *v.* Moore, 37 Ala. 327.

Right of Redemption.—The statutory right of redemption is not subject to the levy of an attachment, but its inclusion in the officer's return does not vitiate the levy on proper subjects; and "equity of redemption" is a proper subject on which to levy an attachment. Central Min., etc., Co. *v.* Stoven, 45 Ala. 594.

It seems that a mortgagor in possession after default has no such interest in the mortgaged premises as will authorize the levy of an attachment thereon, since after default he has neither the legal title nor right to possession. Thompson *v.* Thornton, 21 Ala. 808.

§ 39. Interests of Devisees or Legatees.

As to equitable estates or interests in general, see ante, "Equitable Estates or Interests in General," § 38.

Remainders and Reversionary Interests.—A vested remainder in slaves is not liable to attachment or execution during the particular estate, before the slaves have come to the remainder-man's possession. Goode *v.* Longmire, 35 Ala. 668.

§ 40. Rights of Action in General.

Claims in Pending Actions.—A debt in suit may, under the attachment law of this state, be attached at the suit of a creditor of the plaintiff in the same court, where the suit is pending. Hitt *v.* Lacey, 3 Ala. 104.

A debt in suit in Coosa county can not be attached by a creditor of the plaintiff in Tuskaloosa county, the defendant in attachment controverting the justice of the demand. Bingham *v.* Smith, 5 Ala. 651.

§ 41. Ownership or Possession of Property.

As to record or other notice of transfer, see post, "Priorities between Attachments and Other Liens or Claims," § 108. As to want of ownership as ground for quashing writ, see post, "Ownership of Property Attached," § 139. As to property assigned for benefit of creditors, see the title ASSIGNMENTS FOR BENEFIT OF CREDITORS. As to property fraudulently conveyed by debtor, see the title FRAUDULENT CONVEYANCES. As to remedies of creditors against property in custody of receivers, see the title RECEIVERS. As to remedies of creditors against trust property, see the title TRUSTS. As to rights and remedies of creditors against mortgage chattels on ground of invalidity of mortgage, see the title CHATTEL MORTGAGES. As to rights of creditors to attach property acquired by executor while acting in representative capacity see the title EXECUTORS AND ADMINISTRATORS. As to sufficiency of resale to defeat attaching creditors of seller, see the titles SALES; VENDOR AND PURCHASER. As to title to deposits as affecting right of creditor of deposit to attach, see the title BANKS AND BANKING. As to transfer of bill of lading, see the title CARRIERS. As to transfers of shares of stock, see the title CORPORATIONS. As to concurrent or conflicting jurisdiction of courts, see the title COURTS. As to effect of bankruptcy proceedings, see the title BANKRUPTCY. As to property assigned for creditors, see the title ASSIGNMENTS FOR BENEFIT OF CREDITORS. As to property in hands of receivers, see the title RECEIVERS.

Conditional Sales.—Under a conditional sale, the creditors of the vendee had no right to subject the property to attachment, though they had no notice of the conditional character of such sale. Thornton *v.* Cook, 97 Ala. 630, 12 So. 403.

Payment.—That property attached was part of property purchased by the debtor and another, and that it had been set off to him as his share, and removed by him to his own premises, is sufficient prima facie proof that it was subject to attachment against him, without proof that he had paid for it. Schamragel *v.* Whitehurst, 103 Ala. 260, 15 So. 611.

On a claim in attachment by a third person, there was evidence of a debt from defendant to another corporation, and from the latter to claimant. The books of such corporation showed that defendant was credited with payment of its debt by delivery to claimant of the pig iron attached. It was shown that the iron was delivered to claimants under such agreement for payment, and that claimant was in possession thereof for over a month prior to the levy thereon. Held, that the property was not subject to the attachment. Mary Lee Coal & Railway Co. *v.* Knox, 110 Ala. 632, 19 So. 67.

Proceeds of Property Fraudulently Conveyed or Assigned.—When the debtor's property is purchased by a third person, at a price less than its real value, with intent "to hinder, delay and defraud" creditors, and is afterwards resold by him, the creditor may attach the money in his hands, the proceeds of the resale, by bill in chancery under the act of 1846. Flake *v.* Day & Co., 22 Ala. 132.

§ 42. Property in Custody of the Law.

Property Held under Prior Attachment.—Personal property levied on by attachment is in custodia legis, and is not subject to levy by junior attachment. Powell *v.* Rankin, 80 Ala. 316.

"It has long been a settled law in this state, that, where personal property is levied on under a writ of attachment, or of execution, and is replevied, either by the defendant, by a stranger in his behalf, or by a claimant who is not a party to the suit, and the property is delivered by the sheriff to such person, upon his executing a proper forthcoming bond in the manner prescribed by statute, the property is thus placed in the custody of the law, and a second attachment, or second execution not superior in lien, can not be levied on it by the sheriff, so long as its status remains unchanged. And, if such second levy is made, it will be vacated by the court having jurisdiction, on motion made by a party in interest who is prejudiced. Powell *v.* Rankin & Co., 80 Ala. 316, 317. See Striplin & Co. *v.* Cooper & Son, 80 Ala. 256.

Where property has been replevied, it is nevertheless still in the custody of the law, and the sheriff has no authority to levy an attachment on it. Cordaman *v.* Malone, 63 Ala. 556.

Property Held under Execution.—Where a writ of attachment is levied on lands on which another officer has already levied an execution, the attachment creditor acquires a valid lien subject to the lien of the execution creditor. Johnson *v.* Burnett, 12 Ala. 743.

A sum of money produced by the sale of the effects of a defendant in execution, remaining in the hands of a constable, after satisfying executions against the defendant, is subject to be attached. King *v.* Moore, 6 Ala. 160.

Property Taken from Prisoner.—Money taken by an officer from the person of a prisoner arrested in good faith is subject to attachment in the hands of the officer, under Code, § 2950, permitting sequestered property to be attached while in the hands of the officer; but, in order to be valid the levy must not be procured by fraud or trickery on the part of the creditor or officer, and the money or thing taken from the prisoner must be connected with the offense charged or necessary as evidence on the trial; otherwise the officer has no right to take it from the prisoner, and, if taken, it can not be attached. Ex parte Hurn, 92 Ala. 102, 9 So. 515, 13 L. R. A. 120.

Under Code, § 2950, providing that "money in the hands of an attorney at law, sheriff, or other officer may be attached," money which was taken by the sheriff from the person of a debtor arrested on a criminal charge, and which was attached while in his hands, and by him paid into court, may be attached while in the hands of the clerk of the court. Warren *v.* Matthews, 96 Ala. 183, 11 So. 285.

Where the possession of officers under attachment writs was illegal, the property, which belonged to another than the defendant in the attachment, was not in the custody of the law. Milner & Kettig Co. *v.* De Loach Mill Mfg. Co., 36 So. 765, 139 Ala. 645, 101 Am. St. Rep. 63.

Estates in Process of Administration.—Under the statute authorizing an attachment in favor of a resident citizen against the executor or administrator of a nonresident debtor, the attachment must be levied on property which has not been reduced into possession by the foreign executor, so as to be assets. Loomis *v.* Allen, 7 Ala. 706.

III. PROCEEDINGS TO PROCURE.

As to mandamus to control acts of court or judge in reference to attachment proceedings, see the title MANDAMUS. As to procedure in justices courts, see the title JUSTICES OF THE PEACE.

(A) JURISDICTION AND VENUE.

See, generally, the titles COURTS; VENUE.

As to want of jurisdiction as ground for quashing writ, see post, "Want of Jurisdiction," § 137. As to jurisdiction in justice's court, see the title JUSTICES OF THE PEACE. As to matters affecting jurisdiction or authority of courts in general, see the title COURTS. As to removal of causes, see the title REMOVAL OF CAUSES.

§ 43. Jurisdiction of Courts of Equity.

In General.—The doctrine that the court ought to take jurisdiction in analogy to the proceeding by attachment at law applies only where the complainant's demand is equitable, or there is some special cause for equitable interposition. Smith *v.* Moore, 35 Ala. 76.

Equitable Attachment on Legal Demand against a Nonresident.—Independent of statutory provisions, an equitable attachment does not lie on a purely legal demand, against a nonresident who has property and effects within this state more than sufficient to satisfy the demand, which may be reached and subjected by attachment at law. McKenzie *v.* Bentley, 30 Ala. 139.

§ 44. Place of Bringing Proceedings.

In General.—The statute of 1807, which enacts that "no freeholder of this state shall be sued out of the county of his permanent residence," does not apply to suits commenced by attachment. Herndon *v.* Givens, 16 Ala. 261.

Situs of Property.—Actions commenced by attachment may be instituted in any county of the state where a levy on defendant's property may be made. Such actions are not within Code, § 2640, requiring actions on contracts to be brought in the county in which the defendants or one of them resides, if such defendant has within the state a permanent residence. McPhillips *v.* Hubbard, 97 Ala. 512, 12 So. 711. See Herndon *v.* Givens, 16 Ala. 261; Atkinson *v.* Wiggins, 69 Ala. 190; Home Protection *v.* Richardson, 74 Ala. 468.

A writ of attachment issued and levied on defendant's property in the county where the cause of action arose was made returnable in another county, where plaintiff resided. Defendant was a nonresident, not served with process, and did not appear except specially to object to the jurisdiction. Code, § 526, provides that a writ of attachment, authorized by § 524, subd. 4, when the action sounds in damages merely, may be issued only by a judge of the circuit or probate courts, or chancellor, returnable to any county. Section 4205 requires actions against a resident to be brought in the county of his residence, or where the act or omission complained of occurred, and actions for the recovery of land, or the possession of or trespass thereto, to be brought in the county where the land is situated. Held that, though § 4205 does not relate to suits commenced by attachment, it illustrates the policy of the state as to venue of actions, and an attachment against the property of a nonresident can be made returnable only in a county where the writ is levied, and the court of one county acquires no jurisdiction by a levy of the writ in another county. Kress *v.* Porter, 31 So. 377, 132 Ala. 577.

"For jurisdictional purposes, therefore, the property of a nonresident defendant, who has not been served, or who has not appeared, it seems that the property itself levied on stands in the place of service, to the extent of the levy, for its condemnation to sale, and no further. Being in the nature of a proceeding in rem, it would appear that the situs of the property would determine the jurisdiction of the court to entertain attachment proceedings for its condemnation, there being nothing in the statutes of the state to the contrary. This is in keeping with the policy of our law as to the venue of actions. Code, § 4205, while it does not apply to suits commenced by attachment, may be referred to as showing the policy of the law as to the venue in attachment suits. It provides that all actions on contracts, except as otherwise provided, must be brought in the county in which the defendant, or one of the defendants, resides, if he has a permanent residence in the state; that all other personal actions, if the defendant or one of defendants, has within the state a permanent residence, may be brought in the county of such residence, or in the county in which the act or omission complained of may have been done, or may have occurred; and all actions for the recovery of land, or of the possession thereof, or for trespass thereto, must be brought in the county where the land lies, and a summons issuing contrary to these provisions must be abated on the plea of defendant." Kress v. Porter, 132 Ala. 577, 31 So. 377, 379.

§ 45. Waiver of Objections.

The defense that an attachment was sued out on a demand for which attachment in the particular case would not lie is waived by a plea to the merits. Brown v. Coats, 56 Ala. 439.

The requirement that the record in a judicial attachment shall show that defendant is an inhabitant of the state is not waived by his appearance and replevy of the property. Blair v. Cleveland, 1 Stew. 421.

(B) AFFIDAVITS.

As to want of or defects in affidavits as ground for quashing writ, see post, "Defects or Irregularities in Proceedings," § 138. As to affidavits for attachment to enforce mechanic's lien, see the title MECHANICS' LIENS. As to affidavits in justices courts, see the title JUSTICES OF THE PEACE.

§ 46. Necessity and Purpose.

As to issuance of alias writs without individual affidavit, see post, "Alias Writs," § 90.

In General.—It is the general rule, to require, as a condition to the issuance of an attachment, that the plaintiff shall make an affidavit of the existence of some ground, such as the law authorizes for its issuance. The affidavit is intended as a restraint upon the conscience of the plaintiff, against the wrongful suing out of the attachment. Ex parte Damon, 103 Ala. 477, 15 So. 862, 863.

Code 1852, § 2954, authorizes an attachment in an equity case under the same circumstances and conditions as attachments are issued at law; and § 2506 requires the officer, before issuing an attachment, to require an affidavit. Held, that a proceeding under the former statute could not be maintained where no affidavit was given or an attachment asked, though an injunction is prayed for against the third party in whose hands the property is. Smith v. Moore, 35 Ala. 76.

Though a bill in chancery sets out facts bringing complainant's case within Act 1846, § 8, allowing an attachment to issue, his bill can not be sustained under that act when he has not filed the affidavit required by § 3 thereof. McGown v. Sprague, 23 Ala. 524.

In an action for breach of a special contract, the measure of damages for breach of which is fixed by law, a special affidavit for an attachment, under Code, § 2503, "to determine the amount for which the levy must be made," is unnecessary. Bozeman v. Rose, 40 Ala. 212.

"Section 2989 of said Code enacts that attachments issued without affidavit and bond, as therein provided, may be abated on plea of the defendant, filed within the first three days of the return term. The manifest meaning of this section is, that an attachment may be abated if issued without a sufficient affidavit or bond; it does not require it to be issued without either, to justify a plea in abatement. An affidavit or bond, defective in matter of substance, is in legal contemplation equivalent to no affidavit or bond whatever. If the defect be of form, only, it may be amended, whether it be in the affidavit or bond, or both; but an attachment must not be dismissed for any defect in, or want of, a bond, if the plaintiff, his agent or attorney, is willing to give or substitute a sufficient bond. The affidavit, however, if defective in substance, is not amendable, and the attachment must be abated, on the plea of the defendant. Section 2990, Revised Code." Hall *v.* Brazelton, 46 Ala. 359, 362.

Verified Pleading in Lieu of Affidavit.—Under Sess. Acts 1846, authorizing attachments against nonresidents, it is not necessary that the facts required by the act to be shown should appear by affidavit separate and apart from the bill. It is sufficient if they are clearly alleged in the bill, duly sworn to by the plaintiff or some person in his behalf. Bank of St. Marys *v.* St. John, 25 Ala. 566.

As against the bank, if the bill is verified by affidavit, and alleges that the bank is located in another state, and has property and choses in action in this state, it may also be sustained under the attachment law of 1846; and if it further alleges that the notes were issued and put in circulation in this state by the president, who is charged to be the principal stockholder and a nonresident, it is also well filed against him under that act. Bank *v.* St. John Powers & Co., 25 Ala. 566.

Provision Can Not Be Waived.—Under Code 1876, § 3341, requiring a creditor seeking an attachment to make affidavit that he has just claim to the property attached, such affidavit is necessary to give the court jurisdiction, and can not be waived by the parties. Mobile Life Ins. Co. *v.* Teague, 78 Ala. 147.

Defective Affidavit.—Under § 2989, Rev. Code, an attachment may be abated if issued without a sufficient affidavit. An affidavit, defective in matter of substance, is in legal contemplation equivalent to no affidavit. Hall *v.* Brazelton, 46 Ala. 359, 362.

§ 47. Persons Who May Make.

§ 48. —— Agents or Attorneys.

As to authority to take affidavit, see post, "Authority to Take," § 49.

In General.—Under the provision of the act of February 5, 1846, that an attachment shall issue on the affidavit of "the complainant or complainants or some one of them," the affidavit of the defendant's indebtedness and nonresidence, required for the issuance of the attachment, may be made by an agent or attorney. Flake *v.* Day, 22 Ala. 132.

Averments and Proof of Authority.—The affidavit of one describing himself as agent of the persons for whose use the suit was brought is sufficient to authorize an attachment. Murray *v.* Cone, 8 Port. 250.

§ 49. Authority to Take.

As to amendment where clerk fails to certify affidavit, see post, "Defects Amendable," § 68 (2)

Clerk of Court or Deputy.—An affidavit for an attachment, made before the clerk of the circuit court of B. county, is valid, though the writ is issued by the clerk of the circuit court of M. county. Wright *v.* Smith, 66 Ala. 545.

A deputy clerk—that is, one duly appointed and qualified, has full power to transact all business of his principal (Code, § 676, subd. 2); and an attachment issued by him, or an affidavit administered by him, is not void for want of authority. Minniece *v.* Jeter, 65 Ala. 222.

§ 50. Formal Requisites.

Jurat or Certificate of Officer.—An affidavit actually sworn to is sufficient to support an attachment, although the officer before whom the oath was taken did not make certificate of the fact. McCartney *v.* Branch Bank, 3 Ala. 709; Hyde *v.* Adams, 80 Ala. 111.

If an affidavit for an attachment is in fact made before the officer who issues the writ, it is not necessary that it shall be signed or certified by him; and a plea in abatement, "because it was not signed by the clerk," presents an immaterial issue. Hyde *v.* Adams, 80 Ala. 111.

Special Affidavit.—A special affidavit in an attachment case (Code, § 2503), being made for the single purpose of enabling the judge who grants the writ "to determine the amount for which a levy must be made," does not perform the office of any part of the pleadings, and is not to be construed by the strict rules applicable to pleadings; its definiteness and sufficiency rests in the discretion of the judge, and can not be tested by plea in abatement, nor be a subject of revision on appeal. Bozeman *v.* Rose, 40 Ala. 212.

§ 51. Averments in General.

Showing Commencement of Suit.—Where an attachment is sued out under the act of 1837, "to explain and amend the law in relation to attachments," as auxiliary to a suit then existing, it is not necessary to allege in the affidavit the existence of a previous suit. Hounshell *v.* Phares, 1 Ala. 580.

Sufficiency of Affidavit against Nonresidents.—An affidavit in attachment, made by the agent of nonresident plaintiffs, against the goods and effects of a nonresident debtor, stating that the plaintiffs resided in the state of New York; that the defendant was indebted in a certain sum (describing the demand) that the demand, having been contracted on a credit, was not due; that the defendant was not within the state of Alabama, so that ordinary process could be served on him—being also a resident of New York; that the defendant had not, within the affiant's knowledge, any property, in the state of his residence, sufficient to discharge the debt; and that the process was not prayed with the purpose of vexing or harassing the defendant, or for other improper motive. Held, a sufficient compliance with the requisitions of the statute laws of this state, to authorize the court to sustain the proceeding. Pearsoll *v.* Middlebrook, 2 Stew. & P. 406.

§ 52. Knowledge or Information.

§ 53. —— Necessity of Knowledge.

Averments as to Indebtedness.—An affidavit for attachment, made by the attorney of a nonresident creditor, stating that affiant is "informed and believes, and therefore states" that defendant, who is also a nonresident, is justly indebted, etc., is not defective. Mitchell *v.* Pitts, 61 Ala. 219.

§ 54. —— Necessity of Belief.

As to amendment of affidavit, see post, "Defects Amendable," § 68 (2).

Necessity of Belief in General.—In an attachment by one nonresident against another, the affidavit should show that the defendant has not sufficient property within the state of his residence to answer the debt, within the belief, as well as within the knowledge of the person making the affidavit; and such a defect is sufficient to abate the attachment, when pleaded, Cobb *v.* Force Bros. & Co., 6 Ala. 468; Cobb *v.* Miller, etc., Co., 9 Ala. 499.

§ 55. Averments as to Parties.

In General.—In an action by a partnership, commenced by attachment, if the individual names of the several partners are not stated in the writ, bond, or affidavit, the defect is good matter for plea in abatement. Sims, etc., Co. *v.* Jacobson & Co., 51 Ala. 186.

Proceedings by or against Corporations.—Under Rev. Code, § 2938, relative to attachments against corporations, the affidavit need not state that the corporation against which the attachment is sought is a domestic corporation. Central Mining & Manufacturing Co. *v.* Stoven, 45 Ala. 594.

Averments as to Residence of Parties.—To sustain original attachment against a nonresident, it is not necessary that the affidavit should state that the plaintiff resides in the state. Peters *v.* Bower, Minor 69.

A nonresident, commencing a suit by attachment, need not state the fact of his nonresidence in the affidavit. If such is the fact, and no sufficient bond or affidavit is made, it may be pleaded in abatement. Jackson *v.* Stanley, 2 Ala. 326.

§ 56. Averments as to Cause of Action.

In General.—The special affidavit required by Code, § 2503, is sufficient if it shows prima facie the existence of a "moneyed demand" in favor of plaintiff, without setting forth a cause of action with all the strictness required in pleading. Bozeman *v.* Rose, 40 Ala. 212.

Actions on Written Instruments.—An affidavit that the defendant is indebted to the plaintiff in a certain sum by note, and setting out the note in hæc verba, is sufficient to support an attachment. Alford *v.* Johnson, 9 Port. 320.

§ 57. Averments as to Nature of Demand.

Necessity.—An affidavit for an attachment need not state how the debt accrued, whether on bond, note, etc., but only the amount claimed to be due. Starke *v.* Marshall, 3 Ala. 44; Fleming *v.* Burge, 6 Ala. 373.

Sufficiency of Affidavit.—Under Code 1896, § 524, authorizing the issuance of an attachment by a chancellor in an action for unliquidated damages for breach of contract, or in action sounding in damages merely, and § 529, providing that the chancellor must require plaintiff to make affidavit of the special circumstances in order to determine the amount for which a levy must be made, an affidavit which alleges that defendant unlawfully seized and carried away and converted to his own use lumber, but which fails to show that the attachment was sought for damages for breach of contract or in an action sounding in damages, is insufficient to authorize a writ of attachment. Wiggs Bros. *v.* Ringemann, 45 So. 153, 155 Ala. 189.

§ 58. Averments as to Indebtedness.

§ 59. —— Maturity.

Necessity of Showing Natural Debt.—Although the affidavit states that the defendant will be indebted, yet, if it shows other facts, as by setting out the date and time of payment of the note from which the indebtedness arises, it will be considered as if a present indebtedness was sworn to in direct terms, and will support an attachment. McCartney *v.* Branch Bank, 3 Ala. 709.

Debts Not Due or Due Only in Part.—In an attachment, a note not due when the attachment issued is not admissible in evidence where neither the affidavit nor any part of the proceedings show that fact. Stowe *v.* Sewall, 3 Stew. & P. 67.

The affidavit required to authorize the issuance of an attachment should show what part, if any, of the debt sued on, is not due, and when it will be due. Stowe *v.* Sewall, 3 Stew. & P. 67.

§ 60. —— Amount.

Special Affidavit.—The special affidavit required by statute, as to the particular facts and circumstances of the claim, where an attachment is sued out to recover damages, is intended for the single purpose of enabling the officer granting the writ to determine the amount for which a levy must be made, and its sufficiency can not be tested by plea in abatement. Hadley *v.* Bryars, 58 Ala. 139.

An action for a breach of warranty of title in the sale of personal property is "a moneyed demand, the amount of which can be certainly ascertained," within the meaning of Code, § 3252, subd. 2; and, in order to authorize a writ of attachment to issue, the additional affidavit of "the special facts and circumstances" required by Code, § 3257, to enable the judge to determine the amount for which a levy should be made, is not necessary. Guy *v.* Lee, 81 Ala. 163, 2 So. 273.

§ 61. Averments as to Grounds of Attachment.

§ 62. —— In General.

Showing Facts in Addition to Nonresidence.—In attachment against a nonresident it is not necessary to state in the affidavit that the ordinary process of law can not be served on him. Conklin *v.* Harris, 5 Ala. 213.

§ 63. —— Language of Statute.

In General.—"An affidavit, setting forth the ground of attachment substantially in the words of the statute, is sufficient." Reese *v.* Rugeley, 82 Ala. 267, 2 So. 441, 442. See Gunter *v.* DuBose, 77 Ala. 326.

Nonresidence.—Under a statute providing that an attachment may issue when the defendant "resides out of the state," an allegation, in an affidavit made to obtain an attachment, that the defendant "is a nonresident," is sufficiently certain. Graham *v.* Ruff, 8 Ala. 171.

Under the statute requiring that an affidavit for foreign attachment shall state that the defendant "actually resides out of the state, so that ordinary process of law can not be served on him," an affidavit is insufficient which fails to state that the ordinary process can not be served. A motion to quash did not cure the defects in the attachment. Wilson *v.* Outlaw, Minor 196.

Fraudulent Removal or Disposition of Property.—Under Aik. Dig., § 3, p. 37, authorizing an attachment upon affidavit that defendant "is about to remove his or her property out of the state, and that thereby plaintiff will lose the debt or have to sue for it in another state," an affidavit that, as a consequence of such removal, "the ordinary process of law can not be served" on the defendant, is insufficient. Napper *v.* Noland, 9 Port. 318.

An affidavit that the defendant is "about to abscond himself and his property out of the state" is equivalent to alleging that the defendant is about to remove himself and property out of the state, and therefore, within the statute, sufficient to support an attachment. Ware *v.* Todd, 1 Ala. 199.

An averment in an affidavit for an attachment that defendants are about to dispose of their "goods," etc., is equivalent to an affidavit that they are about to dispose of their "property." Hafley *v.* Patterson, 47 Ala. 271.

Under Rev. Code, § 2928, subd. 6, allowing an attachment "when defendant is about fraudulently to dispose of his property," an affidavit which alleges that defendant "is endeavoring, fraudulently and clandestinely, to dispose of his effects," is sufficient. Free *v.* Hukill, 44 Ala. 197.

§ 64. —— Stating More than One Ground.

In General.—The insertion in the affidavit, or recital in the writ of attachment, of any two of the several grounds embraced in the statute, would be irregular. Cannon *v.* Logan, 5 Port. 77.

Inconsistent Statements.—In an affidavit for an attachment, while it is not permissible to state two or more grounds in the alternative, or disjunctively, two or more grounds may be stated cumulatively, or conjunctively, when they are not inconsistent with each other. Smith *v.* Baker, 80 Ala. 318.

An affidavit of attachment that defendant is about to dispose of his property fraudulently, that he had fraudulently disposed of part of his property, and that he has money and effects liable to satisfy his debts, which he fraudulently withholds, is not self-repugnant and contradictory. Smith *v.* Baker, 80 Ala. 318.

"While the practice is objectionable as unnecessary, we discover no valid reason, why, if two or more consistent grounds exist, the affidavit may not disclose them; or why the averment of two or more statutory causes should vitiate an attachment; which either of them stated singly is sufficient to sustain. When distinct grounds are stated in the alternative, the real ground is uncertain, as it does not clearly appear which is true; but when coupled conjunctively both are verified. The officer, before issuing the attachment, must require an affidavit, that one of the enumerated causes exist. Code, § 3255. The statement of one is essential; but there is no express or implied prohibition, that more than one shall be stated, if the debtor by his conduct has created two or more." Smith *v.* Baker, 80 Ala. 318, 319.

"In Drake on Attachment, § 101, the author observes: 'Usually the plaintiff may allege as many distinct and separate grounds of attachment, within the terms of the law, as he may deem expedient. In doing so, the several grounds should be stated cumulatively.' The rule is subject to the qualification, that the alleged grounds are consistent with each other, and that uncertainty in the affidavit shall not occur." Smith *v.* Baker, 80 Ala. 318, 319.

§ 65. —— Alternative or Disjunctive Statements.

Facts Constituting Distinct Grounds of Attachment.—An affidavit which alleges several grounds for attachment in the alternative is bad for uncertainty. Johnson *v.* Hale, 3 Stew. & P. 331; Watson *v.* Auerbach, 57 Ala. 353.

A party proceeding in attachment, must confine himself, in his affidavit, to some one of the distinct grounds on which the process is authorized, by statute, to issue; and if the affidavit states several grounds, in the disjunctive, the process will be quashed. Johnson *v.* Hale, 3 Stew. & P. 331.

An affidavit for an attachment which states that the defendant has "removed or absconded" is defective, and will vitiate the subsequent proceedings, since it states two distinct grounds of attachment in the alternative. The liberal construction given to the attachment laws, under the act of 1828 (see Aiken's Digest, page 42, § 17), will not aid such a defect. Johnson *v.* Hale, 3 Stew. & P. 331.

Facts of Same Nature or Constituting but One Ground of Attachment.—The allegation, in an affidavit for attachment, that defendant "absconds or secretes himself," etc., states but one ground of attachment, and hence is sufficient, though in the disjunctive. Cannon *v.* Logan, 5 Port. 77.

§ 66. Averm nts as to Purpose of Attachment.

Negativing Purpose of Vexing or Harassing Defendant.—An affidavit for an attachment which omits the statement required by statute, that the writ is not sued out for the purpose of vexing or harassing the defendant, is fatally defective. Saunders *v.* Cavett, 38 Ala. 51, distinguishing Calhoun *v.* Cozzens, 3 Ala. 21; Hall *v.* Brazleton, 40 Ala. 406; Hall *v.* Brazelton, 46 Ala. 359.

When an equitable attachment is sued out by an accommodation endorser on the ground that the principal debtor is fraudulently disposing of his property (Code, §§ 2954, et seq.; Session Acts 1855-6, p. 54), the complainant must make affidavit, as in analogous cases at law, that the writ is not sued out for the purpose of vexing or harassing the defendant. Saunders *v.* Cavett, 38 Ala. 51.

§ 67. Complaint or Other Pleading Accompanying Affidavit.

Necessity.—Under Code, § 2998, requiring plaintiff in attachment to file a complaint, it is error to render final judgment by default, where nothing but an affidavit for attachment is filed. Jones *v.* Howard, 42 Ala. 483; Penn *v.* Edwards, 42 Ala. 655.

§ 68. Amendment and Supplemental Affidavits.

§ 68 (1) In General.

Creation of Lien Affecting Rights of Another Attaching Creditor.—Attachment proceedings may not be amended so as to create a lien affecting the rights of another attaching creditor, previously legally fixed upon the same property. Haas *v.* Cook, 140 Ala. 670, 41 So. 731.

Conformity to Evidence.—Code 1896, § 564, provides that plaintiff in attachment may amend any defect of form or substance in the affidavit, bond, or attachment, and that no attachment must be dismissed for defects in the affidavit or bond, if plaintiff, his agent or attorney, will make a sufficient affidavit. Held to authorize the amendment of an attachment affidavit so as to conform to plaintiff's evidence showing him entitled to enforce a landlord's lien against the attached property. Sloan *v.* Hudson, 24 So. 458, 119 Ala. 27.

§ 68 (2) Defects Amendable.

In General.—Where an affidavit for attachment was defective in matters of form, it was held that it might be amended, but defects of substance, under the statute existing, were incurable. Pearsoll *v.* Middlebrook, 2 Stew. & P. 406; Shield *v.* Dothard, 59 Ala. 595; Hall *v.* Brazleton, 40 Ala. 406; Flexner *v.* Dickerson, 65 Ala. 129. See note on this point in 31 L. R. A. 425.

"In the absence of a statute authorizing it, a court has not power to allow the amendment of an affidavit for an attachment. The statute confers a limited power of amendment. 'The plaintiff, before, or during the trial, must be permitted to amend any defect of form in the affidavit.' etc. Code of 1876, § 3315. It is a defect of form only which is amendable. Defects of substance are not within the words or purposes of the statute." Flexner *v.* Dickerson, 65 Ala. 129, 132. The matters of substance in an affidavit for an attachment, under the general law, are the existence of a debt, its amount, and that it is justly due and owing, and a statutory cause for the issue of the writ, with a negation of a purpose to vex or harass the defendant. All else is matter of form. Flexner *v.* Dickerson, 65 Ala. 129, 132; Sims, etc., Co. *v.* Jacobson & Co., 51 Ala. 186; Tommey *v.* Gamble & Son, 66 Ala. 469.

Where an affidavit in attachment stated, that in consequence of the removal of the goods and effects of defendant, ordinary process could not be served on him, and the writ alleged the same thing—the proceeding was not conformable to the statute, and the defect reaching to the affidavit—could not be amended. Napper *v.* Noland, 9 Port. 218.

The statute now provides that "the plaintiff, before or during the trial, must be permitted to amend any defect or form or substance in the affidavit." Richards *v.* Bestor, 90 Ala. 352, 8 So. 30. See Sloan *v.* Hudson, 119 Ala. 27, 24 So. 458; McCain Bros. *v.* Street, 136 Ala. 625, 33 So. 872; Rosenberg *v.* Claflin Co., 95 Ala. 249, 10 So. 521; Ex parte Nicrosi, 103 Ala. 104, 15 So. 507; Dittman, etc., Shoe Co. *v.* Mixon, 120 Ala. 206, 24 So. 847.

Where pleas in abatement in attachment alleging formal defects in the affidavit were filed, it was proper to allow plaintiff to amend the affidavit before passing on the pleas, under Code 1896, § 564, declaring that the attachment law shall be liberally construed, and authorizing plaintiff to amend for defects of form or substance before or during trial. Simpson *v.* East, 27 So. 436, 124 Ala. 293.

Recitals as to Authority of Affiant.—An affidavit for an attachment made by one who is in fact the agent or attorney of the plaintiff, but which fails to show that fact, may be amended so as to disclose it. Paulhaus *v.* Leber, 54 Ala. 91, cited on this point in note in 31 L. R. A. 425.

Caption, Signature and Jurat.—The failure of the clerk to certify an affidavit for attachment is a defect of form amendable before or during trial. Hyde *v.* Adams, 80 Ala. 111, cited in note in 31 L. R. A. 425.

Under Code, § 564, providing that the plaintiff in attachment shall be permitted to amend any defect of form or substance in the affidavit at any time before or during the trial plaintiff was entitled to amend an unsigned attachment affidavit by filing a new affidavit properly signed. McCain Bros. *v.* Street, 33 So. 872, 136 Ala. 625.

Code, § 527, requires an attachment affidavit to be subscribed by the party making it; and § 564 provides that the plaintiff in attachment before or during the trial shall be permitted to amend any defect in the affidavit. Held that, where an attachment affidavit was not subscribed by the affiant, it was proper to allow it to be amended by adding his signature thereto. Savage *v.* Atkins, 27 So. 514, 124 Ala. 378.

"There are two sections of the Code in which the affidavit required to authorize the issuance of attachment is referred to; these are §§ 2930 and 2961. In the former the oath is required to be reduced to writing and subscribed by the party making it, and in the latter it is only required to be an 'affidavit in writing.' The latter, therefore, may be completed without the signature of the affiant. * * * Then, the signature to the affidavit thus required is a matter of form, rather than substance, as the oath would be sufficient without the subscription. It is then amendable." Watts *v.* Womack, 44 Ala. 605, 608, cited on this point in note in 31 L. R. A. 425.

Averments as to Purpose of Attachment.—Failure to aver that the attachment is not sued out for the purpose of vexing or harassing the defendant is a defect which can not be cured by amendment. Saunders *v.* Cavett, 38 Ala. 51; Hall *v.* Brazleton, 40 Ala. 406; Hall *v.* Brazelton, 46 Ala. 359. See note in 31 L. R. A. 425.

Averments as to Parties.—Under Code 1896, § 564, providing that plaintiff in attachment may amend any defect in the affidavit, it may be amended by inserting the name of an additional party defendant. McKissack *v.* Witz, 25 So. 21, 120 Ala. 412.

Under Code, § 2998, providing that plaintiff, before or during trial, must be permitted to amend any defect of form or substance in the affidavit, and no attachment must be dismissed for any defect therein, if the plaintiff will make a sufficient affidavit, a plaintiff corporation, having stated its name correctly in the original affidavit, may file an amended affidavit averring its corporate character. Rosenberg *v.* H. B. Claflin Co., 95 Ala. 249, 10 So. 521, cited on this point in note in 31 L. R. A. 422.

Under Rev. Code, § 2990, allowing plaintiff in attachment to amend any defect of form in his affidavit, an affidavit in attachment of one firm against another may be amended by inserting the names of the individual members of each firm. Sims *v.* Jacobson, 51 Ala. 186, cited in note in 31 L. R. A. 425.

Since Code, § 2998, permits the affidavit bond and writ in attachment to be amended to cure "any defect in form or substance," the entity of defendant being unquestioned, it is no error to allow an amendment as to the name from "the R. Grocery Company, a corporation," to "E. R., a married woman, doing business" by the duly-recorded consent of her husband, "under the name and style of the R. Grocery Company." Ex parte Nicrosi, 103 Ala. 104, 15 So. 507, cited in note in 31 L. R. A. 422.

The affidavit and writ, in an action commenced by attachment against the W. Sawmill Co., may be amended to make the action against G., doing business as the W. Sawmill; the complaint filed following the amendment. First Nat. Bank *v.* Gobey, 44 So. 535, 152 Ala. 517.

Averments as to Indebtedness and Cause of Action.—The complaint was in three counts, each claiming the statutory penalty of $200 imposed on a mortgagee whose mortgage has been satisfied for failure to enter the satisfaction of record, on request, and each based on a separate request. An affidavit of attachment in the suit, describing the demand as "the sum of $600," was amended so as to describe it as "in the sum of $600, by three statutory penalties of $200 each." Held, that the amendment was justified by Code 1896, § 564, authorizing amendments of "any defect of form or substance in the affidavit, bond, or attachment." George F. Dittman Boot & Shoe Co. *v.* Mixon, 24 So. 847, 120 Ala. 206.

An affidavit for an attachment, which states that the defendants "are or will be justly indebted," may be amended by striking out the words "or will be." Tommey *v.* Gamble, 66 Ala. 469, cited on this point in note in 31 L. R. A. 425.

§ 69. Filing.

Time of Filing Affidavit That Defendant Is an Inhabitant of the State.—The requisite fact that defendant in a judicial attachment is an inhabitant of the state may be shown by affidavit filed in term time or vacation. Blair *v.* Cleveland, 1 Stew. 421.

§ 70. Variance.

As to variance between complaint or petition and writ or warrant, see post, "Variance," § 91.

In General.—A variance between the affidavit and complaint in attachment can not be taken advantage of by demurrer to the complaint. Odom *v.* Shackleford, 44 Ala. 331.

Averments as to Amount of Demand.—There is no variance between an affidavit that defendant is indebted to plaintiff in the sum of $250, for rent of land due November 1, 1885, and a complaint which claims $250, due on defendant's bond, payable November 1, 1885; it not appearing that the bond is a different contract from that set forth in the affidavit. Perkerson *v.* Snodgrass, 85 Ala. 137, 4 So. 752.

§ 71. Defects, Objections, and Waiver.

As to defects as ground for quashing writ, see post, "Defects or Irregularities in Proceedings," § 138.

Right of Objection.—Where defendant in attachment replevied the property and sold it, another attaching creditor, who never acquired any lien or right to the property levied on and replevied, could not question irregularities in the other attachment. Haas *v.* Cook, 148 Ala. 670, 41 So. 731.

Failure to Make Timely Objection.—Defects in the attachment affidavit, unless presented on plea in abatement or on motion to quash, are not reviewable on error. Watson *v.* Auerbach, 57 Ala. 353; Burt *v.* Parish & Co., 9 Ala. 211.

"A variance between the amount of the debt claimed in the affidavit for the attachment, and the amount claimed in the complaint, must be taken advantage of in the trial court. The objection can not be made on appeal for the first time." Fears *v.* Thompson, 82 Ala. 294, 2 So. 719, 720; McAbee *v.* Parker, 78 Ala. 573.

"The question as to a variance between bond and affidavit, if one that the claimants could raise, can not be raised for the first time after appeal to this court." McCain Bros. *v.* Street, 136 Ala. 625, 33 So. 872, 873. See Fears *v.* Thompson, 82 Ala. 294, 2 So. 719.

Where an attachment was issued against a nonresident, and after due notice by publication a judgment by default was given, defendant can not complain on appeal that the amount named in the affidavit for attachment was less than that claimed in the complaint subsequently filed and for which judgment was given. Decatur, etc., Imp. Co. *v.* Crass, 97 Ala. 524, 12 So. 41.

Collateral Attack.—Defects in the affidavit for an attachment, and irregularities in the proceedings, which would prove fatal on error or appeal, do not render the judgment void; and it can not be collaterally imposed on account of such defects and irregularities. Martin *v.* Hall, 70 Ala. 421.

§ 72. Failure to Make.

Ground for Plea in Abatement.—The want of an affidavit, in a suit commenced by attachment, must be taken advantage of by plea in abatement, and it does not vary the case that the attachment is sued out against a non-resident. Jones *v.* Pope, 6 Ala. 154; Kirkman *v.* Patton, 19 Ala. 32.

(C) SECURITY.

§ 73. Necessity and Purpose.

As to issuance of alias writs without additional bond, see post, "Alias Writs," § 90.

Necessity.—Though a bill in chancery sets out facts bringing complainant's case within Act 1846, § 8, allowing an attachment to issue in suits in equity, his bill can not be sustained when he has not filed the bond required by § 3 of such act. McGown *v.* Sprague, 23 Ala. 524.

Code 1852, § 2954, authorizes an equitable attachment under the same circumstances and conditions as attachments are issued at law. Section 2547 provides that, before a legal attachment shall issue, plaintiff shall execute a bond in the manner provided. Held, that an equitable attachment was not authorized without the filing of a bond complying with § 2507. Smith *v.* Moore, 35 Ala. 76.

Code 1852, § 2506, requires the officer, before issuing an attachment, to require a bond. Held, that a proceeding under the former statute could not be maintained where no bond was given, or an attachment asked, though an injunction is prayed for against the third party in whose hands the property is. Smith *v.* Moore, 35 Ala. 76.

Under § 2989, Rev. Code, an attachment may be abated if issued without a sufficient bond. A bond, defective in matter of substance, is in legal contemplation equivalent to no bond whatever. Hall *v.* Brazelton, 46 Ala. 359, 362.

Purpose.—It is the general rule to require, as a condition to the issuance of an attachment, that the plaintiff shall enter into bond, such as the statute prescribes. The bond is intended to impose an additional restraint to the affidavit, against the wrongful suing out of the attachment; by fixing a definite liability upon him and his sureties, as indemnity to the defendant against loss, from the wrongful and vexatious use of the process. Ex parte Damon, 103 Ala. 477, 15 So. 862, 863.

"The bond in attachment, and in garnishment, which is only a species of attachment, is intended to protect defendants against an unnecessary resort to this extraordinary remedy. If there is no ground for such process, damages may be recovered, although the debt claimed is actually due, and is recovered." Bolling *v.* Tate, 65 Ala. 417, 424.

§ 74. Parties by and to Whom to Be Given.

By Whom to Be Given in General.—Plaintiff in an attachment suit by a non-resident need not be a party to the bond. Jackson *v.* Stanley, 2 Ala. 326.

To Whom to Be Given.—In an action against several persons, an attachment bond is properly made payable to defendants jointly, although the writ may be levied on the individual property of one only. Hadley *v.* Bryars, 58 Ala. 139.

§ 75. Form and Requisites of Bond or Undertaking.

Conditions.—It is not necessary that the attachment bond should contain a condition for payment of costs. Peters *v.* Bower, Minor 69.

A bond in original attachment conditioned on plaintiff prosecuting the attachment to effect, and paying defendant the damages he may sustain by the wrongful or vexatious suing out of the attachment, is sufficient under the act of 1814, prescribing the conditions of an attachment bond. Saltmarsh & Beck *v.* Evans, 1 Stew. 132.

Description of Parties.—The addition of the word "Agent" to the name of one of the obligors in an attachment bond does not affect its validity. Hadley *v.* Bryars, 58 Ala. 139.

It was no objection to the validity of an attachment bond, on which suit was brought, that the names of two of the defendants who signed as sureties at the bottom did not appear in the body of the bond. McLean *v.* Wright, 35 So. 45, 137 Ala. 644, 97 Am. St. Rep. 67.

In an action by a partnership, commenced by attachment, if the individual names of the several partners are not stated in the bond, the defect is good matter for plea in abatement. Sims, etc., Co. *v.* Jacobson & Co., 51 Ala. 186.

§ 76. Sufficiency and Justification of Sureties.

Insufficient Security.—A bond must be regarded as defective, when it is insufficient in security, as well as when it is lacking in some particular, which, while it does not render it absolutely void, does render it an imperfect obligation for the purposes intended. Ex parte Damon, 103 Ala. 477, 15 So. 862, 863.

Residence.—The bond of a nonresident in attachment need not show that the sureties reside in the state. Jackson *v.* Stanley, 2 Ala. 326.

A clerk can not refuse to approve an attachment bond because the sureties are not residents of the county, in the absence of any statute requiring the sureties to be residents. Mobile Mut. Ins. Co. *v.* Cleveland, 76 Ala. 321.

§ 77. Approval of Bond or Undertaking.

Indorsement on Bond.—If an attachment bond is in fact approved by the clerk, filed, and the attachment issued on the faith of it, it is not necessary that his approval shall also be indorsed on it. Hyde *v.* Adams 80 Ala. 111.

§ 78. Amendment of Bond or Undertaking.

As to additional or new security, see post, "Additional or New Security," § 79.

In General.—Section 2998 of the Code, which relates to attachment statutes in general, provides that the plaintiff, before or during the trial, must be permitted to amend any defect of form oı substance in the bond. Richards *v.* Bestor, 90 Ala. 352, 8 So. 30. See Hall *v.* Brazelton, 46 Ala. 359, 362.

A defective bond is not a sufficient cause for quashing proceedings by attachment, unless plaintiff declines executing a perfect bond. Planters' & Merchants' Bank *v.* Andrews, 8 Port. 404; Lowe *v.* Derrick, 9 Port. 415; Alford *v.* Johnson, 9 Port. 320.

Under Rev. Code, § 2990, allowing plaintiff in attachment to amend any defect of form in the bond, a bond given by plaintiffs in attachment by one firm again t another may be amended by inserting the individual names of both firms. Sims *v.* Jacobson, 51 Ala. 186.

For a variance between "Abraham" and "Abram," in the Christian name of plaintiff in the affidavit and bond in attachment, the latter may be amended. Alford *v.* Johnson, 9 Port. 320.

Under Code, 1896, § 564, providing that plaintiff in attachment may amend any defect in the bond, it may be amended by inserting the name of an additional party. McKissack *v.* Witz, 25 So. 21, 120 Ala. 412.

Effect of Failure to Amend.—If plaintiff, when required by the court to amend, decline doing so, the attachment may be quashed. Lowry *v.* Stowe, 7 Port. 483.

§ 79. Additional or New Security.

As to amendment of bond or undertaking, see ante, "Amendment of Bond or Undertaking," § 78.

Right to Give Additional or New Security.—When the bond or undertaking given to procure an attachment is insufficient or defective, additional or new security may be given. Lowry *v.* Stowe, 7 Port. 483; Planters' & Merchants' Bank *v.* Andrews, 8 Port. 404; Lowe *v.* Derrick, 9 Port. 415; Jackson *v.* Stanley, 2 Ala. 326. See Ex parte Damon, 103 Ala. 477, 15 So. 862.

"An attachment must not be dismissed for any defect in, or want of, a bond, if the plaintiff, his agent or attorney, is willing to give or substitute a sufficient bond." Hall *v.* Brazelton, 46 Ala. 359, 362. See Richards *v.* Bestor, 90 Ala. 352, 8 So. 30.

"A defective or insufficient bond does not authorize the court to abate an attachment, if the plaintiff is willing to execute another and sufficient bond; though if he declines to do so, the attachment may be abated. (Section 3515.) There is no express statutory requisition, that the bond shall be endorsed approved by the officer issuing the attachment. The reception of the bond by the clerk, the issuing the attachment by virtue thereof, endorsing it filed on the day the attachment was issued, and its retention among the papers of the case on the files of the court, sufficiently manifest his approval. Hyde *v.* Adams, 80 Ala. 111, 113.

There is no difference between a void bond and a defective bond, given for the prosecution of an attachment, and in either case, it is the duty of the court to permit the plaintiff to substitute a sufficient bond. Jackson *v.* Stanley, 2 Ala. 326.

Power of Court to Require New Additional Security.—Code, § 2998, provides that plaintiff in attachment, before or during the trial, may amend any defect of form or of substance in the bond, "and no attachment must be dismissed for any defect in the bond," if a sufficient bond is given. Held, that where the sureties on an attachment bond became insolvent, to the knowledge of the court, it may require an additional bond, with good sureties. Ex parte Damon, 103 Ala. 477, 15 So. 862.

§ 80. Defects, Objections, and Waiver.

As to defects as ground for quashing writ, see post, "Defects or Irregularities in Proceedings," § 138.

In General.—It is the right of the defendant to have the attachment dissolved whenever, at any stage of the cause, the bond shall become defective or insufficient, as an indemnity, on account of the insolvency of its securities; but the plaintiff should be accorded the right of maintaining his cause by repairing a defect brought about by no fault of his. Ex parte Damon, 103 Ala. 477, 15 So. 862, 863.

Where no objection appears on the face of an attachment bond, the court should not quash the proceedings under it for intrinsic objections thereto, unless the plaintiff refuse to remove the objection by the substitution of a perfect bond. Jackson *v.* Stanley, 2 Ala. 326.

Waiver and Objections.—Defects in an attachment bond are waived unless presented on plea in abatement, or on motion to quash. Watson *v.* Auerbach, 57 Ala. 353.

§ 81. Failure to Give.

Objections to Failure to Give Bond.—If an attachment be issued without the affidavit and bond required by the statute, the writ can only be abated by plea of the defendant. Until abated, the writ is valid, and its levy on the property of the defendant creates a lien that can not be displaced or held for naught merely by showing such irregularities in the process as would have entitled the defendant in the writ to abate it on plea. Kirkman *v.* Patton, 19 Ala. 32, 33.

The want of a bond in attachment must be taken advantage of by plea in abatement, even in actions against nonresidents. Jones *v.* Pope, 6 Ala. 154.

IV. WRIT OR WARRANT.

As to quashing or vacating writ or warrant, see post, "Quashing, Vacating, Dissolution or Abandonment," VII. As return, see post, "Return," IX. As to service, see post, "Service of Writ or Warrant," § 99. As to writ or warrant as protection to an officer, see the title SHERIFFS AND CONSTABLES. As to writ or warrant in justices court, see the title JUSTICES OF THE PEACE.

§ 82. Authority to Issue.

Notary Public.—Under a constitutional provision giving notaries public the same jurisdiction as justice of the peace, a notary can not issue writs of attachment, which power is a special statutory authority conferred on justices, and is not included under the term jurisdiction, which means the power to hear and determine causes. Vann *v.* Adams, 71 Ala. 475.

Whatever of jurisdiction is conferred upon justices of the peace, and whatever of power or authority of that jurisdiction they may exercise in the administration of that jurisdiction, are conferred by the constitution on notaries public appointed by the governor to "have and exercise the same jurisdiction as justices of the peace;" but such notaries are not thereby clothed with, nor can they exercise, those special powers granted to justices of the peace, which form no part of their jurisdiction, and which are not necessary to render that jurisdiction effectual. Vann *v.* Adams, etc., Co., 71 Ala. 475.

A notary public, who is ex officio a justice of the peace, has no authority to issue an attachment returnable to the circuit court. Vann *v.* Adams, 71 Ala. 475; Nordlinger *v.* Gordon, 72 Ala. 239.

A notary public with the jurisdiction of a justice of the peace has authority to issue an attachment returnable before himself for the collection of a demand within a justice's jurisdiction. Rice *v.* Watts, 71 Ala. 593.

Clerks of Court.—Under the acts of 1833 (Clay's Dig., p. 54, § 1) and 1845 (Pamph. Acts 1844-45, p. 137), the clerk of the court may issue a judicial attachment against defendant who avoids the service of process, on the filing of the required affidavit, either in vacation or term time. Garner *v.* Johnson, 22 Ala. 494.

Code, §§ 2929, 2931, provide that any civil action may be commenced by attachment, and authorize a clerk of the circuit court to issue such attachment for the collection of "any moneyed demand," the amount of which can be certainly ascertained. But in actions to recover "damages for a breach of a contract, when the damages are not certian or liquidated," or when "the action sounds in damages merely," only the judge or chancellor can issue the attachment, Held, in an action to recover damages for the removal of four bales of cotton on which plaintiff held a landlord's lien for rent and advances, that the clerk had authority to issue an attachment. Atkinson *v.* James, 96 Ala. 214, 10 So. 846.

"The term 'moneyed demand' ordinarily is of comprehensive meaning, and may arise out of contract or breach of duty. Whether its collection be enforced by actions ex contractu or ex delicto does not alter its character as a moneyed demand for which an attachment will lie. The statute limits the authority of the clerk to issue attachments for a moneyed demand to cases in 'which the amount can be certainly ascertained.' The term 'moneyed demand,' as used in § 2739 of the Code—which provides that, 'if suit be brought on any moneyed demand for a less amount than that of which the court has jurisdiction, the suit must be dismissed,' etc., was construed by this court many years ago in King *v.* Parmer, 34 Ala. 416, to apply only to actions ex contractu. In construing that section, the court stated the context controlled the meaning of the phrase, and in the opinion confined the definition given to the term to the section as there employ d." In the same case Chief Justice A. J. Walker, arguendo, held that 'moneyed demand,' as used in § 2503, 1852, which is the same as § 2929 of the present Code, included trover, an action in tort. This decision was reaffirmed in Mills *v.* Long, 58 Ala. 458, and as there construed the act has been readopted into the present Code. Section 2934 of the Code provides that before an attachment shall issue to enforce the collection of a demand 'for a breach of contract, when the damages are not certain or liquidated,' or 'when the action sounds in damages merely,' an additional 'affidavit in writing must be made of the special facts and circumstances,' so as to enable the officer 'to determine the amount for which a levy must be made,' etc. In such cases the clerk has no authority to issue an attachment. Attachment may be issued in trover by the clerk, the recovery in such cases being clearly ascertainable from the value of material things. So in action on the case, if in the particular action the character of the demand is such that the recoverable damages are fixed by a legal standard, such as are ascertainable from the value of material things, the clerk may issue the attachment. This is clearly the meaning of the statute, for it is provided in the third and fourth subdivisions of § 2929 'that, when the damages are not certain or liquidated,' or when the 'action sounds in damages merely,' the clerk can not issue the attachment, while it is expressly provided that to enforce legal moneyed demands, in all other cases, whether ex contractu or ex delicto, he may issue the attachment." Atkinson *v.* James, 96 Ala. 214, 10 So. 846, 847.

A deputy clerk—that is, one duly appointed and qualified—has full power to transact all business of his principal (Code, § 676, subd. 2); and an attachment issued by him is not void for want of authority. Minniece *v.* Jeter, 65 Ala. 222.

An attachment, issued by a deputy clerk who is performing the duties of the office under appointment by his principal, is not voidable, nor subject to be abated on plea, because he has never taken the official oath prescribed by law; his official acts, like those of any other officer de facto, having the same force and effect, so far as the public and third persons are concerned, as the acts of an officer de jure. Joseph *v.* Cawthorn, 74 Ala. 411.

The clerk of the city court of Mobile has no authority to issue original attachments. Stevenson *v.* O'Hara, 27 Ala. 362; Matthews *v.* Sands, 29 Ala. 136; Lewis *v.* Dubose, 29 Ala. 219; Goldsmith *v.* Stetson & Co., 39 Ala. 183; Flash, etc., Co. *v.* Paul, etc., Co., 29 Ala. 141.

Although the city court of Mobile is by statute vested with all the powers of the several circuit courts, except as to actions to try titles to land, yet there is no statute conferring authority on its clerk to issue original attachments, which, being a summary remedy in derogation of the common law, must be specially conferred by statute, or it does not exist; and therefore, where there is a judgment by default, in a suit commenced in that court by such original attachment issued by its clerk, the whole proceeding will be quashed on error. Stevenson *v.* O'Hara, 27 Ala. 362. See Flash, etc., Co. *v.* Paul, etc., Co., 29 Ala. 141.

Issuance on Sunday.—It is irregular to issue an attachment on Sunday, though it may be levied or served on that day; but, if the writ, though actually issued on that day, appears on its face to have been issued on another day, the court can not direct the clerk to amend the date, and then quash the writ, on motion, on account of the irregularity. Matthews *v.* Ansley, 31 Ala. 20.

The issue of an original attachment by a clerk is a judicial act, but its levy or service by a proper officer is a ministerial act. Matthews *v.* Ansley, 31 Ala. 20.

§ 83. Order of Allowance.

Necessity.—Under Code, § 2956, authorizing the issuance of equitable attachments on legal demands; and § 2963, providing that the chancellor, judge, or registrar of the court in which the bill is filed "may make all necessary orders" for the issuing of such attachments—a writ issued without a preliminary order is a nullity, though the allegations of the bill may entitle complainant to the order. McKenzie *v.* Bentley, 30 Ala. 139.

§ 84. Form and Requisites in General.

Clerical Errors.—The test of a writ of attachment being the words, "Witness, W. P. S., clerk of said circuit court," when the writ is returnable to the city court, and recites that complaint on oath had been made "to me, W. P. S., clerk of the city court;" the word circuit will be considered a mere clerical error, cured by the judgment, if not previously objected to. Quere, whether the clerk of the circuit court may not issue an attachment returnable to the city court within his county. Free *v.* Howard, 44 Ala. 195.

§ 85. Direction to Particular Officer or County.

To what Officer Addressed.—Although the proper direction of process of attachment is, to the sheriff, yet, a judgment will not be reversed, because the attachment is directed to any lawful officer, if it is executed by the proper officer. Ware *v.* Todd, 1 Ala. 199.

Under Code, § 2939, declaring that no objection shall be taken to a writ of attachment for any defect in form, if the essential matters are set forth, the direction, "To Any Lawful Sheriff of" a specified county, instead of "To Any Lawful Sheriff of the state of Alabama," as required by law, is an immaterial defect, if the writ is levied in the county named. Blair *v.* Miller, 42 Ala. 308.

To What County Addressed.—The subsequent act of 1837 (p. 65, § 12), which amend and consolidate all the laws relating to attachments, and which authorizes branch writs to as many counties as may be desired, must be considered a legislative exposition of the act of 1833. It follows from this, that under the attachment act of 1833, the writ could be executed only in the county to which it was returnable, though it be addressed to "Any Sheriff of the State." Starke *v.* Marshall, 3 Ala. 44.

§ 86. Description of Parties.

Omission of Individual Name of Partner.—In an action by a partnership, commenced by attachment, if the individual name of the several partners are not stated in the writ, the defect is good matter for plea in abatement. Sims, etc., Co. *v.* Jacobson & Co., 51 Ala. 186.

§ 87. Recital of Cause of Action.

Necessity or Propriety of Recital.—Act 1807 (Aik. Dig. 278), which provides that the cause of action shall be indorsed on the writ, applies only to initiatory process issued from courts in which clerks are necessary officers, and does not extend to attachments issued by a judicial officer. Lowry *v.* Stowe, 7 Port. 483.

The indorsement on a writ of attachment is no part of the record, the cause of action not being required to be indorsed, and will not be looked to to ascertain the nature of the demand forming the basis of the action. Planters' & Merchants' Bank *v.* Andrews, 8 Port. 404.

The form of a writ of attachment, prescribed by the statute, does not recognize the seal of the justice issuing the same, and the seal placed immediately after the signature of the justice is a sufficient compliance with the law. Lowry *v.* Stowe, 7 Port. 483.

§ 88. Directions for Service and Return.

As to service of writ or warrant, see post, "Service of Writ or Warrant," § 99.

Effect of Mistake in Direction.—Under Code, § 2939, declaring that, in attachment proceedings, "no objection shall be taken for any defect in form, if the essential matters are set forth," the writ is not invalidated for failure to insert therein the term of court to which it is returnable. Blair *v.* Miller, 42 Ala. 308.

Where an attachment is issued in one county, returnable to a court in another county, the objection may be taken on error, although it was not made in the court below, if it has not been waived by appearing and pleading to the merits. Brooks *v.* Godwin, 8 Ala. 296.

A clerical mistake in making a writ of attachment issued in L. county, returnable to the court of B. county, arising from the use of a blank, prepared for use in B. county does not render the writ void, where all the other papers show that the writ was issued returnable to L. county, and no one was misled by the mistake, and defendant appeared in the court, and the bond filed by claimant recited that the writ was returnable to L. county. Carter *v.* O'Bryan, 105 Ala. 305, 16 So. 894.

§ 89. Amendment.

In General.—"Section 2998, which relates to attachment suits in general, provides: 'The attachment law must be liberally construed to advance the manifest intent of the law, and the plaintiff, before or during the trial, must be permitted to amend any defect of form or substance in the * * * attachment.'" Richards *v.* Bestor, 90 Ala. 352, 8 So. 30.

Where an attachment is sued as auxiliary to a suit commenced in the ordinary mode, a mistake, in the writ of attachment, of the time when the court is held in which the original writ is pending, is amendable. Scott *v.* Macy, 3 Ala. 250.

Code, § 2941, provides that writs of attachment must be directed to "any sheriff of the state," and be in a form prescribed therein, but that no objection shall be taken for any defect in form, if the essential matters are set forth. Held, that a writ improperly directed "to the sheriff or any constable of said county" is amendable on trial, under Code, § 2998, providing that such writs shall be amended for any defect in form or substance before or during trial. Herring *v.* Kelly, 96 Ala. 559, 11 So. 600.

Parties.—Where the affidavit describes plaintiff by the Christian name of "Abraham," and in the writ he is described as "Abram," the writ may be amended. Alford *v.* Johnson, 9 Port. 320.

Under Code 1896, § 564, providing that plaintiff in attachment may amend any defect in the writ, it may be amended by inserting the name of an additional party. McKissack *v.* Witz, 25 So. 21, 120 Ala. 412.

Under Rev. Code, § 2990, allowing plaintiff to amend any defect of form in the attachment, an attachment of one firm against another may be amended by inserting the names of the individual members of each firm. Sims *v.* Jacobson, 51 Ala. 186.

§ 90. Alias Writs.

As to simultaneous successive attachment, see ante, "Simultaneous and Successive Attachments," § 15.

Issuance of Alias Writs without Additional Affidavit or Bond.—Branch writs of attachment, authorized to be issued to any county of the state in which property of the debtor may be found, by Code, § 545, authorizes the issuance of such writs without an additional affidavit or bond. Simpson *v.* East, 27 So. 436, 124 Ala. 293.

§ 91. Variance.

As to variance between affidavit and complaint or proof, see ante, "Variance," § 70.

In General.—A variance between the writ of attachment and the bond and affidavit, if available at all to defendant, must be peaded in abatement. Goldsticker *v.* Stetson, 21 Ala. 404.

Writ and Affidavit.—Attachment materially variant from the affidavit will be quashed. Woodley *v.* Shirley, Minor 14.

§ 92. Defects, Objections, and Waiver.

As to defects as ground for quashing writ, see post, "Forthcoming or Delivery Bonds," § 195.

Who May Interpose Objections.—A claimant of attached property can not take advantage of defects in the process which do not render it absolutely void. Carter *v.* O'Bryan, 105 Ala. 305, 16 So. 894.

An attachment issued by a notary public, and returnable to the circuit court, being absolutely void, a claimant in a trial of the right of property can take advantage of that defect. Nordlinger *v.* Gordon, 72 Ala. 239.

Waiver of Defects.—An appearance by defendant in an attachment suit is not a waiver of a fatal defect in the writ, on account of the want of jurisdiction on the part of the officer by whom it was issued; nor is it a bar to a subsequent action for damages against the attaching creditor. Stetson *v.* Goldsmith, 30 Ala. 602.

Although Code, § 2571, provides that when a suit is commenced by attachment the fact that plaintiff claims that defendant has waived his statutory exemptions must be indorsed on the writ, yet failure to do so is cured when the complaint alleges such fact, and defendant has appeared and answered. Hutcheson *v.* Powell, 92 Ala. 619, 9 So. 170.

"The purpose of requiring indorsement to be made on the writ of attachment is to provide a mode of presenting this special claim so that defendant may have notice thereof, and an opportunity to contest it. As in suits commenced by attachment the complaint is not required to be filed until the return term of the writ, and as judgment may then be entered without other notice to the defendant than that of the levy of the attachment, unless some special mode of giving notice of the claim of a waiver of exemptions was provided, a recital of such waiver in the judgment entry might be without the defendant having had notice in any manner that the claim of such waiver was made. The indorsement on the writ gives notice in brief form of this special claim, as the statements of the amount of the indebtedness in the affidavit and writ give notice of the plaintiff's claim in that regard. The levy and the statement thereof in writing or by publication to the defendant constitute the statutory notice of the contents of the paper required to be filed prior to the levy." Hutcheson *v.* Powell, 92 Ala. 619, 9 So. 170.

Where a defendant in attachment proceedings appears in court, and files pleas in bar to the suit, he waives all defects in the issuance of the attachment. Carter *v.* O'Bryan, 105 Ala. 305, 16 So. 894.

V. LEVY, LIEN, AND CUSTODY AND DISPOSITION OF PROPERTY.

As to wrongful or excessive levy as ground of action for damages, see post, "Damages," § 211. As to duties to sheriff or constable, see the title SHERIFFS AND CONSTABLES. As to effect of discharge in bankruptcy, see the title BANKRUPTCY. As to fees of officers for levy and return, see the title SHERIFFS AND CONSTABLES. As to levy of property in justices courts, see the title JUSTICES OF THE PEACE. As to liabilities of officer growing out of levy or failure to levy, see the title SHERIFFS AND CONSTABLES. As to detection and enforcement of right of exemption, see the titles EXEMPTIONS; HOMESTEAD. As to right of attaching creditor to redeem from execution sale, see the title EXECUTION.

§ 93. Authority to Levy.

Persons Authorized.—A constable has no authority, in this state, to levy or serve an original attachment, issued for a sum exceeding fifty dollars, and returnable to the circuit court; and a judgment by default, predicated on such void levy, is absolutely void. Martin *v.* Dollar, 32 Ala. 422; Brinsfield *v.* Austin, 39 Ala. 227.

Where a writ of attachment is addressed to "any sheriff" of the state, and is executed by an individual who has no legal deputation, the sheriff can not ratify the levy to the prejudice of other creditors. Perkins *v.* Reed, 14 Ala. 536.

A writ of attachment was directed "to any constable of said county," and was executed by the sheriff. Held that, under section 731, Code Ala. 1876, providing that "the sheriff is authorized to execute all mesne and final process which is required of constables," the sheriff was authorized to execute the writ. Bain *v.* Mitchell, 2 So. 706, 82 Ala. 304.

Property Situated without Limits of County.—An attachment levied by a sheriff on property situated entirely without the limits of his county is void. Jones *v.* Baxter, 41 So. 781, 146 Ala. 620.

§ 94. Mode and Sufficiency of Levy.

§ 95. —— In General.

Service of Garnishment.—The levy of an attachment by the service of a garnishment on a person supposed to be indebted to the defendant, is sufficient to sustain an action on the bond, although the garnishee is discharged on his answer denying any indebtedness, and a judgment against the defendant is thereby defeated. Flournoy *v.* Lyon & Co., 70 Ala. 308.

In attachment, jurisdiction may be acquired by service of garnishment on defendant's debtor, which will be as full and complete as could have been acquired by a levy of the attachment on real estate, or on visible, tangible chattels, capable of manuel seizure; and the garnishment being merely incidental and auxiliary to the attachment, errors intervening therein can not affect the validity of the judgment rendered against the defendant. Betancourt *v.* Eberlin, 71 Ala. 461. See Thompson *v.* Allen, 4 Stew. & P. 184; Tillinghast *v.* Johnson, 5 Ala. 514; Cleaveland *v.* State, 34 Ala. 254.

§ 96. —— Personal Property in General.

Actual Possession or Custody of Property.—To constitute a levy of an attachment on personal property, the officer must assume dominion over the property; he must not only have a view of it, but must assert his title to it by such an act as, but for the protection of the process, would make him liable as a trespasser. Abrams *v.* Johnson, 65 Ala. 465; Goode *v.* Longmire, 35 Ala. 668, 673.

"In levying on merchandise, a part of a stock of goods, and, even in perfecting a levy of an entire stock, the officer must have some time to ascertain what goods are required, or what goods there are, and to make an inventory of them. He must obtain control, to make a levy. Murfree, Sher., § 523. And no matter in whose house they may be, if not in a dwelling, he may, after demand and refusal, forcibly enter and levy if the goods are subject to the process in his hands: and he may remain in such house for a reasonably sufficient time to perfect the levy, and remove the goods." Pollak *v.* Searcy, 84 Ala. 259, 4 So. 137, 138.

Sufficiency of Levy.—An attachment issued against the estate of Charles G. Miller, William J. Wright and Thomas R. Crews; the writ was indorsed thus—"I do hereby authorize R. Thorn, as my special deputy, to execute the within attachment, 10th February, 1841. M. E. Gary, Sheriff S. C." "Levied on four bags marked T. R. C., also twenty-one bags W. J. W., also fifteen bags marked C. G. Miller, as the property of the defendants,

M. E. Gary, S. S. C. by R. Thorn, D. S." Held, that the return sufficiently showed that the property levied on was the defendants. Miller *v.* McMillan, 4 Ala. 527.

An arrangement by a constable levying an attachment with another to gather growing corn held not to constitute a levy. Sells *v.* Price, 3 Ala. App. 534, 57 So. 265.

§ 97. —— Shares of Stock.

Mode of Levy.—Under Code, § 1673, declaring that shares of stock in a corporation may be attached by making the prescribed indorsement on the writ, and giving notice to the custodian of the books of the corporation, oral notice to such officer is sufficient. Abels *v.* Planters' & Merchants' Ins. Co., 92 Ala. 382, 9 So. 423.

§ 98. Property Levied on under Other Process.

Property Levied on by Same Officer.—Where a sheriff having in his hands an attachment at law, which he has not yet levied, receives a writ of seizure issued by the chancery court against the same defendant, he must execute the writ of seizure only, unless he can find property not embraced in it, on which he can levy the attachment at law; otherwise a conflict of authority would arise, and a court of law can not examine chancery process. Read *v.* Sprague, 34 Ala. 101.

§ 99. Service of Writ or Warrant.

See post, "Notice of Levy." As to direction for service in writ or warrant, see ante, "Directions for Service and Return," § 88.

§ 100. Notice of Levy.

Necessity.—Where the attachment is not sued out against a nonresident, but is levied on the defendant's goods and chattels, more than twenty days before the case is placed on the docket, and no garnishee is summoned, there is no law requiring any notice to be given before taking judgment by default. Letondal *v.* Huguenin, 26 Ala. 552.

Mode and Sufficiency in General.—The notice of levy and the mode of giving it prescribed by the amendatory act of March 15, 1857, is intended for the benefit of the defendant, that he may appear and defend. Rice *v.* Clements, 57 Ala. 191.

Notice by Publication.—Code 1886, § 2936, provides that, in case property of a nonresident is attached, a notice thereof should be published once a week in a newspaper for three weeks, and a copy of the paper should be sent to defendant by mail if his residence can be ascertained. A judgment by default recited that a notice to defendant, who was a nonresident, to appear and plead, was published in a newspaper, and a copy was forwarded by mail "to the place of residence of said defendant." No attempt was made to show that any notice of the levy of the attachment in the case was published, or sent to defendant. Held, that the notice sent defendant was a nullity, since it did not contain the statements required by statute, nor did it appear that it was even addressed to the defendant. Wilmerding *v.* Corbin Banking Co., 28 So. 640, 126 Ala. 268.

Code, § 2936, providing for notice by publication of attachment againt the property of a nonresident, applies as well to attachments based on a fraudulent disposition of his property by the debtor as to those based on the fact that he has left the state. Dollins *v.* Pollock, 89 Ala. 351, 7 So. 904.

In an action by original attachment against a nonresident defendant, the recital in the judgment entry that plaintiff made proof "of due and legal service on the defendant of the issuance and levy of the original attachment," is insufficient on appeal to show constructive notice by publication, as provided in Code Ala. 1896, § 2936, the record not showing that publication was made in a newspaper, here naming it, for three consecutive weeks, commencing, etc. Diston *v.* Hood, 83 Ala. 331, 3 So. 746.

"To be sufficient, the record must show, not merely that publication was made as required by law, but the publication was made in a newspaper, naming it, for three consecutive weeks, commencing, etc. The notice being only constructive, the facts constituting a compliance with the statute must be proved to and found by the court to have been done, and the record must show it. And it would be much more satisfactory, if the record also showed that a copy of the notice was sent by mail to the defendant, or that his residence was unknown and could not be ascertained. This latter proposition is not intended to be declared to be an indispensable prerequisite, but the first is, under all our rulings." Diston *v.* Hood, 83 Ala. 331, 3 So. 746, 747.

In an attachment against a nonresident debtor, no publication is necessary, where a judgment is not rendered until more than six months after the suit was commenced. Fleming, etc., Co. *v.* Burge, 6 Ala. 373. See Bickerstaff *v.* Patterson, 8 Port. 245; Murray *v.* Cone, 8 Port. 250; Miller *v.* McMillan, 4 Ala. 527.

Leaving Copy and Notice with Defendant or at Defendant's Residence.—Under Code, § 3260, requiring notice of an attachment levied on land to be left at defendant's residence, if he resides in the county, where the sheriff's return states that h left notice at defendant's residence, it will be presumed to support a judgment by default that defendant resided in the county. McAbee *v.* Parker, 78 Ala. 573.

§ 101. Inventory and Appraisement.

As to inventory and appraisement as evidence in suit by claimant of property, see post, "Admissibility," § 179 (2). As to quashing or vacating writ or warrant, see post, "Quashing, Vacating, Dissolution, or Abandonment," VII.

Necessity.—After the levy of an attachment, the sheriff must in a reasonable time indorse on the process a memorandum of the property seized, or make out an inventory, and file it with the process. Should a loss result to either party from the sheriff's failure to do so, the sheriff would be liable in damages. Toulmin *v.* Lesesne, 2 Ala. 359.

§ 102. Amount of Property Attached, and Excessive Levy.

Levy on Shoes.—The levy of an attachment on a pair of shoes, if really made, and the shoes of any value, is sufficient. If the levy is fictitious or colorable, it would be quashed by the court to which it was returned, on motion. Thornton *v.* Winter, 9 Ala. 613.

§ 103. Quashing or Setting Aside Levy.

Execution of Forthcoming Bond.—The execution of a forthcoming bond by a defendant in attachment to gain possession of his property taken under a void levy was ineffective to validate the levy, and did not deprive the defendant of his right to a vacation of the levy on motion. Jones *v.* Baxter, 41 So. 781, 146 Ala. 620, distinguishing Peebles *v.* Weir, 60 Ala. 413.

§ 104. Operation and Effect of Levy in General.

In General.—The ownership of chattels is not divested by the levy of an attachment. The levy creates an inchoate lien, dependent on the judgment. If the judgment is obtained, the lien relates back to the levy, and is superior to all subsequent liens, alienations or transfers. Scarborough *v.* Malone, 67 Ala. 570; Abels *v.* Mobile Real Estate Co., 92 Ala. 382, 9 So. 423; Cordaman *v.* Malone, 63 Ala. 556; Joseph *v.* Henderson, 95 Ala. 213, 10 So. 843. See however, McRae *v.* M'Lean, 3 Port. 138, 153; McClellan *v.* Lipscomb, 56 Ala. 255; Phillips *v.* Ash, 63 Aa. 414.

"The levy displaces the possession of the defendant, and clothes the officer with a special property. Woolfolk *v.* Ingram, 53 Ala. 11." Phillips *v.* Ash, 63 Ala. 414, 416.

The levy of an attachment on personal property does not divert the right and title of the defendant in the process, nor prevent him from making a valid assignment of the property, subject to the lien of the attachment as determined by the final result of the case. Ware *v.* Russell, 70 Ala. 174.

"The right and title to personal property is not changed by the levy of any attachment, or of an execution. The general property continues in the defendant, and he may alienate it, subject only to the lien of the process. The lien is not a right of property—it is not a jus in re, nor a jus ad rem. It is a simple preference, or priority, created by law, to subject the property, by sale, to the satisfaction of the execution, or other process issuing on the judgment in the attachment suit, if the plaintiff succeeds in recovering judgment." Ware *v.* Russell, 70 Ala. 174, 178.

A levy of an attachment upon realty does not invest the sheriff with a title nor divest the owner of his title, or possession. It only creates a lien, to be made available in the event judgment shall be rendered in favor of plaintiff in the suit. McClellan *v.* Lipscomb, 56 Ala. 255, 258. See Fry *v.* Branch Bank, 16 Ala. 282, 286.

"If the judgment is obtained after the death of the owner, and a revival of the suit against his administrator (as in the present case), the lien can not be enforced, by a sheriff's sale of the realty to satisfy an execution upon that judgment; because the judgment and execution are against the administrator, upon whom, as such, the title to the realty did not descend. On the death of the former owner, the title then in him passed to his heirs; and no man shall be deprived of his land, without an opportunity to defend his title against the claimant. In reference to an execution in the hands of a sheriff at the time of the defendant's death, the statute law has authorized lands subject to it, to be sold to satisfy it, or an alias issued to take its place, without the lapse of a term. Rev. Code, § 2875. But there is no such enactment to carry into effect the lien of a writ of attachment levied on lands." McClellan *v.* Lipscomb, 56 Ala. 255, 258.

Bringing Defendant into Court and Conferring Jurisdiction.—When an attachment is sued out against several persons, it may be levied on the joint property of all the defendants; or on the separate property of one or more; but a levy on separate property only operates to bring in those defendants who have an interest in it, unless they voluntarily appear. Hadley *v.* Bryars, 58 Ala. 139.

An attachment sued out and levied returnable into the circuit court is the commencement of a suit, and may be pleaded in abatement to another suit upon the same debt, although after the levy the papers are destroyed by the direction of the plaintiff upon the supposition that it was irregularly sued out. Dean *v.* Massey, 7 Ala. 601.

In a suit against a nonresident defendant commenced by attachment, if the plaintiff makes a simulated levy on property to which the defendant has no claim of right, the levy will not have the effect of constructive notice, so as to authorize the court to render judgment; a judgment predicated on such levy is no more binding than a judgment rendered upon ordinary process of which the defendant had no notice whatever; and it is immaterial what length of time elapses between the levy and rendition of judgment, since the court has no jurisdiction to render any judgment at all. Grier *v.* Campbell, 21 Ala. 327.

It seems that, upon the authority of Thornton *v.* Winter, 9 Ala. 613, the levy of an attachment in good faith, upon a brass candlestick, really the property of the defendant in the attachment, would be sufficient to sustain a judgment against the defendant, such levy falling within the letter of the statute; but whether such levies conform to the spirit and intent of the statute, and should not be wholly disregarded, upon the maxim "de minimis non curat lex." Grier *v.* Campbell, 21 Ala. 327.

Persons, Property, or Interests Affected.—The levy of an attachment on personalty which is exempt can not affect the defendant's exemption; but the levy, although it be released on that account, will bring the defendant before the court. Hadley *v.* Bryars, 58 Ala. 139.

§ 105. Creation and Existence of Lien.

Commencement of Lien.—According to the statute, "The levy of an attachment creates a lien, in favor of the plaintiff, upon the estate of the defendant so levied on, from the levy." McClellan *v.* Lipscomb, 56 Ala. 255, 257; Abels *v.* Mobile Real-Estate Co., 92 Ala. 382, 9 So. 423; Boswell *v.* Carlisle, etc., Co., 55 Ala. 554, 566; M'Rae *v.* M'Lean, 3 Port. 138, 153; May *v.* Courtnay, etc., Co., 47 Ala. 185, 190.

"The attachment of a debtor's property subjects it, by operation of law, to a lien upon it in favor of the attaching creditor, from the time the writ is executed by a levy; and generally, this is the date at which the lien has its origin in an attachment cause." Boswell *v.* Carlisle, etc., Co., 55 Ala. 554, 566.

§ 106. Property or Interests Affected, and Extent of Lien.

Proceeds of Property Sold.—Where goods are seized under a void attachment, and sold by order of the court as perishable, and the proceeds paid into the hands of the clerk, the plaintiff in attachment has no lien thereon, though he may have obtained a valid judgment by nil dicit. Goldsmith *v.* Stetson, 39 Ala. 183.

§ 107. Priorities between Attachments.

Superior Diligence of Prior Attaching Creditors.—"The rights and equities of the junior attaching creditors were subordinate to the rights and equities the appellees, as prior attaching creditors, had acquired by their superior diligence." Gusdorf & Co. *v.* Ikelheimer & Co., 75 Ala. 148, 157.

§ 108. Priorities between Attachments and Other Liens or Claims.

See the titles ASSIGNMENTS FOR BENEFIT OF CREDITORS; CARRIERS; CHATTEL MORTGAGES; FACTORS; MECHANICS' LIENS; MORTGAGES; TAXATION. As to enforcement of claims or liens prior or superior to an attachment, see post, "Claims or Liens Prior or Superior to Attachment," § 162.

Priority or Subordination of Other Liens and Claims in General.—A lien created by levying an attachment on property is paramount to any subsequent charge thereon or alienation arising either from the debtor's act or by operation of law. Grigg *v.* Banks, 59 Ala. 311.

Effect of Receivership.—Where property has been attached, and a claim of a third person thereto interposed, it is in the custody of the law, and can not be transferred to a receiver appointed on the filing of a creditors' bill at the suit of other creditors of the attachment defendant. Dollins *v.* Lindsey, 89 Ala. 217, 7 So. 234.

"The property which had been attached, and to which statutory claim had been interposed, was in the custody of the law, and it was error to take it away from such custody, and place it in the hands of a receiver. It was alike prejudicial to the rights of the claimants and their sureties, and to the prior acquired jurisdiction of the law court over the res, which was the subject of contention. * * * The only exception to this rule is when the second seizure is under process which has a paramount lien. And, though not necessary to be decided, lest we be misunderstood, we will state it should be a very strong case, sustained by strong affidavit, or affidavits of fact and urgency, to justify the appointment of a receiver, and the dispossession of the owner of his presumptive right to control his own property, with no bond to compensate him for its wrongful seizure, when, as in this case, there was no notice of the application." Dollins *v.* Lindsey, 89 Ala. 217, 7 So. 234.

Pendency of Suits.—Where process in an action by creditors to set aside a fraudulent sale of a stock of goods was served before defendant's attachment was levied, the attachment lien is subordinate to the creditors' lien. Jefferson County Sav. Bank *v.* McDermott, 99 Ala. 79, 10 So. 154.

Attaching Creditor as Bona Fide Purchaser.—An attaching creditor is not a bona fide purchaser for value as against a third person having a prior claim to the property. Tishomingo Sav. Inst. *v.* Johnson, Nesbitt & Co., 40 So. 503, 146 Ala. 691.

Assignment for Benefit of Creditors.—In a contest between an attaching creditor and the trustee in an assignment for the benefit of creditors, there being no proof of actual fraud in the execution of the assignment, and the debt of the attaching creditor not then being in existence, the recitals of the assignment, as to the existence of debts, are sufficient to sustain it; but, if the debt of the attaching creditor was antecedent and existing, the existence of debts must be shown by the assignee by evidence other than the recitals of the assignment, and the existence of other debts than that of the attaching creditor must be proved. Reynolds *v.* Collins, 78 Ala. 94.

Acquirement and Conveyance of Homestead.—Where the owner of a homestead, having made an executory sale in which his wife did not join, afterwards removes from the premises, and an attachment is then levied on the land, a purchaser at sheriff's sale under the attachment acquires a title superior to one to whom a conveyance was executed after levy of the attachment. Striplin *v.* Cooper, 80 Ala. 256.

Judgments or Decrees and Execution.—The lien of an attachment commences from its levy, and can not be divested by a writ of fieri facias subsequently levied on the same chattels, if the writ had no binding effect before the levy of the attachment. Pond *v.* Griffin, 1 Ala. 678.

The lien of an attaching creditor on land is superior to the title of a purchaser under a subsequent judgment, with notice of the levy of the prior attachment. Baldwin *v.* Leftwich, 12 Ala. 838.

A purchaser at sheriff's sale, under a judgment in an attachment case, acquires a title which dates back to the levy of the attachment, and overrides an intermediate conveyance by the defendant. Striplin & Co. *v.* Cooper & Son, 80 Ala. 256.

Assignments of Debts.—A debt to fall due in future, for services to be performed, may be transferred by assignment before the services are rendered, and such transfer, if bona fide, will defeat an attachment subsequently sued out against the transferrer. Payne *v.* City of Mobile, 4 Ala. 333, 37 Am. Dec. 744.

§ 109. Transfers of Property Pending or Subject to Attachment.

Sales and Conveyances in General.—The owner of property attached may sell the same subject to the attachment. Grigg *v.* Banks, 59 Ala. 311; Ware *v.* Russell, 70 Ala. 174, 45 Am. Rep. 82.

The levy of an ancillary attachment upon land operates as a lien; and, where a judgment is rendered in favor of the plaintiff, the creditor's right to have it sold to satisfy his judgment will override and defeat all intermediate conveyances made by the defendant. Randolph *v.* Carlton, 8 Ala. 606.

§ 110. Duration of Lien.

As to death of party discharging lien, see post, "Death of Party," § 158. As to effect of release of property on forthcoming bond, see post, "Delivery of Property on Forthcoming or Delivery Bond," § 114.

Determination of Suit.—The lien in favor of the plaintiff in the attachment upon the estate of the defendant created by the levy, continues until the suit is determined. May *v.* Courtnay, etc., Co., 47 Ala. 185, 190.

§ 111. Waiver, Release, or Abandonment, and Discharge or Extinguishment of Levy or Lien.

As to discharge in bankruptcy and insolvency, see the titles BANKRUPTCY; INSOLVENCY. As to death of party discharging lien, see post, "Death of Party," § 158. As to effect of giving claimant bond, see post, "Security by Claimant for Possession," § 172. As to loss of priorities, see ante, "Priorities between Attachments and Other Liens or Claims," § 108. As to liability of officer for release of levy, see the title SHERIFFS AND CONSTABLES.

Replevy.—"The lien of the attachment created by the levy is not impaired or destroyed by the replevy. Cary *v.* Gregg, 3 Stew. 433; M'Rae *v.* M'Lean, 3 Port. 138; Rives *v.* Wilborne, 6 Ala. 45, 46. Nothing occurring subsequent to the levy can destroy it but the dissolution of the attachment." Woolfolk *v.* Ingram, 53 Ala. 11, 12.

The sheriff levied an attachment on a slave, and, taking a forthcoming bond, restored the slave to the possession of the defendant, making return on the writ that a claim had been interposed, and bond executed for the trial of the right of property. The plaintiff in attachment proceeded to prosecute the claim suit, which, before its final disposition, was continued six times by a general order of the court, and five times by consent of the parties. During its pendency, the plaintiff aided the claimant in procuring security on a claim bond, given by him for other slaves levied upon, under an execution in favor of another creditor of the defendant in attachment, and induced certain persons to become his sureties, by promising to release his lien on the slave attached. Held that, however strongly the facts may tend to show an intent to hinder or delay other execution creditors of the defendant in attachment, it can not be assumed as a conclusion of law that the lien of the attachment was lost. Greene *v.* Tims, 16 Ala. 541.

Judgment Rendered Nugatory.—The lien of an attachment ancillary to an action at law is extinguished where the judgment in such action is rendered nugatory. Hale *v.* Cummings, 3 Ala. 398.

§ 112. Restoration of Lien.

Setting Aside Nonsuit.—Where an attachment is sued out, and plaintiffs suffer a nonsuit, which, however, is set aside on their motion at the same term, the lien of that attachment is left as it was before the nonsuit was granted. Dollins *v.* Pollock, 89 Ala. 351, 7 So. 904.

§ 113. Custody and Care of Property.

As to compensation of custodian, see post, "Expenses of Keeping Property, and Compensation of Custodian," § 116. As to liability of officer for loss or injuries to property, see the title SHERIFFS AND CONSTABLES. As to right to replevy attached property, see the title REPLEVIN.

In General.—When personal property is attached, the officer must take it into possession retaining the custody thereof, unless it is replevied in the mode prescribed by the statute. Phillips *v.* Ash, 63 Ala. 414, 416.

Levy by Constable and Turning Property over to Sheriff.—Under Code, § 2956, providing that, in case of an attachment issued by a justice of the peace for an amount exceeding his jurisdiction, and not more than the amount of the penalty of the constable's bond, the justice may direct that it be executed by the constable, who shall return the same to the court to which it is returnable; and § 2958, providing for the sale of property levied on by order of the court, and that the proceeds of the sale shall be retained by the sheriff; and § 2959, authorizing the sheriff to sell property under certain conditions without an order of court—property levied on by a constable, and delivered to the sheriff, is in the latter's possession as sheriff, and not as mere bailee of the constable, though the statute does not expressly direct the constable to turn the property over to the sheriff. Joseph *v.* Henderson, 95 Ala. 213, 10 So. 843.

"Property claimed by a vendee of a defendant debtor, in some instances, may be rightfully levied upon at the suit of one creditor, and not subject to attachment at the suit of another person. When property of a defendant debtor is in the possession of the sheriff by virtue of a levy of attachment or execution, and subsequent writs of attachment or execution are received by him against the same defendant, returnable to the same court, and to which the property is liable, a second levy by the sheriff, and indorsement thereof on the writ subject to the prior levy, does not disturb or in any manner interfere with the custodia legis under the first levy. If the sheriff should undertake to displace or subordinate the prior lien secured by the first levy, he might render himself liable to the creditors holding the prior lien. * * * This principle, however, is wholly unlike those in which, to prevent a conflict in the jurisdiction of different courts, it is held that property in gremio legis of one court can not be seized under process of another court, or where replevy or other bonds have been executed by the defendant in the suit, or by a stranger, by which the actual custody of the property is taken from the officer, and placed in the possession of the obligors, and held upon condition that the property be returned, etc. In cases of the latter character, the property can not be levied upon by attachment or executions against the original debtor or the claimant." Joseph *v.* Henderson, 95 Ala. 213, 10 So. 843, 845.

Payment into Court.—Where money, which was taken by the sheriff from the person of a debtor arrested on a criminal charge, was attached in the hands of the sheriff, that officer properly paid it into court without waiting for an order to that effect, under Code, § 2950, providing that, "in the case of officers of the court, the money must be paid into court to abide the result of the suit, unless the court otherwise direct." Warren *v.* Matthews, 96 Ala. 183, 11 So. 285.

Money is "paid into court," within the meaning of Code, § 2950, providing that money in the hands of an officer may be attached, and that, in case of officers of the court, the money "must be paid into court to abide the result of the suit, unless the court otherwise directs," when it is paid into the hands of the clerk of the court. Warren *v.* Matthews, 96 Ala. 183, 11 So. 285.

§ 114. Delivery of Property on Forthcoming or Delivery Bond.

As to giving bond as affecting right to attack attachment, see post, "Waiver or Estoppel," § 141. As to giving bond as claimant with notice of claim, see post, "Notice or Demand by Claimant, and Affidavit of Claim," § 171. As to liabilities on bonds, see post, "Liabilities on Bonds or Undertakings," X. As to right of person giving bond to intervene, see post, "Right to Intervene," § 167.

Right to Release of Property and Execution of Bond.—"When property attached has been replevied by a stranger, the defendant has the right to demand of the stranger the possession of it; and on such demand being made, it is the duty of the stranger, either to restore the property to the defendant, or to return it to the sheriff. In the latter event, the defendant may exercise the right of replevying it himself; and in neither event will the right of possession, given by the law to the defendant, be abridged or impaired. No valid objection can exist, in such case, to the return of the property to the sheriff, by the stranger, in the discharge of his bond, should he elect to pursue that course; and it is believed to be sanctioned by authority." Kirk *v.* Morris, 40 Ala. 225, 230. See M'Rae *v.* M'Lean, 3 Port. 138.

When a stranger offers to replevy for the benefit of the defendant, and his offer is improperly refused by the sheriff, he may enforce his statutory right, for the benefit of the defendant, in a court of law; but he has no such interest in the subject matter of the suit as authorizes him to come into equity for relief, although he also alleges that, after refusing his offer, the sheriff allowed the goods to be replevied by other strangers, who therein acted at the instance, and for the benefit of the plaintiff. Kirk *v.* Morris, 40 Ala. 225.

Where two or more strangers offer to replevy goods taken under an attachment in the absence of defendant (Code, § 2536), the sheriff necessarily has a discretion in choosing between them, but should in every instance consult the interest of defendant. Kirk *v.* Morris, 40 Ala. 225.

"The law prescribes no rule by which the officer shall be governed in deciding as to who among them may exercise the right. From the character of the particular duty to be performed, this must necessarily be left very greatly to the discretion of the officer, as is the case in the performance of many ministerial duties by officers, involving as to themselves responsibilities and the risk of pecuniary loss. A contrary rule might lead to contests and litigation, producing delays, and defeating the beneficial purpose intended to be accomplished. In every such case, let whoever may succeed in replevying the property, the duties and responsibilities cast upon him by the law in regard to it are the same. The officer, however, in the exercise of the discretion vested in him, should not abuse it. He should remember that the object of the law, in permitting the property to be replevied, is not to give profit or advantage to any one, at the expense of the defendant; but that it is to relieve the property from the actual custody of the officer, and restore it to the defendant, and thereby to save the expenses, and secure to the plaintiff a return of the property, or the payment of the debt, in the event of a recovery." Kirk *v.* Morris, 40 Ala. 225, 231.

Goods taken in attachment for sums exceeding the jurisdiction of the court are repleviable only by the defendant in the attachment, his attorney or agents. Cummins *v.* Gray, 4 Stew. & P. 397.

Where goods are replevied by a stranger (not being the attorney, agent or factor of the defendant), and a bond is executed—such bond, assigned by the sheriff to the plaintiff in execution, furnishes to the latter no legal cause of action against the obligor. Cummins *v.* Gray, 4 Stew. & P. 397.

Within the meaning of Code, § 2536, providing that goods levied on under an attachment may be replevied by defendant, "or, in his absence, by a stranger," the term "stranger" means a person who is not a party to the suit, and who acts for the benefit of defendant in attachment, whose bailee he becomes. Kirk *v.* Morris, 40 Ala. 225.

"The statute authorizing the replevy of property attached, requires a bond executed by the defendant in attachment, or a stranger, payable to the plaintiff, in double the amount of the demand sued for, with condition that if he fail in the action, he or his sureties wlil return the specific property within thirty days after the judgment. If the property is not delivered, it is the duty of the sheriff, to return the bond forfeited, and execution issues thereon against the obligors for the amount of the judgment and costs. If any of the property replevied, dies, or is destroyed without fault of the obligors, they may tender the value thereof, in discharge of the bond. R. C., §§ 2964-66-67." Woolfolk *v.* Ingram, 53 Ala. 11, 12.

The replevin bond required by the act of December 23, 1837, § 6, "to explain and amend the law in relation to attachments," may be executed by a stranger. Kinney *v.* Mallory, 3 Ala. 626.

Form, Requisites and Sufficiency of Security.—Mistakes in the recital of the attachment and its levy, not being matters of substance, but of inducement, showing the consideration of the bond, will not vitiate it, and may be corrected by parol evidence. Adler *v.* Potter, 57 Ala. 571.

The validity of a forthcoming bond, under Code 1886, § 2523, is not affected by the fact that it erroneously recites the levy of an execution, when the levy in question was that of an attachment, where it shows on its face that it was given for the forthcoming of certain property "levied on," and claimed as exempt, identifying the contest respecting the pendency of which it was given, and showing that the obligors bound themselves to the forthcoming of particular property involved in such contest. Troy *v.* Rogers, 22 So. 486, 116 Ala. 255, 67 Am. St. Rep. 110.

A bond in replevin of property levied on under an attachment writ, providing for the return of the property within twenty days after judgment in the attachment suit, is not a good statutory bond, under Code Ala. 1886, § 3341, providing for such return in ten days. Such defect is not cured by Code, § 3357, providing that a forthcoming bond shall be sufficient, though defective in form. Cobb *v.* Thompson, 87 Ala. 381, 6 So. 373.

A replevin bond taken by an officer levying an attachment, although defective as a statutory bond, may nevertheless be good as a common-law obligation, if supported by a sufficient consideration, and the property levied on is delivered to the obligors by the officers because of its execution. Adler *v.* Potter, 57 Ala. 571.

In a suit against one "Woody," an attachment writ was issued against "Woody," the replevin bond was signed "Woody," and the name "Woody" was in the forthcoming bond, except that in the condition thereof the attachment was referred to as one against "the above-named Moody." Held, that the use of the name "Moody" was, on the face of the papers, a clerical error, which did not affect the instrument as a statutory bond. Friel *v.* North Birmingham Bldg. Ass'n, 6 Ala. App. 223, 60 So. 552.

In an early case it was held that the officer taking the replevy bond in an attachment suit should be made the obligee. Sartin *v.* Weir, 3 Stew. & P. 421.

The bond, authorized by statute, on the replevy of property taken in attachment, must be payable to the sheriff, not to the plaintiff in the attachment. Sewall *v.* Franklin, 2 Port. 493. See Adkins *v.* Allen, 1 Stew. 130.

In a later case it was held that a replevin bond in an attachment case should be made payable to the plaintiff in attachment, and not to the officer by whom the writ is levied. Agnew *v.* Leath, 63 Ala. 345.

Where a sheriff delivered attached property to a third person, who was neither the attachment debtor's agent nor attorney, on receiving a redelivery bond payable to the attaching creditor, instead of the sheriff, it was held that such bond was not recoverable, either as a statute, or common-law obligation. Sewall *v.* Franklin, 2 Port. 493.

When a claim is interposed to property on which an attachment has been levied, the bond required by the statute being intended for the benefit of the plaintiff, he may waive any defects or irregularities therein; and the failure to object, at some proper stage of the proceedings, to any defect or irregularity which might be cured by amendment, is a waiver of it. Rhodes *v.* Smith, 66 Ala. 174.

"The statute confers on a defendant in attachment, or, in his absence, on a stranger, the right of replevying goods or chattels seized under the writ, by executing a bond, with surety, payable to the plaintiff, in double the amount of the demand, with condition that, if the defendant fail in the action, he or his sureties will return the specific property attached, within thirty days after judgment; which bond must be returned, with the other papers of the cause. R. C., § 2964; Code of 1876, § 3289. When replevied by a stranger to the writ, he is presumed to act for the benefit of the defendant; to remedy the inconvenience or hardship which may result from the seizure of his goods in his absence. Of him the defendant may demand possession of the goods; and in that event, it would be his duty to restore them to the defendant, or return them to the sheriff, in the discharge of the bond, that the defendant may for himself exercise his own right of replevy. Kirk *v.* Morris, 40 Ala. 225." Rhodes *v.* Smith, 66 Ala. 174, 176.

"By the execution of the replevy bond, the stranger so far connects himself with the attachment suit, that he must take notice of the judgment therein rendered, and can not, while retaining the goods under the bond, dispute or deny the title of the defendant. If the title resides in him, and the defendant is without an interest therein subject to levy, this will not excuse him from performance of the condition of the bond. The redelivery of the goods, to answer the levy of the writ, is the duty to which the bond obliges him. When he has redelivered them, he may then interpose a claim to them, and demand a trial of the right of property. Braley *v.* Clark, 22 Ala. 361; Cooper *v.* Peck, 22 Ala. 406." Rhodes *v.* Smith, 66 Ala. 174, 176.

Right to Recover for Destruction of Property.—One holding property by virtue of a forthcoming bond in attachment is entitled to sue for its negligent destruction. Louisville & N. R. Co. *v.* Brinckerhoff, 24 So. 892, 119 Ala. 606.

Redelivery of Property.—When personal property, on which an attachment has been levied, is replevied by a stranger in the absence of the defendant, as authorized by the statute (Code, § 3289), he is presumed to act for the benefit of the defendant, and must deliver the property to him on demand, or return it to the sheriff; and he can not, while holding the property under the bond, deny the title of the defendant, or assert title in himself. Rhodes *v.* Smith, 66 Ala. 174.

§ 115. Release of Property on Security.

As to discharge of attachment on security, see post, "Discharge of Attachment on Security," § 153. As to liabilities on bonds, see post, "Liabilities on Bonds or Undertakings," X. As to liability of officer taking insufficient bond, see the title SHERIFFS AND CONSTABLES.

Failure of Bond to Conform to Statute.—Where a replevin bond tendered a sheriff who has levied on the property sought to be replevied does not conform to the statute, it was the duty of the sheriff to perfect it, as he is allowed a fee for taking it, and he can not refuse to accept it for such reason. Chenault *v.* Walker, 14 Ala. 151.

Immaterial Variance.—Where the attachment was for $192.74, and the description of the attachment in the replevin bond was $192, it was an immaterial variance, and was susceptible of explanation by parol proof. Mitchell *v.* Ingram, 38 Ala. 395.

§ 116. Expenses of Keeping Property, and Compensation of Custodian.

Liability for Expenses of Care and Conservation in General.—A plaintiff in an attachment suit, who agrees to release the levy on the property attached, and to give an order to the sheriff for its restoration to the defendants, and, if any have been sold, to deliver the proceeds also to the defendants, and performs this agreement, does not guaranty the good conduct of the sheriff, and is not liable for the expenses incurred in taking care of the property. McPherson *v.* Harris, 59 Ala. 620.

§ 117. Sale or Other Disposition of Property.

§ 118. —— Property Perishable, or Expensive to Keep.

Perishable Property.—Where slaves are

attached and sold under an order of court as "perishable property," the sale is sufficient to pass the title to the purchaser. Millard *v.* Hall, 24 Ala. 209.

A leasehold is not perishable, so as to be subject to sale, under Code, § 2958, in advance of judgment in attachment. First Nat. Bank *v.* Consolidated Electric Light Co., 97 Ala. 465, 12 So. 71.

§ 119. —— Proceedings and Order for Sale.

Jurisdiction of Court.—Under Code, § 2958, authorizing the court, on motion of either party, to order the sale, in advance of judgment, of "perishable" property which has been attached, the court has jurisdiction to order the sale of any property that is subject to attachment. McCreery *v.* Berney Nat. Bank, 22 So. 577, 116 Ala. 224, 67 Am. St. Rep. 105.

Order of Court Authority for Sale.—An order of court directing the sheriff to "proceed to sell" certain property in his hands, which he had attached, and "pay the proceeds into court," is a sufficient authority to him to make the sale, without any process or copy of the order from the clerk. Millard *v.* Hall, 24 Ala. 209.

Collateral Attack on Order of Sale.—The order directing attached property to be sold can not be collaterally attacked for the purpose of defeating the title of the purchaser at the sale. McCreery *v.* Berney Nat. Bank, 22 So. 577, 116 Ala. 224, 67 Am. St. Rep. 105.

§ 120. —— Title and Rights of Purchasers.

Want of Title in Defendant.—Where the defendant in an attachment had no interest in the property levied on, the levy and sale passed no title as against the true owner. Milner, etc., Co. *v.* De Loach Mill Mfg. Co., 139 Ala. 645, 36 So. 765.

Relation of Title Back to Day of Levy.—Where judgment is obtained in an attachment suit, and the attached land is sold pursuant thereto, the title of the purchaser relates back to the day of levy. Grigg *v.* Banks, 59 Ala. 311.

§ 121. —— Disposition of Proceeds.

Rights of Intervenors or Claimants on Sale.—Where the proceeds of a sale of mortgaged personalty which has been seized under an attachment against the mortgagor prior to the registration of the mortgage, and sold as perishable, exceed the amount of the judgment in the attachment suit, and the mortgage has been duly recorded before the rendition of such judgment, the mortgagee may claim the surplus in the hands of the sheriff, or he may interpose a claim to it, and recover it on the trial of a statutory contest with a junior attaching creditor whose attachment was levied on it in the hands of the sheriff after the registration of the mortgage. Hurt *v.* Redd, 64 Ala. 85.

Disposition of Proceeds.—One claiming a lien on personalty, though having priority of right, can not, on summary motion merely, recover from another an amount paid to him by the sheriff out of a fund in the latter's hands to which both parties assert conflicting demands. Garrison *v.* Webb, 107 Ala. 499, 18 So. 297.

Where goods seized on a void attachment were sold by order of the court as perishable, and the proceeds paid into the hands of the clerk, the court had no authority to order the amount to be paid to defendant's landlord for rent claimed, in the absence of any general lien on the goods for the payment of the rent. Goldsmith *v.* Stetson, 39 Ala. 183.

Recovery or Restoration of Proceeds on Invalid Sale.—Where goods seized on a void attachment are sold by the order of the court as perishable, and the proceeds paid into the hands of the clerk, the defendant is entitled to recover the money as his own. Goldsmith *v.* Stetson, 39 Ala. 183.

Estoppel to Claim Proceeds of Sale.—An attaching creditor who pays a judgment in trespass on account of the wrongful attachment by himself and other creditors is not estopped to claim the proceeds of sale thereof, paid to one of the other attaching creditors, by the fact that he did not object to such payment. Griel *v.* Pollak, 105 Ala. 249, 16 So. 704.

VI. PROCEEDINGS TO SUPPORT OR ENFORCE.

As to complaint or other pleading accompanying affidavit, see ante, "Complaint or Other Pleading Accompanying Affidavit," § 67. As to action against executor, see the title EXECUTORS AND ADMINISTRATORS. As to proceedings in justice's court, see the title JUSTICES OF THE PEACE.

§ 122. Prosecution of Action in General.

Time of Trial.—Under Code, § 3000, which declares that no judgment can be rendered against a defendant in attachment when a third person has claimed the attached property until such claim is settled, unless other property has been attached about which no contest has arisen, a defendant in attachment may be compelled to proceed with the trial pending the claim of a third person to only a part of the attached goods. Richards *v.* Bestor, 90 Ala. 352, 8 So. 30.

Under the statute approved December 1, 1873, regulating the trial of attachment cases if the defendant is a resident of the state, and the levy is made and notice thereof given twenty days before the commencement of the term, and the attachment is founded on a debt or demand due, the return term is the trial term. Rice *v.* Clements, 57 Ala. 191.

"Prior to the statute of December 17, 1873 (Pamph. Acts 1873, p. 57), suits commenced by attachment were not triable at the first term after the issue and levy of the attachment. Standifer *v.* Toney, etc., Co., 43 Ala. 70; Letondal *v.* Huguenin, 26 Ala. 552; Napper *v.* Noland, 9 Port. 218. Under that statute, if the defendant is a resident of the state, and the levy is made, and notice thereof given him twenty days before the commencement of the term, and the attachment is founded on a debt or demand which is due, the return term is the trial term. The mode of giving notice is prescribed by the amendatory statute of March 15, 1875 (Pamph. Acts 1875, p. 183)." Rice *v.* Clements, 57 Ala. 191, 192.

Issues and Questions Construed.—Where an attachment is issued on the ground that the tenant, without paying the rent, has removed a portion of the crops, without the landlord's consent, that the crop had not been removed can not be put in issue on the trial of the attachment suit. Tucker *v.* Adams, 52 Ala. 254.

"The cause for which an attachment issues, that can not be made an issuable fact in the attachment suit, is not the relation existing between the plaintiff and the defendant, whether that relation is of landlord and tenant, or of debtor and creditor—nor is it the existence of the debt averred. The relation and the debt may exist, without the existence of any cause for the attachment. The cause of attachment is the state of facts which entitles a party having a debt to resort to this remedy. In this particular case, the cause of attachment was the removal from the rented premises of the crop, or a portion thereof, grown the current year, without the consent of the landlord, and without the payment of the rent. This cause could not be put in issue on the trial of the attachment suit. If it did not exist in fact, the plaintiff could still prosecute his suit to judgment, leaving the defendant to controvert by an action on the bond the truth of this cause, and if untrue, to recover such damages as he suffered from the resort to the attachment. On the trial of the attachment suit, it was matter pleadable in bar, that the relation of landlord and tenant did not exist, and of consequence there was no rent accruing or due to the plaintiff, which could be recovered in that suit, or in a suit commenced in the ordinary mode. If there is not a debt due or owing from the defendant to the plaintiff in the attachment, the attachment wrongfully issues, and the condition of the bond is broken, entitling the defendant to nominal, if there be no actual damage." Tucker *v.* Adams, 52 Ala. 254, 258.

§ 123. Process in Action and Service on Defendant.

§ 124. —— Necessity and Sufficiency of Process.

Replevy or Execution of Bond and Admission of Notice.—The execution of a replevy bond by the defendant, in an attachment case, is an admission of notice, and is sufficient to sustain a judgment by default at the first term (Code of 1876, § 3323), if executed twenty days before the commencement of the term. Peebles *v.* Weir, 60 Ala. 413.

"Attachments, founded on a past-due demand, are triable at the term of the court to which they are returnable, if the levy is made, and notice given, twenty days before the commencement of the term. Code of 1876, § 3323; Rice *v.* Clements, 57 Ala. 191, at last term. Actual notice to the defendant, that he may have the opportunity of appearing and making defense, it is the purpose of the statute to afford him, as the condition on which the plaintiff may proceed to trial and judgment at the return term. The purpose of the statute is fully accomplished, whenever, from the proceedings in the cause, it appears in authentic form that he has had actual notice for the time required. The right to replevy the goods levied on by the writ is conferred by the statute—a right which can not be exercised without notice of the levy. If the right is exercised, it must be by the execution of a bond, with surety, payable to the plaintiff in the writ, in double the amount of the demand, and with condition that, if he fail in the action, he or his sureties will return the specific property within thirty days. If they fail to return it, the bond is forfeited, and execution thereon issues against the principal and sureties, for the amount of the judgment and costs. Code of 1876, §§ 3289-92. By the execution of the bond, the defendant becomes a party to the suit, and his sureties become parties, so far that an execution may issue against them, if he is unsuccessful in the suit, and does not restore the goods to the custody of the proper officer. The execution of the bond is, therefore, an admission of notice of the levy, and of the suit; and if it is executed twenty days before the commencement of the term, as it was in the present case, authorizes the court to proceed to trial. It is a paper belonging to the files and record of the cause, of which the court must take notice." Peebles *v.* Weir, 60 Ala. 413, 415.

Attachment against Absent Defendants.—Notice to the defendant, or advertisement, is not necessary, in a case of attachment against an absent defendant, when the judgment is not rendered until after the expiration of six months from the issuance of the attachment. Bickerstaff *v.* Patterson, 8 Port. 245; Murray *v.* Cone, 8 Port. 250; Miller *v.* McMillan, 4 Ala. 527.

Ancillary Attachments.—It is competent to issue an ancillary attachment under the act of 1837, "when a suit shall be commenced in any circuit or county court," although the leading process shall not have been executed; and the failure to serve the writ upon the defendant will not abate the attachment or impair its efficiency, but the plaintiff may proceed to judgment as in other cases. Morgan *v.* Lamar, 9 Ala. 231.

§ 125. Appearance.

As to right to attachment as to general principles, see post, "Time for Attacking Attachment," § 142.

What Constitutes an Appearance.—The execution of a replevy bond by the defendant in an attachment case is sufficient to sustain a judgment by default, although the levy of the attachment is void, and there was no personal service of process. Peebles *v.* Weir, 60 Ala. 413.

Where a nonresident sued in attachment executes a bond for the release of his property, conditioned that he would have it forthcoming at the next term of the court, such act amounts to an appearance, and charges him with notice of subsequent proceedings in the action. Chastain *v.* Armstrong, 85 Ala. 215, 3 So. 788.

General or Special Appearance.—An appearance for the special purpose of moving to vacate an attachment for irregularity does not constitute a general appearance, where defendant states that the only purposes of his appearance is to urge the motion. Moore *v.* Dickerson, 44 Ala. 485.

Waiver of Irregularity in General.—A defendant in attachment, by filing pleas involving a recognition of the service of the writ, and by going to trial without objection, enters a general appearance, within Code, § 2996, providing that, if the defendant appears and pleads, the cause proceeds as in suits commenced by summons and complaint, and waives defects in the levy, etc. Rosenberg *v.* H. B. Claflin Co., 95 Ala. 249, 10 So. 521.

Waiver of Process Served and of Defects Therein.—The appearance by defendant in an attachment suit dispenses with the service of process. Burroughs *v.* Wright, 3 Ala. 43.

Though Code, § 2995, provides that a suit commenced by attachment is triable at the return term of the writ, if the levy has been made and notice thereof given twenty days before the commencement of such term, defendant, by a general appearance, waives plaintiff's failure to serve the notice within proper time. Rosenberg *v.* H. B. Claflin Co., 95 Ala. 249, 10 So. 521.

Where an attachment is sued out against nonresident defendants, who appear voluntarily and contest plaintiff's claim before a jury, they waive defects in the publication of summons. Corley *v.* Shropshire, 2 Ala. 66.

§ 126. Sufficiency of Complaint or Other Pleading.

As to defects, grounds for quashing or vacating, see post, "Defects or Irregularities in Proceedings," § 138. As to amendment of pleading or setting up new cause of action, see the title PLEADING.

Matters Contained in Affidavit or Bond.—When the suit is commenced by attachment, it is unnecessary to carry into the declaration any of the recitals contained in the bond and affidavit, as these have no connection with the cause of action. Reynolds *v.* Bell, 3 Ala. 57.

Allegation as to Cause of Action.—If the declaration in an attachment case sets forth a substantial cause of action, a demurrer thereto will not be sustained, on the ground that the cause of action does not justify the process of attachment. Cain *v.* Mather, 3 Port. 224.

Allegation as to Parties.—A bill under the act of February 5, 1846, "providing for attachments in chancery," must allege an indebtedness to a specific amount, and there must be an affidavit of a particular sum due. Kirksey *v.* Fike, 27 Ala. 383, 62 Am. Dec. 768.

§ 127. Filing and Service of Pleadings.

Time for Filing Pleadings.—Code 1886, § 2995, which requires plaintiff in attachment to file his complaint "within the first three days of the return term," is directory, and the court may allow such complaint to be filed after the required time. Perkerson *v.* Snodgrass, 85 Ala. 137, 4 So. 752.

§ 128. Trial in General.

Proceeding to Trial.—An attachment suit can not proceed to final judgment until a claimant's right to the attached property is determined. Sloan *v.* Hudson, 24 So. 458, 119 Ala. 27.

§ 129. Appointment and Proceedings of Auditors or Trustees.

Time of Filing Declaration.—When an attachment is sued upon a debt not due, the declaration should not be filed until the maturity of the contract. Beckwith *v.* Baldwin, 12 Ala. 720.

§ 130. Judgment.

As to evidence in action on bond, see post, "Evidence," § 210. As to conclusiveness and effect in action on bond, see post, "Evidence," § 210. As to commencement of lien of judgment and attachment, see the title JUDGMENT. As to default of judgment, see the title JUDGMENT. As to taking judgment for purpose of crediting joint lien, see the title JUDGMENT. As to equitable relief from judgment, see the title JUDGMENT. As to final judgment, decree, or order for sale of attached property, see the title JUDICIAL SALES. As to judgment in rem and attachment proceedings in general, see the title JUDGMENT. As to personal judgments, see the title JUDGMENT. As to validity of judgment to sustain execution, see the title EXECUTION.

Form and Sufficiency in General.—As an attachment under the statute which authorizes such attachment in favor of the nonresident citizen against the executor or administrator of his deceased nonresident debtor can only be levied on the property of deceased within this state which has not come to the possession of his personal representative so as to be assets in his hands, the proper judgment in such case is the condemnation of the property levied on for the satisfaction of the debt, and, if replevied by the executor, then against him personally, to be discharged by the delivery of the property. Loomis *v.* Allen, 7 Ala. 706.

Jurisdiction.—An affidavit in attachment, on the ground of defendant's nonresidence, accompanied by the statutory notice of publication, gave the court jurisdiction of the subject matter, so as to authorize a default judgment against the property attached, though the court had no jurisdiction of defendant's person. De Jarnette *v.* Dreyfus, 51 So. 932, 166 Ala. 138.

Where defendant appears in attachment, further recital in the judgment as to the court's jurisdiction is unnecessary, and may be treated as surplusage. Pacific Selling Co. *v.* Collins (Ala.), 39 So. 579.

Service.—A recital in a judgment entry in attachment that notice was given as required by law is insufficient to sustain a judgment by default. Meyer *v.* Keith, 99 Ala. 519, 13 So. 500.

Attachment proceedings being in rem, and not in personam, no valid personal judgment can be rendered unless the service is personal, whether defendant be a resident or not. De Arman *v.* Massey, 44 So. 688, 151 Ala. 639.

"It is, of course, fundamental that, without jurisdiction of the person obtained, a personal judgment against a defendant can not be validly rendered. To secure such jurisdiction the rule was, prior to Exchange Nat. Bank *v.* Clement, 109 Ala. 270, 19 So. 814, that notice implied in the levy, and service of notice in the manner prescribed of the levy, though such notice was not personally served on the defendant, availed to bring the defendant within the lawful powers of the court. This rule proceeded on the idea that the proceeding in attachment or garnishment was by nature in personam. Whatever may have been the wisdom and soundness of such a rule, long enforced by the courts of this state, the theory of attachment, in keeping with which the mentioned rule obtained, was entirely changed when the supreme court of the United States, in a cause in which a nonresident was the party defendant, declared a proceeding in attachment or garnishment to be in rem, and not in personam. Accordingly, in Bank *v.* Clement, supra, this court, yielding a proper influence to the announcement of the supreme court of the United States in a cause in which that court had superior and controlling jurisdiction, because of the nonresidence of a party therein, accepted the principle, and applied it in that case, viz, that without personal service a judgment in personam against a merely constructively served defendant or garnishee could not be validly rendered, but that the proceeding in attachment or garnishment being, in the absence of personal service, in rem, the power of the court in the given cause was strictly limited to the enforcement of the pressed demand by the subjection, if so entitled, of the property levied on to the satisfaction of the demand." De Arman *v.* Massey, 151 Ala. 639, 44 So. 688.

"So we are now confronted with the alternative whether the rule established to the behoof of nonresidents shall be denied or applied to residents who are not personally served, but whose property is under the ban of process in attachment or garnishment in the courts of this state. The character of proceedings, attachment of garnishment, being fixed in rem, and not in personam, we think that the principle stated compels the conclusion that no jurisdiction to render a personal judgment can be validly acquired unless the service is personal and actual, rather than simply constructive. If any other view was entertained, an incongruous situation would result, to say nothing of the ignoring of the principle upon which the rule as to nonresidents is rested by the supreme court of the United States. To cling to the earlier rule followed in this state would extend to the nonresident an exception which our own courts would deny to our own citizen. Independent of the principle and its consequent rule, common fairness, if its recognition imparts no other principle, demands that we make no insidious distinction against citizens of this state. It would be the creation of an insufferable anomaly to hold that in one class of cases such proceedings were in rem, and in another in personam. And it may be here generally observed that where, in attachment or garnishment proceedings, no personal service was had, the trial court should, in accordance with its practice, ascertain the damages to debt to which the plaintiff is entitled, and then render judgment only in condemnation of the property subject to be sold, the proceeds thereof to be applied to the satisfaction pro tanto of the ascertained debt or damages. Care should be taken to avoid the rendition of a personal judgment in the premises. Exchange Nat. Bank *v.* Clement, 109 Ala. 270, 19 So. 814." De Arman *v.* Massey, 151 Ala. 639, 44 So. 688.

Time of Taking Judgment.—Under the provisions of Rev. Code, §§ 2660, 2661, 2998, in an action commenced by attachment, as in one commenced by summons, a judgment can not be rendered by default against a defendant in any case until the trial term, and judgment rendered at the first term after service of the attachment is erroneous. Standifer *v.* Toney, 43 Ala. 70. See Central Min., etc., Co. *v.* Stoven, 45 Ala. 594.

Under Code 1907, § 2964, providing that an attachment issued without affidavit and bond may be abated on defendant's plea filed within the first three days of the return term, an attachment judgment nil dicit was premature, where taken before the expiration of the third day of the return term. Oliver *v.* Kinney, 173 Ala. 593, 56 So. 203, 206.

Action on Debt Not Due.—Although an attachment may issue in certain cases before the debt is due, judgment can not be rendered in the action before the maturity of the demand. Ware *v.* Todd, 1 Ala. 199; Jones *v.* Holland, 47 Ala. 732.

A judgment can not be rendered before the maturity of the demand, although the statute authorizes an attachment to issue in certain cases, before the debt is due. In such a case the proper course is to stop proceedings until the maturity of the debt, and then to proceed to judgment as in other cases. Ware *v.* Todd, 1 Ala. 199.

Where an attachment is sued out before the maturity of a debt, the cause is continued by operation of law, without formal continuance, until maturity of the debt. Allen *v.* Claunch, 7 Ala. 788.

By Default.—Under Code 1896, § 531, requiring publication of notice to nonresident defendants in attachment proceedings, to sustain a default judgment, it must appear in the judgment entry that such notice has been given. Trammell *v.* Guy, 44 So. 37, 151 Ala. 311.

Operation and Effect.—Where an attachment was taken out under the act of 1837 as ancillary to an action at law, and the record contained the entry of a judgment for plaintiff, it will be considered as having been rendered in the action, and not merely on the ancillary process. Dansby *v.* Johnson, 3 Ala. 390.

Where an attachment is sued out under the act of 1837, as ancillary to an action at law, the irregularity of the attachment or proceedings, on it, will not authorize the reversal of the judgment in the action. Dansby *v.* Johnson, 3 Ala. 390.

If the replevy bond executed on the levy of the attachment, can not, on being returned forfeited, have the effect of a judgment, an execution issued thereupon will be superseded, or enjoined, according as the objection may be. Dansby *v.* Johnson, 3 Ala. 390.

§ 131. Enforcement of Attachment against Property Not Levied On.

§ 132. —— In General.

Jurisdiction in Equity.—When a creditor files a bill in equity against his debtor under the act of 1846, giving an attachment in chancery in certain cases, the jurisdiction of the court is not limited to the condemnation of the property seised under the attachment. If its jurisdiction has once rightfully attached, the court may render it effectual to the complainant's relief, by sending out its process, upon a proper application, or widening the sphere of its action, so as to embrace and subject property enough to satisfy his demand. Shearer *v.* Loftin, 26 Ala. 703.

VII. QUASHING, VACATING, DISSOLUTION, OR ABANDONMENT.

As to the effect of assignment for benefit of creditors as dissolving attachment, see the title ASSIGNMENTS FOR BENEFIT OF CREDITORS. As to attachment in justices court, see the title JUSTICES OF THE PEACE.

§ 133. Nature and Form of Remedy.

Motion to Quash or Plea in Abatement.—Defects and irregularities in a writ of attachment, or apparent on the face of the affidavit or bond, may be taken advantage of by motion to quash, if the motion is interposed within the time prescribed for pleading in abatement. De Bardelebeh *v.* Crosby, 53 Ala. 363. See Planters', etc., Bank *v.* Andrews, 8 Port. 404; Hall *v.* Brazleton, 40 Ala. 406; Steamboat Farmer *v.* McCraw, 31 Ala. 659.

The objection that a suit commenced by attachment is within the law forbidding service of process on Sunday can not be raised by plea, but should be by motion to set aside the process for irregularity. Cotton *v.* Huey, 4 Ala. 56.

Matters in abatement can not be raised by motion, but must be specifically pleaded. Blankenship *v.* Blackwell, 27 So. 551, 124 Ala. 355, 82 Am. St. Rep. 175.

An attachment issued without affidavit and bond can not be quashed on motion; it can only be abated by plea. Free *v.* Howard, 44 Ala. 195; Free *v.* Hukill, 44 Ala. 197.

A plea in abatement is the only method of taking advantage of a variance between a writ of attachment and the bond and affidavit, if the variance is objectionable at all. Goldsticker *v.* Stetson, 21 Ala. 404.

In an action commenced by attachment, a variance between the cause of action stated in the affidavit and attachment and the cause of action described in the complaint may be pleaded in abatement. Wright *v.* Snedecor, 46 Ala. 92.

"The proper mode of taking advantage of any defect in process, or irregularity in the service, is by motion to the court to stay proceedings." Cotton *v.* Huey & Co., 4 Ala. 56, 57.

Remedy Where Nature of Action Will Not Permit of Attachment.—When an attachment is improperly sued out in a case in which that writ is not allowed, the irregularity can be reached only by a rule on the plaintiff to show cause why the writ of attachment should not be dissolved, and neither a plea in abatement, motion to quash, nor a motion to strike out, will reach the defect, and the motion for the rule must precede a plea to the merits. Drakford *v.* Turk, 75 Ala. 339; Adair *v.* Stone, 81 Ala. 113, 1 So. 768; Brown *v.* Coats, 56 Ala. 439; Rich *v.* Thornton, 69 Ala. 473; Watson *v.* Auerbach, 57 Ala. 353.

An attachment having been issued on a cause of action, for which the issue of the process is not authorized by law, the mode of reaching the irregularity is by a rule for the plaintiff to show cause why the attachment should not be dissolved; and on the hearing of the rule the court should receive evidence showing the real nature and character of the demand sought to be enforced, in support, or for the discharge of the rule. Rich *v.* Thornton, 69 Ala. 473.

When an attachment is not rightly sued out, the objection can only be taken by plea in abatement; and when sued out on a demand which does not authorize an attachment, a rule on the plaintiff, to show cause why the attachment should not be dissolved, is the proper mode of reaching the defect; a plea to the merits is a waiver of the objection. Brown *v.* Coats, 56 Ala. 439.

A demurrer to the declaration does not reach the objection that the cause of action is one for which attachment will not lie. The proper mode of presenting that question is by a rule on the plaintiff to show cause why his attachment should not be dissolved. Jordan *v.* Hazard, 10 Ala. 221; Beckwith *v.* Baldwin, 12 Ala. 720; Watson *v.* Auerbach, 57 Ala. 353.

When an attachment is sued out in a case not authorized by law, a motion to quash it is not the proper remedy, nor is the refusal to quash on motion revisable on error. Gill *v.* Downs, 26 Ala. 670.

A motion to dissolve an attachment, on the ground that the cause of action does not warrant that process, can properly be entertained when a new or amended declaration is filed, setting out a cause of action not within the statute, if the motion is made within the time for pleading in abatement. Hazard *v.* Jordan, 12 Ala. 180.

Remedy Where Matters Are Not Apparent of Record.—An original attachment, regular on its face, and supported by affidavit, can not be quashed on the motion of a stranger for matter dehors the record and properly triable by a jury, though he is shown to have an interest in the question and motion. Cockrell *v.* McGraw, 33 Ala. 526, cited on this point in note in 35 L. R. A. 773.

The objections that it does not appear that an attachment against the executor of a deceased nonresident was levied on the property of the debtor within the state which had not been reduced into possession by the foreign executor, and that it did not appear that the attachment was sued out by a resident, must be taken by plea in abatement. Loomis *v.* Allen, 7 Ala. 706.

An affidavit for attachment disclosed a verification by plaintiff and his signature, but the verification was not attested by the justice before whom it was made. Held, that an objection that the affidavit was not verified and subscribed, or that the justice before whom the same purports to have been made was not such in fact, must be presented by plea in abatement. Lowry *v.* Stowe, 7 Port. 483.

§ 134. Grounds for Quashing, Vacating, or Dissolving.

§ 135. —— In General.

Statute Violative of Constitution.—Where a statute authorizing the issuance of an attachment is violative of the constitution, on a proper plea the attachment will be abated. Murphy *v.* Egger, 59 Ala. 639.

§ 136. —— Insufficiency or Want of Grounds of Attachment.

Right to Contradict Affidavit of Plaintiff as to Grounds.—When a judicial attachment is sued out against a defendant who avoids the service of process, he can not by plea put in issue the grounds on which it is issued, as contained in the affidavit. Garner *v.* Johnson, 22 Ala. 494.

Under the acts of 1833 (Clay's Digest, 54, § 1), and 1845 (Pamphlet acts 1844-5 137), the clerk of the court may issue a judicial attachment against the defendant who avoids the service of process, upon the filing of the required affidavit, either in vacation or term time. Garner *v.* Johnson, 22 Ala. 494.

Necessity of Resorting to Attachment Bond as Remedy for False Recitals.—An ancillary attachment sued out in aid of a suit is within Clay's Dig., 1843, p. 61, § 32, providing that defendant must not put in issue the cause for which the attachment issued; his remedy being by a suit on the attachment bond, for the wrongful suing out of the attachment. Jones *v.* Donnell, 9 Ala. 695.

§ 137. —— Want of Jurisdiction.

Motion to Quash Amendment.—A motion to quash the attachment is not the proper manner of raising the question of the court's jurisdiction to issue the writ because of want of personal service. De Jarnette *v.* Dreyfus, 51 So. 932, 166 Ala. 138.

§ 138. —— Defects or Irregularities in Proceedings.

Defective Bond.—An attachment will not be quashed on account of a defective bond, unless the plaintiff is unwilling to execute a good bond. Scott *v.* Macy, 3 Ala. 250.

Want of Lawful Levy.—Though Code 1907, § 2964, provides that an attachment issued without affidavit and bond may be abated on defendant's pleas, the lien could be destroyed for other reasons, as by showing that there had been no lawful levy. Oliver *v.* Kinney, 173 Ala. 593, 56 So. 203.

Mode of Objection.—"The rule is well settled that when an attachment is issued on a cause of action for which such process is not authorized by law, as when sued out by a landlord to enforce a lien for rent on a demand or debt other than for rent, the remedy is by a rule on plaintiff to show cause why it should not be dissolved. The motion made was proper, if the ground existed on which it was based, whether apparent from the face of the proceedings, or established by extrinsic evidence." Harmon *v.* Jenks, 84 Ala. 74, 4 So. 260, 261.

§ 139. —— Ownership of Property Attached.

Want of Ownership of Property.—The fact that the defendant is not the owner of the property attached is not good matter for a plea in abatement. Sims *v.* Jacobson, 51 Ala. 186.

It is not competent for defendant to move the court to set aside a levy under an attachment on the ground that the property levied on does not belong to him. Sims *v.* Jacobson, 51 Ala. 186.

In an action against a nonresident, commenced by attachment, unless the levy is fictitious or merely colorable, the defendant can not, as a ground for abating the action, dissolving the attachment, or vacating the levy, traverse the ownership of the property attached, or deny having a leviable interest therein. Exchange Nat. Bank *v.* Clement, 109 Ala. 270, 19 So. 814.

§ 140. Persons Entitled to Move.

Amici Curiæ.—And, it seems, that the practice of quashing attachments, where the remedy is unauthorized, or the requisitions of the statute not complied with, upon the mere motion of strangers to the record as amici curiæ, has prevailed so long, that it is not now considered irregular. Planters', etc., Bank *v.* Andrews, 8 Port. 404.

§ 141. —— Waiver or Estoppel.

As to claims, see post, "Contest of Attachment by Claimant," § 165.

Execution of Forthcoming Bond.—The affidavit required by statute in attachment proceedings is the foundation of the proceedings, and an abatement of the writ for want of affidavit destroys the lien, though defendant executed a forthcoming bond and bond to discharge the garnishment in order to regain possession of the property taken from him by void process; the execution of such bonds not validating the attachment. Oliver *v.* Kinney, 173 Ala. 593, 56 So. 203.

Effect of Judgment.—Overruling a motion (made after judgment in an attachment), to strike from the levy endorsed upon the writ, whatever relates to lands—held, not to be ground for error. Cannon *v.* Logan, 5 Port. 77.

§ 142. Time for Attacking Attachment.

In General.—Defects in an attachment bond are not available on error, unless the exception has been taken by plea in abatement in the court below. Burt *v.* Parish, 9 Ala. 211.

Time of Making Motion or Plea.—By the thirteenth rule of practice (Code, p. 715), a motion to quash an attachment must be made at the first term at which it can be made, and not afterwards. Hall *v.* Brazleton, 40 Ala. 406.

"There was no error in rejecting the paper purporting to be a plea in abatement. It should have been filed at the return term. Revised Code, § 2989; Vaughan *v.* Robinson, 22 Ala. 519." Free *v.* Howard, 44 Ala. 195, 196.

Motion after General Appearance and Pleading to Merits.—If a motion to quash is the proper remedy when an attachment is sued out in a case not authorized by law, the objection is waived by the failure to make it at the first term, and by afterwards appearing and pleading to the merits. Gill *v.* Downs, 26 Ala. 670.

When an attachment is sued out in the name of the state by the attorney general, it is not necessary that he should exhibit the written instructions of the governor for the institution of the suit (Code, § 2902); if such instructions were not in fact given, the objection should be taken by motion to dissolve the attachment, before joining issue. Wolffe *v.* State, 79 Ala. 201.

In an action commenced against a steamboat by attachment, a party intervened as one of the owners of the boat, was admitted to defend, interposed a plea of not guilty, and moved the court to dismiss the attachment "on the ground that there has been a discontinuance of the suit against the boat by prosecuting the suit against other parties not now before the court, and failing to declare against the boat or otherwise proceeding against it." Held, that the motion to dismiss on account of a discontinuance was made too late. The Farmer *v.* McCraw, 31 Ala. 659.

After a party, who has been allowed to intervene as defendant, has filed the plea of not guilty to the amended declaration, it is too late for him to move to quash the attachment by which the suit was commenced, or to dismiss the proceeding on account of a discontinuance. Steamboat Farmer *v.* McCraw, 31 Ala. 659.

Proceedings after Judgment.—An attachment improperly issued under the statute which authorizes such attachment in favor of the resident citizen against the executor of his deceased nonresident debtor must be abated by plea, and can not be taken advantage of after judgment by default. Loomis *v.* Allen, 7 Ala. 706.

Under Code, §§ 2561, 2562, providing

that where an action is commenced by attachment against a nonresident, and the attachment is issued without affidavit and bond as therein prescribed, the attachment may be abated on plea of defendant filed within the first three days of the term, the objection that the record does not contain the affidavit on which an attachment in the suit issued can not be raised on appeal, since it should have been raised by a plea in abatement. Dow *v.* Whitman, 36 Ala. 604.

§ 143. Proceedings on Motion.

§ 144. —— Application in General.

Motion to Dismiss.—Motions made in the city court of Montgomery, in an attachment suit on the docket of that court, to strike the cause from the docket, and to dismiss, on the ground that it appears from the bond and writ, that the attachment is returnable to, and the cause triable in the circuit court of Montgomery county, are but the equivalent of a motion to quash the attachment because of defects or irregularities in the affidavit, bond and writ; and such a motion is addressed to the sound discretion of the primary court, and may, without error, be overruled, putting the party to a plea in abatement, which is the more appropriate mode of taking advantage of the defect or irregularity, if it exists. Mohr *v.* Chaffe Bros. & Co., 75 Ala. 387. See Free *v.* Howard, 44 Ala. 195; Hall *v.* Brazelton, 46 Ala. 359; De Bardeleben *v.* Crosby, 53 Ala. 363; Watson *v.* Auerbach, 57 Ala. 353; Murphy *v.* Egger, 59 Ala. 639.

§ 145. —— Evidence and Effect of Affidavits.

As to grounds for attachment, see ante, "Evidence as to Grounds," § 29.

Presumption and Burden of Proof.—Upon a motion to quash an attachment, every thing stated in the proceedings must be taken to be true, and nothing beyond, shall be intended prejudicial to the plaintiff. Calhoun *v.* Cozzens, 3 Ala. 21.

In an attachment by a resident creditor against a nonresident debtor, it will not be interferred against a plaintiff, on a motion to quash, that he is a nonresident merely because the affidavit on which the attachment is founded goes further than is necessary, and because the bond is indorsed with the approval of the judge of the county court. Calhoun *v.* Cozzens, 3 Ala. 21.

"On the trial of the motion to quash the writ and of the claim suit, there was no error in allowing the plaintiffs to introduce the attachment writ, the affidavit and bond for attachment, the pleas of the defendant in attachment, the affidavit of the claimant that he was the owner of the property levied on, his claim bond and the agreement of plaintiffs, the defendant and the claimant, as to the levy, return of the sheriff, and the value of the property levied on and claimed. This evidence was within the issues tried. Schamragel *v.* Whitehurst, 103 Ala. 260, 15 So. 611; Guy *v.* Lee, 81 Ala. 163, 2 So. 273; Mayer *v.* Clark, 40 Ala. 259." Carter *v.* O'Bryan, 105 Ala. 305, 16 So. 894.

§ 146. —— Hearing and Determination.

Discretion of Court.—A motion to quash an affidavit for defects apparent on its face, or to quash a writ of attachment for similar defects or irregularities, if made within the time prescribed for filing pleas in abatement, is addressed to the court's sound discretion, and may be entertained or refused, and the moving party put to his plea, at the court's election. Busbin *v.* Ware, 69 Ala. 279.

A motion as to defects and irregularities in a writ of attachment, or apparent on the face of the affidavit or bond, is addressed to the sound discretion of the court, and may be entertained or refused. and the party put to his plea, as the court may elect. The exercise of this discretion is not revisable. De Bardeleben *v.* Crosby, 53 Ala. 363, 364.

Province of Court and Jury.—A motion to dissolve an attachment is for the court, and not for the jury, to decide; but where the jury, instructed by the court, finds thereon, and also on immaterial issues raised by consent of parties on formal but superfluous pleadings and redundant evidence, defendant can not urge such irregularities as grounds to set aside the order dismissing the motion. Harmon *v.* Jenks, 84 Ala. 74, 4 So. 260.

§ 147. Pleading in Abatement, or Traverse of Grounds of Attachment.

§ 148. —— Grounds in General.

As to formal requisites, see post, "Formal Requisites," § 149.

Affidavit Defective in Matter of Substance.—An attachment sued out on an affidavit defective in matter of substance, may be abated on the plea of the defendant. Hall *v.* Brazelton, 46 Ala. 359.

Failure to Show Nonresidence.—Where the fact of the plaintiff's nonresidence does not appear on the proceedings in a sui by attachment, if the defendant would avail himself of it to show their defectiveness, he must plead it in abatement. Calhoun *v.* Cozzens, 3 Ala. 21.

Finding Additional Pleas.—So long as it is open to defendant to file the plea in abatement, prescribed by Code 1907, § 2964, permitting an attachment issued without affidavit and bond to be abated on defendant's pleas, filed within the first three days of the return term, he may also file other pleas having the effect of destroying the writ, provided that he has not already pleaded or otherwise challenged the validity of the lien, in which case the case stands for trial upon the day set by the clerk, pursuant to § 5348, and can not be called before that day, except by consent. Oliver *v.* Kinney, 173 Ala. 593, 56 So. 203.

§ 149. —— Formal Requisites.

As to grounds in general, see ante, "Grounds in General," § 148.

Sufficiency of Plea or Traverse.—Only such parts of a plea in abatement of an attachment as set up defects in the affidavit will be considered, the rest being frivolous. Bell *v.* Allen, 76 Ala. 450.

A plea in abatement in an attachment suit, which craves oyer of the affidavit, bond and writ, and sets them out, but fails to specify or point out any defect or irregularity in either, is fatally defective on demurrer. Mohr *v.* Chaffe Bros. & Co., 75 Ala. 387.

A plea in abatement of an attachment merely denying defendant's right to the property levied on is bad on demurrer; the return can not be contradicted by extrinsic evidence upon a mere allegation of falsity. King *v.* Bucks, 11 Ala. 217.

Where absconding within the state is alone a sufficient ground of attachment, without reference to the domicile of either party, and an attachment is granted on such ground, a plea to the writ, that defendant is a resident citizen of another state and never was within the state of Alabama with the intention of residing therein, is bad on demurrer. Middlebrook *v.* Ames, 5 Stew. & P. 158.

In an action for breach of covenant of seisin, etc., with affidavit in attachment on the ground of defendant's nonresidence, a plea in abatement, alleging defendant's residence and want of personal service, put in issue the ground on which the attachment was issued contrary to Code 1896, § 565, prohibiting defendant from putting in issue the ground on which an attachment was issued. DeJarnette *v.* Dreyfus, 166 Ala. 138, 51 So. 932.

A plea in abatement to an attachment, because it was issued without affidavit, and because the writ, though properly addressed, commands the plaintiff eo nomine to attach the defendant's estate, is bad, because it unites two distinct matters of abatement, and might be stricken out on motion. The defendant, therefore, in such a case, is not prejudiced by the refusal of the court to compel the plaintiff to join issue upon it. Ellison *v.* Mounts, 12 Ala. 472.

A plea of a defective affidavit, in abatement of an attachment, should set out the affidavit on oyer. Banks *v.* Lewis, 4 Ala. 599.

§ 150. —— Issues.

Facts Charged as Ground of Attachment.—It seems, that a defendant in attachment, may not, by plea in abatement, contest the truth of the facts charged as the ground of the attachment, where the affidavit and proceedings on their face, appear regular and sufficient. Middlebrook *v.* Ames, 5 Stew. & P. 158.

§ 151. —— Judgment or Order.

Dismissal of Suit.—Upon the return of a verdict for defendant on a plea in abatement attacking a writ of attachment, the court could not grant a motion to dismiss the suit, where the issue raised only went to the question of the existence of a lien, since under the express provisions of Code 1907, § 4770, plaintiff might still have a recovery of his debt. Pitard *v.* McDowell, 6 Ala. App. 236, 60 So. 555. See Dryer *v.* Abercrombie, 57 Ala. 497.

§ 152. Actions to Set Aside Attachment.

Parties.—The sheriff is a proper party to a bill to set aside an attachment as fraudulent. Cartwright *v.* Bamberger, 90 Ala. 405, 8 So. 264.

Allegations.—Where complainant seeks to set aside an attachment of defendant's property by an alleged creditor on the ground that the debt alleged to be the basis of the attachment is simulated and fraudulent, it is no objection to the bill that it does not allege the absence of any statutory ground for attachments, since, if the debt be fraudulent, it is immaterial whether or not any ground for attachment exists. Henderson *v.* J. B. Brown Co., 28 So. 79, 125 Ala. 566.

§ 153. Discharge of Attachment on Security.

As to appraisal of property as determining amount of bond, see ante, "Inventory and Appraisement," § 101. As to liabilities on bonds, see post, "Liabilities on Bonds or Undertakings," X.

§ 154. —— Right to Release in General.

Effect of Bond as Dissolving Attachment.—In a proceeding to try the right of property levied on under an attachment, the court can not reject an execution (or it seems the attachment) offered in evidence, on the ground that the lien of the attachment was destroyed by the giving of a replevy bond. Perine *v.* Babcock, 8 Port. 131.

The giving of a replevy bond under the attachment law does not discharge the lien acquired on the property under the attachment. McRae *v.* McLean, 3 Port. 138.

A lien is created on property taken in virtue of an attachment, which the right to replevy can not impair, if it be not done by giving a special bail. Cary *v.* Gregg, 3 Stew. 433.

The levy of an attachment on personal property creates a lien, and places the property in the custody of the law, which is neither destroyed nor impaired by the execution of a replevin bond. Cordaman *v.* Malone, 63 Ala. 556. See Scarborough *v.* Malone, 67 Ala. 570.

§ 155. —— Form and Requisites of Security.

Sufficiency of Bond.—A bond given to release a vessel from an attachment, and which the declaration alleged was made payable to a sheriff, did not state, in totidem verbis, that he was such an officer. Held, that the undertaking in the condition that the obligors should perform it to the obligee, or his successor in the office of sheriff, sufficiently indicated his official character. Whitsett *v.* Womack, 8 Ala. 466.

Quære, whether or not the bond be prima facie good, so as to devolve the onus of impeaching it upon the obligors, though it had omitted to show who the obligee was, otherwise than by stating his name. Whitsett *v.* Womack, 8 Ala. 466.

§ 156. Dissolution by Causes Subsequent to Attachment.

As to effect of levying property in possession of debtor, see ante, "Custody and Care of Property," § 113. As to dissolution by adjudication in bankruptcy, see the title BANKRUPTCY.

§ 157. —— Judgment for Defendant.

Discharge of Lien.—A final judgment in favor of a defendant in attachment, unless superseded by writ of error or appeal, discharges the lien of the attachment, thereby entitling defendant to possession of the property. Sherrod *v.* Davis, 17 Ala. 312.

Since a final judgment in favor of a defendant in attachment, unless superseded by writ of error or appeal, discharges the lien of the attachment, if the sheriff, having sold and retained in his hands the proceeds of the goods attached, afterwards, and without notice, pays them over to the defendant, he is not liable, notwithstanding the plaintiff may subsequently sue out a writ of error, procure a reversal of the judgment, and ultimately obtain a judgment in his favor. Sherrod *v.* Davis, 17 Ala. 312.

§ 158. —— Death of Party.

In General.—When an attachment is levied on lands, the death of the defendant before judgment dissolves the attachment, and destroys the lien; and though the action is revived against the administrator, and judgment recovered against him, the lands can not be sold under execution issued on it. Lipscomb *v.* McClellan, 72 Ala. 151; Phillips *v.* Ash, 63 Ala. 414.

"All personal actions, which may be commenced by attachment, or in the course of which an ancillary attachment may issue (except actions for injuries to the person or reputation), survive for and against the personal representatives of the respective parties. Code of 1876, § 2921. The death of the defendant, after the levy of the attachment, causes a temporary suspension, or abatement of the suit, which must be cured by a revivor against his personal representative. The title to all personal property of a deceased person devolves, by operation of law, on his personal representative. Death works a change of the parties to the suit, but, of itself, does not dissolve the attachment, or impair its lien on personal property. For, when the revivor is had against the personal representative, there is before the court the party having the title; and if judgment is rendered against him, it operates directly on the property; and a venditioni exponas, or a fieri facias, may be issued upon it, under which a sale may be made for the satisfaction of the judgment. But, if the estate of the defendant has been judicially declared insolvent, then the lien is lost. The judicial ascertainment of the insolvency takes away all right to execution on the judgment, and transfers to the court ascertaining it exclusive jurisdiction to marshal and distribute the assets, and of all debts and claims chargeable upon them; and the statute intervenes, and declares the order in which debts and claims are to be paid. Woolfolk *v.* Ingram, 53 Ala. 11. But the death of the defendant, pendente lite, of necessity works a loss of the lien created by the levy of the attachment on real estate. If he dies intestate, the lands descend immediately to his heirs; or, if he dies testate, they pass to his devisees. The personal representative takes no estate or interest in them, and a judgment against him will not bind them. No other than real actions, under our statutes, are capable of revivor for or against heirs or devisees. As the title resides in them, and they can not be made parties, no judgment can be rendered by which they are to be divested of their estate, though the levy created a lien, continuing during the life of the ancestor. This is the frailty and uncertainty of the lien, as the statutes have created it. McClellan *v.* Lipscomb, 56 Ala. 255." Phillips *v.* Ash, 63 Ala. 414, 416.

The death of the defendant in attachment, unless attended by the insolvency of his estate, judicially ascertained, does not affect the lien on personal property, or the right to judgment on which process of execution may issue. Woolfolk *v.* Ingram, 53 Ala. 11.

When an attachment is levied on personal property, the death of the defendant before judgment does not destroy the lien nor dissolve the attachment; but if the levy is on lands, and the defendant dies before judgment, and the action is revived and prosecuted to judgment against his administrator, a sale of the lands under execution on such judgment conveys no title to the purchaser as against the heirs. Whether the plaintiff's remedy, in such case, is by scire facias against the heirs, under the statute of Westminster 2 (13 Edw. I. c. 45), as a part of the common law in Alabama, or by bill in equity, quære. McClellan *v.* Lipscomb, 56 Ala. 255; cited in note in 31 L. R. A. 425.

Where a lien on land, arising from the levy of an attachment, is lost by the death of defendant before judgment, equity will not supply the defects of the statutory remedy, by subjecting the land to the satisfaction of plaintiff's claim. Phillips *v.* Ash, 63 Ala. 414, explaining McClellan *v.* Lipscomb, 56 Ala. 255.

Specific Application of Rule.—On the death and the insolvency of the estate of the defendant in a proceeding by attachment to enforce a lien, created by contract, on his crop and stock, for advances to assist in making the crop, the lien is not dissolved as to the property attached as subject to the contract lien, but the court will enforce the lien by ordering a sale of the property, when judgment is rendered for the debt or demand secured by the lien. McKinney *v.* Benagh, 48 Ala. 358.

An administrator may plead the insolvency of the estate committed to his charge, in abatement of a suit by capias, in the lifetime of the intestate, in which an attachment also was sued out as an auxiliary process, and levied on real and personal estate. And the lien of such attachment is only an inchoate right dependent on the judgment, which not being allowed, the lien is gone. Hale *v.* Cummings, 3 Ala. 398.

§ 159. Effect of Dissolution.

Agreement as to Release of Lien.—Where a plaintiff in attachment agreed to release his lien on the property attached in consideration that the sureties on a delivery bond in that suit would go on another bond in a suit by other creditors against the same defendant, such agreement can not be taken advantage of by another claimant of such property, who was not a party to the agreement, and whose interest was not prejudiced thereby. Greene *v.* Tims, 16 Ala. 541.

VIII. CLAIMS BY THIRD PERSONS.

As to necessity to determine claimants right before proceeding to final judgment in attachment suit, see ante, "Trial in General," § 128. As to claims in justices court, see the title JUSTICES OF THE PEACE.

§ 160. Claims under Attachment.

§ 161. —— Rights of Other Creditors.

Different Writs in Attachment.—"When there are writs of attachment subsequent to the first, each differing in date of levy, and all levied in the same property, each subsequent one is levied in subordination to the ones that precede it, and the lien of each dates from the amount of its levy; and, if all are prosecuted to judgment, they must be paid in the order of their respective levies." Bamberger *v.* Voorhees, 99 Ala. 292, 13 So. 305, 306.

§ 162. Claims or Liens Prior or Superior to Attachment.

§ 163. —— Right to Assert.

As to establishment and sufficiency, see post, "Establishment and Sufficiency," § 164.

Right to Intervene or to Become Party in Order to Assert Title.—Third persons, acquiring an interest in the property attached pendente lite, are neither necessary nor proper parties to the suit; and they can not claim the right to intervene for the protection of their interests, by moving a dissolution of the attachment, or a discharge of the levy. McAbee *v.* Parker, 78 Ala. 573, cited on this point in note in 23 L. R. A., N. S., 536.

In case of the liens given by Rev. Code, §§ 1860, 2961, the character of the demand enters into the ground of the attachment. And where an attachment has been sued out to enforce the lien for rent and advances, and levied on crops grown on the rented premises, the person in possession, deriving title from the tenants, may interpose a claim to try the right of property, and defeat the attachment on proof that the debt has been paid, and this, too, without regard to the failure of the debtor to interpose any defense to the attachment suit. Dryer *v.* Abercrombie, 57 Ala. 497.

Defendant in attachment can not complain of a refusal to allow third persons to intervene, and assert an interest in the property, since he can not be prejudiced by such refusal; nor is the refusal revisable on error or appeal, unless duly excepted to. McAbee *v.* Parker, 78 Ala. 573.

Right to Resort to Statutory Action for Trial of Right of Property.—The statutory remedy of trial of right of property levied on by attachment or execution is merely cumulative to the common-law actions of trespass against the officer levying the process, or of trover or detinue against him or those obtaining possession from him, and can be maintained only when one of those actions could be supported at common law. Lehman *v.* Warren, 53 Ala. 535.

A trial of the right of property may be maintained, whenever personal property is seized under legal process, when trespass, trover, or detinue would be against the officer making the seizure. Abraham *v.* Carter, 53 Ala. 8.

Claim by Mortgagee.—On the trial of a claimant's right to certain attached property, the claim being based on a mortgage of the property, the verdict must be for plaintiff in attachment, if claimant has not satisfactorily shown that when the attachment was issued she had a valid, existing, debt, secured by mortgage on the property. Mitcham *v.* Schuessler, 98 Ala. 635, 13 So. 617.

A lien under Rev. Code, §§ 1858-60, for advances to make a crop, which also vests the title to the crops in the claimant, and contains apt words to constitute a mortgage, is sufficient to enable the claimant to maintain a statutory action for a trial of the right of property. Boswell *v.* Carlisle, 55 Ala. 554.

On a trial of the right of property, between a plaintiff in attachment and a third person as claimant, the latter can not, ordinarily, controvert the plaintiff's debt against the defendant, nor can the plaintiff prove title in himself to the property levied on; but, where the plaintiff is seeking by attachment to enforce his statutory lien for advances to make a crop (Rev. Code, §§ 1858-60), and the claimant shows title in himself, by mortgage from the defendant, prior to the levy of the attachment, the plaintiff may, in rebuttal, introduce the instrument creating his lien for advances antecedent to the date of the claimant's mortgage. Boswell *v.* Carlisle, etc., Co., 55 Ala. 554.

An instrument creating a statutory lien for advances to make a crop does not confer on the person making the advances such title to the crop as will enable him to maintain a statutory action for a trial of the right of property therein; but, if it also contains apt words to make it operative as a mortgage, it will be sufficient. Boswell *v.* Carlisle, etc., Co., 55 Ala. 554.

Rights of Pledgee or Bailee.—When the owner of goods transfers to another the possession of them for a particular purpose or use, a bailment is created, the general property residing in the bailor, and the immediate possession and a temporary or qualified right in the bailee; and the goods having been levied on while in the bailee's possession, as the property of the defendant in an attachment, who is not connected with the legal title, the bailee may interpose and maintain a claim under the statute for their recovery. Shahan *v.* Herzberg, etc., Co., 73 Ala. 59.

A bailee of goods has a qualified title thereto, and may recover them from one who has levied an attachment on them, unless a superior title is shown in the defendant in attachment. Shahan *v.* Herzberg, 73 Ala. 59.

Intervention by Sureties on Bond.—If a junior attachment is levied on the property after it has been replevied, the sureties on the replevin bond may interpose a claim, and try the right of property under the statute; and if the sheriff refuses to entertain the claim, on the ground that he has returned the attachment papers to court, the sureties may, by mandamus, compel him to receive and file their affidavit and bond. Cordaman *v.* Malone, 63 Ala. 556.

Effect of Bonded Property on Right to Intervene.—A stranger to an attachment suit, who has replevied the property attached, can not, after the rendition of judgment against the defendant, and a demand of the property on the bond, interpose a claim to the property under the statute, without having first surrendered it to the sheriff according to the condition of his bond. Braley *v.* Clark, 22 Ala. 361, cited in note in 32 L. R. A., N. S., 407.

§ 164. —— Establishment and Sufficiency.

Burden of Proof.—In attachment, where the property is claimed by a third person under a bill of sale from the defendants, and the claimant's evidence is sufficient to establish her case, the fact that she is the mother of the vendors does not cast on her the burden of making any further proof. Troy Fertilizer Co. *v.* Norman, 107 Ala. 667, 18 So. 201.

Sufficiency of Title to Uphold Claims.—A claimant in attachment must fail, unless the facts which support his title existed when the claim was interposed. Seisel *v.* Folmar, 103 Ala. 491, 15 So. 850.

To enable a party to recover in a statutory trial of the right of property in goods attached, he must show a title on which he could support trover, trespass, or detinue. Block *v.* Maas, 65 Ala. 211.

Where two attachments, sued out against the same party, are levied on the same property, and a claim interposed in each case by the same person, the payment by the claimant of the assessed value of the property in the first case does not of itself sustain his claim in the second. Derrett *v.* Alexander, 25 Ala. 265.

Under a joint claim to attached goods, through a bill of sale thereof by defendants in attachment to claimants, plaintiffs in attachment having shown prima facie that the property was subject to the levy, neither claimant can recover, where the evidence shows that the sale was fraudulent and void as to one of them. Cottingham *v.* Armour Packing Co., 109 Ala. 421, 19 So. 842.

In a statutory trial of the right of property, levied upon by attachment, the claimant can not set up outstanding title in a stranger, in which he has no interest and with which he does not connect himself. Wollner *v.* Lehman, 85 Ala. 274, 4 So. 643, 646.

In a statutory trial of the right of property, levied upon by attachment, the claimant must recover on the strength of his own title, not because of the weakness or want of title in the defendant in the process. Seisel *v.* Folmar, 103 Ala. 491, 15 So. 850, 851; Cofer *v.* Reinschmidt, 121 Ala. 252, 25 So. 769, 770.

In a statutory trial of the right of property levied upon by attachment, plaintiff can not be permitted to recover upon the weakness of the title of the claimant unless he shows the property to be the property of the defendant; and subject to his attachment. Cofer *v.* Reinschmidt, 121 Ala. 252, 25 So. 769, 770.

§ 165. —— Contest of Attachment by Claimant.

As to right to intervene, see post, "Right to Intervene," § 167.

In General.—On a statutory trial of the right of property, claimant can not raise objections to mere irregularities in the proceedings under which the attachment writ was issued; but he can defeat plaintiff by showing that the original attachment was void. Wiggs Bros. *v.* Ringemann, 45 So. 153, 155 Ala. 189. See Jackson *v.* Bain, 74 Ala. 328, 330; Nordlinger *v.* Gordon, 72 Ala. 239; Taliaferro *v.* Lane, 2 Ala. 369, 376.

Mortgages.—Persons, who are mortgagees merely, claiming under a mortgage executed after the levy of an attachment on the mortgaged property, and who are strangers to the attachment suit, have not such an interest as gives them a right on motion, as amici curiæ or otherwise, to ask the court in which the attachment suit is pending to dismiss and dissolve the attachment on the ground of irregularities in the affidavit and bond for the attachment, when the motion is made after the suit has been pending for several terms. May *v.* Courtnay, 47 Ala. 185, cited on this point in note in 35 L. R. A. 768, 23 L. R. A., N. S., 536.

§ 166. Intervention to Contest Attachment.

§ 167. —— Right to Intervene.

As to grounds for contest, see post, "Grounds for Contest," § 168. As to choice of remedy, see post, "Nature and Form of Remedy," § 175. As to contest of attachment by claimant, see ante, "Contest of Attachment by Claimant," § 165. As to right as to property conveyed in trust for creditors, see the title ASSIGNMENTS FOR BENEFIT OF CREDITORS.

Claimant of Attached Property.—The right to vacate an attachment under Code, § 563, providing that an attachment issued without affidavit as prescribed may be abated on a plea by the defendant, is limited to the defendant in attachment, and can not be exercised by a claimant of the attached property. McCain Bros. *v.* Street, 33 So. 872, 136 Ala. 625.

Subsequent Attaching Creditor.—A subsequent attaching creditor can not make himself a party defendant to the prior attachment suit, with the view of defending the cause on its merits, his remedy being a bill in equity to contest the lien of the prior attachment on the ground of fraud. Cartwright *v.* Bamberger, 90 Ala. 405, 8 So. 264, cited on this point in note in 35 L. R. A. 772.

"It is the settled practice in this state that in an attachment suit at law, another creditor can not intervene by petition, and be made a party to the suit, in order that he may attack the proceedings on the ground of fraud, or fraudulent collusion between the attaching creditor and the debtor. Cartwright *v.* Bamberger, 90 Ala. 405, 8 So. 264." Bamberger *v.* Voorhees, 99 Ala. 292, 13 So. 305, 306.

§ 168. —— Grounds for Contest.

As to right to intervene, see ante, "Right to Intervene," § 167.

Service of Process.—"The law is well settled that if a writ of attachment is issued by a person not authorized to issue it, or is void upon its face, from any cause, the claimant may avail himself of such a defect." Schamragel *v.* Whitehurst, 103 Ala. 260, 15 So. 611. See Nordlinger *v.* Gordon, 72 Ala. 239; Jackson *v.* Bain, 74 Ala. 328; Taliaferro *v.* Lane, 23 Ala. 369.

In this case it was held that an intervening claimant could not, on a trial of the right of property, assail the validity of the service of process as to a mere irregularity in the designation of the parties, which defect is perfectible by amendment. Dollins *v.* Pollock, 89 Ala. 351, 7 So. 904, cited on this point in note in 23 L. R. A., N. S., 1084.

§ 169. —— Proceedings, Hearing, and Determination.

Errors Available to Claimant.—When a claim is interposed under the statute to property under attachment, the claimant can not, on the trial of the claim suit, take advantage of any mere errors or irregularities in the proceedings against the defendant in attachment. Pace *v.* Lee & Co., 49 Ala. 571.

On a statutory trial of the right of property, the claimant can not take advantage of any defects or irregularities in the process which render it merely voidable at the instance of the defendant; but, if the process is void on its face, he may defeat the plaintiff's claim by setting up such invalidity. Nordlinger *v.* Gordon, 72 Ala. 239.

Issues.—"A 'trial of the right of property,' is a statutory proceeding which answers the purpose of an action of trespass against the sheriff, when it is complained that, under process against one, he has levied on the personal goods of another. The issue of merit in such trial is formed by an allegation on the part of the plaintiff in the process that the goods levied on are subject to it, and a denial by the claimant of the truth of that allegation. Such suit can be resorted to only when there is another suit, or final process in progress, and, in the absence of such suit or process for the enforcement of a judgment recovered, there can be no rightful resort to this statutory remedy. The statutes define its boundaries. 3 Brick. Dig. 776. In such trial the claimant is not concerned in the rightfulness of the levy. His right to litigate is confined to his right to the property, and to his legal right as contrasted with any equitable claim he may assert. 3 Brick. Dig. 776. But if the process under which the condemnation is sought is void, he can take advantage of its invalidity. Of mere irregularities, or reversible errors, he can not complain. 3 Brick. Dig. 777, § 25." Dollins *v.* Pollock, 89 Ala. 351, 7 So. 904, 905.

Record on Appeal.—Under the rule that the interposition of a claim to attached property puts in issue only the claimant's right and title, and that irregularities in the attachment are not available to such claimant, where a claim of attached property is interposed by one partner in the name of his firm, the subsequent proceedings are properly conducted against the partnership as claimant, although the forthcoming bond is given by such partner individually, and recites that he "has filed a claim," etc.; and a recital in the judgment entry in such case that the one by whom the claim was interposed is a member of the firm is sufficient on error to sustain a default judgment against such firm as claimant. Pace *v.* Lee, 49 Ala. 571.

§ 170. Rights of Claimants of Property Attached in General.

Matters Determining Rights.—A right of a claimant of goods attached as the goods of another against the attaching creditor depends on the fact of the levy and not on an excessive levy, which is but an abuse of the process for which a stranger to the writ of attachment can not recover. Brock *v.* Young (Ala. App.), 62 So. 326.

§ 171. Notice or Demand by Claimant, and Affidavit of Claim.

Statement as to Ownership or Possession of Property.—Where the sheriff returns an attachment, levied on certain lands in the possession of a person not a party to the writ, it will be intended, in order to sustain the proceeding, that they were the property of the defendant, and levied on as such. Lucas *v.* Godwin, 6 Ala. 831.

It is no objection to a judgment on an attachment on lands that the return does not show that the lands belonged to defendant, and does show that third persons were in possession. Lucas *v.* Godwin, 6 Ala. 831.

§ 172. Security by Claimant for Possession.

As to liabilities on bonds, see post, "Liabilities on Bonds or Undertakings," X. As to property taken under attachment being subject to replevin, see the title REPLEVIN.

Necessity for Bond.—Under Code 1876, § 3341, et seq., requiring a claimant to property attached to execute a forthcoming bond, such bond is necessary to give the court jurisdiction, and can not be waived by the parties. Mobile Life Ins. Co. *v.* Teague, 78 Ala. 147.

The claimant having made neither affidavit nor bond in the justice's court, and having failed to give any bond in the circuit court, to which the case was removed by appeal, and having withdrawn his claim, by consent of the court; the court has no jurisdiction to render judgment against him for the value of the property, nor any other judgment, except, perhaps, for costs. Mobile Life Ins. Co. *v.* Teague, 78 Ala. 147.

Sufficiency of Bond.—An attachment bond given by a claimant, conditioned that the obligor shall have the property forthcoming for the satisfaction of the judgment, if it be found liable therefor, and shall pay the costs and damages that may be recovered, is sufficient, under Code 1907, § 6039, permitting a person to try the right to the property, upon executing a bond with the condition to have the property forthcoming for the satisfaction of the judgment or claim. Holloway *v.* Burroughs, etc., Co., 4 Ala. App. 630, 58 So. 953.

Amendment of Bond.—Upon the levy of an attachment, third persons, as claimants of the property, filed affidavit of claim, and executed a replevy bond. Before entering on the trial, claimants asked for leave to amend the bond, so as to make it a claim bond. Held, that the amendment was properly allowed. Martin *v.* Mayer, 20 So. 963, 112 Ala. 620.

Waiver of Defects in Bond.—In this case, the bond executed by the claimant being in for and substance a replevy bond, but accepted and treated, without objection, as a regular claim bond; and a trial of the right of property, as if regularly instituted, having been conducted and carried on for eight years, during which there was a mistrial of the cause; held, that the defects in the bond were waived, and the plaintiff could not then have the claim suit struck from the docket, and the bond returned forfeited as an ordinary replevy bond. Rhodes *v.* Smith, 66 Ala. 174.

Effect of Bond.—A stranger may interpose a claim to property on which an attachment has been levied, before it has been replevied by the defendant, on making affidavit, and giving bond conditioned as prescribed by the statute (Code, §§ 3290, 3341); but, in this case, he does not act for the benefit of the defendant, and can not be required, in any event, to restore the property to him; nor can he discharge himself from liability on his bond, by returning it to the sheriff, without the assent of the plaintiff in attachment. Rhodes *v.* Smith, 66 Ala. 174.

Where an attachment is levied on property of plaintiff's debtor, in possession of defendants, claiming it under a prior sale, and on the same day defendants execute a replevy bond, and the sheriff returns the property to them, and on the next day defendants make the required affidavit, and execute a claim bond, which the sheriff accepts and approves, such approval of the claim bond annuls the replevy bond. Roswald *v.* Hobbie, 85 Ala. 73, 4 So. 177.

§ 173. Actions by Claimant for Recovery of Possession.

Detinue.—In detinue for goods seized by a sheriff under writs of attachment and claimed by plaintiff under a mortgage, plaintiff can not raise the question of the duty of the sheriff to first exhaust the debtor's goods not subject to the mortgage. Gillespie *v.* McCleskey, 160 Ala. 289, 49 So. 362.

Where, in detinue for goods seized by a sheriff under attachments, it appeared that the entire property was levied on in each attachment, and there was no rule to determine that any distinct part was liable to one and not to the other, and the jury could be required only to say whether the sheriff was entitled to retain the property, a charge that there were two forms of verdict was not erroneous, because directing the jury to find a verdict according to one or the other of the forms. Gillespie *v.* McCleskey, 160 Ala. 289, 49 So. 362.

In detinue against a sheriff, a plea justifying a seizure of personal property, which sets up several attachments under which he holds the property, does not set up distinct defenses, and, if he may hold under any attachment, the property can not be taken from him. Gillespie *v.* McCleskey, 49 So. 362, 160 Ala. 289.

§ 174. Proceedings for Establishment and Determination of Claims to Property.

§ 175. —— Nature and Form of Remedy.

As to quashing writ by a stranger for matters dehors the record, see ante, "Nature and Form of Remedy," § 133.

Remedy in Equity of One Contesting Attachment.—An attaching creditor, who has acquired a specific lien by levy of his writ, can maintain a bill in equity to set aside as fraudulent a prior attachment of the same property. Cartwright *v.* Bamberger, 90 Ala. 405, 8 So. 264; cited on this point in note in 23 L. R. A., N. S., 536. See Bamberger *v.* Voorhees, 99 Ala. 292, 13 So. 305.

Necessity of Intervention to Maintain Rights.—A justice of the peace, before whom an attachment is returnable, has no jurisdiction to try the right or title to property levied on, at the instance of a third person who claims it, unless a claim is interposed under oath, and proceedings conducted in the manner prescribed by the statute; and consent of the parties can not confer jurisdiction of the subject matter of a contest so initiated and conducted. Walker *v.* Ivey, 74 Ala. 475.

Summary Remedies.—While a circuit court may settle rival claims to funds in the hands of the sheriff, and proceed in such cases in a summary and informal manner, on application of the sheriff, stating the facts, and notice to the parties, such course can only be pursued to protect the sheriff against conflicting claims of suitors; and a claimant who does not claim under legal process is not entitled to litigate in such proceedings with those who do so claim. Gillespie *v.* Bickley, 53 So. 108, 168 Ala. 219.

Nature of Claim Suit.—"A claim suit is not an independent suit, in the sense that it may, in the first instance, be inaugurated as such; but it is, under the statute, consequential or collateral to the main suit against the defendant in attachment. Jackson *v.* Bain, 74 Ala. 328; Cofer *v.* Reinschmidt, 121 Ala. 252, 25 So. 769. Yet, as between the immediate parties to it—the plaintiff and the claimant—it is distinct and independent of the main suit between the plaintiff and defendant in attachment, with distinct and independent issues. Gray *v.* Raiborn, 53 Ala. 40." Wheeles *v.* New York Steam Dye Works, 129 Ala. 393, 29 So. 793.

"A trial of the right to personal property, levied on by legal process, is a statutory proceeding, having all the form and substance of a suit or action at law. It is initiated by the claim of a stranger, making oath in writing to the property, and giving bond as prescribed by the statute. The plaintiff in the process then becomes the actor in the suit, and on him rests the burden of maintaining the affirmative fact asserted by the levy, that the property is subject to the levy. Jacott *v.* Hobson, 11 Ala. 434; McAdams *v.* Beard, 34 Ala. 478. The affidavit and bond of the claimant are returned into the court to which the attachment or execution is returnable, unless the levy is made in another county. When these are returned into the court, it is the duty of the clerk of the court to docket the trial of right of property, as a separate, independent cause, in which an issue, foreign to any involved in the attachment suit, is to be formed, with a stranger to that suit. The affidavit and bond required of the claimant are each intended for the benefit and protection of the plaintiff in attachment, to avoid the making of fictitious claims for delay, or other improper purposes; and to secure him the value of the property, it is adjudged liable to the process. Being intended for the benefit of the plaintiff, he may waive defects or irregularities in both, or in either. Whatever rights or benefits are intended for the advantage or protection of a party to a judicial proceeding, not involving the jurisdiction of the court over the subject matter, he may, at pleasure, renounce or assert; and I apprehend there can be no doubt, that all objections kindred to such as could be made to the want or sufficiency of an affidavit, or a bond for the trial of the right of property, which, when well founded, may be removed and cured by the making of a sufficient affidavit, or a sufficient bond, by order and leave of the court—are waived, if there is an omission to make them at some proper stage of the proceedings. They are not open to inquiry collaterally; do not affect the regularity or the validity of the proceedings, and, even on error, will not be looked into, if not made the matter of specific objection in the primary court. 2 Brick. Dig., 479, §§ 59-62." Rhodes *v.* Smith, 66 Ala. 174, 177.

§ 176. —— Jurisdiction.

What Court Has Jurisdiction.—When an attachment returnable to the county court is levied on property, and a claim is interposed, and bond given to try the right, the trial of the right of property must be had in the same court in which the attachment suit was instituted, and not in the circuit court. Thompson *v.* Evans, 12 Ala. 588.

When an attachment is levied in a county different from that in which it was issued, and a claim to the property is interposed, the statute (Code of 1876, § 3290), requires that the trial of the right of property must be had in the county in which the attachment was levied. Ex parte Dunlap, 71 Ala. 73.

An issue as to the ownership of personal property attached on process made returnable to the circuit court is within the jurisdiction of any circuit court in the state which may acquire jurisdiction of the persons of the plaintiff in attachment and the claimant. Trieste *v.* Enslen, 106 Ala. 180, 17 So. 356.

§ 177. —— Pleading.

Interposition of Claim.—Under Code 1896, § 4145, as amended by Acts 1900-01, p. 106, relating to attachment, and providing that, when the claim interposed is based on a mortgage or lien, the claimant must state in his affidavit the nature of the right which he claims, etc., claims filed in attachment proceedings, not stating the nature of the right set up, but stating that the property attached was not the property of attachment defendant, but of the claimant, and that the latter had a just claim thereto, were sufficient to give the court jurisdiction of the claim suits, and amendments thereto setting forth the nature of the claimant's claims to the property should have been permitted; the evidence showing that claimant had a lien thereon for rent and advances. Witherington *v.* Gainer, 43 So. 117, 149 Ala. 655.

Plea.—A plea in abatement for defects in an attachment bond or affidavit must set out the bond or affidavit; otherwise it is demurrable. Tommey *v.* Gamble, 66 Ala. 469.

A plea in abatement in an attachment case, on account of defects in the affidavit for the writ; is not required to be sworn to (Code, § 2989), since the affidavit is matter of record. Tommey *v.* Gamble & Son, 66 Ala. 469.

§ 178. —— Issues and Questions Considered.

In General.—Under a statutory claim suit (Code, § 4142) the only issue for the jury is whether or not the property claimed is that of the defendant in the writ, and liable to its satisfaction. Schloss *v.* Inman, 30 So. 667, 129 Ala. 424.

On a trial of the right of property, the only proper issue is an affirmation by the plaintiff in the process that the property levied on is subject to the process, and a denial of that fact by the claimant. It was not contemplated that the proceeding should be embarrassed by formal pleadings in the form of complaint, or plea, replication or rejoinder. Lehman, etc., Co. *v.* Warren, 53 Ala. 535.

While it is true that in the statutory action of the trial of the right of property, the claimant will not be permitted to defeat a recovery by the plaintiffs by proving outstanding title in a stranger, this rule extends only to cases where the plaintiff has made out a prima facie case, and the claimant has no privity of estate with the person whose title is set up.

It does not overturn the statutory rule that the burden of proof is on the plaintiff in execution. The proper issue in this action is, an affirmation on the part of the plaintiff that the property in question is subject to his execution or attachment, and a denial of that fact by the defendant, and unless the plaintiff proves prima facie, at least, a title in the defendant, he must fail, though the claimant shows no title to the property in question. Lien, right, or even title in the plaintiff, gives no right to condemn the property under the execution or attachment. Starnes *v.* Allen, etc., Co., 58 Ala. 316.

On trial of the right of property to certain slaves seized on attachment, where no question of adverse title is raised, a charge upon that branch may be properly refused, and, when the claimant takes title under defendant, the only question is as to the bona fides of the transaction. Yarborough *v.* Moss, 9 Ala. 382.

Validity of Levy.—The validity of an attachment levy is immaterial to a claimant of the attached property, since by the execution of the claim bond he is estopped from denying it. Sloan *v.* Hudson, 24 So. 458, 119 Ala. 27.

Service on Defendant.—A claimant of attached property can not object that the attachment suit was not tried before the issue raised by his claim, and hence as to him service on the attachment defendant is immaterial. Sloan *v.* Hudson, 24 So. 458, 119 Ala. 27.

Payment of Debt.—On a statutory trial of right of property attached, the intervening claimant will not be permitted to prove payment of the debt subsequently to the suing out of the attachment, such payment being outside the issue at the time of interposing the claim. Foster *v.* Goodwin, 82 Ala. 384, 2 So. 895.

Indebtedness of Defendant.—In general, on the trial of the right of property, the inquiry, whether the defendant in the process is indebted to the plaintiff, is immaterial and foreign to the issue, the material issue being whether the defendant in the process, had, at the time of the levy, such property in the goods as is subject to levy and sale; and this is so in attachment (under §§ 3252-3 of the Code), which can not be dissolved, quashed or abated, on proof that none of the grounds for suing it out, in fact, existed. Dryer *v.* Abercrombie, 57 Ala. 497.

Hearing and Determination.—In an attachment suit, where a third party claims the property levied on, and the trial of property rights proceeds on that claim, the main issues between plaintiff and defendant are held in abeyance till the property right is determined, and a judgment for the amount of plaintiff's claim, founded on the mere determination of the property right, and at a time when defendant has only made a special appearance, is void. Abraham *v.* Nicrosi, 87 Ala. 173, 6 So. 293.

§ 179. —— Evidence.

See, generally, the title EVIDENCE.

As to admissibility of parol evidence, see the title EVIDENCE.

§ 179 (1) Presumptions and Burden of Proof.

In General.—In a statutory trial for the right of property levied upon by attachment, the plaintiff need only make a prima facie case, which he does by proving that the goods were in the possession and in the control of the defendant at the time of the levy. The burden then shifts to the claimant to establish his right. Wollner *v.* Lehman, 85 Ala. 274, 4 So. 643, 646, See, also, Loeb & Bro. *v.* Manasses, 78 Ala. 555; Jones *v.* Franklin, 81 Ala. 161, 1 So. 199; Foster *v.* Goodwin, 82 Ala. 384, 2 So. 895.

In the trial of the right of property levied on under an execution or attachment, the issue is, whether the property belongs to the defendant and is subject to the process, and the burden of proof is on the plaintiff in the process, who is regarded as the actor. If he makes out a prima facie case, the burden of proof then shifts to the claimant who in that event must show a legal title in himself—such a title as would support trespass, trover or detinue. Shahan *v.* Herzberg, etc., Co., 73 Ala. 59.

Code, § 4141, provides that, when an attachment is levied on personal property, as to which some third person claims the legal or equitable title, or a lien paramount to the interest of the attachment defendant, such person may try the right of property. Held, that the burden of proof is first on the attachment plaintiff to make out a prima facie case of liability of the property to attachment, whereupon the burden is cast on the claimant to show title or lien. British & A. Mortg. Co. *v.* Cody, 33 So. 832, 135 Ala. 622. See Wollner *v.* Lehman, 85 Ala. 274, 4 So. 643, 646; Cofer *v.* Reinschmidt, 121 Ala. 252, 25 So. 769, 770.

Specific Applications of Rule.—Where a claim was dismissed for failure to file the required affidavit, mere proof by plaintiff, in an action on the claimant's bond, that the property was not forthcoming held insufficient to show a breach of the condition; it being necessary to show that claimant was not entitled to the property. Holloway *v.* Burroughs, etc., Co., 4 Ala. App. 630, 58 So. 953.

In a statutory claim suit to try the right to property levied on under an attachment, the burden of proof in the first instance is on plaintiff to show that the property levied on under the attachment was the property of defendant and subject to levy, and when he establishes a prima facie case to that effect the burden is then shifted to the claimant to show ownership in himself. Roberts, Long & Co. *v.* Ringemann, 40 So. 81, 145 Ala. 678.

Under Code 1876, § 3343, providing for the trial of the title to attached property claimed by a third person, the burden of proof is on plaintiff to show a valid seizure and evidence of ownership in defendant before claimant is required to prove his title; and, if the seizure was under a said process, plaintiff can not recover. Jackson *v.* Bain, 74 Ala. 328.

Where, on a trial of the right of property levied on by attachment, the attachment plaintiff introduces the sheriff, who swears that he levied on the property while on the land cultivated by the attachment defendant, the property being a part of defendant's crop, and also testifies as to the value of the property, this makes a prima facie case, and the burden shifts to the claimant. British & A. Mortg. Co. *v.* Cody, 33 So. 832, 135 Ala. 622.

Where, in attachment, a third party interposed a claim, plaintiff in order to make out a prima facie case, must show that defendant in execution was in possession at the time of the levy by the sheriff. Ringemann *v.* Wiggs Bros., 40 So. 323, 146 Ala. 685.

When an attachment is levied by a creditor on goods claimed by a purchaser from his debtor, and his debt antedates the sale or conveyance, the onus is on the purchaser to prove the consideration paid by him. Ellis *v.* Allen, 80 Ala. 515, 2 So. 676.

On trial of the right of property between attaching creditors and a claimant who insists that he holds as a trustee, he must show the existence and bona fides of the secured debts. Elliott *v.* Stocks, 67 Ala. 290.

On trial of the right to property, where it appeared that plaintiffs attached their debtor's property in the hands of defendants, claiming it under a prior sale, the court properly refused to charge that the burden is on defendants to show that such sale was without benefit to the debtor. Roswald *v.* Hobbie, 85 Ala. 73, 4 So. 177.

§ 179 (2) Admissibility.

Evidence as to Ownership.—On the statutory trial of right of property in a stock of attached goods, as tending to show a prior sale by the attachment defendant to the claimant, a witness may testify that he was called in to take an account of the stock, and that at that time defendant said that the stock was to be taken for the purpose of turning it over to the claimant to satisfy a debt due from defendant. Pulliam *v.* Newberry, 41 Ala. 168.

In the trial of the right of property attached, the claimant may put in evidence that, when the claimant got the property from the defendant, all the property owned by the latter was exempt from attachment. Wright *v.* Smith, 66 Ala. 514.

A replevin bond, executed by the defendant in attachment, which did not in express terms assert that the defendant claimed or had an interest in the attached property, is not admissible in evidence against the claimant as proof of the defendant's title to the property at the time of the levy. Wright *v.* Smith, 66 Ala. 514.

In a suit between an attaching creditor and a claimant to try the title to the property attached, the plaintiff may offer evidence showing that, after the date of the supposed mortgage to the claimant, the defendants sold to the plaintiff a part of the goods mortgaged, in the absence of the claimant. But this is admissible only by way of rebuttal, and as explanatory of the possession of the defendant, and not as a circumstance to show the bad faith of the mortgage transaction. Mayer *v.* Clark, 40 Ala. 259.

When the claimant, to disprove plaintiff's prima facie case, introduces in evidence certain transfers under which she claims title, plaintiff may show in rebuttal that, before the levy of the attachment, defendant mortgaged the property to another creditor with the claimant's knowledge and consent, without producing the mortgage. Roberts *v.* Burgess, 85 Ala. 192, 4 So. 733.

In detinue against a sheriff for slaves taken under attachment against A., and claimed by plaintiff as his own property, in order to repel the idea of abandonment by A., and to show title in him, it was admissible to prove that while in possession he had mortgaged them; that when on the steam boat, about to go to California, he declared his intention soon to return; and that plaintiff, after A.'s departure, returned an assessment under oath of his own property, in which said slaves were not included. Rowan *v.* Hutchisson, 27 Ala. 328.

On the trial of the right of property between attaching creditors and a claimant, the creditors must prove that the property in controversy belonged to the defendant, in attachment, at the time of the levy, and, for this purpose, they may trace the title from the original owner to the defendant, and may show the character of the actual possession to disprove the authority of one actually in possession to convey or assign the property to the claimant, and, in such a case, any evidence as to the authority of the person in actual possession to convey the property, or as to the consideration of the conveyance, and its amount, is admissible. Elliott *v.* Stocks & Bro., 67 Ala. 290.

Objections were properly sustained to the introduction by claimant of a receipted bill for the property attached, dated after the levy. Arnold *v.* Cofer, 33 So. 539, 135 Ala. 364.

On a statutory trial of the right of property levied on by attachment, defendant, who was claimant's husband, having appeared as a witness for claimant, and having admitted on cross-examination that he bought the property, was asked on redirect examination for whom the property was bought. Held, that evidence that defendant had listed the property with the tax assessor as his own was properly admitted to weaken the force of the husband's testimony that the property was that of his wife. Arnold *v.* Cofer, 33 So. 539, 135 Ala. 364.

When the parties proceed to trial on an issue whether "the brig levied on was, at the date of the levy, subject to the attachment," a bill of sale bearing date after the levy is, prima facie, irrelevant, as being outside of the issue. But such an issue is itself immaterial. Fontaine *v.* Beers, 19 Ala. 722.

Where a claim is made by one who alleges that he sold the goods attached to defendant because of fraudulent representations as to his ability to pay, collections made and disposition of assets by defendant prior to levy are competent evidence on the trial, but transactions subsequent thereto are not. Wollner *v.* Lehman, 85 Ala. 274, 4 So. 643.

Where the plaintiff is seeking, by attachment, to enforce his statutory lien for advances to make a crop (Rev. Code, §§ 1858-1860), and the claimant shows title in himself, by a mortgage from the defendant made prior to the levy of the attachment, the plaintiff may, in rebuttal, introduce the instrument creating his lien for advances antecedent to the date of the claimant's mortgage. Boswell *v.* Carlisle, 55 Ala. 554.

In attachment, a claim by one who alleges that he sold the goods attached to defendant on fraudulent representations as to his ability to pay, questions by claimant as to whether it is usual or safe to invest so largely in such goods, considering the bad crop year, in the absence of evidence to support the hypothesis, are properly excluded. Woolner *v.* Lehman, 85 Ala. 274, 4 So. 643.

It having been shown in the trial of the

right of property in cotton levied on under an attachment, that the cotton was a part of a crop planted and partly cultivated by the defendant on rented land, but abandoned by him before its maturity, and afterwards gathered by his landlord, who had re-entered, the fact that the landlord, after the crop was abandoned, stated to the plaintiff, who was about to sue out an attachment against the defendant and have it levied on the crop, that he would work out the crop and pay plaintiff's demand against the defendant, on the faith of which the attachment was not then sued out, having no tendency to show that the title to the cotton was in the defendant, or that the cotton was liable to the attachment, is inadmissible for the plaintiff. Shahan *v.* Herzberg, etc., Co., 73 Ala. 59.

Affidavit for Attachment.—The affidavit for attachment is not admissible in evidence on the trial of the claims of third persons who allege that they had purchased the property levied on before the levy. Dollins *v.* Pollock, 89 Ala. 351, 7 So. 904.

Claim Bond.—On the trial of a right of property in an attachment suit, for damages for breach of warranty of title in the sale of personal property, the claim bond given by the claimant for the property levied on is admissible in evidence. Guy *v.* Lee, 81 Ala. 163, 2 So. 273.

When goods have been attached as the property of a debtor, and another person has interposed a claim to them, and has executed a claim bond which recites the levy and the interposition of the claim, and an action had been brought to try the right of property between the attaching creditor and the claimant, the claim bond is evidence for the plaintiff of the levy of the attachment. And if a witness testifies that, on the day on which the attachment is dated, he saw the officer (he having since died) levy an attachment against the defendants in favor of the plaintiff, the attachment and levy may be read in the evidence, although not in the handwriting of the officer. Mayer *v.* Clark, 40 Ala. 259.

Inventories.—When an inventory is attached by the sheriff to a levy of an attachment, and made a part thereof, it is competent evidence in a claim suit instituted to determine the rights of the parties to the property levied upon. Schloss *v.* Inman, 30 So. 667, 129 Ala. 424.

A witness who helped make an inventory of a stock of goods levied upon under an attachment, who has knowledge of the value of a portion of the same, though not of others, can state what the value of the stock as a whole was, as shown in the inventory, as against objection that the testimony, rather than the witness, was incompetent. Schloss *v.* Inman, 129 Ala. 424, 30 So. 667.

Where claimant claims under a bill of sale "per inventory," evidence that the inventory could not have been taken within the alleged time is admissible. Tobias *v.* Treist, 103 Ala. 664, 15 So. 914.

On the trial of the right to property, where the sheriff in levying an attachment on property in possession of defendants, claiming it under a sale from an insolvent debtor, in consideration of a debt to them, makes an inventory of the "reasonable market value" of such property such inventory is admissible, as tending to show an absolute purchase of such property by defendants at a price near its market value. Roswald *v.* Hobbie, 85 Ala. 73, 4 So. 177.

Value of Property.—Where, in proceeding by a claimant to establish his right to attached property, consisting of merchandise, there is evidence of its value six months prior, and of the amount of goods bought subsequent thereto, and that the amount of the sales was always deposited in bank, evidence of the amount of such deposit is admissible to prove the present value of the goods. Tobias *v.* Treist, 103 Ala. 664, 15 So. 914.

Claim of Exemptions. — Defendant's claim of exemptions, which was contemporaneous with her sale of the attached goods to claimant and defendant's failure, was properly admitted in evidence on the trial of the right of property between plaintiff in attachment and claimant. Weinstein & Sons *v.* Yielding Bros. & Co., 167 Ala. 347, 52 So. 591.

Receipt of Money by Defendant Since Marriage with Claimant.—Where claimant of attached property was defendant's wife, and the property consisted of household goods and a cow and a yearling, evidence introduced by plaintiff was properly admitted as to money received by the defendant since his marriage with claimant. Arnold *v.* Cofer, 33 So. 539, 135 Ala. 364.

Marriage of Defendant Immaterial.—In proceedings on a claim by third parties to property levied on by plaintiff in attachment against S. L. W., it was immaterial whether S. L. W. was a man or woman; no question of coverture being involved. Weinstein & Sons *v.* Yielding Bros. & Co., 167 Ala. 347, 52 So. 591.

Declarations and Conduct of Defendants.—On a statutory trial of the right of property in a stock of goods, on which an attachment had been levied, the declarations and conduct of the defendants in attachment proved by the sheriff transpiring after the transfer to the claimant and after the levy, and not accompanying, qualifying, or explaining any material fact in the case, are not admissible in evidence. Pulliam *v.* Newberry, 41 Ala. 168.

On the trial of the right of property in a vessel on which an attachment has been levied, and a claim interposed under the statute, plaintiffs may prove directions given to the captain of the vessel by defendant in attachment, before the levy, under which the former acted. Fontaine *v.* Beers, 19 Ala. 722.

Proof of Identity of Property.—In a suit between an attaching creditor and the person claiming the property by virtue of a sale by defendants, though it may be unnecessary for the plaintiff to prove the identity of the property levied on, the admission of such evidence, at his instance, is not erroneous. Mayer *v.* Clark, 40 Ala. 259.

Proof of Notes as Evidence of Original Debt and Their Consideration.—In a suit between an attaching creditor and the person claiming the property by virtue of a sale by defendants, there was no error in permitting the plaintiff to prove the notes on which his suit was founded or their consideration. Mayer *v.* Clark, 40 Ala. 259.

§ 179 (3) Weight and Sufficiency.

Possession of Defendant Constituting Prima Facie Case against Claimant.—Plaintiff in attachment generally makes a prima facie case as against a claimant of the property levied on by showing that the property was in the possession of defendant at the time of the levy. Roberts, Long & Co. *v.* Ringemann, 40 So. 81, 145 Ala. 678.

Sufficiency of Evidence as to Ownership.—Claim of title by a third person to goods taken in attachment need not be proven beyond a doubt. Wollner *v.* Lehman, 85 Ala. 274, 4 So. 643.

Sufficiency of Proof as to Debt Owing by Defendant.—On the trial of the right of property levied on by attachment, to which a claim has been interposed, under the statute the plaintiff need not produce any other proof of indebtedness than the attachment affords. Butler *v.* O'Brien, 5 Ala. 316.

As between the plaintiff in attachment and a claimant under purchase from the defendant, the attachment itself is sufficient proof of the plaintiff's debt against the defendant. Pulliam, etc., Co. *v.* Newberry, 41 Ala. 168, 169.

Levy of Process.—On the trial of the right of property between a claimant of attached goods and the plaintiff in attachment, plaintiff must prove the levy of process to make out a prima facie case, and was not entitled to recover where no attachment or levy were shown to have been made. M. Weinstein & Sons *v.* Yielding Bros. & Co., 52 So. 591, 167 Ala. 347.

When the claimant's bond and affidavit recite the levy, by a constable named, of an attachment in the suit of plaintiff against the debtor, plaintiff is not bound, on certiorari in the circuit court, to produce other evidence of these facts. Schamragel *v.* Whitehurst, 103 Ala. 260, 15 So. 611.

Notice of Insolvency.—On a claim by a third person in attachment, it appeared that defendant was indebted to a corporation which was indebted to claimant, and that, by mutual agreement, the debts were paid by delivery from defendant to claimant of a quantity of pig iron. There was evidence that defendant was insolvent when the iron was delivered, but that it continued to do business for a month, until an attachment on the iron was levied. Claimant denied notice of insolvency, and it was shown that, though claimant had access to the books of the other corporation, such books did not show the condition of defendant. It was also shown that claimant was a relative of one who had a controlling interest in defendant and the other corporation. Held, that the evidence failed to show notice of insolvency. Mary Lee, etc., R. Co. *v.* Knox, 110 Ala. 632, 16 So. 67.

§ 180. —— Conduct of Trial or Hearing.

Accrual or Release of Action in General.—Where a bond is executed under an order in chancery, conditioned that certain slaves, that had been seized to satisfy such decree as might "be rendered in the suit," should be returned if the decree contemplated their return, the bond is not annulled, or the liability of the obligors restricted or impaired, by an amendment of the bill which merely associates other parties with the complainant (the obligee), without varying the frame of the bill or extending or limiting the liability of the obligors. Falls *v.* Weissinger, 11 Ala. 801.

§ 181. —— Questions for Jury.

In General.—On the trial of a claim interposed to property levied on by attachment, evidence considered, and held that claimant was entitled to a submission of question to the jury. Ringemann *v.* Wiggs Bros., 40 So. 323, 146 Ala. 685.

Fraud.—On a statutory trial of the right of property, where the issue is as to whether the claimant had a right to rescind the sale of goods to the defendant in attachment, and there is evidence from which the jury might have concluded that the purchaser of the goods was insolvent at the time he purchased from the claimant, that he then had no intention of paying for the goods or reasonable expectation of being able to pay for them, and that he failed to communicate these facts to the claimant, and it is further shown that the claimant sought and obtained independent information as to the purchaser's financial condition before shipping the goods, but it does not affirmatively appear that the claimant acted solely upon this independent information, and not upon the alleged fraud of the purchaser, it is a question for the jury to determine as to whether the claimant was induced by the alleged fraud to make the sale, if they believe the purchaser had been guilty of fraud, or by such independent information, and therefore the affirmative charge should not be given. Union Mfg. & Commission Co. *v.* East Alabama Nat. Bank, 29 So. 781, 129 Ala. 292.

§ 182. —— Instructions.

Argumentative Instructions.—An instruction that the jury "may look to the assessment of P. [defendant] of the property, * * * in connection with all the other evidence, to determine whose property it was when levied upon." while argumentative, and perhaps calling for an explanatory charge, was not reversible error. Arnold *v.* Cofer, 33 So. 539, 135 Ala. 364.

An instruction, required by claimant of attached property, that possession of personalty is prima facie evidence of title, and that the jury might "look to the fact, if it be a fact," that claimant was living on her own premises, where the property was also situated, to determine in whose possession it was, was properly refused as argumentative. Arnold *v.* Cofer, 33 So. 539, 135 Ala. 364.

Sale to Innocent Purchaser.—A charge that claimant in attachment can not recover if there has been a sale of the goods by defendant to an innocent purchaser without knowledge of the claim is improper; such sale being no part of the issue. Wollner *v.* Lehman, 85 Ala. 274, 4 So. 643.

Sale without Delivery.—A charge that, if a sale by defendant was without delivery, it passed no title, and claimant was entitled to recover, not only presents an immaterial issue, but does not state the elements essential to claimant's right to recover, and is properly refused. Wollner *v.* Lehman, 85 Ala. 274, 4 So. 643.

Parties.—Where there was evidence to show, in a case of the trial of the rights of property, that claimant did business in St. Louis under the name of "B. & Co.," and sent out circulars claiming a branch house in Chicago, some of which plaintiff received, and plaintiff attached the property in dispute as the property of B. & Co. of Chicago, it was not error to instruct the jury that if they believed B. &

Co. of St. Louis and B. & Co. of Chicago were one and the same firm, and that plaintiff was induced to deal with B. & Co. of Chicago in consequence of such circulars, plaintiff was entitled to recover. Zeiner *v.* Mims, 96 Ala. 285, 11 So. 302.

Excessive Levy.—In an action for conversion, plaintiff, a mortgagee, claimed ownership of goods taken from her by attachment against the mortgagor, against whom the attaching creditor claimed a landlord's lien. The court instructed that the attaching creditor would be liable for the invasion of plaintiff's possession under a bona fide claim of title if the levy of attachment was on property in excess of his claim, and if there was a material excess he would be liable, though he had a just debt and a valid lien and though the property may have exceeded $1,000 in value, the amount of the mortgage debt. Held erroneous for authorizing recovery, though plaintiff's claim, while bona fide, might have been constructively fraudulent and not enforceable as to the attaching creditor because of the value of the goods being unreasonably in excess of the mortgage debt which plaintiff claimed was the sole consideration of a sale of the goods to her by the mortgagor. Brock *v.* Young (Ala. App.), 62 So. 326.

An instruction defining an excessive levy of attachment as on goods of value more than sufficient to satisfy the debt should have included cost of levy, care of goods, etc., Brock *v.* Young (Ala. App.), 62 So. 326.

§ 183. —— Verdict or Findings.

Estimation of Value of Property.—In a trial of the right of property attached, the estimate by the jury of the value of the property contained in the verdict is mere surplusage. Seamans *v.* White, 8 Ala. 656; Powell *v.* Hadden, 21 Ala. 745.

The object of the statute (Code, § 4143) requiring the jury in a claim suit to assess the separate value of each article claimed is to enable the claimant to return the property either in whole or in part, and, if the claimant had disposed of all the goods before the trial, he is not prejudiced by a failure to assess the separate value of each article. Schloss *v.* Inman, 129 Ala. 424, 30 So. 667.

As, in a statutory claim suit, the jury is only required to assess the value of the articles separately when such assessment is practicable, if the jury fail to make such assessment it will be presumed, on a motion in arrest of judgment, that it was impracticable to make it. Jordan *v.* Collins, 107 Ala. 572, 18 So. 137.

Direction of Court.—In a statutory claim suit, a charge that, if the jury find that at the time of the levy of the attachment the property was not in defendant's possession, the verdict must be for claimants, was properly refused. Jordan *v.* Collins, 107 Ala. 572, 18 So. 137.

§ 184. —— Judgment and Enforcement Thereof.

In General.—The claim suit is wholly independent of the attachment suit, at least so long as it is pending. If the claim suit is determined against the claimant, the proper judgment is a condemnation of the property, viz. that it is subject to the levy of the attachment, and may be sold to satisfy the judgment in the attachment suit, if one then exists or is afterwards obtained. Seamans *v.* White, 8 Ala. 656.

Condemnation of Property.—Where the claimant of property levied on under attachment against another is defeated upon trial of the right of property, the proper judgment is the condemnation of the property to the satisfaction of the attachment. Gray *v.* Raiborn, 53 Ala. 40.

It was error to render judgment against the obligors on the claim bond; the appropriate judgment being a condemnation of the property; that it is subject to the attachment, and is condemned to the satisfaction of the judgment which has been or may be rendered. Arnold *v.* Cofer, 33 So. 539, 135 Ala. 364.

On the entry of judgment in favor of an attaching creditor on a trial of the right of property between him and a third person claiming the attached property, judgment of condemnation of the property in suit may be entered, where the attaching creditor has already recovered judgment in the attachment suit. Rogers *v.* Bailey, 25 So. 909, 121 Ala. 314.

"Upon the trial of the right of property levied on by attachment, if the issue be found against the claimant, the appropriate judgment is a condemnation of the property; that it is subject to the levy of the attachment, and is condemned to the satisfaction of the judgment which has been or may be obtained. A judgment that the claimant and his surety or sureties in the claim bond pay the plaintiff in attachment the value of the property, as assessed by the jury, is erroneous. The sureties in the claim bond become liable when the claimant fails to deliver the property to the sheriff. The failure renders it the duty of the sheriff to return the bond forfeited, and then execution thereon may issue against the principal and sureties." Seisel *v.* Folmar, 103 Ala. 491, 15 So. 850, 852.

Judgment When No Judgment Has Been Rendered in Attachment Suit.—Plaintiff, if the issue is found in his favor, is entitled to a judgment that the property is subject to his attachment and to the satisfaction of his judgment, if one has been or shall be obtained, though at the time of trial of the claim suit no judgment had been rendered in the attachment suit. Roberts *v.* Burgess, 85 Ala. 192, 4 So. 733.

Personal Judgment.—Where the verdict is rendered for the attachment plaintiff before he has recovered judgment against defendant, a personal judgment against the claimant is erroneous. Tobias *v.* Treist, 103 Ala. 664, 15 So. 914.

Entering Judgment against Surety or Claim Bond.—A security in a claim bond is not a party to the issue formed to try the right of property; and, unless it is affirmatively shown by the record that he appeared and assented to it, it is error to render judgment against him. Gayle *v.* Bancroft, 17 Ala. 351.

Judgment Where Property Claimed Has Been Destroyed.—The death of the animal attached, before the trial of the claim suit does not affect the right of recovery. Derrett *v.* Alexander, 25 Ala. 265.

Entry of Judgment against Sureties on Replevy Bond.—On trial of a right of property, if it is found subject to an attachment, it is error to render judgment in the claim suit against the sureties on the replevy bond. Derrett *v.* Alexander, 25 Ala. 265.

Failure of Plaintiff to Revive Action against Defendant's Personal Representative.—A plaintiff is not entitled to attach property, as against a statutory claimant, where defendant dies after certiorari by claimant to review a justice's judgment condemning the property to the payment of a judgment for plaintiff, and plaintiff fails to revive the action against defendant's personal representative within the time required by Code 1886, § 2603, in view of § 3013, providing for the issuance of an execution against a claimant, to whom attached property has been delivered, on the recovery of judgment by plaintiff against defendant in attachment. Cofer *v.* Reinschmidt, 25 So. 769, 121 Ala. 252.

Clerical Errors Amendable.—On the trial of right of property attached, judgment against the claimant for the assessed value thereof is a clerical misprision, amendable on motion in the court below. Gray *v.* Raiborn, 53 Ala. 40. See Seisel *v.* Folmar, 103 Ala. 491, 15 So. 850, 852.

Execution.—If the claim suit is determined against the claimant, and judgment entered subjecting the property to the levy of an attachment, though the property may be sold to satisfy the judgment in an attachment suit if one exists or is afterwards obtained, no execution can issue upon the judgment except for the costs of the claim suit. Seamans *v.* White, 8 Ala. 656.

Where attached property is claimed by a third person, who gives the required claim bond, and thereafter the attaching creditor prevails on a trial of the right of property between him and the claimant, it is error to direct the issuance of an execution before the return of the claim bond forfeited. Rogers *v.* Bailey, 25 So. 909, 121 Ala. 314.

§ 185. —— Appeal.

Presumptions on Appeal.—Where the verdict in an action to determine the right of property between an attaching creditor and a claimant describes the property as a sawmill, consisting of a boiler, engines, and fixtures, but does not assess each item of the property as required by Code, § 4143, when practicable, it will be presumed on appeal, in the absence of contrary evidence, that such assessment was impracticable. Massillon Engine & Thresher Co. *v.* Arnold, 32 So. 594, 133 Ala. 368.

Where it appears from a recital in a verdict not assessing each item of property, as required, when practicable, by Code, § 4143, in a trial of the right to property, that there was an agreement of the parties, by which the jury was to be governed in their findings, it will be presumed on appeal, in the absence of a contrary showing, that the agreement dispensed with the necessity of assessing each separate item of the property. Massillon Engine & Thresher Co. *v.* Arnold, 32 So. 594, 133 Ala. 368.

§ 186. Operation and Effect of Determination.

Admissions by Claimant.—By the interposition of a claim suit under the statute (Code, § 4141), where an attachment has been levied, the claimant is held to admit both the indebtedness claimed by the plaintiff in attachment and the fact that a levy was made. Schloss *v.* Inman, 30 So. 667, 129 Ala. 424.

Effect of Judgment on Other Issues.—While a statutory trial of the right of property is a suit dependent or collateral to the main suit in which is issued the process levied upon the property claimed, it is, as between the plaintiff and the defendant, separate and distinct and independent to the main suit, with distinct and independent issues; and, therefore, the judgment in the claim suit is not, in any way, decisive of the right of plaintiff's recovery against the defendant in the main suit. Wheeles *v.* New York Steam Dye Works, 29 So. 793, 129 Ala. 393.

Certain slaves were mortgaged by A. to B., by deed dated in February, 1841, to secure two promissory notes, maturing on the 15th of August of the same year. These slaves were levied on in March, 1841, by attachments at the suit of C. and others, and a claim interposed pursuant to the statute, by the mortgagee, to try the right of property. A trial was accordingly had, and the slaves adjudged liable to the payment of A.'s debts. Afterwards the mortgagee filed his bill in equity, alleging that the validity of the mortgage was not controverted by the plaintiffs in attachment, but was rejected by the court, as evidence, on the trial of the right, at the instance of the plaintiffs, on the ground merely that it did not tend to prove the issue on the part of the claimant, which was whether A. had such an interest in the slaves as was subject to the attachments. The plaintiffs in the attachments and the mortgagor were made defendants to the bill, which prayed a foreclosure of the mortgage, and that the judgment upon the trial of the right of property might be enjoined, etc. Held, that the judgment by which the slaves were determined to be liable to the attachments did not, under the facts alleged, impair the equity of the bill. Ansley *v.* Pearson, 8 Ala. 431.

Quære, where several levies are made upon the same property at the same time, and several trials of the right are had, if upon verdict of condemnation, the jury assess the full value of the property, in each case, and judgments are rendered accordingly, it is not competent for the court, in which the trials are had, to correct its judgment, so that the claimant may not be charged beyond the value of the property. Ansley *v.* Pearson, 8 Ala. 431.

IX. RETURN.

§ 187. Officer Who Must Make.

Successor to Sheriff.—The successor in office to the sheriff who levied a writ of attachment may make the return. Carter *v.* O'Bryan, 105 Ala. 305, 16 So. 894.

§ 188. Form and Requisites.

Description or Schedule of Property or Interest.—An attachment ought not to be quashed because the articles of personal property taken are not specifically described in the return. Green *v.* Pyne, 1 Ala. 235.

The sheriff's return, stating that he had levied the same on four horses, describing their colors, as the property of defendant, is sufficient. Fleming *v.* Burge, 6 Ala. 373.

§ 189. Amendment.

Affecting Established Rights.—The sheriff's return of the levy of an attachment sued out by a landlord against the crop of his tenants may be amended after judgment so as to show that the crop levied on was grown on the rented land. Odom *v.* Shackleford, 44 Ala. 331.

§ 190. Defects, Objections, and Waiver.

Aider by Extrinsic Evidence.—The return of the sheriff is not conclusive as to the amount of goods seized, and it is competent to show that other goods, omitted from the inventory, were also seized. Jefferson County Sav. Bank *v.* Eborn, 84 Ala. 529, 4 So. 386.

In an action on an attachment bond for wrongfully suing out the writ, plaintiff may show what property was seized and delivered to plaintiff in attachment, though the return to the writ is silent as to such property, or has been altered so as to omit it. Hensley *v.* Rose, 76 Ala. 373.

In assumpsit aided by judicial attachment, the sheriff returned on the writ that by virtue thereof he had levied on and taken certain negroes, "and the same were replevied by a bond given by defendant." Held, that the replevin bond was no part of the record, and hence could not be considered for the purpose of explaining or contradicting the rest of the return. Kirksey *v.* Bates, 1 Ala. 303.

§ 191. Construction.

Presumptions.—Where the return properly describes the property, it will be presumed to have been attached as that of defendant. Bickerstaff *v.* Patterson, 8 Port. 245; King *v.* Bucks, 11 Ala. 217.

The sheriff's return stated "that defendant had personal notice of the levy of this attachment." Held that, on the presumption that sworn officers discharge their duty lawfully, the return complies with provisions of Code 1876, § 3260, requiring written notice of levy to defendant. Fears *v.* Thompson, 82 Ala. 294, 2 So. 719.

§ 192. Operation and Effect.

Conclusiveness of Facts Recited in General.—So long as the return of a sheriff is permitted to remain, it must be taken to be true for all purposes, both as it respects the sheriff, and parties claiming rights under it. Clarke *v.* Gary, 11 Ala. 98.

The return of the sheriff to a judicial attachment against three defendants, that, by virtue of the writ he had levied on certain slaves, and that the same were replevied by the bond of "defendant," is conclusive to show that the slaves were the property of all defendants. Kirksey *v.* Bates, 1 Ala. 303.

Effect as to Other Liens or Rights.—The omission of the sheriff to return an ancillary attachment which he had levied, until after the judgment was obtained, will not affect the lien of plaintiff in attachment, he not being privy to, or consenting to, the act of the sheriff. The return, when made, relates back to the time of the levy. Reed *v.* Perkins, 14 Ala. 231.

Contradicting by Extrinsic Evidence.—Where a return of the sheriff fixes on him a liability to plaintiff, it is not competent for him, in a suit by the latter, founded on such return, to prove that it is incorrect. In such case a direct application for leave to amend the return should be made to the court whence the process issued. Governor *v.* Bancroft, 16 Ala. 605.

In an action against the sheriff, for making an insufficient levy on an attachment, he can not show that, by the mistake of a deputy, a return was made on the attachment of an inferior slave not levied on, while a slave valuable enough to satisfy plaintiff's demand was in fact levied on. The return must be taken as true till impeached directly. Clarke *v.* Gary, 11 Ala. 98.

X. LIABILITIES ON BONDS OR UNDERTAKINGS.

As to effect of bankruptcy, see the title BANKRUPTCY. As to liabilities on bonds or undertakings in justices courts, see the title JUSTICES OF THE PEACE.

§ 193. Accrual or Release of Liability by Breach or Fulfillment of Conditions.

§ 194. —— Bonds or Undertakings to Procure Attachment.

As to limitations, see post, "Time to Sue and Limitations," § 207.

Persons Liable.—A corporation may be liable in exemplary damages for wrongful attachment. Jefferson County Sav. Bank *v.* Eborn, 84 Ala. 529, 4 So. 386.

Creditors, acting separately and without concert, though simultaneously, sued out attachments, which were simultaneously levied on property which they were justified in believing had been transferred by their common debtor in fraud of their rights, and, having each indemnified the sheriff, sold the property, and applied the proceeds in payment of their respective demands. The purchaser from the debtor, in an action on the indemnifying bond of one of the attaching creditors, recovered damages for the wrongful taking and sale of the attached property. Held, that the levy of the several attachments was a single tort, and therefore constituted a single cause of action, for which the attaching creditors were jointly and severally liable. Vandiver *v.* Pollak, 107 Ala. 547, 19 So. 180.

"The general rule is that the principal is not responsible for the malice or vexatious conduct of the agent suing out the attachment, unless he procures, authorizes, or ratifies such conduct. In the absence of a statutory ground for the issue of an attachment, the principal would be liable for actual damages, but is not liable for vindictive damages, unless he is without probable cause for believing that grounds for suing out the attachment existed, or had knowledge of the facts relied on, and there is, in truth, no ground for the attachment." Baldwin *v.* Walker, 91 Ala. 428, 8 So. 364, 366, cited on this point in note in 29 L. R. A. 275, 280.

The mere fact that a creditor provides security on an attachment bond by request of his attorney, without knowledge either of the ground on which the attachment was sued out or of any malicious or vexatious conduct on the part of his agent whom he has authorized to collect the debt is not a ratification of such malicious conduct so as to make the creditor responsible for vindictive damages. Baldwin *v.* Walker, 91 Ala. 428, 8 So. 364.

Where the attachment was wrongful and without probable cause, and after levy was made the attaching creditors were informed of all that had been done by their agent, and ratified his conduct, they would be liable for damages, and recovery would not be limited to actual damages. Baldwin *v.* Walker, 94 Ala. 514, 10 So. 391. See S. C., 91 Ala. 428, 8 So. 364.

A creditor who seeks to proceed in the collection of his debt by the use of the harsh process of attachment undertakes to show that some one of the causes which would authorize the issue of an attachment exists. If he fails to do this, the attachment is wrongfully sued out; and, if the property of defendant is seized under authority of process thus issued, it is, in effect, a trespass, and an illegal invasion of defendant's rights of property, for which the party causing the attachment to be sued out is responsible for the damages inflicted. Stewart *v.* Cole, 46 Ala. 646.

Grounds of Action.—If a statutory ground of attachment existed, there is no liability on the attachment bond for wrongful attachment merely because the plaintiff knew that the defendant had no property except such as was exempt. Troy *v.* Rogers, 20 So. 999, 113 Ala. 131, cited on this point in note in 38 L. R. A., N. S., 120.

Vexation without wrong gives no right of action; and hence, in a suit on an attachment bond, no recovery can be had unless the attachment was wrongful. Jackson *v.* Smith, 75 Ala. 97.

Under Code 1896, § 565, providing that at any time within three years of the suing out of the attachment, before or after the suit is determined, defendant may commence suit on the bond, and recover damages actually sustained, if the attachment was wrongfully sued out, such suit may be maintained, though the original suit is still pending. First Nat. Bank *v.* Cheney, 23 So. 733, 120 Ala. 117.

"By force of the statute, whenever an attachment is wrongfully sued out—that is sued out without the actual existence of any one of the grounds on which its issue is authorized, whatever may be the good faith of the party suing it out, and however honest his belief that cause existed. The defendant is entitled to recover in an action on the bond, the actual damage he may sustain. Code of 1876, § 3317; Kirksey *v.* Jones, 7 Ala. 622; Alexander *v.* Hutchison, 9 Ala. 825." Durr *v.* Jackson, 59 Ala. 203, 209.

If, when an attachment is sued our, no

statutory ground for it exists, it is wrongful, no matter how honestly or sincerely the plaintiff may have acted in suing it out; and for such wrongful act, although done by an agent without express direction, the principal and sureties on the attachment bond are liable. Jackson *v.* Smith, 75 Ala. 97.

The nonexistence of the debt for which an attachment issues is a breach of the attachment bond, and entitles defendant to recover in a suit thereon the damages sustained. Tucker *v.* Adams, 52 Ala. 254.

There is a breach of the attachment bond if there was in fact no ground for its issuance, though plaintiff may have had a well-founded belief that a statutory ground existed for suing it out. Pollock *v.* Gantt, 69 Ala. 373, 44 Am. Rep. 519, cited on this point in note in 38 L. R. A., N. S., 120.

§ 195. —— Forthcoming or Delivery Bonds.

Fulfillment of Condition. — Where plaintiff in attachment, after the property has been replevied under the statute, causes a portion of it to be seized and sold under process sued out by him against one of the sureties, and thus prevents a compliance with the condition of the replevin bond for its return, it is a discharge of the bond, to the extent of the property sold. Dunlap *v.* Clements, 18 Ala. 778.

Although a failure to deliver a part of the property replevied in attachment, without the fault of plaintiff, will, under the statute, amount to a forfeiture of the bond, and authorize execution for the entire sum due on the judgment, after crediting it with the proceeds of that delivered, yet if the failure to deliver any portion of it is occasioned by the act of plaintiff, the statute ceases to apply, and the obligors, in default of delivering the residue, can only, as at common law, be held liable for its value. Dunlap *v.* Clements, 18 Ala. 778.

Levy on Slaves.—Where a forthcoming bond stipulates to deliver to the proper officer a certain slave, the death of the slave before forfeiture of the bond discharges the obligors from their liability. Phillipi *v.* Capell, 38 Ala. 575.

Where a bill is filed to subject a slave to the payment of complainant's demand, and defendant executes a bond with surety conditioned for his delivery if complainant is successful, the death of the slave previous to the rendition of the decree or an order requiring his delivery will absolve the obligors from a compliance with the condition. Falls *v.* Weissinger, 11 Ala. 801.

The condition of a bond for the forthcoming of slaves taken under attachment having become, by the abolition of slavery, illegal and impossible of performance, the surety is discharged from liability. Glover *v.* Taylor, 41 Ala. 124.

Release of Attachment Lien.—Plaintiff levied an attachment on defendant's property. Defendant thereupon executed a replevy bond, and the property was delivered to him. The bond was conditioned that, if the defendant failed in the attachment suit, he or his sureties would return the specific property to the sheriff within thirty days after judgment. Defendant personally appeared and consented to judgment against himself, but the property was not returned within the thirty days, and the sheriff returned the replevy bond as forfeited, and the clerk issued an execution against defendant and his sureties, to be levied on their property. Held, that the failure of the court, in rendering the judgment against defendant in the attachment suit, to also render a judgment of sale of the property attached and replevied, did not work a release of the attachment lien, so as to make void the act of the sheriff in returning the bond forfeited and the act of the clerk in issuing the execution. Reynolds *v.* Williams, 44 So. 406, 152 Ala. 488.

"The object of the statute authorizing the replevy of property attached, is its restoration to the possession of the defendant, so that until final judgment is rendered in the attachment suit, determining his liability, and the rights of the plaintiff, he may not be deprived of its use, nor subjected to the expense of its keeping pending suit, if judgment is rendered against him. The purpose is not to free the property from its liability to the attachment. The replevy converts the party making it, into a bailee of the property. His death does not absolve him from the obligation and duty of restoring the property, any more than it would if he was the mere receiptor or bailee of the sheriff. Of him surety is required for the performance of the obligation and duty of restoration, that no detriment may occur to the plaintiff, by the extension to him of the privilege of retaining possession, instead of requiring the officer to take and keep it. The sureties on the replevy bond assume equally with the principal obligor, the duty of restoring the property to enable them to perform this duty, the law invests them with a special property in the chattels replevied, which they may assert if there is any attempt at disposition, so as to prevent them from performing this duty. * * * The condition of the bond is broken, if the property is not restored, unless the failure is caused by the act of God, or of the party plaintiff. Falls *v.* Weissinger, 11 Ala. 801; Dunlap *v.* Clements, 18 Ala. 778. On a breach of the condition, the statute confers on the plaintiff an unquestionable right to an execution against the obligors. 1 Brick. Dig., § 133. The condition is broken when the plaintiff obtains judgment in the attachment suit, and the property is not restored. The death of the principal obligor, can not lessen or impair the obligation of delivery, when the suit is prosecuted to judgment against his personal representatives, on which a venditioni exponas for the sale of such property, or a writ of fieri facias which may be levied on it can issue. If the property had not been replevied, but had remained in the custody of the sheriff, there could be no doubt of its liability to either writ, and of the authority to sell. Notwithstanding the replevy, the liability of the property, is not varied from that to which it would have been subject, if it had remained in the custody of the sheriff. Otherwise than to authorize the party replevying, to keep possession, and to relieve the sheriff from responsibility, if he takes good and sufficient surety, the replevy has no effect." Woolfolk *v.* Ingram, 53 Ala. 11, 13.

§ 196. —— Bonds or Undertakings for Release of Property.

Liability of Surety.—A. attached property of B., who gave a replevin bond for it with C. as surety. Subsequently D. attached the same property, which was taken from C.'s possession by the sheriff, who refused to receive C.'s affidavit of claim, and, with knowledge of the prior attachment, allowed D. to take the property and sell it. A. recovered a judgment. Held, that C. was not liable for a failure to deliver the property, as A.'s remedy was against the sheriff or D. Cordaman *v.* Malone, 63 Ala. 556. See Scarborough *v.* Malone, 67 Ala. 570.

When the property is taken from the sureties on the replevin bond, under a junior attachment, and delivered to the plaintiffs in that attachment, by whom it is removed and sold, the sureties on the replevin bond are discharged from their liability. In such case, the plaintiffs in the first attachment have their remedy against the sheriff, for his unauthorized act in taking the property under the junior attachment, and may, possibly, maintain an action for money had and received against the plaintiffs in that attachment. Cordaman *v.* Malone, 63 Ala. 556.

§ 197. —— Claimants' Bonds for Possession.

Liability for Costs of Trial.—A bond given in conformity with Clay's Dig., 213, § 62, for the trial of the right of property, binds the security, in the event of its condemnation, for the costs of the trial, although the claim may not have been put in for delay. Robertson *v.* Patterson, 17 Ala. 407.

Death of One of the Members of a Partnership.—Code 1886, § 2605, provides that two or more persons associated as partners, transacting business under a common name, may be sued by such name, and, the summons being served on one or more of such partners, the judgment binds the "joint property" of all the partners in the same manner as if all had been defendants, and sued on their joint liability, and served with process. Sections 3012, 3013, provide that personal property on which an attachment has been levied, if claimed by any one not a party to the suit, shall be delivered to such claimant on his executing a bond, etc., and that such bond shall be forfeited if claimant fails to deliver such property to the sheriff within thirty days after judgment against him. Held, that where an attachment was levied on the property of a partnership, and it was delivered to a claimant, not a party to the suit, who failed to redeliver same within thirty days after judgment against her, the fact that one of the partners, against whom judgment was rendered in the attachment suit, died before the rendition thereof, will not invalidate the same, and will not be a ground for the issuance of a writ of supersedeas in an execution on the bond against the claimant. Comer *v.* Reid, 93 Ala. 391, 9 So. 620.

Effect of Transfer of Cause.—The judgment in a suit between plaintiff in attachment and claimants of the attached property rendered by a circuit court which has acquired jurisdiction of the parties by virtue of an agreement between them transferring the cause to such court, is not affected by the fact that the sureties on the claim bonds did not consent to the transfer. Trieste *v.* Enslen, 106 Ala. 180, 17 So. 356.

Effect of Dismissal of Claim.—Where the claim of a third person, who intervened in attachment and executed the forthcoming bond required by Code 1907, § 6039, was dismissed for failure to file the required affidavit, mere proof by the plaintiff, who recovered in the attachment, that the property was not forthcoming is insufficient to show a breach of the condition; it being necessary, in an action on the bond, to show that the claimant was not entitled to the property. Holloway *v.* Burroughs, etc., Co., 4 Ala. App. 630, 58 So. 953.

Code 1907, § 6039, provides that on attachment a third person may try the right to the property, upon making affidavit and executing a bond to have the property forthcoming for the satisfaction of the judgment or claim of plaintiff; and §§ 6040, 6041, 6042, provide for an issue between the claimant and the plaintiff in the writ, and that if the jury or justice find the property levied on to be liable they must assess the value at the time of the claim, and that if judgment is rendered against the claimant, and he fails to deliver the property and pay the costs, execution may be issued against the obligors on the bond. A claimant in attachment executed the required bond, but failed to file the affidavit; and after the property was delivered to him his claim was dismissed and judgment rendered for plaintiff. Held that, no issue having been made up, and the bond having been given in reliance on the making up of such issue, the judgment for plaintiff was not an adjudication which, in an action on the bond, would prevent the claimant from setting up his title to the property as a defense. Holloway *v.* Burroughs, etc., Co., 4 Ala. App. 630, 58 So. 953.

§ 198. Discharge of Sureties.

As to agreement as to trial of causes, not releasing sureties on claim bond, see the title PRINCIPAL AND SURETY.

Acts of Principal.—The sureties on a claim bond are not released by the fact that, by consent of the claimants and plaintiffs in attachment, another claim suit is tried with that of the claimants who are principals in such bond, no prejudice having resulted to the sureties by such action. Triest *v.* Enslen, 106 Ala. 180, 17 So. 356.

An agreement between one who had taken the property of an insolvent debtor out of the hands of the sheriff under a claim bond and the plaintiffs in the attachment suit to assess the value of the property in bulk, and its assessment under such agreement at the amount shown by a previous inventory, did not release the sureties on the claim bond. Jaffray *v.* Smith, 106 Ala. 112, 17 So. 218.

Substitution of New Sureties.—When, by order of the court, new sureties are substituted for those originally given in a claim suit, the former are discharged. Seamans *v.* White, 8 Ala. 656.

Judgment Condemning Property to Satisfaction of Attachment.—Sureties on a claim bond, the undertaking of which is to "have the property forthcoming for the satisfaction of the judgment, if it be found liable therefor," are not discharged because the judgment condemns the property to "the satisfaction of the attachment." Jaffray *v.* Smith, 106 Ala. 112, 17 So. 218.

Taking Property from Sureties and Delivery to Plaintiff.—When the property is taken from the sureties on the replevin bond, under a junior attachment, and delivered to the plaintiffs in that attachment, by whom it is removed and sold, the sureties on the replevin bond are discharged from their liability, and may supersede and quash a summary execution issued against them. Cordaman *v.* Malone, 63 Ala. 556.

§ 199. Extent of Liability.

As to damages, see post, "Damages," § 311.

Injunction against Further Subjection of Property to Payment of Judgments.—Where execution has issued on a forfeited claim bond to satisfy judgments against the claimant's vendor to an amount largely in excess of the agreed value of the property in question, and the claimant has previously paid to the clerk of the court, for the benefit of said judgment creditors, a sum greater than said agreed value, the claimant is entitled to have said creditors and the sheriff enjoined from seeking further to subject his property to the payment of said judgments. Cottingham *v.* Bamberger, 25 So. 771, 121 Ala. 527.

Liability of Sureties.—Where a tenant's crops are replevied after attachment levied by the landlord, and after expiration of the tenancy, and the tenant's removal from the premises, if the crops were replevied with the intention to waste and convert them, and the sureties on the bond had notice of such intent, they are jointly liable with their principal for the conversion. Powell *v.* Thompson, 80 Ala. 51.

While the removal of the tenant's crop from the rented premises, without the consent of the landlord, and without paying the rent, is prima facie a wrongful act, tending to the destruction of the landlord's lien; yet it may be justified by proof of legal right or lawful excuse, as by showing that it was replevied by the tenant after attachment levied at the suit of the landlord, and after the expiration of the tenancy and the tenant's removal from the rented premises; but, if such replevy was made, not in good faith for the preservation of the cotton, but with the intention to waste and convert it, and the sureties on the bond had notice of such wrongful intent, they are liable for the conversion jointly with their principal. Powell *v.* Thompson, 80 Ala. 51.

§ 200. Enforcement in Attachment Suit, or Claimant's Suit.

As to summary remedies, see post, "Summary Remedies," § 201.

Scire Facias.—In a proceeding by scire facias on a replevy bond in attachment, a discontinuance may be entered against the obligors, not served with process, and judgment had against the others. Sartin *v.* Weir, 3 Stew. & P. 421.

Judgment against Defendant Including Sureties on Replevin Bond.—A judgment against an attachment defendant was valid as against him, though it included the sureties on his replevin bond, when by the express provisions of Code 1896, § 556, a judgment is not to be rendered against the sureties until the expiration of thirty days after the judgment against defendant. Stephens *v.* Davis (Ala.), 39 So. 831.

§ 201. Summary Remedies.

As to conclusiveness of judgment in action on bond, see post, "Evidence," § 210. As to enforcement in attachment suit or claimant's suit, see ante, "Enforcement in Attachment Suit, or Claimant's Suit," § 200. As to estoppel to plead defense, see the title ESTOPPEL.

In General.—The statute giving to bonds executed for the forthcoming of property levied on under attachment, when returned forfeited, the force and effect of judgments, and authorizing the issuance of executions thereon for the amount of the recovery in the attachment suits, was intended merely to provide a summary remedy, and not to deprive the obligors of any legal defense which they might have set up against the bonds at common law. Dunlap *v.* Clements, 18 Ala. 778.

"The power to render such summary judgments which involves a waiver of the right of trial by jury on the part of the obligors, is based on the contract of the parties that they will submit to such a remedy, provided the undertaking conforms to the statutory requirements. If it does not, they have the right to assume that the implied agreement is that it will be enforced only by the ordinary common-law remedies, and not by those summarily conferred by statute, and affixed only to statutory undertakings." Cobb *v.* Thompson, 87 Ala. 381, 6 So. 373, 374.

Whether the attached property is replevied by a stranger, or a claim interposed in his own name, and bond given for a trial of the right of property—in either case, if the condition of the bond is broken (Code, § 3291), and it is returned forfeited, it has the force and effect of a judgment, on which an execution may be issued against all the obligors. Rhodes *v.* Smith, 66 Ala. 174.

"In either case, whether the bond is a mere replevy bond, executed in the absence, and for the benefit of the defendant in attachment, or a bond given for the trial of the right of property, the officer making the levy, and taking the bond, must return it, with the attachment, into the court to which the attachment is returnable; and either bond, if its condition is broken, and it conforms to the statute, may have the force and effect of a judgment, on which an execution may issue against all the obligors." Rhodes *v.* Smith, 66 Ala. 174, 177.

The condition of a replevy bond in attachment can only be implied with, after a judgment has been rendered against defendant, by a delivery of the property to the sheriff on his demand; and, if the bond is returned "forfeited" on account of a failure to deliver the property. the statute gives plaintiff in attachment a right to a fi. fa. against all the obligors, without any further action of the courts. Cooper *v.* Peck, 22 Ala. 406.

Right to Forfeiture of Bond and Execution.—"It is settled by the authorities that a forthcoming bond, which provides for the delivery of property on a day different from the day prescribed by law, is not good as a statutory bond, but only as a common-law bond, and it can not be declared forfeited summarily by sheriffs or constables, as only statutory bonds can be." Cobb *v.* Thompson, 87 Ala. 381, 6 So. 373.

A bond in replevin of property attached, providing for the return of the property within twenty days after judgment in the attachment suit, is not a good statutory bond, under Code 1886, § 3341, providing for such return in ten days, and can not be summarily forfeited. Cobb *v.* Thompson, 87 Ala. 381, 6 So. 373.

A statutory execution may issue against a surety on a replevin bond for property attached, on failure to deliver it after judgment in the attachment suit, against the personal representative of the principal obligor dying pending suit. Woolfolk *v.* Ingram, 53 Ala. 11.

Clay's Dig., p. 57, § 11, relative to replevy bonds, provides that, if the bond is foreclosed according to its condition, the officer taking the same shall forthwith enter thereon the necessary indorsement of forfeiture, and the clerk or justice shall immediately issue execution on the same against all obligors thereof. Held, that an execution may issue on a replevy bond in attachment taken under said act which was returned forfeited by the sheriff, and without an assignment by him to plaintiff. Shute *v.* McMahon, 10 Ala. 76.

§ 202. Actions.

§ 203. —— Nature and Form.

Form of Action.—An action of covenant may be maintained on an attachment bond. Hill *v.* Rushing, 4 Ala. 212.

Scire facias is the proper remedy on a replevin bond, under the attachment laws of Alabama of 1807 and 1812. Sartin *v.* Weir, 3 Stew. & P. 421.

§ 204. —— Right of Action.

See post, "Exemplary Damages," § 226.

Attachment Wrongfully Sued Out.—"The defendant, at any time within three years of the suing out of the attachment against him, before or after the suit is determined, may commence suit on the attachment bond, and may recover such damages as he has actually sustained, if the attachment was wrongfully sued out. If sued out maliciously as well as wrongfully, the jury may, in addition, give vindictive damages. Revised Code, §§ 2992, 2993; McKellar *v.* Couch, 34 Ala. 336." Metcalf *v.* Young, 43 Ala. 643, 648, cited on this point in note in 38 L. R. A., N. S., 120.

§ 205. —— Conditions Precedent.

Return of Forfeiture Indorsed on Bond.—A return of "Forfeiture" indorsed on the bond is not necessary to the maintenance of a common-law action of debt on a claim bond. Alexander *v.* Trask, 20 Ala. 805.

Prior Action.—Defendant in attachment may have his action on the attachment bond without having ascertained his damages by a direct action against plaintiff in the attachment. Herndon *v.* Forney, 4 Ala. 243.

§ 206. —— Defenses.

In Action on Bond or Undertaking to Procure Attachment.—In an action on an attachment bond, the defense is not limited to proof of the particular facts stated in the affidavit for the attachment, but may be rested on the existence of any one of the several grounds which authorize the issue of an attachment. Lockhart *v.* Woods, 38 Ala. 631.

It is no justification that one suing out an attachment has good reason to believe the fact to be as he states in his affidavit. If the causes alleged do not exist, he is answerable to defendant in attachment for all the injury he sustains by the suing out of the attachment. Alexander *v.* Hutchison, 9 Ala. 825, cited on this point in note in 38 L. R. A., N. S., 120, 127.

In an action on an attachment bond, the pendency of the attachment suit is not good matter for a plea, either in abatement or in bar, since the statute (Rev. Code, § 2992) authorizes the bringing of the action before the termination of the attachment suit. Swanner *v.* Swanner, 50 Ala. 66.

Reasonable and probable cause to believe that the grounds on which an attachment was sued out were true is not a defense to an action for damages on the attachment bond. Metcalf *v.* Young, 43 Ala. 643.

In an action on an attachment bond, where the attachment was sued out on the ground that defendant in attachment was about to remove his property out of this state, so that plaintiff would probably lose his debt, or have to sue for it in another state, it is a matter provable in defense that defendant in attachment had fraudulently disposed of his property, or was about to fraudulently dispose of his property. Lockhart *v.* Woods, 38 Ala. 631.

Neither indebtedness, pecuniary embarrassment, nor insolvency will justify the wrongful suing out of an attachment. Lockhart *v.* Woods, 38 Ala. 631.

It is no defense to an action for wrongfully suing out an attachment, brought on an attachment bond given by a nonresident creditor on suing out an attachment against a nonresident debtor, that, although the latter had sufficient property in the state of his residence to satisfy the particular debt on which the attachment issued, yet he did not have property in such state sufficient to pay all the debts then owing by him and due therein. Jones *v.* Lawrence, 36 Ala. 618.

Where the parties to an attachment treated the levy as valid, and the property was sold under a venditioni exponas made and executed as on a valid levy, its invalidity is no defense to an action on the attachment bond. Hamilton *v.* Maxwell, 24 So. 769, 119 Ala. 23.

Where an attachment was issued by the clerk on an affidavit which disclosed no statutory ground for the issuance of an attachment, in violation of Code 1896, § 527, such failure was no defense to an action on the bond. McLean *v.* Wright, 35 So. 45, 137 Ala. 644, 97 Am. St. Rep. 67.

It is true § 527 of the Code of 1896 imposed the duty upon the officer, before issuing the attachment in this case, to require the plaintiff to make affidavit that one of the statutory grounds (§ 525, Id.) existed; but his failure to do so, or his issuance of the writ upon an affidavit not complying with the requisitions of the statute, can not relieve the obligors on the bond, also given as required (§ 528, Id.) as the condition to its issuance, of their contractual undertaking to pay plaintiff all such damages as she may sustain by the wrongful or vexatious suing out of the attachment. Their undertaking is valid and binding, although the writ may be quashed upon proper steps taken by defendant in the attachment case, unless the affidavit be amended; which can be done (§ 564, Id.). Indeed, if the statute permitted no amendment of the affidavit so as to cure the defect, and the writ was void, this would not destroy the binding efficacy of the bond. At best, the defect under the Alabama statutes being curable by amendment, it amounts to no more than a mere irregularity, of which the defendants, of course, can not take advantage. McLean *v.* Wright, 137 Ala. 644, 35 So. 45, 46.

In Action on Forthcoming or Delivery Bond or Undertaking.—A plea to an action on a replevin bond, given in attachment, that the property attached and replevied did not belong to defendant in attachment, but to a stranger who had seized it, is bad. Sartin *v.* Weir, 3 Stew. & P. 421.

Sureties in an action on a replevy bond conditioned upon the return of property attached are estopped by the bond from setting up that the property belonged to a third person, and did not belong to the defendant in the attachment proceedings, and a plea setting up such defense is bad. Sartin *v.* Weir & Co., 3 Stew. & P. 421, cited on this point in note in 32 L. R. A., N. S., 406.

The obligors, when sued on a replevy bond, can not take advantage of a variance between its recitals and the indorsement on the writ describing the property levied on; and they are estopped from disputing either the levy or the liability of the property levied on. Adler *v.* Potter, 57 Ala. 571.

In a suit on a replevy bond in attachment against the sureties, it is a good defense that the sheriff was notified to retain the property in his custody by virtue of the proceedings under which it was attached, but that he delivered possession thereof to a stranger, who removed it from the state. McRae *v.* McLean, 3 Port. 138.

Where attachment was levied on defendant's property, and he executed, with sureties, a replevy bond for the forthcoming of the property seized, waiving all rights of exemption, they can not set up the claim of exemptions filed by the defendant as a reason for the granting of a supersedeas restraining the levy against their property, made under execution issued on the forfeiture of the replevy bond. Reynolds *v.* Williams, 44 So. 406, 152 Ala. 488, cited in note in 32 L. R. A., N. S., 407.

In Action on Bond or Undertaking for Release of Property.—A bond conditioned that the obligors should pay to the attaching creditor such judgment as should be rendered in his favor against them binds them to pay one recovered in his favor, not in form against them. Hunter *v.* McCraw, 32 Ala. 518.

§ 207. —— Time to Sue and Limitations.

As to accrual or release of liability by breach or fulfillment of condition, see ante, "Accrual or Release of Liability by Breach or Fulfillment of Conditions," § 193.

Three Years after Suing Out Attachment.—"The defendant, at any time within three years of the suing out of the attachment against him, before or after the suit is determined, may commence suit on the attachment bond." Metcalf *v.* Young, 43 Ala. 643, 648. See McKellar *v.* Couch, 34 Ala. 336.

§ 208. —— Parties.

Parties Plaintiff.—A bond to replevy goods taken in attachment may be assigned by the sheriff to the plaintiff in attachment and may be sued on by the latter. Adkins *v.* Allen, 1 Stew. 130.

A plaintiff in attachment can not sue in his own name on a replevin bond executed by the defendant in attachment, and made payable to the constable. Agnew *v.* Leath, 63 Ala. 345.

A delivery bond in attachment must be assigned to plaintiff therein before such plaintiff can maintain an action thereon in his own name. Sartin *v.* Weir, 3 Stew. & P. 421.

To authorize a recovery on an attachment bond, all of the obligees named therein must join as plaintiffs in the capacity in which they are named, for the use of such as claim to have been injured. Painter *v.* Munn, 23 So. 83, 117 Ala. 322, 67 Am. St. Rep. 170.

A joint recovery may be had on a bond executed to defendants in an attachment suit, though the attachment was levied on the separate property of each defendant, and each employed separate counsel and incurred separate counsel fees in the suit. Weedon *v.* Jones, 106 Ala. 336, 17 So. 454.

In an action on a bond given in an attachment sued out on the ground that plaintiff (defendant in attachment) was about to leave the state, though the property was derived by plaintiff through the will of her husband, and was liable for his debts, yet she had a right to sell it subject to such liability, and could be injured by a wrongful levy of attachment thereon. Baldwin *v.* Walker, 94 Ala. 514, 10 So. 391.

On a bond executed to several, with condition to pay them such costs and damages as they might sustain by the wrongful suing out of an attachment, a joint action may be maintained, though the attachment was levied on the separate property of each, in which they have not a joint interest. Boyd *v.* Martin, 10 Ala. 700.

An action on an attachment bond payable to several persons jointly, and conditioned for the payment to them of all such damages as they may sustain from the wrongful or vexatious suing out of the writ, can only be maintained by all the obligees jointly, although damages may have accrued to only one of them. Masterson *v.* Phinizy, 56 Ala. 336.

There is no statute which requires the sheriff to return "Forfeited" a bond taken in a suit in chancery, conditioned for the forthcoming of property. Consequently, the obligee may maintain an action thereon without showing such a return. Falls *v.* Weissinger, 11 Ala. 801.

In an action on an attachment bond, when it appears from the complaint that all the obligees have not been joined as plaintiffs, the defect will be treated as waived, unless advantage of it is taken by demurrer. Painter *v.* Munn, 117 Ala. 322, 23 So. 83.

§ 209. —— Pleading.

Declaration, Petition or Complaint on Bond or Undertaking to Procure Attachment.—In debt upon an attachment bond, the declaration should show that the attachment was wrongfully or vexatiously sued out, and that thereby the obligee has sustained damages. Flanagan *v.* Gilchrist, 8 Ala. 620.

In an action of debt on the conditionary bond given on suing out an attachment, the declaration must show that the process was wrongfully or vexatiously sued out by plaintiff in attachment, even when it issues on the affidavit of an agent; and the declaration is bad if it asserts the attachment was wrongfully and vexatiously sued out by the obligor in the bond. McCullough *v.* Walton, 11 Ala. 492, cited in note in 38 L. R. A., N. S., 120, 127.

In an action on an attachment bond the breaches assigned were, 1st, that the attachment was wrongfully sued out; 2d, that it was vexatiously sued out; 3d, that it was maliciously sued out; 4th, that it was wrongfully and vexatiously sued out, and 5th, that it was wrongfully, vexatiously and maliciously sued out—held, that the assignments of breaches were sufficient. Dothard *v.* Sheid, 69 Ala. 135.

In an action on attachment bond, plaintiff must aver a breach of the bond in plain terms; and a complaint alleging only inferentially that defendant has not paid all damages sustained by the wrongful or vexatious suing out of the writ is insufficient. Charles Schuessler & Sons *v.* Still, 53 So. 831, 169 Ala. 239.

An averment in a complaint that the attachment was wrongfully sued out, "because the said plaintiffs were not about fraudulently to dispose of their property as alleged in the affidavit," is only an averment of the nonexistence of the particular ground upon which the process issued, and does not show a breach of the bond. Painter *v.* Munn, 23 So. 83, 117 Ala. 322, 67 Am. St. Rep. 170.

A complaint for wrongfully suing out an attachment must aver the falsity of the particular facts stated in the affidavit as the grounds of the attachment. Durr *v.* Jackson, 59 Ala. 203. See Flournoy *v.* Lyon & Co., 70 Ala. 308.

An action on the attachment bond can not be maintained for vexatiously suing out an attachment, without averring that it was also wrongfully sued out. City Nat. Bank *v.* Jeffries, 73 Ala. 183.

In an action on an attachment bond, to recover damages for wrongfully, or wrongfully and vexatiously suing out an attachment, the complaint must negative the truth of the sworn ground on which the process issued. City Nat. Bank *v.* Jeffries, 73 Ala. 183.

It is a sufficient assignment of breaches of an attachment bond, to aver that the attachment bond was sued out—1st, vexatiously; 2d, wrongfully; and that being so vexatiously and wrongfully sued out, it was levied on the goods and effects of the plaintiff, whereby he was injured. Gabel *v.* Hammerwell, 44 Ala. 336, cited in note in 38 L. R. A., N. S., 127.

The declaration distinctly avers, "that said attachment, so sued out as aforesaid, was wrongfully sued out; that by such wrongful suing out of said attachment said plaintiff has sustained damage," etc., going on to lay special damages. This is quite sufficient; since, in suits upon an attachment bond, for the purpose of recovering the actual damages sustained by reason of the wrongful suing out of the writ, it is only necessary to aver that such writ was wrongfully sued out. In such a suit vindictive damages can not be given, and the question of malice in procuring the writ can not arise. It is not, therefore, necessary in the declaration either to negative the ground on which the writ was sued out, or to aver that it was done vexatiously or maliciously. Dickson *v.* Bachelder, 21 Ala. 699, 705. See Wilson *v.* Outlaw, Minor 367; Hill *v.* Rushing, 4 Ala. 212; Herndon *v.* Forney, 4 Ala. 243; McCullough *v.* Walton, 11 Ala. 492; Kirksey *v.* Jones, 7 Ala. 622.

In covenant on an attachment bond, if the damages alleged to have been sustained exceed the penalty of the bond, it is proper to assign the nonpayment of the penalty; if they do not amount to as large a sum as the penalty, then the breach will be the nonpayment of the damages actually sustained. Hill *v.* Rushing, 4 Ala. 212.

In debt on a bond conditioned to indemnify the obligee for all costs and damages he might sustain by the wrongful suing out of a writ of seizure from the chancery court, an averment in the declaration that the bill in the chancery suit was dismissed is sufficient, without stating the grounds for dismissal. Zeigler *v.* David, 23 Ala. 127.

In debt on a bond conditioned to indemnify the obligee for all costs and damages he may sustain by the wrongful suing out of a writ from the chancery court in a cause afterwards dismissed, it is unnecessary to aver notice of the dismissal to the obligors, since they were parties to the record. Zeigler *v.* David, 23 Ala. 127.

In an action on an attachment bond, plaintiff need not allege that the bond was approved by the clerk who issued the writ, nor that the attachment was sued out "without cause," as that is implied in alleging that it was wrongfully sued out, nor that the attachment was levied on plaintiff's property, as that is matter of evidence to establish damages. Dothard *v.* Sheid, 69 Ala. 135.

An allegation that the goods were seized under a writ of detinue issued at the instance of defendant, which was dismissed and the attachment levied, is irrelevant. Jefferson County Sav. Bank *v.* Eborn, 84 Ala. 529, 4 So. 386.

In an action on an attachment bond, an allegation that plaintiff was prevented by the attachment from settling with his creditors by paying them with the goods is not demurrable. Jefferson County Sav. Bank *v.* Eborn, 84 Ala. 529, 4 So. 386.

In an action on an attachment bond, where counsel fees are claimed as special damages, it is not enough to allege merely the employment of an attorney; but he must have rendered services, and plaintiff have incurred liability, and an allegation that plaintiff employed counsel at a certain expense was insufficient. Schuessler & Sons *v.* Still, 169 Ala. 239, 53 So. 831.

In an action on an attachment bond, where the complaint fails to show who are the obligees, and if the bond was in fact payable to others besides plaintiffs, objection may be taken to its introduction in evidence, or a variance may be claimed and proper charges requested. Painter *v.* Munn, 23 So. 83, 117 Ala. 322, 67 Am. St. Rep. 170, cited on this point in note in 38 L. R. A., N. S., 127.

Averments as to Damages.—In an action on an attachment bond, plaintiff can not recover exemplary damages where the complaint fails to allege that the attachment was sued out without probable cause for the belief that the statutory grounds for attachment existed, though it alleges the nonexistence of such grounds. Schloss *v.* Rovelsky, 107 Ala. 596, 18 So. 71, cited in note in 38 L. R. A., N. S., 127.

Where a statute provides that in an action on an attachment bond the damages are actual only, if the attachment was sued out "wrongfully," but may be exemplary also if sued out "vexatiously," and the complaint avers that the attachment was sued out "wrongfully" and "vexatiously," but fails to assign a breach sufficient to recover exemplary damages, the words "and vexatiously" are surplusage, and not grounds for a demurrer to the whole complaint. McLane *v.* McTighe, 89 Ala. 411, 8 So. 70, distinguishing Durr *v.* Jackson, 59 Ala. 203.

"The rule stated in Durr *v.* Jackson. 59 Ala. 203, that in an action on an attachment bond, in order to show a sufficient breach, 'it is necessary for the plaintiff to aver in his complaint the falsity of the particular fact or facts which may be stated in the affidavit as the ground of attachment,' is not of universal application. Though one of the statutory grounds for attachment may exist, if there is no debt or demand to enforce the collection of which an attachment is authorized, the condition of the bond is broken, and the obligee is entitled to recover in an action thereon such actual damages as he may have sustained." McLane *v.* McTighe, 89 Ala. 411, 8 So. 70.

"It may be conceded that, under the decision in City Nat. Bank *v.* Jeffries, 73 Ala. 183, it is requisite, to render a complaint sufficient as a claim for exemplary damages, that it should aver, in addition to negativing the truth of the ground on which the attachment was obtained, that its issue was procured without probable cause for believing the alleged ground to be true." McLane *v.* McTighe, 89 Ala. 411, 8 So. 70.

Where the complaint in an action on a bond in attachment sued out for the collection of rent claims damages of $100, in that plaintiff was put to expense of employing counsel to defend the suit, but does not deny that the rent was due, and fails to show the determination of the attachment suit, but does not show what sum was paid or promised for counsel fee, it is insufficient on demurrer. Crofford *v.* Vassar, 95 Ala. 548, 10 So. 350.

In an action on a bond in attachment sued out for the collection of rent, the allegation that "said attachment was wrongfully, vexatiously, and maliciously sued out, in that no statutory ground existed either for the enforcement of any existing lien or for the purpose of creating a lien," was sufficient to support a recovery of actual damages, but did not authorize vindictive damages. Crofford *v.* Vassar, 95 Ala. 548, 10 So. 350, cited in note in 38 L. R. A., N. S., 120.

A complaint in an action on an attachment bond, which is in substantial compliance with the form prescribed in the Code for suits on bonds with conditions (Code of 1876, § 3009. Form 12), is sufficient; but under such complaint, in the absence of specific averments claiming special damages, only general damages, or such as result necessarily and by implication of law from the issuance of the attachment, can be recovered. Dothard *v.* Sheid, 69 Ala. 135, cited in note in 38 L. R. A., N. S., 127.

In a suit for damages for the wrongful suing out of an attachment, damages resulting from a loss of credit can not be recovered, unless specially pleaded and proved. Lewis *v.* Paull, 42 Ala. 136.

The parties to a bond conditioned that certain property should be forthcoming if the same should be found liable to the attachment are bound to notice the determination of the claim suit, and therefore no averment of notice to them to that effect is necessary. Garnett *v.* Roper, 10 Ala. 842.

Amendment.—The complaint in suit on an attachment bond by one of the payees of the bond may be amended by adding the other payees as coplaintiffs. Weedon *v.* Jones, 106 Ala. 336, 17 So. 454.

§ 210. —— Evidence.

See, generally, the title EVIDENCE.

§ 210 (1) Presumptions and Burden of Proof.

Falsity of Attachment Affidavit.—In an action for the wrongful suing out of an attachment, the burden of proof is on plaintiff to show the falsity of the attachment affidavit; and, if he fails to do so, he can not recover. Calhoun *v.* Hannan, 87 Ala. 277, 6 So. 291. See Flournoy *v.* Lyon & Co., 70 Ala. 308.

"The averment of the falsity of the affidavit, though it may be negative in form, and may involve proof of a negative, casts on the plaintiff the onus of supporting it by evidence either direct, or of circumstances from which the jury may fairly infer untruth of the fact or facts stated in the affidavit." Durr *v.* Jackson, 59 Ala. 203, 204.

Nonexistence of Requisite Facts.—In an action on a bond, which provides in statutory language for "all such damages as he may sustain by the wrongful or vexatious suing out of said attachment," plaintiff is not entitled to recover unless it is shown that the issuance of the writ was wrongful in the sense that the facts on which it was based did not exist. Calhoun *v.* Hannan, 87 Ala. 277, 6 So. 291.

Attachment Wrongful.—To maintain an action under Code, § 3317, for the "vexatious suing out" of an attachment, ill will or vindictiveness need not be proved, but only the want of probable cause, coupled with the unlawful act of suing out the writ. Durr *v.* Jackson, 59 Ala. 203, cited in note in 38 L. R. A., N. S., 120.

An action can not be maintained on an attachment bond without showing that the attachment was wrongful as well as vexatious. City Nat. Bank *v.* Jeffries, 73 Ala. 183, cited in note in 38 L. R. A., N. S., 120, 127.

In an action on an attachment bond, to recover damages for wrongfully or wrongfully and vexatiously suing out an attachment, the burden rests on the plaintiff for proving the nonexistence of the sworn ground on which the process was issued, or, what is the same thing, the falsity of the affidavit. City Nat. Bank *v.* Jeffries, 73 Ala. 183.

§ 210 (2) Admissibility.

Record of Attachment and Proceedings.—The record of the attachment and the proceedings thereon are admissible in evidence in a suit on the attachment bond. Donnell *v.* Jones, 17 Ala. 689, 52 Am. Dec. 194; Dothard *v.* Sheid, 69 Ala. 135; Hundley *v.* Chadick, 109 Ala. 575, 19 So. 845. See note 38 L. R. A., N. S., 120.

In a suit for damages brought on an attachment bond, the record of the proceedings in the attachment suit is not inadmissible on the ground of variance, because the defendant is sued as James Olive, and the record shows that the bond was signed by James A. Olive. A man can not have two Christian names, in law. Adams *v.* Olive, 48 Ala. 551.

Although the defendants, who are sued as partners, can not be held responsible for the separate act of one partner in procuring the levy of another attachment in favor of another creditor; yet, where the attachment on which the action is founded, by the sheriff's return thereon endorsed, shows that the goods had been first taken under the other attachment, the plaintiff may show that the goods levied on were more than sufficient to satisfy that attachment, and may introduce the attachment and levy for this purpose. Goldsmith, etc., Co. *v.* Picard, 27 Ala. 142.

Ownership of Property and Ability to Pay Debts.—A debtor against whom an attachment is sued out on the ground that he has money, property, or effects liable to satisfy his debts, but which are fraudulently withheld by him, may prove in a subsequent suit on the attachment bond that, "at the time the attachment was sued out, he was a man of large means, and had a large amount of property about him and under his control, claiming it openly and notoriously as his own. Burton *v.* Smith, 49 Ala. 293.

In an action for wrongful attachment, defendant having shown in evidence the pecuniary embarrassment of plaintiff at the time of the attachment, plaintiff may rebut by proof of subsisting accounts due to him as a physician, as charged in his books, accompanied with evidence of the correctness of the accounts. Lockhart *v.* Woods, 38 Ala. 631.

Intention of Plaintiff to Remain within the State.—In an action for wrongfully suing out an attachment against plaintiff, on the ground that she was about to leave the state, it is error to permit her to testify as to her uncommunicated intention to remain within the state, or as to the strength of her affection for the place of her domicile within the state. Baldwin *v.* Walker, 91 Ala. 428, 8 So. 364.

Business Broken up Resumed by Assistance of Third Parties.—In an action on a bond to indemnify defendants in attachment, brought by the latter against the obligor in such bond, it is error to allow plaintiffs to prove that their business, which they alleged was broken up by the attachment, had since been resumed through the assistance of third parties. Adams *v.* Thornton, 82 Ala. 260, 3 So. 20.

Seizure and Delivery of Property to Plaintiff.—In an action on an attachment bond for wrongful attachment, plaintiff may show what property of his was seized and delivered to plaintiff in attachment, and by whom converted, though the sheriff's return is silent as to such property. Hensley *v.* Rose, 76 Ala. 373.

Bona Fides of Transfers of Property.—In an action for wrongful attachment, on the examination of a witness, to whom defendants claimed plaintiffs, prior to the attachment, had sold a portion of the goods below cost, it was competent for defendants, in determining the question of plaintiffs' bona fides, to question him as to the price paid, and to refresh his memory by showing him an invoice of the goods. Marx *v.* Strauss, 93 Ala. 453, 9 So. 818.

Prior Offer of Plaintiff to Convey Property in Settlement of Claim.—In an action for wrongfully suing out an attachment on goods in a store, evidence that plaintiff, prior to issue of the attachment, offered to convey certain property at a specified price to defendant in settlement of its claim, is irrelevant. Jefferson County Sav. Bank *v.* Eborn, 84 Ala. 529, 4 So. 386.

Plaintiff's Reason for Attachment.—In an action for wrongful attachment, to allow plaintiff to testify that an assignment made by him, following an attachment of his goods, was made on account of the attachment, when nothing appears to show that this was other than a secret and uncommunicated motive, is error. Adams *v.* Thornton, 82 Ala. 260, 3 So. 20.

Evidence as to Fair Price or Sale under Attachment.—Where plaintiffs claimed that the goods did not bring a "fair price" at the sale under the attachment, the testimony of the auctioneer who had sold the goods, and who had exercised his business for twenty years, was competent in defense. Marx *v.* Strauss, 93 Ala. 453, 9 So. 818.

Price of Goods Purchased by Plaintiff.—It was competent for a witness, the representative of the firm from whom plaintiffs bought the goods, to testify as to the price paid by them therefor. Marx *v.* Strauss, 93 Ala. 453, 9 So. 818.

Evidence as to Notes Showing Indebtedness.—In an action for a wrongful attachment, evidence as to notes signed by plaintiff and another, held by witness at the time of the attachment, is admissible as showing the indebtedness of plaintiff at that time, where the only objection is general, and not made to their introduction without proof of execution. Calhoun *v.* Hannan, 87 Ala. 277, 6 So. 291.

Common Reputation to Prove That Defendant Had Gone to Adjacent State for Business or Pleasure.—In an action for wrongfully and maliciously suing out an attachment against the plaintiff's estate, it is not allowable for him to prove, that by common reputation in the neighborhood in which the defendant and himself resided, it was supposed that he had gone to an adjacent state on a visit of business or pleasure. Pitts *v.* Burroughs, 6 Ala. 733.

Instructions to Deputy Sheriff as to Custody and Control of Property.—In an action on an attachment bond, the instructions of the attorney of the plaintiff in attachment, to the deputy sheriff by whom the writ was levied, "that he might leave the property as he found it until the sheriff came, but to stay there and watch it," are not admissible evidence for the defendant. Floyd *v.* Hamilton, 33 Ala. 235.

Identification of Plaintiff with Obligee of Bond.—In an action by C. on an attachment bond payable to "C. & Co.," the complaint alleging that the bond was made payable to plaintiff under the name of C. & Co., it is proper to admit in evidence the bond subject to proof of the identity of plaintiff with the obligee of the bond. Hundley *v.* Chadick, 109 Ala. 575, 19 So. 845, cited in note in 38 L. R. A., N. S., 120.

Identification of Writ Referred to by Replevin Bond.—Where the replevin bond in attachment is made payable to plaintiff, and describes the writ, parol evidence may be received to identify the particular writ to which it refers. Adler *v.* Potter, 57 Ala. 571.

Declarations and Admissions.—Though neither indebtedness, pecuniary embarrassment, nor insolvency can justify the wrongful suing out of an attachment, in an action on an attachment bond, it having been shown that at the time the attachment was sued out defendant in attachment had been negotiating for a sale of his property at a low price, evidence is admissible of a statement of defendant that he "was involved and broke," as pertinent to the question of the bona fides of the conveyance. Lockhart *v.* Woods, 38 Ala. 631.

In an action on a bond in attachment sued out for the collection of rent, where the complaint was not for the recovery of exemplary damages, it was error to allow plaintiff's witness to testify that defendant had stated that he "intended to get everything plaintiff made on the plantation that year for nothing." Crofford *v.* Vassar, 95 Ala. 548, 10 So. 350.

Where, in an action on an attachment bond, there was a count for wrongful, as well as for vexatious, suing out for the process, and it appeared that the writ was sued out by defendant's attorney, evidence of conversations by the attorney with others prior to issuance of the writ, in reference to defendant's disposition of his property, was admissible, over an objection that it was immaterial, irrelevant, and illegal to establish defendant's liability for actual damages. Louisville Jeans Clothing Co. *v.* Lischkoff, 109 Ala. 136, 19 So. 436.

Evidence of declarations of plaintiff in attachment to his attorney as to his reasons for suing out the writ made at the time of suing it out, is admissible in an action on the attachment bond, as a part of the res gestæ. Wood *v.* Barker, 37 Ala. 60, 76 Am. Dec. 346.

The acts and declarations of defendant's attorney in resisting plaintiff's claims to exemptions in the attachment proceedings, of which acts and declarations defendant was not informed, are not admissible on the question whether or not defendant acted maliciously in suing out the attachment. Baldwin *v.* Walker, 91 Ala. 428, 8 So. 364.

Declarations made by plaintiff anterior to the suing out of the attachment as to her intention of leaving the state for a visit only, are not competent, unless made at the time of leaving, and in explanation of the act. Baldwin *v.* Walker, 91 Ala. 428, 8 So. 364.

What a party said on leaving home, or immediately previous thereto, is admissible in evidence in his favor as a part of the res gestæ on the trial of an action for wrongfully and maliciously suing out an attachment against him in his absence. Pitts *v.* Burroughs, 6 Ala. 733.

In an action on an attachment bond for vexation, the directions of the attaching attorney to the sheriff are declarations inadmissible to show any fact, or to prove or disprove malice in the attachment plaintiff. Floyd *v.* Hamilton, 33 Ala. 235.

It was held that the primary court erred in allowing proof to be made in this case by the plaintiff, (1) when and how he obtained money which he placed on deposit with his surety on a replevy bond executed by him in the attachment suit, the fact of such deposit not having been proved against him; (2) how he had lived after the attachment was levied, it not being in rebuttal to any thing proved against him; and (3) that th laintiff said to witnesses that he was not going to Texas, when it is not shown to have been a part of the res gestæ. Jackson *v.* Smith, 75 Ala. 97.

Intent and Malice.—In a suit by partners on a bond given in attachment against them, and payable to them as partners, evidence that property of one of the partners was seized under the attachment is admissible to show malice as a basis for exemplary damages. Watts *v.* Rice, 75 Ala. 289.

In an action on an attachment bond, a second attachment, sued out by plaintiff therein against defendant one week after the first, is relevant evidence on the question of malice. Ryall *v.* Marx, 50 Ala. 31.

In an action for wrongful attachment, to show that he acted without malice, defendant may show that other attachments were issued against plaintiff one day before this attachment, in connection with evidence that notice thereof was given to him before suing out the process; otherwise as to an attachment of which he had no notice. Lockhart *v.* Woods, 38 Ala. 631.

Since neither embarrassment nor insolvency is ground for suing an attachment, they are immaterial on the question of malice, except so far as they show fraud in the debtor towards his creditors. Floyd *v.* Hamilton, 33 Ala. 235.

In a suit on an attachment bond, assigning as one of the breaches that the attachment was malicious and vexatious, plaintiff's testimony that defendant told him after suing out the writ that he had more money to spend in the lawsuit than plaintiff had is competent to illustrate the quo animo of the attachment proceedings. Dothard *v.* Sheid, 69 Ala. 135.

In a suit on an attachment bond, whether against the principal surety, the unauthorized malice or vexation of the agent not being a ground of recovery, evidence of it should not be allowed to go to the jury. Jackson *v.* Smith, 75 Ala. 97.

Damages.—It is an incompetent method of proving the quantity of goods in the store to show the percentage of profits on the goods sold, and thus approximate the amount on hand. Jefferson County Sav. Bank *v.* Eborn, 84 Ala. 529, 4 So. 386.

The amount of business done by plaintiff since an alleged wrongful attachment is not competent evidence to show the damages arising from the attachment. Adams *v.* Thornton, 82 Ala. 260, 3 So. 20.

In an action on an attachment bond, a witness may testify to the extent of a merchant's business, and the rate or average of his net profits, if within his knowledge, but may not give his opinion as to the loss he will suffer by the breaking up of his business. Pollock *v.* Gantt, 69 Ala. 373, 44 Am. Rep. 519.

Where it appears that the goods seized are the same as those formerly taken in detinue, an officer who made the inventory in such former suit, and testified that it was correct, may give his opinion as to the value of the goods, based on his knowledge thus acquired, in connection with his experience as a deputy sheriff in taking other inventories, and making sales of similar goods. Jefferson County Sav. Bank *v.* Eborn, 84 Ala. 529, 4 So. 386.

While one who has been wrongfully and vexatiously attached, may recover on the attachment bond for his wounded feelings, such suffering is not the subject of direct proof, but is an inference to be drawn by the jury from the manner and carelessness of the wrong; and hence, in such case, it is not competent for the plaintiff to testify that by the issue and levy of the attachment he "was much distressed and harassed in body and mind," or that he "was almost crazy;" or for him to show by other witnesses the apparent distress he suffered in consequence of the attachment. City Nat. Bank *v.* Jeffries, 73 Ala. 183.

Where an attachment is wrongfully sued out, the attachment plaintiff can not show in mitigation of damages that the proceeds of the property were applied by him in payment of a debt due from the attachment defendant. Hundley *v.* Chadick, 109 Ala. 575, 19 So. 845.

In an action for wrongful attachment, it may be shown, in mitigation of damages, that the property was subsequently taken under a second valid attachment issued by another creditor, and sold in satisfaction of the attaching creditor's claim. Grisham *v.* Bodman, 111 Ala. 194, 20 So. 514.

Defendants suing on an attachment bond have the right to show on the subject of exemplary damages that, before their agent sued out the attachment, he was notified that other creditors of plaintiff had on that day sued out attachments against him on the same alleged ground as that set forth in defendant's attachment. Pollock *v.* Gantt, 69 Ala. 373, 44 Am. Rep. 519.

In an action for wrongful attachment, the fact that the property attached brought its full value may be considered only in mitigation of damages. City Nat. Bank *v.* Jeffries, 73 Ala. 183.

Probable cause may be shown in mitigation of damages in an action on the attachment bond for wrongful attachment. Metcalf *v.* Young, 43 Ala. 643.

In an action on attachment bond, it is not competent for the plaintiff to testify that the effect of the attachment on him was to prevent him from making a crop, and from doing any business, and that it ruined him; or to prove that he was a man of limited means. Jackson *v.* Smith, 75 Ala. 97.,

§ 210 (3) Weight and Sufficiency.

Acts and Declarations of Plaintiff.—In an a tion for wrongfully suing out an attachment, evidence of plaintiff's acts and declarations, of which defendant had knowledge, about the time he sued out the writ, and of all circumstances surrounding the parties, and their relations, tending to show, in contradiction of the averments of the affidavit for the writ, that plaintiff was not refusing payment of a debt he knew or believed just, but was resisting a demand he regarded as unjust, is not admissible as being in effect a denial of the validity of the debt on which the attachment issued, and which was conclusively established by the judgment in the attachment suit. Durr *v.* Jackson, 59 Ala. 203.

Indorsement on Bond.—A bond executed by an attachment debtor was declared defective as a statutory undertaking, and was then sued upon as a common-law bond. Without objection, it was admitted in evidence, bearing the following indorsement, signed by the constable: "The property mentioned in this bond not having been returned to me, as required herein, I hereby return it forfeited." Held that, although the indorsement was not competent as evidence of nondelivery, yet, the parties having treated it as competent, it was sufficient, in the absence of opposing testimony, to support a judgment on the bond. Olmstead *v.* Thompson, 91 Ala. 127, 8 So. 346.

Effect of Former Disposition of Cause.—In debt on a bond conditioned to indemnify the obligee for all costs and damages he may sustain by the wrongful suing out of a writ of seizure from the chancery court, the transcript of the record of the chancery suit, showing the dismissal of the bill for want of prosecution, is prima facie evidence that the writ was wrongfully obtained. Zeigler *v.* David, 23 Ala. 127.

A judgment entered on a verdict against plaintiff in an attachment is not conclusive evidence, in a subsequent suit on the bond, that the attachment was wrongfully sued out. Sackett *v.* McCord, 23 Ala. 851.

The mere fact that defendants unsuccessfully attempted to prove fraud, and thereby show probable cause for the issuance of the writ, does not afford a fair inference of malice in a suit on an attachment bond, given on the issuance of an attachment, on the ground that defendants have fraudulently disposed of their property. Flournoy *v.* Lyon, 70 Ala. 308.

Plaintiff in an action on an attachment bond need not offer the original bond in evidence otherwise than by introducing the final record of the attachment suit. Defendant, if he executed the bond, is precluded from disputing its existence or the genuineness of the record. Adams *v.* Olive, 48 Ala. 551.

Damages.—Where, in an action on an attachment bond, plaintiff testified that he employed a certain attorney to defend the suit, and agreed to pay him a certain fee, but there was no proof that he defended it, or that plaintiff had paid or was liable for the fee, there was no evidence of actual damages. Charles Schuessler & Sons *v.* Still, 53 So. 831, 169 Ala. 239.

Assessment of Value of Property.—In an action on the forthcoming bond provided for by Code 1886, § 2523, the obligors are concluded by the assessment of the value of the property in contest in and by the judgment required by § 2532. Troy *v.* Rogers, 22 So. 486, 116 Ala. 255, 67 Am. St. Rep. 110.

§ 211. —— Damages.

See, generally, the title DAMAGES.

As to extent of liability in general, see ante, "Extent of Liability," § 199.

§ 211 (1) Measure of Damages.

On Bond or Undertaking to Procure Attachment.—Where an attachment is wrongful, but there is an absence of malice, the defendant can recover only the actual damages sustained. McCullough *v.* Walton, 11 Ala. 492; Pollock & Co. *v.* Gantt, 69 Ala. 373; City Nat. Bank *v.* Jeffries, 73 Ala. 183; Stewart *v.* Cole & Son, 46 Ala. 646, 651; Dothard *v.* Sheid, 69 Ala. 135, 138; Floyd *v.* Hamilton, 33 Ala. 235; Sharpe *v.* Hunter, 16 Ala. 765, 767; Jackson *v.* Smith, 75 Ala. 97; McLane *v.* McTighe, 89 Ala. 411, 8 So. 70, see note in 29 L. R. A. 275.

In actions on bond for wrongful attachment, the plaintiff may recover the actual damage sustained by him up to the time of the trial. Metcalf *v.* Young, 43 Ala. 643, 648. See Hair *v.* Little, 28 Ala. 236; Jenkins *v.* McConico, 26 Ala. 213; Seay *v.* Greenwood, 21 Ala. 491; Ewing *v.* Blount, 20 Ala. 694.

Where an attachment was sued out by an agent, and it is neither shown that he was thereunto authorized or instructed, nor that the principal ever repudiated the suit, this subjected the principal to actual damages if no cause existed for suing out the process. Pollock & Co. *v.* Gantt, 69 Ala. 373, cited in note in 29 L. R. A., N. S., 280.

Where there is no debt owing from the defendant to the plaintiff in attachment, the condition of the bond is broken, and the obligee is entitled to recover, in an action on the bond, at least nominal damages, or such actual damages as he may have sustained; and if there is no proof whatever of the existence of any debt, the court may instruct the jury, without hypothesis, to find for the plaintiff. Lockhart *v.* Woods, 38 Ala. 631.

In an action on an attachment bond, damages to the time of trial may be recovered, whether plaintiff has paid the expenses and damages incurred or not. Metcalf *v.* Young, 43 Ala. 643. See Hair *v.* Little, 28 Ala. 236; Jenkins *v.* McConico, 26 Ala. 213; Seay *v.* Greenwood, 21 Ala. 491; Ewing *v.* Blount, 20 Ala. 694.

Where, in an action on an attachment bond, given in proceedings under Code 1907, § 3194, relating to seizures in equity, plaintiff showed a dismissal of the bill, he was entitled to nominal damages, though he proved no actual damages. Charles Schuessler & Sons *v.* Still, 53 So. 831, 169 Ala. 239.

If an attachment sued out in a case in which just grounds for it exist is abated, on plea, for a defect in the affidavit, the party against whom it is issued, in a suit on the bond, is not entitled to recover the actual damages he has sustained. Sharpe *v.* Hunter, 16 Ala. 765.

Actions on attachment bond are governed in all respects by the rules applicable to actions on the case for wrongfully suing out attachments, but the recovery can never exceed the penalty of the bond. Hill *v.* Rushing, 4 Ala. 212.

The statute which provides that, "in all actions to recover damages for torts, the plaintiff shall recover no more costs than damages where the damages do not exceed five dollars, unless the presiding judge shall certify that greater damages should, in justice, have been awarded" (Clay's Dig., p. 316, § 25), does not apply to an action of debt on an attachment bond to recover damages for the wrongful and vexatious suing out of the attachment. McAllister *v.* McDow, 26 Ala. 453.

Where the property seized under a writ of attachment is replevied by the defendant, who afterwards sells it, and with the proceeds pays the debt to enforce which the attachment was sued out, these facts may be pleaded in mitigation of damages, in an action on the attachment bond. Painter *v.* Munn, 23 So. 83, 117 Ala. 322, 67 Am. St. Rep. 170.

In a debt on a bond conditioned to indemnify the obligee for all costs and damages he might sustain by the wrongful suing out of a writ of seizure from the chancery court, plaintiff may recover the damages actually sustained, without proof of malice in suing out the process. Zeigler *v.* David, 23 Ala. 127.

In debt on a bond conditioned to indemnify the obligee for all costs and damages he might sustain by the wrongful suing out of a writ of seizure from the chancery court in a suit which was dismissed for want of prosecution, plaintiff may recover, if possession of the slaves seized under the writ is not restored to him, the hire of the slaves down to the time of trial, though after the dismissal of the bill a second bill was filed for the some purpose, and a new bond given, conditioned for the forthcoming of the slaves to abide the final decree. Zeigler *v.* David, 23 Ala. 127.

On Forthcoming or Delivery Bond or Undertaking.—In an action on a replevin bond in attachment, the value of the property at the time it was seized, or at the time at which it should have been delivered in compliance with the condition of the bond, is the measure of the recovery. Adler *v.* Potter, 57 Ala. 571.

On Claimant's Bond or Undertaking for Possession.—When the judgments rendered in favor of several attaching creditors exceed the valuation of the property agreed on between the claimant and such creditors at the beginning of suit, the sureties on the claim bond, on the claimant's failure to return the property to the sheriff, can be held for only the valuation so agreed on, less the necessary expenses of selling, and such amounts as may have been paid to the attaching creditors. Jaffray *v.* Smith, 106 Ala. 112, 17 So. 218.

§ 211 (2) Elements of Compensation.

On Bond or Undertaking to Procure Attachment—In General.—Damages, to be recoverable in an action on an attachment bond, must be the natural and proximate result of the wrongful, or wrongful and vexatious suing out of the attachment; they must not be the accidental, contingent, or speculative consequence resulting therefrom. Jackson *v.* Smith, 75 Ala. 97.

Where an attachment was made against a firm by its firm name, and a bond was given conditioned to pay the partners "all such damage as they might sustain," no recovery could be had in an action on the bond for damage sustained by one partner for wrongful levy on his individual property. Watts *v.* Rice, 75 Ala. 289.

One suing out an attachment wrongfully and also vexatiously is liable for injury to the feelings of defendant. Floyd *v.* Hamilton, 33 Ala. 235.

Damages actually sustained, recoverable where an attachment was only wrongfully sued out against the defendant does not include injury to his wounded feelings. Floyd *v.* Hamilton, 33 Ala. 235, cited in 29 L. R. A., N. S., 275; 38 L. R. A., N. S., 120, 127.

In an action on an attachment bond for the wrongful suing out of the attachment, no recovery can be had for damages caused by the sheriff's selling the goods in quantity, and not in detail; such damages not being the natural and proximate consequence of the act of suing out the attachment. Jefferson County Sav. Bank *v.* Eborn, 84 Ala. 529, 4 So. 386, cited in note in 29 L. R. A., N. S., 275, 280.

The value of time lost and expenses incurred in attending court for the trial may be recovered in an action on the bond for the wrongful or vexatious suing out of the attachment Higgins *v.* Mansfield, 62 Ala. 267.

Damage resulting from the demoralization of the plaintiff's workmen while he was absent from his farm procuring attorneys to defend the suit, or from plaintiff's being compelled to stop a double plow while he was absent, are too remote, and should not be estimated in fixing the value of plaintiff's services. Higgins *v.* Mansfield, 62 Ala. 267.

Same—Expenses in Defense of Action or Attachment.—For wrongful attachment, recovery may be had on the attachment bond for such reasonable and necessary expenses and costs as are incurred by defendant therein in the vindication of his rights. Higgins *v.* Mansfield, 62 Ala. 267.

The sureties in an attachment bond are not liable for the costs accruing on a trial of the right of property between plaintiff and a third person who interposes a claim to the property levied on under the attachment. Thompson *v.* Gates, 18 Ala. 32.

In a suit for wrongfully suing out an attachment, plaintiff can not recover for his voluntary appearance and defense, there having been no levy. Flournoy *v.* Lyon, 70 Ala. 308.

Same—Injury to Business, Credit, or Reputation.—Injury resulting to the credit and business of a defendant in an attachment which has been wrongfully or vexatiously sued out may be recovered as special damages in a suit on the attachment bond. W. F. Vandiver & Co. *v.* Waller, 39 So. 136, 143 Ala. 411. See Durr *v.* Jackson, 59 Ala. 203.

One suing on an attachment bond for damages to his business, credit, and reputation as a merchant can not show that by reason of the destruction of his business and credit he has lost advances made by him, and possible profits on shipments of merchandise, as such damages are too speculative and remote. Pollock *v.* Gantt, 69 Ala. 373, 44 Am. Rep. 519.

Injury to the credit of the defendant in attachment may result from the wrongful or vexatious suing out of the writ, although there was no levy, and may be recovered, as special damages, in an action on the bond. Flournoy *v.* Lyon & Co., 70 Ala. 308. See Gramling-Spalding Co. *v.* Parker, 3 Ala. App. 325, 57 So. 54.

"The damages recoverable for the wrongful or malicious suing out of the writ would, of course, be materially lessened, if there was no levy. There would not be a wrongful seizure and detention of the property of the defendant, and he would not be drawn into the trouble and expense of making defense. But, if special damages accrued to him, such as injury to his credit, which may be a proximate consequence of the wrongful suing out of the writ, these would be recoverable, though it was not levied." Flournoy *v.* Lyon & Co., 70 Ala. 308, 313.

In an action on an attachment bond, in which the only averment of special damage is, that "the plaintiff was engaged in the mercantile business, and had a good reputation, credit, business and good customers; and that by, and in consequence of the levy of said attachment on his property and effects, his business, reputation and credit have been destroyed and lost, and his customers have withdrawn, to the loss and special damage of the plaintiff," etc., it is not competent for the plaintiff to show, that at the time of, and prior to the levy he was making advances to timber-men and others, and that thereby he had become interested in the handling of timber and crops, and that his mercantile business being stopped, he lost these advantages, and lost his advances and the shipment of his timber. Such matters are inadmissible because there is no averment in the complaint authorizing them, and on the further ground, that if there had been such an averment, the damages claimed on account thereof, are speculative and too remote. Pollock & Co. *v.* Gantt, 69 Ala. 373.

Loss of credit and business are natural consequences of an attachment sued out on the ground of fraud, and are properly averred as special damages in a complaint for wrongfully suing out such attachment. Marx *v.* Strauss, 93 Ala. 453, 9 So. 818.

In an action for a wrongful attachment, damages resulting from loss of credit, whereby plaintiffs were prevented from borrowing money from two or three persons, are so remote and speculative that evidence thereof is incompetent. Marx *v.* Strauss, 93 Ala. 453, 9 So. 818.

Same—Attorney's Fees.—In an action on an attachment bond, reasonable attorney's fees paid in defending the attachment suit may be recovered as a part of the damages. Higgins *v.* Mansfield, 62 Ala. 267.

Under an attachment bond conditioned to prosecute the attachment to effect. and to pay defendant such damages as he may sustain from a wrongful or vexatious suing out of the attachment, the attachment defendant may, if the attachment is wrongfully or maliciously sued out, recover counsel fees which were necessitated by the wrongful suing out of the attachment, such as fees paid for services rendered in preparing and filing an exemption declaration and in defending a contest of the declaration by the attachment plaintiff. W. F. Vandiver & Co. *v.* Waller, 39 So. 136, 143 Ala. 411.

Reasonable and necessary counsel fees, incurred in defense of the attachment suit, are recoverable as actual damages in an action on the bond, whether the attachment was merely wrongful, or wrongful and malicious; but counsel fees incurred in defense of a garnishee, although that defense was successful, and a judgment against the defendant in attachment was thereby defeated, are not recoverable in such action. Flournoy *v.* Lyon & Co., 70 Ala. 308.

In an action on an attachment bond, whether brought for the recovery of the actual damages sustained, or for the recovery of vindictive or exemplary damages, reasonable and necessary counsel fees incurred in defending the attachment suit, or in prosecuting or defending an appeal from the judgment rendered in that suit to this court, may be recovered. Such fees, however, while the proximate result of the wrongful suing out of the attachment, are not such damages as necessarily result therefrom, or as are implied by the law; and hence. they can not be recovered, unless they are specifically claimed in the complaint. Dothard *v.* Sheid, 69 Ala. 135.

In an action on an attachment bond, conditioned to "prosecute the attachment to effect, and pay the defendant all such damages as he may sustain from the wrongful or vexatious suing out of such attachment" (Code, § 3256), attorney's fees for services rendered in bringing the action can not be recovered. Copeland *v.* Cunningham, 63 Ala. 394; overruling Burton *v.* Smith, 49 Ala. 293.

Where plaintiff employed an attorney to defend an attachment against her house and lot, which were not sold under the attachment, and of which she was not dispossessed, she can not recover as damages, in an action for wrongful attachment, the amount paid by her as attorney's fees. Baldwin *v.* Walker, 94 Ala. 514, 10 So. 391.

"A defendant in an attachment suit may employ an attorney to look after his interests, and to see that his rights are properly guarded, even though no issue can be made in that case as to the existence of the ground of attachment, though no defense can be made to the claim sued on and though no ground for quashing the attachment may exist. It is not unreasonable for one whose property has been seized under legal process to employ counsel to protect it as far as the law may justify, though there may be no possibility of defeating the proceeding. The question of the propriety of incurring such expense does not depend upon the defendant's ability to make a successful defense. One whose property is in the clutches of the law may seek professional aid to secure whatever measure of protection the law may afford. Though it may not be necessary or proper to undertake a defense of the suit, the defendant may still have counsel to watch its progress, and to see that no undue advantage is taken of him." Baldwin *v.* Walker, 94 Ala. 514, 10 So. 391, 393.

On Bond or Undertaking to Discharge Attachment.—On a bond for the trial of the right of property taken in attachment, the condition of which is that the claimant shall have it forthcoming if it be found liable, and "pay such costs and damages as may be recovered for putting in the claim for delay," the sureties are bound for the costs, though the claim be not put in for delay. McElrath *v.* Whetstone, 89 Ala. 623, 8 So. 7. See Robertson *v.* Patterson, 17 Ala. 407.

When it is determined in a suit by attaching creditors that the claimant, who took the goods from the sheriff, and sold them during the process of the suit, had no title, a sum which such claimant has paid to the insolvent debtor in lieu of the latter's exemption can not be considered in fixing the amount for which the sureties on the claimant's bond are liable. Jaffray *v.* Smith, 106 Ala. 112, 17 So. 218.

§ 211 (3) Exemplary Damages.

On Bond or Undertaking to Procure Attachment.—Exemplary or vindictive damages may be recovered on an action on the bond to procure an attachment where the writ was sued out wrongfully and maliciously. McCullough *v.* Walton, 11 Ala. 492; Baldwin *v.* Walker, 94 Ala. 514, 10 So. 391; Stewart *v.* Cole, 46 Ala. 646, 651; Dothard *v.* Sheild, 69 Ala. 135, 139; City Nat. Bank *v.* Jeffries, 73 Ala. 183; Floyd *v.* Hamilton, 33 Ala. 235; Sharpe *v.* Hunter, 16 Ala. 765, 767; Jackson *v.* Smith, 75 Ala. 97. See notes in 29 L. R. A., N. S., 275, 38 L. R. A., N. S., 120, 127.

"A party may, in extreme eagerness to collect a debt or to obtain security for it, without probable cause, resort to an attachment; and the absence of probable cause, coupled with the unlawful act of suing out the writ, is the vexatious or malicious abuse of the process, against which the statute intends to guard, and for which the jury are authorized to give vindictive damages. Code of 1876, § 3318. The true principle is thus stated in Willis *v.* Noyes, 12 Pick. 328. 'The malice necessary to be shown in order to maintain this action, is not necessarily revenge or other base and malignant passion. Whatever is done willfully and purposely, if it be at the same time wrong and unlawful, and that known to the party, is in legal contemplation malicious. That which is done contrary to one's own conviction of duty, or with a willful disregard of the rights of others, whether it be to compass some unlawful end, or some lawful end by unlawful means, constitutes legal malice.' See, also, Kirksey *v.* Jones, 7 Ala. 622." Durr *v.* Jackson,

59 Ala. 203, 210, cited in note in 29 L. R. A., N. S., 275.

"If it was wrongfully sued out, then the plaintiff is responsible to the extent of the actual injury sustained, but if vexatiously also, the case is one for vindictive damages, only in the event that the plaintiff was wantonly or maliciously resorted to the process." McCullough *v.* Walton, 11 Ala. 492, 497.

In an action on an attachment bond, if the attachment against the defendant was sued out wrongfully and vexatiously, he is entitled to recover vindictive damages. Floyd *v.* Hamilton, 33 Ala. 235. See McLane *v.* McTighe, 89 Ala. 411, 8 So. 70, cited in note in 38 L. R. A., N. S., 120, 127.

Where an attachment is sued out when there is no sufficient evidence or probable cause, the jury may infer malice or vexation from the absence of such proof, and vindictive or exemplary damages may be recovered. Jackson *v.* Smith, 75 Ala. 97.

If an attachment is not vexatious as against defendant himself, the fact that the attaching creditor was actuated by malice against a third person, not a party to the process, is no ground for the recovery of vindictive damages in an action on the attachment bond. Wood *v.* Barker, 37 Ala. 60.

A nonresident creditor, who, acting on the advice of his resident attorney that grounds exist for an attachment, orders one issued without knowledge of the facts and circumstances of the case, is not liable for vindictive damages. City Nat. Bank *v.* Jeffries, 73 Ala. 183.

Where an attachment was sued out by an agent, and it is neither shown that he was thereunto authorized or instructed, nor that the principal ever repudiated the suit, although this subjected the principal to actual damages, if no cause existed for suing out the process, he was not, however, responsible for the malicious and vexatious conduct or wantonness of the agent, unless he caused, or participated in such evil motive or conduct. Pollock & Co. *v.* Gantt, 69 Ala. 373.

If there be no reasonable foundation for believing that a statutory ground for an attachment exists, or if the process be sued out wantonly or recklessly without probable cause, or if it be resorted to in a mere race of diligence to obtain a first lien, when no statutory ground exists in fact, or is reasonably believed to exist, then the attachment is vexatious as well as wrongful; and exemplary or vindictive damages may be recovered. City Nat. Bank *v.* Jeffries, 73 Ala. 183.

If a creditor living in another state entrust a claim against his debtor to a reputable attorney in this state for collection, and that attorney informs him that th re exists a ground for suing out an attachment, and thereupon he orders the attachment issued, and, at the attorney's request, furnishes resident sureties to make the bond, in the absence of other knowledge or information, vexatiousness or malice can not be imputed to the creditor; and he and his sureties on the attachment bond are not liable to exemplary or vindictive damages; but this rule would not apply, if the creditor had actual knowledge of the facts relied on as ground for attachment, and such facts were insufficient, and, in truth, no ground for attachment existed. City Nat. Bank *v.* Jeffries, 73 Ala. 183.

In a suit on an attachment bond for a wrongful attachment, damages resulting from the malice of the person suing out the attachment as agent of the attachment plaintiff are not recoverable. Jackson *v.* Smith, 75 Ala. 97.

A principal is not responsible for the malice, vexation or wantonness of his agent in suing out an attachment, unless he authorized or participated in it; and such authority or participation, to render the principal liable, must be proved; it can not be inferred from the mere relation of principal and agent. Jackson *v.* Smith, 75 Ala. 97.

§ 212. —— Trial.

Instructions.—In an action on an attachment bond, a charge that the fact that plaintiff, when he went beyond the state, left his family in the state, might be considered as evidence of his intention, in reference to removing from the state, was properly refused as argumentative. Troy *v.* Rogers, 20 So. 999, 113 Ala. 131.

In an action on an attachment bond, a

charge that, before the jury could find for defendant, they must find that some statutory ground for attachment existed in fact, "and not in the belief of the defendant," was properly refused. Troy *v.* Rogers, 20 So. 999, 113 Ala. 131.

In an action on an attachment bond, it was error to refuse to charge that if plaintiff was not about to remove permanently from the state, and did not intend to take up a residence in another state, then, though defendant believed that he was about to remove permanently from the state, and had probable cause for such belief, he would still be liable to plaintiff, if there was no other cause for attachment. Troy *v.* Rogers, 20 So. 999, 113 Ala. 131.

Defendant requested a charge that if the attaching creditors' agent, before making the levy, consulted an attorney as to whether there was ground for attaching, and informed such attorney of all the facts, and was advised by him to make the attachment, plaintiff could not recover vindictive damages. Held, that the request was defective in excluding all inquiry as to the agent's diligence in ascertaining the truth of such facts, and as to his good faith in acting on the advice of the attorney. Baldwin *v.* Walker, 94 Ala. 514, 10 So. 391.

Where the debt was $2,723, and the attachment was for $2,770, a charge that, to the extent of the difference between such sums, the attachment was wrongful, was properly refused, since such attachment can not be partially rightful and wrongful. Marz *v.* Strauss, 93 Ala. 453, 9 So. 818.

Where the evidence is such as to leave no room for controversy as to the right of recovery, if the jury were convinced by the evidence there was no debt, the court should charge the jury that, "if they believed from the evidence no demand in favor of plaintiff in the attachment against defendant existed at the time said attachment was sued out, then they must find for plaintiff in this action." Lockhart *v.* Woods, 38 Ala. 631.

In an action on an attachment bond sued out on the ground that plaintiff (defendant in attachment) was about to leave the state, where plaintiff testified that her interview with one R. relative to a sale of her house was prior to the attachment, and R. testified that it was subsequent, the question as to when it occurred should have been submitted to the jury, with instructions not to consider plaintiff's statements to R. as evidence against her, if not made until after the attachment. Baldwin *v.* Walker, 94 Ala. 514, 10 So. 391.

XI. WRONGFUL ATTACHMENT.

As to wrongful attachment as conversion, see the title TROVER AND CONVERSION. As to waste, see the title WASTE. As to wrongful attachments in justices court, see the title JUSTICES OF THE PEACE. As to liability of officer, see the title SHERIFFS AND CONSTABLES. As to malicious attachment, see the title MALICIOUS PROSECUTION. As to wrongful attachment of exempt property, see the title EXEMPTIONS. As to wrongful attachment in actions to collect rent, see the title LANDLORD AND TENANT.

§ 213. Nature and Grounds of Liability.

§ 214. —— Wrongful Suing Out of Attachment.

In General.—Under the attachment law, an action may be sustained either for wrongfully or vexatiously suing out process. Kirksey *v.* Jones, 7 Ala. 622, cited in 29 L. R. A. 274, 279, 38 L. R. A. 120, 127.

An attachment sued out without the existence of any statutory grounds on which to predicate the same is wrongful, and entitles the attachment defendant to recover all actual damages accruing to him therefrom. W. F. Vandiver & Co. *v.* Waller, 39 So. 136, 143 Ala. 411, cited on this point in note in 38 L. R. A., N. S., 120.

If at least one statutory ground for an attachment does not exist, the attachment is wrongful, and the debtor may recover his actual damages, regardless of the good faith of the creditor. Birmingham Dry-Goods Co. *v.* Finley, 26 So. 138, 122 Ala. 534.

"The statute carefully defines specific causes or particular grounds or facts, which will authorize this remedy. If no one of these exists, the attachment is wrongfully sued out, and the plaintiff is liable for the actual injury sustained, though he acted from the purest motives, and had probable cause for believing facts existed, which justified a resort to the remedy. 1 Brick. Dig. 168, § 208. The statutes thus protecting the defendant against the misuse or abuse of the process, to avoid the delays incident to the introduction of collateral issues, not involving the merits of the controversy, and to give the suit the form, character and operation of an ordinary suit, commenced by personal service of process, prohibit the denial, or putting in issue the cause for which the writ issued. R. C., § 2992. The action on the bond, for the recovery of damages, being a plenary remedy for all the injury which could result, if the cause did not exist." Tucker *v.* Adams, 52 Ala. 254, 257.

Malice.—In an action for wrongfully suing out an attachment, it is not necessary to prove malice. Wilson *v.* Outlaw, Minor 368, cited in note in 33 L. R. A., N. S., 120.

Under the Code, to sue out an attachment without probable cause, but in good faith and without malice, is not actionable. McKellar *v.* Couch, 34 Ala. 336.

Under the Code, an action on a case will not lie if sued out on attachment, unless it is sued out maliciously, and without probable cause as well as wrongfully. Hence, in an action to recover damages for the wrongful and malicious suing out of an attachment, the court erred in refusing to give a charge requested by the defendants, that if the defendants did not sue out the attachment with malice, or from a disposition to vex or harass the plaintiff, but honestly believed that they had reasonable and probable cause to sue out the attachment, then the plaintiff was not entitled to recover. Benson & Co. *v.* McCoy, 36 Ala. 710.

To justify an attachment, there must be a debt, due or to become due, and one of the enumerated statutory grounds therefor must exist; and if either of these be wanting in fact, no matter how sincerely the attaching creditor may believe it to exist, the attachment is wrongful. City Nat. Bank *v.* Jeffries, 73 Ala. 183.

Disposition of Property.—An attachment plaintiff is liable to the attachment defendant for wrongfully suing out an attachment where the latter was not about to fraudulently dispose of his property and there was no other cause for the attachment. W. F. Vandiver & Co. *v.* Waller, 39 So. 136, 143 Ala. 411.

A debtor proposed to his creditors a complete surrender of all his property, to be divided pro rata, and pretended that his statement of his financial condition showed a full list of his assets and liabilities. This statement in fact omitted three creditors, for whom the debtor testified he had set aside money to pay their claims in full, but by reason of pressure of business had failed to send it. One of these debts was the final payment of purchase money for a cotton press, but the cotton press was not listed with his assets. Certain assets, which were in the hands of creditors as collateral, were counted as assets, without stating that they were pledged. Held that, under these facts, the debtor had no ground of recovery against a creditor for wrongful attachment. Campbell *v.* Hopkins, 87 Ala. 179, 6 So. 76.

§ 215. Persons Entitled to Damages.

§ 216. —— In General.

Owner of Goods Wrongfully Attached.—The owner of goods wrongfully attached may maintain an action on the case for damages, though at the time of the attachment the goods were in the possession of the sheriff under prior attachments by other of his creditors. Joseph *v.* Henderson, 95 Ala. 213, 10 So. 843.

The owner of goods wrongfully attached can not maintain trespass therefor, where, at the time they were attached, they were not in his actual possession, but were in the possession of the sheriff, under prior attachments by other of his creditors. Joseph *v.* Henderson, 95 Ala. 213, 10 So. 843.

"Any loss or damage sustained by the owner, the result of neglect or misconduct on the part of the sheriff, or the wrongful act of any other person while the goods are rightfully in the possession and under the control of such sheriff as an officer of the court, may be recovered by the owner by an action on the case." Joseph *v.* Henderson, 95 Ala. 213, 10 So. 843, 845.

§ 217. —— Estoppel or Waiver.

Directing Owner to Make Levy.—Where goods are wrongfully levied on as the property of another, the owner is not obliged to make a claim bond and have a trial as to the right of property in the goods, but may allow them to be carried away, and sue in trespass; and the fact that he told the sheriff "to go ahead and levy," stating at the same time that he would hold him responsible as for a trespass, does not confer upon the officer any right which he did not before possess, or estop the owner from the assertion of any right which would otherwise have been his. Smith *v.* Kaufman, 94 Ala. 364, 10 So. 229.

§ 218. Persons Liable.

Attaching Creditors in General. — Creditors of an insolvent attached his stock of goods, which were claimed by a third person as a bona fide purchaser. Other creditors placed attachments on the goods while in the hands of the marshal awaiting sale on the first attachment. The amount of the attachments exceeded the value of the goods, and none of the proceeds went to the previous purchaser. Held, that the creditors first attaching, if liable to the vendee at all, were liable for the whole damages. Stix *v.* Keith, 85 Ala. 465, 5 So. 184.

A party who procures a sheriff to levy an attachment which is void on its face is a trespasser. Stetson *v.* Goldsmith, 30 Ala. 602; S. C., 31 Ala. 649.

Plaintiffs in attachment are not liable with the sheriff for wrongful execution of process by selling at a place other than that named in the advertisement, with part of the property sold not present, and all sold in mass, they having done nothing more than sue out the attachment and place the writ in his hands, and after the levy told him to take the goods out of the house where they were, as they wanted it by a certain time. Brock *v.* Berry, 132 Ala. 95, 31 So. 517.

Liability of Creditor for Acts of Attorney or Agent.—If an attorney, intrusted with a note for collection by suit, wrongfully sue out process under the attachment law, his client will be liable for the actual damage sustained. Kirksey *v.* Jones, 7 Ala. 622.

Administrator.—An administrator who as such wrongfully sues out an attachment is personally liable for damages, since he can not bind the estate by his tortious conduct. Gilmer *v.* Wier, 8 Ala. 72.

§ 219. Recovery or Set-Off of Damages in Attachment Suit.

Sale in Fraud of Creditors.—In attachment on a debt alleged to be due under contract, where the defendant pleads in recoupment, a judgment for defendant is equivalent to a judgment that plaintiff had no cause of action, and hence plaintiff, not being a creditor under such judgment, can not, in an action for wrongful attachment, brought by the vendee of defendant, plead in justification that the sale to the vendee was in fraud of creditors. Grisham *v.* Bodman, 111 Ala. 194, 20 So. 514.

§ 220. —— Nature and Form.

Election of Remedies.—In Alabama, where an attachment is wrongfully and maliciously sued out, the defendant is not confined to his remedy on the bond, but may sue in case for the injury he has sustained. Donnell *v.* Jones, 13 Ala. 490, 48 Am. Dec. 59, cited in this point in note in 29 L. R. A., N. S., 273, 274.

Trespass.—Case lies to recover the damages actually sustained by the wrongful suing out of an attachment. Seay *v.* Greenwood, 21 Ala. 491.

§ 221. —— Defenses.

In General.—It is a full defense to an action, under the attachment law, for wrongfully and vexatiously suing out process, if any one of the causes which warrant the process existed, although a different cause is set out in the affidavit. Kirksey *v.* Jones, 7 Ala. 622.

In an action for the wrongful suing out of an attachment, the defendant is not confined to the particular ground averred in the affidavit, but may show the existence of any statutory ground as a defense. Painter *v.* Munn, 23 So. 83, 117 Ala. 322, 67 Am. St. Rep. 170.

If goods wrongfully levied on by a sheriff belonged to plaintiff, and were in his possession at the time of the levy, his subsequent sale of them to a third person does not affect his right of action for the wrongful act. Ellis *v.* Allen, 80 Ala. 515, 2 So. 676.

Fraudulent Assignment.—In an action for wrongfully and vexatiously suing out an ancillary attachment, a fraudulent assignment, made by the debtor three days afterwards, can not justify the defendant, unless the fraudulent intent on the part of the debtor existed at the time the attachment issued. Donnell *v.* Jones, 17 Ala. 689, cited on this point in note in 30 L. R. A. 481.

§ 222. —— Pleading.

As to pleading in actions on attachment bond, see ante, "Pleading," 209.

Declaration, Complaint or Petition.—A count, in a complaint for wrongful attachment, alleging that "plaintiff claims of defendant $5,000 damages for wrongfully taking the following goods and chattels, the property of plaintiff, viz, a stock of general merchandise formerly owned by A., consisting of dry goods, groceries, hardware," etc., in a certain town and building is a good count in trespass, under the Code of Alabama. Joseph *v.* Henderson, 95 Ala. 213, 10 So. 843.

When exemplary damages are claimed in the complaint for the wrongful suing out of an attachment, it must aver that it was sued out without probable cause for believing the ground to be true. Painter *v.* Munn, 23 So. 83, 117 Ala. 322, 67 Am. St. Rep. 170.

A declaration in case for wrongfully suing out an attachment is bad on demurrer if it does not specially deny the ground set forth in the affidavit for suing out the attachment. Tiller *v.* Shearer, 20 Ala. 527.

A declaration in case for wrongfully and vexatiously suing out an attachment before a justice of the peace in Mississippi, which does not show that such justice had authority by the laws of that state to issue attachments, and which contains no averment connecting the defendant with the levy thereof, discloses no ground of action, and is bad on demurrer. Marshall *v.* Betner, 17 Ala. 832.

A declaration for maliciously and wrongfully suing out an attachment did not aver the termination of the suit by attachment. Held, that the omission was cured by verdict. Rea *v.* Lewis, Minor 382, cited in note in 2 L. R. A., N. S., 950.

In an action for a wrongful attachment on exempt property, evidence as to the amount of attorney's fees paid in asserting the exemption, and as to the expense of hauling the goods back to plaintiff's house, is inadmissible, if such elements of damage are not specially mentioned in the complaint. Boggan *v.* Bennett, 102 Ala. 400, 14 So. 742.

In a suit by a firm for wrongfully suing out an attachment against it, special damages, through loss of reputation, credit, or customers, can not be shown, unless specifically alleged in the declaration. Donnell *v.* Jones, 13 Ala. 490, 48 Am. Dec. 59.

Under a declaration, which avers the wrongful and vexatious suing out of an attachment, and the seizure of the goods of the plaintiffs, whereby they have lost the advantage and benefit of their business as merchants, been forced to abandon the same, and been "wholly ruined in their circumstances," etc., the plaintiffs may recover the actual injury done to the goods by their seizure under the attachment. Donnell *v.* Jones, 17 Ala. 689, 52 Am. Dec. 194.

Plea or Answer.—In an action in trover for levying an attachment against a third person on the property of plaintiff in attachment, a plea failing to deny that defendants had notice of plaintiff's claim of ownership in the property levied on does not state a defense. Mattingly *v.* Houston, 52 So. 78, 167 Ala. 167.

A plea to an action for wrongfully and vexatiously suing out an attachment, which avers that the attachment "was not sued out wrongfully, maliciously, or vexatiously, or without reasonable or probable cause," presents a substantial defense to the action, and is not demurrable. Marshall *v.* Betner, 17 Ala. 832.

§ 223. —— Evidence.

As to evidence in actions on attachment bonds, see ante, "Evidence," § 210. As to damages in action on attachment bonds, see ante, "Damages," § 211. As to damages against officer, see the title SHERIFFS AND CONSTABLES. As to damages for malicious attachment, see the title MALICIOUS PROSECUTION.

Presumptions and Burden of Proof.—In an action to recover damages for the wrongful and malicious suing out of an attachment, the onus is on the plaintiff to prove the falsity of the affidavit on which the attachment was sued out, and not on the defendant to prove its truth. O'Grady *v.* Julian, 34 Ala. 88.

On an issue whether a creditor, at the time an attachment sued out by him was levied on shares of stock standing on the corporate books in the debtor's name, had knowledge of a previous transfer of the stock by the debtor to a third party in payment of a debt, the debtor testified that prior to the levy he told the creditor that he had transferred all his property, and that, though he did not mention the stock, he thought, from what the creditor then said, that the latter knew that the stock was included. The creditor testified that, while he knew that the debtor was indebted to the transferee, he did not know of any transfer of any property whatever being made until after the attachment was sued out, and did not know that the debtor owned the stock in suit until after the levy. Held insufficient to discharge the burden of proof resting on the transferee to show facts which should have put the creditor upon inquiry, so as to charge him with notice of the transfer at the time of the levy. Dittey *v.* First Nat. Bank, 112 Ala. 391, 20 So. 476.

Admissibility.—Where property alleged to have been sold is attached as the property of the sellers, an offer by the attaching creditors to return the surplus over and above their claim is admissible in an action by the purchaser against such creditors for making the levy, in case the sale is found fraudulent, to show that they had no intention to make an excessive levy. Pollak *v.* Searcy, 84 Ala. 259, 4 So. 137.

Evidence of the acts of the sheriff at the time of the levy, and of what passed between him and defendants' attorneys, who directed it, is admissible to show defendants' connection with the levy. Ullman *v.* Myrick, 93 Ala. 532, 8 So. 410.

In an action for a wrongful prosecution of an action of attachment, it being first shown that the goods had been attached in a prior suit, it is admissible to show that they were more than sufficient to satisfy such prior attachment. Goldsmith *v.* Picard, 27 Ala. 142.

In an action by partners, in a mercantile firm, to recover damages for the wrongful and vexatious suing out of an attachment against them, in consequence of which their credit was destroyed, and their business broken up, the record of the attachment, and proceedings thereon, is proper evidence to be submitted to the jury. Donnell *v.* Jones, 17 Ala. 689, 52 Am. Dec. 194.

In an action for the wrongful and malicious suing out of an attachment, evidence is inadmissible, on part of defendant, to show that another attachment was in the sheriff's hands at the time he levied defendant's, and which was also levied, though it might be competent to show the issuance of the other attachment and notice thereof to defendant previous to the issuance of his own, as tending to rebut the presumption of malice. Yarbrough *v.* Hudson, 19 Ala. 653.

In an action for wrongful attachment, where it was shown that no writ of attachment was on file, the admission in evidence of motions by plaintiff in the original suit to substitute the writ of attachment, and for an order directing the sheriff to sell the property levied upon under the writ, and the order of the court thereon, was competent, as showing that plaintiff therein recognized the validity of the levy of the writ of attachment. Hamilton *v.* Maxwell, 32 So. 13, 133 Ala. 233, cited in note in 38 L. R. A., N. S., 127.

In a suit for wrongfully and vexatiously suing out an attachment against the plaintiff, the declaration by the plaintiff, made about a week before the attachment issued, that he was intending to leave the state temporarily, but not in the hearing of the defendant, is not admissible in evidence. Havis *v.* Taylor, 13 Ala. 324.

In a suit for wrongful attachment, evidence that it was generally reputed that plaintiff was about to leave the state is inadmissible in justification. Havis *v.* Taylor, 13 Ala. 324.

In an action for wrongfully and maliciously suing out an attachment, a deed of trust executed by the plaintiff prior to the issuance of the attachment is admissible evidence for the defendant, and also any proof tending to show that it was fraudulent, or that it was part of a plan to enable the plaintiff to dispose of his property fraudulently, or that he was in embarrassed circumstances at the time of its execution, or that the property conveyed by it was subsequently run off by the beneficiary to another state. Yarbrough *v.* Hudson, 19 Ala. 653.

In an action for wrongful attachment, where the writ was sued out on the ground that the debtor was fraudulently withholding her means from the creditor, plaintiff may show what amount she paid on her debts during the year immediately preceding the levy. Birmingham Dry-Goods Co. *v.* Finley, 26 So. 138, 122 Ala. 534.

Where special damages were claimed, in an action for wrongful attachment, because some of plaintiff's customers had left her because of the levy, her manager might testify that some of plaintiff's customers had gone elsewhere to trade after the attachment. Birmingham Dry-Goods Co. *v.* Finley, 26 So. 138, 122 Ala. 534.

On an issue as to the market value of goods wrongfully attached and sold, evidence of what they cost the attachment defendant at some indefinite time in the past was not admissible. Louisville Jeans Clothing Co. *v.* Lischkoff, 109 Ala. 136, 19 So. 436.

Nor was evidence of the amount of plaintiff's profit on similar goods sold to particular persons relevant to the issue. Louisville Jeans Clothing Co. *v.* Lischkoff, 109 Ala. 136, 19 So. 436.

In an action for vexatiously suing out an attachment, it is competent for the defendant to prove, in mitigation of damages, that the plaintiff was indebted to him in Georgia, and that he ran away from that state with his property to avoid the payment of his debts. Melton *v.* Troutman, 15 Ala. 535, cited on this point in note in 29 L. R. A., N. S., 274.

Under a claim of damages for a malicious attachment, the plaintiff can not prove what was the usual profit made by such establishments in the neighborhood of the plaintiff in the same kind of business. O'Grady *v.* Julian, 34 Ala. 88, cited on this point in note in 52 L. R. A. 56.

In an action for wrongful attachment under a writ sued out by defendant's attorney, evidence of conversations held by the attorney with others before the attachment issued, in reference to plaintiff's disposition of his property, is not admissible as ground for exemplary damages. Louisville Jeans Clothing Co. *v.* Lischkoff, 109 Ala. 136, 19 So. 436.

Defendant having denied that he ever heard that the attached property was claimed by third persons, it is competent, as bearing on the question of punitive damages, for plaintiff to contradict him. Ullman *v.* Myrick, 93 Ala. 532, 8 So. 410.

In an action to recover damages for the wrongful and malicious suing out of an attachment, a witness may be asked what, from his own knowledge, was the effect of the attachment upon the business and credit of the plaintiff. O'Grady *v.* Julian, 34 Ala. 88, cited on this point in note in 52 L. R. A. 56.

In an action by partners in a mercantile firm to recover damages for a wrongful attachment, proof of the loss of probable profits, although such loss does not furnish the measure of damages, is, nevertheless, proper to go to the jury, to aid them in arriving at a correct conclusion as to the injury sustained. Donnell *v.* Jones, 17 Ala. 689, 52 Am. Dec. 194, cited in note in 52 L. R. A. 56.

Weight and Sufficiency.—In an action for wrongful attachment it was shown that no writ of venditioni exponas issued in compliance with the judgment for plaintiff in the original suit was on file, and also that the affidavit for the writ of attachment and the bond sued on were dated August 27, 1894; that the writ was issued by a justice of the peace, returnable to the fall term, 1894, of the circuit court. The motions by plaintiff in the attachment suit to substitute the writ of attachment and for an order directing the sheriff to sell the property levied on set forth such facts. Held sufficient to show that the writ of venditioni exponas grew out of the attachment suit mentioned in the bond sued on. Hamilton *v.* Maxwell, 32 So. 13, 133 Ala. 233.

§ 224. —— Damages in General.

As damages in action on bonds for wrongful attachment, see ante, "Damages," § 211.

§ 224 (1) In General.

Injury to Business, Creditor or Reputation.—In an action by a retail merchant against a wholesaler for wrongful attachment of land not connected with plaintiff's business, it was error to permit the jury to consider whether the attachment resulted in loss of customers to plaintiff. Gramling-Spalding Co. *v.* Parker, 3 Ala. App. 325, 57 So. 54.

The extent of damage to credit is an inferential fact, arrived at only by an examination of all the circumstances in a case, and can not be the subject of direct proof. Trammell *v.* Ramage, 97 Ala. 666, 11 So. 916.

A retail merchant can recover damages sustained to his credit by wrongful attachment, though the levy was upon land not connected with his business. Gramling-Spalding Co. *v.* Parker, 3 Ala. App. 325, 57 So. 54.

Plaintiffs can derive no right to recover for consequences not legally entering into their damages, though they are stated in the complaint; and hence, in an action for wrongful attachment, plaintiff can not recover on the theory of loss of customers, though such loss was pleaded, where no loss could have been sustained, since the attachment was levied against land not connected with his business. Gramling-Spalding Co. *v.* Parker, 3 Ala. App. 325, 57 So. 54.

Perishable Goods Injured.—One whose perishable goods have been wrongfully attached may recover damages resulting to such goods by locking them up in a storehouse during warm weather, and failing to give them proper attention. W. F. Vandiver & Co. *v.* Waller, 39 So. 136, 143 Ala. 411.

Injury to Land and Personalty.—In an action for abuse of attachment process, damages may be recovered for injuries to the personalty and to the land on which it was situated, for closing plaintiff's store, and for an excessive levy. Brown *v.* Master, 104 Ala. 451, 16 So. 443, cited in note in 29 L. R. A., N. S., 274, 275, 276.

§ 224 (2) Measure or Amount.

As to evidence, see ante, "Evidence," § 223.

In General.—In trover for the conversion of property sold under a writ of attachment levied against another than the true owner of the property, the measure of damages was the value of the property, with interest, from the date of the levy until the trial. Milner & Kettig Co. *v.* DeLoach Mill Mfg. Co., 36 So. 765, 139 Ala. 645, 101 Am. St. Rep. 63.

Sale Considered in Estimating Damages.—After institution of an action of trespass for a wrongful levy, a sale under the levy does not relate back to the commencement of the suit constituting a cause of action at that time, but, if the levy was wrongful, the sale may be considered in estimating damages. Dunlap *v.* Steele, 80 Ala. 424.

§ 225. —— Costs and Attorney's Fees as Damages.

In General.—As a general rule the costs and reasonable fees paid in the attachment suit are recoverable as damages in an action on the case for wrongfully suing out the attachment. Seay *v.* Greenwood, 21 Ala. 491.

Costs.—In an action for wrongfully and vexatiously suing out an ancillary attachment, the costs incurred in defending the original suit constitute no part of the plaintiff's damages. White *v.* Wyley, 17 Ala. 167.

The costs of the justice's court, before whom the attachment was returnable, are recoverable in case, as part of the damages actually sustained; but where the case is taken by the defendant to the circuit court, by appeal, where he files his pleas, and afterwards withdraws them, for a valuable consideration paid him by the plaintiff, and suffers judgment by nil dicit, he can not recover the costs of the circuit court. Seay *v.* Greenwood, 21 Ala. 491.

Counsel Fees.—Where plaintiff in an action for wrongful attachment did not employ an attorney to defend the attachment suit, but allowed a judgment to be entered by default, he can not recover, as damages, the amount paid to an attorney for making a motion for a new trial of such action. Trammell *v.* Ramage, 97 Ala. 666, 11 So. 916.

Counsel fees paid by the claimant in a suit brought to try the right of property may be taken into consideration by the jury, in assessing his damages, in a subsequent action for damages against the plaintiff in attachment. Roberts *v.* Heim, 27 Ala. 678.

§ 226. —— **Exemplary Damages.**

As to actions on bonds, see ante, "Exemplary Damages," § 211 (3).

Acting in Good Faith and under Advice of Counsel.—A plaintiff is not liable in exemplary or vindictive damages for procuring an attachment, if he acted in good faith, under advice of his attorney, who was on the ground at the place where the attachment was made. Gramling-Spalding Co. *v.* Parker, 3 Ala. App. 325, 57 So. 54.

Failure to State Allegation in Complaint.—Exemplary damages can not be recovered for wrongful attachment where the complaint fails to state that it was sued out without the existence of any statutory ground therefor, and without probable cause. Hamilton *v.* Maxwell, 24 So. 769, 119 Ala. 23.

Recovery before Determination of Attachment Suit.—In trespass on the case to recover damages actually sustained by the wrongful suing out of an attachment, if malice is shown, vindictive damages may be recovered without waiting for the determination of the attachment suit. Seay *v.* Greenwood, 21 Ala. 491.

Attachment Procured by Agent.—Where the suing out of an attachment was wrongful, and it was issued without probable cause, punitive as well as actual damages may be recovered, although the attachment was sued out by an agent, provided the principal, with full knowledge, ratified the agent's act. W. F. Vandiver & Co. *v.* Waller, 39 So. 136, 143 Ala. 411.

Makers of Indemnity Bond.—The makers of an indemnity bond given to induce a sheriff to levy on goods in the possession of a person not a party to the process can not be held liable in trespass for exemplary damages, unless they authorized the sheriff to act wantonly, recklessly, or with circumstances of aggravation, or ratified his unlawful acts, or the acts were consequent on the making of the levy. Lienkauf *v.* Morris, 66 Ala. 406, cited on this point in note in 29 L. R. A., N. S., 275.

§ 227. —— **Questions for Jury.**

Question as to Wrongfully Suing Out Attachment.—In an action for wrongful attachment, the question whether the attachment was wrongfully sued out is for the jury. Hamilton *v.* Maxwell, 32 So. 13, 133 Ala. 233.

§ 228. —— **Instructions.**

Invasion of Province of Jury.—In an action for wrongfully suing out an attachment, a charge that malice can not be testified about by defendants, and that its existence must be determined from the circumstances, is not subject to the objection of precluding the jury from considering letters written by defendants and introduced in evidence on the question of malice. Vandiver & Co. *v.* Waller, 143 Ala. 411, 39 So. 136.

In an action for wrongfully suing out an attachment, charges that the absence of a debtor from his home without his informing a creditor thereof does not authorize the latter to resort to an attachment, and that, if the attachment defendant left his usual place of business with the intention of again returning, and without any fraudulent intent, his absence was not that of absconding within the meaning of the law, were not subject to the objection of invading the province of the jury. W. F. Vandiver & Co. *v.* Waller, 39 So. 136, 143 Ala. 411.

In an action for wrongfully suing out an attachment, a charge that the temporary absence of a debtor from the state, though he does not inform his creditors, does not authorize an attachment against his property, while argumentative and abstract in that there was no evidence that the debtor had left the state, was not subject to the objection of precluding the jury from considering evidence tending to show that the debtor had absconded, and was not reversible error. Vandiver & Co. *v.* Waller, 143 Ala. 411, 39 So. 136.

Correct as to Law and Fact.—In case for an attachment wrongfully sued out on the ground that the debtor was about to remove, it is not error to instruct that the plaintiff may recover the actual damage, unless they believe the plaintiff was about to remove. Hudson *v.* Howlett, 32 Ala. 478, cited in note in 38 L. R. A., N. S., 120.

Where plaintiff in trespass for attaching goods claimed to have been purchased by him from the attachment debtors relies on his own testimony to prove that he was a purchaser in good faith, it is not error for the court to refuse to charge that the failure of plaintiff to produce the sellers as witnesses to prove the consideration is a circumstance of suspicion for the jury to consider. Pollak *v.* Harmon, 94 Ala. 420, 10 So. 156.

In an action for wrongful attachment, it was proper for the court to refuse to charge that if the jury "found from the evidence that in suing out the attachment defendant stated all the facts to his attorney, or his attorney was acquainted with all the facts, and defendant acted under the advice of his attorney in suing out said attachment, then they could not assess exemplary damages," as it pretermitted all inquiry as to defendant's good faith in the action he took. Trammell *v.* Ramage, 97 Ala. 666, 11 So. 916.

In an action for wrongful attachment, a charge that if defendant sued out the attachment under an honest belief that plaintiff was fraudulently disposing of his property, in giving it to his sons, or in giving it to his sons "in any way," exemplary damages could not be recovered, was faulty as assuming that the giving of the property to the sons "in any way" was sufficient to show probable cause. Hamilton *v.* Maxwell, 24 So. 769, 119 Ala. 23.

In trover for levying an attachment against a husband on the property of the wife, where the levy in part was upon the wife's personal apparel and upon furniture in which she had the beneficial ownership subject to the seller's title, retained for security, a charge that if the jury found that the property was in the possession of plaintiff's husband, and he instructed the constable to go and take charge of it, then they should find for defendant, was properly refused, since the husband could not dispose of the wife's property without her consent. Mattingly *v.* Houston, 52 So. 78, 167 Ala. 167.

In trover for levying an attachment on the property of plaintiff, where the evidence required the submission of the questions whether plaintiff was entitled to damages for injured feelings or in the way of smart money, a charge that the measure of damages is the value of the hire or use of the property belonging to plaintiff from the time of the taking to the return of the same, together with the damage to the same, was properly refused. Mattingly *v.* Houston, 167 Ala. 167, 52 So. 78.

In an action for wrongfully suing out an attachment, where the complaint demanded damages equal to the penalty of the bond, a charge that punitive or exemplary damages can not be proven in dollars and cents, but when the proof shows acts of malice and vexation the jury can fix the measure of damages in dollars and cents, and "can fix such punitive damages as may seem right to them, not exceeding the amount of the attachment bond," while informal, is substantially correct, and does not constitute reversible error. Vandiver & Co. *v.* Waller, 143 Ala. 411, 39 So. 136, cited in note in 29 L. R. A., N. S., 275.

Attachment Execution.

See the titles ATTACHMENT; GARNISHMENT. See, also, the title JUSTICES OF THE PEACE.

Attainder.

See the title CONSTITUTIONAL LAW.

Attempt.

As to attempts to commit crime, see the appropriate criminal titles. As to indictments for attempts to commit crime, see the title INDICTMENT AND INFORMATION.

Attendance.

See the titles BANKRUPTCY; CONTEMPT; EXECUTION; SCHOOLS AND SCHOOL DISTRICTS. As to attendance of jurors, see the title JURY.

Attestation.

See the titles ARBITRATION AND AWARD; ASSIGNMENTS FOR BENEFIT OF CREDITORS; CHATTEL MORTGAGES; DEEDS; FRAUD; LANDLORD AND TENANT; MORTGAGES; MOTIONS; PATENTS; WILLS; and other specific titles.

ATTORNEY AND CLIENT.

I. The Office of Attorney.

§ 96. —— Grounds of Action.
§ 97. —— Defenses.
§ 98. —— Time to Sue, and Limitations.
§ 99. —— Evidence.
§ 99 (1) In General.
§ 99 (2) Employment.
§ 99 (3) Value of Services or Amount of Compensation.
§ 100. —— Trial.
§ 100 (1) Questions for Jury.
§ 100 (2) Instructions.
§ 100 (3) Verdict and Findings.

(B) Lien.
§ 101. Nature of Attorney's Lien.
§ 102. Statutory Provisions.
§ 103. Right to Lien.
§ 104. —— In General.
§ 105. Services or Fees Covered.
§ 106. Subject Matter to Which Lien Attaches.
§ 106 (1) In General.
§ 106 (2) Judgment or Proceeds Thereof.
§ 106 (3) Securities and Papers.
§ 106 (4) Land.
§ 107. Time When Lien Attaches.
§ 108. Priorities.
§ 109. Waiver, Loss, or Discharge.
§ 110. Protection against Assignment by Client.
§ 111. —— Protection against Settlement between Parties.
§ 112. —— In General.
§ 113. Remedies of Attorney.
§ 113 (1) In General.
§ 113 (2) Vacation of Settlement and Proceeding with Original Suit.
§ 114. Protection against Set-Off between Parties.
§ 115. Enforcement.
§ 115 (1) In General.
§ 115 (2) Proceedings.

Cross References.

As to the nature of an action against an attorney for neglect of duty, see the title ACTION. As to questioning an attorney's authority in the appellate court where he has appeared without objection in the lower court, see the title APPEAL AND ERROR. As to agreements between attorney and client, whereby the attorney acquires an interest in the subject matter of litigation, see the title CHAMPERTY AND MAINTENANCE. As to the usage of attorneys, at any particular place, to collect money for their clients in bank bills of the State Bank, see the title CUSTOMS AND USAGES. As to the power to require attorneys to take out license, see the titles CONSTITUTIONAL LAW; LICENSES. As to arguments of counsel, see the title TRIAL.

I. THE OFFICE OF ATTORNEY.

(A) ADMISSION TO PRACTICE.

§ 1. Determination of Right to Admission.

It does not rest exclusively with the several courts to determine who is qualified to become or continue an attorney of the court. On the contrary, an attorn y admitted by the supreme court has the legal right to practice "in all the courts in this state," a right of which he can be deprived only in the mode pointed out by law. Withers *v.* Posey, 36 Ala. 252, 268.

§ 2. Oath.

Oath Required by Duelling Act.—So much of the 16th section of the duelling act of Alabama, passed January 7, 1826, as requires attorneys and counselors at law to make oath, before entering upon the practice of the law, according to the form prescribed in that section, that they have not, since the 1st of January, 1826, been engaged, either as principals or seconds, in any duel, and that they will not in future be so engaged (being citizens of that state), either in the state or out of the state, is contrary to the constitution, and void. In re Dorsey, 7 Port. 293.

As the several parts of the oath, required by the 16th section of the duelling act of Alabama, Jan. 7, 1826, to be taken by counsellors and attorneys, can not be disjoined; and as the oath is in part illegal, it can not be imposed. In the Matter of Dorsey, 7 Port. 293, 295.

Prescribed Oath.—Persons licensed to practice law since the adoption of the Code, are not entitled to practice. until they take the oath prescribed by § 735. Withers *v.* Posey, 36 Ala. 252, 260.

§ 3. Certificate or License.

The persons who are entitled to practice in the courts of the state, are those who were regularly licensed under the laws of the state before the adoption of the Code, and those who, since the adoption of the Code, have been admitted by a license from the supreme court, the court of chancery, or a circuit court. Code, § 729. Withers *v.* Posey, 36 Ala. 252, 260.

Those who were regularly licensed to practice law before the passage of the Code, "can practice only in such courts as their license authorizes them." Code, § 730. Withers *v.* Posey, 36 Ala. 252, 260.

(B) PRIVILEGES, DISABILITIES, AND LIABILITIES.

§ 4. Nature and Term of Office.

The office and duty of an attorney at law is the representation of parties in courts of justice. Brewer *v.* Watson, 71 Ala. 299, 304.

The Right to Practice.—The right to practice law is a valuable right, as deserving of protection as property. In the Matter of Dorsey, 7 Port. 293, 296.

The right to practice law, which is obtained upon procuring license and taking the prescribed oath, is a legal right, of which the attorney can not be deprived, except by a judgment of removal or suspension, rendered by the circuit court, on proceedings instituted in conformity with the directions contained in chapter 10, title 9, part 1, of the Code. See §§ 747-761. Withers *v.* Posey, 36 Ala. 252, 266; Thomas *v.* Stepney, 58 Ala. 365.

Official Relation.—A regularly licensed attorney occupies a permanent official relation to the courts in which he has authority to practice, and to the community. Thomas *v.* Stepney, 58 Ala. 365.

Attorneys and counselors at law are part and parcel of the judicial administration of the laws of the commonwealth. They are instrumentalities—necessary instrumentalities—in all judicial contentions. They receive their authority to represent the interests of others, not as a common or natural right, but in consideration of their ascertained legal learning, and good moral character. They thus become a part of the court's machinery; and, although not technically public officers, they are quasi officers. They are called officers of the court; that is, they are instrumentalities, to aid the court in administering the law. So much are they regarded as part of the machinery of the court, that, having business before the court, they are presumed to be present whenever the court is in session. Pinkard *v.* Allen, 75 Ala. 73, 79.

§ 5. Right to Inspect Public Records.

An attorney at law may inspect public records in which his client is interested. Brewer *v.* Watson, 61 Ala. 310.

§ 6. Right to Appear before Mayor or Magistrate.

See ante, "Nature and Term of Office," § 4.

An attorney at law who has been regularly admitted to practice in accordance with the provisions of the Code has a legal right, when employed for that purpose, to appear as counsel for persons on trial before the mayor of Mobile for alleged violations of the city ordinances or for the accused on a preliminary inquiry before him as committing magistrate, although the proceeding before a mayor for an alleged violation of a municipal ordinance is neither a "criminal prosecution," nor a "civil cause," within the meaning of the 10th and 29th sections of the 1st article of the constitution, securing to a party the right "to be heard by himself and counsel." Code, §§ 730, 3403; Withers *v.* Posey, 36 Ala. 252.

§ 7. Acting for Adverse Parties.

§ 8. —— In General.

See post, "What Constitutes a Retainer," § 27.

Counsel, retained under either a general or special retainer, is not at liberty to accept employment or render service adversary to the interest of the client thus retaining him. Agnew *v.* Walden, 84 Ala. 502, 4 So. 672, 673.

The complainant's solicitors in a chancery cause may, without impropriety, prepare and sign formal answers for any of the defendants who admit the allegations of the bill and make no defense. Cargile *v.* Ragan, 65 Ala. 287.

On a bill filed by a widow to compel the settlement of the estate of her deceased husband, the defendant's solicitor can not properly represent the minor heirs, their interests being adverse to that of defendant. Parker *v.* Parker, 99 Ala. 239, 13 So. 520.

§ 9. Acting in Different Capacities.

An attorney at law of a party in obtaining a judgment may act as commissioner in taking a deposition for his client to be used in a claim suit growing out of the judgment, he not being the attorney in the claim suit, and it not being shown that he has any interest in the event of the suit. Taylor *v.* Branch Bank at Huntsville, 14 Ala. 633.

§ 10. Liabilities to Adverse Parties and to Third Persons.

See ante, "Control of Execution," § 50.

Where an attorney, having in his possession moneys of his client, after notice of his client's assignment thereof to a third person, pays them to the client, he is liable to the assignee. Gayle *v.* Benson, 3 Ala. 234.

§ 11. Licenses and Taxes.

Under a statute which provides that all lawyers practicing their profession must pay a license tax, each member of a firm of practicing lawyers must pay the tax. Jones *v.* Page, 44 Ala. 657.

To practice law in a single instance, without a license, is forbidden by law. Pamphlet Acts 1868, pp. 329-30, §§ 105, 111. Cousins *v.* State, 50 Ala. 113, 114.

§ 12. Regulation of Professional Conduct.

If an attorney proceed in the name of a fictitious plaintiff, or without authority, it is contempt punishable by the court. Gaines *v.* Tombeckbee Bank, Minor 50, 51.

Unprofessional or disrespectful conduct on the part of an attorney, though amounting to a contempt and furnishing cause for his removal or suspension, will not justify a court in excluding him from practicing at its bar, no judgment of removal or suspension having been rendered against him. Withers *v.* State, 36 Ala. 252.

For any disrespectful or contemptuous behavior in court, tending to impair the respect due to judicial tribunals, or to interrupt the due course of trial, an attorney may be punished at the time for contempt. Code, §§ 561-563; Withers *v.* State, 36 Ala. 252.

Attorneys Practicing by Comity.—The courts, by comity, permitting attorneys, who have no license and have not taken the prescribed oath, to practice before them, have an inherent power to compel obedience and fidelity to the duties voluntarily assumed by them, as they have to compel it from all their officers. The relation of such attorneys is temporary, and the comity which permits it may at any time be withdrawn. Thomas *v.* Stepney, 58 Ala. 365, 368.

§ 13. Offenses in Exercise of Professional Functions.

A lawyer is liable to the penalty prescribed by Code 1907, § 6218, for sending a threatening or abusive letter, which may tend to provoke a breach of the peace, regardless of the fact that it is sent in an effort to collect an account. Peters *v.* State, 166 Ala. 35, 51 So. 952, 953.

§ 14. Grounds for Suspension or for Striking from Roll.

§ 15. —— Character and Conduct in General.

Willful misconduct of an attorney in his profession, and willful violations of any of the duties enjoined upon him by law, will justify a proceeding in the circuit court for his removal or suspension, and a judgment in either form will deprive him of his right to practice in any court. Withers *v.* Posey, 36 Ala. 252, 266.

One of the duties of attorneys, is "to maintain the respect due to courts of justice and judicial officers;" and among the specified causes for the removal or suspension of an attorney, is any willful violation of this duty. Code, § 748. Withers *v.* Posey, 36 Ala. 252, 266.

§ 16. —— Contempt of Court.

See ante, "Regulation of Professional Conduct," § 12.

After the trial of C., his attorney mailed a letter to the judge, which was delivered at the judge's residence. In the letter the attorney stated that he had been informed that the judge had visited C. in jail at night and expressed sorrow for C., and stated that the judge's conduct toward C. during his trial was because of the judge's dislike for the attorney; that the writer had no patience or respect for a judge who would so far forget his oath as to meet at night during the trial of C. with the solicitor and county solicitors, and feast on partridges, and discuss how and why a certain man should be tried; and that in the future the writer desired the judge to act the gentleman in court toward him, and on the outside of court the judge would have it to do or the writer would know why. Held, that such letter referred to the judge in his official capacity and constituted ground for disbarment. Johnson *v.* State, 152 Ala. 93, 44 So. 671, cited in note in 17 L. R. A., N. S., 586.

§ 17. Proceedings.

§ 18. —— Notice and Preliminary Proceedings.

See post, "Charges and Answers Thereto," § 20; Trial or Hearing," § 21.

Proceedings to remove or suspend an attorney are begun by an accusation in writing, which the attorney is cited to answer. Code, §§ 750-759; Withers *v.* Posey, 36 Ala. 252, 266.

§ 19. —— Nature and Form in General.

A proceeding to remove an attorney is of a criminal nature. Thomas *v.* State, 58 Ala. 365; State *v.* Quarles, 158 Ala. 54, 48 So. 499.

Construction of Statute.—Though the punishment provided for a violation of Code 1896, § 590, subd. 6, and Acts 1900-1, p. 2227, § 1, making it unlawful for an attorney at law to wrongfully encourage litigation is only disbarment, such statutes are penal in character, and must be strictly construed. State *v.* Quarles, 158 Ala. 54, 48 So. 499.

§ 20. —— Charges and Answers Thereto.

An information in statutory proceeding for removing an attorney, under § 882, R. C., must disclose with certainty the facts of misconduct, and that the defendant is amenable to the proceeding. Thomas *v.* Stepney, 58 Ala. 365.

The statutory proceeding for removing an attorney under § 882, Rev. Code, is directed only against attorneys licensed under the laws of the state, who have taken the prescribed oath; hence an allegation in the information that the defendant "is an attorney practicing in the courts of the state of Alabama, in the county of Dallas," is defective for uncertainty because the averment may apply either to a licensed attorney or one practicing by comity. Thomas *v.* State, 58 Ala. 365.

An information for the disbarment of an attorney under Code 1896, § 590, subd. 6, and Acts 1900-1, p. 2227, § 1, is insufficient if it fails to allege that defendant is an attorney at law. State *v.* Quarles, 158 Ala. 54, 48 So. 499.

§ 21. —— Trial or Hearing.

If an attorney denies the accusation filed in proceedings to remove or suspend him, the court proceeds to try the same; the attorney having the right to demand a trial by jury. Witnesses may be summoned, and depositions taken, as in ordinary actions at law. Code, §§ 750-759; Withers *v.* Posey, 36 Ala. 252, 266.

§ 22. —— Judgment or Order.

A judgment of acquittal, in proceedings to remove or suspend an attorney, is final. Withers *v.* Posey, 36 Ala. 252, 266.

§ 23. —— Review.

An attorney may appeal to the supreme court, from a judgment of removal or suspension. Withers *v.* Posey, 36 Ala. 252, 266.

The right to control the discharge of an attorney is within the sound discretion of the court having jurisdiction of the cause, and will not be reviewed on appeal, unless it clearly appears that the discretion was abused. Kelly *v.* Horsley, 147 Ala. 508, 41 So. 902.

§ 24. —— Costs.

Gen. Acts 1903, p. 346, relating to the disbarment of attorneys, makes it the duty of the solicitor to prosecute disbarment proceedings, and provides that the court, on the solicitor's motion and on good cause shown, may at any time require the Alabama State Bar Association to give security for costs of such proceeding, to be approved by the court, etc. Held, that security for costs in such a proceeding could only be required on the motion of the solicitor. Johnson *v.* State, 152 Ala. 93, 44 So. 671.

II. RETAINER AND AUTHORITY.

§ 25. Rights of Litigants to Act in Person or by Attorney.

A party to a suit is not compelled to employ counsel to conduct it, but has the constitutional right to appear in propria persona. May *v.* Williams, 17 Ala. 23.

§ 26. The Relation in General.

Attorney and client sustain to each other, during the time the relation exists, in respect to any matter being conducted for the client by the attorney, the relation of trustee and cestui que trust, and their dealings with each other are subject to the same intendments and imputations as obtain between other trustees and beneficiaries. Yonge *v.* Hooper, 73 Ala. 119; Dickinson *v.* Bradford, 59 Ala. 581; Kidd *v.* Williams, 132 Ala. 140, 31 So. 458.

§ 27. What Constitutes a Retainer.

See ante, "In General," § 8; post, "Employment and Authority of Counsel," § 37; "Nature of Attorney's Duty," § 59.

Two Classes.—There are two classes of retainers by which the services of attorneys, or counselors are secured. Agnew *v.* Walden, 84 Ala. 502, 4 So. 672, 673.

General Retainers.—General retainers have for their object the securing beforehand of the services of a particular attorney or counselor for any emergency that may afterwards arise. They have no reference to any particular service, but take in the whole range of possible future contention which may render attorneyship necessary or desirable. Agnew *v.* Walden, 84 Ala. 502, 4 So. 672, 673.

Special Retainers.—A special retainer has reference to the employment of an attorney in a particular case, or to render a particular service. Agnew *v.* Walden, 84 Ala. 502, 4 So. 672, 673.

§ 28. Proof of Authority.

§ 29. —— Necessity in General.

An attorney representing a corporation as a party to an action can not be compelled by the adverse party to exhibit his warrant of attorney or other authority. Lucas *v.* Bank of Georgia, 2 Stew. 147.

After Pleading of General Issue.—Conceding that an attorney professing to represent a corporation should be required to produce the warrant of his appointment, the right to demand its production is waived by pleading the general issue. Gaines *v.* Bank, Minor 51; Doe *v.* Abbott, 152 Ala. 243, 40 So. 637; Lucas *v.* Bank of Georgia, 2 Stew. 147.

Applicability to Actions by Tenants in Common.—Civ. Code 1896, § 594, providing that the court may, on motion of either party and on a showing of reasonable ground therefor, require the attorney for the adverse party to produce or prove the authority under which he appears, is not applicable to actions by tenants in common for the protection of the common property, since in such actions one tenant in common can use the names of his cotenants with or without their consent; and in an action by two tenants in common for trespass their attorney can not be compelled to prove his authority for adding the name of the third tenant as a plaintiff. Union Naval Stores Co. *v.* Pugh, 156 Ala. 369, 47 So. 48.

Discretion of Court.—Plaintiff's motion to require an attorney appearing for certain defendants to prove his authority was addressed largely to the discretion of the trial court. Beecher *v.* Henderson, 4 Ala. App. 543, 58 So. 805.

§ 30. —— Presumptions.

The authority of an attorney to appear for a client, whom he holds himself out as representing, is presumed. Doe ex dem. Chamberlain, Miller & Co. *v.* Abbott, 152 Ala. 243, 44 So. 637; Cain *v.* Sullivan, Minor 31; Gaines *v.* Tombeckbee Bank, Minor 50; Hill *v.* Lambert Bros., Minor 91, 92; Brewer *v.* Watson, 71 Ala. 299, 304; Brown *v.* French, 159 Ala. 645, 49 So. 255.

It will be presumed that counsel has the authority to make an admission of record, for the purpose of obviating the necessity of proof. Montgomery *v.* Givhan, 24 Ala. 568.

Where an Attorney Is Not Appearing in Court.—When an attorney is not appearing for a party in a court of justice: when his representation is for the transaction of business elsewhere, and business which would lie in the scope of an ordinary agency which any person is capable of transacting, the presumption of authority obtaining in court, arising from his license, and because he is an officer of the court, can not be claimed. Brewer *v.* Watson, 71 Ala. 299, 304.

§ 31. —— Objections to Authority.

See ante, "Necessity in General," § 29.

How Made.—If an attorney's authority to bring suit is questioned, the proper course for determination of the question is by motion, so that the matter may be determined by the presiding judge. Brown *v.* French, 159 Ala. 645, 49 So. 255.

Who May Object.—Makers of promissory notes that have been received from the payees by attorneys at law, in payment of demands in their hands for collection, can not object that the latter transcended their authority, where their clients have approved the transaction. Pond *v.* Lockwood, 8 Ala. 669.

It has been held that the adverse party has no right to question an attorney's authority. Gaines *v.* Tombeckbee Bank, Minor 50, 51.

But in a later case it is said: "the court, of its own motion, or the opposite party may require that the attorney produce evidence of his authority." Brewer *v.* Watson, 71 Ala. 299, 304.

Waiver of Right to Object.—The right, under the express provisions of Code 1896, § 594, to challenge the authority of an attorney, may be waived in like manner as the same right secured by common law. Chamberlain, etc., Co. *v.* Abbott, 152 Ala. 243, 44 So. 637.

Where the authority of an attorney to institute an action was not challenged at the first term after service and before pleading, and not until after the trial thereof had been entered on by selection of the jury, the right to require him to establish his authority was waived. Chamberlain, etc., Co. *v.* Abbott, 152 Ala. 243, 44 So. 637.

A challenge of the authority of an attorney, not by any facts stated showing or tending to show a want thereof, but merely by a denial that he had authority, is insufficient to require him to establish his authorty. Chamberlain, etc., Co. *v.* Abbott, 152 Ala. 243, 44 So. 637.

Proof Necessary to Sustain Objection.—One who would take advantage of an unauthorized appearance in seeking relief in equity from a judgment at law must prove that the appearance was in fact unauthorized. Stubbs *v.* Leavitt, 30 Ala. 352.

§ 32. —— Evidence of Authority.

An appearance by an attorney noted in the dockets of the court is presumptive evidence of his authority to enter appearance for defendant. Ashby Brick Co. *v.* Ely, etc., Dry Goods Co., 151 Ala. 272, 44 So. 96; Daughdrill *v.* Daughdrill, 108 Ala. 321, 19 So. 185.

Under Code 1886, § 868, providing that

"the oath of the attorney is presumptive evidence of his authority," such authority, if in issue, must be proven by legal evidence, when such presumption is overcome; and it is not competent for him, in support of his authority, to prove the contents of letters without accounting for their absence. Daughdrill *v.* Daughdrill, 108 Ala. 321, 19 So. 185.

A record of the supreme court of British Honduras, showing that defendant corporation instituted a suit therein against plaintiff, and that defendant was represented in such action by its solicitor, who continued to so represent it for a considerable time thereafter, is prima facie evidence that the action was instituted by defendant's authority, and is not rebutted by testimony of defendant's vice president that the note on which plaintiff was sued had been turned over to an agent for collection, who took it to Honduras, and died there; that he had searched for the note, and could not find it; and that he never heard of any suit being instituted on it. Christian & Craft Grocery Co. *v.* Coleman, 125 Ala. 158, 27 So. 786.

§ 33. —— Warrant or Other Written Authority.

See post, "Confession of or Consent to Judgment," § 43.

An attorney or solicitor, appearing for a corporation, need not show a warrant of attorney under the corporate seal. Gaines *v.* Tombeckbee Bank, Minor 50, 51; Lucas *v.* Bank, 2 Stew. 280.

The record of a judgment is prima facie evidence that the attorney who confessed judgment was duly authorized therefor. Hill *v.* Lambert, Minor 91.

§ 34. Change and Substitution.

A client may dispense with the services of an attorney at law, subject to the attorney's lien on a fund brought into court through his efforts on a judgment obtained by his services. Kelly & Middleton *v.* Horsley, 147 Ala. 508, 41 So. 902.

§ 35. Termination of Relation.

§ 35 (1) Act of Parties.

The authority of an attorney ceases after he has collected the money due on an execution. Boren *v.* McGehee, 6 Port. 432.

§ 35 (2) Death.

See post, "In General," § 83 (1).

An admission of a mistake in the amount of a judgment, and a consent to its correction, made and given by plaintiff's attorneys after his death, is without authority. Cook *v.* Parham, 63 Ala. 456, cited in note in 34 L. R. A., N. S., 1189.

Where the surviving partner of a firm of attorneys became one of a new firm, a client of the old firm, consenting to their prosecution of his case, waived the right to claim a termination of the contract because it was the understanding that the attorney who died was to give the matter his personal attention. Troy *v.* Hall & Farley, 157 Ala. 592, 47 So. 1035.

§ 35 (3) Determination of Controversy.

See post, "Control of Execution," § 50.

An attorney's authority does not cease with the rendition of the judgment, but continues for the purpose of directing the proceedings under the process of the court, for the collection of the judgment. This authority is subject to revocation by the client, and can not override the control by the plaintiff himself of the proceedings under his judgment. Albertson, etc., Co. *v.* Goldsby, 28 Ala. 711, 718.

§ 36. Scope of Authority in General.

See post, "Bringing or Defending and Dismissal of Action," § 46.

Under U. S. Stat., 39th Cong., p. 143, providing that where a note is made in the United States, in a place where no collection district was established at the time it was made, any party having an interest therein may affix the proper internal revenue stamp thereto, prior to January 1, 1867, an attorney, in whose hands a note is placed for collection, has such an interest, by virtue of his general authority, as authorizes him to affix such stamp to the note, when necessary to protect his client's rights; and such acts will be presumed to be authorized until repudiated by the client. Blunt *v.* Bates, 40 Ala. 470.

An attorney has no authority to determine, for his client, whether or not a claim is reasonable and just, and to bind him to such conclusion. Senn *v.* Joseph, 106 Ala. 454, 17 So. 543.

Attorney's Authority to Sue in Own Name.—The relation of client and attorney, does not authorize the attorney to sue in his own name, not even with the consent of the principal. Bryant *v.* Owen, 1 Port. 201.

The above rule is true, even as regards a note payable to a particular person or bearer. Bryant *v.* Owen, 1 Port. 201.

No Authority in Fact.—"Upon grounds of public policy, the act of an attorney at law is generally considered as the act of the client, if done within the general scope of the business of an attorney, though in point of fact, no authority has ever been given." Kirksey *v.* Jones, 7 Ala. 622, 628.

The exception to above rule is, where the attorney is unable to respond in damages for his unauthorized assumption of authority. Kirksey *v.* Jones, 7 Ala. 622, 628.

Limit of Authority.—An attorney is a special agent, limited in duty and authority to the vigilant prosecution or defense of the rights of the client. Robinson *v.* Murphy, 69 Ala. 543, 547.

It is questionable, whether the general authority implied by the committing of business to an attorney at law, can be limited by special directions to act only in a particular manner, or upon the happening of a particular event; as such directions could not be known to those upon whom the general authority would act, or if known, the other party has no means to control the action of the attorney. Kirksey *v.* Jones, 7 Ala. 622, 628.

§ 37. Employment and Authority of Counsel.

See ante, "What Constitutes a Retainer," § 27.

Defendant sent a claim to a mercantile agency for collection, instructing them that they or their attorneys were authorized to make any arrangements deemed by them necessary to a prompt collection thereof. Subsequently, the attorney of defendant notified plaintiffs, the attorneys in whose hands the claim was placed by the agency, of a settlement thereof, and directed a surrender to the debtor of the papers in their hands. Held, that this did not show an employment of plaintiffs by defendant. Milligan *v.* Alabama Fertilizer Co., 89 Ala. 322, 7 So. 650.

§ 38. Delegation of Authority.

An attorney's authority is in the nature of a personal trust and confidence, incapable of delegation, without the consent of the client. Hitchcock *v.* McGehee, 7 Port. 556; Johnson *v.* Cunningham, 1 Ala. 249, cited in note in 23 L. R. A., N. S., 705; Wright *v.* Evans, 53 Ala. 103, 108.

As to authority of attorney to arbitrate, see ante, "Delegation of Authority," § 38.

§ 39. Disposition of Moneys or Other Property of Client.

Conceding that an administrator d. b. n. might sue under the statute for wrongful death, or succeed to a prosecution by the administrator in chief, it would be a statutory right, given for the assertion of the parents' rights, and not on any legal title to the claim in the administrator, more than in the parents, and after recovery by an administrator, and payment to an attorney, the latter, save as the costs incurred by the administrator, may recognize as an owner of the claim the assignee of the parents, and deal with him as with them, and recognize and pay all liens of other attorneys asserted against the funds in his hands, and thereafter, when proceeded against by the administrator d. b. n., under Code 18 6, § 3810, for the money collected, he should be allowed to show legal disbursement to parties entitled. White *v.* Ward, 157 Ala. 345, 47 So. 166; Jackson *v.* Clopton, 66 Ala. 29.

§ 40. Contracts on Behalf of Client.

See post, "Collection of Demands," § 62.

Transfer of a Note.—Where an attorney takes a bond in payment of his client's judgment, payable to his client or bearer, he can not make a valid transfer thereof without consent of his client. Kirk *v.* Glover, 5 Stew. & P. 340.

An attorney has no authority to transfer a note in his hands for collection, in payment of his own debt, so as to bind his client either at law or in equity. Craig *v.* Ely, 5 Stew. & P. 354.

Giving Day of Payment.—An attorney in the absence of instructions to that effect, has no authority to give day of payment, upon receiving security from his client's debtor. Lockhart *v.* Wyatt, 10 Ala. 231.

An attorney can enter into no bargains or contracts, which bind the client, unless he has specially authorized, or subsequently ratified them. Albertson, etc., Co. *v.* Goldsby, 28 Ala. 711; Robinson *v.* Murphy, 69 Ala. 543, 547.

Counsel have by statute the authority to bind parties by agreements in relation to a cause, and such agreements may not be set aside execpt for fraud, accident, mistake, or some other ground of the same nature. Palliser *v.* Home Telephone Co., 170 Ala. 341, 54 So. 499; Ex parte Hayes, 92 Ala. 120, 9 So. 156.

§ 41. Notice and Demand.

See post, "Satisfaction of Judgment or Execution," § 54.

A demand on the sheriff, by the attorney of record, to pay over money collected by him on a specific execution, is, in law, a demand by the plaintiff. Spence *v.* Rutledge, 11 Ala. 557.

An application by the attorney of defendant to the railroad company for compensation for the loss of the trunks, and presentation of the checks for the same, under implied authority to do anything necessary for the prosecution of the demand, was within the scope of his authority, and was the act of his client. White *v.* State, 86 Ala. 69, 5 So. 674.

§ 42. Submission to Arbitration.

An attorney may submit matters in litigation, in a cause in which he is engaged, to arbitration. Wright *v.* Evans, 53 Ala. 103, 107; Beverly *v.* Stephens, 17 Ala. 701; Ball *v.* Bank, 8 Ala. 590, 599.

Power given to an agent to conduct and manage a suit, or to collect a debt, or to settle a disputed claim, does not embrace an authority to arbitrate. Scarborough *v.* Reynolds, 12 Ala. 252; Huber *v.* Zimmerman, 21 Ala. 488; Wright *v.* Evans, 53 Ala. 103, 108.

As to power of attorney to submit matters to arbitration, see ante, "Submission to Arbitration," § 42.

§ 43. Confession of or Consent to Judgment.

See ante, "Warrant or Other Written Authority," § 33.

Where an attorney appears for a party, he may allow judgment to be entered against him by confession. Beverly *v.* Stephens, 17 Ala. 701; Hill *v.* Lambert & Bros., Minor 91; Caller *v.* Denson, Minor 19; Gayle *v.* Foster, Minor 125.

§ 44. Stipulations and Admissions.

See, generally, the title STIPULATIONS. See post, "Conduct of Trial," § 48.

The garnishee in an attachment suit was induced to file an answer prepared by plaintiff's attorney, under his assurance that she should be protected against certain notes outstanding in the hands of a third person not a party to the suit, the notes being regarded as an attempt to cover up the debt. The garnishee was afterwards compelled to pay the notes. Held, that plaintiff was bound by his attorney's agreement and would be enjoined from enforcing a judgment against the garnishee. Hayes *v.* O'Connell, 9 Ala. 488.

Agreement under Misapprehension of Facts.—It was not error to permit a party to introduce evidence in contradiction of an agreement made between his attorney and the attorney for the adverse party, admitting certain matters relating to the action, where the former attorney had signed the agreement under an entire misapprehension as to the facts, and without consultation with his client, who had given notice before the trial that he would not abide by the agreement. Harvey *v.* Thorpe, 28 Ala. 250.

Agreement as to Pending Litigation.—Under Code 1907, § 2988, an agreement between the attorneys of the parties to a pending litigation, settling the controversy, is binding on the parties and the attorneys. Roden Grocery Co. *v.* MacAfee, 160 Ala. 564, 49 So. 402; Charles *v.* Miller, 36 Ala. 141.

Admissions.—An attorney's solemn admissions made in the progress of the trial are binding upon his client. Starke *v.* Kenan, 11 Ala. 818, 820; Beverly *v.* Stephens, 17 Ala. 701, 705; Rosenbaum *v.*

State, 33 Ala. 354; Saltmarsh *v.* Bower & Co., 34 Ala. 613.

Admissions made by attorneys must be distinct and formal, or such as are termed solemn admissions, made for the express purpose of alleviating the stringency of some rule of practice, or of dispensing with the formal proof of some fact at the trial. In such cases they are in general conclusive. Starke *v.* Kenan, 11 Ala. 818, 820.

Representations made by an attorney as to the ownership of a judgment are binding on the client. McGehee *v.* Gindrat, 20 Ala. 95.

§ 45. Commencement and Conduct of Litigation.

§ 46. —— Bringing or Defending and Dismissal of Action.

See ante, "Scope of Authority in General," § 36.

An attorney may, by reason of his general authority, discontinue a suit. Ball *v.* Bank, 8 Ala. 590, 599.

§ 47. —— Suing Out Attachment.

See ante, "Scope of Authority in General," § 36.

An attorney intrusted with a note for collection is authorized to sue out process of attachment. Kirksey *v.* Jones, 7 Ala. 622, 632.

§ 48. —— Conduct of Trial.

See ante, "Stipulations and Admissions," § 44.

Whatever is done by the attorney in the progress of a trial is considered as done by the authority of the client, and is binding on him. Starke *v.* Kenan, 11 Ala. 818; Riddle *v.* Hanna, 25 Ala. 484; Albertson, etc., Co. *v.* Goldsby, 28 Ala. 711, and authorities cited. See, also, Rosenbaum *v.* State, 33 Ala. 354.

§ 49. —— Control of Judgment.

An attorney can not, without express authority, assign a judgment. Boren *v.* McGehee, 6 Port. 432.

§ 50. —— Control of Execution.

See ante, "Determination of Controversy," § 35 (3).

The statutes of the state plainly manifest the legislative intent, and evidently contemplate, that an attorney's authority continues after the rendition of judgment for the purpose of exercising a general superintendence over the process issued to enforce the payment of the judgment, which he has obtained for his client. Code, §§ 2444, 2451, 2471, 2472, 3602. Albertson, etc., Co. *v.* Goldsby, 28 Ala. 711, 717; Smith *v.* Gayle, 58 Ala. 600.

An attorney has authority to direct a sheriff not to return an execution and to delay the sale under an execution, and a sheriff will be protected from liability by the order of the attorney. McClure *v.* Colclough, 5 Ala. 65; Crenshaw *v.* Harrison, 8 Ala. 342; Walker *v.* Goodman, 21 Ala. 647. See, also, Kirksey *v.* Jones, 7 Ala. 622; Oswitchee Co. *v.* Hope & Co., 5 Ala. 629; Albertson, etc., Co. *v.* Goldsby, 28 Ala. 711, 718.

Instructions as to Levy.—An attorney has authority to give an officer, to whom he delivers an execution on a judgment recovered for a client, instructions as to its levy. Smith *v* Gayle, 58 Ala. 600; Albertson *v.* Goldsby, 28 Ala. 711.

Postponement of Sale.—The lien of an execution may be lost, by the attorney's order to the sheriff, without instructions from his client, to postpone the sale of the property levied on, and to allow the property to remain in the possession of the defendant in execution. Albertson *v.* Goldsby, 28 Ala. 711; Patton *v.* Hayter, etc., Co., 15 Ala. 18; Branch Bank *v.* Broughton, 15 Ala. 127, 132; Wood *v.* Gary, 5 Ala. 43; Campbell *v.* Spence, 4 Ala. 543, 551; Leach *v.* Williams, 8 Ala. 759, 764.

Attorney as Purchaser at Execution Sale.—For an attorney to attend, on behalf of his client, a sheriff's sale under execution, and buy in the property for his client, is not improper. Fabel *v.* Boykin, 55 Ala. 383.

§ 51. —— Prosecution of Appeal or Other Proceeding for Review.

An attorney at law may waive the right of appeal which his client may have. Ball *v.* Bank, 8 Ala. 590, 599.

As to adult complainants, the authority of their solicitor to take an appeal will be presumed. Riddle *v.* Hanna, 25 Ala. 484.

Appeal on Behalf of Minors.—An appeal taken by "the solicitors of the complainants" is not legal where complainants are minors. Riddle *v.* Hanna, 25 Ala. 484.

§ 52. Receiving Payment or Security.

§ 53. —— Mode or Form of Payment or Security.

See post, "In General," § 55 (1); "Ratification by Client," § 56; "Collection of Demands," § 62.

An attorney authorized to collect a debt for his principal can not commute the debt for one due by himself to the debtor. Gullett *v.* Lewis, 3 Stew. 23; Cost *v.* Genette, 1 Port. 212; West, etc., Co. *v.* Ball, 12 Ala. 340, 345. See, also, Cook *v.* Bloodgood, 7 Ala. 683.

Payment in Money.—An attorney who has received a claim for collection has not, in the absence of special authority, power to receive in payment of the claim anything but money. Gullett *v.* Lewis, 3 Stew. 23; Cost *v.* Genette, 1 Port. 212; Craig *v.* Ely, 5 Stew. & P. 354; Ball *v.* Bank, 8 Ala. 590, 599; West, etc., Co. *v.* Ball, 12 Ala. 340, 345; Robinson *v.* Murphy, 69 Ala. 543, 547.

A Bond.—An attorney has no authority to take a bond in payment of his client's claim. Kirk *v.* Glover, 5 Stew. & P. 340.

Depreciated Money.—An attorney has no power to receive depreciated money, in satisfaction of a claim. West *v.* Ball, 12 Ala. 340; Chapman *v.* Cowles, 41 Ala. 103, citing and approving Kirk *v.* Glover, 5 Stew. & P. 340; Craig *v.* Ely, 5 Stew. & P. 354; Gullett *v.* Lewis, 3 Stew. 23; Cost *v.* Genette, 1 Port. 212. See, also, Cook *v.* Bloodgood, 7 Ala. 683.

§ 54. —— Satisfaction of Judgment or Execution.

An attorney has authority to receive payment after judgment is recovered. Ball *v.* Bank, 8 Ala. 590, 599; Henderson *v.* Planters', etc., Bank (Ala.), 59 So. 493; Albertson, etc., Co. *v.* Goldsby, 28 Ala. 711; Frazier *v.* Parks, 56 Ala. 363.

Payment, by a sheriff of money collected on an execution, to the attorney of record would be conclusive against the attorney's client. Spence *v.* Rutledge, 11 Ala. 557, 562. See ante, "Notice and Demand," § 41.

An attorney can not accept anything but money in satisfaction of a judgment of his client. Robinson *v.* Murphy, 69 Ala. 543, 547; Henderson *v.* Planters', etc., Bank (Ala.), 59 So. 493.

§ 55. Settlements, Compromises, and Releases.

§ 55 (1) In General.

See ante, "Mode or Form of Payment or Security," § 53.

An attorney has no authority to discharge a debtor by receiving a less sum than was due his client. Ball *v.* Bank, 8 Ala. 590, 599.

The power to compromise a demand does not arise from the authority of an attorney to sue. It is not incidental, and requires express authority. Robinson *v.* Murphy, 69 Ala. 543, cited in note in 31 L. R. A., N. S., 524. Rosenbaum *v.* State, 33 Ala. 354; Hall, etc., Lock Co. *v.* Harwell, 88 Ala. 441, 6 So. 750; Chapman *v.* Cowles, 41 Ala. 103; West, etc., Co. *v.* Ball, 12 Ala. 340; Charles *v.* Miller, 36 Ala. 141; Harvey *v.* Thorpe, 28 Ala. 250; Ex parte Hayes, 92 Ala. 120, 9 So. 156; Gullett *v.* Lewis, 3 Stew. 23; Senn *v.* Joseph, 106 Ala. 454, 17 So. 543, 544.

A Compromise Judgment.—An attorney, without express authority from his client, has no power to bind the latter by a compromise judgment in a litigated suit for less than the amount demanded. Senn *v.* Joseph, 106 Ala. 454, 17 So. 543, cited in note in 31 L. R. A., N. S., 524, 529.

Remitting a Liability to Remove Interest of Witness.—An attorney can not, in virtue of his retention (by a release or the deposit of money, which will operate as a release, if at all), remit a liability which his client may enforce, for the purpose of removing the interest of a witness, so as to make him competent to testify. Ball *v.* Bank, 8 Ala. 590.

§ 55 (2) Receiving Less than Amount of Judgment.

An attorney has not, by virtue of his general retainer, any authority to accept satisfaction of a judgment for less than the sum due, or for such sum to transfer the judgment. Robinson *v.* Murphy, 69 Ala. 543; Henderson *v.* Planters' & Merchants' Bank (Ala.), 59 So. 493.

§ 56. Ratification by Client.

See ante, "Mode or Form of Payment or Security," § 53.

B. & C., attorneys in Montgomery, collected, by judgment, a debt for a client in New York, and received in payment bank bills of the State Bank of Alabama, with which they purchased a check from the Branch Bank at Montgomery, for the amount of their debt (less their fee), which they remitted to the clients on the 15th June, 1842. On the June 23rd the clients addressed a letter to the attorneys, refusing to receive the check, and denying their right to collect in depreciated funds, and informing them, they had remitted the check to P. & T. at their risk, for the purpose of exchanging it, or adding to it the amount of the exchange on New York. P. T. communicated the contents of the letter to the attorneys, but not offering to do anything, remitted the check to the clients. On the 21st July ensuing, the clients again wrote to the attorneys, informing them that P. & T. had declined acting in the business for them, and had returned the check, and that it was held subject to their order, requiring instructions in regard to it. Alabama bank notes were at a depreciation in Mobile, on May 25, 1842, of 25 per cent, and at the time of the receipt by the plaintiffs, of 30 per cent in New York, at which rate it continued up to the 22d September following, when the clients sold it at this discount. Held, that these facts did not authorize the inference, that the clients had ratified the act of their attorneys—that their silence, when applied to by their clients, was tantamount to a refusal to act, and that after waiting a reasonable time, they had a right to adjust the matter by a sale of the check. West, etc., Co. *v.* Ball, 12 Ala. 340.

A client by acquiescence after full knowledge ratifies an unauthorized delegation by his attorney of the authority to conduct the suit. Hitchcock *v.* McGehee, 7 Port. 556.

Special authority of an attorney to assign a judgment, or a ratification of the assignment, may be inferred from the acquiescence of the client therein for several years. Gardner *v.* Mobile & N. W. R. Co., 102 Ala. 635, 15 So. 271.

By Silence.—Where a client did not obtain notice of an unauthorized delegation by his attorney of the authority to conduct the case until three years after the delegation was made, his silence during such time will not be considered as a ratification. Hitchcock *v.* McGehee, 7 Port. 556.

Accepting a Bond in Payment of Judgment.—Where an attorney takes a bond in payment of his client's judgment, a subsequent confirmation thereof by the client is equal to prior authority. Kirk *v.* Glover, 5 Stew. & P. 340.

An attorney, without authority of his client, accepted a bond in payment of a judgment, payable to the client or bearer, and then transferred the bond in payment of his own debt. Held that, if the client had no knowledge of the bond until after the transfer, he might afterwards ratify the attorney's act in taking the bond, and disaffirm the transfer. Kirk *v.* Glover, 5 Stew. & P. 340.

Receiving Payments on an Execution.—Where an attorney at law, charged with the collection of a judgment, receives money from a stranger on an execution, under an agreement that the execution shall remain open for his benefit, and the money thus received is paid over to the judgment plaintiff, the stranger is entitled to the execution, for his reimbursement, without reference to the attorney's authority to receive the money from him. Leach *v.* Williams, 8 Ala. 759.

Where the attorney for a judgment creditor coerces payments thereon by means of an execution, and the judgment creditor receives the payments, and subsequently the judgment is reversed and the suit dismissed, but the judgment debtor sues for the sums paid, the judgment creditor, to the extent of the payments received by him, must be regarded as having ratified the conduct of his attorney in enforcing payment. Florence Cotton & Iron Co. *v.* Louisville Banking Co., 138 Ala. 588, 36 So. 456.

By Proceeding against Attorney.—If an attorney receives depreciated paper currency, in payment of a judgment, his client, by proceeding against him individually, thereby ratifies the payment. Chapman *v.* Cowles, 41 Ala. 103.

§ 57. **Notice to Attorney.**

General Rule.—If an attorney acquire knowledge, or receive notice of fact, while engaged in the discharge of his duties as such, it will be presumed that it was communicated to his client, or the client is at least chargeable in the same manner as if personal notice was communicated to him. Mundine *v.* Pitts, 14 Ala. 84, 90.

Notice to the attorney of a party, pending a cause, is notice to the party himself. Clay's Dig. 337, § 137; Jefford *v.* Ringgold & Co., 6 Ala. 544, 549. See, also, Jackson *v.* Hughes, 6 Ala. 257; Simington *v.* Kent, 8 Ala. 691, 692.

Notice to Attorney When Subsequently Employed by Another Client.—Notice to an agent or counsel, employed by another person, in another business, at another time, will not be constructive notice to his principal or client, employing him afterwards. Mundine *v.* Pitts, 14 Ala. 84; Pepper & Co. *v.* George, 51 Ala. 190.

After Relation Began.—Notice to an attorney, or knowledge acquired by him, is not notice to his client, unless given or acquired after the relation began. McCormick *v.* Joseph, 83 Ala. 401, 3 So. 796; Lucas *v.* Bank, 2 Stew. 280; Terrell *v.* Branch Bank, 12 Ala. 502; Pepper & Co. *v.* George, 51 Ala. 190; Frenkel *v.* Hudson, 82 Ala. 158, 2 So. 758.

Notice of Unrecorded Deed.—A purchaser is not charged with notice of an unrecorded deed by his grantors by knowledge of his attorney, where the attorney, without the purchaser's knowledge, is also representing the sellers, and is personally interested in making the sale; he receiving the purchase money. Scotch Lumber Co. *v.* Sage, 132 Ala. 598, 32 So. 607.

A purchaser of land is not charged with notice of an unrecorded deed by his grantors because his attorney knew of it; he having acquired his knowledge before he was employed to purchase the land for him, and while representing another. Scotch Lumber Co. *v.* Sage, 132 Ala. 598, 32 So. 607.

III. DUTIES AND LIABILITIES OF ATTORNEY TO CLIENT.

§ 58. **Negligence or Malpractice.**

§ 59. —— **Nature of Attorney's Duty.**

See ante, "What Constitutes a Retainer," § 27; post, "Collection of Demands," § 62.

"An attorney at law is the special agent of his client, whose duties, usually are confined to the vigilant prosecution or defense of the suitor's rights." Gullett *v.* Lewis, 3 Stew. 23, 27.

While an attorney may lawfully perform many of the agencies, lying outside the regular line of professional attorneyship, he is not, in the absence of an express engagement to do so, bound to perform them. They are not among the implied obligations he incurs, when he assumes the relation of attorney for another. Stubbs *v.* Beene, 37 Ala. 627, 630.

In the absence of qualifying terms, a special retainer, such as was given and accepted in this case, imposes on an attorney the following duties and obligations: He must accept no retainer from the opposite side. He must give counsel whenever needed and called for. He must acquaint himself with the case and its wants. Must render all needed professional aid in the preparation of the defense, and must give his earnest, unflagging attention and services to the trial when it comes, and in these several duties he must not relax in zeal until there is a judgment in the trial court, or other termination of the prosecution. Agnew *v.* Walden, 84 Ala. 502, 4 So. 672.

§ 60. —— **Skill and Care Required.**

See post, "Pleading and Evidence," § 79 (2); "Trial," § 79 (3).

An attorney is held to the exercise of reasonable diligence and skill in the particular case in which he is employed, and is liable for ordinary neglect in the discharge of his professional services. Or, as is otherwise expressed in some of the cases, an attorney owes his client ordinary skill and reasonable diligence, and is responsible for all injuries client sustains, which are traceable to want of them. Evans *v.* Watrous, 2 Port. 205; Walker *v.* Goodman, 21 Ala. 647; Goodman *v.* Walker, 30 Ala. 482, 495; Burkham Bros. *v.* Daniel, 56 Ala. 604, 610; Teague *v.* Corbitt, 57 Ala. 529, 543; Jackson *v.* Clopton, 66 Ala. 29; Pinkston *v.* Arrington, 98 Ala. 489, 13 So. 561.

For What Negligence Attorney Is Liable.—A lawyer should be chargeable with gross negligence, or with gross ignorance, in the performance of his duties, to render him liable. Evans *v.* Watrous, 2 Port. 205; Mardis *v.* Shackleford, 4 Ala. 493, 504; Pearson *v.* Darrington, 32 Ala. 227, 260.

There is much inaccuracy in the employment of the phrase, "gross negligence," the court fell into this error in the case of Evans *v.* Watrous, 2 Port. 205. It is there said that an attorney is not liable, "unless he has been guilty of gross negligence." In the same paragraph it is asserted, that he, "is bound to use reasonable care and skill;" and the meaning attributed, by the writer of that opinion to the expression "gross negligence," is the want or absence of "reasonable care and skill." Thus explained, that opinion defines the measure of an attorney's duty and liability. Goodman *v.* Walker, 30 Ala. 482, 496.

§ 61. —— Acts and Omissions of Attorney in General.

An attorney at law is responsible for losses caused by his disregard, in bringing a suit for his client, of a rule of law which was well and clearly defined, both in the text-books and the reports, and which had existed and been published long enough to justify the belief that it was known to the profession. Goodman *v.* Walker, 30 Ala. 482.

If an attorney frames a declaration "so negligently, or skillfully, that his client in the progress of the cause suffers injury by reason of such want of care and skill, the attorney is liable to an action." Goodman *v.* Walker, 30 Ala. 482, 500.

It betrayed gross negligence, or want of skill, for an attorney to change the plaintiff, and declare in a name different from that named in the writ. Goodman *v.* Walker, 30 Ala. 482, 499.

As to liability of attorney for negligence in examining abstract, see ante, "Acts and Omissions of Attorney in General," § 61.

§ 62. —— Collection of Demands.

See ante, "Contracts on Behalf of Client," § 40; "Mode or Form of Payment or Security," § 53; "Ratification by Client," § 56; "Nature of Attorney's Duty," § 59.

If an attorney receives a claim for collection, in the absence of proof to the contrary, he will be presumed to have received it for collection by suit; and that, by the implied terms of such contract, he is required to give his professional skill and attention to all the ordinary stages of the litigation. See Mardis *v.* Shackleford, 4 Ala. 493; Stubbs *v.* Beene, 37 Ala. 627, 629.

If cross litigation be instituted, which bears directly on the further progress of the suit under his control, it is possibly his duty to represent his client in such defensive cross litigation. Stubbs *v.* Beene, 37 Ala. 627, 630.

Where an attorney collects bank bills in lieu of specie, without authority, he is responsible as for a failure to collect. West, etc., Co. *v.* Ball, 12 Ala. 340, 345.

Where attorneys collect and transmit to their clients funds in depreciated bank paper, which the clients refuse to receive, and send back with an offer to return to them, and a request to make up the difference, and the attorneys decline to do anything about it, the clients have a right to sell the paper, and recover the deficiency from the attorneys. West *v.* Ball, 12 Ala. 340.

Personal Use of Securities.—It is the duty of an attorney not to use the securities of his client left with him for collection, in discharge of his own debts. Craig *v.* Ely, 5 Stew. & P. 354, 364.

Claim against Insolvent Estate.—An attorney at law is not liable for a failure to file a note which he has received for collection by suit, as a claim against the estate of the maker upon the death, and declaration of the insolvency of the estate, of the latter, when said facts occurred after he received the note, and without his knowledge. Stubbs *v.* Beene, 37 Ala. 627; Moore *v.* Winston, 66 Ala. 296.

§ 63. —— Unauthorized Appearance.

If an attorney acts without authority he is responsible both to the person whom he represents and to the court. Hill *v.* Lambert & Bros., Minor 91, 92.

An attorney making an unauthorized

appearance can be summarily punished for contempt. Brewer v. Watson, 71 Ala. 299, 304.

An attorney is liable for his unauthorized appearance to any party who may be injured thereby. Wheeler v. Bullard, 6 Port. 352.

§ 64. —— Conduct of Litigation.

See ante, "Skill and Care Required," § 60; post, "Pleading and Evidence," § 79 (2).

A lawyer is not responsible for an error which is the result of neither ignorance, negligence, nor fraud. Pearson v. Darrington, 32 Ala. 227, 260.

Failure to Take an Exception.—The failure of an attorney to reserve a bill of exceptions to an erroneous ruling of the circuit court is not necessarily negligence. Pearson v. Darrington, 32 Ala. 227.

When a lawyer yields to the opinion of the presiding judge, in reference to a question, and forbears to take an exception, he can not be convicted of a want of professional skill, professional knowledge, or professional diligence. Pearson v. Darrington, 32 Ala. 227, 259, cited in note in 52 L. R. A. 883, 886.

Negligently Suing Out Attachment.—While it may not be the duty of an attorney to prepare and sue out a writ of attachment for the enforcement of a claim placed in his hands for collection, yet, if he does undertake to do so, and does it negligently, he will be liable to his client for the damage resulting from the negligence. Walker v. Goodman, 21 Ala. 647.

Releasing an Attachment.—An attorney who releases an attachment without the consent of his client is liable for the damage caused thereby to his client. Walker v. Goodman, 21 Ala. 647.

§ 65. —— Acting for Party Adversely Interested.

The moving to dismiss a case by defendant's attorney, under authorization from plaintiff, is not such a representation of both parties by him as is forbidden. Ex parte Randall, 149 Ala. 640, 42 So. 870.

§ 66. —— Acts and Omissions of Partners and Associates.

An attorney who has received notes for collection is individually responsible for care and diligence in the collection, although he gives his client notice that he has associated with him a partner, who attends to the collecting, unless the client recognize the partnership in the transaction of his business. Mardis v. Shackleford, 4 Ala. 493.

An attorney can not relieve himself from the liabilities he assumed, when his firm undertook the collection of a note by the dissolution of the partnership. The partner, by taking the collection had bound him to the exercise of reasonable skill and diligence in the conduct of the suit, and from that responsibility he could not relieve himself without the consent and act of the client. Goodman v. Walker, 30 Ala. 482, 496.

§ 67. Accounting and Payment to Client.

§ 68. —— Liabilities in General.

Money collected by an attorney for his client belongs to the client—not a part of it merely, but all of it; not a balance after deducting the fee of the attorney, but the total sum collected. The fund may be charged with a lien in favor of the attorney to the extent of his fee, and the attorney may have a right to retain his compensation on a settlement with the client; but the ownership of the entire sum is none the less in the client. McDonald v. State, 143 Ala. 101, 39 So. 257, 259.

Where Property Is Received in Payment of Claim.—Where an attorney holding a note for collection receives payment in property, he may be sued on a parol promise to pay his client, it not being a promise to answer for the debt of another, within the statute of frauds. Cameron v. Clarke, etc., Co., 11 Ala. 259.

Where an attorney holding a note for collection receives payment in property, an action for money had and received may be maintained if the client elects to consider it a payment. Cameron v. Clarke, etc., Co., 11 Ark. 259; Shuart v. Conner, 9 Ala. 803.

Where an attorney charges himself with an amount collected for his client, and charges the client with his fee, the jury, in assumpsit for money received, may infer a promise from the attorney to pay the balance. Cameron *v.* Clarke, etc., Co., 11 Ala. 259.

§ 69. —— Acts or Defaults of Partners and Associates.

In professional partnerships formed for the practice of the law, if one member of the concern acknowledges the receipt of money for a client, the latter need not inquire how the claim was collected, or whether paid at all, or not, but may charge the firm upon the assumption that the receipt expresses the truth; and the partner who had no agency in giving the receipt can not gainsay its truth. Cook *v.* Bloodgood, 7 Ala. 683.

Where one of two attorneys, who were partners, receives his own notes in part payment of a demand left for collection, and gave the receipt of the firm to the debtor for the claim, and a suit was brought against the attorneys for the amount of the demand, it was held that one partner could not show that the other had received his own notes in payment. Cook *v.* Bloodgood, 7 Ala. 683.

§ 70. —— Liability for Interest.

Where an attorney procures a fund in court to be paid to him, and he retains it pending litigation in reference to it, it will be presumed that he used the money while in his possession, and he will be held accountable for interest. Smith *v.* Alexander, 87 Ala. 51, 6 So. 51.

§ 71. —— Persons Entitled.

Client's Creditors.—Where claims are placed in the hands of an attorney, to collect and pay over to the client's creditors, and the creditors are not parties to the arrangement, an action for the failure to collect them and pay over the amount may be maintained by the client; the creditors having no interest, at most, till the claims are collected. Mardis *v.* Shackleford, 6 Ala. 433.

An Attorney's Immediate Principal.—One attorney confided a note to another for collection, and took his receipt therefor, but without giving instructions with respect to the ownership. After the money was collected, it was remitted to the payee of the note, whose name, however, was indorsed on the note. Held, that this remittance (the payee not being the owner) did not discharge the collecting attorney from liability to his immediate principal; and that the action of the latter for the money would not be defeated by proof that he was himself the agent of the indorsee, unless the indorsee had asserted his right to the money as against his agent. Lewis *v.* Peck, 10 Ala. 142.

Owner of Note or His Agent.—Where an attorney collects a note received by him from an agent, he may discharge himself either by paying the proceeds to the agent from whom he received the note, or to the true owner; but he can not discharge himself by payment to the payee of the note, he being neither the owner nor holder of the note. Wallace *v.* Peck, 12 Ala. 768.

Payee of Note.—When a person places a note in the hands of an attorney for collection, and takes from him a receipt for it in his own name, but does not claim it as his own, nor any lien upon it, and the note itself is payable to a third person, and not indorsed, a payment by the attorney of the proceeds of the note to the payee will discharge him from all liability to the person who placed the note in his hands. Peck *v.* Wallace, 19 Ala. 219.

§ 72. Dealings between Attorney and Client.

§ 73. —— In General.

§ 73 (1) In General.

See post, "Value of Services or Amount of Compensation," § 99 (3).

There must be no cause of confidence, with respect to the relation of attorney and client, while it lasts, and as to its subject matter, by which the attorney secures an unjust advantage over the client. Kidd *v.* Williams, 132 Ala. 140, 31 So. 458.

Transactions between attorney and client, as between other persons occupying fiduciary relations, are anxiously and jealously scrutinized by the courts, so that the client may be protected from the influence or ascendency which the relation generates. Dickinson *v.* Bradford, 59 Ala. 581; Ware *v.* Russell, 70 Ala. 174, 179.

Agreement Varying Original Contract.—An agreement between client and counsel, after the latter has been employed, by which the original contract is varied, and greater compensation secured to the counsel, is void. Lecatt *v.* Sallee, 3 Port. 115.

The firmest ground for the support of the principle which affords a client relief from a contract with his attorney for additional compensation by which the original contract is varied, consists in the confidence reposed by a client, in his attorney and the influence which an attorney has, over his client. Confidence is necessarily reposed, by a client in his attorney. The influence of an attorney during the relationship is great. Integrity of character and purety of motive, have never enabled such contracts to stand in full force, against the principle of equity which commonly excludes all inquiry into the fairness of the transactions, and sets them aside as violating policies of justice. Lecatt *v.* Sallee, 3 Port. 115; Kidd *v.* Williams, 132 Ala. 140, 31 So. 458; Dickinson *v.* Bradford, 59 Ala. 581.

The contract which produced the relation between the parties in this case, having ascertained the fee of the defendant, it was as irrevocably settled, as though a rule of law, which tolerated no contract upon the matter, had fixed it. Lecatt *v.* Sallee, 3 Port. 115, 123; Kidd *v.* Williams, 132 Ala. 140, 31 So. 458.

Contracts Foreign to the Relation.—"An attorney is allowed to enter into contracts with his client upon any matter which is not the object of his concern as attorney." Lecatt *v.* Sallee, 3 Port. 115. 120.

After the Relation Has Ceased.—An attorney will not be allowed, during the pendency of a cause, to extort from his client unreasonable compensation for his services. though, after the cause is ended, the court will not interfere in respect to any compensation which the client may make. Lecatt *v.* State, 3 Port. 115; Kidd *v.* Williams, 132 Ala. 140, 31 So. 458.

Contract as to Another Suit.—The employment of attorneys in one suit, does not deprive them, while it is pending, of their right to make a contract for compensation for their services in another, or for any other professional business, with the same client. Lecatt *v.* Sallee, 3 Port. 115, 124; Kidd *v.* Williams, 132 Ala. 140, 31 Ala. 458.

Subsequent Agreements for Compensation.—After an attorney's fiduciary relation has commenced, no subsequent agreement with his client for compensation can be supported, unless it is a fair and just remuneration for his services. Dickinson *v.* Bradford, 59 Ala. 581; Lecatt *v.* Sallee, 3 Port. 115; Ware *v.* Russell, 70 Ala. 174, 179; White *v.* Tolliver, 110 Ala. 300, 20 So. 97.

Consent Decree for Compensation.—The relation between attorney and client is that of trustee and cestui, and a consent decree prepared by an attorney for his services, to be signed by his client, will not be sanctioned beyond a fair and reasonable compensation. Yonge *v.* Hooper, 73 Ala. 119.

§ 73 (2) Conveyances, Mortgages and Assignments.

Transfer of Subject Matter of Litigation.—The contracts between attorney and client, made after the formation of the relation, touching the compensation of the attorney, or by which the client transfers to him an interest in the matter of suit, or a right or interest in and to property involved in litigation, are closely watched, and jealously scrutinized, when as between them, their validity is drawn in question. The confidence the relation involves—the power over the client the attorney naturally acquires, the opportunity and danger of oppression and the exercise of influence, compel courts to a most jealous supervision of all such contracts; and, as between attorney and client, they are supported only when all the circumstances attending them import that they are fair, just, and untainted with an abuse of the relation. Ware *v.* Russell, 70 Ala. 174, 179.

Purchases from Client.—Transactions between attorney and client should be strictly scrutinized, and the attorney must give his client the benefit of all the information he has respecting the value of property purchased by him from the client, but purchases are voidable only on proper and timely application. Dawson *v.* Copeland, 173 Ala. 267, 55 So. 600.

§ 74. —— Payment of or Security for Compensation.

Settlement made between attorney and client for services of the attorney is not invalid because the client did not have independent competent advice, he being a capable and wealthy business man, of unimpaired mind, and the settlement being after performance of the services, and on terms suggested by him, with full understanding of the matters. Kidd *v.* Williams, 132 Ala. 140, 31 So. 458.

Where a bond, or any other security for a greater compensation, is taken from a client, by his attorney, during their connection, it will, upon an application to a court of equity, be either set aside or allowed to stand only as security for the sum to which the attorney would have been entitled if no such security had been given. Lecatt *v.* Sallee, 3 Port. 115, 120.

§ 75. Acquiring Property Adversely to Interest of Client.

An attorney, having recovered a judgment for his client, and having the control thereof, can not, without the consent of his client, express or implied, become the purchaser of lands at a sale under execution issued thereon; and if he does so purchase, he becomes, like any other agent, a trustee for his client. Such a trust arises by operation of law, and continues until barred by lapse of time, or until terminated by an election to ratify the purchase, thereby giving it validity. Pearce *v.* Gamble, 72 Ala. 341.

So long as the relation of attorney and client exists, the attorney is a trustee for his client in and about the cause or the subject thereof and any trade that he makes or benefits that he may derive, resulting from the litigation or a sale of the subject thereof, will inure to the benefit of the client. Singo *v.* Brainard, 173 Ala. 64, 55 So. 603.

§ 76. Summary Remedies of Client.

§ 76 (1) In General.

Attorney's Right of Defense.—The proviso, at the close of Code 1896, § 3810, authorizing a summary remedy against attorneys for money or property recovered and not turned over, that if the attorney doubts the right of the person making the demand, or if there is a dispute as to compensation due him, he may pay the money into court, or turn the property over to the sheriff, and have such questions decided without being liable for interest or damages otherwise provided for, is a mere privilege extended to him, by which he escapes the interest and the statutory penalty, should he be found in the wrong; and hence such section does not, on his failure to comply therewith, deprive him of the right of defense, and every defense is open which would be open in assumpsit against him, whether or not he avails himself of the privilege. White *v.* Ward, 157 Ala. 345, 47 So. 166.

It is clear that the law did not intend that the attorney should pay over on demand to an insolvent and perhaps unprincipled client his commissions or fees, and, therefore, that he would be justified in refusing such a demand, and he would thus not be put in default on such a refusal. And, as the motion must follow the demand, it seems to us that it would be unreasonable to hold that money improperly demanded could be the basis of a motion for a summary judgment, and must be paid into court as preliminary to the allowance of a defense on the merits. White *v.* Ward, 157 Ala. 345, 47 So. 166, 169.

Defense of Set-Off.—In a proceeding against a defaulting attorney for a summary judgment under Code 1896, §§ 3810, 3811, authorizing a summary judgment against an attorney failing to pay over money collected by him as attorney for a client, the attorney can not set up a set-off in defense; the theory of the statute being that no claim of the attorney should be made until he has discharged his duty of putting the fund in the control of the court, and then only for compensation for services rendered in the collection of the fund. McDonald *v.* State, 143 Ala. 101, 39 So. 257.

§ 76 (2) Proceedings and Relief.

In General.—The rule and intent is clear, that the appeal to law for a summary judgment under Code 1896, §§ 3810, 3811, is to enforce a right in one and a duty resting on another. The attorney is supposed to withhold what he has no right to retain, and which it is his duty to pay over to satisfy the correlative right of the client. There can be no procedure without a demand for the performance of the duty. The refusal to satisfy the lawful demand puts the attorney in default and authorizes the motion. The notice and motion is a summons and declaration to enforce the right and duty by judgment. White *v.* Ward, 157 Ala. 345, 47 So. 166.

Sufficient Notice.—A notice for summary judgment, authorized by Code 1896, c. 106, served on an attorney at law, which recited that a motion would be made at a term of court for summary judgment against him for a specified sum, and which stated that the ground of the motion was that the attorney, as attorney for the state in a suit, had received a designated sum in satisfaction of a judgment in favor of the state, and that on demand he had refused to pay over the sum, gave the court jurisdiction of the subject matter. McDonald *v.* State, 143 Ala. 101, 39 So. 257.

Proper Demand.—The proper demand, in proceedings against a defaulting attorney for a summary judgment under Code 1896, §§ 3810, 3811, authorizing summary judgments against an attorney failing to pay over money collected by him "on demand made by the person entitled thereto * * * for the amount collected," and empowering the court to require the party claiming the money to establish his right thereto, is for the gross sum collected by and in the hands of the attorney, though he is entitled on a settlement to retain a part as compensation. McDonald *v.* State, 143 Ala. 101, 39 So. 257.

Reasonable Time before Demand.—In proceedings for summary judgment against an attorney for failure to turn over money collected by him, it was shown that the money was collected in the latter part of 1902 or the early part of 1903, and that demands were made on him for payment in April and May, 1903. Held, as a matter of law, that a reasonable time had elapsed after the collection of the money before the demands were made, authorizing the entry of summary judgment against him. McDonald *v.* State, 143 Ala. 101, 39 So. 257.

Jurisdiction.—Where, in proceedings in a city court for summary judgment against an attorney for failure to pay over money received by him as attorney for a client, the attorney appeared and moved for the dismissal of the proceedings on the ground that the circuit court only had jurisdiction, and filed pleas in set-off, etc., proof that the attorney resided within the territorial jurisdiction of the city court was not necessary in order to confer jurisdiction on the court, and the jurisdiction was shown by the incorporation of the motion for judgment into its records. McDonald *v.* State, 143 Ala. 101, 39 So. 257.

Evidence.—In proceedings for a summary judgment under Code 1896, § 3810, against an attorney failing to pay over money collected by him on a judgment, instituted by a transferee of the judgment, the order of the owner of the judgment directing the attorney to turn over the fund to the transferee is admissible. Boyett *v.* Payne, 141 Ala. 475, 37 So. 585.

Where in proceedings for a summary judgment under Code 1896, § 3810, against an attorney failing to turn over money collected under a judgment, there was evidence tending to show that the attorney had bought the judgment from the owner thereof, it was proper to refuse an instruction that plaintiff was entitled to a verdict. Boyett *v.* Payne, 141 Ala. 475, 37 So. 585.

In proceedings for a summary judgment under Code 1896, § 3810, against an attorney failing to pay over money collected by him on a judgment, evidence of the judgment debtor's financial condition at the time of the collection is relevant to show the value of the attorney's services and the proper amount to be retained by him therefor. Boyett *v.* Payne, 141 Ala. 475, 37 So. 585.

Where in proceedings for a summary judgment under Code 1896, § 3810, against an attorney failing to pay over money collected by him, the evidence tended to show that the attorney, as such, had collected money on a judgment, which he failed to pay over, it was error to give an affirmative charge in favor of the attorney. Boyett *v.* Payne, 141 Ala. 475, 37 So. 585.

Where, in proceedings for summary judgment against an attorney failing to pay over money collected by him in an action by the state against a third person for taxes, a demand on the attorney by the attorney general of the state was shown, the error in admitting evidence of a demand by the tax commissioner was harmless. McDonald *v.* State, 143 Ala. 101, 39 So. 257.

In summary proceedings against an attorney for failure to pay over the money on demand, the finding that the movant demanded of defendant moneys collected, with no further special finding of fact, is insufficient; there being no finding that defendant failed to pay over the money. McCarley *v.* White, 154 Ala. 295, 45 So. 155.

Burden of Proof.—A movant for a summary judgment against an attorney for money collected by him and not paid over, who alleges, as required by Code 1896, § 3810, providing that judgment may be entered summarily against an attorney failing to pay over money collected by him on demand made by the person entitled thereto, a demand on the attorney for payment of the money collected and his refusal, must prove a demand and refusal when the same is denied. McCarley *v.* White, 144 Ala. 662, 39 So. 978.

§ 77. Proceedings for Accounting.

A bill alleged that complainant was the owner of a receipt given by an attorney at law to a firm for certain demands due it from a third party, which receipt had been sold at bankrupt sale by the assignee as a portion of the assets of such firm, and sought to enforce the trust created thereby. Held, that proof of an agreement by such firm with the attorney that he should collect such claims, and pay the proceeds either to the firm or to three firms of which such firm was one, did not sustain the allegations of the bill. Paulding *v.* Lee, 20 Ala. 753.

§ 78. Actions for Money Collected.

Demand and Refusal.—An attorney is not liable, as for money collected by him as attorney, until after a demand and refusal to pay it over, or to remit it, according to instructions, or upon proof of culpable negligence in collecting the same. Mardis *v.* Shackelford, 4 Ala. 493; Kimbro *v.* Waller, 21 Ala. 376.

Although no action can be maintained against an attorney at law for failing to pay over money collected for his client, until he has failed or refused to pay it over after demand made, yet the client can not, by this principle of law, excuse his laches in not making a demand within a reasonable time after the collection and conversion of the money by the attorney. Kimbro *v.* Waller, 21 Ala. 376.

Demand before suit is not necessary where the attorney has agreed to pay over moneys when collected, and has failed to do so. Mardis *v.* Shackleford, 4 Ala. 493.

Time of Demand.—A plaintiff should make his demand in a reasonable time after the money is collected and converted by the attorney, so as to bring his suit within the six years allowed by the statute. Kimbro *v.* Waller, 21 Ala. 376, 378.

Insufficient Replication.—In assumpsit against an attorney at law for money collected as attorney and not paid over, defendant pleaded the statute of limitations, to which plaintiff replied "that the money sued for was collected by defendant, as an attorney at law, in the state of Tennessee, and that no demand was made of him for said money until a short time before the commencement of this suit, and that the statute only began to run from the demand." Held, that the replication was demurrable. Kimbro *v.* Waller, 21 Ala. 376.

Evidence.—In an action by a client against his attorney to recover money retained as fees from the amount collected on a judgment recovered in plaintiff's favor, evidence of the continuance of the plaintiff's suit, occasioned by the necessity of an amendment to the complaint, whereby interest which might have accrued on the judgment, if rendered at the term of continuance, was lost, is inadmissible, if the continuance was not due to the defendant's negligence. Jackson *v.* Clopton, 66 Ala. 29.

Instructions.—In an action to recover a sum retained by attorneys as fees, where the undisputed evidence showed that the contract of employment stipulated for a contingent fee; that defendants were, in the event of recovery, to have a reasonable fee for their services, and if nothing were recovered were to receive no fee; that under such a contract a fee of 50 per cent would be a reasonable and fair fee; that the litigation terminated favorably to the client; and that of the amount collected by defendants as a result of the litigation they received not quite 50 per cent as their fee—an affirmative charge for defendants was proper. German *v.* Browne & Leeper, Ala. 364, 39 So. 742.

§ 79. Actions for Negligence or Wrongful Acts.

§ 79 (1) In General.

Unauthorized Appearance.—The remedy for an unauthorized appearance is against the attorney for his unauthorized act. Beverly *v.* Stephens, 17 Ala. 701, 704. See Gilbert *v.* Lane, 3 Port. 267; Bissell *v.* Carville & Co., 6 Ala. 503.

Action in Assumpsit.—If a declaration in an action against an attorney charged a neglect of duty and impropriety of conduct, and also set out an undertaking by the attorney to collect money, and alleged a promise to make good any loss resulting from a breach of it, the action is in assumpsit. Cook *v.* Bloodgood, 7 Ala. 683, citing Mardis *v.* Shackleford, 4 Ala. 493.

For Failure to Collect a Demand.—If A. place certain demands in the hands of an attorney, who agrees to collect the amount and pay over the proceeds to creditors of A., such creditors being no party to the agreement, A. may maintain an action against the attorney for a failure to collect and pay over the amount of the debts. Mardis *v.* Shackleford, 6 Ala. 433.

Defenses.—When an attorney is sued by his client for negligence and unskillfulness, he can not set up champerty in the contract as a defense to the suit. Goodman *v.* Walker, 30 Ala. 482.

"The attorney's having performed services, could have maintained an action for reasonable compensation. Holloway *v.* Lowe, 1 Ala. 246, approved in Elliott *v.* McClelland, 17 Ala. 206. Being entitled to the benefits of the retainer, it would be monstrous to relieve them from its responsibilities." Goodman *v.* Walker, 30 Ala. 482, 500.

§ 79 (2) Pleading and Evidence.

See ante, "Skill and Care Required," § 60; "Conduct of Litigation," § 64.

In an action against an attorney for failing to collect certain debts and pay the proceeds to "the creditors of B., S., & Co.," the declaration is not bad for not stating such creditors by name, it not appearing that their names were specified in the agreement on which the action was founded. Mardis *v.* Shackleford, 6 Ala. 433.

Sufficient Averments of Negligence.—An averment that an attorney negligently commenced a suit, and improperly dismissed it, contrary to his duty, is a sufficient charge of gross neglect. Evans *v.* Watrous, 2 Port. 205.

In an action against attorneys at law for negligence and unskillfulness, a count is sufficient which alleges that they conducted the suit so negligently and unskillfully, "in not having a certain writ of attachment, affidavit, and declaration, before then prepared by them in said action, prepared, drawn up, and filed, and made out according to the laws of said state and rules of said court, that the said plaintiff, by the said neglect of, etc., was hindered and prevented from recovering judgment, etc., and was forced and compelled to release and dismiss the levy of said writ of attachment," or "by reason whereof the said plaintiff has been prevented from recovering her demand," etc. Walker *v.* Goodman, 21 Ala. 647.

In an action against attorneys for negligence, a count is sufficient which alleges that defendants, through want of care and skill, "did dismiss the levy of a certain writ of attachment" before that time levied on the property of the defendants therein, and "did dismiss, relinquish, and release all liens which had attached or accrued by virtue of said levy," etc., and that, by means of the unskillful management of defendants, the plaintiff "lost her said demand, and the means of recovering and collecting the same." Walker *v.* Goodman, 21 Ala. 647.

The averment of a bill that defendant employed as attorney for complainants to oppose the setting aside of a homestead in proceedings in probate, "did not represent in good faith and to the best of his ability complainants' interest at this time," is insufficient to charge fraud; it not being shown that the decree of probate would not have been the same, had he represented them with great skill and ability. Brainard *v.* Singo, 164 Ala. 353, 51 So. 522.

Evidence of Negligence.—Whether an attorney has been grossly negligent in managing the business of his client, is to be ascertained by the evidence of those who are conversant with the same kind of business. Evans *v.* Watrous, 2 Port. 205, 211.

The receipt of an attorney for notes for collection is not, of itself, sufficient evidence of negligence in collecting them. Mardis *v.* Shackleford, 4 Ala. 493.

But if the receipt is of an old date, and the attorney was informed of the debtor's residence, or upon due inquiry might have been, and did not discharge himself from his engagement to collect the debts, in the absence of countervailing proof, negligence may be inferred. Mardis *v.* Shackleford, 4 Ala. 493, 494.

In an action against an attorney for neglect in the collection of a note, the attorney's receipt describing the note is prima facie evidence of the justness and genuineness of the same. Hair *v.* Glover, 14 Ala. 500, distinguishing Bank *v.* Higgins, 3 Ala. 206.

The receipt in this case was the written evidence of a contract between the attorneys and the plaintiff below, by which the former acknowledged receipt of a note of a third party, for collection, specifying the amount, and the legal effect of the receipt was not only an acknowledgment, that the note existed as a demand against the maker, but that the attorneys would use due diligence in collecting the demand therein specified against the debtor. Hair *v.* Glover, 14 Ala. 500, 503.

In an action by a client against an attorney for negligence and unskillfulness in the collection of a claim, the attorney's receipt for the claim is admissible to show that the relation of attorney and client existed. Goodman *v.* Walker, 30 Ala. 482.

Presumption.—A receipt for notes overdue, given by an attorney at law, raises the presumption that they were received for collection, and implies an agreement on his part to use due diligence for that purpose. Mardis *v.* Shackleford, 4 Ala. 493.

Waiver of Proof.—An attorney may, by his admissions, waive the necessity of proof of facts, which the party would otherwise be compelled to make. Hall *v.* Glover, 14 Ala. 500, 503.

Record of the Suit on a Claim.—In an action by a client against an attorney for negligence and unskillfulness with respect to a claim placed in his hands for collection, the record of the suit on the claim, though conducted by the attorney in the name of another attorney, is admissible in evidence against him to prove the final determination of the suit. Goodman *v.* Walker, 30 Ala. 482.

Proof on Behalf of the Attorney.—Where it appears by the declaration, in an action against an attorney, for improperly dismissing a suit, that there was a good cause of action, the attorney is bound to show some reasonable excuse for not conducting it to a successful termination. Evans *v.* Watrous, 2 Port. 205, 211.

In an action for negligence in the management of a cause, the attorney can not be allowed to prove that he consulted a distinguished attorney respecting the proper course to be pursued by him, or that the arrangement made by him was, in the opinion of the witness, the best that could be made for his client's interest. Goodman *v.* Walker, 30 Ala. 482.

§ 79 (3) Trial.

See ante, "Skill and Care Required," § 60.

Questions for the Jury.—Whether an attorney has been guilty of gross negligence is a question of fact. Evans *v.* Watrous, 2 Port. 205; Mardis *v.* Shackleford, 4 Ala. 493; Walker *v.* Goodman, 21 Ala. 647, cited in note in 38 L. R. A., N. S., 1204.

Where the statute grants registers of court records six months in which to make a final record of causes disposed of, and attorneys who are employed to examine the title to certain land examine all the indexes the law requires the register to keep, and also the trial docket, for causes pending, none of which show the existence of any record affecting such title, and it appears that within less than six months previous to such examination a final decree was rendered, affecting such title, of which the attorneys might have learned by inquiry of the register, or by examination of the trial docket, the question whether such attorneys used reasonable diligence is for the jury. Pinkston *v.* Arrington, 98 Ala. 489, 13 So. 561.

§ 79 (4) Damages and Costs.

The measure of damages to which an attorney is liable, for failing to perform his undertaking with his client, is the loss which has resulted from his negligence. Mardis *v.* Shackleford, 4 Ala. 493, 494; Hair *v.* Glover, 14 Ala. 500.

IV. COMPENSATION AND LIEN OF ATTORNEY.

(A) FEES AND OTHER REMUNERATION.

§ 80. Right to Compensation in General.

"In this state, attorneys and solicitors, are entitled to compensation for their services." Dickinson *v.* Bradford, 59 Ala. 581, 583.

§ 81. Statutory Regulations.

The attorneys appointed under the act of December 30, 1868, in the counties of Mobile, Greene and Pickens, "to attend to all criminal cases wherein the persons prosecuted shall be unable to employ counsel," are entitled to the compensation fixed by the statute in all cases in which they act as such counsel, whether there is a conviction, an acquittal, or dismissal. The disposition of the case does not control the right to compensation. Commissioners' Court *v.* Turner, 45 Ala. 199.

Such compensation is one-half the fees allowed the solicitor on conviction in the case in which the conviction is had, and in case of dismissal or acquittal, one-half the fees that the solicitor would have been entitled to on conviction, to be determined by the character of the offense charged in the indictment. The grade of conviction governs the rate of compensation in case of conviction, and the mode of the indictment when there is no conviction. Commissioners' Court *v.* Turner, 45 Ala. 199.

§ 82. Employment of Attorney.

Contract of Employment Necessary.—An attorney's claim for services must rest on a contract of employment, express or implied, made with the person sought to be charged or his authorized agent. Irvin *v.* Strother, 163 Ala. 484, 50 So. 969; Humes *v.* Decatur Land, etc., Co., 98 Ala. 461, 13 So. 368; Milligan *v.* Alabama Fertilizer Co., 89 Ala. 322, 7 So. 650; Grimball *v.* Cruse, 70 Ala. 534, 544; Tisdale *v.* Troy, 152 Ala. 566, 44 So. 601.

Presumption.—In the absence of proof to the contrary, an attorney appearing for an infant plaintiff will be presumed to have been employed by the plaintiff's guardian or next friend. Hilliard *v.* Carr, 6 Ala. 557.

The presumption acquires increased strength from the fact that the same attorney made the complaint, and conducted the proceedings on the part of the plaintiff before the justice. Hilliard *v.* Carr, 6 Ala. 557, 560.

Employment by the President of a Corporation.—Where the president of a corporation, who is authorized to make contracts for it, employs attorneys to render services in an action to which he is a party, and in which the corporation is also interested, and the interests of both are fully disclosed to such attorneys, and nothing is said as to who is to be liable for such services, both the president and the corporation are liable. Humes *v.* Decatur Land, etc., Co., 98 Ala. 461, 13 So. 368.

Where there are two defendants, and one of them employs an attorney to represent both himself and the other defendant, of which the latter is apprised, he can not recover compensation of the latter. Humes *v.* Decatur Land, etc., Co., 98 Ala. 461, 13 So. 368, 372.

Employment by a Trustee to Obtain the Construction of a Will.—Where, in a bill by a trustee to obtain the construction of the will creating the trust, the cestui que trust having died, a claimant employs counsel to represent his interests, the counsel's fees can not be charged to the estate, nor a portion thereof to another claimant, who did not employ counsel, and who was benefited by the counsel's services through the decision obtained. Grimball *v.* Cruse, 70 Ala. 534.

§ 83. Premature Termination of Relation.

§ 83 (1) In General.

A counsel who, with the consent of his client, withdraws from a case, after having rendered beneficial services, does not thereby lose his right to compensation for the services rendered, unless, at the time of his withdrawal, he waives or abandons his claim to compensation. Coopwood *v.* Wallace, 12 Ala. 790.

Where a client engages a firm to prosecute a case, and one of the firm dies, and the client consents that a new firm into which the surviving partner enters shall continue in the case, and the senior member abandons the case, and the surviving partner of the old firm does nothing except to keep himself informed as to the status of the case for over five years, his conduct is a ratification of the act of the senior member in abandoning the case, and neither the new firm nor the surviving partner of the old firm is entitled to compensation. Troy *v.* Hall, 157 Ala. 592, 47 So. 1035.

§ 83 (2) Under Contract for Contingent Fee.

Where services are performed for a contingent fee, the attorney is not entitled to anything until the claim of his client, or some of it, has been collected, and therefore an abandonment of the case by the attorney before the termination of the case will deprive him of any compensation. Troy *v.* Hall, 157 Ala. 592, 47 So. 1035.

§ 84. Statutory Fees, and Taxed Costs.

For the successful prosecution of a proceeding by scire facias, on a forfeited recognizance, an attorney may claim a fee of six dollars, to be taxed in the bill of costs. Smith *v.* State, 7 Port. 492.

The attorney of the successful party is entitled to the taxed fee in a suit, and not the party himself. Gillis *v.* Holly, 19 Ala. 663.

§ 85. Value of Services.

§ 86. —— In General.

See ante, "What Constitutes a Retainer," § 27.

Where the amount of compensation is not fixed, by the terms of the contract, by which an attorney or solicitor is employed, he will be entitled to be paid such reasonable fees, as are usually paid to others, for similar services. Lecatt *v.* Sallee, 3 Port. 115, 123; Dickinson *v.* Bradford, 59 Ala. 581.

Recovery on a Quantum Meruit.—Where legal services have been performed under a contract providing that the fee should be such as any gentleman of the profession should consider reasonable, and the client has refused to so submit the ascertainment of the value of the services, a recovery can be had on a quantum meruit. Bank of Alabama *v.* Martin, 4 Ala. 615.

The fact that the defendant refused to submit to the arbitrament of a member of the legal profession the ascertainment of the value of the plaintiff's services; as the paper relied on as a contract contemplates, indicated an unwillingness on its part to have the extent of the liability of the bank admeasured, as the plaintiffs proposed; and authorized the latter to recover upon a quantum meruit. Bank *v.* Martin, 4 Ala. 615, 619.

On Proof That Services Are Worth More Than Agreed Fee.—An attorney at law can not recover more than he agreed to receive, by proof that his services were worth more. Coopwood *v.* Wallace, 12 Ala. 790.

Collection of Money under Void Execution.—An execution issued after death of the plaintiff therein is void, and plaintiff's attorney, who controlled the execution, and who knew the fact of her death, is not entitled to compensation out of money collected under it. Smith *v.* Alexander, 80 Ala. 251.

Where Client Was Killed before Trial.—An attorney can only recover pro tanto on a note given as a retainer to defend the maker in a prosecution for homicide, where such maker was killed by a mob before trial. Agnew *v.* Walden, 84 Ala. 502, 4 So. 672.

Considerations in Ascertaining Value of Services.—It is the practice in ascertaining the value of professional services rendered by an attorney to consider the amount, or value involved, in connection with the labor and skill used by the attorney, the reasonable expense incurred, and the benefits received. These may be considered together in forming a conclusion. Humes *v.* Decatur Land, etc., Co., 98 Ala. 461, 13 So. 368, 371.

§ 87. —— Specific Services and Particular Cases.

An agreement to pay $500 out of moneys collected in a specified suit for professional services in said case shown by extrinsic evidence to have been made after the decree is not on condition that future services shall be rendered, and therefore the refusal of the promisees to attend the suit in the appellate court will not impair the right to recover the sum stipulated. Walker *v.* Cuthbert, 10 Ala. 213.

§ 88. Contracts for Compensation.

§ 89. —— Making, Requisites, and Validity.

See ante, "In General," § 73 (1).

An attorney may, before entering on the business of his client, lawfully contract for the measure of his compensation; and any contract then made is as valid and unobjectionable as if made between other persons competent to contract with each other. Dickinson *v.* Bradford, 59 Ala. 581; Lecatt *v.* Sallee, 3 Port. 115.

Where plaintiffs were originally employed to represent the president of a cor oration, personally, a subsequent contract with defendant for their services, which imposed on them no additional duty, is not void for want of consideration, where its interest was many times greater than its president's. Humes *v.* Decatur Land, etc., Co., 98 Ala. 461, 13 So. 368.

Where two persons are jointly indicted and put upon trial, or if only one is upon trial, and either employs counsel to defend him, the fact that an acquittal of the one employing counsel must result in acquittal of the other will not render a contract of employment by the latter null and void. Humes *v.* Decatur Land, etc, Co., 98 Ala. 461, 13 So. 368, 373.

§ 90. —— Construction and Operation.

A written agreement by an attorney to attend to the business of a client, "pending and to be brought before the courts during the remainder of the year," does not oblige the attorney to attend to any business undetermined at the end of the year. Bank of Alabama *v.* Martin, 4 Ala. 615.

The defense of a county, by an attorney, against a bill filed to enjoin the issuance of bonds by it, as authorized by a special act of the legislature, for the building of public roads, was a matter "pertaining to the building and construction of turnpikes or macadamized roads," and a "matter relating thereto," within the meaning of a contract with such county providing that he should be paid a certain sum in full for his services for the county in all matters pertaining to the building of turnpikes or macadamized roads, and in all matters that may come before the county board in relation thereto. Lindsay *v.* Colbert County, 112 Ala. 409, 20 So. 637.

§ 91. Contingent Fees.

§ 92. —— Performance of Contract.

Where a firm of attorneys is retained to procure the granting of a license to sell liquor, under an agreement that they are to be paid a certain sum cash, and the balance "whenever a license to sell liquor is obtained or can be obtained," they can not recover the balance when their efforts to procure a license prove fruitless, but afterwards a license is obtained through the efforts of other parties. Cheney *v.* Kelly, 95 Ala. 163, 10 So. 664.

§ 93. Deductions and Forfeitures.

The failure of an attorney to be present at the final trial of a suit does not deprive him of his right to compensation, in the absence of anything to show that he was employed generally to represent his client's interest in the suit. Pearson *v.* Darrington, 32 Ala. 227.

It is no defense to an action on a promissory note given to an attorney, for services to be rendered by him in a cause in court, that he was absent during a term in which the cause was not reached, and that the case was afterwards compromised. Douglass *v.* Eason, 36 Ala. 697.

§ 94. Allowance and Payment from Funds in Court.

See post, "Services or Fees Covered," § 105.

It is not competent for a court of law, on motion, to order the sheriff to retain, out of money collected for a plaintiff, the charges of an attorney for commission, or compensation for extra services—not being costs or taxed fees. Long *v.* Lewis, 1 Stew. & P. 229.

Compensation Erroneously Granted.—When an attorney receives money, or any articles of value, by virtue of an order of court made in a cause in which he is counsel, and it is decreed, before he turns the same over to his client, that the order was erroneously granted, the court may order and enforce the restoration of the money to its former custodian. Pinkard *v.* Allen, 75 Ala. 73.

From Proceeds of Land Sold for Partition.—It seems too clear for disputation that counsel fees incurred by a complainant can not be allowed, independent of a statute authorizing such allowance, out of the proceeds of lands sold for partition by the chancery court among joint owners. Foster *v.* Foster, 126 Ala. 257, 28 So. 624; Strang *v.* Taylor, 82 Ala. 213, 2 So. 760; Grimball *v.* Cruse, 70 Ala. 534; Jordan *v.* Farrow, 130 Ala. 428, 30 So. 338.

§ 95. Actions for Compensation.

§ 96. —— Grounds of Action.

For all service performed by an attorney, an action for fees may be maintained. Lecatt *v.* Sallee, 3 Port. 115, 123.

Proofs of his original employment, or the performance of services with knowledge of the client, is sufficient to enable an attorney to maintain an action for professional services. Jackson *v.* Clopton, 66 Ala. 29.

§ 97. —— Defenses.

See ante, "In General," § 86, "Construction and Operation," § 90.

A contract with a bank to render legal services to it, and providing that the compensation should be left for future adjustment, since the amount of business was uncertain, but that the attorneys would receive what any gentleman of the bar would consider reasonable, is, at most, only an agreement to arbitrate, and will not bar an action where the bank has refused to submit the question of compensation to a member of the bar. Bank of Alabama *v.* Martin, 4 Ala. 615.

§ 98. —— Time to Sue, and Limitations.

An attorney at law, who, at the instance of the administrators of an estate, has rendered valuable services to the estate, may proceed at once against the estate, in equity, to recover his fee, without previously suing the administrators at law, where one has removed from the state, and the other has become insolvent, and neither of them has made any charge against the estate for the attorney's fee. Coopwood *v.* Wallace, 12 Ala. 790.

§ 99. —— Evidence.

§ 99 (1) In General.

In an action against a corporation to recover for services as associate counsel in an action in which defendant was interested, it is error to admit in evidence a section of defendant's by-laws to show how the general counsel's and president's "compensation was fixed," or for any other purpose, where there is no pretense that plaintiffs had no knowledge of the existence of such by-law. Humes *v.* Decatur Land, etc., Co., 98 Ala. 461, 13 So. 368.

In an action against a corporation to recover for services as an associate counsel, in an action in which the defendant was interested, where it appears that one B was defendant's general counsel, defendant contended that plaintiffs were not employed by it, evidence as to whether or not defendant paid B and its president a salary was properly excluded. Humes *v.* Decatur Land, etc., Co., 98 Ala. 461, 13 So. 368.

Proof of Rendition of Services.—Under a count on an account stated, an attorney's fees for services rendered under a special contract may be recovered on proof of rendition of the services, and defendant's subsequent admission to a third person, not the attorney's agent, of his indebtedness in the specified sum. Wharton *v.* Cain, 50 Ala. 408.

Admissibility of Answer and Cross Bill in Suit in Which the Attorney Appeared.—On an issue of implied contract of defendant to pay for services of plaintiff as attorney for her in a certain suit, the answer and cross bill prepared by plaintiff, signed by defendant and filed therein, are admissible to show not only the nature of services rendered, but knowledge of defendant of their rendition, and her acceptance thereof. Davis *v.* Walker, 131 Ala. 204, 31 So. 554.

§ 99 (2) Employment.

It is not necessary that an attorney should be able to prove the original employment, in order to entitle him to compensation; if he can show a recognition of him, by his client, as attorney in the progress of the suit, it is sufficient. Long *v.* Lewis, 1 Stew. & P. 229, 234.

To support his claim to compensation for professional services, an attorney may prove either his original employment by the client, or the performance of services with the knowledge of the client, and the recognition of the relation by the client during the progress of the cause. Jackson *v.* Clopton, 66 Ala. 29.

A recovery on implied contract may be had on proof of knowledge of defendant that plaintiff was rendering services for her as her attorney, and that she expressed no dissent to their rendition. Davis *v.* Walker, 131 Ala. 204, 31 So. 554.

On the issue whether there was an implied contract by defendant to pay for plaintiff's services as attorney for her in an action, it is immaterial what was the result of the case, what services were to be performed under another contract—the services in issue not being included—or what had been defendant's purpose in employing plaintiff under such other contract. Davis *v.* Walker, 131 Ala. 204, 31 So. 554.

Ratification of Unauthorized Employment.—Conceding that an attorney at law has no authority to employ another attorney to act for his client, yet, if he soon afterwards informs his client of such unauthorized employment, and the latter does not dissent from it, these facts are proper to be submitted to the jury, in an action brought by the second attorney to recover his fees, to enable them to determine whether the client did not assent to the employment. King *v.* Pope, 28 Ala. 601; Hitchcock *v.* McGehee, 7 Port. 556.

Insufficient to Show Employment.—The defendant sent a claim to a mercantile agency for collection, instructing them by letter that they or their attorneys were authorized to make any arrangements deemed by them necessary to a prompt collection thereof. Subsequently the attorney of defendant notified the plaintiffs, the attorneys in whose hands the claim was placed by the agency, of a settlement thereof, and directed a surrender to the debtor of the papers in their hands. Held, that this evidence did not show an employment of plaintiffs by defendant, and that defendant was not liable for the services performed. Milligan *v.* Alabama Fertilizer Co., 89 Ala. 322, 7 So. 650.

In an action by an attorney against a United States marshal for compensation for services rendered in an action to collect claims of his deputies against the government, evidence considered, and held insufficient to show that the attorney was retained by defendant, but that the services were rendered under a contract by which he was not bound. Tisdale *v.* Troy, 152 Ala. 566, 44 So. 601.

§ 99 (3) Value of Services or Amount of Compensation.

See ante, "In General," § 99 (1).

A champertous agreement to pay, as an attorney fee in a suit for slander, one-half of the amount recovered, is not admissible in evidence, as an aid in estimating the value of the services, on a count of quantum meruit. Holloway *v.* Lowe, 1 Ala. 246.

Where an attorney seeks to recover the value of his services in conducting a law suit, it is proper to show to what extent his services were beneficial to the defendant, and what fees are customary in similar cases. Holloway *v.* Lowe, 1 Ala. 246, 248.

In an action for attorney's services, proof as to what plaintiff has charged in other particular matters, varying in nature, was irrelevant. Fuller *v.* Stevens (Ala.), 39 So. 623.

Burden on the Attorney.—Standing in a relation of confidence, which gives the attorney or solicitor an advantage over the client, the burden of proof lies on the attorney or solicitor seeking to recover his fees; and to support the contract for compensation made while the relation existed, he must show the fairness of the transaction, and the adequacy of the consideration. Dickinson *v.* Bradford, 59 Ala. 581, 583.

Admissibility of Evidence to What Would Be a Reasonable Fee.—In an action against a corporation to recover for services as associate counsel in an action in which defendant was interested, but not a party, it is not error to permit defendant to ask plaintiff, on cross-examination, what would be a reasonable fee for such services, "employed at the time your firm was employed, to obtain specific performance of that contract, independent of the value of the land, looking only to the pleadings representing plaintiff's interest in said cause;" especially where there appears to be no contention as to the value of the services. Humes *v.* Decatur Land Improvement & Furnace Co., 98 Ala. 461, 13 So. 368.

§ 100. —— Trial.

§ 100 (1) Questions for Jury.

Conceding that an attorney at law has no authority to employ another attorney to act for his client, yet, if he soon afterwards informs his client of such unauthorized employment, and the latter does not dissent from it, these facts are proper to be submitted to the jury, in an action brought by the second attorney to recover his fees, to enable them to determine whether the client did not assent to the employment. King *v.* Pope, 28 Ala. 601, cited in note in 23 L. R. A., N. S., 708.

In an action by an attorney for compensation for services in conducting litigation, held a question for the jury whether plaintiff was looking to defendant for compensation, and whether defendant understood that he was so doing. Irvin *v.* Strother, 163 Ala. 484, 50 So. 969; Humes *v.* Decatur Land, etc., Co., 98 Ala. 461, 13 So. 368.

§ 100 (2) Instructions.

Where the evidence was conflicting as to whether the consideration of the note sued on was the services of the payee as attorney in the trial court should the maker be indicted, or for his general services in the case, and there had been no trial, but payee had procured bail for the maker by habeas corpus, it was error to instruct that if the parol understanding between the parties was that the note was not to be paid unless the maker was prosecuted before the trial court, and defended by the payee, there could be no recovery, since the evidence of the agreement was admissible only to explain the consideration of the note; and hence if the services rendered formed a part of the consideration of the note, its legal effect could not be varied by the parol agreement. Long *v.* Davis, 18 Ala. 801.

In an action by attorneys to recover for services rendered, it is proper to instruct the jury that in ascertaining, by their verdict, the value of the services, they have no right to go outside of the evidence, and act from their own knowledge, apart from the evidence before them, as their verdict must be rendered "according to the evidence" only. Moore *v.* Watts, 81 Ala. 261, 2 So. 278.

An instruction that proof that the services were performed is not sufficient to render defendant liable, unless there is also proof of knowledge and recognition thereof as having been rendered at the instance and request of defendant, is not erroneous. Humes *v.* Decatur Land Improvement & Furnace Co., 98 Ala. 461, 13 So. 368.

Instructions that defendant is not liable in an action against a corporation to recover for services as associate counsel in an action in which defendant was interested, unless plaintiffs were employed by it, though it was benefited by the services rendered, irrespective of what plaintiffs understood as to its liability, are not erroneous. Humes *v.* Decatur Land Improvement & Furnace Co., 98 Ala. 461, 13 So. 368.

In an action against a corporation to recover services as associate counsel in an action in which defendant was interested, there was evidence that the particular services plaintiffs were to render were originally agreed on, but that they were afterwards required to render greater services than those agreed on; that some of the latter services were rendered at the instance of the president of defendant, who succeeded the one who originally employed them; and that all the services rendered were accepted by it. Held, that instructions which ignored such testimony were erroneous. Humes *v.* Decatur Land Improvement & Furnace Co., 98 Ala. 461, 13 So. 368.

In an action against a corporation to recovery for services as associate counsel in an action in which defendant was interested, where defendant's president was plaintiff in the case, and he employed plaintiffs, it is not error to refuse to charge that if, at the time, nothing was said by either party as to the capacity in which he was acting, plaintiffs "had the right to presume, from all the circumstances of the case, that he was acting for and on behalf of defendant," when the court can not say that there is no evidence, other than the conversation had at that time, tending to rebut the circumstances which tend to show that defendant employed plaintiffs. Humes *v.* Decatur Land Improvement & Furnace Co., 98 Ala. 461, 13 So. 368.

In an action for attorney's services, it was error to refuse to charge that if the jury believed from the evidence that plaintiff made a contract with defendant for all the services, and if the price was agreed on, then it would make no difference how unreasonable the contract was, but that the jury could not charge defendant with any greater fees than those agreed on. Fuller *v.* Stevens (Ala.), 39 So. 623.

In an action for attorney's services, a request to charge that, after hearing all the evidence, it was for the jury to say whether the "charges" were reasonable or not, was properly refused as ambiguous, in that the word "charges" might be understood to refer to the charges of the court. Fuller *v.* Stevens (Ala.), 39 So. 623.

Where, in an action for attorney's services, a set off was pleaded and really litigated at the trial, it was not error to refuse to charge that, taking the evidence in the case as whole, the burden of proof was on plaintiff. Fuller *v.* Stevens (Ala.), 39 So. 623.

§ 100 (3) Verdict and Findings.

In a proceeding to determine the compensation to which an attorney is entitled for collecting certain claims which were compromised by the client, there was evidence tending to show that the attorney distinctly reserved his right to full compensation according to an agreement relating thereto if the client compromised the cause, and it was admitted that the services rendered by the attorney were worth the full amount claimed. Held that, giving the judgment of the court the force and effect of a verdict of a jury, it could not be said that its finding giving the attorney judgment for the full amount claimed was contrary to the evidence, though it was not shown that the compromises was made by the client in opposition to the advice of the attorney. Hall *v.* Gunter & Gunter, 157 Ala. 375, 47 So. 155.

(B) LIEN.

§ 101. Nature of Attorney's Lien.

See post, "Services or Fees Covered," § 105; "Judgment or Proceeds Thereof," § 106 (2); "Securities and Papers," § 106 (3).

The lien of an attorney or solicitor rests on the theory that he is to be regarded as an assignee of the judgment or decree, to the extent of his fee, from the date of the rendition of the judgment or decree, and is subject to all set-offs existing against it at the time. Ex parte Lehman, 59 Ala. 631; Mosely *v.* Norman, 74 Ala. 422.

An attorney's lien is not a general lien, operating as a security for any claim or demand, other than his fees, however meritorious it may be. Mosely *v.* Norman, 74 Ala. 422, 424.

§ 102. Statutory Provisions.

Code 1907, § 3011, giving an attorney at law a lien on his client's papers and money and upon the suit and judgment for his services, does not apply to a suit in progress at the time the section became effective, not being retroactive. Leahart *v.* Deedmeyer, 158 Ala. 295, 48 So. 371.

§ 103. Right to Lien.

§ 104. —— In General.

The courts have long recognized, and summarily enforced, the lien of attorneys and solicitors for fees, or, rather, reasonable compensation for services rendered by them in obtaining judgments or decrees for their clients, or for bringing a fund into court, which the court has power to control. Lehman Bros. *v.* Tallassee Mfg. Co., 64 Ala. 567, 603; Warfield *v.* Campbell, 38 Ala. 527; Jackson *v.* Clopton, 66 Ala. 29, 33; Thornton *v.* Highland Ave., etc., R. Co., 94 Ala. 353, 10 So. 442, 444; Fuller *v.* Clemmons, 158 Ala. 340, 48 So. 101.

For Services Rendered an Insolvent Corporation.—In an action to settle the affairs and marshal and distribute the assets of an insolvent corporation, attorneys who have performed services for the corporation, principally in contesting claims against, have no lien on a fund paid into court by the receivers, nor can they be preferred to other creditors. Lehman Bros *v.* Tallassee Mfg. Co., 64 Ala. 567.

§ 105. Services or Fees Covered.

See ante, "Allowance and Payment from Funds in Court," § 94.

An attorney's lien upon the judgment obtained for his client extends to the fees of counsel not embraced in the taxed costs. Warfield *v.* Campbell, 38 Ala. 527, repudiating what was intimated, to the contrary, in Long *v.* Lewis, 1 Stew. & P. 229, 234.

In Obtaining the Particular Judgment.—It is indispensable to the existence of an attorney's lien, that services should have been rendered or disbursements made, in and about obtaining the particular judgment or decree. A mere general debt due to the attorney is not the foundation of the lien. Jackson *v.* Clopton, 66 Ala. 29; Mosely *v.* Norman, 74 Ala. 422, 424; Higley *v.* White, 102 Ala. 604, 15 So. 141; Warfield *v.* Campbell, 38 Ala. 527; Ex parte Lehman, etc., Co., 59 Ala. 631.

§ 106. Subject Matter to Which Lien Attaches.

§ 106 (1) In General.

In this case the fund in court being the fruit of the litigation in which the attorney represented the claim of the infant, although employed by the guardian of the latter, he had a lien on it for any unpaid balance of his fee in that service, which the court will aid him in making available. Warfield *v.* Campbell, 38 Ala. 527; Ex parte Lehman, etc., Co., 59 Ala. 631; Grimball *v.* Cruse, 70 Ala. 534; Weaver *v.* Cooper, 73 Ala. 318, 320.

In any cause in which an attorney's lien may be declared and enforced, there must be a moneyed judgment or decree to which the lien may attach, or else it can not exist. Higley *v.* White, 102 Ala. 604, 15 So. 141, 143; Kelly *v.* Horsley, 147 Ala. 508, 41 So. 902.

§ 106 (2) Judgment or Proceeds Thereof.

An attorney at law or a solicitor in chancery has a lien upon a judgment or decree obtained for a client to the extent of the compensation agreed on; or if there be no agreement, to the extent to which, he is entitled to recover reasonable compensation of the client for the services rendered. Ex parte Lehman, etc., Co., 59 Ala. 631.

Dissenting from, and disapproving the suggestion in McCaa *v.* Grant, 43 Ala. 262, that the principal stated in Warfield *v.* Campbell, 38 Ala. 527, "needs limitation, before it can be regarded as settled law, and a rule of decision in all the courts of this state, in the language in which the opinion is announced." Warfield *v.* Campbell, 38 Ala. 527; Jackson *v.* Clopton, 66 Ala. 29; Grimball *v.* Cruse, 70 Ala. 534; Weaver *v.* Cooper, 73 Ala. 318; Mosely *v.* Norman, 74 Ala. 422; Higley *v.* White, 102 Ala. 604, 15 So. 141; Fuller *v.* Clemmons, 158 Ala. 340, 48 So. 101.

To Secure Associate Counsel's Fees.—An attorney's lien attaches to a judgment recovered by him for his client, not only to secure his own reasonable fees, but it protects him in the payment of like reasonable fees to other attorneys or counsel who are employed in the same suit by the client. The reason is, that they have jointly a lien on the fund collected under the judgment, which embraces a right to have their fees satisfied out of it, where no intervening equities accrue in favor of third parties to defeat such lien. Jackson *v.* Clopton, 66 Ala. 29.

Attorneys have not lien upon a decree rendered in a probate court on a guardian's final settlement, for services in enforcing the payment of such decree, where the money is not paid to them. McCaa *v.* Grant, 43 Ala. 262.

§ 106 (3) Securities and Papers.

An attorney has a lien on the papers, placed in his hands by his client, for the payment of his fees. Warfield *v.* Campbell, 38 Ala. 527; Blunt *v.* Bates, 40 Ala. 470; Mosely *v.* Norman, 74 Ala. 422.

He therefore has an interest in a note sued on, by virtue of the lien which the law confers. Blunt *v.* Bates, 40 Ala. 470, 473.

§ 106 (4) Land.

A decree fixing defendant's debt to complainant at a certain sum, and charging it as a lien on specified land, which, in default of payment within a fixed time, is to be sold by the clerk, and return made to the court, is not such a judgment for land as to be exempt from complainant's counsel's lien for services in the case. Higley *v.* White, 102 Ala. 604, 15 So. 141.

Lien Limited to Judgment.—An attorney's lien for services is limited to the judgment recovered in the case in which the services were rendered, and does not extend to his client's lands or other like property which was the subject of litigation. McWilliams *v.* Jenkins, 72 Ala. 480; Hinson *v.* Gamble, 65 Ala. 605; Higley *v.* White, 102 Ala. 604, 15 So. 141; Kelly *v.* Horsley, 147 Ala. 508, 41 So. 902.

Defending Title to Land.—An attorney has no lien on his client's land for fees for rendering services defending the land. Lee *v.* Winston, 68 Ala. 402; Hinson *v.* Gamble, 65 Ala. 605.

Defending Title to Separate Estate of Married Woman.—Prior to the passage of the act approved March 1st, 1881, amending § 2711 of the Code (Sess. Acts 1880-81, p. 36), professional services rendered by an attorney at law in defending the title to property belonging to the statutory separate estate of a married woman, were not chargeable upon her estate. Hinson *v.* Gamble, 65 Ala. 605.

Prosecuting Suit for Land.—A solicitor who has successfully prosecuted a suit in equity to establish his client's title to real estate has no lien on such real estate for his fees. McCullough *v.* Flournoy, 69 Ala. 189; Hinson *v.* Gamble, 65 Ala. 605, cited and approved. Carroll *v.* Draughon, 154 Ala. 430, 45 So. 919.

§ 107. Time When Lien Attaches.

An attorney's lien does not arise or attach until the rendition of the judgment or decree. Mosely *v.* Norman, 74 Ala. 422.

§ 108. Priorities.

An administrator and guardian having, on his final account, obtained a decree against the estate for debts contracted in behalf of his wards, the distributees, upon the production of the creditor's receipt, given under an agreement that the decree should inure to the creditor's benefit, and it being shown that the administrator was insolvent, an assignment of the decree to the creditor will be upheld as against an attorney's lien for services in the accounting. Mosely *v.* Norman, 74 Ala. 422.

An attorney is regarded as an assignee of the judgment or decree, pro tanto—to the extent of his fee—from the date of its rendition. It is consequently subordinate to all counterclaims, or set-offs, existing at the time, including, of necessity, such as are allowed prior to the rendition of the judgment. Jackson *v.* Clopton, 66 Ala. 29; Ex parte Lehman, etc., Co., 59 Ala. 631; Warfield *v.* Campbell, 38 Ala. 527; McWilliams *v.* Jenkins, 72 Ala. 480, 487; Mosely *v.* Norman, 74 Ala. 422; Higley *v.* White, 102 Ala. 604, 15 So. 141.

§ 109. Waiver, Loss, or Discharge.

Where attorneys, after having collected a judgment in favor of their client, paid over a certain portion of the fund without any adjustment or agreement as to their fees except the implied contract that they were to receive reasonable compensation, the payments so made were voluntary, and by making the same they released their lien for services on the money so paid. German *v.* Browne, 137 Ala. 429, 34 So. 985.

That the amount of a decree was paid to assistant counsel for plaintiff in the case, who had authority to receive it, having themselves a lien upon the decree for their services as attorneys, could not in equity operate to defeat the lien thereon of plaintiff's principal attorney.

Fuller *v.* Clemmons, 158 Ala. 340, 48 So. 101.

§ 110. Protection against Assignment by Client.

See ante, "Priorities," § 108.

"An assignment of the subject matter of suit, while the suit is pending, or of the judgment or decree after its rendition, ought not to affect, and is not allowed to effect, the lien of an attorney or solicitor upon the judgment or decree; the assignment is subordinate to the lien." Mosely *v.* Norman, 74 Ala. 422, 426.

§ 111. Protection against Settlement between Parties.

§ 112. —— In General.

An attorney's lien is protected against all collusive dealings between the client and the party against whom the judgment or decree is rendered. Mosely *v.* Norman, 74 Ala. 422, 424.

An attorney's lien on a promissory note in his hands for collection gives him no right in a judgment against the defendant on the note for the amount of his fees, after the debt has been paid by the defendant to the plaintiff, either in the name of his client or in his own. Tillman *v.* Reynolds, 48 Ala. 365.

A client, whether he has employed the attorney or not, has a right to make any settlement or compromise he may please with the defendant, and to order the dismissal of the case. Ex parte Randall, 149 Ala. 640, 42 So. 870.

Neither a party or his attorney should be heard to say that an agreement of compromise made by the parties was in actual or legal fraud of the attorney's right to a lien or the attorney at least should be required to show by petition or motion in his own name his right to proceed with the suit, notwithstanding the compromise. Western Ry. of Alabama *v.* Foshee (Ala.), 62 So. 500.

§ 113. —— Remedies of Attorney.

§ 113 (1) In General.

After a decree had been rendered, on bill filed in equity by a judgment creditor against the debtor, ordering a sale of the defendant's property for the payment of complainant's demand, the parties came together, and entered into a compromise, the complainant, in consideration of small sum paid by the defendant, executing a receipt in full of her demand. Afterwards, the complainant's solicitors filed a petition in the cause, alleging the insolvency of their client, and the compromise made by the parties, and praying a reference to ascertain what would be a reasonable compensation to them for their services in the cause, and directions to the register to proceed with the sale for the payment of such compensation. Held, that no ground for the interference of a court of equity is shown, and that a decree of the chancery court, granting the relief prayed in the petition, was erroneous. Connor *v.* Boyd. 73 Ala. 385.

§ 113 (2) Vacation of Settlement and Proceeding with Original Suit.

Plaintiff, in a decree of the probate court, rendered on final settlement of the guardianship, employed certain attorneys to collect the money mentioned in said decree, at a stipulated fee for their services. The attorneys had had no connection with the case before the decree was rendered, but succeeded in enforcing the payment of the money thereon, which did not come into their hands or into the possession of the court. Held, that said attorneys could not, under such circumstances, go into the probate court, and by motion therein, in their own name, as plaintiffs against defendant in the decree, have set aside an entry of satisfaction in full, except costs, which had been made by order of plaintiff on an execution issued to the sheriff while the same was in his hands. McCaa *v.* Grant, 43 Ala. 262.

§ 114. Protection against Set-Off between Parties.

See ante, "Priorities," § 108.

An attorney's lien upon the judgment which he has recovered to secure his counsel fees will prevail over a set-off acquired by the judgment debtor, after the rendition of the judgment. Warfield *v.* Campbell, 38 Ala. 527.

§ 115. Enforcement.

§ 115 (1) In General.

An attorney's lien, when he has a lien,

can not be enforced by an involuntary judgment against the defendant, in a court of law. McCaa *v.* Grant, 43 Ala. 262; Tillman *v.* Reynolds, 48 Ala. 365, 368.

An attorney's lien has in it much of an equity, especially in its operation upon judgments or decrees; and in its protection and enforcement, a court of law exercises its inherent powers to regulate and control its own process, often denominated the equitable powers of the court. Mosely *v.* Norman, 74 Ala. 422, 425.

§ 115 (2) Proceedings.

Petition.—In an equitable proceeding by a solicitor of a creditor of an insolvent estate, to establish a lien on the funds in the hands of the register for his fees, the same particularity is not required in the petition as would be required in a bill filed for the same purpose, since the parties and the record of the proceeding are constructively before the court. Weaver *v.* Cooper, 73 Ala. 318.

If the amount of a decree were paid into the registry of the court, the more orderly procedure by an attorney to enforce a lien thereon for attorney fees would be by petition to the chancellor, instead of by an original bill. Fuller *v.* Clemmons, 158 Ala. 340, 48 So. 101.

Filing of Bill.—A bill to enforce an alleged lien for attorney's fees on a money decree is not a bill to alter or disturb that decree, and need not be filed at the term of court at which the decree was rendered. Fuller *v.* Clemmons, 158 Ala. 340, 48 So. 101.

When Notice Dispensed with.—The only necessary party defendant to the petition, of an attorney seeking to establish a lien on funds of his client, the party for whose benefit the services were rendered, having appeared and answered, notice of the petition was thereby dispensed with. Weaver *v.* Cooper, 73 Ala. 318.

Defenses.—On petition by a solicitor of a creditor of an insolvent estate, in administration suit in equity, to establish a lien on the funds in the hands of the register, it is no defense that some of the services were rendered in the probate court from which the case was removed to chancery. Weaver *v.* Cooper, 73 Ala. 318.

ATTORNEY GENERAL.

Cross References.

See the titles APPEAL AND ERROR; APPEARANCE; CERTIORARI; CONSTITUTIONAL LAW; COURTS; DISMISSAL AND NONSUIT; DISTRICT AND PROSECUTING ATTORNEYS; MANDAMUS; MUNICIPAL CORPORATIONS; OFFICERS; PUBLIC LANDS; QUO WARRANTO; STATES; TERRITORIES; UNITED STATES.

As to authority of attorney general to sue in name of state, see the title STATES.

As to nature of proceedings upon writ of habeas corpus, see the title HABEAS CORPUS.

§ 1. Powers and Duties.

§ 2. —— In General.

Supervisory Power over Accounts of United States Marshals.—The attorney general of the United States has vested in him by § 368, Rev. St. U. S., a general supervisory power over the accounts of the United States marshals, and his decision of any point connected with the subject is conclusive, and not subject to collateral attack by the courts. Schloss *v.* Hewlett, 81 Ala. 266, 1 So. 263. See, also, Dowling *v.* Blackman, 70 Ala. 303.

Certificate of Acknowledgment to Tax Deed.—Code, § 594, requiring the attorney general to furnish the auditor with suitable forms of certificates of purchase and deeds to purchasers at tax sales, does not authorize him to furnish a form of certificate of acknowledgment to a tax deed, so as to validate it, contrary to the form prescribed by statute. Jackson *v.* Kirksey, 110 Ala. 547, 18 So. 304.

Attorney in Fact.

See the title PRINCIPAL AND AGENT.

Attorneys' Fees.

See the title ATTORNEY AND CLIENT.

Attornment.

See the title LANDLORD AND TENANT.

AUCTIONS AND AUCTIONEERS.

Cross References.

See the titles JUDICIAL SALES; PRINCIPAL AND AGENT; SALES; VENDOR AND PURCHASER.

As to whether auction sales are within statute of frauds, see the title FRAUDS, STATUTE OF. As to whether signing of contract of sale by the auctioneer, is a sufficient signing, within statute of frauds, see the title FRAUDS, STATUTE OF. As to rights of a purchaser at sheriffs' sale, see the title JUDICIAL SALES. As to passing of legal title by a deed made in name of auctioneer under a power given in mortgage, see the title MORTGAGES.

§ 1. Statutory Regulations.

See post, "Licenses and Taxes," § 3.

§ 2. Persons Subject to Regulation.

See post, "Licenses and Taxes," § 3.

§ 3. Licenses and Taxes.

Acts 1896-97, p. 1505, § 35, dividing cities and towns into classes according to population, and imposing license taxes on auctioneers engaged therein, the amount being different for each class, is not unconstitutional as discriminating between persons engaged in the same occupation. O'Hara *v.* State, 121 Ala. 28, 25 So. 622.

§ 4. Agency of Auctioneer.

See, generally, the title PRINCIPAL AND AGENT.

An auctioneer is the agent of the purchaser, of either lands or goods, at auction, to sign a contract for him, as the highest bidder. Adams *v.* McMillan, 7 Port. 73.

§ 5. Conduct and Validity of Sale.

As to rights and liabilities of seller and

buyer, see post, "Rights and Liabilities of Seller and Buyer," § 6.

§ 6. Rights and Liabilities of Seller and Buyer.

Who May Object to Defective Memorandum of Sale.—Only the parties to the sale can take advantage of any defects or irregularities in the memorandum made by the auctioneer; and if they complete the sale without objection, by payment of the purchase money, and execution and acceptance of a deed, it does not lie in the mouth of the mortgagor, whose lands were thus sold under a power contained in the mortgage, when sued by the purchaser, to object to the sufficiency of the memorandum made by the auctioneer, or to the fact that the mortgagee's agent acted as auctioneer at the sale. Lewis *v.* Wells, 50 Ala. 198.

To authorize awarding as damages the difference between the price at which the land was first bid off, and the price at which it was sold on resale, it must appear that the second sale was conducted fairly. Adams *v.* McMillan, 7 Port. 73.

Attempt to Prevent Bidding.—An association formed to prevent competition at auction sales of public lands, and to purchase such lands and resell same at an increased price, is illegal. Carrington *v.* Caller, 2 Stew. 175, cited in note in 20 L. R. A. 547.

The mere attempt of a purchaser to prevent another person from bidding for it will not render the purchase invalid; to have this effect, the attempt must have been successful. Haynes *v.* Crutchfield, 7 Ala. 189, cited in note in 20 L. R. A. 551.

§ 7. Compensation and Lien of Auctioneer.

Where an auctioneer was employed by an administrator to sell property belonging to the estate, and made sales to the amount of $75,981.08, a register's finding that the reasonable value of his services was 1½ per cent, or $1,139.71, was improperly modified by the chancellor, so as to increase the same to 3 per cent of the gross sales and interest. Andrews *v.* Frierson, 144 Ala. 470, 39 So. 512.

§ 8. Actions by or against Auctioneers.

As to rights and liabilities of seller and buyer, see ante, "Rights and Liabilities of Seller and Buyer," § 6.

AUDITA QUERELA.

Cross References.

See, generally, the titles EXECUTION; JUDGMENT; SUPERSEDEAS.

Nature and Scope of Remedy.—The practice of granting summary relief on petition or motion has practically superseded the remedy by audita querela. Edwards *v.* Lewis, 16 Ala. 813; Bruce *v.* Barnes, 20 Ala. 219.

The proceeding by petition and supersedeas has been substituted for that by audita querela. Dunlap *v.* Clements, 18 Ala. 778.

The writ of audita querela has been supplanted in Alabama by a proceeding by supersedeas. Henderson *v.* Planters' & Merchants' Bank of Ozark (Ala.), 59 So. 493; Thompson *v.* Lassiter, 86 Ala. 540, 6 So. 33.

Auditing Claims.

See the titles COUNTIES; MUNICIPAL CORPORATIONS; SCHOOLS AND SCHOOL DISTRICTS; STATES; TOWNS.

Auditor.

See the titles ACCOUNT; COUNTIES; REFERENCE; TOWNS; and other appropriate titles.

Auditor of the State.

See the title STATES.

Authentic Acts.

See the titles CHATTEL MORTGAGES; DEEDS; MORTGAGES.

Authentication.

As to authentication of particular papers, instruments, etc., see the appropriate titles.

Authorities.

See the titles APPEAL AND ERROR; COURTS.

Authority.

As to authority to perform particular acts, duties and functions, in individual or official capacity, see the appropriate titles.

Automatic Appliances.

See the titles CARRIERS; MASTER AND SERVANT; RAILROADS.

Automobiles.

As to licensing, regulating, etc., automobiles, see the titles CONSTITUTIONAL LAW; HIGHWAYS; LICENSES; MUNICIPAL CORPORATIONS. As to rights, duties, and liabilities, civil and criminal, see the titles CRIMINAL LAW; HIGHWAYS; MASTER AND SERVANT.

Autopsy.

See the titles CORONERS; DEAD BODIES; HOMICIDE.

Autrefois Acquit.

See the title CRIMINAL LAW.

Avocation.

See the titles EXEMPTIONS; LICENSES.

Avoidance.

As to avoidance of particular instruments, contracts, conveyances, etc., see the appropriate titles. As to pleading matter in avoidance, see the title PLEADING.

Avulsion.

See the title NAVIGABLE WATERS.

Award.

See the title ARBITRATION AND AWARD. As to award for maintenance, support, etc., of wife or child, see the titles BASTARDS; GUARDIAN AND WARD; HUSBAND AND WIFE; INFANTS; PARENT AND CHILD. As to award of costs, see the title COSTS.

Award of Contracts.

See the titles COUNTIES; MUNICIPAL CORPORATIONS; STATES.

Badge of Fraud.

See the titles FRAUD; FRAUDULENT CONVEYANCES.

Baggage.

See the titles CARRIERS; INNKEEPERS.

BAIL.

Cross References.

As to liability of officers as bail, see the title SHERIFFS AND CONSTABLES. As to review of decision relating to bail, see the titles APPEAL AND ERROR; CERTIORARI; CRIMINAL LAW; HABEAS CORPUS. As to execution of bail bond on Sunday, see the title SUNDAY. As to bail for appearance of witnesses, see the title WITNESSES. As to recognizances in general, see the title RECOGNIZANCES. As to validity of contract to indemnify bail, see the title CONTRACTS. As to attorney as sureties on bail bonds, see the title ATTORNEY AND CLIENT. As to bail in bastardy proceedings, see the title BASTARDS.

I. IN CIVIL ACTIONS.

§ 1. Application.

Affidavit.—It is not important at what time an affidavit, which may be made in an application for bail, be filed—so it be made before the order for bail. But where, in a case where such issue arose, a jury interposed between the issue and the judgment, it was held, that this court would regard the verdict as a nullity, in respect to the sufficiency of the affidavit, and presume that judgment of the court, upon the affidavit, was given. Magee *v.* Erwin, 5 Stew. & P. 54. See the title AFFIDAVITS.

§ 2. Bond, Undertaking, or Recognizance.

As to criminal proceedings, see post, "Bond, Undertaking, or Recognizance," § 27; "Bonds, Undertaking, or Recognizance on Appeal," § 34.

§ 3. —— Recitals.

A bail bond with the condition that the principal shall appear at the court indicated by the writ, and answer the plaintiff, is good, although it contains no recital that the party was arrested. Walker *v.* Massey, 10 Ala. 30.

§ 4. —— Conditions and Obligations.

The condition of a bail bond for the appearance of the defendants in the original cause, at the return term, for their attendance, from term to term, until discharged, is sufficient to charge the obligees as special bail. Embree *v.* Norris, 2 Ala. 271.

A bond conditioned for appearance at a term not appointed by law for the holding of the court is void. Allen *v.* White, Minor 289.

§ 5. —— Errors and Irregularities.

"All irregularities, as to taking bail, may be taken advantage of, on motion, at the return term. Whether it can afterwards, is questionable. Glidden *v.* Leonard, 4 Port. 194, 197.

§ 6. Extent of Liability.

"In all cases where the principal is liable for interest, the bail are so likewise, and also for the costs of the sci. fa." Kenan *v.* Carr, 10 Ala. 867, 874.

§ 7. Proceedings for Fixing Liability or Foreclosure.

General Rule.—"At common law, it was necessary, in order to charge the bail, that a capias ad satisfaciendum should be sued out, and directed to the sheriff of the county in which the defendant was arrested, and be returned 'non est inventus.'" Kennedy *v.* Spencer, 4 Port. 428, 432; Woodward *v.* Harbin, 4 Ala. 534, 536; Brown *v.* Simpson, 3 Stew. 331.

"Our statute directs, that the plaintiff shall not proceed against the bail, 'until execution hath been returned, that the defendant is not to be found in his proper county." Kennedy *v.* Spencer, 4 Port. 428, 432.

Irregularities in Issuance or Return.—Mere irregularities in the issuance of the ca. sa., as that there were not fifteen days between its teste and return, or that it did not remain in the sheriff's office a number of days, can not be urged as a defense by bail. Kenan *v.* Carr, 10 Ala. 867.

The return of a capias ad satisfaciendum "Not found" is the foundation of the liability of bail given in an action of debt, but the surety is not liable after such a return on a ca. sa., which by mistake of the clerk was returnable at a time prior to the date of issuance. Brown *v.* Simpson, 3 Stew. 331.

When Principals Moves to Another County.—In scire facias against bail, it need not be shown that a ca. sa. issued to the county to which the principal may have removed after his arrest. Kennedy *v.* Spencer, 4 Port. 428.

Where a ca. sa. issues to the county to which the principal has removed after his arrest, a return of non est is not necessary to charge the bail. Kennedy *v.* Spencer, 4 Port. 428.

§ 8. Relief from Liability or Foreclosure.

As to criminal proceedings, see post, "Relief from Liability or Forfeiture," § 42.

§ 9. —— In General.

Where the sheriff takes insufficient bail, and, on motion of the plaintiff, he is substituted for the bail so taken by him, the bail is entitled, on motion, to have an exoneretur entered on the bail piece. Smith *v.* Dennis, 3 Ala. 248.

§ 10. —— Surrender of Principal.

Bail are liable for the debt on the return of non est inventus to a ca. sa. properly sued out, and are authorized to arrest and surrender their principal in discharge of themselves, in the same manner as before the act. Kennedy *v.* Rice, 1 Ala. 11.

§ 11. Action or Scire Facias on Bond, Undertaking or Recognizance.

As to criminal proceedings, see post, "Action or Scire Facias on Bond, Undertaking, or Recognizance," § 45.

§ 12. —— Defenses.

Nothing can be pleaded by bail, which could have been used by his principal, in defense to the action against him. Toulmin *v.* Bennett, 3 Stew. & P. 220.

Cause of Action—Affidavit.—Bail will not be allowed to dispute the cause of action or the truth of the affidavit filed by the plaintiff, as a prerequisite to the demand of bail. Kennedy *v.* Rice, 1 Ala. 11.

Failure of Plaintiff to Comply with Statute.—In debt on sci. fa. against bail, the bail will be permitted to show by plea that the plaintiff did not comply with the requirements of the statutes before demanding bail. Kennedy *v.* Rice, 1 Ala. 11.

It is a good plea to scire facias, against bail, that the plaintiff has not given security for costs, as required by the statute. Toulmin *v.* Bennett, 3 Stew. & P. 220.

Invalidity of Bond.—In sci. fa. against bail, it is competent for the bail to show by plea that the plaintiff has not given security for costs, and that therefore the bail bond is void. Wood *v.* Yonge, 9 Port. 208.

§ 13. —— Process.

Sufficiency.—The affidavit or order for bail need not be set forth in the sci. fa. Glidden *v.* Leonard, 4 Port. 194.

In scire facias against bail, it is not necessary to insert an entire copy of the bail bond. A reasonable certainty in describing the record upon which the action is founded is all that is required. Toulmin *v.* Bennett, 3 Stew. & P. 220; Kennedy *v.* Spencer, 4 Port. 428.

Under the practice, it is unnecessary to set out, in a scire facias against bail, that the principal appeared to the action against him. Kenan *v.* Carr, 10 Ala. 867.

§ 14. —— Pleading.

Sufficiency.—In an action against bail, it is unnecessary to show in the declaration, the return on the scire facias. Kenan *v.* Carr, 10 Ala. 867.

It is not a sufficient assignment of a breach of a bond for special bail to allege that the defendants have failed to deliver their bodies to the court or the sheriff, and that the sureties have also failed to do so, "and otherwise to discharge the bond," without also alleging a failure to satisfy the condemnation of the court. Embree *v.* Norris, 2 Ala. 271.

Variance.—In declaring in scire facias against bail, it is no ground of objection to the proceedings that the writ vouches the record for the affidavit to warrant the ca. sa., and for the ca. sa. itself, but the declaration contains an averment that these papers had been lost since the writ was issued. Kenan *v.* Carr, 10 Ala. 867.

A plea in abatement in dispute against bail must allege the existence of facts which authorized them as bail to defend suit. Deforest *v.* Elkins, 2 Ala. 50.

§ 15. —— Judgment and Enforcement Thereof.

Judgment by Default.—Where all the proceedings against the principal are set out in the scire facias against the bail, and the bond is executed to the sheriff as sheriff, conditioned as a bail bond, this is sufficient to warrant a judgment by default, although no declaration is filed. Walker *v.* Massey, 10 Ala. 30.

II. IN CRIMINAL PROSECUTION.

§ 16. Nature and Scope of Remedy.

"**Bail signifies** a guardian, or keeper, etc. A man bailed is, where any one arrested, or in prison, is delivered to others as his bail, who ought to keep him to be ready to appear at a time assigned, or otherwise to answer for him." Hammons *v.* State, 59 Ala. 164, 168.

"Bail is a delivery of a person to his sureties, upon their giving, together with himself, sufficient security for his appearance; he being supposed to continue in their friendly custody instead of going to jail." Bearden *v.* State, 89 Ala. 21, 7 So. 755.

"The undertaking of bail binds the parties for the appearance of the defendant. Code of 1876, §§ 4852, 4853; State *v.* Weaver, 18 Ala. 293; State *v.* Eldred, 31 Ala. 393." Peck *v.* State, 63 Ala. 201, 203.

"'The undertaking of bail, binds the parties thereto, jointly and severally, for the appearance of the defendant, on the first day of the court, from day to day of such term, and from day to day of each term thereafter, until he is discharged by law.' Code, § 4427." State *v.* Crosby, 114 Ala. 11, 22 So. 110, 111.

At common law, when bail was given, and the principal relieved from the custody of the law, he was regarded, not as freed entirely, but as transferred to the "friendly custody" of his bail. They had a dominion over him, and it was their right, at any time, to arrest and surrender him again to the custody of the law, in discharge of their obligation. They were sometimes said to be his jailors. This right of bail is of such importance that it has been introduced into, affirmed, and regulated by the Alabama statutes. Cain *v.* State, 55 Ala. 170, 173.

§ 17. Right to Release on Bail.

§ 18. —— In General.

Admission to bail at common law was not a matter of right, but rested in a sound judicial discretion, and its allowance was the exercise of judicial power. In this state it has been controlled by constitutional and statutory provisions. Hammons *v.* State, 59 Ala. 164.

Capital Cases—Constitutional Provisions.—The fortieth section of the eighth chapter of the Penal Code (Clay's Dig., p. 444), by which it is enacted that, if the defendant in capital cases is not tried at the first term at which he is properly triable, on account of any of the causes therein specified, he shall not be entitled to bail as a matter of right, but that he may claim to be discharged on bail if he is not tried at the second term, unless the failure is occasioned by his own fault or misfortune, or on his application, or with his assent, is not repugnant to the seventeenth section of the first article of the constitution, by which it is declared that "all persons before conviction shall be bailable by sufficient securities, except for capital offenses where the proof is evident and the presumption great." Ex parte Croom, 19 Ala. 561.

Continuances in General.—The defendant in a capital case is not entitled to bail as a matter of right on account of continuances which were four in number, where they were twice on account of defects in the venire or its service, once for want of time, and the remaining time on account of the sickness of the presiding judge. Ex parte Carroll, 36 Ala. 300.

Where a prisoner, indicted for murder, after the case has been continued by the state and at the same term, applies for and obtains a change of venue, the continuance is necessarily set aside, and will not authorize him, upon the case being continued by the state in the court to which it is transferred, to claim, as a matter of right, that he be admitted to bail on the ground that the state has twice continued the cause. Ex parte Johnson, 18 Ala. 414.

Where the trial of a party charged with a capital offense is continued at one term on account of the incompetency of the presiding judge to try him, and at the succeeding term by the state, without his fault or assent, he is entitled as a matter of legal right to be admitted to bail, and this notwithstanding the cause had been previously continued at his instance. Ex parte Stiff, 18 Ala. 464, cited in note in 39 L. R. A., N. S., 769.

A prisoner may insist on his right to be

discharged on bail on account of a premature unauthorized adjournment at the first term of which he was properly triable, although, at the time of adjournment, he was confined in the custody of the sheriff, at a place several miles distant from the courthouse, and the sheriff was advised by physicians that it was unsafe to remove him on account of his wounds, and although he made no application for a trial, and might have continued his trial on account of his situation. Ex parte Croom, 19 Ala. 561.

Continuances Due to Absent Witnesses.—The right to bail in capital cases, on account of continuances by the state (Code, §§ 3671-72), is confined to cases which have twice been continued "for the testimony of absent witnesses." Ex parte Carroll, 36 Ala. 300; Ex parte Johnson, 18 Ala. 414.

A person committed for a felony, if not tried at the next term of the court where the offense is cognizable, is entitled to be set at liberty on bail, unless it appear that the witnesses for the state could not be produced, or that the defendant assented to the delay. Ex parte Simonton, 9 Port. 390, 33 Am. Dec. 320.

The fortieth section of the eighth chapter of the Pénal Code, which declares that no person charged with an offense capitally punished shall, as a matter of right, be admitted to bail, when he is not tried at the term of the court at which he was first triable, if the failure to try proceeded from the nonattendance of the state's witnesses, "where an affidavit is made satisfactorily accounting for their absence," does not make it imperative upon the supreme or any other court to admit the accused to bail because such an affidavit was not made and acted on by the court in which the indictment is pending, but it is competent for the judge or court which directs the prisoner to be brought up on habeas corpus to allow the affidavit to be made. Ex parte Chaney, 8 Ala. 424; cited in note in 39 L. R. A., N. S., 757.

Where bail is applied for because of a continuance on the unsworn statement of the prosecutor, if the statement is verified before the hearing of the application for bail such application may be denied. Ex parte Campbell, 20 Ala. 89.

Failure to Indict.—Where a prisoner is committed for an assault with intent to kill and murder, and it is shown that the person wounded is in danger of dying before the expiration of a year and a day from the time the wound was inflicted, the prisoner is not entitled to bail as a matter of right, because no indictment has been found against him, although two terms of the court at which he might have been indicted have elapsed since his commitment, unless it is also shown that he would be entitled to bail if death should ensue within the year and day. Ex parte Andrews, 19 Ala. 582; cited in note in 39 L. R. A., N. S., 768.

§ 19. —— Bailable Offense.

"By the common law, all offenses, however high, including murder and other felonies, and treason, were and still are bailable, before indictment found; though not as matter of right in cases of capital felonies, but as matter of judicial discretion." Ex parte McAnally, 53 Ala. 495, 496, cited in note in 39 L. R. A., N. S., 753, 754, 760, 775, 784.

Under the constitution and laws of Alabama, every person charged with crime, whether before or after indictment found, is entitled to bail before conviction as matter of right, except when the offense may be punished capitally; and even then, if the proof is not evident or the presumption great, of defendant's guilt, he should be enlarged on bail. Ex parte McAnally, 53 Ala. 495; Ex parte Croom, 19 Ala. 561, 570.

Capital Cases.—Murder is bailable except when the proof is evident or the presumption strong. Ex parte Banks, 28 Ala. 89; Ex parte Dykes, 83 Ala. 114, 3 So. 306; Ex parte King, 86 Ala. 620, 5 So. 863. See note in 39 L. R. A., N. S., 755, 756, 782.

Where, from all the evidence, the proof is not "evident" that a capital crime has been committed by defendant, he should be admitted to bail. Ex parte Bryant, 34 Ala. 270, cited in note in 39 L. R. A., N. S., 753, 757, 772, 784.

A prisoner accused of homicide is, under Const., art. 1, § 17, entitled to bail, where the evidence against him is all circumstantial, unless it excludes, to a moral certainty, every other reasonable hypothesis but that of his guilt. Ex parte Acree, 63 Ala. 234, cited in note in 39 L. R. A., N. S., 757.

Although, since the adoption of the Penal Code, the jury have the power, in all cases of murder in the first degree, of determining whether the punishment shall be death or imprisonment for life in the penitentiary, yet this does not make the offense less capital than before. The inquiry before the magistrate, on a question of bail, still is whether the offense charged may be capitally punished; if it may, and the proof is evident or the presumption great, it is not bailable. Ex parte McCrary, 22 Ala. 65, cited in note in 39 L. R. A., N. S., 772, 774.

Determination of Question.—Generally, bail should be denied whenever the trial court would sustain a verdict of conviction for a capital offense, if rendered on the same evidence introduced on the application for bail. Ex parte McAnally, 53 Ala. 495, 25 Am. Rep. 646; Ex parte Nettles, 58 Ala. 268; Ex parte Brown, 65 Ala. 446; Ex parte Sloane, 95 Ala. 22, 11 So. 14; Ex parte Richardson, 96 Ala. 110, 11 So. 316; Ex parte Alfen, 55 Ala. 258; Ex parte Warrick, 73 Ala. 57. See note in 39 L. R. A., N. S., 755, 780.

If the offense may be punished capitally, the only inquiry is—"Is the proof evident or the presumption great" of defendant's guilt? If the evidence is clear and satisfactory, leading a well-guarded judgment to the conclusion that the offense has been committed by the person charged; and that being tried he would probably be punished capitally, bail is not a matter of right. Ex parte McAnally, 53 Ala. 495.

It is a rule of the common law, that before indictment found, a defendant charged with murder will be admitted to bail, whenever, upon examination of the testimony under which he is held, the presumption of guilt is not strong; while, on the other hand, bail is always refused after an indictment for murder has been found by a grand jury. Ex parte Bryant, 34 Ala. 270, 274.

Instances Where Bail Granted.—On indictment for murder, the prisoner is entitled to bail where the evidence introduced by him leaves it doubtful whether deceased came to his death by accident, suicide, or violence at the hands of another, no evidence being introduced by the prosecution. Ex parte Hammock, 78 Ala. 414.

Under the evidence set out in the bill of exceptions, the defendant is held to be entitled to bail, because the proof is not evident, nor the presumption great, that he is guilty of murder in the first degree. Ex parte Dykes, 83 Ala. 114, 3 So. 306.

Defendant was indicted for killing deceased; and on an application for bail the evidence, without conflict, showed that deceased struck defendant with a stick or piece of wood. The evidence was conflicting as to whether, after the parties had grappled, deceased undertook to draw a weapon before he was shot and killed by defendant. Held, that an order admitting defendant to bail in the sum of $1,000 was not error. State *v.* Dixon, 5 Ala. App. 271, 59 So. 313.

Defendant, having been indicted for first-degree murder, applied for bail. The only evidence connecting him with the crime, or indicating criminal responsibility, consisted of threats, made a short time before the homicide, and certain circumstances indicating guilty agency. This evidence was conflicting, however, and there was no positive testimony connecting defendant directly with the physical act causing decedent's death. He denied all connection with and participation in the homicide, and induced several witnesses to testify to his whereabouts at or about the time the crime was committed, whose testimony, if believed, made it improbable that he could have been personally present at the place where deceased was killed, or close enough to the locality at the time to have participated in the murder. Held, that an order letting him to bail was not erroneous. State *v.* Cole, 5 Ala. App. 286, 59 So. 681.

Under Const., art. 1, § 17, granting bail, except for capital offenses "when the proof is evident or the presumption great," one committed for murder is entitled to bail, where the evidence shows that deceased was the aggressor, was violent and boisterous, and had struck defendant with sufficient force to stagger him, when defendant shot him; and that defendant first endeavored to allay deceased's anger, though there was also evidence that defendant had previously said that, if deceased "ever made a break at him, he would kill him." Ex parte King, 86 Ala. 620, 5 So. 863, cited in note in 39 L. R. A., N. S., 779.

Instances Where Bail Refused.—An order of the probate judge refusing bail to a party indicted for murder will not be reversed where the homicide was committed with a deadly weapon, unless the testimony which proved the killing proved also that justification. Ex parte Warrick, 73 Ala. 57.

Where there is evidence that petitioner, indicted for murder, and others, conspired to do an unlawful act the execution of which made it probable, under the circumstances, that a homicide not specially designed would be committed, and that in the execution of such conspiracy the homicide was committed, bail will be refused, though petitioner was not present when the homicide was committed. Ex parte Bonner, 100 Ala. 114, 14 So. 648.

Where Accused Acquitted of First Degree Murder.—Where accused, under an indictment charging murder in the first degree, has been found guilty of murder in the second degree only, that conviction operates as an acquittal of the greater crime, and entitles him to admission to bail. Ex parte Spivey, 175 Ala. 43, 57 So. 491.

Homicide of Slave.—A prisoner in custody under an indictment for the homicide of a slave, framed in reference to § 3296 of the Code, is entitled to bail as a matter of right. Ex parte Howard, 30 Ala. 43.

Misdemeanor.—On an indictment for a misdemeanor, bail is a matter of right, and on the sheriff in whose custody the defendant may be, is devolved the duty unconditionally of discharging him on sufficient bail. Hammons *v.* State, 59 Ala. 164.

§ 20. —— Pending Appeal or Error.

Under Gen. Acts. Sp. Sess. 1909, p. 62, conferring the right to bail pending appeal, except to those under sentence of death or under sentence for terms longer than five years, one convicted of murder in the second degree and sentenced to imprisonment for fifteen years is not entitled to bail pending his appeal. State *v.* Weaver, 52 So. 638, 167 Ala. 672.

Code 1907, c. 162, art. 1, treats of appeal, and art. 2 treats of writs of error. Section 6249, part of art. 1, provides that when any question of law is reserved in case of felony, and the court is informed that the defendant desires to take an appeal, judgment must be rendered against the defendant, but the execution thereof must be suspended pending the appeal, and the defendant held in custody. Section 6050 provides for admitting to bail for misdemeanors. Acts 1909, p. 62, approved August 24, 1909, amending § 6262, part of art. 2, allows bail in all cases where the imprisonment does not exceed five years, and directs that the judge or court must also direct the clerk of the court in which conviction was had to admit the defendant to bail. Held, that the section, as amended, being still part of art. 2, treating of writs of error, the amended section has no application to appeals in cases of felony. Ex parte Byrd, 172 Ala. 179, 55 So. 203.

§ 21. —— After Reversal on Appeal or Error.

Where one charged with a criminal offense was, prior to trial, released on bail, he has not the right, after conviction and sentence, and on reversal of such judgment, to be released from custody by virtue of the former bail bond. Ex parte Williams, 114 Ala. 29, 22 So. 446, cited in note in 20 L. R. A., N. S., 862.

§ 22. Jurisdiction and Authority to Admit to Bail.

§ 23. —— Courts and Judicial Officers.

Under Acts 1909, p. 62, amending Code 1907, § 6262, providing for bail in all cases where the imprisonment does not exceed five years, and directing that the judge or court must also direct the clerk of the court in which conviction was had to admit the defendant to bail, held, that the judge or court mentioned refers to the supreme judge or court issuing the writ of error. Ex parte Byrd, 172 Ala. 179, 55 So. 203.

Probate Judge.—Under Rev. Code, § 4264, a probate judge had no jurisdiction, on habeas corpus, to grant bail to a person who was confined under a charge of a capital felony; but under the act approved March 20, 1873, amending that section (Sess. Laws 1872-73, p. 120), he has equal jurisdiction in such cases, within the limits of his county, with circuit judges and chancellors. Hale *v.* State, 24 Ala. 80; Ex parte Keeling, 50 Ala. 474.

Under Rev. Code, § 4264, allowing petitions for habeas corpus to be brought before the probate judge where the prisoner is confined in the county jail on charge of felony or under a commitment for felony, probate judges may, on writ of habeas corpus, admit to bail before conviction in all cases of felony except felonies punishable by death or by imprisonment in the penitentiary for life, where the accused is confined in the county jail; but, if confined in the penitentiary, or under a sentence, judgment, or decree or order of the supreme court, the court of chancery, the circuit court, or a city court, the probate judge has no jurisdiction. Ex parte Ray, 45 Ala. 15.

City Court of Mobile.—Under Pamph. Acts, pp. 30, 31, § 4, conferring upon the city court of Mobile jurisdiction coextensive with the circuit court of Mobile, and making him a conservator of the peace, etc., the judge of the city court has power to take a bond conditioned that the principal obligor "make his personal appearance before the city court, now in session, instanter, and from day to day during the term, and from term to term thereafter, to answer the state of Alabama on a charge of an assault to murder." Arnold *v.* State, 25 Ala. 69.

Right to Delegate Power.—A judicial officer, clothed with the power to admit to bail persons charged with criminal offenses, can not delegate the power to another. Butler *v.* Foster, 14 Ala. 323; Antonez *v.* State, 26 Ala. 81, 84.

§ 24. —— Clerks, Sheriffs, and Other Ministerial Officers.

Sheriff.—"The power and duty of a sheriff, to take recognizance in criminal cases, is derived from, and imposed by statute. A recognizance, taken by him without authority, is void. Governor *v.* Jackson, 15 Ala. 703; Antonez *v.* State, 26 Ala. 81; Gray *v.* State, 43 Ala. 41." Jones *v.* State, 63 Ala. 161, 162.

A sheriff has no authority to admit to bail a party committed to jail by a justice of the peace, on a charge of burglary, unless said justice indorses on his warrant of commitment the amount of bail required, and a bail bond so taken is void. Evans *v.* State, 63 Ala. 195.

Where a justice of the peace issues a warrant for the arrest of a party for an offense of which he has no final jurisdiction, the sheriff has no authority to take said party's recognizance, conditioned to appear before the justice on the day named in the warrant; such recognizance is, therefore, void. Jones *v.* State, 63 Ala. 161.

The order, by a circuit judge, provided for in Code, § 4849, for the sheriff to take bail in vacation, may be granted without any return to the writ, or any hearing under it, and without the presence of the prisoner. Callahan *v.* State, 60 Ala. 65.

An order of the court, in a prosecution for felony, which merely determines that the offense is bailable, and fixes the sum, can not, under a statute authorizing the sheriff to take bail in vacation, give him authority, in term time, to admit the party to bail and take a recognizance. Gray *v.* State, 43 Ala. 41.

A sheriff has no power under the Code to admit to bail a person charged with a felony after indictment found, nor can that power be delegated to him by an order of the circuit court in these words: "And it appearing to the court that the offense with which the prisoner stands charged, namely, murder in the second degree, is bailable, it is ordered that, upon the prisoner giving good and sufficient bail, according to law, for his appearance at the next term of this court, in the sum of $1,000, then said prisoner be discharged from custody until the next term of this court." Antonez *v.* State, 26 Ala. 81.

A recognizance taken by the sheriff from a defendant, whom he has arrested, under a capias, on a charge of felony, is void. Governor *v.* Jackson, 15 Ala. 703; Antonez *v.* State, 26 Ala. 81.

Deputy Sheriff.—Under the statute, the deputy sheriff, when he arrests a party on a capias for a misdemeanor, is authorized to take his recognizance; and such recognizance need not be certified by the officer. Shreeve *v.* State, 11 Ala. 676.

§ 25. Proceedings to Admit to Bail.

In General.—An undertaking of bail,

approved and taken by the sheriff under the order of a chancellor, is not void because the application for bail was not verified; nor because proper notice was not given to the solicitor, and no writ of habeas corpus or precept to the sheriff to produce the body of the prisoner was issued. These requirements are directory, though they ought not to be omitted. Merrill *v.* State, 46 Ala. 82.

Withdrawal of Motion.—Where a prisoner moves the circuit court for bail, and the court proceeds to examine fully the facts and circumstances attending the commission of the alleged offense, it is not error to refuse to permit the prisoner, after having submitted all the evidence, to withdraw his motion, since the state as well as the prisoner is interested in it. It is the duty of the court to proceed with the case and either bail the prisoner, and thereby rid the state of the expense of his custody, or remand him, as the facts may require. Ex parte Campbell, 20 Ala. 89.

Taking in Vacation.—On an indictment for a felony if the defendant does not give bail in open court, it must make an order and cause the same to be entered of record, fixing the amount of bail required. This the sheriff may take in vacation and discharge the defendant. Hammons *v.* State, 59 Ala. 164.

Hearing after Term.—Applications for bail will not be heard after the expiration of the time allotted for the regular business of the term, though the minutes have not been signed, unless public interest should require a hearing of the case after that time. Ex parte Wreford, 40 Ala. 378.

Burden of Proof.—The production of an indictment for murder casts on defendant the burden of introducing exculpatory evidence. Ex parte Hammock, 78 Ala. 414, cited in note in 39 L. R. A., N. S., 773, 775, 777, 779, 782.

On an application for bail by a prisoner, who is shown to be under indictment for murder, he is presumed to be guilty of the charge in the highest degree, and that presumption must be overcome by proof. Ex parte Vaughan, 44 Ala. 417, cited in note in 39 L. R. A., N. S., 773, 775.

One who applies for bail or discharge on habeas corpus, and is under indictment for murder, must, upon production of the indictment, rebut the presumption arising therefrom, for the purposes of such application, that he is guilty of murder in the first degree. Ex parte Rhear, 77 Ala. 92, cited in note in 39 L. R. A., N. S., 774.

Order.—An order in habeas corpus proceedings, for admission to bail of one who has been transferred from the county in which he is to be tried to the jail of another county, is properly directed to the sheriff of the latter county, who has the prisoner in custody. Holcombe *v.* State, 99 Ala. 185, 12 So. 794.

Second Application.—Where the record of the court shows that the facts and circumstances attending the commission of the offense with which a prisoner is charged have been inquired into, on an application by the prisoner for bail, the court, although not bound to do so, may well decline to hear another application based on the same facts. Ex parte Campbell, 20 Ala. 89.

A party can not make a second application for bail to a circuit judge, or, on such application, introduce evidence, or take such exceptions as will bring before the appellate court the evidence and judgment on the first application. Ex parte Carroll, 36 Ala. 300.

The discretion of the lower court in refusing to hear a second application for release on bail will not be controlled by mandamus. Ex parte Campbell, 20 Ala. 89. See the title MANDAMUS.

Where Indictment Found before Bail Given.—On a preliminary examination before a magistrate, defendant was admitted to bail, and, on failure to give bail, was committed to jail. A second warrant was issued, and a second preliminary examination was had before the city court, and defendant was committed without bail, and subsequently an indictment was found against him for murder. Held, that accused was not entitled to a release on giving the bail fixed at the first preliminary examination. Ex parte Robinson, 108 Ala. 161, 18 So. 729, ov rruling Skelton *v.* Robinson, 104 Ala. 98, 16 So. 74, cited in note in 39 L. R. A., N. S., 773, 783.

Review of Proceedings in General.—See the title CRIMINAL LAW.

Habeas Corpus to Review Refusal.—See the title HABEAS CORPUS.

§ 26. Amount of Bail.

See post, "Approval and Filing," § 32.

§ 27. Bond, Undertaking, or Recognizance.

§ 28. —— Requisites and Validity in General.

"A recognizance is an obligation of record entered into before some court of record or magistrate, duly authorized, with a condition to do a particular act. (Tidd's P. 984.)" Lloyd *v.* State, Minor 34.

"A recognizance as such, does not derive its efficacy so much from the form of its execution, as from the occasion upon which it was taken, the object of it, and the competency of the tribunal or officer who takes the acknowledgment of the recognizors." Hall *v.* State, 9 Ala. 827, 829.

The omission of a party's name in the body of a recognizance will not make it inoperative as to him if he has regularly acknowledged it. Hall *v.* State, 9 Ala. 827.

Where a recognizance taken before a justice of the peace has been signed and sealed by the principal and his surety, its validity is not affected by the failure to insert the name of the latter in a blank left for that purpose in the body of it. Badger *v.* State, 5 Ala. 21, cited in note in 38 L. R. A., N. S., 318.

Omission of Principal's Name.—An appearance bond, which, after setting out the names of four persons, then recites that they "agree to pay to the state of Alabama, unless ——— appear at the next term of the said court," a certain sum, is insufficient to support a judgment upon the defendant forfeiting such bond, since it does not appear by reason of the blank in said bond who was the principal obligor. State *v.* Fuller, 30 So. 506, 128 Ala. 45.

Signature.—Parties may sign an undertaking of bail with their initials or mark. Hammons *v.* State, 59 Ala. 164, 31 Am. Rep. 13.

Seal.—A bail bond to which a scroll which contains the word "Seal" is attached, opposite the name of each signer, is sufficiently sealed. Lindsay *v.* State, 15 Ala. 43.

Statutory Form.—Where an undertaking of bail for a person charged with murder is given in the form of a penal bond, with a condition which if performed will avoid the bond, it can not be enforced, under Rev. St., § 4239, which provides a form for "an undertaking of bail" when not taken in open court. Dover *v.* State, 45 Ala. 244.

Scire facias can not be maintained on a recognizance in a criminal action which possesses none of the statutory requisites. Lloyd *v.* State, Minor 34.

Term of Court—Charge by Statute.—A recognizance to appear at the next term of the court, "to be holden on the 4th Monday of March," is not avoided by a statute changing the time of holding the court to the first Monday. Walker *v.* State, 6 Ala. 350.

Execution on Sunday.—See the title SUNDAY.

§ 29. —— Defects in Antecedent Proceedings.

Manner of Arrest.—The sureties can not object to the manner of arrest if the bond was taken by the proper officer. Peck *v.* State, 63 Ala. 201.

Illegal Imprisonment.—To scire facias on a forfeited recognizance, it is a good plea by the sureties that their principal, at the time of its execution, "was illegally and by force imprisoned and restrained of his liberty, and that, under such illegal and forcible imprisonment, and to procure a release and discharge therefrom, defendants made and subscribed said writing." State *v.* Brantley, 27 Ala. 44.

Recitals in Minutes—New Indictment.—Where the judgment is arrested and a nol. pros. entered in a county to which the prisoner has had the case removed, and the court has bound him to appear at the circuit court of the proper county to answer a new indictment for the same offense, the validity of the recognizance is not impaired because the minutes fail to recite the specific cause for which the indictment was arrested, or that the court ordered another indictment to be preferred or the defendant to give bail. Gooden *v.* State, 35 Ala. 430.

Irregularities in Grand Jury—Sufficiency of Indictment.—In a proceeding by sci. fa. to fix the liability of the principal and sureties on a forfeited bail bond, said sureties can not object to the irregularities in drawing the grand jury or the sufficiency of the indictment, if the bond was taken by the proper officer. Peck *v.* State, 63 Ala. 201.

§ 30. —— Description of Offense.

A recognizance given by a person, charged with an offense, to appear at a term of court, must set out the kind of offense for which he is to answer. Goodwin *v.* Governor, 1 Stew. & P. 465, cited in note in 38 L. R. A., N. S., 310.

A recognizance to appear and answer an indictment, to be preferred at a future time against the principal recognizor, need not set out the offense charged with the technical accuracy required in the indictment, but it will be sufficient if the offense be substantially described. State *v.* Weaver, 18 Ala. 293, cited in note in 38 L. R. A., N. S., 318.

Burglary.—Under the statute prescribing the form of bail bonds, and making them read to answer "for the offense of burglary," or whatever the crime may be, it is sufficient if a bond reads to answer "for burglary." Holcombe *v.* State, 99 Ala. 185, 13 So. 794, cited in note in 38 L. R. A., N. S., 325.

Burglary and Grand Larceny.—It is no objection to a bail bond, binding defendant to answer for burglary and grand larceny, that the indictment is for either or both separately, and not jointly. Holcombe *v.* State, 99 Ala. 185, 12 So. 794.

"To Answer to Any Indictment."—If an undertaking of bail stipulates that the person charged with an offense shall appear "to answer to any indictment found against him," these words are not an incorrect description of an offense, within the meaning of section 3679 of the Code, admitting parol evidence in case there is an incorrect description. State *v.* Whitley, 40 Ala. 728.

Malicious Mischief—Telegraph Wires.—A demurrer does not lie to a scire facias against bail, on the ground that the indictment was for intentionally injuring telegraph wires, while the bail bond and scire facias describe the offense as malicious mischief. Welch *v.* State, 36 Ala. 277.

Conspiracy.—A recognizance, by which the recognizors stipulate that the principal shall appear and answer to a charge of conspiracy, is sufficient, although it does not designate, in terms of the indictment, the particular act which he conspired to do. Hall *v.* State, 15 Ala. 431, cited in note in 38 L. R. A., N. S., 317.

Carrying Concealed Weapons.—A recognizance, by which the recognizors stipulate that the principal shall appear and answer a charge to be exhibited against him on behalf of the state, for carrying concealed weapons, is sufficient, although the offense is not described in the terms of the statute. Hall *v.* State, 9 Ala. 827.

Resisting Process.—An undertaking to answer to a charge for "resisting process" is sufficiently significant in a recognizance to indicate the offense intended to be charged, although the statute makes the offense consist in "knowingly and willfully resisting or opposing any officer of this state in serving or attempting to serve or execute any legal writ or process whatsoever." Browder *v.* State, 9 Ala. 58, cited in note in 38 L. R. A., N. S., 318.

Carrying on Lottery.—Where the indictment charges the defendant, in proper form, with setting up or carrying on a lottery not authorized by law, and also with selling tickets in such unauthorized lottery (Rev. Code, § 3616), an undertaking of bail, conditioned for the appearance of the defendant "to answer an indictment pending against him for selling lottery tickets," contains a substantial description of the offense. Keipp *v.* State, 49 Ala. 337, cited in note in 38 L. R. A., N. S., 317.

Effect of Misdescription.—The misdescription, or the want of a proper description, of the offense in the recognizance, will not avoid a judgment on it, as it is forfeited by the nonappearance of the party. Shreeve *v.* State, 11 Ala. 676, cited in note in 38 L. R. A., N. S., 318.

"Section 3679 of the Code provides,

that an undertaking of bail is 'forfeited by the failure of the defendant to appear, although the offense, judgment, or other matter, is incorrectly described in such undertaking; the particular case, or matter to which the undertaking is applicable, being made to appear to the court.'" State *v.* Whitley, 40 Ala. 728, 730.

But see Howie *v.* State, 1 Ala. 113, where it is held that if the charge which the accused was called to answer varies from that described in the condition of the recognizance, no sufficient breach is shown, and the judgment nisi is erroneous.

§ 31. —— Conditions and Obligations.

"Every recognizance, when drawn in a correct form, contains three distinct conditions: 1 To appear—2. To answer a particular offense; and 3. Not to depart without the leave of the court." Shreeve *v.* State, 11 Ala. 676, 678.

Superadded words of condition, beyond what are authorized by statute, do not invalidate the recognizance, but they have precisely the same effect as if they had been omitted. Howie *v.* State, 1 Ala. 113.

Place of Appearance.—A recognizance, taken by a justice of the peace, conditioned for the prisoner's appearance on a day certain, before him, or some other justice, is void for uncertainty, no place for the party's appearance being specified. State *v.* Allen, 33 Ala. 422.

A recognizance taken by the court, in which the indictment is found, simultaneously with an order changing the venue to another county, and which is conditioned for the appearance of the accused, to answer the charge, at the ensuing circuit court of the county to which the cause is transferred, is not liable to objection on that account. Hall *v.* State, 15 Ala. 431.

Where the judgment is arrested, and a nol. pros. entered in a county to which the prisoner has had the case removed, the court can bind him to appear at the circuit court of the proper county to answer a new indictment for the same offense. Gooden *v.* State, 35 Ala. 430.

§ 32. —— Approval and Filing.

A statement made by a justice of the peace preceding a recognizance, which shows the manner of executing it, and who are the recognizors, is equivalent to a formal certificate of such facts at the foot of it. Badger *v.* State, 5 Ala. 21.

It is not indispensable to the validity of a recognizance, which the recognizor has entered into before some court or officer authorized to take his acknowledgment, that it should be sealed by him. Hall *v.* State, 9 Ala. 827.

Amount of Bail.—Section 3408 of the Code, requiring the magistrate to indorse on the warrant of commitment the amount of bail required, applies only to preliminary proceedings before indictment found, and not to commitments after indictment. Antonez *v.* State, 26 Ala. 81.

§ 33. —— Construction and Operation.

A bail bond, being conditioned as the statute requires, has the effect to bind the defendant to appear at the first day of the next term, and "from day to day of such term, and from term to term thereafter," until discharged by law. Cohely *v.* State, 129 Ala. 660, 30 So. 905.

Where a defendant charged with the same felony in three separate cases is, upon preliminary investigation, bound over to await the action of the grand jury in each of the cases, and the bail bond for each case is identical, except in one respect as to one of such bonds, and the grand jury prefers an indictment against him in each case, in the absence of some identifying mark by which the clerk of the court could tell to which indictment the bail bond should be applied, it is not improper for him to apply said bond to the cases indiscriminately. State *v.* Fuller, 30 So. 506, 128 Ala. 45, cited in note in 38 L. R. A., N. S., 313.

Joint and Several Liability.—"The undertaking of bail binds the parties thereto, jointly and severally, for the appearance of the defendant to answer the indictment or prosecution mentioned therein." Keipp *v.* State, 49 Ala. 337, 339.

When the parties acknowledge themselves bound in the sum of $500, to be levied severally and individually of their goods, etc., respectively, this is a joint and several recognizance, and not the several recognizance of each of the parties for that sum. Ellison *v.* State, 8 Ala. 273.

§ 34. Bond, Undertaking, or Recognizance on Appeal.

§ 35. —— Requisites and Validity in General.

Stating Term of Court.—Under Cr. Code, § 4640, allowing persons convicted before a justice to appeal on giving bond to appear, etc., and § 4362, prescribing the form of bail bonds, and making a statement of the term of court at which the principal is to appear a part thereof, a bond on appeal from a conviction before a justice which does not state the term of court at which the principal is to appear is not a statutory bond, and hence can not be enforced by the summary remedy for the enforcement of statutory bonds. Tolleson *v.* State, 139 Ala. 159, 35 So. 997.

§ 36. —— Amendments, and New or Additional Bonds.

Where one charged with a criminal offense was, prior to trial, released on bail, he has not the right, after conviction and sentence, and on reversal of such judgment, to be released from custody by virtue of the former bail bond. Ex parte Williams, 22 So. 446, 114 Ala. 29.

§ 37. Deposit in Lieu of Bail.

A sheriff has no right to receive money to the amount of the bail, and discharge a prisoner in his custody. Butler *v.* Foster, 14 Ala. 323.

§ 38. Rights of Sureties over Principal.

"'The bail may keep the person committed to them in their custody for their indemnity. Or, if he be at large, they may reseize him and bring him before a justice to find new bail, or to be committed to prison. And this they may do upon a Sunday.' 2 Com. Dig. 3; Cain *v.* State, 55 Ala. 170." Hammons *v.* State, 59 Ala. 164, 168.

§ 39. Discharge of Sureties.

See post, "Relief from Liability or Forfeiture," § 42.

§ 39 (1) In General.

Lack of Indictment and Information.—The obligation of the sureties on a bail bond is for the appearance of their principal, and, if he fails to appear, the bond is forfeited, whether there was an information or indictment against him or not. State *v.* Kyle, 99 Ala. 256, 13 So. 538.

Arrest in Another State.—When one released on a bail bond goes into another state, and is there confined in the penitentiary for another crime, whereby his bond is forfeited, his bail are not exonerated. Cain *v.* State, 55 Ala. 170; State *v.* Crosby, 114 Ala. 11, 22 So. 110. See note in 23 L. R. A., N. S., 140.

When defendant is ordered to give a new bail bond because the first is insufficient, and is ordered into custody under Code, § 4862, for failure to do so, his sureties are discharged for any future default. State *v.* Posey, 79 Ala. 45.

Reversal of Judgment.—If the undertaking of bail, instead of being conditioned as required by the statute, is conditioned for the defendant's appearance at the next term, "to abide the judgment rendered at this term," the reversal of that judgment by the appellate court would probably discharge the sureties; but this defense must be set up by the plea of nul tiel record, craving oyer of the undertaking, and sustained by evidence from the record, and can not be taken by demurrer to the sci. fa. Williams *v.* State, 55 Ala. 71.

Agreement in Undertaking.—Under Code Ala. 1886, § 4428, providing that no bail is discharged by reason of there not being the requisite number of bail, or by reason of any other agreement than is expressed in the undertaking, an understanding at the time a bail bond is given that it was to have effect only until a second one was given is of no avail. Matthews *v.* State, 92 Ala. 89, 9 So. 740.

Where Principal Indicted for Different Offense.—A recognizance to answer to an indictment for perjury will not warrant a judgment against the sureties for the failure of their principal to appear and answer to an indictment for burglary. Sureties, in such a case, have a right to stand upon the terms of their contract. Gray *v.* State, 43 Ala. 41, cited in note in 38 L. R. A., N. S., 327.

The sureties of one bound over to answer a charge of manslaughter are liable for his appearance to an indictment for murder. Gresham *v.* State, 48 Ala. 625.

The death of the principal releases the surety from a compliance with the obligation of bail. Pynes *v.* State, 45 Ala. 52, cited in note in 23 L. R. A., N. S., 137.

When accused is taken into custody by the proper officer, he is no longer in the custody of his bail, who are thereby discharged. Miller *v.* State, 48 So. 360, 158 Ala. 73, 20 L. R. A., N. S., 861.

Subsequent Irregular Arrest.—When one has been arrested on a magistrate's warrant and bail taken for his appearance in court, a subsequent irregular rearrest for the same offense will not discharge the bail. Ingram *v.* State, 27 Ala. 17.

Where a person accused of a criminal offense has been arrested and given bail, his subsequent arrest, on another charge, or his delivery (after escaping from his bail) by the authorities of another state, on the requisition of the governor, when the demand does not appear to be founded on the same charge, does not discharge his bail. Ingram *v.* State, 27 Ala. 17.

Sureties on a bail bond, who do not surrender the principal after his conviction and imprisonment on another indictment, are liable where he escapes and does not appear for trial on the charge on which such bond was given; Code, §§ 4427, 4429, providing that bail are bound for the appearance of the principal from day to day until he is discharged, and that they may at any time exonerate themselves by surrendering the principal. State *v.* Crosby, 22 So. 110, 114 Ala. 11.

Erasure of Co-Surety's Name.—The sureties in a bond for the appearance of one under indictment having become such on condition that the acting sheriff, who had the prisoner in charge, should also sign as surety, they are discharged by his erasing his own name before he approved the bond, and released the prisoner. King *v.* State, 81 Ala. 92, 8 So. 159.

§ 39 (2) Continuance or Postponement of Case.

If a person recognize for his appearance at a particular time of court, to answer, etc., and no proceedings are had in the case at such term, the accused is discharged from his recognizance. Goodwin *v.* Governor, 1 Stew. & P. 465.

Where a person is bound over on preliminary examination to appear at the next term of the circuit court, and from term to term thereafter until discharged by law, if no indictment is found against him at that term of court, no forfeiture taken, and the case not continued for further investigation, the sureties on the recognizance are discharged. Rogers *v.* State, 79 Ala. 59.

Where Case Regularly Entered and Continuance Duly Made.—When a defendant, upon a preliminary investigation, is bound over to await the action of the grand jury, and his recognizance is continued for his appearance at the next term of the court, and from term to term thereafter until discharged by law, the failure of the grand jury at the next term of said court to prefer an indictment against him does not discharge the sureties, when it appears that the case against the defendant was regularly entered on the docket, and the order of continuance was duly made. State *v.* Fuller, 30 So. 506, 128 Ala. 45.

An undertaking of bail, under Rev. Code, § 4305, on suspension of judgment of conviction pending error or appeal, binding the defendant to appear at the next term to "abide the judgment rendered," in effect binds him to appear, not only at the next succeeding term, but at any subsequent term to which the case may be continued until decided by the appellate court. Williams *v.* State, 55 Ala. 71.

Where Indictment Found.—A recognizance conditioned that the party charged will appear and answer to the indictment to be preferred against him at a named term of the court, and not depart therefrom without leave, may be extended at any subsequent term, if an indictment is preferred and found at that term. Ellison *v.* State, 8 Ala. 273.

§ 40. Breach or Fulfillment of Condition of Bond, Undertaking or Recognizance.

Sureties on a bail bond can only be discharged from liability by the appearance of their principal according to the condition of the recognizance, or by some intervening act of God, or of the law of the state, or of the obligee, which renders performance of the condition impossible. Ringeman *v.* State, 34 So. 351, 136 Ala. 131; State *v.* Crosby, 114 Ala.

11, 22 So. 110, 111. See note in 23 L. R. A., N. S., 137.

Sureties can be finally discharged only in one of two ways—they must pay the amount of the bond, or the judgment of the court must be pronounced in their favor. Bearden *v.* State, 89 Ala. 21, 7 So. 755.

Extent of Obligation.—The appearance of the defendant at court for trial, or his presence during trial, or a mistrial, will not operate to discharge the bail. The obligation of a proper bail bond binds the sureties, at least, until after the verdict of the jury; but, when the sentence of the law is pronounced, the officer of the law is charged with its due execution. The bail have no further control over the custody of their principal, and can not be longer held responsible. Hawk *v.* State, 84 Ala. 466, 4 So. 690; Cain *v.* State, 55 Ala. 170; Robinson *v.* Dickerson, 108 Ala. 161, 18 So. 729; Ex parte Williams, 114 Ala. 29, 22 So. 446.

Where accused was in court at the rendition of a verdict and judgment against him for a felony, he thereby immediately passed from the custody of his bail to that of the sheriff under an implied order of the court by which his bail were discharged; nor could they be again bound by the subsequent vacation of the judgment and the granting of a new trial, and an order that defendant be held on his former bond until discharged by due process of law. Miller *v.* State, 158 Ala. 73, 48 So. 360.

"The fact that the defendant appeared and entered on the trial was neither the fulfillment of either of the terms of the bond, nor did it answer the requirements of the statute, and that his escape before the trial was completed authorized the forfeiture." Hawk *v.* State, 84 Ala. 466, 4 So. 690; Cook *v.* State, 91 Ala. 53, 8 So. 686; Cohely *v.* State, 129 Ala. 660, 30 So. 905.

§ 41. Proceedings for Fixing Liability or Forfeiture.

§ 41 (1) In General.

As to civil proceedings, see ante, "Proceedings for Fixing Liability or Foreclosure," § 7.

Code, §§ 4863, 4868, providing for a conditional judgment on an undertaking of bail, does not clothe the court with an absolute power of discharging or fixing the liability of bail; nor does it confer the power to determine questions of fact without the intervention of a jury, on which the validity of the undertaking or the liability may depend. Hammons *v.* State, 59 Ala. 164.

Evidence—Admissibility. — Physician's certificate that defendant was sick on a day other than the trial day was properly excluded at the hearing, under Code 1907, § 6355, to determine whether the forfeiture of his bail should be made absolute. Carson *v.* State, 5 Ala. App. 283, 59 So. 719.

Sufficiency.—Under the evidence, held, that the trial court's judgment, making absolute the forfeiture of defendant's undertaking of bail, could not be disturbed. Carson *v.* State, 5 Ala. App. 283, 59 So. 719, 720.

§ 41 (2) Judgment or Record of Foreclosure.

A judgment nisi on a forfeited undertaking of bail should state the offense for which the accused was indicted. Gresham *v.* State, 48 Ala. 625.

It is no objection to a judgment nisi on a forfeited bail bond that it does not show that any indictment has been found against defendant, where the heading recites, "State *v.* H. [Defendant]. Indictment for burglary"—since under Code, § 4431, great particularity is not required. Holcombe *v.* State, 99 Ala. 185, 12 So. 794.

A judgment nisi in the form prescribed by Code, § 3691, to which is prefixed the name of the case, with a description of the offense charged, and which recites that the recognizance was conditioned for the principal defendant's ap earance "to answer the case," sufficiently describes and identifies the case. Cantaline *v.* State, 33 Ala. 439.

A judgment nisi, on a forfeited recognizance, which does not specify the charge that the principal recognizor was called to answer, is insufficient to support a judgment final. Hall *v.* State, 15 Ala. 431.

A judgment nisi on a forfeited recognizance recited that the recognizance was entered into on "Tuesday, the 8th day of the term." After a sci. fa. was issued and dismissed, leave was granted on the solicitor's motion to amend the judgment nisi, nunc pro tunc. By direction of the court, the clerk referred to the judgment nisi of the preceding term, and erased therefrom with his pen the recital as to the date, and interlined, "Wednesday, the 9th day of the term." Held that, while there should have been a new entry referring to the original, the mode of amendment did not annul the first judgment in toto. State *v.* Craig, 12 Ala. 363.

Where a recognizance states the offense for which the principal recognizor has undertaken to appear and answer, a judgment nisi rendered thereon should substantially describe the offense, or refer to it so that the recognizance may be identified. Unless it is thus special, it would not support the final judgment, and the latter, if it conformed to the recognizance, would vary from the judgment nisi. Faulk *v.* State, 9 Ala. 919.

A judgment nisi on a recognizance, reciting the charge to be "the exhibition of a circus without first obtaining a license according to law," can not be supported under a statute against exhibiting "a circus for hire, pay, or emolument, without a license." Badger *v.* State, 5 Ala. 21.

It is unnecessary to recite the recognizance in the judgment nisi. It is only necessary to show that the accused was required in court to answer the charge which his recognizors have stipulated he should answer, and the consequent forfeiture of the recognizance. Therefore a misrecital of the recognizance will not avoid the judgment. Howie *v.* State, 1 Ala. 113.

A recital, in a judgment nisi, that the accused was called to answer to an indictment for forgery, is not a sufficient averment of the breach of a recognizance conditioned that the accused should appear and answer a charge for counterfeiting a certain draft purporting to be drawn, etc. Howie *v.* State, 1 Ala. 113.

Necessity of Forfeiture against Principal.—Code 1876, §§ 4866, 4867, authorize a conditional judgment to be taken in proceedings to enforce a forfeiture, under certain circumstances, "against the parties to the undertaking," a form for which is given, and provide that such judgment may be made final by a notice of its rendition to each of defendants, or in case of two returns of "Not found" by the sheriff, which are made equal to personal service. Section 4852, relating to the same subject matter, provides that "the undertaking of bail binds the parties thereto jointly and severally," for the appearance of defendant. Held, that a forfeiture may be taken against any one or more of the obligors in an undertaking of bail, with or without the principal. Kilgrow *v.* State, 76 Ala. 101.

Amendment—Entry Nunc Pro Tunc.—A judgment nisi on a forfeited recognizance may be amended even after a scire facias has been issued thereon, and the appropriate judgment may be entered nunc pro tunc. Browder *v.* State, 9 Ala. 58; State *v.* Craig, 12 Ala. 363.

A judgment nisi rendered on a recognizance, when it does not conform to the recognizance, may be amended nunc pro tunc. Governor *v.* Knight, 8 Ala. 297.

§ 42. Relief from Liability or Forfeiture.
See ante, "Discharge of Sureties," § 39.

§ 43. —— In General.

§ 43 (1) In General.

When Relief Granted.—The power of the court to determine the sufficiency of the excuse for the default at a former term of the principal in a bail bond is intended to be exercised only when the principal appears, submits to the orders of the court, and can be held to answer the indictment. Hammons *v.* State, 59 Ala. 164, 31 Am. Rep. 13.

Where Judgment against Principal Set Aside.—If a judgment nisi on a forfeited recognizance is set aside as to the principal, on his plea of pardon, it can not be enforced against the surety. Hatch *v.* State, 40 Ala. 718.

Mitigation.—The imprisonment of accused in another state would authorize the court to mitigate the judgment against bail. Cain *v.* State, 55 Ala. 170.

On making final a judgment against bail the court may reduce it according to circumstances. Cain *v.* State, 55 Ala. 170.

Remitting Forfeiture.—The court has

power to remit a forfeiture. Hammons *v.* State, 59 Ala. 164, 31 Am. Rep. 13.

§ 43 (2) Application and Proceedings for Relief.

Plea—Sufficiency—Sickness.—A plea, in answer to a judgment nisi against a principal and the sureties in a bail bond, which avers that the principal's condition of health prevented his return to the jurisdiction when the forfeiture of the bond was taken but does not aver that he could not have appeared without imminent peril to his life at the time of the return term of the scire facias, is bad. Ringeman *v.* State, 34 So. 351, 136 Ala. 131.

In answer to a judgment nisi, the sureties on a bail bond filed a plea alleging that after the execution of the bond the principal therein was so ill of consumption that it became necessary to the preservation or prolongation of his life for him to go to another state; that at the time forfeiture was taken a return could not have been made without serious detriment to his health, nor without imminent danger to his life. Held not to aver impossibility of appearance by the principal, resulting from an act of God, as illness, however severe and critical, is not the act of God in legal contemplation. Ringeman *v.* State, 34 So. 351, 136 Ala. 131.

Sufficiency of Evidence—Sickness.—Physician's certificate, not stating that defendant was sick on date of trial, and testimony of defendant alone that he was sick on the day of the trial, held not to require forfeiture of his bail to be set aside. Carson *v.* State, 5 Ala. App. 283, 59 So. 719.

§ 44. —— Surrender of Principal.

"Bail may, at any time, before they are finally discharged, exonerate themselves by surrendering the defendant." Bearden *v.* State, 89 Ala. 21, 7 So. 755; Cherokee County *v.* Kyle, 99 Ala. 256, 13 So. 538, 539.

Sureties had a common-law right to arrest accused at pleasure without process and surrender him. Gray *v.* Strickland, 50 So. 152, 163 Ala. 344.

Code 1907, § 6351, authorizing bail to arrest their principal on a certified copy of the undertaking, is not cumulative, but exclusive of the common-law remedy, authorizing bail to arrest their principal without process. Gray *v.* Strickland, 163 Ala. 344, 50 So. 152.

Under Code 1886, § 4429, providing that bail may at any time exonerate themselves by surrendering the defendant, and § 4430, providing that, to exonerate the bail, the surrender of the defendant must be to the sheriff, and the sheriff may discharge him on his giving new bail, a surety can not be discharged by the giving of a second bond without the surrender of the defendant Matthews *v.* State, 92 Ala. 89, 9 So. 740.

Surrender after Forfeiture.—Where, after forfeiture for failure to appear, accused is surrendered and tried, the surety on the bond must be discharged. Bearden *v.* State, 89 Ala. 21, 7 So. 755.

To Whom Surrender—Violation of Ordinance.—A surety on an appeal bond, given after conviction of violating a municipal ordinance, was not released by surrendering the principal to the sheriff, instead of to the court to which the principal was bound to appear; the common law, and not the statutes relating to the surrender of the principal in criminal cases, being determinative of the surety's procedure to secure release from such bond. House *v.* Anniston, 5 Ala. App. 357, 59 So. 686.

Where, after conviction in the recorder's court of violating a municipal ordinance, defendant appealed to a city court, where the trial was to be de novo, the recorder's court no longer had any jurisdiction; and a surety on defendant's appeal bond was not released by delivering him to the city authorities. House *v.* Anniston, 5 Ala. App. 357, 59 So. 686.

§ 45. Action or Scire Facias on Bond, Undertaking, or Recognizance.

§ 46. —— Nature and Form of Remedy.

Nature of Proceedings.—A scire facias, brought to recover the forfeiture on a recognizance, is a civil proceeding. Hatch *v.* State, 40 Ala. 718; Hunt *v.* State, 63 Ala. 196; Peck *v.* State, 63 Ala. 201.

Form of Remedy.—A scire facias is the proper remedy to recover the penalty on a forfeited recognizance. Lloyd *v.* State, Minor 34.

A scire facias on a forfeited recognizance is a mere notice to the recognizor to show case why the judgment nisi should not be made final. Hall *v.* State, 15 Ala. 431. See post, "Process and Appearance," § 51.

"The scire facias is regarded as a mere notice to the parties to the recognizance, to show cause why they should not be subjected to the payment of its penalty; the state may call upon such of the parties as its prosecuting officer may select, to show cause and allow the proceedings to be silently discontinued as to the others. See Howie *v.* State, 1 Ala. 113." Robinson *v.* State, 5 Ala. 706, 708.

§ 47. —— Right of Action.

The remedy by sci. fa. upon a recognizance estreated is given by statute, and only maintainable upon the supposition that the liability which it seeks to redress is authorized by a legislative act. The hypothesis failing, the defendant can not be charged. Whitted *v.* Governor, 6 Port. 335.

§ 48. —— Defenses.

See ante, "Discharge of Sureties," § 39; "Relief from Liability or Forfeiture," § 42.

§ 49. —— Jurisdiction and Venue.

See ante, "Proceedings for Fixing Liability or Forfeiture," § 41.

As Dependent on Conditions in Bond.—The power of the court to try a defendant in a criminal case at a certain time is not affected by the fact that the sheriff has accepted a bail bond providing for his appearance at court on a day later than that on which he is put on his trial, since the jurisdiction of the court is not dependent on the condition of the bail bond. Ex parte Chandler, 114 Ala. 8, 22 So. 285.

§ 50. —— Parties.

See post, "Appeal and Error," § 57.

Joint and Several Liability.—Where judgment nisi is rendered on a forfeited recognizance, the scire facias may be either joint or several. Howie *v.* State, 1 Ala. 113; Keipp *v.* State, 49 Ala. 337, 339.

"The proceeding by scire facias on a forfeited recognizance is not governed by the rules which apply to actions prosecuted by individuals. Every joint judgment, bond, etc., is declared by statute to be joint and several in its legal effect, and process may be sued out against any one or more of the parties liable thereon, yet, if suit is brought against all, and service of process perfected, there can be no discontinuance as to one without putting an end to the entire case. This enactment has never been considered as applicable to a recognizance of bail in a criminal case, whether joint or several, nor has the more stringent rule of the common law which regulates proceedings on contracts between individuals." Robinson *v.* State, 5 Ala. 706, 707.

§ 51. —— Process and Appearance.

As to civil proceedings, see ante, "Process and Appearance," § 51.

Form—Setting Out Judgment.—A scire facias on a judgment nisi on a forfeited undertaking of bail should set out the judgment or recite it substantially. Gresham *v.* State, 48 Ala. 625.

Service — Sufficiency.—Under Code 1876, § 4866, providing that, "if the notice is not served on any of the parties to the undertaking, such other notices as are necessary may from time to time be issued; but two returns of 'Not found' by the proper officer are equivalent to personal service," final judgment can not be rendered against the principal on a bail bond, where only one scire facias has been issued, and, as to said principal, returned "Not found." Hunt *v.* State, 63 Ala. 196.

By the third section of the statute of 1833 (Aik. Dig. 122), personal service of a scire facias issued on a recognizance against bail in a criminal case is required to enable the state to recover. Hayter *v.* State, 7 Port. 156. But see, Badger *v.* State, 5 Ala. 21.

§ 52. —— Pleading.

§ 52 (1) In General.

Conformity to Code Forms.—In proceedings against a surety on a bail bond, an exact or literal conformity with the forms set forth in § 703, 704, and 707 of the Code is not required. Grund *v.* State, 40 Ala. 709.

A scire facias on a recognizance following the precedent of the Code is sufficient. Gooden *v.* State, 35 Ala. 430.

In scire facias against bail on a forfeited recognizance, if the undertaking of bail is described in the judgment nisi according to its legal effect, though not according to its literal terms, there is no such variance as will support a demurrer to the sci. fa. setting out the undertaking on oyer. Williams *v.* State, 55 Ala. 71.

Oyer—Variance.—Under the Alabama statutes, which allow a sci. fa. without setting out the recognizance, the defendant is entitled to crave oyer of the recognizance upon which the proceedings are based, and to demur if there is a variance. Ellison *v.* State, 8 Ala. 273.

After judgment, it is too late to object that there is a variance in the recognizance entered into and that set out in the judgment nisi or sci. fa. Shreeve *v.* State, 11 Ala. 676.

Demurrer.—The sureties on a forfeited recognizance can not, by a demurrer to the scire facias, test the legal sufficiency of the indictment against their principal. A demurrer to the scire facias can reach no further than the recognizance on which the judgment nisi is founded. State *v.* Weaver, 18 Ala. 293; Williams *v.* State, 20 Ala. 63. See note in 38 L. R. A., N. S., 314.

A demurrer will not lie to a scire facias against the sureties on a bail bond because the offense charged in the indictment is intentionally injuring telegraph wires, while it is described in the capias, bail bond, and scire facias as malicious mischief. Welch *v.* State, 36 Ala. 277, cited in note in 38 L. R. A., N. S., 325.

Under the provisions of the Code, a demurrer does not lie to a scire facias against bail on account of an incorrect description of the offense in the undertaking of bail, when the undertaking sufficiently identifies the pending indictment. State *v.* Eldred, 31 Ala. 393, cited in note in 38 L. R. A., N. S., 311.

Where a judgment nisi has been rendered against joint and several recognizors, some of whom have regularly executed and acknowledged the recognizance, the question whether the others are bound as recognizors can not be raised upon a joint demurrer to a scire facias against all the parties to the judgment nisi. Hall *v.* State, 9 Ala. 827.

§ 52 (2) Plea, or Answer, Cross Complaint and Reply.

Plea—Nul Trial Record.—In scire facias against bail on a forfeited recognizance, if the undertaking of bail is described in the judgment nisi according to its legal effect, though not according to its literal terms, there is no such variance as will support a plea of nul tiel record. Williams *v.* State, 55 Ala. 71.

Plea—Arrest of Principal.—A plea against the rendition of a judgment absolute on a forfeited undertaking of bail, that the accused appeared at the court, and was arrested on a capias issued by the clerk after indictment found, without more, is subject to demurrer. Merrill *v.* State, 46 Ala. 82.

§ 52 (3) Amendment.

"In Governor *v.* Knight, 8 Ala. 297, it was held that a judgment nisi which did not conform to the recognizance, may be amended nunc pro tunc, so that a second scire facias might issue after the lapse of a term, and after one issue on the defective judgment, had been quashed. So in Browder *v.* State, 9 Ala. 58, it was determined that an irregular judgment nisi upon a recognizance may be vacated and set aside even after a scire facias has been issued thereon, and the appropriate judgment may be entered nunc pro tunc. These citations very fully establish that a judgment on a recognizance, like all others, is amendable, where the record furnishes anything to amend by." State *v.* Craig, 12 Ala. 363, 365.

§ 53. —— Evidence.

See ante, "Application and Proceedings for Relief," § 43 (2).

Admissibility—Approval of Bond.—The fact of the approval of an undertaking of bail may be proved otherwise than by the indorsement thereon "Approved," as by proving that it was signed in the presence of the magistrate, who took possession thereon and discharged the accused from custody, and that the undertaking was subsequently found on file in the court to which it bound the principal to appear. Ozeley *v.* State, 59 Ala. 94.

To Show Matter to Which Undertaking Applicable.—Where an undertaking of bail stipulates that the principal shall appear at the next term of the circuit court, and then from term to term until discharged, "to answer to an indictment in said court against him," but does not otherwise describe the indictment, the state may, under Code, § 3679, providing for forfeiture of a recognizance, prove to the court "the particular case or matter" to which the undertaking is applicable. Vasser *v.* State, 32 Ala. 586, cited in note in 38 L. R. A., N. S., 310.

On scire facias against bail, where the offense charged in the indictment is for intentionally injuring telegraph wires, while that described in the capias, bail bond, and scire facias is malicious mischief, the capias and bail bond are admissible in evidence, as also is parol testimony showing their connection with the indictment. Welch *v.* State, 36 Ala. 277, cited in note in 38 L. R. A., N. S., 325.

Where a recognizance, or undertaking of bail, taken by a justice of the peace, is conditioned for the appearance of the principal at the next term of the circuit court, "to answer any indictment found against him," not specifying or referring to any particular offense, parol evidence can not be received, in a proceeding by scire facias against the bail, to connect the recognizance or undertaking with any particular case. State *v.* Whitley, 40 Ala. 728, distinguishing State *v.* Eldred, 31 Ala. 393, and Vasser *v.* State, 32 Ala. 586, cited in note in 38 L. R. A., N. S., 310.

Sufficiency—Execution of Bond.—On the rendition of judgment final against obligors on a forfeited bail bond, taken and approved by a justice of the peace for the appearance of the principal at the circuit court, sci. fa. having duly issued to them to appear and show cause why judgment final should not be rendered, no further proof of the execution of the bail bond is required, where it is in proper form, than the bond itself, properly signed by the justice who took and approved it. Gresham *v.* State, 48 Ala. 625.

§ 54. —— Damages.

Rev. Code, § 4258, authorizes the court, when judgment is made final against bail, to make it absolute for the full amount of the penalty, or for any part thereof, according to the circumstances of the particular case. Cain *v.* State, 55 Ala. 170.

Judgment can not be rendered against the sureties on a recognizance for a sum greater than the penalty. State *v.* Hinson, 4 Ala. 671.

A judgment may be rendered for the penalty of a recognizance, although it exceed the forfeiture which the law imposes, upon the conviction of the principal recognizor of the offense charged. Badger *v.* State, 5 Ala. 21.

§ 55. —— Trial.

Discontinuance.—A scire facias on a forfeited recognizance is not discontinued by an unexplained failure of the court to take action for one or more terms. Hunt *v.* State, 63 Ala. 196.

In a proceeding on a forfeiture of bail there is no discontinuance if the court chooses to make the judgment final against the sureties served with notice of the judgment nisi, without waiting for two returns of "Not found" against the principal. Keipp *v.* State, 49 Ala. 337.

Determination of Issues.—In scire facias on a forfeited bail bond, the issues are to be decided by the court. Code, §§ 4867, 4868. State *v.* Posey, 79 Ala. 45.

§ 56. —— Judgment and Enforcement Thereof.

Validity in General.—If a judgment on a forfeited recognizance describes it so that the particular sum for which each recognizor is bound and the nature of his undertaking is shown, and the judgment charges each to the extent of his liability, and no further, there is no error. Smith *v.* State, 7 Port. 492.

An indictment for adultery described the defendant as "Caroline T." The recognizance was signed "Lucinda Katherine T." The judgment nisi recited that the court was satisfied that Caroline T. had signed her bond as "Lucinda Katherine T." The scire facias issued on the judgment was directed to "Cornelia T.," and the final judgment was rendered against "Caroline T., who signed her bond 'Lucinda Katherine T.'" Held, that there was no such error in the proceedings as would be available to the recognizors, on a motion to have the judgment set aside. Tolison *v.* State, 39 Ala. 103.

Where the judgment final recites the issue of an alias scire facias, returnable to the term at which said judgment was rendered, which was the term next after that at which the original scire facias was returned, as "Not found," this is sufficient to support the final judgment, although the alias writ is not set out in the record, and the date of its issue is left blank in the judgment. Cantaline *v.* State, 33 Ala. 439.

Showing Default of Sureties.—In scire facias against bail for the failure of the principal to appear in accordance with the condition of their bond, it is not necessary that a final judgment should show that the sureties were called and made default. Richardson *v.* State, 31 Ala. 347.

As to Trial of Principal.—The judgment upon a recognizance should show that the party charged with an offense was required to answer the charge specified therein. Farr *v.* State, 6 Ala. 794.

Particularity Required — Indictment Found.—It is no objection to a judgment nisi and scire facias on a forfeited bail bond that they do not show that any indictment has been found against defendant, where the heading recites, "State *v.* H., [defendant]. Indictment for burglary"—since, under 2 Code, § 4431, great particularity is not required. Holcombe *v.* State, 99 Ala. 185, 12 So. 794.

Nisi Prius Proceedings.—Final judgment can not, under Code 1876, § 4863, be rendered against the sureties on a bail bond, unless they have had a chance to appear to show cause why the judgment nisi should not be made absolute, and the sci. fa. should be so framed. Hunt *v.* State, 63 Ala. 196.

A judgment nisi on a forfeited bond which recites, that the defendant, to secure whose appearance such bond was executed, "being called, came not, but made default," without specifying the particular charge that he was called to answer, is fatally defective, and a judgment final rendered thereon is erroneous. Lindsay *v.* State, 15 Ala. 43.

Joint and Several Judgment.—Final judgment on a forfeited recognizance must be joint or several, according to the liability of the parties. Howie *v.* State, 1 Ala. 113.

Although a sci. fa. issued upon a judgment nisi on a recognizance be served upon all the recognizors, the state may take judgment against a part only, and allow the proceedings to be silently discontinued as to the others. Robinson *v.* State, 5 Ala. 706.

Compromise after Final Judgment.—After rendering of a final judgment on a forfeited bail bond, the prosecuting attorney can not make any compromise in settlement. Dunkin *v.* Hodge, 46 Ala. 523.

§ 57. —— Appeal and Error.

Parties to Writ of Error.—Where recognizors are bound in several sums in one recognizance, and several judgments are rendered against them, they can not join in the prosecution of a writ of error; but where a joint writ is sued out by them, it may be amended under the act of 1843. "To authorize the amendments of writs of error," by striking out one of their names, and then it will remove the cause as to the other. Farr *v.* State, 6 Ala. 794.

On final judgment being rendered on a forfeited recognizance, all subsequent proceedings, including a writ of error, must be either joint or several, according to the form of judgment. Howie *v.* State, 1 Ala. 113.

Record.—The undertaking of bail, unless made so by plea or by bill of exceptions, is no part of the record, in sci. fa. against bail on a forfeited recognizance. Hendon *v.* State, 49 Ala. 380.

Where a judgment by default has been rendered against bail in a criminal case, a revising court will not look to a recognizance found in the transcript, as a part of the record. Robinson *v.* State, 5 Ala. 706.

A recognizance copied into the transcript by the clerk, but not made part of the record by exceptions or appropriate reference, can not be looked to as a part of the record of the proceedings against bail on their forfeited undertaking. Cantaline *v.* State, 33 Ala. 439.

Presumptions on Appeal.—After judgment without objection on a forfeited undertaking of bail in case of felony, which was approved by the sheriff, it will be presumed that he was authorized to do so by the proper court. Dunkin *v.* Hodge, 46 Ala. 523.

Questions Not Raised in Lower Court.—Upon an application, after issue of a scire facias, for judgment final against obligors in a forfeited bail bond taken by a justice of the peace, no other proof of execution of the bond is necessary, in the first instance, than the production of the bond itself, signed and approved by the justice. If the obligors did not execute it, this is matter of affirmative defense, which must be pleaded and proved below, and can not be set up for the first time on appeal. Gresham *v.* State, 48 Ala. 625.

Prejudicial Error—Minutes of Clerk.—When an undertaking of bail is forfeited, and a sci. fa. thereon is returned executed as to the sureties, but not found as to the principal; and a judgment final is thereupon rendered against the sureties, which is set aside on a subsequent day of the term; and neither said final judgment, nor the order setting it aside, is entered on the minutes by the clerk—the refusal of the court, at a subsequent term, to require the clerk to enter these matters on the record is not a matter of which the sureties can complain, on appeal from a final judgment afterwards rendered against them. Hendon *v.* State, 49 Ala. 380.

Affirmance—Absence of Transcript.—The judgment in proceedings for forfeiture of bail on defendant's failure to appear at the time fixed in the bond can not be affirmed merely on a certificate taken out by the state, in the absence of a transcript of the proceedings in the record. State *v.* Lowry, 29 Ala. 44.

Reversal—Judgment—Joint Liability.—When a judgment is erroneously entered severally against the parties bound by a joint recognizance, the entire proceedings as to all the parties will be reversed upon a writ of error sued out by one only, and the cause remanded, that its unity may be preserved. Ellison *v.* State, 8 Ala. 273, 274.

§ 58. —— Costs.

An action, brought in the name of the state for the use of a county, to recover on a forfeited bail bond, is a civil action, and, on judgment against it, costs may be taxed against the county, under Code Ala. 1886, §§ 2837, 3128, which provides for the taxation of costs in favor of the successful party in all civil actions. Coosa Co. *v.* Parker, 83 Ala. 269, 3 So. 552.

Clay's Dig., p. 236, provides for certain fees of counsellors, etc., for prosecuting or defending a suit in a county court, etc., and Id., p. 575, relative to county taxes, in § 94, provides that, for the purpose of providing a fund to defray county expenses the sum of etc., shall be taxed in the bill of costs on all suits hereafter commenced, etc., and paid into the treasury, etc. Held, that it is irregular to tax an attorney's fee and the county tax upon a judgment nisi on a recognizance in a criminal case, when the judgment is afterwards, at the same term, set aside on condition that all costs shall be paid. Weissinger *v.* State, 11 Ala. 540.

BAILMENT.

Cross References.

See the titles BANKS AND BANKING; DEPOSITARIES; PLEDGES; TROVER AND CONVERSION; WAREHOUSEMEN.

As to particular species of bailments, and bailments incident to particular occupations, see the titles BANKS AND BANKING; CARRIERS; DEPOSITARIES; FACTORS; INNKEEPERS; PLEDGES; SLAVES; WAREHOUSEMEN. As to conditional sales, see the title SALES. As to embezzlement of bailees, see the title EMBEZZLEMENT. As to larceny by bailee, see the title LARCENY. As to detinue for recovery of property, see the title DETINUE. As to conversion of animals hired, see the title ANIMALS. As to liens, see the title LIENS.

§ 1. Nature and Elements in General.

Definition and Nature.—Bailment is a term of very large signification, and is defined as "a delivery of goods in trust, upon a contract, express or implied, that the trust shall be executed, and the goods returned by the bailee, as soon as the purposes of the bailment shall be answered." 2 Kent 559. Watson *v.* State, 70 Ala. 13, 14.

Judge Story defines a bailment as "a delivery of a thing in trust for some special object or purpose, and upon a contract, express or implied, to conform to the object or purpose of the trust." Watson *v.* State, 70 Ala. 13, 14.

A bailment is qualified, limited, or special property, in a thing capable of absolute ownership. Magee *v.* Toland, 8 Port. 36. See Cartlidge *v.* Slone, 124 Ala. 596, 26 So. 918.

A bailment is treated in equity as a trust, but the reason seems to be to enable the beneficiary to recover the fund which, in law, he might not be able to do on account of want of privity in the contract. Henry *v.* Porter, 46 Ala. 293, 295.

Contract Essential.—"A bailment is a contract, and its terms, and the rights and liabilities of the bailor, and bailee, depend on the agreement of the parties. As the third persons, a special property is incident to the possession of the bailee, which enables him to protect the thing bailed, from injury by mere wrongdoers, or to recover it from them." Calhoun *v.* Thompson, 56 Ala. 166, 171.

To make out a case of bailment, there must be a contract, either expressed or implied, and the mere taking, by an overseer, of cotton seed left by the former occupant on the plantation of the employer of the overseer, and the use of it by his direction, will not support a declaration by the owner of the cotton seed against the overseer, for the value of it, as upon a bailment to him. Bohannon *v.* Springfield, 9 Ala. 789.

Bailment Distinguished from Other Transactions.—When a landlord purchases a mule, and delivers it to his tenant, to be used in the cultivation of crops on the rented lands; promising to sell the mule to the tenant when the latter may be able to buy it, but specifying no time or price; the transaction is not a conditional sale, but is a mere bailment, with a privilege to the tenant of purchasing, which he may or may not exercise at his option; and a purchaser from the tenant, without notice of the bailment, acquires no title. McCall *v.* Powell, 64 Ala. 254. See the title SALES.

What Constitutes a Bailment in General.—"A person becomes a bailee for hire when he takes property into his care and custody for a compensation." Prince *v.* Alabama State Fair, 106 Ala. 340, 17 So. 449, 450.

Where title to goods has passed, but they remain in the custody of the seller, he is presumptively a mere bailee and liable for their safe keeping and delivery as a bailee. Cook & Laurie Contracting Co. *v.* Bell (Ala.), 59 So. 273.

An administratrix, who was the sole distributee of her intestate's estate, delivered a part of it to her married daughter, and took from her and her husband a receipt reciting that: "Said property to be used and employed by us for our sole use and benefit, but nevertheless to be subject to her order, and to be returned whenever she may make demand of us, until the day of final settlement of said estate. Without recourse to said property being rendered necessary in order to pay off the debts and claims against said estate, and when the rights of said [administratrix] as sole heir to said estate shall accrue to her, she will substitute for this instrument such other conveyance as she may deem proper." Held, that the transaction was a mere bailment, determinable on the administratrix's demand at any time before the final settlement of the estate, subject to the provision for the substitution of another conveyance, if the property was not needed for the payment of debts. English *v.* McNair, 34 Ala. 40.

Since, to constitute a bailment, there must be a contract, either express or implied, evidence of the mere taking, by an overseer, of cotton seed left by the former occupant on a plantation of the overseer's employer, and the use of it by his employer's direction, will not support a declaration by the owner of the cotton seed against the overseer for the value of it, as upon a bailment to him. Bohannon *v.* Springfield, 9 Ala. 789.

Vendee Disaffirming Sale.—A vendee, seeking the rescission of a contract for fraud, who retains the possession of the property after an offer to return or a tender with a view to redelivery, is merely the bailee of the vendor. Dill *v.* Camp, 22 Ala. 249.

Vendor in Possession after Sale.—A vendor who, after the payment of the purchase money, agrees to store and protect the property sold, and, when called upon, to deliver it at a specified place, is a bailee. Oakley *v.* State, 40 Ala. 372.

Title of Parties.—Neither the bailor or

bailee of a personal chattel has an absolute property in the chattel. The property in both is qualified, and each of them is entitled to his action, if the goods be damaged or taken away. The bailee, on account of his possession, and the bailor because the possession of the bailee is immediately his possession. Magee *v.* Toland, 8 Port. 36.

§ 2. Particular Forms of Bailment.

Mutuum.—"A mutuum is created, when the identical thing bailed is not to be returned, but another thing of the same nature, kind or value." Derrick *v.* Baker, 9 Port. 362, 363.

Hiring.—"Hiring is a known species of bailment, and one of its distinguishing characteristics is that it is never gratuitous; it is always a reward or compensation." Learned-Letcher Lumber Co. *v.* Fowler, 109 Ala. 169, 19 So. 396, 398.

"The hirer of chattels for a term is a bailee, doubtless, but of a particular class or kind. The trust created is not exclusively for the benefit of the bailor, but rather for his own benefit." Watson *v.* State, 70 Ala. 13, 15.

Questions of Law and Fact.—Where the evidence showed that no charge was customarily made by a steamboat for carrying cash letters unless a receipt was demanded, it was proper to leave to the jury the question whether the letters involved in the suit were of the paid class. Knox *v.* Rives, 14 Ala. 249, 68 Am. Dec. 97.

§ 3. Validity in General.

Recording Contract.—Although the borrower may have had the continuous possession of chattels for more than three years, without the registration required by the second section of the statute of frauds, yet, if the owner resumes the possession of them before a creditor acquires a lien upon them, they can not be subjected to the payment of the borrower's debts. Pharis *v.* Leachman, 20 Ala. 662.

In trover for goods loaned by plaintiff which had come into possession of defendant through the death of the borrower, who was his tenant, a receipt given by the borrower, on receiving the goods, more than three years before the action was brought, is not inadmissible in evidence, under Code 1876, § 2173, which provides that all loans in writing under which possession is suffered to remain for three years with the party entitled to the use shall vest an absolute estate in the loanee "as to creditors and purchasers of such person," unless such loan is recorded. Butler *v.* Jones, 80 Ala. 436, 2 So. 300.

Estoppel of Bailees to Assert Illegality.—Where an administrator makes an illegal bailment of property belonging to his intestate's estate, he is estopped from setting up a title in avoidance of it, though he may recover the property by suit after the termination of the bailment according to its terms. English *v.* McNair, 34 Ala. 40.

§ 4. Delivery and Acceptance.

Acceptance.—The general rule, whenever property is committed to another, to be held for the use of, or to deliver to, a third person, is that such person shall signify to the mandatary his assent to it, or the conditions of the mandate. Lockhart *v.* Wyatt, 10 Ala. 231, 44 Am. Dec. 481.

§ 5. Title and Rights to Property.

§ 6. —— In General.

Rights of Bailee.—"In a bailment by way of mutuum, the chattel bail becomes the absolute property of the bailee to do what he pleases with it." Henry *v.* Porter, 46 Ala. 293, 295.

Special Title or Rights of Bailees.—A bailee for hire can not make a valid sale of the subject of the bailment, "even to bona fide purchaser who may buy in ignorance of the vendor's want of title." Medlin *v.* Wilkerson, 81 Ala. 147, 1 So. 37; Boozer *v.* Jones, 169 Ala. 481, 53 So. 1019. See Singer Mfg. Co. *v.* Belgart, 84 Ala. 519, 4 So. 400; Milner, etc., Co. *v.* DeLoach Mill Mfg. Co., 139 Ala. 645, 36 So. 765.

Unless authorized by the terms of the bailment, a bailee can not make a sale which will alter the general property of the bailor, and divest him of the right to maintain trover for its conversion against the bailee, the purchaser, or any one claiming under such sale. Calhoun *v.* Thompson, 56 Ala. 166, 28 Am. Rep. 754.

To enable a bailee to assert an adverse

possession against his bailor, he must do some open unequivocal act evincing such intention, and this must be brought to the knowledge of the bailor. Knight *v.* Bell, 22 Ala. 198; Lucas *v.* Daniels, 34 Ala. 188.

Three years' possession of personal property, under a loan, does not render such property liable to the debts of the bailee, contracted before the expiration of the three years. Durden *v.* McWilliams, 31 Ala. 206.

Possession of personal property for three years, under a loan, does not subject it to the debts of the party who has possession, unless his creditor, while it is thus held, acquires a lien on it by reducing his debt to judgment, and taking out execution. McCoy *v.* Odom, 20 Ala. 502.

§ 7. —— Estoppel of Bailee to Deny Title of Bailor.

See post, "Evidence," § 24.

In General.—The bailee can not defend against the bailor unless the latter's possession was tortious. The privity of contract and rules of public policy alike estop the bailee from disputing the bailor's title. Crosswell *v.* Lehman, etc., Co., 54 Ala. 363, 365, cited in note in 33 L. R. A., N. S., 684, 685.

As a general rule, the bailee can not set up the title of a third person, in defense of an action by his bailor; but, if the bailor in fact had no valid title, the bailee may deliver the goods to the rightful owner on demand, or hold them subject to his order on notice and demand, the onus of providing that defense resting on him. Young *v.* East Alabama R. Co., 80 Ala. 100; Calhoun *v.* Thompson, 56 Ala. 166; Powell *v.* Robinson, 76 Ala. 423; Crosswell *v.* Lehman, etc., Co., 54 Ala. 363; Jackson *v.* Jackson, 97 Ala. 372, 12 So. 437. See note in 33 L. R. A., N. S., 684.

Specific Applications of Rule.—Where a bailee violates his contract of bailment by suffering the property to be sold on execution for his debt, the purchaser at the sale acquiring an absolute title, he becomes upon acquiring the property again from such purchaser, as between the lender and himself, a mere bailee as before, and can not defend against the lender under the title of the purchaser at the execution sale. Knight *v.* Bell, 22 Ala. 198, cited in note in 33 L. R. A., N. S., 684.

A bailee employed for a compensation to keep possession of property can not show as a defense to an action against him for its conversion that he repudiated his trust, and was holding possession of such property for himself. Plummer *v.* Hardison, 6 Ala. App. 525, 60 So. 502.

§ 8. Care and Use of Property, and Negligence of Bailee.

§ 9. —— In General.

Care of Property in General.—The degree of care required of a bailee is proportioned to the nature, intrinsic value, etc., of the article entrusted to his keeping. A man will not be expected to take the same care of a bag of oats, as of a bag of dollars; of a bale of cotton as of a box of diamonds or other jewelry; of a load of wood as a box of rare painting; of a rude block of marble as of an exquisite sculptured statue. The bailee there ought to proportion his care, to the injury or loss which is likely to be sustained by any improvidence on his part, and to the watchfulness necessary to the preservation of the article. Hatchett & Bro. *v.* Gibson, 13 Ala. 587.

When a bailee undertakes to perform some act in respect to the property of another, he is not bound to do it; but if the act is performed, it must be done with some degree of care, and the bailee will be held responsible for any injury or loss that may result from a want of due care in what he does. Melbourne *v.* Louisville, etc., R. Co., 88 Ala. 443, 6 So. 762.

Insurance and Storage.—Where one obtains an insurance on the property of another in his possession, without instructions so to do, the owner may adopt the policy at any time before or within a reasonable time after a loss. Watkins *v.* Durand, 1 Port. 251.

§ 10. —— Bailments for Sole Benefit of Bailor.

Duty in General.—When the bailment is for the sole benefit of the bailor, the law requires only slight diligence or ordinary care on the part of the bailee, and makes him answerable only for gross neglect. Henry *v.* Porter, 46 Ala. 293.

The trust and confidence reposed on the bailor in the gratuitous bailee is regarded as a sufficient consideration to support the obligation, which the law implies, that the bailee will bestow the degree of care and diligence required by the law. The law deems the trust and confidence of the bailor, and the bailee's obligation of care and diligence, as reciprocal stipulations of the contract of bailment, like mutual promises, each constituting a consideration of the other. Morris *v.* Lewis, 33 Ala. 53, 56.

A mandatary or bailee who undertakes, without reward, to take care of, or perform some duty or labor affecting, the subject of the bailment, is required to use such care as men of common sense and prudence ordinarily take of their own affairs, and is only liable for bad faith or gross negligence. Haynie *v.* Waring, 29 Ala. 263.

§ 11. —— Bailments for Mutual Benefit.

In General.—Where the bailment is for the mutual benefit of both parties, the law imposes upon the bailee the duty of exercising that degree of care in respect to the property which the man of average prudence and diligence would bestow upon his own like property under like conditions, and which the law denominates "ordinary care." Higman *v.* Camody, 112 Ala. 267, 20 So. 480, 482. See Louisville, etc., R. Co. *v.* Buffington, 131 Ala. 620, 31 So. 592.

"The bailee of a horse for hire is bound to take the same care of it that a prudent man would of his property, and i responsible for all injuries that result from his neglect. If the horse becomes sick or exhausted, it is his duty to abstain from using it; and, if he pursued his journey, he is liable for all the injury occasioned thereby." Higman *v.* Camody, 112 Ala. 267, 20 So. 480, 482, cited in note in 43 L. R. A., N. S., 1186.

Where plaintiff delivered to cotton ginners certain cotton in controversy to be ginned and stored for hire, the ginners were bailees for hire, chargeable with the exercise of ordinary care. Hackney *v.* Perry, 44 So. 1029, 152 Ala. 626, cited in note in 43 L. R. A., N. S., 1171.

Care of Goods Delivered for Manufactures.—Where defendant agreed to gin plaintiff's cotton in preference to all other, but ginned other cotton before a part of plaintiff's, and the gin and plaintiff's cotton were burnt, he is liable for the loss, though there was no negligence as to the fire. Pattison *v.* Wallace, 1 Stew. 48.

Care of Property Delivered for Exhibition.—In an action against a corporation for the value of a picture lost by it while engaged in carrying on a public fair, it appeared that the article was shipped by plaintiff upon invitation of defendant, issued in pursuance of its general purpose to augment its receipts, and lost, after the close of the exhibition, by reason of the failure of defendant's agent to return the picture to plaintiff. Held, that the transaction was a lucrative bailment, and the defendant is liable for the loss. Prince *v.* Alabama State Fair, 106 Ala. 340, 17 So. 449, 28 L. R. A. 716. See 43 L. R. A., N. S., 1171.

Loss by Accident or Unavoidable Causes.—An action of trover can not be sustained for goods taken by an armed force, without any negligence or complicity on the part of the bailee. Abraham *v.* Nunn, 42 Ala. 51.

Defendant was driving plaintiff's mare, attached to a harrow, preparing the soil of a field which had been previously planted to corn; and while the mare was being driven in a careful manner she was injured by the end of a cornstalk piercing her breast. The work was not dangerous or hazardous. Defendant immediately unhitched the mare, gave her proper attention, and a few hours thereafter returned her to plaintiff, and assisted him in caring for her. Held, that defendant was not liable for negligence because of such injury, though he had agreed not to use the mare for such work. Cartlidge *v.* Slone, 26 So. 918, 124 Ala. 596.

Repair of Hired Chattels.—In an action against a bailee for hire for damages to a barge, it appeared that, when hired, the plaintiff had represented the barge to be in good condition. After one trip, defendant discovered that it was leaking badly. Held, that defendant had no right to rely upon the representations of plaintiff in making a second voyage with the barge, but should either repair the barge or notify the owner of its condition. Higman *v.* Camody, 112 Ala. 267, 20 So. 480.

Negligence of Servants of Bailee.—Where cotton was sent to be ginned, and was destroyed by a fire that burned the gin house, through the negligence of the bailee's servants he was held liable to the owner. Maxwell *v.* Eason, 1 Stew. 514.

A bailee for reward may maintain an action in his own name against a steamboat company, for the loss of his reward and damages paid by him to the owner of the goods, for injuries thereto caused by the negligence of the servants of the company after he had placed the goods in their charge to be carried to their place of destination. McGill *v.* Monette, 37 Ala. 49.

§ 12. Conversion by Bailee.

See the title TROVER AND CONVERSION.

What Constitutes Conversion.—If the thing bailed is used in a different manner, or for a different purpose, or for a longer time, than was agreed by the parties, the hirer is guilty of a conversion, and is answerable for all damages, and even for a loss which due care could not have prevented. Hooks *v.* Smith, 18 Ala. 338; Moseley *v.* Wilkinson, 24 Ala. 411; Wilkinson *v.* Moseley, 30 Ala. 562; Fail *v.* McArthur, 31 Ala. 26; Jones *v.* Fort, 36 Ala. 449. See note in 43 L. R. A., N. S., 1192.

"If a horse is hired as a saddle horse, the hirer has no right to use him in a cart, or to carry loads, or as a beast of burden; and one who borrows jewels, to wear to a ball, will be responsible if he wear them to the theatre, or to a gaming house." Fail *v.* McArthur, 31 Ala. 26, 32.

Where a bailee puts the goods intrusted to him beyond his control, he is liable for a conversion. St. John *v.* O'Connel, 7 Port. 466.

Under an agreement by which stock is placed with another to be fed during the winter, the stock to be liable for the expenses of keeping them, the bailee's implied power to sell them to pay the expense of their keeping does not authorize a sale of more than sufficient to do so. Such a sale would be a conversion. Whitlock *v.* Heard, 13 Ala. 776, 48 Am. Dec. 73.

An absolute sale of a chattel by one who has possession under a contract of hiring does not transfer to his vendee the right to the unexpired term, but is a violation of the contract of hiring, and gives the owner the immediate right to take peaceable possession if he can. Hair *v.* Little, 28 Ala. 236.

Where the hirer of a chattel exchanges it for another during the term of the bailment, there is a conversion authorizing immediate suit. Atkinson *v.* Jones, 72 Ala. 248.

A purchase by the bailee himself, at a public sale by auction, is not absolutely void, but voidable at the election of the party whose title is sought to be divested by such sale. Whitlock *v.* Heard, 13 Ala. 776.

It is the duty of the bailee on the termination of the bailment, to restore the property to the person from whom he received it; and if he delivers it, by negligence or design, to another, who is not entitled to it, it amounts to a conversion, for which he is responsible. Where he has notice that he property does not belong to his principal, a delivery to him will be a conversion, for which the true owner can hold him liable. The bailee has no higher or better right than his bailor, and is not exempted from liability to the true owner, because he holds the property as bailee, claiming no title. In such case, he may refuse to deliver it to his principal, and surrender it to the rightful claimant, but he assumes the burden of establishing a paramount title. Powell *v.* Robinson, 76 Ala. 423. See Crosswell *v.* Lehman, etc., Co., 54 Ala. 363; Calhoun *v.* Thompson, 56 Ala. 166.

Where a person hires an animal for a specified kind of work and for a definite time, and in violation of the bailment such person uses it for other and different labor, or for a time longer than that specified for, such unauthorized use by the bailee is a conversion of the animal, for which the bailor may maintain trover for its value. Ledbetter *v.* Thomas, 30 So. 342, 130 Ala. 299.

In an action of trover to recover damages for the alleged conversion of a mule, the evidence showed that the plaintiff had rented said mule, together with its mate, to the defendant, for the purpose of plowing them, at the rate of 25 cents per hour, and the plaintiff was to furnish a driver; that after three days the driver furnished by the plaintiff was taken sick, and the defendant sent the team back to the plaintiff, with a note in which he said that "if you can let me have the team for balance of week I will let" a person the defendant had hired plow it. The team was sent back. It was not returned at the end of the week, but was plowed a part of the day on Monday. That evening the mule involved in the controversy was taken sick and died. Held, that the acceptance by the plaintiff of the terms proposed in the note extended the operation of the bailment until Saturday night, and no longer; that the use of the mule by the plaintiff on the following Monday, in the absence of all proof of consent by plaintiff of its use on that day, was unauthorized, and therefore constituted a conversion, for which the defendant is liable in an action of trover. Ledbetter *v.* Thomas, 30 So. 342, 130 Ala. 299.

Demand.—A demand of goods bailed is not always necessary to support an action by the bailor against the bailee, as in case of their tortious conversion or destruction. Cothran *v.* Moore, 1 Ala. 423.

A bailee becomes liable to an action without any previous demand, whenever he coverts the thing bailed to his own use or it is lost or destroyed by gross negligence on his part. Stewart *v.* Frazier, 5 Ala. 114.

Def nses.—If, when demand is made by a third person, in whose hands the writing was placed for that purpose, the bailee does not call on him to produce his authority, but places his refusal upon the ground that the chattel had been removed from his possession by some other person, he can not object, in his defense to an action of trover, that the agent did not show an authority when the chattel was demanded. Spence *v.* Mitchell, 9 Ala. 744.

A bailee who refuses to deliver the goods to the bailor or to a buyer from him, and who did not deliver them to any one having a superior right, could not question bailor's right to dispose of the goods, and relieve himself of liability for conversion. Blair *v.* Riddle, 3 Ala. App. 292, 57 So. 382.

§ 13. Compensation and Lien of Bailee.

Waiver or Loss of Lien.—If a bailee refuses to deliver the goods except to the consignee or person holding the transportation receipt, but asserts no lien for storage paid by him, he can not afterwards set up that claim to defeat an action by the owner, but must be held to have waived it. Leigh *v.* Mobile & O. R. Co., 58 Ala. 165.

Where, in conversion against a public ginner for plaintiff's cotton, it appeared that, if a demand for the cotton was made, there was an unqualified refusal to deliver, such refusal operated as a waiver of defendant's lien, if any, for ginning. Alabama Cotton Oil Co. *v.* Weeden, 43 So. 926, 150 Ala. 587.

Enforcement of Lien.—Under an agreement by which stock is placed with another to be fed during the winter, the stock to be liable for the expenses of keeping them, the bailee has power to sell them to pay the expense of their keeping. Whitlock *v.* Heard, 13 Ala. 776.

§ 14. Compensation of Bailor for Use of Property.

Right to Compensation.—Four .pars were hired for an indefinite period to aid in raising a steamboat that was sunk. For the use of each the owner of the boat was ‘o pay one dollar a day, and, if they were "lost or injured," he was to pay $25 each for three, and $10 for the other. Held that, although the spars were not lost or injured, the owner of the boat might pay $85, the price of the spars, and avoid the payment of the hire. Pope *v.* Murray, 6 Ala. 489.

If the owner resumes the possession of his hired chattel during the term, from a subhirer, without legal cause, and refuses to surrender him on the demand of the hirer, he is guilty of a breach of the contract, and can not recover any portion of the hire; nor can he excuse such breach of contract, as against the hirer, on the ground that his own unlawful act amounted to a tort as against the subhirer. Harris *v.* Maury, 30 Ala. 679.

If the owner retakes the possession of his chattel before the expiration of the stipulated time of hiring, and against the objection of the hirer, he can not afterwards recover any portion of the hire. Farrow *v.* Bragg, 30 Ala. 261.

§ 15. Rights and Liabilities as to Third Persons.

See post, "Actions by or Against Third Persons," § 28.

In General.—In an action for conversion, it is immaterial whether plaintiff was the owner or bailee of the property. Baker *v.* Troy Compress Co., 21 So. 496, 114 Ala. 415.

Bailor's Rights.—The wrongful seizure under an attachment of goods in the hands of a bailee, and taking from him a forthcoming bond for their delivery, is such a conversion as will support an action of trover by the owner against the sheriff. Abercrombie *v.* Bradford, 16 Ala. 560.

A bailor, with the immediate right of repossession, may maintain trespass against a tortious taker from the gratuitous bailee. Walker *v.* Wilkinson, 35 Ala. 725, 76 Am. Dec. 315.

Bailee's Rights.—Parties who have entered into a bond as bailees of property that had been levied on by deputy sheriff can not object that the deputy transcended his powers, where the sheriff himself affirms the act. Whitsett *v.* Womack, 8 Ala. 466.

The bailee of a sheriff, to whom the property of a third person is delivered, upon a contract to return it at the sale day, has such a property in the thing bailed as will authorize him to sue a wrongdoer, for depriving him of the possession. Cox *v.* Easley, 11 Ala. 362.

A bailee for hire may maintain an action for negligent injuries to the subject of the bailment while in his possession. Montgomery Gaslight Co. *v.* Montgomery & E. Ry. Co., 86 Ala. 372, 5 So. 735.

The plaintiff had possession as bailee for hire, and owned such a special property in the cars as to authorize an action in its name against a third person, for negligently or tortiously injuring them. Such bailee may maintain an action on the case for an injury to the bailed property, as well as in action of trespass, trover, or detinue against a wrongdoer, in a proper case. Montgomery Gaslight Co. *v.* Montgomery, etc., R. Co., 86 Ala. 372, 5 So. 735, 738.

A bailee of goods for hire may maintain an action against a steamboat for negligently towing a barge containing the goods, so that he lost his compensation as bailee, and was compelled to pay a sum of money to the bailor. McGill *v.* Monette, 37 Ala. 49.

Liabilities to Third Persons.—If a bailee, asserting no title in himself in good faith restores the property to the bailor, in accordance with the express or implied terms of the bailment, before he is notified that the true owner will look to him for it, no action can be maintained against him, either for the property or its value. Nelson *v.* Iverson, 17 Ala. 216.

A bailee of property, after notice from a purchaser of such property from the bailor of his acquisition thereof, stands in the same relation to the purchaser as he did to the original bailor, and can not deny such purchaser's title and justify his conversion of the property by his refusal to deliver to the purchaser on the theory that the property belonged to another. Riddle *v.* Blair, 42 So. 560, 148 Ala. 461, cited in note in 33 L. R. A., N. S., 684, 685, 686, 694.

§ 16. Termination.

In General.—A bailment terminates when its objects are accomplished. Lay *v.* Lawson, 23 Ala. 377.

Rights of Bailor.—The right of a bailor to terminate a bailment is not restricted to the lifetime of the bailee because it was accompanied with the declaration that he gave or loaned the property to the latter, but subject to his call at any time. McGehee *v.* Mahone, 37 Ala. 258.

On the bailee's failure to return the property at the expiration of the term, the bailor may either treat the bailment as ended, and bring his action, or, where the hiring is from year to year, may consider the bailment as continuing or renewed; and in this class of cases the question whether the bailment continues is for the jury to determine. Benje *v.* Creagh, 21 Ala. 151.

Option of Parties.—Where the duration of a bailment for hire is not expressed in the contract, it may be terminated at the will of either party. Learned-Letcher Lumber Co. *v.* Fowler, 109 Ala. 169, 19 So. 396.

Delivery of Shipper's Cotton by Compress Company.—Where a shipper delivered cotton to a compress company and then, in accordance with arrangements between the compress company and a railroad company, delivered the compress company's receipts to the railroad company, and received bills of lading, neither the contract between the shipper and the railroad company for carriage nor the assignment of that contract to a consignee of the cotton, will affect the right of the shipper to have the compress company deliver the cotton to the railroad company, and a constructive delivery to the railroad company will not be sufficient to relieve the compress company of liability to the shipper. Southern Ry. Co. *v.* Jones Cotton Co., 52 So. 899, 167 Ala. 575.

§ 17. Redelivery of Property.

Bailee's Obligation to Return.—As a general rule, it is the duty of the hirer, in the absence of any express stipulation, to return a chattel when the bailment is determined. Benje *v.* Creagh, 21 Ala. 151.

When a bailment terminates the bailee should return the property on demand. Lay *v.* Lawson, 23 Ala. 377.

A party who seeks to rescind a contract of hiring on the ground of fraud must offer to return the property hired within a reasonable time if the parties live at a distance from each other, or by an actual delivery or a tender with a view to delivery if they reside near each other, and the property is susceptible of easy transportation. Camp *v.* Dill, 27 Ala. 553.

Persons Entitled to Return.—Surrender by a bailee or possession under a judgment by default, wherein he failed to give his bailor statutory notice to defend, will render him liable for the goods, unless he has delivered them to the real owner. Powell *v.* Robinson, 76 Ala. 423.

Time of Return.—Where one receives a chattel from another, under a stipulation, in writing, that he will return it "whenever called for, in good repair, and free from expense," he must deliver it on demand. Spence *v.* Mitchell, 9 Ala. 744.

Property Returnable.—Where the gratuitous bailee of a naked deposit of bank bills deposited them with a person of due credit, who made a general deposit of them with a bank of good credit, and, when called on to return them, delivered the proper sum in bills of the same bank, but not the identical ones received by him, equity will not hold him responsible for the depreciation of the bill on account of the failure of the bank which issued them. Henry *v.* Porter, 46 Ala. 293.

§ 18. Actions between Bailor and Bailee.

As to nature of an action for putting a slave to a different work than that to which he was hired, see the title ACTION.

§ 19. —— Nature and Form.

Election of Remedies.—See the titles ACTION; ASSUMPSIT, ACTION OF; TROVER AND CONVERSION.

When a bailee fails to return the goods on demand, the principal has an election of remedies. He may sue in assumpsit for a breach of the contract, or in case for negligence, or, if there has been a conve sion of the goods, in trover for the conversion. Davis *v.* Hurt, 114 Ala. 146, 21 So. 468, 469; Hackney *v.* Perry, 152 Ala. 626, 44 So. 1029.

Whenever a contract includes a bailment, and it is broken by the bailee, either case or assumpsit may be brought by the bailor. Bank *v.* Huggins, 3 Ala. 206.

Assumpsit.—Where money is deposited in the hands of a trustee or bailee, for the use and benefit of a minor, under a contract authorizing him to defray out of it the charges of the schooling, clothing and other probable expenses which he might deem necessary, the minor may, on attaining majority, maintain an action against him for money had and received, if a balance had been ascertained against him on settlement, or if he never entered on the discharge of the duties imposed on him by the contract; but, if such trustee assumed the fiduciary duties which devolved on him under the contract, and has never had a settlement of accounts with the beneficiary, an action at law can not be maintained. Vincent *v.* Rogers, 30 Ala. 471, 472.

Detinue.—Detinue lies against one having actual possession of a chattel, or such control thereover that he could surrender possession without breach of a legal duty, so that the action was maintainable against the bailee of a mule who had placed it in possession of another under an attempted sale thereof, under an agreement that it should be returned in case the bailee had to account to the bailor therefor. Boozer *v.* Jones, 53 So. 1018, 169 Ala. 481. See Stoker *v.* Yerby, 11 Ala. 322.

Detinue will lie by the trustees and deacons of a religious society, to recover a deed which they had deposited with the defendant, and which he refused to redeliver. Stoker *v.* Yerby, 11 Ala. 322.

§ 20. —— Conditions Precedent.

Demand.—If a bailee fails to return the property on demand after the bailment terminates, he is liable for damages in detinue, without a special demand. Lay *v.* Lawson, 23 Ala. 377.

§ 21. —— Defenses.

Failure to Redeliver Property because of Other Claims.—A bailee charged with conversion, can not defend a refusal to deliver the property to plaintiff because others claimed it, where he did not deliver the property to any one who claimed it, but either converted it himself or allowed others to do so. Riddle *v.* Blair, 163 Ala. 314, 51 So. 14, cited in note in 33 L. R. A., N. S., 684, 687.

Acts 1880-81, p. 121, provides that when a person has possession of personal property to which he asserts no claim and which is claimed by two others adversely to each other, he may notify each of the claim of the other, and require them to litigate between themselves their rights to such property; and that such notice shall be a full defense to the person in possession against any action brought against him by either of such claimants, on account of the property, and against any liability for the loss, injury, or destruction of it except when it occurs from the failure to take care of the property. Held that, where an action brought against a party in possession by the party claiming adversely to his bailor, defendant waives the benefit of such statute if he neither defends the suit by showing that he has given the statutory notice, nor notifies his bailor of the institution of the suit; and that on such waiver he is remitted to his common-law liability as bailee, and his surrender of the property under judgment by default recovered against him is no defense to a subsequent action against him by his bailor. Powell *v.* Robinson, 76 Ala. 423.

Proof that a bailee, alleged to have converted bailed property, refused to deliver it to plaintiff because he doubted his right thereto, may rebut the presumption of malice which might otherwise arise, but does not amount to a complete defense. Riddle *v.* Blair, 51 So. 14, 163 Ala. 314.

Subsequent Return and Acceptance of Property after Misuse.—"The subsequent return of the property after its misuse, and its acceptance by the bailor, bar an action for the conversion, but its redelivery will only go in mitigation of damages." Cartlidge *v.* Slone, 124 Ala. 596, 26 So. 918, 920.

Property in Possession of Compress Company Constructively Delivered to Railroad Company.—Where cotton was injured by the negligence of a compress company while still in its actual possession, the fact that there had been a constructive delivery to a railroad company by delivery of the compress receipts did not relieve the compress company from liability for its negligence. Gulf Compress Co. *v.* Jones Cotton Co., 172 Ala. 645, 55 So. 206.

§ 22. —— Time to Sue, and Limitations.

See generally, the title LIMITATION OF ACTIONS.

When Statute Begins to Run.—"In an action of trover brought by a bailor against his bailee, the statute of limitations does not begin to run in favor of the bailee against the bailor until the bailee, to the knowledge of the bailor, does some act in repudiation of the bailment. Until the bailor has notice—or at least facts putting him on notice—to the contrary, he has a right to presume that the possession by the bailee, if he continues in possession, is in accordance with the terms of the bailment." Plummer *v.* Hardison, 6 Ala. App. 525, 60 So. 502, 503. See Knight *v.* Bell, 22 Ala. 198; Benje *v.* Creagh, 21 Ala. 151.

§ 23. —— Pleading.

Declaration or Complaint.—Since pleadings are to be construed most strongly against the pleader, an allegation that plaintiff "let" defendant have the use, etc., of his mare, and that she died by reason of defendant's negligence, is equivalent to an allegation of a hiring of plaintiff's mare for a reward. Cartlidge *v.* Slone, 26 So. 918, 124 Ala. 596.

In an action against a bailee to recover an alleged deposit of bank notes, it is not necessary to state by what bank the notes were issued, a general description being sufficient. Moody *v.* Keener, 7 Port. 218.

Since an allegation that defendant so recklessly, carelessly, and wantonly used plaintiff's mare that she died is repugnant, and, being strictly construed against him, charges negligence only, where the complaint showed no duty on defendant to care for the mare, nor facts from which such duty could be implied, it did not state facts sufficient to constitute a cause of action. Cartlidge *v.* Slone, 26 So. 918, 124 Ala. 596.

Counts alleging that plaintiff delivered to defendant certain cotton to be kept for hire, and that defendants received the cotton and agreed to redeliver it to plaintiff on demand; that the cotton, though received by defendants, had never been returned to plaintiff, though she had demanded the same before the bringing of the suit; and that defendants negligently lost, misplaced, or delivered the cotton to some person, and thus failed on account of such negligence to del'ver the cotton or the proceeds thereof, which was thereupon lost to plaintiff,. to her damage, etc., were counts in the case and contained sufficient averments of negligence. Hackney *v.* Perry, 44 So. 1029, 152 Ala. 626.

Where, in a suit against cotton ginners and B., to whom it was alleged they wrongfully delivered plaintiff's cotton, counts in the complaint charged a contract relation, from which the alleged duty to redeliver the cotton to plaintiff arose, as to both the ginners and B., but there was a failure of proof of any contract relation between plaintiff and B., there was a fatal variance as to such counts, notwithstanding the rule that in actions for tort, where two or more are jointly sued, a recovery may generally be had, according to the proof, as to all or any number less than all. Hackney *v.* Perry, 152 Ala. 626, 44 So. 1029.

§ 24. —— Evidence.

Presumptions and Burden of Proof.—Where a bailee of goods, on demand made, fails to redeliver or account for such failure, negligence will be prima facie imputed to him, and he is bound to prove that the loss was not caused by his want of ordinary care. Hackney *v.* Perry, 44 So. 1029, 152 Ala. 626; Seals *v.* Edmondson, 71 Ala. 509; First Nat. Bank *v.* First Nat. Bank, 116 Ala. 520, 22 So. 976. See Prince *v.* Alabama State Fair, 106 Ala. 340, 17 So. 449.

Where, however, there is a full explanation of the failure to deliver on demand, and is shown that the goods were lost by a cause not involving the bailee in liability, as by fire, the attending circumstances being known to the bailor before demand, and the demand being merely formal, it can not be presumed from the failure to deliver that the bailee had been wanting in care, or had been negligent, and his negligence was the proximate cause of the loss; and hence, upon the bailor, in a suit by him for damages resulting from the loss, rests the burden of offering some evidence tending to show that defendant had been guilty of negligence, causing or contributing to the destruction of the goods. Seals *v.* Edmondson, 71 Ala. 509.

It being the duty of one in possession of property on which he has a lien to take such care of it as a prudent man takes of his own similar property, the burden is on him to account for its not being forthcoming when demanded, after the lien has been discharged. Haas *v.* Taylor, 80 Ala. 459, 2 So. 633, cited in note in 43 L. R. A., N. S., 118.

In an action against a bailee for hire for damages to a barge, where the evidence as to the condition of the barge at the time of hiring was conflicting, it was error to charge that, for the plaintiff to recover, it must appear that defendant had failed to use ordinary care; such instruction placing the burden on plaintiff to show negligence on the part of defendant, irrespective of the condition of the barge. Higman *v.* Camody, 112 Ala. 267, 20 So. 480.

The burden of proof, where a conversion by the bailee for a misuse is relied upon for a recovery, is upon the plaintiff, just as it is in any other action for a conversion. The mere proof by the plaintiff that the mare was uninjured when delivered to the defendant, and was injured when returned by him, did not make out a prima facie case. It was incumbent upon him to prove to the reasonable satisfaction of the jury that the defendant made use of her in a way in violation of the terms of the bailment. Cartlidge *v.* Slone, 124 Ala. 596, 26 So. 918, 921.

Admissibility.—In an action against a bailee for hire for damages to a barge, a witness testified that the barge was defective in construction, in that it was not strengthened by rift bolts, without which it was liable to swag and open the seams. Held, that it was not admissible for plaintiff to show, on cross-examination of the witness, that greater care should be used in loading a barge thus defective than one supplied with rift bolts. Higman *v.* Camody, 112 Ala. 267, 20 So. 480.

§ 25. —— Damages.

Loss of Goods Due to Negligence of Seller after Sale and Payment of Price.—Where a buyer has paid the purchase price, and the title to goods has passed to him, and they are afterwards injured or destroyed through the negligence of the seller, acting as bailee, the buyer may recover the value of the goods, or the amount of the injury thereto. Cook & Laurie Contracting Co. *v.* Bell (Ala.), 59 So. 273.

§ 26. —— Trial.

Instructions.—Where the evidence was conflicting as to whether plaintiff delivered his mare to defendant to do heavy or light work, and the mare was injured in doing heavy work, an instruction in an action for such injury that plaintiff made out a prima facie case by proving to a reasonable certainty that the mare was not injured when defendant received her, and was injured when he returned her, was proper, since the burden was on plaintiff to show a violation of the terms of the bailment. Cartlidge *v.* Slone, 26 So. 918, 124 Ala. 596.

Where, in a suit for injuries received by plaintiff's mare while in defendant's possession, the evidence was conflicting as to whether the bailment was gratuitous or for hire, the refusal of an instruction that the contract of the parties was one of hiring was proper. Cartlidge *v.* Slone, 26 So. 918, 124 Ala. 596.

Where plaintiff claimed that his mare received injuries by reason of defendant's conversion, the refusal of instructions that, if the jury believed the mare died from plaintiff's improper treatment or doctoring after the injury, they must find for the defendant, or if they believed that the mare died from erysipelas or blood poison, and not from the injury, defendant was not liable, was proper, since plaintiff's right of action was complete when the conversion took place, and the condition of the mare when returned was only to be considered by the jury in fixing the amount of plaintiff's damages, and erysipelas or blood poisoning might have been the result of the injury. Cartlidge *v.* Slone, 26 So. 918, 124 Ala. 596.

Where plaintiff's mare was injured while in defendant's possession, and the evidence was conflicting as to whether plaintiff delivered the mare to do light work, or to do farm work generally, or whether the bailment was gratuitous or for hire, instructions that if defendant got the mare to do a particular kind of work, and did other work with her, he was liable for a conversion; or if he borrowed or hired her to do light work, and did heavy work with her, and while so engaged she received an injury from which she died, he was liable, though the injury occurred without his fault; or if defendant used the mare at different work from that agreed on, if any was agreed on, and she received an injury while so used, from which she died, defendant was liable, whether borrowed or hired—were proper. Cartlidge *v.* Slone, 124 Ala. 596, 26 So. 918.

§ 27. —— Judgment and Review.

Effect of Judgment.—In case of a claim of property the bailee might refuse the demand of the adverse claimant, and await an action at law by him; and on such action being brought, he might notify his bailor, and require him to defend the suit; in which case, the bailor would be bound by the judgment rendered, whether he appeared and defended it or not; but, if he was not notified, and did not appear, his rights would not be affected by the judgment. Powell *v.* Robinson, 76 Ala. 423.

§ 28. Actions by or against Third Persons.

Right of Action.—A bailee of hogs running at large in the range may maintain an action of trespass for injury to them. Hare *v.* Fuller, 7 Ala. 717. See ante, "Defenses," § 21.

Effect of Judgment.—A recovery by either the bailee or the owner for injury of hogs running at large in the range, would oust the other of his right of action. Hare *v.* Fuller, 7 Ala. 717, 718.

Balance.

See the titles ACCOUNT; ACCOUNT STATED.

Ballots.

See the title ELECTIONS.

Bankable Paper.

See the titles BANKS AND BANKING; CONTRACTS.

Bank Check.

See the title BANKS AND BANKING.

Bank Deposit.

See the title BANKS AND BANKING.

Banker's Lien.

See the title BANKS AND BANKING.

Banking Customs.

See the title BANKS AND BANKING.

Bank Notes.

See the title BANKS AND BANKING.

BANKRUPTCY.

Cross References.

As to assignments for benefit of creditors, see the title INSOLVENCY. As to acknowledgment and power of attorney to creditor's proxie, see the title ACKNOWLEDGMENT. As to admissions by bankrupt, see the title EVIDENCE. As to the abandonment of provisional receiver of bankrupt's property as deprivation of property without due process of law, see the title CONSTITUTIONAL LAW. As to the assignment of mechanic's lien by bankrupt to trustee, see the title MECHANICS' LIENS. As to waiver of garnishment, see the title GARNISHMENT. As to the best and secondary evidence of proceedings, see the title EVIDENCE. As to champertous sale of bankrupt's proceedings, see the title CHAMPERTY AND MAINTENANCE. As to conspiracy to commit offenses as being against bankrupt act, see the title CONSPIRACY. As to contract to prevent competition at sale of bankrupt's property, see the title CONTRACTS. As to the election of remedy by creditors of bankrupt, see the title ELECTION OF REMEDIES. As to estoppel of bankruptcy by assertion of title in another, see the title ESTOPPEL. As to estoppel to claim tax liens against bankrupt's estate, see the title ESTOPPEL. As to immunity to bankrupt giving incriminating testimony, see the title CRIMINAL LAW. As to interpleader by receiver in bankruptcy, see the title INTERPLEADER. As to jurisdiction of federal supreme court to review decisions of state courts involving bankruptcy acts, see the title COURTS. As to insolvency under local insolvent laws, see the title INSOLVENCY. As to landlord's lien on bankrupt's property, waiver or forfeiture of lien, see the title LANDLORD AND TENANT. As to the power of bankruptcy court to re-examine fact tried by jury, see the title JURY. As to presumption of regularity of bankruptcy proceedings, see the title EVIDENCE. As to the right of assignee to purchase at tax sale, see the title TAXATION. As to state laws as rules of decision in courts of bankruptcy, see the title COURTS. As to summary proceedings to compel surrender of bankrupt property by officer of state court, as denial of due process of law, see the title CONSTITUTIONAL LAW. As to the taxation of bankrupt's property, see the title TAXATION. As to the organization, etc., of courts having jurisdiction in bankruptcy, see the title COURTS.

I. CONSTITUTIONAL AND STATUTORY PROVISIONS.

§ 1. Bankruptcy Acts.

It is undeniably competent for congress to declare a decree in bankruptcy invalid, when irregularly or unfairly obtained, whenever and wherever it may be drawn in the question; to allow it to be impeached for fraud, or other kindred cause; and upon the allegation being established, to authorize all courts to pronounce it invalid. The Bankrupt Act of 1841 has done this, almost in totidem verbis. Mabry *v.* Herndon, 8 Ala. 848, 862. See post, "Appeal and Revision of Proceedings," VI.

§ 2. —— Construction and Operation in General.

The United States supreme court having held that the language of the Bankrupt Act of 1841, excepting from discharge debts "created in consequence of any defalcation as a public officer," "or while acting in any other fiduciary capacity," related to cases of express trust, and did not embrace cases of mere agency, the same construction must be given to the equivalent expressions in the Bankrupt Act of 1867. Woolsey *v.* Cade, 54 Ala. 378.

In construing the terms used in the bankrupt law, giving or excluding its benefits, resort must be had to their meaning in the common law, and not in the local law of the state where the bankrupt is domiciled. Austill *v.* Crawford, 7 Ala. 335.

II. PETITION, ADJUDICATION, WARRANT, AND CUSTODY OF PROPERTY.

(A) JURISDICTION AND COURSE OF PROCEDURE IN GENERAL.

§ 3. Jurisdiction of Courts of Bankruptcy in General.

The court of bankruptcy, by the filing of the voluntary petition, acquires full and exclusive jurisdiction of the bankrupt and his estate. Steele *v.* Moody, 53 Ala. 418.

District Courts of United States—Extent of Jurisdiction.—"The district courts of the United States, are not, by the general Bankrupt Act, invested with jurisdiction over all bankrupts, but only over such as petition to be discharged in the district where he shall reside or have his place of business at time of filing the petition." Stiles *v.* Lay, 9 Ala. 795, 799.

State Courts.—When a state court has acquired jurisdiction of person and subject matter before bankruptcy proceedings are instituted, and permitted to prosecute the suit until judgment is rendered, such judgment is conclusive upon the assignee, and upon all other persons. There are many categories to which this principle applies. Among them are stated cases in which the suitor has acquired a lien by execution or attachment more than four months before the adjudication in bankruptcy. So, also, when the assignee makes himself a party to a suit by or against the bankrupt, or, having notice fails to make himself a party, and the suit is prosecuted to a final determination. As a settlement of the matters involved in the issue, such judgment is conclusive upon the assignee, and upon all persons claiming in his right. In such cases, in the absence of fraud or kindred defense, it would seem the assignee could accomplish nothing by intervening. Sullivan *v.* Rabb, 86 Ala. 433, 5 So. 746, 749.

§ 4. Persons Subject to Jurisdiction.

§ 5. —— Place of Business, Residence, or Domicile.

Where Petition Must Be Filed.—Under the bankrupt law, the petition must be filed in the district where the supposed bankrupt, at the time of filing it, shall reside, or have his place of business, and if the district granting his discharge has not jurisdiction of the person by reason of residence, or place of business, the discharge is void. Stiles *v.* Lay, 9 Ala. 795.

One living with his family in New Hampshire, and carrying on business there, is a resident of that state within the act, although the spring previous, and for some years before, he had a commercial establishment in Alabama, acted as a citizen, and intended to remove his family there the next season. Stiles *v.* Lay, 9 Ala. 795.

§ 6. Rules, Forms, and Orders as to Procedure.

As to courts of bankruptcy in general, see ante, "Jurisdiction of Courts of Bankruptcy in General," § 3.

"The 10th section of the bankrupt law required the justice of the supreme court of the United States to frame general orders for regulating the practice and procedure of the district courts in bankruptcy and generally for carrying the provisions of the law into effect. These orders they were required to report to congress. In obedience to this requisition, general orders were framed and forms prescribed for the various proceedings in bankruptcy." Steele *v.* Moody, 53 Ala. 418, 424.

§ 7. Commencement of Proceedings.

In bankruptcy, the commencement of the proceeding is the filing of the petition. Griel *v.* Solomon, 82 Ala. 85, 2 So. 322.

(B) VOLUNTARY PROCEEDINGS.

§ 8. Nature of Proceedings.

"An adjudication of bankruptcy is in the nature of a statute execution for all creditors. The assignee, as the representative of creditors, stands in the relation of a judgment creditor, capable of enforcing every right such creditor could enforce." Steele *v.* Moody, 53 Ala. 418, 424.

§ 9. Persons Who May Become Voluntary Bankrupts.

§ 10. —— In General.

Under § 1 of the United States bankrupt law of 1841 declaring that its provisions shall not extend to one whose debt has been created while acting in a fiduciary capacity, a factor who has converted to his own use proceeds of goods consigned to him for sale is not prohibited from taking advantage of the act, the fiduciary capacity meant being a trust proper. Austill & Marshall *v.* Crawford, 7 Ala. 335, cited on the point in note in 42 L. R. A., N. S., 1094.

§ 11. —— Partners.

A partnership may be adjudged a bankrupt in voluntary or involuntary proceedings, irrespective of any adjudication as to individual members. Lacey *v.* Cowan, 162 Ala. 546, 50 So. 281.

§ 12. Adjudication.

The adjudication of a debtors bankruptcy is the pivotal period of all bankrupt proceedings, from which flow all of his disabilities, as well as the attendant rights of creditors conferred by the law; being, as it is, a judicial ascertainment of the fact that an act of bankruptcy was committed at some antecedent period, which is fixed, by relation, at the commencement of the bankrupt proceedings, which is the filing of the petition. Griel *v.* Solomon, 82 Ala. 85, 2 So. 322, 325.

The bankrupt court, in proceedings to declare one partner a bankrupt, can not declare the partnership or the other partner a bankrupt. Lacey *v.* Cowan, 162 Ala. 546, 50 So. 281.

Effect of Adjudication on Relationship of Landlord and Tenant.—The relation of landlord and tenant is not severed by adjudication in voluntary bankruptcy of the tenant under Act July 1, 1898, c. 541, 30 Stat. 544 (U. S. Comp. St. 1901, p. 3418). Shapiro *v.* Thompson, 160 Ala. 363, 49 So. 391.

(C) INVOLUNTARY PROCEEDINGS.

§ 13. Acts of Bankruptcy.

§ 14. —— Fraudulent Disposition of Property.

"The fraud and concealment of property by a bankrupt, it is held, must be deliberate and intentional to affect him; but it is said where property is discovered belonging to the bankrupt's estate, subsequent to the issuing of the decree, which has not been accounted for; the intention of the bankrupt being apparent, his discharge and certificate will be disallowed." Hargroves *v.* Cloud, 8 Ala. 173, 175.

§ 15. Persons Who May Be Adjudged Bankrupt.

§ 16. —— Corporation in General.

Name in Which a Corporation May Be Proceeded against.—A corporation may lawfully be proceeded against in bankruptcy in the name which it has acquired by usage, though its charter name is different. Jones *v.* Watkins, 1 Stew. 81.

§ 17. Petition.

§ 18. —— Requisites and Sufficiency.

Insufficiency of Allegation.—A petition in bankruptcy alleged that the petitioners were creditors of the company in a requisite sum, and that its principal place of business was within the jurisdiction of the court, and that the bankrupt had committed a specified act of bankruptcy within four months of filing the petition, and prayed the appointment of a receiver to take possession of the property; but it did not appear that the bankrupt was such a corporation as could be declared an involuntary bankrupt. Held that this omission was merely descriptive of the alleged bankrupt, and was amendable, so that the petition was sufficient to invoke the jurisdiction of the court. McAfee *v.* Arnold & Mathis, 155 Ala. 561, 46 So. 870; McAfee *v.* Wallenhaupt, 156 Ala. 665, 46 So. 873.

§ 19. Adjudication.

Conclusiveness of Decree.—A decree

adjudging one a bankrupt is not conclusive on the issue of the precise amount which he owed to any one creditor, or that he was indebted to any particular creditor in any sum; and one who has received a gift from the bankrupt is not cut off by the decree from contesting with the trustee the validity of the claim of every creditor asserted by him, and for whose benefit a suit is prosecuted by the trustee to set aside gifts made by the bankrupt in fraud of creditors. Cartwright *v.* West, 155 Ala. 619, 47 So. 93.

Nature and Conclusiveness of Adjudication.—An adjudication in bankruptcy is in the nature of a decree in rem, and is conclusive on the issues of the bankrupt's insolvency and of existing creditors at the date of its rendition; but it is not proof that such creditors existed a year or more prior thereto. Cartwright *v.* West, 155 Ala. 619, 47 So. 93.

(D) WARRANT AND CUSTODY OF PROPERTY.

§ 20. Possession and Control Pending Proceedings in General.

Though a bankrupt can do nothing in derogation of the estate, an agreement between a bankrupt insured and an insurer made after the commencement of the bankruptcy proceedings that the investigation of a loss should not constitute a waiver of the avoidance of the policy for failure to take an inventory will bind the bankrupt estate, where the agreement was signed by the insured in the presence of and with the advice of the receiver. Day *v.* Home Ins. Co. (Ala.), 58 So. 549.

The agreement was not invalid as an act by the bankrupt in derogation of the interests of the bankrupt estate, since it operated for the benefit of the estate. Day *v.* Home Ins. Co. (Ala.), 58 So. 549.

§ 21. Warrant and Seizure Pending Proceedings.

§ 22. —— Liabilities on Bonds.

Sufficiency of Pleas.—In an action against a surety on the forthcoming bond of an alleged bankrupt, pleas charging that after the bankruptcy adjudication a writ of error was duly sued out to review the same but failing to show whether or not, or when the decree was finally confirmed, or whether the writ was still pending and undetermined, or had been dismissed, were insufficient, either in abatement or in bar, since under Bankr. Act July 1, 1898, c. 541, § 1, subd. 2, 30 Stat. 544 (U. S. Comp. St. 1901, p. 3418), providing that the adjudication shall mean the date of the entry of the decree that defendant is a bankrupt, or, if such decree is appealed from, then the date when such decree is finally confirmed, as the mere taking of an appeal and the dismissal thereof, either by the appellant or the appellate court, would not change the date of the adjudication from the time it was taken to the time of dismissal of the appeal. Moore Bros. *v.* Cowan, 173 Ala. 536, 55 So. 903.

Defenses.—Where certain bankrupts were so adjudged in involuntary proceedings and executed a forthcoming bond to retain possession of their assets, and sued out a writ of error to review the adjudication, it was no defense to a subsequent action on the bond that after its execution the property was taken from the alleged bankrupts pursuant to voluntary bankruptcy proceedings instituted by them, it not being denied that the voluntary proceedings were instituted for the bankrupts benefit, and it not being shown that the assets were returned to and accepted by the person to whom they were surrendered, as receiver in the bankruptcy proceedings. Moore Bros. *v.* Cowan, 173 Ala. 536, 55 So. 903.

Estoppel.—Where a forthcoming bond in bankruptcy was executed by defendant surety to two persons named "the receivers in the above cause," they were thereby estopped from questioning the validity of the receiver's appointment. Moore Bros. *v.* Cowan, 173 Ala. 536, 55 So. 903.

§ 23. Appointment and Authority of Receiver or Marshal Pending Proceedings.

It is properly within the province of the judge to take possession and release the property of the bankrupt. Yet the referee is clothed with this power, provided the clerk issues a certificate showing the absence of the judge from the judicial district, or the division of the district, or his sickness or inability to act. This language evidently means that the referee has the same power to act in cases properly referred to him as the judge has when no reference is made. The referee may appoint a receiver or the marshal, upon application of parties in interest, in case it shall be necessary for the preservation of the state, to take charge of the property of the bankrupt at any time after the filing of the petition and until it is dismissed or the trustee is qualified. McAfee *v.* Arnold, 155 Ala. 561, 46 So. 870, 872.

Jurisdiction of Federal Courts.—The federal court having exclusive jurisdiction to adjudge a person a bankrupt and to appoint a receiver, such appointment may not be collaterally attacked in a suit on the forthcoming bond. Moore Bros. *v.* Cowan, 73 Ala. 536, 55 So. 903.

III. ASSIGNMENT, ADMINISTRATION, AND DISTRIBUTION OF BANKRUPT'S ESTATE.

(A) ASSIGNMENT, AND TITLE, RIGHTS, AND REMEDIES OF TRUSTEE IN GENERAL.

§ 24. Property and Rights Vesting in Trustee.

§ 25. —— In General.

As to rights of purchasers at a trustees' sale, see post, "Rights of Purchasers," § 67.

§ 26. —— Personal Property in General.

Nature in General.—A. executed several notes payable to B., guardian of C., with D. as his surety. D. married the ward, and became and was declared a bankrupt. Suit being instituted on the notes against A. by the assignee in bankruptcy of D., it was held that, as it did not appear that the notes ever passed from the guardian to the bankrupt, or that he had ever come to a final settlement with the guardian, or how the account stood between the guardian and his ward, as the ward herself could not have sued at law upon the notes, no such right passed to the assignee in bankruptcy of her husband. Chilton *v.* Cabiness, 14 Ala. 447.

§ 27. —— Real Property and Interest Therein.

Where the vendee of lands has become bankrupt, whatever interest he had in the lands passes to his assignee in bankruptcy, who becomes a proper party to a suit to enforce a vendor's lien on the lands. McDonald *v.* McMahon, 66 Ala. 115.

Right to Enforce Parol Contract for Sale of Land.—A purchaser of lands under an executory parol contract, having afterwards obtained a certificate of discharge in bankruptcy, can not maintain a bill in equity for the specific performance of the contract. His assignee is the only party who can sue. Rea *v.* Richards, 56 Ala. 396.

When Vendor May Recover in Ejectment.—The assignment in bankruptcy of a vendor of land who had contracted to convey the title on payment of the purchase money is a complete bar to his recovery in ejectment on the nonpayment of the price, his assignee taking all his rights. Clements *v.* Taylor, 65 Ala. 363.

§ 28. —— Property Fraudulently Conveyed.

As to the right of trustees to avoid transfers, see post, "Rights of Trustee as to Transfers," § 46.

The rights of property of a bankrupt, to which the assignee succeeds, are those rights to which the bankrupt had either a legal or equitable title, which could be enforced in a court of justice. No right, therefore, to property of which the bankrupt has made a fraudulent assignment would pass to his assignee. To whom such right would belong, whether to the creditors, generally, who assert a title to it, or only to those who refuse to come in under the commission, quære. Reavis *v.* Garner, 12 Ala. 661.

§ 29. —— Property Capable of Transfer or Subject to Process.

§ 29 (1) In General.

The Bankrupt Act of congress includes the franchise of a toll bridge as property within its contemplation, and passes it over to the assignee in bankruptcy. Stewart *v.* Hargrove, 23 Ala. 429. See, also, Lewis *v.* Gansville, 7 Ala. 85.

§ 29 (2) Mortgaged Property.

Equity of Redemption.—Under the Bankrupt Act of 1867, an assignee in bankruptcy acquires the equity of redemption of the bankrupt in real estate, subject to an outstanding mortgage. Robinson *v.* Denny, 57 Ala. 492.

§ 29 (3) Property of Wife or Children of Bankrupt.

A father subscribed for shares of stock in the name of his daughter, and executed his note for them, and a mortgage securing it. Before the payments were due the note and mortgage were canceled, and a firm of which he was a member became bound for the installments, and afterwards paid them. Held that, the daughter's husband having become a bankrupt, she had no such interest in the stock that would pass to the assignee of her husband. Butler *v.* M. Ins. Co., 14 Ala. 777.

§ 29 (4) Estate in Wife's Land.

The rents of a wife's separate estate accruing after her death intestate become the absolute property of the husband, and the right to collect them passes to his assignee in bankruptcy. Gayle *v.* Randall, 71 Ala. 469.

Statutory Separate Estate of Wife—What Right Bankrupt Acquires.—The allowance, under Rev. Code, § 2379, to the husband, upon his wife's death, of the use of her realty during his life, passes to his assignee in bankruptcy. Conoly *v.* Gayle, 54 Ala. 269.

§ 29 (5) Property Passing by Succession or Will.

Where a testator devises property, part of which is severable and part not, to his son for the use of the latter and his family jointly, with the provision that it is not to be subject to the son's debts, the provision is ineffectual as to the severable portion of the property, the son's interest in which will pass to his assignee in bankruptcy, to be subjected to his debts. Rugely *v.* Robinson, 10 Ala. 702.

Property may be given to a man until he shall become bankrupt; but a disposition to a man until he shall become bankrupt and after his bankruptcy, over, is quite different from an attempt to give to him for his life, with a proviso that he shall not sell or alien it. If the condition is expressed so as to amount to a limitation, neither the man or his assignees can have it beyond the period limited; but while it is his property, it must be subject to the incidents of property, and therefore to debts. Rugely *v.* Robinson, 10 Ala. 702, 717.

§ 30. —— Rights of Action.

As to right of bankrupt to sue, see post, "Actions by Bankrupt," § 90. As to rights pending actions, see post, "Rights as to Pending Actions," § 35.

A bankrupt, by the adjudication of bankruptcy, becomes incapable of enforcing, in his own name, any property rights which belonged to him at the time of the adjudication; but upon the appointment of an assignee by the bankrupt court, and the execution and delivery of an assignment to him, all the property rights of the bankrupt, except such as were specially excepted from the operation of the Bankrupt Act, of March 2, 1867, c. 176, 14 Stat. 517, vest in the assignee, with the exclusive right to sue for the same. Gayle *v.* Randall, 71 Ala. 469. See, also, Cain *v.* Sheets, 77 Ala. 492.

For Tort.—A claim for damages, for negligence in keeping a ferry, against the keeper and his sureties on his statutory bond, constitutes a part of a bankrupt's assets. Borden *v.* Bradshaw, 68 Ala. 362.

§ 31. —— After-Acquired Property.

See, also, post, "Debts Not Duly Scheduled," § 109.

Where creditors seize, on execution, property acquired by one after he has been decreed a bankrupt under the law of the United States, and before it is decided whether his certificate of discharge shall be granted, a court of equity will interfere, by injunction, to protect his rights, and will restrain proceedings until the question of his discharge is decided. Mosby *v.* Steele, 7 Ala. 299.

§ 32. —— Partnership and Individual Property.

Where one or more partners, not including all, are adjudged bankrupt, the partnership property can not be administered in the proceeding, unless by consent of the other partners. Lacey *v.* Cowan, 162 Ala. 546, 50 So. 281.

Proceeds of property of a bankrupt firm should be appropriated to pay partnership debts, and if the partners are adjudged bankrupts proceeds of each individual estate should be appropriated first to pay individual debts, and if surplus remains in the partnership case it may be appropriated to pay individual's debts, and in the other case it may be appropriated to pay partnership debts. Lacey *v.* Cowan, 162 Ala. 546, 50 So. 281.

When Trustee May Sue to Subject Funds of the Partnership.—A trustee in bankruptcy of the estate of one partner can not sue to subject funds of the partnership, so long as the partnership remains unsettled. Lacey *v.* Cowan, 162 Ala. 546, 50 So. 281.

Dissolution of Partnership by Bankruptcy.—Where a decree of bankruptcy is awarded against a member of a firm under Act 1841 or Act 1867, the partnership is thereby dissolved and the partnership effects are vested in the assignee and the solvent partner as tenants in common. McNutt *v.* King, 59 Ala. 597.

§ 33. Title Acquired by Trustee in General.

"The bankrupt's discharge does not affect the assignee's title to the property, by law vested in him. This vestiture of title is absolute, and no conduct of the bankrupt can defeat it. Then, neither the examination of the bankrupt, nor opposition to his discharge by a creditor, nor the final discharge of the bankrupt, can operate as a bar to a recovery by the assignee against a creditor, in an action of ejectment, for lands fraudulently conveyed by the bankrupt to such creditor." Bradley *v.* Hunter, 50 Ala. 265, 270.

A trustee in bankruptcy is not a purchaser of the property of the bankrupt, and he acquires only the title of the bankrupt, and can sell only such title as he has. F. A. Ames Co. *v.* Slocomb Mercantile Co., 166 Ala. 99, 51 So. 994.

§ 34. Equities of Third Persons.

"An assignee in bankruptcy is not a purchaser for a valuable consideration, entitled to protection against equities to which the estate of the bankrupt is subject. In the absence of fraud, such an assignee succeeds merely to such rights and interests as the bankrupt had, and was capable of asserting at the time of the bankruptcy. Whatever equities affect the bankrupt, or his estate, affect the assignee, as if the bankrupt himself were still clothed with the rights and interests the law compelled him to surrender." Smith *v.* Perry, 56 Ala. 266, 268. See, also, Crowe *v.* Reid, 57 Ala. 281.

§ 35. Rights as to Pending Actions.

See post, "Actions by Bankrupt," § 90.

Where, after an action was brought in a state court to cancel deeds in which a debtor fraudulently attempted to transfer his property, the debtor was adjudged a bankrupt, and a trustee in bankruptcy appointed, the state court upon setting aside such conveyances will not decree a sale of property, since upon the cancellation the title vested in the trustee in bankruptcy. Dickens *v.* Dickens, 174 Ala. 305, 56 So. 806.

Trustee May Be Made Party Defendant.—Under Bankr. Act July 1, 1898, c. 541, § 70, 30 Stat. 565 [U. S. Comp. St. 1901, p. 3451], vesting the trustee with title to property of the bankrupt, etc., a trustee appointed pursuant to an adjudication in bankruptcy, made after the institution of a suit to set aside a fraudulent conveyance made by the bankrupt, may be added by amendment as a party defendant to the suit. Davis *v.* W. F. Vandiver & Co., 143 Ala. 202, 38 So. 850.

The Bankrupt Act of 1841, in virtue of the decree of bankruptcy, divests the bankrupt of all property and rights of property, except as therein provided, and declares that all suits pending to which he is a party shall be prosecuted or defended by the assignee to their final conclusion, in the same way, and with the same effect, as they might have been by the bankrupt himself; consequently the assignee must be made a party to the litigation which may be pending in favor of or against the bankrupt, or it can not progress to a trial. Lacy *v.* Rockett, 11 Ala. 1002.

The assignee in bankruptcy may be made a party by motion, or perhaps by sci. fa. to a suit in which the bankrupt was a party when he was declared such. And perhaps, where the assignee, in a proper case, fails to come in as a plaintiff, the defendant may suggest the plaintiff's bankruptcy, and upon the production of the decree the court may order the assignee to make himself a party within a limited time, and, in default thereof, the suit to abate for want of prosecution. But, however this may be where the fact of bankruptcy is not controverted, it is competent for the defendant to plead in bar to an action by the bankrupt himself the decree declaring the plaintiff to be a bankrupt. The effect of this plea may be avoided by the assignee's making himself a party, but if he replies, and the issue is found against him, or he demurs, and his demurrer is overruled, and he does not plead further, judgment will be rendered for the defendant. Lacy *v.* Rockett, 11 Ala. 1002.

Where, on bankruptcy of complainant after judgment, leave was given the assignee to revive the suit on his being indemnified against costs, and subsequently counsel agreed that certain depositions could be opened in court, which agreement stated the title of the case as the assignee against defendant, objection can not thereafter be taken that the assignee was improperly made a party. Brandon *v.* Cabiness, 10 Ala. 155.

The assignee in bankruptcy of an executor who has been removed may be made a party to proceedings in the probate court on final settlement of the executor's accounts, and may have a decree in his favor for any balance that may be found due to the executor from the estate. Appling *v.* Bailey, 44 Ala. 333.

Pending Suits Vest in Assignee.—Bankrupt Act 1841, § 3, vests in a bankrupt's assignee all pending suits in law or in equity. One having brought suit to enjoin the collection of a judgment because it was paid, and a temporary injunction having been issued, the latter was dissolved, and the cause continued to a hearing on the merits. In the meanwhile complainant assigned in bankruptcy. Held, that the assignee took the bankrupt's right in the action, and was entitled to revive it. Brandon *v.* Cabiness, 10 Ala. 155.

Motion against Sheriff Must Be Made in Name of Assignee.—A motion against a sheriff for failing to make money on an execution which had issued in favor of a plaintiff, who, after the rendition of the judgment, had been declared a bankrupt, must be made in the name of the assignee in bankruptcy. Gary *v.* Bates, 12 Ala. 544.

(B) PREFERENCES AND TRANSFERS BY BANKRUPT, AND ATTACHMENTS AND OTHER LIENS.

§ 36. Preferences Voidable.

§ 37. —— In General.

See post, "Grounds for Refusal of Discharge," § 98.

"If a bankrupt shall have given a preference, and the person receiving it or to be benefited thereby, or his agent acting therein, shall have had reasonable cause to believe that it was intended thereby to give a preference, it shall be voidable by the trustee, and he may recover the property or its value from such person." Herzberg *v.* Riddle, 171 Ala. 368, 54 So. 635, 637.

§ 38. —— Insolvency of Debtor.

If a creditor accepts only that part of his debt to which he would be entitled if all the property liable to the debtor's debts should be apportioned among the creditors, there is no preference in violation of Bankr. Act July 1, 1898, c. 541, § 60 (a, b), 30 Stat. 562 (U. S. Comp. St. 1901, p. 3445), though the debtor be hopelessly insolvent. Herzberg *v.* Riddle, 171 Ala. 368, 54 So. 635.

"To suspect preference denounced by the statute implies insolvency or the belief therein, because the former can not exist without the latter, though the latter can exist without the former. If a man's debtor who is solvent pays him his debt in full, surely there is no ground to suspect a preference because every other creditor can compel payment; but if he accepts all of his debt, or a large part thereof, from a debtor known or suspected to be hopelessly insolvent, then he may know or have reasonable cause to believe that a preference is made in violation of the statute. But, if he accepts only that part of his debt to which he would be entitled if all the property liable to the debts should be appropriated among the creditors, then, of course, there is no preference such as is prohibited by the statute, though the debtor may be hopelessly insolvent." Herzberg *v.* Riddle, 171 Ala. 368, 54 So. 635, 637.

§ 39. —— Time of Giving Preference.

§ 39 (1) In General.

Where the payee of an order sells the same before his bankruptcy, but indorses it thereafter, the purchaser takes title, and may maintain an action in her own name. Smoot *v.* Morehouse, 8 Ala. 370.

§ 39 (2) Effect of Prior Agreement or Promise to Give Security or to Make Transfer.

The preference given by a bankrupt by payment or assignment of effects to a creditor, to be void under the bankrupt act, must be a voluntary preference, not induced by an agreement between the parties for the creditor's security. Smoot *v.* Morehouse, 8 Ala. 370.

§ 40. —— Procuring or Suffering Judgment.

When Person Shall Be Deemed to Have Given a Preference.—"A person shall be deemed to have given a preference if, being insolvent, he has within four months before the filing of the petition or after the filing of the petition and before the adjudication, procured or suffered a judgment to be rendered against himself in favor of any person, or made a transfer of any of his property, and the effect of the enforcement of such judgment or transfer will be to enable any one of his creditors to obtain a greater percentage of his debt than any other of such creditors of the same class." Herzberg *v.* Riddle, 171 Ala. 368, 54 So. 635, 637.

§ 41. —— Knowledge and Intent of Parties.

§ 41 (1) In General.

Under Act Cong. July 1, 1898, c. 541, § 60b, 30 Stat. 562 [U. S. Comp. St. 1901, p. 3445], providing that a preference by a bankrupt is voidable by the trustee when received by a person having reasonable cause to believe that it was intended to give a preference, and § 67e, 30 Stat. 564 [U. S. Comp. St. 1901, p. 3449], providing that transfers by a bankrupt within four months prior to the filing of the petition, with intent to defraud creditors shall be void except as to purchasers in good faith, in order to constitute a fraudulent preference it must be an advantage actually given to a creditor over others, with knowledge of his situation and the intent to accomplish this end. Bacon *v.* Merchants' Bank of Florence, 146 Ala. 521, 40 So. 413, cited on this point in note in 33 L. R. A., N. S., 560.

§ 41 (2) Knowledge of Insolvency by Creditor.

Under Bankr. Act July 1, 1898, c. 541, § 60 (a, b), 30 Stat. 562 (U. S. Comp. St. 1901, p. 3445), defining voidable preferences, before a trustee in bankruptcy can recover money paid by the bankrupt as an unlawful preference, he must show that the creditor had reasonable cause to believe the bankrupt was insolvent when he received the money, and that the payment was made with intent to defeat the bankrupt law. Herzberg *v.* Riddle, 171 Ala. 368, 54 So. 635, cited on this point in note in 33 L. R. A., N. S., 560.

§ 42. Transfers in General.

§ 43. —— Validity as against Trustee.

Insolvent Estate—Claim Filed by Creditor Afterwards Becoming Bankrupt—Respective Rights of Transferee and Assignee in Bankruptcy.—When a claim against an insolvent estate is duly filed and verified, by a creditor who afterwards becomes a bankrupt, but is transferred by him, by deed of assignment, before the proceedings in bankruptcy are instituted, the decree allowing the claim should be in favor of the assignee in bankruptcy, and not in favor of the transferee or trustee under the deed. Miller *v.* Parker, 47 Ala. 312.

§ 44. Fraudulent Transfers.

§ 45. —— Nature and Form of Transaction.

§ 45 (1) In General.

Where a husband conveys, by way of release, to his wife, for her sole use and

[illegible]

What Facts Are Proof of Fraud.—[illegible]

§ 45 (2). Assignments for Benefit of Creditors.

[illegible] ... the property vested in the assignee in bankruptcy ... [illegible]

§ 46. Rights of Trustee as to Transfers.

Code [illegible], § [illegible], which makes unrecorded conveyances inoperative as to judgment creditors, etc., without notice, does not entitle a trustee in bankruptcy to sue to annul a conveyance as in fraud of a creditor represented by him, if that creditor had acquired no lien on the property. Cowan v. Staggs (Ala.), 59 So. 158.

It is the duty of a trustee in bankruptcy to represent the unsecured creditors, and he is not entitled to sue to annul a conveyance as in fraud of a creditor having a lien on the property conveyed. Cowan v. Staggs (Ala.), 59 So. 158.

§ 47. Liens in General.

§ 48. —— Validity as against Trustee.

§ 48 (1). In General.

[illegible]

Paramount Lien Created by Bill Filed to Reach and Condemn Property.—[illegible]

§ 48 (2). Equitable Assignments or Liens.

[illegible] Nevlin v. McAfee, [illegible]

§ 49. Statutory Liens.

§ 50. —— In General.

Exempt Property—Lien for Rent.—A lessee obtained a lease for a renewal term, but before the beginning thereof, he filed a petition in bankruptcy. After the commencement of the term he was adjudged a bankrupt, and the goods on the leased premises were set apart to him as exempt. Held, that under Code 1896, § [illegible], et seq., creating a lien for rent, the goods were subject to a lien for the entire rent to become due during the term. Shapiro v. Thompson, 160 Ala. 363, 49 So. 391, cited on this point in note in 33 L. R. A., N. S., 747.

§ 51. Liens Acquired by Legal Proceedings Prior to Bankruptcy.

§ 52. —— In General.

See post, "Rights of Purchasers," § 67.

The effect of the proviso of the second section of the Bankrupt Act of 1841, upon a lien acquired by the institution of the proceedings in a state court, has been elaborately and learnedly considered.

The court, speaking of the effect of proceedings in bankruptcy upon suits pending against the petitioner, remarks, that where the court has jurisdiction of the cause and the parties, the suit will not abate because the defendant has filed a petition in bankruptcy, nor by reason of his having obtained a certificate. That certificate must be pleaded, that its validity may in some way, be contested. Marry v. Hermon, 8 Ala. 848, 851.

"Well considered decisions declare that the bankrupt law does not discourage diligence in the collection of debts, and that creditors who have obtained a lien, by a legitimate effort to collect an honest debt, must be permitted to enjoy the advantages gained by their diligence." Trimble v. Williamson, 49 Ala. 525, 528.

After the lien upon the realty of the debtor, by a judgment, or upon his personal estate, by a fieri facias, a decree in bankruptcy subsequently rendered cannot defeat it. Doremus, etc., Co. v. Walker, 8 Ala. 194, 200.

Discharge Pleaded as Bar to Suit.—If the debtor should be decreed a bankrupt, and receive a discharge under the act, that dischage could be pleaded as a good bar to the suit, in the nature of a plea puis darrein continuance; and therefore under such circumstances ought to prevent the plaintiff from obtaining a priority of lien over the general creditors of the defendant, on the property attached in his suit. Consequently the creditor ought to be enjoined against farther proceedings in his suit, except so far as the district court should allow until it should be ascertained whether the debtor obtained his discharge or not. Doremus, etc., Co. v. Walker, 8 Ala. 194, 199.

§ 53. —— Judgment or Execution and Proceedings Thereon.

The levy of an execution, issued after the defendant has made application for the benefit of the bankrupt law, will be quashed by the court out of which it issued, on motion. McDougald v. Reid, 5 Ala. 810.

A judgment obtained bona fide before the petition is filed is a valid lien under Act 1841, § 2. Doremus v. Walker, 8 Ala. 194.

Effect of Execution Lien.—The lien of an execution creditor whose judgment was rendered before the defendant obtained a discharge in bankruptcy, though no execution was then in the hands of the sheriff, is not destroyed by the bankruptcy, and may be enforced by an alias. Steele v. Davis, [illegible] Ala. [illegible].

Code 1876, § [illegible], provides that an execution may be levied after defendant's death, or an alias issued and levied, if there has not been the lapse of an entire term. An execution defendant was adjudged a bankrupt before the expiration of a term after the return of the execution, and about a year thereafter died. Several terms elapsed after his death, when an execution was issued, and the land sold. Held, that the bankruptcy of defendant, though it bridged over the lapse of time thereafter up to his death because under the bankrupt law the lien was preserved, did not bridge over the time after defendant's death, so as to render unnecessary the issuing of alias and pluries executions to keep the lien alive. Brown v. Newman, 66 Ala. 275.

§ 54. Dissolution of Liens of Attachments and Other Proceedings by Adjudication.

§ 55. —— In General.

An adjudication in bankruptcy, and assignment of bankrupt's property to the assignee, did not, by their unaided force, dissolve attachments levied on the bankrupt's property less than four months before the commencement of the bankruptcy proceedings, but that it required the action of the court to effect that result. The decision was pronounced in 1874. Sullivan v. Rabb, 86 Ala. 433, 5 So. 746, 749.

Dissolution—Attachment.—Rev. St. U. S., § 5044, providing that an adjudication in bankruptcy and an assignment of the bankrupt's estate shall vest the title in the assignee, though it is already attached on mesne process against the bankrupt, and shall "dissolve any attachment made within four months next preceding the commencement of the bankruptcy proceedings," has the effect to dissolve an attachment levied within the time mentioned, though no order of disbenefit, all the right, title, and interest he had acquired, by virtue of their marriage, to certain stock in an incorporated company, as also the right to sue the company for permitting the unlawful transfer thereof, such a conveyance will be inoperative at law; and the rights of the husband attempted to be released, will, upon his being declared to be a bankrupt, vest in the assignee in bankruptcy. Butler *v.* Merchants' Ins. Co., 8 Ala. 146.

What Facts Are Proof of Fraud.—A transfer by a father, largely indebted, and who afterwards is adjudged a bankrupt, to his son, of valuable property, is not necessarily fraudulent, but should be carefully scrutinized, and, if made in good faith to pay an actual indebtedness, should be sustained. Barnard *v.* Davis, 54 Ala. 565. See the title FRAUDULENT CONVEYANCES.

§ 45 (2) Assignments for Benefit of Creditors.

Where a bankrupt conveyed property before filing his petition, by a deed of assignment fraudulent as to his creditors, it was held that the property vested in the assignee in bankruptcy, if the preferred creditors have not expressly assented to it, and it is the duty of the bankrupt, if he retains the property, to surrender it. Ashley *v.* Robinson, 29 Ala. 112, cited on this point in note in 45 L. R. A. 179.

§ 46. Rights of Trustee as to Transfers.

Code 1907, § 3383, which makes unrecorded conveyances inoperative as to judgment creditors, etc., without notice, does not entitle a trustee in bankruptcy to sue to annul a conveyance as in fraud of a creditor represented by him, if that creditor had acquired no lien on the property. Cowan *v.* Staggs (Ala.), 59 So. 153.

It is the duty of a trustee in bankruptcy to represent the unsecured creditors, and he is not entitled to sue to annul a conveyance as in fraud of a creditor having a lien on the property conveyed. Cowan *v.* Staggs (Ala.), 59 So. 153.

§ 47. Liens in General.

§ 48. —— Validity as against Trustee.

§ 48 (1) In General.

"The liens protected and preserved by the bankrupt law are not the technical liens of the common law only, of which possession was an element, and often an indispensable element, but charges on realty or personalty, recognized in law or equity." Trimble *v.* Williamson, 49 Ala. 525, 528.

Paramount Lien Created by Bill Filed to Reach and Condemn Property.—A judgment creditor, who six months before the debtor's bankruptcy, and after execution returned nulla bona, has filed a summons and bill under Rev. Code, § 3446, to condemn equitable assets which have been fraudulently conveyed by the debtor, acquires a lien paramount to those of the assignee. Pool *v.* Ragland, 57 Ala. 414, cited on this point in note in 45 L. R. A. 194.

§ 48 (2) Equitable Assignments or Liens.

The provisions of the bankrupt act, saving all liens or mortgages on the property of the bankrupt, real or personal, embraces equitable as well as other mortgages. Newlin *v.* McAfee, 64 Ala. 357.

§ 49. Statutory Liens.

§ 50. —— In General.

Exempt Property—Lien for Rent.—A lessee obtained a lease for a renewal term, but, before the beginning thereof, he filed a petition in bankruptcy. After the commencement of the term, he was adjudged a bankrupt, and the goods on the leased premises were set apart to him as exempt. Held, that under Code 1896, § 2716, et seq., creating a lien for rent, the goods were subject to a lien for the entire rent to become due during the term. Shapiro *v.* Thompson, 160 Ala. 363, 49 So. 391, cited on this point in note in 33 L. R. A., N. S., 747.

§ 51. Liens Acquired by Legal Proceedings Prior to Bankruptcy.

§ 52. —— In General.

See post, "Rights of Purchasers," § 67.

The effect of the proviso of the second section of the Bankrupt Act of 1841, upon a lien acquired by the institution of the proceedings in a state court, has been elaborately and learnedly considered.

The court, speaking of the effect of proceedings in bankruptcy, upon suits pending against the petitioner, remarks, that where the court has jurisdiction of the cause and the parties, the suit will not abate because the defendant has filed a petition in bankruptcy, nor by reason of his having obtained a certificate. That certificate must be pleaded, that its validity may, in some way, be contested. Mabry *v.* Herndon, 8 Ala. 848, 859.

"Well considered decisions declare that the bankrupt law does not discourage diligence in the collection of debts, and that creditors who have obtained a lien, by a legitimate effort to collect an honest debt, must be permitted to enjoy the advantages gained by their diligence." Trimble *v.* Williamson, 49 Ala. 525, 528.

After the lien upon the realty of the debtor, by a judgment, or upon his personal estate, by a fieri facias, a decree in bankruptcy subsequently rendered can not defeat it. Doremus, etc., Co. *v.* Walker, 8 Ala. 194, 200.

Discharge Pleaded as Bar to Suit.—If the debtor should be decreed a bankrupt, and receive a discharge under the act, that dischage could be pleaded as a good bar to the suit, in the nature of a plea puis darrein continuance; and therefore under such circumstances ought to prevent the plaintiff from obtaining a priority of lien over the general creditors of the defendant, on the property attached in his suit. Consequently the creditor ought to be enjoined against farther proceedings in his suit, except so far as the district court should allow until it should be ascertained whether the debtor obtained his discharge or not. Doremus, etc., Co. *v.* Walker, 8 Ala. 194, 199.

§ 53. —— Judgment or Execution and Proceedings Thereon.

The levy of an execution, issued after the defendant has made application for the benefit of the bankrupt law, will be quashed by the court out of which it issued, on motion. McDougald *v.* Reid, 5 Ala. 810.

A judgment obtained bona fide before the petition is filed is a valid lien under Act 1841, § 2. Doremus *v.* Walker, 8 Ala. 194.

Effect of Execution Lien.—The lien of an execution creditor, whose judgment was rendered before the defendant obtained a discharge in bankruptcy, though no execution was then in the hands of the sheriff, is not destroyed by the bankruptcy, and may be enforced by an alias. Sheffey *v.* Davis, 60 Ala. 548.

Code 1876, § 3213, provides that an execution may be levied after defendant's death, or an alias issued and levied, if there has not been the lapse of an entire term. An execution defendant was adjudged a bankrupt before the expiration of a term after the return of the execution, and about a year thereafter died. Several terms elapsed after his death, when an execution was issued, and the land sold. Held, that the bankruptcy of defendant, though it bridged over the lapse of time thereafter up to his death because under the bankrupt law the lien was preserved, did not bridge over the time after defendant's death, so as to render unnecessary the issuing of alias and pluries executions to keep the lien alive. Brown *v.* Newman, 66 Ala. 275.

§ 54. Dissolution of Liens of Attachments and Other Proceedings by Adjudication.

§ 55. —— In General.

An adjudication in bankruptcy, and assignment of bankrupt's property to the assignee, did not, by their unaided force, dissolve attachments levied on the bankrupt's property less than four months before the commencement of the bankruptcy proceedings, but that it required the action of the court to effect that result. The decision was pronounced in 1874. Sullivan *v.* Rabb, 86 Ala. 433, 5 So. 746, 749.

Dissolution—Attachment.—Rev. St. U. S., § 5044, providing that an adjudication in bankruptcy and an assignment of the bankrupt's estate shall vest the title in the assignee, though it is already attached on mesne process against the bankrupt, and shall "dissolve any attachment made within four months next preceding the commencement of the bankruptcy proceedings," has the effect to dissolve an attachment levied within the time mentioned, though no order of dissolution is entered in the court wherein the attachment is pending. Sullivan *v.* Rabb, 86 Ala. 433, 5 So. 746. See the title ATTACHMENT. See, also, post, "Attachment or Garnishment," § 114 (1).

Attachment of Goods Omitted from Schedule.—Where a creditor attaches in the hands of the fraudulent vendee goods omitted from the bankrupt's schedule, and pursues them through a protracted and expensive litigation for three or four years, without any intervention or claim on the part of the assignee or trustee, the latter can not then have the attachment dissolved because it was sued out within four months before the commencement of proceedings in bankruptcy, and claim the goods or their proceeds as part of the bankrupt's estate. Jacobson *v.* Sims, 60 Ala. 185.

Effect of Validity of Lien Four Months Prior to Proceedings in Bankruptcy.—Under Act 1867, § 14, which enacts that the register shall convey to the assignee all the estate, real and personal, of the bankrupt, and that such assignment shall relate back to the commencement of the proceedings in bankruptcy, "and shall dissolve any such attachment made within four months next preceding the commencement of said proceedings," and attachment which, under state laws, is a valid lien, laid more than four months previous to the beginning of the proceedings in bankruptcy, is not dissolved by the transfer to the assignee in bankruptcy. Crowe *v.* Reid, 57 Ala. 281; Martin *v.* Lile, 63 Ala. 406.

§ 56. —— Time of Proceeding.

§ 56 (1) In General.

Dissolution of Garnishment Proceedings by Adjudication of Bankruptcy.—Adjudication of the principal defendant to be a bankrupt of itself dissolves the garnishment proceedings in a state court, begun within four months of the bankruptcy proceedings, authorizing its dismissal on motion of garnishee. Hobbs *v.* Thompson, 160 Ala. 360, 49 So. 787.

§ 56 (2) Attachment or Garnishment.

Effect of Prior Attachments and Garnishments.—Proceedings in bankruptcy do not affect the lien of attachments or garnishments acquired more than four months preceding the bankruptcy. Bloch Bros. *v.* Moore (Ala.), 39 So. 1025.

§ 56 (3) Judgment or Execution and Proceedings Thereon.

The lien of an execution on a bankrupt's property, valid at the adjudication of bankruptcy, is preserved, though executions are not sued out from term to term. Crowe *v.* Reid, 57 Ala. 281.

§ 57. Remedies to Establish or Enforce Rights or Liens.

§ 58. —— Nature and Form.

See, also, post, "In General," § 72 (1).

After the discharge of a bankrupt, his creditor, who had no lien upon his property, can not file a bill for the purpose of setting aside a voluntary conveyance made by him before his bankruptcy; such a suit being maintainable only by the assignee as the representative of the creditors defrauded. Bolling *v.* Munchus, 59 Ala. 482.

§ 59. —— Conflicting Jurisdiction of Courts of Bankruptcy and State Courts.

Defendant had been appointed trustee of the property of a bankrupt by a United States court, and had taken possession. Plaintiff claimed some of the property, and brought detinue therefor in a state court. Held, that the state court had no jurisdiction, since the United States court had previously acquired jurisdiction of the assets of the bankrupt and his creditors, and no proceeding affecting such assets in the hands of the trustee could be brought in a state court without permission of the district court. Turrentine *v.* Blackwood, 125 Ala. 436, 28 So. 95.

§ 60. —— Enforcement of Liens in General.

When Assignee's Claim Is Based.—Where property of the bankrupt is incumbered with a lien at the time of adjudication, which is preserved by the bankrupt law, and the assignee takes no steps to bring the property within the jurisdiction of the bankrupt court to have the lien adjusted, but leaves it with the creditor incumbered with the lien, and he obtains a sale under process from the state courts in enforcement of his lien, and the assignee allows more than two years to elapse from his appointment before the sale by the sheriff, it operates as an acknowledgment of the superiority of the lien of the creditor, and is a bar to any claim by the assignee. Crowe *v.* Reid, 57 Ala. 281.

§ 61. —— Enforcement of Rights and Liens Acquired by Legal Proceedings.

In a suit by a judgment creditor, whose lien was not discharged by the debtor's discharge in bankruptcy, to subject assets of the bankrupt to the satisfaction of the lien, the assignee is a necessary party. Rugely *v.* Robinson, 10 Ala. 702.

A suit against one who subsequently becomes a discharged bankrupt, instituted by attachment in 1866, which has been levied in that year on the lands of the defendant, may proceed to judgment in favor of the plaintiff, unless the same is stayed by order of the court of bankruptcy. May *v.* Courtnay, 47 Ala. 185.

Right of Judgment Creditor to Redeem, Not Affected by Bankruptcy of Debtor.—The right of a judgment creditor, under Rev. Code, §§ 2513-2521, to redeem lands sold under judicial process against his debtor, is not taken away by the bankruptcy of the debtor, occurring after the rendition of the judgment, and before the offer to redeem. Trimble *v.* Williamson, 49 Ala. 525.

Validity of Execution Issued on Judgment Rendered before Final Discharge.—An execution issued on a judgment, which has been rendered against a bankrupt, before he obtains his certificate of final discharge, is not void, but voidable only, at the instance of the bankrupt. Cogburn *v.* Spence, 15 Ala. 549.

A., by deed, conveyed certain lands to a trustee, to indemnify his securities on a debt due to the bank, and subsequently availed himself of the benefit of the bankrupt act. Pending the application, and before his final discharge, B., having recovered a judgment, and sued out execution against him, paid the debt due to the bank, and procured a sale of the lands under and pursuant to the deed of trust, at which sale she became the purchaser. Held, that the execution issued on the judgment in favor of B. was voidable merely, and was sufficient, until avoided, to entitle her under the statute (Clay's Dig., p. 256, § 36) to discharge the debt secured by the deed of trust, and have the lands sold under it for her use and benefit; and that such sale vested in B. both the legal and equitable title to the land. Roden *v.* Jaco, 17 Ala. 344.

What Constitutes a Sufficient Return on Ca. Sa.—It is no sufficient return on a ca. sa. that the defendant, after it was placed in the officer's hands, applied for the benefit of the bankrupt law of 1841. Robb *v.* Powers, 7 Ala. 658.

§ 62. Representation of Creditors by Trustee.

Representative Character of Trustee.—While ordinarily the trustee in bankruptcy is a representative of both the bankrupt and the creditors, on a bill to set aside fraudulent conveyances made by the debtor, he represents the interests of the creditors alone. Cartwright *v.* West, 173 Ala. 198, 55 So. 917.

§ 63. Collection of Assets.

In General—Rights of Creditors against Trustee.—While the trustee in bankruptcy has the legal title to the estate of the bankrupt, the creditors are nevertheless interested in a realization upon the assets of the bankrupt, and the trustee can not complain of the institution by creditors of suits to reduce to control assets which the trustee might intentionally or unintentionally permit to escape. Davis *v.* W. F. Vandiver & Co., 143 Ala. 202, 38 So. 850.

§ 64. Sale of Property.

§ 65. —— In General.

The authority of an assignee in bankruptcy to sell the property of the bankrupt under the bankrupt law of 1867, may be reduced substantially to two methods: First, a sale without an order of court, in which case the assignee sells simply the unascertained interest of the bankrupt, leaving to the purchaser the right and duty of settling and determining all controversies as to disputed ownership, and all litigation that may grow out of such disputed ownership; and second, a sale of the entire property, and the entire title to it, freed from all conflicting claims and liens, under § 5063 of the U. S. Rev. Stat., thereby placing and leaving its proceeds in its stead, as the subject of contention and litigation; and between these two methods there is no middle ground, to which the assignee is authorized to resort. Tennessee, etc., R. Co. *v.* East Alabama R. Co., 75 Ala. 516. See ante, "Rights of Action," § 30.

§ 66. —— Order of Court.

Heirs and Administrator as Parties.—Where a bankrupt surrenders possession of land which he has brought, but for which he has not paid, having only received a bond for title, a sale of the land by his assignee under order of court does not affect the title of the heirs of such deceased vendor who were not made parties, though his administrator was brought in. Cain *v.* Sheets, 77 Ala. 492.

Effect upon Rights of Third Persons as Parties.—A sale of land by an assignee in bankruptcy, under an order of court, can not affect the rights of third persons, who are not made parties, and who have no notice, although their rights would have been concluded if they had been brought in. Cain *v.* Sheets, 77 Ala. 492.

Effect upon Bankrupt's Title.—A decree rendered at the instance of an assignee in bankruptcy, ordering a sale of all the lands included in the bankrupt's schedule, does not affect the bankrupt's title to lands mentioned in the schedule which were allotted to him as a homestead. Walker *v.* Carroll, 65 Ala. 61.

Effect of Sale of Land by Assignee without Order.—When the title to lands surrendered by a bankrupt is in litigation, and the assignee has not acquired possession, he can not sell them without an order of the court of bankruptcy, made on his petition, after notice to the parties claiming adversely; and a sale by him without such an order is a nullity. Shaw *v.* Lindsey, 60 Ala. 344.

§ 67. —— Rights of Purchasers.

A purchaser at a bankrupt sale acquires no greater rights than the bankrupt himself had in the property sold. A sale, therefore, by the assignee, of a chose in action, does not divest him of the legal title, and authorize the purchaser to sue in his own name. Camack *v.* Bisquay, 18 Ala. 286.

An assignee in bankruptcy succeeds to all the rights and interests of the bankrupt, to precisely the same extent that the bankrupt himself had, subject to and affected by all the equities, liens, and incumbrances existing against them in the hands of the bankrupt; and the same rule applies to the purchaser at an assignee's sale of the bankrupt's effects. Smith *v.* Perry, 56 Ala. 266.

A partnership had, under an agreement, been furnishing one C. with supplies at the request of a corporation, to which it charged the same; the corporation in turn charging the same to C. On a settlement, the corporation gave its notes to the firm for the balance due on account. Thereafter the corporation became bankrupt, and a member of the firm, acting as receiver, took a note for the balance of the supplies, and a mortgage securing the same, from C. to the firm, instead of to himself as receiver. As to this balance there had been no settlement between the corporation and the firm, and it was not included in the note executed to the firm by the corporation, nor in a note executed to the latter by C. By order of court all the bankrupt's property, including the debt from C., was sold and bought by the complainant. Held that, as the mortgage did not pass into the estate by the mortgage to the firm it could not be sold at the bankruptcy sale, and did not pass thereby to the complainant, and the latter could not foreclose the mortgage. Winter, Loeb & Co. *v.* Montgomery Cooperage Co., 169 Ala. 628, 53 So. 905.

Purchaser's Title in Case of Execution Sale.—"The lien of a creditor obtaining judgment in the state court, acquired by the delivery of a fi. fa. to the sheriff, was not affected by the subsequent bankruptcy of the debtor before a levy was made. Notwithstanding the bankruptcy, the sheriff could proceed to levy and sell, and the purchaser would acquire a valid title, prevailing over any claim of the assignee." Crowe *v.* Reid, 57 Ala. 281, 286. See ante, "Liens Acquired by Legal Proceedings Prior to Bankruptcy," § 51.

Purchaser Acquires No Title to Chose in Action Sold by Bankrupt Nor Assignee.—Under the bankrupt act of 1841, clothing the assignee with all the rights, title, and powers in and over the assets that the bankrupt possessed, as a sale by the bankrupt of a chose in action would not vest the legal title in the purchaser, and authorize him to sue in his own name, a sale by the assignee conveys no such power. Camack *v.* Bisquay, 18 Ala. 286.

Limitation of Two Years No Defense by Purchaser.—The limitation of suits by and against an assignee to two years, prescribed by the bankrupt law, is not available as a defense in an ejectment suit in a state court by a purchaser to recover from the bankrupt lands sold by the assignee. Steele *v.* Moody, 53 Ala. 418.

Right of State Courts to Inquire as to Exemption after Sale to Third Person by Assignee.—Where an assignee in bankruptcy sells to a third person property in which the bankrupt had title at the time of adjudication of bankruptcy, no state court can inquire whether such property was exempt from the assignment in bankruptcy. Steele *v.* Moody, 53 Ala. 418.

Where a debtor of the bankrupt has hypothecated to the latter as security certain corporate stock, the right of action to compel a transfer of such stock on the corporate books is subject to the prescribed limitation; and, the assignee having sold such stock over two years after his appointment, the purchaser can not maintain such action. Moses *v.* St. Paul, 67 Ala. 168. See, also, Lacy *v.* Southern Mineral Land Co. (Ala.), 60 So. 283.

(C) ACTIONS BY OR AGAINST TRUSTEE.

§ 68. Actions by Trustee.

§ 69. —— In General.

Power of Trustee.—See post, "Defenses," § 73.

A trustee in bankruptcy can not maintain a bill for the benefit of less than all the creditors. Stephenson *v.* Bird, 168 Ala. 422, 53 So. 93.

§ 70. —— Relating to Property or Proceeds Thereof.

A trustee in bankruptcy, who sues in a state court to reach land sold by the bankrupt prior to the adjudication in bankruptcy, on the ground that the conveyance is void under Code 1907, § 3383, providing that conveyances are void as to judgment creditors without notice unless recorded before the accrual of the right of such judgment creditors, must show that he has or represents a judgment creditor with a lien and without notice, and since a mere judgment does not operate as a lien, and since under § 4093 an execution operates as a lien from the time only that it is received by the sheriff, a trustee neither has nor represents creditors who have a lien, and he may not maintain the suit. Sparks *v.* Weatherly (Ala.), 58 So. 280.

Bankruptcy Act, § 47, as amended by Act June 25, 1910, § 8, held not to authorize a trustee in bankruptcy to recover land conveyed by the bankrupt prior to the adjudication in bankruptcy on the mere ground that the deed has not been recorded. Sparks *v.* Weatherly (Ala.), 58 So. 280.

Name in Which Bill May Be Maintained.—A bill to set aside an alleged fraudulent transfer of property by an insolvent debtor may be maintained in the name of a trustee in bankruptcy. Exchange Nat. Bank of Montgomery *v.* Stewart, 158 Ala. 218, 48 So. 487.

Right of Assignee to Recover Lands Fraudulently Conveyed by Bankrupt.—The assignee of a bankrupt's estate, regularly appointed, may sue for and recover, by action at law, lands conveyed by the bankrupt in fraud of the bankrupt act; and neither a contest of the bankrupt's right to a discharge by a creditor, nor the bankrupt's examination on that contest, nor his final discharge by the bankrupt court, is conclusive on the assignee in such action, as to the conveyance of the lands by the bankrupt. Bradley *v.* Hunter, 50 Ala. 265.

Effect of Neglect of Assignee to Institute Proceedings.—Where an assignee, for more than five years, neglected to institute proceedings to obtain the condemnation of the bankrupt's interest, in certain trust property, though he continued to contest the right of a creditor, who had ferreted out the interest, and, after a long litigation, had obtained a decree subjecting the property to the satisfaction of his debt, such assignee will be presumed to have abandoned his claim, and can not arrest it against such creditor. Rugely *v.* Robinson, 19 Ala. 404.

§ 71. Leave to Sue.

Though a trustee in bankruptcy must have authority from the bankrupt court to bring suit to set aside a conveyance by the bankrupt as fraudulent, it is not necessary for the trustee to allege in his bill the special orders authorizing him to sue. Chisolm *v.* Wallace, 146 Ala. 683, 40 So. 219.

Right of Trustee to Sue in State Court without Obtaining Leave.—A trustee in bankruptcy may sue in a state court without first obtaining leave of the court appointing him. Cartwright *v.* West, 155 Ala. 619, 47 So. 93.

§ 72. Nature and Form of Remedy.

§ 72 (1) In General.

Action to Set Aside Fraudulent Transfer.—Where a bill by a bankrupt's trustee to recover an alleged fraudulent preference averred that a mortgage was fraudulently given, and also showed that the mortgage had been fully paid and discharged before the bill was filed, and was therefore functus officio, the bill was not maintainable, under Code 1896, § 818, as a bill to set aside a fraudulent conveyance or transfer. Brock & Spight *v.* Oliver, 149 Ala. 93, 43 So. 357.

§ 72 (2) Suits in Equity.

Suit by Trustee to Set Aside Fraudulent Conveyances.—Bankr. Act 1898, § 70e, providing that the trustee may avoid any transfer by the bankrupt which a creditor of the bankrupt might have avoided, and may recover the property so transferred, or its value, from the person to whom it was transferred, does not limit the trustee to an action at law; but he may, at least in the state court, maintain a suit in equity, under Code, § 818, authorizing suit by a creditor to subject to his debt property fraudulently conveyed by the debtor. Andrews *v.* Mather, 134 Ala. 358, 32 So. 738.

§ 73. Defenses.

On a bill by a trustee in bankruptcy to set aside as fraudulent certain conveyances by the debtor, the defendants were entitled to set up by way of plea that certain creditors named in the bill had not presented their claims within the time required in the bankruptcy proceedings, and were barred as creditors entitled to participate in the disposition of the estate. Cartwright *v.* West, 173 Ala. 198, 55 So. 917.

If the bankrupt obtains his discharge it would be no defense to the due execution and discharge of that judgment, in the regular course of proceedings thereon; for the debtor, after judgment, has no day in court to plead any bar of defense. Doremus, etc., Co. *v.* Walker, 8 Ala. 194, 199.

§ 74. Jurisdiction.

§ 75. —— Courts of Bankruptcy.

"There is not discoverable any suggestion countenancing the proposition, that an adjudication in bankruptcy strips other tribunals of jurisdiction adready existing, and transfers to the court of bankruptcy exclusive jurisdiction of the estate of the bankrupt." Martin *v.* Lile, 63 Ala. 406, 409.

A claim of exemption to personal property by a bankrupt must be asserted in the court of bankruptcy; and if not asserted and allowed by that court, it can not be afterwards asserted in a state court. Gayle *v.* Randall, 71 Ala. 469. See post, "Exemptions," § 93.

§ 76. —— State Courts.

Under the Bankrupt Acts of 1841 and 1867, the assignee in bankruptcy could sue in the state courts to collect assets vesting in him by the assignment, and to set aside payments, or transfers fraudulent under the bankruptcy laws or under the state laws or at common law. Barnard *v.* Davis, 54 Ala. 565.

As Code 1896, § 818, providing that a creditor may file a bill in chancery to subject to the payment of his debt any property which has been fraudulently conveyed, gives the right to sue to set aside a fraudulent conveyance, but does not authorize setting aside conveyances operating only as a preference under the federal bankruptcy act, a trustee in bankruptcy can not resort to equity to avoid a conveyance which is not fraudulent, but which is a preference under Bankr. Act July 1, 1898, c. 541, § 60, 30 Stat. 562 [U. S. Comp. St. 1901, p. 3445]; the remedy given by the bankruptcy act, giving the trustee the right to pursue property conveyed as a preference in any state court which would have jurisdiction if bankruptcy had not intervened, affording relief only against that class of conveyances which would be invalid under the laws of the state. Redd *v.* Wallace, 145 Ala. 209, 40 So. 407.

Chancery Jurisdiction to Set Aside Fraudulent Transfers by Bankrupt Prior to Adoption of Revised United States Statutes.—Prior to the adoption of the Revised Statutes of the United States, the chancery courts of this state had jurisdiction to entertain a bill filed by an assignee in bankruptcy, to assail and set aside transfers of property made by the bankrupt in fraud of the rights of his creditors, or in fraud of the assignee as their trustee, or fiduciary representative. Pollock & Co. *v.* Hill, 69 Ala. 515.

Since the Adoption of the Revised Statutes, Federal Courts Have Jurisdiction.—Since June 22, 1874, when the Revised Statutes of the United States became operative, exclusive jurisdiction of all suits by an assignee in bankruptcy, for the recovery of assets belonging to the bankrupt's estate, is vested in the federal courts (§§ 711 [U. S. Comp. St. 1901, p. 577], 4972); except that, under the provisions of an amendatory law, adopted on the same day (18 U. S. Statutes at Large, 178), the bankrupt court may authorize the assignee to sue in a state court for the recovery of a debt not exceeding $500; and any suit brought by him in a state court, without such permission or direction, without the jurisdiction of the court. Glover *v.* Love, 68 Ala. 219; Pollock & Co. *v.* Hill, 69 Ala. 515.

In such cases the state courts may take jurisdiction, under the exception created by the amendment, when the amount in controversy does not exceed five hundred dollars, and the federal court in which the proceedings in bankruptcy are pending, has authorized or directed the assignee to sue in the state courts. Pollock & Co. *v.* Hill, 69 Ala. 515.

Interpretation of Bankrupt Act, 1898, § 23, in Regard to Jurisdiction—Jurisdiction of State Courts.—Suit by trustee in bankruptcy to recover property fraudulently conveyed may be brought in the state court, under Bankr. Act 1898, § 23, entitled "Jurisdiction of the United States and state courts," and providing (a) the United States circuit court shall have jurisdiction of all controversies at law and in equity, as distinguished from proceedings in bankruptcy, between trustees and adverse claimants, concerning the property acquired or claimed by the trustees, in the same manner, and to the same extent only, as though bankruptcy proceedings had not been instituted and such controversies had been between the bankrupt and such adverse claimants; and (b) suits by trustees shall only be brought in the courts where the bankrupt might have brought or prosecuted them if proceedings in bankruptcy had not been instituted. Andrews *v.* Mather, 134 Ala. 358, 32 So. 738.

§ 77. —— Concurrent and Conflicting Jurisdiction of United States Courts and State Courts.

"The district court of the United States, sitting in bankruptcy, could not interfere with, or oust the state court from which the attachment issued, of jurisdiction to proceed to a judgment of condemnation of the property levied on, to the satisfaction of the lien." Crowe *v.* Reid, 57 Ala. 281, 286.

§ 78. Time to Sue and Limitations.

As to commencement of actions, see the title LIMITATION OF ACTIONS.

"No suit, either at law or in equity, shall be maintainable in any court, between an assignee in bankruptcy and a person claiming an adverse interest, touching any property transferable to, or vested in such assignee, unless brought within two years from the time when the cause of action accrued for or against such assignee." Moses *v.* St. Paul, 67 Ala. 168, 171.

When Assignee Must Intervene in Attachment Suit.—A debtor, within four months before his assignment in bankruptcy, transferred property to a third person, which transfer was claimed, but not proven, to be fraudulent as to creditors. A creditor attached such property, and the litigation thereover continued nearly four years, during which time the assignee in bankruptcy asserted no title against the transferee or the attaching creditor. The bankrupt did not include such property in his schedule of assets. Held, that the assignee could not have the attachment dissolved, because sued out within four months before bankruptcy proceedings, the limitation prescribed by § 2 of the bankrupt law being applicable. Jacobson *v.* Sims, 60 Ala. 185.

Fraudulent Concealment.—Where an assignee in bankruptcy files a bill in equity to enforce a claim which had accrued more than two years previously, a general averment of fraudulent concealment is insufficient to avoid the bar of Rev. St. U. S., § 5057; he must aver the facts constituting such fraudulent concealment, and show when he first came to a knowledge of the facts which put him on inquiry. Toney *v.* Spragins, 80 Ala. 541; Mohr *v.* Lemle, 69 Ala. 180; Evans *v.* Richardson, 76 Ala. 329.

Under Rev. St. U. S., § 5057, where a debtor of the bankrupt had hypothecated to the latter certain corporate stocks as security, the bar of the statute to the right of action to have the stock transferred on the corporate books is not removed either as to the assignee, or as to a purchaser from him, because the bankrupt, without fraud or collision by the debtor, fraudulently failed to schedule the debt or the pledge of the stock. Moses *v.* St. Paul, 67 Ala. 168.

Defect Appears in Complaint—It May Be Reached by Demurrer.—If the defect in not bringing the action within two years after the decree in bankruptcy, or from the time when the cause of action accrued, appears by the declaration, it may be reached by demurrer. Harris *v.* Collins, 13 Ala. 388.

If Cause of Action Had Accrued at the Time of Declaration or Decree.—An assignee in bankruptcy can not sue in the state or federal courts, after the lapse of two years from the time of the declaration and decree in bankruptcy, if the cause of action had then accrued, to recover the property of the bankrupt. Comegys *v.* McCord, 11 Ala. 932.

§ 79. Injunction and Receiver.

In an action by an assignee in bankruptcy to set aside a transfer of a judgment by the bankrupt to his son, the collection of the judgment should not be enjoined, but payment directed to be made to the register pending the final disposition of the cause, a receiver being unnecessary. Barnard *v.* Davis, 54 Ala. 565. See the title RECEIVERS.

§ 80. Pleading.

§ 80 (1) Declaration, Complaint, Petition, or Bill.

When Assignee May Sue without Proof of Debt.—When an assignee in bankruptcy files a bill in equity to set aside fraudulent conveyances by the bankrupt, he is not obliged to show that debts have been proved against the estate. Donegan *v.* Davis, 66 Ala. 362.

When Complaint Is Demurrable.—A complaint by a trustee in bankruptcy was demurrable where it did not point out whether the action was for money paid by the bankrupt to a creditor or for specific property purchased by the creditor from the bankrupt in payment of a preexisting debt. Herzberg *v.* Riddle, 171 Ala. 368, 54 So. 635.

A complaint in an action by a trustee in bankruptcy on a bond executed by the bankrupts and sureties held bad on demurrer for failing to show the trustee's beneficial ownership of the bond, or that it was made for the benefit of the estate of the bankrupts. A. Dreher & Co. *v.* National Surety Co., 174 Ala. 490, 57 So. 34.

A complaint, in an action on a bond for the benefit of the trustee in bankruptcy of the principals in the bond, held bad on demurrer notwithstanding Bankruptcy Act, § 64, subd. 3. Dreher & Co. *v.* National Surety Co., 174 Ala. 490, 57 So. 34.

Suit to Set Aside—Sufficient Allegations.—A bill by a trustee in bankruptcy to set aside, as fraudulent against creditors, gifts made by the debtor more than a year prior to the filing of the petition for bankruptcy, must allege and prove the facts essential to a recovery in a suit by the creditors to set aside the gifts; the trustee being the representative of the creditors. Cartwright *v.* West, 155 Ala. 619, 47 So. 93.

A bill by a trustee in bankruptcy to set aside, as fraudulent against creditors, gifts made by the bankrupt more than a year prior to the adjudication of bankruptcy, must allege and prove, either that the debts of the creditors accrued prior to the making of the gifts, or that the gifts were made with a fraudulent intent. Cartwright *v.* West, 155 Ala. 619, 47 So. 93.

§ 80 (2) Plea, Answer, Affidavit of Defense, and Demurrer.

Sufficiency of Answer.—Where a paragraph of a bill by a bankrupt's trustee to set aside fraudulent conveyances described the subjects thereof, and alleged that the bankrupt was seized and possessed of the land within four months prior to the filing of the bankruptcy petition, an answer denying all the paragraphs of the bill and every allegation therein contained, and calling for strict proof thereof, did not traverse the allegations of the bill, but had the effect of admitting, not only that the conveyance was made to hinder and defraud the bankrupt's creditors, but also the allegation that the bankrupt was seised and possessed of the land described within four months prior to the filing of the bankruptcy petition. Prestridge *v.* Wallace, 155 Ala. 540, 46 So. 970.

§ 81. Evidence.

§ 81 (1) Presumptions and Burden of Proof.

Fraudulent Sale—Seizure of Goods—Liability of Vendee.—Where a bankrupt conveyed a stock of goods to defendant, from which she sold various amounts in due course of business, and which she replenished with new goods purchased, and the bankrupt's trustee seized the stock after his appointment, and sold the same as a part of the bankrupt's estate, he was not entitled to recover from defendant for the goods sold by her in the absence of proof of the difference in value of the stock received by defendant and the goods seized. Wallace *v.* Boggan, 137 Ala. 535, 34 So. 824.

§ 81 (2) Admissibility.

Property in Hands of Trustee in Bankruptcy.—In detinue to recover property claimed to belong to plaintiff, in the hands of a trustee in bankruptcy, it was not error to refuse to allow proof that, at the time the trustee took possession, plaintiff notified him that the property sued for belonged to him, and that it was his property at the time the bankrupt court ordered the trustee to take charge thereof. Turrentine *v.* Blackwood, 125 Ala. 436, 28 So. 95. See the title DETINUE.

§ 81 (3) Weight and Sufficiency.

In an action by a trustee in bankruptcy to recover a preference, evidence held to sustain judgment for plaintiff. Bacon *v.* Merchants' Bank of Florence, 146 Ala. 521, 40 So. 413.

(D) CLAIMS AGAINST AND DISTRIBUTION OF ESTATE.

§ 82. Claims Provable.

§ 83. —— In General.

Debts, to be provable against bankrupt estate, must be in existence when the petition in bankruptcy is filed, and those not provable are not effected by the discharge. Leader *v.* Mattingly, 140 Ala. 444, 37 So. 270, 271.

A demand for unpaid subscription to stock, payable on call, is not a provable demand against a bankrupt stockholder's estate. Sayre *v.* Glenn, 87 Ala. 631, 6 So. 45

A debt created by a loan to the bankrupt by a creditor after adjudication in bankruptcy to be used in complying with the terms of a composition, the bankrupt agreeing to pay to such creditor when the composition was confirmed the balance of such loan after deducting therefrom the creditor's share of the consideration of the confirmation, was not a provable debt in the bankruptcy proceedings within Bankr. Act (Act July 1, 1898, c. 541, 30 Stat. 550 [U. S. Comp. St. 1901, p. 3428]), § 17a. Zavelo *v.* J. S. Reeves & Co., 171 Ala. 401, 54 So. 654.

§ 84. —— Instruments in Writing Made before Filing of Petition.

§ 84 (1) Contingent Demands and Liabilities.

Bankr. Act July 1, 1898, c. 541, § 63, 30 Stat. 562 [U. S. Comp. St. 1901, p. 3447], makes no provision for proving contingent liabilities against a bankrupt's estate. Leader *v.* Mattingly, 140 Ala. 444, 37 So. 270.

§ 84 (2) Claims of Indorsers, Guarantors, or Sureties.

Under the Bankrupt Act of 1867, a surety's liability on an administrator's bond, before there has been any settlement of the estate, or any decree fixing the administrator's liability, is not a provable debt. Steele *v.* Graves, 68 Ala. 21, overruling Jones *v.* Knox, 46 Ala. 53.

§ 85. Time for Proof of Claims.

See ante, "Time to Sue and Limitations," § 78.

Section 5057, Rev. Stat., applies the two years bar to suits "touching property or rights of property transferable to, or vested in the assignee," and extends no further; and hence, where the bankrupt had no property or right of property in the subject of litigation, it neither vesting in nor being transferable to the assignee, the provisions of the statute do not apply. Tennessee, etc., R. Co. *v.* East Alabama R. Co., 75 Ala. 516.

Where a decree in bankruptcy proceedings established the priority of the lien of one creditor over all other creditors, a creditor who was not made a party to the proceedings, and who had no notice thereof, is not barred by Rev. St., § 5057, from presenting his claim in the bankrupt court after the expiration of two years from the date of the decree. Tennessee & C. R. Co. *v.* East Alabama Ry. Co., 75 Ala. 516.

§ 86. Allowance or Disallowance of Claims.

See post, "Appeal and Revision of Proceedings," VI.

A decree in bankruptcy allowing a claim on a contract is binding on both the creditor and the bankruptcy, and in a subsequent action to enforce the contract a reply setting up such decree is a complete answer to a plea that the contract was ultra vires. Elmore, Quillian & Co. *v.* Henderson-Mizell Mercantile Co. (Ala.), 60 So. 820.

IV. COMPOSITION.

§ 87. Operation and Effect.

Trustee's Title in Bankrupt's Property.—Where the bankrupt's title is defeasible, such title only vests in the trustee, he having no better title than that of the bankrupt, and on confirmation of a composition effected with the bankrupt's creditors, and dismissal of the bankruptcy proceedings, the same defeasible title reverts to the bankrupt. Zavelo *v.* Cohen Bros., 156 Ala. 517, 47 So. 292.

Discharge of Debt by Confirmation.—The Bankr. Act (act July 1, 1898, c. 541, 30 Stat. 550 [U. S. Comp. St. 1901, p. 3428]), § 14c, provides that the confirmation of a composition shall discharge the bankrupt from his debts, other than those agreed to be paid by the terms of the composition and those not effected by a discharge. After adjudication, but before confirmation of the composition, the bankrupt procured a loan of plaintiff, a creditor with which to satisfy the terms of a composition, agreed to pay it and the excess of the whole debt over the sum of the dividend paid plaintiff under the composition when confirmed. The loan was not extorted to induce plaintiff to consent to the composition. Held that, as the loan would not have been affected by a formal discharge of the bankrupt, it was not discharged by the confirmation of the composition, so that it could be thereafter enforced. Zavelo *v.* Reeves & Co., 171 Ala. 401, 54 So. 654.

The confirmation of a composition has the same effect as a discharge, and may be pleaded against liabilities which would have been affected by a formal discharge. Zavelo *v.* Reeves & Co., 171 Ala. 401, 54 So. 654.

§ 88. New Promise to Pay Debt.

It is now settled by the great weight of authority, with comparatively few decisions to the contrary, that an expressed promise to pay a debt made by a bankrupt before his discharge, but if it is adjudicated, is just as effective to revive the debt against him and to waive his expected discharge, as would a promise made after obtaining his certificate of discharge. Greil *v.* Solomon, 82 Ala. 85, 2 So. 322, 325; Torrey *v.* Kraus, 149 Ala. 200, 43 So. 184; Zavelo *v.* Reeves & Co., 171 Ala. 401, 54 So. 654.

§ 89. Pleading.

Sufficiency of Allegations.—"As a plea of discharge in bankruptcy must show the jurisdiction of the court granting it, a plea of composition should also show that it is binding on the party against whom it is pleaded. Binding only on creditors who were shown by the statement of the bankrupt, produced at the meeting of creditors passing the resolution of composition, the plea must aver that such statement included the name and debt of the plaintiff. This is as essential to the efficacy of the composition, as is jurisdiction to the efficacy of a discharge." Shulman *v.* Graves, 63 Ala. 402, 405. See post, "Pleading Discharge," § 116.

Intendments—Effect of Omission to State a Material Fact.—"Intendments are not made to support pleadings, when assailed by demurrer. The pleader is presumed to state the case as strongly for himself, as the facts will authorize. The omission to state a material fact justifies the court, in pronouncing judgment, in assuming the fact does not exist." Shulman *v.* Graves, 63 Ala. 402, 406.

Necessary Allegations.—In an action by a creditor against his bankrupt debtor, a plea of composition must aver that the plaintiff's name and claim were included in the statement of the bankrupt, produced at the meeting of the creditors who passed the resolution of composition, or it will be demurrable. Shulman *v.* Graves, 63 Ala. 402.

V. RIGHTS, REMEDIES, AND DISCHARGE OF BANKRUPT.

§ 90. Actions by Bankrupt.

"Where a party to a suit pending in a state court applies to be declared a bankrupt under the act of congress of 1841, the proceedings must be suspended for a reasonable time, to enable him to file the decree, when the assignee must be made a party. As soon as the decree in bankruptcy is pronounced, the bankrupt in relation to all actions for and against him, except such as the statute prescribes, is legally dead, and can only be represented by the assignee." Lacy, etc., Co. *v.* Rockett, 11 Ala. 1002, 1007. See ante, "Rights as to Pending Actions," § 35.

Sufficiency of Allegations.—A plea by the defendant, that the plaintiff was declared a bankrupt pendente lite, need not allege anything in respect to the jurisdiction of the court in which the proceedings in bankruptcy were had; for it will be inferred that these were in the proper tribunal. Lacy, etc., Co. *v.* Rockett, 11 Ala. 1002. See the title ABATEMENT AND REVIVAL.

Insufficiency of Allegations.—A suggestion by the plaintiff's counsel of the bankruptcy of the party who instituted the suit, and the substitution of the assignee in bankruptcy as plaintiff, render inoperative a plea of the defendant previously filed, alleging the bankruptcy of the plaintiff. Brooks *v.* Harris, 12 Ala. 555.

Defenses.—The adjudication in bankruptcy of one of two partners suing for a conversion of the property of the firm is a good plea in bar to the action. McNutt *v.* King, 59 Ala. 597.

Quære, is it not a good plea that some of the plaintiffs, all of whom were a partnership, were declared bankrupts pendente lite? Lacy, etc., Co. *v.* Rockett, 11 Ala. 1002, See the title ABATEMENT AND REVIVAL.

§ 91. Actions against Bankrupt.

§ 91 (1) In General.

When Discharge as a Defense Is Good Bar to an Action.—"A right of action to recover a debt is not wholly extinguished, for all purposes, by a discharge in bankruptcy. The effect of a discharge in bankruptcy is very much like the effect of the statute of limitations. It extinguishes and bars an action thereon only when it is set up as a defense or bar at the proper time and in the proper manner. Its efficacy may be lost or waived by a failure to assert it. It is a defense personal to the bankrupt, and what he must plead specially in the manner and time prescribed. It would not be available to him on a mere motion, and not by a third party, and certainly not (as in this case) by one who claims against, and not through, him. Because a bankrupt is or may be discharged from debt is no sufficient reason why his debtors are discharged from their debts due him or due his estate in case of his death or bankruptcy." Hobbs *v.* Thompson, 160 Ala. 360, 49 So. 787, 788.

Custody of Property.—Where an estate was in the custody of a federal district court as a bankrupt estate at the time property of the estate was garnished, the garnishment proceedings could not be maintained without the previous consent of the bankruptcy court. McAfee *v.* Arnold & Mathis, 155 Ala. 561, 46 So. 870; McAfee *v.* Wallenhaupt, 156 Ala. 665, 46 So. 873.

Rights of Creditors to File Bill to Set Aside Conveyance after Discharge.—After the discharge of a bankrupt, his creditor who had no lien upon his property can not file a bill for the purpose of setting aside a voluntary conveyance made by him before his bankruptcy. Bolling *v.* Munchus, 59 Ala. 482.

The Rights of Debtor of Bankrupt.—"The debtor of a bankrupt, or the man who contests the right to real or personal property with him, loses none of those rights by the bankruptcy of his adversary. The same courts remain open to him in such contests, and the statute has not divested those courts of jurisdiction in such actions." Crowe *v.* Reid, 57 Ala. 281, 287.

Construction of Allegations.—In assumpsit to recover a sum loaned defendant, the replication alleged that defendant after his adjudication in bankruptcy promised that, if plaintiff would lend him such sum to use in paying the consideration of the composition with his creditors, he would upon confirmation of such composition pay plaintiff the balance of the demand sued on after deducting plaintiff's share of the consideration of the composition, and that plaintiff loaned defendant such sum for such purpose, and also alleged that, after the adjudication, defendant promised to pay what he owed plaintiff, which was the demand sued on herein, when his composition was confirmed. Held, that the replication could not be construed as alleging that the agreement to repay the loan was to induce plaintiff to consent to the composition. Zavelo *v.* J. S. Reeves & Co., 171 Ala. 401, 54 So. 654.

The replication did not allege extortion of the loan to procure plaintiff's assent to the composition within the meaning of Bankr. Act (Act July 1, 1898, c. 541, 30 Stat. 554 [U. S. Comp. St. 1901, p. 3433]), § 295b, penalizing one who attempts to extort, or extorts money from a person as a consideration for acting or forbearing to act in a bankruptcy proceeding. Zavleo *v.* Reeves & Co., 171 Ala. 401, 54 So. 654.

Postponement of Action, When Properly Done.—Where the complaint stated a cause of action for embezzlement within Bankruptcy Act, § 17, and defendant asserted that his liability, if any, was on contract, the action held properly postponed pending determination against defendant in the bankruptcy court. Ex parte Butler-Kyser Mfg. Co., 174 Ala. 237, 56 So. 960.

Continuance on Account of Bankruptcy—When Will Be Presumed to Be Rightfully Done.—When the record shows that a cause was continued as to part of several defendants on their plea of bankruptcy, the appellate court will presume that the plea was sufficiently proven, unless the contrary be shown. Melvin *v.* Clark, 45 Ala. 285. See the title ABATEMENT AND REVIVAL.

Effect of Mere Filing without an Adjudication.—The mere filing of a petition in bankruptcy without an adjudication of bankruptcy does not bar the prosecution of a suit against the debtor in a state court, and is no ground of staying the proceedings. Givens *v.* Robbins, 5 Ala. 676; Stewart *v.* Sonneborn, 51 Ala. 126. See the title ABATEMENT AND REVIVAL.

§ 91 (2) In Case of Appeal.

Where, after the submission of a cause in the supreme court, a party thereto becomes bankrupt, the judgment will not be set aside, but will be rendered as of the date of the submission. A mere suggestion, on information and belief, by the appellant, that the appellee has become bankrupt since the appeal, but before judgment rendered affirming that of the court below, will not authorize any action by the supreme court. Booker *v.* Adkins, 48 Ala. 529. See the titles ABATEMENT AND REVIVAL; APPEAL AND ERROR.

§ 92. Privilege from Arrest.

The court will not discharge without giving the party arresting, time to show that the certificate was fraudulently obtained; and any of the reasons mentioned in the statute may be given in opposition to his discharge; and wherever it is shown that the validity of the certificate is to be disputed, the court will not discharge in a summary manner; and it has, when necessary, directed the commission to be tried on a feigned issue. Mabry *v.* Herndon, 8 Ala. 848, 858.

When Officer Has Power to Discharge.—An officer arresting has no power to discharge a bankrupt, upon the mere production of his certificate, and that if he do so, the court will not stay proceedings against him for an escape. Mabry *v.* Herndon, 8 Ala. 848, 858.

§ 93. Exemptions.

§ 94. —— In General.

A claim for damages resulting from negligence in the conduct of the ferry against a keeper of a ferry and securities on a bond executed by him under the statute (Code of 1876, § 1680) may be claimed and allowed as an exemption to the bankrupt, under the statute of this state exempting one thousand dollars worth of personal property. Borden *v.* Bradshaw, 68 Ala. 362.

In order to revest in a bankrupt property claimed by him as exempt, the assignee must acquiesce in the claim. Borden *v.* Bradshaw, 68 Ala. 362.

§ 95. —— Property Exempt.

§ 95 (1) Application of State and Federal Laws in General.

A. attached land belonging to B. more than four months before the latter was adjudged a bankrupt, and recovered a judgment which was not satisfied by the sale of the land to him. B., who had never occupied the land, had a homestead exemption allowed him by the bankruptcy court, and conveyed it to C. Held, that C. could claim no interest in the land, as B.'s homestead claim was valid against his assignee only, who had acquired no interest in the land. Martin *v.* Lile, 63 Ala. 406.

§ 95 (2) Pension Money and Life Insurance.

Code 1896, § 2607 (Act Feb. 18, 1897, § 32 [Acts 1896-97, p. 1393]), provides that, where any person insures his life for the sole benefit of his estate, the amount becoming due shall be exempt from all creditors of the assured or beneficiary. Bankr. Act July 1, 1898, c. 541, § 70, 30 Stat. 565 (U. S. Comp. St. 1901, p. 3451), provides that, when any bankrupt shall have an insurance policy which has a cash surrender value payable to himself, his estate, or personal representatives, he may pay to the trustee such value and continue to hold the policy free from the claims of creditors; otherwise, the policy shall pass to the trustee. But the same section, in enumerating the items of property which are to be turned over to the trustee, makes a special exception of "property which is exempt;" and § 6 provides that the act shall not affect the exemptions given by the state laws then in force. Held, that a trustee was not entitled to receive, either from the bankrupt or the insurance company, the cash surrender value of a policy payable to the bankrupt, or his estate, which he had transferred to his wife, as the surrender value of the policy, as well as the amount due at the death of the insured, is the sum or amount of insurance becoming due and payable by the terms of the application and policy, within the meaning of § 2607. Chandler *v.* Traub, 159 Ala. 519, 49 So. 240, cited on this point in note in 26 L. R. A., N. S., 455.

A policy of insurance on the life of a bankrupt which is exempt from liability for the bankrupt's debts under the state law is also exempt under Bankr. Act 1898. Young *v.* Thomason (Ala.), 60 So. 272.

§ 95 (3) Homestead Exemptions.

What Can Be Asserted in State Court.—A mere claim of homestead exemption, made by the bankrupt to his assignee, but not incorporated in the schedules to his petition, and not allowed by the assignee, or certified by the judge or register, can not be asserted, in a state court, against a purchaser from the assignee. Steele *v.* Moody, 53 Ala. 418.

§ 96. —— Setting Apart and Report of Exempt Property.

§ 96 (1) Claim of Exemption, and Allowance or Determination in General.

Under the bankruptcy statute, the

bankrupt's property passes to the trustee, unless the bankrupt complies with the state law as to claiming exemptions, and when he does so the trustee must set aside the exempt property, subject to exceptions by creditors. Northern Alabama R. Co. *v.* Feldman, 1 Ala. App. 334, 56 So. 16.

§ 96 (2) Appraisement, Selection, Allotment or Setting Apart.

Where the bankrupt included in his schedule all his lands, claiming, as a homestead exemption therein, "real estate to the value of $500," but without designating any particular portion, it is an amendable defect, of which advantage can not be taken in a subsequent collateral proceeding; and the assignee having set apart to him, as exempt, the homestead on which he was then residing, and which did not exceed, in quantity or value, more than was then allowed by law, and reported his action to the bankruptcy court, this action was conclusive until set aside by that court in a proceeding of which the bankrupt had notice. Walker *v.* Carroll, 65 Ala. 61.

Homestead — How Set Apart.—The quantity and value of land to be set apart as a homestead in Alabama should be ascertained from Rev. Code, § 2884, notwithstanding the owner of the land (the mortgagor) has become bankrupt, and has purchased the property, subject to the mortgage, at sale by his assignee in bankruptcy. Ray *v.* Wragg, 48 Ala. 52.

§ 96 (3) Objections and Exceptions to Report or Determination, and Proceedings Thereon.

The records are the best evidence on the questions of a compliance by the bankrupt with the requirements of the state law in respect to claiming the exemptions, and of the action of the trustee in setting aside the exempt property, and it is not proper, against objections duly and seasonably made, to admit the testimony of witness, in regard to these matters. Northern Alabama R. Co. *v.* Feldman, 1 Ala. App. 334, 56 So. 16, 17.

§ 97. Right to Discharge in General.

"Fiduciary debts not proved under the proceedings in bankruptcy, were not extinguished by the discharge and certificate under the act, and that a misapplication of fiduciary funds deprived the party of all right to a discharge from them, only, if made before the passage of the act, but if made after the passage, such misapplication deprived him of all right to a discharge from any debts." Pinkston *v.* Brewster, etc., Co., 14 Ala. 315, 322.

§ 98. Grounds for Refusal of Discharge.

§ 99. —— In General.

See ante, "Right to Discharge in General," § 97.

§ 100. —— Offenses against Bankrupt Act.

Where property is discovered belonging to bankrupt's estate subsequent to the issuing of the decree which has not been accounted for; the intention of the bankrupt being apparent, his discharge and certificate will be allowed. Hargroves *v.* Cloud, 8 Ala. 173, 175.

§ 101. Petition for Discharge.

Although by the terms of the act of congress the applicant for the discharge as a bankrupt is required to set forth in his petition a list of his creditors, and their respective places of residence, as well as the sums due to each, yet this is permitted to be stated according to the best of the petitioner's knowledge and belief. It seems evident these requirements are to be construed as directory only, not merely from the latitude given by the act itself, but by reason of the great difficulty there is to comply with certainty and precision in all cases. Fox *v.* Paine, 10 Ala. 523, 525.

§ 102. Notice of Application for Discharge.

"This court has decided, that the omission of a bankrupt to state a debt, and his failure to notify the creditor of his application for discharge, do not, together, render the discharge inoperative against the omitted debt. Fox *v.* Paine, 10 Ala. 523." Milhouse *v.* Aicardi, 51 Ala. 594, 597.

§ 103. Proceedings in Opposition to Discharge.

Form, Requisites, and Sufficiency of Specifications.—"The opposition to the discharge, authorized by the law, must be made on 'a specification in writing of the grounds' of objection; and this must be tried as a question of fact at a stated session of the district court, and not by the register, as may be done on the examination." Bradley *v.* Hunter, 50 Ala. 265, 270.

§ 104. Revoking Discharge.

§ 104 (1) Grounds.

The payment of money, or any other thing, by the bankrupt, to a creditor, to induce him to consent to the allowance of a certificate, is a fraud on the act, which avoids the discharge. Fox *v.* Paine, 10 Ala. 523, 526.

§ 104 (2) Jurisdiction.

Where and When Certificate of Discharge May Be Impeached.—The validity of a discharge, under the United States bankruptcy act, can only be contested by application in the United States district court within two years, as provided by Act 1867, § 34 (Rev. St., § 5120). Milhous *v.* Aicardi, 51 Ala. 594.

"The power to set aside and annul the discharge being vested by law in the federal courts, it can not be exercised by the state courts, because the jurisdiction is exclusive." Oates *v.* Parish, 47 Ala. 157, 161.

If a bankrupt's motion be resisted on any of the grounds specified in the bankrupt act, the facts relied on to impeach his certificate must be stated with certainty to a common intent. Stewart *v.* Hargrove, 23 Ala. 429.

"A discharge, obtained under the bankrupt law of 1841, could be impeached for fraud in any court before which it was pleaded. Mabry *v.* Herndon, 8 Ala. 848. But, under the bankrupt law of 1867, the discharge could be impeached, for any cause which would have prevented it from being granted, only in the court in which the adjudication was had, and within two years after the date thereof. Oates *v.* Parish, 47 Ala. 157; Milhous *v.* Aicardi, 51 Ala. 594." Shulman *v.* Graves, 63 Ala. 402, 405.

§ 105. Conclusiveness and Effect of Discharge in General.

In General.—"A discharge and certificate, duly granted to a bankrupt, under the act of congress of 1841, for the establishment of a uniform system of bankruptcy, shall, in all courts of justice, be deemed a full and complete discharge of all debts, contracts and other engagements of such bankrupt, which are provable under the act, and shall be and may be pleaded as a full and complete bar to all suits brought in any court of judicature whatever, the same shall be conclusive evidence of itself in favor of such bankrupt, unless the same shall be impeached for some fraud or willful concealment, by him, of his property, or rights of property, contrary to the provisions of this act, on reasonable notice specifying in writing such fraud or concealment." Hargroves *v.* Cloud, 8 Ala. 173, 175.

The bankrupt is regarded as civiliter mortus, as to all previous dischargeable debts and liabilities, from the date of such adjudication, so long as it continues unrevoked by the court of bankruptcy in which the proceedings originated. Griel *v.* Solomon, 82 Ala. 85, 2 So. 322.

A bankrupt who, after his discharge, becomes the bona fide holder of a note, payable to himself, which had been returned in his schedule and sold by the assignee, is remitted to his original title, and may transfer it by indorsement so as to vest the right of action in his indorsee. Birch *v.* Tillotson, 16 Ala. 387.

Earning of Debtor after Discharge in Bankruptcy.—The earnings of a debtor after his discharge in bankruptcy are not subject to a debt contracted prior to such discharge; the debt being extinguished by the discharge. J. B. Ellis & Co. *v.* Mobile, J. & K. C. R. Co., 166 Ala. 187, 51 So. 860.

Effect of Discharge on Trustee from Recovering Property Fraudulently Conveyed.—A discharge in bankruptcy, being personal, does not preclude the trustee from recovering property fraudulently transferred by the bankrupt. Stephenson *v.* Bird, 168 Ala. 363, 53 So. 92.

Since under Bankr. Act July 1, 1898, c. 541, § 14, par. 4, 30 Stat. 550 (U. S. Comp. St. 1901, p. 3427), as amended by

Act Feb. 5, 1903, c. 487, § 4, 32 Stat. 797 (U. S. Comp. St. Supp. 1909, p. 1310), a fraudulent conveyance must have been made within four months preceding filing of the petition, to be ground for refusing a discharge, a discharge over objection on that ground does not preclude a subsequent bill by the trustee to declare a transfer by the bankrupt fraudulent, where it does not appear that the transfers involved in the objection to the discharge, or that the transfers sought to be vacated, were made within that period. Stephenson *v.* Bird, 168 Ala. 363, 53 So. 92.

§ 106. Collateral Attack on Discharge.

Jurisdiction as to Attack on Discharge.—A discharge in bankruptcy may be assailed in any court where pleaded, on the ground that the bankrupt court had no jurisdiction to grant it. Stiles *v.* Lay, 9 Ala. 795.

Bank Act, Second Section, Construed.—Under the Bankrupt Act of August 19, 1841 (§ 2), the execution by a voluntary bankrupt, after January 1, 1841, of a deed of trust, giving a trust to some of his creditors, does not invalidate his discharge, unless the act was "done in contemplation of the passage of a bankrupt law." Pearsall *v.* McCartney, 28 Ala. 110.

When Bankrupt's Certificate of Discharge Can Not Be Avoided.—A bankrupt's certificate of discharge can not be avoided by his having given money or property to a creditor, who had filed objections to his discharge for cause assigned, in order to induce him to withdraw his opposition. Fox *v.* Paine, 10 Ala. 523.

Grounds for Impeaching Discharge.—"The omission of the name and demand of a creditor from the schedule of a bankrupt, if inadvertent, is not ground for impeaching the discharge. If fraudulent, it may be ground for its vacation in the bankrupt court, but would not be available collaterally. The case is different with a composition, which the statute limits in operation to creditors whose names and addresses, and the amounts of whose debts, are shown in the statement produced by the bankrupt to the meeting of creditors accepting it." Shulman *v.* Graves, 63 Ala. 402, 406.

"A discharge in bankruptcy, granted by a court of competent jurisdiction, like judgments and decrees operating in personam, can not be collaterally impeached for mere defects or irregularities in the proceedings." Shulman *v.* Graves, 63 Ala. 402, 404.

A discharge in bankruptcy can not be impeached in a state court on the ground that it was obtained by fraud upon the creditors seeking to set it aside, as proper relief can, under United States Bankrupt Act 1867, § 34, be obtained in the federal court. Oates *v.* Parish, 47 Ala. 157.

A mere omission to include in his schedule an interest in trust property, bequeathed to the bankrupt by his father, is not such a "fraud or willful concealment" as will necessarily vacate a discharge; nor is a charge in a bill by his creditors, to subject the bankrupt's property to a discharge of their debt, that the failure of the debtor to render in such interest, in his schedule, "amounted in law" to a fraud which would vacate his discharge, equivalent to a charge of "fraud or willful concealment" of his property. Rugely *v.* Robinson, 19 Ala. 404.

Where a defendant in execution sets up his discharge and certificate as a bankrupt, by a petition, upon which a supersedeas is awarded, it is competent for the plaintiff to impeach the same for any of the causes provided by the act, and make up an issue to try the facts. Mabry *v.* Herndon, 8 Ala. 848.

Whether the discharge and certificate of a bankrupt may not be impeached for fraud by one not a party to the proceedings in bankruptcy, according to the principles of the common law, without reference to the provisions of the bankrupt act, quære. Mabry *v.* Herndon, 8 Ala. 848.

Rights of Creditors When Bankrupt's Discharge is Impugned for Fraud.—When a bankrupt's discharge is impugned for fraud, the creditor may prove the possession of the property by the bankrupt four years after the bankruptcy, and the jury must determine whether the property was fairly acquired, or by a fraudulent concealment of his effects. Gilbert *v.* Bradford, 15 Ala. 769. See McBride *v.* Thompson, 8 Ala. 650.

Decree of Discharge—Conclusiveness.—A decree of discharge on sufficient notice to creditors of the bankruptcy proceedings, and where the bankruptcy court had jurisdiction over the subject matter of the petition, and exercised it according to law, is conclusive, and can not be impeached in a collateral proceeding, however irregularly the court may have proceeded. Jones *v.* Knox, 51 Ala. 367.

§ 107. Debts and Liabilities Discharged.

§ 108. —— In General.

§ 108 (1) In General.

See ante, "Claims Provable," § 82.

A note given by a bankrupt, two days before the filing of his petition, reciting that it was given for "cash bona fide advanced to enable him to take the benefit of the bankrupt law, and without such advance it would be impossible for him to do so," is barred by his subsequent discharge. Nelson *v.* Stewart, 54 Ala. 115.

Effect of Discharge on Nonprovable Debts.—Under Bankr. Act July 1, 1898, c. 541, § 17, 30 Stat. 551 (U. S. Comp. St. 1901, p. 3428), providing that a discharge shall release the bankrupt from his provable debts, a discharge does not discharge a nonprovable debt, nor from liability for rent to accrue, which is not a fixed liability, and not provable in bankruptcy. Shapiro *v.* Thompson, 160 Ala. 363, 49 So. 391.

Under Bankr. Act July 1, 1898, c. 541, §§ 17, 63, 30 Stat. 550, 562 (U. S. Comp. St. 1901, pp. 3428, 3447), declaring that a discharge in bankruptcy shall release the bankrupt from provable debts, except judgments for fraud, and providing that unliquidated claims may be liquidated, and may thereafter be proved, a claim for unliquidated damages for breach of contract is provable, and is released by a discharge in bankruptcy. Jim Pearce & Co. *v.* Fisher, 170 Ala. 456, 54 So. 164.

When a Set-Off Is Defeated by Subsequent Discharge.—A set-off bona fide acquired by the maker against the payee of a note, before notice of its assignment to a third person, is not defeated by the subsequent discharge of the payee as a bankrupt. Harwell *v.* Steel, 17 Ala. 372, cited on this point in note in 55 L. R. A. 71. See the title SET-OFF AND COUNTERCLAIM.

Effect of Discharge in Bankruptcy on Judgment.—A judgment against a bankrupt is barred by his discharge in bankruptcy subsequent to the rendering of the judgment. Otto Young & Co. *v.* Howe, 150 Ala. 157, 43 So. 488.

When Judgment Is Extinguished.—A judgment is extinguished by a subsequent discharge in bankruptcy of the judgment defendant. J. B. Ellis & Co. *v.* Mobile, J. & K. C. R. Co., 166 Ala. 187, 51 So. 860.

The lien of a judgment, which has attached before the commencement of the bankruptcy proceedings, is not effected by the discharge. Rugely *v.* Robinson, 10 Ala. 702, 703, cited on this point in note in 42 L. R. A., N. S., 294.

Effect of Discharge upon Contingent Liability.—The contingent liability of the principal in a bond given to indemnify a constable against damage possible to result from levy of an execution placed in his hands is not affected by his discharge under Bankr. Act July 1, 1898, c. 541, § 63, 30 Stat. 562 [U. S. Comp. St. 1901, p. 3447]. Leader *v.* Mattingly, 140 Ala. 444, 37 So. 270.

Effect of Discharge on Covenant of Warranty Made Prior to His Bankruptcy.—A discharge in bankruptcy does not discharge, release, or annul the obligation of a bankrupt upon a covenant of warranty made prior to his bankruptcy, where the breach is subsequent to his discharge. Abercrombie *v.* Conner, 10 Ala. 293. See the title COVENANTS.

§ 108 (2) Claims of Sureties for Bankrupt.

A surety may prove his contingent liability, upon his principal's application for a discharge in bankruptcy; and, if he fails to make such proof, he is barred, by the certificate of discharge, from further action against the bankrupt. Jones *v.* Knox, 46 Ala. 53.

Under the Bankrupt Act of 1867 the

liability of a surety on an administrator's bond, before there has been any settlement of the estate, or any decree fixing the liability of the administrator to the estate, is not a provable debt, and a discharge in bankruptcy does not relieve the surety from liability for decrees subsequently rendered against his principal. Steele *v.* Graves, 68 Ala. 21.

§ 108 (3) Claims against Bankrupt as Surety.

A discharge in bankruptcy will not protect the surety of a guardian of a minor on his official bond, against a statute judgment obtained against him as such surety, by the return of "No property" to an execution against his principal, though made after he obtained his discharge in bankruptcy. Turner *v.* Esselman, 15 Ala. 690.

The liability of a surety on a guardian's bond, which liability attaches when the guardian receives property of his ward, is a contingent liability, within the meaning of Bankrupt Law 1867, § 19, and provable against the estate of the surety, who has been adjudged a bankrupt, and the obligation is relieved on the latter's discharge. Jones *v.* Knox, 46 Ala. 53. See the title GUARDIAN AND WARD.

§ 109. —— Debts Not Duly Scheduled.

A bankrupt's discharge will not release him from any debt omitted from the schedule annexed to his petition, where the omitted creditor had no notice or knowledge of the bankruptcy proceedings in time to have proved his claim. Karter *v.* Fields, 140 Ala. 352, 37 So. 204.

§ 110. —— Debts Created by Fraud, Embezzlement, Misappropriation, or Defalcation in Official or Fiduciary Capacity.

§ 110 (1) Debts Created by Fraud.

"Debts created by the fraud or embezzlement of the bankrupt, or by his defalcation as a public officer, or while acting in any fiduciary character" (Bankrupt Law of 1867, § 33), are not affected by a discharge in bankruptcy, and are not within the exclusive jurisdiction of the bankrupt court. Broadnax *v.* Bradford & Co., 50 Ala. 270.

What Constitutes Fraud.—False representations by the bankrupt as to the pecuniary condition of the partnership of which he is a member, made with the intent to procure goods on credit, and by means of which goods were thus obtained, constitute a fraud, within the meaning of § 33 of the bankrupt act, and avoid his discharge as to the debt so created; but his representations as to the pecuniary circumstances of his copartner, though false, are not fraudulent, unless they were known by him to be false, or were made with the intent to deceive; and, if his statements as to the pecuniary circumstances of his co-partner were true, his failure to notify the creditor of an assignment subsequently made by said partner would not constitute a fraud. Broadnax *v.* Bradford & Co., 50 Ala. 270.

§ 110 (2) Debts Created in Official or Fiduciary Capacity.

In General.—The obligation of a surety upon a guardian's bond is not a fiduciary obligation, within Rev. St., § 5117, and is released by the discharge of the surety in bankruptcy. Jones *v.* Knox, 46 Ala. 53, cited on this point in note in 42 L. R. A., N. S., 1099. See the title GUARDIAN AND WARD.

A debt due a planter from a cotton factor and commission merchant for the proceeds of cotton sold, is not a "debt created by his defalcation, while acting in a fiduciary character," within the meaning of the bankrupt law, and is barred by his subsequent discharge in bankruptcy. Woolsey *v.* Cade, 54 Ala. 378, cited on this point in note in 42 L. R. A., N. S., 1098, 1099.

A trustee under a deed of assignment, who wrongfully retained the trust fund, or paid it over to another not entitled to it, was not released from liability to creditors by his discharge in bankruptcy. Pinkston *v.* Brewster, 14 Ala. 315, cited on this point in note in 42 L. R. A., N. S., 1100.

The liability of a surety on an administrator's bond for the defaults of his principal is not a fiduciary debt within the meaning of the Bankrupt Act. Steele *v.* Graves, 68 Ala. 21.

Under Bankr. Act 1898, § 17, providing that a discharge shall release the bankrupt from all provable debts, except such as were created by his fraud, while acting in a fiduciary capacity, a bankrupt was not released from a debt created by the collection of certain notes for defendant under an agreement reciting their receipt as trustee for collection. Williams *v.* Virginia-Carolina Chemical Co. (Ala.), 62 So. 755.

What Fiduciary Capacity Consist of.—Factors and commission merchants, when exercising their functions of receiving, selling, taking their commissions, and accounting to their principals, are not acting in a fiduciary capacity, within the bankrupt law, and are relieved by a discharge in bankruptcy from obligations contracted in that capacity. Austill *v.* Crawford, 7 Ala. 335; Woolsey *v.* Cade, 54 Ala. 378.

Husband's Liability to Account as Trustee.—A husband's liability as trustee under an antenuptial contract to account to the deceased wife's personal representative for trust moneys is a "fiduciary" one. Donovan *v.* Haynie, 67 Ala. 51, cited on this point in note in 42 L. R. A., N. S., 1099.

§ 111. Effect of Discharge as to Codebtors, Guarantors, and Sureties.

§ 112. —— Guarantors.

The discharge in bankruptcy of one surety or guarantor did not release his codebtors, though the creditor failed to prove his claim against the bankrupt's estate. Gurley *v.* Robertson (Ala.), 59 So. 643.

§ 113. —— Sureties.

See ante, "Claims against Bankrupt as Surety," § 108 (3).

Effect of Discharge as to Sureties.—Under Code 1896, § 493, authorizing a judgment against sureties on an appeal bond only in case the judgment appealed from is affirmed, the sureties on an appeal bond can not be proceeded against, where the judgment was barred by the discharge in bankruptcy of the judgment debtor. Otto Young & Co. *v.* Howe, 150 Ala. 157, 43 So. 488.

Sureties are not discharged under the bond of their principal by his discharge under Bankr. Act July 1, 1898, c. 541, § 63, 30 Stat. 562 [U. S. Comp. St. 1901, p. 3447]. Leader *v.* Mattingly, 140 Ala. 444, 37 So. 270.

The bankruptcy of the principal obligor in a penal bond does not discharge the sureties. Garnett *v.* Roper, 10 Ala. 842.

§ 114. Effect of Discharge as to Sureties and Liens.

§ 114 (1) Attachment or Garnishment.

Where plaintiff had an attachment lien, which was not dissolved by the bankruptcy of the defendant, and the court said: "Such attachment being recognized as valid by the Bankrupt Act (Rev. St., § 5044), a discharge in bankruptcy does not prevent the attaching creditors from taking judgment against the debtor in such limited form as may enable them to reap the benefit of their attachment. When the attachment remains in force, the creditors, notwithstanding the discharge, may have judgment against the bankrupt, to be levied only upon the property attached." Otto, etc., Co. *v.* Howe, 150 Ala. 157, 43 So. 488, 489.

Plea of Bankruptcy—When Good.—A discharge in bankruptcy obtained by defendant after the levy of an attachment may be pleaded in abatement of the attachment suit. Sims *v.* Jacobson, 51 Ala. 186, overruled. Sullivan *v.* Rabb, 86 Ala. 433, 5 So. 746.

Effect of Attachment Levied before Bankruptcy Act.—An attachment levied on the defendant's property in 1866 is not dissolved by the discharge of the defendant on his petition in bankruptcy, under the Bankruptcy Act of 1867. In such a case the attachment lien of the plaintiff remains unimpaired; and the court may ascertain by its judgment the amount of plaintiff's debt, notwithstanding defendant's discharge in bankruptcy. May *v.* Courtnay, 47 Ala. 185.

§ 114 (2) Mortgages.

A mortgage is not released or discharged by the discharge of the mortgagor as a bankrupt. Stewart *v.* Anderson, 10 Ala. 504, cited on this point in note in 42 L. R. A., N. S., 295.

Rights of Assignee of Mortgage.—Where a mortgage was given by a principal debtor to his surety, who transferred it to the creditor for a valuable consideration, the subsequent discharge in bankruptcy of the principal and surety does not destroy the lien of the mortgage or affect the holder's right to foreclose it. Carlisle *v.* Wilkins, 51 Ala. 371, cited on this point in note in 42 L. R. A., N. S., 295.

§ 114 (3) Judgments or Executions and Proceedings Thereon.

Where a judgment is discharged by defendant's discharge in bankruptcy, any process dependent thereon is vacated. Ewing *v.* Peck, 26 Ala. 413.

Effect of Execution on Judgment after Discharge.—Where execution is issued on a judgment after defendant has obtained a certificate of discharge in bankruptcy, he can not move to have the discharge entered of record for the purpose of preventing the issuance of the execution before the writ has been actually sued out. Brown *v.* Branch Bank at Montgomery, 20 Ala. 420.

On a motion by a bankrupt to have his discharge entered of record, where the record does not purport to set out all the evidence, and the motion itself is wanting, the appellate court can not presume that there was no proof before the court below that an execution had issued, nor that the motion did not allege such to be the fact; and the rule laid down in Brown *v.* Branch Bank, 20 Ala. 420, does not apply to the case. Stewart *v.* Hargrove, 23 Ala. 429.

The lien of a judgment which has attached before the commencement of the bankruptcy proceedings is not affected by the discharge. Freeny *v.* Ware, 9 Ala. 370; Rugely *v.* Robinson, 10 Ala. 702; Martin *v.* Lile, 63 Ala. 406. See note on this point in 42 L. R. A., N. S., 294.

Supersedeas of Execution. — Where, after judgment is recovered, the judgment debtor is discharged in bankruptcy, an execution, subsequently issued on the judgment, may be quashed and superseded on petition in the court from which it issued. Ewing *v.* Peck, 17 Ala. 339; Brown *v.* Branch Bank of Montgomery, 20 Ala. 420; Milhous *v.* Aicardi, 51 Ala. 594.

Judgment Recovered Pending Proceedings Is Discharged by Certificate.—A judgment recovered pending the proceedings in bankruptcy, and before the granting of the certificate of discharge upon a debt due at the time of the adjudication in bankruptcy, is discharged by the certificate. McDougald *v.* Reid, 5 Ala. 810.

Effect of Appeals Pending.—The discharge in bankruptcy of defendant in unlawful detainer pending appeal by him to the circuit court is no bar to the action, though plaintiff has regained possession, and the action is only prosecuted for damages and costs. Lomax *v.* Spear, 51 Ala. 532. See the title FORCIBLE ENTRY AND DETAINER.

Defendant's Right to Recover Money Paid on Pluries Execution.—Where, pending a motion by a judgment defendant to quash an execution on the ground of his discharge in bankruptcy, plaintiff issues a pluries execution, which defendant voluntarily pays, under no mistake as to his rights, he can not recover it. Ewing *v.* Peck, 26 Ala. 413.

When Lien of a Judgment Is Recognized as Operative against the Assignee.—"The lien of a judgment is recognized as operative against the assignee, as it respects the real property of the bankrupt, and the personalty will be bound by the execution. In either case the lien is preserved according to the rights of the creditor at the time the bankruptcy is established. If the lien is then absolute, it completely overrides the decree, and the creditor will be let into the enjoyment of its fruits." Crowe *v.* Reid, 57 Ala. 281, 289; Doremus, etc., Co. *v.* Walker, 8 Ala. 194, 202.

Rights of Creditor Who Has Reduced His Debt to Judgment, before Bankrupt Is Discharged.—If a creditor of one who has taken the benefit of the bankrupt act has reduced his debt to judgment, before the bankrupt obtains his certificate of final discharge, he will not be compelled to bring a new suit on the judgment, but may, after discharge, cause execution to issue thereon, subject to be set aside or quashed on the application of the bankrupt. Cogburn *v.* Spence, 15 Ala. 549.

Where Execution Is Attempted, How Bankrupt May Avail Himself of the Discharge.—It is settled, by the decisions of the supreme court, that where an execution is attempted to be enforced against the bankrupt, he may avail himself of his discharge, by superseding and quashing the execution. Mabry *v.* Herndon, 8 Ala. 848; Cogburn *v.* Spence, 15 Ala. 549; Turner *v.* Esselman, 15 Ala. 690, 693.

Where an execution is levied on land, and the defendant in execution was discharged as a certificated bankrupt, after the judgment, but previous to the levy, the execution and levy can not regularly be quashed on the motion. Freeny *v.* Ware, 9 Ala. 370. See the title EXECUTION.

Rights of Creditor—Proceedings in Bankruptcy after the Judgment.—"The proceedings in bankruptcy, after the judgment, can have no effect whatsoever upon the judgment, or upon the property attached in the suit. The creditors right is then made perfect, being no longer conditional, or contingent, but has attached absolutely to the property; and the court has no authority to deprive him, or by an injunction to obstruct the proceedings on his execution." Doremus, etc., Co. *v.* Walker, 8 Ala. 194, 199.

§ 115. New Promise to Pay Debt Discharged.

See ante, "Debts and Liabilities Discharged," § 107.

The promise must be express. Evans *v.* Carey, 29 Ala. 99.

Under former bankrupt laws, a distinction was taken between promises made after the adjudication of bankruptcy, and those made after the filing of the petition, and it was held that a new promise, to overcome the effect of a discharge, must appear to have been made after the party was decreed to be a bankrupt; or, in other words, after the adjudication. Under the law of 1867, there is no difference practically between the date of the fiat or adjudication and the date of the petition, because the first, extended by relation back to the latter date, as does also the discharge when duly obtained. Griel *v.* Solomon, 82 Ala. 85, 2 So. 322, 325.

It is now settled by the great weight of authority, with comparatively few decisions to the contrary, that an express promise to pay a debt made by a bankrupt before his discharge, but after his adjudication, is just as effective to revive the debt against him, and to waive his expected discharge, as would a promise made after obtaining his certificate of discharge. Griel *v.* Solomon, 82 Ala. 85, 2 So. 322, 325.

Where, after his discharge in bankruptcy, a judgment debtor makes a new promise to pay the judgment, such promise will inure to the benefit of an assignee of the judgment. Wolffe *v.* Eberlein, 74 Ala. 99.

Conditional Promise.—In an action upon a conditional promise made by a bankrupt to pay a debt discharged by his bankruptcy, it must be alleged that the condition has been performed. Griel *v.* Solomon, 82 Ala. 85, 2 So. 322.

A subsequent promise to pay "as soon as the bankrupt is able" is a valid condition, and not void for uncertainty. Griel *v.* Solomon, 82 Ala. 85, 2 So. 322.

New Promise Sufficient Replication to the Plea of Bankruptcy.—It is sufficient to declare upon the original undertaking of a bankrupt and to set up a new promise by him by way of replication to the plea of bankruptcy. Wolffe *v.* Eberlein, 74 Ala. 99, 104; Dearing *v.* Moffitt, 6 Ala. 776; Branch Bank *v.* Boykin, 9 Ala. 320.

What Is Sufficient Consideration to Support Subsequent Promise.—A count in a declaration against a bankrupt on a pre-existing liability, as the indorser of a promissory note, upon which he had been charged by regular proceedings against the maker, which, after stating that the makers, on bill filed, etc., obtained an order enjoining the parties that, on the final hearing, said injunction was, by decree of the chancellor, made perpetual, and that from this decree an appeal was taken to the supreme court, avers "that after the discharge of said defendant in bankruptcy, and whilst the said appeal was pending in the supreme court, the said defendant undertook and faithfully promised the plaintiff that, if plaintiff should lose said case in the supreme court, he would make it good to him, and plaintiff should lose nothing by said indorsement of the note; and that the said decree of the chancellor was subsequently by said supreme court in all things affirmed"—sets out a sufficient consideration to support a subsequent promise. Herndon *v.* Givens, 16 Ala. 261.

By a debtor's discharge in bankruptcy, he becomes civiliter mortuus as to all dischargeable debts, though his moral obligation, coupled with an antecedent valuable consideration, will support an unequivocal new promise to pay. Anthony *v.* Sturdivant, 174 Ala. 521, 56 So. 571.

No Recovery on Conditional unless Condition Is Performed.—There can be no recovery upon a conditional promise to pay a debt from which defendant has been discharged in bankruptcy, unless it is shown that the condition has been performed or the contingency has happened, in which case it is binding. Branch Bank at Mobile *v.* Boykin, 9 Ala. 320; Griel *v.* Solomon, 82 Ala. 85, 2 So. 322; Dearing *v.* Moffitt, 6 Ala. 776.

Where a discharged bankrupt said he did not intend to avail himself of his discharge, but had some work engaged, from the proceeds of which he intended to pay the plaintiff, the promise was held to be conditional, and not absolute, and that, to recover thereon, the state of things upon the happening of which event the payment depended must be shown. Dearing *v.* Moffitt, 6 Ala. 776. See the title CONTRACTS.

Definiteness of New Promise.—A promise by a bankrupt to pay as soon as he is able a debt barred by discharge is enforceable. and not void for uncertainty. But, to be available, the promise must be averred in proper form, and satisfactory proof of the defendant's ability to pay; that is, of the fact that he has sufficient property or means to pay. Kraus *v.* Torry, 146 Ala. 548, 40 So. 956.

Necessary Allegations and Proof to Sustain a New Promise.—Where a bankrupt promises that as soon as he is able he will pay a debt barred by his discharge, it is necessary for plaintiff, in an action on the promise, to allege and prove that defendant is able to pay, and proof of ability to borrow money is not sufficient. Torrey *v.* Kraus, 149 Ala. 200, 43 So. 184.

What Defendant Is Entitled to Show.—In an action on a promise made by a bankrupt to pay as soon as he is able a debt barred by his discharge, defendant is entitled to show what portion of his earnings it is necessary for him to use for the support of himself and family, and, if the residue is insufficient to pay the debt, ability to pay is not shown. Kraus *v.* Torry, 146 Ala. 548, 40 So. 956.

Effect of New Promise upon Debtor after Being Adjudged a Bankrupt.—After a debtor has been adjudicated a bankrupt, he may, by a new promise to pay a discharged debt, if clear, distinct, and unequivocal, become liable therefor in an action at law. Torrey *v.* Kraus, 149 Ala. 200, 43 So. 184.

Extent of Debtor's Liability on New Promise.—A debtor, liable on a new promise to pay a debt discharged by bankruptcy, is not required to gauge his family expenditures so as to obtain the means to meet the obligation. Torrey *v.* Kraus, 149 Ala. 200, 43 So. 184.

What May Be Excluded.—In an action against a bankrupt on a new promise to pay a debt barred by discharge, it was not error to exclude an inquiry as to the defendant's earnings two years subsequent to the commencement of the suit. Torrey *v.* Kraus, 149 Ala. 200, 43 So. 184.

When Debtor Is Entitled to an Affirmative Charge.—In an action against a bankrupt on a new promise to pay a debt barred by his discharge, where there was no showing that the defendant had any means apart from his salary, which the undisputed proof showed was required to support himself and family, he was entitled to a general affirmative charge, if he requested it; and it was not prejudicial error to exclude evidence of his ability to borrow money. Torrey *v.* Kraus, 149 Ala. 200, 43 So. 184.

Creditor's Rights of Action upon New Promise.—Where a debtor, absolved from liability on a debt by a discharge in bankruptcy, becomes liable on a new promise to pay, the creditor may sue directly on the new promise, or he may sue on the original debt, and reply the new promise to a plea of discharge in bankruptcy. Torrey *v.* Kraus, 149 Ala. 200, 43 So. 184.

Where a debt barred by bankruptcy has been revived by a new promise, the creditor may sue on the new promise, or sue on the old debt, and reply the new promise to the plea of discharge in bankruptcy. Wolffe *v.* Eberlein, 74 Ala. 99.

What Constitutes a New Promise.—Neither payment of interest nor part payment of the principal constitutes a new promise to pay a debt from which the bankrupt has been discharged. Griel *v.* Solomon, 82 Ala. 85, 2 So. 322.

Promise to Pay After Decree of Bankruptcy.—A new promise to pay a debt, which otherwise would have been discharged by proceedings in bankruptcy, made after the decree of bankruptcy, and before the certificate of discharge, is valid and binding upon the party making it. Griel *v.* Solomon, 82 Ala. 85, 2 So. 322.

Effect of Word Constituting New Promise When Spoken to Third Person.—"An express promise by a bankrupt, to pay a particular debt to a creditor, would 'avoid the effect of such discharge, as well when the words constituting such promise are spoken to a third person, as when they are spoken to the creditor personally, or to his agent.'" Wolffe *v.* Eberlein, 74 Ala. 99, 106; Evans *v.* Carey, 29 Ala. 99.

Subsequent Promise after Filing Petition but before Discharge, Is Void.—In an action on an indebtedness against a discharged bankrupt, where the discharge is pleaded as a defense, and the replication alleges a subsequent promise since the filing of the petition in bankruptcy, an offer to prove that the defendant promised to pay the debt sued on after his adjudication, but before his discharge as a bankrupt. Held, improperly excluded. Griel *v.* Solomon, 82 Ala. 85, 2 So. 322.

§ 116. Pleading Discharge.

"A discharge in bankruptcy is not pleadable in an action ex delicto, unless, perhaps, in an action for the wrongful taking or conversion of personal property. The form of the action is the decisive test of the propriety of the plea." Lomax *v.* Spear, 51 Ala. 532, 534.

Distinction between Discharge under a Statute and Discharge by Reason of Statutes of Limitations.—There is no distinction between a discharge under a statute of bankruptcy and a discharge by reason of the statute of limitations, so far as the rules of pleading are involved. Ivey *v.* Gamble, 7 Port. 545.

Bankruptcy Pleaded to Scire Facias to Revive a Judgment.—Bankruptcy may be pleaded to a scire facias to revive a judgment, and, when it is pleaded "in short by consent," the appellate court will presume that it was well pleaded. Duncan *v.* Hargrove, 2 Ala. 150.

Where Bankrupt Omits to Plead Discharge before Justice, It Is a Good Defense on Appeal.—Where a bankrupt is sued before a justice of the peace, and omits then to plead his discharge, it is, notwithstanding, a good defense on an appeal by him to the circuit court of Alabama. McCary *v.* Mabe, 7 Ala. 356.

Bankruptcy a Personal Defense and Must Be Pleaded.—A discharge in bankruptcy does not expunge the debt, but merely bars its recovery, and is a personal defense, which must be pleaded, or it is waived. Collins *v.* Hammock, 59 Ala. 448.

Discharge in Bankruptcy Pleaded as a Bar in Suit to Set Aside Fraudulent Conveyances.—Where, in a suit to set aside certain fraudulent conveyances, defendants pleaded defendants' discharge in bankruptcy as a bar, such plea was properly met by an amendment to the bill alleging that the lien under the judgment sought to be enforced was acquired more than four months before the filing of the bankruptcy petition. Brunson *v.* Joseph Rosenheim & Son, 149 Ala. 112, 43 So. 31.

It is a good replication that the debt was created by fraud, etc.; and the court in which the action is brought has jurisdiction to try the issue. Broadnax *v.* Bradford, 50 Ala. 270.

A replication to a plea of discharge alleging a fraudulent conveyance in avoidance must contain a description of the property alleged to have been transferred as to kind and quantity, and a statement as to whom it was conveyed. Stewart *v.* Hargrove, 23 Ala. 429.

Plea—Intendment—What May Be Presumed.—No intendments being indulged in favor of a plea of a decree of discharge in bankruptcy in defense to a creditor's bill to subject choses in action charged to have been fraudulently transferred, the bill can not be presumed to have been filed within four months before the petition in bankruptcy. Stephenson *v.* Bird, 168 Ala. 422, 53 So. 93.

Amendments to Meet Defense.—The specifications of fraud, of which notice has been given to defendant, are amendable, but the refusal of the court to allow an amendment, after the case has gone to the jury, is not revisable. Ashley's Adm'r *v.* Robinson, 29 Ala. 112.

Specifications contesting a bankrupt's discharge on the ground of fraud are within the statute allowing amendments on terms after a demurrer is sustained. Stewart *v.* Hargrove, 23 Ala. 429.

Right of Creditor to Contest Certificate upon Grounds Not Stated in Written Notice.—"Prior reasonable notice, specifying in writing the fraud or concealment, for which a bankrupt's certificate of discharge is assailed, is expressly required by the act of congress. 5 U. S. Statutes at Large, 444. A creditor, therefore, can not be permitted to contest such certificate upon any ground not stated in the written notice previously given. Stewart *v.* Hargrove, 23 Ala. 429; Petty *v.* Walker, 10 Ala. 379." Ashley *v.* Robinson, 29 Ala. 112, 121.

Construction of Bankrupt Act of 1841.—The Bankrupt Act of 1841 does not restrain a creditor of one, who has availed himself of its benefits, from suing on his demand, but merely arms the bankrupt with a complete defense to the suit, until it is shown that his certificate was obtained by fraud, or that the debt comes within some one of the exceptions mentioned in the act. Cogburn *v.* Spence, 15 Ala. 549.

Under the bankrupt act of 1841 (§ 4), requiring a plaintiff who relies upon a fraud or concealment of property, to avoid a plea of discharge in bankruptcy, to give reasonable notice in writing thereof, specifying the grounds of fraud, etc., it is not an available objection, on error, that notice of an intention to impeach a bankrupt's discharge and certificate was not given until after the commencement of the term of the court where the cause was triable. The act of congress does not prescribe the time when the notice must be given, and, if too short to allow the necessary preparation to be made for trial, a continuance should be asked. Mabry *v.* Herndon, 8 Ala. 848.

Sufficiency of Plea.—Defendant pleading a discharge in bankruptcy, need not aver that plaintiffs debt was scheduled; the failure so to do being a matter for special replication to the plea setting up the discharge. B. F. Roden Grocery Co. *v.* Lessley, 169 Ala. 579, 53 So. 815.

In an action on a judgment, a plea averring that, since the commencement of the suit, the plaintiff has become a bankrupt, and has obtained a certificate of discharge in bankruptcy, if verified as a plea puis darrein continuance (Rev. Code, § 2640), is a good plea in bar. Penn *v.* Edwards, 50 Ala. 63.

A plea alleging that a lien was created in favor of the contesting creditor before the bankrupt's application for the benefit of the act, by the delivery of an execution to the sheriff of a county in which there were slaves, the property of the defendant, is defective in substance if it does not allege that the lien was continued up to the rendition of the decree. Stewart *v.* Hargrove, 23 Ala. 429.

An allegation which does not give the amount of a decree alleged to have been fraudulently omitted, nor the time of its rendition, is demurrable for want of certainty and precision. Stewart *v.* Hargrove, 23 Ala. 429.

An allegation, in general terms, that the bankrupt had not filed a full schedule of his notes and accounts, without naming those omitted, is but a statement of a legal conclusion, and is demurrable for want of precision and certainty. Stewart *v.* Hargrove, 23 Ala. 429.

§ 117. Evidence as to Discharge or New Promise.

§ 117 (1) Presumption and Burden of Proof.

"The possession of property by a bankrupt, at the time of his discharge, or immediately after, which by industry he might reasonably have acquired, does not warrant the presumption that he did not make a full surrender of his estate; but if the value of the property is so great, as to make it improbable that it was earned since the filing of the petition in bankruptcy, it devolves upon the bankrupt to show how he became the proprietor of such property, when his discharge is impugned for fraudulent or willful concealment." Gilbert *v.* Bradford, 15 Ala. 769, 778; Hargroves *v.* Cloud, 8 Ala. 173; Powell *v.* Knox, 16 Ala. 364.

When Burden of Proof Is on Defendant and When on Plaintiff.—Whenever the possession of property by a bankrupt is not referred to the time of the application, or so recently afterwards, that no business or industry could reasonably have created a fund by which to obtain the property in possession, the onus is upon the defendant to show how the property was acquired, to rebut the presumption of fraud, which otherwise, and when there are no other circumstances to repel it, may arise. In all other cases, it rests with the plaintiff to create the presumption of fraud, by showing that the business or industry of the defendant could not reasonably furnish the means to acquire the property held by him as owner. Petty *v.* Walker, 10 Ala. 379, 383.

Presumption of Law—When Arises.—Where, upon the trial of an issue vel non in obtaining a discharge in bankruptcy, it is shown that, five years before the filing of his petition, the bankrupt was the owner of a certain slave, which was not rendered in his schedule, and that, four years after his discharge, the same slave was in his possession, the law raises the presumption that he was the owner of the slave during the interim, and devolves upon him the necessity of showing by competent proof that such was not the fact. Powell *v.* Knox, 16 Ala. 364.

When Presumption of Fraud Is Raised.—The mere fact that a bankrupt, at some time prior to the filing of his petition, was owner of certain property, which is not returned in his schedule, raises no such presumption of fraud as will cast upon him the burden of explanation. Powell *v.* Knox, 16 Ala. 364.

Certificate of Discharge Presumptive Evidence.—A certificate of discharge under the Bankrupt Act of 1841 is presumptive evidence that notice was given, and conclusive where nothing appears to the contrary. Jones *v.* Knox, 51 Ala. 367.

What May Be Explained and Shown in Evidence.—In an action upon a note or claim which the defendant maintains has been discharged in bankruptcy, it is competent to identify the note or claim sued on as one scheduled, and also to show in evidence that, although the schedule described the creditor as "B. F. R. & Co.," it was the "B. F. R. Grocery Company." B. F. Roden Grocery Co. *v.* Lessley, 169 Ala. 579, 53 So. 815.

§ 117 (2) Admissibility.

The creditor having proved that one S., a few years after the bankruptcy, hired two slaves of L. G., who represented himself as the agent of the bankrupt in hiring the slaves, and that S. subsequently paid a part of the hire, as hire to the bankrupt, and the residue to another person; held, that this testimony was competent, there being no specific objection to that portion of it, which established the agency of L. G. Gilbert *v.* Bradford, 15 Ala. 769.

On an issue as to whether G. had fraudulently obtained a discharge in bankruptcy, the creditor showed that G., in the year in which he applied for his discharge, had hauled a quantity of wood, which he sold for a considerable sum, and G. offered to prove that S., at the time of said hauling, had declared in G.'s presence that the hauling was done for S. Held, that such declarations were inadmissible. Gilbert *v.* Bradford, 15 Ala. 769.

Where the issue is that the defendants did not surrender a large sum in cash, evidence that one of them, from two to four years after their discharge, was in possession of property of considerable value, may be excluded, unless connected with other proof raising the presumption that the property was not acquired by the business or industry of that defendant. Petty *v.* Walker, 10 Ala. 379.

Where, in an action by a judgment creditor to recover the amount due on the judgment against one who pleads his discharge in bankruptcy, the plaintiff replies fraud in the fraudulent concealment of assets, if a judgment was paid off to the defendant about the time of filing his petition in bankruptcy, or before that time, and the facts are such as to show that he had not parted with the money at that time, evidence would be admissible, as affecting the question whether he had money at the time he filed his petition; but, if the judgment was paid off after the institution of proceedings in bankruptcy, such evidence would be totally irrelevant. Ashley *v.* Robinson, 29 Ala. 112.

Admissibility of Evidence as to Bankrupt's General Good Character.—When a bankrupt's certificate of discharge is impeached for fraud, evidence of his general good character is not admissible for him. Pearsall *v.* McCartney, 28 Ala. 110.

Proof of Fraud.—On the issue of fraud in the creation of a debt by a bankrupt, by false representations as to the pecuniary circumstances of his co-partner and the partnership, whereby he procured goods on credit, the evidence of indebtedness must be confined to debts existing at the time the representations were made; but subsequent transactions, indicating antecedent indebtedness, would be competent evidence. Broadnax *v.* Bradford, 50 Ala. 270.

The fact that a bankrupt has made a fraudulent conveyance, which does not come within the provisions of Bankrupt Act 1841, § 2, does not of itself affect the validity of his discharge, nor does his omission to surrender the property thus situated necessarily prove a fraud or willful concealment, under § 4 of such act; but these facts are admissible as evidence, affecting the question of a fraudulent or willful concealment of the bankrupt's property. Ashley *v.* Robinson, 29 Ala. 112.

Where bankruptcy is pleaded, and the issue is the fraud of the defendants in obtaining their discharge, the inquiry is confined to the matters of which notice is given; and when the notice is that certain property, "described in a deed of trust," executed, etc., "recorded in the office of the county clerk," was not surrendered to the assignee or included in the schedule, the deed itself must be produced, or its absence accounted for. An office copy is not sufficient without such preliminary proof. Petty *v.* Walker, 10 Ala. 379.

Ability to Pay—Promise before Bankruptcy.—Where there was a new promise to pay as soon as the bankrupt should be able, and an action is instituted on such promise, evidence offered by the plaintiff that, at the time the account sued on was contracted, the plaintiff knew that the defendant was of doubtful solvency, and that the defendant stated that, no matter what happened, he would not let the plaintiff lose anything by him, is inadmissible. Griel *v.* Solomon, 82 Ala. 85, 2 So. 322.

What Bankrupt Whose Discharge Is Attacked for Fraud May Show.—A bankrupt whose discharge in bankruptcy is attacked for fraud can not show, to rebut evidence, that since his discharge he has purchased cotton to a large amount, that merchants in the neighboring city were in the habit of employing persons to buy cotton for them in the place where he resided on commission, it not appearing that he was so employed. Edgar *v.* McArn, 22 Ala. 796.

An effort being made to establish that A had obtained a discharge in bankruptcy fraudulently, he offered to prove that, six months before the institution of the proceedings in bankruptcy, one C applied to him to borrow money; that he informed him he had none of his own, but had some belonging to one B, which he had no doubt C could get if B did not want it. At the termination of this conversation, B rode up, and A handed him a roll of money supposed to be $100. Held, that this testimony was properly rejected. Gilbert *v.* Bradford, 15 Ala. 769.

Evidence by Bankrupt of Losses Sustained by Others in Same Business Not Admissible.—When a bankrupt's certificate is attacked on an allegation of fraud in withholding moneys in his hands, after the defendant has introduced evidence to show that the business in which he was engaged for several years prior to the filing of his petition in bankruptcy was generally disastrous to those engaged in it at the same time, evidence of the amount of losses sustained by another individual, wholly disconnected from him, is not admissible evidence for the defendant. Edgar *v.* McArn, 22 Ala. 796.

But after plaintiffs have proved that defendant had received considerable sums of money before filing his petition, that he was engaged in merchandising, and had purchased cotton, etc., defendant may repel any inference which might be drawn from this evidence prejudicial to him, by showing that all those who were engaged in the purchase of cotton at the same time and place with himself had failed; and this, notwithstanding it is shown that he sold his goods for cash, while the others had sold on a credit. Edgar *v.* McArn, 22 Ala. 796.

When plaintiffs have proved that defendant purchased cotton to a very large amount during the three years immediately preceding the trial, which was several years after obtaining his discharge in bankruptcy, defendant can not rebut this evidence by showing that nine-tenths of those engaged in that business during the same time were insolvent. Edgar *v.* McArn, 22 Ala. 796.

Evidence of Recklessness Admissible to Rebut Presumption of Fraud.—Where the certificate of a bankrupt is attacked for fraud, and it is shown that he had received considerable sums of money shortly before the filing of his petition, evidence that he had been reckless in his business of buying cotton is admissible on his behalf to rebut the inference of fraudulent acts. Edgar *v.* McArn, 22 Ala. 796.

Credibility of Witness—Impeachment.—No predicate can be laid by the answer of a witness as to the fact that plaintiff proved the debt against the estate, for impeaching him by contradiction, as that fact is immaterial to the issue. Griel *v.* Solomon, 82 Ala. 85, 2 So. 322.

§ 117 (3) Weight and Sufficiency.

Plaintiffs sued on a joint note, describing themselves as doing business under the firm name and style of the "Bank of Camp Mill." The notes aggregated $1,049.59, without interest. One of the defendants had been discharged in bankruptcy, and the schedule of liabilities showed, the "Bank of Camp Mill, Camp Mill, Ala., accounts and notes, $1,100." Held, a sufficient prima facie showing that such joint maker's liability on the notes in the suit was scheduled, and so fell with the degree of discharge. Anthony *v.* Sturdivant, 174 Ala. 521, 56 So. 571.

No Fraud Inferred from Omission to State Debt or Notification to Creditors.—The omission of a bankrupt to state the debt sued for, and the failure to notify the creditors of his application for a discharge, in the absence of circumstances evincing the intention to deceive, is not evidence from which fraud can be inferred. Fox *v.* Paine, 10 Ala. 523.

§ 118. Reversion of Property or Surplus to Debtor on Dismissal, Composition, or Discharge.

If, after all the debts proved against a bankrupt's estate have been paid, there remains a surplus consisting of rights of action, the assignee alone can maintain suits thereon, before the court has decreed their transfer to the bankrupt. Robinson *v.* Denny, 57 Ala. 492.

VI. APPEAL AND REVISION OF PROCEEDINGS.

§ 119. Taking and Perfecting.

As to right of congress to declare a decree in bankruptcy invalid, see ante, "Bankruptcy Acts," § 1.

Where an assignee in bankruptcy appeals from an allowance of a claim to the assignee of one of the creditors of the bankrupt without notice to such assignee, the appeal will be dismissed. Miller *v.* Parker, 47 Ala. 312.

§ 426 (2). As to debts created in an official or fiduciary capacity, see ante, "Debts Created in Official or Fiduciary Capacity," § 111 (2).

Bank.

As to banks of streams, lakes, etc., both navigable and nonnavigable, see the titles NAVIGABLE WATERS; WATERS AND WATERCOURSES.

BANKS AND BANKING.

Cross References.

As to the banking powers of building and loan associations, see the title BUILDING AND LOAN ASSOCIATIONS. As to bankruptcy proceedings against banks, see the title BANKRUPTCY. As to certificates of deposit being negotiable instruments, see the title BILLS AND NOTES. As to the negotiability of checks, see the title BILLS AND NOTES. As to embezzlement by officers and agents, see the title EMBEZZLEMENT. As to the taxation of banks and bank property, see the titles MUNICIPAL CORPORATIONS; SCHOOLS AND SCHOOL DISTRICTS; TAXATION.

I. CONTROL AND REGULATION IN GENERAL.

§ 1. Right of Banking in General.

At Common Law.—Private banking is not prohibited by the constitution, and, being a common-law right, may be exercised until prohibited by law. Nance *v.* Hemphill, 1 Ala. 551; McGehee *v.* Powell, 8 Ala. 827, 828; Durr *v.* State, 59 Ala. 24, cited in note in 15 L. R. A. 478.

Since the adoption of the constitution in this state, the right to exercise banking powers is a franchise. State *v.* Stebbins, 1 Stew. 299. See post, "Power to Control and Regulate," § 2.

2. Power to Control and Regulate.

See post, "Power to Control and Regulate," § 123.

Power of State.—It is not now, if it ever has been, seriously denied that the states have the power to charter banks; whether congress possesses that power, has been fiercely contested, and can not be considered as a settled question, notwithstanding the decisions of the supreme court of the United States affirming the right. No one however contends, that congress can directly interfere with the state authorities in the creation or management of the state banking institutions. Owen *v.* Branch Bank, 3 Ala. 258, 272.

§ 3. Constitutional and Statutory Provisions.

Constitutional Provisions for the Establishment of State Banks.—See Nance *v.* Hemphill, 1 Ala. 551; Owen *v.* Branch Bank, 3 Ala. 258.

Statutory Provisions.—Acts 1900-01, pp. 2685-2688, regulating the business of money lenders in certain counties, but exempting "banking and loans" where the sum let is over $75, does not apply to banking concerns, regardless of the size of the loan. Wright *v.* Bush, 51 So. 635, 165 Ala. 320.

§ 4. Charter Provisions.

A bank charter is a contract between the state and the stockholders, and its obligation can not be impaired by a subsequent law. Logwood *v.* Planter's, etc., Bank, Minor 23; Judson *v.* State, Minor 150, 155; State *v.* Tombeckbee Bank, 2 Stew. 30, 37. See, generally, the title CONSTITUTIONAL LAW.

§ 5. Safety Funds and Deposits of Securities.

Necessity.—Under the free-banking law of 1868 (Rev. Code, pt. 2, tit. 1, c. 1, § 1644, et seq.), an association, not claiming the right to issue or circulate its own notes, need not deposit money or transfer stock to the auditor, to authorize it to carry on other banking business. Marion Sav. Bank *v.* Dunkin, 54 Ala. 471.

II. BANKING CORPORATIONS AND ASSOCIATIONS.

(A) INCORPORATION, ORGANIZATION, AND INCIDENTS OF EXISTENCE.

§ 6. Nature and Formation in General.

See post, "Nature and Status," § 122; "Organization and Corporate Existence," § 124.

Nature.—"A bank, created by the government for its own uses, whose stock is exclusively owned by the government, is, in the strictest sense, a public corporation. But a bank, insurance, canal, bridge, or turnpike company, etc., whose stock is owned by private persons, is a private corporation, although it is erected by the government, and its objects and operations partake of a public nature." Logwood *v.* Planter's, etc., Bank, Minor 23, 24.

Sufficiency of Organization. — Under the provisions of the Revised Code (Part 2, Tit. 1, Chap. 1, § 1644, et seq.) as amended by the act of 1868, "supplementary to the corporation laws of Alabama," a corporation is sufficiently organized to carry on the business of a bank of discount and deposit and loaning money, when the certificate of the associates (properly acknowledged and recorded) for the purpose of carrying on such banking business, shows the name selected by the associates; the town where its business is to be conducted; the amount of capital stock (within the limits prescribed) and the number of shares into which it is divided; the name and place of residence of the stockholders; the shares held by them respectively, and the time when the association is to begin and terminate. Marion Sav. Bank *v.* Dunkin, 54 Ala. 471.

§ 7. Partnerships and Joint-Stock Companies.

See post, "Criminal Prosecutions," § 105.

Partnership.—There can be no limited partnership for the purpose of banking or making insurance, and an association formed in 1838, for the purpose of issuing bills to circulate as money, was not prohibited by the statute from doing the act. The only consequence resulting from the act is to make all the partners alike responsible. McGehee *v.* Powell, 8 Ala. 827, 828.

§ 8. Special Charters or Acts.

See the title CONSTITUTIONAL LAW.

The act of 1823 incorporating the Bank of the State of Alabama, is constitutional. Lyon *v.* State Bank, 1 Stew. 442.

(B) CAPITAL, STOCK, AND DIVIDENDS.

§ 9. Reduction of Capital Stock.

Purchase of Bank's Own Stock.—Where a solvent banking corporation, not in contemplation of insolvency, purchases its own stock in payment of a previously existing debt due from a stockholder, such stock does not constitute a reduction pro tanto of the bank's capital; the shares under such circumstances being treated as the property of the bank, subject to be sold or held for the benefit of creditors and the remaining stockholders, together with any dividends earned thereon. Draper *v.* Blackwell & Keith, 35 So. 110, 138 Ala. 182. See post, "Purchasing and Holding Bank's Own Stock," § 34.

§ 10. Subscription to and Issue of Stock.

See the title FRAUD.

Compelling Issue.—In a suit against a bank to compel it to register plaintiff as a stockholder for forty shares of stock, or pay the value of the stock and the dividends declared thereon, as compensation in lieu of the stock, the defendant demurred, on the ground that plaintiff had a complete remedy at law. Held, that plaintiff could, in equity, enforce a specific performance by having the stock registered in his name, and compel the issue of certificates to him, or in the alternative, if the corporation was unable to perform its contract, have his remedy by compensation in damages. Birmingham Nat. Bank *v.* Roden, 97 Ala. 404, 11 So. 883.

§ 11. Transfer of Stock.

See the title CORPORATIONS.

Misrepresentations by Vendor.—Where a bank had made two issues of stock, a representation by one selling stock that it was of the original issue was a representation of a material fact, and, if false, the buyer could decline to accept a subsequent issue. Feore *v.* Avent, 4 Ala. App. 551, 58 So. 727.

One who contracted to buy twenty shares of stock for a specified sum, relying on the seller's representation that he would transfer his certificate of stock originally issued by the bank, which originally issued $25,000 of stock divided into shares of $50 each, and which subsequently and before the contract increased its stock, could not be compelled to take any except the original stock. Feore *v.* Avent, 4 Ala. App. 551, 58 So. 727.

Parties.—In a suit against a bank to compel it to transfer certain stock to plaintiff on its books, the cashier of the bank was not a necessary party. Johnson *v.* Hume, 36 So. 421, 138 Ala. 564.

Process.—Where, in a suit to compel a bank to transfer certain stock to plaintiff on its books, the president of the bank was a defendant, and the bill at issue as to him, it was sufficient, for the execution of the compulsory process under a decree in favor of plaintiff, that the process be directed to him. Johnson *v.* Hume, 36 So. 421, 138 Ala. 564.

Variance.—Where a wife assigned her bank stock to her husband, who sold it to another, and the latter sued the bank to compel a transfer of the stock on the books to him, and the bill alleged various facts tending to show a reduction of the stock to the possession of the husband, the mere fact that plaintiff failed to show certain of the acts relied on as showing a reduction to possession did not constitute a fatal variance between the allegations and the proof. Johnson *v.* Hume, 36 So. 421, 138 Ala. 564.

§ 12. Lien of Bank on Stock or Dividends.

See, generally, the titles CORPORATIONS; LIENS.

Lien on Stock.—A bill for an accounting, brought by a bank against the administrator of its deceased cashier, contains equity in so far as it seeks, as incidental thereto, to declare and enforce a lien against the stock of respondent's intestate under Code 1907, § 3476, conferring the lien without designating or naming any court or tribunal in which it shall be enforced, but providing for foreclosure without suit or action. Wynn *v.* Tallapoosa County Bank, 53 So. 228, 168 Ala. 469.

(C) STOCKHOLDERS.

§ 13. Liability for Debts and Acts of Bank.

§ 14. —— Nature and Extent.

See post, "Liability of Stockholders or Officers," § 109. See the titles CONSTITUTIONAL LAW; PARTNERSHIP; SUBROGATION.

Liability on Insolvency.—Where a bank had been adjudged insolvent, and a receiver appointed at the attorney general's suit, in which the corporation was in effect dissolved, the depositors could maintain a creditor's suit to reach unpaid stock subscriptions; Code 1907, § 3744, authorizing bill in equity by judgment creditors of the corporation having an execution returned "no property found," not being applicable. Drennen *v.* Jenkins (Cr.) App.), 60 So. 856. See, generally, the title CREDITORS' SUIT.

Liability as Partners.—See ante, "Partnerships and Joint-Stock Companies," § 7.

§ 15. —— Actions and Proceedings to Enforce.

A creditor's bill to subject the unpaid subscription of a bank stockholder to payment of the bank's debts, which alleged that plaintiffs were not preferred creditors, and that the bank's assets, without the subscriptions, were insufficient to pay the claims of preferred creditors, so that it was necessary to subject the unpaid subscriptions, was not demurrable for not showing liability of the stockholders. Drennen *v.* Jenkins (Ala.), 60 So. 856. See, generally, the title CREDITORS' SUIT.

Defenses.—Where the charter of a bank makes the stock a fund pledged for the security of depositors, a subscriber who has paid a portion of his subscription, and acquiesced in the bank's carrying on business, is estopped to withdraw his assent, to the prejudice of other depositors, or deny the corporate existence of the bank. Lehman *v.* Warner, 61 Ala. 455.

(D) OFFICERS AND AGENTS.

§ 16. Election or Appointment, Qualification, and Tenure.

See post, "Evidence as to Authority," § 50.

Appointment.—A bank may appoint an agent to transact any business which it may lawfully do, and such appointment may be made by a mere corporate vote. Bates *v.* State Bank, 2 Ala. 451.

Compensation and Special Agents.—Act Feb., 1839, providing that the several attorneys of the Bank of the State of Alabama, and its branches, shall hereafter receive an annual salary of $1,000, and no more, does not prohibit the banks from employing such other legal assistance as their interests may require. Bank of Alabama *v.* Martin, 4 Ala. 615.

§ 17. Rights and Liabilities as to Bank and Stockholders.

§ 18. —— Nature and Extent.

See post, "Nature and Extent," § 21.

Generally.—"The president and directors of our state banks are but the agents of the state for the purpose of managing the affairs of the corporation. The charters of incorporation are in some sense letters of attorney under which they act, and are not only enabling, but are also restraining acts. Branch of the Bank *v.* Collins, 7 Ala. 95." Spyker *v.* Spence, 8 Ala. 333, 339.

A cashier is liable to account to the bank in equity, but only for losses occasioned by his lack of or failure to exercise reasonable care and diligence, and not for losses the result of mere errors of judgment. Wynn *v.* Tallapoosa County Bank, 168 Ala. 469, 53 So. 228.

A cashier is liable for losses, the result of negligence or fraud, but not for his dereliction or fault when there is no loss in consequence thereof. Wynn *v.* Tallapoosa County Bank, 168 Ala. 469, 53 So. 228.

Directors can not, by neglecting to perform any duties, and imposing all on the cashier, make him an absolute insurer of the bank against all loss merely because, to carry on its business successfully, he must ignore or fail to observe the by-laws, or fail to confer with them. Wynn *v.* Tallapoosa County Bank, 168 Ala. 469, 53 So. 228.

Acts Done under Lawful Authority.—A bank can act only by or through its officers or agents, and if directors themselves can do an act, so far as they or the bank is concerned, they can authorize the cashier to do it; and, if he acts under their lawful authority, he is not liable to them or the bank. Wynn *v.* Tallapoosa County Bank, 168 Ala. 469, 53 So. 228.

If directors place on the cashier the duty of carrying on the bank's business, and they as a body, or the committees thereof, fail to meet, or to instruct, help, and supervise him, absenting themselves from the bank and its business, and thus put on him the whole burden, neither they nor the bank can hold him responsible for not consulting with them, as required by the by-laws, as to discounts and loans. Wynn *v.* Tallapoosa County Bank, 168 Ala. 469, 53 So. 228.

Estoppel to Assert Liability of Cashier.—Stockholders, directors, committees, and officers must be presumed to have known of and consented to a cashier's course of business as to overdrafts, loans, and discounts which continued for a period of seven years without suspicion or complaint, and after allowing it for that time and profiting thereby, they must be presumed to have ratified his acts. Wynn *v.* Tallapoosa County Bank, 168 Ala. 469, 53 So. 228.

Misappropriation of Funds.—Though a cashier is a quasi trustee, he is not such strictly speaking, and though in his dealings with the public he is the agent of the bank, he is held as to the bank like a trustee; yet, if he wrongfully acquires its funds and invests them in his own name, it cannot fasten a trust or lien on the property, as in case of a real trustee, since the acquisition of the funds being wrong in such case, the trust does not exist. Wynn *v.* Tallapoosa County Bank, 168 Ala. 469, 53 So. 228.

Negligence of Cashier in Respect to Loans and Overdrafts.—A cashier is not absolutely liable for an overdraft if it is really a loan on sufficient security. Wynn *v.* Tallapoosa County Bank, 168 Ala. 469, 53 So. 228. See post, "Overdrafts," § 73.

When the whole duty and responsibility as to a bank's business is intentionally or negligently imposed on the cashier, he will be liable to the bank for improper loans, discounts or overdrafts where he fails to make reasonable inquiry into the financial standing of those making the same, or knowingly or negligently fails to take proper security, but he is not an insurer against loss in such cases, and is not liable merely because he did not observe the by-laws, unless negligent or inexcusable in not doing so. Wynn *v.* Tallapoosa County Bank, 168 Ala. 469, 53 So. 228.

Where a cashier allows numerous drafts to accumulate, and afterwards closes up the transaction by taking secured notes therefor, the wrong, if any, for which he is liable to the bank was in the original transactions, and not in taking the notes, which could not of itself injure it. Wynn *v.* Tallapoosa County Bank, 168 Ala. 469, 53 So. 228, 231.

The mere fact that notes taken by the cashier are entered on the books as bills receivable, is not sufficient to render him liable for not accounting for the proceeds, where there is no proof that they were ever paid. Wynn *v.* Tallapoosa County Bank, 168 Ala. 469, 53 So. 228.

Liability of Cashier for Acts of Sub-

ordinates.—A cashier need not examine and supervise every act of his subordinates, but as to such acts need only use such care and diligence as an ordinary man would exercise in his own business affairs. Wynn *v.* Tallapoosa County Bank, 168 Ala. 469, 53 So. 228.

A cashier is not liable for errors or improper acts of his subordinates, but to render him liable therefor he must in some way have contributed to their wrongs. Wynn *v.* Tallapoosa County Bank, 168 Ala. 469, 53 So. 228.

Order of Directors as Defense.—A cashier is responsible for all losses suffered directly from his failure in any respect in his official duty, and it does not avail that the directors ordered or authorized him so to act, if they had no authority to do so, nor to do the act themselves which they authorized him to do, and he knew or ought to have known the act done or authorized was unlawful. Wynn *v.* Tallapoosa County Bank, 53 So. 228, 168 Ala. 469.

Compensation.—Under the statute fixing the compensation of directors of the State Bank, a director of a branch bank, receiving the compensation provided by law, can be allowed no compensation by the board for extra services while he continues a director. Mobile Branch Bank *v.* Collins, 7 Ala. 95; Mobile Branch Bank *v.* Scott, 7 Ala. 107; Godbold *v.* Branch Bank at Mobile, 11 Ala. 191.

Where work was done by mechanics for a bank, under the superintendence of one of the directors, the board might lawfully direct their compensation to be paid to him for their use. Mobile Branch Bank *v.* Collins, 7 Ala. 95.

The giving compensation to a member of the board of directors, for extra services as an agent of the bank, though unlawful, is not such an act as will expose the directors to liability, if done in good faith, and with the honest intent of benefitting the bank. Godbold *v.* Bank at Mobile, 11 Ala. 191, 46 Am. Dec. 211.

§ 19. —— Actions and Proceedings to Enforce.

Right of Action.—In so far as a bill by a bank against the administrator of its deceased cashier seeks an accounting against the agent, it contains equity. Wynn *v.* Tallapoosa County Bank, 168 Ala. 469, 53 So. 228.

Pleading.—A bill by a bank against an administrator of a deceased cashier for an accounting averred various claims and demands covering transactions extending over more than seven years, but did not inform the court or respondent as to the time a liability accrued, except that it was within such period, and as to many transactions there was no other description of the liability or demand than that it was for allowing an overdraft, or for taking insufficient security for a loan, or for making a loan in violation of the bylaws, or without consulting the board of directors. Held, that the description of the various claims and demands was not sufficiently specific. Wynn *v.* Tallapoosa County Bank, 168 Ala. 469, 53 So. 228.

Variance.—In a suit for an accounting against the administrator of a deceased cashier, based on wrongful acts as to loans, discounts, and overdrafts, it was alleged that a great number were made or allowed by him to certain parties named, for certain amounts, without fixing any dates or otherwise identifying them, while the proof showed losses, discounts, overdrafts, etc., of different amounts, and several times to different parties, and in a number of instances the wrongful act alleged was the making of a loan to a certain person, and the taking of notes therefor without sufficient security, while the proof showed that the transactions alleged were not a loan, but the closing up of a previous indebtedness of such person to the bank, by notes and security, or making a past-due and existing indebtedness more secure, by extending the time of payment and taking notes and collateral security. Held, that the variances were material, though a mere difference in an amount would not be if it was shown to be the same transaction. Wynn *v.* Tallapoosa County Bank, 168 Ala. 469, 53 So. 228

Evidence held to conclusively show that a loss to a bank on account of overdrafts allowed by its deceased cashier, whose administrator is sued therefor, was the fault of the bank or its officers after his death. Wynn *v.* Tallapoosa County Bank, 168 Ala. 469, 53 So. 228.

§ 20. Liability for Debts and Acts of Bank.

§ 21. —— Nature and Extent.

See ante, "Nature and Extent," § 18.

Errors of Judgment.—Directors of a bank are not responsible for an injury to the bank, caused by their act, originating in an error of judgment, unless the act be so grossly wrong as to warrant the imputation of fraud, or the want of the necessary knowledge for the performance of the duty assumed by them, on accepting the agency. Godbold *v.* Bank at Mobile, 11 Ala. 191, 46 Am. Dec. 211.

Withdrawal of Stock Subscriptions.—If a bank allows its stockholders to withdraw its funds to the amount of their subscriptions, and to use them, without security, in their private business, such conduct is a fraud on its creditors, which renders the directors liable in equity for the amount so withdrawn, and each agent who participated in the fraud individually responsible for the amount traced to his hands and all profits made from its use. Bank of St. Marys *v.* St. John, 25 Ala. 566.

(E) INSOLVENCY AND DISSOLUTION.

§ 22. Voluntary Liquidation and Dissolution.

Surrender of Charter.—The object of the act of February 12, 1843, " for the final settlement of the affairs of the Planters' and Merchants' Bank of Mobile," was to obtain a dissolution of the bank's charter agreeably to law; and although it provides for the institution of judicial proceedings against the bank, to obtain a judgment of forfeiture of its charter, and declares, "that, if no cause of forfeiture shall be found, this act shall have no force or validity," yet the bank might dispense with the judicial proceeding by surrendering its charter and accepting the provisions of the act, and it was competent for the state, with the assent of the bank, to resume its franchises at any time. Savage *v.* Walshe, 26 Ala. 619.

§ 23. Grounds for Forfeiture of Franchise or Dissolution.

The act of 1821, declaring the charter of the Tombeckbee Bank liable to forfeiture for a failure to pay specie on demand for its notes, did not affect the bank, as its charter contained no such provision. State *v.* Tombeckbee Bank, 2 Stew. 30.

§ 24. Effect of Dissolution.

See post, "Power of Discount," § 92.

On Right to Contract.—The Planters' & Merchants' Bank of Mobile had no power, after the judgment of the circuit court, declaring its charter forfeited, to make a contract, except so far as it was authorized to act by the statute providing for the ascertainment of the fact, whether its charter was forfeited or not. Saltmarsh *v.* Planters' & Merchants' Bank, 14 Ala. 668; S. C., 17 Ala. 761.

On Right to Sue.—The act of 1823, declaring a forfeiture of the charter of the Huntsville Bank to ensue from a failure to pay specie for its notes, did not take from the bank the right to sue in its corporate capacity. Huntsville Bank *v.* McGehees, 1 Stew. & P. 306. See post, "Capacity to Sue and Be Sued," § 111.

On Prior Judgment.—Where the affairs of a bank are, by statute, placed in the hands of trustees for settlement, after a judgment has been rendered on quo warranto against the bank declaring its charter forfeited, the subsequent reversal of that judgment does not affect a suit previously instituted by the trustees against a debtor of the bank, so as to protect the debtor against the rendition of judgment. Jemison *v.* Planters' & Merchants' Bank, 23 Ala. 168.

§ 25. Transfers and Preferences Affected by Insolvency.

If a bank, on the eve of insolvency, having notes out which it can not redeem, and a large claim on a solvent stockholder for money lent, extends his debt by taking his notes, payable at two and three years, with its president as sole surety, this is a fraud on its creditors, and they may proceed in equity directly against such debtor, without a judgment at law or process of garnishment. Bank of St. Marys *v.* St. John, 25 Ala. 566.

§ 26. Assets and Receivers on Insolvency.

§ 26 (1) Appointment and Removal.

Statutory Receivership.—Code 1907, §

3560, providing that, whenever the treasurer finds a bank or corporation doing a banking business is not in a solvent condition, the attorney general shall institute proceedings to put the bank in the hands of some competent person, who shall collect its assets and pay off its liabilities, creates a statutory receivorship for banks subject to the general principles of receivorship and § 3509, providing that the assets of insolvent corporations constitute trust funds for the payment of creditors. Oates *v.* Smith (Ala.), 57 So. 438.

Superintendent of Banks.—Under Act 1911, p. 59, § 10, providing that the affairs of banks in default shall be turned over to the superintendent, who is authorized to collect moneys due and do such other acts as necessary to conserve its assets and business and liquidate the affairs thereof, the superintendent is in reality a receiver, and there is no change in the ownership or legal title of the property. Montgomery Bank, etc., Co. *v.* Walker (Ala.), 61 So. 951.

The inhibition of Const. U. S., amend. 14, against the deprivation of property without due process of law requires that the substance of property rights be preserved and that opportunity be given to invoke the equal protection of the law by some judicial proceeding adequate and appropriate, but does not deprive the state of the power to determine by what process legal rights may be asserted or legal obligations enforced, consequently Act 1911, p. 59, § 10, providing that, before the banking board shall declare a bank in default or turn its affairs over to the superintendent of banks, the superintendent must first submit to the board matters of default or misconduct in its affairs of which the bank shall have notice and upon which it may be heard in person or by counsel, and further authorizing a bank feeling aggrieved by the action of the board to apply for an injunction, does not work a deprivation of property without due process of law. Montgomery Bank, etc., Co. *v.* Walker (Ala.), 61 So. 951.

§ 26 (2) Operation and Effect.

The appointment of a receiver under Code 1907, § 3560, providing that, when a bank is found to be insolvent, the attorney general shall institute proceedings in a court having jurisdiction to put the bank into the hands of some person, to wind up its affairs, operates as an adjudication of insolvency fixing the status of corporate assets and qualifying the rights of creditors. Oates *v.* Smith (Ala.), 57 So. 438.

§ 26 (3) Powers and Duties of Receivers in General.

Power to Contract.—Under the powers conferred by the acts of the 13th of February, 1843, for the final settlement of the affairs of the Planters' & Merchants' Bank of Mobile, and of the 24th January, 1845, amendatory thereof, the trustees appointed by virtue of the latter act may lawfully enter into a contract with a third person, without the consent of the debtor, to secure the payment of a doubtful debt due to the bank, and transfer the debt for that purpose to such third person. Saltmarsh *v.* Planters' & Merchants' Bank, 17 Ala. 761.

Power to Discount Bills.—Act Feb. 13, 1843, for the final settlement of affairs of the Planters' & Merchants' Bank after declaring its charter forfeited, and providing for the exhibition of an information in the nature of a quo warranto and the appointment of commissioners, provides that it shall be lawful for said commissioners to submit to arbitration contested claims, "to compound any doubtful or bad debt," etc. Pamph. Acts 1845, p. 46, provides that the trustee may use the corporate name of said bank in the collection of debts due it, and may use all the modes and powers given to the bank for the collection of its debts, in the same manner as if the charter had never been forfeited. Held, that these provisions do not authorize discounting or purchasing bills except in payment or as security for a debt that is bad or doubtful. Saltmarsh *v.* Planters' & Merchants' Bank, 14 Ala. 668.

As the trustees of the Planters' & Merchants' Bank of Mobile had authority, on the final settlement of the affairs of the bank, to take a note in settlement of a debt due to the bank, the fact that a note taken by the trustees after the surrender of the bank's charter was made "negotiable and payable at said bank" does not raise a legal presumption that it was unlawfully discounted by the trustees, instead of being taken in settlement of a debt due, so as to defeat an action brought thereon by one who purchased the note at the trustees' sale of the bank's assets. Savage *v.* Walshe, 26 Ala. 619.

Power to Transfer Negotiable Paper.—Under the act of 1850, relative to the final settlement of the affairs of the Planters' & Merchants' Bank of Mobile, etc., and providing that within thirty days after, etc., the trustees of said bank shall sell for cash all remaining property, claims, etc., belonging to said bank, and realize the same for the purpose of final settlement, the trustees, by necessary implication, had the power to transfer negotiable securities so as to pass the legal title by their assignment, and enable the purchaser to sue in his own name. Savage *v.* Walshe, 26 Ala. 619.

Power to Take Individual Notes.—Act 1845 authorizes the appointment of trustees to settle the affairs of the Planters' & Merchants' Bank, whose charter had been declared forfeited, and gave them power to compromise bad or doubtful debts, and to use all the remedies which the bank might have used, while in existence, for the collection and securing of its claims. Held, that the trustees were authorized to take individual notes to secure a balance due from another bank that had suspended specie payment, as such debt must be considered bad or doubtful. Jemison *v.* Planters' & Merchants' Bank, 23 Ala. 168.

Power of Suit.—Under Act 1911, p. 59, § 10, providing that, in case a bank is in default, its affairs shall be turned over to the superintendent of banks who is authorized to collect all debts due and claims belonging to the bank and to do all acts necessary to conserve its assets and business, the superintendent has power to sue in the name of the bank to avoid a fraudulent transaction made by its officials. Montgomery Bank, etc., Co. *v.* Walker (Ala.), 61 So. 951.

§ 26 (4) Collection and Protection of Assets.

Regardless of Code 1907, § 3509, providing that the assets of insolvent corporations constitute a trust fund for the payment of creditors, the assets of an insolvent bank must be regarded as a trust fund for the payment of creditors, and the stockholders, directors, and agents of the bank are trustees for their benefit, and as such may be made to discover and account in chancery. Montgomery Bank, etc., Co. *v.* Walker (Ala.), 61 So. 951.

Where the superintendent of banks wished to avoid a transaction whereby the officers of an insolvent institution pledged collateral to another bank for an antecedent debt as well as one presently created, and challenged the authority of the officers but offered to do equity, he had no plain adequate remedy at law, and the jurisdiction of equity was properly invoked. Montgomery Bank, etc., Co. *v.* Walker (Ala.), 61 So. 951.

Where the superintendent of banks filed a bill to set aside a pledge of the assets of a bank made by the president averring that he had no authority to so act, the bill need not negative special authority which should be set up as an affirmative defense. Montgomery Bank, etc., Co. *v.* Walker (Ala.), 61 So. 951.

§ 26 (5) Sale or Other Disposition of Assets.

Sale of Assets.—The clause in the second section of the act of 1850, which requires the trustees to sell the remaining property and assets of the Bank "within thirty days from the first Monday in November next," is not mandatory, but directory merely; and therefore, a sale made after the expiration of the time specified is sufficient to pass a good title to the purchaser. Savage *v.* Walshe, 26 Ala. 619.

The act of 1850, which directed a sale of the remaining assets of the Planters' & Merchants' Bank of Mobile, does not repeal, by implication, the act of 1845, which authorized the appointment of trustees to settle its affairs, and gave them power to use all the remedies to which the bank, while in existence, was entitled; and a sale, pursuant to the act, of notes then in suit, does not affect the further prosecution of it for the benefit of the purchaser. Jemison *v.* Planters' & Merchants' Bank, 23 Ala. 168.

§ 27. Rights of Holders of Circulating Notes.

Right to Proceed in Equity.—The note holders of a foreign banking corporation, which has suspended payment, and become insolvent, may, without first obtaining a judgment at law, proceed in equity against the bank, its directors, stockholders, and agents, charging them with fraud and misapplication of the assets, and seeking a discovery and account. Such a bill may be maintained under the general powers and jurisdiction of the court, which regards the capital stock of the company and all its assets as a trust fund for the payment of its creditors, and the directors, stockholders, and agents as trustees. Bank of St. Mary s *v.* St. John, 25 Ala. 566.

Right to Set Off.—The bank notes of the Pennsylvania Bank of the United States can not be set off to a note sued upon by the trustees of the bank, to whom it had been assigned for the payment of its creditors. Gee *v.* Bacon, 9 Ala. 699.

§ 28. Presentation and Payment of Claims.

Priorities.—A holder of a bank's certificate of deposit, payable on a fixed date with interest, is a creditor of the bank on a loan made to it for a fixed period on which interest is stipulated for, and is not a depositor, within Const., § 250, giving depositors who have not stipulated for interest a preference in case of the bank's insolvency. Taylor *v.* Hutchinson, 40 So. 108, 145 Ala. 202.

Where a Texas bank sent its note for collection to an Alabama bank, but it did not appear that the amount collected was to be credited to the Texas bank, the latter was not within Const. 1901, § 250, providing that depositors shall be entitled, in case of insolvency, to a preference of payment over creditors. Nixon State Bank *v.* First State Bank of Bridgeport (Ala.), 60 So. 868.

Right to Set Off.—Code 1907, § 5858, providing that mutual debts subsisting between the parties at the commencement of the suit may be set off, does not give one indebted to an insolvent bank, which has been placed in the hands of a receiver, the right to offset an obligation acquired since insolvency, for it refers to a debt to and a claim against the same legal person, each of which must equally afford the obligee a right of action against the obligor. Oates *v.* Smith (Ala.), 57 So. 438.

Where a receiver was appointed under Code 1907, § 3560, to collect the assets and pay off the liabilities of an insolvent bank, a debtor can not offset a debt due the bank with an obligation acquired after its insolvency, for § 3509, provides that the assets of insolvent corporations constitute a trust fund for the payment of creditors, and, while the changed status wrought by insolvency does not impair or defeat existing rights of set-off, debtors are not required to have offset against their debt claims which they have acquired subsequent to insolvency, for, after insolvency is established, a creditor is only entitled to file his claim and share ratably in the distribution of the assets, and so his assignee has no greater rights. Oates *v.* Smith (Ala.), 57 So. 438.

Deposits Made by Husband.—In proceedings for the allowance of a claim against an insolvent bank, based on a deposit in claimant's name, the cashier stated that claimant's husband, when he deposited the money, stated that it was the proceeds of land claimed by his wife. The testimony of claimant showed that it was her money. The husband deposited the money in claimant's name, and in her absence told the cashier that it would be used as a credit on a debt due by him and her, and the deposit was entered as a credit thereon. When claimant saw the entry, her husband told her that the credit was not to be made. Held, that no agreement made by the husband in the wife's absence would bind her, and the claim of the wife was properly allowed. Peach *v.* Grubbs, 40 So. 110, 145 Ala. 685.

Proof Required.—Where a bank induced collections and deposits by false representations of solvency, creditors can not have a trust declared in their favor in the assets of the bank in the hands of a receiver without showing that the receiver has or ever had collected them, or deposited money or property in which such money was invested. St. Louis Brewing Ass'n *v.* Austin, 100 Ala. 313, 13 So. 908. See note in 25 L. R. A. 547, 34 L. R. A. 536.

§ 29. Criminal Responsibility on Insolvency.

§ 30. —— Offenses.

Cause of Insolvency.—On an issue as to whether a banker received deposits while insolvent, it is immaterial whether the bank became insolvent by his fault or by accident, and whether the insolvency consisted in inability to pay depositors or other creditors, or both. Carr *v.* State, 104 Ala. 4, 16 So. 150, cited in note in 31 L. R. A. 125.

Liability as Affected by Partnership.—The liability of a private banker, under Code, § 3797, for fraudulently converting a special deposit of money, is none the less that his bank, which used the money, is a partnership, and such case is covered by an allegation of conversion "to his own use." Carr *v.* State, 104 Ala. 43, 16 So. 155.

Liability of One Officer for Act of Another.—Under the act (Acts 1892-93, p. 95) making guilty of a misdemeanor a bank officer or agent who shall receive for deposit any money, knowing at the time that the bank is insolvent, a manager who keeps his bank open for business, knowing it to be insolvent, is guilty in respect to a deposit received by the teller in the course of business, though the manager himself be not present, or even in town, and the teller himself have no guilty knowledge. Carr *v.* State, 104 Ala. 4, 16 So. 150, cited in note in 26 L. R. A., N. S., 1072.

§ 31. —— Prosecution and Punishment.

See ante, "Offenses," § 30.

Punishment.—Act Dec. 12, 1892, declaring a banker who receives a deposit, knowing his insolvency, to be guilty of a misdemeanor, punishable by fine of double the deposit, half to go to the depositor, with imprisonment in case of nonpayment, but payment back to depositor of amount of deposit before conviction to be a defense, violates Const., art. 1, § 21, declaring that no person shall be imprisoned for debt. Carr *v.* State, 106 Ala. 35, 17 So. 350. See, generally, the title CONSTITUTIONAL LAW.

III. FUNCTIONS AND DEALINGS.

(A) BANKING FRANCHISES AND POWERS, AND THEIR EXERCISE IN GENERAL.

§ 32. What Are Banking Powers in General.

See ante, "Partnerships and Joint-Stock Companies," § 7; post, "Banking Powers," § 126.

Steamboat Company.—Act Feb. 10, 1818, incorporating the St. Stephen's Company, authorized it to purchase and hold lands, goods, etc., and to dispose of the same, and, in general, to do all the acts usually incident to bodies corporate. Through the entire grant of powers, there was no intimation of any important object to be effected, or enterprise to be pursued, for which a corporate capacity was necessary. Held, that the charter did not, by implication, grant banking powers to the corporation. State *v.* Stebbins, 1 Stew. 299.

§ 33. Customs and Usages.

See, generally, the title CUSTOMS AND USAGES.

Effect of Observance.—"A course of dealing between the bank and a single person may establish obligations as to its continuance, and, if nothing is provided to the contrary, will govern subsequent transactions of the same nature between them." Tobias *v.* Morris, 126 Ala. 535, 28 So. 517, 522.

A custom of passing checks payable to a person "or bearer" by delivery only does not affect the operation of Code, § 1761, requiring such checks to be construed as payable to a person "or order." First Nat. Bank *v.* Nelson, 105 Ala. 180, 16 So. 707.

Effect of Abandonment.—Plaintiffs, doing a banking business, after abandoning a practice to give notice of the dishonor of notes by mail notwithstanding that the indorser and holder lived in the same town, could not rely on such custom, even though it continued to prevail among other banks. Isbell *v.* Lewis, 98

Ala. 550, 13 So. 335, cited on this point in note in 21 L. R. A. 441.

§ 34. Purchasing and Holding Bank's Own Stock.

See ante, "Reduction of Capital Stock," § 9.

In the absence of statutory restriction, a solvent banking corporation, not in contemplation of insolvency or dissolution, as against creditors, may purchase its own stock in payment of a previously existing debt due from the stockholder. Draper *v.* Blackwell & Keith, 35 So. 110, 138 Ala. 182.

§ 35. Property and Conveyance.

§ 36. —— In General.

Personal Property.—The twentieth section of the act of incorporation of the State Bank provides that the "bank shall not deal in articles of goods, wares, or merchandise, in any manner whatever, unless it be to secure a debt due the said bank, incurred by the regular transactions of the same, as is provided for in this act." The meaning is that the bank shall not buy and sell goods, wares, or merchandise for the purpose of gain, or do the ordinary business of a merchant or trader, or engage in the business of broker or commission merchant. Bates *v.* State Bank, 2 Ala. 451.

A contract, by which the State Bank lent a large sum of money, taking bills of exchange at nine months for payment thereof, and receiving at the time, and as one of the conditions of the loan, a quantity of cotton, with authority to ship it to a foreign port, and sell it for the account and at the risk and expense of the owners, and to credit his bill with the amount of the net proceeds, adding the difference of exchange between this state and the place where the cotton was sold, is not dealing in "goods, wares, or merchandise," within the twentieth section of the charter. Bates *v.* State Bank, 2 Ala. 451.

The purchase of cotton in this state with Confederate notes by a banking corporation of Louisiana, in 1862, was not the exercise of the privilege of banking in this state within the meaning of § 939 of the Code, which requires such corporations to exercise that privilege "by the exclusive use of gold and silver coin and bank bills issued by the authority of the state," but such contract was void under the laws of the United States and the proclamations of the president, the banking corporation being at the time of the purchase of the cotton located in New Orleans, which was in the federal possession. Morris *v.* Hall, 41 Ala. 510.

§ 37. —— Real Property.

Under the joint resolution of the general assembly of the 31st December, 1842, the State Bank and its branches have the power to purchase real estate sold under executions in their favor. Martin *v.* Branch Bank at Decatur, 15 Ala. 587, 50 Am. Dec. 147.

§ 38. Contracts in General.

A bank agreed to receive in payment of debts, and to put into circulation, such bonds or notes as a railroad company might lawfully issue. The bank accordingly received some of the paper emitted by the railroad, and again loaned it out in the purchase of bills of exchange, upon one of which suit was brought, and payment resisted upon the ground that the contract between the bank and the railroad was illegal. Held, that the contract was not illegal upon its face, as it only stipulated that the bank should receive such bills or notes as the railroad company might lawfully issue under its charter; but if this contract was a mere contrivance to aid the railroad company in evading the prohibition contained in the proviso to the second section of the charter, "forbidding it to remit any bills or notes for circulation," it would be unlawful, and would vitiate a contract made by the bank, of which the paper of the railroad constituted the consideration. Whetstone *v.* Bank at Montgomery, 9 Ala. 875, affirming Crocheron *v.* Bank of Alabama, 5 Ala. 251.

An agreement by the Branch Bank to receive such bills as a certain railroad company could lawfully issue, and to pay the same out as circulation, will not avoid a recovery on bills of exchange given for the loan by the bank of such bills, as being contrary to the policy of the laws of the state with reference to its banking institutions. Branch Bank *v.* Crocheron, 5 Ala. 250.

§ 39. Borrowing Money.

"A board of directors, authorized to conduct the affairs of the company, may empower the president and cashier to borrow money, but the president, under an authority thus conferred upon the cashier and himself, can not borrow money." Spyker *v.* Spence, 8 Ala. 333, 340.

(B) REPRESENTATION OF BANK BY OFFICERS AND AGENTS.

§ 40. Disposition of Property.

The rule that the president of a corporation has no ex officio power to sell or mortgage the corporate property applies to bank presidents, and such officers have no right to pledge the assets of the bank, particularly to secure an antecedent and questionable debt. Montgomery Bank, etc., Co. *v.* Walker (Ala.), 61 So. 951.

While the cashier of a bank is the chief executive officer and his authority exceeds that of the president, he has no inherent power to pledge the assets of the bank for the payment of an antecedent debt; his power only extending to the disposal of the bank's negotiable securities in the ordinary course of business. Montgomery Bank, etc., Co. *v.* Walker (Ala.), 61 So. 951.

In the absence of authority by its charter, the president of a banking corporation can not use its cash or credits, etc., for the purpose of effecting a settlement of the demands of its creditors; and an assignment by him of property of the bank to a third person for that purpose will not be valid, though the seal of the corporation be affixed. Gibson *v.* Goldthwaite, 7 Ala. 281, 42 Am. Dec. 592.

"It has been held that the president has not, ex officio, authority to transfer the property or securities of a bank; but must have express authority to that effect, from the corporation at large, or the directors, as the case may be." Spyker *v.* Spence, 8 Ala. 333, 340.

§ 41. Contracts.

A cashier's act within the scope of the ordinary course of business is binding upon the bank, though he was acting beyond the scope of the express authority conferred by it. First Nat. Bank *v.* First Nat. Bank, 22 So. 976, 116 Ala. 520.

"The acts of the cashier, done in the ordinary course of the business, actually confided to such an officer, may well be deemed prima facie evidence that they fell within the scope of his duty." Everett *v.* United States, 6 Port. 166, 181.

§ 42. Deposits.

"The president or cashier can not charge a bank with any special liability, for a deposit contrary to its usage, without the previous authority of subsequent assent of the corporation." Spyker *v.* Spence, 8 Ala. 333, 340.

§ 43. Collections.

Generally.—The cashier is the executive officer of the bank, and his acts, if apparently within the regular course of business, in respect to the collection of its debts, will be presumed to be within the scope of his official authority, until the contrary is shown. Spyker *v.* Spence, 8 Ala. 333, 340.

"It may be declared as a matter of law that the receipt, for collection, by a bank engaged in transacting a general banking business, of paper transferable by indorsement, which, although not of themselves evidence of an indebtedness, show by the indorsements thereon that the persons sending them must hold them as collateral security for an indebtedness, and which are, in fact, held as such collateral security, is within the usage, custom, and ordinary course of business of banking institutions; and therefore that the act of receiving such papers by the cashier of such bank is within the scope of his authority, and not his individual act, but that of the bank, in the absence of any knowledge or notice on the part of the sender of any express limitation on the authority of the cashier with respect to the character of the papers which he may receive for collection." First Nat. Bank *v.* First Nat. Bank, 116 Ala. 520, 22 So. 976, 980.

"The cashier of a bank has a general authority to suspend the collection of notes under protest, and to make such arrangements as may facilitate that object, and to do any thing in relation thereto that an attorney might lawfully do." Spyker *v.* Spence, 8 Ala. 333, 340.

To Accept Partial Payments.—It was not within the scope of the authority or duty of an agent for the collection of a check to accept a partial payment. Lowenstein *v.* Bresler, 109 Ala. 326, 19 So. 860.

§ 44. Bills, Notes, and Securities.

§ 44 (1) President.

"An agreement by the president and cashier of a bank that an indorser shall not be liable on his indorsement is not binding on the bank." Spyker *v.* Spence, 8 Ala. 333, 340.

§ 44 (2) Cashier.

A cashier of a bank has prima facie authority to indorse negotiable paper belonging to the bank. Everett *v.* United States, 6 Port. 166, 30 Am. Dec. 584.

"This inference, however, would not be conclusive, and it would still be competent for the party sued, to controvert the fairness of the transfer, by showing that it was not made in the regular course of business, but in prejudice of the rights and interests of the bank. Where this is the case, no title could pass to the assignee, and consequently no action could be maintained by him." Everett *v.* United States, 6 Port. 166, 181.

§ 45. Actions.

See post, "Parties," § 112 (2); "Use of Name of Bank or Officer," § 115.

Power of President to Stay Execution.—The president of a banking corporation, the charter of which does not confer the power either expressly or incidentally, is not authorized, without the permission of the directors, to whom is intrusted the management of the concerns of the institution, to stay the collection of an execution against the estate of one of its debtors; and if a sheriff omits to levy an execution, in consequence of such an order from the president, it will not become dormant, so as to lose its lien. Spyker *v.* Spence, 8 Ala. 333.

Defending Suit.—It is not within the scope of the powers ordinarily conferred upon a cashier to appear and defend suits against the bank. An answer, therefore, by the cashier, when the bank is garnished, will not support a judgment against the bank. Branch Bank *v.* Poe, 1 Ala. 396; Bank of Mobile *v.* Leavens, 4 Ala. 753.

Such an answer should be made under the common seal of the bank, either by the express authority of the directors, or president, who thus far, is the executive officer of the board. Branch Bank *v.* Poe, 1 Ala. 396.

§ 46. Representations or Admissions.

The president of a bank can not charge it with a debt by his admissions. Henry *v.* Northern Bank of Alabama, 63 Ala. 527.

§ 47. Estoppel to Deny Authority of Officer or Agent.

The performance of a construction contract for a bank was in the hands of the president in so far as it was concerned. Orders by the contractor on the bank were taken to the president, who ordered them paid. Some payments were in violation of the construction contract, which required payments to be made only on certificates and estimates of the architect. Held, that the bank, claiming credit for such payments, could not deny the authority of the president to make them. First Nat. Bank *v.* Fidelity & Deposit Co. of Maryland, 40 So. 415, 145 Ala. 335, 5 L. R. A., N. S., 418, 117 Am. St. Rep. 45.

§ 48. Ratification.

Power to Ratify and Acts Constituting Ratification.—Directors can ratify whatever acts of the cashier they can do in the first instance, and they will be held to have ratified his acts where they impose on him a duty which they should perform, and fail to object to his course of business when they know, or could easily know, all the facts. Wynn *v.* Tallapoosa County Bank, 53 So. 228, 168 Ala. 469.

Where defendant's cashier declined to make a loan until proper security should be given, and during his absence plaintiff applied to the acting cashier, and by fraudulently representing that the cashier had agreed to make the loan for the bank obtained a cashier's check to the borrower, which the borrower transferred to plaintiff, and as soon as the cashier returned he attempted to repudiate the transaction, and took steps to protect the bank and himself by taking the mortgage from the payees, such attempt did not constitute a ratification of the transaction by the bank. Bank of Coffee Springs *v.* W. A. McGilvray & Co., 52 So. 473, 167 Ala. 408.

Evidence held to show ratification by a bank and its directors of the acts of its cashier in making loans and allowing over drafts in violation of its by-laws. Wynn *v.* Tallapoosa County Bank, 53 So. 228, 168 Ala. 469.

§ 49. Notice to Officer or Agent.

See post, "Officers and Agents," § 134.

Cashier.—Notice to the cashier of a bank that its modification of the proposals of a party are acceded to by him is notice to the bank. Branch Bank at Huntsville *v.* Steele, 10 Ala. 915.

President and Cashier.—Knowledge of a president and cashier of a bank of a proposed loan, and their conduct in assisting to procure it, was the knowledge and act of the bank. Harris *v.* American Building & Loan Ass'n, 25 So. 200, 122 Ala. 545.

Notice Acquired in Dual Capacity.—A bookkeeper's knowledge of a firm's dissolution, acquired because of his position, was not notice to a bank of which he was assistant cashier and bookkeeper. Morris *v.* First Nat. Bank, 50 So. 137, 162 Ala. 301.*

The agent of an insurance company obtained a promissory note from defendant by false representations, and transferred it in the usual course of business to a bank, the cashier of which was the agent's partner in the insurance business. The cashier had no actual knowledge of the fraud. Held, that the bank was a bona fide holder; the notice which the law imputed to the cashier, as partner, of the manner in which the agent acquired the note not being imputable to him as cashier. Scott *v.* Choctaw Bank, 4 Ala. App. 648, 59 So. 184.

Notice of Officer's Own Fraud.—The maker of a note for a blank amount handed it to a bank director to be filled up with a certain amount to use in renewal of another note. The director fraudulently filled up the note for a larger amount, and discounted it for his own use at the bank. The director did not communicate the facts to any other director, but sat as one of the discount board. Held, that the bank was not charged with knowledge of his fraud. Terrell *v.* Branch Bank, 12 Ala. 502, cited on this point in note in 29 L. R. A., N. S., 559.

§ 50. Evidence as to Authority.

That an assistant bank cashier had charge of the bank, and represented it in all negotiations for the erection of a bank building, of which the bank subsequently took possession, was sufficient to raise a presumption of authority in him to contract for the construction of the building. Merchants' Bank *v.* Acme Lumber & Mfg. Co., 49 So. 782, 160 Ala. 435.

Neither a remittance of money to one as the agent of a bank by another party, and his consent to receive it as such, nor his admissions, or the fact that he is a director of the bank, have any tendency to prove that he is the agent of the bank. The consent of the bank that he should so act is necessary. Holman *v.* Bank of Norfolk, 12 Ala. 369.

(C) DEPOSITS.

§ 51. Relation between Bank and Depositor in General.

See the title TRUSTS. See post, "In General," § 58.

Nature of Deposit.—A deposit in bank is a peculiar species of contract. It is not like an ordinary "bill receivable," but is classed as the depositor's cash on hand. It is subject to his draft and control at any moment, and he is not expected to give notice of his intention to draw. The bank is expected to be at all times ready to meet its customers' checks, drawn on deposits, and its credit is seriously impaired, if not ruined, if it fail to do so. It does not stand in the category of an ordinary debt between man and man, for money had and received. Concurring opinion of Stone J. in Henry & Co. *v.* Northern Bank, 63 Ala. 527, 546.

"A deposit is a matter of contract between the depositor and bank, and the depositor may stipulate at the time as to the manner, or by whom (there being no statute or by-law to the contrary) the money may be drawn out; and when payment is thus made the bank is discharged from further liability." Sayre *v.* Weil, 94 Ala. 466, 10 So. 546, 548.

General and Special Deposits.—See post, "In General," § 58.

§ 52. Power and Duty to Receive Deposits.

A corporation, authorized by its charter "to receive deposits on trust," may receive money on deposit and give certificates therefor; and this power is not affected by a proviso prohibiting the corporation from issuing bills, bonds, notes, or other securities to circulate in the community as money. Talladega Ins. Co. *v.* Landers, 43 Ala. 115.

§ 53. Deposits Other than Money.

§ 54. —— Checks and Drafts on Depositor's Bank.

Where a bank was not accustomed to receive checks for collection drawn on itself by its depositors, and a check was so drawn by one depositor in favor of another, presented by the latter, credited on his pass book as a deposit, and placed on the file of paid checks entered to his credit on the books of the bank, the check was paid, and the amount of it could not be withheld by the bank on discovering that it was an overdraft and the drawer was insolvent. City Nat. Bank *v.* Burns, 68 Ala. 267, 44 Am. Rep. 138, cited in note in 23 L. R. A., N. S., 1093.

§ 55. —— Entry to Credit of Depositor.

Where one has a deposit account at a bank, in which he is accustomed to deposit checks payable to himself, foi entry on his pass book, and to be drawn against, an indorsement by him on a check of the words "For deposit" is a direction to deposit such a sum to his credit. National Commercial Bank *v.* Miller, 77 Ala. 168, cited on this point in note in / L. R. A., N. S., 700.

§ 56. —— Title and Rights of Bank.

In an action by a bank to recover money advanced on a draft, for goods sold, deposited with it by the vendor, where it claims that the deposit was made for collection, and the depositor that it was a sale, it is proper to instruct that, if it was a sale, the bank could not recover, though there is evidence that the vendee, after the deposit, paid part of the price for which the draft was drawn directly to the vendor. Bank of Guntersville *v.* Webb, 108 Ala. 132, 19 So. 14, cited on this point in note in 7 L. R. A., N. S., 695.

Where a bank cashier, in receiving from an illiterate person a draft sold to the bank, fraudulently makes out his deposit slip for him so as to show a deposit for collection, it is error to admit evidence that the bank required the cashier to pay the draft on failure to collect it, on the issue as to whether the bank was liable as purchaser or as a receiver for collection only. Bank of Guntersville *v.* Webb, 108 Ala. 132, 19 So. 14.

Where a bank cashier, in receiving from an illiterate person a draft in his favor sold to the bank, fraudulently makes out his deposit slip for him so as to show that this draft was deposited for collection, statements subsequently made by the depositor to another officer of the bank on discovering the fraud, though inadmissible to vary the written contract evidenced by the deposit slip, are admissible to show a repudiation of it by the depositor. Bank of Guntersville *v.* Webb, 108 Ala. 132, 19 So. 14.

Where a bank cashier, in receiving from an illiterate person a draft sold to the bank, fraudulently makes out his deposit slip so as to show a deposit for collection, and the depositor subsequently, on discovering the fraud, repudiates the transaction as a deposit for collection, and, on an issue as to whether the transaction was a purchase or a deposit for collection, the bank admits that the slip was a receipt for the draft, and the depositor claims that it was one for the proceeds, it is proper to refuse to instruct for the bank that the retention of the slip by the depositor after repudiation, and using it as evidence of a demand against the bank, rendered it binding on him. Bank of Guntersville *v.* Webb, 108 Ala. 132, 19 So. 14.

§ 57. Title to and Disposition of Deposits.

§ 58. —— In General.

See, generally, the titles BAILMENT; TRUSTS.

"The relation of banker and customer, in respect to deposits is that of debtor and creditor. The money becomes the property of the banker, and he becomes liable to pay it on demand of the depositor." Moore & Co. *v.* Meyer, 57 Ala. 20, 21.

Relation of Debtor and Creditor.—A bank became the owner of money deposited and credited to the account of the depositor, whose debtor it became. Batson *v.* Alexander City Bank (Ala.), 60 So. 313.

The relation between a bank and a general depositor is that of debtor and creditor, respectively. Southern Hardware & Supply Co. *v.* Lester, 52 So. 328, 166 Ala. 86; Alston *v.* State, 92 Ala. 124, 9 So. 732.

A deposit of bank bills with a banking company, unless special, creates a debt, not a bailment. Wray *v.* Tuskegee Ins. Co., 34 Ala. 58.

The rule is clearly settled, that in the ordinary transactions of banks, when they receive moneys on general deposits, the money thereby becomes the property of the bank, and the bank becomes debtor to the depositor for the amount, as so much money had and received; and any subsequent loss of the money, or destruction of its value, falls on the bank. The depositor is only a creditor; and if the bank fail, and be unable to pay its debts in full, he comes in only as a general creditor, and must be content to receive his pro rata of the assets. Concurring opinion of Stone, J., in Henry & Co. *v.* Northern Bank, 63 Ala. 527, 543.

Until an actual application of the customer's deposits to the credit of the owner of the bill, the relation of debtor and creditor existed between the banker and his customer, and he could have countermanded his instructions and otherwise appropriated the money. It was the customer's duty to make payment, and after the deposit by the customer in his own name the banker could not so appropriate but by virtue of the instructions given by the customer, in carrying out which the banker was his and not the creditor's agent. Moore & Co. *v.* Meyer, 57 Ala. 20.

General and Special Deposits.—"Deposits made with bankers are either general or special. In the case of a special deposit, the bank merely assumes the charge or custody of property, without authority to use it, and the depositor is entitled to receive back the identical money or thing deposited. In such case, the right of property remains in the depositor, and, if the deposit is of money, the bank may not mingle it with its own funds. The relation created is that of bailor and bailee, and not that of creditor and debtor. * * * When a money deposit is made, it is to be regarded as a general deposit, unless there is evidence to show that it was the bank's duty, by agreement, express or clearly implied, to keep it separate and apart from its own funds, and to return that identical money to the depositor. Money received by a bank on general deposit becomes the property of the bank, and can be loaned or otherwise used by it, as other moneys belonging to it. The bank becomes the debtor of the depositor, and its obligation is satisfied by honoring the depositor's checks to the amount of his deposit. The depositor's claim is a mere chose in action for so much money. He becomes a creditor of the bank." Alston *v.* State, 92 Ala. 124, 9 So. 732, cited on this point in note in 16 L. R. A. 517.

"There are two kinds of deposits—one called a general, and the other a special deposit. A special deposit is where the special money, the very silver or gold coin, or bills deposited, are to be returned, and not an equivalent. A general deposit is where the money deposited is not itself to be returned, but an equivalent in money (that is, a like sum is to be returned); such a deposit is said to be equivalent to a loan. The title to a special deposit remains, notwithstanding the deposit, in the depositor; in a general deposit, the money deposited becomes the money of the depositary." Talladega Ins. Co. *v.* Landers, 43 Ala. 115, 138.

A deposit with a bank is special when it is a deposit, like stocks, bonds, and other securities, and sometimes money, to be specially kept and returned to the owner, or money deposited for a fixed period of time or on unusual conditions, which is mingled in the general funds like a general deposit and repaid therefrom, or money which is to be applied by the bank at the depositor's request for specific purposes. First Nat. Bank *v.* Henry, 49 So. 97, 159 Ala. 367.

§ 59. —— Funds of Person Other than Depositor.

Presumption.—The fact that money is deposited in a bank to the individual credit of the depositor shows, prima facie, that it belonged to him, but not conclusively so. Bessemer Sav. Bank *v.* Anderson, 32 So. 716, 134 Ala. 343, 92 Am. St. Rep. 38.

One who had money in his possession before and at the time he deposited it in bank in the name of his wife was presumptively the owner of the money. First Nat. Bank *v.* Taylor, 142 Ala. 456, 37 So. 695.

Deposit by Register.—Where money in the hands of a register was deposited by him in a bank in his name as register, the deposit became a part of the funds of the bank, creating the relation of debtor and creditor between the bank and the depositor. Clisby *v.* Mastin, 43 So. 742, 150 Ala. 132.

§ 60. Repayment in General.

Code, § 1530, which provides that deposits by married women of their earnings shall be paid only to such married women, does not apply to a deposit made by defendant in the name of his wife. Sayre *v.* Weil, 94 Ala. 466, 10 So. 546, 15 L. R. A. 544.

In the absence of fraud, a depositor of an insolvent bank can not claim to rescind a contract, evidenced by a bill of exchange drawn in his favor by the bank on a business correspondent, with whom it has funds on deposit, because such bill has been dishonored on presentation in consequence of the bank's subsequent assignment. Ex parte Jones, 77 Ala. 330.

The crediting of a bank depositor's account, with an amount deposited was not payment of a consideration to him by the bank for the deposit, so as to preclude one receiving an order thereon from the depositor in satisfaction of a valid claim from asserting such claim; the bank not having appropriated the deposit to any valid claim by it against depositor. Batson *v.* Alexander City Bank (Ala.), 60 So. 313.

§ 61. Application of Deposits to Debt Due Bank or Set-Off by Bank.

Right to Set-Off.—A bank may not set off a claim against a depositor against such deposit unless the claim is certain, definite, and liquidated, or capable of liquidation by calculation without the intervention of a jury to estimate the sum. Tallapoosa County Bank *v.* Wynn, 173 Ala. 272, 55 So. 1011.

Where a bank, on being garnished, answers that it has paid the debtor's claim by giving him credit on his note for the amount on deposit, and the evidence shows that the note was not due at the time the garnishment was levied, a judgment for plaintiff is proper. Birmingham Nat. Bank *v.* Mayer, 104 Ala. 634, 16 So. 520, cited on this point in note in 27 L. R. A., N. S., 813.

Applying Deposit to Liability as Surety.—A deposit in bank by the principal, is subject only to the check of the person deposited and can not be pleaded by the security as a payment or set off. Lyon *v.* State Bank, 1 Stew. 442.

Application of Funds Deposited as Trustee.—Defendant deposited money in a bank to the credit of himself as "trustee for G. children," and had also made another deposit in the name of his wife, and it was understood by the bank that he could check against this deposit. He subsequently checked against the deposit, but his wife had not drawn on it. Defendant afterwards directed the bank to apply the trust fund to the payment of a note which he owed the bank, and also directed that enough be taken from the deposit in the name of his wife to pay the balance due on the note. The bankers agreed to this, and the wife ratified the act of defendant. Held, that this agreement bound the bankers. Sayre *v.* Weil, 94 Ala. 466, 10 So. 546, 15 L. R. A. 544, cited on this point in note in 32 L. R. A. 374, 29 L. R. A., N. S., 68.

Defendant deposited money in a bank to the credit of himself as "trustee for G. children." Defendant owed the bankers on his note, and directed them to apply such trust fund towards the payment of the note. They agreed to do that, and to deliver the note as soon as their cashier could make the proper entries. Before the note was delivered, they assigned for the benefit of creditors. Defendant knew nothing of their financial embarrassment, or that they intended to assign. Held, in an action on such note by the assignees, that the agreement to apply such trust fund bound the bankers. Sayre *v.* Weil, 94 Ala. 466, 10 So. 546, 15 L. R. A. 544.

The assignees were invested with no higher or more extensive authority than the bankers, but were bound by those agreements equally with the bankers. Sayre *v.* Weil, 94 Ala. 466, 10 So. 546, 15 L. R. A. 544.

§ 62. Lien of Bank on Deposits.

A bank has a lien on all funds deposited in due course of business for any balance of general account due from the depositor. Batson *v.* Alexander City Bank (Ala.), 60 So. 313.

The word "lien" is inaptly applied to a general deposit which is the property of the bank itself, but can be properly applied to special specific deposits of chattels, choses in action, valuables, etc. Wynn *v.* Tallapoosa County Bank, 168 Ala. 469, 53 So. 228.

When Lien Arises.—The lien of a bank for any advance or loan made to the depositor arises when the advance is made, entitling the bank to apply the funds of the depositors to the payment of such indebtedness. Batson *v.* Alexander City Bank (Ala.), 60 So. 313.

As to a general deposit the bank has a right to set-off as for the balance of the depositor's general account, and so long as that is in his favor, its lien or right thereon has neither existence nor validity; but the moment an advance or loan is made to the depositor in the form of an overdraft, a discount, acceptance, etc., the lien or right is born, and may be applied by the bank alone to the payment of such indebtedness till fully discharged. Wynn *v.* Tallapoosa County Bank, 168 Ala. 469, 53 So. 228.

Statute in Equity.—The lien or claim which a bank has on a deposit can not be enforced in equity against the depositor, though in a proper sense it may be declared or recognized. Wynn *v.* Tallapoosa County Bank, 53 So. 228, 168 Ala. 469.

§ 63. Payment of Checks.

§ 64. —— Duties and Liabilities of Bank to Depositor.

Money Used in Payment.—The currency delivered by a bank in payment of a check is the money of the debtor bank, and not the money of the drawer creditor. Southern Hardware, etc., Co. *v.* Lester, 166 Ala. 86, 52 So. 328.

Effect of Payment.—If free from fraud or other vitiating circumstance affecting its rights, a bank, by paying checks on it, extinguishes its liability to the depositor to the extent of the sums so paid. Southern Hardware & Supply Co. *v.* Lester, 52 So. 328, 166 Ala. 86.

§ 65. —— Notice Not to Pay or Revocation of Check.

Notice of Check.—Plaintiff, in an action by a depositor against a bank in which the defense was payment of a check, may prove a verbal notice given by him before the payment to defendant's receiving teller not to pay it, though afterwards on the request of the teller he reduced the notice to writing. People's Sav. Bank & Trust Co. *v.* Lacey, 40 So. 346, 146 Ala. 688.

It is no defense to an action by a depositor against a bank that it paid his check; payment having been after notice from him not to pay it. People's Sav. Bank & Trust Co. *v.* Lacey, 40 So. 346, 146 Ala. 688.

Revocation.—A check is revoked by the death of its drawer at any time before its acceptance by the drawee. National Commercial Bank *v.* Miller, 77 Ala. 168, cited in note in 20 L. R. A. 291, 9 L. R. A., N. S., 698. See, generally, the title BILLS AND NOTES.

§ 66. —— Obligation of Bank to Payee or Holder.

See, generally, the title BILLS AND NOTES.

"'The bank,' says Judge Story, 'is not bound to pay unless it is in full funds; and it it not obliged to pay, or to accept to pay, if it has partial funds only; for it is entitled to the possession of the check on payment; and, indeed, in the ordinary course of business, the only voucher of the bank for any payment is the production and receipt of the check, which the holder can not safely part with, unless he receives full payment, nor the bank exact, unless under the like circumstances. The holder is not bound to accept part payment, even if the bank is willing to pay in part; for he has a claim to the entirety.'" Industrial Trust, etc., Co. v. Weakley, 103 Ala. 458, 15 So. 854, 855.

"A check or bill, payable to order, is authority to the banker only to pay it to the payee, or to a person who becomes the holder by a genuine indorsement." Russell v. First Nat. Bank, 2 Ala. App. 342, 56 So. 868, 870.

§ 67. —— Mode and Sufficiency of Payment.

Where a check indorsed "For deposit" is deposited by a customer of a bank, and the amount is entered in his pass book to his credit, against which he draws checks, the bank becomes more than the mere agent for collection; and where, instead of collecting, the bank has the check certified by the drawee, such certification is a payment, as between the depositor and the bank, and therefore the deposit is subject to garnishment for the depositor's debt. National Commercial Bank v. Miller, 77 Ala. 168, 54 Am. Rep. 50, cited on this point in note in 23 L. R. A. 165.

§ 68. —— Liability of Bank to Drawer for Refusal to Pay.

A bank's failure to pay a check of a depositor drawn in favor of another does not render it liable, unless the check was presented at the proper time and place, properly indorsed, and, if transferred by the payee, properly indorsed by the transferee. Harden v. Birmingham Trust & Savings Bank, 55 So. 943, 1 Ala. App. 610.

§ 69. Notes Payable at Bank.

A depositor's parol direction to a bank to apply his deposit in payment of a note payable at the bank is sufficient to authorize such application. First Nat. Bank v. Hall, 24 So. 526, 119 Ala. 64.

§ 70. Certified Checks or Notes.

Nature.—A certified check has a distinctive character as a species of commercial paper, the certification constituting a new contract between the holder and the certifying bank; the funds of the drawer are, in legal contemplation, withdrawn from his credit, and appropriated to the payment of the check, and the bank becomes the debtor of the holder as for money had and received. National Commercial Bank v. Miller & Co., 77 Ala. 168.

Presumption from Certification.—The statement in writing upon a check on a bank, payable to a bearer, by the proper officer, that it was "good," is prima facie an admission by the bank that the money drawn for is in the bank, subject to the order of the drawer. The presumption may be repelled by proof, as that the admission was made by mistake. Smith v. Branch Bank at Mobile, 7 Ala. 880.

Liability of Bank.—The liability under which a bank is to one of its depositors upon a check left with it by him "for deposit," and which it has had certified by the bank upon which it is drawn, may be reached by process of garnishment. National Commercial Bank v. Miller, 77 Ala. 168, 54 Am. Rep. 50. See post, "Attachment or Garnishment," § 117.

§ 71. Payment of Forged or Altered Paper.

§ 72. —— Liabilities of Bank to Depositor, Payee, or Owner.

Forged Checks.—If banks on which checks were drawn had no notice of fraud in procuring their issuance by the drawer, they are not negligent in honoring them, and the checks are not in such case forgeries in such sort as to render the banks liable for paying them when sued by the drawer. Southern Hardware & Supply Co. v. Lester, 52 So. 328, 166 Ala. 86.

Forged Indorsement.—Payment by the bank on which it is drawn of a check with the payee's indorsement forged is not an acquittance, though it also bears the indorsement of other banks through which it has passed; it having used no diligence to ascertain whether the payee's indorsement was genuine, and not having shown the other banks had used any. Russell v. First Nat. Bank, 2 Ala. App. 342, 56 So. 868, cited on this point in note in 38 L. R. A., N. S., 1113.

The rule that, where one, by representing that he is a certain other person, induces another to draw a check in his favor in the name of the person he represents himself to be, the drawer can not complain of its payment by the bank on which it is drawn, when indorsed by such impositor in the name assumed by him, does not apply where a check, payable to a certain person is delivered to another on his false representation that he is the payee's agent, and is paid on said impositor's forged indorsement of the payee's name. Russell *v.* First Nat. Bank, 2 Ala. App. 342, 56 So. 868.

Negligence of Depositor.—It is the duty of a depositor, by himself or an authorized agent, to examine the account and vouchers or checks returned with his bank book, and to denounce any check that has been forged; and, where such examination is left to a clerk, his knowledge will be the knowledge of the depositor, and it is then his duty to make it known. The fact that such clerk was the forger is immaterial. First Nat. Bank *v.* Allen, 100 Ala. 476, 14 So. 335, 46 Am. St. Rep. 80, 27 L. R. A. 426, cited on this point in note in 27 L. R. A. 635, 20 L. R. A., N. S., 82.

Defenses.—In an action against a bank on a cashier's check assigned to plaintiffs, pleas that plaintiffs, or one of them, procured the check to be issued by false representations as to the security given or to be given to the bank to secure a loan by the bank to the payees of the check, which the check represented, and that, as a part of the scheme to defraud the bank, plaintiffs, or one of them, had the check indorsed and assigned to him, stated a complete defense. Bank of Coffee Springs *v.* W. A. McGilvray & Co., 52 So. 473, 167 Ala. 408.

Where a bank claimed that a cashier's check, representing a loan, had been procured from it by plaintiff's fraud and then transferred to plaintiff, the act of the bank's cashier in taking a mortgage from the payees of the check to secure a loan, which the check represented, did not estop the bank from setting up plaintiff's fraud as a defense to the check. Bank *v.* McGilvray & Co., 167 Ala. 408, 52 So. 473.

Measure of Liability.—In an action against a bank to recover a deposit, it appeared that the money was paid out by defendant upon checks to which plaintiff's name, was forged by his clerk; that the forgeries covered a period of six months; and that monthly during this period defendant furnished plaintiff a statement of his account, and returned him all checks that it had paid on the account. Held, that the bank was only liable for payments made before the furnishing of the first monthly statement. First Nat. Bank *v.* Allen, 100 Ala. 476, 14 So. 335, 46 Am. St. Rep. 80, 27 L. R. A. 426.

Upon plaintiff's discovery of the forgeries, he caused his clerk's arrest, who then had upon his person eight forged checks, and defendant, in ignorance of the fact that it had been paying forged checks, made good the amount of the eight checks to plaintiff. Held that, as defendant was only liable for payments made before the furnishing of the first monthly statement, it could counterclaim the amount made good to plaintiff for the eight checks. First Nat. Bank *v.* Allen, 100 Ala. 476, 14 So. 335, 46 Am. St. Rep. 80, 27 L. R. A. 426.

Though, in an action against a bank to recover a deposit paid out by defendant upon checks to which plaintiff's name was forged by his clerk, it appeared that it was plaintiff's custom, on signing a check, to enter the amount and number of the check on the stub of the check, and that the checks as paid by defendant were "raised" by the clerk after they had been so signed, entered, and numbered, defendant's liability is not to be determined, the checks themselves having disappeared, by charging it with the amount a check as paid exceeded the amount as entered on the stub, where the evidence showed that the clerk made out several checks, and then destroyed them because the signature was bad, leaving the amount on the stubs; and that plaintiff was unable to distinguish between the genuine and the forged stubs. First Nat. Bank *v.* Allen, 100 Ala. 476, 14 So. 335, 46 Am. St. Rep. 80, 27 L. R. A. 426, cited on this point in note in 7 L. R. A., N. S., 746.

§ 73. Overdrafts.

"Subject to some exception, it is a correct general proposition, that a bank has no right to allow drawers of checks to overdraw their balances, and pay checks out of funds of other depositors, or the money of the stockholders. Overdrawing, even to persons of good standing with the bank, does not find sanction in sound usage, except under special conditions. Culver *v.* Marks, 122 Ind. 554, 23 N. E. 1086; Bank *v.* Woodward, 18 Pa. St. 357. As to overdrafts, Mr. Morse says, there is power in the bank to allow them; that a customer by negotiating with the authorized and proper officials, may make a legal and binding arrangement by which his overdrafts to a certain amount named, and under the circumstances agreed upon, shall be honored; that such a dealing is in the nature of a loan, and is placing money at his disposal or control. 1 Morse, Banks, § 358." Industrial Trust, etc., Co. *v.* Weakley, 103 Ala. 458, 15 So. 854, 855.

Bank directors may allow overdrafts, and they can authorize the cashier to do so. Wynn *v.* Tallapoosa County Bank, 168 Ala. 469, 53 So. 228.

§ 74. Certificates of Deposit.

Nature.—The certificate of deposit is evidence of money had and received. Talladega Ins. Co. *v.* Landers, 43 Ala. 115, 139.

Code 1876, § 2094, provides that notes and bills payable at a bank, or some other designated place, are commercial paper; and § 2100 declares that all contracts other than bills of exchange, notes payable at a bank, and paper issued to circulate as money are subject to all defenses prior to notice of transfer. Held, that a banker's certificate of deposit, payable on its return properly indorsed, with the banker's name and address at its heading, contained no sufficient designation of a place of payment to render it commercial paper, and hence it was subject to defenses. Renfro *v.* Merchants' & Mechanics' Bank, 83 Ala. 425, 3 So. 776.

Distinction between Issuing Certificates of Deposit and Money.—"The power of issuing certificates of deposit is distinct and distinguishable from that of issuing paper for circulation as money. Certificates of deposit may be somewhat assimilated to paper money, in their susceptibility of transfer; but they are different, and the discrimination between them is as easy as between ordinary promissory notes and bank bills." Bliss *v.* Anderson, 31 Ala. 612, 623. See post, "Power to Issue or Circulate," § 100.

§ 75. Special Deposits.

What Constitutes.—A bank receiving certain transfers of land certificates with instructions to deliver them to a certain person upon payment of a certain sum, is not a gratuitous bailee thereof, and must use ordinary care in keeping them. First Nat. Bank *v.* First Nat. Bank, 22 So. 976, 116 Ala. 520.

A member of a firm made a deposit in its favor of his own money, receiving therefor a deposit slip reciting that the deposit was to be protected for his benefit by compress receipts and bills of lading sufficient to cover the amount, the receipts to be deposited with the bank in like manner as other similar accounts. On the same date he took from his firm a note for the amount of the deposit, payable through the bank. Held, that the note was simply the promise of the firm to repay the money which they were to get under the terms of the contract between the bank and the depositor, without effect on the transaction between the latter and the bank, and the effect of the whole transaction was a loan from him to the firm on their note, the money in the bank to be turned over to them when they deposited collateral for his benefit, so that he held the double obligation of the firm for the money, if the firm got it from the bank, and the obligation of the bank not to let the firm have it without the collaterals. First Nat. Bank *v.* Henry, 49 So. 97, 159 Ala. 367.

By its contract, in such case, the bank agreed in substance that it would protect the deposit for the benefit of the depositor by taking from his firm compress receipts and bills of lading sufficient to cover the amount thereof, or that it would have and hold at all times either that amount or compress receipts or bills of lading deposited by his firm sufficient to cover it, or so much thereof as the bank let them have, and it was bound thereby unless released. First Nat. Bank *v.* Henry, 159 Ala. 367, 49 So. 97, 108.

Distinction between General and Special Deposits.—See ante, "In General," § 58.

Showing Special Deposit to Be General.—Though a banker marks a credit in a customer's pass book "Special Deposit," and gives her a form of check so marked by him, it may be shown that the deposit is a general one. Carr *v.* State, 104 Ala. 43, 16 So. 155, cited on this point in note in 39 L. R. A., N. S., 849.

§ 76. Actions by Depositors or Others for Deposits.

Grounds.—In an action by a married woman against a bank for money had and received, the following facts were disclosed: A check was drawn payable to the order of the plaintiff and delivered to her husband. The husband presented the check at the defendant bank unindorsed by the payee. Upon his attention being called to this fact, the husband, pretending to have authority to indorse the paper for and in the name of his wife, wrote on the back of the check his wife's name, per himself. Thereupon the defendant bank cashed the check, and put the money to the credit of the husband. Subsequently the money so put to his credit was drawn out by the husband, and used in the payment of his own debts and for other purposes of his own. The husband was without authority to indorse the check for and in the name of his wife. The check was given by the lender of the money to the wife, and the money collected on it was the proceeds of a loan which was secured by a mortgage upon the wife's property, which mortgage was duly executed by her. The purpose of the wife in obtaining the loan was to raise money to pay off her husband's debt and enable him to carry on his business, and she knew that her husband had gotten the money on the loan for such purpose. Held, that the wife can not maintain an action against the bank for money had and received. First Nat. Bank *v.* Moragne, 128 Ala. 157, 30 So. 628.

Conditions Precedent.—A formal demand is a condition precedent to the maintenance of an action against a banker for a deposit, which must be alleged in the complaint; and where the money counts do not aver a demand, nor any excuse for not making it, they are insufficient. Tobias *v.* Morris, 28 So. 517, 126 Ala. 535.

"The bringing of the suit does not amount to a demand in such cases." Tobias *v.* Morris, 126 Ala. 535, 28 So. 517, 520.

Parties.—Where a banking firm is sued to recover money deposited, a member of the firm can not intervene as administrator of an estate claiming such deposit, under Code, § 2610, giving such right to one "not a party to the suit, without collusion with him." Jackson *v.* Jackson, 91 Ala. 292, 10 So. 31.

Admissibility of Evidence.—In an action for money, it appeared that plaintiff's husband had, from his own funds, made a deposit in plaintiff's name in defendant bank, and received the pass book which plaintiff got possession of before her husband's death. In his lifetime the husband had checked out the money without plaintiff's authority. Held, that defendant could show, as proving no completed transfer of the money to the absolute ownership and control of plaintiff, that, at the time the deposit was made, the husband instructed defendant to honor either his own or his wife's checks. Anniston Nat. Bank *v.* Howell, 22 So. 471, 116 Ala. 375.

Where H., falsely claiming to be F.'s agent, delivered to R. a deed of land, F.'s signature to which as grantor was forged, and received from R. a check, payable to F., the bank on which it was drawn, being sued by R., on the ground that it was liable for payment of the check on the forged indorsement of F.'s name, may not introduce the deed in evidence for comparison of the signature thereto with that of the indorsement of the check; it being immaterial whether or not they are the same. Russell *v.* First Nat. Bank, 2 Ala. App. 342, 56 So. 868.

Sufficiency of Evidence.—Plaintiff, who was a depositor of defendant bank, denied signing a certain check and obtaining the money thereon, for the reason that the check was signed with her initials, contrary to her custom; and an expert witness stated that, in his opinion, the check was not signed by the same person who wrote plaintiff's signature for comparison, admitted to be genuine. The bank's cashier and one of its employees, who were both acquainted with plaintiff, testified that they saw her sign the check and get the money, and that plaintiff had previously signed checks, in her dealings with other banks, using her initials only. Other experts testified that the signature was genuine. Held, that a verdict finding that plaintiff did not sign the check was contrary to the weight of evidence. People's Sav. Bank, etc., Co. *v.* Keith, 136 Ala. 469, 34 So. 925.

Question of Fact.—Plaintiff sued defendants, bankers, to recover on a deposit, and the defense was payment. The plaintiff testified that she took a draft which had been sent her, and with her husband and J. went to defendants' bank, where J. or her husband handed the draft to the receiving teller, asking that it be deposited to plaintiff's credit; that the teller examined the draft, and handed it back to J., saying that plaintiff must indorse it first, which plaintiff did, returning it to J., who handed it to the teller; and that nothing else occurred. Defendants' teller testified that at the time the account was opened he had all the negotiations with plaintiff's husband, and was not aware that plaintiff was present; that plaintiff's husband deposited the draft to plaintiff's credit, and stated that it would be checked out in his wife's name by him; and that the husband wrote in the record of signatures that of his wife; and that all the money then or thereafter deposited was paid out on checks signed "B. T., by M. S. T." Held, that it was error to charge, if the jury believed the evidence, to find for defendants, since the question whether plaintiff was estopped by her conduct from disputing her husband's authority to draw on her account was a question of fact for the jury. Tobias *v.* Morris, 28 So. 517, 126 Ala. 535.

(D) COLLECTIONS.

§ 77. Relation between Bank and Depositor for Collection.

See post, "Title to Paper Received for Collection," § 80.

Relation of Principal and Agent.—A bank, or banker, receiving paper for collection, is the agent of the creditor, and not of the debtor. The loss resulting from the omissions or defalcations of the agent, must be borne by his principal, who trusted him, and not by those dealing with him while in the line of his duty and authority. Moore & Co. *v.* Meyer, 57 Ala. 20, 21.

A bank which receives a check for collection, and enters the value of it as a deposit credit to the owner, is an agent for collection, and if the collection is made the relation of banker and depositor is consummated, and if the bank fails to collect through his own fault it is liable for the resulting damages. Jefferson County Sav. Bank *v.* Hendrix, 39 So. 295, 147 Ala. 670, 1 L. R. A., N. S., 246.

A holder of a draft sent it to a bank for collection, with instructions to collect and remit the proceeds to a banker for the holder's credit. Held that, in view of the instructions, the relation between the bank and holder was that of principal and agent, and not that of creditor and debtor or general depositor, and the bank could not, without the consent of the holder, change the relation by any conduct in dealing with the proceeds. Hutchinson *v.* National Bank of Commerce, 41 So. 143, 145 Ala. 196.

§ 78. Power and Duty to Make Collections.

Power and Duty of Bank.—"Not only do banks organized to do a general banking business have the power and authority to receive paper for collection, but it is a matter of common, and therefore of judicial, knowledge, that it is their general usage and practice to engage in this branch of business; and this power necessarily carries with it authority to receive collaterals accompanying, and given to secure the payment of, such paper, to be delivered to the debtor when he takes up the paper." First Nat. Bank *v.* First Nat. Bank, 116 Ala. 520, 22 So. 976, 979.

"The taking of paper for collection is a regular and customary part of the banking business, to engage in which requires no special authorization in the bank charter, and the making of collections by a bank is no more a gratuitous undertaking than the transaction of any part of its business. Whether any charge is made for the collection or not in a particular case, it is well settled that the indirect profit and benefit derived by the bank from the use of the money collected for the time it may be left in its hands, the advantage of settling its accounts with distant banks without being compelled to send money to and fro between them, and the development and extension of its business by serving the convenience of its customers, constitute a sufficient and valuable consideration for the undertaking to collect paper left with it for that purpose. * * * The same consideration will support the implied contract of bailment with respect to the papers sent for collection, and collaterals accompanying it, and prevent the bank from availing itself of the defense that it undertook the care of the same as a mere gratuitous favor." First Nat. Bank *v.* First Nat. Bank, 116 Ala. 520, 22 So. 976, 979.

Where a bank is authorized by its charter to deal in bills of exchange, and discount notes made negotiable and payable at the bank, with two or more good and sufficient securities, it may, under this power, undertake to collect bills of exchange on other places; the restriction, if one, extending only to promissory notes. Branch Bank *v.* Knox, 1 Ala. 148.

If a bank is authorized by its charter to receive money on deposit, quære, whether, under this power, it may not lawfully undertake to collect moneys on all negotiable commercial securities, when no other act is necessary to be done than to forward the securities to their place of payment, and demand and receive the money. Branch of the Bank *v.* Knox & Co., 1 Ala. 148.

Power and Duty of Cashier to Receive Paper for Collection.—See ante, "Collections," § 43.

§ 79. Making, Receipt, and Entry of Deposit for Collection.

The contract of agency arising from the deposit of a note with a bank for collection, and an entry in the bank book of the depositor, is not revoked by canceling the entry in the bank book. The only effect of such cancellation is to show that the note has been returned to the depositor, who is authorized to deal with it as he pleases. Bank *v.* Huggins, 3 Ala. 206.

§ 80. Title to Paper Received for Collection.

See ante, "Relation between Bank and Depositor for Collection," § 77.

A bill indorsed "For account," which has been remitted by one bank to another, accompanied by a letter of advice that it was for the benefit of the remitting bank, remains the property of the latter. Williams, Deacon & Co. *v.* Jones, 77 Ala. 294.

Where a draft was drawn to the order of the cashier of a bank to enable it to collect the same, and the cashier indorsed it, "Pay to the order of M. & Co.," and signed the indorsement in his capacity as cashier, and inclosed it to M. & Co. for "collection and credit," M. & Co. took the paper in the capacity of a collecting agent for the forwarding bank, and not as a purchaser. Josiah Morris & Co. *v.* Alabama Carbon Co., 36 So. 764, 139 Ala. 620.

Plaintiff purchased a car load of hay from B., who drew on plaintiff for the price, attaching a bill of lading to the draft. The draft was payable "on the arrival of car of hay" to the order of C., "cashier," and was indorsed "For the collection account of Missouri National Bank," and was collected through a bank where plaintiff resided. Plaintiff, for cause, rescinded the sale. Held, that the Missouri National Bank, in an action against it by plaintiff for money had and received, could not deny being the owner of the draft, not on the ground that such denial would be contradicting a written instrument by parol, but because plaintiff acted and acquired his rights without knowledge that the bank was only a collecting agent. Eufaula Grocery Co. *v.* Missouri Nat. Bank, 24 So. 389, 118 Ala. 408.

§ 81. Authority and Acts in Making Collection.

§ 82. —— Banks in General.

Effect of Customs and Usages.—A custom authorizing a bank to which a check is sent for collection to send it to the drawee for collection is unreasonable and void, and the bank so sending it is liable for any damages to the payee resulting from such action. Farley Nat. Bank *v.* Pollock & Bernheimer, 39 So. 612, 145 Ala. 321, 117 Am. St. Rep. 44, cited on this point in note in 18 L. R. A., N. S., 442, 443. See ante, "Customs and Usages," § 33; post, "Failure to Collect," § 89.

§ 83. —— Agents and Correspondents.

See post, "Failure to Collect," § 89.

Power to Employ.—In an action to recover money paid by mistake of fact on a draft for the price of a car load of hay, where the draft, which was sent to a bank where the drawee resided for collection, was payable "on the arrival of car of hay," to the order of C., "cashier," and was indorsed, "For collection account of Missouri National Bank," the principle that when the owner of a security deposits it for collection, in a bank located remotely from the place of payment, he thereby impliedly authorizes such bank to employ another reputable bank located at or near the place of payment to make the collection, does not apply. Eufaula Grocery Co. *v.* Missouri Nat. Bank, 24 So. 389, 118 Ala. 408.

Termination of Agency.—Where a forwarding bank made an assignment and ceased to do business prior to the collection of a draft sent to defendant for collection, such assignment terminates defendant's agency for the forwarding bank. Josiah Morris & Co. *v.* Alabama Carbon Co., 36 So. 764, 139 Ala. 620.

§ 84. What Constitutes Collection.

Where it was the course of business between a banker and his customer for the bank to pay all claims sent for collection out of the customer's deposits if he had any, charging the payment in the account when balanced, and a particular claim was sent for collection, to pay which and others the customer deposited money in his own name with the banker, with directions to pay the claims, the customer remained liable on the bill, if the banker failed before thus applying the money. Moore *v.* Meyer, 57 Ala. 20.

§ 85. Rights and Liabilities as to Proceeds.

§ 86. —— In General.

Where a draft was drawn in favor of the cashier of a bank to enable the latter to collect and apply the proceeds thereof to the drawer's credit, the execution of such draft did not divest the drawer's equitable ownership of the debt for which the draft was drawn. Josiah Morris & Co. *v.* Alabama Carbon Co., 36 So. 764, 139 Ala. 620.

§ 87. —— Insolvency of Collecting Bank.

Effect.—The mere fact that a bank has, as agent, collected money which it failed to account for, is not sufficient, on the bank becoming insolvent, to impress the general assets with a trust for the payment of the money. Bank of Florence *v.* United States Savings & Loan Co., 104 Ala. 297, 16 So. 110, cited on this point in note in 32 L. R. A. 719.

A holder of a draft sent it to a bank for collection, with instructions to collect and remit the proceeds to a banker for the holder's credit. The drawee of the draft paid it by his draft on a third person, which was sent by the bank to its correspondent. The correspondent collected the money from the third person, and afterwards paid the proceeds to the assignee of the bank, which was insolvent at the time it received the draft for collection. Held, that the holder traced the proceeds into the hands of the assignee, and showed that such proceeds constituted trust property for his benefit. Hutchinson *v.* National Bank of Commerce, 41 So. 143, 145 Ala. 196, cited on this point in note in 38 L. R. A., N. S., 149.

§ 88. —— Insolvency of Transmitting Bank.

Where, prior to the collection of a draft, the forwarding bank made an assignment, the drawer of the draft was entitled to recover the amount subsequently collected from the collecting bank as money had and received. Josiah Morris & Co. *v.* Alabama Carbon Co., 36 So. 764, 139 Ala. 620.

Where a bank forwarding a draft for collection inclosed a letter of the drawer, directing the forwarding bank to collect the draft and place the proceeds to the drawer's credit, such letter was notice to the collecting bank that the drawer was the beneficial owner of the claim sought to be collected, notwithstanding the form of the draft and the indorsement were such as to transfer the legal title to the claim, and hence, on the failure of the forwarding bank, the collecting bank was not entitled to credit the proceeds of the draft against the debt of the forwarding bank to it. Josiah Morris & Co. *v.* Alabama Carbon Co., 36 So. 764, 139 Ala. 620.

§ 89. Failure to Collect.

Liability for Failure to Collect.—A bank which receives a check for collection and fails to collect through its own fault is liable for the resulting damages. Jefferson County Sav. Bank *v.* Hendrix, 147 Ala. 670, 39 So. 295.

Where a bank, with which a check was deposited for collection, presented it for payment, gave notice of its dishonor, and charged it back to the depositor, it was then the property of depositor, so that he alone could file it against estate of bankrupt bank on which it was drawn, and the collecting bank can not be held bound to have filed it, and liable for its full amount, on the ground that it had made the check its own, because it did not return it to the depositor; it having at all times remained in the possession of the bankrupt bank and its receiver in bankruptcy. Hendrix *v.* Jefferson County Sav. Bank, 45 So. 136, 153 Ala. 636.

Negligence in Sending Paper Directly to Debtor.—"It may be the drawee of a check is not a suitable agent to be intrusted with its collection; and it may be that the Bank of Commerce, in selecting the banking company as the agent to collect the check and to remit the collection, rendered itself liable to the plaintiffs for whatever of loss might result to them from the unsuitable selection." Lowenstein *v.* Bresler, 109 Ala. 326, 328, 19 So. 860, 861; Farley Nat. Bank *v.* Pollock, 145 Ala. 321, 39 So. 612. See note in 18 L. R. A., N. S., 443.

It is prima facie negligence in a bank receiving a check for collection to send it to the drawee bank for payment, especially when the paper is a cashier's check. Jefferson County Sav. Bank *v.* Hendrix, 147 Ala. 670, 39 So. 295, 1 L. R. A., N. S., 246, cited on this point in note in 18 L. R. A., N. S., 442.

Failure to Present or Delay in Presenting Paper.—Where a bank, on presenting a draft which it has for collection, receives a check drawn on a bank in the same place, it is bound to present the check on the same day, and, failing in this, is liable to the drawer thereof for the loss occasioned thereby, the bank drawn on having suspended at the end of the day. Morris *v.* Eufaula Nat. Bank, 106 Ala. 383, 18 So. 11.

"The plaintiffs having received the check, were under the duty to defendant of making due presentment of it for payment, and, if not paid, of giving due notice of its dishonor. Laches in the performance of this duty, resulting in loss or damage to the defendant, to the extent of such loss or damage would operate a satisfaction of the original indebtedness. But if there was not loss or damage, the laches would not be material." Lowenstein *v.* Bresler, 109 Ala. 326, 328, 19 So. 860, 861.

Where a note is deposited with a bank for collection, without any special arrangement, it is the duty of the bank to present the note at the time and place fixed for payment, and to take such steps as are necessary to fix the liability of the parties; and, in case of neglect of this duty, it will be liable for the actual loss sustained by the owner by reason of the neglect. Bank of Mobile *v.* Huggins, 3 Ala. 206.

Duty to Give Notice of Nonpayment—Check.—It is the duty of a collecting bank to give the depositor notice of the dishonor of a check deposited with it for collection. Jefferson County Sav. Bank *v.* Hendrix, 147 Ala. 670, 39 So. 295, 1 L. R. A., N. S., 246; Lowenstein *v.* Bresler, 109 Ala. 326, 328, 19 So. 860.

Same—Note.—Where payment of a note is refused on presentment by a bank with which it has been deposited for collection, the bank is bound to notify the owner thereof, in order that he may take measures for his own security. Bank of Mobile *v.* Huggins, 3 Ala. 206.

In the absence of any local custom, it is not incumbent on the agent to notify the indorsers, unless he is directed by his principal to do so; nor to cause the note to be protested, unless this is necessary to fix the liability of other parties; or to give his principal some advantage, which, otherwise, the law would not accord to him. Bank *v.* Huggins, 3 Ala. 206.

Same—Bill of Exchange.—A bank which receives a bill of exchange for collection is bound to demand payment of the maker, and to cause notice of nonpayment to be given to all of the indorsers. Branch Bank of Alabama *v.* Knox, 1 Ala. 148.

Where Paper Given in Payment Is Not Paid.—A check given by a drawee of a draft to a collecting bank on presentation of the draft, being only conditional payment, leaving the drawer of the check liable to the drawer of the draft, where the bank on which the check was drawn failed before the check was presented, payment thereafter by the drawer of the check to the collecting bank of the amount of his debt will not prevent his suing the collecting bank for failure to make timely presentment of the check. Morris *v.* Eufaula Nat. Bank, 106 Ala. 383, 18 So. 11.

Waiver of Neglect of Bank.—The withdrawal from a bank of a bill of exchange which had been sent in for collection, after the bank had failed to demand payment and notify indorsers of nonpayment, is not a waiver of the holder's right of action against the bank for such neglect. Branch Bank of Alabama *v.* Knox, 1 Ala. 148.

§ 90. Actions for Negligence or Default.

§ 90 (1) Nature and Form of Remedy.

The liability of a bank negligently failing to collect a check received for collection is enforceable in assumpsit, for breach of its implied undertaking to use diligence in making the collection; or in case, for damages resulting from negligence in the performance of duties imposed by law. Jefferson County Sav. Bank *v.* Hendrix, 147 Ala. 670, 39 So. 295, 1 L. R. A., N. S., 246. See, generally, the title ASSUMPSIT, ACTION OF.

§ 90 (2) Pleading.

Complaint.—A complaint in an action against a bank negligently failing to collect a check received for collection which sets up the common counts is fatally bad. Jefferson County Sav. Bank *v.* Hendrix, 147 Ala. 670, 39 So. 295, 1 L. R. A., N. S., 246.

A count of a complaint against a bank for failure to present plaintiff's check in time is demurrable where it fails to show any damage. Morris *v.* Eufaula Nat. Bank, 106 Ala. 383, 18 So. 11.

A complaint which alleges that plaintiff deposited with the bank a check for collection, that the bank agreed to use good faith in the selection of subagents for collection, that the bank sent the check for collection to the drawee bank, which suspended without paying, and that defendant bank by proper agency could have collected the check, is bad on demurrer, for failing to allege that plaintiff suffered damages from failure to collect. Jefferson County Sav. Bank *v.* Hendrix, 147 Ala. 670, 39 So. 295, 1 L. R. A., N. S., 246.

A complaint which alleges a deposit of the check for collection; that the check was presented by the bank, but was dishonored, of which dishonor the bank failed to give plaintiff any notice until nine days later, when it mailed him a notice which he received two days later, at which time the drawee bank had failed; and that because of want of timely notice plaintiff was deprived of an opportunity to collect the check—is bad on demurrer, for failing to allege that plaintiff suffered damages from the failure to collect. Jefferson County Sav. Bank *v.* Hendrix, 147 Ala. 670, 39 So. 295, 1 L. R. A., N. S., 246.

§ 90 (3) Evidence.

Burden of Proof.—The burden is upon a bank losing paper sent to it for collection to show that it was not negligently lost. First Nat. Bank *v.* First Nat. Bank, 22 So. 976, 116 Ala. 520.

Plaintiff, suing a bank for the expenses incurred in substituting what purported to be transfers of land certificates, which the bank negligently lost, need not prove the execution and contents of the certificates. First Nat. Bank *v.* First Nat. Bank, 116 Ala. 520, 22 So. 976.

Sufficiency.—Plaintiff sent certain papers to a bank by mail, and in reply received a postal card acknowledging receipt, in the handwriting of a clerk, who was under the cashier's direction. The card was a printed form used by the bank in acknowledging the receipt of papers, and had the cashier's name printed upon it. Held sufficient to show that the papers were received by the cashier. First Nat. Bank *v.* First Nat. Bank, 22 So. 976, 116 Ala. 520.

§ 90 (4) Damages.

Measure of Damages.—The damages which the holder of a bill or note is entitled to receive of a bank guilty of negligence or default as a collecting agent is the actual loss, which is prima facie the amount of the bill or note placed in its hands; but evidence is admissible to reduce it to a nominal sum. First Nat. Bank *v.* Henry, 49 So. 97, 159 Ala. 367.

Where a bank neglects to fix the liability of the parties to a note or bill left with it for collection, it is liable to the owner for the actual damage sustained; and it rests with such owner to show that the parties discharged are solvent, and that the party or parties who remain liable are unable to pay. Bank of Mobile *v.* Huggins, 3 Ala. 206; Hendrix *v.* Jefferson County Sav. Bank, 153 Ala. 636, 45 So. 136.

The liability of a bank, with which a check is deposited for collection, for negligence in not collecting it and not giving notice of nonpayment till after the bank on which it was drawn suspended payment because of insolvency, is only for such amount as the depositor will lose thereby, which he must allege and prove. Hendrix *v.* Jefferson County Sav. Bank, 45 So. 136, 153 Ala. 636.

The amount of the recovery in an action against a bank for its negligent failure to collect a check received for collection is not necessarily the amount of the check, for the owner may secure all or a part of the debt for which the check was given, as by subsequent voluntary or enforced payment by the drawee bank when solvent, or by dividends when insolvent. Jefferson County Sav. Bank *v.* Hendrix, 39 So. 295, 147 Ala. 670, 1 L. R. A., N. S., 246.

"It is apparent, that a mere agency is created when a note is deposited for collection, and we find it difficult to imagine any circumstances which can cast on one standing in this relation, a liability to a greater extent than the actual amount of injury sustained by the principal. To permit a recovery for more, would be to inflict damages on the agent, as a penalty for his misconduct merely; and beyond the damage sustained, the principal would seem to have no better title than an indifferent person." Bank *v.* Huggins, 3 Ala. 206, 213.

If a bank receives a bill for collection, and omits to present it at the proper time and place, for payment, and a loss is sustained in consequence of this omission, the bank is liable to the extent of the loss. Branch of the Bank *v.* Knox & Co., 1 Ala. 148.

"If this were a suit between the plaintiff and the Bank of Commerce, founded on the averments of a want of care and diligence in intrusting the check to the payee for collection, the measure of recovery would be the actual loss the plaintiffs had suffered." Lowenstein *v.* Bresler, 109 Ala. 326, 328, 19 So. 860, 861.

A bank negligently losing transfers of land certificates sent to it to collect the sum for which they were given as collateral security is liable for the expenses of prosecuting suits to establish them, though such expenses would not have been necessary if the sender had recorded them before sending. First Nat. Bank *v.* First Nat. Bank, 22 So. 976, 116 Ala. 520.

One sending transfers of land certificates to a bank to collect the sum for which they were given as collateral security may recover of the bank for negligently losing them, the expenses of procuring substitutes, consisting of legal advice, an investigation of land-office records, a trip to a distant city to obtain a portion of them from the only person able to give them, and the costs, expenses, and attorney's fees paid in prosecuting litigation to establish the other portion. First Nat. Bank *v.* First Nat. Bank, 22 So. 976, 116 Ala. 520.

Where a customer of a state bank, located within the Confederate States, deposited notes and drafts with it for collection at various dates during 1861 and 1862, when practically no circulating medium except Confederate notes existed there, giving no instructions as to the kind of funds to be received, and made no demand for the proceeds until after the close of the war, he can recover not more than the value of the amount due in Confederate currency when the demand was made. Henry *v.* Northern Bank of Alabama, 63 Ala. 527.

(E) LOANS AND DISCOUNTS.

§ 91. In General.

Definition and Distinctions.—"The term 'discount,' as a substantive, signifies the interest allowed in advancing upon bills of exchange or negotiable securities; and 'to discount a bill is to buy it for a less sum than that, which upon its face is payable.'" Saltmarsh *v.* P. & M. Bank, 14 Ala. 668, 678.

"The terms 'discount' and 'loan' are employed in the books indiscriminately and synonymously in all cases where compensation for the use of money advanced is retained out of the gross sum at the time of the advancement. Thus, it is said: 'Discounting or loaning money, with a deduction of the interest in advance, is a part of the general business of banking,' etc. 2 Amer. & Eng. Enc. Law, p. 92. And a discount is thus defined: 'By the language of the commercial world, and the settled practice of banks, a discount by a bank means, ex vi termini, a deduction or drawback made upon its advances or loans of money upon negotiable paper, or other evidences of debt, payable at a future day, which are transferred to the bank. The term "discount," as a substantive, means the interest reserved from the amount lent at the time of making the loan; as a verb, it is used to denote the act of giving money for a note or bill of exchange, deducting the interest.' 5 Amer. & Eng. Enc. Law, pp. 678, 679. A distinction between 'discount' and 'loans' is sometimes enforced by the terms of statutes obtaining in the premises; but, in the absence of any element of this kind—whenever the words stand alone upon the signification accorded them in the general law—every loan upon evidences of debt, where the compensation for the use of money till the maturity of the debt is deducted from the principal and retained by the lender at the time of making the loan, is a discount." Youngblood *v.* Birmingham Trust, etc., Co., 95 Ala. 521, 12 So. 579.

§ 92. Power of Discount.

The Tombeckbee Bank is not authorized by its charter to discount a note, unless it be expressed on the face of the note that the same shall be negotiable at such bank. United States *v.* Fay, 9 Port. 465.

In Excess of Charter Provisions.—The fortieth section of the act of incorporation of the State Bank of Alabama, declaring it unlawful for the bank to discount or purchase a bill of exchange for a larger amount than $5,000, is directory merely; and, if they do discount a bill for a larger amount, the contract is not, therefore, void. Bates *v.* State Bank, 2 Ala. 451.

Although the issuance of bills of a less denomination than three dollars was prohibited at the time when a contract for the loan of the bills of an unchartered association was made, yet the mere fact that bills for less than three dollars were received does not avoid the contract. McGehee *v.* Powell, 8 Ala. 828.

Effect of Insolvency.—Act Feb. 13, 1843, for the final settlement of the affairs of a certain bank, after declaring its charter forfeited for failure to pay its debts, and providing for the exhibition of an information in the nature of a quo warranto by the solicitor of the circuit court on the requisition of the governor, and the appointment of commissioners to take charge of its effects, with power to sue, etc., provides that it shall be lawful for said commissioners to submit to arbitration contested claims, either those against or held by the bank, and "to compound any doubtful or bad debt," etc. Pamph. Acts 1845, p. 46, provides that the trustees may use the corporate name of said bank in the collection of debts due it, and may use all the modes and powers given to the bank by its original charter, or any subsequent act of the legislature, for the collection of its debts, in the same manner as if the charter had never been forfeited. Held that, though the statute authorizes the bank to exert all the powers conferred by the charter for the purpose of collecting its debts, it has no power to discount or purchase a bill of exchange as a business transaction; and an averment, therefore, in a plea in an action on a bill due the bank, that such bill was acquired by the bank by discounting it is sufficient prima facie to show that the transaction was unauthorized. Saltmarsh *v.* Bank, 14 Ala. 668.

§ 93. Requisites and Validity of Loan or Discount.

Essential Element.—"One material element of a discount in connection with the loan of money is the taking out of the principal sum, and the retention by the lender, at the time of the loan, of the interest charged for the use of the principal." Planters,' etc., Bank *v.* Goetter, 108 Ala. 408, 19 So. 54, 55. See ante, "In General," § 91.

Effect of Usury.—The amount of a thirty-days draft, made by S. & T. on defendant, and payable to plaintiff bank, was, after acceptance, paid by plaintiff, less 1 per cent of its face, which was retained as compensation for the money till maturity. Held, that the transaction by which plaintiff became the owner of the paper was a "discounting," within the meaning of Code 1886, § 4140, providing that any banker who discounts any note or draft at a higher rate of interest than 8 per cent is guilty of a misdemeanor. Youngblood *v.* Birmingham Trust, etc., Co., 95 Ala. 521, 12 So. 579.

Where money is loaned by a bank at a usurious rate of interest, and notes taken for the amount of the principal and interest, payable at a future day, the transaction is not a discounting, within the meaning of Code, § 4140, prohibiting the discounting of any note at a greater rate of interest than 8 per cent. Planters' & Merchants' Bank *v.* Goetter, 108 Ala. 408, 19 So. 54. See post, "Interest or Rate of Discount, and Usury," § 95.

§ 94. Collateral Security.

The receipt by a bank of transfers of land certificates was within the scope of the ordinary course of banking business, where they were transferable by indorsement, and showed by the indorsements thereon that the sender held them for collateral security, and were sent with instructions to deliver to a certain person upon receipt of a certain sum. First Nat. Bank *v.* First Nat. Bank, 22 So. 976, 116 Ala. 520.

§ 95. Interest or Rate of Discount, and Usury.

See, generally, the titles INTEREST; USURY. See ante, "Requisites and Validity of Loan or Discount," § 93.

Method of Calculating Interest.—The rules of the bank, whereby interest is taken in advance, and taking interest on renewals on the old and new note, both for the day of renewal, and also, calculating interest for a day as 1-360th part of a year, etc., are legal; being sanctioned by universal banking usage. Lyon *v.* State Bank, 1 Stew. 442, cited on this point in note in 29 L. R. A. 763.

A discount of a note, made by calculating the interest for one year, and multiplying this sum by the number of years the note has to run, and deducting the amount thus ascertained from the amount of the note, is illegal, whether made by a bank, or by an individual. Branch Bank at Mobile *v.* Strother, 15 Ala. 51.

What Law Governs.—Notwithstanding the charter of the United States Bank of Pennsylvania prohibits it from taking more than at the rate of 6 per cent per annum interest on its loans, yet where it enters into a contract of loans in a state where laws allow a greater rate of interest, the contract will not be vitiated if the bank receives the rate of interest allowed by law in the state where the contract is made. Hitchcock *v.* United States Bank, 7 Ala. 386.

Rate Allowable.—Though the interest to be taken by the bank is limited by statute to 6 per cent, yet there is no usury unless more than 8 per cent be taken. Lyon *v.* State Bank, 1 Stew. 442.

Banks can not discount notes or bills at the rate of 8 per cent per annum, having a longer period to run than twelve months; nor can they extend a debt due them, and charge interest, by way of annual discount, in advance. They may discount a bill or note having more than twelve months to run by ascertaining the present worth of the note or bill at 8 per cent for the time it has to run. Branch Bank at Mobile *v.* Strother, 15 Ala. 51.

Same—After Maturity.—A note discounted by the bank carries interest at the rate of 8 per cent per annum after its maturity. Kitchen *v.* Branch Bank at Mobile, 14 Ala. 233; Branch Bank at Mobile *v.* Strother, 15 Ala. 51.

An agreement entered into by the bank to receive payment by installments of 20 per cent annually, but without consideration, has no effect upon the rate of interest which by law the note bears after maturity. Kitchen *v.* Branch Bank at Mobile, 14 Ala. 233.

Contracts Affected by Change of Rate.—The charter of the Bank of Mobile was in force until 1859, and allowed 7 per cent discount. In 1852 the legislature passed an act to extend the privileges of the bank for twenty years beyond the expiration of its charter, with a proviso that it should not take more than 6 per cent. This proviso was held to apply only to the privileges granted by the extension, and not to affect loans made while the original charter was in force. Pearce *v.* Bank of Mobile, 33 Ala. 693.

Usury.—Where, on the issue whether plaintiff was guilty of reserving interest in excess of the 8 per cent allowed by Code 1886, § 4140, to bankers for discounting commercial paper, the evidence shows an excess of five cents only, the maxim, "De minimis non curat lex," obtains, and the issue need not be submitted. Slaughter *v.* First Nat. Bank, 109 Ala. 157, 19 So. 430, cited in note in 56 L. R. A. 681.

Code 1886, § 4140, made it a misdemeanor for any banker to discount any note at a higher rate than 8 per cent. Plaintiff sued to have a mortgage made to defendant canceled as a cloud on her title, alleging a usurious consideration. Held, that she was not entitled to relief without tendering the amount actually borrowed, with lawful interest, since the loan, though prohibited by the act, was not in itself wrong, and he who asks equity must do equity. Turner *v.* Merchants' Bank, 28 So. 469, 126 Ala. 397.

Since Code 1886, § 4140, provides that any banker who discounts any note or draft at a higher rate of interest than 8 per cent per annum is guilty of a misdemeanor, cashing a thirty-days draft at a discount of 1 per cent of its face renders the draft absolutely void, and defeats an action thereon against the acceptor. Youngblood *v.* Birmingham Trust & Savings Co., 95 Ala. 521, 12 So. 579, 20 L. R. A. 58, cited on this point in note in 5 L. R. A., N. S., 877.

§ 96. Repayment of Loans.

A stockholder in a bank may sell or convey slaves by mortgage to the bank in payment of a debt he owes the bank. Governor *v.* Baker, 14 Ala. 652.

Where a note is made for the payment of a debt due a bank in one, two, and three years, under the provisions of the second section of the act of 1837, it does not become due in toto upon a failure to pay the first installment. Lightfoot *v.* Branch Bank, 2 Ala. 345.

§ 97. Actions on Loans or on Paper Discounted.

Evidence of Discount.—"In Findley *v.* State Bank, 6 Ala. 244, we held that when the bank refused to discount a note, unless additional security was given, the mere possession of the note, no additional security being given, was not evidence that the bank had afterwards discounted it." Colgin *v.* State Bank, 11 Ala. 222, 227.

A banking company with whom a foreign bank has made a general deposit of bills of the foreign bank, in using and paying out those bills, acts in its own right as with its own money, and not as the agent of the depositor. Therefore, in an action by the local bank against the indorser of a bill discounted by plaintiff with the foreign bills, defendant can not urge that plaintiff violated its charter by acting as the agent of the foreign bank in unlawfully issuing its bills for circulation. Wray *v.* Tuskegee Ins. Co., 34 Ala. 58.

Where an accommodation drawer of a bill of exchange did not know that the acceptor intended to discount it at a certain bank, and was not present and took no part in the negotiation, he is not estopped, in a suit against him on the bill, to deny the proper organization of the bank. Marion Sav. Bank *v.* Dunkin, 54 Ala. 471.

(F) EXCHANGE, MONEY, SECURITIES, AND INVESTMENTS.

§ 98. Loans and Investments by Bank for Others.

In an action against a bank for failure

to take warehouse receipts for cotton and bills of lading as collateral security for an indebtedness of a third person to plaintiff, on account of money deposited by plaintiff to pay such person on deposit of collateral for plaintiff's benefit, it could not avail the bank to show that there had been a shrinkage in the value of cotton, unless it showed that it had taken receipts or bills sufficient to cover the amount. First Nat. Bank *v.* Henry, 49 So. 97, 159 Ala. 367.

(G) CIRCULATING NOTES.

§ 99. Nature and Requisites.

Bank notes issued by a state bank are not bills of credit, within the meaning of Const. U. S. art. 1, § 10, prohibiting any state from emitting such bills. Owen *v.* Branch Bank, 3 Ala. 258.

Merchandise Checks.—The prohibition, in Code, § 4433, of the emission of any paper, etc., without authority of law, to answer the purposes of money, or for general circulation, does not apply to a paper of the form: "Let A. have —— dollars trade at store," dated and signed, and the words "Not transferable" written across its face. Durr *v.* State, 59 Ala. 24.

§ 100. Power to Issue or Circulate.

Meaning of "Issue" and "Circulate."—The word "issue," when used in reference to bank bills, is the antithesis of circulation. Chief-Justice Marshall, in his decision in the case of Craig *v.* Missouri, 4 Pet. 410 (7 L. Ed. 903), treats "emit," in that article of the constitution which prohibits a state "to emit bills of credit," as synonymous with "issue." Then, to "issue" bills to circulate as money is to "emit" them—to send them out. It is an act antecedent to the circulation of the bills, and different from it. If the bank, by loan or deposit, transferred the property in its bills to the T. Co.—deprived itself of the ownership of the bills, and made them the property of the plaintiff; and the plaintiff thereby became a debtor to the bank for the bills so received, the bills were issued by the bank itself when they were delivered. When they passed from the bank, and became the property of the plaintiff, they were issued, or emitted; and the subsequent use of them by the plaintiff was a circulation, not an issue of them. Wray *v.* Tuskegee Ins. Co., 34 Ala. 58, 64.

Certificates of Deposit.—In Bliss *v.* Anderson, 31 Ala. 612, 623, the court, in spe·king of certificates of deposit, said: "The power to issue paper which may be transferred, is not a power to issue paper to circulate as money."

The charter of the Gainesville Insurance Company, in authorizing the company to receive money on deposit, "and to give acknowledgments for deposits in such manner and form as they may deem convenient and necessary to transact such business," does not authorize the company to issue certificates of deposit to circulate as money, and with the intent that they shall so circulate. Bliss *v.* Anderson, 31 Ala. 612, 70 Am. Dec. 511.

Distinction between Issuing Certificates of Deposit and Money.—See ante, "Certificates of Deposit," § 74.

§ 101. Restrictions upon Issue or Circulation.

Power to Restrict.—The legislature has the power to limit at all times the issuance and circulation of paper currency, when not issued under previous express authority. State *v.* Stebbins, 1 Stew. 299.

Purpose of Restriction.—The purpose of the statute (Code of 1876, § 4433) forbidding the emission of change bills to circulate generally, as money, was intended to suppress the evils of an unauthorized paper currency. Durr *v.* State, 59 Ala. 24.

The statute is not directed against paper of any particular form of character. If the purpose of its emission be, that it shall pass and circulate generally as money for an indefinite period, it falls within the statutory prohibition. Durr *v.* State, 59 Ala. 24.

§ 102. Deposit of Security.

See ante, "Safety Funds and Deposits of Securities," § 5.

§ 103. Unauthorized Issue.

§ 104. —— Operation and Effect of Notes.

The violation of its charter by an incorporated bank, in circulating as currency notes or bills not payable on demand, does not vitiate a contract made by the bank with other parties, involving the circulation of such notes or bills. Cannon *v.* McNab, 48 Ala. 99.

§ 105. —— Criminal Prosecutions.

Nature of Offense.—To constitute the statutory offense of making, emitting, or circulating change bills to be used as money (Rev. Code, §§ 3643, 3644), it is immaterial what name was given to the paper, to what extent it was circulated, what considerations of convenience prompted it, or what benefit accrued from it to the accused or any one else. Norvell *v.* State, 50 Ala. 174.

Intent.—It is the purpose for which paper is issued or circulated, and the absence of legal authority therefor, and not the character or form of such paper, which constitute the offense denounced by § 3643 of the Revised Code; and although the form and contents of such paper may be evidence to establish or negative the criminal purpose, such unlawful intent is not inferred therefrom as matter of law, but is a question of fact for the determination of the jury; and any description of the paper identifying it is sufficient. Barnett *v.* State, 54 Ala. 579.

On a prosecution for the statutory offense of making, emitting, or circulating change bills to be used as money (Rev. Code, §§ 3673, 3674), the criminal intent, necessary to be proved, can not be avoided by showing that the act was done through indifference, thoughtlessness, or mechanical compliance with the orders of some other person. Norvell *v.* State, 50 Ala. 174.

Indictment.—An indictment under Rev. Code, § 3643, alleging that defendants, being members or partners of a private company or corporation known as the Tallassee Manufacturing Company, emitted, without authority of law, a certain paper to answer the purposes of money, or for general circulation, is not bad, on demurrer, in not setting forth with sufficient certainty whether the defendants are charged as individuals or as a private corporation. Barnett *v.* State, 54 Ala. 579.

An indictment under Rev. Code, § 3643, for emitting bills to circulate as money, is not bad, on demurrer, because it charges the defendants disjunctively as members of a corporation or of an association of partnership. Barnett *v.* State, 54 Ala. 579.

Evidence.—On a prosecution under Rev. Code, § 3643, for emitting change bills to circulate as money, evidence that the paper emitted was circulated and used as money, it being given and accepted in exchange for merchandise or for marketable articles, is admissible as tending to show its adaptation to circulate and use as money. Barnett *v.* State, 54 Ala. 579.

Instructions.—On a prosecution under Rev. Code, § 3643, "for countersigning a paper," etc., "issued without authority of law for purposes of money, or for general circulation," a charge that the defendant could not be convicted "unless there was proof by an eyewitness to the signature, or proof that defendant admitted the signature to be his, or that the signature was in his handwriting," is erroneous. Jordan *v.* State, 45 Ala. 188.

Variance.—On a prosecution under Rev. Code, § 3643, for emitting change bills to circulate as money, the difference between the word "cents," as written in the paper offered in evidence, and its abbreviation "cts.," as written in the indictment, is not a material variance. Barnett *v.* State, 54 Ala. 579.

Question for Jury.—On a prosecution under Rev. Code, § 3643, for emitting change bills to circulate as money, it is proper to refuse to permit a witness to state the purpose for which the paper was emitted, it being the province of the jury to determine from the evidence whether it was issued for general circulation or for the purpose of money. Barnett *v.* State, 54 Ala. 579.

§ 106. Payment or Redemption.

§ 107. —— In General.

What Constitutes.—The surrender to a bank agent of its notes, and the acceptance from him of his draft on a third person, is but the substitution of one security for another, and does not extinguish the original liability on the notes, unless the draft is drawn in good faith, and accepted as an absolute payment and discharge of the notes; and even if it is, through the fraud of the agent, accepted as an absolute payment, the fraud would prevent it from so operating. Bank of St. Marys *v.* St. John, 25 Ala. 566.

§ 108. —— Penalties for Failure to Pay.

When defendants are held liable on the original bank notes held by complainants, they are liable only for the amount of the bills and interest, and not for statutory damages on a draft which was substituted for the notes, and was protested for nonpayment. Bank of St. Marys *v.* St. John, 25 Ala. 566.

§ 109. Liability of Stockholders or Officers.

See ante, "Nature and Extent," § 14.

An officer or stockholder of a foreign banking corporation, who issues and puts in circulation its notes, is individually liable for their payment. Clay's Dig., p. 133, § 3. Bank of St. Marys *v.* St. John, 25 Ala. 566.

In an action against an insolvent bank and its stockholders under a statute making them personally liable for notes issued by it, an allegation in the bill that plaintiffs were the holders of $200,000 in bills purporting to have been issued by the bank, payable on demand, and that they presented said bills for payment at the bank, and payment was at first refused, and then made, by delivering a draft to plaintiffs on a person claimed to have funds of the bank, but payment of which was thereafter refused, sufficiently shows an indebtedness due plaintiffs from the bank and its stockholders to sustain an attachment issued against the bank and its president, who was the principal stockholder. Bank of St. Marys *v.* St. John, 25 Ala. 566.

§ 110. Actions on Notes or for Nonpayment Thereof.

Nature and Form of Remedy.—Code, § 2151, providing that "suit may be brought on a bond, note, bill of exchange, or other mercantile instrument which has been lost or destroyed by accident, and, if affidavit is made by plaintiff of such loss and destruction, and the contents thereof, * * * and accompanies the complaint, it must be received as presumptive evidence, * * * unless defendant under oath denies the execution of the bond, note, or bill, * * * but this section must not be so construed as to authorize a suit for the recovery of a note or bill issued by an incorporated bank to pass as money, and alleged to be lost or destroyed," merely furnishes a cumulative remedy, and does not abrogate the common-law remedy for the recovery of lost or destroyed bank notes. Bank of Mobile *v.* Meagher, 33 Ala. 622.

Nor does the proviso to that act, declaring that "it must be so construed as to authorize a suit for the recovery of a note or bill issued by any incorporated bank to parties as named and alleged to be lost or destroyed," amount to an inhibition to an action at law on such note or bill. Bank of Mobile *v.* Meagher, 33 Ala. 622.

Where a bank note has been destroyed, thus rendering it impossible that the bank can be made to pay it a second time, the owner at the time of the loss may maintain an action at law against the bank for its value, and need not go into chancery. Bank of Mobile *v.* Meagher, 33 Ala. 622.

An action at law does not lie against a bank to recover the value of a lost note or bill, which, passing from hand to hand by delivery merely, and which might be presented to the bank by the finder for payment. Bank *v.* Meagher & Co., 33 Ala. 622.

A recovery may be had upon the common counts in assumpsit, against a bank, for the value of notes of the bank, proved to have been destroyed, without an affidavit of loss previous to the institution of the suit. Bank of Mobile *v.* Williams, 13 Ala. 544.

Parties.—The holder of bank bills issued by an unchartered banking association, payable to the persons named therein, or bearer, may sue the bank in his own name, though the bills are not indorsed; Act June 30, 1837, providing that "all bonds, bills, or notes" payable to the persons named therein, or bearer, shall have the effect of creating a liability to the payee only, expressly named, and no one but such payee or his indorsee "shall have a right to maintain, in his own name, an action on any such bond, bill, or note," applies only to paper made by persons in the course of their ordinary business transactions, and not to bank bills. Kemper & Noxubee Navigation & Real-Estate Banking Co. *v.* Schieffelin, 5 Ala. 493.

Pleading.—It is sufficient to describe the bills as 14 $100 bank bills of that bank. Bank of Mobile *v.* Meagher, 33 Ala. 622.

In an action at law to recover from the bank the value of destroyed bank notes, the complaint, in describing the notes, need not aver their dates, or the time when they were payable. The court will take judicial notice of the fact that they were payable on demand. Bank of Mobile *v.* Meagher, 33 Ala. 622.

Burden of Proof.—In an action to recover the value of destroyed bank notes, plaintiff must first prove the existence and destruction of the notes, and adduce proof of their contents. Mere proof of their aggregate amount, and issue by the bank, is not sufficient to authorize a recovery. Bank of Mobile *v.* Meagher, 33 Ala. 622.

Damages.—Where bank bills are at a discount, but the bank is liable to pay them in gold and silver, the damages properly accruing on the breach of a contract, of which such bills formed the active consideration, can not be reduced by reason of the depreciation. Bell *v.* Real-Estate Banking Co., 3 Ala. 77. See the title DAMAGES.

(H) ACTIONS.

§ 111. Capacity to Sue and Be Sued.

"The act of 1837, legalizing the suspension of specie payments by the banks, was merely intended to prevent a forfeiture of their charters, and to save them from the effects of the penalty consequent upon the refusal to pay specie on demand. It was not intended to prevent any one, who thought proper, from suing the bank, and recovering his debt in specie; nor, if such had been the intention, would the law have been obligatory." Owen *v.* Branch Bank, 3 Ala. 258, 274.

§ 112. Summary Remedies.

§ 112 (1) In General.

Remedy Strictly Construed.—In pursuing the summary remedy given to the banks by the Alabama statute, the terms of the statute must be strictly observed. Logwood *v.* Planters', etc., Bank, Minor 23.

The summary remedy given by its charter to the Branch Bank at Mobile, to recover judgment against the maker or indorser of a note, on thirty days' notice, must be strictly construed. Murphy *v.* Branch Bank at Mobile, 5 Ala. 421; Alexander *v.* Branch Bank of Montgomery, 5 Ala. 465.

When Applicable.—The remedy of judgment on summary motion, given to parties, bound for the payment of any bill of exchange, the property of the Bank of Alabama, or any of its branches, by Act 1830, § 2, does not extend to ordinary business paper, but is confined to accommodation paper discounted by said bank or its branches. Edgerly *v.* Butler, 3 Port. 344.

The eighteenth section of the charter of the Bank of Alabama, authorizing proceedings by and against it, by notice and motion, on a bill, bond, etc., does not authorize such proceeding by an agent of the bank to recover stipulated wages while employed as such. Wrigglesworth *v.* State Bank, 1 Ala. 222.

Act June 30, 1837, giving banks the right to sue under their charters by summary remedy on bills, notes, etc., applies only to such as are acquired after its passage. Levert *v.* Planters' & Merchants' Bank, 8 Port. 104.

The charter of a bank provides that if any person shall be indebted to the corporation as maker or indorser of any note expressly made negotiable and payable at said bank, and shall delay payment thereof, the bank may, after giving notice, move for judgment and execution. Act June 30, 1837, provides that if any person shall become indebted to any of said institutions (including said bank) by note or other contract for the payment of money, and shall delay payment thereof, the said banks may sue for and collect the same by summary remedy, as in other cases under the charter of said banks. Held, that such act applies only to future acquisitions of such bank, and therefore, to be entitled to such summary remedy, it must appear either that the note on which claim is made was expessly made negotiable and payable at said bank, or that it was acquired after June 30, 1837. Levert *v.* Planters' & Merchants' Bank, 8 Port. 104.

Under the statute of 1837 "to extend the time of indebtedness to the State Bank," etc., it is not necessary that a note should be negotiable at the bank, to authorize the bank to institute the summary remedy given by its charter. Hancock *v.* Branch Bank, 5 Ala. 440.

Where a note is payable to the maker, and is not indorsed by him, and the holder is a bank, it can not maintain proceedings by notice, under the statute, on the certificate of the president that the note is bona fide the property of the bank. Lea *v.* Branch Bank of Mobile, 8 Port. 119.

§ 112 (2) Parties.

See ante, "In General," § 112 (1).

Parties Plaintiff.—The trustees of the Planters' & Merchants' Bank of Mobile, appointed under the act of 1845, were authorized to take individual notes to secure a balance due to the bank from a suspended bank of another state, and to institute suit thereon by the summary remedy of notice and motion. Jemison *v.* Planters' & Merchants' Bank, 23 Ala. 168.

Parties Defendant.—The summary remedy provided by statute in favor of banks will not lie against the representative of a deceased debtor of a bank. Andrews *v.* Branch Bank at Mobile, 10 Ala. 375.

The summary remedy given by its charter to the Branch Bank at Mobile can not be used against the representatives of a deceased maker or indorser. Alexander *v.* Branch Bank, 5 Ala. 465.

Where a bank gave notice, under the statute, of a motion for judgment against four persons, and judgment was taken against two only which was set aside, and at a subsequent term judgment rendered against all, such judgment was held erroneous as to all, because it did not appear that a motion was submitted at the first term for judgment against all. Crawford *v.* Planters' & Merchants' Bank, 4 Ala. 313.

§ 112 (3) Notice of Motion.

Functions of Notice.— The notice issued at the suit of a bank requiring its debtor to answer to an allegation of indebtedness is process to bring the latter into court; but, after the motion for judgment has been submitted, it may be regarded as a motion in writing, identifying the debt, to which the defendant may either demur or plead to issue. Griffin *v.* Bank, 6 Ala. 908; Jemison *v.* Planters', etc., Bank, 17 Ala. 754.

"It has heretofore been decided by this court, in the case of Lyon *v.* State Bank, 1 Stew. 442, that the notice does not occupy the place of a declaration; that it is principally intended to bring the defendant into court. Indeed, it can not be considered as the declaration, because it is the act of the plaintiff, performed out of court—not governed by the rules which control the pleadings in a cause. Walker *v.* Bank, 4 Stew. & P. 215, 220.

In proceedings to take summary judgment against one indebted to the State Bank, a declaration is not necessary, though the record must show every material fact to have been proven. Lyon *v.* State Bank, 1 Stew. 442. See, also, Bates *v.* Planters', etc., Bank, 8 Port. 99.

In summary proceedings by notice and motion against bank debtors, this notice serves the double purpose of a writ and declaration, and prevents the statute of limitations from creating a bar, although the motion for judgment is afterwards delayed. Stanley *v.* Bank of Mobile, 23 Ala. 652.

Form and Requisites.—This summary process by notice, etc., is remedial, and does not require technical nicety. Branch of State Bank *v.* Harrison, 2 Port. 540.

A notice of a motion for summary judgment by the State Bank and the certificate of indebtedness are sufficient if they identify the debt with reasonable certainty, though they have not the technical precision of a declaration. Lyon *v.* State Bank, 1 Stew. 442.

The notice which the statute requires to be given in summary proceedings is sufficient if it describe the debt upon which the motion is to be made with reasonable certainty. Colgin *v.* State Bank, 11 Ala. 222.

A notice of a motion for judgment in a suit by a bank requiring its debtor to answer to an allegation of indebtedness need not be dated, unless the date is made material by a reference to it as indicating the time when the motion will be made. Griffin *v.* State Bank, 6 Ala. 908.

In a proceeding by a bank by notice, the notice need not allege that the debt is due and unpaid, if the note or bill is set out in hæc verba, from which it appears to be overdue. Sale *v.* Branch Bank, 1 Ala. 425.

Notice of a motion for judgment by the Huntsville Bank must be under its corporate seal. Logwood *v.* Planter's, etc., Bank, Minor, 23. But the notice to the maker or indorser of a bill or note, which is authorized by the act incorporating the Branch of the Bank of the State of Alabama at Montgomery, need not be under the corporate seal. Branch of State Bank *v.* Harrison, 2 Port. 540.

An allegation, in the notice of a motion for summary judgment in favor of the State Bank, that the president, etc., are "holders and owners of the bill" of exchange sued on, is tantamount to an averment that the bill is the property of the bank. Walker *v.* Bank of Alabama, 4 Stew. & P. 215.

Under the act of December 4, 1841, providing that all notes, bills, etc., held by the State Bank or Branch Banks, payable to the cashier, may be sued and collected in the name of the several banks, in the same manner as if made payable directly to such bank or Branch Banks, a note payable to B. G., cashier, and described in a notice under the statute by the State Bank or Branch Banks, is sufficient to show that the title is in the bank. Crawford *v.* Branch Bank at Mobile, 7 Ala. 383; Blackman *v.* Branch Bank of Mobile, 8 Ala. 103; Ewin *v.* Branch Bank, 14 Ala. 307, 314.

In a summary proceeding by notice and motion at the suit of a bank, where the notice recites that the bank will move for judgment on a bill dated January 4, 1840, payable six months after date, and that "it was purchased under the first section of the act of 1843," the recital as to the purchase may be treated as surplusage, since the only effect of the fact, if established, would be to entitle the bank to a penalty. State Bank *v.* Dent, 12 Ala. 187.

In a suit by a branch of the State Bank of Alabama against one of its debtors, upon motion and notice under its charter, the notice was received by the sheriff in April, 1842, and served on the 7th of May thereafter, and informed the defendant that the plaintiff would move for judgment against him "at the next term," etc., "to be holden," etc., in 1841. In May, 1842, the defendant appeared and pleaded. Held that, the fair inference being that the motion was to be submitted at the next term of court succeeding the time when the notice was issued, so much of the notice as particularized the time when the court was to sit might be rejected as surplusage. Crawford *v.* Bank at Mobile, 7 Ala. 205.

Where a notice of a motion for judgment in favor of a bank states the time when the note was discounted, so as to show that it was before it bears date, this statement, as it is unnecessary, may be treated as surplusage. Griffin *v.* Bank, 6 Ala. 908.

On a plea of non assumpsit to a notice by a bank requiring its debtor to answer to an allegation of indebtedness, if the note sought to be recovered is misdescribed as to the time of its maturity, the variance will be fatal to the motion. Griffin *v.* State Bank, 6 Ala. 908.

In a summary proceeding by the State Bank against its debtor, the notice alleged that the drawer and indorser were indebted to the plaintiff by a bill of exchange, purchased under the first section of the act of 1843, and informed them that a motion would be made against them for the amount of money due and unpaid on the bill, together with the interest and damages at the rate of 30 per cent, which shall have lawfully accrued thereon. The damages prescribed by the statute on one description of bill to which it referred was 30, and on another 5, per cent. Held, that as the plaintiff, upon proof of default and notice, might recover at least 5 per cent damages, the notice was not bad on demurrer. Riggs *v.* State Bank, 11 Ala. 183.

The acts of February 13, 1843, for the final settlement of the affairs of the Planters' & Merchants' Bank of Mobile, not having reserved to the bank the power to sue after the forfeiture of its charter, but having vested it first in commissioners, and then in trustees, to be by them exercised in the name of the bank, a notice in its name against one of its debtors, which fails to show that the proceeding is instituted by direction or for the use of the trustees, is bad on demurrer. Jemison *v.* Planters' & Merchants' Bank, 17 Ala. 754.

§ 112 (4) Who May Give.

See post, "Execution and Return of Process," § 112 (8).

President and Directors.—In a summary proceeding for judgment at the suit of a bank, a notice by the president "and directors" of the bank is sufficient, where its charter requires the notice to be given by the president of the bank. Crawford *v.* State Bank, 5 Ala. 679.

De Facto President.—A notice for judgment, by motion, made by one assuming to be president of the bank, is sufficient, whether he be president of the bank de jure or not, if the act is adopted by his successor, who is legally president of the bank. Blackman *v.* Branch Bank at Mobile, 8 Ala. 103.

Agent of President.—"The charter requiring the president of the bank to give notice, does not contemplate that he should do it in person, but that notice shall be given under his direction." Blackman *v.* Branch Bank, 8 Ala. 103, 104.

Attorney.—"In Curry *v.* Bank, 8 Port. 360, 373, we held, that the notice of an intended motion for judgment, might be given by an attorney of the corporation." Blackman *v.* Branch Bank, 8 Ala. 103, 104.

§ 112 (5) Length of Notice.

The statute of 1821, authorizing summary judgment against banks on ten days' notice, was repealed, as to the time of notice by the charter of the Branch Bank at Decatur, requiring thirty days' notice. Branch Bank *v.* Jones, 5 Ala. 487.

In a summary proceeding by motion at the suit of a bank, it is not necessary that the notice should be served thirty days before the commencement of the term of the court, or that the motion should be made on any certain day, unless, perhaps, the notice in this respect is special. Ticknor *v.* Branch Bank, 3 Ala. 135.

§ 112 (6) Objections to Notice.

In a summary proceeding by notice issued at the instance of a bank against its debtor, the notice, after it has served the purpose of bringing the debtor into court, may be treated as a declaration, to which the defendant may either demur or plead. Jemison *v.* Planters' & Merchants' Bank, 17 Ala. 754.

Where a debtor of a branch of the State Bank of Alabama, against whom the summary remedy by motion for judgment, provided by its charter, has been prosecuted, pleads to the merits, and a verdict and judgment are rendered against him, an objection that the notice is defective can not be allowed if it show, prima facie, that he is indebted to the plaintiff. Crawford *v.* Branch Bank at Mobile, 7 Ala. 205.

§ 112 (7) Amending Notice.

Where the notice in a summary proceeding, under the statute, by a bank, the charter of which has been forfeited, and the affairs of which have been placed in the hands of trustees for settlement, is defective for the want of an averment that the suit was instituted by authority of the trustees, it may be amended by annexing the trustees' certificate to the notice, averring that the bank, "by its trustees, named in the certificate annexed hereto, appointed under the act therein specified, will move," etc. Jemison *v.* Planters' & Merchants' Bank, 23 Ala. 168.

§ 112 (8) Execution and Return of Process.

The agents of the State Bank and its branches, appointed under the statute, possess the same powers in executing process in favor of the bank conferred on sheriffs, and are bound to observe the same rules. Branch Bank at Mobile *v.* Darrington, 14 Ala. 192; Morgan *v.* Ramsey, 15 Ala. 190.

Such notice may be served by the sheriff or a private person. Lyon *v.* State Bank, 1 Stew. 442.

The act of 1841 (Clay's Dig., p. 118, § 86) authorizes the State Bank and its several branches to appoint an officer to serve notices and writs and perform other duties which hitherto have appertained to the office of sheriff. Held, that the courts will ex officio take notice of the returns made by the bank agents in the same manner as they do returns by sheriffs. Crawford *v.* Branch Bank at Mobile, 7 Ala. 383.

§ 112 (9) Certificate as to Indebtedness to Bank.

See post, "Record and Judgment," § 112 (12).

Necessity of Certificate.—To sustain a judgment on notes recovered by the Huntsville Bank, or the Tombeckbee Bank, on motion pursuant to the provisions in their respective charters, the record must show that the certificate of the president was produced, stating that the bank was owner of the notes. Logwood *v.* Huntsville Bank, Minor 23; Duncan *v.* Tombeckbee Bank, 4 Port. 181.

In a proceeding by motion by the Planters' & Merchants' Bank of Mobile for judgment against the indorser of a note held by it, the president must file a certificate that the debt sued for was really and bona fide its property. Bates *v.* Planters' & Merchants' Bank, 9 Port. 376. See, also, Gazzam *v.* Bank of Mobile, 1 Ala. 268.

In order to authorize proceedings by a bank on a note by notice, the certificate of the president of the bank of the indebtedness of defendant must show that the note declared on is bona fide the property of the bank. Roberts *v.* State Bank, 9 Port. 312.

In a summary proceeding on a bank notice, when the record does not show that the certificate of the president of the bank was produced and shown to the court, it has no jurisdiction, and the judgment can not be rendered. Bates *v.* Planters' & Merchants' Bank, 8 Port. 99.

Filing a declaration in support of a motion for summary judgment by a chartered bank is unnecessary, and does not so alter the proceeding as to dispense with the necessity of the certificate of the president of the bank that the debt is bona fide, as required by the charter. Duncan *v.* Tombeckbee Bank, 4 Port. 181; Bates *v.* Planters' & Merchants' Bank, 8 Port. 99, 102.

Who May Make.—The president pro tem. of the Branch Bank at Mobile may certify, under the charter, that a note sued on is bona fide the property of that branch. Bancroft *v.* Branch Bank, 1 Ala. 230.

To authorize the rendition of judgment by motion in favor of the Planters' & Merchants' Bank of Mobile, it is not sufficient to produce to the court the certificate of one assuming to be the president of the bank, or a commissioner, under the act of 1843, that the debt is the property of the bank, but the official character of the persons assuming to act must be proved, and the genuineness of their signature. Crawford *v.* Planters' & Merchants' Bank, 6 Ala. 289. See ante, "Who May Give," § 112 (4).

Time of Making.—On motion for judgment by a bank on a bill of exchange, the certificate, required by statute to be made by the bank, that the bill is bona fide its property, may be made at the time of the trial or at any time before judgment. Ford *v.* Branch Bank, 6 Ala. 286.

Requisites.—In a summary proceeding by a bank against one of its debtors to recover the amount of a promissory note as authorized by the special act of June, 1837, the certificate of the president of the bank as to the title of the note must identify it with reasonable certainty by some other description than by merely stating its amount. Sale *v.* Branch Bank at Decatur, 1 Ala. 425.

Where the certificate of the president of the bank contains no reference to the instrument sued on, other than its amount, it is insufficient to give the court jurisdiction, and too loose and indeterminate to be received. Roberts *v.* State Bank, 9 Port. 312.

Effect of Certificate.—The certificate of the president of the bank, of the indebtedness of defendant, is conclusive as to the right of the bank to sue, and prima facie evidence of the genuineness of the signature. Roberts *v.* State Bank, 9 Port. 312.

In a summary proceeding by notice and motion against a bank debtor, if the proper certificate is appended to the notice that the note is really and bona fide the property of the bank, the certificate is proof of the jurisdictional fact to the end of the suit, although the note is sold or assigned before judgment. Jemison *v.* Planters' & Merchants' Bank, 23 Ala. 168.

On motion of a bank for judgment against its debtor, the certificate required by statute that the debt is bona fide the property of the bank is intended merely to give the court jurisdiction, and can not cure a defect in the notice. Jemison *v.* Planters' & Merchants' Bank, 17 Ala. 754.

Use as Evidence.—On motion by the Bank of Mobile for judgment, the certificate of the president of the bank that the note sued on is bona fide the property of the bank is necessary to give the court jurisdiction, but can not be used for any other purpose, or looked to by the jury as evidence. Gazzam *v.* Bank of Mobile, 1 Ala. 268.

The object of the certificate of the president of the bank is to prove property in the bank, but it does not establish the debt. Lyon *v.* State Bank, 1 Stew. 442.

§ 112 (10) Trial by Jury.

The statute authorizing summary proceedings by the banks, in collecting claims due them, requires the court to impanel a jury to try the issue, where the claim is contested. Curry *v.* Bank, 8 Port. 360.

§ 112 (11) Burden of Proof.

The plea of non assumpsit to a notice of a motion for judgment at the suit of a bank requiring its debtor to answer to an allegation of indebtedness, throws upon plaintiff the onus of proving the material facts stated in the notice. Griffin *v.* State Bank, 6 Ala. 908.

§ 112 (12) Record and Judgment.

See ante, "Certificate as to Indebtedness of Bank," § 112 (9).

What Record Should Show.—In a summary proceeding on a bank notice, everything necessary to give the court jurisdiction, and to sustain its judgment, must appear on the record. Bates *v.* Planters' & Merchants' Bank, 8 Port. 99; Lyon *v.* State Bank, 1 Stew. 442. See, also, Jemison *v.* Planters' & Merchants' Bank of Mobile, 17 Ala. 754.

Where a judgment by default, or nil dicit, is rendered upon motion in favor of a bank, the record must show the liability of the defendant for the debt or demand, and that the facts were proved which gave the court jurisdiction. Andrews *v.* Branch Bank at Mobile, 10 Ala. 375.

In cases where bank debtors are proceeded against summarily by notice, the judgment, whether by default or otherwise, must show affirmatively every fact necessary to give the court jurisdiction; and in judgments by default the liability of the defendant for the debt must be also shown. Curry *v.* Bank of Mobile, 8 Port. 360; Roberts *v.* State Bank, 9 Port. 312.

"In Smith *v.* Branch Bank, 5 Ala. 26, it is said, the result of all the cases in this court, where judgments had been rendered on motion, is, that when the judgment is by default, it must appear by the judgment, that the defendant had the notice which the law requires, and that the facts were proved which gives the court jurisdiction, and show the liability of the defendant for the debt, or penalty. If the defendant appear, it will be evidence of notice, and if an issue is made up and submitted to a jury, it is then like any other cause, commenced in the ordinary mode, except that it must appear upon the record, that the court had jurisdiction to entertain the motion. See Curry *v.* Bank, 8 Port. 360." Riggs *v.* Bank, 11 Ala. 183, 186.

To charge one as acceptor of a bill of exchange, under the process prescribed, by which the State Bank takes summary judgment against its debtors, the record must show that positive proof was given that he accepted the bill. A default in this sort of cases is not an admission of the cause of action. Walker *v.* Bank of Alabama, 4 Stew. & P. 215.

To sustain a summary judgment of the State Bank for thirty per cent damages upon the dishonor of a bill of exchange, it must be shown by the record that it was purchased by the bank to make a remittance in payment of the state bonds. The statement of a fact from which such an inference might be drawn is not sufficient. Leigh *v.* State Bank, 10 Ala. 339. See, also, Riggs *v.* State Bank, 11 Ala. 182.

In a summary proceeding by a bank, the judgment entry, if the judgment is by default, must show a legal title in the bank to maintain the action; and if the note is described as payable to A. A., cashier, or bearer, the legal title will not be presumed to be in the bank, unless the judgment entry avers the note to have been indorsed by the bank, or avers that the note was payable to the bank by the name of A. A., cashier. McWalker *v.* Branch of State Bank, 3 Ala. 153; Huntington *v.* Branch of State Bank, 3 Ala. 186.

The judgment on a bank notice must disclose that the instrument sued on was negotiable and payable at the bank. Sayre *v.* Bank of Mobile, 9 Port. 423; Ford *v.* Bank of Mobile, 9 Port. 471.

To sustain a judgment by default on a motion by a bank, under Act 1837, p. 9, authorizing a joint judgment against all the parties liable on any bill or note to the state bank or any of its branches, the liability of the defendant must be shown by the judgment entry, as well as the notice and certificate which authorized the court to exercise the summary jurisdiction. Clements Hall, Gindrat & Steele *v.* Branch Bank at Montgomery, 1 Ala. 50.

Notice of a motion for judgment must be given under the corporate seal, and the record must show that the president's certificate was produced, and was under that seal; but it need not appear that the defendant was called before judgment. Logwood *v.* Huntsville Bank, Minor 23.

Where the judgment in a summary proceeding at the suit of a bank recites that a notice and certificate as to ownership were produced to the court, it will be intended that the notice and certificate found in the transcript were those on which the court acted. Jordan *v.* Branch Bank at Huntsville, 5 Ala. 284.

A judgment in a summary proceeding at the suit of a bank against the drawer of a bill of exchange is sufficiently certain when it recites that the bill was presented for payment at "maturity," without specifying the day. Crawford *v.* Branch Bank at Decatur, 6 Ala. 574.

In a proceeding by notice and motion, at the suit of a bank against its debtor, if no issue is made up, and a verdict is returned for the plaintiff, it is not necessary that the judgment should affirm with particularity the proof of every fact which was necessary to have authorized their verdict. It is enough if it distinctly sets forth the facts which are essential to the exercise of the summary jurisdiction. Riggs *v.* State Bank, 11 Ala. 183.

Notice as Part of Record.—In summary proceeding on a bank notice, the notice issued to defendant and attached to the transcript is not considered as part of the record, so as to show the bank entitled to recover judgment on motion. Levert *v.* Planters' & Merchants' Bank, 8 Port. 104.

Certificate as Part of Record.—In a summary proceeding on a bank notice, the certificate of the president of the bank, appended to a notice to defendant, attached to the transcript, is no part of the record, unless the court has acted on it. Bates *v.* Planters' & Merchants' Bank, 8 Port. 99. See, also, Curry *v.* Bank of Mobile, 8 Port. 360.

Judgment—Amendment.—In a summary proceeding by a bank against the indorsers of a note, the notice described the note as payable to J. C. W., by him indorsed to J. W. W., and by him indorsed to the bank. The judgment described the note as in the notice, except that it recited that it was indorsed to the bank by J. C. W. Held, that the misrecital was amendable by a referance to the notice. Jordan *v.* Branch Bank at Huntsville, 5 Ala. 285.

Where a judgment is rendered in favor of "The President of the Bank," etc., omitting the words "and Directors," which are a part of the corporate name, the omission is a mere clerical misprision, amendable at the costs of plaintiff in error. Snelgrove *v.* Branch Bank at Mobile, 5 Ala. 295.

§ 112 (13) Review on Appeal.

In a summary proceeding at the suit of a bank against its debtor, an appellate court will not look to the notice sent up with the record, for the purpose of contradicting the recital in the judgment, where there has been no contestation in the trial court. Snelgrove *v.* Branch Bank at Mobile, 5 Ala. 295.

Where the record in a suit by a bank against an indorser of a promissory note, by motion, recites that the certificate of W. R. H., its president, was produced that the debt was really and bona fide the property of the bank, and no objection was made in the court below to the testimony by which the fact that W. R. H. was the president was established, it will, on appeal, be held sufficient. Lester *v.* Bank of Mobile, 7 Ala. 490.

§ 113. Parties.

§ 114. —— In General.

See ante, "Parties," § 112 (2).

§ 115. —— Use of Name of Bank or Officer.

Use of Name of Bank.—The cases of McWalker *v.* Bank, 3 Ala. 153, and Smith *v.* Branch Bank, 5 Ala. 26, which decide that a bank can not maintain an action upon a note payable to its cashier, without showing an indorsement was determined by the primary courts, and the former in the supreme court previous to the passage of the act of December, 1841. The statute declares that all notes, etc., thus payable "may be sued and collected in the name of the several banks, in the same manner, as if they had been made payable directly to the said bank, or branch banks by which the paper has been taken or discounted." Clay's Dig. 112, § 47. In Crawford *v.* Branch Bank, 7 Ala. 383, it was held under the act cited that a note payable to "B. Gayle, Cashier," authorized the branch bank to sue thereon, and the inference was, that it had the legal title. Caldwell *v.* Bank, 11 Ala. 549, 551, See, also, the early case of Gazzam *v.* Bank, 1 Ala. 268, 270, where it was held that where a note was not payable to the bank, it could derive a legal title to the instrument, only by proof of an indorsement, and without such proof, it could maintain no action at law, in its own name, upon the note.

Since the act of 1841, a note payable to the cashier of a bank may be sued on in the name of the corporation. Caldwell *v.* Branch Bank at Mobile, 11 Ala. 549.

Act 1841 (Clay's Dig., p. 112, § 47), declaring that a note payable to the cashier of the State Bank or Branch Banks, may be sued on and collected as a note payable to the bank, applies to notes made since the passage of the act, as well as to those which had been executed at the time of its passage. Davis *v.* Branch Bank of Mobile, 12 Ala. 463.

An allegation in the declaration that the note sued on was payable to A., cashier, or bearer, in consideration thereof the defendant promised to pay the plaintiff, etc., is sufficient, upon demurrer, to show that the bank was entitled to maintain the action, under the statute of 1841. Erwin *v.* Branch Bank at Mobile, 14 Ala. 307.

A bank may, in its own name, recover on a note payable to "Andrew Armstrong, Cashier," on an averment that it was made to the corporation by that name and description. Smith *v.* Branch Bank of Mobile, 5 Ala. 26.

A bank may maintain an action in its own name upon a note given to its cashier, upon an averment that it was made to the corporation by that name. Smith *v.* Branch Bank of Mobile, 5 Ala. 26.

The State Bank may sue in its own name on a lease of its real estate, when, by the terms of the lease, the rent is reserved to it, although the demise is in the name of an assistant commissioner. Douglass *v.* Branch Bank at Mobile, 19 Ala. 659.

A bank may sue as payee on a note payable to its cashier, alleging either that the promise was made to the cashier for it, or that the cashier's name was used by adoption for that of the bank. Darby *v.* Berney Nat. Bank, 97 Ala. 643, 11 So. 881.

Use of Name of Holder of Legal Title.—Where the bank has not the legal title to a note, it may sue in the name of the person who has the legal title to its use. Moore *v.* Penn, 5 Ala. 135.

§ 116. Process and Appearance.

Service of Process.—An agent, appointed by the Bank of the State, or one of its branches, under the statute of 1843, to execute the process, is the sheriff of the bank, and is invested with the power and authority to perform the duties of his office by deputy. Draine *v.* Smelser, 15 Ala. 423. See ante, "Who May Give," § 112 (4).

§ 117. Attachment and Garnishment.

See, generally, the titles ATTACHMENT; GARNISHMENT.

Attachment.—Banks may proceed against a debtor by attachment. Planters' & Merchants' Bank *v.* Andrews, 8 Port. 404.

The right conferred on the Alabama banks to sue out attachment in the county of their location is a privilege conferred on them, and does not abridge the power they previously possessed of suing out attachments in the county of the residence of the defendant. Pearson *v.* Gayle, 11 Ala. 278.

Under Act 1840, § 1, authorizing the State Bank and its branches to take out attachments on the oath of an officer, etc., and § 2, providing that "said banks are hereby severally authorized to take out attachments according to the first section of this act, on the application of any indorser or surety to the bill, note or other demand, and on satisfactory showing of such indorser or security, on oath or otherwise, that either of the grounds specified in this act exists," an officer of the bank need not reaffirm the ground stated by an indorser or security; but, if the showing is satisfactory to the bank, and the oath is sufficient in form, and duly made, the bank may take out an attachment thereon, as provided in § 1. Faver *v.* State Bank, 10 Ala. 616.

Garnishment.—A bank may be garnished by a creditor of a depositor without first demanding payment, of the bank, of the depositor's debt. Birmingham Nat. Bank *v.* Mayer, 104 Ala. 634, 16 So. 520. See ante, "Certified Checks or Notes," § 70.

§ 118. Pleading.

Illegal Circulation of Notes.—In an action on a bill of exchange, brought by a corporation having power "to purchase, discount, and sell bills of exchange," and prohibited from making or issuing any bills, etc., to circulate as money, the plea alleged that plaintiff procured from a foreign bank a loan or deposit of a large amount of its notes for the unlawful purpose of putting said notes in circulation in this state, "under an express agreement that said bank should redeem said notes as the same shall be returned to the counter of said bank by which they were issued;" that plaintiff, with the bank notes thus obtained, "made discounts, purchased bills, and did other business pertaining to banking," and put said notes into circulation as money; that the bill of exchange sued on was made for the benefit of defendant, "and with intent to have the same discounted by plaintiff, either with said foreign bank bills or some other bank bills, as plaintiff might see fit and proper;" that it was presented at plaintiff's banking house for discount, "and was then and there discounted by plaintiff with said foreign bank bills;" that plaintiff, in thus using said foreign bank bills in the purchase and discount of said bill, "did emit and put them into circulation in this state;" and that this was the only consideration given by plaintiff for said bill of exchange. Held that, though Code, § 939, provides that no foreign corporation invested with the privilege of banking must exercise the same by agent in this state except by the exclusive use of gold or silver coin, etc., yet that the plea did not show any illegality of consideration for the contract by which plaintiff obtained the bill of exchange, the averments not being sufficient to show the existence of an agency between plaintiff and the foreign bank, within the meaning of said section, nor a violation of plaintiff's charter. Wray *v.* Tuskegee Ins. Co., 34 Ala. 58.

Plea of Estoppel.—Where, in an action against a bank on a cashier's check transferred to plaintiff, the bank pleaded plaintiff's fraud in procuring the check, replications not denying the fraud, nor confessing and avoiding the effect thereof, but alleging that after the check had been transferred to plaintiff he had, in consideration thereof, released the payees from their indebtedness to him and delivered up a note and mortgage securing the indebtedness, and that defendant's ashier procured from the payees of the check a note and mortgage to a partnership of which the cashier was a member to secure the loan made by the bank evidenced by the check, and that the bank was therefore estopped from setting up such fraud, or that, after discovering it, defendant had ratified the transaction, were insufficient and demurrable. Bank of Coffee Springs *v.* W. A. McGilvray & Co., 52 So. 473, 167 Ala. 408.

§ 119. Evidence.

Admissibility.—Where a bank does not hold the legal title to a note, and sues in the name of the person who has the legal title to its use, evidence that the bank has no interest in the note is not relevant unless offered as the foundation of a defense against the real owner. Moore *v.* Penn, 5 Ala. 135.

An indorsement on a note of the sum for which it was discounted, and the date of the discount, is an admission, on the part of the bank discounting, of the sum lent upon the note, of which the defendant may avail himself; as otherwise the inference would be that the bank was entitled to recover the entire amount. Colgin *v.* State Bank, 11 Ala. 222.

§ 120. Judgment.

See ante, "Record and Judgment," § 112 (12).

In a suit by the Bank of the State, or any of its branches, on a joint and several promissory note or bill of exchange, judgment may be rendered, under the statute of 1840, requiring all the parties to be sued in the same action, against any defendant whom the jury shall, by their verdict, find liable on it, although other defendants may make a successful defense, and defeat a recovery against them. Bussey *v.* Branch Bank at Montgomery, 15 Ala. 216.

§ 121. Costs.

Under the statute of February 13, 1843, the judge of the county court of Tuscaloosa was authorized to tax a fee of two dollars on bank suits, although no jury trial was had. Ex parte State Bank, 6 Ala. 498.

IV. NATIONAL BANKS.

§ 122. Nature and Status.

See ante, "Nature and Formation in General," § 6.

National banks are agents of the general government to aid in the administration of a branch of the public service, and are constitutionally authorized as a proper exercise of the incidental or implied powers of Congress. Tarrant *v.* Bessemer Nat. Bank (Ala.), 61 So. 47.

National banking corporations are agencies or instruments of the general government, designed to aid in the administration of an important branch of the public service, and are an appropriate constitutional means to that end. Pollard *v.* State, 65 Ala. 628.

§ 123. Power to Control and Regulate.

See ante, "Power to Control and Regulate," § 2.

It has often been held "that the national banks organized under the acts of congress are subject to state legislation, except where such legislation is in conflict with some act of congress, or where it tends to impair or destroy the utility of such banks as agents or instrumentalities of the United States, or interferes with the purposes of their creation." Winter *v.* Baldwin, 89 Ala. 483, 7 So. 734, 735.

§ 124. Organization and Corporate Existence.

It will be assumed that a bank entitling itself a "national bank" was duly organized as such. Slaughter *v.* First Nat. Bank, 109 Ala. 157, 19 So. 430.

A copy of the organization and certificate of a national bank, duly certified by the comptroller of currency of the United States, and authenticated by his official seal, and the deposition of the cashier of said bank, is sufficient evidence of its corporate existence. Hanover Nat. Bank *v.* Johnson, 90 Ala. 549, 8 So. 42.

§ 125. Rights and Liabilities of Stockholders in General.

Code 1886, § 1677, which provides that stockholders of all private corporations have the right to have access to, and inspection and examination of, the books, records, and papers of the corporation, at all reasonable and proper times, applies to national banks located within the state. Winter *v.* Baldwin, 89 Ala. 483, 7 So. 734.

The rights of stockholders conferred by the above statute are not curtailed by, nor is the statute in conflict with, Rev. St. U. S., §§ 5240, 5241, which provide that national banks are subject to examination by an officer appointed by the comptroller of the treasury for that purpose, and that they shall not be subject to visitorial powers other than those authorized by congress, or vested in the courts of justice. Winter *v.* Baldwin, 89 Ala. 483, 7 So. 734.

§ 126. Banking Powers.

"'A national bank can purchase notes and bills; rediscount notes or collateral security; borrow on its own notes; deal in national bonds; compromise a debt; pay money and take securities in settlement; receive special deposits, besides those usually received by banks; endorse and guarantee paper, and issue a certificate of deposit.' In that respect its powers seem to be as ample as other banks." First Nat. Bank *v.* Henry, 159 Ala. 367, 49 So. 97, 100.

§ 127. Effect of Acts Ultra Vires.

A national bank can not escape liability to a depositor for money which he placed in its hands by pleading that it made with him an ultra vires agreement to pay out the money to some third person on deposit of collaterals for his benefit, when the evidence shows it paid out the money without taking the collaterals agreed on. First Nat. Bank *v.* Henry, 49 So. 97, 159 Ala. 367.

§ 128. Collections.

An officer of a national bank has no authority to agree to receive anything but money in payment of a nonnegotiable note indorsed to it. First Nat. Bank *v.* Alexander, 44 So. 866, 152 Ala. 585.

Where a bank to which a forged check has been forwarded for collection credits the person sending it with the amount thereof, without actually remitting the money, it may, on discovering the forgery, charge back such amount to such person. Birmingham Nat. Bank *v.* Bradley, 103 Ala. 109, 15 So. 440.

§ 129. Interest or Rate of Discount, and Usury.

See ante, "Interest or Rate of Discount, and Usury," § 95.

What Law Governs.—A state law imposing a penalty on banks exacting usurious discounts does not apply to national banks, the penalty imposed on such banks by federal laws in regard to usurious discounts being exclusive. Florence R. R. & Imp. Co. *v.* Chase Nat. Bank, 106 Ala. 364, 17 So. 720, cited on this point in note in 56 L. R. A. 676, 677.

Code 1886, § 4140, making it a misdemeanor for any banker to discount commercial paper at a higher rate than 8 per cent per annum, does not apply to national banks. Slaughter *v.* First Nat. Bank, 109 Ala. 157, 19 So. 430, cited on this point in note in 56 L. R. A. 676, 680, 700.

Penalty.—It is only where usurious interest has been actually paid a national bank that a remedy by a suit to recover twice the amount so paid is afforded by Rev. St. U. S., § 5198 (U. S. Comp. St. 1901, p. 3493), so that where usury has been charged, but not paid, the penalty, to wit, forfeiture of the entire interest, is the same under both such section and Code 1907, § 4623. First Nat. Bank *v.* Clark, 49 So. 807, 161 Ala. 497.

Application of Usury to Principal.—Usurious interest paid can not be set off against the principal in an action by the creditor to recover the balance of the loan. Or as stated in another case: "Usurious interest paid a national bank on renewing a series of notes can not, in an action by the bank on the last of them, be applied in satisfaction of the principal of the debt." First Nat. Bank *v.* Denson, 115 Ala. 650, 22 So. 518, 524, cited on this point in note in 56 L. R. A. 681, 702, 706.

§ 130. Actions by or against National Banking Associations.

§ 131. —— Parties.

See ante, "Use of Name of Bank or Officer," § 115.

A mortgage given to the cashier of a bank as security for a loan made by the bank may be enforced by suit in the name of the bank, without assignment or indorsement; and a suit to foreclose such a mortgage can not be maintained by the cashier alone, but the bank should be joined with him as a necessary party. Moore *v.* Pope, 97 Ala. 462, 11 So. 840.

§ 132. —— Attachment and Garnishment.

See ante, "Attachment and Garnishment," § 117.

Application of State Laws.—"Section 5242, Rev. St. U. S. (U. S. Comp. St. 1901, p. 3517), among other things provides: 'No attachment, injunction or execution, shall be issued against such association (national banks) or its property before final judgment in any suit, action or proceeding, in any state, county or municipal court.' Whatever opinion a state court might entertain as to a correct construction of this provision of the statute of the United States, is immaterial, since these courts are bound by the construction placed upon the act by the supreme court of the United States. That court, in the case of Pacific N. Bank *v.* Mixter, 124 U. S. 721, 8 Sup. Ct. 718, 31 L. Ed. 567, has plainly and pointedly construed the act to be 'a prohibition upon all attachments against national banks under the authority of the state courts.' Chief Justice Waite, delivering the opinion for the court says: 'It stands now, as it did originally, as the permanent law of the land, that attachments shall not issue from state courts against national banks, and writes into all state attachment laws an exception in favor of national banks. Since the act of 1873, all the attachment laws of the state must be read as if they contain a provision in express terms that they were not to apply to suits against a national bank. * * * In our opinion the effect of the act of congress is to deny the state remedy altogether, so far as suits against national banks are concerned, and in this way it operates as well on the courts of the United States as on those of the states. Although the provision was evidently made to secure equality among the general creditors in the division of the proceeds of the property of an insolvent bank, its operation is by no means confined to cases of actual or contemplated insolvency. The remedy is taken away altogether and can not be used under any circumstances. So it is held, that the state courts are without jurisdiction to entertain such a case.'" Merchants' Laclede Nat. Bank *v.* Troy Grocery Co., 144 Ala. 605, 39 So. 476.

Under Rev. St. U. S. § 5242 [U. S. Comp. St. 1901, p. 3517], providing that no attachment shall be issued against a national bank or its property before final judgment in any suit in any state court, a state court has no jurisdiction of an attachment against a national bank before final judgment, even by consent of the parties or by waiver of the want of it. Merchants' Laclede Nat. Bank *v.* Troy Grocery Co., 39 So. 476, 144 Ala. 605.

See, however, the earlier case of First Nat. Bank *v.* Colby, 46 Ala. 435, where it was held that the property of a national bank is subject to attachment issued by a state court and that an action in attachment against a national bank is to be conducted and governed by the laws of the state applicable to attachment suits against natural persons.

Dismissal of Attachment.—The attachment of the property of a national bank in an action against it will not be dissolved, dismissed, or abated, or the levy quashed, because the bank had committed an act of insolvency before the institution of the suit, and its charter had afterwards been dissolved and its franchises forfeited by decree of the federal court, and a receiver properly appointed to take charge of its assets under the act of congress. First Nat. Bank *v.* Colby, 46 Ala. 435.

§ 133. Transfers and Preferences Affected by Insolvency.

Notes given in renewal of other notes held by a national bank, the original notes not being returned to the maker, are not "evidences of debt," or "assets," within Rev. St. U. S., § 5242, declaring void all transfers of "evidences of debt" owing to any national bank made after insolvency or in contemplation thereof, to prevent the application of the assets to the bank, as required by law, or with a view to prefer creditors. First Nat. Bank *v.* Johnston, 97 Ala. 655, 11 So. 690, cited on this point in note in 25 L. R. A. 547.

"By its terms it operates only upon notes, and other evidences of debt, owing to any national bank, and which are assets of such bank. Preferential transfers of such notes, only, are avoided by this statute. Transfers by the bank of notes and other evidences of debt in its possession, which are not part of its assets, but the property of another, are not within the letter of influence of this statute, and the validity of such transfers must be determined independently of its provisions." First Nat. Bank *v.* Johnston, 97 Ala. 655, 11 So. 690, 691. See ante, "Notice of Officer or Agent," § 49.

V. LOAN, TRUST, AND INVESTMENT COMPANIES.

§ 134. Officers and Agents.

Notice.—Where the cashier and bookkeeper of a trust company assisted in the hypothecation of certain shares of its stock to a bank as security for a loan made by the bank to one of its stockholders, and had full knowledge that such stock had been so pledged, such knowledge is the knowledge of the company, and it can not thereafter refuse to transfer the stock to the bank on the nonpayment of the loan on the ground that it had a lien on the stock for an indebtedness to it, created subsequent to the pledge, and this although such indebtedness was created after the cashier's death by officers having no knowledge of the loan by the bank. Birmingham Trust & Savings Co. *v.* Louisiana Nat. Bank, 99 Ala. 379, 13 So. 112, 20 L. R. A. 600.

The cashier is the executive officer, held out to the public as having authority to act according to the general usage, practice, and course of business of such institutions; and his acts and dealings within the scope of such usage, practice, and course of business bind the corporation in favor of those dealing with him, not having other knowledge. Notice received, or knowledge acquired by him, while engaged in the transaction of business according to such usage and practice, is substantially notice to and the knowledge of the corporation. Birmingham Trust, etc., Co. *v.* Louisiana Nat. Bank, 99 Ala. 379, 13 So. 112, 114.

Barbers.

See the titles HEALTH; LICENSES.

Barns.

See the title NUISANCE.

Barratry.

See the titles CHAMPERTY AND MAINTENANCE; INSURANCE.

Barriers.

See the title HIGHWAYS.

Barter.

See the title EXCHANGE OF PROPERTY.

Base Fee.

See the titles DEEDS; ESTATES; WILLS.

BASTARDS.

Cross References.

See the titles DESCENT AND DISTRIBUTION; GUARDIAN AND WARD; HUSBAND AND WIFE; INCEST; INFANTS; MARRIAGE; SEDUCTION.

I. ILLEGITIMACY IN GENERAL.

§ 1. Who Are Illegitimate.

"Illegitimate children, commonly called bastards, are those persons who are begotten and born out of lawful wedlock. 2 Kent's Com., 4th Ed. 208." Lingen *v.* Lingen, 45 Ala. 410, 413, cited in note in 65 L. R. A. 178, 180, 183.

§ 2. Evidence.

As to evidence in a prosecution under bastardy laws, see post, "Evidence," § 37, et seq.

§ 3. —— Presumption of Legitimacy.

If filiation is established, the law raises a presumption of legitimacy. Lay *v.* Fuller (Ala.), 59 So. 609; Weatherford *v.* Weatherford, 20 Ala. 548.

Failure of Presumption.—When the evidence, by which filiation is established, also proves illegitimacy, the presumption of legitimacy fails. Weatherford *v.* Weatherford, 20 Ala. 548.

§ 4. —— Burden of Proof.

The burden of proof is on the one asserting illegitimacy. Lay *v.* Fuller (Ala.), 59 So. 609.

When filiation is once established, the law raises the presumption of legitimacy, and the burden of proof is cast upon those who assert the illegitimacy. Weatherford *v.* Weatherford, 20 Ala. 548.

§ 5. —— Admissibility.

General Reputation. — General reputation and common report in the neighborhood is admissible to prove legitimacy. Lay *v.* Fuller (Ala.), 59 So. 609.

Facts Showing Impossibility of Mother's Husband Being Father.—Finally, the simple rule has been recognized that a child is a bastard, though born, or begotten and born, during marriage, when it is impossible that its mother's husband could have been its father; and that every species of legal evidence tending to this conclusion is admissible on the trial of the issue as to its legitimacy. Bullock *v.* Knox, 96 Ala. 195, 11 So. 339, 340, cited in note in 36 L. R. A., N. S., 262.

Same—That Child, of White Woman with White Husband, Is Mulatto.—On the question of the legitimacy of a child born during the wedlock and cohabitation of its mother with her husband, they both being white persons, evidence that the child is a mulatto, and that, in the course of nature, a white man and woman can not procreate a mulatto, is admissible. Bullock *v.* Knox, 96 Ala. 195, 11 So. 339.

§ 6. —— Sufficiency.

In ejectment, where the legitimacy of plaintiff was in issue, evidence held to conclusively establish legitimacy. Lay *v.* Fuller (Ala.), 59 So. 609.

Filiation.—Filiation may be established at common law, by a satisfactory combination of facts, indicating the connection of parent and child between an individual and the family to which he claims to belong; and the principal of these facts are that he has always borne the name of the person whom he claims as his father; that the father has treated him as his child, and in that character has provided for his education, his maintenance, and his establishment; that he has been uniformly received as such in society; and that he has been acknowledged as such by the family. Weatherford *v.* Weatherford, 20 Ala. 548.

Rebuttal of Presumption of Legitimacy.—"The modern authorities sustain the propositions that the presumption of legitimacy from the birth of a child during marriage may be rebutted by evidence which clearly and conclusively shows that the procreation by the husband was impossible; and that it is competent to show that, according to the course of nature, the husband could not be the father of the child." Bullock *v.* Knox, 96 Ala. 195, 11 So. 339, 340.

§ 7. Legitimation.

§ 8. —— Legislative Act.

"Blackstone says, 'a bastard may be made legitimate and capable of inheriting, by the transcendent power of an act of parliament, and not otherwise, as was done in the case of John of Gant's bastard children by a statute of Richard the Second.' Wendell's Blackstone, 459." Lingen *v.* Lingen, 45 Ala. 410, 414.

§ 9. —— Marriage of Parents.

"The marriage of the mother and reputed father of a bastard child renders it legitimate, if recognized by the father as his child." Marriage, however, without recognition, is not sufficient. Section 5199. Lingen *v.* Lingen, 45 Ala. 410, 414; McBride *v.* Sullivan, 155 Ala. 166, 45 So. 902.

Statutory Provisions.—"'Where a man having by a woman a child, or children, shall afterwards intermarry with such woman, such child or children, if recognized by him, shall be thereby legitimated.' Clay's Dig. 168, § 3." Hunter *v.* Whitworth, 9 Ala. 965, 968.

"The act of 1811, 'concerning bastardy,' provides, that if the mother of a bastard child and the imputed father shall, at any time after its birth, intermarry, the child shall in all respects be deemed and held legitimate, conformably to the maxim of the civil law. Clay's Dig. 134, § 6. See, also, Croke on Illegitimacy, 95." Hunter *v.* Whitworth, 9 Ala. 965, 968.

§ 10. —— Recognition or Acknowledgment.

"The father of a bastard child may legitimate it, and render it capable of inheriting his estate, by making a declaration in writing, attested by two witnesses, setting forth the name of the child proposed to be legitimated, its sex, its supposed age, and the name of the mother; and that he thereby recognizes it as his child and capable of inheriting his estate, real and personal, as if born in wedlock; the declaration being acknowledged by the maker, before the probate judge of the county of his residence, or its execution proved by the attesting witnesses, filed in the office of the probate judge, and recorded on the minutes of its court, has the effect to legitimate such child." Lingen *v.* Lingen, 45 Ala. 410, 415.

Sufficiency of Recognition When Parents Marry.—The object of Code 1896, § 364, providing that the marriage of the mother and "reputed" father of a bastard renders it legitimate, if recognized by the father as his child, is to enable parents by marrying to clothe their offspring with legitimacy, and a publication before marriage of the parentage of the child is not required, but if the child is regarded by the parents themselves as their child, either before or after marriage, it is legitimate; the use of the word "reputed" being intended merely to dispense with absolute proof of paternity. McBride *v.* Sullivan, 155 Ala. 166, 45 So. 902.

II. CUSTODY, SUPPORT, AND PROTECTION.

§ 11. Duty to Support.

In the absence of statutory regulations, the father is under no legal obligation to support his illegitimate child. The statute prescribes the only legal mode by which this support can be obtained. Simmons *v.* Bull, 21 Ala. 501.

The father's duty of maintenance, under the statute, continues for a period of ten years, which, in no case, we apprehend, is to extend beyond the time of the child's minority, or legal infancy. Washington *v.* Hunter, 67 Ala. 81, 83.

III. PROCEEDINGS UNDER BASTARDY LAWS.

§ 12. Nature and Form of Remedy.

As to bastardy proceedings not misdemeanor under statute of limitations, see post, "Limitations," § 24.

Proceedings under the statute in a bastardy case are sui generis. State *v.* Hunter, 67 Ala. 81; Dorgan *v.* State, 72 Ala. 173.

"A proceeding under the statutes to compel a putative father to the support and education of a bastard child, during the helplessness of mere infancy, has some of the characteristics of a civil action and of a criminal prosecution. It is commenced by a complaint on oath, on which a warrant of arrest issues in the name of the state. A preliminary examination is had before a justice of the peace of the county in which the woman is pregnant or delivered of the child, and if sufficient evidence appears, the accused is recognized to appear at the next term of the circuit court. If he fails to enter into the recognizance with sufficient sureties, he is held in custody. Entering into the recognizance and failing to appear in obedience to it, a forfeiture is incurred, and a writ of arrest issues against him, as in criminal cases on indictment. On his appearance in the circuit court, an issue is made up to which he and the state are the parties, to ascertain whether he is the real father of the child. If this issue is found against him, judgment is rendered against him for the costs, and he is required to give bond and security payable to the state, conditioned for the payment annually, for the period of ten years, of such sums not exceeding fifty dollars a year, as the court may prescribe, for the support and education of the child. Failing to give the bond, the court renders a judgment against him of necessity, in the name of the state, for such sum as at legal interest will produce the sum he is required to pay yearly, and 'he must also be sentenced to imprisonment for one year, unless in the meantime he execute the bond required, or pay the judgment and costs.' R. C., §§ 4396-4406. The proceeding is certainly penal in its character, if not strictly criminal. On the trial in the circuit court the accuser and accused are alike competent witnesses. It can be commenced only on the complaint of the mother. No indictment or presentment by a grand jury is necessary to support it. It abates on the death of the child, and the marriage of the mother and putative father vacates the proceeding, though it has progressed to final judgment. It is a penal proceeding, intended to relieve the state from the duty of maintaining the illegitimate child, rather than to inflict punishment for the violation of law. It is founded on the hypothesis, that it is a duty due to society from the putative father to maintain and educate his illegitimate child, and the purpose is to compel performance of this duty. Judge of County Court *v.* Kerr, 17 Ala. 328; Satterwhite *v.* State, 28 Ala. 65." Paulk *v.* State, 52 Ala. 427, 428, cited in Dorgan *v.* State, 72 Ala. 173, 174.

Bastardy Proceedings Quasi Criminal.—A bastardy proceeding under the statute is penal, but is strictly neither criminal nor civil, partaking, as it does, somewhat of the nature of both. Dorgan *v.* State, 72 Ala. 173, cited in Collins *v.* State, 78 Ala. 433, 434; Shows *v.* Solomon, 91 Ala. 390, 391, 8 So. 713; Ex parte Charleston, 107 Ala. 688, 690, 18 So. 224; Smith *v.* State, 73 Ala. 11; Washington *v.* Hunter, 67 Ala. 81; Miller *v.* State, 110 Ala. 69, 20 So. 392; Judge of County Court *v.* Kerr, 17 Ala. 328; Satterwhite *v.* State, 28 Ala. 65; Paulk *v.* State, 52 Ala. 427.

"Proceedings in bastardy are said to be quasi criminal, but they are not strictly so. In their nature they partake somewhat of the qualities of a civil suit, and, to some extent, of a criminal prosecution. Washington *v.* Hunter, 67 Ala. 81; Smith *v.* State, 73 Ala. 11." Shows *v.* Solomon, 91 Ala. 390, 8 So. 713.

Not Public Offense.—"While a proceeding in a case of bastardy partakes of the nature of both a criminal prosecution and a civil suit, and is regarded as quasi criminal, bastardy is not a public offense, as public offenses are defined and classified by the statutes. Washington *v.* Hunter, 67 Ala. 81; Smith *v.* State, 73 Ala. 11; Satterwhite *v.* State, 28 Ala. 65." Collins *v.* State, 78 Ala. 433, 434.

Assignment of Error Not Dispensed with.—A proceeding in bastardy is not a criminal case, within Cr. Code 1886, § 4509, which dispenses with an assignment of errors in criminal cases taken to the supreme court by writ of error or appeal. Williams *v.* State, 117 Ala. 199, 23 So. 42.

Number of Challenges Allowed Defendant.—The statute does not prescribe the number of peremptory challenges to which the defendant shall be entitled in bastardy proceedings, and he can not complain that he was allowed only four challenges, as in civil cases, instead of six, as in criminal cases. Dorgan *v.* State, 72 Ala. 173.

Comment on Defendant's Failure to Testify.—A bastardy proceeding, though penal in character, is not a criminal prosecution, within Code, § 4473, forbidding counsel to comment on defendant's failure to testify in his own behalf. Miller *v.* State, 110 Ala. 69, 20 So. 392.

§ 13. Grounds of Proceeding in General.

Maintenance and education of illegitimate offspring, born or to be born, are the purpose and policy of bastardy proceedings. Shows *v.* Solomon, 91 Ala. 390, 8 So. 713.

Bastardy proceedings are chiefly intended for the public indemnity, and to coerce the putative father to support and maintain the unfortunate child. 2 Kent's Com., p. 215. Washington *v.* Hunter, 67 Ala. 81, 83.

§ 14. Bar or Abatement of Proceeding in General.

As to nonappearance not a ground for suspending action, see post, "Appearance by Defendant," § 30.

§ 15. —— Effect of Previous Proceedings.

The acquittal or discharge by a justice of the peace of one charged with bastardy does not bar a subsequent prosecution on the same charge, as a justice has no jurisdiction to try such charge. Nicholson *v.* State, 72 Ala. 176, cited in note in 1 L. R. A., N. S., 470.

§ 16. —— Settlement or Release Pending Proceedings.

See post, "Dismissal before Trial," § 47.

A bona fide compromise by the mother of a bastard, after she has commenced proceedings against the putative father, is a bar to the further maintenance of the prosecution. Martin *v.* State, 62 Ala. 119.

Validity of the Settlement.—A release given by the mother of a bastard, while under age, is not binding, and, if afterwards repudiated by her, can not be insisted on in bar of her rights. Wilson *v.* Judge of County Court, 18 Ala. 757.

A plea to a promissory note that it was made on Sunday, in order to procure the discharge of the principal maker, who had been arrested on the same day, upon a charge of bastardy, is good; and a replication that the makers, with a knowledge of the facts alleged, "did ratify and acknowledge the note," and then "promise to pay the same," is not a sufficient answer to the plea. Shippey *v.* Eastwood, 9 Ala. 198.

Validity of Note Given in Settlement.—Dismissing or ceasing to prosecute a compliant of bastardy is a good consideration for a note from the father to the mother of the bastard. Robinson *v.* Crenshaw, 2 Stew. & P. 276; Ashburne *v.* Gibson, 9 Port. 549; Merritt *v.* Flemming, 42 Ala. 234.

A promissory note executed by one, in compromise of proceedings against him, for bastardy, is valid. The fact that the note was made payable to the mother of the plaintiff in the bastardy proceeding, and the offspring of the illicit intercourse, comes into the world, stillborn, after the compromise has been affected, can not defeat a recovery on such a note. Merritt *v.* Flemming, 42 Ala. 234.

Must Be Pleaded.—After the jury has been impaneled to try the question of paternity, the court, on the production of a release from the mother of the bastard, is not bound, on the motion of the defendant, to dismiss the proceeding, but may refuse to do so, and, in that event, the defendant, if he wishes to insist on it, should plead the release in bar, and request of the court appropriate charges to the jury. Wilson *v.* Judge of County Court, 18 Ala. 757, cited in Frank *v.* State, 40 Ala. 13; Martin *v.* State, 62 Ala. 119, 121.

§ 17. —— Defects in Proceedings.

Where defendant in bastardy, on being bound over by a justice to the city court, appears for trial, the proceedings will not be quashed because of any defect in the bond. Williams *v.* State, 21 So. 463, 113 Ala. 58.

In a bastardy proceeding instituted by a complaint before a notary public having the jurisdiction of a justice of the peace which reached the circuit court, there was no error in requiring defendant, who was personally present, to join in the issue required to be formed, though the warrant under which he was arrested had been stricken from the files. Douglass *v.* State, 23 So. 142, 117 Ala. 185.

§ 18. —— Intermarriage of Prosecutrix and Defendant.

The marriage of the mother and putative father vacates the bastardy proceeding, though it has progressed to final judgment. Paulk *v.* State, 52 Ala. 427, 428.

§ 19. —— Marriage of Prosecutrix to Third Person.

As to right of married woman to maintain proceedings, see post, "Who May Maintain Proceedings," § 21.

The marriage of the relator in an information for bastardy after the information will not abate the proceedings in a prosecution for bastardy; nor will a marriage in fact be inferred when the relator is afterwards called by another name, as late of the name set out in the information. Austin *v.* Pickett, 9 Ala. 102.

§ 20. —— Death of Child.

Upon the death of the illegitimate child pending a proceeding in bastardy, the defendant has no right to demand from the court a dismissal of the proceeding. After issue joined it would be matter for a plea puis darrein continuance. Satterwhite *v.* State, 32 Ala. 578.

In a bastardy proceeding, it need not appear of record that the bastard was born alive, and is still living. Trawick *v.* Davis, 4 Ala. 328.

§ 21. Who May Maintain Proceedings.

Parties on appeal, see post, "Appeal," § 62.

As to marriage to third person as bar to proceedings, see ante, "Marriage of Prosecutrix to Third Person," § 19.

The infancy of the mother in bastardy proceedings does not render it necessary that she prosecute such proceeding by next friend, although costs may be adjudged against her if the verdict is for the defendant. Hanna *v.* State, 60 Ala. 100; Miller *v.* State, 110 Ala. 69, 20 So. 392.

Married Women.—A married woman can not prefer a complaint, under the statute, against the alleged father of a bastard, of which she has been delivered. Judge of County Ct. of Limestone *v.* Kerr, 17 Ala. 328, cited in Paulk *v.* State, 52 Ala. 427, 429; State *v.* Hunter, 67 Ala. 81, 82.

§ 22. Jurisdiction.

Justice of the Peace.—The jurisdiction of a justice of the peace upon a proceeding in bastardy depends upon the existence of the following facts: First, that a woman should make a complaint on oath to him, accusing a particular person of being the father of a bastard child, with which she is pregnant, or of which she has been delivered; second, that the woman making the complaint is a single woman; third, that she is so pregnant, or has been so delivered, in the county in which the justice acts as justice. But if the complaint, does not assert their existence, and he is satisfied by other evidence, he should recite their existence in his warrant, in order that his jurisdiction may appear upon the face of his proceedings. Williams *v.* State, 29 Ala. 9; Collins *v.* State, 78 Ala. 433, 434.

Notary Public.—A notary public, with ex officio powers of a justice of the peace, has the same jurisdiction in bastardy proceedings as a justice of the peace. Bell *v.* State, 27 So. 414, 124 Ala. 94.

Under Cr. Code 1886, §§ 4842-4851, providing for the institution of proceedings in bastardy before a justice of the peace, such proceedings were legally instituted where the complaint was made before a notary public appointed by the governor, under authority of Const., art. 6, § 26, empowering him to "appoint one notary public for each election precinct in counties, and one for each ward in cities, * * * who, in addition to the powers of notary, shall have and exercise the same jurisdiction as justices of the peace." Douglass *v.* State, 23 So. 142, 117 Ala. 185.

City Court.—A city court has jurisdiction to try bastardy proceedings arising within its territorial jurisdiction. Williams *v.* State, 21 So. 463, 113 Ala. 58.

Circuit Court.—In bastardy proceedings, that the bond given by defendant for his appearance before the circuit court was defective does not affect the jurisdiction of the circuit court to try the case. Walker *v.* State, 108 Ala. 56, 19 So. 353.

Probate Court.—In proceedings under the bastardy act, the court of probate has but a limited jurisdiction, to be exercised in a special manner; and this jurisdiction attaches when a party is bound to appear before it, on the charge of being the father of a bastard child, at its session next after the bond is taken; but it has no power to take cognizance and proceed ex parte with a cause brought before it in a different manner. Seale *v.* McClanahan, 21 Ala. 345.

When Too Late to Object to Jurisdiction.—Where the defendant in a bastardy proceeding appears before the county court, pleads guilty to the accusation, and acknowledges himself to be the father of the child, and, in pursuance of the judgment rendered, executes a bond, which recites that the mother is a single woman, and was delivered of the child in the county wherein the proceedings were had, the jurisdiction of the court is sufficiently shown, and it is then too late to object to defects in the original complaint, or in the process of the justice of the peace. Pruitt *v.* Judge of County Court, 16 Ala. 705.

§ 23. Venue.

In bastardy proceedings authorized by Code 1886, § 4842, "when any single woman, pregnant with, or delivered of, a bastard child, makes complaint, on oath, to any justice of the county where she is so pregnant or delivered," etc., no jurisdiction is given where prosecutrix was delivered of the child in another county than that in which the proceeding is instituted, and prior thereto. State *v.* Woodson, 99 Ala. 201, 13 So. 580.

It is clear that the bastardy charges must be preferred in the county in which the mother resides, if made before the birth of the child, or if after, then in the county in which the child was born. Clay's Dig. 133; Wilson *v.* Judge of County Court, 18 Ala. 757, 759; Pruitt *v.* Judge of County Court, 16 Ala. 705.

§ 24. Limitations.

Formerly it was held that there was no statute of limitation in this state, which would bar a proceeding under the statute to charge the reputed father of a bastard child with its support, unless, in analogy to the doctrine of prescription, it would be barred by presumption, after a period of twenty years from the birth of the child. State *v.* Hunter, 67 Ala. 81. Now, however, the law is different. Under the Code of 1886, § 4848, it is declared that "no proceeding shall be instituted under this chapter after the lapse of one year from the birth of the child, unless the defendant has, in meanwhile, acknowledged or supported the child." State *v.* Woodson, 99 Ala. 201, 13 So. 580, 581.

A proceeding to charge a person as the reputed father of a bastard child is not a misdemeanor, within the statutes, so as to be barred within "twelve months after the commission of the offense," under section 4644 of the Code. State *v.* Hunter, 67 Ala. 81.

§ 25. Preliminary Proceedings.

§ 26. —— In General.

Notice.—When a party is bound to appear before the court of probate on the charge of being the father of a bastard child, no further notice to him is required. Seale *v.* McClanahan, 21 Ala. 345.

§ 27. —— Complaint or Affidavit.

As to failure of record to show that prosecutrix was a single woman—Effect on appeal, see post, "Appeal," § 62.

As to effect on appeal of affidavit failing to show prosecutrix was single, see post, "Appeal," § 62.

A proceeding under the statutes to compel a putative father to support and educate a bastard child, during the helplessness of mere infancy, is commenced by a complaint on oath, on which the warrant of arrest issues in the name of the state. Paulk *v.* State, 52 Ala. 427, 428.

Allegations of an affidavit that prosecutrix was a single woman and in a pregnant condition, that defendant was the cause of her pregnancy, and that he did impregnate her, sufficiently charged that defendant was the father of the unborn child, within Code 1896, § 4381. Allred *v.* State, 44 So. 60, 151 Ala. 125.

Allegations of an affidavit that prosecutrix was a single woman and in a pregnant condition, that defendant was the cause of her pregnancy, and that he did impregnate her, were equivalent to an averment that she was pregnant with a bastard child, within Code 1896, § 4381, providing that, when any single woman pregnant with a bastard child makes complaint to a justice accusing any one of being the father, the justice must issue a warrant against such person, etc. Allred *v.* State, 151 Ala. 125, 44 So. 60.

When Affidavit May Not Be Objected to.—One charged with bastardy, and bound over by a justice to a court of jurisdiction to determine the case, may not object to the sufficiency of the affidavit, when his objections are raised for the first time in such court. State *v.* Rowell, 4 Ala. App. 207, 58 So. 1007.

Failure to Allege That Prosecutrix Was Single.—The affidavit in bastardy proceedings before a justice which fails to state that the prosecutrix was a single woman is not subject to demurrer on appeal to the circuit court, as the affidavit is in no sense pleading. Smith *v.* State, 73 Ala. 11, cited in Walker *v.* State, 108 Ala. 56, 19 So. 353; Laney *v.* State, 109 Ala. 34, 19 So. 531.

In bastardy proceedings, that the affidavit of prosecutrix before the justice is defective, for failure to allege that she is a single woman and resident of the county, does not deprive the circuit court of jurisdiction, but it may allow the prosecuting attorney to file an unsworn complaint setting up these facts, no objection having been made to the affidavit before the justice. Walker *v.* State, 108 Ala. 56, 19 So. 353.

Complaint May Be Oral.—Proceedings in bastardy are statutory, and must originate before a justice of the peace, on the complaint of a single woman that she is pregnant with, or has been delivered of, a bastard child, in the county in which the complaint is made and must accuse a particular person of being the father of such child. The complaint before the justice is not required to be in writing. It may be oral or written. It serves all the purposes intended if it induces the issue of process for the arrest of the defendant. Laney *v.* State, 109 Ala. 34, 19 So. 531, 532; Pruitt *v.* Judge of County Court, 16 Ala. 705; Smith *v.*

State, 73 Ala. 11; Austin *v.* Pickett, 9 Ala. 102.

§ 28. —— Examination of Complainant.

A preliminary examination is held before a justice of the peace of the county in which the woman is pregnant or delivered of the child. Paulk *v.* State, 52 Ala. 427, 428.

§ 29. —— Warrant or Other Process.

As to failure of warrant to show that prosecutrix was single—Effect on appeal, see post, "Appeal," § 62.

A warrant of arrest issued by a justice of the peace under Code, § 4071, for bastardy, reciting merely that the offense of bastardy has been committed, and that B. is guilty thereof, is void, and will not support the proceeding. Collins *v.* State, 78 Ala. 433, cited in Walker *v.* State, 108 Ala. 56, 19 So. 353.

A recital by the justice in his warrant that the mother is a single woman, and is pregnant, or has been delivered in the county where the justice acts, must be taken as evidence that he did determine the existence of such facts, and, in the absence of any evidence showing it to be erroneous, is certainly conclusive between the parties. Williams *v.* State, 29 Ala. 9, cited in Collins *v.* State, 78 Ala. 433.

§ 30. —— Appearance by Defendant.

Defendant's Appearance Not Indispensable.—The appearance of the reputed father in a bastardy proceeding is not indispensable to authorize the court to determine the question of filiation. Trawick *v.* Davis, 4 Ala. 328, cited in Yarborough *v.* Judge of County Court, 15 Ala. 556, 558.

The court may investigate the charge and render judgment against defendant in his absence; his nonappearance furnishes no reason for suspending or thwarting the action of the court. Seale *v.* McClanahan, 21 Ala. 345.

When Proceedings Are Defective.—If the proceedings before a justice of the peace in a case of bastardy are defective, the defendant should move the county court to quash them before he appears, and thus impliedly admits himself regularly in court. Trawick *v.* Davis, 4 Ala. 328.

Where the putative father of a bastard appears, and submits, without objecting, to a trial in the county court on the merits, it is too late to object to the regularity of the recognizance taken by the justice. Wilson *v.* Judge of County Court, 18 Ala. 757.

Where there is a mittimus showing the commitment of a party upon a prosecution for bastardy, and subsequently a petition for a habeas corpus, and a recognizance executed in due form by the reputed father, a motion to quash the proceedings before the justice will not be maintained by the county court on the ground that there is no warrant in the papers showing the arrest; all the papers reciting that the proceedings before the examining justices were regular. The warrant might be substituted by another, conforming to it as nearly as practicable; or if it was shown that no warrant ever issued, or its production was necessary, the court might protect the party by making a suitable order. Berryman *v.* Judge of County Court, 9 Ala. 455.

§ 31. —— Record and Return to Higher Court.

Section 3801 of the Code requires the justice to return the bond and complaint to the clerk of the circuit court by the first day of the term at which the accused is bound to appear; and the warrant also may be returned when it is expressly referred to in the bond, and recites the existence of those jurisdictional facts which are by law referred to his determination. Williams *v.* State, 29 Ala. 9, cited in Collins *v.* State, 78 Ala. 433.

§ 32. Security for Appearance.

As to bond for appearance pending appeal, see post, "Appeal," § 62.

If sufficient evidence appears, the accused is recognized to appear at the next term of the circuit court. If he fails to enter into recognizance with sufficient sureties, he is held in custody. Entering into recognizance and failing to appear in obedience to it, a forfeiture is incurred, and a writ of arrest issues against him, as in a criminal case on indictment. Paulk *v.* State, 52 Ala. 427, 428.

"A party charged with bastardy, may

be arrested, and carried before a justice of the peace, and if, on examination, it appear there is probable cause for believing him to be guilty, he must be required to give bond for his appearance at the next term of the circuit court, and in default of giving bond and surety required, he must be committed to jail. The duty of the justice in such a case, as it is in many offenses with which parties are charged before him, is purely preliminary. Imprisonment follows, in default of a bond, in the same way, just as surely and effectually as in a purely criminal case, and it may be as unlawful in the one as the other. Collins *v.* State, 78 Ala. 433, 434; Smith *v.* State, 73 Ala. 11." Ex parte Charleston, 107 Ala. 688, 18 So. 224, 225.

A bond conditioned for one's appearance "to answer to a prosecution and complaint in bastardy" held to be sufficient, on having served its purpose; the affidavit and warrant returned therewith showing to what case the bond referred. Hanna *v.* State, 60 Ala. 100.

The statute of December 20, 1824, requiring an assignment of breaches in an action on a bond, does not apply to a bond given by defendant in bastardy to appear and answer the charge. Lake *v.* Governor, 2 Stew. 395.

Effect of Continuance.—If a proceeding under the bastardy act was continued by the defendant at the first term to which he was bound to appear, the county court had jurisdiction to compel him to enter into recognizance for his personal appearance from term to term, and for his good behavior; and, if the recognizance contained any superadded condition, it was void only as to that condition, and valid as to the remaining obligations. State *v.* Castleberry, 23 Ala. 85, cited in Ellis *v.* Smith, 42 Ala. 353.

The bond entered into to answer to a charge of bastardy, is binding upon the obligors until the case is disposed. of, though it may be continued for several terms. Be this as it may, the continuance of the case on the defendant's affidavit will keep it in court as to him. Trawick *v.* Davis, 4 Ala. 328.

Failure to Appear When Not Convicted.—On a bond given by defendant to appear he is liable on failure to appear, though he was not convicted. Lake *v.* Governor, 2 Stew. 395.

Disposition of Proceeds of Forfeited Bond.—Money collected on a forfeited bail bond given by defendant in bastardy proceedings as required by Code, §§ 4844, 4849, can not be held as a part of the fine and forfeiture fund where it does not appear whether or not a trial was had, or the hild is living, or the parents intermarried, or any part of the money had been paid to the child, or whether a bond has been given, under Code, § 4854, for the support of the child. Shows *v.* Solomon, 91 Ala. 390, 8 So. 713.

Effect of Bond Not Conforming with Statute.—If the bond does not conform to the statute in requiring the defendant to appear at "the next term" after it is taken, it is void, and the proceedings dependent on it are coram non judice. Seale *v.* McClanahan, 21 Ala. 345.

To Whom Payable.—The bond given by the defendant for his appearance in a bastardy proceeding should be made payable to the governor. Lake *v.* Governor, 2 Stew. 395; Trawick *v.* Davis, 4 Ala. 328; Chaudron *v.* Fitzpatrick, 19 Ala. 649.

§ 33. Pleading and Indictment.

§ 34. —— Indictment.

No indictment or presentment by the grand jury is necessary to support bastardy proceedings. Paulk *v.* State, 52 Ala. 427, 428.

In an information for bastardy, the recital in the caption that the relator is a single woman is sufficient. Austin *v.* Pickett, 9 Ala. 102, cited in Dorgan *v.* State, 72 Ala. 173, 176.

§ 35. —— Amendment.

As to amendment of judgment, see post, "Award for Support and Expenses," § 56.

A complaint averring, in the words of the statute, that the prosecutrix "was pregnant with or delivered of a bastard child," though not objectionable, may be amended by striking out the words "or delivered of." Miller *v.* State, 110 Ala. 69, 20 So. 392.

§ 36. —— Issues, Proof, and Variance.

Evidence that prosecutrix was delivered of a child before the trial was admissible, though the complaint merely averred pregnancy. Miller *v.* State, 110 Ala. 69, 20 So. 392.

§ 37. Evidence.

As to the establishment of illegitimacy, see ante, "Evidence," § 2, et seq.

§ 38. —— Presumptions and Burden of Proof.

In bastardy, the evidence must reasonably satisfy the jury of the guilt of accused, and to this extent the burden of proof is on the prosecution. White *v.* State, 170 Ala. 229, 54 So. 430.

§ 39. —— Admissibility in General.

Offer to Compromise.—The fact that the putative father of a bastard child compromised, or offered to compromise, the charge against him without any admisson of its truth, can not be given in evidence in a subsequent proceeding in bastardy, to prove him to have been the father. Martin *v.* State, 62 Ala. 119.

Same—Offer to Marry Prosecutrix.—On a trial for bastardy, testimony that, after defendant was arrested, he promised to marry prosecutrix, was not inadmissible on the ground that it was on offer to compromise the suit; it not appearing that the promise was accompanied with the requirement that the prosecution should be abandoned. Laney *v.* State, 109 Ala. 34, 19 So. 531.

Letters.—A letter from defendant to prosecutrix, admitted to be genuine by defendant, and tending to show affection and intimacy between them, is admissible. Williams *v.* State, 113 Ala. 58, 21 So. 463.

Same—Letters from Prosecutrix to Defendant.—Letters written by prosecutrix in a bastardy proceeding to defendant, indicating a fondness of prosecutrix for defendant, were properly excluded as immaterial, where defendant denied having had intercourse with prosecutrix near the period of gestation, and letters were not written during that period. Allred *v.* State, 151 Ala. 125, 44 So. 60.

Same—Contents of Destroyed Letter from Defendant to Prosecutrix.—In a prosecution for bastardy it was competent for the state to prove the contents of a letter written to prosecutrix by defendant in which he advised her how to procure an abortion, though the letter itself had been destroyed by her. Miller *v.* State, 110 Ala. 69, 20 So. 392.

Defendant's Offer to Procure Miscarriage.—On trial for bastardy, where defendant denied the intercourse at the time alleged, but admitted subsequent intercourse and opportunities for intercourse at the time alleged, it was proper to admit evidence that during the pregnancy of prosecutrix he offered to pay for a miscarriage, though he professed that his offer was made in the interest of a third person. Nicholson *v.* State, 72 Ala. 176.

§ 40. —— Testimony of Prosecutrix.

Formerly, it was held that the mother of a bastard child was a competent witness only to prove the paternity of the child, for she is clearly interested under the Alabama statutes in the prosecution, and can only be examined touching the question of the child's paternity. Clay's Dig. 134, § 2. Wilson *v.* Judge of County Court, 18 Ala. 757, 759. But by a later decision it is held that the mother of the alleged bastard is made a competent witness by the statute (Code, § 6375), and her competency is not affected by the death of the child before the trial. Satterwhite *v.* State, 32 Ala. 578.

On the trial in the circuit court the accuser and the accused are alike competent witnesses. Paulk *v.* State, 52 Ala. 427, 428.

Where the mother, being made a witness by the statute (Code, § 6375), is examined on the trial, her testimony must be weighed by the jury like that of other witnesses. Satterwhite *v.* State, 28 Ala. 65, cited in Washington *v.* Hunter, 67 Ala. 81, 82; Dorgan *v.* State, 72 Ala. 173, 174.

§ 41. —— Character and Conduct of Prosecutrix.

Character for Truth and Veracity.—The fact that witnesses in bastardy proceedings give evidence of unchaste acts of prosecutrix, in contradiction to her testimony on that issue, does not render evidence as to her character for truth and veracity admissible where no predicate has been laid for its admission; such evidence for defendant being defensive and not impeaching evidence. Bell *v.* State, 124 Ala. 94, 27 So. 414.

In a bastardy proceeding, where the prosecutrix, after having testified to the material facts charged, further testified, on cross-examination, that, covering the time inquired about with reference to the defendant, she had been visited by and associated with other men, and, further, that she had stated on preliminary trial before the justice of the peace that she "had never kept company with any other young man but the defendant," and there was other evidence introduced by the defendant showing that the prosecutrix was visited by and associated with other men than the defendant, it is competent for the state, in rebuttal, to support her credibility, to introduce evidence of the prosecutrix's general good character, and of her good character for truth and veracity; such attempt to impeach her supplying the predicate for rebutting character evidence. Lusk *v.* State, 129 Ala. 1, 30 So. 33.

The attempt to impeach prosecutrix supplied the predicate for rebutting character evidence, which was lacking in the case of Bell *v.* State, 124 Ala. 94, 27 So. 414, and in other cases of that line of authority; and the evidence was properly admitted on the principles recognized in those cases. Lusk *v.* State, 129 Ala. 1, 30 So. 33, 34.

Associates.—Evidence that prosecutrix was at one time seen to associate with another person, who had previously given birth to an illegitimate child, was properly excluded as irrelevant. Miller *v.* State, 110 Ala. 69, 20 So. 392.

Where the state, on a prosecution for bastardy, had proved the defendant's association with the prosecutrix about the time of probable conception, it was error to exclude evidence offered by the defendant that prosecutrix had also associated with other men during that period, and that she was in the company of another man, under circumstances affording opportunity for sexual intercourse, about that time. Kelly *v.* State, 133 Ala. 195, 32 So. 56.

On a trial for bastardy, evidence as to whether another was going with prosecutrix at a time not within the period of gestation was properly excluded, as being immaterial. Allred *v.* State, 151 Ala. 125, 44 So. 60.

Intercourse by Prosecutrix with Third Persons.—On a trial for bastardy, defendant may show that prosecutrix had intercourse with others than defendant within the period of gestation. Allred *v.* State, 151 Ala. 125, 44 So. 60.

On denial by prosecutrix of intercourse with others named, at certain times and places, the time being within the period of gestation, such intercourse may be proved as a fact. Williams *v.* State, 113 Ala. 58, 21 So. 463.

Evidence to contradict the statement of prosecutrix in a bastardy proceeding that she had never had intercourse with witness, or any other man than defendant, as to acts of intercourse outside the period of gestation, was inadmissible. Allred *v.* State, 151 Ala. 125, 44 So. 60.

§ 42. —— Admissions and Declarations of Defendant.

Where the officer who arrested defendant under warrants charging bastardy and seduction told him that the girl's father spoke of killing defendant, the latter's statement that "he did not know that he could blame him" was admissible against him in the bastardy trial. Miller *v.* State, 110 Ala. 69, 20 So. 392.

§ 43. —— Intimacy and Illicit Intercourse.

As to admissibility of letters, see ante, "Admissibility in General," § 39.

Evidence that the prosecutrix was on one occasion seen alone with defendant was admissible for what it was worth. Miller *v.* State, 110 Ala. 69, 20 So. 392.

Instruction.—In a bastardy proceeding, where it was shown the bastard child was born December 20, 1899, and there was evidence on the part of the state that the defendant had been criminally intimate with the prosecutrix many times between November, 1898, and April 23, 1899, and the defendant testified that he had no criminal relations with prosecutrix from January 4, 1899, to April 23, 1899, a charge is erroneous, and properly refused, which instructs the jury that "the fact that the defendant had sexual intercourse with the prosecutrix on and before January 4, 1899, and on April 23, 1899, is not sufficient to convict the defendant; and, if the state has not reasonably satisfied you that the defendant had sexual intercourse with prosecutrix between these dates, you should acquit the defendant." Lusk *v.* State, 129 Ala. 1, 30 So. 33.

In a bastardy proceeding, where criminally intimate relations are shown to have existed between defendant and the prosecutrix, a charge is properly refused, as being a mere argument, which instructs the jury that "the fact that the defendant had sexual intercourse with the prosecutrix makes no difference if the defendant is not the father of the child." Lusk *v.* State, 129 Ala. 1, 30 So. 33.

§ 44. —— Resemblance of Child to Defendant.

On a prosecution for bastardy, it was proper to permit the bastard child to be introduced in evidence by the state, for the purpose of showing the likeness of the child to the defendant. Kelly *v.* State, 133 Ala. 195, 32 So. 56.

The issue being as to the paternity of the bastard child, the defendant may prove that the child bears no likeness to him, or that it resembles another man, who had opportunities of illicit intercourse with the mother; but proof that the child resembled the children of another man, without showing in what particular, or that such children resembled their father rather than their mother, is too vague and indefinite, and is properly excluded. Paulk *v.* State, 52 Ala. 427.

§ 45. —— Degree of Proof.

In bastardy proceedings it is not required that the evidence shall satisfy the jury to a moral certainty or beyond a reasonable doubt that defendant is the father of the child. A reasonable certainty only is required. Bell *v.* State, 124 Ala. 94, 27 So. 414; Miller *v.* State, 110 Ala. 69, 20 So. 392.

It is not required that the evidence should place the defendant's guilt beyond a reasonable doubt, before authorizing a conviction in bastardy proceedings. Satterwhite *v.* State, 28 Ala. 65; Washington *v.* Hunter, 67 Ala. 81; cited in Bell *v.* State, 124 Ala. 94, 27 So. 414.

If, upon the whole evidence in a bastardy trial, defendant's guilt is doubtful or uncertain, or he can not be reasonably said to be guilty, he must be acquitted. Allred *v.* State, 151 Ala. 125, 44 So. 60.

Instructions as to Degree of Proof.—It is not error to refuse to instruct the jury, at the request, of the defendant in proceedings under bastardy laws "that they ought to acquit, unless the proof showed beyond a reasonable doubt that he was guilty;" but it is erroneous to instruct them, "that, if the state produced a preponderance of evidence, they might upon such preponderance of proof find the defendant guilty." Satterwhite *v.* State, 28 Ala. 65, cited in Paulk *v.* State, 52 Ala. 427, 429; Dorgan *v.* State, 72 Ala. 173, 174; Collins *v.* State, 78 Ala. 433, 434.

In a bastardy proceeding, a charge which instructs the jury that, if they "reasonably believe the weight of the evidence is on the side of the state, and that the defendant is the father of the child, they should find that the defendant is the father of the child," is free from error, and properly given at the request of the state. Lusk *v.* State, 129 Ala. 1, 30 So. 33.

In such a case, a charge which instructs the jury that "the burden is on the state to convince you that the defendant is the father of the child, and if, on considering the whole of the testimony, you are not satisfied of this fact, you should return a verdict for the defendant," is erroneous, and properly refused, in that it exacts too high a degree of conviction on the part of the jury. Lusk *v.* State, 129 Ala. 1, 30 So. 33.

§ 46. —— Sufficiency.

An instruction that the mere fact that prosecutrix comes into court, and testifies as to her pregnancy, of itself was a fact which the jury should consider in determining whether she was pregnant, is erroneous. Williams *v.* State, 113 Ala. 58, 21 So. 463.

Intercourse Must Be Proved.—A defendant in a bastardy proceeding can not be convicted unless intercourse with prosecutrix be shown within the period of gestation. Allred *v.* State, 151 Ala. 125, 44 So. 60.

§ 47. Dismissal before Trial.

See ante, "Settlement or Release Pending Proceedings," § 16.

The law is settled in this state, that the mother of a bastard, after she has instituted proceedings against the putative father can compromise the cause and dismiss the prosecution. Wilson *v.* Judge of County Court, 18 Ala. 757, 758; Martin *v.* State, 62 Ala. 119.

§ 48. Trial.

§ 49. —— Conduct in General.

Under the statute providing that the judge shall submit the issue to the jury whether the defendant is the father of "the bastard child," the court submitted as an issue whether the defendant was the father "of the said child." On defendant's being obliged to plead over, he pleaded not guilty. The verdict followed the language of the issue submitted. Held, that the plea and verdict should be referred to the complaint, and the irregular issue disregarded. Austin *v.* Pickett, 9 Ala. 102, cited in Dorgan *v.* State, 72 Ala. 173; Smith *v.* State, 73 Ala. 11; L ney *v.* State, 109 Ala. 34, 19 So. 531.

§ 50. —— Questions for Jury.

Under the act of 1811, as modified by the act of 1816, the question of paternity need not be presented to the jury, unless the reputed father demand it. Trawick *v.* Davis, 4 Ala. 328, cited in Berryman *v.* Judge of County Court, 9 Ala. 455.

As to instructions as to degree of proof, see ante, "Degree of Proof," § 45.

§ 51. —— Instructions.

It is proper to refuse a charge in bastardy proceedings that in weighing the credibility of the prosecutrix the jury are restricted to "her testimony and all the evidence tending to contradict her," since such excludes testimony tending to corroborate her. Miller *v.* State, 110 Ala. 69, 20 So. 392.

A charge that the testimony of the prosecutrix, "who is shown to be unworthy of credit," must be corroborated, etc., was properly refused as containing an unwarranted assumption. Miller *v.* State, 110 Ala. 69, 20 So. 392.

A charge that if defendant's failure to testify was because of the pendency of an indictment for seduction against him, and not because of a consciousness that he was the father of the child, it could not be considered as a circumstance against him, was properly refused. Miller *v.* State, 110 Ala. 69, 20 So. 392.

A charge that if the prosecutrix on a former occasion made a sworn statement inconsistent with her present testimony, and inconsistent with defendant's guilt, and the jury are unable to find to a reasonable certainty which of said statements is correct, their verdict should be for defendant, is properly refused, as it takes from the jury the consideration of all evidence save that of the prosecutrix. Miller *v.* State, 110 Ala. 69, 20 So. 392.

On trial for bastardy it was proper to refuse an instruction that, where one witness swears to a fact, and another witness swears to its nonexistence, the fact is not proved unless there is other satisfactory proof of it, which, standing alone, would be sufficient to establish the probability of its truth. Dorgan *v.* State, 72 Ala. 173.

Argumentative Instructions — Examples of.—An instruction in a bastardy proceeding that, if the jury believe the defendant has a good moral character, they may look to such facts and circumstances, whether testimony is sufficiently reasonable to satisfy them that defendant is the father of the child, is objectionable as being involved and argumentative. Bell *v.* State, 27 So. 414, 124 Ala. 94.

A charge that defendant was not called upon to explain the suspicious circumstances against him was properly refused as argumentative. Miller *v.* State, 110 Ala. 69, 20 So. 392.

§ 52. —— Verdict or Findings.

A verdict which affirms that defendant is the real father of the bastard child of the woman by whom he was charged is sufficient. Berryman *v.* Judge of County Court, 9 Ala. 455, cited in Quinn *v.* State, 121 Ala. 39, 25 So. 694.

§ 53. Judgment or Order.

§ 54. —— In General.

A judgment in a bastardy suit, by which the defendant is condemned to pay the sum of $50 a year, for 10 years, towards the maintenance and education of the bastard child, and that he enter into bond and security for the due and faithful payment of the said sums of money, as by statute required, is regular. Austin *v.* Pickett, 9 Ala. 102, cited in Yarborough *v.* Judge of County Court, 15 Ala. 556; Seale *v.* McClanahan, 21 Ala. 345; Quinn *v.* State, 121 Ala. 39, 25 So. 694.

Providing for Issue of Execution in Default of Payment of Sums Adjudged.—Notwithstanding a different remedy is provided by statute, a direction, in a judgment against the father of a bastard child, that an execution issue thereon for each default in the payment of the sums adjudged to be paid, is regular. Trawick *v.* Davis, 4 Ala. 328, cited in Yarborough *v.* Judge of County Court, 15 Ala. 556; State *v.* McClanahan, 21 Ala. 345.

In Whose Favor Judgment Rendered.—A judgment rendered by the court of probate under the bastardy act, though not in favor of any person by name as plaintiff, is nevertheless sufficient, since the statute points out with certainty who is the plaintiff. Seale *v.* McClanahan, 21 Ala. 345.

The bond consequent upon the judgment in bastardy proceedings is required to be payable to the county court; and this, in the absence of more explicit legislation on the point, may serve to show that the judgment should be considered to be in favor of the judge of that court, as the representative of the county. Yarborough *v.* Judge of County Court, 15 Ala. 556, 557; Trawick *v.* Davis, 4 Ala. 328; Austin *v.* Pickett, 9 Ala. 102.

§ 55. —— Rendition and Entry.

Where entries by the trial judge on his docket show that in bastardy proceedings the jury rendered a verdict for the state, and the court fixed the amount to be contributed by defendant to the bastard's support at a certain sum, judgment may be entered thereon nunc pro tunc at a subsequent term. Kuehlthan *v.* State, 92 Ala. 91, 9 So. 394.

The proceedings before the justice against the putative father of a bastard are a part of the record of the cause, and if, from them, the facts necessary to sustain the jurisdiction of the county court appear, it will be sufficient, notwithstanding the judgment entry may fail to disclose them. Wilson *v.* Judge of County Court, 18 Ala. 757.

A judgment in a bastardy proceeding will not be reversed because the judgment entry omits to state in whose favor the judgment is rendered. The statute determines with unerring certainty who is the plaintiff. Yarborough *v.* Judge of County Court, 15 Ala. 556, cited in Seale *v.* McClanahan, 21 Ala. 345.

In Vacation.—A probate judge has no jurisdiction, except when sitting as a court in term time, to take a confession of judgment from the defendant in a bastardy proceeding. Such a judgment, in vacation therefore, is coram non judice, and void. Moore *v.* McGuire, 26 Ala. 461.

§ 56. —— Award for Support and Expenses.

If defendant is found to be the father, judgment is rendered against him for the costs, and he is required to give bond and security payable to the state, conditioned for the payment annually, for the period of ten years, of such sums not exceeding fifty dollars a year, as the court may prescribe, for the support and education of the child. Paulk *v.* State, 52 Ala. 427, 428.

A judgment in favor of the prosecutrix in bastardy proceeding "for her costs in this behalf expended," and requiring the defendant to enter into bond "conditioned that he pay to the judge of probate fifty dollars on the 1st day of January in each year for the term of ten years," etc., is materially different from a judgment requiring him to enter into bond "conditioned to pay fifty dollars a year for the period of ten years, on the first Monday in January in each year," etc. Williams *v.* State, 26 Ala. 85, cited in Satterwhite *v.* State, 28 Ala. 65.

A judgment which condemns the defendant to the payment of the sum prescribed by law as a consequence of the paternity, and directs a bond to be executed with surety for the annual payment of the sum adjudged, though not entirely formal, will be sustained. Berryman *v.* Judge of County Court, 9 Ala. 455; Quinn *v.* State, 121 Ala. 39, 25 So. 694.

A judgment against the father of a bastard that he pay "the sum of forty dollars annually, for ten years, to wit, forty dollars now, and forty dollars every year for ten years afterwards," is erroneous; but, as the judgment shows upon its face that the defendant was condemned to pay "forty dollars annually, for ten years," the latter portion of the judgment entry must be treated as a clerical misprision, and here amended. (Parsons, J., dissenting, thought the judgment was not amendable, and should be reversed. Wilson *v.* Judge of County Court, 18 Ala. 757, cited in Quinn *v.* State, 121 Ala. 39, 25 So. 694.

Must Go to Support of Child.—The money required to be paid by one found to be the father of a bastard must go to the maintenance and education of the child, and no part can be paid to the informer. Bell *v.* State, 124 Ala. 94, 27 So. 414.

Period Bastard to Be Supported.—The correct construction of the bastardy act is not that the father shall be compelled to support the child until it arrives at the age of ten years, but for ten years from the judgment of condemnation. Pruitt *v.* Judge of County Court, 16 Ala. 705, cited in Washington *v.* Hunter, 67 Ala. 81.

Amendment of Judgment.—In a proceeding in bastardy, judgment was entered against the defendant, and a motion was subsequently made to amend the judgment nunc pro tunc, so as to require the annual payments to be made on "the first Monday in January," as the statute requires, instead of "the first day of January." Held, that there was no error in allowing the judgment to be amended. Williams *v.* State, 29 Ala. 9, cited in Moore *v.* Leseur, 33 Ala 243.

§ 57. Enforcement of Order for Support.

§ 58. —— In General.

A judgment that the "defendant pay not exceeding $50," sustained by no evidence of a bond except the clerk's testimony that none could be found in his office, but that the defendant's sureties said they had executed one, was held not to authorize an execution. Isaacs *v.* Judge of County Court, 5 Stew. & P. 402.

§ 59. —— Requiring Security.

Under Code, §§ 4396, 4397, providing that a defendant convicted of bastardy, and sentenced for failure to give a bond for support may procure a discharge by paying costs and giving such bond, to be approved by the court, where a proper bond is offered for approval it is the judge's duty to approve it, though defendant is not entitled to a discharge until he pays the costs. Bell *v.* State, 124 Ala. 77, 27 So. 271.

§ 60. —— Imprisonment.

Failing to give bond, the court renders judgment against defendant in bastardy proceedings of necessity, in the name of the state, for such sums as at legal interest produce the sum he is required to pay yearly, and "he must also be sentenced to imprisonment for one year, unless in the meantime he execute the bond required, or pay the judgment and costs." Paulk *v.* State, 52 Ala. 427, 428.

The sections of the Revised Code which require the imprisonment of the putative father in bastardy proceedings, if he fail to give bond for the support of the child, are not violative of the constitutional inhibition against imprisonment for debt. Paulk *v.* State, 52 Ala. 427.

Where a defendant in a bastardy proceeding is in custody when a judgment is rendered against him, it is not erroneous for the court to order that he remain in custody until he gives the bond required by the statute. Yarborough *v.* Judge of County Court, 15 Ala. 556.

§ 61. Review of Proceedings.

§ 62. —— Appeal.

Bastardy proceedings should not be scanned with two much strictness, but it should be rather intended, where the reverse is not shown, that everything material was proved in the county court. Trawick *v.* Davis, 4 Ala. 328, 332, cited in Austin *v.* Pickett, 9 Ala. 102, 104.

"Proceedings in bastardy are statutory, and to them the statutes which give a writ of error or appeal in criminal cases do not extend. The statute prescribing the course of proceeding confers on either party (the state or the defendant) the right of appeal, if taken within thirty days after judgment, and either party must give security for the costs of appeal. Cr. Code 1886, § 4866." Williams *v.* State, 117 Ala. 199, 23 So. 42, 43.

Where there is no record evidence of a motion in bastardy proceedings in a justice court, and the evidence in the circuit court as to the fact of such motion having been made is conflicting, the finding of the court on the question will not be disturbed. Bell *v.* State, 124 Ala. 94, 27 So. 414.

Appearance Bond Awaiting Appeal.—Since there is no statute allowing an appearance bond to await a decision on appeal from a judgment in bastardy proceedings, the offer of such bond, with security for costs on appeal, does not entitle defendant to a discharge from custody, which he could procure under Code, §§ 4396, 4397, by giving bond for support and paying costs. Bell *v.* State, 124 Ala. 77, 27 So. 271.

Security for Costs.—From a judgment of the circuit court, in a proceeding under the bastardy act, an appeal may be taken by merely giving security for costs —either a bond or an acknowledgment in writing. Satterwhite *v.* State, 28 Ala. 65, cited in Dunham *v.* Hatcher, 31 Ala. 487; Marshall *v.* Croom, 50 Ala. 479; Williams *v.* State, 117 Ala. 199, 23 So. 42.

Failure of Record to Show That Prosecutrix Was Single Woman.—Where a complaint for bastardy alleges that prosecutrix was a single woman, and the jury finds that defendant was the father of the child, a conviction will not be reversed because the record fails to show affirmatively that prosecutrix was a single woman. Dorgan *v.* State, 72 Ala. 173.

Failure of Affidavit and Warrant to Show That Prosecutrix Was Single.—Objection that the affidavit and warrant in a bastardy proceeding before a justice does not aver that the prosecutrix was unmarried can not be made for the first time on appeal to the circuit court. Smith *v.* State, 73 Ala. 11, cited in Walker *v.* State, 108 Ala. 56, 19 So. 353; Laney *v.* State, 109 Ala. 34, 19 So. 531.

Parties on Appeal.—In a writ of error by the putative father of a bastard child and his surety on the order of the county court requiring him to give bond and security, the judge of the county court, and not the mother of the child, should be made defendant. Brown *v.* McLane, Minor 208.

On error by the reputed father, the mother of a bastard child should not be made a party to a writ of error in a bastardy proceeding. The judge of the county court, being considered the legal plaintiff, is the proper party in the writ of error. Trawick *v.* Davis, 4 Ala. 328.

§ 63. Costs.

As to bond for costs on appeal, see ante, "Appeal," § 62.

The woman making the complaint in a case of bastardy, if she fail to make it good is made liable for costs. Clay's D. 134, § 5. Berryman *v.* Judge of County Court, 9 Ala. 455, 459.

A party on whom the paternity of a bastard child is established by judgment is liable to pay costs. Berryman *v.* Judge of County Court, 9 Ala. 455.

IV. PROPERTY.

§ 64. Statutory Provisions.

Code 1907, §§ 3760, 3761, relating to inheritance of bastards, are a part of the statutes of descent and distribution, and should be construed in pari materia. Foster *v.* Lee, 172 Ala. 32, 55 So. 125.

§ 65. Inheritance by Bastards.

§ 16. —— In General.

The word "children," as used in Code 1907, § 3754, prescribing the descent and distribution of real and personal property, means legitimate children only having inheritable blood. Williams *v.* Witherspoon, 171 Ala. 559, 55 So. 132.

§ 67. —— From or Through Father.

Bastards have no inheritable blood, and are incapable of inheriting as heirs of their putative fathers. 2 Kent's Com., 4th Ed. 212. Lingen *v.* Lingen, 45 Ala. 410, 413.

A bastard born in France and legitimated there, can not inherit the estate of his father in Alabama; nor can he inherit his personal property, if his father, at the time of his death, was domiciled in this state. Lingen *v.* Lingen, 45 Ala. 410.

§ 68. —— From or Through Mother.

"By the laws of this state, a bastard may inherit from his mother, but not from his father. Rev. Code, § 1894." Lingen *v.* Lingen, 45 Ala. 410, 414.

Mississippi Law.—Under the Mississippi statute regulating the descent and distribution of the estates of intestates, an illegitimate child takes equally with legitimate children in the estate of their deceased mother. Alexander *v.* Alexander, 31 Ala. 241.

§ 69. Inheritance from or Through Bastards.

At Common Law.—At common law, bastards could have no heirs except the heirs of their own bodies. 2 Kent's Com., 4th Ed. 212; Lingen *v.* Lingen, 45 Ala. 410.

"Blackstone, speaking of the incapacity of bastards, says: 'The incapacity of a bastard consists principally in this, that he can not be heir to any one, neither can he have heirs, but of his own body; for, being nullius fillius, he is therefore of heir to nobody, and has no ancestor from whom any inheritable blood can be derived. 1 Wendell's Blackstone, 459.'" Lingen *v.* Lingen, 45 Ala. 410, 413.

Under Statute.—Under Code 1907, § 3760, providing that every illegitimate child shall be the heir of his mother, and may inherit her estate in whole or in part as if born in wedlock, and section 3761, providing that the mother or kindred of an illegitimate child by the mother are, in default of children of such illegitimate child or their descendants, entitled to inherit his estate, bastards are legitimated for the purpose of heirship and succession, so that the legitimate children and grandchildren of a bastard can inherit from his mother as he could have done had he survived her. Foster *v.* Lee, 172 Ala. 32, 55 So. 125.

Code, § 1460, provides that the mother or kindred of an illegitimate child on the part of the mother, in default of children of such illegitimate child or their descendants, is entitled to inherit his estate. Id. c. 35, art. 1, provides that, on the death of an intestate leaving a parent or parents, his property shall descend to the parents in equal portions, but, in case only one parent survives, then he or she shall be entitled to one-half, and the other half shall descend to the brothers and sisters of the deceased. Held that, on the death of an illegitimate child intestate, the mother is entitled to one-half of the estate, and the remainder should be divided among the half-brothers and sisters of the decedent. Ward *v.* Mathews, 122 Ala. 188, 25 So. 50.

A bastard died seised of land, without issue, leaving a bastard half-brother and their mother surviving him. Code 1886, § 1922, provides that "the mother, or kindred of an illegitimate child on the part of the mother, are, in default of children of such illegitimate child, or their descendants, entitled to inherit his estate." Held, that the statute must be construed with others in pari materia, and the established rules of descent; and the half-brother will take to the exclusion of the mother. Butler *v.* Elyton Land Co., 84 Ala. 384, 4 So. 675.

Bastard Offsprings of Same Mother.—One illegitimate child can inherit from another of the same mother. Butler *v.* Elyton Land Co., 84 Ala. 384, 4 So. 675.

§ 70. Effect of Recognition, Acknowledgment, or Legitimation.

Under Rev. Code, §§ 2404, 2405, regulating the legitimation of bastards, a child of parents never married, legitimated by the laws of a foreign country, can not inherit real estate in Alabama. The fact that the child was begotten in Alabama can not alter the case. Lingen *v.* Lingen, 45 Ala. 410.

Battery.

See the title ASSAULT AND BATTERY.

Bawdy House.

See the titles DISORDERLY HOUSE; NUISANCE.

Bearing Arms.

See the title WEAPONS.

Beasts.

See the title ANIMALS.

Beer.

See the title INTOXICATING LIQUORS.

Bench Warrant.

See the titles CONTEMPT; CRIMINAL LAW; WITNESSES.

BENEFICIAL ASSOCIATIONS.

Cross References.

See, generally, the titles ASSOCIATIONS; BUILDING AND LOAN ASSOCIATIONS; CORPORATIONS; INSURANCE; RELIGIOUS SOCIETIES.

As to the authority of a grand lodge of free-masons to lend money, see the title ASSOCIATIONS. As to an action to determine the right to the proceeds of a policy of insurance by a fraternal order, see the title INSURANCE.

§ 1. Nature and Status in General.

Where the members of a beneficial association create a fund for their own benefit by mutual contributions, equity has no jurisdiction over such association and fund on the ground of partnership, since the members inter se are not partners. Burke *v.* Roper, 79 Ala. 138.

§ 2. Name.

The corporate name of the "Grand Lodge" being, "Most Worshipful Grand Lodge of Ancient Free Masons of Alabama and its Masonic Jurisdiction," it was held that a charter granted by the "Grand Lodge of the State of Alabama" to a lodge, authorizing their organization by the name of Yorkville Lodge, No. 131, was properly issued, and that the charter was admissible in evidence. Burdine *v.* Grand Lodge, 37 Ala. 478.

§ 3. Powers of Societies in General.

Execution of Promissory Note in Consideration of a Loan.—Where the charter of a beneficial association does not authorize it to loan money, a promissory note made to it in consideration of a loan is void. Grand Lodge of Alabama *v.* Waddill, 36 Ala. 313.

§ 4. Superior, Subordinate, and Affiliated Bodies.

A corporation whose name is the "Most Worshipful Grand Lodge of Ancient Freemasons of Alabama and its Masonic Jurisdiction" is sufficiently identified by the name of the "Grand Lodge of the State of Alabama," as given in a charter which it issued for the formation of a subordinate lodge. Burdine *v.* Grand Lodge of Alabama, 37 Ala. 478. See McWalker *v.* Branch of the Bank, 3 Ala. 153; Crawford *v.* Planters', etc., Bank, 4 Ala. 313; Smith *v.* Branch Bank, 5 Ala. 26; Hancock *v.* Branch of the Bank, 5 Ala. 440; Snelgrove *v.* Branch Bank, 5 Ala. 295; Crawford *v.* Branch Bank, 7 Ala. 383; Caldwell *v.* Branch of the Bank, 11 Ala. 549; Davis *v.* Branch Bank, 12 Ala. 463; Smith *v.*

Tallassee, etc., Plank Road Co., 30 Ala. 663.

§ 5. Property and Funds.

Jurisdiction of Court of Equity.—The jurisdiction of equity over beneficial associations and their funds is based on the trust nature of the fund, the charitable uses for which it is designed, and the inadequacy of legal remedies. Burke *v.* Roper, 79 Ala. 138.

Decree of Distribution—When Granted.—On a bill in equity for the distribution of the funds of a relief association among the members, a decree of distribution will not be granted unless it clearly appears that the operations of the association have entirely ceased, and its objects been abandoned. Roper *v.* Burke, 83 Ala. 193, 3 So. 439.

§ 6. Dissolution.

When the operation of a voluntary association has been discontinued, its objects and purposes have been abandoned by common consent, a court of equity has jurisdiction to decree a dissolution, and to distribute the common fund among the several contributors in proportion to the amount contributed or paid by them respectively. Burke *v.* Roper, 79 Ala. 138.

Beneficiaries.

See the titles CHARITIES; INSURANCE; POWERS; TRUSTS.

Benefits.

As to effect of acceptance of benefits, see the titles APPEAL AND ERROR; CORPORATIONS; ESTOPPEL; PRINCIPAL AND AGENT. As to resulting benefits and deductions from compensation or damages, see the titles DAMAGES; EMINENT DOMAIN; MUNICIPAL CORPORATIONS.

Benevolent Organizations.

See the titles CHARITIES; TAXATION.

Bequests.

See the titles CHARITIES; EXECUTORS AND ADMINISTRATORS; TRUSTS; WILLS.

Best Evidence.

See the titles CRIMINAL LAW; EVIDENCE.

Betterments.

See the titles EJECTMENT; IMPROVEMENTS; LIFE ESTATES; PARTITION.

Betting.

See the titles ELECTIONS; GAMING.

Beverages.

See the titles FOOD; INTOXICATING LIQUORS.

Bicycles.

See the titles HIGHWAYS; LICENSES; MUNICIPAL CORPORATIONS.

Bids.

See the titles AUCTIONS AND AUCTIONEERS; CONTRACTS; COUNTIES; EXECUTION; HIGHWAYS; JUDICIAL SALES; MORTGAGES; MUNICIPAL CORPORATIONS; PUBLIC LANDS; STATES; TAXATION.

BIGAMY.

Cross References.

See the titles ADULTERY; CRIMINAL LAW; CURTESY; DEATH; DIVORCE; DOWER; EVIDENCE; HUSBAND AND WIFE; LEWDNESS; MARRIAGE; SLAVES.

As to admissibility of testimony of a just and lawful wife against husband in trial for bigamy, see the title WITNESSES.

§ 1. Nature and Elements of Offense.

Intent.—No other intent is necessary to support a conviction for bigamy than that which must be inferred from the second marriage, knowing the first wife to be living, or not having a reasonable belief of her death; and a charge which, unexplained, would lead the jury to the conclusion that some other intent was necessary, is properly refused. Dotson *v.* State, 62 Ala. 141, 34 Am. Rep. 2, cited in note in 27 L. R. A., N. S., 1098.

Cohabitation.—Cohabitation under the second marriage is not necessary to complete the offense of bigamy; it is complete when the unlawful marriage is consummated. Beggs *v.* State, 55 Ala. 108.

Same—Intercourse.—Under the last clause of Cr. Code 1896, § 4406, which in its entirety provides that "if any person having a former husband or wife living marries another, or continues to cohabit with such second husband or wife in this state, he or she must, on conviction, be imprisoned," etc., it is unnecessary, to constitute the crime of bigamy, that sexual intercourse should continue during the whole time the parties live together, but the crime is committed when they live under the same roof, and acknowledge each other as husband and wife, although they are prevented, by incapacity, from committing the carnal act. Cox *v.* State, 23 So. 806, 117 Ala. 103, 41 L. R. A. 760, 67 Am. St. Rep. 166.

Existence of Former Marriage.—To find defendant guilty, it must be shown that his former wife was living at the time he contracted the second marriage. Parker *v.* State, 77 Ala. 47, 54 Am. Rep. 43.

Same — Common-Law Marriage.—A marriage entered into merely by the consent of the parties, followed by cohabitation, is valid, though no license was obtained from the judge of probate, and though not solemnized by any person authorized by statute. Beggs *v.* State, 55 Ala. 108.

Same—When Void.—Bigamy can not be predicated of a second marriage where the first marriage is void, and not merely voidable. Beggs *v.* State, 55 Ala. 108; Cooley *v.* State, 55 Ala. 162.

Same—When Voidable Only.—One whose marriage is only voidable may be prosecuted for bigamy upon his contracting a second marriage before the former has been disaffirmed. Beggs *v.* State, 55 Ala. 108.

Same—When Party under Age of Consent.—As a marriage of a person under the age of consent is a marriage until disaffirmed, a subsequent marriage by such person, before the former has been set aside, is bigamy. Beggs *v.* State, 55 Ala. 108; Cooley *v.* State, 55 Ala. 162.

Same — When Dissolved.—Defendant, after marrying in Alabama, went to Mississippi to live, and from there to Arkansas, leaving his wife in Mississippi. After obtaining a divorce in Arkansas, on publication he returned to Alabama, and married again, his former wife still living. He had been bona fide a resident of Arkansas for over a year before filing his bill, as provided by the Arkansas statutes. Held, that the divorce was a defense to the prosecution. Thompson *v.* State, 28 Ala. 12.

The ordinance of 1867, § 1, recognizes as husband and wife all freedmen then living together as such. The act of 1868 authorizes the dissolution of the connection by mutual consent of the parties. Held, that the act of 1868 was no defense to a prosecution for bigamy of one whose marriage was regularly solemnized under license from the probate judge, and who, after dissolution of the marriage by mutual consent, married another. McConico *v.* State, 49 Ala. 6, cited in note in 27 L. R. A., N. S., 1103.

Same—Restrictions on Marriage in Divorce.—It was no defense in a bigamy case that within six months prior to the offense a decree of divorce between defendant and his wife was granted in Oklahoma, where such decree was inoperative on its face until after six months. Witt *v.* State, 5 Ala. App. 187, 59 So. 715.

§ 2. Defenses.

As to presumption of death from absence, see post, "Presumptions and Burden of Proof," § 7.

Absence of Spouse.—It is no defense, on one's trial for polygamy, that on her second marriage her former husband had been absent for more than a year, and was rumored, and by her believed, to be dead. Jones *v.* State, 67 Ala. 84, cited in note in 27 L. R. A., N. S., 1098, 1099, 1102.

Where defendant left his wife in the state in which they were married, her continued residence there is not an absence, within Code, § 4186, which provides that one who does not know that his former wife is living may marry a second time, where she has remained absent from him for the last five years preceding. Parker *v.* State, 77 Ala. 47, 54 Am. Rep. 43.

§ 3. Indictment or Information.

§ 4. —— Requisites and Sufficiency.

An indictment against a man for bigamy was not demurrable because it failed to allege that the other party was a woman. Witt *v.* State, 5 Ala. App. 187, 59 So. 715.

Necessity of Averring Marriage Is Unlawful.—An indictment which avers that defendant, "having a former wife living," married a certain woman, is insufficient. As it fails to aver that the second marriage was unlawful. Parker *v.* State, 77 Ala. 47, 54 Am. Rep. 43.

Where Indictable.—The offense of bigamy under the statute (Rev. Code, § 3599) is indictable only in the county in which the second marriage is solemnized; while subsequent cohabitation under the second marriage, which is a distinct offense, may be indicted and punished in any county in which it is committed; but, under an indictment for bigamy, a conviction can not be had on proof only of subsequent cohabitation, in the county in which the indictment was found, when the second marriage took place in another county, or in another state. Beggs *v.* State, 55 Ala. 108; Williams *v.* State, 44 Ala. 24.

§ 5. —— Issues, Proof, and Variance.

There is no variance between an indictment for bigamy, alleging the name of the alleged second wife as "Lydia E.," and the proof, showing her name as "Liddie E." Caldwell *v.* State, 41 So. 473, 146 Ala. 141.

It is necessary to aver in an indictment for bigamy, and prove on the trial, that the accused married his second wife or cohabited with her in the county in which the indictment was found. Williams *v.* State, 44 Ala. 24.

§ 6. Evidence.

§ 7. —— Presumptions and Burden of Proof.

Presumption of Death of Absent Spouse.—"Absence, from which death is presumed, is absence abroad; absence from the former place of abode, where nothing has been heard of the absent person by those who would naturally have heard of him, if alive." Parker *v.* State, 77 Ala. 47, 52.

"To constitute the statutory exception, an available defense, continuous absence for the last preceding five years, and ignorance of the life or death of the former husband or wife, must concur." Parker *v.* State, 77 Ala. 47, 51.

Same—Length of Absence.—"Whoever marries a second time, having a former husband or wife living, absent for a less period than five years, violates the statute, and is subject to punishment." Parker *v.* State, 77 Ala. 47, 52.

Cases may arise in which death will be presumed from unexplained absence for a less period than five years. Questions of conflicting presumptions may arise; and the accompanying circumstances as to age, or health, or condition may be such, that the presumption of innocence will overcome the presumption of the continuance of life. Parker *v.* State, 77 Ala. 47, 52.

Same—When Deserted.—"A husband can not create absence by abandoning his family, and then invoke the presumption of innocence to destroy the presumptive proof of continuing life. On such facts, there can be no inference of death, available as a defense; and the presumption of innocence only avails as in other criminal cases—that each essential ingredient of the offense must be proved beyond a reasonable doubt." Parker *v.* State, 77 Ala. 47, 52.

Same—When Proved That Spouse Was Alive within Time.—Where the prosecution has shown that the former wife was living at the specified time before the second marriage, the burden is on defendant to rebut the presumption that she is still alive. Parker *v.* State, 77 Ala. 47, 54 Am. Rep. 43.

Proof that the former wife, abandoned by the defendant, was living at a specified time before the second marriage, raises a presumption that she was living at the date of the second marriage. Parker *v.* State, 77 Ala. 47, 54 Am. Rep. 43.

§ 8. Admissibility in General.

On a trial under an indictment for bigamy, evidence that at the time of the second marriage the defendant had made inquiries to ascertain whether or not his former wife was dead, and that he had received a letter stating that she was dead, is irrelevant, illegal, and properly excluded. Rand *v.* State, 29 So. 844, 129 Ala. 119, cited in note in 27 L. R. A., N. S., 1099, 1102.

§ 9. —— Previous Marriage.

How Proved.—"On trial for bigamy, marriage, like any other fact involved in a judicial inquiry, may be proved by circumstances; direct or positive proof of the fact is not necessary. 1 Bish. Mar. & Div., § 487; 2 Whart. Ev., § 1297; 2 Greenl. Ev., § 461; Langtry *v.* State, 30 Ala. 536; Campbell *v.* Gullatt, 43 Ala. 57; Williams *v.* State, 54 Ala. 131; Parker *v.*

State, 77 Ala. 47." Bynon *v.* State, 117 Ala. 80, 23 So. 640.

Same—By Parol Evidence.—Oral proof of the marriage is admissible on the trial of an indictment under Code, § 4185, for either the offense of bigamy or that of continuing to cohabit in the county, etc. Brewer *v.* State, 59 Ala. 101.

Same—Admissions.—Where, on a trial for bigamy, a witness proved a prior marriage of accused, it was competent to prove acts, declarations, or admissions of accused in recognition of the alleged first wife as his legal wife. Caldwell *v.* State, 41 So. 473, 146 Ala. 141.

"In Parker *v.* State, 77 Ala. 47, it was held, that the weight of authority is in support of the proposition, that, 'in the absence of local laws prescribing formalities and ceremonies to validate a marriage, the first marriage may be proved by the admissions of the accused.' Citing Miles *v.* United States, 103 U. S. 304, 26 L. Ed. 481. There are no formalities or ceremonies in this state necessary to establish a marriage, and, in this case, the admissions of the defendant of the first marriage are clear and uncontroverted." Williams *v.* State, 151 Ala. 108, 44 So. 57, 58.

Same—Admissions and Cohabitation.—By way of dictum in an early case it was said that in trials for bigamy marriage must be proved by the record or the testimony of a witness to the ceremony. Admissions, reputation, and cohabitation are not sufficient. Ford *v.* Ford, 4 Ala. 142. This doctrine is overruled, however, by subsequent cases. Langtry *v.* State, 30 Ala. 536, 537; Williams *v.* State, 151 Ala. 108, 44 So. 57.

In prosecutions for bigamy, the first marriage may be proved by evidence of cohabitation and the confessions of the prisoner; and such evidence, if full and satisfactory, is sufficient to authorize a conviction, without the production of the record, or the testimony of a witness who was present at the ceremony. Langtry *v.* State, 30 Ala. 536.

Evidence that a man and woman lived and cohabited together for more than ten years; that they were the parents of eight children; that the woman and children were known by his name; and that she, described as his wife, joined him in the execution of a deed, is competent to prove the previous marriage on trial for bigamy. Bynon *v.* State, 117 Ala. 80, 23 So. 640.

In prosecutions for bigamy, marriage may be proved by cohabitation and the confessions of the party; and if the proof of marriage be full and satisfactory, it is not absolutely necessary that the prosecution shall produce either the record of the marriage, or the testimony of some person who witnessed the ceremony. See Morgan *v.* State, 11 Ala. 289; Langtry *v.* State, 30 Ala. 536, 538; Parker *v.* State, 77 Ala. 47.

Same—Bill for Divorce.—A bill in equity for a divorce, not verified by the oath of the complainant, is, like any other unsworn bill regarded as the mere suggestion of counsel; and is not competent evidence against the complainant therein, in a subsequent prosecution for bigamy, to prove his marriage with the defendant as therein alleged. Cooley *v.* State, 55 Ala. 162.

Same—Marriage License.—On a trial for bigamy, certified copies of marriage licenses issued to defendant, and of the marriage certificates appended to the licenses, and referring to them for the names of the parties, are admissible, under Code, §§ 2846, 2847, requiring registry of such license and certificates, and making certified copies presumptive evidence. Eldridge *v.* State, 28 So. 580, 126 Ala. 63.

Degree of Proof.—In a prosecution for bigamy (Code, § 4185), the fact of a former marriage, valid by the laws of the country in which it was contracted, must be proved by competent evidence, and beyond a reasonable doubt. Parker *v.* State, 77 Ala. 47.

"Marriage, even in prosecutions for bigamy, may be proved by cohabitation and the confessions of the party; but the testimony, to justify a conviction, must be clear, strong and convincing. See able opinion by C. J. Gibson, in Forney *v.* Hallacher, 8 Serg. & R. 159; Com. *v.* Murtagh, 1 Ashm. 272; Ham's Case, 11 Me. 391; Cayford's Case, 7 Greenl. Ev. 57; The State *v.* Hilton, 3 Rich. Law, 434; Roscoe's Cr. Ev. 311, 312." Langtry *v.* State, 30 Ala. 536, 537.

§ 10. —— Illegal Marriage or Cohabitation.

"The alleged second marriage of defendant having been solemnized by a justice of the peace without a license, and not followed by cohabitation, was not valid either as a statutory or common-law marriage. Beggs *v.* State, 55 Ala. 108. With the evidence of the second marriage, excluded, there remained no evidence on which the defendant could be convicted of bigamy." Ashley *v.* State, 109 Ala. 48, 19 So. 917, 918.

§ 11. Trial.

§ 12. —— Questions for Jury.

In a prosecution for bigamy, whether there was a common-law marriage in the state between defendant and one who had formerly been his wife held, under the evidence, a question for the jury. Williams *v.* State, 44 So. 57, 151 Ala. 108.

Where there was evidence from which the jury could infer that the wife of one indicted for bigamy was alive when the second marriage was solemnized, an affirmative charge for defendant, requested on the theory that there was no evidence that she was alive, was properly refused, though there was no direct evidence that she was living at the time of the second marriage. Eldridge *v.* State, 28 So. 580, 126 Ala. 63, cited in note in 27 L. R. A., N. S., 1098, 1102.

§ 13. —— Instructions.

On a prosecution for bigamy, where the only testimony is that of an ignorant negro woman that, after defendant had been married to and separated from a certain man, a marriage ceremony was performed between her and another man by a person named, "a colored man, who read the testimony to them," without any attempt to produce evidence of a marriage license, or to account for its nonproduction in reference to either ceremony, and without any proof that the one who performed the second ceremony was, or pretended to be, or was supposed to be, a preacher, minister, or officer of any kind, or that the ceremony performed by him was followed by cohabitation, an instruction that "marriage in cases of this kind could be proved by cohabitation, living together, or the confession of the parties; that it was like any other civil contract in this respect, and that it was not necessary to show by proof that the requirements of the statute were conformed to to establish a marriage in either case; that it was not necessary to show the authority of the parties who solemnized the marriage," etc.—is erroneous. Brown *v.* State, 52 Ala. 338.

Bill.

See the titles ACCOUNT; ACCOUNT STATED. As to statutes, see the title STATUTES.

Bill of Cost.

See the title COSTS.

Bill of Credit.

See the titles BANKS AND BANKING; CONSTITUTIONAL LAW; STATES.

Bill of Discovery.

See the title DISCOVERY.

Bill of Exceptions.

See the title EXCEPTIONS, BILL OF.

Bill of Exchange.

See the title BILLS AND NOTES.

Bill of Interpleader.

See the title INTERPLEADER.

Bill of Lading.

See the titles CARRIERS; EVIDENCE; SALES; SHIPPING.

Bill of Particulars.

See the titles CONTEMPT; INDICTMENT AND INFORMATION; JUSTICES OF THE PEACE; PLEADING.

Bill of Peace.

See the titles EQUITY; INJUNCTION; QUIETING TITLE.

Bill of Review.

See the title EQUITY.

Bill of Rights.

See the titles BAIL; CONSTITUTIONAL LAW; CRIMINAL LAW; EMINENT DOMAIN; INDICTMENT AND INFORMATION; JURY; SEARCHES AND SEIZURES; WEAPONS; WITNESSES.

Bill of Sale.

See the title SALES.

Bill Quia Timet.

See the title QUIETING TITLE.

BILLS AND NOTES.

Cross References.

See the titles ASSOCIATIONS; BANKRUPTCY; BANKS AND BANKING; COMPROMISE AND SETTLEMENT; CONSTITUTIONAL LAW; CONTRACTS; CORPORATIONS; COUNTIES; CUSTOMS AND USAGES; DISMISSAL AND NONSUIT; EVIDENCE; EXECUTORS AND ADMINISTRATORS; GARNISHMENT; GIFTS; GUARANTY; GUARDIAN AND WARD; HUSBAND AND WIFE; INFANTS; INSANE PERSONS; INTEREST; INTERNAL REVENUE; INTOXICATING LIQUORS; JOINT-STOCK COMPANIES; JUDGMENT; LIMITATION OF ACTIONS; LOST INSTRUMENTS; MORTGAGES; MUNICIPAL CORPORATIONS; NOVATION; PARTNERSHIP; PAYMENT; PLEADING; PLEDGES; PRINCIPAL AND AGENT; PRINCIPAL AND SURETY; SALES; SCHOOLS AND SCHOOL DISTRICTS; SET-OFF AND COUNTERCLAIM; SIGNATURES; STATES; SUBROGATION; SUNDAY; TOWNS; TROVER AND CONVERSION; TRUSTS; USURY; VENDOR AND PURCHASER; WITNESSES.

I. REQUISITES AND VALIDITY.

(A) FORM AND CONTENTS OF BILLS OF EXCHANGE, DRAFTS, CHECKS, AND ORDERS.

§ 1. Nature and Essentials in General.

A bill of exchange is an order for the payment of money absolutely. Waters *v.* Carleton, 4 Port. 205, 206.

An order drawn by one person on another in favor of a third person for a specific amount is a "bill of exchange." Faircloth-Byrd Mercantile Co. *v.* Adkinson, 52 So. 419, 167 Ala. 344; Anderson *v.* Jones, 102 Ala. 537, 14 So. 871.

An order drawn on another to pay a sum certain to the order of the drawer and to charge the same to the drawer's account is a bill of exchange. H. T. Woodall & Son *v.* People's Nat. Bank of Leesburg, Va., 45 So. 194, 153 Ala. 576.

Where a writing is capable of being interpreted as a bill of exchange or promissory note, the person who receives it may, at his option, treat it as a bill of exchange or as a note against the maker. Brazelton *v.* McMurray, 44 Ala. 323.

§ 2. What Law Governs.

The liability of the drawer of a bill of exchange is governed by the law of the place where he drew the bill. Crawford *v.* Branch Bank, 6 Ala. 12, 41 Am. Dec. 33, cited in note in 61 L. R. A. 213, 215.

§ 3. Original Parties.

"A bill of exchange has usually three parties—the drawer, the drawee (who after acceptance is the acceptor), and the payee (after endorsement the endorser) —Chitty on Bills, 1, 19. The acceptor is primarily liable to pay the bill, and the drawer and endorser, if the proper steps are taken to charge them, are liable on his default—Ibid. 182, 183. And in no instance is the endorser under any liability to the acceptor, unless it be in the case of an acceptance for his honor—Ibid. 142." Inge *v.* Branch Bank, 8 Port. 108, 115.

It is not necessary that the various parties to a negotiable instrument should be different persons in order to render it a bill of exchange. Randolph *v.* Parish, 9 Port. 76.

A bill of exchange may be drawn payable to the order of the maker. Hart *v.* Shorter, 46 Ala. 453.

A bill drawn by a party upon himself is a bill of exchange in the hands of an indorsee. Randolph *v.* Parish, 9 Port. 76.

An order drawn by the president of a corporation on the treasurer, payable on demand, may be declared on, when dishonored, as a bill of exchange. Wetumpka & C. R. R. *v.* Bingham, 5 Ala. 657.

An instrument drawn by one partner payable to the firm is not complete as a bill of exchange until indorsed by the payees. Capital City Ins. Co. *v.* Quinn, 73 Ala. 558.

Action at law is not sustainable on a bill single, payable to a firm of which one of the obligors is a partner. Tindal *v.* Bright, Minor 103.

§ 4. Form of Order or Request.

An order for a definite sum, payable generally, and not out of any particular fund, is not an assignment of moneys due the drawer, but is a bill of exchange, within Code, § 1766, providing that no person must be charged as the acceptor of a bill of exchange unless his acceptance is in writing, signed by himself or agent. Anderson *v.* Jones, 102 Ala. 537, 14 So. 871.

§ 5. Designation of Parties.

"Every bill of exchange should specify to whom it is payable, to enable the acceptor to discharge himself from liability by payment to the proper person." Prewitt *v.* Chapman, 6 Ala. 86, 88.

"It is not, however, necessary that the name of the payee should be inserted when the bill is drawn. If a blank is left for that purpose, it will be considered an authority to the holder to fill it up. Cruchley *v.* Clarance, 2 M. & S. 90; Crutchly *v.* Mann, 5 Taunton, 529." Prewitt *v.* Chapman, 6 Ala. 86, 89.

An instrument purporting to be a bill of exchange, which does not direct to whom payment shall be made, may be the foundation of a suit by the person from whom the consideration moved, but has not the effect of a bill payable to bearer. A third person can not maintain an action thereon. Prewitt *v.* Chapman, 6 Ala. 86.

§ 6. Designation of Medium of Payment.

An order payable in "funds current in the city of New York" is a bill of exchange. Lacy *v.* Holbrook, 4 Ala. 88.

A written order by a person to whom cotton is due, to the party from whom it is due, to deliver to a third party "cotton to the value of $271," is not a bill of exchange within the meaning of Code, § 2101, requiring such bill to be accepted in writing, and an oral acceptance is sufficient. Auerbach *v.* Pritchett, 58 Ala. 451.

§ 7. Inland or Foreign Bills.

A bill of exchange drawn by a person in one state of the union upon a person residing in another, and payable there, is a foreign bill. Donegan *v.* Wood, 49 Ala. 242, 20 Am. Rep. 275; Todd *v.* Neal, 49 Ala. 266; Turner *v.* Patton, 49 Ala. 406, cited in note in 61 L. R. A. 217.

A bill of exchange, drawn in Alabama, on parties in Louisiana, and payable there, is a foreign bill (Rev. Code, § 1857). Todd *v.* Neal, 49 Ala. 266; Donegan *v.* Wood, 49 Ala. 242, 247.

The statute providing that the remedy on bills of exchange, foreign and inland, and on promissory notes payable in bank, shall be governed by the rules of the law merchant as to days of grace, protest, and notice, does not destroy any distinction recognized by the law merchant between foreign and inland bills and promissory notes, but its intention is that the law merchant as applicable to each class shall prevail. Quigley *v.* Primrose, 8 Port. 247.

§ 8. Checks as Bills of Exchange.

"Randolph defines a 'check' to be, 'a bill of exchange drawn on a banker, payable on demand.' Rand. Com. Paper, § 8. The authorities and text-books, as a general thing, class them among commercial instruments. 'All checks are bills, but all bills are not checks,' is the sum of the conclusion of the authorities. Id., and authorities there cited. Morse, Banks, §§ 363, 393; 2 Daniel, Neg. Inst., § 583; Byles, Bills, 13; 1 Edw. Bills & N., § 19; 2 Pars. Bills & N. 57; Story, Prom. Notes, 487; 3 Am. & Eng. Enc. Law 211, note 1." First Nat. Bank *v.* Nelson, 105 Ala. 180, 16 So. 707, 708.

Code, § 1761, providing that all bills or notes payable to an existing person or bearer must be construed as if payable to such person or order, applies to checks. First Nat. Bank *v.* Nelson, 105 Ala. 180, 16 So. 707.

§ 9. Orders Payable on Contingency or Out of Particular Fund.

An order payable out of a particular fund or upon a contingency that may never happen is not a bill of exchange. It is an essential to a bill of exchange that it involve the personal responsibility of the drawer. Waters *v.* Carleton, 4 Port. 205.

A written order, requesting the person to whom it is addressed to pay a specified sum out of the proceeds of a certain judgment when collected, is not a bill of exchange. Gliddon *v.* McKinstry, 28 Ala. 408, cited in note in 35 L. R. A. 648.

A written order to pay a certain sum and interest, "the demand I have against the estate of D. Y., deceased," is neither a bill of exchange nor such a written instrument for the payment of money as, under the statute, may be assigned so as to entitle the assignee to sue on it in his own name. West *v.* Foreman, 21 Ala. 400, cited in note in 35 L. R. A. 648.

An order, signed by a firm, directing its clerk to pay the bearer a certain amount whenever a certain amount of the firm's change tickets should be presented at the clerk's office, which order was accepted by the clerk merely for the firm's accommodation, was held intended to circulate as a bank note, and not as a bill of exchange. Dillahunty *v.* Parry, 1 Stew. 251.

§ 10. Nature of Contract and Liability of Drawer.

A party drawing a bill on himself, payable at the same place, is liable for damages if the bill be dishonored. Randolph *v.* Parish, 9 Port. 76.

The fact that a bill was drawn and indorsed for the accommodation of the acceptors without consideration, and that when it was transferred the acceptors were indebted to the drawer, is a good defense against the transferee, who took the bill after maturity. Battle *v.* Weems, 44 Ala. 105.

§ 11. Refusal of Drawee to Accept or Pay.

§ 12. —— Liability of Drawee.

Where the funds are insufficient, the drawee of a check is under no obligation to make a partial payment thereon. Lowenstein *v.* Bresler, 109 Ala. 326, 19 So. 860.

§ 13. —— Liability of Drawer.

The drawees in a bill of exchange, who refuse to accept the same, may acquire it by indorsement, and sue thereon as indorsees. Desha *v.* Stewart, 6 Ala. 852.

The holder of a bill of exchange does not waive his right of action for its nonacceptance by afterwards having it presented and protested for nonpayment. Decatur Branch Bank *v.* Hodges, 17 Ala. 42.

Inland bills of exchange carry damages when protested for nonacceptance. Moore *v.* Bradford, 3 Ala. 550.

By statute damages are recoverable against the drawer on a foreign bill protested for nonpayment. Murphy *v.* Andrews, 13 Ala. 708.

Act Dec. 21, 1832, reducing the damages on bills of exchange purchased by the State Bank or its branches, applies only to bills of which the State Bank or one of its branches is the owner, and not to bills owned by private persons. Moore *v.* Clements, 4 Port. 227.

(B) FORM AND CONTENTS OF PROMISSORY NOTES AND DUE BILLS.

§ 14. Nature and Essentials in General.

"Though, according to the law merchant, a promissory note is not confined to any set form of words, whatever are the words employed, they must import an unconditional promise to pay to another's order or to bearer a certain sum of money at a time therein specified. Story, Prom. Notes, § 1. To these essential requisites of a promissory note, certainty in obligation, certainty in the money to be paid, and certainty in the time of payment, the statute adds certainty of the place of payment. To be negotiable and governed by the commercial law, the statute requires that the note be payable 'at a bank, or private banking house, or a certain place of payment therein designated.' Code, § 1756." Anniston Loan, etc., Co. *v.* Stickney, 108 Ala. 146, 19 So. 63.

"It is one of the essentials of a promissory note that it shall be based upon the personal credit and liability of the maker. 4 Am. & Eng. Enc. Law 89; Munger *v.* Shannon, 61 N. Y. 251." Heflin Gold Min. Co. *v.* Hilton, 124 Ala. 365, 27 So. 301.

Failure to fill certain blanks left for pronouns in the printed waiver of exemptions in a note is immaterial. Lesser *v.* Scholze, 93 Ala. 338, 9 So. 273.

§ 15. What Law Governs.

See post, "What Law Governs," § 76.

§ 16. Form of Promise.

"The promise to pay must be absolute, and without restriction to particular funds. Chit. Bills, 132-134; Blackman *v.* Lehman, etc., Co., 63 Ala. 547." Heflin Gold Min. Co. *v.* Hilton, 124 Ala. 365, 27 So. 301.

A writing in form: "I., B. R., do sertify that I give the girle Mary R. the sum of $500 at my death, pable onely after my death to the said Mary R., onela to the said Mary R., and I here forwarne every persones or person for traden for said note pable after my death," signed, but without attesting witnesses, and delivered to said Mary R.—held not to be a promissory note, there being no promise, nor a will, and there being no consideration, to be nudum pactum. Rice *v.* Rice, 68 Ala. 216. See the title WILLS.

§ 17. Designation of Parties.

Designation of Payee.—A bill or note must be certain as to the payee, though it is not necessary that the payee should be named. The instrument must, on its face, afford an indication or designation by which he can be ascertained. Blackman *v.* Lehman, 63 Ala. 547, 35 Am. Rep. 57.

A sealed note payable to "J. W. C., for the benefit of A. T., may be declared on as payable to J. W. C. Turner *v.* Eldridge, 6 Ala. 821.

A note acknowledging a certain indebtedness to be "due J. F., * * * which I promise to pay T. C., sheriff, * * * to satisfy an attachment," gives a right of action to J. F. against the maker thereof. Bowie *v.* Foster, Minor 264.

"A promise in writing made by A, to pay a specified sum of money to his own order, is not a note, until endorsed by him; for the reason, that, until then, no legal obligation is created." Murdock *v.* Caruthers, 21 Ala. 785, 788.

Promise by Firm to Pay Another Firm Both Having a Common Partner.—A promise in writing by one firm to pay a sum certain, on a specified day, to another firm, both having a common partner, is not a promissory note until assigned. When assigned by the latter firm, the assignee must be regarded, as between himself and the makers, as the real payee, and may maintain an action in his own name against the makers. Murdock *v.* Caruthers, 21 Ala. 785.

A promissory note payable to "R. C. & Co.," is only evidence of a promise to pay. It must be shown by other evidence who composed the firm. Bell *v.* Rhea, 1 Ala. 83.

Bill Single Payable to Firm of Which One of Obligors Is a Partner.—An action at law is not sustainable on a bill single payable to a firm, of which one of the obligors is a partner. Tindal *v.* Bright, Minor 103.

Upon a note made payable to "treasurer of the Manual Labor Institute of South Alabama," a suit can not be maintained by Madison College without an averment that it is the same corporation, and that the name had been changed since the making of the note, and before the institution of the suit. Madison College *v.* Burke, 6 Ala. 494.

A note made payable to "the estate of" a deceased person is evidence of the existence of a debt, which the executor may recover as assets of the estate. Hendricks *v.* Thornton, 45 Ala. 299.

Note Payable to Administrator in Representative Character.—An administrator can not maintain an action on a note payable to himself in his representative character, and signed by him as surety for the principal maker. Moore *v.* Randolph, 70 Ala. 575.

An instrument which is in the form of a note, but which in addition is addressed to a third person, who accepts it, is a promissory note, and may be so declared on. Brazelton *v.* McMurray, 44 Ala. 323.

§ 18. Designation of Time for Payment.

Installments.—A note payable in installments, and providing that the whole amount shall become due on failure to pay any installment, is valid as a note. Martin *v.* Jesse French Piano & Organ Co., 44 So. 112, 151 Ala. 289.

§ 19. Designation of Place for Payment.

Under Code 1886, § 2954, a promissory note, made payable at a designated place, is commercial paper, and an action thereon is properly instituted in the name of the holder of the legal title. Carmelich *v.* Mims, 88 Ala. 335, 6 So. 913.

An instrument in the form of a promissory note, payable at a bank, but with the seal of the maker attached, does not come within Code, § 2094, by which "bills of exchange and promissory notes, payable in money at a bank, * * * are governed by the commercial law." Muse *v.* Dantzler, 85 Ala. 359, 5 So. 178. See post, "Sealed Instruments," § 23.

§ 20. Designation of Medium of Payment.

C. sold land to P., and took a writing by which the latter promised by a specified time "to pay C., or bearer, the amount of cotton raised on fifty acres of land, more or less, raised on the lands sold by C. to P., cultivated to the best of my skill and ability, as second payment on the said tract of land," the cotton to be hauled to the gin by P. Held, that such writing was not a promissory note, nor one of the contracts specified in Code, § 2890, on which actions "must be prosecuted in the name of the party really interested, whether he has the legal title or not." Auerbach *v.* Pritchett, 58 Ala. 451.

An instrument for the payment of a sum of money "in the common currency of Alabama" can not be declared upon as a promissory note. Carlisle *v.* Davis, 7 Ala. 42.

§ 21. Due Bills or Other Acknowledgments of Indebtedness.

A writing in the words, "Due J. J., or bearer, the sum," etc., "money borrowed," etc., and signed by the maker, is a note. Johnson *v.* Johnson, Minor 263.

The writing, "Due J. F. $145.75, which I promise to pay T. C., sheriff, to satisfy an attachment," etc., signed "J. B.," is a promissory note. Bowie *v.* Foster, Minor 264.

A writing acknowledging that there is due from the subscriber to the person therein named a specified sum of money for the keeping of stage horses in the subscriber's possession, is a promissory note, on which final judgment by default may be rendered. Fleming *v.* Burge, 6 Ala. 373.

§ 22. Certificates of Deposit.

Though there are respectable authorities holding otherwise, it may be regarded as supported by the great weight of authority that a certificate of deposit, possessing the essential elements—an acknowledgment of a present debt, and a promise to pay—is, in legal effect and operation, a promissory note. Renfro *v.* Merchants', etc., Bank, 83 Ala. 425, 3 So. 776.

Under Code Ala. 1876, § 2094, providing that notes and bills of exchange payable at a banking house, or some certain place of payment designated therein, are commercial paper, a certificate of deposit payable on its return properly indorsed, with the name and address of the bankers at its heading, does not sufficiently describe the place of payment to come within the statute. Renfro *v.* Merchants', etc., Bank, 83 Ala. 425, 3 So. 776.

§ 23. Sealed Instruments.

"At common law, sealing was an essential and distinctive requirement to constitute a bond; and, under the mercantile law, sealing an instrument, though otherwise corresponding in form, deprived it of the character of a promissory note. Though an instrument under seal for the payment of money, without condition, at a specified time, is sometimes designated as a note under seal, there is a well-defined distinction between such instrument and a promissory note. Early after the Code of 1852 took effect it was said substantially that the distinction between sealed and unsealed instruments is not altogether destroyed by the Code. In Reed *v.* Scott, 30 Ala. 640, the complaint described the instrument sued on as a promissory note. The instrument offered in evidence under the complaint was in form a promissory note, except that it was under seal. It is said: 'A bond can not, with strict legal propriety, be termed a promissory note, and they have always been distinguished in the incidents which attach to them. The instrument sued upon, being described as a promissory note, was not the instrument offered in evidence, because the latter is a bond.' The same ruling was reaffirmed in McCrummen *v.* Campbell, 82 Ala. 566, 2 So. 482." Muse *v.* Dantzler, 85 Ala. 359, 5 So. 178, 179.

Under Rev. Code, § 1585, making a writing a sealed instrument when it imports on its face to be such, a promissory note containing only the word "Seal," surrounded by a scroll, appended to the signature of the maker, is not a sealed instrument. Blackwell *v.* Hamilton, 47 Ala. 470, cited in note in 35 L. R. A. 608.

A promissory note with a scroll, in which is written the word "Seal" at the end of the name of the party signing it, is not a sealed instrument, unless it appears from its body that the parties intended to give it that character. Carter *v.* Penn, 4 Ala. 140.

§ 24. Instruments Payable after Death of Maker.

A written instrument, whereby the maker promised to pay a sum certain in money at his option before his death or to be collected from his estate thereafter, is not invalid as a testamentary instrument or a promise to make a future gift, but is a good promissory note; the expressed consideration taking it out of the classes mentioned. Dorsey *v.* Hudmon (Ala.), 60 So. 303.

A written instrument whereby the maker, for value received, promised to pay a sum certain in money at his option before his death, and, if not paid before, to be then collected from his estate, is a valid promissory note; it not being void because of uncertainty as to time of payment, the ultimate time being absolutely fixed. Dorsey *v.* Hudmon (Ala.), 60 So. 303.

"In the case of In re Beatty's Estate *v.* Western College, 177 Ill. 280, 52 N. E. 432, 42 L. R. A. 797, 69 Am. St. Rep. 242, the court reviews and cites the authorities on the subject. It is there said: 'A note payable "on demand after my decease" has been held to be valid. Bristol *v.* Warner, 19 Conn. 7. A note payable "one day after date or at my death" has been held valid. Conn *v.* Thornton, 46 Ala. 587; 1 Randolph, Com. Paper, § 113. The mere fact that a note is payable upon the death of the maker, or at a certain day after the death of the maker, does not make it a testamentary paper, nor constitute it a will in such sense as to require its execution in accordance with the statute of wills. It is an obligation to pay, and, being delivered to the payee as an evidence of debt, and being made payable to order, it is a promissory note. Bristol *v.* Warner, 19 Conn. 7. In Price *v.* Jones, 105 Ind. 543 [5 N. E. 683], 55 Am. Rep. 230, is was insisted that a note payable one day after the death of the maker was invalid as being an attempt to make a testamentary disposition of property. The court there said: "There is no attempt to make a testamentary disposition of property, for the instrument contains no provisions resembling those of a will. It is a promise to pay money. It differs from an ordinary promise in the single particular that it fixes the time of payment at a period subsequent to the promisor's death. It is nevertheless a promise to pay money, absolutely and at all events, to a person named, and it has therefore all the essential features of a promissory note." See, also, Carnwright *v.* Gray, 127 N. Y. 92, 27 N. E. 835, 12 L. R. A. 845, 24 Am. St. Rep. 424.'" Dorsey *v.* Hudmon (Ala.), 60 So. 303, 304.

A writing in these words: "One day after date I promise to pay, or at my death, W. G. Conn, or bearer, the sum of," etc.—may be sued as a promissory note. Conn *v.* Thornton, 46 Ala. 587, cited in note in 27 L. R. A., N. S., 1018.

§ 25. Recitals and Provisions Affecting Character of Instrument.

A written promise by a corporation to pay a certain sum, but containing a provision that it shall not be chargeable against the stock interest of certain of the stockholders, is not a note enforceable in an action at law against the corporation. Heflin Gold Min. Co. *v.* Hilton, 27 So. 301, 124 Ala. 365.

A contract in the form of a promissory note for the hire of a slave may be declared on as a promissory note, notwithstanding, besides the promise to pay a sum certain in money, there is also a promise in the same instrument to furnish the slave with certain articles of clothing, pay his taxes, and return him to the owner at a stipulated time. Gaines *v.* Shelton, 47 Ala. 413.

§ 26. Nature of Contract and Liability of Maker.

Accommodation Maker.—If an accommodation note is made to the order of a bank for the purpose of raising money by procuring its discount by the bank, but a third person discounts the note after the refusal of the bank to do so, the accommodation makers are liable to such third person. Thompson *v.* Armstrong, 5 Ala. 383.

Estoppel to Deny Rights of Payee.—Where a promissory note is payable to the plaintiff generally, this is an admission of his right to receive the amount, and estops the defendant from insisting that the beneficial interest is in others; especially, when it is admitted on the record that the plaintiff was authorized to take the note in the form he did. Grigsby *v.* Nance, 3 Ala. 347.

(C) EXECUTION AND DELIVERY.

§ 27. Signature.

Place of Signature.—"The name of the drawer or maker of a note, bill, or of an order for the payment of money may appear in any part of the writing; it is sufficient that he sign in the capacity of maker or drawer. 1 Daniel, Neg. Inst., § 74." Lampkin *v.* State, 105 Ala. 1, 16 So. 575, 576.

One may bind himself as maker of a note by writing his name on the back thereof. Eudora Mining & Development Co. *v.* Barclay, 26 So. 113, 122 Ala. 506.

"While it is true, that generally the makers' names are signed to a note at its foot, and the indorsers, if any, on its back, and without more the names of those appearing on the back would be presumed to have been placed there as indorsers, and not as makers, yet, we know of no rule of law which requires that the makers may not place their names on any part of the note where they may prefer to write them, and thus bind themselves as makers. It is immaterial, in other words, upon what part of a note the name of a maker may be written. Quin *v.* Sterne, 26 Ga. 223, 71 Am. Dec. 204; Story, Prom. Notes, §§ 34, 121, 152." Eudora Min., etc., Co. *v.* Barclay, 122 Ala. 506, 26 So. 113, 114.

A signature to a bill of exchange made by mark without an attesting witness is

insufficient to bind the person sought to be charged thereby. Flowers *v.* Bitting, 45 Ala. 448.

"At the common law, a note may be signed by a mark, and a person may adopt a mark as his signature." Jackson *v.* Tribble, 156 Ala. 480, 47 So. 310, 313.

A note executed by an illiterate promisor by his mark is sufficient, and need not be attested. Civ. Code 1896, § 1, defining "signature" or "subscription" as including mark when one can not write, his name being written near it and witnessed by one who writes his own name as a witness, is inapplicable to the execution of notes; and a note is validly executed by one who can not write his name by his affixing thereunto an X-mark between an initial of his own name and his surname, written by the payee, the name of a witness, who also could not write his name, being written by the payee. McGowan *v.* Collins, 46 So. 228, 154 Ala. 299. See, also, Jackson *v.* Tribble, 156 Ala. 480, 47 So. 310, 313.

An objection to the validity of a note, that it was signed by mark and without an attesting witness to the signature, was not valid, where at the time the objection was made it was not shown that the person claiming to have signed the note by mark could not read. Jackson *v.* Tribble, 47 So. 310, 156 Ala. 480.

Payee of Note Can Not Sign Maker's Name and Make His Mark.—The promisee can not become the agent of the promisor for the purpose of signing his name to a contract, and hence the payee of an instrument in the form of a note could not sign the maker's name and make his mark; the maker touching the pen staff. Penton *v.* Williams, 51 So. 35, 163 Ala. 603.

Principal's Name Written by Surety at His Request.—Where the testimony of a surety who claimed against her principal on a note which had been paid by and indorsed to her showed that no antagonistic relation existed, that her principal could not write, and that at his request she wrote his name on the note, after which he made his mark, and she signed as surety, which testimony was corroborated by several witnesses who were present, a finding that she was authorized to sign her principal's name to the note was sufficiently supported; and it was not error to render judgment in her favor, though the statutory requirement that such mark be attested by a witness who could write was not complied with, and the note contained a clause waiving exemptions as to personal property, since, when the surety so signed her principal's name to the note, the contract was complete, and the principal's mark thereafter added did not affect its validity. Wright *v.* Forgy, 28 So. 198, 126 Ala. 389.

§ 28. Attestation.

The attorney of the payee of a note is a competent subscribing witness thereto. Sowell *v.* Bank of Brewton, 24 So. 585, 119 Ala. 92.

A signature by mark to a note and mortgage to a bank, and the attestation thereof, are not invalidated by the fact that the attesting witness was an agent or employee of the mortgagee. Morris *v.* Bank of Attalla, 38 So. 804, 142 Ala. 638.

§ 29. Affixing Revenue Stamps.

When Revenue Law Became Effective.—A promissory note made after the passage of the internal revenue law, but before any collection district was organized, or stamps prepared and placed on sale, within the state, is valid, and may be read in evidence, although unstamped. McElvain *v.* Mudd, 44 Ala. 48, 4 Am. Rep. 106.

Mode and Time of Stamping.—A promissory note not stamped as required by the internal revenue act of 1864 can not be stamped in open court, and thus stamped be read in evidence. Such note may be made available as evidence only by having it stamped by the collector of the revenue of the proper district, under § 158 of that act. Whigham *v.* Pickett, 43 Ala. 140.

But under the act of congress approved July 13, 1866 (U. S. Stats. at Large, 1865-67, pp. 143-4, §§ 163, 165), a promissory note, dated and delivered in December, 1867, and payable one day after date, on which suit is brought in January, 1871, may be stamped when offered in evidence at the trial, unless the stamps were designedly omitted with intent to evade the Revenue Laws of the United States. Foster *v.* Holley, 49 Ala. 593.

An indorsement on a promissory note is competent as evidence if properly stamped before it is offered, though the stamp was affixed after the date of the indorsement. Rowland *v.* Plummer, 50 Ala. 182.

Authority to Affix Stamp.—An attorney at law, in whose hands a note is placed for collection, has such an interest therein, by virtue of his general authority, as will authorize him to affix an internal revenue stamp to the note, when necessary to protect the interest of his client. Blunt *v.* Bates, 40 Ala. 470.

What Constitutes a Sufficient Cancellation of Stamp.—Under the revenue act, providing that the person using or affixing a revenue stamp shall write thereon the initials of his name, and the date, so that the same may not again be used, where a promissory note made by three or more has the requisite stamps on it, and is canceled by the initials of the first in the order of signers and the date of the instrument, there is a sufficient cancellation. Spear *v.* Alexander, 42 Ala. 572.

Effect of Failure to Stamp.—The fact that a promissory note sued on is not properly stamped, is not sufficient to authorize its rejection as evidence, unless it be shown that the omission to stamp was with the intent to evade payment of revenue. Bibb *v.* Bonds, 57 Ala. 509.

Effect of Failure to Cancel Stamp Until Trial of Action on Note.—The fact that the revenue stamp on a promissory note was not canceled as required by law until the trial of an action thereon, and then in the presence of the court, does not affect its competency as evidence. Foster *v.* Holley, 49 Ala. 593.

§ 30. Signature Added after Delivery.

A party who, for a sufficient legal consideration, signs his name to a promissory note after it is due, may be declared against as a maker. Tiller *v.* Shearer, 20 Ala. 596.

The signing of a note by a person after delivery to enable the payee to negotiate it does not affect the liability of the maker of the note. Rudolph *v.* Brewer, 96 Ala. 189, 11 So. 314.

One signing a note after delivery to enable the payee to negotiate it can not set up in a suit on the note that there was no consideration for his signature. Rudolph *v.* Brewer, 96 Ala. 189, 11 So. 314.

§ 31. Partial Execution and Failure of Others to Sign.

A note signed by one as surety, on condition that another person also signs it as surety, and left with the payee for that purpose, can not be enforced against the surety, unless executed also by the person indicated as cosurety. Jordan *v.* Loftin, 13 Ala. 547.

§ 32. Persons Liable Whose Names Are Not Subscribed or Inserted.

To hold one liable as the drawer of a bill, his name must be either inserted in it or subscribed to it. May *v.* Miller, 27 Ala. 515.

"A bill of exchange may be drawn upon a person, natural or artificial, by a name different from the proper name of such person, and may be accepted by a name variant from the proper name of the acceptor. Edwards on Bills, 251, 91." Alabama Coal Min. Co. *v.* Brainard, 35 Ala. 476, 479.

§ 33. Execution in Blank.

If one signs or endorses a blank or note, and parts with its possession, with the view of its being filled up and made a negotiable security, and it afterwards and before maturity comes to the hands of a bona fide holder for a valuable consideration without notice, he will be held to its payment, without regard to the authority of the person by whom the blank was filled. Robertson *v.* Smith, 18 Ala. 220.

Person Signing Liable to Bona Fide Holder for Amount Filled in.—When the maker of a note signs it in blank as to the amount and returns it to the payee, the latter is authorized to fill in the blank, so as to make the note enforceable in the hands of an indorsee for value, without notice, and before maturity. Prim *v.* Hammel, 32 So. 1006, 134 Ala. 652, 92 Am. St. Rep. 52.

When a note is signed and sent out in blank, the person signing is bound for the amount inserted in the note to one having no notice of the facts, although it was understood that the sum should be less than that inserted. Brahan *v.*

Ragland, 3 Stew. 247; Herbert *v.* Huie, 1 Ala. 18, 34 Am. Dec. 755.

"It is true, that when a blank note is signed and delivered to another, for the purpose of being filled up, authority must of necessity be conferred to do the act, without which the note could be of no value; but to deduce from this presumption an argument that the note when filled up and in the hands of a bona fide holder, can be sustained alone on this ground, is not correct. The rule by which a recovery in such a case is allowed, stands on a much broader ground, and may be thus stated. That where one of two innocent persons must sustain a loss, he must bear it who is most in fault. If, by misplaced confidence, one enables another to commit a fraud, it is but just he should pay the penalty of his own indiscretion; and that the loss should not be visited on another who has vested his money on the faith of the genuineness of his signature, without the means of ascertaining the fraud which had been committed. These being the principles which governs the case, it follows that, the implied authority is given to the holder to fill up the note, with any amount which he may have advanced on it, in good faith, and without the knowledge of any fact which might lead to an inquiry and expose the fraud. This principle, as has been stated, is well settled, and to permit it now to be questioned, would be of most mischievous consequence. See Brahan *v.* Ragland, 3 Stew. 247; Putnam *v.* Sullivan, 4 Mass. 45 [3 Am. Dec. 206]; Violett *v.* Patton, 5 Cranch 142; Russell *v.* Lanstuffer, Doug. 496; and Roberts *v.* Adams, 8 Port. 297, and cases there cited [33 Am. Dec. 291]." Herbert *v.* Huie, 1 Ala. 18.

Where a note is signed in blank for the purpose of being filled up for a particular amount, and to be used in a particular mode, and it is filled up afterwards for a different sum, or employed in a different manner, a bona fide holder or purchaser may recover on it of the maker, although he knew it was signed in blank, if he was ignorant of the purpose for which it was made. Huntington *v.* Branch Bank, 3 Ala. 186, cited in note in 35 L. R. A. 468.

"No rule can be better settled than the one which determines that he who signs his name to a blank piece of paper, with intent to be filled up as a note or endorsement will be liable, although the person entrusted therewith shall violate the confidence reposed in him, by filling it up with another sum, or using it for another purpose than the one intended. Collis *v.* Emett, 1 Hen. Black. 313; Russell *v.* Langstaffe, Doug. R. 496; Snaith *v.* Mingay, 1 M. & S. R. 87; Crutchly *v.* Mann, 5 Taunt. R. 529; Pasmore *v.* North, 13 East. R. 517; Crutchley *v.* Clarence, 2 M. & S. R. 90; Brahan *v.* Ragland, 3 Stew. 247; Violett *v.* Patton, 5 Cranch, 142 [3 L. Ed. 61]; Mitchell *v.* Culver, 7 Cow. 336; Putnam *v.* Sullivan, 4 Mass. 45 [3 Am. Dec. 206]." Roberts *v.* Adams, 8 Port. 297, 301.

Such a blank is a letter of credit to any amount which the person to whom the same is confided may choose to insert in it. Roberts *v.* Adams, 8 Port. 297.

"When an individual instrusts another with his signature to a blank note, he certainly intends it should be filled up for some amount of money, and used for some purpose. If the sum of money and the object to which it is to be applied are agreed on, it is obvious that the faith of the person intrusted with it is relied on to carry the proposed design into effect. If he violates the trust reposed in him, who should sustain the loss? Most certainly he who enabled the fraud to be practiced. This is a familiar principle of law, and it appears to us this is a correct application of it. The supposition that the knowledge of the fact that the note is not filled up, should put any one taking the note on inquiry as to the authority of the agent, assumes as true, the proposition to be established. It by no means follows that the possessor of a blank signature holds it under an agreement to fill it up for a particular amount, or dispose of it in a particular mode; a much more natural presumption is, that he is vested with a discretion in relation to it, and that in the language of Lord Mansfield, in Russel *v.* Langstaffe, cited from Douglass—'it is a letter of credit for an indefinite sum.' As therefore, the transaction may be what the holder of the blank represents it to be, or at least, as there is nothing in the mere possession of a blank note, which would lead to a suspicion of unfairness or fraud; with no propriety whatever, could an innocent purchaser be so affected with notice of the transaction as to put him on inquiry of the maker." Huntington *v.* Branch Bank, 3 Ala. 186, 188.

A party who signs his name to a note in blank, with the understanding that it shall be filled up with a particular amount, or be used in a particular mode, is liable upon the note, to a party who receives it in ignorance of the agreement, and pays a valuable consideration for it, whether it be an advance of money or the extinguishment of a debt. Decatur Bank *v.* Spence, 9 Ala. 800.

Filling Blank with Name of Bank Where Payable.—Where a person executing a note leaves a blank space after the printed words "payable at the bank of," it is no defense against a bona fide purchaser before maturity that some one, without his knowledge, and before the purchase, had filled in the space with the name of a bank. Winter *v.* Pool, 104 Ala. 508, 16 So. 543, cited in note in 35 L. R. A. 468. See the title ALTERATION OF INSTRUMENTS.

Name of Payee Left Blank.—It is no defense to an action on a note that the name of the payee was left blank, since, between the maker and innocent third parties, the person to whom it was intrusted must be deemed the agent of the maker, with full authority to fill out such blank. First Nat. Bank *v.* Johnston, 97 Ala. 655, 11 So. 690.

Promissory Note Written over a Signature without Authority.—If a man writes his name upon a blank piece of paper, and another person obtains possession of the same, and, without authority to use it for any purpose, writes a promissory note over the name, and negotiates it, such note is not valid, in the hands of an innocent holder, against the person whose name is subscribed to it. Nance *v.* Lary, 5 Ala. 370.

§ 34. Ratification of Instrument Defectively Executed.

Ratification of the unauthorized execution of a note does not ratify stipulations therein to pay attorney's fees and to waive exemptions, unless the putative maker had knowledge of such stipulations when he ratified the note. Brown *v.* Bamberger, 110 Ala. 342, 20 So. 114.

§ 35. Delivery.

§ 36. —— Necessity and Sufficiency in General.

A note made to be discounted in a bank, though not discounted, but afterwards put in circulation, may be binding on the parties. Thompson *v.* Armstrong, 5 Ala. 383.

§ 37. —— Conditional Delivery.

Where a written instrument, in form a conditional note, is signed by the maker with the distinct admission on the part of the payee that it does not contain the terms of their contract, and with the understanding that they will meet again at a convenient time, and execute another instrument truly setting out the contract, the writing has not the force of a contract good and complete in law for want of an absolute unconditional delivery, and, if suit is instituted on it as a note, it is not evidence as such for any purpose. Hopper *v.* Eiland, 21 Ala. 714, cited in note in 43 L. R. A. 474.

§ 38. —— Operation and Effect.

A note takes effect from delivery only, and not from the day it was dated or signed. Flanagan *v.* Meyer, 41 Ala. 132; Burns *v.* Moore, 76 Ala. 339, 52 Am. Rep. 332.

(D) ACCEPTANCE.

§ 39. Oral Acceptance.

"An order drawn by one person, upon another, in favor of a third person, for a specific amount, is a "bill of exchange," and an acceptance, to be binding, must be in writing and signed as the statute requires. Anderson *v.* Jones, 102 Ala. 537, 539, 14 So. 871; Code 1886, § 1766; Code 1896, § 880." Faircloth-Byrd Mercantile Co. *v.* Adkinson, 167 Ala. 344, 52 So. 419, 420.

§ 40. Implied Acceptance.

Where the drawee of a bill of exchange, by permission of the payee's agent, retains the bill for examination from Saturday until the following Monday, no legal obligation is thereby created against him as acceptor during that time. Sands *v.* Matthews, 27 Ala. 399, cited in note in 17 L. R. A., N. S., 1267.

§ 41. Acceptance for Honor or Supra Protest.

Where a bill of exchange is directed to a particular person, no other person can accept it, but for the honor of the drawer. May *v.* Kelly, 27 Ala. 497.

§ 42. Revocation of Acceptance.

"'When an acceptance is once made, if the bill has been delivered to the holder, the transaction is complete, and the acceptance "irrevocable."' Ragsdale *v.* Gresham, 141 Ala. 308, 37 So. 367." Gresham *v.* Ragsdale, 145 Ala. 683, 40 So. 99.

§ 43. Nature of Contract and Liability of Acceptor.

§ 44. —— In General.

The acceptor of a bill is the principal debtor, and the drawer the surety, and nothing will discharge the acceptor but payment or a release. He is bound, though he accepted without consideration, and for the sole accommodation of the drawer. Wilson *v.* Isbell, 45 Ala. 142.

The acceptance of a bill of exchange drawn by one partner in favor of the partnership, in payment of a pre-existing debt due by the acceptors to the payee, imports an engagement on the part of the acceptor to pay the bill to the payee, or the rightful owner thereof, when, according to its terms, it becomes due and payable; and he thereby becomes the primary, principal debtor, his obligation being similar to that of the maker of a promissory note. Capital City Ins. Co. *v.* Quinn, 73 Ala. 558.

Acceptor of Order Becomes Principal Debtor without Regard to Negotiability.—Where the drawee of an order for the payment of money accepts the same, he assumes to pay the order, and becomes the principal debtor, without regard to the negotiability of the order. Ragsdale *v.* Gresham, 37 So. 367, 141 Ala. 308; Gresham *v.* Ragsdale, 145 Ala. 683, 40 So. 99.

The acceptance is an admission of everything essential to the existence of such liability. Gresham *v.* Ragsdale, 145 Ala. 683, 40 So. 99; Ragsdale *v.* Gresham, 141 Ala. 308, 37 So. 367.

Where, at the time an order sued on was drawn, the acceptor was indebted to the drawer for rent of a mill, which indebtedness the order was signed to pay, and the acceptor was also bound by a lease, under which rent would accrue in behalf of the drawer in the future to an amount sufficient to pay the entire order, the acceptor became absolutely bound to pay the same, and could not defend on the ground that by reason of the acts of a mortgagee of the mill the lease was abandoned, and a new lease executed by the mortgagee. Ragsdale *v.* Gresham, 37 So. 367, 141 Ala. 308.

Damages Not Recoverable.—In Alabama, damages can not be recovered of an acceptor of an inland bill of exchange. Hanrick *v.* Farmers' Bank, 8 Port. 539.

The acceptor of a bill of exchange is not, in general, liable for damages for his refusal to pay, in an action thereon by the payee. Manning *v.* Kohn, 44 Ala. 343.

Damages, other than interest, are never given by the law merchant against an acceptor of a bill as such merely. Hanrick *v.* Farmers' Bank, 8 Port. 539.

Under an unqualified acceptance of a bill of exchange, the acceptor is liable only for interest, as on a promissory note, and not for the damages of protest prescribed in Rev. Code, § 1845. Trammell *v.* Hudmon, 56 Ala. 235.

But, in Ticknor *v.* Branch Bank, 3 Ala. 135, it was held that if the acceptor of a bill fail to pay it at maturity, so that it is necessary to protest it, in order to charge the drawer and indorser with damages, the acceptor is liable to refund the notarial fees.

§ 45. —— Accommodation Acceptor.

The liability of an acceptor of a bill is not affected by the fact that it was accommodation paper. Steiner *v.* Jeffries, 24 So. 37, 118 Ala. 573.

§ 46. —— Discharge of Acceptor.

The failure of the owner of an accommodation bill of exchange, who had obtained judgments thereon against the maker and indorser, to collect the judgments during the existence of the Confederate government, until such judgment debtors became insolvent, held not to discharge the acceptor. The law does not require one to attempt a probable impossibility, as to enforce the collection during the suspension of the executions. Wilson *v.* Isbell, 45 Ala. 142.

§ 47. Acceptance of Orders Made Payable on Contingency or Out of Particular Fund.

Where one accepts an order payable out of a certain note, when collected, but dies before the money is collected, and it is afterwards received by his personal representatives, they are liable in their representative character upon the contract of their testator. Swansey *v.* Breck, 10 Ala. 533.

The acceptor of an order to pay a certain sum out of the proceeds of a certain judgment may prove the consideration on which his acceptance was based, and for this purpose may show that the money collected on the judgment was paid to other persons who had prior claims on the fund, and that the balance was not collected. Gliddon *v.* McKinstry, 28 Ala. 408.

§ 48. Conditional or Qualified Acceptance.

See ante, "Acceptance of Orders Made Payable on Contingency or Out of Particular Fund," § 47.

On presentation of an order by plaintiffs to defendants for acceptance, defendants denied owing the drawer the amount therein specified, but admitted a less indebtedness, and said they would pay the amount "when the money was due" the drawer, and retained the order with the acquiescence of plaintiffs. Afterwards defendants wrote to plaintiffs that they would pay them "what might become due" to the drawer. Held, that plaintiffs did not unconditionally accept the order, and were not liable thereon. Williams *v.* Gallyon, 107 Ala. 439, 18 So. 162.

The receipt of indemnity for his liability by an accommodation acceptor of a bill, whose acceptance was conditional, authorizes the drawer to use it contrary to the conditions of the acceptance only where the indemnity was given in exchange for the acceptance, and not as collateral security therefor. Farley Nat. Bank *v.* Henderson, 24 So. 428, 118 Ala. 441.

An accommodation acceptor of a bill, whose acceptance was conditional, before its maturity sued the drawer on notes, one of which was given him as security for the acceptance; and, on learning that the drawer had breached the conditions of the acceptance, he instructed his attorney to strike from the suit the note given for it, which the attorney neglected to do, and the note was included in the judgment, on which less than the debt, exclusive of the amount of the note, was realized. When sued on the acceptance, he offered to remit the judgment against the drawer, to the extent of the note. Held, that there was no ratification of the drawer's diversion of the acceptance. Farley Nat. Bank *v.* Henderson, 24 So. 428, 118 Ala. 441.

If a bill is accepted, "to be paid when in funds," and the holder does not object to such acceptance, he can not resort to the drawer till the acceptor refuses to pay, after he has funds. Andrews *v.* Baggs, Minor 173.

§ 49. Promise to Accept.

§ 50. —— Requisites and Validity.

A promise in writing to accept a bill of exchange not in esse, is, in law, a sufficient acceptance, if the bill be taken on the faith of such promise. Kennedy *v.* Geddes & Co., 8 Port. 263.

"In Coolidge *v.* Payson, 2 Wheat. 66 [4 L. Ed. 185], Chief Justice Marshall thus states the law: 'Upon a view of the cases which are reported, this court is of the opinion, that a letter written within a reasonable time before or after the date of a bill of exchange, describing it in terms not to be mistaken, and promising to accept it, is, if shown to the person who afterwards takes the bill on the credit of the letter a virtual acceptance, binding the person who makes the promise.' So, in the case of McEvers *v.* Mason, Hodgson & Co., 10 Johns. 207, it was held, that a promise in writing to accept a bill of exchange, will not, in law, amount to an acceptance, unless the bill was taken on the faith of such promise. See, also, Goodrich & De Forest *v.* Gordon, 15 Johns 6; Schimmelpennich *v.* Bayard, 1 Pet. 283 [7 L. Ed. 138]; Mayhew *v.* Prince, 11 Mass. 54; Banorgee *v.* Hovey, 5 Mass. 11 [4 Am. Dec. 17]; Parker *v.* Greele, 2 Wend. 545."

Kennedy *v.* Geddes & Co., 8 Port. 263, 267.

Any form of written words clearly showing an intention to accept unconditionally a bill of exchange to be subsequently drawn is a sufficiently compliance with Code, §§ 2101, 2102, requiring such acceptance to be made in writing. Whilden *v.* Merchants' & Planters' Nat. Bank, 64 Ala. 1, 38 Am. Rep. 1, cited in note in 26 L. R. A. 621.

Verbal Promise.—Under Code, §§ 1532, 1535, no right can accrue to any one from a verbal promise to pay or accept a bill of exchange, unless the party to whom such promise is made negotiates the bill on the faith of it. Sands *v.* Matthews, 27 Ala. 399.

Before the enactment of this statute it was held that a mere verbal promise to accept a bill, made after it is drawn, may amount to an acceptance; but that a mere verbal promise to accept a bill of exchange, not yet drawn, is not such an acceptance, as will in law bind the acceptor, even if made to the person in whose favor the bill is drawn. Kennedy *v.* Geddes & Co., 8 Port. 263, cited in note in 26 L. R. A. 622.

Promise Binding Though Amount and Time for Payment Not Fixed.—A promise to accept a bill before it is drawn is binding in law as an acceptance, although, at the time the promise is made, the amount of the bill and time for payment are not fixed. Kennedy *v.* Geddes, 3 Ala. 581, 37 Am. Dec. 714, cited in note in 26 L. R. A. 621, 622.

Where one promised to accept a bill of exchange for the price of goods to be sold by the drawer to a third person, and a sale is made on the faith of such promise, the promisor will be liable on a bill, drawn within reasonable time thereafter, which was payable four months after date, with interest on the account after sixty days; such being the custom in sales like the one made, and the promisor having made no objection to the bill on such grounds when presented to him for acceptance. Kennedy *v.* Geddes, 3 Ala. 581, 37 Am. Dec. 714.

A letter authorizing the person to whom it is addressed to draw on the writers for any cotton he may buy in a named city, provided the draft is accompanied by a bill of lading of the cotton, and does not in amount exceed three-fourths of the market price of the cotton, binds the writers, as in favor of any person who, on the faith of the letter, advances the money to buy the cotton, for a draft which conforms to the prescribed conditions, although the accompanying bill of lading is not genuine. Young *v.* Lehman, 63 Ala. 519.

Letters Held to Be Letters of Credit.—Letters from a commission firm to a cotton buyer, "Should you feel inclined to try this market, either in the way of speculation, or with a portion of your own crop, it will afford us pleasure to serve you, and your drafts will meet with due honor at our hands;" and, "If you can ship any more, you can draw at sight; your own cotton we are holding"—are letters of credit. Smith *v.* Ledyard, 49 Ala. 279.

Though, in a letter, the drawee says, "I shall accept," yet this is not an acceptance, if from the whole letter it appears that an acceptance was not intended. Musgrove *v.* Hudson, 2 Stew. 464.

§ 51. —— Construction and Operation in General.

Defendant orally agreed to accept a draft to be given by a third person in payment of goods to be sold such person by plaintiff. Thereupon plaintiff sold the goods to such person without obtaining the draft, which the latter refused to give. Held, that plaintiff could not recover the value of the goods from the defendant, as he had only agreed to accept the draft, and not to pay for the goods. Pake *v.* Wilson, 28 So. 665, 127 Ala. 240.

On presentation of an order by plaintiffs to defendants for acceptance, defendants denied owing the drawer the amount therein specified, but admitted a less indebtedness, and said they would pay the amount "when the money was due" the drawer, and retained the order with the acquiescence of plaintiffs. Afterwards defendants wrote to plaintiffs that they would pay them "what might become due" to the drawer. Held, that plaintiffs did not unconditionally accept the order, and were not liable thereon. Williams *v.* Gallyon, 107 Ala. 439, 18 So. 162.

§ 52. —— **Effect as Absolute Acceptance.**

A letter to a broker, inquiring the price of cotton, adding, "If we see a margin, will authorize you to draw for the cost," and a subsequent telegram, on being informed of the price, "Will advance cost if you buy strict good ordinarily at sixteen," constitute "an unconditional promise in writing to accept a bill before it is drawn," and under a statute "amount to actual acceptance." Whilden *v.* Merchants' & Planters' Nat. Bank, 64 Ala. 1, 38 Am. Rep. 1.

§ 53. —— **Actions for Breach.**

A promise to accept a bill of exchange is a chose in action, on which no one but the immediate promisee can maintain a suit in his own name. Kennedy *v.* Geddes, 8 Port. 263, 33 Am. Dec. 289.

(E) CONSIDERATION.

§ 54. **Necessity.**

A note given voluntarily, without any consideration, can not be enforced by the original payee. Oldacre *v.* Stuart, 25 So. 38, 122 Ala. 405.

Where A., defendant's agent, who personally owed plaintiff a debt evidenced by notes, sent plaintiff orders on defendant of the amount of the debt, signed by defendant's treasurer and countersigned by A. as its agent, and plaintiff marked the notes paid, he can not recover on the orders, defendant not having been indebted to plaintiff or A., and not having received consideration from either of them for the orders. Smith *v.* Southern Exp. Co., 36 So. 621, 139 Ala. 519.

The written acknowledgment, of a husband, of a note, executed by his wife; though the note may originally have been void in itself; becomes, by such acknowledgment, under the statute of this state, the note of the husband; and it is not necessary to set out in the declaration any consideration on the part of the husband, for such acknowledgment. Phillips *v.* Scoggins, 1 Stew. & P. 28.

Where a drawee of an order accepts the same unconditionally, he is absolutely liable to the payee, without regard to the consideration, as between himself and the drawer, which moved him to accept the order. Gresham *v.* Ragsdale, 145 Ala. 683, 40 So. 99; Wilson *v.* Isbell, 45 Ala. 142; Capital City Ins. Co. *v.* Quinn, 73 Ala. 558.

§ 55. **Sufficiency.**

§ 56. —— **In General.**

§ 56 (1) **In General.**

Consideration Held Sufficient.—Payment by a third person, at the request of a surety, of a judgment against the principal and surety, is a sufficient consideration to support a note and mortgage given by the surety for the repayment of the money. Frazier *v.* Parks, 56 Ala. 363.

Though Const., art. 14, § 6, provides that all fictitious increase of stock by corporations shall be void, where a fictitious increase is authorized before any stock is issued, and all of the certificates are issued at the same time, and purport to represent a gross capital, double in amount to the actual capital, each certificate entitles the holder to share in the assets of the corporation in the proportions his certificate sustains to the whole issue, and the whole issue sustains to the actual capital, so that a note given for such certificates, at 50 cents on the dollar, by one with knowledge of the fictitious issue, is not void for want of consideration. Beitman *v.* Steiner, 98 Ala. 241, 13 So. 87, distinguishing Williams *v.* Evans, 87 Ala. 725, 6 So. 702.

A., being indebted to B., who had died, executed his note for the amount to C., who was about to administer on the estate of B., C. promising to execute a receipt for the money as administrator, after his qualification as such. He became the administrator of B., and afterwards, brought a suit against A. on the note. Held that, as he could give a valid receipt for the money, there was a sufficient consideration for the note, and, no demand having been made of the receipt, that there was no failure of the consideration. Nelson *v.* Lovejoy, 14 Ala. 568.

A note executed after the close of the Civil War, in consideration of Confederate treasury notes collected during the war by the maker for the payee, and converted to the maker's own use, is upon a sufficient consideration, and a recovery thereon will not be limited to the value of the converted Confederate treasury notes. Massie *v.* Byrd, 87 Ala. 672, 6 So. 145.

A promissory note for the prices of slaves given upon a sale between citizens of a seceded state, embraced in the emancipation proclamation of President Lincoln, made after the date of the proclamation, but before it was actually and practically carried into effect by the success of the national forces, is not invalid for want of consideration. The proclamation was a war measure, and did not operate absolutely to destroy property in slaves until the national forces were able to enforce it. McElvain *v.* Mudd, 44 Ala. 48, 4 Am. Rep. 106.

It is no defense to an action on a note that the consideration thereof was the loan to defendant of the proceeds of a share of stock which was a voluntary gift from him to plaintiff. Rice *v.* Rice, 106 Ala. 636, 17 So. 628.

G., having large transactions with the Pennsylvania Bank of the United States, by borrowing money, made a settlement with an agent of the bank, and discharged the principal of his indebtedness, and, for the payment of usurious interest, transferred notes on three persons, and executed a guaranty for their payment. These notes were, by the bank, transferred to trustees, for the payment of creditors, and B., as the agent of the trustees, reduced the notes to judgment. G. then made an agreement with B., by which he obtained the control of the judgments, and took up his guaranty, and executed his own note for the amount due, B. being ignorant of the usury. Held, that there was a sufficient consideration for the note. Gee *v.* Bacon, 9 Ala. 699.

Consideration Held Insufficient.—A note executed by the promisor to his son, in lieu of the conveyance of lands promised if the latter would not remove from the state, the evidence failing to show that the son contemplated removing, and had abandoned that purpose in consideration of the promise, is without consideration, and void. Head *v.* Baldwin, 83 Ala. 132, 3 So. 293.

A note without other consideration than the transfer, by delivery, of a certificate of the register of the United States land office, to the effect that the person to whom it was issued had taken the preliminary steps towards entering as a homestead the land described therein, which land had, before the making of such note, been abandoned by such entryman before he was entitled to a final certificate or patent therefor, is invalid for want of consideration. McCollum *v.* Edmonds, 109 Ala. 322, 19 So. 501.

In a contract between A. and B., A. was to receive B.'s note, without surety, and the note was made and received. Afterwards A. called on B. for a surety, who accordingly had the note subscribed by a third person, and returned it to A. Held, that there was no new consideration between A. and B., or any between A. and the surety, which would support his undertaking. Jackson *v.* Jackson, 7 Ala. 791.

A promise to pay a sum of money for the delivery of a valuable paper, to which the person in possession has no claim, but which belongs to another, can not be enforced; nor will it vary the case that the note which was given for the production of the paper was made payable to a third person. McCaleb *v.* Price, 12 Ala. 753.

A note given for the purchase money of land sold at a public sale by an administrator, without an order of court, under the erroneous supposition that the will conferred on him authority to sell, is without consideration; and if an assignee of such note, for the purpose of avoiding that defense, induces the maker to substitute a new note, the substituted note is also without consideration. Stark *v.* Henderson, 30 Ala. 438.

§ 56 (2) Waiver of Rights and Surrender or Release of Lien or Security.

A note given to a corporation by its treasurer, who acted without compensation, and in his name, as such treasurer, deposited funds in a reputedly solvent bank, where they were lost through the bank's failure, in consideration of the corporation releasing him and the sureties on his fidelity bond, and the bank from all claims for such funds, is founded on a sufficient consideration. Booth *v.* Dexter Steam Fire-Engine Co. No. 1 of Montgomery, 24 So. 405, 118 Ala. 369.

A note given by a purchaser of a subdivision of the public lands, as a compensation to one who, previous to the purchase, had settled upon and improved the same, is not supported by a consideration which will authorize its recovery. Duncan *v.* Hall, 9 Ala. 128.

§ 56 (3) Forbearance.

Where, pending proceedings to compel settlement of a guardian's account, one of the sureties on the guardian's bond gave his note, with sureties, for his share of the estimated liability of the guardian in consideration that his co-surety would take no proceeding against his property, he being about to remove from the state, the consideration is sufficient to support the note as against the surety thereon. Blankenship *v.* Nimmo, 50 Ala. 506.

§ 56 (4) Contract to Convey or Deliver.

A vendee of land, who takes and retains possession, under a parol contract of purchase, can not defeat a recovery on his note, given for the purchase money, on the ground of want or failure of consideration, it not appearing that the vendor has failed or refused to comply with his contract. Gillespie *v.* Battle, 15 Ala. 276.

§ 56 (5) Mutual Promise.

The endorsement of a promissory note is a sufficient consideration for a promise by the endorsee to pay the endorser an equivalent sum. Litchfield *v.* Falconer, 2 Ala. 280.

§ 57. —— For Acceptance.

The consideration for the acceptance of a draft is not sufficient in that it moves from the drawer, and not from the payee. Hunt *v.* Johnson, 96 Ala. 130, 11 So. 387.

An accommodation acceptor of a bill, whose acceptance procures the release of the drawer's property from a lien asserted by the payee, is liable on the bill, though he does not know what the consideration of the acceptance is. Dunbar *v.* Smith, 66 Ala. 490.

§ 58. —— Pre-Existing Indebtedness or Liability.

§ 58 (1) In General.

Promise of Debtor.—"An existing indebtedness is a consideration for a promise by the debtor himself." Rutledge *v.* Townsend, etc., Co., 38 Ala. 706, 714.

This is so because a past consideration is sufficient as to the party at whose request, expressed or implied, it was incurred. Rutledge *v.* Townsend, etc., Co., 38 Ala. 706, 714.

An antecedent debt of the maker is sufficient consideration for a note. Gates *v.* Morton Hardware Co., 40 So. 509, 146 Ala. 692.

A note taken in payment of an antecedent debt is taken for value in due course of business. Carter *v.* Odom, 25 So. 774, 121 Ala. 162.

"It is well established, that when a promissory note is given for a subsisting debt, and the note is payable at a future day, the remedy upon the original debt is suspended; and that suspension is a consideration for the new promise. Addison on Contracts 1117, 1118; Baker *v.* Walker, 14 M. & W. 465; Simson *v.* Lloyd, 2 C., M. & R. 184." Rutledge *v.* Townsend, etc., Co., 38 Ala. 706, 715.

Where a widow is sued on a note made by her when a feme covert, and she pleads her coverture in bar, it is not a good replication that, after her husband's death, she promised to pay the note, unless some new consideration or previous moral obligation is shown to support the promise. Vance *v.* Wells, 6 Ala. 737.

Where A. gave his note to B. for services rendered in a suit in which A. was surety for C., without knowledge that the amount of B.'s fee had been fixed by arbitration, and that C. had given his note therefor, secured by a mortgage, held, that A.'s note was without consideration. Edwards *v.* Logan, 66 Ala. 506.

Promise of a Third Party.—Where defendants had given a note for an antecedent debt of another, without any new consideration moving to them, it was without consideration. Richardson *v.* Fields, 26 So. 981, 124 Ala. 535.

Where a third person joins with a debtor in the execution of a promissory note, payable to the creditor, and to be delivered as collateral security for the original indebtedness, the note is without consideration as to him; but a valid promise by the debtor, contemporaneously made, to indemnify him against liability on the note, forms a sufficient consideration to support the note as to the surety. Rutledge *v.* Townsend, etc., Co., 38 Ala. 706.

"Where one thus makes a promise to pay the pre-existing debt of another, for the purpose of its security, there is no element, either of detriment to the promisee, or of benefit to the promisor; and upon principle it seems clear, that there is no consideration. It is the case of a promise made for a consideration wholly, past, and not founded upon the request of the promisor; and can not be distinguished, in principle, from the case where a third person subscribes to an existing note, or guaranties the payment of a subsisting debt, or where an administrator executes his note for a debt of the intestate; in all of which cases it is held, that there is no consideration. Jackson *v.* Jackson, 7 Ala. 791, 792; 1 Parsons on Contracts, 391; Chitty on Contracts, 53, 61, 62, 426; Hester *v.* Wesson, 6 Ala. 415; Williams *v.* Sims, 22 Ala. 512. We accordingly find, as the principle would lead us to expect, numerous adjudications, that the promise to pay the pre-existing debt of another, founded upon no other consideration than the debt, no matter what form it may assume, is nudum pactum. Leonard *v.* Vredenburgh, 8 Johns. 29 [5 Am. Dec. 317]; Clark *v.* Small, 6 Yerg. 418; Commercial Bank *v.* Norton, 1 Hill 501; Rix *v.* Adams & Throop, 9 Vt. 233 [31 Am. Dec. 619]; Littlefield *v.* Shee, 2 Barn. & Ad. 811; Meyer *v.* Haworth, 8 Ad. & El. 467; Bates *v.* Sturges, 2 Moore & Scott, 172 (28 E. C. L. 284); French *v.* French, 2 M. & G. 644 (40 E. C. L. 555); Russell *v.* Buck, 11 Vt. 166; Barker *v.* Bucklin, 2 Denio 45 [43 Am. Dec. 726]; Gilman *v.* Kibler, 5 Humph. 19; Hopkins *v.* Logan, 5 Mees. & W. 241; Deeson *v.* Gridley, 15 C. B. 295; 1 Amer. Leading Cases (Hare & Wallace's notes), 146; Chitty on Contracts, 53; Salmon *v.* Brown, 6 Blackf. 347; Blunt *v.* Boyd, 3 Barb. 209." Rutledge *v.* Townsend, etc., Co., 38 Ala. 706, 712.

A promissory note given for the debt of another, on the assurance of the payee that the agent of the debtor will pay it on request, but without the knowledge or assent of such debtor or his agent, is without consideration, notwithstanding the note is made payable some time after the transaction, and the claim against the debtor is receipted and delivered to the maker. Stoudenmire *v.* Ware, 48 Ala. 589.

The fact that a widow remains in possession of all the real and personal estate of her deceased husband, such possession not being derived from a creditor of his to whom she gives a promissory note, forms no consideration therefor. Watson *v.* Reynolds, 54 Ala. 191.

The widow of one who had died insolvent, induced by the false representations of a judgment creditor of the estate, namely, that her having used a certain work horse of the estate without administration rendered her liable to pay the judgment, gave her promissory note with surety in settlement thereof; and the creditor thereupon, without her consent, receipted the judgment on the docket. Held, that the note was without consideration and void, both as to the principal and surety. Maull *v.* Vaughn, 45 Ala. 134.

The surrender to a widow of a claim against her deceased husband, and the release of the husband's estate from all liability thereon, is a sufficient consideration to uphold a promissory note given by the widow in payment of the claim, though the husband's estate may have been absolutely insolvent at the time. Nowlin *v.* Wesson, 93 Ala. 509, 8 So. 800.

A. having purchased from B. "a claim on public land" for $50, and B. being indebted to C. in that amount, due by open account, by mutual agreement between the three A. executed his note to C. "in payment of" B.'s indebtedness. Held, that this was a sufficient consideration to support an action on the note by C. or his assignee. Hughes *v.* Young, 25 Ala. 483.

B. executes his note to O., in satisfaction of a supposed demand due from the son-in-law of B., to O., when in fact no such demand existed. Held, that the note was without consideration. Bullock *v.* Ogburn, 13 Ala. 346.

§ 58 (2) Settlement of Claims in General.

If a creditor and his debtor entertain doubts about the validity of the debt, and make an honest compromise of it, a note given in consideration of such compromise is valid; and, on suit on such a note, the invalidity of the claim compromised can not be set up. Curry *v.* Davis, 44 Ala. 281. See the title COMPROMISE AND SETTLEMENT.

A compromise in good faith, of certain notes made in 1863, in consideration of the purchase of slaves in the same year, and after the emancipation proclamation of the president of the United States, whereby the amount of the first claim was largely abated, and a new note executed in consideration of such compromise, is a sufficient legal consideration to sustain such note; and this, even if the third section of ordinance No. 38 of the convention of 1867 was not unconstitutional. The fact that said third section is unconstitutional, places the question beyond doubt. Curry *v.* Davis, 44 Ala. 281. See the title CONSTITUTIONAL LAW.

§ 58 (3) Settlement of Claims in Litigation.

A compromise of matters in dispute and litigation between the parties is a sufficient consideration, in the absence of fraud, to support a promissory note given in pursuance of the settlement. Wyatt *v.* Evins, 52 Ala. 285.

In an action on a promissory note given in settlement of a pending attachment suit against the maker, which was founded on a debt for the loan of Confederate money, and the price of goods sold, the defendant can not defeat a recovery on account of the invalidity of the Confederate money as a consideration. Bozeman *v.* Rushing, 51 Ala. 529.

§ 59. Failure of Consideration.

See post, "Want or Failure of Consideration," § 284 (3).

§ 59 (1) In General.

A. executed her note to B. for future services to be rendered by him as an overseer, but, before the note was delivered, told him that she could not employ him, unless he brought a recommendation from C. B. promised to procure the recommendation, but failed to do so, and the services were never rendered. B. brought suit on the note, and proved that he had been ready to enter upon the service at the time agreed on, and that A. then refused to employ him. Held, that the procuring of C.'s recommendation formed part of the consideration of the note, and, having failed to procure it, B. could not recover on the note. Corbin *v.* Sistrunk, 19 Ala. 203.

Where a drawee of an order accepts the same unconditionally, he is absolutely liable to the payee, without regard to the consideration, as between himself and the drawer, which moved him to accept the order, or to the failure of that consideration. Gresham *v.* Ragsdale, 40 So. 99, 145 Ala. 683.

The fact that whiskey sold by plaintiff to defendant did not meet the wants of defendant's trade as plaintiff represented it would, did not amount to a failure of consideration of a note given by defendant for the price of the whiskey. Shiretzki *v.* Kessler & Co., 147 Ala. 678, 37 So. 422.

§ 59 (2) Partial Failure.

A note was given as a retainer to attorneys in a prosecution against the maker for homicide. Before trial, the maker was killed by a mob. Held, that there was a partial failure of consideration. Agnew *v.* Walden, 84 Ala. 502, 4 So. 672.

A donee of bank stocks, in which the donor reserved a life estate, agreed that the undivided surplus earned by the stock during the donor's lifetime should be paid to his executor. At the death of the donor, a settlement was had on the supposition that the surplus earned by the stock was a certain amount, for which the donee made notes secured by a mortgage. It was afterwards ascertained that the surplus was in fact very much less. Held, that there was a pro tanto failure of consideration for the notes and mortgage. Thompson *v.* Hudgins, 22 So. 632, 116 Ala. 93.

§ 60. Estoppel to Deny Consideration or Allege Failure of Consideration.

Repeated promises to pay do not prevent the maker from insisting that there was no consideration for his note. Oldacre *v.* Stuart, 25 So. 38, 122 Ala. 405.

(F) VALIDITY.

§ 61. Validity of Assent.

§ 62. —— In General.

It is no defense to a note that the defendant signed it under such intoxication that he could not give proper attention to it, since intoxication is not a defense unless the contracting party does not know what he is doing. Wright *v.* Waller, 29 So. 57, 127 Ala. 557, 54 L. R. A. 440.

§ 63. —— Mistake.

Where a person signs an instrument without reading it, or, if he can not read, without asking to have it read to him, the legal effect of the signature can not be avoided by showing his ignorance of its contents, in the absence of some fraud, deceit, or misrepresentation having been practiced upon him. Burroughs *v.* Pacific Guano Co., 81 Ala. 255, 1 So. 212.

Where one voluntarily executed a note without reading it, and there were no false representations as to its contents, he is entitled to no relief if the document proves different from what he thought it to be. Martin *v.* Smith, 22 So. 917, 116 Ala. 639.

In an action on a note, payable to a partnership, the maker can not defeat a recovery under the plea of non est factum, because he did not read it, and did not know that it was made payable to the partnership, and not to the individual partner with whom he was dealing; no fraud, deceit, or misrepresentation being alleged. Cannon *v.* Lindsey, 85 Ala. 198, 3 So. 676.

Where the maker of a note which contains no waiver of exemptions, executed, on request of the payee, a new one, which contained such a waiver, the maker in an action thereon can not, under a plea denying the waiver, show that he did not read the note except as to the amount, he being fully able and having ample opportunity to read it, and the payee having been guilty of no fraud or deceit. Goetter *v.* Pickett, 61 Ala. 387.

§ 64. —— Fraud and Misrepresentation.

§ 64 (1) In General.

Note Void Where Execution Obtained by Misrepresentation of Contents.—Where a person signs a note without reading it, or, if he can not read, without asking to have it read to him, the legal effect of the signature can not be avoided by showing his ignorance of its contents, in the absence of some fraud, deceit, or misrepresentation having been practiced upon him. But the rule is otherwise, and the instrument will be held void, where its execution is obtained by a misrepresentation of its contents; the party signing a paper which he did not know he was signing, and did not really intend to sign. Burroughs *v.* Pacific Guano Co., 81 Ala. 255, 1 So. 212.

Where a person who could neither read nor write was by fraud induced to sign a note giving the payee a lien on the promisor's property, when he supposed he was signing simply an ordinary note, the instrument is invalid. Davis *v.* Snider, 70 Ala. 315.

If the debtor has given his note for the balance of an account fraudulently overcharged, he can defend on the notes, they being then sued on by the payees. Dickinson *v.* Lewis, 34 Ala. 638.

If a creditor, for the purpose of obtaining his debtor's note for a debt already due, falsely and fraudulently promises to supply him with goods for a specified future time, this constitutes no defense to an action on the note. Overdeer *v.* Wiley, 30 Ala. 709.

Contract Growing Directly Out of an Immoral Act.—It is a good defense to an action on a promissory note that the note was given in compromise of actions prosecuted by the payee against the maker, in behalf of others, whose agent he falsely and fraudulently represented himself to be; the contract growing directly out of an immoral act, and connected with and depending upon it. Wyatt *v.* Ayres, 2 Port. 157.

The drawer of a bill induced the acceptor to believe that the latter signed only as surety, and that writing his name across the face was "only a peculiar way of signing." Held, that the acceptor should be relieved to the extent of the injury done by the fraud, as against a party with notice. Ross *v.* Drinkard, 35 Ala. 434.

False Representations as to Nature of Contract.—Where defendant's evidence tended to show that, at the time of signing the notes sued on, plaintiff, who had handed them to defendant, fraudulently represented them to contain the contract agreed on, and that defendant, relying on such representations, signed the notes, which contained a different agreement, it was proper to charge that if defendant, relying on plaintiff's representations that they were as agreed, signed the notes, whereas in fact they contained a different agreement, the jury should find for defendant. Folmar *v.* Siler, 132 Ala. 297, 31 So. 719, 720.

Immaterial Whether Maker Could Read or Write.—If defendant was induced to execute a note by false representations that he was signing an application for an insurance policy, upon which he relied, whether or not he could read and write would not affect his right to rely upon the fraud. Gillespie *v.* Hester, 49 So. 580, 160 Ala. 444, cited in note in 35 L. R. A., N. S., 776.

§ 64 (2) Fraudulent Representations as to Consideration.

A plea in an action on a note alleging that it was a renewal of one originally executed in payment of a subscription to stock; that three certain persons were interested in selling said stock; that one of said persons, acting for himself and his associates, induced defendant to sign said note, by representing that certain other persons had agreed to take a large amount of said stock, that others had contracted to take a large quantity of the product of the corporation, and that the property of the corporation was then marketable; but that said representations were wholly false—imports liability on said three persons for said false representations, and the averments thereof are sufficient to avoid the original note and all mere renewals thereof, as between defendant and said persons and their assigns with notice. Alabama Nat. Bank *v.* Halsey, 109 Ala. 196, 19 So. 522.

A., a nonresident, having an account against B. for materials furnished in building his house misrepresented to C., upon the advice of an attorney, that such account constituted a lien on the house. Held, that this was not such a misrepresentation as would render voidable a note given by C. for the account. Davis *v.* Betz, 66 Ala. 206.

§ 65. —— Duress.

Checks are utterly void as between payee and drawer if their issuance be procured by duress in obtaining their issuance by an officer of the drawer, a corporation. Southern Hardware & Supply Co. *v.* Lester, 52 So. 328, 166 Ala. 86.

A note is not procured by a coercion or other undue means where it appears that plaintiff, after judgment in his favor in ejectment, procured a writ of restitution, and, accompanied by the sheriff, went to the premises, which were in defendant's possession, for the purpose of executing the writ, when plaintiff told defendant that if he did not rent the premises the sheriff would have to put him out, and that rather than have himself and family turned out he did so, and executed the note in question in payment of the rent. Davis *v.* Rice, 88 Ala. 388, 6 So. 751.

§ 66. Legality of Object or of Consideration.

"If a part of the consideration of a note involves the violation of a penal statute, no recovery can be had on said note. Cotten *v.* McKenzie, 57 Miss. 418; Widoe *v.* Webb, 20 Ohio St. 431, Derring *v.* Chapman, 22 Me. 488; Wadsworth *v.* Dunnam, 117 Ala. 661, 23 So. 699; Patton *v.* Gilmer, 42 Ala. 548; Wynne *v.* Whisenant, 37 Ala. 46." Long *v.* Holley (Ala.), 58 So. 254.

Where the consideration of a note was a number of sacks of fertilizers, a portion of which were sold without being inspected, branded, etc., as required by a statute then in force, and the rest after the repeal of the statute, held, that there could be no recovery on the note. Pacific Guano Co. *v.* Mullen, 66 Ala. 582.

It is no defense to an action on a promissory note that a part of its consideration consisted of a sum of money advanced by one of the payees to a third person, at the request of the maker, in payment of an illegal wager, which such third person had won from the maker. White *v.* Yarbrough, 16 Ala. 109.

A railroad corporation, by its charter, was prohibited from emitting for circulation any notes or bills, or from making contracts for the payment of money except under its corporate seal, and then alone for debts contracted by it. The company and a bank made an agreement whereby the bank was to receive in payment of debts, and pay out in circulation, such notes as the company should issue in payment of its debts. The company issued bills single, in sums from $1 to $20, engraved as bank notes, in payment of its debts; and the bills were received by the bank, under its contract with the company. A third company applied to the bank for a loan, agreed to take the bills single issued by the railroad company, and gave as the consideration certain bills of exchange. Held, that these transactions were not on their face illegal.. so as to prevent the bank from recovering on the bills of exchange. It was a question for the jury whether the bills were lawfully issued by the railroad company in payment of its debts, or as a means of evading its charter prohibition against issuing bills for circulation. Branch Bank at Montgomery *v.* Crocheron, 5 Ala. 250; Whetstone *v.* Bank at Montgomery, 9 Ala. 875.

G. having large transactions with the Penn. B. U. S. by borrowing money, made a settlement with an agent of the bank, and discharged the principal, and for the payment of usurious interest, transferred notes on three persons, and executed a guaranty for their payment. These notes were by the bank transferred to trustees, for the payment of creditors, and B., as the agent of the trustees, reduced the notes to judgment. G. then made an agreement with B., by which he obtained the control of the judgments, and took up his guaranty, and executed his own note for the amount due, B. being ignorant of the usury. Held, that the note was not affected by the usury in the original contract. Gee *v.* Bacon, 9 Ala. 699.

§ 67. Notes in Which Payee Joins with Principal Maker as Surety.

If the payee in a promissory note join with the principal maker as surety, the note is void, and an action at law can not be maintained against either principal or surety. Ramsey *v.* Johnson, Minor 418, overruled in Lea *v.* Branch Bank, 8 Port. 119.

§ 68. Legality of Particular Provisions.

§ 69. —— As to Payment or Default.

A provision in a note that the payee shall take live stock from the maker in payment if they can agree upon the price is not enforceable, because of indefiniteness. Buford *v.* Ward, 108 Ala. 307, 19 So. 357.

§ 70. —— As to Attorney's Fees and Costs.

See the title USURY.

"It is well settled by our decisions that an agreement to pay the reasonable attorney's fees which the payee of a note would have to pay if forced to collect by suit, in addition to the legal interest, does not render the contract usurious." Williams *v.* Flowers, 90 Ala. 136, 7 So. 439.

A stipulation in a note that if the debt evidenced thereby is not paid at maturity, and it becomes necessary to employ an attorney to enforce it, the promisor will pay a certain per cent in addition to the debt, to reimburse the promisee for the amount expended for the attorney's services, when not a mere cloak for usury, will be enforced. Stephenson *v.* Allison, 26 So. 290, 123 Ala. 439.

"An agreement to ten per cent of the amount recovered, in addition to the legal interest, is not itself usurious. The amount stipulated must be reasonable, or at least not obviously excessive; for no form which may be given to the contract —no device—can evade the statute against usury, if the intent appears, or is shown, to secure a profit in addition to the legal interest and the reimbursement of the creditor of the expenses which he may incur in collecting the note." Williams *v.* Flowers, 90 Ala. 136, 7 So. 439.

"In Munter *v.* Linn, 61 Ala. 492, 494, the agreement was to pay, if it became necessary to institute legal proceedings to recover the amount of the notes, the fee of the attorney employed, 'such fee to be 10 per cent of the amount sued for and recovered,' an unconditional agreement to pay 10 per cent. It was held that this stipulation does not constitute the contract usurious, but that the creditor could recover only a reasonable fee, though he stipulated for a larger sum or per cent." Williams *v.* Flowers, 90 Ala. 136, 7 So. 439.

A promissory note for the payment of money, "and 10 per cent attorney's fees," will support a judgment by default for the amount due, including 10 per cent on the amount of the note as attorney's fees. Code Ala. 1886, § 2470. Wood *v.* Winship Mach. Co., 83 Ala. 424, 3 So. 757.

§ 71. Effect of Invalidity.

§ 72. —— Partial Invalidity.

Where part of the consideration of a promissory note is illegal, the whole note is void. Wynne *v.* Whisenant, 37 Ala. 46.

A note taken to secure an account, items of which for sales on Sunday and for liquors illegally sold are blended with legal items, is entire and indivisible, and hence there can be no recovery thereon. Wadsworth *v.* Dunnam, 23 So. 699, 117 Ala. 661.

In an action upon several notes given for various shipments of fertilizer, each consisting of several sacks, it was error to instruct that if one sack did not have the tag attached, as required by law, plaintiff could not recover on any of the notes. Alabama Nat. Bank *v.* C. C. Parker & Co., 40 So. 987, 146 Ala. 513.

A negotiable promissory note, the consideration of which is partly a loan of Confederate treasury notes and partly a sale of goods, is void as between the immediate parties to it, but it is valid in the hands of an innocent indorsee, who is a bona fide holder for valuable consideration, without notice of the illegality, unless it be made wholly void by statute in the hands of such indorsee. Bozeman *v.* Allen, 48 Ala. 512.

§ 73. Estoppel or Waiver as to Defects or Objections.

The maker may waive the illegality, in a suit on the note, and rely on a failure of the consideration. Wynne *v.* Whisenant, 37 Ala. 46.

The maker of a note payable at Tuscaloosa Fence Factory is estopped in a suit thereon by an innocent purchaser for value to deny the existence of such a place. Brown *v.* First Nat. Bank, 103 Ala. 23, 15 So. 435.

Where, in an action on a note given for a stock subscription, there was no evidence that, at the time defendant denied his liabliity on another ground before suit brought, he knew that plaintiff's representations inducing him to subscribe were false, the contention that he thereby waived the fraud is without merit. Alabama Foundry & Machine Works *v.* Dallas, 29 So. 459, 127 Ala. 513.

When a person who is about to purchase a note given for the hire of a slave applies to the maker for information concerning it, and is assured by the latter that he has no defense against it, this does not preclude the maker, when sued by the purchaser, from setting up a subsequent failure of consideration, arising out of the payee's conduct in receiving the slave who ran away before the expiration of the term of hiring, and refusing to deliver him up on demand. Maury *v.* Coleman, 24 Ala. 381.

§ 74. Ratification or Recognition of Validity.

Where a note is purchased by a third person, before maturity, on the faith of a promise by one of the makers that it shall be paid at maturity, such promise imposes on the maker a personal liability to pay the note, and he can not join with his comakers in a bill of interpleader against the purchaser and one claiming the proceeds of the note. Plant *v.* Voegelin, 30 Ala. 160.

One who purchases a wager note, on the admission of the maker that it is good, and he will pay it, can not recover if the note itself discloses the illegality of the consideration. Givens *v.* Rogers, 11 Ala. 543.

A promise by the maker, to pay a note founded on a gaming consideration to the holder, after he had acquired it, with knowledge of its illegality, will not enable him to recover upon it, although after such promise the holder released a debt due from another person to him, to secure which he had previously received the note. Finn *v.* Barclay, 5 Ala. 626.

When a promissory note is given in consideration of the transfer of an account against a third person, which is falsely represented to be a statutory lien on his house, for materials furnished and used in its construction, the contract is not void on account of the fraud or misrepresentation, but voidable at the election of the party defrauded, seasonably expressed; and if, on the discovery of the fraud, he does not offer to restore the account, but retains it, and attempts to collect it by suit, he can not set up the fraud to defeat a subsequent action on the note. Davis, etc., Co. *v.* Betz, 66 Ala. 206.

§ 75. Right to Contest Validity.

See ante, "Estoppel or Waiver as to "Defects or Objections," § 73; "Ratification or Recognition of Validity," § 74.

II. CONSTRUCTION AND OPERATION.

§ 76. What Law Governs.

Law in Force at Time of Execution and Indorsement Governs.—The liability of the parties to a promissory note is governed by the law in force at the time the note was made and indorsed. Cook *v.* Mutual Ins. Co., 53 Ala. 37.

Laws of State Where Payable Govern.—In general, commercial paper executed in one state, and made payable in another, is governed by laws of the state in which it is payable. Todd *v.* Neal, 49 Ala. 266.

Where defendants, residents of Alabama, purchase of W., a resident of Georgia, a fertilizer, to be delivered in Alabama, giving their note therefor, it is an Alabama contract. Hanover Nat. Bank *v.* Johnson, 90 Ala. 549, 8 So. 42.

What Law Governs Rate of Interest.—Where a note is made in and payable in a state it is governed by the interest laws of such state. Kraus *v.* Torry, 146 Ala. 548, 40 So. 956.

A note executed in one state, and made payable in another, must bear interest according to the law of the latter state when no rate of interest is specified in the note. Hunt *v.* Hall, 37 Ala. 702.

Where a bill is drawn in New York, payable in Alabama, which does not contemplate the payment of interest on its face, and interest accrues only in default of payment at maturity, the rate of interest will be governed by the laws of Alabama. Hanrick *v.* Andrews, 9 Port. 9.

In an action on a promissory note, payable in a different state, judgment can not be entered for interest, unless the rate of interest allowed by such state be proved. Peacock *v.* Banks, Minor 387.

A jury have not a right to allow the legal interest of this state on a note shown to have been given in South Carolina; but, if the plaintiff would recover interest on uch a note, he should show what is the legal interest in South Carolina. Evans *v.* Clark, 1 Port. 388.

§ 77. Parties.

§ 78. —— Joint or Several.

See post, "Principals and Sureties or Guarantors," § 79.

Where a note runs to two payees, the presumption is of a joint and coequal interest in them; but this presumption does not preclude proof that their interests were separate and unequal. Tisdale *v.* Maxwell, 58 Ala. 40.

§ 79. —— Principals and Sureties or Guarantors.

See post, "Accommodation Parties," § 80.

Persons who sign their names to a note will be presumed to be joint makers, and not principal and surety, in the absence of anything to the contrary on the face of the note. Johnson *v.* King, 20 Ala. 270.

The order in which the makers sign a promissory note of itself raises no presumption of the relation of principal and surety between them. Summerhill *v.* Tapp, 52 Ala. 227.

Where two names are signed to a note, the presumption is that the signers are comakers, and equally bound; and therefore, in the absence of proof that they were not comakers, the executrix of one is not entitled to a credit for money paid the other to reimburse him for a payment of one-half the note. Jackson *v.* Wood, 108 Ala. 209, 19 So. 312.

One of two joint and several makers of a note can not show, in abatement of a suit against him, that he is surety merely, and that the principal, his comaker, has deceased, and that the time has not elapsed within which his representatives can not be sued. Rice *v.* Brantley, 5 Ala. 184.

One who unites with another, as his surety, in drawing a bill, in the absence of proof limiting his liability, is to be considered as assuming all the duties and liabilities of drawer to each of the parties to the bill, and is consequently liable to the accommodation acceptor, not only for the amount of the bill, in case the acceptor has it to pay, but for the usual commissions incident to its acceptance and payment. Swilley *v.* Lyon, 18 Ala. 552.

§ 80. —— Accommodation Parties.

Accommodation drawers, acceptors, and indorsers are not made co-sureties by Rev. Code, § 3070, where there is no agreement, express or implied, to render them liable as such. Moody *v.* Findley, 43 Ala. 167.

When parties stand on a note in relation of principal and surety, the mere fact that both signed the note for the accommodation of a third person, whose name also appears as surety, will not repel the presumption created by the form of the paper, so as to constitute them joint sureties. Ragland *v.* Milam, 10 Ala. 618.

§ 81. —— Representative or Fiduciary Capacity.

§ 81 (1) In General.

There being nothing on the face of a draft, nor any evidence in the record to show that it was the intention of the parties, in the execution of the draft, not to bind the drawer personally, but the drawee alone; there is no error in a charge, that in determining whether the drawer (defendant) acted for himself, or as the agent of the drawee, "nothing could be looked to but the draft itself, and that the legal effect of the draft was, that the defendant (the drawer) was personally bound." Knott *v.* Venable, 42 Ala. 186.

Where the owner of a steamboat authorizes the captain to accept a bill of exchange for him by writing his own name, with the addition of the word "Captain," across the face of the bill, an acceptance so made is binding on the owner. May *v.* Hewitt, 33 Ala. 161.

§ 81 (2) Signature as or by Agent of Named Principal.

Instrument Signed "A., Agent for B."—An instrument containing nothing in the body of it to show that it is made by an agent on behalf of a principal, but signed, "A, agent for B.," will be deemed the personal contract of A. Dawson *v.* Cotton, 26 Ala. 591.

Sealed Note Signed by One as Agent for Another.—A promissory note signed by one, with a seal placed after his name, who designates himself as agent for another, does not create, prima facie, any obligation on the latter. Dawson *v.* Cotnon, 26 Ala. 591.

Note Signed by President of Corporation.—A promissory note containing the words, "Twelve months after date, we promise to pay," etc., and signed, "For the Montgomery Iron Works. I. S. W., President; S. J., Secretary," held to be prima facie the contract of the principal, and not that of I. S. W. personally. Roney *v.* Winter, 37 Ala. 277.

Note Signed by Secretary of College.—A promissory note, signed by the defendant in his own name, with the addition of the words, "Secretary Auburn Masonic Female College," prima facie imposes a personal obligation on him. Drake *v.* Flewellen & Co., 33 Ala. 106.

Note Signed by Chairman and Secretary of Board of Trustees.—Where a note given for school furniture, bought on credit extended to the board of trustees as such, was signed "Board of Trustees," with the signature of "W., Chairman," and "M., Secy.," beneath, and no consideration passed to W. or M. as individuals, and the payee's agent knew they had no intention to bind themselves personally, it was not enforceable against them personally, and the court properly gave a general charge in their favor on their plea of want of consideration. Peabody School Furniture Co. *v.* Whitman, 6 Ala. App. 182, 60 So. 470.

The acceptance of a bill of exchange by the captain and master of a steamboat, in his own name, as captain, does not bind the owner as acceptor. May *v.* Kelley, 27 Ala. 497.

A bill drawn on "steamer C. W. D. and owners," and accepted by "steamer C. W. D., per A. B., Agent," binds the owners, A. B.'s principals, and they can be sued by their proper names, the bill being properly described. Alabama Coal Min. Co. *v.* Brainard, 35 Ala. 476.

A promissory note, given by an executor, is his personal contract, and will not support an action against him in his official capacity, although words descriptive of his representative character are added to his signature. Christian *v.* Morris, 50 Ala. 585.

Bill Signed as "Executor of" Person Named.—A bill of exchange drawn by G. S., with the addition of the words "executor of S. S.," is the personal contract of the drawer, and does not bind the estate; and an accommodation acceptor, who pays the bill, has no claim against the estate. Kirkman *v.* Benham, 28 Ala. 501, cited in note in 37 L. R. A., N. S., 785.

§ 81 (3) Instruments Made to Persons in Representative Capacity.

Where a promissory note is made to one as agent, he may bring an action in his own name on the note, the addition of his official character being but descriptio personæ. Preston *v.* Dunham, 52 Ala. 217.

Where a bill single is described in the declaration, as made and delivered to the plaintiff, by the name and description of J. D. F. agent for G. A. K. or bearer, the suit is properly brought, and the words agent, etc., will be considered merely as descriptio personæ. Castleberry *v.* Fennell, 4 Ala. 642.

A note payable to the "president and directors of the Planters' and Merchants' Bank of Mobile" is a note payable to the corporation, and may be declared on as such. Hazard *v.* Planters' & Merchants' Bank, 4 Ala. 299.

A promissory note, payable "to the Treasurer of the Manual Labor Institute of South Alabama," is a contract with the corporation, and no action can be sustained thereon in the name of the treasurer; and the law would be the same, even if the association was not incorporated. Alston *v.* Heartman, 2 Ala. 699.

A note payable to A. B., administrator or executor of C. D., is payable to A. B. personally, the word "executor," etc., being merely descriptive. Duncan *v.* Stewart, 25 Ala. 408.

§ 82. Amount.

The general rule is that, where a note for a certain sum of money may be discharged by the payment of a less sum, the greater sum will be considered as a penalty, and the lesser as the debt actually due. Plummer *v.* McKean, 2 Stew. 423.

But where a note is payable at a specified date, for a sum certain, which may be discharged by the payment of a less sum at an earlier date, the greater sum is not in the nature of a penalty, but is the debt actually due, and is recoverable if the less sum is not paid according to the terms of the note. Carter *v.* Corley, 23 Ala. 612; Jordan *v.* Lewis, 2 Stew. 426.

Where a note for $2,000 provided; "which, if paid in par money at New Orleans, may be discharged by $1,600," the greater sum was the sum actually due, and not a penalty. Plummer *v.* McKean, 2 Stew. 423.

Where the figures in a margin of a note do not correspond to the amount written in the body, parol evidence is inadmissible to show that the note should be construed as one for the amount appearing in the margin. Bell *v.* Birmingham (Ala.), 62 So. 971.

§ 83. Interest.

"**Interest runs on a note payable on demand** only from the time when demand is made or suit upon it brought. Macey *v.* Knight, 18 Ala. 300; Dodge *v.* Perkins, 9 Pick. 369; Breyfogle *v.* Beckley, 16 Serg. & R. 264; Dillon *v.* Dudley, 1 A. K. Marsh. (Ky.) 66. And it makes no difference that the note was given * * * for money received at the time it was made. Schmidt *v.* Limehouse, 2 Bailey, 276; Pullen *v.* Chase, 4 Ark. 210." Hunter *v.* Wood, 54 Ala. 71, 72.

A promissory note, payable at a future day, "with interest" at a specified rate, bears interest from date, since it would, without these words, bear interest from maturity. Campbell Printing Press, etc., Co. *v.* Jones, 79 Ala. 475.

A promissory note, made payable at a future day, with interest from date if not punctually paid, carries interest only from maturity. Fugua *v.* Carriel, Minor 170; Henry *v.* Thompson, Minor 209; Boddie *v.* Ely, 3 Stew. 182; Dinsmore *v.* Hand, Minor 126.

Peculiar Provisions as to Time from Which Notes Bear Interest Construed.—Where one, in December, 1834, promised to pay money on the 1st day of January, 1836, "with interest from 1835," it was held that the intention of the contracting parties was that interest was to be paid from the 1st day of January, 1835. Evans *v.* Sanders, 8 Port. 497, 33 Am. Dec. 297.

Where a note is payable on a specified day, and contains a stipulation not to bear interest until another specified day after maturity, a judgment entered thereon after maturity, and before the date fixed for accrual of interest, must be for the principal only. Billingsley *v.* Billingsley, 24 Ala. 518.

The defendant made his promissory note, by which, about twenty-seven months after date he promised to pay to plaintiff, as attorney, etc., of the Connecticut Asylum, etc., "at Hartford, for the education and instruction of the deaf and dumb, the sum of three thousand three hundred and thirty-nine dollars and eighteen cents, at the Mechanics' Bank, in the city of New York, with lawful interest from date till paid (but if the principal sum shall be punctually paid when due, then, in that case and not otherwise, the interest is to be deducted), value received, Tuscaloosa, State of Alabama, 3d February, 1841." Held that the fair intendment is, that the contract, which occasioned the making of the note, required the payment of interest from its date, but the high rate of exchange (of which, the history of the times afford ample evidence) on the North Eastern cities, and the risk in effecting a remittance thither, induced the payee to agree to remit the interest, if payment was promptly made. And the defendant not having paid the principal at maturity, was liable to pay interest from the date of the note. Ely *v.* Witherspoon, 2 Ala. 131.

Statutory Rate Applicable as Well to Time after as before Maturity.—When it was provided by statute that notes given for the purchase money of certain public lands should bear interest at a specified rate, less than the rate in ordinary cases, and the same rate is stated in a note of that kind, it was held that the rule applied as well in computing the interest for the time after as before maturity of the note. Branch Bank *v.* Harrison, 1 Ala. 9.

Note and Mortgage Construed Together Show Note Bears Interest.—The body of a note made no reference to interest, but in the margin were figures representing both principal and interest from date to maturity. A mortgage, executed as part of the same transaction, recited that it was given to secure the payment of this note, "with interest from its date to maturity." Held that, construing the two instruments together, they sufficiently show that the note bears interest from date. Prichard *v.* Miller, 86 Ala. 500, 5 So. 784.

The act of November 17, 1862, to regulate the interest upon debts, being limited by its terms to contracts for the payment of money, does not apply to promissory notes payable in Confederate treasury notes. Toulmin *v.* Sager, 42 Ala. 127.

§ 84. Attorney's Fees and Costs.

A provision in a note for an attorney's fee, not stating the amount, means a reasonable attorney's fee. Gates *v.* Morton Hardware Co., 40 So. 509, 146 Ala. 692.

Agreement Covering Reasonable Attorney's Fee for Collecting.—A stipulation in a note that the maker shall pay all costs of collection will be construed as an agreement to pay a reasonable attorney's fee for the collection of the note, since the law provides for the recovery of court costs. Reeves *v.* Estes, 26 So. 935, 124 Ala. 303; McGhee *v.* Importers', etc., Nat. Bank, 93 Ala. 192, 9 So. 734.

Stipulation Held to Refer to an Attorney's Fee.— A stipulation in a note to pay "costs for collecting above, not less than 10 per cent., on failure to pay at maturity," refers to an attorney's fee, since the parties are liable for court costs without any stipulation. Williams *v.* Flowers, 90 Ala. 136, 7 So. 439, 24 Am. St. Rep. 772; Montgomery *v.* Crossthwait, 90 Ala. 553, 8 So. 498, 24 Am. St. Rep. 832, 12 L. R. A. 140.

Stipulation Including Attorney's Fee for Bringing Suit.—A stipulation in a note to pay "all costs for collecting the above not less than ten per cent," includes an attorney's fee for bringing suit. Williams *v.* Flowers, 90 Ala. 136, 7 So. 439, 24 Am. St. Rep. 772.

Facts Not Depriving Payee of Right to Collect Attorney's Fees.—Where notes provided for attorney's fees in case of collection by attorney on default, the mere fact that attachments were sued out on such notes before maturity, there being no evidence as to the time of levy, on the ground that the maker was about to fraudulently dispose of his property, does not deprive the payee of the right to collect the fees in case of nonpayment on maturity. Munn *v.* Planters' & Merchants' Bank, 109 Ala. 215, 19 So. 55.

§ 85. Place and Time of Execution.

Where a note is declared on as made in "Kemper County Mississippi," the place must be read as Kemper county, state of Mississippi. Dunn *v.* Clement, 2 Ala. 392.

The date of a note is only prima facie evidence of the day on which it was executed. Aldridge *v.* Branch Bank, 17 Ala. 45.

In an action on a promissory note, which bears date on Sunday, it is competent to allege and prove that it was in fact executed and delivered on a different day. Aldridge *v.* Branch Bank, 17 Ala. 45.

§ 86. Place of Payment.

Sufficiency of Description of Place of Payment under Statute Relating to Commercial Paper.—Under Code 1876, § 2094, providing that notes and bills of exchange payable at a banking house, or some certain place of payment designated therein, are commercial paper, a certificate of deposit payable on its return properly indorsed, with the name and address of the bankers at its heading, does not sufficiently describe the place of payment, but is subject, under Code, § 2100, to all payments, set-offs, and discounts had against it before notice of assignment or transfer. Renfro *v.* Merchants' & Mechanics' Bank, 83 Ala. 425, 3 So. 776.

A note payable only in a certain town is not payable at a certain place, within Code, § 2094, declaring what instruments are governed by commercial law. Haden *v.* Lehman, 83 Ala. 243, 3 So. 528.

A note headed "Hayneville, Ala.," and payable at "J. L. H.'s office," is payable at "a certain place of payment therein designated," within Code, § 1756. Rudolph *v.* Brewer, 96 Ala. 189, 11 So. 314.

It may be shown by parol that a note payable at "Anniston Loan & Trust Company, of Anniston, Ala.," complies with Code, § 1756, providing that a note to be governed by the commercial law shall be payable "at a bank * * * or at a certain place of payment therein designated." Anniston Loan & Trust Co. *v.* Stickney, 108 Ala. 146, 19 So. 63.

A note headed "Hayneville, Ala," was prima facie executed there, and is payable there. Rudolph *v.* Brewer, 96 Ala. 189, 11 So. 314.

A note promising to pay a certain sum "in work or cash after my arrival in San Francisco" is not merely a contract to be performed only in California. It is payable wherever payment is demanded after maturity. Schuessler *v.* Watson, 37 Ala. 98.

No Presumption That Place Stated Is in Another State.—Where a promissory note is dated at "Macon," and "payable at either of the banks in Macon," it can not, in the absence of an allegation or proof, be presumed that "Macon" is in another state, so as to devolve upon the plaintiff the necessity of proving the rate of interest abroad, especially as there is a county, and perhaps several villages, called "Macon," although there is no incorporated bank in either. Smith *v.* Robinson, 11 Ala. 270.

§ 87. Time of Maturity.

A note payable at bank "seventy-five after date" will be construed as payable in so many days. Boykin *v.* Mobile Bank, 72 Ala. 262, 47 Am. Rep. 408.

A note payable "by" the 1st day of November, 1870, is payable on that day. Preston *v.* Dunham, 52 Ala. 217.

A note dated in May, 1837, and made payable January 1, "one thousand forty," was held sufficient of itself to determine the day of payment to be the 1st of January, 1840. Evans *v.* Steel, 2 Ala. 114.

A note dated the 4th of December, 1820, and made payable the "25th of December next," does not become due until the 25th of December, 1821. Wallace *v.* Hill, Minor 70.

Note Made Payable "Six Months Fixed after Date."—A note which is executed on "November 11, 1899," and is made payable "six months fixed after date," matures on the 11th day of May following. Doyle *v.* First Nat. Bank, 30 So. 880, 131 Ala. 294, 90 Am. St. Rep. 41.

A bill of exchange, dated the 13th October, and payable ninety days after date,

falls due on the 11th January next. Bradley *v.* Northern Bank, 60 Ala. 252.

A bill drawn within, and payable within this state, nine months after sight, is payable nine months after it is presented for sight. Brown *v.* Turner, 11 Ala. 752.

Note to Mature When Certain Work Is Completed.—A note for a subscription to railroad stock provided that it should mature whenever the directors "shall decide that the railroad has been finished" to a certain point, and that if the company should fail to complete the work "necessary to make this obligation binding by October 1st, 1890," the note should be void. Held, that the note matured before October 1st, if the work was completed before that date. Garner *v.* Hall, 21 So. 835, 114 Ala. 166, cited in note in 30 L. R. A., N. S., 44.

Notes Falling Due on Sunday.—The rule that notes falling due on Sunday are payable on the Saturday previous does not apply to a note made on Saturday, payable one day after date, without grace. Such note becomes payable on Monday. Sanders *v.* Ochiltree, 5 Port. 73, 30 Am. Dec. 551; Mahoney *v.* O'Leary, 34 Ala. 97.

§ 88. Days of Grace.

A bill drawn and payable within the state nine months after sight is entitled to days of grace. Brown *v.* Turner, 11 Ala. 752.

A bill of exchange payable twelve months after date, when the nominal day of payment falls on Sunday, is, notwithstanding, allowed three days of grace, and is properly protestable on the Wednesday following. Wooley *v.* Clements, 11 Ala. 220.

Bill of exchange payable at sight is entitled to days of grace. Hart *v.* Smith, 15 Ala. 807.

"Judge Story, in his treatise on bills, says, 'that days of grace are allowed on all bills, whether payable at a certain time after date, after sight, or even at sight. And although there has been some diversity of opinion, whether bills payable at sight, are entitled to days of grace, it is now settled by the decisions, both in England and America, that days of grace are allowable on such bills:' § 342, p. 429. 'To the same effect, see Chit. on Bills, 10th Ed., 376; Bayl. on Bills, 5th Ed., 244, 245; Selwyn's N. P., 9th Ed., 351; Coleman *v.* Sayre, 1 Barn. (K. B.) 303; Dehers *v.* Harriot, 1 Show. 165; Stephens' N. P. 876." Hart *v.* Smith, 15 Ala. 807.

"We hold the doctrine to be, at least under our statute, that on a check, bill or note, expressed to be payable on demand, or when no time of payment is expressed, payment may be demanded at any time, without any allowance of days of grace." Sommerville *v.* Williams, 1 Stew. 484, 486.

§ 89. Mode and Form of Payment.

Stipulation Clearly for Benefit of Maker.—If a stipulation as to the manner of payment of a note is clearly for the benefit of the maker, and the maker neglects to avail himself of the privilege inserted for his benefit, according to its terms, the note becomes an absolute promise to pay money. Weaver *v.* Lapsley, 42 Ala. 601, 94 Am. Dec. 671.

When a note promises to pay a certain amount in cash or work after a certain time, the maker, if he wishes to benefit by the option, must offer to do the work when the time arrives and an opportunity is afforded; otherwise, the note becomes absolute for the payment of money. Schuessler *v.* Watson, 37 Ala. 98.

A note payable at a specified time, "which may be discharged in good leather," at a fixed price, becomes an absolute contract to pay money if the payee does not give notice of his intention to pay in leather. Plowman *v.* Riddle, 7 Ala. 775.

A stipulation, in a promissory note, that it may be discharged in cotton of a fair quality, at seven cents per pound, delivered at a particular place, is for the benefit of the defendant, and he must show that he delivered or offered to deliver it in payment of the note. Love *v.* Simmons, 10 Ala. 113.

Note for a Certain Number of "Dollars."—A promissory note made in Alabama on October 31, 1863, for a certain number of "dollars," and payable January 1, 1864, is not, prima facie, subject to be discharged by a payment in Confederate treasury notes. In such a note the word "dollars" means dollars in lawful money of the United States. Wilcoxen *v.* Reynolds, 46 Ala. 529.

A promissory note for the payment of "dollars," dated in January, 1865, is presumed to be payable in lawful money, and not in Confederate currency; but this presumption may be rebutted by proof of an agreement or understanding, express or implied, that it should be paid in Confederate currency. Hightower *v.* Maull, 50 Ala. 495.

A promissory note to pay a sum in "current money of the state of Alabama," is, in legal effect, an undertaking to pay in gold or silver coin. Carter *v.* Penn, 4 Ala. 140.

Promise to Pay "in the Common Currency of Alabama."—But it was held that a writing, in the form of a promissory note, for the payment of a sum of money "in the common currency of Alabama," was not an undertaking to pay the sum expressed in coin, but in bank notes, which were the common currency of the state when the writing was made. Carlisle *v.* Davis, 7 Ala. 42.

A promise to pay a sum of money in "Alabama Bank or branch notes" is a promise to pay in notes of the Bank of the State of Alabama or its branches; and it is proper for a court to charge a jury that such is the proper construction, without evidence of the meaning of the terms used. Wilson *v.* Jones, 8 Ala. 536.

A bill payable in "funds current in the city of New York" was held to be payable in gold and silver, or their equivalent. Lacy *v.* Holbrook, 4 Ala. 88.

Promise to Pay in Confederate Currency.—Where the agreement of the parties was that the note sued on should be discharged in Confederate currency, the measure of the plaintiff's recovery is the value of the stipulated amount of such currency at the time of maturity. If it is of no value at that time, only nominal damages can be recovered. Powe *v.* Powe, 42 Ala. 113; Thomas *v.* Thomas, 42 Ala. 120; Toulmin *v.* Sager, 42 Ala. 127; Marshall *v.* Marshall, 42 Ala. 149.

In an action since the war on a note payable during the war, given in consideration of the loan of Confederate currency, and intended to be discharged in "dollars" of that currency, the measure of recovery is the value of the currency at the time of the loan. Whitfield *v.* Riddle, 52 Ala. 467.

A note payable "in solvent notes or accounts of other men" is not equivalent to a note payable in money, but is a contract to pay the sum expressed in the note, at or before maturity, dollar for dollar, "in solvent notes and accounts of other men," or, if paid after maturity, the value in money of that amount of such "solvent notes and accounts," at the time of the maturity of the note. Williams *v.* Sims, 22 Ala. 512.

Obligation to Pay in Coin or Cotton.—An obligation in writing to pay a specified sum of money on a day certain in coin or cotton, at the option of the creditor, does not require of him an election and notice to the maker in order to maintain an action to recover the coin. Russell *v.* McCormick, 45 Ala. 587, 6 Am. Rep. 707.

Where there is a condition in a note that it may be discharged in specific articles within a certain time, the time is of the essence of the contract, and after its expiration it becomes an absolute contract for the payment of money. Nesbitt *v.* Pearson, 33 Ala. 668.

§ 90. Conditions.

See post, "Collateral Agreements," § 92.

Performance of Services a Condition Precedent.—Where an obligation is to pay $100 nine months after date, on the condition that the obligee perform certain services, the performance is a condition precedent. Taylor *v.* Rhea, Minor 414.

Peace as Condition Precedent to Payment.—A promissory note by its terms was made payable at a certain date, provided peace was declared between the United States and the Confederate States at that time, but stipulated that it should in no event become due or payable until peace had been concluded and declared. Held, that the note became due upon the cessation of hostilities between the two sections, and not upon the formal making of a treaty of peace. Nelson *v.* Manning, 53 Ala. 549.

Note to Be Void if "Conscript Should Take" Maker.—R. was conscripted and mustered into the service of the Confederate States. L. agreed to, and did, enter the service as a substitute for R., who, in consideration thereof, paid L. $1,300 in cash, and executed the following note: "By the 25th of December next, we or either of us promise to pay to L., or bearer, the sum of seven hundred dollars. The condition of this note is that, if the conscript should take R., the note to be void; if the conscript does not take him, this note to remain in full force and virtue." About a year afterwards R. was enrolled and discharged, on the ground that he was a miller, and continued to be so exempted up to the time of the commencement of this suit. Held, that the contingency on which the contract was to become invalid had not happened. Lively *v.* Robbins, 39 Ala. 461.

Condition in Note Given in Purchase of Land.—A. having sold to B., three quarter-sections of land for $1,000 each, executed to him a title bond for 280 acres, and a deed for the balance; and B., to secure the purchase money, gave his three notes, each for $1,000, and payable at different times—the two first due absolutely, and the last on condition that full title should be made. A. afterwards conveyed to B. 120 acres of the land embraced in the bond, transferred all the notes for valuable considerations, became insolvent, and left the state without making, or being able to make, title to the remaining quarter-section of the land. Held, that the fair inference, from the circumstances was that the parties understood and intended the condition annexed to the note last due as an indemnity against any damage which B. might sustain by the failure of A. to make title to the residue of the land. Graham *v.* Nesmith, 18 Ala. 763.

Conditions in Note Given for Payee's Interest in Mail Contract.—Where a promissory note, given in consideration of the payee's interest in a contract with the United States for carrying the mail on a specified route, contained the express conditions "that said route is not abolished, nor the pay by the United States diminished," the failure of the principal contractor, under whom the payee of the note derived his interest in the contract, to pay over to the maker his proportion of the compensation received from the United States, is no defense to an action on the note. Blackman *v.* Dowling, 63 Ala. 304.

§ 91. Marginal Memoranda and Figures.

A pointed stipulation on the back of a note is as much a part of the instrument as if set out in its body. Seymour *v.* Farquhar, 93 Ala. 292, 8 So. 466.

Where the figures in the margin of a note do not correspond to the amount written in the body, the latter controls. Bell *v.* Birmingham (Ala. App.), 62 So. 971.

§ 92. Collateral Agreements.

Nonperformance of Agreement No Defense to Action on Note.—The nonperformance of an agreement collateral to the execution of a note furnishes no defense to an action on the note. The remedy is by action for breach of the collateral agreement on rescission of the principal contract. McNair *v.* Cooper, 4 Ala. 660, cited in note in 43 L. R. A. 483.

Where a party recovered several judgments, and took the defendant's note for the aggregate amount, with the understanding that satisfaction should immediately thereafter be entered, it is no defense to an action on the note that satisfaction of the judgments had neither been entered by the defendant, nor ordered to be entered by the clerk upon the record, it not appearing that any injury had resulted to the defendant from the failure of the plaintiff to perform his undertaking, and it being competent for the court in which the judgments were rendered to cause satisfaction to be entered upon the motion of either party. Childs *v.* Franklin, 10 Ala. 79.

The maker of a promissory note can not avoid it on the ground of a parol promise, made by the payee before the note was made, that payment would be accepted in depreciated railroad notes then in circulation as money. Hair *v.* La Brouse, 10 Ala. 548, cited in note in 43 L. R. A. 459.

Agreement Held to Be Independent of Note.—Where a note is made in consideration of the purchase of a brickyard in the town of Catawba, and the vendor agrees, in consideration of the sale, not to make bricks there, the promises are independent, and the maker can not plead a breach of the agreement in bar of an action on the note by the payee. Comelander *v.* Bird, 11 Ala. 913.

Agreement of Partnership No Part of Consideration of Note.—In an action upon a note, it appeared from a written contract between the parties that the consideration was an undivided moiety of a tract of land upon which was a sawmill, and that the parties were to hold the mill in partnership. Held, that the agreement of partnership was no part of the consideration of the note, and the breach, therefore, no defense to the action. Durden *v.* Cleveland, 4 Ala. 225.

Agreement That Other Notes Might Be Substituted.—An agreement between the principal, the accommodation makers of a note, to secure the debt, and the creditor, made when the note was signed, that the principal might substitute other notes of responsible parties, and that said note should not be sued by the creditor, with an averment that the principal had tendered and brought into court good notes, etc., was held no defense on a demurrer to the answer. Collins *v.* Seay, 35 Ala. 347.

Where the maker of a note subscribes a contemporaneous writing, in which he recognizes the note, and promises, on the same consideration, to pay an additional sum on a contingency, the writing will be regarded as the last expression of the understanding of the parties, and merge all prior stipulations; hence it is not admissible to prove what either party may have said some months previously in respect to the consideration. Cuthbert *v.* Bowie, 10 Ala. 163.

An oral agreement that a note is to be paid in corporate stock of the maker, so long as it remains unperformed, is inoperative, and no defense to an action on the note. Tuscaloosa Cotton-Seed Oil Co. *v.* Perry, 85 Ala. 158, 4 So. 635, cited in note in 43 L. R. A. 458, 485.

An agreement that payment of a note should be in a currency which afterwards depreciated does not of itself constitute a defense to an action upon the note. It merely gives a right to reduce the recovery to the value of the stipulated sum in such currency at the maturity of the note. Powe *v.* Powe, 42 Ala. 113.

Where A. indorses a bill of exchange in blank, with an understanding that it is to be accepted by B., and this understanding is communicated to C., who purchases the bill, before his purchase, and the bill is not accepted by B., but by some other person, A., the indorser, is not liable on his indorsement to C., the holder. Inge *v.* Branch Bank, 8 Port. 108.

Facts Not Making Bill Conditional or Payable on Contingency.—A., in consideration of a purchase made of B., gave to him his promissory notes therefor, and his own acceptance of a bill drawn on him by C., taking back a receipt, reciting that the bill was to be given up on the payment of the notes of A. Held, that these facts only showed the consideration of the bill, and did not make it conditional or payable on a contingency. Goodwin *v.* McCoy, 13 Ala. 271.

Payment of a Note Not a Condition Precedent to Payee's Right to Recover.—H., in consideration of the promise of L. to pay a certain note due from H. to A., made his note to L. for the same sum. Held, that the payment of the note due to A. was not a condition precedent to L.'s right to recover on the note payable to him. Logan *v.* Hodges, 6 Ala. 699.

A note was given in settlement of a suit on a firm debt, under an agreement that the plaintiffs should prosecute to judgment an action for the same debt, begun against the estate of a deceased partner, and assign the judgment to defendants. Thereafter, in an action for a settlement of the partnership affairs, a consent decree was entered, providing that the accounts of the partners between themselves were balanced, and defendants agreed thereby to release all claims they had, or might thereafter have, against the estate of the deceased copartner. Held, that plaintiffs' failure to prosecute the suit to judgment against the estate of the deceased partner was no defense to an action on the note. Bain *v.* Handley, 104 Ala. 399, 16 So. 58.

Where a mortgage to secure notes contemporaneously executed provides that all the notes shall become due on default in the payment of either of them, or in the payment of taxes, or for insurance, on such default the notes become due, not merely for foreclosure proceedings, but for general purposes, so that suit may be brought on any of them. Chambers v. Marks, 93 Ala. 412, 9 So. 74.

Agreement to Exchange Note for Other Notes.—An agreement, entered into without consideration, by the maker of a note, with one who at the time is the owner of the note, to exchange it for other notes, then held by the maker against him, can not be enforced against a subsequent plaintiff, for whose use suit is brought on the note. Sawyer v. Hill, 12 Ala. 575.

Waiver of Condition.—In an action on a note, it appeared that defendant had arranged with his creditors to execute to each his note payable a certain time in futuro, provided they all, as a condition precedent, would sign an agreement granting extensions on their claims. Held, that the execution and delivery by defendant of a note before the signing of such agreement constituted a waiver of the condition, and the subsequent failure of certain creditors to sign was immaterial. Garner v. Fite, 93 Ala. 405, 9 So. 367, cited in note in 43 L. R. A. 458.

III. QUALIFICATION, RENEWAL, AND RESCISSION.

§ 93. Modification by Parties in General.

The maker and holder of a note may change the rate of interest which the maker shall pay by a subsequent parol agreement, if it is based on a sufficient consideration. Hunt v. Hall, 37 Ala. 702.

A plea in an action on a note averred "that the note sued on was made payable to A. or order, and, at the time said note was made payable, it was agreed that it should not be transferred except to S., and afterwards, by consent of the parties to said note, in pursuance of said agreement, and to carry out the same, said agreement * * * was indorsed on said note, and the indorsement was made while said A. was still the owner." Held, that the subsequent indorsement of such agreement on the note, being without consideration, imposed no binding obligation. Johnson v. Washburn, 98 Ala. 258, 13 So. 48.

A contract for the sale of a slave was completed by the delivery of a bill of sale to the buyer, and the taking of his personal note for the consideration, the slave to be delivered the next morning. On the next day the seller insisted on having a new note, with sureties, as originally suggested by the buyer. The buyer went to find sureties, but the slaves committed suicide while in the seller's possession, before the making of the new note. Held, that the completion of the contract by the bill of sale and note on the first day invested the buyer with the title to the slaves, and waived all prior parol agreements. Therefore the new promise to make a note with sureties was without consideration and void, and did not estop the seller from recovering on the original note. Thomason v. Dill, 30 Ala. 444.

§ 94. Extension and Agreements to Extend.

The time of payment of a promissory note may be extended by parol. Ferguson v. Hill, 3 Stew. 485, 21 Am. Dec. 641.

§ 95. Consideration for Extension or Renewal.

§ 95 (1) Extension in General.

An agreement that no suit shall be brought on a note within five years is founded on a sufficient consideration, where, before the maturity of the note, the principal debtor conveys to the holder property apparently sufficient to satisfy the debt. Branch Bank of Mobile v. James, 9 Ala. 949.

§ 95 (2) Payment of or Promise to Pay Interest as Consideration for Extension.

Payment by the maker of a note of accrued interest and costs of a suit which had been commenced by the holder constitutes a sufficient consideration for an agreement to extend time of payment. David v. Malone, 48 Ala. 428.

A mere promise by the maker of a note to pay usurious interest is no consideration for an agreement to extend time of payment. Cox v. Mobile & G. R. Co., 37 Ala. 320.

§ 95 (3) For Renewal.

Renewal notes are without consideration, where the original note was without it. Cochran v. Perkins, 40 So. 351, 146 Ala. 689.

Effect of Original Note Being Given upon an Illegal Consideration.—"We may concede it to be the settled law that while no number of mere renewals, and consequent extensions of the time for payment, of a promissory note given upon an illegal consideration, will eliminate that infirmity, yet, if there be a consideration for the new note other than the renewal of, and extension of the time for payment of the debt evidenced by, the old one, such other consideration, whether of benefit to the promisor or of detriment merely to the promisee, will support the new contract, and entitle the payee therein to recover upon it, notwithstanding the illegality of the original note, and that the release of an indorser of the original illegal paper would ordinarily constitute a new and sufficient consideration for the renewal note; since, in the absence of participation by the indorsee in the illegal transaction out of which the consideration for the note arises, he may recover against the indorser, notwithstanding the illegality of the paper indorsed, and this, it seems, though he had notice of the illegality of the consideration of the note when he purchased it. Tied. Com. Paper, §§ 199, 259; 2 Rand. Com. Paper, §§ 536, 756; 1 Daniel, Neg. Inst., §§ 205, 206, 669a, 669b; 2 Am. & Eng. Enc. Law, p. 385; Copp *v.* M'Dugall, 9 Mass. 1; Torbett *v.* Worthy, 1 Heisk. 107; Cuthbert *v.* Haley, 8 Term. R. 390; Calvert *v.* Williams, 64 N. C. 168; Ware, etc., Co. *v.* Morgan, 67 Ala. 461, 468." Alabama Nat. Bank *v.* Halsey, 109 Ala. 196, 19 So. 522, 528.

A plea in an action on a note alleging that it was a renewal of one originally executed in payment of a subscription to stock; that three certain persons were interested in selling said stock; that one of said persons, acting for himself and his associates, induced defendant to sign said note, by representing that certain other persons had agreed to take a large amount of said stock, that others had contracted to take a large quantity of the product of the corporation, and that the property of the corporation was then marketable; but that said representations were wholly false—imports liability on said three persons for said false representations, and the averments thereof are sufficient to avoid the original note and all mere renewals thereof, as between defendant and said persons and their assigns with notice. Alabama Nat. Bank *v.* Halsey, 109 Ala. 196, 19 So. 522.

A note made in Alabama since the war of the secession, in renewal of a note given during that war for a loan of Confederate treasury notes, is illegal and void. Lawson *v.* Miller, 44 Ala. 616, 4 Am. Rep. 147.

Where the parties to a note given for a loan of Confederate money ascertained the actual value thereof in gold and United States currency, a new note given by the maker for the amount thus ascertained is void, under Rev. Code 1867, §§ 3643, 3644, prohibiting any person, private corporation, or association from making or emitting any paper to circulate as money and prescribing a punishment for any one who circulates any paper issued without authority of law to answer the purposes of money. Wilson *v.* Bozeman, 48 Ala. 71.

Renewal of Note Usurious in Its Inception.—The renewal of a note, or change of the form of the contract, does not alter the character of the original transaction. If it is usurious in its inception, the taint abides in it, and will affect it throughout all its renewals and mutations, and follow it into whose hands soever it may go, unless the holder receives it through the fraud of the maker. Pearson *v.* Bailey, 23 Ala. 537, 542.

Note Not Violated by Invalidity of Original Contract between Maker and Another and the Payee.—A and B, in exchange for bonds payable at a future day, of the Alabama Life Insurance & Trust Company (a corporation whose charter does not authorize it to lend its credits), executed to the company their individual bond, secured by mortgage, which they afterwards took up by transferring to the company the notes of C, given to them for land. C, before the transfer of his notes, had made a payment on one of them, which A and B neglected to enter; and, in consideration thereof, they gave him their note for the amount of the payment, which he transferred to the company in part discharge of his notes. and which was subsequently taken up by A's substitution of his own note therefor, payable to the company. Held, that the note of A is not vitiated by the invalidity of the original contract between him and B and the company, but is founded on a sufficient consideration. Gee *v.* Alabama Life Ins. & Trust Co., 16 Ala. 637.

A note taken by a partner in his own name, on giving up to the maker a note taken from him by his copartner, which is void by statute, is also void for want of consideration. Bragg *v.* Channell, 3 Ala. 275.

Surrender of Note by Indorsee to Maker Thereby Releasing Indorsee.—Where an indorsee of a note which was illegal in its inception has a right of action against the indorser, a surrender of such note by the indorsee to the maker, thereby releasing the indorser, is a sufficient consideration for a renewal note made by the maker; but the rule does not apply where the transfer to the indorsee was part of the illegal execution of the original note, so as to give the indorsee no right against the indorser. Alabama Nat. Bank *v.* Halsey, 109 Ala. 196, 19 So. 522.

In an action on a note given to a bank in renewal of a note originally executed for a subscription to stock in double the amount of the note, it appeared that the original note was discounted by the bank for the corporation, and the certificate of stock was attached to the note when the latter was discounted, as collateral security for the payment of said note, and that said stock was to be delivered to defendant on payment of the note. Held that, as there was evidence that plaintiff participated in the illegal issuance of said stock, it was not entitled to an affirmative charge that the subsequent renewals of said note for defendant constituted a new consideration, by reason of plaintiffs having relinquished its right to sue the corporation as indorser. Alabama Nat. Bank *v.* Halsey, 109 Ala. 196, 19 So. 522.

Renewal Note Held to Be Given upon a Sufficient Consideration.—Where a widow, in exchange for notes of her husband, which were of value and enforceable in her hands against his estate, gave her own notes, secured by a mortgage, thereby obtaining an extension of the time of payment, in the absence of fraud, duress, or mistake of fact, such transaction was valid. The surrender of a note, founded on a valuable consideration to the maker, and the acceptance by the payee of a smaller note, with a postponement of the time of payment, are sufficient consideration to sustain the second note. Hixon *v.* Hetherington, 57 Ala. 165, overruling 46 Ala. 297.

§ 96. Operation and Effect of Extension or Renewal.

An agreement by parol, extending the day of payment on a promissory note, is binding, so that suit can not be brought, until the time of forbearance has expired. Ferguson *v.* Hill, 3 Stew. 485.

If the maker of a note give a new note in payment of the whole amount of the first note, without objecting to the consideration, this is a waiver of any defense arising out of the consideration. Cameron *v.* Nall, 3 Ala. 158.

The giving a new note, even to the vendor's assignee, but without a new consideration, does not debar the vendee from setting up misrepresentations of the vendor as to the land, as a defense to a suit on the second note. Kelly *v.* Allen, 34 Ala. 663.

§ 97. Renewal Bills and Notes.

See ante, "For Renewal," § 95 (3); "Operation and Effect of Extension or Renewal," § 96.

IV. NEGOTIABILITY AND TRANSFER.

(A) INSTRUMENTS NEGOTIABLE.

§ 98. Negotiability in General.

Recovery of judgment against the maker of a note destroys its negotiable quality, and it can not be afterwards transferred so as to enable the holder to maintain an action in his name against an indorser. Brown *v.* Foster, 4 Ala. 282.

When a judgment is obtained upon an assigned note, the note has lost its negotiable quality, and can not again be assigned, so as to enable the assignee to sue in his own name. Sawyer *v.* Bradford, 6 Ala. 572.

§ 99. What Law Governs.

The law in force when a promissory note is made and indorsed, regulates and defines the liabilities of the parties. Cook *v.* Mutual Ins. Co., 53 Ala. 37.

The act of April 8, 1873, converting

promissory notes payable in money at a designated place, into negotiable instruments governed by the commercial law, has no application to notes made before its passage. Cook *v.* Mutual Ins. Co., 53 Ala. 37.

The negotiability of a note executed in a foreign state will be determined according to the common law, where the statutes of such state relating thereto are not pleaded. Holmes *v.* Bank of Ft. Gaines, 24 So. 959, 120 Ala. 493.

§ 100. Nature and Form of Instrument.

§ 101. —— Bills of Exchange, Checks, and Drafts.

An accepted sight draft for the price of a bale of cotton, with bill of lading attached, indorsed and negotiated by the payee, is governed by commercial law. Bank of Guntersville *v.* Jones Cotton Co., 46 So. 971, 156 Ala. 525.

§ 102. —— Promissory Notes.

In General.—Promissory notes are, under the common law, negotiable instruments. Dunn *v.* Adams, 1 Ala. 527, 35 Am. Dec. 42.

Under the statute of 1812, promissory notes were not negotiable, except so far as to allow an assignee to sue in his own name. Smith *v.* Pettus, 1 Stew. & P. 107.

A note payable absolutely at a designated bank for a sum certain, and at a definite time, is governed by the commercial law, and negotiable. First Nat. Bank *v.* Slaughter, 98 Ala. 602, 14 So. 545, 39 Am. St. Rep. 88.

A note reading: "Mt. Sterling, Ala., March 9, 1903. On December 5, after date, I promise to pay B., or order, $163.81, with cost of collection and attorney's fee. Value received. Payable at their office, Mobile, Alabama. To secure the payment of this debt, the right of exemption existing under the laws of the state of Alabama or any other state is hereby expressly waived"—possesses all the elements of commercial paper under Code 1896, § 869, providing that promissory notes and bonds payable in money at a bank or private banking house, or a certain place of payment therein designated, and bills of exchange, are governed by the commercial law. Dumas *v.* People's Bank, 40 So. 964, 146 Ala. 226.

A chattel mortgage given to secure payment of the note did not impair the character of the note as commercial paper. Dumas *v.* People's Bank, 40 So. 964, 146 Ala. 226.

A note negotiable under Code 1876, § 2094, is not rendered nonnegotiable by the fact that it is payable to the order of the maker, and by him indorsed in blank. Mayberry *v.* Morris, 62 Ala. 113.

§ 103. —— Instruments Payable from Particular Fund.

An order directing the person to whom it is addressed to pay a certain amount out of any moneys he may collect in a certain action is payable out of a particular fund, and therefore not negotiable. Waters *v.* Carleton, 4 Port. 205, cited in note in 35 L. R. A. 647.

§ 104. Certainty as to Place of Payment.

A note specifying no place of payment is not commercial paper as defined by Code 1896, §§ 869, 870, and hence whether transferred before or after maturity is subject to defenses. Holloway *v.* Darden, 53 So. 187, 168 Ala. 256.

Under Code 1896, § 869, providing that a note payable at a bank or private banking house or any certain place of payment is governed by the commercial law, a note not made payable at a certain place is not governed by the commercial law. Walston *v.* Davis, 40 So. 1017, 146 Ala. 510.

§ 105. Certainty as to Time of Payment.

That a note contains an agreement that the note is to be extended six months from maturity, if so desired by the makers and indorsers, does not render it nonnegotiable. Anniston Loan & Trust Co. *v.* Stickney, 108 Ala. 146, 19 So. 63.

The negotiability of a note is not destroyed by a clause authorizing the payee bank to appropriate on the note, whether or not due, at any time, at its option, without notice or legal proceedings, any money which the maker may have in the bank on deposit or otherwise, on the ground that the date of payment is thereby made uncertain. Louisville Banking Co. *v.* Gray, 26 So. 205, 123 Ala. 251, 82 Am. St. Rep. 120, cited in note in 35 L. R. A., N. S., 393.

§ 106. **Certainty as to Amount Payable.**

§ 107. —— **In General.**

The negotiability of a note is not destroyed by a clause authorizing the payee bank to appropriate on the note, whether or not due, at any time, at its option, without notice or legal proceedings, any money which the maker may have in the bank, on deposit or otherwise, on the ground that the amount to be paid at maturity is uncertain. Louisville Banking Co. *v.* Gray, 26 So. 205, 123 Ala. 251, 82 Am. St. Rep. 120.

§ 108. —— **Attorneys' Fees and Costs.**

A stipulation in a note to pay costs for collecting on failure to pay at maturity does not destroy its negotiability. Montgomery *v.* Crossthwait, 90 Ala. 553, 8 So. 498, 24 Am. St. Rep. 832, 12 L. R. A. 140.

A provision in a note by which the maker agrees to pay the expenses of collection, including attorney's fees, does not destroy its negotiability. Bledsoe *v.* City Nat. Bank (Ala. App.), 60 So. 942.

Under Code 1907, § 4959, par. 5, providing that the sum payable by a note is a sum certain, a provision in a note for the payment of costs of collection or attorney's fees in case the note is not paid at maturity does not affect its negotiability. Ex parte Bledsoe (Ala. App.), 61 So. 813.

A note payable absolutely at a designated bank, for a sum certain, at a definite time, is "paper governed by the commercial law," which, if negotiated before maturity, is, under Code 886, § 2684, free from set-off or recoupment, though it also waive exemptions, and provide for attorney's fees. First Nat. Bank *v.* Slaughter, 98 Ala. 602, 14 So. 545.

§ 109. **Medium of Payment.**

Notes made payable in "cash notes" are payable in money, and negotiable. Goading *v.* Britain, 1 Stew. & P. 282.

A note does not lose negotiability, as allowing payment by another note instead of money, by a provision that, if desired, the indebtedness could be extended by the makers and indorsers giving a new note. Anniston Loan & Trust Co. *v.* Stickney, 108 Ala. 146, 19 So. 63.

A bank check payable in currency is not an instrument payable in money, and is not negotiable paper, within the meaning of the law merchant. Mobile Bank *v.* Brown, 42 Ala. 108.

§ 110. **Conditions and Restrictions in Instrument.**

A note by which the maker, four months after date, promised to pay at a bank, to the order of M., a certain sum of money, with interest from maturity until paid, containing a waiver of exemptions, etc., and retaining title to certain mules, was negotiable. First Nat. Bank *v.* Alexander, 50 So. 45, 161 Ala. 580.

An instrument given for the purchase price of an automobile, by which the maker promised to pay, on or before a day specified, to the seller or order a specified sum with interest at 8 per cent payable at a bank named, and also containing a waiver of exemption, and agreement to pay attorney's fees, and a provision retaining title to the automobile, was negotiable. Bledsoe *v.* City Nat. Bank (Ala. App.), 60 So. 942.

Note for purchase price of automobile held negotiable notwithstanding a number of collateral provisions relative to retaining title to the automobile, etc. Ex parte Bledsoe (Ala. App.), 61 So. 813.

Provisions in note for purchase price of automobile, for the retention of the title, and that the loss in case of destruction should be that of the maker of the note, held not to amount to an order or promise to do an act in addition to the payment of money, within Code 1907, § 4962; the provision relative to loss being permissible under paragraph 3 of that section. Ex parte Bledsoe (Ala. App.), 61 So. 813.

An order directing the person to whom it is addressed to pay a certain amount out of any money he may collect in an action at law is payable on a contingency, and therefore not negotiable. Waters *v.* Carleton, 4 Port. 205.

§ 111. **Recitals and Provisions as to Collateral Securities.**

Where a note sued on possesses all the requisites of commercial paper, being made payable absolutely at a designated bank, for a sum certain, and at a definite time, the fact that it contains a provision for the retention of the legal title to the property for which it is given as a security for its payment, does not impede its circulation or impair its validity as negotiable paper. First Nat. Bank *v.* Slaughter, 98 Ala. 602, 14 So. 545, 546.

A note, secured by a chattel mortgage, attached thereto, on a cotton crop, providing for delivery to the mortgagee of the entire crop as rapidly as it could be prepared for market, to be sold by him, as agent of the maker, and the proceeds applied on the note, is not negotiable. Affirmed by a divided court. Commercial Bank *v.* Crenshaw, 103 Ala. 497, 15 So. 741, cited in note in 32 L. R. A., N. S., 859.

§ 112. Effect, as to Negotiability, of Indorsement or Other Transfer.

A note originally negotiable continues so in the hands of an indorsee, unless restricted by indorsement forbidding it by the payee. Robinson *v.* Crenshaw, 2 Stew. & P. 276.

A qualified indorsement does not affect the negotiability of a note, but simply qualifies the obligation of the indorser. Hailey *v.* Falconer, 32 Ala. 536, cited in note in 36 L. R. A. 118.

An indorsement, "Pay B. or order for account of L.," is restrictive, and destroys the negotiability of the draft. People's Bank of Lewisburg *v.* Jefferson County Sav. Bank, 106 Ala. 524, 17 So. 728.

§ 113. Effect of Payment.

"Until a bill or note has been paid by the maker or acceptor, it has not discharged its functions, and may be reissued, after it is due and after it has been paid by an endorser. See Byles on Bills of Exchange, 97, and Callow *v.* Lawrence; 3 Manuel & Selwyn, 97." Kirksey *v.* Bates, 1 Ala. 303, 311.

A promissory note may be reissued by an endorsee after it is due, and after it was discounted in bank, and paid by him at its maturity with his own funds. Kirksey *v.* Bates, 1 Ala. 303.

The payment of a promissory note or bill, will not destroy its negotiability when made by the last indorser; or when made by a prior indorser, if the subsequent indorsements are struck out, before it is again negotiated. Wallace *v.* Branch Bank, 1 Ala. 565.

Where the maker of a promissory note becomes the proprietor of it in the regular course of trade (after it had been in circulation), it is extinguished ipso facto. Wallace *v.* Branch Bank, 1 Ala. 565.

(B) TRANSFER BY INDORSEMENT.

§ 114. Indorsement as Inception of Instrument.

§ 115. —— Notes Payable to Order of Maker.

A promissory note payable to the order of the maker is of no validity until indorsed by him. When indorsed, the note becomes perfect, and he is liable as maker. Lea *v.* Branch Bank, 8 Port. 119.

The legal title to a bill or note payable to order can be transferred only by indorsement. Alday *v.* Jamison, 3 Port. 112.

§ 116. What Law Governs.

An indorsement of a promissory note, made in the state of Georgia, must be governed by the law of that state. Dunn *v.* Parmeter & Co., 1 Ala. 527.

§ 117. Formal Requisites.

Where a torn note has been pasted upon another piece of paper, an indorsement of the note may be made on such paper. Crutchfield *v.* Easton, 13 Ala. 337.

B by a contract in writing, transferred to A a note made by C, which was past due, stipulating that it should be first paid from the proceeds of certain lands, etc., which C bought from B, and for the sale of which B had filed a bill in chancery; and, if the lands did not bring enough to cover the note on the chancery sale, B was to pay the deficiency. Held, that the contract, being independent of the note, could not be treated as an indorsement thereof so that B would be entitled to the rights of an indorser. Brown *v.* Isbell, 11 Ala. 1009.

The indorsement of a receipt given by an attorney for a note placed in his hands for collection will not pass the legal title to the note, although the attorney, by an indorsement on the receipt, promised to pay the proceeds when collected. Gookin *v.* Richardson, 11 Ala. 889, 46 Am. Dec. 232.

§ 118. Consideration.

Where defendants remit a bill, indorsed

by them, to a correspondent house, to whom they are indebted, with instructions to credit them on account, and that house procures the bill to be discounted, and credits the remitters with the proceeds, and advises them of the facts, these circumstances constitute a sufficient consideration for the indorsement to enable the correspondent house to maintain an action on the bill, when subsequently paid by them as indorsers, against the remitters. Sheffield *v.* Parmlee, 8 Ala. 889, cited in note in 46 L. R. A. 764.

§ 119. Indorsement in Blank.

"It is well settled that it is competent for the holder of paper indorsed in blank to insert the name of the indorsee. Kennon *v.* M'Rea, 7 Port. 175, 181." Bancroft *v.* Paine, 15 Ala. 834, 838.

The holder of a note endorsed in blank may fill it up with any name he pleases. Agee *v.* Medlock, 25 Ala. 281.

Where a suit is brought for the use of another, on a note which at the trial appears to be indorsed in blank by several indorsers, and also by the nominal plaintiff, the several indorsements may be filled up at the trial, so as to correspond with the declaration, and that of the nominal plaintiff stricken out. Pickett *v.* Stewart, 12 Ala. 202.

Where a note is indorsed in blank, the indorsement will be regarded as filled up, in an action by the holder. Miller *v.* Henry, 54 Ala. 120.

It is unnecessary to fill up a blank indorsement, though the declaration alleges that the note was indorsed to plaintiff. Riggs *v.* Andrews, 8 Ala. 628; Sawyer *v.* Patterson, 11 Ala. 523; Bancroft *v.* Paine, 15 Ala. 834.

§ 120. Operation and Effect as to Title.

§ 121. —— In General.

It will be intended that the payee and indorser of a promissory note are the same person, where the only difference in the names is the insertion of the initial of a middle name in the indorsement. Hunt *v.* Stewart, 7 Ala. 525.

Thus, an indorsement by Irvine P. Hunt of a note payable to Irvine Hunt will be regarded as an indorsement by the payee. Hunt *v.* Stewart, 7 Ala. 525.

The transfer of a due bill for a valuable consideration, by an insolvent, who subsequently indorses the same after his discharge in bankruptcy, vests the right of action thereon in the transferee. Smoot *v.* Morehouse, 8 Ala. 370.

§ 122. —— Representative or Fiduciary Character of Parties.

The indorsee of a bill of exchange belonging to a firm, holding under the indorsement of one partner only, has an equitable title, which, under Code, § 2129, will sustain an action thereon in his own name. Alabama Coal Min. Co. *v.* Brainard, 35 Ala. 476.

A bill of exchange payable to the drawer's own order may be properly indorsed by the drawer and payee to executors as such, and by such indorsement a legal title to the bill, and a right of action thereon against the acceptor, are vested in the indorsees as executors. Hart *v.* Shorter, 46 Ala. 453.

§ 123. —— Conditional and Restrictive Indorsements.

Plaintiff bank indorsed a draft to the C. bank "for account of" plaintiff, and the indorsee forwarded it to defendant bank in a letter which stated that it was sent for collection and credit. The C. bank was indebted to defendant in a sum greater than the amount of the draft, and, having collected the draft, defendant credited it to the C. bank, and sent notice thereof to the latter, which, on the same day, became insolvent, defendant having no knowledge of its failing condition before sending such notice. There was an understanding between plaintiff and the C. bank that, when drafts sent by the former to the latter were collected, and the amounts reported, and credited to plaintiff—but not before—plaintiff might draw for such amounts. No report was made by the C. bank of the collection of the draft in suit, nor was the amount thereof ever placed to plaintiff's credit. Held, that defendant was liable to plaintiff for the proceeds of the draft, the restrictive indorsement being notice of the latter's ownership. People's Bank *v.* Jefferson County Sav. Bank, 106 Ala. 524, 17 So. 728.

(C) TRANSFER WITHOUT INDORSEMENT.

§ 124. Transfer by Delivery.

§ 125. —— In General.

To transfer a promissory note at common law without delivery, an indorsement on the paper itself, or at least on one attached to it, is necessary. Borum *v.* King, 37 Ala. 606.

The legal title to a bill or note payable to order can be transferred only by indorsement. Alday *v.* Jamison, 3 Port. 112; Gookin *v.* Richardson, 11 Ala. 889, 46 Am. Dec. 232, cited in note in 36 L. R. A. 119.

§ 126. —— Instruments Payable to Bearer.

A note payable to bearer may be transferred by mere delivery, without indorsement. Town of Brewton *v.* Glass, 22 So. 916, 116 Ala. 629.

But, under the act of June 30, 1837, which prohibited a holder of a note payable to a person named, "or bearer," from suing thereon, unless indorsed by the payee, such a holder could not use an unindorsed note as a set-off in an action against him by the maker. Carew *v.* Northrup, 5 Ala. 367.

This statute had no operation on notes in existence at the time of its enactment. Sprowl *v.* Simpkins, 3 Ala. 515, 516.

Before the enactment of the act of June 30, 1837, a note payable to a person named "or bearer" passed by delivery, so as to vest the legal interest in the holder, and authorize him to sue upon it in his own name. Carroll *v.* Meeks, 3 Port. 226. See, also, Robinson *v.* Crenshaw, 2 Stew. & P. 276.

A note under seal, payable to A. or bearer, is not transferable by delivery, so as to enable the holder to maintain an action in his own name. Sayre *v.* Lucas, 2 Stew. 259, 20 Am. Dec. 33, cited in note in 35 L. R. A. 608.

§ 127. —— Instruments Indorsed in Blank.

A note indorsed in blank is transferable by delivery only. Carter *v.* Lehman, Durr & Co., 90 Ala. 126, 7 So. 735.

§ 128. Assignment.

An assignment of a note by a separate instrument, without indorsement or delivery of the note, and without notice to the maker, is valid as between assignor and assignee. Planters' & Merchants' Ins. Co. *v.* Tunstall, 72 Ala. 142.

To constitute a holder of notes a purchaser for value, it is not necessary that the notes should be delivered to him, if they are assigned by a separate instrument. Boykin *v.* Mobile Bank, 72 Ala. 262, 47 Am. Rep. 408.

The assignment of a note by a separate instrument without indorsement or delivery, is not void for champerty or maintenance, though at the time the note is held adversely to the assignor. Planters' & Merchants' Ins. Co. *v.* Tunstall, 72 Ala. 142. See the title CHAMPERTY AND MAINTENANCE.

The transfer of negotiable notes by the payee, by a separate assignment, and without indorsement, will not vest the legal title in the assignee, but is merely an assignment of a chose in action. Hull *v.* Planters' & Merchants' Bank, 6 Ala. 761, cited in note in 17 L. R. A., N. S., 1109, 36 L. R. A. 118.

Assignment Sufficient to Transfer Legal Title to Note.—An assignment in these words, "this note has been transferred to L. M. Guy by J. Weathereby" is sufficient to transfer the legal title to the note to Guy, if made by Weatherby, and being declared on as such, is under the statute of this state, prima facie evidence of the fact, unless the assignment is questioned by a sworn plea. Deshler *v.* Guy, 5 Ala. 186.

Letter Held Not a Present Assignment of Notes.—A letter from a landlord to third persons stated that he wrote to know about his tenant's rent, that most of the time he just got a check for it when it was due, and that he thought possibly this would suit them; that the tenant's note was for a certain amount, which would be due about a certain time, and if this suited them the tenant could start shipping cotton to them as soon as he got it out, and, as the writer did not care to handle any cotton, all the notes the tenant had turned over to him, he would turn to them through his banker, and would see that they turn their cotton over to them on the tenant's account; and that he wanted them to do the best they could for the tenant in price, etc. Held, that there was nothing therein to indicate that a present assignment of the notes was thereby intended. Strickland & Co. *v.* Lesesne, 160 Ala. 213, 49 So. 233.

An assignment made by one partner, in his name, of a note payable to the firm, does not transfer the legal interest, so as to authorize the assignee to sue at law in his own name; yet, as the partner's authority will be presumed, a right to the note passes to the assignee, who may maintain an action on the note in the name of the payees. Planters' & Merchants' Bank *v.* Willis, 5 Ala. 770.

Assignment by Indorsee Who Has Paid Note.—An indorsee, who, after execution, and return of "No property," against the maker, pays the note upon judgment against himself, and takes it up, can transfer a good title, under which his assignee can recover of the maker, upon averment of all these steps through which his title is made. Smith *v.* Harrison, 33 Ala. 706.

St. 1837, providing that notes payable to bearer must be assigned by **the person whose name is mentioned on the face,** before suit can be maintained in the name of the holder, does not apply to notes in existence at the time the statute was enacted. Sprowl *v.* Simpkins, 3 Ala. 515.

The indorsement of a receipt given by **an attorney at law for a note placed in his hands for collection** will not pass to the assignee the legal title to the note, although the attorney, by an indorsement on the receipt, promised to pay him the proceeds when collected. Gookin *v.* Richardson, 11 Ala. 889, 46 Am. Dec. 232.

An agreement contained in the body of a note, purporting to be in consideration of the hire of slaves, to return the slaves clothed as slaves usually are, is not assigned by the indorsement of the note; nor can the assignee maintain an action for the breach of it when suing for the amount of the note. Winston *v.* Metcalf, 6 Ala. 756.

§ 129. Sale.

A sale of two specified promissory notes, at a specified price, not exceeding $200, may be so made as to invest the purchaser with the equitable title and ownership of them, without writing, without delivery at the time of sale, and without the payment of any part of the price at that time. Hudson *v.* Weir, 29 Ala. 294.

§ 130. Operation and Effect as to Title.

Transfer for Collection.—A transfer of paper for collection without indorsement does not pass the title. Carter *v.* Lehman, 90 Ala. 126, 7 So. 735.

V. RIGHTS AND LIABILITIES ON INDORSEMENT OR TRANSFER.

(A) INDORSEMENT BEFORE DELIVERY TO OR TRANSFER BY PAYEE.

§ 131. Nature and Construction of Contract in General.

An indorsement made by a person not a party to the note imposes upon him a liability to his indorsee which is strictly analogous to the liability upon a regular indorsement. The same diligence in attempting to collect the note of the maker is required. Price *v.* Lavender, 38 Ala. 389.

§ 132. What Law Governs.

Sureties, endorsers and guarantors are liable according to the law of the place of their contract. Walker *v.* Forbes, 25 Ala. 139.

Where a note payable at the Western Bank of Georgia was indorsed in Alabama, the indorsement was governed by the laws of Alabama, although the note and indorsement were made with the intention that the note should be negotiated and paid in Georgia. Lowry *v.* Western Bank of Georgia, 7 Ala. 120.

§ 133. Consideration.

Where it was averred in the complaint that the defendants indorsed the note sued on as makers by agreement with the payees at the time the note was executed, a plea that there was no consideration moving to or from the payees of the note nor to or from the plaintiffs was bad, since a contract may be supported by a consideration moving from a third person as well as from the promisee. Carter *v.* Long, 28 So. 74, 125 Ala. 280.

The contract of one who indorses a

draft for accommodation of the payee is supported by the consideration which moves to the payee from the person to whom he negotiates the draft. Alabama Nat. Bank *v.* Rivers, 22 So. 580, 116 Ala. 1, 67 Am. St. Rep. 95.

§ 134. Accommodation Indorsement.

§ 135. —— In General.

If the maker gets an indorsed note discounted, the transaction, on its face, shows that it was indorsed for the accommodation of the maker. Wallace *v.* Branch Bank, 1 Ala. 565.

If a prior indorser offer a note to a bank to be discounted on his own account, the transaction imports upon its face that the subsequent indorsement was made for the accommodation of the prior indorser. Mauldin *v.* Branch Bank, 2 Ala. 502.

§ 136. —— Accommodation or Identification of Payee.

The liability of one who indorses a draft for accommodation of the payee is the same as that of a regular indorser, and hence payment by the drawee is a defense to an action on the indorsement. Alabama Nat. Bank *v.* Rivers, 22 So. 580, 116 Ala. 1, 67 Am. St. Rep. 95.

§ 137. Indorsement Unauthorized, Procured, by Fraud, or Forged.

Where an accommodation indorsement is procured by the fraud of the maker in concealing a condition annexed to the prior indorsement, the accommodation indorser is liable to the payee who accepts the note without notice of such fraud in payment of an antecedent debt. Marks *v.* First Nat. Bank, 79 Ala. 550, 58 Am. Rep. 620.

§ 138. Nature of Liability on Indorsement.

§ 139. —— As Indorser.

An indorsement of a note before its delivery subjects the indorser merely to the same obligations as an ordinary indorsement, unless it is shown that the one making such indorsement did it as a maker. Carrington *v.* Odom, 27 So. 510, 124 Ala. 529.

One who, for the accommodation of the maker, indorses his name on the back of a note before it has been indorsed by the payee, who never puts it in circulation, is liable to the payee as an indorser. Marks *v.* First Nat. Bank, 79 Ala. 550, 58 Am. Rep. 620.

A person who writes his name in blank on the back of a note, negotiable and payable in bank, before it has been endorsed or put in circulation by the payee, is bound as though he made a perfect endorsement to another person. Hooks *v.* Anderson, 58 Ala. 238; Milton *v.* De Yampert, 3 Ala. 648.

§ 140. —— As Surety.

An indorser is not a surety, within the act for the relief of sureties (Ark. Dig. 385), although he became such for the accommodation of the maker. Bates *v.* Branch Bank, 2 Ala. 689.

§ 141. Time of Indorsement.

An indorsement of a bill or note after it has been protested for nonpayment is to be construed according to the intention of the party making it, and if it be clear that he intended by the act to bind himself as a regular indorser, whose liability is fixed, he may be sued and a recovery had against him as such. Hullum *v.* State Bank, 18 Ala. 805.

§ 142. Mode or Form of Indorsement.

Where one draws a bill of exchange, and directs it to himself, he must be regarded as both drawer and drawee, so that one that writes his name across the face of such a bill is not an acceptor, but an indorser, and consequently entitled to notice of demand, nonpayment, and protest. Walton *v.* Williams, 44 Ala. 347.

§ 143. Indorsement on Condition.

One who indorses a note on the express condition that it shall not be delivered unless another signs as comaker is not liable to the payee taking it without knowledge of the condition, or of the forgery of the comaker's signature. Sharp *v.* Allgood, 100 Ala. 183, 14 So. 16.

Where an accommodation indorsement of a note is made on condition that it be not used until two others have signed it as co-sureties, one acquiring the note with knowledge of the condition does so at his peril, where the names of the other sureties are signed as successive indorsers, with nothing to show a joint liability as between themselves. First Nat. Bank *v.* Dawson, 78 Ala. 67.

Where the indorsement of a bill of exchange was on condition that the drawer placed under the control of the holder certain property, to be sold by him, and the proceeds applied to the payment of the bill, before the indorser should be called upon, and the holder agreed to do so, it was held that the holder could not recover of the indorser without first complying with that agreement, or showing that he had been prevented from doing so by the destruction of the property, etc. State Bank *v.* Whitlow, 6 Ala. 135.

§ 144. Diversion to Unauthorized Purpose.

Where the proceeds of notes were used in redeeming collaterals pledged for a debt of the maker, according to the agreement between him and persons indorsing the notes, and the collaterals were delivered to the indorsers pursuant to the agreement, the mere fact of a sale of the notes to another than the pledgee did not constitute a fraudulent diversion of the notes, and a breach of the agreement on which the indorsements were obtained. Bunzel *v.* Maas, 22 So. 568, 116 Ala. 68.

§ 145. Order of Liability.

In the absence of an express or implied agreement changing the liability of indorsers inter se, they will be bound to pay in the order in which their names appear on the paper; and this although they may have indorsed for the accommodation of the maker, or some other person. Spence *v.* Barclay, 8 Ala. 581, 583; Brahan *v.* Ragland, 3 Stew. 247; Moody *v.* Findley, 43 Ala. 167, 168.

Where several persons indorse a bill for the accommodation of the drawer, or acceptor, they will be liable as between themselves in the order in which they indorsed; unless there was some agreement, express or implied, to be liable otherwise. Abercrombie *v.* Conner, 10 Ala. 293.

A and B signed as indorsers under the name of C, which was already on the paper being then blank, but afterwards filled up and made payable to A and B; and the indorsements were filled, making A and B the first indorsers. The holder of the note recovered judgments thereon against C and A and B. C paid the judgment against him, and took an assignment of the judgment against A and B, who filed their bill for relief against it. C showed that the indorsement in his name was a forgery. Held, that the judgment against C, although conclusive upon him as to the holder of the note, was not evidence as between him and A and B, they being strangers; that, whether the signature of C was a forgery or not, A and B had no equity against him; that their liability was as first indorsers; and that C was entitled in equity to be substituted to the judgment against them, on payment of the debt. Brahan *v.* Ragland, 3 Stew. 247, cited in note in 28 L. R. A., N. S., 1040.

§ 146. Necessity, to Charge Indorser, of Proceeding against Maker.

Necessity of Suing Maker.—In order to hold an indorser for accommodation, suit against the maker of the note must have been brought to the first term. Bates *v.* Ryland, 6 Ala. 668.

Under Code 1876, §§ 2112, 2116, providing that, to charge an indorser of certain instruments, suit must be brought against the maker at the first court after making the indorsement to which suit can be brought, to hold an indorser on a note payable "at call," which, by custom, means on demand, suit must be brought at the first court after the indorsement, not the first court after demand for payment. Mobile Sav. Bank *v.* McDonnell, 83 Ala. 595, 4 So. 346.

A note not indorsed by the payee was indorsed by A, not a party to the note, and transferred by him to B. In an action brought in the name of the payee, for the use of B, against A, it was held that the action should be commenced against the maker at the first term of court after the note matured, unless he is insolvent. Jordan *v.* Garnett, 3 Ala. 610.

Failure to Sue Maker before Action Barred by Limitations.—In case of an indorsement of noncommercial paper by the payee, "I indorse the within until paid," the indorser is discharged, if suit be not brought against the maker before the statute of limitations bars an action on the note. Thomason *v.* Cooper, 57 Ala. 560, cited in note in 18 L. R. A., N. S., 554.

The consent of the endorser of a note, not payable in bank, that suit may be delayed against the maker, does not discharge the other statutory condition requiring that the maker shall first be prosecuted to insolvency. Bates *v.* Ryland, 6 Ala. 668, cited in note in 18 L. R. A., N. S., 554.

Under Code 1896, § 894, subd. 7, providing that the holder of an indorsed contract is excused from bringing suit when by any act or promise of the indorser the plaintiff is induced to delay bringing the suit, it was error to give the general affirmative charge for defendant, in an action on a note against the indorser, where there was evidence that defendant expressly promised to pay the note immediately after its maturity, and from time to time thereafter; leaving it open to inference that the promise induced the payee to forego suit against the maker. Marshall *v.* Bishop, 37 So. 324, 140 Ala. 206, cited in note in 18 L. R. A., N. S., 554.

Effect of Insolvency and Death of Maker.—Acts 1827-28, p. 37, requires, as a condition precedent to a suit against the indorser of a note not payable in bank, that the maker shall be prosecuted to insolvency. Held, that the insolvency and death of the maker before the holder is bound to bring suit against him excuses the holder from the condition. Bates *v.* Ryland, 6 Ala. 668.

A note payable "at call" is not embraced in the statutory exceptions in Code 1876, § 2112, providing that "on all contracts assigned by writing, except bills of exchange or other instruments, and notes payable in money at a bank or private banking-house, or a certain place of payment therein designated, to charge the indorser or assignor, suit must be brought against the maker * * * to the first court to which suit can properly be brought." Mobile Sav. Bank *v.* McDonnell, 83 Ala. 595, 4 So. 346, cited in note in 18 L. R. A., N. S., 540.

Guaranty Not within Statute Relative to Liability of Indorsers.—A guaranty in the words, "I bind myself to pay this note if T. M. L. [the maker] does not," made upon the back of a note by one not a party to it, is not within the statute relative to the liability of indorsers. Insolvency of the maker fixes the liability of the guarantor without suit against the maker. Nesbit *v.* Bradford, 6 Ala. 746.

§ 147. Extent of Liability.

A waiver of exemptions contained in a note applies to persons who write their names on the back of the note with intent to bind themselves as makers. Eudora Mining & Development Co. *v.* Barclay, 26 So. 113, 122 Ala. 506.

§ 148. Discharge of Indorser.

See ante, "Necessity, to Charge Indorser, of Proceeding against Maker," § 146.

Where the holder of a note or bill, without the indorser's consent, gives time to the maker, so as to preclude himself from suing the latter, the indorser is discharged. Inge *v.* Branch Bank of Mobile, 8 Port. 108.

Agreement by Holder of Bill of Exchange for Delay of Payment.—Every party to a bill of exchange is in the nature of a surety. for all those whose liability on the bill is precedent to his; and therefore a valid agreement, entered into by the holder with such prior party for delay of payment, will be a discharge of the liability of all parties subsequent to him on the bill. Abercrombie *v.* Knox. 3 Ala. 728, 731.

"To produce this result, there must be an agreement, on sufficient consideration, by which the holder disables himself from suing or proceeding to collect the money; the mere omission to sue or failing to sue out execution, will not have this effect." Abercrombie *v.* Knox, 3 Ala. 728, 731.

Agreement to Give Time to Acceptor of Bill.—An agreement between the holder of a bill and the acceptor that the holder will not look to the acceptor for payment of the bill until the holder has exhausted, without success, the legal remedies against the indorsers, will operate to discharge the indorser. Inge *v.* Branch Bank, 8 Port. 108.

But there is no obligation to active

diligence on the part of the holder in suing the acceptor, and he may forbear the employment of coercive measures as long as he chooses, if he does not agree to give time so as to suspend his remedy against the acceptor, to the prejudice of the parties who are secondarily liable. Inge *v.* Branch Bank, 8 Port. 108, 117.

"It is said there are two points of view in which, agreeing to give time to an acceptor, will discharge the indorser. According to the one, the creditor, in prolonging the day of payment, is considered as having disentitled himself to proceed against the acceptor, until the time agreed to be given has expired. Such an agreement is inconsistent with the obligation of a creditor to sue the principal debtor, at any moment when required by the surety to do so; and the creditor's voluntary disablement of himself for the performance of any obligation which he is under to the surety, discharges the latter. According to the other, the creditor is regarded as having, in point of good faith towards the debtor, obliged himself not to proceed against the surety; because if he were to proceed against the surety, and the surety to pay, the surety would be instantly entitled to his remedy against the debtor; and so, through the medium of the surety he would deprive the debtor of the time he had agreed to give him—and therefore, to preserve good faith, he will not be allowed to proceed against the surety. English *v.* Darley, 2 Bos. & Pul. 61; Boultbee *v.* Stubbs, 18 Ves. R. 20; Maltby *v.* Carstairs, 1 M. & R. 562, note —Bowmaker *v.* Moore, 3 Price, 214. See, also, Theobold on Prin. & Surety, 123, et post, and 180, et post—Chitty on Bills, 289, et post." Inge *v.* Branch Bank, 8 Port. 108, 116.

Agreement by Bank, Holder of Bill, with Acceptor, Discharging Indorser.— An agreement entered into by a bank, the holder of a bill of exchange, with the acceptor, that, if the bill is not paid at maturity, his credit shall not suffer in bank, will discharge an indorser on the bill who has no knowledge of, and does not consent to, the arrangement. Posey *v.* Decatur Bank, 12 Ala. 802.

No Valid Contract for Definite Extension of Time Releasing Indorsers.— Where the maker of an overdue note proposes to pay it at a future day in state bonds, and the creditor agrees to the proposition, the debtor is not bound to deliver the bonds. There is, therefore, no valid contract for a definite extension of time, since both parties must be bound, or neither, and indorsers are not released. Branch Bank of Huntsville *v.* Steele, 10 Ala. 915.

§ 149. Rights of Indorser.

§ 150. —— As against Maker.

Where plaintiff has recovered separate judgments against the maker and indorser of a promissory note, the payment of the judgment against the indorser does not annul that against the maker. The indorser may, in equity, have the advantage which it there affords for his reimbursement. Lyon *v.* Bolling, 9 Ala. 463, 44 Am. Dec. 444.

Where there are several accommodation indorsers upon a note, one of whom is compelled to pay the note, it is no defense to an action by him against the maker to recover the amount that the maker, before the note became due, placed in the hands of another indorser funds to pay the note. The indorsers are not joint creditors or payees. Meek *v.* Black, 4 Stew. & P. 374, cited in note in 37 L. R. A., N. S., 788.

Where a debtor sent a first and second bill of exchange to his creditor, who, without authority of the debtor, altered the second part to an only bill by drawing a line through the word "second," and writing the word "only" above it, and by tearing off the words "second of," and as thus altered it was negotiated by an accommodation indorser, who paid the amount, he can not recover the same of the drawer. Fontaine *v.* Gunter, 31 Ala. 258, cited in note in 35 L. R. A. 470.

§ 151. ——Indorsement for Accommodation or Identification of Payee.

Equitable defenses to a bank check are not available to the maker, as against one indorsing for the accommodation of the payee, in ignorance of such defenses, and who has been compelled to pay it, as he occupies the position of a bona fide holder in due course. Andrews *v.* Meadow, 31 So. 971, 133 Ala. 442.

§ 152. —— As against Other Indorsers.

Where all the indorsers of a bill are accommodation indorsers, and the last two are secured by a deed of trust, the first indorser can not have the collection of the bill enjoined against those secured, on the ground that they refuse to have the trust property sold to pay the bill. He can be subrogated to their rights under the trust only by paying the bill. Dunlap *v.* Clements, 7 Ala. 539, cited in note in 28 L. R. A., N. S., 1040.

§ 153. Contribution.

"The doctrine of contribution does not apply as between accommodation indorsers, unless there was an express or implied agreement to bear parts of the loss as joint sureties, in the event of the liability of the maker, or drawer to pay." Spence *v.* Barclay, 8 Ala. 581, 583; Brahan *v.* Ragland, 3 Stew. 247.

Accommodation endorsers as such merely, are not liable as cosureties to contribution. To constitute that relation between successive accommodation endorsers, there must be an agreement to that effect between them, or some fact or circumstance must exist from which such an agreement can be inferred. Sherrod *v.* Rhodes, 5 Ala. 683.

Accommodation drawers, acceptors, and endorsers, are not made cosureties by § 3070 of the Revised Code. There must be some agreement, express or implied, to be such, to render them liable as such. Moody *v.* Findley, 43 Ala. 167, cited in note in 28 L. R. A., N. S., 1040, 1042.

Although bills are drawn and indorsed for the accommodation of a corporation, it is competent for one party, when sued for money paid, etc., to show by parol that the agreement was to contribute jointly in case of loss; and this although the names, as indorsed on the bills, indicate a different liability. Rhodes *v.* Sherrod, 9 Ala. 63.

The circumstance that a party to a bill, sued by another party to the same bill, stands upon it as the last indorser, is not conclusive that he is not liable to contribute otherwise, when there is evidence before the jury of a collateral agreement. Rhodes *v.* Sherrod, 9 Ala. 63, cited in note in 28 L. R. A., N. S., 1040, 1045.

A bill of exchange was indorsed by the payee and by M. and by C. in the order named. All were accommodation indorsers, under an agreement to contribute. The bill was not paid at maturity, and after due protest the holder brought several actions against the acceptor and indorsers. Judgments were recovered in these actions, and the bill was thereupon fully paid by the payee, who took an assignment of the judgments, and sought to enforce contribution from C. by an execution issued on the judgment against C. Held, that payment by the payee operated to discharge all the judgments, and contribution could therefore be only enforced by a separate action by the payee against C. Abercrombie *v.* Conner, 10 Ala. 293, cited in note in 28 L. R. A., N. S., 1040.

(B) INDORSEMENT FOR TRANSFER.

§ 154. Nature and Construction of Contract in General.

The indorsement of a negotiable note is a separate and independent contract that the indorser will pay the note on due presentment and notice of dishonor, that the indorsement and signatures of prior parties to the note are genuine, that the indorsement is valid according to its purported effect, that the parties thereto are competent to contract, and that he himself has title and right to transfer. Scarbrough *v.* City Nat. Bank, 48 So. 62, 157 Ala. 577.

The contract of an indorser is conditional, and the conditions must be strictly complied with by the holder, to render the liability absolute. Lockett *v.* Howze. 18 Ala. 613.

The indorsement of a promissory note is a sufficient consideration for a promise by the indorsee to pay the indorser an equivalent sum. Litchfield *v.* Falconer, 2 Ala. 280.

§ 155. What Law Governs.

The indorsement of a note or bill is a new, distinct contract, which is governed, as to its nature, validity, interpretation, and effect, by the law of the state where it is made. Dunn *v.* Adams, 1 Ala. 527, 35 Am. Dec. 42; Walker *v.* Forbes, 25 Ala. 139, 60 Am. Dec. 498.

St. 1828-29, defining the liability of indorsers of promissory notes, affect the nature of the contract, and not the remedy upon it merely, and, therefore, do not apply to a note indorsed prior to their passage. Bloodgood *v.* Cammack, 5 Stew. & P. 276, cited in note in 18 L. R. A., N. S., 540.

§ 156. Modification or Rescission of Contract.

The indorser and indorsee may, by a contract subsequent to the indorsement, rescind or modify the contract evidenced by the indorsement, and it will control the indorsement, so far as it may conflict with it. Young *v.* Fuller, 29 Ala. 464.

§ 157. Nature and Validity of Instrument.

§ 158. —— Nonnegotiable Instruments.

See post, "Necessity to Charge Indorser, of Proceeding against Maker," § 169.

"While there is considerable conflict and confusion among the cases, as well as the text-books, as to the liability of the indorser of a nonnegotiable note, we are disposed to follow the line of decisions holding that the indorser of a note not negotiable is liable to the indorsee to the same extent as the indorser of a negotiable note (Byles on Bills, 146, and note; Jones *v.* Fales, 4 Mass. 245; Sanger *v.* Stimpson, 8 Mass. 260); the only distinction being, not as to extent of liability, but as to the action of the indorsee to fasten the liability after default by the maker." Bank *v.* Sharpe, 152 Ala. 589, 44 So. 871, 872.

An indorser of a nonnegotiable note is liable to an indorsee for value before maturity, notwithstanding the maker can not be held liable because of a failure of consideration. Bank of Luverne *v.* Sharpe, 44 So. 871, 152 Ala. 589.

An irregular indorsement on paper not negotiable is not embraced by the act of 1828, and the liability thereby created is that the indorser will pay it, if, by the use of proper diligence, the money can not be collected from the maker. Fulford *v.* Johnson, 15 Ala. 385.

Where a nonnegotiable note is transferred without indorsement, it can not be allowed to go to the jury as evidence under the money counts in a declaration in the name of the holder, without proof of a promise to pay him the note. Taylor *v.* Acre, 8 Ala. 491.

§ 159. —— Accommodation Paper.

A blank indorsement of a note by one not a party thereto is, so long as the note remains in the hands of the payee, void under the statute of frauds, as an undertaking to answer for the debt, default, or miscarriage of another, for which no consideration was expressed. Hood *v.* Robbins, 98 Ala. 484, 13 So. 574.

§ 160. —— Instruments Paid and Reissued.

When the payee and indorser of a bill of exchange regains possession of it after it has matured and been dishonored, and reissues it, the nature and extent of his contract is a question of fact, dependent on the agreement made with his transferee, to be ascertained by the jury. Montgomery & E. R. Co. *v.* Trebles, 44 Ala. 255.

§ 161. Nature of Liability on Indorsement in General.

A note not indorsed by the payee was indorsed by A, not a party to the note, and transferred by him to B. In an action brought in the name of the payee, for the use of B, against A, it was held that the liability created was that the indorser should pay the debt, if it could not be obtained from the maker after due diligence. Jordan *v.* Garnett, 3 Ala. 610, cited in note in 18 L. R. A., N. S., 542.

§ 162. Mode, Form, or Purpose of Indorsement.

§ 163. —— Special Indorsement.

An indorsement of a promissory note before due in these words, "For value received this 28th Feb., 1850, I transfer unto J. P. H. all my right and title in the within note, to be enjoyed in the same manner as may have been by me," discharges the indorser of personal liability. Hailey *v.* Falconer, 32 Ala. 536.

An indorsement of a note by the payee thus, "For value received, I indorse the within note to H. & B., and warrant the payment of the same," does not impose an unconditional liability, but only in the event that the maker is unable to pay. Douthitt *v.* Hudson, 4 Ala. 110.

§ 164. —— Conditional or Restrictive Indorsement.

A restrictive indorsement by the payee, after acceptance, does not render him liable thereon to a remote indorsee. Erskine *v.* McLendon, 1 Stew. 30.

By the indorsement of a promissory note, the indorser was to be liable, "should the maker fail." Held, that the effect of this indorsement was different from a general one, and must be specially declared on; the word "fail" being equivalent to the insolvency of the principal. Davis *v.* Campbell, 3 Stew. 319.

Where a special indorsement on a note imposed the obligation of trying to collect the amount from one of the makers as a prerequisite to the liability of the indorser, such obligation is fulfilled by a suit brought by the indorsee against such maker, within a reasonable time, in the state where he resided, although by mistake the suit was not brought in the proper name. Brown *v.* Johnson, 42 Ala. 208, cited in note in 18 L. R. A., N. S., 562.

Plaintiff bank indorsed a draft to the C. Bank "for account of" plaintiff, and the indorsee forwarded it to defendant bank in a letter which stated that it was sent for collection and credit. The C. Bank was indebted to defendant in a sum greater than the amount of the draft, and, having collected the draft, defendant credited it to the C. Bank, and sent notice thereof to the latter, which, on the same day, became insolvent, defendant having no knowledge of its failing condition before sending such notice. There was an understanding between plaintiff and the C. Bank that, when drafts sent by the former to the latter were collected, and the amounts reported, and credited to plaintiff—but not before—plaintiff might draw for such amounts. No report was made by the C. Bank of the collection of the draft in suit nor was the amount thereof ever placed to plaintiff's credit. Held, that defendant was liable to plaintiff for the proceeds of the draft, the restrictive indorsement being notice of the latter's ownership. People's Bank of Lewisburg *v.* Jefferson County Sav. Bank, 106 Ala. 524, 17 So. 728.

Where defendant, payee of a note, indorses it for a limited amount, he can not be held liable for attorney's fees, provided for in the note, in addition to the amount indorsed. Cole *v.* Tuck, 108 Ala. 227, 19 So. 377.

§ 165. —— Indorsement for Collection.

Where the holder of a note for collection, having bound himself by written contract to account for it to the owner, recovers judgment on it in his own name, and by private agreement with the sheriff, after sale under execution, takes the property at the purchaser's bid, he thereby becomes liable to the owner of the note for the amount in money. Hudson *v.* Crow, 26 Ala. 515.

Where the holder of a note for collection having bound himself by written contract to account for it to the owner, recovers judgment on it in his own name, and, by private agreement with the sheriff after sale under execution, takes the property at the purchaser's bid, he being thereby rendered liable to the owner of the note for the amount in money, he is not entitled to a deduction for expenses incurred by him in pursuing defendant in execution, who had secretly left the country, taking his property with him, when such expenses are not shown to have been necessarily incurred, nor to have been such as the bailor would be bound to pay. Hudson *v.* Crow, 26 Ala. 515.

§ 166. —— Indorsement with Guaranty.

An indorsement of a note, overdue, in these words, "I assign and guaranty the payment of this note, waiving demand and notice," is not an absolute and unconditional promise to pay the amount of the note presently. The effect of the indorsement is that the indorser is liable on the indorsement, on the ascertainment of the fact of the inability of the maker to pay. Grannis *v.* Miller, 1 Ala. 471.

§ 167. Express and Implied Warranties.

A party indorsing a promissory note

impliedly affirms its genuineness, as well as that of all previous indorsements; and though his indorsee, in declaring against him, may, in usual form, allege the making of the note, and its indorsement to the defendant, yet he can not be required to prove it. Woodward *v.* Harbin, 1 Ala. 104.

The payee of a forged check, who indorses it, and receives full value therefor, guaranties its genuineness; and as to him the indorsee is under no obligation to discover that it is forged, and may recover back the money so paid. Birmingham Nat. Bank *v.* Bradley, 103 Ala. 109, 15 So. 440, cited in note in 10 L. R. A., N. S., 71.

§ 168. Time When Liability Attaches.

The liability of an indorser is complete whenever the indorsee has exhausted his remedy against the maker. Lockett *v.* Howze, 18 Ala. 613.

§ 169. Necessity to Charge Indorser of Proceeding against Maker.

All Remedies Must be Exhausted against Maker.—Under the statute of 1828, all remedies must be exhausted against the maker before the indorser can be held liable. Chapman *v.* Arrington, 3 Stew. 480.

The liability of an indorser is complete when the indorsee has exhausted his remedies against the maker. Lockett *v.* Howze, 18 Ala. 613.

The receipt of a note before its maturity, upon which there is a solvent indorser, as collateral security for the payment of a debt, imposes on the creditor the necessity of doing those acts which will preserve the liability of the indorser, and if he fails to do so, and the maker is insolvent, he is responsible for the injury thereby sustained, to the person from whom he received it. Russell *v.* Hester, 10 Ala. 535, cited in note in 18 L. R. A., N. S., 553, 68 L. R. A. 487.

Contract of Indorser Conditional.—Under St. 1828, providing that, in order to hold an indorser, recovery shall be had against the maker by suit prosecuted as soon as may be after the maturity of the indorsed paper, the contract of the indorser is conditional, depending upon the performance of the conditions imposed by the statute. Ivey *v.* Sanderson, 6 Port. 420.

Diligence Required of Indorsee.—Under Code 1896, § 892, providing that on all contracts not governed by commercial law, to charge the indorser, suit must, on default, be brought against the maker within a fixed time after default, and § 893, providing that the time for bringing suit may be extended or waived by the indorser, and section 894, providing that the indorsee shall be excused from bringing suit for the reasons therein prescribed, an indorsee, to charge an indorser, is bound to exercise the diligence required to first recover of the maker, unless there be a waiver by the indorser, or show an excuse for not doing so. Bank of Luverne *v.* Sharpe, 44 So. 871, 152 Ala. 589, cited in note in 18 L. R. A., N. S., 564.

When the note of a third person is assigned by an irregular indorsement, in consideration of a pre-existing debt, due from the indorser to the indorsee, plaintiff, whether he sues on the indorsement or the pre-existing debt, is equally bound to show proper diligence in endeavoring to collect the note from the maker. Fulford *v.* Johnson, 15 Ala. 385.

Time of Bringing Suit against Maker.—In the case of an irregular indorsement of nonnegotiable paper, to constitute such diligence as will bind the indorser, the maker must be sued to the first court after the maturity of the paper, unless it is dispensed with by the insolvency of the maker, or some such valid reason. Fulford *v.* Johnson, 15 Ala. 385.

If a note for more than $50 is indorsed and delivered by the holder to a third person, suit must be brought against the maker to the first circuit or county court to which he can be sued, next after the maturity of the note; and if the indorsee remits a part of the demand, so as to bring it within the jurisdiction of a justice of the peace, a suit in a justice's court, though prosecuted to a return of "No property," is insufficient to charge the indorser. Fulford *v.* Johnson, 15 Ala. 385.

The fact that an indorser of a note was previously liable to the one to whom he indorsed it does not entitle the latter to recover against the indorser without showing that he brought suit against the maker in the first court to which suit could be brought, which was necessary to charge an indorser. Bradford *v.* Haggerthy, 11 Ala. 698.

Code, § 1543, prescribing the term of court to which an indorser of a note must sue the maker in order to hold indorsers, is not a statute of limitation within the meaning of the ordinance of Sept. 21, 1865, suspending the statute of limitation. McDaniel *v.* Dougherty, 42 Ala. 506.

Action Must Be Prosecuted to Return of Execution "No Property Found."—In order to hold an indorser on an indorsement in this state, there must have been suit against the maker, and a return of no property found in the absence of a valid excuse for not bringing suit. Woodward *v.* Harbin, 1 Ala. 104; Howze *v.* Perkins, 5 Ala. 286, cited in note in 18 L. R. A., N. S., 549.

Under St. 1829 (Aik. Dig. 330), in order to sustain an action against an indorser of a bill single, not payable and negotiable at bank, an action must be prosecuted against the drawer to return of execution "No property found," which return must be made before the commencement of the suit against the indorser, and it is not sufficient that it is before judgment merely. Riddle *v.* Rourke, 1 Ala. 394, cited in note in 18 L. R. A., N. S., 549.

The return by the sheriff of "No property," to an execution at the suit of the indorsee against the maker of a note, is conclusive to fix the liability of the indorser, where the other requisitions of the statute have been complied with. Reese *v.* White, 2 Ala. 306, cited in note in 18 L. R. A., N. S., 548.

Statutory Requirement Not Sufficiently Complied with to Charge Indorser.—The return of non est inventus by a constable on a warrant against the maker of a promissory note, the same day on which it is issued, is not sufficient to charge an indorser, under the statute, which requires the holder of a promissory note for a sum not exceeding $50 to sue the maker within thirty days after it becomes due, and use due diligence to recover the amount of him, in order to charge the indorser. Cavanaugh *v.* Tatum, 4 Stew. & P. 204, cited in note in 18 L. R. A., N. S., 546.

The mere circumstance that the maker of a note not negotiable has a set-off against the payee does not dispense with the necessity for the indorsee to sue to the first court, in order to charge an indorser who is not the payee. Hagerthy *v.* Bradford, 9 Ala. 567.

Effect of Insolvency of Maker.—In an action by the holder against the indorser of a note not negotiable, the insolvency of the maker is not a sufficient excuse for failing to procure a return of "No property" on an execution against him. Bishop *v.* Bradford, 16 Ala. 769, cited in note in 18 L. R. A., N. S., 547.

Suit Impossible or Impracticable.—The law requiring a suit against the maker to first court after due, and return of nulla bona to an execution thereon, in order to charge the indorser, does not contemplate cases where, from absence from the state, his absconding, or other cause, it is impossible or impracticable to bring suit. Roberts *v.* Kirkpatrick, 5 Stew. & P. 96, cited in note in 18 L. R. A., N. S., 563.

Maker a Nonresident.—Where at the time of the execution and indorsement of a note, and from then continuously to the institution of a suit against the indorser, the maker has been a nonresident, it is not necessary, in order to charge the indorser, that a suit against the maker be brought at the first term of court. Bradley *v.* Patton, 51 Ala. 108.

Failure to sue the maker is excused where the maker was when the note was executed, and still is, a nonresident and notoriously insolvent. Miller *v.* McIntyde, 9 Ala. 638.

Acts 1828 and 1829, requiring the indorsees of negotiable paper to sue the maker thereof to the first court after due, in order to charge an indorser, does not embrace a case where the maker has removed beyond the jurisdiction of the courts of the state, and so remains during the period which he may be sued. Woodcock *v.* Campbell, 2 Port. 456, cited in note in 18 L. R. A., N. S., 560.

If the maker of a note resides out of the state when the endorsement is made, and this fact is known to the endorsee, he can not maintain an action against his endorser without averring some diligence to obtain the sum due from the maker. Bristow *v.* Jones, 1 Ala. 159, cited in note in 18 L. R. A., N. S., 561.

In an action against the indorser of a note which was indorsed while the maker was a nonresident, if plaintiff allege that the maker is a nonresident, as an excuse for not suing him, the court will not presume that the plaintiff was ignorant of the maker's place of residence at the time of indorsement. Bristow *v.* Jones, 1 Ala. 159.

Inability to Ascertain Residence of Maker.—In order to fix the liability of the indorser of a note not negotiable at a bank, Aiken's Dig. 329, 330, requires the holder to sue the maker in the county of his residence at the first court at which suit can properly be brought after the note falls due. Held, that where the holder was ignorant of the maker's residence, and could not ascertain it by the exercise of reasonable diligence in time to sue at the first court, the indorser will not be discharged by such failure. Lindsay *v.* Williams, 17 Ala. 229.

Where Writ Sued Out against Maker Is Returned "Not Found."—Where a writ is sued out by the holder of a note against the maker at the first term after the note became due, which is returned "Not found," it is sufficient, in order to hold the indorser, to sue out a new writ at the next subsequent term, and the old writ need not be kept alive, under the statute. Pearson *v.* Mitchell, 2 Ala. 736, cited in note in 18 L. R. A., N. S., 542.

Maker Having No Known Place of Residence in State.—Under Code, §§ 1543, 1546, providing that the holder of a note must sue the principal before he can hold the indorser, no suit need be brought against a maker who has no known place of residence within the state, even though occasionally he is here on a visit. Goggins *v.* Smith, 35 Ala. 683, cited in note in 18 L. R. A., N. S., 562.

The mere absence of the maker from the county will not excuse the prosecution of a suit against him to a return of nulla bona, in order to charge the indorser, if he has a known residence in any part of the state. Roberts *v.* Kilpatrick, 5 Stew. & P. 96.

Where the maker of a note removed from the county a few days before suit was brought, but it does not appear that such removal was open and notorious, or known to the plaintiff, or that the maker became a freeholder in the county to which he removed, or exempt from suit in the county in which the action was brought, the suing out of a writ of attachment in the county from which the removal was made, and a return thereof of nulla bona, was sufficient to charge an indorser. Weed *v.* Brown, 13 Ala. 449, cited in note in 18 L. R. A., N. S., 548.

Where a writ is properly sued out against the maker of a note, and execution issued on the judgment in the cause returned nulla bona, it is sufficient to charge the indorsers, though after the institution of the suit the maker removed to another county. Weed *v.* Brown, 13 Ala. 449.

The absence of the holder of a note from the state constitutes no excuse for the failure to sue the maker, according to the provisions of the statutes of 1828 and 1829, to the first term of court to which a writ may be made returnable. Rathbone *v.* Bradford, 1 Ala. 312, cited in note in 18 L. R. A., N. S., 563.

Note Payable Out of State.—Where an indorsement was made in this state, the fact that the note was payable out of the state does not excuse suit against the maker in order to hold the indorser. Howze *v.* Perkins, 5 Ala. 286.

Effect of Continuance of Cause.—After suit begun by the holder against the maker to the first term of court after the note falls due, the continuance of the cause by consent or other legal delay of the trial is not such an improper suspension of the remedy against the maker as will discharge the indorser. Hays *v.* Myrick, 47 Ala. 335, cited in note in 18 L. R. A., N. S., 545.

In assumpsit against the maker and indorser of a promissory note, if the case is continued as to the maker final judgment by default can not be rendered against the indorser. Chapman *v.* Arrington, 3 Stew. 480.

The omission by an indorsee, for nearly two years, to sue out an alias execution upon a judgment obtained by him against the maker, the sheriff having failed to return the original execution, in the absence of any excuse for such neglect, discharges the indorser from liability. Bradford *v.* Bishop, 14 Ala. 517, cited in note in 18 L. R. A., N. S., 547.

Effect of Verdict in Suit Against Maker.—When an indorsee sues the maker of an indorsed note, and notifies the indorser of the pendency of the suit, or advises him of any defense interposed, this will make the verdict conclusive against the indorser, if the maker is discharged, and it can not be controverted when the indorser is sued. Hagerthy *v.* Bradford, 9 Ala. 567.

Where the suit against the maker was determined in his favor, it must appear, in order to hold the indorser, that the judgment was upon the merits. Murphy *v.* Gee, 9 Ala. 276.

The word "waive," as used in the statute (Rev. Code, §§ 1851, 1853) providing that the time for bringing a suit on a promissory note may be extended or waived by consent of the indorsers, does not mean that the suit is waived, but only the time for bringing it. The suit must still be brought during the running of the statute of limitations. Walker *v.* Wigginton, 50 Ala. 579.

If the indorser waive suit against the maker of a promissory note to the first court, apprehending there was not time after the indorsement to bring suit to the next succeeding court in the county of the maker's residence, the statutory obligation on the indorsee is not revived. It is only necessary to prosecute to insolvency at some time after the expiration of the period of the stipulated delay. Lodor *v.* Gayle, 29 Ala. 412, cited in note in 18 L. R. A., N. S., 554.

Where the payee of a note, not payable in bank, assigns it for value, and binds himself "for the payment of the same until paid," the necessity of suit against the maker at the first court to which the suit can be brought is thereby waived, and his liability is complete whenever the indorsee shall have exhausted his legal remedy against the maker. Lockett *v.* Howze, 18 Ala. 613, cited in note in 18 L. R. A., N. S., 554.

An indorsement of a nonnegotiable note in these words, "For value received, I indorse the within note to B. W., and waive suit to be brought to the next term of the circuit court, when suit should be brought," is an absolute and unconditional waiver of the time of bringing suit against the maker, and does not impose on the indorsee the duty of bringing suit to the second ensuing term (Rev. Code, §§ 1851, 1853); but he must nevertheless bring suit against the maker before the statute of limitations has effected a bar, and prosecute it to insolvency. Walker *v.* Wigginton, 50 Ala. 579, cited in note in 18 L. R. A., N. S., 554.

Under Code, § 894, providing that a holder of a note is excused from bringing the suit required by § 892 at the next term of court after the maturity of the note against the maker, in order to fix the liability of the indorser, when by any act or promise of the indorser the plaintiff is induced to delay bringing such suit, where delay has been so induced an action may be maintained against the indorser, without suing the maker, at any time. Brown *v.* Fowler, 32 So. 584, 133 Ala. 310.

An indorser of a note wrote on the back of it: "I bind myself and my representatives not to take advantage of the statute by which indorsers are relieved from liability after the first court ensuing the maturity of the note." Held, in an action against such indorser, that such writing was unambiguous, and its terms could not be varied by parol proof. Foster *v.* Stafford, 14 Ala. 714.

The true interpretation of such contract was that the indorser dispensed with the bringing of suit to the first court to which it might be brought, and with the prosecution of the maker to insolvency, as required by the statute of 1828 (Clay's Dig. 383, § 12), which is the only statute applicable. Foster *v.* Stafford, 14 Ala. 714, cited in note in 18 L. R. A., N. S., 554.

Form of Indorser's Consent to Delay in Bringing Suit.—The provision of the act of 1828 requiring the written consent of the indorser, to authorize delay in the indorsee in suing the maker of a note, applies only where the sum due does not exceed $50. In other cases a verbal consent is binding on the indorser. Litchfield *v.* Allen, 7 Ala. 779.

Under Code, § 894, providing that the holder of a note is excused from suing the maker in order to fix the liability of an indorser, when by any act or promise of the indorser the holder is induced to delay such suit, where such delay was induced by an express promise to pay the note the promise need not have been in writing. Brown *v.* Fowler, 32 So. 584, 133 Ala. 310.

Consideration Not Necessary for Indorsers Promise to Pay Note.—Where the complaint in an action against the indorsers of a note alleges that the holder was induced to delay suing the maker by the express promise of the indorsers to pay the note, a demurrer to a plea denying that there was any consideration for such promise was properly sustained. Brown *v.* Fowler, 32 So. 584, 33 Ala. 310.

Evidence of Question of Waiver of Action Requiring Reversal of Judgment for Plaintiff.—In an action to recover from an indorser on a note, where it is admitted that no action was brought against the maker within thirty days after maturity, as required by statute, and plaintiff's testimony leaves it in doubt as to whether or not such action was waived by defendant, while defendant's testimony denies a waiver, a judgment for plaintiff will be reversed. Cole *v.* Tuck, 108 Ala. 227, 19 So. 377, cited in note in 18 L. R. A., N. S., 554.

Indorsers' Promise to Pay Not Waived.—Where the holder of a note was induced to delay suit against the maker by a promise of the indorsers to pay, the fact that the holder afterwards recovered judgment against the maker was not a waiver of such promise. Brown *v.* Fowler, 32 So. 584, 133 Ala. 310.

Where the maker of a note, in a suit against him, yields to the jurisdiction, it is a waiver of any irregularities which may exist; and the indorser of the note, when sued on his indorsement, can not take advantage of it. Schaefer *v.* Adler, 14 Ala. 723, cited in note in 18 L. R. A., N. S., 542.

Objection That Maker Was Sued Prematurely Must Be Raised by Plea in Abatement.—The payee of a one-day promissory note transferred it by indorsement, and below the indorsement, and of the same date, wrote: "Also, this note is not to be sued for three months. I will stand good for the payment of the same, waiving all demands and notices." Two months after the transfer the indorsee sued the maker, and after judgment, and return of an execution "No property found," sued the indorser. Held, that the indorser could not urge in bar that the maker was sued prematurely. If so, the indorser was merely subjected to an action too soon, and the objection should have been raised by a plea in abatement. Herndon *v.* Garrison, 5 Ala. 380.

Suit upon Indorsement Made in Another State.—Where the indorsee sues the indorser of a bill single, and the indorsement was made in another state, the presumption is that the common law obtains there; and the indorsee must show a statutory modification of the common law, or that he has exhausted his remedy against the obligor, or did not sue him, because he was and has continued notoriously insolvent. Miller *v.* McIntyre, 9 Ala. 638.

Where a special indorsement on a note imposed the obligation of trying to collect the amount from one of the makers as a prerequisite to the liability of the indorser, such obligation was fulfilled by a suit brought by the indorsee against such maker, within a reasonable time, in the state where he resided, although by mistake the suit was not brought in the proper name. Brown *v.* Johnson, 42 Ala. 208.

§ 170. Extent of Liability.

An indorsee is entitled to recover of his immediate indorser only the amount actually paid for the transfer of the note, with interest. Cook *v.* Cockrill, 1 Stew. 475, 18 Am. Dec. 67; Hutchins *v.* McCann, 7 Port. 94.

"Where the consideration passing between the endorsee and his endorser is not equal to the amount of the note, the endorsee in an action against the endorser can only recover the consideration which he has already paid." Cook *v.* Cockrill, 1 Stew. 475.

An indorsee of a note can not recover of the indorser usurious interest, which, in a suit by the indorsee against the makers of the note, had been deducted from it; the indorsee being a party to the contract by which the usury was reserved. Lloyd *v.* Pace, 12 Ala. 637.

An indorser is not responsible to the indorsee for any improper allowance made to the makers of the note, upon their plea, in a suit against them by the indorsee. Lloyd *v.* Pace, 12 Ala. 637.

In an action against the payee and endorser of an inland bill of exchange, duly protested for nonpayment, the mere fact that the bill was addressed to, and accepted by the defendant, does not relieve him from the payment of damages. McKenzie *v.* Clanton, 33 Ala. 528.

§ 171. Discharge of Indorser.

See ante, "Necessity to Charge Indorser, of Proceeding against Maker," § 169.

Laches on Part of Holder.—A party to a bill, once discharged by laches on the part of the holder, is always discharged, and can not again be made liable, unless by his own voluntary act. Smith *v.* Rowland, 18 Ala. 665.

Indorsee's Refusal to Receive Part Payment from Maker.—If, even pending a suit by the indorsee of a promissory note against the maker, the indorsee refuse to receive part payment thereof from the maker, such refusal relieves the liability of an indorser, to the amount refused, though the indorsee does not obtain the same afterwards. Hightower *v.* Ivy, 2 Port. 308.

Where a further day of payment is given by deed to the drawer of a bill of exchange, but a reservation is made in the deed that nothing contained in it shall bar or affect the right of the creditor to sue on the bill at the request of any of those secondarily liable on the bill, the contract does not discharge the indorsers. Prout *v.* Branch Bank at Decatur, 6 Ala. 309.

The discharge of the maker of a promissory note, when arrested on a ca. sa., by his creditor, is not such a satisfaction of the debt as to relieve the indorser from his liability to the creditor upon the indorsement. Quarles *v.* Glover, 4 Ala. 674, cited in note in 18 L. R. A., N. S., 549.

Where a bank accepts a proposition from the drawer of a bill to take into its possession a stock of goods, to be applied pro rata to all his debts, it is not a discharge of the indorsers, although the goods are afterwards taken and sold by the bank, but the sum received is an extinguishment pro tanto. Ford *v.* Branch Bank, 6 Ala. 286.

The discharge, by the holder of a note, of slaves of the maker sufficient to pay the debt, seized under an attachment at his suit, does not operate in law or in equity to relieve the indorser. Caller *v.* Vivan, 8 Ala. 903.

The release of an indorser does not operate a discharge of any previous party to a promissory note; every endorsement of a paper being a new and substantive contract, and the liability of each endorser, as it respects the holder, being separate and distinct from the others. Kennon *v.* M'Rea, 7 Port. 175.

That the second indorser of a promissory note had neglected to pay it within three years, after maturity—held to be no discharge of the first indorser, in an action by the former against the latter. Worsham *v.* Goar, 4 Port. 441.

The deliberate cancellation by the holder, of an endorsement on a note, discharges the liability of such endorser to the holder, and so operating, it will also discharge from liability to the holder, the subsequent endorser. Curry *v.* Bank, 8 Port. 360.

§ 172. Rights of Indorser.

§ 173. —— In General.

The indorser of a bill pays a judgment against himself on his indorsement, and takes from the holder an assignment of a separate judgment against the acceptor. Afterwards it is ascertained, in a suit in chancery between the holder and acceptor, that the latter is entitled to a credit on the judgment against himself for $968.72, which decree is in full force. To the extent to which the judgment against the acceptor is made unavailable by the acts or omissions of the holder, the holder is liable to the indorser in an action for money had and received. Knox *v.* Abercrombie, 11 Ala. 997.

§ 174. —— As against Original Parties.

The payee and first indorser of a note may pay it at any time after maturity, and maintain an action thereon against the maker. Tuscaloosa, etc., Oil Co. *v.* Perry, 85 Ala. 158, 4 So. 635.

A forwarded a bill of exchange to B, with instructions to negotiate it, and with the proceeds discharge a bond held by C against A. B indorsed the bill, and took an assignment of the bond. Held, that the transaction operated as a discharge of the bond, and that B's remedy was upon the bill, if he should become liable as indorser. Cox *v.* Robinson, 2 Stew. & P. 91.

§ 175. Rights and Liabilities as between Indorsers in General.

Where the holder of a bill obtains judgment against a prior indorser, he has no right to have the judgment satisfied on payment by the last indorser, as the latter has a right either to have the judgment assigned to him, or prosecuted for his benefit against such prior indorser. Hall *v.* Dargan, 4 Ala. 696.

The payment of a judgment rendered against a prior indorser on a bill of exchange by a subsequent indorser does not extinguish the bill, as between him and such prior indorser, but gives him a right to maintain an action against the parties prior to him. Cotten *v.* Bradley, 38 Ala. 506.

A, an indorser on a bill of exchange, paid the amount to the bank which held it, under the agreement with the bank, which was to be secret, that the bank should by suit collect the same of B, a subsequent indorser, for the benefit of A. The bank recovered the same of B, and paid the amount to A. Held, that B was entitled to recover the amount so paid of A, in an action of assumpsit. Boyd *v.* Taliaferro, 13 Ala. 424.

In an action by the holder of a note against an indorser, the plaintiff can not be permitted to strike out the name of any indorser prior to the defendant. Curry *v.* Bank of Mobile, 8 Port. 360.

Though, it seems, that in such case, the situation of the endorser, whose name is stricken out, might be explained—as, that he was an accommodation endorser, and not responsible to his immediate endorsee, in any event. Curry *v.* Bank, 8 Port. 360.

(C) ASSIGNMENT OR SALE.

§ 176. Nature and Construction of Contract in General.

Where a promissory note is transferred by delivery merely, without indorsement, the transferror is liable only to answer for the genuineness of the note, and his right to transfer it. Bankhead *v.* Owen, 60 Ala. 457, cited in note in 36 L. R. A. 92.

The vendor of a promissory note which has been paid is liable to the vendee for the amount, though there be no special contract, or fraud on his part. Ellis *v.* Grooms, 1 Stew. 47.

The term "discount," as a substantive, signifies the interest allowed in advancing on bills of exchange and negotiable securities; and "to discount a bill" is to buy it for a less sum than that which, upon its face, is payable. Anderson *v.* Timberlake, 22 So. 431, 114 Ala. 377, 62 Am. St. Rep. 105.

Where a bill single, not rendered negotiable by indorsement, is given by the payee to an agent for collection, and he sells it for a fair consideration to a third person, and he to another, who sues thereon in the name of the payee to his use, a court of equity will hold him as trustee for the payee, and compel him to account for the proceeds of the judgment. May *v.* Nabors, 6 Ala. 24.

Where a railroad company, for the purpose of settling a debt, prepared a statement of the claim in the form of an approved account, having thereon a receipt in blank, together with a statement that when said voucher is properly signed, it becomes a draft, without exchange, on the treasurer of the company, and this paper is sent to the creditor in whose favor it is drawn, and one pretending to have authority to represent said creditor, but who was without such authority, assigned the receipt attached to said statement in the name of the creditor, and obtained money thereon from the person to whom it was assigned, and the assignee subsequently deposited such voucher in the bank, by which bank the amount of the voucher was collected from the railroad company, such railroad company, upon discovering the forgery of the voucher, can not maintain an action of assumpsit against the person to whom it was originally assigned by the person representing himself as the agent of the original creditor of the railroad company; it not being shown that there existed between the railroad company and such person to whom the voucher was originally assigned a privity of contract created by express promise or by implication of law. Louisville & N. R. Co. *v.* Johnson, 30 So. 580, 128 Ala. 634.

§ 177. Statutory Provisions.

Act 1837, which inhibits the assignment of a promissory note by delivery merely, so as to permit the assignee to maintain an action thereon as the bearer, can not be extended by construction to blank indorsements, or to an indorsement which directs the contents to be paid to the bearer, without indicating him by name. Sawyer *v.* Patterson, 11 Ala. 523.

§ 178. Rights of Assignee or Purchaser.

An assignee of a promissory note succeeds to all the rights of his assignor at the time of the transfer, and will be entitled to prior satisfaction against a subsequent assignee of other notes out of a fund provided for the payment of all the notes. Bank of Mobile *v.* Planters' & Merchants' Bank, 9 Ala. 645.

Where a note loses its assignable quality by a judgment having been recovered thereon against one of the makers in the name of the assignee, the insertion of the name of another person in the indorsement of the payee, which was previously blank, is a nugatory act, and the name thus inserted may be stricken out at the trial of a suit brought by the assignee against another maker. Sawyer *v.* Patterson, 11 Ala. 523.

§ 179. Equities and Defenses against Assignee.

§ 180. —— In General.

Statement of General Rule.—The assignee for value of a negotiable instrument, who takes it even before due, and without notice of any equities between prior parties thereto, will hold it subject to all equities or counterclaims between the original parties existing at the time of the assignment. Teague *v.* Russell, 2 Stew. 420; Smith *v.* Pettus, 1 Stew. & P. 107, cited in note in 46 L. R. A. 757, 769.

Failure of Consideration.—Where a nonnegotiable note has been given by the vendee of land for the purchase money, equity will interpose against its recovery, even in the hands of an assignee, if the vendor, through insolvency, is unable to make titles of the land sold. Smith *v.* Pettus, 1 Stew. & P. 107.

Assignee a Trustee for Amount of Hire of Slaves.—A father, by deed, conveyed certain slaves to a trustee, for the use of his daughter during her life, to be hired out, and the monthly or annual proceeds to be paid to her, and at her death the slaves to vest in her children. The daughter married, and the husband took possession of the slaves, and hired them out for a year, taking the note for the hire, payable to himself, and transferred it by assignment to one Kernodle; in the month of March of that year, his wife died. Held, that under the statute of this state, the assignee of the husband, though a bona fide purchaser without notice, was in no better situation than his assignor, and affected by all equities which would bind him, and must therefore be considered a trustee for the amount of the hire of the slaves, which accrued after the death of the owner of the life estate. Lucas *v.* Kernodle, 2 Ala. 199.

Where the payee of an attorney's fee note assigns it to her attorney, who has collected everything due thereon, except the attorney's fees, the fact that the payee is relieved by the attorney from further liability for such fees in consideration of the assignment is not a defense to an action on the note by the attorney to recover the attorney's fees. Cowan *v.* Campbell, 31 So. 429, 131 Ala. 211.

Set-Offs.—In June, 1840, A sold a plantation and slaves to B on credit, taking from B eleven notes, to become due one in each of the next eleven years. In October, 1840, A assigned the four notes falling due in the years 1844, 1845, 1846, and 1847 to C as collateral security for a debt from A to C. The three notes first falling due were paid by B to A at maturity; and, in an action by C against B on one of the notes assigned to him, it was held that B could not set off any matter of offset which he held against A at the time of paying the prior notes. Nelson *v.* Dunn, 13 Ala. 259.

Estoppel to Set Up Defenses.—Where a note is purchased by the assignee on the faith of a promise by the maker to pay it, the latter is thereby estopped from asserting the invalidity of the note as between himself and the payee, either on the ground of fraud or subsequent failure of consideration. Cloud *v.* Whiting, 38 Ala. 57.

§ 181. —— Defenses Existing before Transfer or Notice Thereof.

The rule that a bona fide holder of negotiable paper is not affected by prior equities, of which he has no notice, does not apply if he receives the paper from the original payee by assignment or delivery instead of indorsement. He thus obtains no title superior to that of the payee, in whose name only he can sue, and the maker is therefore not precluded from asserting equities that would have been valid as against the payee. Andrews *v.* McCoy, 8 Ala. 920, 42 Am. Dec. 669. See post, "Bona Fide Purchasers," V, (D).

If a note under seal is assigned by indorsement after maturity, the assignee takes it subject to all equitable defenses existing in favor of the maker prior to notice of the assignment, whether they grow out of the same or of a different transaction. Carroll *v.* Malone, 28 Ala. 521, cited in note in 46 L. R. A. 796.

Equity Existing against Vendor.—An assignee of notes given upon the purchase of a tract of land, who is cognizant of all the facts, takes them subject to the equity which exists against the vendor. Griggs *v.* Woodruff, 14 Ala. 9.

Note Procured by Fraudulent Representations and without Consideration.—The maker of a negotiable note, given without consideration, and procured by means of fraudulent representations of the payee, is not liable thereon to a purchaser thereof, unless such purchaser is a bona fide holder. Bomar *v.* Rosser, 26 So. 510, 123 Ala. 641.

Payment of Debt by Maker as Surety for Payee.—When suit is brought on a promissory note, in the name of the payee, for the use of his assignee, against the maker, the latter may defend by showing that, before the assignment of the note sued on, he was surety for the payee on a note to the bank, that the payee became and continued to be insolvent, and that afterwards, on account of the payee's insolvency, he had been compelled to pay the bank debt, if he also shows that such payment was made before the transfer of the note sued on, and notice thereof. Gildersleeve *v.* Caraway, 19 Ala. 246.

Usury.—To cut off the defense of usury against a noncommercial promissory note in the hands of a person who was not a party to the original transaction, there must be more than a transfer to him in good faith and without notice of the usury. There must be a renewal of the debt, by giving a new security payable to him. McCullough *v.* Mitchell, 64 Ala. 250.

A promise by the maker of a note to the assignee, after the assignment, that he will pay it, will not preclude him from making any defense which existed previous to notice of the assignment; being without consideration. Clemens *v.* Loggins, 1 Ala. 622.

§ 182. —— Set-Offs Existing before Transfer or Notice.

Where a note has been assigned, the maker may plead, in a suit by the assignee, any matter as set-off existing against the payee at the time of the assignment, and before notice thereof. Carroll *v.* Malone, 28 Ala. 521.

"A right of set-off against a note or bond, under our statute, does not exist for demands subsisting against intermediate assignees through whose hands such note or bond may have passed by blank indorsement or otherwise." Sykes *v.* Lewis, 17 Ala. 261, 267.

In an action on a promissory note not payable at a bank or banking house (Rev. Code, § 1839), brought by an assignee against the maker, the defendant may set off another note which the assignor owed him at the time of the assignment, and notice thereof, although the assigned note was not due at that time. Russell *v.* Redding, 50 Ala. 448.

P. and W. are joint makers, and J. the payee, of a note. J. assigns the note to M. Before notice of the assignment to the makers, P. acquired a note made by J., payable to J. P., and by him assigned to P. Held, in a suit brought by M. against W. on the note, that W. was entitled to set off the note against J. held by P., on producing the note at the trial with the consent of P. to use it as a set-off. Winston *v.* Metcalf, 6 Ala. 756.

In an action on a promissory note by the payee for the use of a bona fide transferee from a prior beneficial holder, the maker can not set off a demand against the latter, although the note was delivered to him, and he was the real owner of it at the time of its execution. Sykes *v.* Lewis, 17 Ala. 261.

§ 183. —— Set-Offs Arising after Transfer or Notice.

The maker of a note can not acquire a set-off against an assignee of the same after notice of the assignment. Wray *v.* Furniss, 27 Ala. 471.

Where the payee of a note assigns it by delivery merely, so as to make it necessary to sue in the name of the party beneficially interested, the maker can not set off a demand acquired against the payee after he had notice of the assignment. Crayton *v.* Clark, 11 Ala. 787, cited in note in 17 L. R. A., N. S., 1109.

Account to Be Applied Where Collected, to Payment of Note.—The maker of a note not negotiable transferred to the payee an account, to be applied, when collected, to the payment of the note. After the note was assigned, the payee collected the account. Held, that the account could not be offset by the maker in an action by the assignee of the note. Chilton *v.* Comstock, 4 Ala. 58.

Assignment of Note Held as Collateral Security to Surety of Payee.—A bank debtor having transferred to the bank, as collateral security, a note held by him against a third person, and his surety having paid the debt to the bank, and taken from it, by agreement with him, an assignment of the note held as collateral, held, in suit on the note by the surety, that the maker could not set off a demand against the payee or principal debtor acquired after notice of the transfer to the bank; that the assignment to the surety related back to the time when the note was transferred to the bank, and clothed the assignee with the rights then held by the bank, against which subsequent equities could not be asserted. Lewis *v.* Faber, 65 Ala. 460, cited in note in 46 L. R. A. 786, 796.

§ 184. —— Parties Affected by Defense or Set-Off.

The assignee of nonnegotiable paper takes it subject only to those equities to which it was subject in the hands of the assignor, as between the original parties, not to those arising between other parties in the course of its transfer. Goldthwaite *v.* National Bank, 67 Ala. 549.

In an action by the assignee of a promissory note given for money borrowed from a slave, debts due from the slave to one of the makers, who is not sued, do not constitute a valid set-off. Broadhead *v.* Jones, 39 Ala. 96.

Under the statute of set-off, where A and B make a note jointly to C, which he assigns to D, who brings an action upon it against A alone, a note made by C, and assigned to B before notice of the assignment of the former note, can be used in set-off. Winston *v.* Metcalf, 7 Ala. 837.

A set-off due to the maker of a note, by one who has become beneficially interested in it, without the legal title by indorsement, can not be enforced to defeat the right of a subsequent holder to recover on the note. Pitts *v.* Shortridge, 7 Ala. 494.

§ 185. Recourse by Assignee to Assignor.

§ 186. —— In General.

The assignor of a note is liable to the assignee for costs of the suit prosecuted against the maker of the note as a condition precedent to fixing the assignor's liability. Hammett *v.* Smith, 5 Ala. 156.

§ 187. —— Necessity of Proceeding against Maker.

Necessary Averments in Action by Assignee against Assignor.—In an action by an assignee against the assignor of a note not mercantile, it is necessary to aver that suit was brought against the maker at the first term to which suit could be brought after maturity of the note, or an excuse for not bringing it. Ryland *v.* Bates, 4 Ala. 342, cited in note in 18 L. R. A., N. S., 540.

Averment of Sufficient Diligence.—In an action on an irregular assignment of a note against the assignor, an averment that, when the note became due, diligent search and inquiry were made after the maker in the county and state which was his ordinary place of residence, to present the note for payment, but that he could not be found, and that his place of residence was unknown to the plaintiffs, and that suit was commenced against him in the first court to which he could be sued, but that he could not be found, was held an averment of sufficient diligence. Hall *v.* Chilton, 3 Ala. 633, cited in note in 18 L. R. A., N. S., 561.

Action against Maker during Civil War.—The requirement of Rev. Code, § 1851, that, in order to fix the liability of the assignor of a note, suit must be first brought against the maker, is complied with by an action against the maker of a nonnegotiable note instituted and prosecuted to judgment with reasonable diligence in the courts of this state during the late Rebellion. Sugg *v.* Winston, 49 Ala. 586, cited in note in 18 L. R. A., N. S., 542.

Where the judge of the county court is assignor of a note, it is sufficient to charge him if the assignee bring suit against the maker at the first term of the circuit court after maturity. Holt *v.* Moore, 4 Ala. 394, cited in note in 18 L. R. A., N. S., 542.

Record Sustaining Allegation That Plaintiff Commenced Suit against Maker.—In a suit against the assignor of a note by the assignee, the allegation that the plaintiff commenced a suit against the maker, to the first court to which suit could be brought, etc., is sustained by the production of the record of a suit, commenced in the name of the payee, for the use of the plaintiff, if the judgment is still in force, unreversed. Kain *v.* Walke, 12 Ala. 184.

Allegation Sufficiently Showing That Fi. Fa. Had Been Issued and Returned.—In an action by an assignee against an assignor of a note, an allegation that execution issued on a judgment against the maker, and was returned "No property found," sufficiently shows that a fi. fa. had been so issued and returned. Hammett *v.* Smith, 5 Ala. 156.

The death and insolvency of the maker of a note is a sufficient excuse for the failure of the assignee to prosecute a suit against him to judgment, execution, and a return of "No property found." Kain *v.* Walke, 12 Ala. 184, cited in note in 18 L. R. A., N. S., 558.

If the maker of an assigned nonnegotiable note is dead at the time of the assignment, and his estate is declared insolvent after the institution of a suit against his personal representative, this excuses the assignee (Rev. Code, § 1854, cl. 6) from prosecuting the suit to a return of "No property found" on an execution. Walker *v.* Wigginton, 50 Ala. 579.

An assignment of a note to A, "with said A to try the insolvency of B" (the maker of the note), imposes on the assignee the burden of establishing the insolvency of B by an action on the note against him. Hines *v.* Mullikin, 11 Ala. 634.

§ 188. Express and Implied Warranties.

Where a note is assigned without recourse, the assignor is liable for fraudulent representations as to the solvency of the maker. Harton *v.* Scales, Minor 166.

(D) BONA FIDE PURCHASERS.

§ 189. Nature and Grounds of Protection.

"A negotiation, or a transfer of a negotiable instrument, bona fide, before its maturity, in the usual course of business, for a valuable consideration, and without notice, is by the law merchant esteemed as a creation in the indorsee of an original and paramount right of action against the previous parties; and in his hands the instrument is discharged of all legal and equitable defenses to which it may have been subject before it came to him. 1 Amer. Lead. Cases, 420; Pond *v.* Lockwood, 8 Ala. 669; Winston *v.* Westfeldt, 22 Ala. 760." Capital City Ins. Co. *v.* Quinn, 73 Ala. 558, 560.

"It is a principle of general recognition, that a purchaser of commercial paper in the usual course of business, before its maturity, for a valuable consideration, having no notice of defenses that existed between the original parties, or have subsequently arisen, is a 'bona fide holder for value,' and, as such, takes the instrument free from defenses which were available between the original parties. Randolph on Com. Paper, § 14; 2 Daniel on Neg. Instr. 769." Woodall & Son *v.* People's Nat. Bank, 153 Ala. 576, 45 So. 194, 195; Bluthenthal *v.* Columbia, 175 Ala. 398, 57 So. 814, 815; Pond *v.* Lockwood, 8 Ala. 669; Merchants Nat. Bank *v.* Norris, 163 Ala. 481, 51 So. 15.

"Mr. Randolph, in his work of Commercial Paper, and Mr. Daniel in his work on Negotiable Instruments, both say that such a paper is in some respects like the currency of the country, a circulating credit, and that before maturity the genuineness of the obligation and the solvency of the parties are the sole matters to be considered in determining its value, and that such a paper has been aptly called a courier without language, which carries on its face its own history, and that the policy of the law requires that it shall tell its own history, and have effect in the hands of innocent holders for value according to what appears on its face. Daniel, Neg. Instr., § 1, 769a; Randolph, Com. Paper, § 14; Brown *v.* First Nat. Bank, 103 Ala. 123, 15 So. 435." Bluthenthal *v.* Columbia, 175 Ala. 398, 57 So. 814, 815.

"It is laid down by elementary writers, as well as in the adjudged cases, that a bona fide holder for value, without notice, is entitled to recover upon any negotiable instrument, which he has received before its maturity, notwithstanding any defect or infirmity in the title of the person from whom he derived it; although such person may have acquired it by fraud, or even by theft or robbery. The same doctrine is in general applicable to one thus becoming the holder of negotiable paper, where the note or bill, or the indorsement thereof, is founded on an illegal consideration. The law upon this point is founded in public policy, and there is no distinction between a case of illegality, where the consideration is tainted with moral crime, which is malum in se, or where it violates the positive prohibition of a statute, which is malum prohibitum; for in each case the innocent holder may be otherwise exposed to the most ruinous consequences, and the circulation of negotiable instruments would be materially obstructed, if not altogether stopped. The only exception is, where the statute creating the prohibition has, at the same time, either expressly or by necessary implication, made the instrument absolutely void in the hands of every holder, whether he has notice of the illegality or not. There are few cases in which any statute has created a positive nullity of such instruments. The most important seems to be the statutes against gaming and usury. Neither is it any defense, that the note or bill was known to the holder to have been made, drawn or endorsed for accommodation, as between the other parties, if he takes it bona fide, for value, before it becomes due. The reason is, that the object of accommodation paper is to enable the parties thereto, by a sale, or negotiation thereof, to obtain for it a free credit and circulation; and this object would be frustrated, unless the purchaser or other holder for value could hold such paper by as valid a title, as if it were founded in a real business transaction. In fact the parties to every accommodation note or bill, hold themselves out to the world, by their signatures, to be absolutely bound to every person who shall take the same for value, to the same extent as if that value were personally advanced to them, or on their account, and at their request. Story on Prom. Notes, § 191 to 197; Smith's Mer. Law, H. & G. ed. 261 to 263, and citations in notes." Saltmarsh *v.* Tuthill, 13 Ala. 390, 404.

Under Code 1907, § 5007, defining a "holder in due course" of a negotiable note, so as to require that it shall have been "negotiated" to him, and § 4985, defining "negotiated" so as to require transfer from a prior holder, the payee of a note can not be its holder in due course, within § 5013, as to defenses to negotiable instruments. Stone *v.* Goldberg, 6 Ala. App. 249, 60 So. 744.

§ 190. Character of Instrument.

See post, "Want or Failure of Consideration in General," § 219; "Set-Off or Counterclaim," § 227.

A note dated "Hayneville, Ala.," and made payable "at H.'s office," which office was in said town, comes within the purview of Code, § 1756, providing that promissory notes payable "at * * * a certain place of payment therein designated, * * * are governed by the commercial law;" and a purchaser of such note before maturity, for value, and without notice, takes it free from the equities between the original parties. Rudolph *v.* Brewer, 96 Ala. 189, 11 So. 314.

§ 191. Mode or Form of Transfer.

To enable the holder to rely on the rules of the law merchant, as to the transfer of negotiable securities, the legal title to the paper must be vested in him by an indorsement. Andrews & Bros. *v.* McCoy, 8 Ala. 920.

The statute of 1812, which provides that in actions upon promissory notes, etc., by an indorsee, the defendant shall have the benefit of all offsets, etc., against the same, had before notice of the indorsement, does not apply to a note payable to bearer, and transferred by delivery. Robinson *v.* Crenshaw, 2 Stew. & P. 276.

§ 192. Actual Notice.

§ 193. —— In General.

A note indorsed as collateral security was returned to the indorsers for collection. They had agreed with a creditor to procure and turn it over to him in payment of his demand, and informed him that it was then held as collateral security by a firm to whom they had telegraphed to send it, and with whom they had an arrangement for the return thereof, and represented that they in fact owned it. On its arrival no further questions were asked, and the note was accepted without notice that it was sent and receipted for, for collection only. Held, that the creditor was not a purchaser without notice of the rights of the indorsee so sending it. Carter *v.* Lehman, Durr & Co., 90 Ala. 126, 7 So. 735.

§ 194. —— Implied from Relation between Parties.

A corporation purchased from a firm composed of persons, who afterwards became stockholders and officers of the corporation, a negotiable note executed by a city for liquors purchased for the dispensary, which note was illegal in the hands of the firm because executed in violation of the dispensary law. Held, that the corporation was not a bona fide holder; knowledge of the partners being imputed to the corporation. Bluthenthal *v.* Columbia, 175 Ala. 398, 57 So. 814.

The maker of a note for a blank amount handed it to a bank director, to be filled up with the sum of about $500, and used in the renewal of another note of the maker held by the bank. The director, in violation of the trust, filled up the note for a much larger sum, and got the bank to discount it for his own use. The director did not communicate the facts to any other director, but sat as one of the board when the note was taken by the bank. Held, that the bank was a bona fide purchaser without notice, and hence the maker was liable on the new note. Terrell *v.* Branch Bank at Mobile, 12 Ala. 502.

§ 195. —— Operation and Effect.

"If * * * the holder of a negotiable instrument, at the time he acquired it, knew that circumstances existed which rendered it improper that payment should be enforced, he will not acquire any better interest in the same than the party had, who transferred it to him. A person, therefore, who receives a bill with notice that it is to be negotiated only upon certain terms, or for a particular purpose, holds the bill subject to such terms. Chitty on Bills, 264, 9th Am. Ed." Saltmarsh *v.* Tuthill, 13 Ala. 390, 399.

If the holder of a note received it

knowing that the person passing it to him obtained it surreptitiously, he can not recover on the instrument. McKenzie *v.* McRae, 8 Port. 70.

An action can not be maintained, by an indorsee with knowledge, on notes given for the purchase price of a fertilizer sold in violation of Code 1886, §§ 4153, 4154, which makes it a penal offense to sell a fertilizer without first submitting it to the commissioner of agriculture, and having the parcels tagged according to law. Johnson *v.* Hanover Nat. Bank, 88 Ala. 271, 6 So. 909.

§ 196. Constructive Notice, and Facts Putting on Inquiry.

§ 197. —— Good Faith in General.

Where A loses at gaming the note of B, given for A's accommodation, and the winner loses it in the same way to C and D, or transfers it to them in discharge of a gambling debt, C and D not being bona fide holders, can not, by an arrangement between themselves, confer upon the note a validity which it did not previously possess. Whitlock *v.* Heard, 16 Ala. 336.

§ 198. —— Character or Capacity of Persons Dealing with Paper.

A bona fide holder without notice of an accommodation note, indorsed with the name of a firm, by one of the members for his own benefit, and without the assent of the others, may collect it of the firm. Mauldin *v.* Branch Bank, 2 Ala. 502.

The rule that a note given by one partner in the partnership name for his individual debt is good against the firm in the hands of a bona fide holder applies only to notes of mercantile partnerships, and does not apply to those of partnerships for keeping tavern. Cocke *v.* Branch Bank, 3 Ala. 175.

One who, in payment of A's debt, knowingly takes a note purporting to have been executed by the firm of A & B, but shown to have been signed by A in renewal of one given for the debt of A and C, is not a bona fide holder, and can not enforce it against B. Tyree *v.* Murphy, 67 Ala. 1.

Money being deposited in bank by a tax collector, to the credit of "I. H. Vincent, treasurer," and checked out by him in the purchase of exchange on New York, the draft being made payable to himself as treasurer, and indorsed in the same way; these facts are sufficient to charge the indorsee with notice of the official character in which the treasurer held the funds, and, if he applies the money in payment of an individual indebtedness of the treasurer to him, he becomes liable to the state, as a trustee in invitum, in an action for money had and received. Wolffe *v.* State, 79 Ala. 201.

§ 199. —— Relation to Instrument of Persons Dealing Therewith.

A purchaser of an accepted bill of exchange from the drawer is chargeable with notice that it is accommodation paper, which, until negotiated, is no evidence of indebtedness against the acceptor. Farley Nat. Bank *v.* Henderson, 24 So. 428, 118 Ala. 441.

Where the drawer of a bill, accepted or indorsed for his accommodation, offers it for discount, this is notice to the purchaser of the character of the acceptance or indorsement. Noble *v.* Walker, 32 Ala. 456.

If a bill of exchange is indorsed for the accommodation of the acceptor, for a special purpose, and it is used for a different purpose, the receiver takes it with implied notice of the fact and purpose of the accommodation indorsement, and subject to any defense which would be available against the acceptor himself. McKenzie *v.* Branch Bank, 28 Ala. 606, 65 Am. Dec. 369, cited in note in 31 L. R. A., N. S., 292, 297.

B., being indebted to a life insurance and trust company, obtained from friends certain blank bills of exchange drawn and indorsed by them—he being the acceptor—which blanks were to be used by him only in the renewal of the debt due the company. In violation of the agreement, he filled up one of the blanks for $6,000 and sold it to W. for $5,000. W. afterwards transferred the bill to a bank. Held, in an action by such bank against one of the indorsers, that the bill's being in the hands of the acceptor was evidence to charge the indorsee that it was drawn and indorsed for the accommodation of the acceptor. Saltmarsh *v.* Planters' & Merchants' Bank, 14 Ala. 668.

§ 200. —— Knowledge as to Consideration or Collateral Agreements or Securities.

Though a deed of trust, if properly executed, is constructive notice of the lien in all contests respecting the property, yet this constructive notice does not run with mercantile paper secured by the deed, so as to charge a bona fide holder thereof, before maturity, with knowledge of its recitals. Minell *v.* Reed, 26 Ala. 730.

If there is not on the face of a note secured by trust deed anything which could give a bona fide holder of such note notice of the recitals of the trust deed, or to put him on inquiry, he can not be affected by any payments, discounts, set-offs, or equities existing between the antecedent parties. Minell *v.* Reed, 26 Ala. 730.

§ 201. Taking after Maturity.

§ 202. —— Title and Rights Acquired.

Where accommodation paper is not made for a specified purpose, and there is no understanding between the parties that its use shall be restricted, the fact that a holder has acquired it after maturity does not affect his title thereto. Connerly *v.* Planters' & Merchants' Ins. Co., 66 Ala. 432.

§ 203. —— Defenses as against Purchasers after Maturity.

Doctrine Stated.—Where a note, check, or bill is transferred after maturity, the transferee takes it subject to all the defenses that are available as between the original parties. Robertson *v.* Breedlove, 7 Port. 541; Glasscock *v.* Smith, 25 Ala. 474; Battle *v.* Weems, 44 Ala. 105.

"The indorsee of commercial paper acquiring it after maturity, * * * takes it subject to all defenses which the maker could prefer against the payee, if he had remained the holder. Glasscock *v.* Smith, 25 Ala. 474; Fenouille *v.* Hamilton, 35 Ala. 319; McKenzie *v.* Branch Bank, 28 Ala. 606; Cullum *v.* Bank, 4 Ala. 21. The rule has been sometimes limited to defenses affecting the instrument itself, as a want, or illegality, or failure of consideration. But in Carroll *v.* Malone, 28 Ala. 521, it was after very careful consideration of our statutes, from which the provisions of the Code do not materially vary, held, that the indorsee was subject to set-off, and discounts, as well as to defenses, affecting the instrument itself." Bank *v.* Poelnitz, 61 Ala. 147, 149, cited in note in 46 L. R. A. 757, 796.

It had formerly been held that the maker of a note transferred after maturity can plead only such defenses and counterclaims as are connected with the note and not such as grow out of independent or collateral transactions. Robertson *v.* Breedlove, 7 Port. 541; Sheffield *v.* Parmlee, 8 Ala. 889, cited in note in 46 L. R. A. 760, 761, 765, 788, 790.

A transfer by the payee of past-due commercial paper carries with it no greater rights than the payee has; and the purchaser or indorsee of a note and the mortgage securing it, after the maturity of the note, takes it subject to all defenses which the maker could prefer against the payee if he had remained the holder, and such purchaser or indorsee can not claim to be a bona fide purchaser without notice. Marshall *v.* Shiff, 30 So. 335, 130 Ala. 545.

An indorsee who acquires a note after maturity takes it subject to all defenses existing in favor of the maker as against the party for whose accommodation it was made. Glasscock *v.* Smith, 25 Ala. 474, cited in note in 46 L. R. A. 757, 773; 11 L. R. A., N. S., 1036.

"A note in circulation after it is due, carries suspicion upon its face. It suggests inquiry, and places the purchaser in privity with his indorser, and subject to any defense available against him. Sylvester *v.* Crapo, 15 Pick. 92; Burroughs *v.* Moss, 10 Barn. & Cresw. 563." Atkins *v.* Knight, 46 Ala. 539, 548.

"It is better to require one who would purchase a negotiable note after its maturity to ascertain whether it is a subsisting demand, than to subject the antecedent parties to the necessity of tracing to him a knowledge that it is not." Atkins *v.* Knight, 46 Ala. 539, 548.

The fraud of the maker and payee of a note in antedating it, for the purpose of practicing a deceit on a third person, and making it appear an absolute promise to pay, when in fact its payment depends on the success of the deceit, can give no protection to the maker, nor aid to the indorsee after maturity, in a suit for its collection. Atkins *v.* Knight, 46 Ala. 539, cited in note in 46 L. R. A. 755, 762, 768, 769.

Doctrine Illustrated.—In a suit by an endorsee against the maker of a promissory note, it is a valid defense that it was given in consideration of the notes and accounts of another person, and payable when they were collected, which had not been done, and that the plaintiff obtained it after maturity. Atkins *v.* Knight, 46 Ala. 539.

Defendants remitted a bill, indorsed by them, to a correspondent house, to whom they were then indebted, with instructions to credit them in account. That house procured the bill to be discounted, and credited the remitters with the proceeds, and advised them of the facts. Held, that a holder to whom the house indorsed the bill after its maturity, and subsequent to its having been taken up by them as indorsers, was not affected by a set-off then held by defendants against their correspondents. Sheffield *v.* Parmlee, 8 Ala. 889.

Where a creditor, holding his debtor's note and also the note of another person as collateral, transfers them after maturity to different persons, the rights of the transferees depend on the priority of the transfers. A first transfer of the collateral extinguishes the original debt pro tanto, and the party taking a subsequent transfer of the original note takes it subject to a credit pro tanto. But, if the original note is first transferred, the collateral will follow it into whosesoever hands it passes, being subject in them to any defense the maker might have made in first hands. Ware *v.* Russell, 57 Ala. 43, 29 Am. Rep. 710, cited in note in 46 L. R. A. 779.

§ 204. Consideration in General.

§ 205. —— Payment of Less than Face Value.

A executed several notes to C, amounting in the whole to $319, and C indorsed them to B for the accommodation of A, and received $200 of B, which he passed over to A. A paid to B $200. In an action by B against C it was held that he was not entitled to recover, on the ground of a failure of consideration for the residue. Hutchins *v.* McCann, 7 Port. 94.

§ 206. —— Usurious Consideration.

Doctrine Stated.—The rule obtains in this state, that a holder of a negotiable instrument, acquired by transfer or indorsement before maturity, upon a usurious consideration, though in the usual course of business, and without notice, is not a bona fide holder; and, in his hands, the instrument is subject to the equities or defenses which would have been available against the antecedent parties. Capital City Ins. Co. *v.* Quinn, 73 Ala. 558; Saltmarsh *v.* Tuthill, 13 Ala. 390, 410.

"The doctrine is well settled in this court that the holder of commercial paper, acquiring it on a usurious consideration, is not a bona fide holder, and is not protected against the infirmities of the paper, nor against transactions between the makers or indorsers with third persons, dealing with them without notice, in good faith, on a valuable consideration. Saltmarsh *v.* Tuthill, 13 Ala. 390; Carlisle *v.* Hill, 16 Ala. 398; Smith *v.* Lehman, etc., Co., 85 Ala. 394, 5 So. 204. In Saltmarsh *v.* Tuthill, supra, the court quotes the terse sentence in the opinion of Cowen, J., in Ramsdell *v.* Morgan, 16 Wend. 574: 'There is a solecism on the face of the expression, "a bona fide purchaser on usury."'" Hart *v.* Adler, 109 Ala. 467, 19 So. 894, 895.

Purchase of a note at a discount greater than the legal rate of interest does not affect the bona fides of the purchaser. Holmes *v.* Bank of Ft. Gaines, 24 So. 959, 120 Ala. 493.

"'A note or bill, which in the hands of the holder is a valid debt, may be bought or sold as any other chattel at its real or supposed value, and the transfer of such a note or bill at a discount beyond the legal rate of interest is not usurious, although the holder may indorse it, unless the transaction was a mere device to evade the statute against usury.' Saltmarsh *v.* Planters', etc., Bank, 17 Ala.

761, 768." Capital City Ins. Co. *v.* Quinn, 73 Ala. 558, 561; Woodall & Son *v.* People's Nat. Bank, 153 Ala. 576, 45 So. 194, 196; King *v.* People's Bank, 127 Ala. 266, 28 So. 658, 659.

"A sale at any rate of discount, unless the transaction originated in a treaty for the loan of money, of which the sale or discount was the consummation, is not a loan of money, or the forbearance of a debt, and is not consequently offensive to the statute against usury." Capital City Ins. Co. *v.* Quinn, 73 Ala. 558, 561.

The fact that the indorsements on a note were without consideration, or were procured by fraud, or that the notes were misapplied by the maker, constitutes no defense where plaintiff was a bona fide purchaser without notice of such fact, though the purchase was at usurious rates. Bunzel *v.* Maas, 22 So. 568, 116 Ala. 68.

Where the acceptor of a bill of exchange, drawn for his accommodation, disposes of it at a rate of discount greater than the legal rate of interest, the contract is usurious, and, being thus infected, the purchaser can not be regarded as a bona fide holder. Carlisle *v.* Hill, 16 Ala. 398.

"The principle is thus stated by Mr. Parsons: 'If no party to the note who is prior to the holder could himself bring an action upon it against the maker, then no prior party ever owned the note, and the holder, being the first owner, must be held to have loaned the money to the maker, through the prior parties, who were only agents of the maker; and on the other hand, if either prior party could have maintained an action, he owned the note and sold it to the holder.' 2 Parsons on Bills, 426. The principle is stated in substantially the same language by Mr. Daniel in his work on 'Negotiable Instruments' (1 Daniel's Neg. Ins., § 751); and of itself forms the test by which a sale of a bill or note at a greater rate of premium than legal interest, is distinguished from a usurious loan of money. Williams *v.* Reynolds, 10 Md. 57; Durant *v.* Banta, 27 N. J. Law 624; Gaul *v.* Willis, 26 Pa. 259; Saltmarsh *v.* Planters', etc., Bank, 17 Ala. 761." Capital City Ins. Co. *v.* Quinn, 73 Ala. 558, 562.

Doctrine Illustrated.—A drew a bill on B, in favor of C, which was indorsed by C and D on Sunday, and handed to B, who delivered it to E as a substitute for another bill held by E against B for the same amount, on which he had paid usurious interest, and extending the time of payment; E taking it without notice that they were indorsed on Sunday. Held, that E was not a bona fide holder, receiving the bill in the usual course of trade, so as to preclude a defense, in his hands, which would have been available as between the original parties, and that, as the indorsements were in violation of law, the bill was void in his hands. Saltmarsh *v.* Tuthill, 13 Ala. 390.

In an action on notes, it was a good plea that they were transferred by payee to plaintiff as collateral, and that the collateral debt bore usurious interest, or was usuriously discounted, and that before suit defendant paid the notes without knowing that they had been transferred. Stewart *v.* Bibb County Banking & Trust Co. (Ala.), 58 So. 273.

A purchase of notes by a third person from the payee at a discount of 10 per cent is not a usurious contract, under Code 1896, §§ 2626, 2630, which provide that contracts for the payment of interest on a loan of money at a higher rate than 8 per cent per annum are usurious. Orr *v.* Sparkman, 120 Ala. 9, 23 So. 829.

Under Code, § 2630, declaring that all contracts for the payment of interest on a loan or any contract at a higher rate than 8 per cent per annum can not be enforced save as to the principal, the fact that the holder of a note purchased the same from the payee at a discount, at a greater rate of interest than 8 per cent per annum, did not deprive him of protection against defenses existing between the maker and payee, on the ground that he was not a bona fide purchaser. King *v.* People's Bank, 28 So. 658, 127 Ala. 266.

§ 207. —— Crediting Proceeds.

The crediting by a bank of the amount of a check to the account of a depositor indebted to it does not make the bank a bona fide holder for value of the check. First Nat. Bank *v.* Nelson, 105 Ala. 180, 16 So. 707.

A bank, which discounts paper for a depositor and gives him credit for the proceeds, is not a "bona fide holder" for value, so as to be protected against infirmities in the paper unless some other consideration passes, such transaction merely creating the relation of debtor and creditor between the bank and the depositor; and so long as that relation continues and the deposit is not withdrawn the bank is subject to the equities of the prior parties, though the paper is taken before maturity and without notice. Alabama Grocery Co. *v.* First Nat. Bank, 48 So. 340, 158 Ala. 143.

§ 208. Taking as Collateral Security in General.

The taking of negotiable paper as collateral security for a debt presently created, is acquiring it in the usual course of business, upon a valuable consideration, entitling the holder to protection against equities or defenses existing between the original parties, of which he does not have notice. Connerly & Co. *v.* Planters,' etc., Ins. Co., 66 Ala. 432, 434; Miller & Co. *v.* Boykin, 70 Ala. 469; Boykin *v.* Bank, 72 Ala. 262, 271.

One who honestly receives a negotiable note before maturity as collateral security for a debt contracted simultaneously, or takes it as collateral in pursuance of a previous agreement made at the time the debt was contracted, is a bona fide purchaser. Thompson *v.* Maddux, 23 So. 157, 117 Ala. 468; Miller *v.* Boykin, 70 Ala. 469.

To constitute a purchaser for value, of notes or paper agreed to be transferred as collateral security for a debt contemporaneously contracted, it is not necessary that the notes or paper should be particularly described at the time. When the securities are subsequently transferred, in execution of the agreement, it is rendered specific and certain, and the creditor becomes a holder for value. Boykin *v.* Bank, 72 Ala. 262; Miller & Co. *v.* Boykin, 70 Ala. 469.

An agreement to give collaterals would be sufficient to include any particular collateral afterwards delivered in execution of such promise; the delivery when made would relate back to the time of the agreement, and it would be immaterial to the validity of the agreement or transfer, whether the collateral afterwards transferred was, at the time the agreement was made, in the city where the parties then were, or elsewhere. Miller & Co. *v.* Boykin, 70 Ala. 469.

Where notes are pledged to secure a debt, and the pledgee takes them as a bona fide purchaser for value, other notes afterwards substituted for these notes by agreement will also be held free from equities between the original parties. First Nat. Bank *v.* Johnston, 97 Ala. 655, 11 So. 690.

§ 209. Taking as Collateral Security for Pre-Existing Debt.

Doctrine Stated.—Whatever may be the general weight of authority elsewhere, it is the settled law of this state that a holder of negotiable paper as collateral security for a pre-existing debt is not a bona fide holder for value, and is not entitled to protection against equities and defenses existing between prior parties, of which he had no notice. Connerly & Co. *v.* Planters', etc., Ins. Co., 66 Ala. 432; Fenouille *v.* Hamilton, 35 Ala. 319; Thompson *v.* Maddux, 117 Ala. 468, 23 So. 157, 160; Miller & Co. *v.* Boykin, 70 Ala. 469, cited in note in 31 L. R. A., N. S., 292, 299; First Nat. Bank *v.* Johnston, 97 Ala. 655, 11 So. 690, 692; Stewart *v.* Bibb County, etc., Co. (Ala.), 58 So. 273; Andrews & Bros. *v.* McCoy, 8 Ala. 920, cited in note in 31 L. R. A., N. S., 292.

The indorsee of commercial paper, acquiring it before maturity merely as collateral security for a pre-existing debt, takes it subject to all the defenses which the maker could prefer against the payee, if he had remained the holder. Bank *v.* Poelnitz, 61 Ala. 147; First Nat. Bank *v.* Johnston, 97 Ala. 655, 11 So. 690, 691; Boykin *v.* Bank, 72 Ala. 262.

And under the decisions of the supreme court, contrary to the weight of authority, accommodation paper is not an exception to this rule. Boykin *v.* Bank, 72 Ala. 262; Miller & Co. *v.* Boykin, 70 Ala. 469.

And this right exists as to matters of set-off and discount, as well as to defenses affecting the instrument itself. Bank *v.* Poelnitz, 61 Ala. 147.

And the fact that the assignee afterwards grants indulgence, or forbears to enforce his remedies for the collection of his debt, when it is not shown that such indulgence or forbearance was an element of the contract by which he acquired the paper, does not affect the principle. Fenouille *v.* Hamilton, 35 Ala. 319, cited in note in 31 L. R. A., N. S., 292, 299.

"But if there be any additional consideration, such as forbearance or extension of the time of payment of the pre-existing debt for which the note was transferred as collateral security, the rule is different, and in such case the transferee becomes entitled to the same protection and to the same extent, under the commercial law, as any other bona fide holder for value." Stewart *v.* Bibb County, etc., Co. (Ala.), 58 So. 273.

Where negotiable paper is transferred to secure a pre-existing debt, in consideration of an extension of the time of payment of the debt, the transferee is a bona fide holder for value, and is not subject to equities between prior parties, of which he had no notice. First Nat. Bank *v.* Johnston, 97 Ala. 655, 11 So. 690.

Thus, a note transferred to secure a pre-existing debt, in consideration of an extension of the time of payment of the debt, makes the transferee a bona fide holder, and not subject to equities between the original parties of which he had no notice. Prim *v.* Hammel, 134 Ala. 652, 32 So. 1006; Louisville Banking Co. *v.* Howard, 123 Ala. 380, 26 So. 207, 208, cited in note in 31 L. R. A., N. S., 292, 298, 299.

In such a case, notes afterwards substituted by mutual agreement of the parties, without any new consideration, to take the place of the collateral originally taken, will be held in the same condition as the collateral whose place it took. First Nat. Bank *v.* Johnston, 97 Ala. 655, 11 So. 690.

Doctrine Illustrated.—If the indorsee takes the note as an indemnity for a pre-existing liability as surety for the payee, it is not in the usual course of business, and he will hold it subject to the equities of the maker against the indorser. Bank of Mobile *v.* Hall, 6 Ala. 639, 41 Am. Dec. 72.

Where a note given for the purchase money of land is transferred as collateral security for a pre-existing debt of the payee, the maker may set up as defense in an action by the holder a breach of a covenant against incumbrances. Cullum *v.* Branch of State Bank, 4 Ala. 21, 37 Am. Dec. 725, cited in note in 31 L. R. R., N. S., 292.

A mortgagee delivered to plaintiff, without indorsement, a mortgage note as collateral security for a debt. The mortgagor paid the mortgage to, and procured its cancellation by, the mortgagee, without notice of the transfer of such note. There was evidence that the transfer of the note to plaintiff was in consideration of an indulgence by him to such mortgagee on an antecedent debt. Held, that he was not a bona fide holder, where such evidence did not show such a definite agreement as to the forbearance as to constitute an independent consideration for the transfer. Vann *v.* Marbury, 100 Ala. 438, 14 So. 273, 46 Am. St. Rep. 70, 23 L. R. A. 325, cited in note in 31 L. R. A., N. S., 292.

§ 210. Taking in Payment of Pre-Existing Debt.

Doctrine Stated.—One who receives a bill, or negotiable note, before its maturity, in payment of a debt, is a bona fide holder. Barney *v.* Earle, 13 Ala. 106.

When a creditor takes his debtor's check on a bank in payment of his debt, he is a holder for a valuable consideration. Mobile, etc., R. Co. *v.* Felrath, 67 Ala. 189.

"The transfer of negotiable paper in payment of a pre-existing debt, is according to the known and usual course of business, and is founded on a valuable consideration, entitling the transferee to protection against equities and defenses, to which the paper may have been subject between the original parties. Swift *v.* Tyson, 16 Pet. 1; Bank *v.* Hall, 6 Ala. 639; Barney *v.* Earle, 13 Ala. 106." Mayberry & Co. *v.* Morris, 62 Ala. 113, 116.

The act of 1828, places promissory notes in respect to the remedy, on the same footing with bills of exchange, and declares that they shall all be governed by the rules of the law merchant, etc.; consequently, where such a note is indorsed before its maturity in payment of a pre-existing debt, its collection may be enforced by the indorsee against the maker, though the latter may have a defense which implicates its validity, as between himself and the payee. Pond *v.* Lockwood, 8 Ala. 669.

A negotiable instrument received before it is due, in payment of a pre-existing debt, is received in the usual course of trade between merchants, and will protect the holder against a latent equity between the original parties, of which he had no notice. Bank *v.* Hall, 6 Ala. 639.

A creditor who takes the note of his debtor, with accommodation indorsements, in payment of an antecedent debt, is a purchaser for value in due course of business, and may hold the indorser. Marks *v.* First Nat. Bank, 79 Ala. 550, 58 Am. Rep. 620.

Rationale of Doctrine.—"There is no sensible distinction between receiving a bill in payment of a pre-existing debt, and purchasing it with money or property. In either case, the consideration is a valuable one; and all the reasons which apply to protect the holder against latent equities between the original parties of which he had no notice, apply with the same force in the one case as in the other." Bank *v.* Hall, 6 Ala. 639, 644.

Doctrine Illustrated.—One who receives a bill, or negotiable note, before its maturity, in payment of a debt, is not affected by any force, or fraud in obtaining the bill, of which he had no notice. Barney *v.* Earle, 13 Ala. 106.

The transferee, before maturity, of an accepted bill of exchange in payment of an antecedent debt, from one to whom it was given for another purpose, acquires a good title, unless he took it with knowledge of the conditions of the acceptance. Farley Nat. Bank *v.* Henderson, 118 Ala. 441, 24 So. 428.

A party who signs his name to a note in blank, with the understanding that it shall be filled up with a particular amount or be used in a particular mode, is liable upon the note to a party who receives it in ignorance of the agreement and pays a valuable consideration for it, whether it be an advance of money or the extinguishment of a debt. Decatur Bank *v.* Spence, 9 Ala. 800.

§ 211. Knowledge of or Notice to Immediate Indorser as to Defenses.

An indorsee of a note before maturity with notice of payment to a third person, pursuant to an order of the payee, may transfer the note to an innocent purchaser for value before maturity, who may enforce the note notwithstanding such payment. Snead *v.* Barclift, 2 Ala. App. 297, 56 So. 592.

The bona fide holder of a bill of exchange, who took it before maturity, without notice of any defect in the title of his indorser, may recover thereon, though such indorser acquired it by fraud. Saltmarsh *v.* Tuthill, 13 Ala. 390.

§ 212. Purchasers from Bona Fide Holders.

An innocent holder for value of an acceptance, improperly made by a member of a firm, by his indorsement of the bill, transfers all his rights to his indorsee, who will not therefore be required to show when he acquired the bill, or that he gave value for it. Pearson *v.* Howe, 11 Ala. 370.

Where the defendants remitted a bill, indorsed by them, to a correspondent house, to whom they were then indebted, with instructions to credit them in account, and that house procured the bill to be discounted, and credited the remitters with the proceeds, and advised them of the facts, these circumstances constitute a sufficient consideration for the indorsement to enable the correspondent house to maintain an action on the bill, when subsequently paid by them as indorsers, against the remitters; and a holder to whom this house indorsed the bill after its maturity, and subsequent to its being taken up by them, is not affected by a set-off then held by the defendants against their correspondents. Sheffield *v.* Parmlee, 8 Ala. 889.

§ 213. Defenses as against Bona Fide Purchasers.

§ 214. —— In General.

§ 214 (1) In General.

Commercial paper, in the hands of a bona fide purchaser for value before maturity, is not subject to defenses which would be available against the original payee, unless it is shown that such purchaser had notice of such defenses. Merchants' Nat. Bank *v.* Norris, 163 Ala. 481, 51 So. 15. See ante, "Nature and Grounds of Protection," § 189.

In an action on notes, special pleas setting up fraud in securing the signature, suretyship, failure of consideration, and breach of warranty, were completely answered by replication averring that the notes were commercial paper, and the purchase by plaintiff in the regular course of business for value and without notice. Merchants' Nat. Bank *v.* Norris, 163 Ala. 481, 51 So. 15.

§ 214 (2) Estoppel to Set Up Defense.

Where the payee of a note was inquired of by a prospective purchaser as to whether there existed any defenses against it, and answered that he had none, he did not thereby preclude himself from making any defense growing out of the original transaction of which he had no knowledge at the time. Clements *v.* Loggins, 2 Ala. 514.

§ 214 (3) Waiver of Defenses.

Where a note is expressly made negotiable and payable at bank, the right of set-off or other like defense is thereby waived, not only as against the bank, but as against any innocent holder. Knapp *v.* McBride, 7 Ala. 19.

§ 215. —— Incapacity or Want of Authority of Parties in General.

Where the wife, as comaker with her husband, signs a note payable at a bank, and hence governed by the commercial law, and it is sold before maturity, for value, to a purchaser having no notice of defenses existing between the original parties, the wife can not escape liability by showing that she was a mere surety on the note, within Code, § 2349, providing that a wife shall not become surety for her husband. Scott *v.* Taul, 22 So. 447, 115 Ala. 529.

If one signs or indorses a blank bill or note, and parts with its possession, with the view of its being filled up and made a negotiable security, and it afterwards and before maturity comes to the hands of a bona fide holder for a valuable consideration without notice, he will be held to its payment, without regard to the authority of the person by whom the blank was filled. Robertson *v.* Smith, 18 Ala. 220. See post, "Defective Execution," § 217.

Where one partner affixes the partnership name to a note, as security for a debt of a third person, without his partner's assent, an innocent holder of the note, by the Alabama statute of 1812, takes it subject to the same defense as the original payee. Rolston *v.* Click, 1 Stew. 526.

§ 216. —— Powers of Corporations or Corporate Officers.

Where a corporation issues commercial paper when not authorized to issue any commercial paper, such paper is void, even in the hands of a bona fide purchaser for value before maturity. Stouffer *v.* Smith-Davis Hardware Co., 154 Ala. 301, 45 So. 621.

But where a corporation, having the power to accept drafts for some purposes, accepts a draft for goods which it has no power to deal in, it can not defend a suit on such note by a bona fide holder for value before maturity on the ground that the transaction was ultra vires; nothing appearing on the face of the draft to show for what purpose it was issued. Stouffer *v.* Smith-Davis Hardware Co., 45 So. 621, 154 Ala. 301.

A private corporation can not defend an action on its accommodation note on the ground of ultra vires, as against a bona fide holder. Florence R. R. & Imp. Co. *v.* Chase Nat. Bank, 106 Ala. 364, 17 So. 720.

"The doctrine is thus stated in 29 Am. & Eng. Ency. of Law (2d Ed.), p. 66: 'If the corporation is authorized to issue negotiable paper for any purpose, the defense of ultra vires will not be available to it in a suit by a bona fide indorsee, although the particular contract might have been really unauthorized; the reason being that the corporation, by giving the note, has virtually represented that it was given for some legitimate purpose, and the indorsee could not be presumed to know the contrary. This doctrine is applied to commercial paper made by a corporation for the accommodation of a third person when in the hands of a bona fide holder, who has taken it before maturity on the faith of its being business paper. But if the corporation is not authorized to issue negotiable paper under any circumstances, such paper is void, not only in the hands of the original payee, but in those of any subsequent holder as well; and this for the reason that all persons dealing with a corporation are bound to take notice of the extent of its charter powers.' See note 1 on page 67, where the cases are collated in support of the doctrine." Stouffer *v.* Smith-Davis Hardware Co., 154 Ala. 301, 45 So. 621, 622.

§ 217. —— Defective Execution.

"'There is a general principle which pervades the universal law merchant, respecting alterations (which, when they are material, will, as we have seen, vitiate the will or note even in the hands of a bona fide holder without notice); a principle necessary to the protection of the innocent and prudent from the negligence and fraud of others. That is, that when the drawer of the bill or the maker of the note has himself, by careless execution of the instrument, left room for any alteration to be made, either by insertion or erasure, without defacing it, or exciting the suspicions of a careful man, he will be liable upon it to a bona fide holder without notice, when the opportunity afforded has been embraced, and the instrument filled up with a larger amount or different terms than those which it bore at the time he signed it.' 2 Daniel, Neg. Inst., § 1405; Tied. Com. Paper, § 397; Angle *v.* Insurance Co., 92 U. S. 330; Garrard *v.* Haddan, 67 Pa. St. 82; Young & Son *v.* Lehman, etc., Co., 63 Ala. 519, 523; Toomer *v.* Rutland, 57 Ala. 379, 384." Winter *v.* Pool, 104 Ala. 508, 16 So. 543.

Where a person executing a note leaves a blank space after the printed words "payable at the bank of," it is no defense against a bona fide purchaser before maturity that some one, without his knowledge, and before the purchase, had filled in the space with the name of a bank or other place. Winter *v.* Pool, 16 So. 543, 104 Ala. 508.

"When one intrusts another with his signature to a note in blank, upon an agreement between them, that it is to be filled up with a certain amount, or to be used in a particular mode, and this contract is violated, either by the insertion of a larger amount, or by using the instrument in a way not contemplated by the party signing it, if the person receiving it is ignorant of the fraud which has been committed, and gives a valuable consideration for the paper, he may recover upon it. This principle has been so frequently decided in this court, that it is only necessary to refer to the cases in which the rule is expounded. See Roberts *v.* Adams, 8 Port. 297; Herbert *v.* Huie, 1 Ala. 18; Huntington *v.* Branch Bank, 3 Ala. 186; Nance *v.* Lary, 5 Ala. 370." Decatur Bank *v.* Spence, 9 Ala. 800, 801.

Where a note is indorsed before it is signed, and delivered to the maker without any understanding as to how it is to be signed, the maker can sign the name of a firm of which he is a member, so as to bind the indorser to an innocent holder. Montgomery *v.* Crossthwait, 90 Ala. 553, 8 So. 498, 24 Am. St. Rep. 832, 12 L. R. A. 140.

§ 218. —— Conditions or Collateral Agreements.

It is no defense against a note in the hands of a bona fide holder that the note as signed was delivered to the payees under agreement that it should not take effect unless other persons should sign. Norris *v.* Merchants' Nat. Bank, 2 Ala. App. 434, 57 So. 71.

Where a negotiable note is transferred for value before maturity, without notice that one of the signers is a surety, that fact can not defeat the collection of the note. Sherrer *v.* Enterprise Banking Co., 49 So. 779, 160 Ala. 329.

In an action on notes, a special plea setting up suretyship, was completely answered by replications averring that the notes were commercial paper, and the purchase by plaintiff in the regular course of business for value and without notice. Merchants' Nat. Bank of La Fayette, Ind. *v.* Norris, 51 So. 15, 163 Ala. 481.

Where respondent's signature to a note was apparently that of a comaker, the indorsee could presume that he signed in such capacity, and not as a surety, until it obtained knowledge to the contrary. Alabama Nat. Bank *v.* Hunt, 28 So. 488, 125 Ala. 512.

The fact that notes which B. took for purchase money of goods sold to customers were impressed with a trust in favor of C. by reason of B.'s contract with C. to hold them in trust for it till his debt to it was satisfied, and the transfer of the notes by B. to L., do not, as matter of law, charge L. with notice of the trust, so as to make it accountable to C. Bank of Luverne *v.* Birmingham Fertilizer Co., 39 So. 126, 143 Ala. 153.

§ 219. —— Want or Failure of Consideration in General.

Partial or total failure of consideration is not a defense to counts on a negotiable instrument alleging ownership in plaintiff through an indorsement before maturity, in due course of business without notice of any defense. Bledsoe *v.* City Nat. Bank of Selma (Ala. App.), 60 So. 942.

In an action on notes, a special plea setting up failure of consideration, was completely answered by replications averring that the notes were commercial paper, and the purchase by plaintiff in the regular course of business for value and without notice. Merchants' Nat. Bank of La Fayette, Ind. *v.* Norris, 51 So. 15, 163 Ala. 481.

Where, in an action on a note, defendant's plea set up both failure of consideration and that the holder was not a bona fide purchaser, in that he had discounted the note at a usurious rate of interest, the plaintiff was entitled to judgment, where the first defense was made out but the second was not. King *v.* People's Bank, 28 So. 658, 127 Ala. 266.

Under the statute of Alabama in force in 1831, Aik. D. 69, providing that, in an action by the assignee of a promissory note, the defendant shall be allowed the benefit of all discounts, etc., had against the same, previous to notice of the assignment, the maker may show a failure of consideration of a note, in an action by an indorsee, although the note was indorsed before maturity. Hudson *v.* Tindall, 1 Stew. & P. 237.

An instrument in the form of a promissory note payable at a bank, but with the seal of the maker attached, does not come within Code, § 2094, by which "bills of exchange and promissory notes, payable in money at a bank, * * * are governed by the commercial law," and failure of consideration may be shown by the maker, in a suit by a bona fide holder, who took for value and before maturity. Muse *v.* Dantzler, 85 Ala. 359, 5 So. 178.

At the request of the payee of a note, who said that he desired to trade it with plaintiff, but that plaintiff would not take it unless it was payable at a bank, and contained a waiver of exemption, the maker executed an instrument in the form of a negotiable note, but under seal, payable at a bank, and containing the waiver, which the payee transferred to plaintiff. Held, that the maker was not estopped to set up a failure of consideration which arose out of the original contract on which the note was made, and which was unknown to him at the time. Muse *v.* Dantzler, 85 Ala. 359, 5 So. 178.

§ 220. —— Accommodation Paper.

See post, "Usury," § 223.

Where a party consents to make notes for the accommodation of the party named as payee in them, and to intrust the latter with their negotiation in his business, he must be deemed the maker upon valuable consideration, as regards every holder of the notes for value to whom no fraud can be imputed; and when sued on the notes he can not show that he could have protected himself from loss if he had been notified that the notes were unpaid, since the payee was solvent at the time of their maturity. Connerly *v.* Planters' & Merchants' Ins. Co., 66 Ala. 432.

As paper executed without consideration for the payee's accommodation becomes obligatory only when the latter negotiates it, whereupon the transferee becomes the real payee as against the maker, Code 1886, § 2594, giving the payor of notes or bonds the same defenses against a transferee which he had against the payee before notice of the assignment, does not apply to accommodation paper. Talmadge *v.* Milliken, 24 So. 843, 119 Ala. 40.

§ 221. —— Fraud in Inception.

Fraud of the payee of a note in procuring its execution held not available as a defense to the note in the hands of a bona fide holder. Norris *v.* Merchants' Nat. Bank, 2 Ala. App. 434, 57 So. 71.

In an action on notes, a special plea setting up fraud in securing the signature was completely answered by a replication averring that the notes were commercial paper and the purchase by plaintiff in the regular course of business for value and without notice. Merchants' Nat. Bank of La Fayette, Ind. *v.* Norris, 51 So. 15, 163 Ala. 481.

Where the consideration of a note is the assignment of a patent right, and the payee fraudulently obtains possession without making the assignment, a bona fide transferee before maturity, for a valuable consideration, in the usual course of business, will be protected. Wildsmith *v.* Tracy, 80 Ala. 258, cited in note in 20 L. R. A. 606, 36 L. R. A. 439.

§ 222. —— Illegality in General.

When a part of the consideration of a contract is illegal, the contract is void as between the immediate parties to it, who have knowledge of the illegality, and as between these it can not be enforced. But if such contract be a negotiable promissory note in the hands of an indorsee who is a bona fide holder for valuable consideration, without knowledge of the illegality, this rule of law does not apply. Such indorsee may recover on such note, notwithstanding the illegality, unless the contract is declared by statute a nullity from the beginning. Bozeman *v.* Allen, 48 Ala. 512.

A note which is expressly made illegal and void by statute is void in the hands of even otherwise bona fide holders without notice of illegality, but if the statute merely, expressly or impliedly, makes the consideration illegal, the note will be valid in the hands of a bona fide purchaser without notice. Bluthenthal *v.* Columbia, 175 Ala. 398, 57 So. 814.

"Chitty, in his Treatise on Bills, says, that unless the legislature has expressly declared that the illegality of the contract or consideration, shall make the security, whether bill or note, void, illegality of consideration will be no defense in an action at the suit of a bona fide holder, without notice of the illegality, unless he obtained the bill after it became due. Thus, in an action by the indorsee against the maker of a promissory note, the defense insisted on was, that the note had been given for hits against the defendant in a lottery insurance. Lord Kenyon observed, that the innocent indorsee of a gaming note, or note given on an usurious contract, could not recover, but that in no other case could the innocent indorsee be deprived of his remedy on the note; and that a contrary determination would shake paper credit to the foundation. The ground upon which gaming and usury are made an exception, is, that the statute declare the securities void; and the law in respect to these, under the influence of commercial policy, has been modified in England, and perhaps some of the states of the union. Chit. on B. 9th Am. Ed. 110 to 117. This distinction has been repeatedly recognized. Thus, the statute of 7 Geo. 2, c. 8, makes wagers and contracts in nature of wagers, etc., void, yet it has been held, that as it does not avoid bills, notes, and securities, but only the contracts, a bill or note on such a contract is valid in the hands of a bona fide indorsee, receiving it without notice, before it was due. Day *v.* Stuart, 6 Bing. 109; 2 Man. & R. 422; Amory *v.* Merewether, 2 B. & Cresw. 573; Brown *v.* Turner, 7 T. Rep. 630; Steers *v.* Lashley, 6 T. Rep. 61; Aubert *v.* Maze, 2 Bos. & P. 374; Story on Bills, § 189, and note 2; 3 Kent's Com. 4th Ed. 79, 80." Saltmarsh *v.* Tuthill, 13 Ala. 390, 405.

Gambling Contracts.—Notes given in gambling contracts are void not only as to the parties but as to innocent purchasers for value, and it is immaterial what form the contract may assume, whether a note or a bill of exchange, and it is void though negotiated before maturity to an innocent purchaser for value. Birmingham Trust, etc., Co. *v.* Curry, 160 Ala. 370, 49 So. 319.

Where a person purposing neither to buy nor sell cotton, but simply to stake margins to cover differences in price, and, on final settlement, merely to receive or pay the difference between the contract price and the market price at the time fixed for delivery, gave a broker, who knew of his purpose, his acceptance of a bill of exchange, to be discounted in making such contracts. Held, that the consideration of the bill was a wager, and that by Code, § 2131, it was void, even in the hands of a bona fide holder. Hawley *v.* Bibb, 69 Ala. 52.

Under Code, § 2163, declaring that all contracts founded wholly or in part on a gambling consideration are void, a sale of slot machines, where the vendor, as an inducement to the purchase, places some of the machines, and protects their use by a reward for conviction of any one tampering with them, the contract of sale is absolutely void, and consequently notes given in consideration for it are void in the hands of an innocent holder for value. Kuhl *v.* M. Gally Universal Press Co., 26 So. 535, 123 Ala. 452, 82 Am. St. Rep. 135.

An innocent holder of a security won at gaming can not recover of the indorser who lost it, though the indorsement was made before the security was lost, unless he was induced to take it by the representations of the indorser. Ivey *v.* Nicks, 14 Ala. 564.

Where fertilizers were sold without being tagged as required by law, notes given for the price were invalid, even in the hands of a bona fide holder for value. Alabama Nat. Bank *v.* C. C. Parker & Co., 40 So. 987, 146 Ala. 513.

Under Code 1886, § 141, providing that a sale or exchange of fertilizer not tagged as provided by statute is void, a sale of fertilizer in sacks not tagged is void, and a note given for the price can not be collected though in the hands of a bona fide purchaser without notice and before maturity. Hanover Nat. Bank *v.* Johnson, 90 Ala. 549, 8 So. 42.

Notes Executed on Sunday.—"We think it safe to hold, as stated by Mr. Herman (Estoppel and Res Judicata, vol. 2, § 1027), that it is 'a general rule of law' that all notes executed and delivered on Sunday are void between the parties; yet, if falsely dated as of another day, and such an instrument comes to the hands of an innocent holder, who takes it for value, before maturity, without notice, the maker is estopped, in an action on such instrument by the innocent holder, from setting up that it is not truly dated, and is a Sunday contract, and therefore void. To hold otherwise would be to invite fraudulent collusion between makers and payees of negotiable instruments, who at their will could give a false date to a negotiable note and invite its use in the commercial world, and then defeat its enforcement in the hands of an innocent purchaser for value, before maturity, by pleading their own perfidy." Moseley *v.* Selma Nat. Bank, 3 Ala. App. 614, 57 So. 91, 95.

"The act of 1803, inhibits all 'worldly business' or employment, or servile work (works of necessity or charity excepted), and goes quite beyond the English statute, which applies to the business of one's 'ordinary calling.' Now the indorsement of a bill, and delivery of it to the acceptor, to be used for his accommodation, is certainly 'worldly business,' although the acceptor may not negotiate it until Monday, or some subsequent day. The transaction on the part of the indorser, is not the mere writing his name, but includes an authority to the acceptor to negotiate. If the manual act of indorsement is not in itself the performance of 'worldly business,' it certainly becomes such when coupled with the authority to transfer; and is not the less so, though the authority be verbal, or can only be implied from the indorsement, and intrusting the paper to the acceptor. See Clough *v.* Davis, 9 N. H. 500. It has been repeatedly determined, that a penalty inflicted by statute upon the doing of an act, is equivalent to a prohibition, and a contract relating to it is void. See Shippey *v.* Eastwood, 9 Ala. 198, 200. Under the influence of this rule, it has been decided that a contract made on a Sunday is void, and a security founded on it, is not recoverable at the suit of a party to the illegal consideration. But as the act does not declare that both the contract and security are void, the authorities clearly indicate that a bona fide indorsee of negotiable paper, founded upon such a contract, who acquires it before maturity, without notice of the illegality, for value, may enforce its payment. See, also, as to contracts, etc., made on Sunday, Peirce *v.* Hill, 9 Port. 151; O'Donnell *v.* Sweeny, 5 Ala. 467; Dodson *v.* Harris, 10 Ala. 566, 567; Butler *v.* Lee, 11 Ala. 885; Sayles *v.* Smith, 12 Wend. 57; Drury *v.* DeFontaine, 1 Taunt. 131; 56 Law Lib. (top page) 86; Smith *v.* Sparrow, 4 Bing. 84; Williams *v.* Paul, 4 M. & P. 532; Boynton *v.* Page, 13 Went. 425; Tracy *v.* Jenks,

15 Pick. [Mass.] 465; Clap *v.* Smith, 16 Pick. [Mass.] 250; Lyon *v.* Strong, 6 Vt. 219; Fox *v.* Abel, 2 Conn. 541; Kepner *v.* Keefer, 6 Watts 231; Northup *v.* Foot, 14 Went. 248; Blaxsome *v.* Williams, 3 B. & C. 232; Fennell *v.* Ridler, 5 B. & C. 406; Myers *v.* The State, 1 Conn. 502; Story on Con., 2d Ed. 543." Saltmarsh *v.* Tuthill, 13 Ala. 390, 405.

"By intentionally giving a negotiable note a false date, so as to make it appear valid on its face, the maker holds it out and represents it to be a valid instrument, and invites all parties to deal with and treat it as his legal act and binding obligation. Giving the note a false date for this purpose, if not an express representation of its validity that would estop the maker from denying its legality of date as against an innocent holder, is a representation necessarily implied from the circumstance, and there is no real difference between the express and implied representation. As said by Mr. Story (Story's Eq. Jur., § 384): 'There can be no real difference between an express representation and one that is naturally or necessarily implied from the circumstances.' The representation or assertion, to create an estoppel, need not be express, but may be implied. Bigelow on Estoppel, vol. 1, § 6. If the false representation, either express or implied, induced the one who becomes the innocent holder to be deceived and part with a valuable consideration for what he honestly believes to be the legal obligation of another, then it is to protect such a one that the law of estoppel operates to close the mouth of the other party against setting up his own fraudulent act to defeat the right of the one who has innocently acted on the false representation and put himself in a position of disadvantage." Moseley *v.* Selma Nat. Bank, 3 Ala. App. 614, 57 So. 91, 93.

Where a note and chattel mortgage securing it were executed on Sunday, but dated as of a secular day, and an innocent purchaser took them for value, without notice, before maturity, the maker was estopped to defeat an action thereon by the purchaser. Moseley *v.* Selma Nat. Bank, 3 Ala. App. 614, 57 So. 91.

§ 223. —— Usury.

The fact that there was usury in a note, as between maker and payee, or that the maker signed the note without reading it, and in ignorance of a waiver of exemption and provision for attorney's fee contained therein, is not a defense to a suit on the note by an innocent purchaser for value before maturity. Orr *v.* Sparkman, 23 So. 829, 120 Ala. 9.

The mere renewal of a note between the original parties to a usurious contract, does not purge the transaction of the taint of usury; but the illegal taint may be eliminated, by a renewal of the note after it has passed into the hands of a bona fide purchaser for value without notice. Masterson *v.* Grubbs, 70 Ala. 406; Mitchell *v.* McCullough, 59 Ala. 179.

But in Pearson *v.* Bailey, 23 Ala. 537, it was held that the taint of usury follows a note or renewal thereof even into the hands of a bona fide holder, unless he received it through the fraud of the maker. Pearson *v.* Bailey, 23 Ala. 537.

Promise by Maker to Pay if Indulgence Is Given.—A promise by the maker to an innocent holder of usurious paper to pay it, if indulgence is given, is binding on him, and may be enforced, if the delay is given. Palmer *v.* Severance, 8 Ala. 53.

Accommodation Note Tainted with Usury in Its Inception.—A note made for the special accommodation of an individual, to enable him to raise money by its discount, which provides for a rate above legal interest, is usurious and void in the hands of an innocent purchaser. Metcalf *v.* Watkins, 1 Port. 57.

A note made for purpose of raising money for the maker at a usurious rate of interest, and sold at a discount beyond the legal interest, is usurious, and the buyer, though ignorant of the original taint, can not recover on it. Faris *v.* King, 1 Stew. 255.

Accommodation Bill of Exchange Sold at a Usurious Discount.—B., being indebted to the L. Ins. & T. Co., obtained from his friends, certain blank bills of exchange, drawn and indorsed by them, he being the acceptor, which blanks were to be used by him, only in renewal of the debt due the L. Ins. & T. Co. In violation of this agreement, he filled up one of the blanks for $6,000, and sold it to W. for $5,000, being about at the rate of 20 per cent discount. W. afterwards transferred the bill to the P. & M. Bank, by which, suit was brought against one of the indorsers. Held, as W. purchased the bill at 20 per cent discount, he could only recover the $5,000 advanced him, from the acceptor, and the statute of usury of this state, avoiding the bill as to all but the principal sum, as between the original parties, it is void to the same extent into whose ever hands it may afterwards go. Saltmarsh *v.* P. & M. Bank, 14 Ala. 668.

§ 224. —— Alteration.

See the title ALTERATION OF INSTRUMENTS.

Where the maker of a negotiable note left room so that it might be materially altered without defacing it, such alteration is no defense as against a bona fide purchaser before maturity, nothing appearing on its face to excite suspicion. Holmes *v.* Bank of Ft. Gaines, 24 So. 959, 120 Ala. 493.

A purchaser of a note in due course before maturity could recover thereon according to its original tenor, under the express provisions of Negotiable Instruments Act (Acts Sp. Sess. 1909, p. 146), § 124, notwithstanding a material alteration of which it had no notice, and in which it did not participate. Bledsoe *v.* City Nat. Bank (Ala. App.), 60 So. 942.

§ 225. —— Fraudulent Diversion.

M. became the indorser for L. of certain bills of exchange, upon an agreement that they should be used in the purchase of the stock of a particular bank, in which both were equally interested, and both to be equally bound for the payment of the bills. L., pursuant to an arrangement with H., transferred the bills to C., in payment of a debt due by H. to C., the latter being ignorant of the agreement between M. and L., relating to the indorsement of the bills. Held, first, that C. could recover of M., the indorser, though L., in the transfer to C., had violated the contract by which the indorsements were made. Second, that if L. was the dupe of H. in the contract by which the bills were transferred to C., the fraud could not be visited on C., who was ignorant of it, and did not participate in it. Clapp *v.* Mock, 8 Ala. 122.

§ 226. —— Payment or Discharge.

It is no defense to an action on a note or bill of exchange by a bona fide transferee before maturity that the maker or acceptor paid the original payee. Prim *v.* Hammel, 134 Ala. 652, 32 So. 1006; Capital City Ins. Co. *v.* Quinn, 73 Ala. 558.

A payment of a promissory note to the payee, made before maturity, but after the note has been assigned for valuable consideration, or made after maturity, but with notice or knowledge of the assignment, is not available as against the assignee. Barbour & Son *v.* Washington Fire, etc., Ins. Co., 60 Ala. 433.

"It is a general rule that, when the maker pays a negotiable promissory note before its maturity and fails to take it up, he does so at his peril. If, when such payment is made, the note is in the hands of an innocent holder thereof for value, or if, after such payment, the note is indorsed before maturity to an innocent purchaser for value, without notice of such payment, such payment is, as to such owner, no payment, and such innocent holder for a valuable consideration is entitled to enforce its payment." Snead *v.* Barclift, 2 Ala. App. 297, 56 So. 592.

§ 227. —— Set-Off or Counterclaim.

In an action on a bill of exchange by the assignee the court properly charged as to set-off that, unless defendant owned the note sought to be set off before the indorsement of the bill to plaintiff, and that at or before the transfer plaintiff knew the same, defendant would not be entitled to set it off against the bill. Manning *v.* Maroney, 87 Ala. 563, 6 So. 343.

A note payable in bank, assigned before it is due, is not subject to an offset against the original payee. O'Hara *v.* Bank, 2 Ala. 367.

Where a promissory note, payable either in a bank of this or some other state, is endorsed before maturity, under the act of 1828, a set-off is not admissible to an action brought thereon by a bona fide indorsee. Beal *v.* Wainwright, etc., Co., 6 Ala. 156.

A note made negotiable and payable at bank, is not subject to offset in the hands of a bona fide indorsee, who has acquired it previous to maturity, although it has never been negotiated at the bank where it is made payable. McDonald *v.* Husted, 3 Ala. 297.

Where one makes a promissory note negotiable at bank, and the bank becomes its purchaser—no set-off can be allowed against it in favor of the maker against the payee. In such a note, the maker impliedly stipulates that he will forego every defense against the payee, and all intervening holders, and it would be a fraud on the bank to set up offsets against a note, under such circumstances. Emanuel *v.* Atwood, 6 Port. 384.

Where a note is made payable to a bank, and by a separate agreement in writing made at the same time the maker agrees that it may be negotiated to any other person as well as the bank, no set-off can be allowed against the note in favor of the maker against the payee. Emanuel *v.* Atwood, 6 Port. 384.

A note payable absolutely at a designated bank, for a sum certain, at a definite time, is "paper governed by the commercial law," which, if negotiated before maturity, is, under Code 1886, § 2684, free from set-off or recoupment, though it also waive exemptions, and provide for attorney's fees and retention of title to the property bought with it, as security for its payment. First Nat. Bank *v.* Slaughter, 98 Ala. 602, 14 So. 545, 39 Am. St. Rep. 88.

VI. PRESENTMENT, DEMAND, NOTICE, AND PROTEST.

§ 228. What Law Governs.

The demand, protest, and notice of nonpayment of a negotiable instrument is governed by the law of the place where it is made payable, in the absence of an agreement of the parties to the contrary. Todd *v.* Neal, 49 Ala. 266.

Thus, a bill of exchange, drawn in Alabama, on parties in Louisiana, and payable there, is a foreign bill (Rev. Code, § 1857), and is governed, as to demand, protest, and notice thereof, by the law of Louisiana. Todd *v.* Neal, 49 Ala. 266.

§ 229. Presentment for Acceptance.

Necessity.—A bill payable at a given time after date need not be presented for acceptance. Evans *v.* Bridges, 4 Port. 348.

Where a bill is payable at sight, a demand of payment and notice to the drawer, without previous presentation for acceptance, are insufficient to charge him. Hart *v.* Smith, 15 Ala. 807, 50 Am. Dec. 161.

Presentment of a bill of exchange for acceptance is not necessary to fix the liability of one who has promised in writing unconditionally to accept the bill before it was drawn. Whilden *v.* Merchants' & Planters' Nat. Bank, 64 Ala. 1, 38 Am. Rep. 1.

On plaintiff's requirement of security for the purchase price of machinery, defendants made a written proposition to give their acceptance if the machinery were fully guarantied, which plaintiff accepted. Thereupon defendants wrote, "You can make him [the purchaser] the shipment, comply with your contract with him, and the paper will be forthcoming." Held, that defendants were bound to furnish the acceptance on plaintiff's compliance with the contract, and he need not make a presentation of the purchaser's draft for acceptance. Maas *v.* Montgomery Iron Works, 88 Ala. 323, 6 So. 701.

The want of funds in the hands of the drawee of a bill, furnishes a sufficient excuse for the failure of the holder to present it for acceptance. Tarver *v.* Nance, 5 Ala. 712.

§ 230. Necessity of Demand for Payment and Notice of Nonpayment.

§ 231. —— In General.

The drawer of a bill of exchange is entitled to notice of nonpayment, wherever it appears that he has any funds whatever in the hands of the acceptor. Hill *v.* Norris, 2 Stew. & P. 114.

So, if there be a running account between the drawer and drawee; and the former has a bona fide reason to believe that his draft will be honored, he has a right to notice. Hill *v.* Norris, 2 Stew. & P. 114.

§ 232. —— Nature of Instrument or Obligation.

Promise to Pay on Demand.—An action may be brought without a previous request, where a party promises to pay on demand. Branch Bank at Montgomery *v.* Gaffney, 9 Ala. 153.

Note Constituting an Absolute Indebtedness Not Requiring Demand.—A note reciting that the maker had received from the payee a certain amount of money, "which I am to account for," constitutes an absolute indebtedness, on which action may be maintained without previous demand. Cleaver *v.* Patterson, 14 Ala. 387.

Unconditional Promise to Accept Bill before It is Drawn.—To charge a party as acceptor, on a unconditional promise in writing to accept a bill before it is drawn, presentment for payment is not necessary. Whilden & Sons *v.* Merchants', etc., Nat. Bank, 64 Ala. 1.

The unconditional acceptor of a draft is the primary debtor thereon, and as such is not entitled to presentation or demand for payment. Hunt *v.* Johnson, 96 Ala. 130, 11 So. 387.

The holder of a negotiable accommodation note, knowing its nature, and that no consideration passed between the maker and the payee, is charged with the duty of notifying the maker of nonpayment of the note at its maturity. Connerly *v.* Planters' & Merchants' Ins. Co., 66 Ala. 432, cited in note in 46 L. R. A. 772.

A drawer for the accommodation of the acceptor, and with the knowledge of the payee, is entitled to notice of dishonor, although he has not funds in the acceptor's hands. Shirley *v.* Fellowes, 9 Port. 300; Sherrod *v.* Rhodes, 5 Ala. 683.

The fact that the drawer of a bill of exchange was indebted to the acceptor for whose use the bill was drawn in a sum equal to the amount of the bill will not dispense with notice to the drawer of the dishonor of the bill, unless the bill was drawn in payment of the debt. Sherrod *v.* Rhodes, 5 Ala. 683.

Acceptance for Accommodation of Drawer.—A firm signed a paper writing directing its clerk to pay bearer a certain amount whenever a certain amount of the firm's change tickets should be presented at the clerk's office. The clerk had no office other than the firm's store, and accepted the writing merely for the firm's accommodation. Held, that no demand of the drawers was necessary before bringing suit. Dillahunty *v.* Parry, 1 Stew. 251.

The drawer of a bill which was accepted for his accommodation is not entitled to notice of nonpayment. Evans *v.* Norris, 1 Ala. 511.

An accommodation acceptor of a bill is not entitled to a demand for payment before suit brought. Steiner *v.* Jeffries, 24 So. 37, 118 Ala. 573.

Where a bank check is drawn by a partnership on one of the partners individually, the drawers are not entitled to notice of dishonor. New York & A. Contracting Co. *v.* Meyer, 51 Ala. 325.

When a bill of exchange is drawn by one firm on another, and accepted by the latter, and the two firms have a common partner, notice of dishonor is not necessary to charge the drawers. New York & A. Contracting Co. *v.* Selma Sav. Bank, 51 Ala. 305, 23 Am. Rep. 552.

§ 233. —— Condition Precedent to Liability of Indorser.

Under the act of 1812 (Laws Ala., p. 69), demand and notice of nonpayment were essential to fix the liability of indorsers, unless waived. Ward *v.* Gifford, Minor 5; Crenshaw *v.* McKiernan, Minor 295. See post, "Waiver of Presentment, Protest, or Notice," § 258.

Repeal of Act of 1812.—St. 1828, providing that, in order to hold an indorser, recovery must be had against the maker by suit prosecuted as soon as may be after the maturity of the indorsed paper, repeals by implication so much of the act of 1812 as provides that, to charge an indorser, demand must be made of the maker, and notice given to the indorser, as in cases of inland bills of exchange. Ivey *v.* Sanderson, 6 Port. 420, cited in note in 18 L. R. A., N. S., 561.

An indorser of an inland bill of exchange is entitled to notice of nonpayment at maturity. Winter *v.* Coxe, 41 Ala. 207.

A note payable in bank is, by statute, made subject "to the rules of the law merchant, as to days of grace, demand, and notice, in the same manner that inland bills of exchange" are; and where such paper is indorsed, either regularly or irregularly, the indorser must be charged by a demand and notice. Branch Bank at Montgomery *v.* Gaffney,

9 Ala. 153, cited in note in 46 L. R. A. 804, 805.

Absolute, Unconditional Guaranty of Payment.—An indorsement on a note, made before its maturity, in the following words, viz. "I assign and guaranty the within note to J. C., for value received," is an absolute, unconditional guaranty of the payment of the note at maturity, and no notice is necessary to perfect the guarantor's liability. Donley *v.* Camp, 22 Ala. 659, 58 Am. Dec. 274.

Blank Indorsement before Note Is Indorsed or Put in Circulation by Payee.—A person who writes his name in blank on the back of a note, negotiable and payable in bank, before it has been indorsed or put in circulation by the payee, is bound as though he made a perfect indorsement to another person; and the payee can not recover of him without proof of a demand for payment at maturity and due notice of nonpayment. Hooks *v.* Anderson, 58 Ala. 238, 29 Am. Rep. 745.

When an indorser before maturity puts a bill of exchange into circulation after its dishonor, if his liability is by virtue of his second indorsement only, the holder must demand payment of the acceptor, and give notice within a reasonable time of the latter's failure to pay, before proceeding against the indorser; but, if the indorser intended to stand in reference to the bill as an indorser whose liability was already fixed, no subsequent demand and notice is necessary. Montgomery & E. R. R. Co. *v.* Trebles, 44 Ala. 255.

An indorser for whose accommodation the note was drawn, and who has received the benefit of it, is not entitled to notice of its nonpayment. Holman *v.* Whiting, 19 Ala. 703.

Where a creditor, on account of his debt, accepts the note of a third person from, and endorsed by, his debtor, the creditor, upon its dishonor, is entitled to declare either on the endorsement or for the precedent debt; but in either case he is bound to show the same degree of diligence. Bates *v.* Ryland, 6 Ala. 668.

§ 234. —— Excuses for Failure to Make Demand or Give Notice.

Where a note was executed by a corporation, by one as agent, payable to, and indorsed by, the latter, it is insufficient to relieve the holder from giving the indorser notice of dishonor to show that he was the sole agent of the corporation, without showing that he was the sole agent to pay it at maturity, and that none of the other officers were authorized to do so. Winter *v.* Coxe, 41 Ala. 207.

"A drawer, who has no funds in the hands of the drawee, is not entitled to notice of the dishonor of a bill, because he can not be prejudiced by want of notice." Stewart *v.* Desha, etc., Co., 11 Ala. 844, 848; Tarver *v.* Nance, 5 Ala. 712, 715.

Where the drawees of a bill had no effects of the drawer in their hands from the time it was drawn up to the time of its maturity, in an action against the drawer, the holder will be excused from proving, that a presentment was made when the bill became due, and that notice of the dishonor was promptly given, to the drawer; and such is the law, notwithstanding the bill may be drawn in good faith, and if duly presented would have been honored. Foard *v.* Womack, 2 Ala. 368.

A. M. & Co. draw on J. G. L., in April, at sight; the drawee having no funds of theirs in hands. The bill presented only in August and acceptance refused. The payee entitled to recover of drawers, though demand and notice not in reasonable time; and although, if demanded in due time, it might perhaps have been paid and although drawers thought drawee would pay. They having no right to expect drawee would pay, and the bill being drawn for their accommodation. Armstrong, etc., Co. *v.* Gay, 1 Stew. 175.

H. being indebted to D. & Co., procured S., who was indebted to him, to draw a bill in his favor, on D. & Co., which he indorsed to them, and which they received in payment of the debt of H. Held, that S. was not entitled to notice of the dishonor of the bill (no funds being provided for its payment). Stewart *v.* Desha, etc., Co., 11 Ala. 844.

Failure of Consideration Owing to Fraud of Indorser.—Where there is a failure of consideration for a note in the hands of the indorsee, owing to the fraud of the indorser, demand and notice are not necessary to bind the indorser. Gee *v.* Williamson, 1 Port. 313.

False Representation by Indorser That Note Is Good.—If the purchaser of goods indorse in payment a promissory note, representing it to be good, when the indorser knew it to be worthless, such indorser is not entitled to notice of nonpayment, on account of the fraud. Alexander *v.* Dennis, 9 Port. 174.

Note Indorsed for Accommodation of Maker and Indemnity Given Indorser.—Where it was admitted that a note was indorsed for the accommodation of the maker, and not made for the accommodation of the indorser, and no demand or notice of dishonor was alleged or proved, the holder could not recover from the indorser on a mere showing that he had received indemnity from the maker, since such showing was no legal excuse for failure to allege and prove demand and notice. Moody *v.* Keller, 127 Ala. 630, 29 So. 68.

"**Neither the bankruptcy, or known insolvency of the drawee of a bill, or maker of a note,** will excuse the necessity of demand of payment, and notice thereof. 1 Saund. Pl. & Ev. 293, and authorities cited thereon." Hightower *v.* Ivy, 2 Port. 308, 313.

Where a promissory note, payable in bank, is transferred by indorsement, after maturity, to entitle the indorsee to charge the indorser, he should demand payment of the maker within a reasonable time after he became the proprietor of the paper, and if refused, give notice of nonpayment to the indorser; and the insolvency of the maker at the time of the transfer will not excuse the indorsee's neglect thus to proceed. Adams *v.* Torbert, 6 Ala. 865, cited in note in 46 L. R. A. 804, 806.

Where A receives a note on another person, to be applied to the payment of a debt due to him by B, the mere insolvency of the maker of such note will not dispense with due diligence to collect it. A is bound to demand payment in a reasonable time, of the maker, and to give notice to B if payment is refused even if the maker of the note be insolvent. Stocking *v.* Conway, 1 Port. 260, cited in note in 19 L. R. A., N. S., 557.

Maker of Note a Nonresident.—The fact that at the time of the execution and indorsement of a note, and from then continuously to the institution of suit against the indorser, the maker has been a nonresident, but has had a known place of residence in another state, will not excuse the holder from demanding payment of the maker and giving an indorser notice of dishonor. Bradley *v.* Patton, 51 Ala. 108, cited in note in 18 L. R. A., N. S., 561.

Note Payable at Bank Which Has Ceased to Exist.—If a note is made payable at a particular bank, and if such bank before maturity ceases to exist, a demand, in order to hold an indorser, is excused. Roberts *v.* Mason, 1 Ala. 373.

Absence of Lights and Failure to See One in House.—Failure to give notice of the dishonor of a note at the indorser's residence is not excused by the fact that an agent of the bank, in casually passing the indorser's house at 6 P. M., in May, found no lights in the windows, and saw no one in the house; such agent not stopping at the house, or making any inquiry as to whether the indorser was in. Isbell *v.* Lewis, 98 Ala. 550, 13 So. 335.

§ 235. —— Effect of Failure to Make Demand or Give Notice.

Failure to demand payment of a note at the place where it is payable is a defense by the maker only when he has sustained damages, and then only to the extent of the damages. Clark *v.* Moses, 50 Ala. 326.

A party to a bill, once discharged for the want of notice or other laches on the part of the holder, is always discharged, and can not again be made liable, unless by his own voluntary act. Smith *v.* Rowland, 18 Ala. 665.

The indorser of a note, made for his accommodation, is not discharged from liability on his indorsement by failure of the holder to demand payment of the maker, and to give such indorser notice of nonpayment. Morris *v.* Birmingham Nat. Bank, 93 Ala. 511, 9 So. 606.

The first indorser of a bill, whose liability had not been fixed by the holder, can not, by notice of its dishonor, charge a subsequent indorser, whose liability had been discharged by the laches of the holder. Boggs *v.* Branch Bank at Mobile, 10 Ala. 970.

§ 236. Sufficiency of Presentment for Payment and Demand.

§ 237. —— Diligence in General.

Where the holder of a note, on coming near the last place of residence of the maker, in order to make a demand on him, perceived that the house was closed, and was told that the maker had left the country, it was held that this was sufficient to hold the indorser. Goading *v.* Britain, 1 Stew. & P. 282.

§ 238. —— Persons Who May Make.

The son of the holder, who is a notary, may demand payment. Eason *v.* Isbell, 42 Ala. 456.

A notary can not present a foreign bill and demand payment by his clerk or deputy. Donegan *v.* Wood, 49 Ala. 242.

§ 239. —— Persons on Whom to Be Made.

The acceptor of a bill of exchange may appoint an agent to pay it, or to refuse payment, and a presentment of the bill to such agent is a sufficient presentment to charge the drawer and indorsers. Phillips *v.* Poindexter, 18 Ala. 579.

Where a notary presented a bill for payment at the drawee's place of business to a competent clerk, no member of the drawee firm being present, and was told by the clerk that the bill could not be paid, such acts constitute a sufficient presentment to warrant the protest of the bill. Bradley *v.* Northern Bank of Alabama, 60 Ala. 252.

Where the drawees of a bill of exchange absent themselves from their place of business and make no provision for its payment, a presentment there to their bookkeeper is a sufficient presentment to charge the drawers. Decatur Branch Bank *v.* Hodges, 17 Ala. 42.

When a bill of exchange has been accepted by two persons as partners, who, at the maturity of the bill, have dissolved their partnership, and are also absent from Mobile, the place of their residence, a demand of payment made of the agent of one of the partners is sufficient. Brown *v.* Turner, 15 Ala. 832, cited in note in 36 L. R. A. 704.

On a note payable at a bank, demand of the cashier is sufficient. Crenshaw *v.* McKiernan, Minor 295.

§ 240. —— Place.

Note Payable at a Particular Place.—A demand of payment of a note made payable at a particular place, at such place, is not necessary to enable the holder to maintain an action against the maker, though it may be matter of defense, for the defendant, if he was ready to pay at the time and place appointed. Evans *v.* Gordon, 8 Port. 142.

But as against the endorser, when a note is payable at a certain place, it must be there presented for payment. Roberts *v.* Mason, 1 Ala. 373, 375.

Where a note is made payable at a named place, demand at such place, at maturity, is sufficient to hold the indorser. Crenshaw *v.* McKiernan, Minor 295; Evans *v.* St. John, 9 Port. 186; Eason *v.* Isbell, 42 Ala. 456.

If a note is made payable at a particular bank, a personal demand on the maker is not necessary to charge an indorser, but presentment for payment on maturity, at the bank, is sufficient. Roberts *v.* Mason, 1 Ala. 373.

"Though it is clearly settled, that as against the indorser, when a note is payable at a certain place, it must be there presented for payment, yet, when it is made payable at bank, and the note is placed in the hands of the cashier of that bank for collection, there is no necessity for his making a specific or clamorous demand. The legal requirements as to presentment and demand, are complied with if the note is in bank at the time it falls due, in the hands of the cashier, who was ready to receive the money. Shaw *v.* Reed, 12 Pick. 132; Ogden et al. *v.* Dobbin & Evans, 2 Hall. 129." Roberts *v.* Mason 1 Ala. 373, 375.

"The maker of a promissory note, payable at a banking house, is not discharged, if the holder omits to present it there at maturity, though he sustains damages by such neglect, unless it is made payable 'there only,' or 'not otherwise, or elsewhere.' Chitty on Bills, 354." Clark *v.* Moses, 50 Ala. 326.

But if the maker had funds at the appointed place, at the time, to pay the note, and it was not duly presented, he will, in the suit, be exonerated; not, indeed, from the payment of the principal sum, but from the payment of all damages and costs in that suit. Clark *v.* Moses, 50 Ala. 326, 327.

Where a note is negotiable and payable at a particular bank, and such bank ceases to exist before the note matures, if another bank is established at the same place, and is the agent for closing the concerns of the former bank, a demand there is sufficient; a personal demand not being necessary. Roberts *v.* Mason, 1 Ala. 373.

On a note payable at any bank in a specified city, a demand at any bank in that city is sufficient to charge the indorser. Boit *v.* Corr, 54 Ala. 112.

§ 241. —— Time.

§ 241 (1) In General.

Limitations, but not mere laches in demanding payment of a note, is a defense to an action thereon. Stewart *v.* Bibb County Banking & Trust Co. (Ala.), 58 So. 273.

Where a note is payable on demand, or if no time of payment is expressed, it must be presented for payment by the holder within a reasonable time, in order to charge an indorser. Sommerville *v.* Williams, 1 Stew. 484.

Where commercial paper, past due, is indorsed, it can not be assumed as a legal conclusion, that a demand of payment should be made by the holder within any precise time; but in such case, all that can be said is, that the demand must be made in a reasonable time. The facts must be ascertained by the jury, and their verdict should be influenced by such legal analogies as are established. Branch of the Bank *v.* Gafney, 9 Ala. 153; Adams *v.* Torbert, 6 Ala. 865, 867; Kennon *v.* M'Rae, 7 Port. 175, 184.

Demand on Last Day of Grace.—A demand on the maker of a note on the last of the three days of grace, is sufficient to charge an indorser. Crenshaw *v.* McKiernan, Minor 295.

Note Payable on Sunday.—The demand for payment of a note made payable on Sunday is properly made on the succeeding day. Brennan *v.* Vogt, 97 Ala. 647, 11 So. 893.

§ 241 (2) Bill of Exchange.

To charge the endorser of a bill of exchange, demand must be made of the acceptor within the three first days after the maturity of the bill. Eldridge *v.* Rogers, Minor 392.

An agent to collect a draft, to whom the acceptor gave a check for the amount in payment, as between himself and the acceptor has until the close of banking hours on the next secular day in which to present the check for payment; and hence, where the acceptor paid the check after the failure of the bank on which it was drawn before the expiration of such time, he can not recover the amount from the agent. Morris *v.* Eufaula Nat. Bank, 25 So. 499, 122 Ala. 580.

Defendant drew his check in favor of N., in payment of a note. At the time, the bank was indebted to him, for services and for checks in his hands, to an amount which, with his balance, was more than the check was for. Before drawing the check, defendant arranged with the cashier of the bank that it would be paid. When defendant gave the check to N., on June 16th, he directed him to go to the bank, which was across the street, and get his money. Instead, defendant indorsed the check to plaintiffs, and sent it to them in another state, and the bank suspended June 22d, before it was presented for payment. Held, that the delay was unreasonable. Industrial Trust, Title & Savings Co. *v.* Weakley, 103 Ala. 458, 15 So. 854.

A check on a bank at Greenville, Ala., was received by the payee in Philadelphia on December 12th, after banking hours, and deposited the next day in a local bank for collection; but said bank, instead of sending the check directly to the drawee bank, which would have received it on December 16th, presented it to a bank in South Carolina, whence it went to another bank in Montgomery, Ala., and was not presented at the place of payment till December 19th, one day after the drawee had failed. There was no proof that the method adopted by the Philadelphia bank was according to custom, or to any previous course of dealing between the parties. Held, that the loss fell on the payee. Watt *v.* Gans, 21 So. 1011, 114 Ala. 264, 69 Am. St. Rep. 99.

As between endorsee and endorser a promissory note is a bill of exchange, and a demand of payment and notice, etc., on the last day of grace is good. Crenshaw *v.* McKiernan, Minor 295.

§ 242. —— Form and Mode.

The process by which a suit is begun on a note which was indorsed after maturity does not authorize the officer serving the process to receive the money, nor contemplate payment otherwise than by legal coercion; hence a service is not a demand of payment, so as to render availing a consequent notice to the indorser. Branch Bank at Montgomery *v.* Gaffney, 9 Ala. 153.

The facts that a note was in the hands of the cashier of the bank fixed as the place for presentment for payment, and that he was also a notary, together with his certificate of presentment, were sufficient to show that he was authorized to receive payment, and that the note was at the bank at maturity; and it was immaterial that it was not presented at the bank. Carrington *v.* Odom, 27 So. 510, 124 Ala. 529.

§ 243. —— Effect of Delay.

Proof of undue delay in the presentation of a check, and of the failure of the drawee bank after the expiration of the period within which, with due diligence, the check would have been presented, raises a presumption of loss to the drawee from such delay, and casts on the holder the burden of proving otherwise. Watt *v.* Gans, 21 So. 1011, 114 Ala. 264, 62 Am. St. Rep. 99.

Where a bank, on presenting a draft which it has for collection, receives a check drawn on a bank in the same place, it is bound to present the check on the same day, and, failing in this, is liable to the drawer thereof for the loss occasioned thereby, the bank drawn on having suspended at the end of the day. Morris *v.* Eufaula Nat. Bank, 106 Ala. 383, 18 So. 11, cited in note in 1 L. R. A., N. S., 247.

Defendant drew his check in favor of N. in payment of a note. At the time, the bank was indebted to him, for services and for checks in his hands, to an amount which, with his balance, was more than the check was for. Before drawing the check, defendant arranged with the cashier of the bank that it would be paid. When defendant gave the check to N., on June 16th, he directed him to go to the bank, which was across the street, and get his money. Instead, defendant indorsed the check to plaintiffs, and sent it to them in another state, and the bank suspended June 22d, before it was presented for payment. Held, that defendant was discharged from liability on the check. Industrial Trust, Title & Sav. Co. *v.* Weakley, 103 Ala. 458, 15 So. 854.

The presumption of loss to the drawer of a check, arising from want of diligence in the presentation thereof by the holder, and the intervening failure of the drawee bank, may be rebutted by proof that the drawer had no available funds to meet the check, or that he withdrew them before the failure. Watt *v.* Gans, 21 So. 1011, 114 Ala. 264, 62 Am. St. Rep. 99, cited in note in 10 L. R. A., N. S., 1153; 53 L. R. A. 432.

Where it appears that no degree of diligence would have resulted in the payment of the check, the laches, if any, of the payee sending it to the drawee for collection, is no defense to a subsequent action by him against the drawer for the amount of the check. Lowenstein *v.* Bresler, 109 Ala. 326, 19 So. 860.

§ 244. Protest and Certificate Thereof.

§ 245. —— Necessity of Protest and Notice Thereof.

No formal protest of a note, aside from notice of dishonor, is necessary to fix the liability of the indorser. Quigley *v.* Primrose, 8 Port. 247.

Where an accommodation note is made payable to the president of a bank and discounted by the bank, protest is unnecessary. Sale *v.* Branch Bank of Decatur, 1 Ala. 425.

Inland Bills.—A protest is not necessary, by the law merchant, to fix the liabilities of the parties to an inland bill. A demand of acceptance or payment, and notice of refusal, are sufficient. Knott *v.* Venable, 42 Ala. 186.

Protest of an inland bill is unnecessary to fix the liability of the indorser. Winter *v.* Coxe, 41 Ala. 207.

An inland bill need not be protested to entitle the holder to recover its face, with interest. Leigh *v.* Lightfoot, 11 Ala. 935.

A Bank Check Payable in Confederate Currency.—A bank check drawn by a bank in Mobile, on a bank in New Orleans, on the 23d April, 1862, payable in currency, is not an instrument payable in money, and is not negotiable paper, within the meaning of the law merchant, and a protest is not necessary to fix the liability of the drawer. Bank *v.* Brown, 42 Ala. 108, cited in note in 26 L. R. A. 571.

An instruction by the drawer to the drawee not to pay a bill will excuse a failure to protest it. Manning *v.* Maroney, 87 Ala. 563, 6 So. 343, 13 Am. St. Rep. 67.

The fact that the drawer joined the Confederate army before maturity of the bill does not deprive him of the right to notice or protest. Tyson *v.* Oliver, 43 Ala. 455.

§ 246. —— Requisites and Sufficiency.

The term "protest," in its popular significance, means "those acts which are necessary to charge an indorser." White *v.* Keith, 97 Ala. 668, 12 So. 611.

Where Note Is Subject to Protest.—A note which is executed on "November 11, 1899," and is made payable "six months fixed after date," matures on the 11th day of May following, and such note is subject to protest for nonpayment on that date. Doyle *v.* First Nat. Bank, 131 Ala. 294, 30 So. 880.

"The holder of a bill of exchange is not bound to rely on the agency of a notary public, in order to have his bill protested upon its dishonor, though this is the most usual and convenient practice. If there be no legal notary, then, on demand and refusal of payment, it is sufficient, if the protest be made out and drawn up by a respectable inhabitant of the place where the bill is payable in the presence of two witnesses; and it should be made out and drawn up in the form required by the law or usage of the place where it is made. Story on Bills, § 276; Kyd on Bills, pp. 136, 137; Chitty on Bills, pp. 362, 363; 2 Parsons on Notes & Bills, p. 633; Burke *v.* McKay, 2 How. 66 [11 L. Ed. 181]." Todd *v.* Neal, 49 Ala. 266, 273.

Notary an Officer of a Seceding State.—It is no ground of objection to a protest that "the notary before whom it was executed was an officer of" a seceding state. Tyree *v.* Rives, 57 Ala. 173, in effect overruling Todd *v.* Neal, 49 Ala. 266.

Time of Protest.—A ninety-days bill, dated October 13th, was properly protested on January 14th. Bradley *v.* Northern Bank of Alabama, 60 Ala. 252.

"A notarial protest of a bill of exchange for nonacceptance, or for nonpayment, usually states the name and place of residence of the notary; that he was duly qualified; the time, manner, and place that he made demand of the acceptance, or of the payment of the bill; describing or identifying, usually by reference to a copy written upon the reverse of the certificate, the names of the parties of whom the demand was made, the refusal, and the name of the party at whose request acceptance or payment was demanded. It is not unusual now to embody in the protest a statement of the parties notified, or to embody such statement in a separate certificate." Martin, etc., Co. *v.* Brown, etc., Co., 75 Ala. 442, 447.

The protest of a note made payable on Sunday was properly made on the succeeding day. Brennan *v.* Vogt, 97 Ala. 647, 11 So. 893.

Location of Bank at Which Demand Was Made.—The protest of a note payable "at any bank in Savannah, Ga.," showed that the note was presented for payment "at the Southern Bank of the State of Georgia," but did not expressly state that such bank was in the city of Savannah. The caption showed that the protest was made in the city of Savannah, Ga., and the protest recited that the notary resided in that city, and, after showing demand and refusal of payment, concluded, "done and protested in the city of Savannah, aforesaid." Held, that the protest sufficiently showed that the bank at which the demand was made was located in the city of Savannah. Boit *v.* Corr, 54 Ala. 112.

Description of Place of Notice.—Where the parties live in the same town, and notice is left at the place of business of the indorser, it is sufficient to describe it in the certificate of the notary as the office of the person so notified. Curry *v.* Bank of Mobile, 8 Port. 360.

Where a notice is sent by mail to a distant post office, the place to which the letter containing the notice is directed must be stated in the certificate of the notary. Curry *v.* Bank of Mobile, 8 Port. 360.

Time of Protest.—Where, from the date of a bill of exchange and the evidence offered, it appeared to have been protested twelve months after its maturity—held, that the indorser was discharged. Hudson *v.* Bank, 3 Port. 340.

Time of Certifying to Notice of Dishonor.—A certificate made by a notary public, that he had given the parties to the bill notice of its dishonor, must be made at the time and as a part of the protest. Such a certificate, made four and one-half years after the date of the protest, is not proof of notice. Boggs *v.* Branch Bank at Mobile, 10 Ala. 970.

Certificate Not Showing Facts Sufficient to Constitute Notice to Indorser.—A notarial certificate of the protest of a bill, stating that "notice of the protest was left at the boarding house" of the indorser, etc., without showing the circumstances under which it was left, nor that the indorser was not there, nor whether inquiry was made for him or notice handed to any person to be delivered to him, or whether any person was at the house or not, does not show facts sufficient to constitute notice to the indorser. Rives *v.* Parmley, 18 Ala. 256.

A recital in the notary's certificate of protest that "notice of the protest had been left at the offices of the indorsers" is not, of itself, sufficient to charge an indorser with notice. Coster *v.* Thomason, 19 Ala. 717.

Recital of Notice to Indorser Written Below Signature and Seal.—That, in a notary's certificate of protest, the recital of notice to an indorser was written below his signature and official seal, does not render the certificate bad in any part. Jordan *v.* Long, 109 Ala. 414, 19 So. 843.

Authentication of Certificate.—Where the certificate of protest is not authenticated except by a deposition of the notary, it is not sufficient evidence of itself of dishonor and notice thereof. Stewart *v.* Russell, 38 Ala. 619.

A notary's signature and a circular indentation, without wax, wherein the words, "Notary Public, New Orleans," were visible, held, 17 years after the date of the certificate, sufficient to establish the authenticity of the protest. Bradley *v.* Northern Bank of Alabama, 60 Ala. 252.

§ 247. —— Certificate as Evidence.

Statute Making Notary's Certificate Evidence Applies to Certificates of Foreign Notaries.—The statute which makes a notary's certificate "of the presentment for acceptance, or demand of payment, or protest for nonacceptance or nonpayment, of any instrument governed by the commercial law," etc., "evidence of the facts contained in such certificate" (Rev. Code, § 1089; Code of 1876, § 1336), although improperly placed in the chapter which relates to the appointment, etc., of notaries public in this state, equally applies to the certificates of foreign notaries, when offered in evidence in the courts of Alabama. Bradley *v.* Northern Bank, 60 Ala. 252.

Protest of Notes Made in Another State.—Since negotiable notes are not protestable at common law, a protest in a sister state of a note made and indorsed there is not evidence, without proof, that it is made so by statute of that state. Dunn *v.* Adams, 1 Ala. 527, 35 Am. Dec. 42.

Certificates Not Conclusive Evidence.—The certificate in the protest of a notary setting forth the demand and refusal of an inland bill, etc., and notice to the drawer and indorsers, is made evidence by statute, yet it is not conclusive; and it is competent for the party to show such a state of facts, as prove that the certificate is untrue. Bank *v.* Marston, 7 Ala. 108.

The certificate of the notice of the dishonor of a note by the notary, is prima facie evidence only of the fact recited; and if left at the wrong place, the fact may be controverted. Curry *v.* Bank, 8 Port. 360.

The certificate of a notary in his protest, that he had given notice to the endorser of a note, of its nonpayment, by depositing a letter, containing the notice, in the postoffice, and directed to him, is only prima facie evidence of the fact of notice, and may be contradicted by other evidence. Booker *v.* Lowry, 1 Ala. 399.

Sufficient Evidence of Demand Unless Controverted by Other Testimony.—The protest on a bill of exchange is sufficient evidence of a demand, unless such fact is controverted by other testimony. Moore *v.* Clements, 4 Port. 227.

Where the statute makes the protest of nonpayment of a bill evidence of presentment, plaintiff, in an action on a bill payable at a bank, need not affirmatively prove that the demand was made during banking hours, where defendant puts in no evidence. Moore *v.* Clements, 4 Port. 227.

Evidence of Names of Parties to Whom Notice of Protest Was Sent.—A statement in the notary's certificate of protest, of the names of the parties to whom notice of protest was sent by him, is made by statute competent evidence of the facts stated (Code, § 1336); but such statement is not an essential part of the protest, and the fact of notice may be proved otherwise. Martin, etc., Co. *v.* Brown, etc., Co., 75 Ala. 442.

No Proof That Notices of Dishonor Were Properly Directed.—The statement contained in a notarial protest, that the notary had sent notices of the dishonor of the paper, addressed to the parties at a particular place, is no proof, even on a demurrer to evidence, that the notices were properly directed; this fact must be shown by proof independent of the protest. Bank of Mobile *v.* King, 9 Ala. 279.

The protest of a notary public, stating that notice was given, "to the agent" of a party, of the protest of his paper, is not evidence of such agency, so as to make the notice sufficient; such agency must be proved aliunde before the protest can be produced as evidence of notice. O'Connell *v.* Walker, 1 Port. 263.

Under Act 1828, declaring the effect of notarial protests, the recital in a protest that a bill was presented to F. & F., agents of the drawees, is not evidence of their agency. Castles *v.* McMath, 1 Ala. 326.

Certificate Held Admissible to Prove Notice to Indorser.—Under Clay's Dig., p. 280, § 9, making a notarial protest of a bill or note evidence of notice of dishonor to indorsers, when it certifies that such notice was legally given, "personally or through the postoffice," a notice left at the indorser's residence or place of business, in a proper manner, is to be deemed "personal," and hence a notarial protest, certifying that notice was thus given, is admissible in evidence to prove notice to the indorser. Rives *v.* Parmley, 18 Ala. 256.

Certificate Held Sufficient Proof of Notice by Mail.—Under Code, § 1110, making the certificate of a notary public, under his hand and seal, evidence of the demand for payment of the note, of the notice of protest, and the mode of giving it, where the certificate gives the number of notices mailed, to whom and where addressed, and a charge for postage, and defendant gives no evidence to the contrary, there is sufficient proof of the giving of notice by mail. Brennan *v.* Vogt, 97 Ala. 647, 11 So. 893.

Meaning of Certificate as to Character of Notice.—A notary certified in a protest as follows: "Notice of protest given to the drawer and to first indorsers same day." Held to mean that the notice was in writing and given personally. Roberts *v.* State Bank, 9 Port. 312.

Testimony Not Rendering Certificate Inadmissible.—A protest is not inadmissible in evidence because a witness testifies that he is acquainted with the handwriting of the notary whose name is subscribed to the protest, and believes that such subscription is not in the handwriting of the notary. Bank of Alabama *v.* Whitlow, 6 Ala. 135.

Effect of Misnomer.—In an action against an indorser, plaintiff ordered in evidence the protest of a bill, agreeing in all respects with that described in his declaration, save that the bill in the protest purported to be addressed to "Gamble and Murrah," and the original bill was addressed to "Gamble and Murray." Held, that the protest was admissible, on plaintiff's showing by parol that "Murrah" and "Murray" were identical, and that the drawer had inadvertently written "Murray" for Murrah" Branch Bank of Decatur *v.* Rhodes, 11 Ala. 283.

§ 248. Sufficiency of Notice of Nonpayment and of Protest.

§ 249. —— Diligence in General.

If the residence of the drawer is not known to the holder, and he can not ascertain it by reasonable diligence, he is relieved from giving notice of protest. Robinson *v.* Hamilton, 4 Stew. & P. 91.

Where absence from the indorser's place of business, when it was visited for the purpose of giving notice, is relied on as an excuse for not giving notice, it must be shown that the visit was made during business hours, at a time when it is reasonable to suppose the party may be found. John *v.* City Nat. Bank, 57 Ala. 96.

Failure to give notice of the dishonor of a note at the indorser's residence is not excused by the fact that an agent of the bank, in casually passing the indorser's house at 6 p. m., found no lights in the windows, and saw no one in the house; such agent not stopping at the house, or making any inquiry as to whether the indorser was in. Isbell *v.* Lewis, 98 Ala. 550, 13 So. 335.

§ 250. —— Persons Who May Give.

A notary who protests a bill of exchange is authorized to give notice of its nonpayment to the various parties to the bill. Greene *v.* Farley, 20 Ala. 322

An agent of the holder, having a bill for presentment, need not give notice of its dishonor to an indorser, but may notify his principal, and seasonable notice from him will be sufficient to charge him. But, if the agent give the necessary notice, this is sufficient. Foster *v.* McDonald, 3 Ala. 34.

The relation which exists between a notary and the holder of commercial paper, with regard to the protest thereof, and notice to the drawer or endorser, is that of principal and agent; and a son of the holder of such paper, if he be a notary, may act as agent of his father in his notarial capacity. Eason *v.* Isbell, 42 Ala. 456.

The notary protesting a bill may send notices to the holder, to be given to the prior parties; but the person to whom the notices are so sent must appear to be the holder or his agent. Crawford *v.* Branch Bank at Mobile, 7 Ala. 205.

§ 251. —— Persons to Whom to Be Given.

By the law merchant, personal notice of dishonor need not be given presently and directly to the indorser, but the notice may be left with any person in charge of his place of business, whether such person is his agent or not, or with any person found on and belonging to the place where he resides apparently capable of transmitting the notice to the indorser. Isbell *v.* Lewis, 98 Ala. 550, 13 So. 335.

To charge a party with notice of the dishonor of a bill of exchange because notice was given to another person as his agent, it must appear that it was within the scope of the agent's duties to receive such notice. The mere fact that he was "the financial agent" of his principal is not enough. New York & A. Contracting Co. *v.* Selma Sav. Bank, 51 Ala. 305, 23 Am. Rep. 552.

It can not be intended, because one is authorized to indorse notes, that he is also an agent for the purpose of receiving notices of their dishonor. Bank of Mobile *v.* King, 9 Ala. 279.

When a bill indorsed by a partnership is dishonored after a dissolution of the firm, notice of protest to any one of the late partners is sufficient to bind all. Coster *v.* Thomason, 19 Ala. 717.

§ 252. —— Place.

Residence or Nearest Postoffice.—Notice of the nonpayment of a bill of exchange may be sent to the residence, or nearest postoffice, of the party to be charged, at the time of his signing the bill, unless he, at that time, specifies another place, to which he requires it to be sent. Tyson *v.* Oliver, 43 Ala. 455.

The name of the place where the bill was signed, appearing on it, is not alone sufficient evidence of the residence, or postoffice, of the party to be charged. Tyson *v.* Oliver, 43 Ala. 455.

Where an indorser of a note has a permanent residence, it is such for the purpose of serving him with notice of dishonor, notwithstanding the temporary absence of his family. Isbell *v.* Lewis, 98 Ala. 550, 13 So. 335.

If a notice of protest is left at the office of an indorser, who is an attorney, and keeps no clerk, on the evening of the day on which it is required to be given, the law presumes that he received it, and it is sufficient to charge him. Stanley *v.* Bank of Mobile, 23 Ala. 652.

A room to which a man is accustomed to resort, but in which it is not shown that he carried on any regular business, can not be considered his place of business for the purpose of serving notice of protest. Stephenson *v.* Primrose, 8 Port. 155, 33 Am. Dec. 281.

Where it is proper to give notice of nonpayment of a note to an indorser through the postoffice, notice must be sent to the office nearest to the indorser's residence, or that at which he is in the habit of receiving his letters; or, his residence not being known, and due diligence being used to discover it, notice sent to his supposed residence will be sufficient. Worsham *v.* Goar, 4 Port. 441.

Diligence Required Where Notice Is Sent by Mail.—When notice of the nonpayment of a bill is sent by mail, the holder of the bill is bound to exercise diligence in ascertaining whether there is a postoffice at the place to which the notice is addressed. Tyson *v.* Oliver, 43 Ala. 455.

Notice to the drawer and indorser of protest, directed to a postoffice which had formerly been the one where he got his mail, but which had been discontinued, the mail service there having been suspended on account of the Civil War, is insufficient. Tyson *v.* Oliver, 43 Ala. 455.

The name of the place where a bill was signed, as it appears on the instrument itself, is not sufficient evidence of the postoffice address of the party to be charged to authorize the holder to send notice of nonpayment of the bill to such address. Tyson *v.* Oliver, 43 Ala. 455; Sprague *v.* Tyson, 44 Ala. 338.

Where a bill is dated at a particular place, the drawer can not be charged by a notice of nonpayment deposited in a postoffice and addressed to him at that place, unless that was the postoffice nearest his residence, or unless, upon diligent inquiry, his residence could not be ascertained. Foard *v.* Johnson, 2 Ala. 565, overruling Robinson *v.* Hamilton, 4 Stew. & P. 91.

Where the holder of negotiable paper is ignorant of the residence of an indorser, there is reasonable diligence in endeavoring to ascertain his address for the purpose of notice of protest, if the notary makes inquiries of different persons living at the place where the note is payable, whom he may suppose most likely to give the information. Branch Bank of State of Alabama *v.* Peirce, 3 Ala. 321.

Where the maker of a bill had resided within eighteen miles of a certain town, and had been in the habit of receiving his letters there, but during a period of three months preceding the service of the notice had received his letters at another office, within fourteen miles of his residence, a notice of dishonor sent to him at the first postoffice was sufficient. McGrew *v.* Toulmin, 2 Stew. & P. 428.

Where the drawer of a bill, before its maturity, removed with his family from his plantation in A. to another county, leaving his slaves in A., on his plantation, which he visited occasionally, it was held that notice of the dishonor of the bill, it not appearing that the holder knew of the removal, sent to the postoffice at A., was sufficient to fix the drawer's liability, it also not appearing that he had permanently changed his residence. Goodwin *v.* McCoy, 13 Ala. 271.

§ 253. —— Time.

Notice of nonpayment must be given within a reasonable time after protest. Eldridge *v.* Rogers, Minor 392.

"Notice of the dishonor of a note may be given on the same day protest is made, and must be given on the next day, or placed in the postoffice, to be sent by the next mail, in the ordinary course of business." Curry *v.* Bank, 8 Port. 360, 370.

Each party to a bill of exchange or note, whether by indorsement or mere delivery, has, in all cases, until the day after he has received notice to give or forward notice to his prior indorser, and so on till it reaches the drawer. Whitman *v.* Farmers' Bank, 8 Port. 258.

Where the parties to a bill of exchange reside at a distance, and the ordinary mode of communication is by general post, the holder, or party to give notice of its nonacceptance or nonpayment, must forward notice by the post of the next day after the dishonor, or after he receives notice of such dishonor; and, if there be no post on the next day, then he must send notice by the very next post that occurs after that day; but he is not legally bound, on account of there being no post on the day after he receives notice, to forward it on the very day he receives it; and, if such notice be placed in the proper postoffice in due time, it is legal diligence, the holder or party to give the notice not being responsible for the irregularities of the mail. Knott *v.* Venable, 42 Ala. 186.

Where payment is refused when the note is presented on the day of payment, the holder is not bound to wait until the last moment of that day, but may forthwith protest for nonpayment, and give notice thereof to the indorser, though notice given the following day would be sufficient. Crenshaw *v.* McKiernan, Minor 295.

A ninety days' bill, dated October 13th, was properly protested on January 14th. Bradley *v.* Northern Bank of Alabama, 60 Ala. 252.

Delay Rendering Notice Insufficient to Charge Drawer.—Notice of the dishonor of a bill, payable on the 12th of November, in Mobile, given on the 27th of the month, to the drawer, in Washington county, Ala., is insufficient to charge him, unless some satisfactory excuse is made for such long delay. Brown *v.* Turner, 11 Ala. 752.

Where commercial paper, past due, is indorsed, it can not be assumed as a legal conclusion that a demand of payment should be made by the holder, and notice of its dishonor given, within any precise time. Branch Bank at Montgomery *v.* Gaffney, 9 Ala. 153.

§ 254. —— Excuses for Delay.

Where the holder of a bill of exchange, residing in one seceding state, failed to give notice of protest to the indorser, residing in another, until nearly a year after military operations had ceased, and over two months after re-establishment of the regular United States mails between the two places, there was not sufficient diligence to bind the indorser. Turner *v.* Patton, 49 Ala. 406.

§ 255. —— Form and Requisites.

A verbal notice of dishonor to the indorser of a note is sufficient. Martin, etc., Co. *v.* Brown, etc., Co., 75 Ala. 442, 448; Abels *v.* Mobile Real-Estate Co., 92 Ala. 382, 9 So. 423; Stephenson *v.* Primrose, 8 Port. 155, 159; Scarborough *v.* City Nat. Bank, 157 Ala. 577, 48 So. 62, 63.

And this is so, though it is given to an agent of the indorser. Scarborough *v.* City Nat. Bank, 157 Ala. 577, 48 So. 62, 63.

No Particular Form of Notice Necessary.—No particular form of notice of dishonor of a negotiable note is necessary; it being sufficient that the party liable is informed of its dishonor and notified that he will be held for payment. Scarborough *v.* City Nat. Bank, 157 Ala. 577, 48 So. 62.

"The law does not prescribe any form of notice to an indorser; all that is necessary is, that it should be sufficient to put the party on inquiry, and to prepare him to pay it or to defend himself. Even if there be some uncertainty in the description of the bill or note, if it does not tend to mislead the party, it will be good. Reedy *v.* Seixas, 2 Johns. Cas. 337; Mills *v.* Bank of the United States, 11 Wheat. 431 [6 L. Ed. 512]; Forster *v.* Jurdson, 16 East. Rep. 105; Chitty on Bills, 9th Am. Ed. 501, et post & notes." Crawford *v.* Bank, 7 Ala. 205, 211.

Notice May Be Either in Writing or Verbal.—"Notice of the dishonor of a bill of exchange, foreign or domestic, may be given in writing, or may be given verbally. The form of notice is not material; all that is necessary is, that within a reasonable time after dishonor, the party liable and intended to be charged should be apprised of the dishonor, and that he is looked to for payment. Byles on Bills, 412. True, as is often said in the books, it is more prudent to give the notice in writing, because thereby the evidence of it will be the better preserved, in the event the fact becomes matter of dispute. But this is far from saying that notice in writing is indispensable. Wade on Law of Notice, § 831." Martin, etc., Co. *v.* Brown, etc., Co., 75 Ala. 442, 448.

Description of Bill.—A notice of the dishonor and protest of a bill is prima facie sufficient if it describes the bill correctly, although it does not mention the date or time of payment. Saltmarsh *v.* Tuthill, 13 Ala. 390.

The notice of a notary, describing himself officially, to which his name is printed, is good. In such case it may be intended, from the similarity of names, that the person who made the protest was the one also who gave the notice, though no official seal be attached to the notice. Crawford *v.* Branch Bank at Mobile, 7 Ala. 205.

Notice Sufficient as a Presentment of Note as a Claim against Indorsee's Estate.—A notice of the nonpayment of a note personally served on the executor of the indorser, or shown to have come to his hands, where it describes the note with accuracy, and informs the executor who the holder is, and that he looks to him for payment, is sufficient as a presentment of the note as a claim against the indorser's estate. Hallett *v.* Branch Bank at Mobile, 12 Ala. 193.

Effect of Misnomer in Notice of Protest.—In an action against the indorser, where the notice of protest described the name of a subsequent indorser as "Pyron," when the bill sued on showed his name to be "Byron," it was held that this was sufficient to charge the prior indorser. Moorman *v.* Bank of Alabama, 3 Port. 353.

§ 256. —— Mode of Giving or Service in General.

By the law merchant, personal notice of dishonor need not be given presently and directly to the indorser, but the notice may be left with any person in charge of his place of business, whether such person is his agent or not, or with any person found on and belonging to the place where he resides, apparently capable of transmitting the notice to the indorser. Isbell *v.* Lewis, 98 Ala. 550, 13 So. 335.

Notice of protest left at the boarding house of the drawer is insufficient to charge him, where it is not shown whether the drawer or any other persons were at the house at that time, or whether inquiry was made for him, or that the notice was handed to some person to be delivered to him. Rives *v.* Parmley, 18 Ala. 256.

A notice of dishonor of a note at the indorser's place of business, not during business hours, is insufficient. Stephenson *v.* Primrose, 8 Port. 155, 33 Am. Dec. 281.

§ 257. —— Notice by Mail.

See ante, "Place," § 252.

When Notice May Be Given Through the Postoffice.—Notice of dishonor of a note, given by mail, was sufficient where the parties lived in different towns. Carrington *v.* Odom, 27 So. 510, 124 Ala. 529. See, also, Carson *v.* Bank, 4 Ala. 148, 152.

Notice of protest and nonpayment of a bill of exchange deposited in the postoffice of the place of the indorser's residence, where the bill was payable and protested, is sufficient to charge him, where it is not shown that the holder also resided there. Shelton *v.* Carpenter, 60 Ala. 201.

Notice of the protest of a note or bill of exchange may be given to an indorser through the post office, notwithstanding the place where payment was to be made and where demand and protest were made was that of his residence, when the holder who is the owner lives elsewhere. Philipe *v.* Haberlee, 45 Ala. 597.

Where the holder of a bill of exchange and the parties sought to be charged on its dishonor reside in different towns, notice of nonpayment may be given through the postoffice, although the agent of the holder and the party to be notified reside in the same town. Gindrat *v.* Mechanics' Bank, 7 Ala. 324, explaining Foster *v.* McDonald, 5 Ala. 376, and correcting head note thereto.

At the maturity of the bill its payee and owner resided in the state of Florida. The drawer resided in the city of Montgomery, Ala. The bill was left with a person in Montgomery, who held it for the payee, and had it protested for nonpayment and notice of protest was sent to the drawer through the postoffice at Montgomery. Held, that the notice was properly sent. Bibb *v.* McQueen, 42 Ala. 408.

Where an indorser lives in the place of protest, and it is a town or city having 10,000 or more inhabitants, or having a free delivery of mail, it is not necessary that the certificate of protest should show that he was sought for at his place of business or at his residence for the purpose of giving notice; for Code, § 1777, provides that in such case notice of protest may be given through the mail, the postage being prepaid. Brennan *v.* Vogt, 97 Ala. 647, 11 So. 893.

In a city of less than 10,000 inhabitants, not having free mail delivery, and which is not within Code, § 1777, permitting notice of dishonor to be given by mail, although the indorser and holder live in the same town, personal notice must be given. Isbell *v.* Lewis, 98 Ala. 550, 13 So. 335.

By the law merchant which governed the question in this state prior to the enactment of the act of December 10, 1878, p. 172, now incorporated into the Code as § 1777, where the residence of the holder of a bill or note and that of the party to be notified of its dishonor was in the same town, it was not sufficient to put a notice into the postoffice; personal notice must have been given, or the notice must have been left at his residence or place of business. Stephenson *v.* Primrose, 8 Port. 155; Tyson *v.* Oliver, 43 Ala. 455; Carson *v.* Bank, 4 Ala. 148, 152; Foster *v.* McDonald, 3 Ala. 34.

Rev. Code, § 1850, authorizing the transmission of notice by mail to the residence or post office nearest the residence of the drawer, maker, or indorser, at the time he became a party to the bill, did not change the rule of the law merchant that, when the holder and indorser of the bill reside in the same city, it is necessary, to bind the indorser, that he must have notice of the default on the day of dishonor or on the succeeding day, given him in person, or left at his residence or place of business. John *v.* City Nat. Bank, 57 Ala. 96.

This statute merely converted notice (in cases where it was transmissible by mail) addressed to the postoffice nearest the residence of the party to be charged at the time he became a party into sufficient notice, without regard to his postoffice at the time of dishonor. John *v.* City Nat. Bank, 57 Ala. 96.

But it has been held that the notary who protests a bill of exchange, is authorized to give notice of its nonpayment; and such notice may be given by mail, although the actual holder, and the party to be charged, reside in the same place. Greene *v.* Farley, 20 Ala. 322.

And when the drawer resides in the vicinity of a town or city, a letter giving notice of nonpayment deposited in the postoffice, and directed to him at the same town or city where the letter is deposited, is sufficient to charge him. Carson *v.* Bank, 4 Ala. 148.

Where the holder and indorser of a draft reside in the same place, the indorser is ordinarily entitled to personal notice of dishonor, but this is excused where the notary, on the day of dishonor, called at the indorser's place of business, during business hours, to give him notice, but found it locked and no one present to receive notice, and deposited the notice properly addressed, in the postoffice on the same day. John *v.* City Nat. Bank, 62 Ala. 529.

It is competent for a bank to establish a rule that notice of the dishonor of bills holden by the bank may be given through the post office to parties resident in the same place, and the rule would be binding on parties to all bills made payable at that bank. Gindrat *v.* Mechanics' Bank, 7 Ala. 324.

Notice Sent by Mail Controlled by Confederate Government.—Rev. Code, § 1850, providing that notice by mail of the nonpayment of a bill of exchange is sufficient if directed to the residence of the one sought to be charged, includes only a notice sent by the regular mail of the United States government, so that where it was sent by a mail controlled by the Confederate government it must be proved to have been received. Todd *v.* Neal, 49 Ala. 266.

§ 258. Waiver of Presentment, Protest, or Notice.

§ 258 (1) In General.

"**Waiver of protest before default** binds the indorser by way of estoppel on time to deny notice of dishonor, and obviates the necessity for such notice." White *v.* Keith, 97 Ala. 668, 12 So. 611.

Indorser Indemnified or Taking Collateral Security.—An endorser who is fully indemnified, is not entitled to notice of its nonpayment. Holman *v.* Whiting, 19 Ala. 703; Carlisle *v.* Hill, 16 Ala. 398, 408.

If an endorser has used the precaution to obtain an assignment to all the effects of the drawer or maker, to be applied to the payment of the paper endorsed, he can not claim an exemption from liability, because he has not had regular notice of the dishonor of the bill or note. Stephenson *v.* Primrose, 8 Port. 155.

So, if he has protected himself by taking collateral security, sufficient, to cover the endorsement, he impliedly waives his legal right to notice. Stephenson *v.* Primrose, 8 Port. 155.

Where the indorser of a bill of exchange has been fully indemnified by the drawer, for whose use the bill was made, indorsed and accepted he can not avail himself of the want of notice of the dishonor of the bill. Posey *v.* Decatur Bank, 12 Ala. 802.

Where the indorser of a negotiable note, after its protest for nonpayment, upon the note being shown to him by the maker, with the false assurance that it was paid, delivered up to the latter a security which he held for his indemnity, the fact that such a security existed when the note was protested, will not excuse the neglect to give notice of the dishonor to the indorser. Marston *v.* Bank, 10 Ala. 284; Bank *v.* Marston, 7 Ala. 108.

Where an endorser of a negotiable note has received from the maker effects of sufficient value to discharge it, and in consideration thereof, promises to pay it, proof of demand and notice is not necessary to charge him, whether the promise was made before or after the maturity of the note. Cockrill *v.* Hobson, 16 Ala. 391.

A, as attorney, recovered judgment against B & C for $900, but could not obtain satisfaction by legal process. C proposed to give his individual note, with a good indorser, for about $300, in full satisfaction of the judgment. He also afterwards proposed to give his note for the same amount, with D, who was his mother, as indorser, and that A should assign the judgment to her. A accepted the later proposition, and executed an assignment of the judgment to D. The assignment was delivered to C, who thereupon gave his note for the required amount, indorsed by D, payable in bank. A indorsed the note to E, who brought assumpsit on it against D. Held, not sufficient to justify the inference that D. assented to the assignment of the judgment to her or that she was informed of it, so as to deprive her of the right to notice of the nonpayment of the note. Holman *v.* Whiting, 19 Ala. 703.

Indemnity Received by Accommodation Drawer.—If ample indemnity against his liability on a bill is received by the accommodation drawer from the acceptor, notice of nonpayment is not necessary to bind him, but a partial indemnity is insufficient to excuse want of notice. Carlisle *v.* Hill, 16 Ala. 398.

§ 258 (2) By Waiver in Indorsement.

Where a note payable to a named individual, or bearer, is indorsed by a third person to plaintiffs before its maturity, and its due payment guarantied, waiving the suit and diligence required by law, such indorsement binds the indorser, if the note is not paid by the makers at its maturity, without any further action by plaintiffs. Burt *v.* Parish, 9 Ala. 211.

The words, "I waive protest of the within note," on the back of a note, signed by an indorser on the last day of grace, are a waiver of demand and notice, and fix his liability. Fisher *v.* Price, 37 Ala. 407.

§ 258 (3) By Separate Agreement.

An agreement waiving the bar of limitations, which acknowledges the justness of all bills and notes held by the creditor on which the debtor is drawer, acceptor, indorser, or maker, and waiving the debtor's right to be discharged from any obligation on any of such bills and notes indorsed or accepted by him, by reason of any failure to have them protested, is sufficiently broad to cover bills and notes which, at the date of the agreement, were not subsisting obligations on account of failure to give the debtor notice of nonpayment when they fell due. Pollak *v.* Billing, 131 Ala. 519, 32 So. 639.

The indorser of a note, who was not given notice of dishonor, stated that he allowed the note to go to protest so as to bind the maker; that he did not desire to shirk any liability, but that his attorney had advised him that he was not liable; and he disclaimed liability. He offered to indorse a note for half of the amount if the holder would apply to the payment of the other half certain money previously paid by the maker, and also offered to pay half of the note, and be relieved from further liability. These offers were declined. Held, that the indorser had not waived the failure to give him notice of dishonor. Isbell *v.* Lewis, 98 Ala. 550, 13 So. 335.

§ 259. New Promise or Waiver after Discharge.

New Promise or Acknowledgment of Liability.—"The promise or acknowledgment must be such as shows that the endorser assumes a liability, or admits it to be continuing. If conditional, the performance of the terms of the condition must be proved, before the promise or acknowledgment becomes absolute. Dennis *v.* Morris, 3 Esp. N. P. 158; Cumming *v.* French, 2 Camp. 106, n.; Standage *v.* Creighton, 5 C. & P. 406; Bonodaile *v.* Lowe, 4 Taunt. 93." Kennon *v.* M'Rea, 7 Port. 175, 184.

"It will make no difference that a promise or acknowledgment were made under a misapprehension of the law, for every man must be taken to know the law; otherwise, a premium is held out to ignorance, and there is no telling to what extent this excuse might be carried. Bilbie *v.* Lumley, 2 East. 469." Kennon *v.* M'Rea, 7 Port. 175, 184.

If a promise or acknowledgment, to charge the endorser of a promissory note, be made under a misapprehension of facts, to wit, under an impression that a demand had been made of the maker of a note, or that notice had been regularly sent through the postoffice, and the endorser promised payment or acknowledged his liability—the consequence of the laches is not waived. Kennon *v.* M'Rea, 7 Port. 175.

"If a promise or acknowledgment is made to the holder of endorsed paper—any party to it, who afterwards takes it up, may avail himself of such promise or acknowledgment, and maintain an action against the party making it. Potter *v.* Rayworth, 13 East, 417; Brahan *v.* Ragland, 3 Stew. 247. And this, upon the ground that by the payment of a note by an endorser, he is remitted to all the rights of the holder against the previous parties." Kennon *v.* M'Rea, 7 Port. 175, 186.

"The consequences of a neglect to make a demand of the maker or drawer of a note or bill, and give notice to an endorser or drawer, may be waived by the person authorized to take advantage of it, by a promise to pay, or an acknowledgment of a liability to pay. Vaughan *v.* Fuller, 2 Strange, 1246; Horford *v.* Wilson, 1 Taunt. 12; Lundie *v.* Robertson, 7 East, 231; Brett *v.* Levett, 13 East, 213; Wood *v.* Brown, 1 Starkie, 217; Hopes *v.* Alder, 6 East, 16; Whitaker *v.* Morris, 1 Esp. N. P. 60; Rogers *v.* Stephens, 2 T. R. 713; Dixon *v.* Ellison, 5 C. & P. 437; Margetson *v.* Aitken, 3 C. & P. 338; Gibbon *v.* Coggon, 2 Camp. 188; Greenway *v.* Hindley, 4 Camp. 52; Hodge *v.* Fillis, 3 Camp. 463; Potter *v.* Rayworth, 13 East. 417; Wilks *v.* Jacks, Peake, 202; Walker *v.* Laverty, 6 Munf. 487; Hall *v.* Freeman, 2 Nott & McC. 479; Fotheringham *v.* Price's Ex'rs, 1 Bay, 291; Lawrence *v.* Ralston, 3 Bibb, 102; Ladd *v.* Kenney, 2 N. H. 340; Hopkins *v.* Liswell, 12 Mass. 52; May *v.* Coffin, 4 Mass. 341; Duryee *v.* Dennison, 5 Johns. 248; Miller *v.* Hackley, 5 Johns. 375." Kennon *v.* M'Rea, 7 Port. 175, 182.

"If the plaintiff show a sufficient promise or acknowledgment, he can not be deprived of its benefit, because it may appear to have been made after suit brought; for the reason, that it is supposed the plaintiff had a good cause of action, of which the promise or acknowledgment furnishes but evidence; or if there was no cause of action, when it was commenced, the defendant, for proper reasons, has admitted it, by waiving his defense." Kennon *v.* M'Rea, 7 Port. 175, 185; Bolling *v.* McKenzie, 89 Ala. 470, 7 So. 658.

Where defendant indorsed a draft for accommodation of the apparent payee, by whom it was negotiated to plaintiff, who mailed it for collection, and several days afterwards notified defendant of the fact that the draft had been fraudulently altered by changing the name of the original payee, and by raising the amount, and there was evidence that defendant promised to pay it, the question whether he made such promise should have been submitted to the jury, with instructions that, if he made it with knowledge that demand, protest, and notice of dishonor had been omitted, such promise was a waiver of plaintiff's laches, and that a promise to pay would cast on defendant the burden of proving laches and his ignorance thereof. Alabama Nat. Bank *v.* Rivers, 22 So. 580, 116 Ala. 1, 67 Am. St. Rep. 95.

A promise by the accommodation drawer of a dishonored bill of exchange to pay the acceptors a debt, independent of the bill, due from the drawer to the acceptors, in order to enable the acceptors to pay the bill, is not a waiver of a want of notice of the dishonor. Sherrod *v.* Rhodes, 5 Ala. 683, cited in note in 28 L. R. A., N. S., 1040, 29 L. R. A. 312.

A mere waiver of protest and notice after a negotiable note has been dishonored does not preclude the indorser from insisting on such protest and notice. White *v.* Keith, 97 Ala. 668, 12 So. 611.

Receiving Indemnity.—When the liability of an indorser has not been fixed by notice, the fact that he has taken an indemnity from the maker, after the maturity of the note, will not have the effect to charge him on the indorsement. Lowry *v.* Western Bank, 7 Ala. 120.

Waiver of notice of nonpayment by the drawer of a bill can not be implied from his receiving of the acceptor, after he has been discharged for want of notice, ample indemnity against his general liabilities for him. Carlisle *v.* Hill, 16 Ala. 398.

Acts of Indorser Held Not to Constitute Waiver of Failure to Give Notice of Dishonor.—The indorser of a note, who was not given notice of dishonor, stated that he allowed the note to go to protest so as to bind the maker; that he did not desire to shirk any liability, but that his attorney had advised him that he was not liable; and he disclaimed liability. He offered to indorse a note for half of the amount if the holder would apply to the payment of the other half certain money previously paid by the maker, and also offered to pay half of the note, and be relieved from further liability. These offers were declined. Held, that the indorser had not waived the failure to give him notice of dishonor. Isbell *v.* Lewis, 98 Ala. 550, 13 So. 335.

VII. PAYMENT AND DISCHARGE.

§ 260. Nature and Modes of Discharge in General.

A note is extinguished where the maker obtains possession thereof in the regular course of trade. Wallace *v.* Branch Bank, 1 Ala. 565.

§ 261. Persons by Whom Payment May Be Made and Effect.

A promissory note discounted in bank may be paid by an indorser with his own funds at maturity, and be reissued by him, the maker having provided no funds for its payment. Kirksey *v.* Bates, 1 Ala. 303.

Where an accommodation indorser paid the discounting bank the amount of the note, and received the note, it was a payment and extinguishment of the note by the indorser, and not a purchase by him. Borland *v.* Phillips, 3 Ala. 718.

A person paying a note, without the request of the maker, which he was not bound mediately or immediately to pay, can not recover the amount of the maker in an action of indebitatus assumpsit in his own name. Stephens *v.* Brodnax, 5 Ala. 258.

§ 262. Persons to Whom Payment May Be Made.

See post, "Payment and Discharge," § 363 (7).

§ 262 (1) To Actual Holder in General.

Payment of the amount of a note, the property of the estate of a decedent, made to his widow, the sole legatee of the estate, during life or widowhood, when the estate was not in debt, and there was no pending administration, held valid. Hannah *v.* Lankford, 43 Ala. 163.

Payment to a guardian of a note held by him as such is an extinguishment of the debt, though the note is not given up, so that the ward can not, after the guardian's death, again collect the same. Bradley *v.* Graves, 46 Ala. 277.

The custodian of a note involved in litigation held not to have prejudiced the parties entitled to it by accepting payment, so as to be chargeable with interest after that time. Rutledge *v.* Cramton, 173 Ala. 306, 56 So. 128.

§ 262 (2) To Another than Actual Holder in General.

Where one bank discounts a bill, and sends it to its correspondent bank to collect, which latter bank, on the faith of the acceptance of the bill, advances the amount to the first bank, the first bank has no right to accept payment of the bill from the drawer. Williams *v.* Jones, 77 Ala. 294.

Where a bank has discounted a bill of exchange for the drawer thereof, still retaining ownership and control of it, though it has transferred it for collection, an acceptance by it from the drawer of a conveyance, in absolute discharge of his liability, extinguishes the bill as between the drawer and the discounting bank. Williams *v.* Jones, 77 Ala. 294.

§ 262 (3) Notice of Transfer.

Payment by the maker to the payee of a note after notice of its assignment or transfer to a third person does not discharge the maker. Gildersleeve *v.* Caraway, 19 Ala. 246; Barbour *v.* Washington Fire & Marine Ins. Co., 60 Ala. 433.

§ 262 (4) Payment without Notice of Assignment.

Payment made to an intermediate holder of a note transferred by delivery without notice of the transfer, such holder being the real owner of the note, is good. Richardson *v.* Farnsworth, 1 Stew. 55.

It is a good defense to a suit by the transferee of a note given for land that, before notice of the transfer, the money due thereon was deposited with a third person, by request of the payee, to be paid to him on his conveying the land to the purchaser. Eads *v.* Murphy, 52 Ala. 520.

Where a bill of exchange drawn by one partner in favor of the partnership was accepted by a debtor of the firm in payment of a pre-existing debt which he owed the partnership, and afterwards, and before maturity, the payees sold and indorsed the bill to a bona fide purchaser, a payment by the acceptor to the partnership, made after maturity, and without notice of the sale and indorsement, is no defense to the bill in the hands of the indorsee. Capital City Ins. Co. *v.* Quinn, 73 Ala. 558.

§ 262 (5) Payee as Agent of Holder.

A payment of a promissory note to the payee, made before maturity, but after the note has been assigned or transferred for valuable consideration, is not available as against the assignee. Barbour *v.* Washington Fire & Marine Ins. Co., 60 Ala. 433.

§ 263. Mode and Sufficiency of Payment.

See post, "In General," § 264; "New Bills or Notes," § 265; "Property or Services," § 266.

§ 264. —— In General.

See post, "Satisfaction Otherwise than by Payment," § 269.

The maker of a note deposited money in a national bank, where it was payable, and instructed the cashier to apply it in payment of the note. On the day it matured the maker tendered the bank his check in payment of the note, but was told it had been charged to his account, and that the check was unnecessary. The note, stamped "Paid," was shown him hanging on a canceling spindle, and was subsequently delivered to him. The bank was insolvent at the time, and failed before remitting the proceeds to the owner of the note, though at the time of payment it had sufficient funds for that purpose. Held not to constitute a valid payment of the note, under Rev. St. U. S., § 5242, providing that all transfers of moneys by a national bank, and payments of money or deposits to creditors, in contemplation of insolvency, with a view to prevent the application of its assets as provided, or to prefer any creditor, shall be null and void, though, except for such statute, it would have been a valid payment. First Nat. Bank *v.* Hall, 24 So. 526, 119 Ala. 64.

H. sold to S. a tract of land which he had previously purchased from A., and for the payment of which A. held three notes on H., and it was agreed that S. should execute three notes for the same amount, and to fall due at the same time with those held by A. on H., which H. agreed to substitute for those held by A. on him. Held, that if H. failed to substitute one of the new notes for one of the old ones, and S. paid one of the notes thus held by A., it was a valid defense to one of the notes executed to H. by S., when sued on by H. for the use of another. Honeycut *v.* Strother, 2 Ala. 135.

On payment of a note to the payee, the note, having been indorsed to another person, was not delivered up, but a receipt was given which showed the payment of the principal of the note only, and contained an obligation by the payee to pay the interest. Held, that the payment of the principal was not a composition of the whole debt. Hart *v.* Freeman, 42 Ala. 567.

The collection by an attorney of the principal and interest on an attorney's fee note after it has matured does not preclude the attorney to whom the note is assigned from maintaining a suit against the maker to recover the attorney's fee. Cowan *v.* Campbell, 31 So. 429, 131 Ala. 211.

§ 265. —— New Bills or Notes.

Where the payee of a promissory note, payable in cash notes, delivered the same to the maker, on the receipt from him of other notes by indorsement, it was held that this transaction did not operate to discharge such note, there being no express agreement to that effect. Crocket *v.* Trotter, 1 Stew. & P. 446.

§ 266. —— Property or Services.

In General.—Where there is a contemporaneous oral agreement that a promissory note is to be discharged by boarding and caring for the payee for a given time, so long as the agreement remains executory, it is wholly inoperative as a defense to a suit on the note; but when it has been performed it becomes a complete defense, and if performed in part, and full performance is prevented by the death of the payee of the note, it amounts to payment pro tanto, without presentation as a claim against the estate. Patrick *v.* Petty, 83 Ala. 420, 3 So. 779.

An oral agreement that a promissory note is to be discharged by receiving corporate stock of the maker in payment, so long as it remains neither wholly nor partially performed, is inoperative, and no defense to an action on the note. Tuscaloosa, etc., Oil Co. *v.* Perry, 85 Ala. 158, 4 So. 635.

In a suit between the payee of a note and one who had assumed the debt, the issue was whether goods sold by the maker to the payee's sister were a payment on the note. Held, that it was not error to charge that the goods were not a payment on the note unless it was agreed that they should be so taken, though the payee would not have given the order but for the indebtedness on the note. If it was feared that the charge would be construed as excluding an implied agreement, an explanatory instruction should have been asked. McPherson *v.* Foust, 81 Ala. 295, 8 So. 193.

Valid.—In debt on a promissory note it is a good bar that, after making and before maturity of the note, the parties agreed that the maker should buy and deliver specific articles to the payee in satisfaction, and that the maker bought and tendered the articles accordingly, and the payee refused to receive them; and it is not necessary to aver the defendant yet has them ready to deliver, or that he has abandoned. Garrard *v.* Zachariah, 1 Stew. 272.

Not Valid.—A promissory note can not be discharged by an executory parol agreement to receive property in payment. Walker *v.* Greene, 22 Ala. 679.

An agreement that a note may be paid in work is not binding so long as it is executory. First Nat. Bank *v.* Alexander, 152 Ala. 585, 44 So. 866.

An agreement between the maker and the payee of a note that it is to be paid in work is not binding on a bank to which the note is indorsed, and which does not receive any benefit from the work, and the bank is not bound to accept payment in anything but money. First Nat. Bank *v.* Alexander, 152 Ala. 585, 44 So. 866.

§ 267. Indorsement of Payments.

See post, "Payment and Discharge," § 340; "Payment and Discharge," § 363 (7).

The holder of a note may erase credits entered on it by mistake. Tubb *v.* Madding, Minor 129.

§ 268. Recovery of Payments.

A person who discounts a negotiable instrument which is forged, and to which he is not a party, may recover back the money so paid; but, when he is a party to the instrument, and stands in such a relation to the other parties that he ought to know whether it is genuine or not, he can not recover money paid on it. Young & Son Lehman, etc., Co., 63 Ala. 519.

Plaintiffs authorized J., by letter, to draw on them for any cotton he might buy in a certain city, provided the draft was accompanied by a bill of lading of the cotton, and did not exceed three-fourths of the market price of the cotton; and on the faith of this letter defendants advanced money to J. upon a draft conforming to the prescribed conditions, and were repaid by plaintiffs. Held, that plaintiffs could not, on discovering that the bill of lading was fraudulent, recover the amount so paid. Young *v.* Lehman, 63 Ala. 519.

In an action on a note which contains a stipulation that, in case it is not paid at maturity, the maker will pay 10 per cent as an attorney's fee, it is not necessary for the attorneys bringing the action to introduce evidence to show their employment or services, as their appearance will be presumed authorized, and prove their services. Stephenson *v.* Allison, 26 So. 290, 123 Ala. 439.

§ 269. Satisfaction Otherwise than by Payment.

See ante, "In General," § 264.

Remitting a check to the drawee for collection does not constitute payment. Lowenstein *v.* Bresler, 109 Ala. 326, 19 So. 860.

The discharge of the maker of a promissory note, when arrested on a ca. sa., by his creditor, is not such a satisfaction of the debt as to relieve the indorser from his liability to the creditor upon the indorsement. Quarles *v.* Glover, 4 Ala. 674.

A debtor to a decedent's estate, whose debt has been compromised by the administrator by taking the debtor's note, payable to himself individually, can not set up in defense of an action on the note by the administrator, in his own name, a transfer by the debtor to the administrator of a note on a third person as collateral security for the debt, and an agreement by the administrator to collect it, and apply a part of the proceeds on the original debt, and the administrator's failure to do so. McGehee *v.* Slater, 50 Ala. 431.

§ 270. Discharge.

See post, "In General," § 271; "Cancellation or Surrender of Instrument," § 272; "Payment or Satisfaction by Other Parties," § 273.

§ 271. —— In General.

Recovery of judgment against the maker of a note discharges the indorsers from liability on the instrument. Brown *v.* Foster, 4 Ala. 282.

A gratuitous agreement by the holder of a bill with the acceptor, made on the last day of grace, to look to him alone for the payment, and not to present the bill or notify the drawer, does not relieve the drawer if the protest is made and notice given. De Witt *v.* Bigelow, 11 Ala. 480.

Where the defendants signed a note as principals, the fact that plaintiff agreed with other joint obligors to sue the defendants alone in the first instance, and to assign the judgment recovered against the defendants to the other joint obligors, in order to avoid the necessity of suits for contribution, did not amount to a release of the joint obligors not sued, and consequently did not release the defendants. Carter *v.* Long, 125 Ala. 280, 28 So. 74.

§ 272. —— Cancellation or Surrender of Instrument.

If a payee surrenders to the maker his original note, and receives as payment in its stead, without indorsement, a note of a stranger to the original debt, the original debt is extinguished. Dennis *v.* Williams, 40 Ala. 633.

If the owner of a promissory note give it up to one of the makers, with the understanding that another note is to be executed in its stead, this will discharge either one of the makers. Smith *v.* Awbrey, 19 Ala. 63.

§ 273. —— Payment or Satisfaction by Other Parties.

The payee of a bill of exchange, drawn by a firm of which he was a member, indorsed the same to his creditor in trust to pay certain other creditors. He afterwards assigned all his property to the indorsee for the benefit of all his creditors, with a stipulation for a release from them. The assignee, in his private capacity, executed such release to the debtor. Held, that this did not release his claim, as indorsee of the bill, upon the other members of the partnership. Hazlehurst *v.* Pope, 2 Stew. & P. 259.

§ 274. Rights of Parties on Payment or Discharge.

A party to a bill, once discharged by laches on the part of the holder, is always discharged, and can not again be made liable, unless by his own voluntary act. Smith *v.* Rowland, 18 Ala. 665.

If the acceptor of a bill of exchange, after it has come to his hands, put it again in circulation, he admits it to be a subsisting bill, and can not be allowed to allege, in an action against him, that it was paid before that time. Hinton *v.* Bank of Columbus, 9 Port. 463.

VIII. ACTIONS.

§ 275. Right of Action.

See post, "Nature and Grounds in General," § 276; "Title to Sustain Action," § 277; "Conditions Precedent," § 278; "Time of Accrual," § 279; "Option of Holder," § 280.

§ 276. —— Nature and Grounds in General.

See post, "Issues Raised and Evidence Admissible in General," § 319 (1).

§ 277. —— Title to Sustain Action.

See post, "Parties Plaintiff," § 286; "In General," § 287.

§ 277 (1) In General.

The transfer of a note pending suit does not abate the action. Dalberry *v.* Trice, 49 Ala. 207.

Beneficial Owner.—Under Code 1907, § 2489, a beneficial owner of a nonnegotiable instrument may sue thereon in his own name. A. Dreher & Co. *v.* National Surety Co., 174 Ala. 490, 57 So. 34.

Party in Interest.—Under Code, § 2129, an action on a bill or note payable in bank or at a private banking house must be prosecuted in the name of the party in interest, though he has not the legal title. Crook *v.* Douglass, 35 Ala. 693.

On a writing acknowledging indebtedness to F. and promising to pay C., F. has a right of action. Bowie *v.* Foster, Minor 264.

Equitable Owner.—Under Code, §§ 2129, 2240, an equitable owner of promissory notes may sue on them or use them in set-off, although he has not the legal title to them. Hudson *v.* Weir, 29 Ala. 294.

W. and P. were joint administrators, having given joint administration bond. P. and others executed a note for purchase money of land of the estate, payable to "W. and P., administrators," etc. W. took upon himself the sole administration, and upon final settlement was charged with the amount of the note as cash. Some of the decrees rendered on this final settlement were paid; others remained unpaid. Before P. settled his administration, W. brought suit on the note in his individual name. Held that, under the facts, the sole equitable title to the note vested in W., and that he could maintain the action. Waldrop *v.* Pearson, 42 Ala. 636.

Holder of Legal Title.—Under Code 1886, § 2594, a promissory note, made payable at a designated place, is commercial paper, and an action thereon is properly instituted in the name of the holder of the legal title. Carmelich *v.* Mims, 88 Ala. 335, 6 So. 913; First Nat. Bank *v.* Slaughter, 98 Ala. 602, 14 So. 545; Holmes *v.* Bank, 120 Ala. 493, 498, 24 So. 959; Cowan *v.* Campbell, 131 Ala. 211, 31 So. 429.

"Under the letter of Code, § 2489, the holder of the 'legal title' to such an obligation is the proper party to institute the action. Hanna *v.* Ingram, 93 Ala. 482, 9 So. 621; Berney *v.* Steiner, 108 Ala. 111, 19 So. 806; Bibb *v.* Hall, 100 Ala. 79, 95, 14 So. 98." Coats *v.* Mutual Alliance Trust Co., 174 Ala. 565, 56 So. 915, 916.

An action can be maintained on notes or obligations only by those in whom the legal title is vested. Moore *v.* Penn, 5 Ala. 135.

Blank Indorsement.—It is unnecessary to fill up a blank indorsement of a promissory note, even when the description in the declaration is that the note was indorsed to the plaintiffs. Riggs *v.* Andrews, 8 Ala. 628; Sawyer *v.* Patterson, 11 Ala. 523; Bancroft *v.* Paine, 15 Ala. 834.

Bearer.—Under the statute of 1837, the bearer of a note payable to A. or bearer, and not indorsed, can not maintain an action upon it in his own name for the use of the payee. Clark *v.* Field, 1 Ala. 468; White *v.* Joy, 4 Ala. 571.

The bearer of a promissory note can not sue in his own name, in consequence of the prohibition arising out of the act of 1837, entitled an "act to prevent the institution of illegal and oppressive suits in the United States courts of this state."

Nor can the right to sustain an action be derived from the indorsement of one who holds a note as bearer. Clark *v.* Field, 1 Ala. 468.

The holder of a promissory note, into whose hands it goes by delivery, after several indorsements, can not maintain an action thereon, in his own name, against the first indorser, the payee, on the evidence of the paper alone; though such action be commenced in a justice's court. Alday *v.* Jamison, 3 Port. 112.

The holder of bills on an unincorporated banking association, payable to different individuals by name or to bearer, may maintain an action against the members of the association in his own name, though the bills have not been indorsed. Kemper & Noxubee Navigation & Real-Estate Banking Co. *v.* Schieffelin, 5 Ala. 493.

The right of the bearer of a promissory note, payable to a certain person or bearer, to sue thereon, is not affected by an intermediate indorsement by the payee to another person. Carroll *v.* Meeks, 3 Port. 226.

Holder in Name of Payee.—The holder of a note may maintain an action thereon against the maker in the name of the payee, though the note never went into the payee's hands, the presumption being that he is a bona fide holder. Bird *v.* Wooley, 23 Ala. 717.

Endorser.—It is competent for an endorser of a note, on again coming into possession of the note, to maintain an action thereon, without producing extrinsic proof of ownership. Earbee *v.* Wolfe, 9 Port. 366.

An action on a note executed to the order of, and indorsed in blank by, the maker, may be maintained against the maker by one who indorsed the note for him, though the note had not been paid by said indorser, and was obtained from the person beneficially interested therein merely for the purpose of suit. Berney *v.* Steiner, 108 Ala. 111, 19 So. 806.

Plaintiffs indorsed a note made by defendant, payable to himself, and indorsed by him in blank, and delivered it to a firm under an agreement that it should not be negotiated; that, if the maker failed to pay the same, plaintiffs were first to exhaust their remedies under the note, and the securities pledged by the maker as collateral thereto; and that, if there should be any balance due, plaintiffs should pay the same. Held, that on the maker's failure to pay the note, and on redelivery thereof by the firm to plaintiffs, with the securities, plaintiffs could sue on the note. Berney *v.* Steiner, 108 Ala. 111, 19 So. 806.

Endorser of a note can not maintain an action against the maker, for the use of the endorsee, his endorsement appearing on the note. In such case, the presumption that the endorsee has no interest in the note is rebutted and destroyed. Stone *v.* English, 1 Stew. 169.

Agent.—Where an agent place notes, belonging to his principal, in the hands of an attorney for collection, and takes a receipt therefor to himself, he may, when the money is collected, maintain an action for it in his own name. Moore *v.* Henderson, 18 Ala. 232.

On a promissory note payable to "W. A. M., agent of M. W., executrix of J. H. W., deceased," an action may be maintained in the name of the agent. Goodman *v.* Walker, 30 Ala. 482, 68 Am. Dec. 134.

Where an agent was employed to sell land, and took from the purchaser the note of another individual, indorsed by the purchaser, it is no defense, in a suit on the indorsement in the name of the agent, to show that the principal has received the amount of the purchase money, unless it is also shown that it came from the maker or indorser of the note. The agent, paying the money to his principal, acquired such an interest in the note as to entitle him to sue upon it. Tankersley *v.* Graham, 8 Ala. 247.

Receiver.—Where the members of a partnership have been enjoined by the chancery court from collecting a note, and the maker from paying it to them, a receiver appointed by such court and ordered to collect the note is the party really interested, within the meaning of Code, § 2129, and so entitled to bring the action in his own name. Leonard *v.* Storrs, 31 Ala. 488.

Executrix.—On a promissory note payable "to W. M., agent of A. B., executrix of C. D., deceased," the executrix may maintain an action in her own name, as executrix, averring that the demand is assets of her testator's estate. Goodman *v.* Walker, 30 Ala. 482, 68 Am. Dec. 134.

Distributee of Estate.—On the division of the property of a decedent by the parties interested under the will of the deceased, by agreement, without probate of the will, the distributee to whom a promissory note has been allotted may maintain an action at law on it in his own name. Carter *v.* Owens, 41 Ala. 217.

Owner of Note Transferred as Security.—Where a note is transferred to a trust company as collateral security for certain interest payments which the owner of the note has guarantied, the owner can not, without the consent of the trust company, sue on the note in his own name, since he is not the party really interested, within Code, § 2594. Alabama Terminal, etc., Co. *v.* Knox, 115 Ala. 567, 21 So. 495.

Successors of Trustees.—Trustees were appointed to sell town lots and empowered to appoint successors. Held, that successors could not maintain an action on a note taken to the trustees. Bumpass *v.* Richardson, 1 Stew. 16.

§ 277 (2) Payees.

One to whom a note is made as trustee for another may sue on the note in his own name, though Code, § 2594, provides that such suits must be brought by the real party in interest. Rice *v.* Rice, 106 Ala. 636, 17 So. 628.

An administrator may sue in his own name on a promissory note or bill of exchange payable to himself individually, which he has taken in settlement or compromise of a debt due to the estate; and his removal pending the suit is no defense to the action, unless it is shown that he has been in some way discharged from the liability thus incurred. McGehee *v.* Slater, 50 Ala. 431.

Where a note was transferred by the payee to his assignee for the benefit of creditors, but, after a settlement with the creditors, was returned to the payee, he was the real party in interest, within Code 1896, § 28, and entitled to sue thereon without any written assignment from the assignee for creditors. Brown *v.* Johnson Bros., 33 So. 683, 135 Ala. 608.

A guardian, appointed by a probate court in June, 1861, may sue in his own name on a promissory note made payable to him, and given for the hire of his ward's property. Hightower *v.* Maull, 50 Ala. 495.

The payee of a note can not maintain an action thereon, where an indorsee is the owner, without his direction or consent. Bullock *v.* Ogburn, 13 Ala. 346.

In an action on a note in the name of the payee for the use of an assignee of the note, if the assignment is stricken out pending suit the legal title does not revest in the payee so as to enable him to recover. Bullock *v.* Ogburn, 13 Ala. 346.

Where a suit is brought in the name of the payee of a promissory note for the use of another to whom it appears to have been regularly indorsed, the form of the action is an acknowledgment that the indorser is the owner of the note, and the suit can not be supported by the payee. Hunt *v.* Stewart, 7 Ala. 525.

§ 277 (3) Indorsees and Assignees in General.

An assignee of a note as collateral security is the proper party to sue under Code 1907, § 2489. Coats *v.* Mutual Alliance Trust Co., 56 So. 915, 174 Ala. 565.

The indorsee of a note payable to bearer may maintain an action thereon in his own name. Kimmey *v.* Campbell, 1 Ala. 92.

A receipt, promising to return or account for a note, was indorsed, in blank, by the promisee to the payee of the note, and by him delivered, without further indorsement, to the plaintiff. Held, that the plaintiff could maintain an action on the receipt in his own name. Henley *v.* Bush, 33 Ala. 636.

When a note payable to the order of the maker has been indorsed by him, the holder, in an action against a subsequent indorser, may derive title through the indorsement of the maker. Lea *v.* Branch Bank, 8 Port. 19, distinguishing Tindal *v.* Bright, Minor 103.

The delivery of a note to the party in whom resides the beneficial interest is sufficient, notwithstanding the legal title is vested in another, to enable a bona fide transferee of such beneficial owner to recover thereon. Sykes *v.* Lewis, 17 Ala. 261.

The drawee of a bill can, before dishonor, receive the same by indorsement, and sue the drawer and indorser on it. Desha *v.* Stewart, 6 Ala. 852.

§ 277 (4) Indorsees and Assignees for Collection.

Where a note is indorsed to an administrator, as such, he may maintain an action thereon in his own name. Evans *v.* Gordon, 8 Port. 142.

The indorsee of a bill or note made by a firm, payable to one of its members, and indorsed by him, may maintain an action against the firm. Hazlehurst *v.* Pope, 2 Stew. & P. 259; Smith *v.* Strader, 9 Port. 446.

Promissory notes payable to township trustees or their successors in office, under the free public school system, for money loaned by them that had accrued from the sale of the sixteenth section of their respective townships, must, under the present educational system, be turned over to the county superintendent of education of the proper county, and may be collected by suit in his name as such superintendent. Yerby *v.* Sexton, 48 Ala. 311.

The assignee of a note may bring an action on it in his own name. Barclay *v.* Moore, 17 Ala. 634; Morris *v.* Poillon, 50 Ala. 403.

Where the consideration of a note is effects belonging to an estate of which plaintiff is executor, the contract is made with the individual, and he need not declare in his representative capacity in a suit on the note. Evans *v.* Gordon, 8 Port. 346.

Where a note is indorsed to one person, with the assent of all interested, in payment of debts due the indorsee and several others, the indorsee may maintain an action thereon in his own name, and no defense can be interposed to avoid its payment which would not avail if the note had been indorsed and the suit brought in the names of all who were entitled to receive portions of the sum collected. Pond *v.* Lockwood, 8 Ala. 669.

The assignee of a note not negotiable can not maintain an action thereon in his own name; it must be brought in the name of the payee. Howell *v.* Hallett, Minor 102.

§ 278. —— Conditions Precedent.

An action on a note may be brought without a request to pay. Henderson, *v.* Howard, etc., Co., 2 Ala. 342; Montgomery *v.* Elliott, 6 Ala. 701; Cleaver *v.* Patterson, 14 Ala. 387, 389.

Suit on a note payable on demand may be brought without a previous request for payment. Hunter *v.* Wood, 54 Ala. 71.

A note of the following tenor: "Received of R. B. P., six hundred and fourteen dollars ninety cents, which I am to account for, 4th December, 1843. [Signed] William Cleaver"—indicates an absolute indebtedness, on which a suit may be instituted without a previous demand. Cleaver *v.* Patterson, 14 Ala. 387.

It is not necessary to protest an inland bill of exchange to enable the holder to sue. The only effect of the protest is to entitle the holder to damages. Leigh & Co. *v.* Lightfoot, 11 Ala. 935; Boyd *v.* McIvor, 11 Ala. 822, 826.

It is unnecessary to fill up a blank indorsement of a promissory note, even when the description in the declaration is that the note was indorsed to the plaintiffs. Riggs *v.* Andrews, 8 Ala. 628; Sawyer *v.* Patterson, 11 Ala. 523; Bancroft *v.* Paine, 15 Ala. 834.

In suit on a note, where defendant has denied an assignment to plaintiff, plaintiff must prove the execution of the indorsement, to put himself within Code, § 2594, providing that "such suit must be instituted in the name of the person holding the legal title." Slaughter *v.* First Nat. Bank, 109 Ala. 157, 19 So. 430.

§ 279. —— Time of Accrual.

Suit on a promissory note can not be commenced on the day on which it becomes due. Randolph *v.* Cook, 2 Port. 286.

In a suit on a bill or check payable on demand, or where no time of payment is expressed, it is no defense that the action was commenced immediately; no grace being allowed on such bill. Sommerville *v.* Williams, 1 Stew. 484.

Though a note, payable on a specified day, contains a stipulation that it shall not bear interest until another specified day after maturity, an action can be brought on its nonpayment at maturity. Billingsley *v.* Billingsley, 24 Ala. 518.

Where a note, given upon a defective consideration, is endorsed on a valid consideration, a right of action to the extent of the defect accrues to the indorsee immediately. Gee *v.* Williamson, 1 Port. 313, 27 Am. Dec. 628.

The drawer and the indorser are liable to an action by the holder, immediately after the bill is refused acceptance and before it is payable, on giving due notice of nonacceptance. Evans *v.* Bridges, 4 Port. 348.

Where a note is payable to a corporation on demand, subject to call, a cause of action does not accrue thereon until the call has been made. Brockway *v.* Gadsden Mineral Land Co., 102 Ala. 620, 15 So. 431.

Under Code, § 894, providing that a holder of a note is excused from bringing the suit required by § 892 at the next term of court after the maturity of the note against the maker, in order to fix the liability of the indorser, when by any act or promise of the indorser the plaintiff is induced to delay bringing such suit, where delay has been so induced an action may be maintained against the indorser, without suing the maker, at any time. Brown *v.* Fowler, 133 Ala. 310, 32 So. 584.

An agreement by a debtor promising to pay all the notes and bills held by the creditor against him at the date of the agreement, "as shown by the same, and in the manner shown by same," and admitting that all such bills are just and unpaid, furnishes the means by which the amount of the indebtedness can be ascertained with sufficient definiteness to render the agreement effectual as a removal of the bar of limitations. Pollak *v.* Billing, 131 Ala. 519, 32 So. 639.

§ 280. —— Option of Holder.

Code, § 1779, provides that the time of bringing suit against the maker of assigned nonnegotiable paper, in order to hold the assignor or indorser, as required by the preceding sections, may be extended or waived by the indorser or assignor in writing. Held, that anything which will constitute a waiver of demand and notice by the indorser of commercial paper will constitute a waiver of suit by the assignor of paper not commercial, if in writing. Caulfield *v.* Finnegan, 21 So. 484, 114 Ala. 39.

Code, §§ 1778-1780, provide that where the amount due on nonnegotiable paper assigned exceeds $100, the assignment may be converted into an absolute undertaking by suit against the maker at the first term of court, unless the time for bringing it has been extended or waived by the indorser in writing, and that suit is excused "when, by any act or promise of the indorser, the plaintiff is induced to delay bringing" it, etc. Held, that a "promise" is not shown by evidence that one of the holders told the indorser that nothing could be made out of the maker, and the indorser said he did not expect them to make anything out of him, but wanted them to wait until the maker died, and see if the maker's wife would not pay it out of the insurance money she would then receive. Caulfield *v.* Finnegan, 21 So. 484, 114 Ala. 39.

§ 281. Nature and Form of Remedy.

Debt lies on a promissory note for a certain sum payable at a day certain, or in merchandise; and it is not necessary to aver a failure to pay in merchandise. Henry *v.* Gamble, Minor 15.

Debt lies by the bearer against the maker of a promissory note payable to bearer; and it is not ground of reversal of judgment in such action that it is entered as in assumpsit, it being for the proper sum. Carroll *v.* Meeks, 3 Port. 226.

Recovery may be had on a bill or note under the common money counts in assumpsit. Catlin *v.* Gilders, 3 Ala. 536.

Debt does not lie by an indorsee against the indorser of a promissory note. Whiting *v.* King, Minor 122.

An action of debt will not lie on a promise under seal to pay a sum of money in current bank notes; the value is not stable. Young *v.* Scott, 5 Ala. 475.

Debt can not be maintained by the bearer of a sealed note payable to bearer. Howell *v.* Hallett, Minor 102.

An accommodation indorser of a bill of exchange is not entitled to a summary judgment, on motion against his principal, under the act of 1821 (Clay's Dig. 531, § 3). Stodder *v.* Cardwell, 20 Ala. 223.

§ 282. Defenses.

See post, "Issues, Proof, and Variance," § 319.

§ 283. —— In General.

§ 283 (1) In General.

As between the parties and all others not bona fide holders, a negotiable note occupies the same position in an action for its collection as one not negotiable: and is subject to the same defenses. Stone *v.* Goldberg & Lewis, 6 Ala. App. 249, 60 So. 744.

Where one who is not a bona fide holder acquires a bill of exchange from the acceptor, he takes it, in respect to the other parties to the bill, subject to any defense which they could set up against the party from whom he received it. Carlisle *v.* Hill, 16 Ala. 398.

In an action by a payee on a note given for life insurance it is of no consequence that it contains a stipulation waiving all defenses against it, where there is no consideration therefor. Parker *v.* Bond, 25 So. 898, 121 Ala. 529.

Where the payee of an attorney's fee note assigns it to her attorney, who has collected everything due thereon, except the attorney's fees, the fact that the payee is relieved by the attorney from further liability for such fees in consideration of the assignment is not a defense to an action on the note by the attorney to recover the attorney's fees. Cowan *v.* Campbell, 131 Ala. 211, 31 So. 429.

A surety on a promissory note on which the payee or indorsee brings an action at law can not go into equity to enjoin the action and to obtain the benefit of a set-off, when such set-off was due at the commencement of the action, and is of such a nature as to be made available at law without difficulty; and the fact that the payee is insolvent is immaterial, and furnishes no ground for resort to equity. Bank of Mobile *v.* Poelnitz, 61 Ala. 147.

To an action on a note, a plea setting up a parol understanding at the time of contracting, and not embraced in the note given, is bad. Caldwell *v.* May, 1 Stew. 425.

§ 283 (2) Facts Necessary to Establish Defense.

Where the payee of a note procured by a life insurance agent accepts it, and sues thereon the defense of want of consideration is available to defendant, whether or not such person was in fact plaintiff's agent in taking the note. Parker *v.* Bond, 25 So. 898, 121 Ala. 529.

§ 284. —— Particular Grounds.

§ 284 (1) In General.

In an action against the drawer by an indorsee, defendant can not set off the note of an indorser of the bill to a firm of which defendant is a member, there being no mutuality. Manning *v.* Maroney, 87 Ala. 563, 6 So. 343, 13 Am. St. Rep. 67.

Set-Off—In General.—The right of set-off, against a note or bond, under the Alabama statutes, does not exist for demands subsisting against intermediate assignees, through whose hands such note or bond may have passed, by blank indorsement, or otherwise. Stocking *v.* Toulmin, 3 Stew. & P. 35.

As against the assignee or holder of a promissory note, suing the maker, the doctrine of set-off has never been carried further than to put him in the place of the payee, or party having the beneficial interest. Goldthwaite *v.* National Bank, 67 Ala. 549.

A set-off by the maker of a promissory note against an intermediate indorser can not be allowed unless there is a contract between the parties, so as to allow it, founded on some new consideration. Kennedy *v.* Manship, 1 Ala. 43.

The maker of a note in a suit by the holder can not set off a claim against an intermediate holder, unless there is an agreement between them, founded on a new consideration. Goldthwaite *v.* National Bank, 67 Ala. 549.

It is not necessary that the assignee of a note by indorsement or delivery should give notice, by himself or an agent, that he is the holder of the paper, to exclude set-offs acquired subsequently to the assignment; but it is sufficient if the maker is informed of the transfer by one who has knowledge of the fact, and speaks understandingly. Crayton *v.* Clark, 11 Ala. 787.

When Set-Off Available.—Where the

payee of a note agrees that any note of his that the maker may obtain shall be a good set-off, a note against the payee, though not indorsed, if obtained by the defendant before notice that his note had been transferred, will be a good set-off against it when sued for the use of another. Gary *v.* James, 7 Ala. 640.

When Set-Off Not Available.—A set-off against a prior indorsee of a promissory note can not be maintained in an action against the maker by a subsequent indorsee, the provisions of the Code in that respect being substantially the same with those of the act of 1812. McKenzie *v.* Hunt, 32 Ala. 494.

In an action upon a promissory note, brought by an indorser against the maker, the maker can not claim in offset the amount of any debt which he may hold against a prior indorsee, under the statute providing that he shall have the benefit of all offsets, etc., which he may have against such note before the indorsement. Stocking *v.* Toulmin, 3 Stew. & P. 35.

In an action on a promissory note by a second indorsee or transferee against the maker, a promissory note made by the plaintiff's immediate indorser and another person, payable to a stranger, is not available to the defendant as a set-off (Rev. Code, § 2642), on proof that it was in his possession at the time the note sued on was transferred to the plaintiff. Bostick *v.* Scruggs, 50 Ala. 10.

Other Defenses Available — Satisfaction of Judgment.—When a note is given to one assuming to act for another, for a debt already owing, and the agreement is that it shall remain with a third person until the concurrence of the creditor is obtained, an attachment afterwards levied, upon such concurrence, will authorize the maker to resist the payment, on showing satisfaction of the judgment on the garnishee process. McClure *v.* Litchfield, 11 Ala. 337.

Estoppel.—The maker of a sealed note, having admitted to the transferee thereof that he was indebted thereon, and having promised to pay the same, is not thereby estopped from setting up payment as a defense in an action by the transferee. First Nat. Bank *v.* Chaffin, 118 Ala. 246, 24 So. 80.

Other Defenses Not Available—Oral Agreement.—An executory oral agreement, made contemporaneously with the execution of a promissory note, is not available as a defense to an action on the note, without proof of its performance; and this, notwithstanding its performance is proved to be impossible. Thompson *v.* Rawles, 33 Ala. 29.

Usury—Renewal.—The plea of usury is no defense to a suit on a note, when the maker renewed it in the hands of a subsequent holder, who gave full value for the note and had no knowledge of the usury. Mitchell *v.* McCullough, 59 Ala. 179.

Failure to Read Note.—Where one voluntarily executed a note without reading it, and there were no false representations as to its contents, he is entitled to no relief if the document proves different from what he thought it to be. Martin *v.* Smith, 116 Ala. 639, 22 So. 917.

The fact that there was usury in a note, as between maker and payee, or that the maker signed the note without reading it, and in ignorance of a waiver of exemption and provision for attorney's fee contained therein, is not a defense to a suit on the note by an innocent purchaser for value before maturity. Orr *v.* Sparkman, 120 Ala. 9, 23 So. 829.

§ 284 (2) Want of Title or Interest.

Where a note is given on a consideration moving entirely from a third person to one assuming to act for him, any defense of the maker against the party in interest is admissible where no interest in the note is disclosed by the person to whom it is made. McClure *v.* Litchfield, 11 Ala. 337.

In an action upon a note in the name of the person having the legal interest, to the use of a bank, the defendant can not be allowed to show that the bank has no interest in the note, without laying a foundation for it, as an offer to prove an offset against the true owner. Moore *v.* Penn, 5 Ala. 135.

Where a vendee of real estate executes a note in consideration of the purchase money, and receives a bond for title from the vendor, with possession, he can not resist a recovery upon the note, on the ground of the want of title in the vendor; no fraud being imputed or rescission claimed; and no effort made to place the vendor in statu quo, by a return of the premises. Wade *v.* Killough, 3 Stew. & P. 431.

If the defendant makes a note payable to the plaintiff generally, he is estopped to set up in defense that the plaintiff was only the agent for others in whom is the beneficial interest. Grigsby's Ex'rs *v.* Nance, 3 Ala. 347.

Where the purchaser of land gave a note for the price to a third person, he admitted the latter was entitled to the money, and could not afterwards be heard to allege the contrary. Lowrie *v.* Stewart, 8 Ala. 163.

It is not a valid objection to a suit against a surety upon a promissory note that it is brought for the benefit of the principal in the note and two others, as executors of an estate. Hampton *v.* Shehan, 7 Ala. 295.

Although the admission of a vendor of land that he has no title may furnish good ground for abandoning the possession and rescinding the contract, yet the retention of possession by the vendee. no fraud being shown, estops him from insisting that the contract is a nullity, and that the note given by him for the purchase money is without consideration. Gillespie *v.* Battle, 15 Ala. 276.

§ 284 (3) Want or Failure of Consideration.

See post, "Evidence Admissible under General Issue," § 319 (5); "Payment and Discharge," § 340.

In General.—In an action on a note given for an illegal consideration against the maker, he may waive the illegality, and prove as a defense that the payee violated an agreement on his part which formed the consideration. Wynne *v.* Whisenant, 37 Ala. 46.

Laches can not be attributed to one setting up a partial failure of consideration to a note for the price of land: he need not set it up till suit is brought. Kelly *v.* Allen, 34 Ala. 663.

The giving of notes for a running account does not waive the maker's right, when sued on such notes, to set up as a defense that part of the goods were sold in violation of the statute. Wadsworth *v.* Dunnam, 23 So. 699, 117 Ala. 661.

Where the vendor of a negro receives from the vendee a promissory note indorsed by the latter for an amount larger than the purchase money, and gives his own note payable at a day certain for the excess, to entitle the vendor to insist upon the want of consideration when sued on his note it is not necessary that the vendor should release the vendee from his indorsement to a corresponding extent. Litchfield *v.* Allen, 7 Ala. 779.

It is no defense to an action on a note that the consideration thereof was the loan to defendant of the proceeds of a share of stock which was a voluntary gift from him to plaintiff. Rice *v.* Rice, 106 Ala. 636, 17 So. 628.

Defenses Available.—In an action on a note against the maker, he may prove what the real consideration was and that it was in whole or in part illegal. Wynne *v.* Whisenant, 37 Ala. 46.

Where a vendor takes an indorsed note for a greater amount than the purchase money of property, and gives his own note for the excess, he may show, in defense to an action on his note, that the maker of the indorsed note is insolvent, although no action may have been brought against him. Litchfield *v.* Allen, 7 Ala. 779.

Where the vendor of a slave receives from the vendee a promissory note indorsed by the latter for an amount larger than the purchase money, and gives his own note, payable at a certain day, for the excess, the pendency of a suit by the vendor (as indorsee) against the indorser will not in any manner prejudice the vendor's defense of want of consideration when sued upon the note. Litchfield *v.* Allen, 7 Ala. 779.

Where a defendant, in an action on a promissory note, can maintain a cross action for damages on account of a partial failure of the consideration for such note, such damages will avail, pro tanto, as a defense to the action. But it seems this rule does not apply where the consideration of the note is real estate. Peden *v.* Moore, 1 Stew. & P. 71, 21 Am. Dec. 649; Evans *v.* Murphy, 1 Stew. & P. 226.

A person who was president and treasurer of a local board of trustees of an insurance company, gave a certificate that the insurance company had on deposit with him a certain number of dollars, and signed it "H., president and treasurer, local board of trustees." Held, the certificate, in legal effect, was H.'s promissory note, and in a suit at law against him by the insurance company, he could show in defense that the contract of which it formed a part had been rescinded, or that the contract was of mutual stipulations, and the payee had not performed on his part. Hart *v.* Life Ass'n, 54 Ala. 495.

Defenses Not Available.—Where, upon the purchase of a plantation and slaves, on credit, a number of notes are executed, falling due during a period of years, if the maker discharges or pays the note first falling due to the payee, he will be presumed to have availed himself of any payment or offset which then existed, and will not be permitted to make such defense against the assignee of notes subsequently falling due. Nelson *v.* Dunn, 13 Ala. 259.

When an administrator sues on a note given for the price of property sold by him under an order of the probate court, he is estopped from denying the validity of a contemporaneous parol agreement, set up in defence, that the note might be discharged in Confederate currency. Riddle *v.* Hill, 51 Ala. 224.

The acceptance of a deed with warranty prevents the purchaser from setting up failure of consideration, at law, in defense of an action on a note given for the purchase money of the land. Starke *v.* Hill, 6 Ala. 785.

Where several notes are given to a plaintiff, for a consideration which, with the assent of the defendant, fails in part, the failure can not be set up against all the notes—plaintiff may recover on the first note sued on, the amount due him for past performance. Hansford *v.* Mills, 9 Port. 509.

§ 284 (4) Fraud.

A misrepresentation of a material fact by the vendor of personal property, made at the time of the sale, or pending the preliminary negotiations, on which the purchaser has a right to rely, and does in fact rely, as inducement to the contract, is a fraud, and is available as a defense to an action upon a promissory note given for the purchase money of the property so sold. Hooper *v.* Whitaker, 30 So. 355, 130 Ala. 324.

Fraud can not defeat the recovery at law on a note given for the price of land, when a deed containing covenants of warranty running with the land has been accepted by the purchaser, his relief is in a court of equity. Starke *v.* Hill, 6 Ala. 785.

§ 285. —— Persons as to or against Whom Defenses Are Available.

See ante, "Property or Services," § 266; "Title to Sustain Action," § 277.

Available.—A vendor of land took several negotiable notes for the payment of the purchase money, one of which was negotiated in the usual course of trade, and the others were not. Held that, although the holder of the note so negotiated was not subject to an equity existing against the vendor, such equity could be enforced against the holders of the other notes, and that the vendor could not be required to apportion the loss. Andrews *v.* McCoy, 8 Ala. 920, 42 Am. Dec. 669.

Not Available.—In a suit by the payee of a note made by a debtor at request of the creditor, payable to a third person, the maker can not dispute the existence of the consideration moving between the creditor and the payee. Lea *v.* Cassen, 61 Ala. 312.

The payer of a note can not defend a suit by the transferee on the ground of inadequacy of the consideration paid for the transfer, and the action of the transferee in taking advantage of the transferror's weak mental condition, and overreaching him. Walker *v.* Winn, 39 So. 12, 142 Ala. 560, 110 Am. St. Rep. 50.

Usury is a defense personal to the party known as the borrower. He can not transfer to another the right he has to allege and prove a demand to be usurious. Cain *v.* Gimon, 36 Ala. 168.

In an action upon a note given for the purchase money of mules warranted sound by the payee, brought by the indorsee against the maker, the purchaser may recover damages sustained by a breach of the warranty. Weaver *v.* Shropshire, 42 Ala. 230.

If, in pursuance of an award made pending a suit, the defendant, at the request of the plaintiff, executes a promissory note to a third person, he can not, when sued on the note, defeat the action by showing that no consideration passed between the plaintiff and the payee; nor can he raise any question as to the application of the money due on the note to the payment of attorney's fees of plaintiff's counsel in the original suit. Yeatman *v.* Mattison, 59 Ala. 382.

P. purchased some slaves of H., for $1,400, upon which A. and B. had mortgages—the latter being the eldest—paid down $1,000, and executed his note for $400. H. agreeing to satisfy both mortgages. At the time of the sale the slaves were in the possession of A., to whom H. delivered the note of $400, and obtained possession of the slaves, which he delivered over to P. H. did not satisfy the mortgage of B., and P. was compelled to pay upon it a larger sum than the amount of the note, suit being brought on the note in the name of H., for the use of A., against P. Held, that if P. was privy to and assented to the agreement between H. and A., by which the former obtained possession of the slaves from A., he could not defend himself against the payment of the note by proving that he had been compelled to pay a larger sum for H., but, in the absence of such proof, A. must be understood as having delivered up the slaves on the responsibility of H., and had, therefore, no greater rights than H. would have if suing for his own benefit. Pippin *v.* Huntington, 9 Ala. 228.

§ 286. Parties Plaintiff.

See ante, "Right of Action," § 275; "Title to Sustain Action," § 277; post, "In General," § 287; "Joinder," § 288.

§ 287. —— In General.

A bona fide holder of a note may sue thereon in the name of the payee. Herndon *v.* Taylor, 6 Ala. 461.

Where the note of a banking partnership was made payable to one of the partners or bearer, and put in circulation, without indorsement, the rule that a partner can not sue a copartner did not apply to prevent the holder from bringing action in the name of the payee against the other partners. Elliott *v.* Montgomery, 4 Ala. 600.

When a suit is improperly commenced in the name of the party to whom a note not negotiable is transferred without indorsement, instead of using the name of the person having the legal interest, and the cause is afterwards appealed to the circuit court, the defect can not then be cured by substituting the name of the proper party in the declaration. Taylor *v.* Acre, 8 Ala. 491.

The payee of a note made to him by a wrong name may sue upon it in his right name, alleging that the note was made payable to him by the name therein inserted, and may show by evidence on the trial that he was the person intended. Taylor *v.* Strickland, 1 Ala. Sel. Cas. 571, 37 Ala. 642.

When an action under the Code (§ 2129), founded on a "writing obligatory" for the payment of money, is brought in the name of one person, for the use of another, a demurrer lies to the complaint, because it shows on its face that the action ought to have been brought in the name of the beneficial plaintiff. Dwyer *v.* Kennemore, 31 Ala. 404.

When suit is brought on a promissory note, in the name of the payee, for the use of another, and is produced in evidence at the trial, it ought not to be excluded, although it appears, from an indorsement upon it, to have been assigned to one not connected with the suit; the legal presumption in such a case is that the note has been returned by the assignee to his assignor. Woodward *v.* Taylor, 6 Ala. 461.

The act of June, 1837, inhibits the bearer of a bond or note from suing thereon in his own name, unless he can deduce a title to the same by indorsement; consequently, where a note was payable to S. L. or bearer, an action could not be maintained upon it by J. J. or bearer, for the use of S. L.—the same not appearing to have been indorsed to J. J. or any one else. White *v.* Joy, 4 Ala. 571.

§ 288. —— Joinder.

Under Code 1886, § 2594, providing that actions upon notes payable at a bank must be instituted in the name of the person having the legal title, an action on such note was properly brought in the name of the payees thereof, although one of them had assigned his interest therein. Hanna *v.* Ingram, 93 Ala. 482, 9 So. 621.

§ 289. Parties Defendant.

See post, "In General," § 290; "Joinder," § 291.

§ 290. —— In General.

See post, "Joinder," § 291.

The holder of a bill of exchange may maintain, at the same time, separate actions against the acceptor, the drawer and the payee, their liability being fixed by proper protest and notice, and nothing but a payment of the judgment against one will discharge the others; and where the bill is held as collateral security for prior advances made to the payee, he may maintain an action against the acceptor in the name of the payee. Williams, etc., Co. *v.* Jones, 79 Ala. 119.

A joint and several note, made by several persons, may be declared on as made by one of such persons alone. Miller *v.* Sneads, Minor 27.

An indorsee of promissory notes may sue the indorser before suing the makers, and the latter are not necessary parties to the suit. McGhee *v.* Importers' & Traders' Nat. Bank, 93 Ala. 192, 9 So. 734.

Under the provisions of Code, §§ 2129, 2143, a payee of a promissory note, who is also one of the joint makers, and who has assigned his interest in the note to the other payees, is not a necessary party defendant in a suit on the note. The action may be maintained against the other maker. Willis *v.* Neal, 39 Ala. 464.

§ 291. —— Joinder.

The holder of a bill or note may sue all the parties thereto, or either of them, but he can have but one satisfaction. Abercrombie *v.* Knox, 3 Ala. 728, 37 Am. Dec. 721.

A law allowing all the indorsers of a note to be joined in one action affects the remedy merely, and does not follow the contract. Givens *v.* Western Bank, 2 Ala. 397.

While the payee of a negotiable promissory note may sue both the maker and indorser at the same time in separate actions, in absence of statute he can not sue them jointly. Scarbrough *v.* City Nat. Bank, 48 So. 62, 157 Ala. 577, distinguishing Abercrombie *v.* Knox, 3 Ala. 728, 37 Am. Dec. 721.

The executor or administrator of a deceased joint maker of a note can not be sued jointly with the surviving maker. Murphy *v.* Branch Bank of Mobile, 5 Ala. 421.

§ 292. Declaration, Complaint, or Petition.

See post, "Form and Requisites in General," § 293; "Execution and Delivery of Instrument," § 294; "Description of Instrument," § 295; "Consideration," § 296; "Nature of Contract," § 297; "Transfer and Ownership," § 298; "Maturity and Performance of Conditions," § 299; "Presentment, Demand, Protest, and Notice," § 300; "Nonpayment," § 301; "Amount Due, Interest, and Attorneys' Fees," § 302.

Where a complaint sets out an agreement, made a year before the suit was instituted, whereby defendant promised to pay all the bills and notes held by plaintiff against him on that date, a demurrer on the ground that the cause of action founded on such notes was barred by six years' limitations will be overruled, regardless of whether the complaint showed that the bills and notes were outstanding at the date of the agreement, since, if the bill does not show this, it necessarily does not show that the bills and notes were of six years' standing, and, if it does show that they were outstanding at such date, then they are designated by the promise to pay with sufficient definiteness to remove the bar. Pollak *v.* Billing, 131 Ala. 519, 32 So. 639.

§ 293. —— Form and Requisites in General.

§ 293 (1) In General.

In General.—Since a party may declare for any cause consistent with or embraced by the indorsement on his writ, if the writ be indorsed with a bill or note the declaration may embrace the common counts, under which a bill or note may be given in evidence. Kirkpatrick *v.* Bethany, 1 Ala. 201.

Under Code, § 3292, providing that actions on contracts for the payment of money may be united in the same action, drafts sued on may be described in one count. H. T. Woodall & Son *v.* People's Nat. Bank of Leesburg, Va., 45 So. 194, 153 Ala. 576.

A single count on several notes made by the same person is good. Dade *v.* Bishop, Minor 263; Bird *v.* Daniel, 9 Ala. 302.

An agreement in certain notes to pay attorney's fees is additional to the obligation of the note, and hence there is no objection to embodying in one count a claim for all attorney's fees claimed in the suit. Boyett *v.* Standard Chemical & Oil Co., 41 So. 756, 146 Ala. 554.

A note is in itself a legal liability, and needs no distinct substantive allegation in the declaration to entitle plaintiff to recover a part from a description of the note and an allegation of nonpayment. Adams *v.* McMillan, 8 Port. 445.

In an action by an assignee of a note against the maker, a promise by the maker to pay the assignee need not be alleged. Conklin *v.* Harris, 5 Ala. 213.

In a declaration on a bill single, it is a sufficient excuse for the omission to make profert to allege that defendant wrongfully and illegally obtained possession of the bill from plaintiff's attorney, and, on demand, refused to return it to plaintiff. The statute requiring an affidavit to be filed when suit is commenced on a lost instrument does not apply. Robinson *v.* Curry, 6 Ala. 842.

A transferee of a note purporting to be payable to "Aaron Formey" may aver a promise to pay Aaron Formby by the name of Aaron Formey, and may show by evidence that Formby was the person really meant. Taylor *v.* Strickland, 37 Ala. 642.

Sufficient.—The complaint in an action by the payee on a note, being in the form prescribed by Code 1907, § 5382, form No. 1, is sufficient. Stone *v.* Goldberg & Lewis, 6 Ala. App. 249, 60 So. 744.

A complaint in the form prescribed by the Code "on promissory note, by payee against maker," is sufficient to support a judgment by default; and its legal effect is the same as if it contained an averment, in express terms, that the note was payable to plaintiff. Letondal *v.* Huguenin, 26 Ala. 552; Cumming *v.* Richards, 32 Ala. 459; Beggs *v.* Arnotte, 80 Ala. 179.

In an action by a prior against a subsequent indorser, who has been compelled to pay a note, a declaration which alleges the making of the note, its indorsement, protest for nonpayment, and notice to defendant, and thence deduces his liability, if sustained by proof, entitles plaintiff to recover, especially if a count is added for money paid, laid out, and expended. Spence *v.* Barclay, 8 Ala. 581.

A count on eight notes is sufficiently precise which alleges that they all bear the same date (which is stated), and that plaintiff is the payee—three of them payable on the 1st day of December, 1842, for the sum of $45 each; four others, for the same amount, payable 12 months thereafter; the eighth, payable on the latter day, for $25. Bird *v.* Daniel, 9 Ala. 302.

Where a complainant alleges that defendants indorsed a note, which is set out in full, and that between its maturity and the next term of court they each requested him not to sue the maker, and promised to pay the debt, and thereby induced him to delay suit, wherefore he now sues to recover of them the amount of the note and the costs of a suit against the maker, with interest, the action is properly against the indorsers as such. Brown *v.* Fowler, 32 So. 584, 133 Ala. 310.

Insufficient.—A complaint on a note, not due when suit is brought, does not state a "substantial cause of action," within Code 1907, § 4143. Ritter *v.* Hoy, 1 Ala. App. 643, 55 So. 1034.

§ 293 (2) Acceptance.

In declaring against a party as the acceptor of a bill of exchange, it is not necessary to aver that the acceptance was in writing; and in declaring on a promise to accept, made before the bill was drawn, it is not necessary to aver that it was in writing and unconditional, though the proof of these facts on the trial may be necessary to entitle plaintiff to recover. Whilden *v.* Merchants' & Planters' Nat. Bank, 64 Ala. 1, 38 Am. Rep. 1.

In declaring against the principal, on a bill accepted by his agent, the agent's authority to accept must be averred. It is not sufficient to aver he was the agent, and, as such agent, accepted for the principal. May *v.* Kelly, 27 Ala. 497.

An averment that an accommodation acceptor of a bill ratified a use thereof contrary to the conditions of the acceptance by the maker states a mere conclusion, and is bad on demurrer. Farley Nat. Bank *v.* Henderson, 24 So. 428, 118 Ala. 441.

§ 293 (3) Inability to Recover of Maker.

See ante, "In General," § 293 (1).

In General.—"When the holder relies on an excuse for the nonperformance of a prerequisite to the absolute liability of an endorser, the declaration must aver the facts which constitute the excuse. Chitty's Pl. 329; Glover *v.* Tuck, 24 Wend. 153." Lindsay *v.* Williams, 17 Ala. 229, 231.

Although a note is payable in the city of New York, yet, if made and endorsed in this state, in an action against the endorser, the declaration must aver a suit against the maker, and return of no property found as the statute requires, or a sufficient excuse for not bringing such suit. Howze, etc., Co. *v.* Perkins, 5 Ala. 286.

Where an indorsement is made in the state in an action brought in that state against the indorser by the holder, plaintiff must allege suit against the maker, and a return of nulla bona, or show sufficient excuse for not bringing suit. It is not an excuse that the note was made payable out of the state. Woodward *v.* Harbin, 1 Ala. 104; Howze *v.* Perkins, 5 Ala. 286.

Sufficient.—A declaration against the indorser discloses a good cause of action which shows that the debt is past due; alleges the indorsement, in the state, of a bill single, that the obligor was then, and still is, a resident of another state; and that he then was, and still continues, wholly and notoriously insolvent, so that no part of the debt could be collected of him by suit. Miller *v.* McIntyre, 9 Ala. 638.

In an action by the holder of a note against the indorsers, the refusal of the court to strike out allegations of the complaint that plaintiff had recovered against the maker, and that execution thereon had been returned, "No property found," was not reversible error. Brown *v.* Fowler, 32 So. 584, 133 Ala. 310.

Insufficient.—The words, "used the legal means to try to collect out of the maker" of a note is not a sufficient averment of the necessary diligence to bind an indorser. Alday *v.* Jamison, 3 Port. 112.

When the suit is against the indorser of a note not negotiable, after a failure to recover in a suit against the maker, commenced with the statutory diligence, the declaration must show that the suit against the maker was decided by a judgment on the merits of the note, and a declaration is defective if it alleges only the determination of the suit in favor of the maker. Murphy *v.* Gee, 9 Ala. 276.

An averment in a declaration on an irregular indorsement, that suit was commenced against the maker, "in the county where he ordinarily resided, but that he could not, on diligent search and inquiry, there and elsewhere in said state, be found," is not an averment of such diligence as will charge the indorser. Fulford *v.* Johnson, 15 Ala. 385.

Where the holder of a note not negotiable at a bank failed to sue the maker at the first court after it matured, as required by Aik. Dig., pp. 329, 330, in order to hold the indorser an averment in a declaration against the indorser that the court at which suit was brought against the maker was the first at which it could be brought "after plaintiff, by prompt and diligent inquiry, ascertained the maker's residence," is insufficient, since the facts constituting the excuse should be specially averred, and not left to implication. Lindsay *v.* Williams, 17 Ala. 229.

§ 294. —— Execution and Delivery of Instrument.

See post, "Verification," § 315.

It is not necessary in a declaration in debt on a single bill to allege delivery of the writing to the payee, although such delivery is essential to its validity. Brown *v.* Hemphill, 9 Port. 206.

Where the declaration stated that the note sued on, was made in "Kemper County, Mississippi," it was held that the meaning of the averment was, that the note was made in the state of Mississippi. Dunn *v.* Clement, 2 Ala. 392.

A complaint averring that, though the names of the defendants appeared on the back of the note, the contract between defendants and the payees, at the time it was made, was that defendant should sign it jointly with the maker, and that their names were written on the back as makers, and not as indorsers, sufficiently declares against the defendants as makers of the note. Carter *v.* Long, 28 So. 74, 125 Ala. 280.

An allegation that defendant, president of a corporation, refused to guarantee on certain proposed terms the notes and loans made by plaintiff bank to the corporation, but stated that he would sign any paper in connection with the notes or loans which the bank held against the company, was not an averment that defendant agreed to sign a particular note on which suit was brought, but only an allegation of a negotiation for additional security which failed to ripen into a contract. Briel *v.* Exchange Nat. Bank, 172 Ala. 475, 55 So. 808.

An allegation in the declaration, that the note on which the suit was brought "was made by A, acting for himself. and as joint owner with B of the boat," is not an allegation that A had authority, as the agent of B, to execute the note in his name, so as to make the note evidence under the statute, unless contradicted by a sworn plea. Brooks *v.* Harris, 12 Ala. 555.

An allegation in the declaration, in a suit on a note, that it was delivered to defendant, is a mere clerical misprision. Allen *v.* Claunch, 7 Ala. 788.

§ 295. —— Description of Instrument.

See post, "Variance," § 319 (7).

In declaring on the acceptance of a bill of exchange, it is not necessary to allege that it is in writing, though written acceptance must be proved. Faircloth-Byrd Mercantile Co. *v.* Adkinson, 52 So. 419, 167 Ala. 344.

Where a note was executed by one partner in the name of a firm, which was then in dissolution, and described in the note as in liquidation, it is sufficient in a declaration by an indorsee against the indorser to describe the note as made by the firm. Riggs *v.* Andrews, 8 Ala. 628.

When plaintiff styles himself executor or administrator, and declares on a note payable to himself in that capacity, but the declaration does not aver that the note is assets of the estate, the words "executor," etc., are a mere descriptio personæ. Arrington *v.* Hair, 19 Ala. 243.

§ 296. —— Consideration.

In an action on a note a consideration need not be alleged. Allen *v.* Dickson, Minor 119; Bowie *v.* Foster, Minor 264; McMahon *v.* Crockett, Minor 362; Hunley *v.* Lang, 5 Port. 154; Jones *v.* Rives, 3 Ala. 11; Thompson *v.* Armstrong, 5 Ala. 383.

A writing acknowledging a sum of money to be due for corn and fodder, used by the party, may be declared on as a promise to pay that sum immediately, and without noticing that it was due for corn and fodder. Carlisle *v.* Davis, 9 Ala. 858.

Every writing, which is the foundation of an action, being made by the statute of 1811 (Clay's Dig., p. 340, § 152) 'evidence of the debt or duty for which it was given," it is not necessary, in declaring on a note, to allege the consideration. The fact that the note appears on its face to have been given for the debt of another can not affect the principle. Thompson *v.* Hall, 16 Ala. 204.

A bill to charge the estate of A, deceased, alleged that A and one B made their note to complainant for a valuable consideration, payable at a certain bank; that the note was discounted at such bank, and A received the money obtained; and that complainant was compelled to buy up the note from the bank. Held, that this allegation did not show any indebtedness originally from A to complainant, but must be understood to mean that the note was made to raise money on, and was indorsed by complainant, in which capacity he was compelled to pay the note. Borland *v.* Phillips, 3 Ala. 718.

Where, in counting on a note under seal, plaintiff, without setting out the note in hæc verba, inserted the words "Value received," which were not in the note, it was held that the words were not descriptive of the note, but merely an unnecessary allegation, and therefore did not vitiate the declaration. James *v.* Scott, 7 Port. 30.

§ 297. —— Nature of Contract.

See ante, "In General," § 293 (1).

Where the indorser of a promissory note holds himself liable to the indorsee, "should the maker fail," this is a different contract from a general indorsement, and must be specially declared on. The word "fail" in such indorsement, is of larger import than "feruse," and is equivalent to inability or insolvency of the principal; and such fact must be shown by the indorsee, as ascertained by suit or otherwise. Davis & Co. *v.* Campbell, 3 Stew. 319.

An allegation that a note sued on was payable in money to the order of "R," sufficiently shows that it was negotiable at common law. Holmes *v.* Bank of Ft. Gaines, 24 So. 959, 120 Ala. 493.

A count on a note alleging that "plaintiff claims of defendant $300, due by note made by him for the Winter Iron Works, payable at the office of the Montgomery Insurance Company; that said note was indorsed by defendant, and that the Winter Iron Works are insolvent, and were insolvent at the time said note became due and payable; that said note is payable to the order of defendant"—is against defendant as indorser, and not as maker, and is insufficient to charge him. Winter *v.* Coxe, 41 Ala. 207.

§ 298. —— Transfer and Ownership.

See post, "Verification," § 315.

§ 298 (1) Necessity of Alleging Indorsement, Assignment, and Ownership.

In an action on a note by the transferee against the maker, the complaint must aver the assignment, or contain some other allegation to show plaintiff's ownership. Browder *v.* Gaston, 30 Ala. 677; Douglas *v.* Beasley, 40 Ala. 142.

A beneficial owner of a nonnegotiable instrument suing thereon in his own name, under Code 1907, § 2489, should aver in what manner he became owner. A. Dreher & Co. *v.* National Surety Co., 174 Ala. 490, 57 So. 34.

In an action by G. for the use of "S., sheriff of T. County, and successor of G.," on a note described as payable to "G., sheriff, and administrator of the estate of J. C.," if S. was the legal proprietor of the note as administrator de bonis non, that fact should have been pleaded by defendant. King *v.* Griffin, 6 Ala. 387.

The declaration should state the inducement or consideration for the indorsement and tranfer. McInnis *v.* Rabun, 1 Port. 386.

The bearer of a promissory note, payable to a certain person or bearer, may maintain an action thereon against the maker, without setting out any title through an assignment, but may claim merely as bearer. Carroll *v.* Meeks, 3 Port. 226.

In an action on a note by the assignee against the maker, if the complaint fails to aver the assignment, or containing some other averment showing plaintiff's ownership, the defect is available on error, after judgment by default. Douglas *v.* Beasley, 40 Ala. 142.

In an action against an indorser, an averment in the declaration, "that by the laws of the state of Georgia, where said indorsement was made, the said defendant became liable to pay said sum of money, in said note specified, to said plaintiff," is but the statement of a conclusion as to the effect of the foreign law, and the rights and liabilities of the parties under that law, and is therefore demurrable. McDougald *v.* Rutherford, 30 Ala. 253.

Counts in complaint on a bill of exchange held demurrable for failure to allege indorsement by payee, or that plaintiff was the legal holder or owner. Jefferson County Savings Bank *v.* Interstate Savings Bank, 59 So. 348, 5 Ala. App. 368.

§ 298 (2) Sufficiency of Allegations as to Indorsement, Assignment, and Ownership.

In General.—An averment that a note was regularly indorsed to plaintiff includes the averment that it was indorsed by the payee. Snelgrove *v.* Branch Bank, 5 Ala. 295.

The summons and complaint in an action by an administrator on a note payable to himself were in the name of such administrator, followed by the words "who sues by the name and description of administrator of H., deceased." Held, that the words added to plaintiff's name were mere descriptio personæ, and the action is his individual suit. Wright *v.* Rice, 56 Ala. 43.

Sufficient.—An allegation in a bill that complainant is the bona fide holder and transferee of a note, and that the same is unpaid, is, in connection with a copy of the note exhibited, a sufficient allegation of title. Owen *v.* Moore, 14 Ala. 640.

In an action by the assignee against the maker of a note, an averment that the sum therein mentioned is due plaintiff is a sufficient averment of his ownership. Nesbitt *v.* Pearson, 33 Ala. 668.

In an action on a note by an assignee against the maker, an allegation that the note, which is described, is now plaintiff's property, is sufficient. Clark *v.* Moses, 50 Ala. 326; Morris *v.* Poillon, 50 Ala. 403.

A complaint alleging that "plaintiffs claim of defendant $29,05, with interest thereon, due on a bill of exchange drawn by one S. * * * on defendant, and accepted by it, payable to plaintiff, which bill is due and unpaid," sufficiently alleges that plaintiff is the owner of the bill. Town of Woodlawn *v.* Purvis, 108 Ala. 511, 18 So. 530.

In an action against indorsers of a note, an allegation in the complaint, as to the indorsement that on the day of the date of the note "the defendant indorsed a written obligation executed" by the maker "in words and figures following (setting out the note) is sufficient. Brown *v.* Fowler, 32 So. 584, 133 Ala. 310.

Not Sufficient.—Under Code 1896, § 28, providing that a suit on a note payable at a bank shall be brought in the name of the party holding the legal title, a complaint in a action on such a note, alleging that the note is "the property of plaintiff," but containing no allegation showing that plaintiff has the legal title, is insufficient. Young *v.* Woodliff-Dunlap Furniture Co., 40 So. 656, 147 Ala. 686.

Where a suit is brought, in the name of the payee of a note, for the use of A. and B., against an indorser, and the declaration does not state who indorsed the same to defendant, or to whom he indorsed it, nor allege any transfer to or from him, nor any inducement or consideration for the indorsement, the declaration is bad on demurrer. McInnis *v.* Rabun, 1 Port. 386.

§ 299. —— Maturity and Performance of Conditions.

See ante, "In General," § 293 (1).

In General.—The error of misstating the day on which the note was payable is cured by judgment by default. Crawford *v.* Camfield, 6 Ala. 153.

Where the note was given for a cotton gin, which defendant had the privilege of trying and returning if it was not good, it was held that this was a condition for the benefit of defendant, which he must take advantage of by plea, and that the note might be declared on, as an absolute promise to pay, without noticing the condition. Lockhard *v.* Avery, 8 Ala. 502.

Sufficient.—In an action on a note, payable on a contingency, plaintiff alleged that the contingency had happened, but did not state at what time. Held sufficient. Allen *v.* Dickson, Minor 119.

A court in a declaration by the indorsee against the personal representatives of the indorser of a negotiable note avers that, by an agreement between the maker and indorser, the surplus value of certain slaves, held by the latter as an indemnity, was, after the payment of the sum of $4,646.13, to be applied to the discharge of several notes, of which the note sued on was one, and, in the event the indorser should keep the slave, etc., the surplus should be ascertained by three disinterested persons, etc., and further avers that the said surplus was sufficient fully to indemnify the indorser, etc.,

Held, that the count is not defective because it fails to aver that the surplus had been ascertained in the mode designated by the agreement. Cockrill *v.* Hobson, 16 Ala. 391.

In an action on a note against an indorser, a declaration alleging that the note was presented for payment when the same was due and payable, "to wit, on the 3d of August," etc., the note being before described as payable on the 4th of November, is good on demurrer. Crawford *v.* Camfield, 6 Ala. 153.

A declaration, on a note to be paid on a contingency, that averred that the contingency had happened, as appeared by an indorsement thereon, was held sufficient to warrant a judgment by default. McGehee *v.* Childress, 2 Stew. 506.

A declaration describing a promissory note as bearing date in November, 1836, and payable on the 1st day of March, eighteen hundred and twenty-nine, meaning thirty-nine, must be considered as containing a sufficient cause of action, after a judgment by default. Cater *v.* Hunter, 3 Ala. 30.

Not Sufficient.—In a suit on an unmatured note, an allegation that complainants previous to the suit offered to discount the note, which offer defendant accepted, is insufficient to show that the date of maturity was changed. Freider *v.* Leinkauff, 92 Ala. 469, 8 So. 758.

§ 300. —— Presentment, Demand, Protest, and Notice.

In General.—In an action against an indorser, demand of payment from maker, refusal and notice to indorser, or the facts which will excuse or be equivalent to it, must be alleged. Mims *v.* Central Bank, 2 Ala. 294.

In an action by an indorsee against the indorser of a note, indorsed after it is overdue, the indorsee must allege a demand of payment of the maker, and notice to the indorser. Kennon *v.* McRea, 3 Stew. & P. 249.

In an action against an indorser of a note, made in another state, which has dispensed with the necessity of demand and notice by statute, such facts must be alleged. Mims *v.* Central Bank, 2 Ala. 294.

In an action on a note, an averment in the declaration of protest is necessary to authorize damages. Jordan *v.* Bell, 8 Port. 53.

In declaring against the indorser of a note, at common law, it was necessary to aver a demand and notice, or an excuse for the omission of either; while, under the statute of this state, respecting notes not payable in bank, it is necessary to aver the institution of a suit against the maker, and its prosecution to a return of "No property" on an execution. McDougald *v.* Rutherford, 30 Ala. 253.

In an action against the drawer of a bill of exchange, who was also the acceptor, it is not necessary to allege a demand and notice. Smith *v.* Paul, 8 Port. 503.

Where a note payable to a named individual or bearer is indorsed by a third person to plaintiffs before its maturity, and its due payment guarantied, waiving the suit and diligence required by law, it is unnecessary to aver notice to the indorser that the makers had not paid the note. Burt *v.* Parish, 9 Ala. 211.

In an action by an indorser against an indorser, plaintiff need not allege a continued refusal to pay, by the maker, up to the time of suit brought. Crenshaw *v.* McKierman, Minor 295.

The declaration or complaint in an action against the maker of a note, payable at a certain time and place, need not allege presentation for payment at such time and place. Irvine *v.* Withers, 1 Stew. 234; Montgomery *v.* Elliott, 6 Ala. 701; Clark *v.* Moses, 50 Ala. 326.

Where the custom of a particular bank to give notice through the post office of the dishonor of bills holden by the bank, to parties residing at the same place, is relied on in a suit against such parties, the special custom need not be averred in the declaration. Gindrat *v.* Mechanics' Bank, 7 Ala. 324.

Sufficient.—In an action on a note against the indorser, averments of "due" presentment, protest, and notice are sufficient. Winter *v.* Coxe, 41 Ala. 207.

In an action against an indorser of a note payable at bank, an allegation of presentment at the bank when due is a sufficient averment of demand of payment. Smith *v.* Raymond, 9 Port. 459.

In an action by the holder of a bill of exchange against the drawer or indorser, the words "duly protested," in the complaint, must be considered equivalent to an averment that the bill was presented at maturity, at the place of payment named in it. Battle *v.* Weems, 44 Ala. 105.

An averment that the note sued on was duly and legally presented for payment is sufficient, without stating that it was presented at the place designated in the note. Carrington *v.* Odom, 27 So. 510, 124 Ala. 529.

In an action by the indorsee against the indorser, the declaration alleged that after the note became due and payable according to its tenor, to wit, on, etc., the note was duly presented for payment. Held that, though the time stated under the videlicet was a day previous to the maturity of the note, yet that the generality of the declaration would control it, and be sufficient. Smith *v.* Robinson, 11 Ala. 270.

In a summary proceeding by a bank against the drawer of a bill of exchange, it is sufficient to allege that the bill was presented for payment at maturity, without stating the day. Crawford *v.* Branch Bank, 6 Ala. 574.

It is sufficient to allege demand of payment to have been made at the place of business of the drawee, without alleging such place to be in the place of his alleged residence. Cullum *v.* Casey, 9 Port. 131, 33 Am. Dec. 304.

A count averred that, since the protest of the bill, "defendant, with knowledge that the usual steps of demand, protest, and notice were not duly taken, acknowledged his liability as indorser on said bill, and promised plaintiffs, to pay the same." Held that, although the allegation of a promise to pay was insufficient because the promise was not alleged to have been made before the bringing of the suit, the acknowledgment of continuing liability was good without such allegation. Bolling *v.* McKenzie, 89 Ala. 470, 7 So. 658.

An allegation that notice of dishonor was given to one who was present at the indorser's place of business and in his employment was a sufficient allegation of notice to the indorser. Scarborough *v.* City Nat. Bank, 48 So. 62, 157 Ala. 577.

In an action by the holder against an indorser of a bill, an averment that the bill was presented to the drawee for acceptance, but that he refused to accept the same, of which the defendant had notice, is sufficient. Cullum *v.* Casey, 9 Port. 131, 33 Am. Dec. 304.

An allegation in a declaration "that the notary, at," etc., "aforesaid, made diligent search, and inquiry for the said acceptor," is a sufficient allegation that inquiry and search were made in Mobile, it having been previously alleged that the bill was directed to Charles Byrem, Esq., Mobile. Hazzard *v.* Shelton, 15 Ala. 62, 48 Am. Dec. 129.

Not Sufficient.—Where a note was made by a corporation, by one as agent, to whom it was payable, and who indorsed it, an allegation that the indorser was the sole agent of the corporation, and that no other person was authorized to pay the note for the corporation, is sufficient to show that the indorser was the sole agent to pay the note for the corporation at maturity, so as to raise the inference that he had notice of its dishonor. Winter *v.* Coxe, 41 Ala. 207.

An averment in a declaration on an irregular indorsement that the maker was at the time of the indorsement of the note, and has continued since, a nonresident, and that the fact of his nonresidence was at the time unknown to plaintiff, is an insufficient averment to charge the indorser. Fulford *v.* Johnson, 15 Ala. 385.

Defects Cured.—The statement of demand in an action on a note, which omits the date thereof, is not fatal after trial and verdict. Cater *v.* Hunter, 3 Ala. 30.

In an action on a note, failure to aver protest so as to authorize assessment of damages is cured by judgment. Jordan *v.* Bell, 8 Port. 53.

Where a declaration on a note payable at a particular place contains no averment of a special demand at that place, the defect, if any, will be cured by verdict. Irvine *v.* Withers, 1 Stew. 234.

§ 301. —— Nonpayment.

In an action by G. for the use of "S., sheriff of T. county, and successor of G.," on a note described as made payable to "B., sheriff and administrator of the estate of J. C.," the allegation of nonpayment to plaintiff without negativing payment to S. was a sufficient assignment of the breach. King *v.* Griffin, 6 Ala. 387.

§ 302. —— Amount Due, Interest, and Attorneys' Fees.

A complaint in an action on a note, by the payee against the maker, alleging that "plaintiff claims of defendants the sum of $400 due by note made by them on March 7, 1853, and payable on January 1, 1854, with interest thereon," is sufficient. Cumming *v.* Richards, 32 Ala. 459.

The writ and declaration on a note payable at a future day, with interest from date of note, should not claim the principal and interest to day appointed for payment, in an aggregate sum, as debt. Butler *v.* Limerick, Minor 115.

The declaration in an action on a note under seal, payable at a day certain, with interest, setting out the amount of principal and interest, as the debt claimed, is bad, as the principal and interest should be specified separately. Butler *v.* Limerick, Minor 115.

Where a note is declared on as made at Fayetteville, it is to be intended that Fayetteville is in the state where suit is brought, and hence that interest should be recovered under the laws of that state. Garner *v.* Tiffany, Minor 167.

In debt on a note payable at a future day, with interest from date if not punctually paid, when such interest was demanded in the declaration, yet, not being demanded as a part of the debt itself, the declaration is sufficient. Boddie *v.* Ely, 3 Stew. 182.

The complainant in an action on an attorney's fee note after it has matured is not required to allege that a ten per cent attorney's fee, as stipulated in the note, is reasonable compensation for the attorney's services in collecting the note. Cowan *v.* Campbell, 31 So. 429, 131 Ala. 211.

A complaint in an action on a note which demands $15 or so much thereof as may be reasonable attorney's fees, and which avers that the note stipulates that if it is not paid at maturity the maker will pay expenses of collection, including attorney's fees, demands a reasonable attorney's fee not exceeding $15, and sufficiently alleges the amount of recovery on account of attorney's fees. Phillips *v.* Holmes, 51 So. 625, 165 Ala. 250.

§ 303. Plea, Answer, or Affidavit of Defense.

See post, "Form and Requisites in General," § 304; "Traverses or Denials and Admissions in General," § 305; Execution and Delivery of Instrument," § 306; "Want or Failure of Consideration," § 307; "Mistake, Fraud, or Duress," § 308; "Illegality," § 309; "Transfer and Ownership in General," § 310; "Good Faith and Payment of Value," § 311; "Presentment, Demand, Protest, and Notice," § 312; "Extension of Time and Agreement Not to Sue," § 313; "Payment and Discharge," § 314; "Verification," § 315; Issues, Proof, and Variance," § 319.

§ 304. —— Form and Requisites in General.

The plea in an action on a note in the form prescribed by Code 1907, § 5331, for the general issue in such form of action, is sufficient as such. Stone *v.* Goldberg & Lewis, 6 Ala. App. 249, 60 So. 744.

In an action on a bill single, payable to a firm of which one of the obligors is a partner, defendant may plead non est factum, and a special plea that the name and seal of one of the obligors have been canceled without his consent. Tindal *v.* Bright, Minor 103.

When the defendant is sued on a note by the name signed to it, and he does not deny the execution of the note by him, he can not plead in abatement on account of an alleged misnomer. Comer *v.* Jackson, 50 Ala. 384.

§ 305. —— Traverses or Denials and Admissions in General.

Where the payee of a note procured by a life insurance agent accepts it, and sues thereon, and defendant pleads want of consideration he need not allege that such agent had no interest in the note. Parker *v.* Bond, 25 So. 898, 121 Ala. 529.

A promissory note was made payable to the "Nashville Bank," and, in an action thereon by the bank, it was held, that the defendant, by pleading the general issue, prima facie admitted the capacity of the bank to contract and sue. Herbert *v.* Nashville Bank, 1 Stew. & P. 286.

§ 306. —— Execution and Delivery of Instrument.

See post, "Verification," § 315.

A plea in an action under a note by an indorsee which alleges that the indorsee is not a bona fide holder, and that the note was delivered on condition, and the conditions were not complied with, states a valid defense under Code 1907, § 4793. Bank of Cartersville *v.* Gunter, 4 Ala. App. 539, 58 So. 757.

A plea to an action on a note, stating that the defendant authorized his agent, by writing, to sign a note in the name of his principal, to be binding on him if the payee gave notice thereof to the principal in thirty days, and alleging that no notice was given, is equivalent to a plea denying the execution of the note. Sorrelle *v.* Elmes, 6 Ala. 706.

One sued on a note is not compelled to plead non est factum generally with an absolute affidavit of facts supporting, but he may state in a special plea the particular facts and circumstances which amount to a denial of the legal effect or validity of the note, or deny the authority of the agent who made it. Martin *v.* Dortch, 1 Stew. 479.

§ 307. —— Want or Failure of Consideration.

§ 307 (1) In General.

See post, "Mistake, Fraud, or Duress," § 308.

Sufficient.—A special plea that the negotiable note sued on was "without consideration" was sufficient. Cochran *v.* Burdick Bros. (Ala.), 61 So. 29.

In an action on a note, a plea that "said note was given by defendant's intestate, wholly without consideration," is good. Milligan *v.* Pollard, 112 Ala. 465, 20 So. 620.

Where, in assumpsit on a note by the payee, defendant pleaded "that plaintiff was not a bona fide holder for value," and "that the note was without consideration," and the first clause was struck out, it was not prejudicial error; the latter clause implying the former. Cunyus *v.* Guenther, 96 Ala. 564, 11 So. 649.

A plea by the acceptor of a bill of exchange that the drawer requested defendant to accept a bill for his accommodation, to be used for a specific purpose, and with the understanding that it should be so used, and, in consideration of the promise to so use it, he accepted the bill in suit, sufficiently shows defendant to be an accommodation acceptor. Farley Nat. Bank *v.* Henderson, 24 So. 428, 118 Ala. 441.

Such plea is not demurrable as failing to show a want of consideration for the acceptance. Farley Nat. Bank *v.* Henderson, 24 So. 428, 118 Ala. 441.

Not Sufficient.—A plea in an action on a note, which merely states as a conclusion of the pleader that defendant does not owe the demand sued on, without the statement of any facts, is demurrable, since it fails to inform plaintiff of what he is to meet. Scott & Sons *v.* Rawls, 159 Ala. 399, 48 So. 710.

In an action on a promissory note made by defendant with others who are not sued, the plea of no consideration to defendant is demurrable, as it fails to negative consideration moving to defendant's co-makers. McAfee *v.* Glen Mary Coal & Coke Co., 97 Ala. 709, 11 So. 881.

Where it was averred in the complaint that the defendants signed the note sued on as makers by agreement with the payees at the time the note was executed, a plea that there was no consideration moving to or from the payees of the note to or from the plaintiffs was bad, since a contract may be supported by a consideration moving from a third person as well as from the promisee. Carter *v.* Long, 125 Ala. 280, 28 So. 74.

§ 307 (2) Failure of Consideration.

Failure of consideration must be specially pleaded. T. J. Scott & Sons *v.* Rawls & Rawls, 48 So. 710, 159 Ala. 399.

A plea of failure of consideration, in an action on a note, should show what the consideration was, and how it failed. Carmelich *v.* Mims, 88 Ala. 335, 6 So. 913; McAfee *v.* Glen Mary Coal & Coke Co., 97 Ala. 709, 11 So. 881.

In an action on a note, by the transferee against the maker, defendant pleaded that at the time of the execution of the note there were mutual unsettled accounts between the parties, and that the note was given to cover only the balance that should be found due the payee on a settlement of the accounts, and that "only a few dollars was in fact due" Plaintiff demurred to the plea (1) that "the maker attempted to show by a parol agreement that a different amount was to be paid than that specified in the note, at an indefinite time;" and (2) that "the plea attempted to change a written agreement by parol testimony." Held, that the demurrer was properly overruled. Baker *v.* Boon, 100 Ala. 622, 13 So. 481.

In an action on a note, a plea that a cotton press, for which the note was partly given, has never been delivered to defendant, is insufficient in failing to show that plaintiff undertook to deliver the press, or that it was sold by him to defendant. Maness *v.* Henry, 96 Ala. 454, 11 So. 410.

A plea, which states that the note sued on was given in consideration of slaves sold by the plaintiff to the defendant in 1860, is bad on demurrer. Ward *v.* Hudspeth, 44 Ala. 215.

A plea, in an action on a note, which alleges that the maker purchased certain property, relying on the representation of the payee that the same belonged to him, that the payee did not own the property which constituted a large part of the value of the note, and that the consideration for which the note was given failed, is demurrable. Noble *v.* Anniston Nat. Bank, 41 So. 136, 147 Ala. 697.

A plea, in an action on a note, which alleges that the note was given to the payee for a part of the purchase price of property which he sold to the maker, that the payee guaranteed that the property was of a specified value, and that the maker would receive that amount therefor, and that he could not realize from the property such sum, is demurrable as setting up a plea of failure of consideration. Noble *v.* Anniston Nat. Bank, 41 So. 136, 147 Ala. 697.

§ 308. —— Mistake, Fraud, or Duress.

See post, "Issues Raised and Evidence Admissible in General," § 319 (1).

A plea, in an action on bills of exchange by a transferee thereof against the acceptor, that defendant was induced to sign the same by fraudulent representations of the payee, presents prima facie a good defense and puts it on the transferee to reply that he purchased the bills in good faith, for value, before maturity, and without notice. H. T. Woodall & Son *v.* People's Nat. Bank of Leesburg, Va., 45 So. 194, 153 Ala. 576.

Where, in an action on an accepted draft, fraud is alleged as a defense, but the facts showing the fraud are not set out, the plea is faulty, and subject to demurrer. Stouffer *v.* Smith-Davis Hardware Co., 154 Ala. 301, 45 So. 621.

A plea alleging that defendant executed a note and mortgage on plaintiff's promise to loan to defendant, which he failed to do, does not show fraud in the execution of the note and mortgage, but want of consideration. Lewis *v.* Simon, 101 Ala. 546, 14 So. 331.

In an action on a note, the plea setting up false representations of a third person as to the value of certain stock in insurance companies held demurrable. Mizell *v.* Farmers' Bank (Ala.), 61 So. 272.

A plea, in an action on a note, that it was given on a rescission of a sale made ostensibly to plaintiff, but in fact to one B., and that, after delivery of the note, defendant ascertained that B., his agent, was a party to the purchase, which was thereby fraudulent, does not sufficiently allege the interest of B., and is demurrable. Webb *v.* Ward, 25 So. 48, 122 Ala. 355.

A plea, in an action on a note, which alleges that the maker purchased property from the payee in reliance on his representation that he was the owner thereof, that the representation was untrue, and by reason of the untrue statements as to the ownership of the property for which the note was given the same is void, is demurrable. Noble *v.* Anniston Nat. Bank, 41 So. 136, 147 Ala. 697.

In an action on notes of L., brought by an indorsee against indorsers, defendants in one plea alleged that the indorsements were made on L.'s promise to use them to redeem certain collaterals pledged for his debt, promising to "pay off" the debt "by the use of said indorsements," and to deliver the collaterals to defendants; that L. also promised to procure, as further indemnity for the indorsements, the written guaranty of a certain firm, which L. "falsely and fraudulently assured these defendants" said firm had agreed to make; that relying on said promises, for the purpose stated, they indorsed said notes; and that L. fraudulently diverted the indorsements, and failed to keep said promises. Held, that the plea was bad, in that it failed to state the facts constituting the supposed fraud of L., or to show that defendants were not accommodation indorsers without restriction on the use of the notes. Bunzel *v.* Maas, 22 So. 568, 116 Ala. 68.

Another plea alleged the indorsement for L.'s accommodation, and on his promise to use the notes with the creditor holding said collaterals, and on his promise to deliver the collaterals so taken up to defendants for their indemnity; that L. did not so use the notes, but fraudulently diverted them, by discounting them with a firm named, at a usurious rate of interest; and that plaintiff did not acquire them before maturity in the usual course of business. Held bad, in that there was no averment how the notes were to be used with such creditor, whether by discount or otherwise, nor how the proceeds of the discount actually made were used. Bunzel *v.* Maas, 22 So. 568, 116 Ala. 68.

§ 309. —— Illegality.

A plea by the defendant, in an action on a note given for the purchase price of fertilizers, alleging failure to comply with Act March 2, 1871, requiring the inspection, stamping, and branding of fertilizers, need not allege that the sale was made in this state; if made elsewhere, that fact is matter for replication. Renfro *v.* Loyd, 64 Ala. 94.

§ 310. —— Transfer and Ownership in General.

See post, "Verification," § 315.

In General.—The genuineness of an endorsement of the note sued on can only be denied by a sworn plea. Savage *v.* Emanuel, 26 Ala. 619, 620.

Sufficient.—In assumpsit on a promissory note by an indorsee thereof, a plea that plaintiff was not, at the commencement of the action, the legal owner of the note, puts in issue only the genuineness of the indorsement. Agee *v.* Medlock, 25 Ala. 281.

A plea to an action by an indorsee of a note, denying that the note is the property of the plaintiff, and asserting it to be in a different right, is a plea denying the indorsement. Frazer *v.* Brownrigg, 10 Ala. 817.

A plea averring who is the real owner of the note sued upon, and that the suit is instituted for his benefit, and pleading an offset against him, is a good plea, although a different person is indicated on the record as the beneficiary of the note in suit. Bowen *v.* Snell, 9 Ala. 481.

Code, § 2594, requires suits upon bills of exchange and promissory notes payable at a bank or banking house to be brought in the name of the person having legal title. Held, that a plea which averred want of legal title in plaintiff, but failed to aver that the note was payable at a bank or banking house, was not demurrable, when that fact appeared from the complaint. Lakeside Land Co. *v.* Dromgoole, 89 Ala. 505, 7 So. 444.

Not Sufficient.—In an action on a note by an assignee thereof, an affidavit verifying a plea, and reciting that "the note was not at any time indorsed and delivered to the plaintiff, nor had he any equitable or legal interest in it," is insufficient as a denial of the factum of the assignment. Bancroft *v.* Paine, 15 Ala. 834.

In an action on a note, a plea that it was received by plaintiff from the payee as collateral for the payment of a preexisting debt, and that defendant maker has paid the note, without notice of the transfer, to the payee, is insufficient, without negativing the presumption that the transfer was for value. Louisville Banking Co. *v.* Howard, 26 So. 207, 123 Ala. 380, 82 Am. St. Rep. 126.

Code 1886, § 2594, provides that actions on bonds for the payment of money must be prosecuted in the name of the party really interested, whether he has the legal title or not, subject to any defense the payor may have had against the payee, previous to notice of assignment or transfer. Held, that a plea which averred "that the note sued on was made payable to A. or order, and at the time said note was made payable it was agreed that it should not be transferred except to S., and afterwards, by consent of the parties to said note, in pursuance of said agreement, and to carry out the same, said agreement * * * was indorsed on said note, and the indorsement was made while said A. was still the owner," was demurrable, since it did not negative the fact that the note was traded first to S., and afterwards by him to plaintiff, or that plaintiff could maintain a suit in his own name under the statute. Johnson *v.* Washburn, 98 Ala. 258, 13 So. 48.

Though such agreement imposed on A. a binding obligation not to transfer the note except to S., there was nothing stated in the plea which showed that defendant was cut out of any defense, or otherwise injured, by A.'s alleged breach thereof. Johnson *v.* Washburn, 98 Ala. 258, 13 So. 48.

§ 311. —— Good Faith and Payment of Value.

In an action by the assignee of a negotiable note against the maker, pleas alleging a failure of consideration need not allege that plaintiff had notice of such facts when he acquired the note. Cochran *v.* Burdick Bros. (Ala.), 61 So. 29.

A plea in an action on a note alleging that it was a renewal of one originally executed in payment of a subscription to stock; that three certain persons were interested in selling said stock; that one of said persons, acting for himself and his associates, induced defendant to sign said note, by representing that certain other persons had agreed to take a large amount of said stock, that others had contracted to take a large quantity of the product of the corporation, and that the property of the corporation was then marketable; but that said representations were wholly false. Held, that such pleas, without averment of notice to plaintiff of the infirmity of the note, prima facie present a good defense, and put it upon plaintiff to reply that it purchased the note in good faith, for value, before maturity, without notice of the alleged fraud. Alabama Nat. Bank *v.* Halsey, 109 Ala. 196, 19 So. 522.

§ 312. —— Presentment, Demand, Protest, and Notice.

Where the complaint on a note alleges its due protest and notice thereof to an indorser, a special plea by the latter that he was never legally notified of the protest is demurrable where he also pleads the general issue, since, the allegation of notice in the complaint having been necessary, the special plea was merely a repetition of the plea of the general issue. Carter *v.* Odom, 25 So. 774, 121 Ala. 162.

In an action on a note for the costs of protest and notice, a plea that protest was waived on the day of maturity, and before protest by the notary, is demurrable, since the term "protest," in its popular significance, means "those acts which are necessary to charge an indorser," and with this significance the plea is open to the construction that the alleged waiver was subsequent in point of time to the dishonor of the note. White *v.* Keith, 97 Ala. 668, 12 So. 611.

§ 313. —— Extension of Time and Agreement Not to Sue.

Where the complaint in an action against the indorsers of a note alleged that the holder was induced to delay suing the maker by the express promise of the indorsers to pay the note, a demurrer to a plea denying that there was any consideration for such promise was properly sustained. Brown *v.* Fowler, 133 Ala. 310, 32 So. 584.

§ 314. —— Payment and Discharge.

In General.—Payment must be specially pleaded. Scott & Sons *v.* Rawls, 159 Ala. 399, 48 So. 710.

A plea that the note was part of a sum agreed on as an account stated, and that the amount was paid, in a manner set forth, though bad for failure to aver that the payment was made before the commencement of the suit, was good as against a demurrer alleging that the plea was double, that it did not show the fact from which the indebtedness arose, and does not show that the order on a third person, as set forth in the plea, was given in payment. Scott & Sons *v.* Rawls, 159 Ala. 399, 48 So. 710.

Sufficient.—In an action on a note, a plea that, since the execution of the note, there has been a novation of the same, in that plaintiffs agreed that they would release defendants from their liability, and accept a corporation as their debtor, to which agreement such company was a party, and that the consideration therefor was the fact that such company received and used the machinery, which was the consideration for the note, and got the benefit thereof, is sufficient. Moragne *v.* Richmond Locomotive & Machine Works, 27 So. 240, 124 Ala. 537.

In suit on a negotiable note by indorsee, a plea alleging it was agreed that it was to be paid by proceeds of work done, etc., and maker paid plaintiff by proceeds of work all that was due prior to commencement of suit, and plaintiff received full benefit thereof, the proceeds being in money, constituted a plea of payment in money, the source from which it was derived being immaterial. First Nat. Bank *v.* Alexander, 50 So. 45, 161 Ala. 580.

Where the complaint in an action on a note claimed $5 as attorney's fees, a demurrer to a plea averring payment of the note prior to the commencement of the suit was properly overruled, since the plea was to be taken as affirming a payment of the debt, and under the averment of the complaint such fee being due, just as the principal and interest would have been, had it not been paid. Rarden *v.* Salter, 55 So. 456, 1 Ala. App. 569.

A plea, in a suit on a note, alleging that the defendant had been garnished in a court of the state of Louisiana, and a judgment rendered against him on his answer, condemning the debt in favor of a creditor of the plaintiff, setting out the proceedings fully, and alleging that they were conducted according to the law of Louisiana, and that he had paid, and satisfied the judgment so rendered, is good. It is not necessary in such a plea to allege, in totidem verbis, that the defendant had no notice of the transfer of the note, when he answered the garnishment. Mills & Co. *v.* Stewart, 12 Ala. 90.

Not Sufficient.—In an action on a note, a plea that, since the execution and delivery thereof to plaintiff, she has, without the knowledge and consent of the defendant, an indorser, erased and changed the same, for the purpose of releasing another indorser, whereby he was released, is demurrable, as being too general and indefinite. Scharf *v.* Moore, 102 Ala. 468, 14 So. 879.

In an action on a note, a plea that plaintiff has released defendant from all liability on the note is merely the statement of a conclusion. Maness *v.* Henry, 96 Ala. 454, 11 So. 410.

In an action against an indorser, a plea setting up the release of another indorser, which does not aver a consideration for the release, is demurrable. Scharf *v.* Moore, 102 Ala. 468, 14 So. 879.

A plea alleging that, before suit brought, defendant notified plaintiffs that he demanded a cancellation of the insurance policy for which the note sued on was given, and notified plaintiffs that he would not further abide by the policy of insurance, and returned the same to plaintiffs, was bad in failing to show either that plaintiffs agreed to the cancellation of the policy, or that defendant had a right to demand the cancellation. Hatcher *v.* Branch, Powell & Co., 37 So. 690, 141 Ala. 410.

Conceding that the policy was returned and the return accepted, the plea was further defective in failing to show the date of the return and acceptance, or that the return was accepted in extinguishment of the note sued on. Hatcher *v.* Branch, Powell & Co., 37 So. 690, 141 Ala. 410.

A plea asserting that the note sued on was indorsed to the plaintiff by the payee for the sole purpose of discharging a particular note made by him to a third party, and that the payee, after the maturity, directed the maker to pay the money to the third party, which was done, is bad, without averring that the payment was made to the third party in discharge of the particular note which it was the object of the indorsement to discharge. Alsobrook *v.* Deshler, 10 Ala. 698.

§ 315. —— Verification.

See post, "Evidence Admissible under Plea or Answer in General," § 319 (3); "In General," § 326 (1); "Indorsement," § 326 (3).

Sufficiency of Affidavit.—If, to an action on a note made by their intestate, administrators plead non est factum, the affidavit verifying the plea may be upon the knowledge and belief of the administrators. Martin *v.* Dortch, 1 Stew. 479.

The oath of defendant's attorney, affixed to a plea, and sworn to before the clerk of the court, even though the plea states in its body that "defendant, for answer to the complaint, saith that he did not sign the note sued on," etc., and he makes oath that this plea is true, etc., is a sufficient affidavit, under § 2279 of the Alabama Code, providing that the execution of an instrument shall not be denied except by plea verified by affidavit. McCoy *v.* Harrell, 40 Ala. 232.

Under Toulmin's Dig., p. 454, § 33, providing that no plea of non est factum shall be admitted unless accompanied by an affidavit of its truth, a plea of non est factum is admissible on an affidavit stating special facts from which the truth of the plea may be inferred. Tindal *v.* Bright, Minor 103.

Necessity of Verification.—The consideration of a note may be inquired into and impeached without a sworn plea. Holt *v.* Robinson, 21 Ala. 106, 107.

In an action by an indorsee or assignee against the maker, the indorsement or assignment can only be denied by a sworn plea. Deshler *v.* Guy, 5 Ala. 186; Frazer *v.* Brownrigg, 10 Ala. 817; Agee *v.* Medlock, 25 Ala. 281; Savage *v.* Walshe, 26 Ala. 619; Smith *v.* Harrison, 33 Ala. 706.

A special plea averring facts amounting to nothing more than a denial of the execution of the note sued, in such a manner as to make it binding on the defendant, is bad on demurrer, unless verified by affidavit. Bryan *v.* Wilson, 27 Ala. 208.

A plea, averring that the plaintiff was not at the commencement of the suit, the legal owner of the note sued on must be verified by affidavit. Agee *v.* Medlock, 25 Ala. 281.

In assumpsit by the assignee of a note, a plea which puts in issue the fact of the assignment must be verified by affidavit, or be sworn to in open court. Beal *v.* Snedicor, 8 Port. 523; Bancroft *v.* Paine, 15 Ala. 834.

Under Code 1886, § 2594, providing that actions on notes must be prosecuted in the name of the party really interested, the defense to an action on a note by the payees named therein, that one of them has assigned his interest, can be made available only by filing a verified plea denying his interest. Hanna *v.* Ingram, 93 Ala. 482, 9 So. 621.

In an action on a note, a plea averring that the note sued on is not the one signed by the defendant is insufficient when unverified. Lesser *v.* Scholze, 93 Ala. 338, 9 So. 273.

A plea that the date of the note sued on has been altered must be verified. Lesser *v.* Scholze, 93 Ala. 338, 9 So. 273.

Although a promissory note declared on does not on its face purport to have been executed by the defendant, yet, if its execution by him is averred, he can not deny it, whether it was by mark, initial, or other designation, except by a sworn plea under section 2682 of the Revised Code. Wimberly *v.* Dallas, 52 Ala. 196.

In a suit by the holder of a bill of exchange against the payee and indorser, an averment in the complaint that the defendant—a corporation—indorsed the bill by its president can not be objected to on demurrer; the allegation must be traversed by a sworn plea. Montgomery & E. R. Co. *v.* Trebles, 44 Ala. 255.

Where, in an action against an acceptor, the plea denies that the acceptance was the act of defendant, the plea must be supported by an affidavit, as required by Aik. St., p. 283, § 137. McWhorter *v.* Lewis, 4 Ala. 198.

Under a rule providing that, when plaintiff in an action on a contract to pay money avers that he is the party really interested in such contract, his right to maintain the action shall be disputed only by plea verified by affidavit, the right of a widow to sue on a note payable to her deceased husband, where she alleges facts showing her right to such note under the exemption statute, can be disputed only by verified plea. Howle *v.* Edwards, 20 So. 956, 113 Ala. 187.

"Under §§ 1801, 1802, Code 1896, if the making or assignment of a note be alleged in the complaint, or if it purports on its face to be signed, neither the making nor the assignment can be denied except by a sworn plea. Alabama Coal Min. Co. *v.* Brainard, 35 Ala. 476, 480; Montgomery, etc., R. Co. *v.* Trebles, 44 Ala. 255, 258; Oxford Iron Co. *v.* Spradley, 46 Ala. 98, 105; Wimberly *v.* Dallas,

52 Ala. 196, 197; Ledbetter, etc., Loan Ass'n *v.* Vinton, 108 Ala. 644, 646, 18 So. 692; Carter *v.* Long, 125 Ala. 280, 290, 28 So. 74." International Harvester Co. *v.* Gladney, 157 Ala. 548, 47 So. 733.

In a suit by an indorsee of a bill, a plea denying that the plaintiff is the sole owner, and alleging that the bill is owned by an association of individuals of whom the plaintiff is one, must be verified by affidavit. Tarver *v.* Nance, 5 Ala. 712.

Administrators who plead non est factum to an action on the note made by their intestate must verify the plea by affidavit. Martin *v.* Dortch, 1 Stew. 479.

Under Code, § 1801, providing that pleas denying the execution or assignment of any instrument in writing which is the subject of suit must be verified, plaintiff's ownership of the note in suit must be denied by a sworn plea, and can not be raised on demurrer. Henderson *v.* J. B. Brown Co., 28 So. 79, 125 Ala. 566.

Code, § 3037, requiring a denial of the execution of an instrument to be verified by affidavit, applies to a note which purports to be signed by the maker's mark only, and is not attested by witnesses. Walker *v.* Bentley, 64 Ala. 92.

Verification Not Required.—A plea by the acceptor of a bill of exchange that the drawer requested defendant to accept for his accommodation and for a specific purpose need not be verified by affidavit. Farley Nat. Bank *v.* Henderson, 24 So. 428, 118 Ala. 441.

Where, in an action on a promissory note by the indorsee against the maker, the defense set up is a want of legal title in the plaintiff, a plea verified by affidavit is not necessary, but evidence appropriate to the issue may be introduced under the plea of nonassumpsit. Birch *v.* Tillotson, 16 Ala. 387.

Rules of Evidence Not Affected by Verification.—Under circuit court rule 29 (Code 1896, p. 1200), providing that, when an action is brought by the assignee or indorsee of a contract for the payment of money, the interest of plaintiff in such a contract and his right to maintain the action shall not be disputed, except by a verified plea, the filing of a verified plea denying plaintiff's right to maintain an action on a note does not change any rule of evidence or impose on plaintiff any greater or less burden of proof than in other cases. Hughes *v.* Black (Ala.), 39 So. 984.

The rule of practice adopted at the January term, 1863, which provides that, in an action "by any transferee, assignee, or indorsee, the plaintiff shall not be required to prove his interest in the cause of action, unless the same is put in issue by plea, verified by affidavit," does not change any rule of evidence, nor relieve the plaintiff, when such sworn plea is filed, from the necessity of proving his cause of action as before. Jarrell *v.* Lillie, 40 Ala. 271.

Effect of Absence of Verification.—A plea that the plaintiff is not owner of the note sued on, if not verified by affidavit, is bad on demurrer, in Alabama. Jennings *v.* Cummings, 9 Port. 309.

Where, in an action on a note, an unverified plea is filed denying plaintiff's title, it is subject to a motion to strike. Stouffer *v.* Smith-Davis Hardware Co., 45 So. 621, 154 Ala. 301.

Under statutes relating to practice in actions on written instruments, it is not necessary for plaintiff to prove the execution of a promissory note, unless its execution is denied under oath. Tuscaloosa Cotton Seed Oil Co. *v.* Perry, 85 Ala. 158, 4 So. 635.

The note sued on purporting to have been signed by defendant is by provision of Code 1907, § 3967, embracing all written instruments, admissible without proof of its execution, in the absence of sworn plea denying its execution. Stone *v.* Goldberg, 6 Ala. App. 249, 60 So. 744.

In a suit on a promissory note, where the only pleas were the general issue and that there was no consideration for the note, it was properly admitted in evidence over the objection that attesting witnesses were not called or their absence accounted for, in view of Code 1896, § 1801, providing that a written instrument, the foundation of a suit, purporting to be signed by the defendant, must be admitted in evidence without proof of its execution, unless the execution is denied by verified plea. Gates *v.* Morton Hardware Co., 40 So. 509, 146 Ala. 692.

Where plaintiff, in an action on a bill

of exchange, avers that he is the owner by indorsement, and his ownership is not denied under affidavit, as provided by Code 1886, § 2770, it is proper to admit the bill in evidence, though it shows an indorsement by plaintiff to a third person. Manning *v.* Maroney, 87 Ala. 563, 6 So. 343, 13 Am. St. Rep. 67.

When an indorsement is alleged, which the defendant fails to controvert by a sworn plea, if the signature of the defendant appears upon the note which is averred to be an indorsement, the note must be allowed to go to the jury, without proof that such signature was designed to pass title. Bragg *v.* Nall, 14 Ala. 619.

Under Code, § 1801, which requires that the denial of execution of a written instrument which is the foundation of the suit must be verified, where the complaint averred that the defendants signed their names on the back of the note sued on as makers in accordance with an agreement with the payees, and the plea filed thereto was not under oath, the defendants were not entitled to show that they signed the note otherwise than as makers. Carter *v.* Long, 28 So. 74, 125 Ala. 280.

By provision of Code 1907, § 3966, embracing all written contracts, the note sued on, purporting to have been signed by defendant, is, in the absence of sworn plea impeaching its consideration, prima facie evidence of sufficient consideration. Stone *v.* Goldberg, 6 Ala. App. 249, 60 So. 744.

In Alabama, in an action on a note, the burden of showing a consideration for the note can not be thrown upon the plaintiff except by a sworn plea. A mere plea denying consideration is not sufficient. Parkman *v.* Ely, 5 Ala. 346.

It is not necessary, in an action upon the indorsement of a bill single, for the indorsee to prove the consideration which moved from him to the indorser. The statute makes the writing evidence of the debt or duty, and requires the defendant to deny it by plea, supported by affidavit; and this although the paper indorsed was not negotiable at common law, and the indorsement was made in another state. Miller *v.* McIntyre, 9 Ala. 638.

§ 316. Replication or Reply and Subsequent Pleadings.

In General.—The maker of a note sued thereon by its assignee having pleaded any defense valid against the payee, plaintiff, desiring to invoke the aid of the law merchant, must do so by special replication. Stone *v.* Goldberg & Lewis, 6 Ala. App. 249, 60 So. 744.

Where counts of the complaint averred that the notes were negotiable, replications to pleas, in so far as they answer such counts, need not aver that the notes were negotiable or commercial. Merchants' Nat. Bank of La Fayette, Ind. *v.* Norris, 51 So. 15, 163 Ala. 481.

In a suit on a note, plaintiff must aver that he is a purchaser without notice, and the fact is properly pleaded in his replications to defendant's pleas. Slaughter *v.* First Nat. Bank, 109 Ala. 157, 19 So. 430.

In an action against O. & B. on notes in which, as alleged, they had waived their rights of exemption, B.'s plea of non est factum was confessed by plaintiff, who attempted to avoid it by replying that, though B. had not authorized the making of the notes, he had subsequently ratified them, by promising payment. To this replication B. rejoined that after the execution of the notes he neither signed, nor authorized the signing of, any writing waiving his right of exemption; and on such rejoinder plaintiff took issue, instead of demurring thereto. Held, that proof of the rejoinder eliminated the replication, leaving the case to stand on the plea of non est factum, confessed without avoidance, entitling defendant to a verdict. Brown *v.* Bamberger, 110 Ala. 342, 20 So. 114.

In a suit on a note, where plaintiff joins issue on defendant's pleas of breach of warranty, failure of consideration, fraud, and others, he thereby waives the protection of the law merchant, and the issues must be submitted to the jury. Slaughter *v.* First Nat. Bank, 109 Ala. 157, 19 So. 430.

To a plea of non est factum in an action on a negotiable note, plaintiff replied that the plea was based on an alleged material alteration, and then averred facts to avoid its effect. Held, not an admission that the note was altered, but that, if it was, that fact was not a defense, as against plaintiff. Holmes v. Bank of Ft. Gaines, 24 So. 959, 120 Ala. 493.

Sufficient.—In an action on a note, where special pleas had been filed, setting up failure of consideration, want of consideration, payment, and fraud in procuring the execution of the note, a replication that plaintiff purchased the note for a valuable consideration, that he was induced to purchase the same by assurances made him by defendant that the note was all right, and would be paid, and that, if the statements in the special pleas were true, plaintiff was ignorant of them at the time he made the purchase, is not demurrable as constituting no answer to the special pleas. Kimball v. Penney, 22 So. 899, 117 Ala. 245.

In an action on a note in which defendant pleaded that the note was given for a premium on life insurance policies issued by an association of which plaintiff was agent, and that plaintiff, before the execution of the note, made certain false representations as to the policies, the plea sufficiently showed that plaintiff was a party or privy to the policies, so that a replication that defendant was estopped from pleading such false representations by a provision in the application that no statement made by the person soliciting the application should be binding on the association unless reduced to writing and presented to its officers, was not objectionable for failure to show plaintiff's privity to the contract. Blanks v. Moore, 36 So. 783, 139 Ala. 624.

Special pleas in an action on a note set up that the payee was a foreign corporation, which had not performed the conditions required by Const., art. 14, § 4, and Code, § 1209, before business could be done in the state; and replications were filed confessing the facts so pleaded, but alleging, in avoidance, that the consideration of the note was the purchase by defendant from a foreign corporation of certain articles of interstate commerce. Held that, since the replication merely set up facts relied on as an answer to the plea, there was no departure from the theory of the complaint, which contained no allegation as to interstate commerce. Culberson v. American Trust & Banking Co., 107 Ala. 457, 19 So. 34.

Where the complaint alleged ownership of the note in suit, and the plea denied the same, a replication alleging that plaintiffs indorsed the note for defendant; that the note was delivered to a certain firm, under an agreement that it should not be negotiated, and that, if defendant failed to pay the same, plaintiffs were first to exhaust their remedies under said note and the securities pledged by defendant as collateral thereto, and that, if there should be a balance due, plaintiffs were to pay the same; that defendant failed to pay said note; and that said firm before the commencement of the action redelivered said note and securities to plaintiffs—did not constitute a departure from the complaint. Berney v. Steiner, 108 Ala. 111, 19 So. 806.

Not Sufficient.—Where the replication sets out that the note in controversy was purchased for a valuable consideration, and in reliance on statements made by defendant, a rejoinder that said statements, if made by defendant, were made under an erroneous impression as to the amount of the note, and that the note was purchased with full knowledge of all the facts, and at a greatly reduced rate, after it was due and payable, and that the contract set out in the replication was void because not in writing, signed by defendant, is insufficient. Kimball v. Penney, 22 So. 899, 117 Ala. 245.

In a suit by the indorsee against the indorser of a bill, where the latter denies demand and notice, a replication that the indorser was the real debtor, the consideration being goods sold to him, is insufficient, in that it does not negative the presumption that the bill was given to the indorser, who was the payee, for a debt due him by the drawer, or, in other words, it does not show that the bill was accommodation paper. Bolling v. McKenzie, 89 Ala. 470, 7 So. 658.

Where, in an action on a bill against the indorser, the latter denies demand and notice, a replication averring that, with knowledge of the want of demand and notice, the indorser promised to pay the bill, is insufficient, without alleging that such promise was made before suit brought. Bolling v. McKenzie, 89 Ala. 470, 7 So. 658.

Where, in a suit against an indorser of a bill of exchange, the complaint simply averred nonpayment and notice, and notice was denied, a replication that defendant was the real debtor, "owing the debt represented by the bill of exchange, the consideration thereof being goods and merchandise sold by plaintiffs to defendant," is a departure, and a demurrer thereto was properly sustained. Bolling *v.* McKenzie, 89 Ala. 470, 7 So. 658.

§ 317. Amended and Supplemental Pleadings.

In General.—In an action on a note by the payee, where only the general issue has been filed, it is in the discretion of the court to deny defendant's request, made during the trial, to file a plea denying plaintiff's title, so as to allow the introduction of an indorsement on the note by payee to a third party. Anniston *v.* Pipe Works *v.* Mary Pratt Furnace Co., 94 Ala. 606, 10 So. 259.

Proper Amendments.—To an original complaint on a promissory note, in the form prescribed by Code, p. 701, Form No. 4, an amendment setting out the instrument in full, in form a promissory note, with express conditions, and averring that the conditions had not happened, is proper. Dowling *v.* Blackman, 70 Ala. 303.

In an action on a note, the complaint may be amended by adding averments that plaintiff sues, not as payee, but as assignee and owner. Long *v.* Patterson, 51 Ala. 414.

In an action on a promissory note, payable to a third person as guardian of the plaintiff, if the complaint does not show that the note is the property of the plaintiff the defect may be remedied (Rev. Code, § 2809) by amendment. Robinson *v.* Darden, 50 Ala. 71.

Where a complaint, in an action on a note, did not allege to whom the note was payable, an amendment averring that it was made payable to a certain person who had assigned it to the plaintiff may properly be allowed. Ricketts *v.* Weeden, 64 Ala. 548.

In an action against an administrator, the complaint set forth a promissory note made by "him." Held, that the complaint might be amended by striking out "him" and inserting the name of the intestate, even after the argument to the jury had commenced. Burch *v.* Taylor, 32 Ala. 26.

In an action against two defendants on notes alleged to have been made by "him," it was not error to allow plaintiff to amend by inserting in lieu of the word "him" the word "them." Thompson Foundry & Machine Works *v.* Glass, 33 So. 811, 136 Ala. 648.

In a suit by the indorsee against the maker of a note, where the count alleged the assignment to have been before the date of the note it may be amended by the indorsement of the writ. Davis *v.* Chester, Minor 385.

Where the original complaint in an action contains a single count seeking to recover upon a promissory note, which is averred to contain a waiver of exemptions and a promise to pay reasonable attorney's fees, it is permissible to amend the complaint by adding a second count, which seeks to recover upon a promissory note, without the conditions as alleged in the original complaint; such amendment not being the substitution of an entirely new cause of action. Tanscott *v.* Gibson, 30 So. 23, 129 Ala. 503.

Amendment of complaint alleging that the notes sued on were made payable to plaintiff, so as to declare that they were made payable to others, but were the property of the plaintiff, does not set up a new cause of action; and does not give defendants the absolute right to file during the trial the additional plea of usury. Lytle *v.* Bank of Dothan, 26 So. 6, 121 Ala. 215.

Not Proper Amendments.—It is not error to refuse to allow a complaint in a single count on a note to be amended by the addition of counts on an account stated, and for goods sold and delivered, where the record does not show that the common counts were not intended to represent different causes of action. Mahan *v.* Smitherman, 71 Ala. 563.

§ 318. Setting Out, Annexing, Filing, or Production of Instrument, and Profert and Oyer.

Where the plaintiff declares in one count upon several notes, it is not indispensable to his right to recover that he should produce them all at the trial, but he may claim a verdict upon so many as he adduces. Bird *v.* Daniel, 9 Ala. 302.

§ 319. Issues, Proof, and Variance.

§ 319 (1) Issues Raised and Evidence Admissible in General.

See ante, "Verification," § 315.

Where the issue is whether the place of payment was inserted in a note after delivery, evidence that other notes executed by other persons to the same payee were left blank as to the place of payment is inadmissible. Winter *v.* Pool, 100 Ala. 503, 14 So. 411.

Where, in an action on notes under seal, the complaint described the notes as payable to a third person, and alleged that they had been duly transferred to plaintiff, and there was no plea denying their execution or indorsement, or averring that they were not the property of plaintiff, their exclusion as against the objections that they were not properly transferable, and that the legal title thereto remained in the third person, was erroneous, under Code 1896, §§ 1801, 1802, providing that the denial of the execution or assignment of an instrument sued on must be verified. International Harvester Co. *v.* Gladney, 47 So. 733, 157 Ala. 548.

In an action on an instrument in the form of a note, where the only claim to recover for an attorney's fee was under the instrument, which was not admissible in evidence, because not legally executed, testimony as to what was a reasonable attorney's fee was properly excluded. Penton *v.* Williams, 51 So. 35, 163 Ala. 603.

The defense that the intestate arranged with the holder of the note for an extension of the time of payment is not available as a defense when it is not set up by plea. Tuscaloosa, etc., Oil Co. *v.* Perry, 85 Ala. 158, 4 So. 635, 636.

A plea, of a drawer of a bill of exchange accepted by L. & Co., alleging that she drew the bill to secure a debt of her husband, L., does not on its face show that she drew the bill to secure L. & Co., and that she is estopped to assert that her husband was the sole proprietor of the firm of L. & Co.; and hence the issue of such estoppel can be raised only by replication, and not by demurrer. First Nat. Bank *v.* Leland, 122 Ala. 289, 25 So. 195.

Where an action is brought upon the indorsement of a promissory note, the plaintiff's right to recover can not be made out by proof of a fraudulent concealment or misrepresentation by the indorser in respect to the ability of the maker to pay. To make such a fraud available as a ground of action, it must be specifically declared on in a suit brought by the party defrauded. Branch Bank at Montgomery *v.* Gaffney, 9 Ala. 153.

§ 319 (2) Evidence Admissible under Declaration or Complaint.

Facts which excuse demand and notice may be proved, in an action against an indorser, under a declaration in the usual form. Kennon *v.* McRae, 7 Port. 175.

In an action on a bill of exchange by an indorsee against the acceptor, under a general replication to the pleas of non assumpsit, fraud, and want or failure of consideration, the plaintiff can not adduce evidence showing that he is an innocent holder for value, but is confined to evidence negativing the pleas. Trammell *v.* Hudmon, 56 Ala. 235.

§ 319 (3) Evidence Admissible under Plea or Answer in General.

In an action on a note alleged to have been executed by plaintiff's intestate for defendant's accommodation, the defense that the intestate arranged with the holder for an extension of time is not available unless pleaded. Tuscaloosa Cotton-Seed Oil Co. *v.* Perry, 85 Ala. 158, 4 So. 635.

Evidence that the payee of a note was insane at the time he transferred the same to plaintiff is competent under a sworn plea denying that plaintiff was the party really interested in the note sued on. Walker *v.* Winn, 39 So. 12, 142 Ala. 560, 110 Am. St. Rep. 50.

Where, in an action on a note, defendant pleaded in bar a contract whereby he was entitled to return the piano for which the note was given, that plaintiff had declined to receive it, and that defendant was ready to deliver it to him, and the execution of the contract was not denied by verified replication, it was error to exclude proof of defendant's offer and readiness to deliver the piano to plaintiff. Alley *v.* Jesse French Piano & Organ Co., 42 So. 623, 148 Ala. 303.

Defendants rented lands from plaintiffs for a year, entered into possession, and remained undistributed, executing to plaintiffs, individually, a note, stating that it was given for rent of certain described lands. Held that, under plea denying plaintiff's ownership of the note, defendants might show by parol that plaintiffs had been school trustees of a fractional township in which the lands (which were the sixteenth section school lands) were situated, and that before the renting, but unknown to the parties, who contracted under the common mistake that plaintiffs were still school trustees, the legislature had incorporated the lands into another township, the trustees of which claimed the debt. Borland *v.* Box, 62 Ala. 87.

The defendant may contest the authority of the plaintiff to sue on a promissory note, upon which action is brought, under a plea, upon which issue is joined, that the plaintiff is not the legal holder of such note. Bryant *v.* Owen, 2 Stew. & P. 134.

Under a plea, by the maker of a note, that it was procured by false and fraudulent representations of the payee, it is error to admit evidence showing he made like representations to a third party. Bomar *v.* Rosser, 123 Ala. 641, 26 So. 510.

§ 319 (4) Evidence Admissible under Plea of Non Est Factum.

In an action on a note, a special plea of non est factum, alleging a material alteration admits the execution of the note, so that it may be admitted in evidence without preliminary proof of its execution. Brown *v.* Johnson Bros., 135 Ala. 608, 33 So. 683.

Under plea of failure and want of consideration, it may be proved that a note sued on, though absolute in its terms, was given as an indemnity to the plaintiff against loss as surety. Laroqen *v.* Russell, 7 Ala. 798.

Since the adoption of the Code, the defense of fraud is available, under the plea of set-off, to a note given for the purchase money of land. Kannady *v.* Lambert, 37 Ala. 57.

In an action on a promissory note by an assignee against the maker, the latter may show, under a plea of payment, that judgment was rendered against him as garnishee for the amount of the note, as debtor of one to whom the note had been transferred, and that he had paid such judgment, to prove which defense the record of the garnishment suit, together with parol proof of payment of the judgment and transfer of the note, is admissible. Ross *v.* Pitts, 39 Ala. 606.

In an action on a note made for the purchase money of lands, where plaintiff consents to receive pleas stated on the papers as "failure of consideration; fraudulent representation, by which defendant was induced to make the purchase," and merely denies their truth by replications, on which issues are submitted to the jury, it will be intended that the defenses were open to defendant, and that the pleas severally alleged such facts as established them; therefore evidence on the part of defendant which does not support such issues must be rejected. Knight *v.* Turner, 11 Ala. 636.

§ 319 (5) Evidence Admissible under General Issue.

Evidence that the plaintiff, in an action on a note, is not the owner of the note, may be given under the general issue. Evans *v.* Gordon, 8 Port. 142.

In assumpsit on a promissory note by the indorsee against the maker, want of legal title in the plaintiff may be shown under the plea of nonassumpsit. Birch *v.* Tillotson, 16 Ala. 387.

In assumpsit by the indorsee of a promissory note, the fact that plaintiff is not the owner of the note is not a good defense under the general issue. Agee *v.* Medlock, 25 Ala. 281.

In an action on a note given for the purchase money of land, a promise by the vendor to cancel and destroy the note, in consideration of the fact that the land was subject to overflow, when he had represented that it was not, is available as a defense under the general issue. Kannady *v.* Lambert, 37 Ala. 57.

In an action on a note for the costs of protest and notice, evidence of waiver of protest and notice before maturity is not admissible under a general denial. White *v.* Keith, 97 Ala. 668, 12 So. 611.

The fact that a signer of a note is a surety of one of the other signers is not available under a plea of general issue; there being nothing on the face of the note to show the relations between the signers. Sherrer *v.* Enterprise Banking Co., 160 Ala. 329, 49 So. 779.

Where the defense that a note was given for a gambling consideration is relied upon, it must be pleaded specially, when the note is in the hands of an indorsee. Baldwin *v.* Brogden, 2 Stew. 9.

§ 319 (6) Matters That Must Be Proved.

Where, in assumpsit against the maker of a note, the plaintiff's note was offered in evidence under a general plea of set-off, it was necessary to prove its execution. Taylor *v.* Morgan, 6 Ala. 893.

The fact that a lease, not alleged in the complaint in an action on rent notes, is alleged in the replication as a part of the same transaction as the making of the notes, does not make it admissible without proof of its execution, as it was not made the foundation of the suit. Thompson Foundry & Machine Works *v.* Glass, 136 Ala. 648, 33 So. 811.

The general issue merely throws upon the plaintiff, in an action by an indorsee against an indorser, the burden of proving that execution against the maker is unsatisfied, under the statute. Woodward *v.* Harbin, 4 Ala. 534.

Where in a suit on a note the answer was not verified, and there was no plea denying the execution of the note, or that the same had been materially altered since its execution, an objection to the introduction of the note in evidence on the ground that defendant had not executed it, and that it had been altered in a material respect, was not sustainable. Noble *v.* Gilliam, 136 Ala. 618, 33 So. 681. On this point the court cites the following cases: Dreyspring *v.* Loeb, 119 Ala. 282, 24 So. 734; Henderson *v.* Brown Co., 125 Ala. 566, 567, 28 So. 79; Smith *v.* Hiles-Carver Co., 107 Ala. 272, 18 So. 37; Paige *v.* Broadfoot, 100 Ala. 610, 13 So. 426. The cases of McGhee *v.* Importers,' etc., Nat. Bank, 93 Ala. 196, 9 So. 734, and Clements *v.* Motley, 120 Ala. 575, 24 So. 947, in conflict with these cases on this point, are overruled.

§ 319 (7) Variance.

See ante, "Persons to Whom to Be Given," § 251.

In General.—The omission to set out in a declaration on a promissory note the specific consideration, and that it might be discharged by other paper, can not be taken advantage of as a variance, there being no attempt to set it out in hæc verba. McRae *v.* Raser, 9 Port. 122.

It is not necessary to fill up a blank indorsement by inserting the plaintiff's name although the declaration describes him as an indorsee. Sawyer *v.* Patterson, 11 Ala. 523.

In a suit on a note in which the complaint is founded upon the note alone, the plaintiff can recover only the face interest of the note, notwithstanding a subsequent valid agreement to pay a higher rate. Hunt *v.* Hall, 37 Ala. 702.

In an action on a certificate of deposit, if there should appear upon the trial a variance in the description of the certificate, plaintiff may recover on the count for money had and received. Talladega Ins. Co. *v.* Landers, 43 Ala. 115.

It seems that an actual variance in the description of a name, notwithstanding the statute of eighteen hundred and eleven, will still be fatal. Dew *v.* Garner, 7 Port. 503.

Fatal Variance.—A variance between the description of a bill or note, and the one produced in evidence, is fatal. May *v.* Miller, 27 Ala. 515.

As a writing in the form of a promissory note for the payment of a sum of money "in the common currency of Alabama," is not an undertaking to pay the sum expressed in coin, but in bank notes, it is inadmissible under a declaration describing it as a promissory note for the payment of a sum in numero. Carlisle *v.* Davis, 7 Ala. 42.

A protest describing a bill as dated the 26th January is not admissible as evidence to show the protest of a bill dated the 28th January. Bank at Decatur *v.* Hodges, 9 Ala. 631.

No recovery can be had by an indorsee against the acceptor of a bill under a complaint alleging a transfer to plaintiff of the legal title by indorsement, where the indorsement on the bill offered in evidence conveyed only an equitable right. Alabama Coal Min. Co. *v.* Brainard, 35 Ala. 476.

Where, in an action on a note by the indorsee thereof, defendant pleaded illegality, averring that the cotton future contract on which the note was based was made by defendant with plaintiff, but the evidence showed that the alleged contract was made with other parties, there was a fatal variance. Birmingham Trust & Savings Co. *v.* Curry, 160 Ala. 370, 49 So. 319.

In an action on a promissory note, the complaint averred that the "plaintiff claims of the defendants the sum of $3,030, due by promissory note made by G. H. H. and H. T. H. on the 8th day of November, 1853, and payable on the 1st of March, 1854, with interest thereon; said note being indorsed by defendants on the day of its date, and before the same was accepted by the plaintiff, and received and held by the plaintiff on the faith and credit of their said indorsement, they having indorsed the same for the makers thereof, and thereby induced the plaintiff to take and accept the same." Held, that a promissory note payable to plaintiff "or order," negotiable and payable at the bank of Mobile, for value received, and indorsed by the defendants, was not admissible in evidence. Clancy *v.* Hilliard, 39 Ala. 713.

Under a declaration against one as indorser of a promissory note, evidence of a subsequent promise is not admissible. Davis *v.* Campbell, 3 Stew. 319.

Under a complaint on a promissory note, an instrument under seal, corresponding in other respects with the note declared on, is not admissible evidence. Reed *v.* Scott, 30 Ala. 640.

Under a declaration which describes a note for the payment of a sum of money at an appointed day, it is not allowable to give in evidence a note which conforms to the description in the declaration, and contains the additional stipulation to pay "interest from the date." Sawyer *v.* Patterson, 11 Ala. 523.

Where the declaration on a note sets out an indorsement, and the note does not correspond with the allegation, the variance is fatal. Strader *v.* Alexander, 9 Port. 441.

A complaint declaring on a written order in which defendants were instructed to pay over to plaintiff, or order, all sums of money for lumber, is fatally variant from an order offered in evidence directing defendants to pay to the order of plaintiff an amount due him on lumber shipped, and no recovery can be had. Leatherbury *v.* Spotswood, Turner & Co., 145 Ala. 655, 39 Ala. 588.

Where a bill averred that defendant got the note in question as a gift from his father, plaintiff's intestate, but the proof showed that the note was surrendered by the father to defendant in consideration of a new contract entered into between them, the variance was fatal to any relief under the bill. Sellers *v.* Sellers (Ala.), 39 So. 990.

Where, in an action on a life policy, the defendant pleaded forfeiture by reason of the failure of the insured to pay a premium note "payable at Central National Bank, New York City," such plea was not sustained by the production of a note "payable at the Lowery Banking Company, Atlanta, Ga." New York Life Ins. Co. *v.* McPherson, 137 Ala. 116, 33 So. 825.

When the complaint describes a promissory note, and the instrument offered in evidence at the trial proves to be under seal, there is such a variance as to lead to its rejection. Reed *v.* Scott, 30 Ala. 640; McCrummen *v.* Campbell, 82 Ala. 566, 2 So. 482.

On a note made payable to the "treasurer of the Manual Labor Institute of South Alabama," a suit can not be maintained by "Madison College," without an averment that it is the same corporation, and that the name had been changed since the making of the note and before the institution of the suit. Madison College *v.* Burke, 6 Ala. 494.

On a plea that an indorsement was conditioned on the maker's wife signing it as comaker, evidence that the condition was that she sign as maker was a variance. Glover *v.* Jefferson County Savings Bank, 6 Ala. App. 195, 60 So. 548.

In an action by the assignee against the assignor on an assigned note, where the form of complaint is used which is given by the Code (page 552), and the complaint contains no express statement of the amount of the note, the amount must be taken to be that claimed in the commencement of the complaint, and proof of a note for a different amount is a variance. Fournier *v.* Black, 32 Ala. 41.

When the plea, in an action on two notes, alleged that the consideration of both notes was plaintiff's promise to keep sufficient money in the hands of a brokerage company to prevent a future contract for cotton from being sold, and the evidence was that one of the notes was given for money loaned defendant to cover losses on the cotton theretofore sustained by him, there was a fatal variance, and plaintiff was entitled to recover on both notes. Emmett *v.* Hooper, 157 Ala. 586, 47 So. 1006.

A note made payable at a particular bank will not support a declaration upon a note described as payable generally. Puckett *v.* King, 2 Ala. 570; Clancy *v.* Hilliard, 39 Ala. 713; Clark *v.* Moses, 50 Ala. 326; Morris *v.* Poillon, 50 Ala. 403.

Where the signature to a note is not illegible, and is not that of defendant, and the declaration, without recitals or averments, misdescribes the note; it can not authorize a recovery against the defendant. Dew *v.* Garner, 7 Port. 503.

A declaration upon a promissory note, not stating when it was made payable, is not supported by a note payable nine months after date. Caller *v.* Boykin, Minor 206.

In an action on a promissory note, defendant alleged that plaintiff's intestate agreed to take stock in the defendant corporation in payment of all his claims against the same. The evidence showed that he agreed to subscribe for additional stock, and pay for the same by satisfying accounts which he held, or might thereafter hold, against the corporation, and the note in question was executed subsequent to such agreement. Held, that the allegations were not supported by the evidence. Tuscaloosa, etc., Oil Co. *v.* Perry, 85 Ala. 158, 4 So. 635.

Immaterial Variance.—Where, in an action, by the indorsee of a note against the maker, the declaration described it as payable to A. B., or order, and the note was payable alone to A. B., it was held to be an immaterial variance. Harrison *v.* Weaver, 2 Port. 542.

The misdescription of the name of an indorser in the certificate appended to the protest, certifying that the notice was sent to one "Chomason," when the indorser's name was "Thomason," is not sufficient to exclude the protest as evidence, the true name appearing in the copy of the bill. Bank at Decatur *v.* Hodges, 9 Ala. 631.

In an action on a promissory note, it is set out, in the declaration, "the own proper hand of the defendant being thereto subscribed." The declaration is supported by a note, subscribed "S. B., executrix of W. B., by her agent, F. G. H." Baldwin *v.* Stebbins, Minor 180.

Where the note sued acknowledges indebtedness to A., and promises to pay the amount thereof to B., sheriff, to satisfy an attachment against A., the failure of the declaration to aver the capacity in which B. was to receive the money, or the purpose to which he was to apply it, is not a material variance. Bowie *v.* Foster, Minor 264.

The declaration stated that "Frederick W. C." made his promissory note. The note offered in evidence was signed "F. W. C." Held, that it was sufficiently described to make it admissible evidence. Chandler *v.* Hudson, 8 Ala. 366.

A bill of exchange drawn by "Ebenezer Hearn," may be given in evidence under a declaration on a bill alleged to have been drawn by "Ebenezer Hearne." Coster *v.* Thompson, 19 Ala. 717.

In an action against an indorser, where the day on which demand was made is erroneously alleged, plaintiff is not thereby prevented from proving on the proper day. Quigley *v.* Primrose, 8 Port. 247; Crawford *v.* Camfield, 6 Ala. 153; Smith *v.* Robinson, 11 Ala. 270.

If a declaration on a note state that it was given at a particular time, this is not descriptive of the note, and a variance between it and the date of the note is not material. Lawson *v.* Townes, 2 Ala. 373.

Where the copy of the bill indorsed on the protest differs in some one or more words from that declared on, and produced at the trial, the protest should, notwithstanding, be allowed to go before the jury, that the plaintiff may show, by other testimony, the identity of the copy with the original adduced. Leigh *v.* Lightfoot, 11 Ala. 935.

Where a note contains a stipulation for the benefit of the maker as to the manner of payment, and the maker neglects to avail himself of the privilege, the complaint in an action on the note may describe it as an absolute promise to pay money. Weaver *v.* Lapsley, 42 Ala. 601.

When the declaration sets out a note payable "one day after date," and the note offered in evidence is payable "one day after," the word "date" being omitted, the variance is immaterial, and the omission will be supplied by intendment. White *v.* Word, 22 Ala. 442.

Not Variance.—A duebill may be declared on as a promissory note. Johnson *v.* Johnson, Minor 263.

Averments of due presentment or demand are sustained by showing excuse for failure to present. Taylor *v.* Branch, 1 Stew. & P. 249, 23 Am. Dec. 293.

Where the complaint in an action against two indorsers of a note alleges that they each promised to pay the note, the plaintiff may recover on proof of a separate promise by each; a joint promise not being necessary. Brown *v.* Fowler, 32 So. 584, 133 Ala. 310.

There is no variance between "Formey" and "Formby" in the name of the payee of a note. Taylor *v.* Strickland, 37 Ala. 642.

An action on rent notes was brought against "Julius Thompson and wife, May Thompson, doing business as 'Thompson Foundry & Machine Works.'" The notes were signed "Thompson F. & M. Wks. Julius Thompson." Held, that an objection that the notes were inadmissible on the ground of variance was no merit. Thompson, etc., Mach. Works *v.* Glass, 136 Ala. 648, 33 So. 811.

In an action on a promissory note, against the maker, the declaration alleged that the note was made by "John" C., and the note offered in evidence was signed by "J." C. Held, that this was not a variance. Cantly *v.* Hopkins, 5 Stew. & P. 58.

In an action against the defendant, as maker of a promissory note, to which the signature is illegible, and is not attempted to be described in the declaration, there is not such a variance between the note and declaration as can operate to defeat the action. It is like a signature evidenced by a mark. Dew *v.* Garner, 7 Port. 503.

§ 320. Presumptions and Burden of Proof.

See ante, "Verification," § 315; post, "In General," § 321; "Execution, Delivery, and Identity of Instruments," § 322; "Consideration," § 323.

§ 321. —— In General.

Presumptions.—Promissory notes being negotiable at common law, in the absence of proof to the contrary, they are presumed to be negotiable in a sister state. Dunn *v.* Adams, 1 Ala. 527, 35 Am. Dec. 42; Beal *v.* Wainwright, 6 Ala. 156.

The legal presumption arising from the drawing of a bill of exchange is that the drawer is indebted to the payee. Bolling *v.* McKenzie, 89 Ala. 470, 7 So. 658.

In an action on a bill of exchange, where it is averred that the bill bears a certain date, but it is not stated when it matures, it will be presumed that it was payable on presentment. Bolling *v.* McKenzie, 89 Ala. 470, 7 So. 658.

It will be presumed that the amount for attorney's fees stipulated for in a note on failure to pay at maturity is a reasonable amount. Stephenson *v.* Allison, 26 So. 290, 123 Ala. 439.

An intent to defraud the government by the omission of a stamp from a promissory note will not be presumed, but such intent must be proved as any other fraud is proved. Whigham *v.* Pickett, 43 Ala. 140.

Plaintiff's Burden of Proof.—Where the payee of a written order, requesting defendant to pay out of the proceeds of a certain judgment, when collected, brings suit, after acceptance, for defendant's negligence in collecting and failing to pay when collected, the burden of proving negligence is no plaintiff, and not on defendant to prove diligence. Gliddon *v.* McKinstry, 28 Ala. 408.

Where, in an action on a note payable in another state, plaintiff offers no evidence as to the interest laws of that state, he can not recover any interest. Kraus *v.* Torry, 40 So. 956, 146 Ala. 548.

When a bill is drawn payable at a place beyond the limits of the state, interest and damages can not be recovered of the acceptor, on its dishonor, without proving the law of the place of payment, giving such damages and interest. Dickinson *v.* Branch Bank at Mobile, 12 Ala. 54.

Defendant's Burden of Proof.—Where the holder declares on one of a set of exchange, it is not necessary to account for the nonproduction of the rest. Any ground of defense which may arise in reference to another of the set it devolves on defendant to make. Hazzard *v.* Shelton, 15 Ala. 62.

An accommodation acceptor of a bill of exchange, to be used by the drawer for a special purpose, need not show, in an action thereon by one to whom the drawer transferred it contrary to the terms of the acceptance, that he would not have accepted it for the purpose for which it was used. Farley Nat. Bank *v.* Henderson, 24 So. 428, 118 Ala. 441.

Nor that by diverting it the drawer failed to receive as much benefit as he would have received had it been used in accordance with the terms of the acceptance. Farley Nat. Bank *v.* Henderson, 24 So. 428, 118 Ala. 441.

Nor that he has not ratified the diversion. Farley Nat. Bank *v.* Henderson, 24 So. 428, 118 Ala. 441.

Nor that he was not indemnified against loss as such acceptor. Farley Nat. Bank *v.* Henderson, 24 So. 428, 118 Ala. 441.

He need not show that he was injured by the diversion. Farley Nat. Bank *v.* Henderson, 24 So. 428, 118 Ala. 441.

§ 322. —— Execution, Delivery, and Identity of Instruments.

See ante, "Verification," § 315.

Presumptions.—The mere fact that the same name appears as that of the maker and of an indorser of a note does not raise the presumption that it was made and indorsed by the same person. Curry *v.* Bank of Mobile, 8 Port. 360.

When the place of drawing is not disclosed in an action on a bill of exchange, it will, on demurrer, be inferred to be that stated in the margin of the declaration. Moore *v.* Bradford, 3 Ala. 550.

Plaintiff's Burden of Proof.—Upon a plea of non est factum in an action on an instrument in the form of a note, the burden is on plaintiff to prove the execution of the instrument before it is admissible in evidence. Penton *v.* Williams, 51 So. 35, 163 Ala. 603; Himes Supply Co. *v.* Parker, 157 Ala. 512, 47 So. 794.

Under Code 1907, § 3967, requiring a written instrument which is the foundation of a suit to be received without proof of execution, unless its execution is denied by plea, when the burden is on plaintiff to show its execution, the burden was upon plaintiff to show the execution of the note, under the plea of non est factum. Gillespie *v.* Hester, 49 So. 580, 160 Ala. 444.

If, in an action on a note, defendant denies, by plea, that he made the note, plaintiff may read it to the jury, it he show prima facie that defendant made the note, authorized it, or adopted it as his own. Knapp *v.* McBride, 7 Ala. 19.

Under Code, § 2769, providing that every written contract, the foundation of the suit, purporting to be executed by the party sought to be charged, is evidence of its own execution, it was not necessary, on default in an action on a note, to offer proof of the execution of the note in the manner alleged in the complaint. Ledbetter, etc., Loan Ass'n *v.* Vinton, 108 Ala. 644, 18 So. 692.

In an action against a firm on a note given by one partner in the name of the firm as security for the debt of a third person, the burden of proving the assent of the other partners is on plaintiff. Rolston *v.* Click, 1 Stew. 526.

In an action on a note dated on Sunday, the burden is on plaintiff to show that it was in fact executed on a day which was not Sunday. Hauerwas *v.* Goodloe, 101 Ala. 162, 13 So. 567.

Where a note was shown to have been signed on Sunday, but not in the presence of plaintiffs, and it bore date on a different day, the burden was held not to be on plaintiffs to show that it was not delivered on Sunday. Flanagan *v.* Meyer, 41 Ala. 132.

Defendant's Burden of Proof.—Where in an action on a note defendant interposes a general plea of non est factum, and plaintiff proves signature, the note itself giving no indication of alteration since signature, the burden of showing such alteration is on defendant. Bouldin *v.* Barclay, 25 So. 827, 121 Ala. 427.

"Where, to an action on a note or bond, the defendant interposes a special plea of non est factum, not denying his signature, but setting up alteration after execution, the burden is upon him to show such alteration, unless the paper itself furnishes some evidence or indication of having been tampered with—some badge of the alleged fraud, so to speak. Montgomery *v.* Crossthwait, 90 Ala. 553, 8 So. 498; Barcliff *v.* Treece, 77 Ala. 528. This upon the presumption, in favor of good faith and against fraud, where the paper bears no evidence to the contrary, that the paper is as it was when it was signed." Bouldin *v.* Barclay, 121 Ala. 427, 25 So. 827, 828.

In an action on a note, where defendant's evidence was sufficient to raise grave suspicions that it had been altered, a charge that the burden of proof was on defendant to show, to the reasonable satisfaction of the jury, that the note had been changed without the payor's consent, was erroneous, as misplacing the burden of proof. Glover *v.* Gentry, 104 Ala. 222, 16 So. 38.

When a note is presented collaterally, and not as the foundation of the action, the party asserting or relying on it must prove its execution. Garrett *v.* Garrett, 64 Ala. 263.

In an action on a note signed by a firm by one of the partners, against the other partner, where defendant pleads non est factum, the burden is on plaintiff to show the existence of the partnership, and the execution of the note by authority of one or more of the partners; but, where such proof is made, a prima facie liability is established against the partnership, which shifts the burden of proof to defendant to establish any defense which is admissible under his pleas. Guice *v.* Thornton, 76 Ala. 466.

On the trial of an issue before the probate court between the distributees and administrator of an estate, respecting the genuineness of the intestate's signature to a note, payable to the administrator, the burden of proof is on him, and a mere preponderance of evidence does not necessarily entitle him to a verdict. Kirksey *v.* Kirksey, 41 Ala. 626.

§ 323. —— Consideration.

§ 323 (1) Presumptions as to Consideration in General.

A negotiable instrument is presumed to be based on a valid and sufficient consideration. Allen *v.* Dickson, Minor 119; Bowie *v.* Foster, Minor 264; McMahon *v.* Crockett, Minor 362; Hunley *v.* Torg, 5 Port. 154; Jones *v.* Rives, 3 Ala. 11; Thompson *v.* Armstrong, 5 Ala. 383; Thompson *v.* Hall, 16 Ala. 204; Bird *v.* Wooley, 23 Ala. 717; Martin *v.* Foster, 83 Ala. 213, 3 So. 422.

The execution of a note raises a presumption of a settlement of accounts between the maker and payee prior to its date; hence a receipt for goods delivered by the maker to be accounted for by the payee, dated two years before the execution of the note, can not be proved as a set-off thereto, in the absence of evidence showing that it was not included in the settlement. Copeland *v.* Clark, 2 Ala. 388.

§ 323 (2) Presumptions as to Consideration and Burden of Proving Consideration.

The onus of proof of the consideration of a promissory note, can not be thrown on the plaintiff by any mode of pleading. Jones *v.* Rives, 3 Ala. 11.

In an action on a note, a charge that, if the note was given to secure future advances, the burden of proving that advances were made, and that there was a balance due on the note, was upon plaintiff, was properly refused; the note being prima facie evidence of sufficient consideration. Brown *v.* Johnson Bros., 33 So. 683, 135 Ala. 608.

Where suspicion is cast upon a mercantile security, the holder must prove that he gave a valuable consideration for it, and acquired it before it was dishonored. Boyd *v.* McIvor, 11 Ala. 822.

In an action on a bill of exchange, by an endorsee, the acceptor, proof by the defendant that the bill was procured by fraud, or that there was a want or failure of consideration, casts on the plaintiff the burden of proving that he paid a valuable consideration for it. Ross *v.* Drinkard, 35 Ala. 434.

§ 323 (3) Presumptions as to Consideration and Burden of Proving Want or Failure.

In General.—When a note is given in payment of the debt of another, and a recepit for the payment of the debt taken in the name of the debtor, the payee can not recover on the note against the maker, on proof of these facts only; the privity or assent of the debtor must also be shown. Williams *v.* Sims, 22 Ala. 512.

Where a firm note is given in discharge of a separate debt of one of the partners, the burden is on the holder or creditor to repel the presumption of fraud, by showing the consent of the other partners to the transaction. Guice *v.* Thornton, 76 Ala. 466.

Presumptions.—A promise in writing indorsed on a note, to pay the amount thereof if the maker does not, imports a consideration until the contrary is shown. Nesbit *v.* Bradford, 6 Ala. 746.

When suit is brought on a note in the name of the payee for the use of another person, if the defendant does not by plea deny its execution, the note itself imports a consideration, and this presumption is not repelled by showing that the payee "never was the owner of the note, and never put it in circulation or authorized it to be done." Bird *v.* Wooley, 23 Ala. 717.

Where the evidence leaves the question as to the consideration of a note in doubt, the presumption that there was a sufficient consideration created by the note must prevail. Martin *v.* Foster, 83 Ala. 213, 3 So. 422.

Burden of Proving Want of Consideration.—Where a consideration is expressed, or there is a presumption of consideration, the burden of showing want or failure of consideration is on defendant. Jones *v.* Rives, 3 Ala. 11; Martin *v.* Foster, 83 Ala. 213, 3 So. 422.

A note sued on is prima facie evidence of consideration therefor, and the burden is on defendant to show there was no consideration. Gates *v.* Morton Hardware Co., 40 So. 509, 146 Ala. 692.

In an action against the acceptor of an order the burden was on the latter to show want of consideration. Ragsdale *v.* Gresham, 37 So. 367, 141 Ala. 308.

Where an unconditional note is made for professional services to be rendered by the payee as an attorney at law, payable on a day certain, the payee's breach of the stipulations which were the consideration for the note is a matter of defense, and must be proved by the maker. Douglass *v.* Eason, 36 Ala. 687.

§ 324. Validity.

In an action on notes given for fertilizers, the burden of proving that the bags were not tagged as required by law was on defendant. Alabama Nat. Bank *v.* C. C. Parker & Co., 40 So. 987, 146 Ala. 513.

§ 325. —— Nature of Liability.

Where two names are signed to a note, there is an evidential, rebuttable presumption that they are comakers and equally bound. Smith *v.* Pitts, 52 So. 402, 167 Ala. 461.

It will be presumed that indorsements were made in the order in which they appear on the note. Price *v.* Lavender, 38 Ala. 389.

§ 326. —— Transfer and Ownership in General.

§ 326 (1) In General.

Presumptions.—The payee of a note is presumed to be the owner thereof until the contrary is shown. Grigsby *v.* Nance, 3 Ala. 347; Turnley *v.* Black, 44 Ala. 159.

In trover for a note which plaintiff "traded off to defendant," with a reservation that he should have the privilege of redeeming it by paying $55 at any time before it became due, it was held that the court could not infer it was indorsed absolutely to defendant, so as to vest in him the legal title, and judgment was rendered for plaintiff. Trulove *v.* Brown, 21 Ala. 544.

Burden of Proof.—The onus of proving the beneficial ownership of a note is not cast on plaintiff without a sworn plea. Broadhead *v.* Jones, 39 Ala. 96; Nesbitt *v.* Pearson, 33 Ala. 668.

In an action by a bank on a note against a surety, proof that the note was offered for discount to the bank, and refused, without another surety, which was not obtained, was held sufficient to compel the bank, in order to show title, to prove that the note was afterwards discounted. Findley *v.* State Bank, 6 Ala. 244.

Where the will in question did not show an original indebtedness from the deceased to the complainant, evidenced by the note, but only that the note was made to be discounted in the bank for the purpose of raising money, and that the complainant paid it to the bank as endorser, proof of the note, merely, would not establish the liability of the maker of the note, but it was necessary to go further, and prove the payment of the money to the bank. Borland *v.* Phillips, 3 Ala. 718.

The statute of 1819, exempting plaintiffs in suits on assigned notes from proving the assignment, unless defendant makes an affidavit that the same is forged, is not applicable to cases where an indorsed note is produced by defendant as a set-off. Cass *v.* Northrop, 1 Stew. & P. 89.

§ 326 (2) Possession.

Presumptions.—The holder of a note may maintain an action thereon against the maker in the name of the payee, though the note never went into the payee's hands, the presumption being that he is a bona fide holder. Bird *v.* Wooley, 23 Ala. 717.

The legal presumption arising from the possession of the bill by the drawee before its maturity, or after its dishonor, is, that a consideration has been paid by him to some other lawful holder, but this presumption may be rebutted by showing that he took up the bill as drawee, or obtained it from the drawer. Desha, etc., Co. *v.* Stewart, 6 Ala. 852.

Where a note is in the possession of one who appears to have previously transferred it, the legal presumption is that it has been regularly returned to him. Price *v.* Lavender, 38 Ala. 389.

Plaintiff's Burden of Proof.—Under Code 1886, § 1761, providing that a negotiable instrument payable to a person or bearer shall be construed as payable to such person or order, a person other than the payee, who brings suit on such instrument without indorsement, and who is shown to have been the agent of the payee, and originally brought the suit in that capacity, but amended by striking out the name of his principal, has the burden of proving, if his beneficial ownership is denied, by evidence other than the mere possession of the note, that he is the beneficial owner. Cobb *v.* Bryant, 86 Ala. 316, 5 So. 586.

Defendant's Burden of Proof.—While a blank indorsement of a note vests title to the note in the holder thereof, yet if the note, after having been indorsed, gets back into the possession of the payee or the indorser, his possession shows a prima facie legal title to the note upon which suit may be predicated, and the burden is on defendant in such suit to show plaintiff's actual want of title. Hughes *v.* Black (Ala.), 39 So. 984.

§ 326 (3) Indorsement.

Presumptions.—Where the complaint in an action against two indorsers of a note alleges that they indorsed it, the presumption is that they indorsed separately, and evidence that either promised to pay the note is good, as against him. Brown *v.* Fowler, 32 So. 584, 133 Ala. 310.

Plaintiff's Burden of Proof.—In an action on promissory notes, where trial was had upon issues raised by a complaint alleging that the notes were negotiable and pleas of non est factum and one denying plaintiff's ownership, the notes were not admissible in evidence until plaintiff proved their execution and his legal title thereto by indorsement at the time of the commencement of the action. Peevey *v.* Tapley, 42 So. 561, 148 Ala. 320.

To recover on a bill of exchange, plaintiff must prove such of the indorsements as carry title to him, and it is error to receive the bill in evidence without proof of the payee's indorsement. Jefferson County Savings Bank *v.* Interstate Savings Bank, 59 So. 348, 5 Ala. App. 368.

If the defendant does not, by sworn plea, controvert either the making of an irregular indorsement on a note, or that it was made to the plaintiff, proof of the execution of the indorsement is not necessary. Price *v.* Lavender, 38 Ala. 389.

Defendant's Burden of Proof.—Where an indorsed note is relied on as a set-off, the indorsement must be proved. Cass *v.* Northhop, 1 Stew. & P. 89.

The statute providing that plaintiffs in suits brought by assignees of bonds, notes, or other writings need not prove the assignments, unless defendants make affidavit that they believe them forged, does not apply to a case where an indorsed note is relied on as a set-off, and hence the indorsement must be proved. Cass *v.* Northrop, 1 Stew. & P. 89.

§ 327. —— Good Faith and Payment of Value.

§ 327 (1) Presumptions as to Bona Fides in General.

The transferee or holder of a negotiable instrument is presumed to have obtained it in good faith, before maturity, and for value. Minell *v.* Reed, 26 Ala. 730; Lehman *v.* Tallassee Mfg. Co., 64 Ala. 567.

Where a note was transferred before maturity, and the payee indorsed it, waiving protest and guarantying prompt payment, it will be presumed that the transfer was for a valuable consideration. First Nat. Bank *v.* Sproull, 105 Ala. 275, 16 So. 879.

In assumpsit by the payee of a check payable to plaintiff "or bearer," for money received thereon from the drawee by defendant, without the indorsement of the payee, and without her knowledge or consent, a custom of passing such checks by delivery can not affect the operation of Code, § 1761, requiring such checks to be construed as if payable "to order." Therefore, though the check was received by defendant before maturity, it can not be presumed that it was obtained bona fide and for a valuable consideration. First Nat. Bank *v.* Nelson, 105 Ala. 180, 16 So. 707.

§ 327 (2) Burden of Proof as to Bona Fides in General.

See ante, "Presumptions as to Consideration and Burden of Proving Want or Failure," § 323 (3).

Plaintiff's Burden of Proof.—Where a valid defense is shown to exist between the original parties to a negotiable instrument, and the holder claims protection against it, the burden is on him to show that he acquired the paper in good faith, for a valuable consideration, without notice of such defect before maturity. Chambers *v.* Falkner, 65 Ala. 448.

The indorsee of negotiable paper, in order to relieve himself from any discounts, cross demands, or failure of consideration which the maker could have set up against the payee, must show that he purchased it for value before maturity. Johnson *v.* Hanover Nat. Bank, 88 Ala. 271, 6 So. 909.

In an action by an indorsee against the maker of a negotiable note, payable in bank, plaintiff must show that he received the note before maturity, for a valuable consideration, to avoid the defense of a want or failure of consideration in the origin of the note. Marston *v.* Forward, 5 Ala. 347.

In an action by the indorsee of a bill against the drawer, who had also indorsed it, proof that it was so drawn and indorsed for the accommodation of the acceptor, without consideration, is sufficient to throw the burden on plaintiff to show that he is a holder before maturity, for value. Battle *v.* Weems, 44 Ala. 105.

It is incumbent on an indorsee of negotiable paper, if he would prevent usury from being set up against him, to show that he became the innocent holder of the paper for a valuable consideration before its maturity. Hanrick *v.* Andrews, 9 Port. 9.

Where, to a plea that defendant was induced to sign the acceptance of bills of exchange sued on by fraudulent representations of payee, the transferee replied that he was a purchaser for value, before maturity, and without notice, the burden was on the transferee to show that the bills were purchased by him before maturity and for a valuable consideration. H. T. Woodall & Son *v.* People's Nat. Bank of Leesburg, Va., 45 So. 194, 153 Ala. 576.

If payment is made by the maker to the payee, and the note is not delivered up at the time of payment, and suit is afterwards brought thereon against the maker by another holder claiming to be the indorsee or transferee of the note, the burden of proof rests on plaintiff in the action (defendant having proved the payment) to show that defendant had notice of the transfer or indorsement before the payment was made. Hart *v.* Freeman, 42 Ala. 567.

The doctrine has been long settled in the supreme court, as to negotiable paper, that when fraud or illegality in putting it in circulation is shown, or any defense addressed to its consideration, the onus is cast on the holder to prove that he acquired it in good faith, before maturity, upon a valuable consideration, and in the usual course of business. Wetumpka *v.* Wetumpka Wharf Co., 63 Ala. 611.

Where a negotiable instrument has been wrongfully parted with by one holding it as trustee, one claiming protection against the real owner must show that he took it for a valuable consideration, in the usual course of trade, before maturity, and without knowledge of any defect in title of his transferror. Reid *v.* Bank of Mobile, 70 Ala. 199.

Where a note is put in circulation by fraud, the holder is bound to show himself a bona fide possessor, and if he fail to do so, it will be a question for the jury, whether his possession is not mala fide. Wallace *v.* Branch Bank, 1 Ala. 565.

Defendant's Burden of Proof.—One seeking to impeach the bona fides of the holder of a negotiable instrument assumes the burden of proof. Lehman *v.* Tallassee Mfg. Co., 64 Ala. 567; First Nat. Bank *v.* Dawson, 78 Ala. 67.

One who seeks to defend an action on a negotiable instrument by a transferee, by reason of some payment, set-off, or equity against the payee or some intermediate holder, is required to show that the holder did not give value for it, or to raise a presumption of that fact sufficient to require an explanation from the holder of the manner in which he received it. Minell *v.* Reed, 26 Ala. 730.

In an action by an indorsee of notes before maturity against accommodation indorsers, the burden is on defendants to prove that plaintiff had notice of certain infirmities, invalidating the indorsements. Bunzel *v.* Maas, 22 So. 568, 116 Ala. 68.

On a bill to enjoin collection of a note on the ground of usury, the burden of proving a defense of bona fide purchase is on defendant, where he alleges it. Thompson *v.* Maddux, 23 So. 157, 117 Ala. 468.

The purchaser of a negotiable note, before maturity, and for valuable consideration, is not bound to enquire of the maker whether there is any defect in it, or defense against it; but is entitled to protection, unless there was bad faith in his purchase or such gross negligence as is evidence of bad faith; and his purchase for value before maturity being shown, the onus of proving notice is on the maker. Wildsmith *v.* Tracy, 80 Ala. 258.

§ 327 (3) Consideration for Indorsement or Transfer.

"The general rule is that mercantile paper in the hands of the holder, imports a consideration passing between the original parties. When, however, this presumption is repelled and it is shown that the instrument is made without consideration or has been fraudulently or improperly put into circulation, the holder will be required to prove that he gave value for the note, or bill, and that he acquired it before it was due, or he can not recover. Chitty on Bills, 79; Collins *v.* Martin, 1 B. & P. 650; Marston *v.* Forward, 5 Ala. 347; Wallace *v.* Branch Bank, 1 Ala. 565." Thompson *v.* Armstrong, 7 Ala. 256.

In an action on the indorsement of a bill single, the indorsee need not prove the consideration which moved from him to the indorser. The statute (Clay's Dig., p. 340, § 152) declares that, where suit is founded on any written instrument, the writing shall be evidence of the debt, and requires defendant to deny it by plea, supported by affidavit. Miller *v.* McIntyre, 9 Ala. 638.

On the question of notice vel non by the holder, of conditions or restrictions imposed by the indorser, the burden of proof is on the defendant; and a charge which instructs the jury, "that where valid defenses are shown to exist against negotiable paper, if the holder would protect himself against them, he is required to show that, in good faith, for a valuable consideration, without notice of its infirmities, he acquired the paper before maturity," misplaces the burden of proof as to notice, and is therefore erroneous. First Nat. Bank *v.* Dawson, 78 Ala. 67.

§ 327 (4) Fraud in Inception or Transfer.

The fact that there was fraud or illegality in the inception of a negotiable instrument places the burden on the holder of showing bona fides. Thompson *v.* Armstrong, 7 Ala. 256; Boyd *v.* McIvor, 11 Ala. 822; Ross *v.* Drinkard, 35 Ala. 434.

When a note, based on insufficient consideration, has been obtained from a person under the influence of liquor at the time of its execution, and enfeebled in mind and body by long-continued disease and drunkenness, a presumption of fraud arises, which must be countervailed by proof of a fair consideration, and fair and honest dealing on the part of him who seeks to enforce payment of the note. Holland *v.* Barnes, 53 Ala. 83, 25 Am. Rep. 595.

§ 328. —— Presentment, Demand, Protest, and Notice.

See post, "Presentment, Demand, Protest, and Notice," § 353.

Presumptions.—The presumption is that the holder of a bill resided at the place where the bill was dishonored and protested, the burden being on him to show otherwise. Tyson *v.* Oliver, 43 Ala. 455.

The fact that, five years after the protest of a bill, the drawer was living at a certain place, raises no presumption that he was living there when protest was made. Tyson *v.* Oliver, 43 Ala. 455.

Burden of Proof.—"In an action by an indorsee against the drawer or indorser of a bill of exchange for nonpayment, no recovery can be had without showing that the bill was presented for payment, at maturity, or due diligence used for that purpose, and timely notice of its dishonor given to them, or some legal excuse shown, why such notice was not given. Story on Bills, §§ 323, 326; Roberts *v.* Mason, 1 Ala. 373; Irvine *v.* Withers, 1 Stew. 234." Battle *v.* Weems, 44 Ala. 105, 106.

Where notice of nonpayment is sent through the post office, addressed to the drawer of a bill at a particular place, it must be shown that he resided there, or that it was the place at which notice should have been addressed to him. Crawford *v.* Branch Bank at Mobile, 7 Ala. 205.

In an action against the drawer or indorser of a bill, the onus of showing due diligence is on plaintiff, and is a prerequisite, to his right of recovery. If the proof, therefore, be too uncertain to enable the court to see that due diligence has been used, he must fail in his action. Rives *v.* Parmley, 18 Ala. 256.

In assumpsit by the indorsee against the indorser, the court must, if required, order a nonsuit, if notice and refusal be not proved. Ward *v.* Gifford, Minor 5.

It need not be shown as preliminary proof, before admitting in evidence the bill sued on, that there was a demand, protest, and notice, or waiver of them. Manning *v.* Maroney, 87 Ala. 563, 6 So. 343, 13 Am. St. Rep. 67.

Upon a suit on a note payable on demand, at a particular place, it is not necessary that the plaintiff should prove a demand at the place before suit brought. It is a matter of defense for the defendant, if he was ready at the place, to pay. Montgomery *v.* Elliott, 6 Ala. 701.

§ 329. —— Payment.

Presumptions.—The possession of a negotiable instrument by the maker or acceptor after maturity raises a presumption that it has been paid. Hill *v.* Gayle, 1 Ala. 275; Potts *v.* Coleman, 67 Ala. 221; Lipscomb *v.* De Lemos, 68 Ala. 592.

Possession of a note by maker, and of a receipt from the payee for the amount of the note, to be credited on the note, is sufficient to create a presumption of payment of the note. Penn *v.* Edwards, 50 Ala. 63.

It is well settled that a presumption of payment of a debt arises from the possession by the payee of the note or other security given therefor, after its maturity; and when such presumption of payment arises, the inference is necessary that the payment was made to one lawfully authorized to receive the money. Lipscomb *v.* De Lemos, 68 Ala. 592.

Lines drawn across a note raise the presumption that it has been satisfied; but such presumption may be rebutted by evidence, to be determined on by a jury. Pitcher *v.* Patrick, 1 Stew. & P. 478.

Where a note is declared on as made in another state, it must be presumed that it was payable there. Dunn *v.* Clement, 2 Ala. 392.

The presumption of payment of a note arising from the maker's possession does not arise where he has been appointed the payee's administrator, in view of Code, § 115, entitling an administrator to take possession of his intestate's evidence of debt. Arnold *v.* Arnold, 27 So. 465, 124 Ala. 550, 82 Am. St. Rep. 199.

Defendant had a claim against a corporation the property of which was purchased and debts assumed by a new corporation. Defendant pledged said claim, as collateral security for his notes, to one who was the president and principal stockholder of the new corporation, and also a partner in a bank. Held, in an action on said notes by the assignee of said bank, which afterwards became the owner of said notes, that, even if there had been an obligation on the president of said corporation to pay the claim which was pledged as collateral, that obligation rested on him individually, and not on the bank of which he was a member, and therefore it would not be presumed that the payment of the collateral operated as payment of the note. Sampson *v.* Fox, 109 Ala. 662, 19 So. 896.

Where a note payable to two persons, not partners, is found by the executor of one of them among his testator's effects, it will be presumed that the note was unpaid. Tisdale *v.* Maxwell, 58 Ala. 40.

Burden of Proof.—The burden of proving payment of a note sued on is on the defendant. Walston *v.* Davis, 40 So. 1017, 146 Ala. 510; Sampson *v.* Fox, 109 Ala. 662, 19 So. 896; Engelbert *v.* Taylor, 55 So. 442, 1 Ala. App. 553.

Where a series of notes payable at different dates were given for the price of a plantation, and the maker paid the first of the series, the burden is on him to show, as against an assignee, that the note was assigned prior to such payment, and, when paid, was in the hands of the assignee. Nelson *v.* Dunn, 15 Ala. 501.

That a note was lost after suit does not alter the rule that the burden is on defendant to prove payment; plaintiff not being required to prove that the lost paper has not reached the hands of an innocent purchaser. Walston *v.* Davis, 40 So. 1017, 146 Ala. 510.

§ 330. Admissibility of Evidence.

See ante, "Issues, Proof, and Variance," § 319; post, "In General," § 331; "Execution, Delivery, and Identity of Instrument," § 332; "Consideration," § 333; "Nature of Liability, and Relations of Parties to Instrument and to Each Other," § 334; "Mistake, Fraud, or Duress," § 335; "Legality of Object and of Consideration," § 336; "Transfer and Ownership in General," § 337; "Good Faith and Payment of Value," § 338; "Presentment, Demand, Protest, and Notice," § 339; "Payment and Discharge," § 340; "Competency of Parties or Intermediate Holders as Witnesses," § 341; "In Actions on Acceptances, Drafts, or Orders," § 342; "In Actions on Contracts of Indorsement," § 343.

§ 331. —— In General.

See ante, "Amount," § 82.

In an assumpsit on a note, under a count on an account stated, the note is admissible in evidence, without proof of its consideration. Catlin *v.* Gilders, 3 Ala. 536.

Where the execution of a promissory note is put in issue by plea, if it is correctly described in the declaration, it may be read to the jury, without any additional evidence, in order that the plaintiff may offer proof of its genuineness. Catlin *v.* Gilders, 3 Ala. 536.

Where non est factum is pleaded to a suit on a promissory note, the note itself is admissible in evidence, if there is other evidence, proper for the jury, tending to show that the defendant made the note. Morris *v.* Varner, 32 Ala. 499.

In an action on a note by the payee against the maker, the payee makes out a prima facie case by showing possession, and he need not therefore set out in the complaint or establish by evidence indorsements on the back of it in order to introduce the note in evidence. Anniston Pipe Works *v.* Mary Pratt Furnace Co., 94 Ala. 606, 10 So. 259.

Where, in an action on a note given for an option to buy land, the payors put in issue the legality of the contract granting an option, such contract is relevant, and admissible in evidence. Hanna *v.* Ingram, 93 Ala. 482, 9 So. 621.

Another note between the same parties, though not in suit, may, when shown to be connected with the note sued on, being in part consideration of the purchase for which the latter was given, be read in evidence as a part of the transaction. Weaver *v.* Lapsley, 42 Ala. 601, 94 Am. Dec. 671.

Where an action is brought upon a promissory note, with an affidavit of its loss, if the plaintiff has it at the trial, it may be read to the jury. Carlisle *v.* Davis, 7 Ala. 42.

§ 332. —— Execution, Delivery, and Identity of Instrument.

In an action on a note alleged to have been given by defendant's intestate for a loan by plaintiff, the execution of which was denied, evidence that plaintiff, between the time of the making of the note and decedent's death, tried to borrow money, was competent; his pecuniary condition, and ability to lend money to decedent, being a subject of legitimate inquiry. Glover *v.* Gentry, 104 Ala. 222, 13 So. 38.

Where defendant pleaded non est factum, it was error to refuse him permission to testify as to whether he signed the paper in suit. Mizell *v.* Farmers' Bank (Ala.), 61 So. 272.

In an action by a bank on a note dated on Sunday, it is not error to admit evidence that the note is in the handwriting of the bank's cashier, and that he was not in the employ of the bank until after the date of the note, and that the note is a renewal note, and dates back. Hauerwas *v.* Goodloe, 101 Ala. 162, 13 So. 567.

A question asking a witness to describe notes referred to in certain letters attached as exhibits to a deposition of another witness is not subject to the objection that the notes are the best evidence, where the notes are not the foundation of the action, since in such cases, coming up collaterally, they need not be produced. Bunzel *v.* Maas, 116 Ala. 68, 22 So. 568.

Parol evidence is inadmissible to show that a note signed by the makers as "Board of Business Managers" was the obligation of a corporation of which they were the board of business managers, and not their individual note, the words used being mere descriptio personæ. Richmond, etc., Mach. Works *v.* Morgagne, 119 Ala. 80, 24 So. 834.

In an action by a bank on a note dated on Sunday, its "discount register" is not admissible in evidence to show that the note in suit was a renewal of a note which matured on Sunday, and that the renewal note was made on a certain week day after its date, and dated back to the date of the maturity of the first note, according to the custom of the bank. Hauerwas *v.* Goodloe, 101 Ala. 162, 13 So. 567.

§ 333. —— Consideration.

See ante, "Presumption as to Consideration in General," § 323 (1); post, "Good Faith and Payment of Value," § 338; "Payment and Discharge," § 340.

Admissible for Plaintiff.—In a suit at law on a promissory note, in which the consideration is stated, plaintiff may show by parol evidence a valuable consideration for the note, differing from that expressed therein. Ramsey *v.* Young, 69 Ala. 157.

In an action on a note for the price of a slave, defended on the ground of fraud, and want and failure of consideration, the bill of sale is competent evidence for the plaintiff. Ward *v.* Reynolds, 32 Ala. 384.

In a suit on a note, where the maker testified that he had denied liability for the debt of a third person when he made the note, and that he gave the note for the account of such third person, evidence was admissible to show when he first denied liability, and that he gave the note for his own account. Gates *v.* Morton Hardware Co., 40 So. 509, 146 Ala. 692.

In a suit on a note, evidence that an account for goods furnished to a third person was never presented to him, but only to the maker of the note, was admissible. Gates *v.* Morton Hardware Co., 40 So. 509, 146 Ala. 692.

Where the defendant, the maker of a promissory note, introduced a witness who stated that there was no consideration passing from the plaintiff, the payee, and that the latter was unknown to the former, it is competent for the plaintiff to ask the witness if the note was made at the instance of a third person, and whether there was any consideration passing from that person to the maker, on which the note was founded, and what it was. Moore *v.* Ponders, 11 Ala. 815.

Admissible for Defendant.—"In reference to bills of exchange and promissory notes, it is said in 1 Parsons on Notes and Bills, 194, 'that any statement in a bill or note respecting the consideration may be explained or contradicted by parol evidence. It may be shown, notwithstanding any such statement, either that there was no consideration at all, or that the consideration was different from that stated.'" Ramsey *v.* Young, 69 Ala. 157, 158.

"The maker of a promissory note. notwithstanding the usual expression of consideration, such as 'for value received,' etc., may show as against the payee, or other person standing in the same situation, that the note was given without consideration, or that the consideration failed, etc., 3 Phil. Ev. 1458, et seq." Nicholas *v.* Krebs, 11 Ala. 230, 232.

"As between the original parties to a negotiable promissory note, and of paper not negotiable as between those standing in privity, the consideration is always open to inquiry. The making of the paper with full knowledge of all the facts relied on as showing a want, or illegality, or failure of consideration, total or partial, or of any valid defense, though it may be a set-off, or in the nature of a set-off, will not preclude the defense. Ware, etc., Co. *v.* Morgan, 67 Ala. 461; Stark *v.* Henderson, 30 Ala. 438; Holt *v.* Robinson, 21 Ala. 106; Finn *v.* Barclay, 15 Ala. 626; Clemens *v.* Loggins, 1 Ala. 622." Foster *v.* Bush, 104 Ala. 662, 16 So. 625, 627.

While parol testimony may not be received to contradict or vary the terms of a note, yet the consideration for which it was given may be established by parol testimony. Long *v.* Davis, 18 Ala. 801; Ramsey *v.* Young, 69 Ala. 157; Folmar *v.* Siler, 132 Ala. 297, 31 So. 719, 720.

When the consideration of a note is not stated in it, parol proof is admissible to show what it was, and that the contract of which the note formed a part had been rescinded by the parties. Newton *v.* Jackson, 23 Ala. 335.

In an action on a promissory note, defendant may prove its consideration by parol testimony as preliminary to the introduction of evidence to show that the consideration has failed. Cuthbert *v.* Bowie, 10 Ala. 163.

In a suit by a bank, against the maker of a promissory note, purporting, on its face, to have been given for the amount of the maker's indebtedness to the bank, evidence is admissible to show that the agreement which constituted the consideration of the note was the extinguishment of the debt of another person to the bank, and that the proceeds were so applied. Murrah *v.* Branch Bank at Decatur, 20 Ala. 392.

Where a promissory note is made for a specified sum "for work done on a saw and grist mill," the statement of the consideration does not conclusively indicate that the note is a complete expression of the contract; and, when sued on the note, the maker may show what was the contract between the parties, and that the payee stipulated that the work should be well done, and answer the purpose for which it was intended. Self *v.* Herrington, 11 Ala. 489.

The consideration of a note from A to B was the transfer by B to A of certain notes and an account against C, with the agreement that if A could not use such claims in offset against C to whom he was indebted, they were to be returned to B, and the note given up. Held, that this agreement might be proved by parol, it being not a varying of the written contract, but only proof of the consideration. Simonton *v.* Steele, 1 Ala. 357.

In a suit on a note, testimony of a third person as to whether he had ever offered to pay the payee for certain goods was admissible as tending to show whether he was to pay for the goods, or was looking to the maker of the note to pay for them. Gates *v.* Morton Hardware Co., 40 So. 509, 146 Ala. 692.

In a suit against a firm on a note signed in the firm name by an individual partner, parol evidence by the other partner that he instructed his partner to sign the firm name in order to avoid attachment of the firm goods by the latter's creditors, and that plaintiff, the payee of the note, was aware of the purpose, is admissible to show want of consideration. Guice *v.* Thornton, 76 Ala. 466.

The maker of a note, in order to show a want or failure of consideration, may prove the inducements to the making of the note. Litchfield *v.* Falconer, 2 Ala. 280.

In an action by a bank on a note defended on the ground that the note was given under the impression that it was in consideration of stock in a corporation, the application by defendant for the purchase of such stock is properly admitted. Mizell *v.* Farmers' Bank (Ala.), 61 So. 272.

A woman who drew a bill of exchange accepted by a firm may show by parol that it was drawn by her to secure a debt of her husband, who was a member of the firm. First Nat. Bank *v.* Leland, 122 Ala. 289, 25 So. 195.

Where the defense to a note sued on is that there is a failure of consideration, evidence that the consideration of a note similar to that in suit has failed is admissible, it being for the jury to decide upon the identity. Smith *v.* Armistead, 7 Ala. 698.

Not Admissible for Defendant.—In an action on a note expressed to be given for certain described lands, parol evidence is inadmissible that it was given in payment of a debt for other consideration different from that expressed. Adams *v.* Thomas, 54 Ala. 175.

In an action on a promissory note which purports on its face to have been given "for the rent of land," the defendant can not introduce parol proof to show that the payee also agreed to repair the fencing around the land, and that he failed to do so, in consequence of which failure defendant's crop was damaged by the breaking in of stock. Evans *v.* Bell, 20 Ala. 509.

In an action on a note given to the agent of the insurer for the first premium on life insurance policies, the applications for which contained an agreement that no statement made by the person soliciting the application should be binding on the insurer, unless reduced to writing and presented to the insurer, and that the application and policy should constitute the entire contract, defendant could not show that plaintiff, in soliciting the insurance, represented that the policies would contain a certain provision which they did not contain; such evidence having the effect of varying the written contract. Blanks *v.* Moore, 139 Ala. 624, 36 So. 783.

§ 334. —— Nature of Liability, and Relations of Parties to Instrument and to Each Other.

See ante, "In General," § 287.

Where a person other than the payee writes his name on the back of a note at its inception, the nature of the transaction, and the relation of the person so indorsing, whether as maker, guarantor, or indorser, and the intention of the parties, may be shown by parol evidence. Carter *v.* Long, 125 Ala. 280, 28 So. 74.

Admissible for Plaintiff.—In an action against an administrator, on a note made by his intestate to the maker "or bearer," parol evidence is admissible to show that the note was intended to be made to plaintiff. Hellen *v.* Wideman, 10 Ala. 846.

In an action upon a promissory note by persons as commissioners, the fact that they are the promisees may be proved by parol, and they need not produce the record evidence of their appointment. Mundine *v.* Crenshaw, 3 Stew. 87.

Defendant subscribed the written memorandum, "Good for three hundred dollars. Jan'y 15th, 1829." Held, that parol evidence was admissible to show that it was delivered to, and intended to acknowledge a liability to, plaintiff. Nicholas *v.* Kerbs, 11 Ala. 230.

Where the complaint in an action on notes stated that they were subject to the conditions of a lease, and the evidence showed that the notes and lease were executed with reference to each other, as a part of the same transaction, it was not error to admit the lease in evidence, though it did not bear the same date as the notes. Murphy *v.* Farley, 27 So. 442, 124 Ala. 279.

In an action on a note signed by a corporation, followed by defendant's name and the word "Priest," in which it was in issue whether the note was defendant's personal obligation, a question as to whether the note was sent to defendant by plaintiff for his individual signature, in accordance with an agreement to sign it, was proper. Briel *v.* Exchange Nat. Bank (Ala.), 61 So. 277.

If it be doubtful whether a bill drawn by the president of a corporation on the treasurer thereof was drawn by the president in his private character or as agent of the corporation and by its authority, parol evidence is admissible to show the true nature of the transaction. Wetumpka & C. R. R. *v.* Bingham, 5 Ala. 657.

Not Admissible for Plaintiff.—Where the written instrument, which is the foundation of the suit, is unstamped, and excluded as evidence for that reason, the contract evidenced by such written instrument can not be proved by oral evidence. Mobile, etc., R. Co. *v.* Edwards, 46 Ala. 267.

Admissible for Defendant.—Where, from the face of a note, it is doubtful whether the party making it acted for himself or as the agent of another, parol evidence is admissible to show the character of the transaction. Deshler *v.* Hodges, 3 Ala. 509.

A contract, for the sale of a horse, which is not reduced to writing, but for the price of the horse a note is given, is not affected by the rule that written contracts can not be explained by parol evidence. In such a case it is competent to prove by parol that the note was to be returned if the horse died. Barlow *v.* Flemming, 6 Ala. 146.

Parol proof is admissible to show the intention of the parties to a note at the time the contract was entered into, with regard to their several liabilities among themselves, and the relation which they were to bear to the note. Branch Bank at Mobile *v.* Coleman, 20 Ala. 140.

Parol evidence is admissible to show that a bill drawn on the owner of a steamboat, and accepted by the captain, as such, was intended to bind the owner, and that he authorized the acceptance to be made in that name and form. May *v.* Hewitt, 33 Ala. 161.

"When it is doubtful from the face of a contract, not under seal, whether it was intended to operate as the personal engagement of the party signing, or to impose an obligation upon some third person as his principal, parol evidence is admissible to show the true character of the transaction; especially, if the right of a bona fide endorsee is not prejudiced thereby. Lazarus *v.* Shearer, 2 Ala. 718; Deshler *v.* Hodges, 3 Ala. 509; McWhorter *v.* Lewis, 4 Ala. 198; Mott *v.* Hicks, 1 Cow. 513." May *v.* Hewitt, etc., Co., 33 Ala. 161, 166.

Where it is doubtful from the face of a note whether it was intended to operate as the personal engagement of the party signing it, or to impose an obligation upon some third person as his principal, parol evidence is admissible to show the true character of the transaction. Lazarus *v.* Shearer, 2 Ala. 718.

Although the signers of a note are apparently joint promisors, and each is liable for a ratable proportion of the debt, it may be shown by parol evidence, as between the signers, that one was surety for the other. Summerhill *v.* Tapp, 52 Ala. 227.

Not Admissible for Defendant.—Parol evidence is not admissible, in an action on a bond or note, to show that the instrument was delivered to the payee (or obligee) himself as an escrow, to take effect upon a condition; nor is it admissible, in the absence of fraud or mistake, to show a delivery to the payee (or obligee) upon the condition that it was not to have any binding force at all. Guice *v.* Thornton, 76 Ala. 466.

A parol agreement, made when a right to vend a churn was sold, and notes were given for the price, that the maker of the notes need not pay them if he was unable to sell enough churns to do so, is inadmissible in an action on the notes. Rice *v.* Gilbreath, 119 Ala. 424, 24 So. 421.

§ 335. —— Mistake, Fraud, or Duress.

When a promissory note is, by mistake, made payable to Aaron Formey, instead of Aaron Formby, the latter may sue upon it in his own name, alleging that it was made payable to him by the name therein inserted, and may prove on the trial, by parol evidence, that he was the person intended. Taylor *v.* Strickland, 37 Ala. 642.

In the absence of any proof of false representations as to the contents of an instrument made for the purpose of securing defendant's signature thereto, evidence that his signature to another instrument of the same kind, between the same parties, had been secured by such false representations, shortly before the signing of the one in question, is inadmissible. Martin *v.* Smith, 116 Ala. 639, 22 So. 917.

§ 336. —— Legality of Object and of Consideration.

Where, in an action by the indorsee, defendant set up that the note was based on a gaming transaction, any circumstances from which knowledge or consent of the payee as to the transaction could be reasonably inferred was competent evidence. Birmingham Trust & Savings Co. *v.* Curry, 49 So. 319, 160 Ala. 370.

§ 337. —— Transfer and Ownership in General.

See ante, "Verification," § 315.

The fact that plaintiff knew the maker was insolvent when he bought the notes is proper evidence to be considered by the jury on the question of actual purchase by plaintiff. Bunzel *v.* Maas, 22 So. 568, 116 Ala. 68.

Where it is a question before the jury whether the note sued on is the note of the defendant or of a third person, the fact that the plaintiff had sued and recovered judgment on the note against such third person is not irrelevant, but is a circumstance proper for the consideration of the jury. Clealand *v.* Huey, 18 Ala. 343.

In an action on notes, on the issues raised by a complaint declaring upon the notes as nonnegotiable and pleas denying plaintiff's ownership, the notes were inadmissible, in the absence of proof of plaintiff's ownership. Peevey *v.* Tapley, 42 So. 561, 148 Ala. 320.

In an action on a promissory note, made payable to L. and W., by the payees against the maker, evidence that they were then transacting business in partnership with a third person, who is yet alive, is not admissible. Cotton *v.* Lane, Minor, 320.

§ 338. —— Good Faith and Payment of Value.

See ante, "Consideration," § 333.

On an issue as to whether a note was transferred to a bank as collateral security for an existing debt or for a new loan, evidence that no portion of the money loaned was drawn out of the bank till after the transfer of the note is competent. Boykin *v.* Bank of Mobile, 72 Ala. 262, 47 Am. Rep. 408.

Where plaintiff purchased a draft from the apparent payee, who had fraudulently altered it, and who paid part of the proceeds to defendant in payment of an alleged debt, evidence to show that the debt was secured was competent, as tending to show that defendant gave value. Alabama Nat. Bank *v.* Rivers, 22 So. 580, 116 Ala. 1, 67 Am. St. Rep. 95.

A note, indorsed in blank, was delivered to H. by the payee to secure the payment of a debt owing by the payee to him. Held, in an action by H. on the note, that the evidence that the payee was indebted to H. & Co. was inadmissible. Prim *v.* Hammel, 32 So. 1006, 134 Ala. 652, 92 Am. St. Rep. 52.

§ 339. —— Presentment, Demand, Protest, and Notice.

It is permissible to prove a custom or usage, at a particular place where the parties to a bill of exchange reside, as to the mode of giving notice of protest for nonpayment of the bill. Ray *v.* Porter, 42 Ala. 327.

Where the protest of a note made payable at any bank in a designated city, although showing that it was presented for payment at a certain named bank in the state, does not expressly state that the bank was in such city, parol evidence is admissible, in connection with the protest, to show that a bank of the name of that mentioned therein was located in such city at the date of the protest. Boit *v.* Corr, 54 Ala. 112.

As the statute makes the certificate of a notary, in the protest of an inland bill, that he had mailed a notice of the dishonor, addressed to the drawer, at a certain post office evidence of the fact, if the protest and notice recited therein are regular, the holder may prove, on the trial, that the post office to which the notice was addressed was the one at which the drawer usually received his letters. Leigh *v.* Lightfoot, 11 Ala. 935.

Although protests are excluded from the jury, yet the deposition of the notary is proper to prove notice sent to the indorsers. Bank at Decatur *v.* Hodges, 9 Ala. 631.

Though a notarial certificate is by statute competent evidence of the facts stated therein, notice may be proved otherwise. Martin *v.* Brown, 75 Ala. 442.

Notice sent to an indorser by mail of the dishonor of a bill of exchange need not be produced in order to be able to give proof of its contents. John *v.* City Nat. Bank, 62 Ala. 529, 34 Am. Rep. 35.

As promissory notes were not required, when dishonored, to be protested, at common law, it can not be presumed, in the absence of proof of a change of the common law in the state of Georgia, that promissory notes are protestable in that state; and therefore, the protest of a notary public is not evidence. Dunn *v.* Adams, etc., Co., 1 Ala. 527.

§ 340. —— Payment and Discharge.

Payment—Fact of Payment.—When a note has been paid and delivered up, it will not be presumed that the maker afterwards retains it in his possession; and therefore parol evidence is admissible to prove a payment, when it becomes a material inquiry, without calling upon the party to whom the writing was delivered to produce it. Mead *v.* Brooks, 8 Ala. 840.

The maker's possession of the note being only presumptive evidence of payment, evidence is admissible that another note of the same tenor has been substituted for it. Potts *v.* Coleman, 67 Ala. 221.

A witness can not be allowed to state that he saw a credit of $400 entered upon a note, without producing the note, unless there is evidence that perhaps the note has been fully paid off, so as to warrant the inference that it has been destroyed, or unless he could swear to the payment from his own knowledge. Scarborough *v.* Reynolds, 12 Ala. 252.

Admissions that a note has been paid, made by the holder of a note while he is the owner, are admissible in evidence in an action by such holder for the use of another. Remy *v.* Duffee, 4 Ala. 365.

The custom of the merchants of Mobile to retain notes and bills of their country customers, after they are paid, until the end of the year, for settlement, may be given in evidence to explain why a paid note was not given up. Remy *v.* Duffee, 4 Ala. 365.

Where defendant claimed that at a specified time he made a payment on a note with money borrowed from a third person, to whom he had given his note therefor, the note so given, and the testimony of such third person as to the date and amount of the loan, are competent in rebuttal. Turrentine *v.* Grigsby, 23 So. 666, 118 Ala. 380.

In an action of assumpsit by the representative of a deceased father against his son on promissory notes, made by the latter in 1837, and payable to the intestate, the defendant relied on payments and set-off to a greater amount than the sum sought to be recovered. To show that the set-off had been allowed on some other indebtedness to the testator, the plaintiff adduced evidence tending to prove that the defendant had been unsuccessful in business as a merchant some years previous to making the notes; that he afterwards resided at his father's house, without any visible means, and then engaged in a business which required a considerable cash capital, and when he ceased to do that business, in 1835, money could not be made of him on execution. Held, that this testimony did not tend to prove the fact it was intended to establish, that it was prima facie irrelevant, and should therefore have been excluded. Sorrelle *v.* Craig, 9 Ala. 534.

In a suit between the payee of a note and one who had assumed the debt, the issue was whether goods sold by the maker to the payee's sister and on his credit, were a payment on the note. The maker having been a witness for the payee, the clerks of the former testified for the other side that the maker of the note told him to sell the sister all the goods she wanted, and that it had been agreed that her account should be a credit on the note. Held, that the statements, testified to were not part of the res gestæ and were admissible only to impeach the testimony of the maker of the note. McPherson *v.* Foust, 81 Ala. 295, 8 So. 193.

Mode of Payment.—Where, in suit by a bank on a note, defendant claimed that it had been paid with proceeds of work on a railroad grade, evidence as to the work, introductory to testimony that it was paid for and the money appropriated to defendant's debt, due plaintiff, was admissible. First Nat. Bank *v.* Alexander, 50 So. 45, 161 Ala. 580.

In an action on a note, parol evidence is admissible to prove an agreement to receive, in part payment, a debt due from another person. Murchie *v.* Cook, 1 Ala. 41.

In an action of debt on a note, for "dollars," given to secure the purchase money of lands of a decedent sold in one of the seceded states in the year 1863, under an order of the probate court for the payment of debts, the defendant can not show, after the return and confirmation of the sale in the probate court, that the sale was for Confederate treasury notes, and not for "dollars" in some lawful currency of the United States. Hill *v.* Erwin, 44 Ala. 661.

It is inadmissible to show by parol that a promissory note was not to be paid in money. Such evidence clearly contradicts the legal terms of the written agreement. Clark *v.* Hart, 49 Ala. 86.

Where a note was made payable "at the Branch Bank at Montgomery," parol evidence to prove that at the time the note was made it was agreed that, if the note was sent to the bank, the maker should be exonerated from payment, is inadmissible, because it contradicts one of the terms of the note. Montgomery R. Co. *v.* Hurst, 9 Ala. 513.

Time of Payment.—In an action by the payee on a promissory note, payable unconditionally, and at a time certain, it is incompetent to prove by parol testimony any promise by the plaintiff, contemporaneous with or antecedent to the execution of the note, stipulating for a postponement of the time of payment. Doss *v.* Peterson, 82 Ala. 253, 2 So. 644; Litchfield *v.* Falconer, 2 Ala. 280.

Place of Payment.—Where a bond or note fails to designate the place of payment, parol evidence is admissible to show that it was, by agreement between the parties, to be paid at a place different from that of the contract. Moore *v.* Davidson, 18 Ala. 209.

§ 341. —— Competency of Parties or Intermediate Holders as Witnesses.

Party to Vote in General.—The mere fact, that a witness is a party to a negotiable paper, does not disqualify him. Griffing *v.* Harris, 9 Port. 225; Adams *v.* Moore, 9 Port. 406.

"In later cases (than Whatley *v.* Johnson, 1 Stew. 498), the doctrine has frequently been laid down, that 'the mere fact, that the witness is a party to a negotiable paper, does not disqualify him. Such is the established law in this state.' Adams *v.* Moore, 9 Port. 406; Griffing *v.* Harris, 9 Port. 225; Dawidson *v.* Love, 1 Ala. 133." Thompson *v.* Armstrong, 5 Ala. 383, 386.

The mere fact of a witness being a party to the note, independently of other testimony, goes to his credit—not to his competency. Thompson *v.* Armstrong, 5 Ala. 383.

A party to a negotiable instrument is inadmissible as a witness, after the instrument has been negotiated, to show it void at the time of its execution. Ross *v.* Wells, 1 Stew. 139.

Maker.—The mere fact that the maker of a note is a party to the paper does not render him incompetent to testify in an action by an indorsee against an indorser. Adams *v.* Moore, 9 Port. 406.

"The general policy of the country forbids that any one should join as one of the makers in the note, and afterwards be admitted by his testimony to impeach it. 1 Term 296; 3 Term 34, 36; 7 Term 597; 1 H. Black. 308; 2 Dal. 194; 2 John. 165; 15 John. 270; 1 Caines, 258. The cases cited on the other side are, where makers or endorsers have been permitted to testify as to facts which occurred after and not before they had put their names to the note." Ross *v.* Wells, 1 Stew. 139, 140.

Payee.—The payee of a bill is a competent witness for the drawer, in a suit against him by the indorsee, to impeach its validity. State Bank *v.* Seawell, 18 Ala. 616.

In an action against the maker of a note, by the bearer, the payee is not competent to prove the making of the note, under the plea of non est factum. Carroll *v.* Meeks, 3 Port. 226.

Indorser.—An indorser who has no interest in the note, nor liable in any manner upon it, is a competent witness in favor of the indorsee, against the maker. Boyd *v.* McIvor, 14 Ala. 593.

An indorser, who has assigned a note without recourse, which was made payable to him as the agent of the indorsee, for a debt due the indorsee, is a competent witness for the latter in a suit upon the note. Boyd *v.* McIvor, 14 Ala. 593.

Assignor.—When the assignee of a promissory note is the defendant in an action, and seeks to establish it as a set-off, he may render his assignor a competent witness for him, to prove the time when the assignment was made, by releasing him from all liability on account of the note. Section 2290 of the Code does not apply to such a case. Grayson *v.* Glover, 33 Ala. 182.

Transferee.—In an action on a note alleged to have been executed by defendant's intestate, it appeared that plaintiff had transferred the note to his wife in consideration of her agreement to pay a debt her brother owed plaintiff, and that after suit was brought he caused the clerk to enter the cause on the docket to the use of his wife, and so notified defendant. The wife testified that, a few minutes before she was called to testify, she "formally recanted" the agreement with her husband, without the advice of her attorney; but it was not shown that the husband was present, or was a party to the "recantation," or on what consideration it was done. Held, that no bona fide retransfer took place, and that the wife was disqualified to testify. Glover *v.* Gentry, 104 Ala. 222, 16 So. 38.

But an intermediate indorsee who returns the note to the payee, before the latter delivers it to a bearer, is a competent witness for the plaintiff, in such an action. Carroll *v.* Meeks, 3 Port. 226.

§ 342. —— In Actions on Acceptances, Drafts, or Orders.

In an action by an indorsee against accommodation acceptors of a bill, where the defense was payment by the drawer, a list of the drawer's liabilities to the indorsee, prepared by the drawer's bookkeeper on his order, and at the request of the indorsee, several months after the alleged payment, containing the acceptance sued on, was proper evidence for plaintiff. Steiner *v.* Jeffries, 24 So. 37, 118 Ala. 573.

Where, in an action on a draft accepted by defendant, defense is made that the acceptance was conditional on the doing of certain work by the drawer, evidence that at maturity defendant asked for an extension is admissible to negative such defense. Hunt *v.* Johnson, 96 Ala. 130, 11 So. 387.

In an action by an indorsee against accommodation acceptors of a bill, where the defense was payment by the drawer, plaintiff might show that several months after the alleged payment the drawer executed to the acceptors a note which included the amount of the bill sued on. Steiner *v.* Jeffries, 24 So. 37, 118 Ala. 573.

In an action to charge defendant as accommodation indorser of a draft purchased by plaintiff from the apparent payee, after he had fraudulently substituted his name as payee, and raised the amount, it was competent to ask by whom defendant was requested to indorse. Alabama Nat. Bank *v.* Rivers, 22 So. 580, 116 Ala. 1, 67 Am. St. Rep. 95.

On presentation of an order to defendants for acceptance, defendants retained the order, apparently with plaintiffs' acquiescence. Held, in an action to hold defendants liable as acceptors thereof, that it was error to overrule a general objection to the introduction by defendants of a letter purporting to be the order in controversy, and defendants' letter to plaintiffs agreeing to pay what might become due. Williams *v.* Gallyon, 107 Ala. 439, 18 So. 162.

§ 343. —— In Actions on Contracts of Indorsement.

Admissible.—It may be shown by parol that an indorsement in blank by the payee of the note in suit, and its delivery to plaintiff's collector, were in fact a transaction in which the latter was to act as the agent of the payee to get the note discounted, and to apply a portion of the proceeds in payment of a debt due to plaintiff. Avery & Sons *v.* Miller, 86 Ala. 495, 6 So. 38.

Where, in an action against the indorsers of a note, they denied having induced the holder to delay suit against the maker, a corporation, by promising to pay the note, it was proper to show on cross-examination of one of the defendants that he and the other defendant owned the majority of the stock of the maker. Brown *v.* Fowler, 32 So. 584, 133 Ala. 310.

On an issue as to whether defendants had promised to pay a note on which they were indorsers, a letter subsequently written by one of them containing an individual promise to pay, and stating that they wanted the plaintiff to hold the paper, was admissible. Brown *v.* Fowler, 133 Ala. 310, 32 So. 584.

Where, in an action against the indorsers of a note, they denied having induced the holder to delay suit against the maker by promising to pay the note, testimony that they said to witness that they told the holder that either of them was worth the debt, and that they had offered to give him a mortgage on the maker's property, and pay $300 per month until the debt was paid, was properly received. Brown *v.* Fowler, 133 Ala. 310, 32 So. 584.

In an action brought by the assignee against the maker of a promissory note, the defendant seeking to establish as a set-off a note executed by the assignor to a third person, and transferred by the latter to the defendant, a memorandum written on the latter note by the plaintiff's assignor, stating that said note, if "taken up" by the defendant, should be credited on the note of the latter to him, is competent evidence for the defendant, if shown to have been made before the transfer of the note sued on. Grayson *v.* Glover, 33 Ala. 182.

If payment of a note is made by the maker to the payee, the note having been indorsed without notice to the maker, and suit is afterwards brought upon it by the indorsee against the maker, the defendant, in proving the fact of payment, may also prove the declarations of both himself and the payee, made at the time of the payment, in relation thereto, as a part of the res gestæ. Hart *v.* Freeman, 42 Ala. 567.

In an action of assumpsit at the suit of a subsequent against a prior indorser, to authorize the admission of the note as evidence it is sufficient to prove the signature of the maker and the defendant; and the recital in a joint judgment rendered upon the note, at the suit of a bank, against the defendant, the plaintiff, and maker, is evidence, in such an action, to charge the defendant. Spence *v.* Barclay, 8 Ala. 581.

In an action by the indorsee against the drawer of a bill of exchange, drawn at Mobile by a bank on a bank in New Orleans, in August, 1862, after the capture of the latter place by the Federal forces, "payable in currency," and which was not represented for payment until May 11, 1865, after the close of the war, and then duly protested for nonpayment, evidence is admissible on behalf of the defendant, under § 3 of Ordinance No. 26, adopted September 28, 1865, to show that it was understood and agreed between the defendant drawer and the payee, at the time of drawing the bill, that if it could not be sent to New Orleans in a short time it should be returned to the defendant, and the same amount of money that the payor had paid for it, which was Confederate treasury notes, should be returned to him; and evidence also was admissible showing that this agreement was communicated to the plaintiff indorsee at the time he purchased the bill. Tarleton *v.* Southern Bank, 41 Ala. 722.

In a suit by an indorsee of a promissory note against the indorser, the record of the suit against the maker was held admissible in evidence, notwithstanding the declaration in such former suit described the note as maturing on the 1st day of May, 1843, when in fact it was payable January 1, 1843; the note being correctly described in the indorsement on the writ, and in a subsequent part of the same declaration. Randolph *v.* Jones, 10 Ala. 228.

Not Admissible.—Evidence of a parol agreement varying the legal effect of the indorsement of a promissory note is inadmissible. Hightower *v.* Ivy, 2 Port. 308; Holt *v.* Moore, 5 Ala. 521; Preston *v.* Ellington, 74 Ala. 133; Tankersley *v.* Graham, 8 Ala. 247.

Where the payee of a bill or note has

duly indorsed the same for value, and before maturity, parol evidence is inadmissible for the purpose of showing a contemporaneous parol agreement with the indorsee that the indorsement was only for the purpose of passing the title, and that the indorser should be relieved from all other liability. Day *v.* Thompson, 65 Ala. 269.

In an action by an indorsee against the drawer of a bill, a written admission of the payee, discharging the liability of the drawer, is inadmissible in evidence. Carmichael *v.* Brooks, 9 Port. 330.

Where the holder of a note was induced to delay suit against the maker by the request of the indorsers, and their promise to pay the note, in a suit against them thereon evidence of the solvency and property of the maker of the note at its maturity is irrelevant. Brown *v.* Fowler, 32 So. 584, 133 Ala. 310.

In an action by indorsee and purchaser against the drawer and payee of a bill of exchange, drawn against a consignment of cotton from Mobile to Liverpool, and protested for nonacceptance, held, that evidence of the quality of the cotton was entirely irrelevant. Martin *v.* Brown, 75 Ala. 442.

The declarations of the payee of a note, through whom plaintiff derives title as indorsee, are not admissible to charge the maker, though his admissions made on a previous day have been introduced by the maker to show a discharge; the two admissions not having been parts of the same conversation. Perry *v.* Graves, 12 Ala. 246.

A question as to why plaintiff required a certain indorsement of defendants' note is objectionable as calling not for a fact, but merely for a reason. Lytle *v.* Bank, 121 Ala. 215, 26 So. 6, 7.

§ 344. Weight and Sufficiency of Evidence.

See post, "In General," § 345; "Execution, Delivery, and Identity of Instrument," § 346; "Consideration," § 347; "Nature and Extent of Liability," § 348; "Mistake, Fraud, or Duress," § 349; "Legality of Object and of Consideration," § 350; "Transfer and Ownership in General," § 351; "Possession as Evidence of Ownership," § 352; "Presentment, Demand, Protest, and Notice," § 353; "Payment and Discharge," § 354; "In General," § 356; "Interest," § 357; "Costs of Protest," § 358; "Questions for Jury," § 363.

§ 345. —— In General.

Plaintiff's introduction of a negotiable note entitles him prima facie to recover the face value of the note, with interest and reasonable attorney's fees. Chilton Warehouse & Mfg. Co. *v.* Lewis, 3 Ala. App. 464, 57 So. 100.

In assumpsit against the payee as indorser of a promissory note, payable at bank, where defendant pleads the general issue, plaintiff makes out a case by producing the note indorsed, and showing presentment at the bank for payment, nonpayment, and that defendant was seasonably advised thereof by notice given personally or by mail. Tarver *v.* Boykin, 6 Ala. 353.

In an action on a note, evidence considered, and held sufficient to sustain a judgment for plaintiff. Cochran *v.* Perkins, 40 So. 351, 146 Ala. 689.

Defendant in an action on a note is not required to establish the defense beyond doubt, nor even beyond reasonable doubt. Walston *v.* Davis, 40 So. 1017, 146 Ala. 510.

Where plaintiff sues the indorser, on his indorsement of a note, his right to recover can not be made out by proof of a fraudulent concealment or misrepresentation by the indorser of the maker's ability to pay. Fulford *v.* Johnson, 15 Ala. 385.

§ 346. —— Execution, Delivery, and Identity of Instrument.

Sufficient.—The evidence, in an action on acceptances of bills of exchange, that the son of defendant, signing defendant's name to the acceptances, was in charge of defendant's mercantile business, that the goods for which the bills were drawn were shipped to defendant and put in the store, and that the son drew checks in defendant's name to pay bills for the store, sufficiently showed the execution of the acceptances. Wooten *v.* Federal Discount Co. (Ala.), 62 So. 263.

Proof of the execution and required registration of an instrument obviates the necessity of proving the execution of the note attached to the instrument, which the latter was intended to secure. Steiner *v.* McCall, 61 Ala. 413.

One of two subscribing witnesses to a note may be called to prove its execution without calling or accounting for the absence of the other. Sowell *v.* Bank of Brewton, 24 So. 585, 119 Ala. 92.

Evidence held to justify a finding that notes set up as a foundation of a bill to sell lands of the maker were not executed as alleged. Jackson *v.* Grisham, 171 Ala. 553, 55 So. 165.

In an action on a note it appeared that plaintiff shipped defendants certain goods, and sent a draft, with the bill of lading attached, to a bank, for collection; that defendants refused to pay the draft, and wrote plaintiff, "Will accept goods on these terms only: 30 days, or 2 off at ten days, or a 30-day acceptance:" that on April 8th plaintiff replied, "Send us 30 days' acceptance;" that on April 9th defendant forwarded plaintiff the note sued on, and on April 10th defendants received from plaintiff a draft for acceptance at 30 days, dated April 9th; that defendants then wrote plaintiff that it [plaintiff] had not accepted their proposition, and that the goods were subject to its disposal; that after mailing this letter, on the same day, defendants received a telegram from plaintiff that the bank would release the bill of lading, and on the same day defendants received a letter acknowledging the receipt and acceptance of defendants' note. Held, that the evidence showed that plaintiff accepted the note, and duly notified defendants. Tatnall *v.* Rome Foundry & Machine Works, 98 Ala. 532, 13 So. 271.

A transferee of a bond for title, who had assumed payment of the original purchase-money notes, received a deed from the vendor, to whom he gave a mortgage; the parties contemporaneously executing a written agreement extending time of payment, which agreement expressly preserved the rights of the original vendee as surety for the transferee of the bond. Each of these instruments referred to notes as having been executed by the latter, which notes were dated several months before the instruments. One was payable six months from its date, and the other in semiannual installments, at intervals of six months from the date of the note. Held, to show that the notes were delivered on the day they bore date, and not when the subsequent agreement was executed. Elyton Co. *v.* Hood, 25 So. 745, 121 Ala. 373.

On an issue as to whether a married woman signed a note purporting to be signed by her jointly with her husband, a witness testified that in his opinion the signature was genuine. Four other witnesses testified that the signature, though closely resembling defendant's, was not hers. Other evidence showed that when the note was handed to the husband, to procure his wife's signature thereto, he took it towards the room occupied by himself and wife, and returned with her name signed to it. Held, that the evidence was sufficient to sustain a finding that the signature of the wife was forged, and that therefore her separate estate was not to be charged with the amount of the note. Starke *v.* Blackwell, 36 Ala. 154.

Not Sufficient.—In an action against defendant as indorser of a note, his admission of his signature as joint maker is not sufficient to support the action, on a plea of non est factum. Adams *v.* Moore, 9 Port. 406.

In an action by the payee against the maker of a note, it appeared that the note was made for the accommodation of the payee, to enable him to obtain money at a particular bank, but it did not appear that the note had been discounted. Held, that plaintiff was not entitled to recover. Allen *v.* Matthews, 1 Stew. 273.

A was indebted to B, by note, in the sum of $280. As an offset against this note, C transferred to A a note which he held on B for $300, but B was not present, nor was A acquainted with the handwriting of B. A handed back the note of B to C, that he might exchange it with B for the note of A for $280, and a few days thereafter C handed to A his note for $280. Held, that this testimony was not sufficient to establish the genuineness of the signature of B. to the note of $300. Hopper *v.* Ashley, 15 Ala. 457.

§ 347. —— Consideration.

See ante, "Verification," § 315.

§ 347 (1) In General.

A promissory note, prima facie, carries on its face, evidence of a consideration. Thompson *v.* Armstrong, 5 Ala. 383.

A note payable to the cashier of a bank, in the hands of one who does not derive title from the bank, imports on its face that it was made without consideration to be negotiated in bank. Thompson *v.* Armstrong, 7 Ala. 256.

In a suit on a note, it appeared that defendant had written a new note for a certain sum to be given plaintiff in renewal, which he afterwards refused to sign. Held, that the note was prima facie an admission that defendant was indebted to plaintiff for that amount. Turrentine *v.* Grigsby, 118 Ala. 380, 23 So. 666.

In an action on a note the jury were properly instructed that if the parties had a settlement three years after its date, and defendant then had a credit indorsed on it, these facts tended to show a valid consideration. Martin *v.* Foster, 83 Ala. 213, 3 So. 422.

In an action on a note by an indorsee, which was given for the price of a slave, with warranty of soundness, it was held that proof of the unsoundness of the slave at the time of sale, amounting to a total failure of consideration, was sufficient to entitle defendant to a verdict, without showing that the vendor knew of the unsoundness, and without proof of an offer to return the slave, the slave dying so soon after the sale as to render a return impracticable. Morehead *v.* Gayle, 2 Stew. & P. 224.

Evidence held to justify a finding that notes set up as a foundation of a bill to sell lands of the maker were without consideration. Jackson *v.* Grishan, 171 Ala. 553, 55 So. 165.

§ 347 (2) Accommodation Obligation.

If a maker of a promissory note carries it to a bank to get it discounted on his own account, with the name of a third person indorsed thereon; the transaction, on its face, shows that it is a mere accommodation indorsement, or the note would not be in the hands of the maker. Wallace *v.* Branch Bank, 1 Ala. 565.

§ 348. —— Nature and Extent of Liability.

Evidence held to support a finding that the note was intended as the personal obligation of defendant, and not that of a corporation of which he was an officer, though signed by the corporation and followed by defendant's name and the word "Prest." Briel *v.* Exchange Nat. Bank (Ala.), 61 So. 277.

§ 349. —— Mistake, Fraud, or Duress.

Where, in an action on certain rent notes, defendant pleaded fraudulent representations by plaintiff's agent that a street car line was projected through or near the land leased, but there was no proof as to when the representations were made, or as to the authority of the agent to make them, that the notes were given on the faith of such representations, or as to whether the car line would add to the value of the property, the defense of fraud was not sustained. Tribble *v.* Crestline Land Co., 52 So. 600, 167 Ala. 398.

§ 350. —— Legality of Object and of Consideration.

Evidence of illegality of consideration of the contract on which the note in suit was based is sufficient if it produces the amount of conviction essential in civil cases. It need not remove all reasonable doubt as in criminal cases. Ware *v.* Jones, 61 Ala. 288.

§ 351. —— Transfer and Ownership in General.

See post, "Possession as Evidence of Ownership," § 352.

In an action on a note, where plaintiff introduced the note, with an indorsement transferring it to him, and testified that he bought it in due process of business, before maturity, for its face value, he made out a prima facie case. Tapia *v.* Baggett, 52 So. 834, 167 Ala. 381.

When a note is offered to a bank for discount, and refused, unless an additional surety is given, which is not done, and afterwards, the note is put in suit by the bank—held, that the bank, to show title in the note, must prove that it was afterwards discounted, and the money received by the principal, or carried to his credit, in the extinction of an old debt, and proof that the old debt was extinguished, would be evidence prima facie of the acceptance and discount of the note by the bank. Findley *v.* State Bank, 6 Ala. 244.

Where there is added to the payee's name, in a note given for the rent of a wife's land, payable to the husband, the words "trustee for" his wife, the addition is insufficient to show that the note belonged to her. Westmoreland *v.* Foster, 60 Ala. 448.

The mere indorsement of the payees' names in blank remaining on a bill of exchange, when introduced as evidence in a suit on the bill, does not show that the legal title was not in them. Beeson *v.* Lippman, 52 Ala. 276.

§ 352. —— Possession as Evidence of Ownership.

See ante, "Possession," § 326 (2); "Presentment, Demand, Protest, and Notice," § 328.

The possession of a negotiable instrument is sufficient prima facie evidence of ownership. Jarrell *v.* Lillie, 40 Ala. 271; Lakeside Land Co. *v.* Dromgoole, 89 Ala. 505, 7 So. 444.

Possession of a note by the payee is prima facie evidence that it is his property, and that it is unpaid. Anniston Pipe Works *v.* Mary Pratt Furnace Co., 94 Ala. 606, 10 So. 259.

Possession of a note transferable by delivery only, or indorsed in blank, is prima facie proof of title. Alabama & M. R. Co. *v.* Sanford, 36 Ala. 703.

In an action on a note against the maker, plaintiff's introduction of the note corresponding with the allegation in the complaint established a prima facie case. Deleon *v.* Walter, 50 So. 934, 163 Ala. 499.

Where the holder of a note is the payee, he is presumed to be the owner of it although it has an indorsement to another, until the contrary appears. Pitts *v.* Keyser, 1 Stew. 154; Stone *v.* English, 1 Stew. 169.

Plaintiff producing a note payable to him, is presumed owner of it; though it appears endorsed by him to another, but this is but a presumption, and may be rebutted by proof; and if the interest be really in such endorsee, the plaintiff can not recover. Pitts *v.* Keyser, 1 Stew. 154.

When a note payable to the order of an intestate, and bearing his indorsement, is found in the possession of his administratrix, the presumption is that the note was regularly returned to her, and she is entitled to maintain an action thereon. Tuscaloosa, etc., Oil Co. *v.* Perry, 85 Ala. 158, 4 So. 635.

Where a note payable to two persons, not partners, is found by the executor of one of them among his testator's effects, and produced by the executor on the trial, the presumption is that he owns the note in his representative capacity. Tisdale *v.* Maxwell, 58 Ala. 40.

The possession of a promissory note by the maker, or one who succeeds to his rights, or estate, tends to show that it has been paid, or that such person has acquired the beneficial ownership of it. Potts *v.* Coleman, 67 Ala. 221.

§ 353. —— Presentment, Demand, Protest, and Notice.

Prima Facie Evidence.—The recital of a notary public, that he had "given due notice by notice addressed to the party, by the first mail to Lafayette, Chambers county, Alabama," is prima facie sufficient evidence under the statute of notice. Dunn *v.* Adams, etc., Co., 1 Ala. 527.

A memorandum on the face of a bill, in form a noting of the bill for protest, in the absence of explanatory proof, is prima facie evidence of protest for nonacceptance. Riggs *v.* McDonald, 1 Ala. 641.

The postmark on a letter is not evidence, per se, that the letter was deposited in the post office on the day indicated by it; but, its genuineness being proved, it is prima facie evidence, to fix the liability of a drawer of a protested bill, of the time when the notice was mailed. Crawford *v.* Branch Bank at Mobile, 7 Ala. 205.

Not Sufficient.—In an action on a note against the indorser, testimony of plaintiff that he mailed to defendant a notice of protest, at F., which place he "understood" to be the address of defendant, in the absence of any proof that F. was defendant's post-office address, or any evidence as to inquiries made by plaintiff to ascertain his address, is insufficient to prove notice of protest. German Security Bank *v.* McGarry, 106 Ala. 633, 17 So. 704.

An admission by an indorser of a bill of exchange of his indebtedness thereon is not evidence of his having received notice of protest thereof, unless such admission was preceded by a legal protest. Todd *v.* Neal, 49 Ala. 266.

Where the holder of a bill resided in Mobile, and the indorser in Tuskaloosa, though the deposit in the post office of the latter place, by an agent, of notice of the dishonor of the bill will not be sufficient to charge the indorser, unless it actually comes into his hands, yet on proof of these facts a jury might infer that the indorser received notice, if no countervailing fact is shown to destroy the presumption, and, on a demurrer to the evidence, the court will so decide. Foster *v.* McDonald, 5 Ala. 376.

In an action on a note, against an indorsee, testimony of plaintiff that he mailed to defendant notice of protest, "about" a certain time, is insufficient to prove that the notice was promptly given, the burden of proof being on plaintiff to prove notice. German Security Bank *v.* McGarry, 106 Ala. 633, 17 So. 704.

Question for Jury.—The cashier of a bank which was the holder of a bill payable in another state testified that the bill, at the time of maturity, was at the place of payment; that, in due course of mail thereafter, he received a package containing a large number of protests; that he had no distinct recollection of the one in question, but does not doubt it was regularly received; that notices were enclosed, enveloped, addressed, and mailed to the drawer and indorsers on the same day, as such was his constant practice; and, if he had received the protest under circumstances indicating that it had not been transmitted from the place of payment in due season, it would have been noted according to the invariable mode of doing business in the bank. Held, that the refusal to instruct the jury that the evidence of the cashier was insufficient to charge the indorser with notice of the dishonor of the bill was not an error, and that the evidence was such as might well have been left to the jury to determine its effect. Ball *v.* Bank of Alabama, 8 Ala. 590, 42 Am. Dec. 649.

§ 354. —— Payment and Discharge.

In General.—An indorsement of a payment on a promissory note, if legible, is prima facie evidence of such payment, although an attempt has been made to obliterate it by drawing a pen through the lines. Clark *v.* Simmons, 4 Port. 14.

Where defendant in a suit on a note pleads that judgment was rendered against him in a foreign state, as garnishee in an action against the payee of the note, and that such judgment had been satisfied, a statement by the clerk of the court rendering said judgment. of its amount, and payment by the garnishee, though certified as part of the record in the garnishment proceedings, is not evidence of the fact of payment, in the absence of any proof of the laws of such foreign state making it a part of the proceedings. Mills *v.* Stewart, 12 Ala. 90.

A, being indebted to B in a sum of money secured by note, left the amount in the hands of C to take up the note. On being written to by the attorneys of B for the money, A informed them of the deposit with C, and requested them to call on C, and receive the money. After this, the attorneys of B brought suit against C, and recovered judgment, but the judgment was not satisfied, C being insolvent. Held, that these facts did not establish a payment of the debt. Sledge *v.* Tubb, 11 Ala. 383.

Where the uncontradicted evidence in an action on a note showed that it had not been paid, the mere assertion of one of the makers that he had paid the payee all he owed him, and that the payee had stated that the indebtedness had been paid, did not sustain the plea of payment, and justify a finding of payment. Engelbert *v.* Taylor, 55 So. 442, 1 Ala. App. 553.

In an action on a note, evidence held to so clearly preponderate against the verdict for the maker on the defense of payment as to necessitate a new trial. Engelbert *v.* Taylor, 1 Ala. App. 553, 55 So. 442.

In a proceeding by an administrator de bonis non to compel the former administrator to account for the amount of three notes executed by the latter in the intestate's favor, the latter's wife testified that he had possession of the notes in December, 1894, prior to intestate's death, and before one of the notes was due. She did not know how he had obtained money to pay the notes, and there was evidence of an admission by him that the notes had not been paid. There was evidence that a firm of which he was a member had paid certain sums to intestate subsequent to December, 1894, and that the firm was under obligations to pay intestate something for personal services and the rent of a sawmill. Held, that the evidence was too indefinite to show any payment. Arnold *v.* Arnold, 124 Ala. 550, 27 So. 465, 466.

§ 355. Amount of Recovery.

See post, "In General," § 356; "Interest," § 357; "Costs of Protest," § 358; "Damages for Dishonor," § 359; "Attorney's Fees," § 360.

§ 356. —— In General.

Where a bank was indebted to a customer, for services, and for checks held by the customer, and for a balance on account, in an amount exceeding a check drawn by the customer, which check the bank agreed it would pay, the damages sustained by the drawer for failure to present the check were held to be the amount thereof, and not merely the balance on account due him. Industrial Trust, Title & Savings Co. *v.* Weakley, 103 Ala. 458, 15 So. 854.

In assumpsit on a promissory note, if the defendant, after appearance, withdraws his plea, the court may render judgment for the amount of the note and interest thereon, without regard to the amount of damages laid in the declaration. Kennedy *v.* Young, 25 Ala. 563.

In an action since the war on a note payable during the war, given in consideration of the loan of Confederate currency, and intended to be discharged in "dollars" of that currency, the measure of recovery is the value of the currency at the time of the loan. Whitfield *v.* Riddle, 52 Ala. 467.

The measure of damages for the breach of the contract of payment of several promissory notes payable in Confederate money, a part of which became due before the overthrow of the Confederate government in Alabama, and a part afterwards, is the value of the Confederate currency at the maturity of the notes, respectively. Kirtland *v.* Molton, 41 Ala. 548.

§ 357. —— Interest.

On a note payable at a future day, with interest from the date, if not punctually paid, judgment may be properly rendered for principal, with the interest from maturity. Boddie *v.* Ely, 3 Stew. 182.

Where a bill drawn in this state is payable abroad, if dishonored either by nonacceptance or nonpayment, the drawer is liable to pay interest according to the laws of this state. Crawford *v.* Branch Bank, 6 Ala. 574.

A person entitled to a life estate in a note, and to the interest accruing thereon during her life, may, upon maturity of the note, recover both principal and interest, as the demand for principal and interest is an entire one, and can not be split so as to allow a recovery for interest alone. Ellerbe *v.* Troy, 58 Ala. 143.

§ 358. —— Costs of Protest.

In an action on a bill of exchange against the drawer, the bill being made payable in a sister state, and protested there, plaintiff can not recover the notarial fees, without proof of the notary's legal fees in such sister state. Crawford *v.* Branch Bank, 6 Ala. 574.

§ 359. —— Damages for Dishonor.

Damages on a bill of exchange accrue only on protest, which, in an action on the bill, must be averred in order to recover damages. Jordan *v.* Bell, 8 Port. 53.

The damages on a protested bill of exchange, drawn within this state, and payable in a sister state, is ten per cent. Murphy *v.* Andrews & Bros., 13 Ala. 708.

A bill of exchange drawn in one state upon a person therein, but made payable in another state, is not entitled to the statute damages in such other state, on protest for nonpayment. Crawford *v.*

Branch Bank at Mobile, 6 Ala. 12, 41 Am. Dec. 33; Crawford *v.* Branch Bank at Decatur, 6 Ala. 574.

A drawee of a bill of exchange can not maintain an action for damages against the holder for having the bill protested after waiver of protest by the drawer and indorser. Bellinger *v.* Glenn, 80 Ala. 190, 60 Am. Rep. 980.

§ 360. —— Attorney's Fees.

An agreement to pay a note, "with all legal or other expenses of or for collection," covers a reasonable attorney's fee for collection. McGhee *v.* Importers, etc., Nat. Bank, 93 Ala. 196, 9 So. 734.

The plaintiff, in a suit on a promissory note providing for the payment of an attorney's fee in case of suit, is not entitled to have such fee included in the judgment, without proving what a reasonable fee would be. Camp *v.* Randle, 81 Ala. 240, 2 So. 287; Orr *v.* Sparkman, 23 So. 829, 120 Ala. 9.

§ 361. Trial.

See post, "Conduct in General," § 362; "Questions for Jury," § 363; "Instructions," § 364; "Verdict and Findings," § 365.

§ 362. —— Conduct in General.

When it becomes necessary to prove the consideration of a note, the most regular mode of proceeding is to introduce the note in evidence first, and then go on to show its consideration. Pennington *v.* Woodall, 17 Ala. 685.

Where the common counts are added to a count on a bill of exchange, in an action thereon, the clerk may compute the damages without there being a nol. pros. entered to the common counts. Hanrick *v.* Farmers' Bank, 8 Port. 539, overruling Moreland *v.* Ruffin, Minor 18.

When an action is brought by summons and complaint, under the Code, on a promissory note and an open account for work and labor done, it is error to render judgment final by default for the aggregate amount of the sums claimed, without the intervention of a jury, or the execution of a writ of inquiry. Beville *v.* Reese, 25 Ala. 451.

In an action on a note, where defendant pleaded non est factum, a remark of the plaintiff's attorney that, if the plea was true, it charged plaintiff with forgery, was but an expression of opinion, and not a statement of a fact not in evidence, and that overruling of an exception to the remark was not error. Brown *v.* Johnson Bros., 135 Ala. 608, 33 So. 683.

§ 363. —— Questions for Jury.

§ 363 (1) In General.

The question as to whether certain facts existed, invalidating a bill for usury, is for the jury. Saltmarsh *v.* P. & M. Bank, 14 Ala. 668.

In a suit on a note, where plaintiff has joined issue on defendant's plea that he did not sign it "as a waive note or contract," the only question raised is the waiver of exemption, and it must be submitted to the jury. Slaughter *v.* First Nat. Bank, 109 Ala. 157, 19 So. 430.

In an action on a note given for the price of a circular saw, defendant pleaded that plaintiff had agreed that any sum which defendant should be obliged to pay to one holding any patent covering such saw should be deducted from the amount of the note, and that an agent of the patentee, claiming that the patent covered the saw in suit, had demanded and received without suit a sum equal to the amount of the note. Held, that the question whether the saw in suit was covered by the patent was one of fact for the jury. Orr *v.* Burwell, 15 Ala. 378.

§ 363 (2) Execution and Delivery.

In an action on a note in which defendant pleaded non est factum, but, as a witness, admitted signing the instrument in suit, an affirmative charge as to that plea was proper. Mizell *v.* Farmers' Bank (Ala.), 61 So. 272.

Where, in a suit on a renewal note, there was evidence that the note had not been changed in terms from the original note, defendant was not entitled to an affirmative charge on the plea of non est factum. Cochran *v.* Perkins, 40 So. 351, 146 Ala. 689.

Where a note was shown to have been signed on Sunday, but bore date of a different day, it is for the jury to determine, under all the circumstances, on what day it was delivered. Flanagan *v.* Meyer, 41 Ala. 132.

§ 363 (3) Consideration.

Where, in a suit on a bond or bill single, issue was taken on plaintiff's replication that the bond was given in settlement of certain controversies between the parties, such allegation became material, and, it being proved without dispute and beyond adverse inference, plaintiff was entitled to an affirmative charge thereon. Union Fertilizer Co. *v.* Johnson (Ala.), 39 So. 684.

Where, in an action on a note, pleas of failure of consideration were fully established, and it also appeared in support of a plea of non est factum that the note had been materially altered without defendant's consent, it was not error to give a general charge in favor of defendant. Carroll *v.* Warren, 37 So. 687, 142 Ala. 397.

Where, in an action on a note, defendant set up that the same was without consideration for the reason that he had acted as agent only for plaintiff in the sale of stock, and that the note was given for losses on such sales, for which he was not liable, but there was evidence from which the jury could have inferred that defendant had something as agent belonging to plaintiff when he executed the original note, of which the one sued on was a renewal, the refusal to give the affirmative charge for defendant was not error. Cochran *v.* Perkins, 40 So. 351, 146 Ala. 689.

In an action on a note, which the maker claimed was void because given for a horse which the seller intended should be used in the Confederate service, the question whether the seller did so intend is for the jury. Thedford *v.* McClintock, 47 Ala. 647.

§ 363 (4) Title and Ownership of Instrument.

Where plaintiff did not prove when the note sued on was transferred to him or that he was a bona fide purchaser, his request for the general affirmative charge was properly denied. Darden *v.* Holloway, 1 Ala. App. 661, 56 So. 32.

Where there is some evidence tending to impeach the conclusion that plaintiff paid anything for the notes, it is a question for the jury to determine whether or not plaintiff was a purchaser or a formal holder for other persons. Bunzel *v.* Maas, 22 So. 568, 116 Ala. 68.

§ 363 (5) Good Faith and Payment of Value.

Where the testimony as to the bona fides of the purchase of a note, the only fact in controversy, is undisputed, it is proper for the court to direct the verdict. Scott *v.* Taul, 22 So. 447, 115 Ala. 529.

§ 363 (6) Presentment, Demand, Protest, and Notice.

See post, "Demand and Notice," § 364 (4).

The seasonableness of notice of nonpayment of a note is a question of fact for a jury. Brahan *v.* Ragland, Minor 85; Branch Bank at Montgomery *v.* Gaffney, 9 Ala. 153.

The question of diligence in the case of an irregular indorsement of nonnegotiable paper is for the jury. Fulford *v.* Johnson, 15 Ala. 385.

In an action against an indorser, parol evidence being given in support of the certificate of notice annexed to the protest, that he kept no clerk, and that the notice was left at his office on the day of protest, the whole evidence should be referred to the jury, to determine whether he had actually received the notice. Stanley *v.* Bank of Mobile, 23 Ala. 652.

Where it is sought to charge an indorser of commercial paper, who indorsed it after maturity, it is a question for the jury, considering the residence of the parties, facilities for communication, etc., whether the holder demanded payment within a reasonable time. Branch Bank at Montgomery *v.* Gaffney, 9 Ala. 153.

The interpretation of notice of dishonor and protest is for the court, and should not be referred to the jury. Saltmarsh *v.* Tuthill, 13 Ala. 390.

The court is to determine, as a matter of law, the sufficiency, in itself, of a written notice of dishonor. Stanley *v.* Bank of Mobile, 23 Ala. 652.

§ 363 (7) Payment and Discharge.

Whether credits on a note were indorsed by mistake is a question for the jury. Tubb *v.* Madding, Minor 129.

In an action on a promissory note, the evidence examined, and held that the issue of payment was properly left to the jury. Englehart *v.* Richter, 33 So. 939, 136 Ala. 562.

Defendant indorsed a draft for the accommodation of the apparent payee, who had without his complicity fraudulently changed the name of the original payee, and raised the amount, and who negotiated the draft to plaintiff bank. Plaintiff sent the draft for collection to its agent, who entered the amount to its credit, but the draft was afterwards returned. It did not appear directly whether payment had been refused on presentment, or whether the draft had been paid, and the money refunded by the agent to the drawee on discovery of the forgery. The draft, when offered in evidence by plaintiff, was stamped "Paid" by the agent, and was mutilated in the manner employed by the drawee for cancellation of paid drafts. Held, that plaintiff was entitled to have the question of payment submitted to the jury, since from plaintiff's possession of the draft it was to be presumed that it had been regularly returned, and that the title was in plaintiff, which was possible only on the supposition that, on discovery of the forgery, the agent had refunded the money, received the draft in return, charged back the credit to plaintiff, and returned to it the draft, and such facts would be proof of nonpayment. Alabama Nat. Bank *v.* Rivers, 22 So. 580, 116 Ala. 1, 67 Am. St. Rep. 95.

§ 364. —— Instructions.

§ 364 (1) In General.

Pleading.—In an action on a promissory note, the defendant pleaded a readiness to pay the note on maturity, and also a readiness to pay but a part. On the trial of the case, the judge charged the jury that the two pleas admitted a balance to be due. Held, that the charge was erroneous, and that each plea must stand on its own distinct admissions and merits. Cowan *v.* Harper, 2 Stew. & P. 236.

Issues.—Where a note bore date April 25th, but showed evidence of having been changed from April 15th, and the sole issue raised by the pleadings was as to whether the alteration was before or after the note was executed, a charge directing a verdict for defendant if the jury should find that the instrument actually bore date April 15th was properly denied, as raising an issue not in the case. Lesser *v.* Scholze, 93 Ala. 338, 9 So. 273.

Inapplicable.—Where, in a suit on a note, a plea of non est factum is interposed, and plaintiff replies that he is a bona fide purchaser, and issue is joined on the replication, an instruction that, if there was a material alteration of the note by the payee after delivery, no recovery can be had, is inapplicable and erroneous. Winter *v.* Pool, 100 Ala. 503, 14 So. 411.

Burden of Proof.—In an action by the assignee of a note and open account, the plaintiff's ownership of the cause of action being put in issue by plea verified by affidavit, it is error to instruct the jury "that, if the evidence between the parties was equally balanced, they must find for the plaintiff." Jarrell *v.* Lillie, 40 Ala. 271.

Justified by Evidence.—Where, in an action on notes signed by husband and wife, there was evidence that they were partners, a charge that a wife can not become surety for her husband, and was not liable unless she was a partner, was proper, though they were sued as individuals. Compton *v.* Smith, 25 So. 300, 120 Ala. 233.

Not Justified by Evidence.—In an action on a note defended on the ground of a material alteration, an instruction that if defendant, after being fully informed thereof, authorized an entry of credits on the note, which he claimed to be entitled to for past payments, he thereby ratified and confirmed the alteration, is properly refused, where it does not appear that the payments referred to were made at a time when defendant had full knowledge of the alleged alteration. Payne *v.* Long, 25 So. 780, 121 Ala. 385.

An instruction that "if the agreement between the plaintiff and defendants, which included the signing of the notes sued on, is equally capable of two constructions, one legal and the other criminal, the jury should rather hold to the construction making the agreement legal," was properly refused, as misleading, and because excluding from the jury all the evidence in the case except the agreement itself. United States Fidelity & Guaranty Co. *v.* Charles, 31 So. 558, 131 Ala. 658, 57 L. R. A. 212.

§ 364 (2) Ownership and Transfer of Note.

In an action on an unindorsed note payable to a person other than plaintiff, in which defendant filed a sworn plea that plaintiff had no interest or title in the note, and the evidence was conflicting on the issue raised thereby, it was error to refuse to instruct, on defendant's request, that, the note being payable to a third person, the law presumes that person to be the owner until the evidence shows his title to have terminated. Turnley *v.* Black, 44 Ala. 159.

§ 364 (3) Consideration.

Where, in an action on a note, defendant set up that it was without consideration, in that it was given for losses arising on a sale of stock in which sale he had acted as plaintiff's agent only, an instruction that, if the jury believed that defendant received the stock from plaintiff under an agreement that defendant was to be paid one-half of the profit made by a sale of them, after the payment of expenses, and that there were no profits, but a loss arising on the sale, defendant was not liable for any portion of such loss, and any note given by him was without consideration, was properly refused, as ignoring the conditions existing when the note was given, as, while defendant would not be liable on the original contract for any loss sustained, or if the sole consideration of the note was the assumption of the loss, yet there may have been stock, proceeds for the sale of the same in excess of expenses, or debts owing for the same at the time to provide a valuable consideration for the note, and from the instruction the jury might have inferred that the note was without consideration, if a loss was sustained in the sale of the stock. Cochran *v.* Perkins, 40 So. 351, 146 Ala. 689.

Where, in an action on a note, defendant set up that the same was without consideration, in that it was given for losses sustained by plaintiff on the sale of stock, in making which sale defendant acted as plaintiff's agent merely, and was not liable for such losses, the jury could have inferred from the evidence a valuable consideration for the note, whether defendant agreed to buy the stock or not, as he might have had proceeds of the sale of the same, or notes representing debts for the same, to which plaintiff was entitled when the note was made, and the relinquishment of which claims would afford a valuable consideration of the note, an instruction that, unless the jury found from the evidence that defendant agreed to buy the stock or some of it from plaintiff, the verdict must be for defendant, was properly refused. Cochran *v.* Perkins, 40 So. 351, 146 Ala. 689.

Where, in an action on a note, defendant pleaded that the same was without consideration, in that he had acted only as plaintiff's agent in the sale of stock, and that the note was given for losses occurring on such sales, for which he was not liable, but there was evidence from which the jury could infer that defendant had something as agent that belonged to plaintiff when he executed the note, the court properly refused to charge that defendant was not liable for any loss sustained by plaintiff on the stock, as the relinquishment of plaintiff's claim would have supported the note, and the jury might have inferred from the charge that they could not find for plaintiff, even if there was a valuable consideration for the note. Cochran *v.* Perkins, 40 So. 351, 146 Ala. 689.

§ 364 (4) Demand and Notice.

See ante, "Presentment, Demand, Protest, and Notice," § 353.

Where plaintiff averred, and the evidence showed, that the note sued on was duly presented for payment, and legal notice of dishonor given, the error, if any, in instructing that presentment was unnecessary unless there were funds of the maker at the bank where it was payable, and that notice by mail was sufficient, was not injurious to defendants. Carrington *v.* Odom, 27 So. 510, 124 Ala. 529.

In an action on a bill of exchange by the indorsee against the indorser, there was produced what was testified to as a copy of the protest, which did not appear to have been a certified copy, nor to have been authenticated otherwise than by certain depositions of the notary and witnesses of the protest to which the copy was attached as an exhibit. The court charged the jury that "the exhibit, together with the depositions accompanying the same, were sufficient evidence, of themselves, of the protest of the bill." Held, that the charge was erroneous, as it assumed that as a fact which it was the province of the jury to find. Stewart *v.* Russell, 38 Ala. 619.

In an action on a bill of exchange against the drawer, the court charged the jury "that the bill of exchange which had been read to them, and the certificate thus admitted, was testimony for them to consider as evidence of the protest of said bill and notice to the defendant." Held that, as the protest was admissible evidence, though perhaps insufficient in itself, the charge was not erroneous. Leigh *v.* Lightfoot, 11 Ala. 935.

§ 364 (5) Payment and Discharge.

In an action on a note, a charge that it is the duty of the plaintiff to satisfy the jury that the debt sued for has not been paid, and that until they are satisfied of this they can not find for the plaintiff, was properly refused for failure to use the word "reasonably" as qualifying "satisfied," and as misplacing the burden of proof. Walston *v.* Davis, 40 So. 1017, 146 Ala. 510.

§ 365. —— Verdict and Findings.

Where two makers of a note are sued jointly, it is error to charge that if the evidence warrants a verdict against one only the verdict must be for defendants generally, since a general verdict would bar plaintiff's several action against the defendant really liable to him. A verdict should be permitted according to the evidence, leaving it afterwards to the parties to move for judgment, or to annul it, as they may be advised. Palmer *v.* Severance, 10 Ala. 346.

A finding that the indorser of a note was duly notified of its protest, based on proof of the service of protest by mail, and evidence that in the town where the note was protested that manner of giving notice was customary, will not be disturbed on the ground that, the payee and indorser residing in the same town, personal notice was necessary, where the objection was by demurrer to the evidence, which admits the competency of the evidence, and merely presents the question of its sufficiency for determination. Carter *v.* Odom, 25 So. 774, 121 Ala. 162.

§ 366. Judgment.

See post, "Execution," § 367.

Under the statute (Code of 1876, §§ 2905, 2919), written obligations and promises of any description are several as well as joint; and in a suit against the obligors or promisors a recovery may be had against one or more of them, as the facts in evidence may justify. Steed *v.* Barnhill, 71 Ala. 157.

It is no objection that interest and damages for nonpayment, on a bill of exchange, are included in the same entry of judgment, without specifying the amount of each separately. Dickinson *v.* Branch Bank at Mobile, 12 Ala. 54.

By Default.—In an action against the drawer or an indorser of a bill of exchange, a final judgment may be rendered, by default, against the defendant. Henderson *v.* Howard, 2 Ala. 342.

When, in an action of assumpsit, the common counts are added to a count on a promissory note, it is allowable to take a judgment by default, without causing a nolle prosequi to be entered as to the former; but the judgment in such case must not exceed the amount of the note. Granberry *v.* Wellborn, 4 Ala. 118.

In an action against an indorser, it is competent to render a judgment final by default, without the intervention of a jury. Smith *v.* Robinson, 11 Ala. 270.

A note containing a stipulation for attorney's fees will support a judgment by default which includes such fees, without a writ of inquiry. Ledbetter, etc., Loan Ass'n *v.* Vinton, 108 Ala. 644,

18 So. 692; Wood *v.* Winship Mach. Co., 83 Ala. 424, 3 So. 757.

A judgment by default, in an action on a promissory note, will be reversed on error, when the record shows that a plea of non est factum, duly verified by affidavit, was on file. McCoy *v.* Nichols & Co., 40 Ala. 232; Crow *v.* Decatur Bank, 5 Ala. 249.

By statute of 1828, in an action against the maker and indorser jointly, where one appears and continues the case as to him, and there is judgment by default against the other, this judgment can not be rendered final. Chapman *v.* Arrington, 3 Stew. 480.

§ 367. —— Execution.

A writ is properly sued out, so as to charge the indorser, although the maker removed from the county a few days previous to the institution of the suit; it not appearing, that such removal was open, visible, and notorious, or that the indorsee had knowledge of the fact, or that the maker was a freeholder of the county to which he removed, or was exempt from suit in the county in which he was sued. Weed & Co. *v.* Brown, 13 Ala. 449.

When a writ is properly sued out against the maker of a note, judgment obtained, and the statutory return of "no property found," made by the sheriff, it will be sufficient to charge the indorser, though it be shown, that the maker removed to another county after the institution of the suit. Quære, if the indorsee is informed of such removal and that an execution would be more likely to be availing there, than if issued in the county in which the judgment was obtained, would it not be his duty to send it to such county. Weed & Co. *v.* Brown, 13 Ala. 449.

§ 368. Appeal and Error.

See ante, "Necessity of Alleging Indorsement, Assignment, and Ownership," § 298 (1); "Verification," § 315.

That suit is brought on a cause of action before the same is past due is available in error, even after appearance and judgment by nil dicit. Randolph *v.* Ellis, 2 Port. 286.

A declaration against defendant, as drawer of a bill, which does not allege presentment for payment, and the notice of refusal, is not a defect available in error. Smith *v.* Paul, 8 Port. 503.

In an action by an indorsee against the maker of a note, the omission to set out the name of one of the indorsers is not available after verdict. Strader *v.* Alexander, 9 Port. 441.

In an action on a promissory note, where the record shows that the parties went to trial on an issue joined, but it does not appear what the issue was, an objection to the admissibility of evidence, offered by the defendant, that the note sued on was given for the sole consideration of negro hire, in the year 1864, without stating why it was inadmissible, may be properly overruled. Tracey, etc., Co. *v.* Warren, 45 Ala. 408.

In an action against the indorsers of a note which purported to have been indorsed under a power of attorney, where the defendants deny the indorsement and demur to the evidence, which recites that the execution of the power, as well as the note on which the plaintiff sought to recover judgment, was proved, it will be intended, as the making of the note was not a point in issue, that the indorsement, and not the execution of the note, was in fact proved. Bank of Mobile *v.* King, 9 Ala. 279.

Where the plea which denied the execution of a note as averred in the complaint was not verified, and on that account could have been stricken out on motion, error in striking out such plea on an insufficient demurrer was harmless. Carter *v.* Long, 125 Ala. 280, 28 So. 74.

In an action on a note dated in another state, and containing a waiver of exemptions, defendant contended that the waiver referred only to the laws of such state. Held, that the exclusion of evidence offered by defendant to show that the note was executed and delivered at the place of its date, and that he was then living in the state where suit was brought, if error, was harmless. Holland *v.* Bergan, 89 Ala. 622, 7 So. 770.

Bill to Enforce Decree.

See the titles EQUITY; JUDGMENT.

Bill to Impeach Decree.

See the titles EQUITY; JUDGMENT.

Bill to Perpetuate Testimony.

See the title DEPOSITIONS.

Bill to Remove Cloud.

See the titles EQUITY; QUIETING TITLE.

Binding Out.

See the title APPRENTICES.

Binding Over.

See the titles BAIL; BREACH OF THE PEACE. And see the title WITNESSES.

Birds.

See the title GAME.

Birth.

See the title ABORTION.

As to determining descent of property, see the title DESCENT AND DISTRIBUTION. As to evidence as to birth, see the title EVIDENCE. As affecting question of domicile, see the title DOMICILE. As to bastard children, see the title BASTARDS.

Blackmail.

See the titles CONSPIRACY; THREATS.

Blanket Policy.

See the title INSURANCE.

Blanks.

As to blanks in particular instruments, see the particular titles, such as BILLS AND NOTES; CONTRACTS; DEEDS; MORTGAGES; etc. As to filling blanks, see the titles ACKNOWLEDGMENT; ALTERATION OF INSTRUMENTS; FORGERY. As to indorsement in blank, see the title BILLS AND NOTES.

Blasphemy.

See the title DISORDERLY CONDUCT.

Blasting.

As to care required by persons blasting and injuries received therefrom, see the titles EXPLOSIVES; MASTER AND SERVANT.

Blind Persons.

See the titles NEGLIGENCE; RAILROADS.

Block Signals.

See the titles MASTER AND SERVANT; RAILROADS.

Blood.

As determining right of inheritance and right of persons to take under will, see the titles BASTARDS; DESCENT AND DISTRIBUTION; WILLS. As evidence, see the title CRIMINAL LAW.

Boarding Houses.

See the titles INNKEEPERS; LICENSES.

Boards.

As to particular classes of boards, such as boards of agriculture, aldermen, assessors, etc.; see the particular titles throughout this work, such as AGRICULTURE; MUNICIPAL CORPORATIONS; TAXATION; etc. As to municipal department in general, see the title MUNICIPAL CORPORATIONS. As to officers in general, see the title OFFICERS. As to prohibiting acts and proceedings of public boards, see the title PROHIBITION. As to compelling performance of public duties, see the title MANDAMUS.

Bodily Conditions.

See the titles DAMAGES; EVIDENCE.

Bodily Fear.

See the titles DAMAGES; HOMICIDE; RAPE; ROBBERY.

Bodily Harm.

See the titles ASSAULT AND BATTERY; HOMICIDE; MAYHEM; RAPE; ROBBERY. As to particular causes or manners of injuries, see the particular titles throughout this work, such as ANIMALS; ASSAULT AND BATTERY; ELECTRICITY; NEGLIGENCE; RAILROADS; STREET RAILROADS. As to particular classes of persons injured, see the particular titles, such as HUSBAND AND WIFE; MASTER AND SERVANT; PARENT AND CHILD; etc.

Body.

As to dead bodies, see the title DEAD BODIES. As to heirs of the body, see the titles DEEDS; DESCENT AND DISTRIBUTION; WILLS.

Bona Fide Purchasers.

As to assignees in general, see the titles ASSIGNMENTS FOR BENEFIT OF CREDITORS; MORTGAGES. As to bona fide purchasers of particular rights, instruments and property, see the particular titles throughout this work.

Bondholders.

See the titles BONDS; CORPORATIONS; COUNTIES; MUNICIPAL CORPORATIONS.

BONDS.

I. Requisites and Validity.

II. Construction and Operation.

III. Negotiability and Transfer.

IV. Performance or Breach of Condition.

V. Actions.

Cross References.

As to actions for the recovery of the amount of a lost bond, see the title LOST INSTRUMENTS. As to acknowledgment of bond by obligor as preventing the running of the statute of limitations, see the title LIMITATION OF ACTIONS. As to bonds conditioned for the conveyance of real estate, see the title VENDOR AND PURCHASER. As to bonds of clerks, see the title CLERKS OF COURTS. As to bonds required or incident to particular remedies or legal proceedings, see the titles APPEAL AND ERROR; ARREST; ATTACHMENT; BAIL; COSTS; GARNISHMENT; INJUNCTION; REPLEVIN; SHERIFFS AND CONSTABLES. As to bonds given to a sheriff to save him harmless upon the levy of property of a stranger to the judgment, see the title SHERIFFS AND CONSTABLES. As to bonds delivered in escrow, see the title ESCROW. As to bonds by particular classes of persons, see the titles INFANTS; INSANE PERSONS; and other specific heads. As to bonds by corporations, see the title CORPORATIONS; by governments, see the titles STATES; UNITED STATES; and by other political or municipal bodies, see the titles COUNTIES; MUNICIPAL CORPORATIONS; SCHOOLS AND SCHOOL DISTRICTS; TOWNS. As to bonds secured by mortgage, see the title MORTGAGES. As to bottomry and respondentia bonds, see the title SHIPPING. As to bonds for performance of particular classes of fiduciary or official duties, see the titles EXECUTORS AND ADMINISTRATORS; GUARDIAN AND WARD; OFFICERS; TRUSTS; and titles of specific officers. As to certiorari bonds, see the title CERTIORARI. As to demurrer to declaration on a bond, see the title PLEADING. As to distinct rights and liabilities of sureties, see the title PRINCIPAL AND SURETY. As to extent to which a wife is bound by joining with husband in a covenant in a bond to convey title, see the title HUSBAND AND WIFE. As to execution of bonds by one member of a partnership, and parol ratification by the others—effect of, see the title PARTNERSHIP. As to injunction bonds, see the title INJUNCTION. As to liability of principal whose agent, having authority to fill in blanks, converts the instrument into a bond by sealing, see the title PRINCIPAL AND AGENT. As to liability of agent signing a bond, see the title PRINCIPAL AND AGENT. As to mandamus to compel judges to approve bonds, see the title MANDAMUS. As to plea to action upon bond conditioned to execute title, see the title VENDOR AND PURCHASER. As to requisites and mode of affixing seal to bonds, see the title SEALS. As to subrogation to rights of obligee, see the title SUBROGATION.

I. REQUISITES AND VALIDITY.

§ 1. Nature and Essentials in General.

"A bond can not, with strict legal propriety, be termed a promissory note, and they have always been distinguishable in the incidents which attach to them. Reed *v.* Scott, 30 Ala. 640; Muse *v.* Dantzler, 85 Ala. 359, 5 So. 178; McCrummen *v.* Campbell, 82 Ala. 566, 2 So. 482." Davis *v.* McWhorter, 122 Ala. 570, 26 So. 119.

§ 2. Parties.

§ 3. —— Sureties.

If a surety is permanently absent from the state during much of each year, and the facts as to his residence leave his domicile in doubt, he may properly be declared insufficient. Ex parte Buckley, 53 Ala. 42.

§ 4. Form and Contents.

§ 5. —— In General.

The obligors of a bond will be personally liable thereon, though the word "ourselves," in the clause "bind ourselves, our heirs," etc., was omitted. Wood *v.* Coman, 56 Ala. 283.

§ 6. —— Designation of Parties.

One executing a bond is bound by it, though he is not named in the body thereof. Martin *v.* Dortch, 1 Stew. 479; Grimmet *v.* Henderson, 66 Ala. 521.

Whether the promise in a bond be in the singular or plural, is believed to be immaterial; it applies to each person whose signature is covered by it, and under the Alabama statute binds them jointly and severally. Martin *v.* Dortch, 1 Stew. 479, 482.

To bind parties as obligors, when their names are signed to the bond, it is not necessary that they should also appear in body thereof. Grimmet *v.* Henderson, 66 Ala. 521, citing Hatch *v.* Crawford, 2 Port. 54.

§ 7. —— Designation of Amount or Penalty.

An action can not be maintained upon a bond, the penalty of which is for "—— dollars," as the defect can not be supplied by oral proof of the amount intended. Copeland *v.* Cunningham, 63 Ala. 394. See McKellar *v.* Couch, 34 Ala. 336; Garrow *v.* Carpenter, 1 Port. 359; Hamner *v.* Cobb, 2 Stew. & P. 383; Mead *v.* Stegar, 5 Port. 498; Sanford *v.* Howard, 29 Ala. 684, 68 Am. Dec. 101.

§ 8. —— Condition.

"Incorrect recitals in the condition may sometimes vitiate the bond, as in case of misdescription of a judgment in a writ of error." Walker *v.* Chapman, 22 Ala. 116, 124; Curry *v.* Barclay, 3 Ala. 484; Wiswell *v.* Munroe, 4 Ala. 9.

§ 9. Execution in General.

Proof that a bond was executed and subsequently a contract to which it had reference, and simultaneous delivery, as supporting an averment that at the time of the execution of the bond a contract was entered into. See Forst *v.* Leonard, 116 Ala. 82, 22 So. 481. See post, "Weight and Sufficiency," § 76.

§ 10. Signature.

Even though a clause in a written instrument for the payment of money waiving the right of homestead exemption is void for lack of execution of the agreement according to statute being by mark in place of signature, the contract may still stand as a promise to pay. Penton *v.* Williams, 43 So. 211, 150 Ala. 342, 20 So. 114.

§ 11. Seal.

Sealing is an essential requisite to constitute a perfect bond. Skinner *v.* McCarty, 2 Port. 19.

The term "bond," or "obligation," or "writing obligatory," ex vi termini, imports a sealed instrument. Skinner *v.* McCarty, 2 Port. 19.

One seal on a bond may serve for all the signers, and where a bond contains the clause, "Sealed with our seals," it will be presumed that all the signers adopted one seal. Martin *v.* Dortch, 1 Stew. 479.

What Constitutes.—To make a sealed instrument or bond, the intention to make it so must be expressed in the body of the writing. Attachment of a seal to the signature is not enough. Lytle *v.* Bank of Dothan, 26 So. 6, 121 Ala. 215.

A writing with a scroll inclosing the word "Seal," but having no expression in the body of the instrument indicating that it is sealed, is not a sealed instrument. Lee *v.* Adkins, Minor 187.

A bond signed by "A. [L. S.] for B., C., and D.," is sufficiently executed as the bond of B., C., and D., by their agent, although only one seal is used. Martin *v.* Dortch, 1 Stew. 479.

The fact that an instrument concludes with, "Sealed with my seal," "Witness my hand and seal," does not make it a sealed bond, in the absence of a scrawl or seal attached to the signature. Williams *v.*, Young, 3 Ala. 145, citing Lee *v.* Adkins, Minor 187.

Where a contract in writing professes to be sealed by the obligors, although they have omitted to affix their seals, yet, by the act of 1839 (Clay's Dig., p. 158, § 41), it will be held to be a sealed instrument. Bancroft *v.* Stanton, 7 Ala. 351.

Where an instrument has a scroll attached to the name of its signer, and the word "Sealed" written within, and contains a clause that the parties "bind and oblige themselves," it imports on its face to be under seal, and will be deemed to be a sealed instrument. Lindsay *v.* State, 15 Ala. 43. See, also, Foster *v.* Ross, Minor 421; Lee *v.* Adkins, Minor 187; Carter *v.* Penn, 4 Ala. 140.

A contract between the parties by which the principal duty was to be performed by A. G., defendant, in favor of J. W., plaintiff, concluded and was subscribed as follows: "In testimony of which, we have hereunto annexed our respective signatures. J. W. [L. S.] A. G." Held, that the contract was not a sealed instrument, even under Act 1839, which provides that all contracts in writing "which import on their face to be under seal" shall be deemed sealed instruments without regard to scrawls or seals. Waddell *v.* Glassel, 11 Ala. 568, citing, Lee *v.* Adkins, Minor 187. As to sealing of certiorari bonds, see the titles CERTIORARI; SEALS.

§ 12. Partial Execution, and Failure of Others to Sign.

Where sureties sign a bond on condition that three of four other good men, unnamed, shall sign it before its delivery to the obligee, they are not bound thereby unless the other signatures are procured. White Sewing-Mach. Co. *v.* Saxon, 121 Ala. 399, 25 So. 784.

Where sureties sign a bond on condition that others shall also sign it before delivery by their principal to the obligee, they are not bound, where no other signatures are procured, though the bond provides for their liability, notwithstanding such a condition, and contains other provisions inconsistent therewith. White Sewing-Mach. Co. *v.* Baxon, 121 Ala. 399, 25 So. 784.

Where sureties sign a bond on condition that others shall also sign it before delivery, knowledge that the principal is proceeding with the business the bond was intended to secure is insufficient to put them on notice that the bond has been delivered in violation of the condition. White Sewing-Mach. Co. *v.* Saxon, 121 Ala. 399, 25 So. 784.

§ 13. Execution in Blank.

One who executes a bond and delivers it to another, knowing that there are blanks therein, consents, by implication, that the blanks may be filled. Boardman *v.* Gore, 1 Stew. 517.

Defendant, by signing a blank paper and handing it to another to be filled up for a sum of money, did not thereby authorize the person to whom he delivered it to seal and deliver it as defendant's bond. Manning *v.* Norwood, 1 Ala. 429. See post, "Necessity and Sufficiency," § 15.

An authority to perfect a bond by filling it up, given by parol, may be revoked in the same manner. Gibbs *v.* Frost, 4 Ala. 720.

Authority to an agent to fill in blanks in a bond may be by parole. Boardman *v.* Gore, 1 Stew. 517.

§ 14. Delivery.

§ 15. —— Necessity and Sufficiency.

Delivery is essential to the validity of a bond. Bibb *v.* Reid, 3 Ala. 88.

"The delivery must be by the obligor himself or by some one authorized to act for him." Bibb *v.* Reid, 3 Ala. 88, 91.

Delivery is a question of fact evidenced by acts and declarations at the time, or inferred from the silence of the party; as where the obligor without any formal act or declaration permits the obligee to take possession of the bond. Bibb *v.* Reid, 3 Ala. 88, 90.

Defendant, by signing a blank paper and handing it to another to be filled up for a sum of money, did not thereby authorize the person to whom he delivered it to seal and deliver it as defendant's bond. Manning *v.* Norwood, 1 Ala. 429. See ante, "Execution in Blank," § 13.

What Constitutes Delivery.—"It rarely happens that when a deed is delivered, it is formally placed in the hands of the obligee, with the declaration that it is delivered. The mere permission of the obligor to the taking possession of the deed by the obligee is a delivery." Gibbs *v.* Frost, 4 Ala. 720, 729.

The delivery of a bond to the holder of the equitable interest is sufficient, notwithstanding the legal title to the bond is in another. Sykes *v.* Lewis, 17 Ala. 261.

"A formal delivery to the obligee in any case, even in respect to the most solemn instruments, is unnecessary. If no condition be annexed, if nothing remains to be performed to give effect to the instrument, its signing, sealing and attestation as a valid instrument between the parties will make it complete, it is said, even though it may remain in the hands of the grantor or bargainor." Sykes *v.* Lewis, 17 Ala. 261, 269.

Conditional or Absolute Delivery.—If an obligor seal a bond and deliver it to the other party to the instrument, the delivery is an absolute one, regardless of the words used or the conditions imposed. Bibb *v.* Reid, 3 Ala. 88.

Where a bond is delivered conditionally to a co-obligor, it is not the bond of the person delivering it until the condition is performed. Bibb *v.* Reid, 3 Ala. 88.

§ 16. Consideration.

§ 17. —— Effect of Seal.

"The omission of the recital of the consideration which induced the execution of the bond, does not impair the obligation, or impose upon the obligee the necessity of proving it by evidence aliunde—if the consideration is not impugned, it will be intended to be sufficient." Holman *v.* Crane, 16 Ala. 570, 579; Holman *v.* Bank, 12 Ala. 369.

A executed to B a bond, on the face of which no consideration was expressed, but conditioned to make him a quitclaim deed to certain lots of land in two years. Held that, under the laws of this state, the bond imported a consideration sufficient to support it. Holman *v.* Crane, 16 Ala. 570.

§ 18. —— Want of Consideration.

Where the contestant of an election of tax collector gave a bond for $250 for costs, under Code 1886, § 398, providing that a bond of $500 may be required of such contestant, and, after the institution of the action, the bond for $250 proving insufficient, the court required another bond for $250, such second bond was not invalid for want of consideration. McThirter *v.* Frazier, 129 Ala. 450, 29 So. 445.

Where A, having executed a mortgage of slaves to B, entered into a bond, with C and D as his sureties, conditioned to be void if A surrendered the property mentioned therein to B, if equity should decree the same of right to belong to B, and that A further abides the decree of equity on a foreclosure, such bond is valid, and not void for want of consideration. Barnes *v.* Peck, 1 Port. 187.

§ 19. Statutory Bonds and Bonds Taken by Officers.

§ 20. —— In General.

A bond which contains all the conditions required by statute, and also conditions in excess of those specified by statute, is valid, so far as it imposes obligations authorized by the statute, and the stipulations which are in excess of it may be rejected as surplusage. Sanders *v.* Rives, 3 Stew. 109; Walker *v.* Chapman, 22 Ala. 116. See, also, Howie *v.* State, 1 Ala. 113. See post, "Partial Invalidity," § 27.

Where authority to take a bond is wholly derived from a statute, if it be taken in a larger sum, or on conditions not required by the statute, and be not voluntarily given by the obligors, it is wholly void. Whitsett *v.* Womack, 8 Ala. 466. See post, "Legality of Condition or of Consideration," § 24.

Where the statute prescribing a bond declares all bonds not taken pursuant to it void, the statute must be strictly pursued, as bonds which do not conform to it are void by express enactment. Whitsett *v.* Womack, 8 Ala. 466.

Although the condition of a bond is more specific than the statute prescribes, yet, if it substantially conforms to the requirements of the law, and imposes no additional obligations, it will be considered good as a statutory bond. Boring *v.* Williams, 17 Ala. 510.

Where the condition of a bond given under a statute varies from that prescribed by the statute, the bond is not void, if the conditions contained in the bond are more beneficial to the obligor than those prescribed by the statute. Rouse *v.* Jayne, 14 Ala. 727. See, also, Bell *v.* Thomas, 8 Ala. 527, 528.

Where a statute requires a bond to be executed in a prescribed form, and not otherwise, no recovery can be had on a bond professedly taken under the authority of the act, if it does not conform to it; but if a statute merely prescribes the form, without prohibiting any other, a bond which varies from it may be good at common law. So, if part of the condition of a bond conform to the statute, and part does not, a recovery may be had for the breach of the former, where so much of the condition as is illegal is not malum in se. Whitsett *v.* Womack, 8 Ala. 466. See, also, Bates *v.* Bank, 2 Ala. 451, 487.

§ 21. —— Sureties.

See ante, "Sureties," § 3.

§ 22. —— Validity as Common-Law Bonds.

A bond, entered into voluntarily by competent parties and for a lawful purpose, not prohibited by law, and founded upon a sufficient consideration, is good and valid at common law. Munter *v.* Reese, 61 Ala. 395; Sewall *v.* Franklin, 2 Port. 493; Hester *v.* Keith, 1 Ala. 316; Butler *v.* O'Brien, 5 Ala. 316; Whitsett *v.* Womack, 8 Ala. 466; Gayle *v.* Martin, 3 Ala. 593; Miller *v.* Vaughan, 78 Ala. 323; Stow *v.* City Council, 74 Ala. 226.

A statutory bond, not duly executed, or not conditioned as required by statute, may be sustained as a common-law bond. Sugg *v.* Burgess, 2 Stew. 509; Reed *v.* Brashers, 3 Port. 378; Butler *v.* O'Brien, 5 Ala. 316; Whitsett *v.* Womack, 8 Ala. 466; Mitchell *v.* Ingram, 38 Ala. 395; Russell *v.* Locke, 57 Ala. 420; Adler *v.* Potter, 57 Ala. 571.

Where the obligor has executed as a statutory bond a bond not required by statute, and acts thereunder, the obligation will be sustained as a common-law bond. Williamson *v.* Woolfe, 37 Ala. 298, citing Sprowl *v.* Lawrence, 33 Ala. 674, 692; Alston *v.* Alston, 34 Ala. 24, 25.

If a bond for the delivery of a boat seized under process in a libel suit, is good as a common-law bond, it may be proceeded on as a stipulation, although it does not conform to the statute. Bell *v.* Thomas, 8 Ala. 527.

Where a boat, libeled and seized, is claimed by a third person subsequent to the decree of condemnation and order of sale, who executed a bond to prosecute a writ of error, it was held that, as the bond had no effect but to arrest the proceedings until the decision in error, a bond subsequently executed to the libelants, in consideration of relinquishing their lien, conditioned to pay the judgments in their favor should they not be reversed, was good at common law. Gayle *v.* Martin, 3 Ala. 593. See the title COUNTIES.

§ 23. —— Bonds Exacted without Authority or under Color of Office.

A bond extorted from the principal obligor and his sureties, colore officii, can not be enforced. Whitsett *v.* Womack, 8 Ala. 466.

Under Code, §§ 4005, 4021, requiring an officer executing a search warrant to carry the property before the magistrate, he has no authority to take a forthcoming bond; and, if he takes such bond, and the warrant is void, the bond is without consideration, and can not be sustained as a common-law bond. Counts *v.* Harlan, 78 Ala. 551, citing, Noles *v.* State, 24 Ala. 672; Cary *v.* State, 76 Ala. 78.

§ 24. Legality of Condition or of Consideration.

If a bond be given on a legal consideration, and free from usury in its origin, no subsequent illegal contract, in which it may be transferred, can impair the holder's right of action against the original debtor. McCausland *v.* Drake, 3 Stew. 344, 352; Faris *v.* King, 1 Stew. 259. See ante, "Validity as Common-Law Bonds," § 22.

§ 25. Effect of Invalidity.

§ 26. —— In General.

See ante, "Validity as Common-Law Bonds," § 22.

§ 27. —— Partial Invalidity.

The rule in regard to bonds or other deeds, void in part, by common law, or by statute, is, that they are void as to such conditions, covenants or grants, as are illegal, and good as to all others which are legal and unexceptionable. Whitted *v.* Governor, 6 Port. 335.

Where the condition of a bond consists of several different parts, some of which are lawful and others not, it is good for so much as is lawful, and void for the rest. Whitted *v.* Governor, 6 Port. 335.

If, however, the illegality was for something malum in se, or if the statute has not confined its prohibitions to the illegal conditions, covenants or grants; but has expressly or by necessary implication, avoided the whole instrument, to all intents and purposes, then there could be no recovery upon any part of it. Whitted *v.* Governor, 6 Port. 335.

II. CONSTRUCTION AND OPERATION.

§ 28. General Rules of Construction.

A bond should be so construed as to effectuate the reasonable intention of the parties. Loeb *v.* Montgomery (Ala.), 61 So. 642.

"In giving a construction to a bond, the court will look to the intention of the parties at the time it was executed, and expound it as the law then was." Whitsett *v.* Womack, 8 Ala. 466, 480.

"The court may depart from the letter of the condition of a bond, to carry into effect the intention of the parties. Whitsett *v.* Womack, 8 Ala. 466, 481.

"The condition of the bond ought to be construed, by rejecting insensible words, as to fulfill the intent of the parties." Whitsett *v.* Womack, 8 Ala. 466, 481.

All deeds are to operate according to the intention of the parties, unless that is unlawful. And it is proper to look to the subject matter of a contract, and the inducement that led to it, for the purpose of ascertaining what the parties intended. Rives *v.* Toulmin, 19 Ala. 288, 293; Bates *v.* Bank, 2 Ala. 451.

A bond should be construed against the party on whom rests the obligation involved. Loeb *v.* Montgomery (Ala.), 61 So. 642.

Doubtful language in a bond should be so construed as to support rather than defeat the instrument, if that can be fairly done. Loeb *v.* Montgomery (Ala.), 61 So. 642.

§ 29. What Law Governs.

A bond substituted for, and containing the same stipulations as, another bond, which was executed in another state for the purchase money of slaves, under a contract entered into and consummated therein, is governed by the laws of that state. Broughton *v.* Bradley, 36 Ala. 689, citing, Wright *v.* Burt, 5 Ala. 29; Moore *v.* Davidson, 18 Ala. 209; Evans *v.* Kittrell, 33 Ala. 449; Hanrick *v.* Andrews, 9 Port. 9, 25; Pearson *v.* Bailey, 23 Ala. 537; Jackson *v.* Jones, 13 Ala. 121.

§ 30. Parties.

§ 31. —— Joint or Several.

Signers of a bond for admission of a person to the insane hospital as a paying patient (Code, § 1238), conditioned to pay all charges against such patient, are principals so far as the hospital is concerned, and jointly and severally liable. Enslen *v.* Alabama Insane Hospital, 21 So. 74, 113 Ala. 658. See Elliott *v.* Mayfield, 4 Ala. 417.

§ 32. Amount or Extent of Liability.

See ante, "Joint or Several," § 31.

§ 33. Time of Performance or Payment.

Where the bond is conditioned for the payment of money at a certain day, the whole debt accrues from the day mentioned in the condition, and does not wait the damnification, although it may appear that the bond was given by way of indemnity. Hogan *v.* Calvert, 21 Ala. 194.

§ 34. Collateral Agreements.

Where there is a sufficient reference in a bond to a contract, the reference makes all the stipulations of the contract a part of the bond, and they may be read together without a recital in the bond that the contract was a written one. Forst *v.* Leonard, 112 Ala. 296, 20 So. 587.

The fact that a building contract was signed by the contractors only, while a bond conditioned on its proper performance was signed by the contractors and others, is no objection to the taking of the two papers together to determine the liability under the bond. Forst *v.* Leonard, 112 Ala. 296, 20 So. 587.

III. NEGOTIABILITY AND TRANSFER.

§ 35. What Law Governs.

The indorsement of a bond is in itself a distinct and substantive contract, and, if it does not look to any other place, will be governed by the lex loci contractus; and where it is made in another state, in which the common law is presumptively in force, to fix a liability upon the indorser, it is incumbent upon the indorsee to show, by a suit prosecuted against the obligor, that the amount of the specialty could not be collected of him, or else excuse the prosecution of such a suit by proof of the obligor's insolvency, or the production of a statute modifying the common law. Miller *v.* McIntyre, 9 Ala. 638.

§ 36. Statutory Provisions.

Act Dec. 15, 1870, authorizing the Tallassee Mfg. Co., No. 1, on a vote of two-thirds of its shareholders in value, to issue its bonds for a sum not exceeding one-third of its capital stock paid in, in bonds of $1,000 each, payable in gold, with legal interest, and coupons for interest attached, payable in gold, semiannually at such place as it may appoint, contemplates the issue of instruments having all the qualities, elements, and characteristics of negotiable paper, which could be introduced into the commercial markets, circulating and passing as such paper in the usual course of business; and the bonds issued under the authority of this statute, being payable to bearer at the office of the company in Montgomery, with coupons for interest attached, payable semiannually at a designated bank in New York, are negotiable instruments. Lehman *v.* Tallassee Mfg. Co., 64 Ala. 567.

§ 37. Words of Negotiability.

Corporate bonds payable to bearer are transferable by delivery, so as to enable the holder to maintain an action in his own name. Reid *v.* Bank, 70 Ala. 199. See the title CORPORATIONS.

§ 38. Nature and Form of Instrument.

A provision in a bond for payment of money, payable to bearer, issued and put in circulation by a corporation, that the bond might "be registered and made payable by transfer only on the books of the company," does not, of itself, make such bonds nonnegotiable by mere manual transfer. Savannah & M. R. Co. *v.* Lancaster, 62 Ala. 555.

§ 39. Transfer without Indorsement in General.

Title to a bond passes by delivery. Savannah & M. R. Co. *v.* Lancaster, 62 Ala. 555.

A bond to convey land, on the obligee's establishing the obligor's claim thereto, under the pre-emption laws, and paying the purchase money to the United States, is assignable under the act of 1828, and the assignee may maintain an action thereon in his own name, by showing a performance of the condition by the obligee. Brown *v.* Chambers, 12 Ala. 697. See, also, Burt *v.* Henry, 10 Ala. 874. See post, "Assignment," § 40.

§ 40. Assignment.

"The assignee of a bond takes it at his peril, and stands in the place of the obligee, so as to let in every defence which the obligor had against the obligee at the time of notice of assignment." Brown *v.* Chambers, 12 Ala. 697, 707.

In a suit by an assignee upon a bond to convey lands upon the payment of a certain note, it must be averred that the obligor had notice of the assignment. Burt *v.* Henry, 10 Ala. 874. See, also, Williams *v.* Harper, 1 Ala. 502. See post, "Declaration, Complaint, or Petition," § 69.

Who May Maintain Action.—"It is well settled that bonds can not be assigned at common law, so as to entitle the assignee to an action in his own name thereon. But courts of law will recognize the assignment of a bond, so as to refuse to give effect to a subsequent release of the debt by the original obligee." Brown *v.* Chambers, 12 Ala. 697, 706.

"The assignment, it has been held, amounts to a contract that the assignee shall receive the money to his own use, entitles him to sue in the assignor's name, and is a sufficient consideration for a promise by the obligor to pay the assignee." Brown *v.* Chambers, 12 Ala. 697, 706.

Where a bond is assigned to the executrix of the obligor and another, and the executrix assigns her interest therein to her co-assignee, the latter may maintain a bill in equity on the bond against the executor and executrix of the obligor. Crawford *v.* Childress, 1 Ala. 482. See post, "Parties," § 67.

§ 41. Sale.

See post, "Parties," § 67.

§ 42. Rights and Liabilities on Indorsement or Other Transfer in General.

Under the statute of 1828, the contract of an indorser is a conditional one, it being necessary in an action against him for recovery upon it, that an unsuccessful attempt has been made to recover from the original obligor, this being a prerequisite to his liability. Ivey *v.* Sanderson, 6 Port. 420.

Under the statute of 1828, it must appear that a suit against the obligor has proved unproductive, in order to support an action by an indorsee against the indorser of a bond. Ivey *v.* Sanderson, 6 Port. 420. See, also, Woodcock *v.* Campbell, 2 Port. 456; Cavanaugh *v.* Tatum, 4 Stew. & P. 204; Roberts *v.* Kilpatrick, 5 Stew. & P. 96.

In an action against the indorser of a bond, the allegation "that the instrument was duly presented to the maker thereof" is supported by proof that on diligent search he could not be found, and it is not necessary to aver these facts specially. Taylor *v.* Branch, 1 Stew. & P. 249.

Under Act Feb. 1, 1870, providing that, after the completion of the first twenty miles of a railroad, its bonds should be indorsed by the state, to be applied in the further construction of the road, the state is simply an accommodation indorser, and is not liable, where the bonds were used to pay debts incurred in constructing the first twenty miles, except to a bona fide holder for value. Gillman *v.* New Orleans & S. R. Co., 72 Ala. 566, citing, Plock & Co. *v.* Cobb, 64 Ala. 127.

§ 43. Rights and Liabilities on Assignment or Sale.

§ 44. —— In General.

One of two joint assignees of a penal bond can not, by his separate assignment, transfer to a third person the legal title to his moiety. Skinner *v.* Bedell, 32 Ala. 44, citing Brown *v.* Chambers, 12 Ala. 697.

§ 45. —— Equities and Defenses against Assignee.

To an action on an assigned bond, in the name of the assignee, it is not a good plea that the assignment was extorted from the obligee by threats, though the obligor had notice from the obligee, and was required not to pay to the assignee. McCausland *v.* Drake, 3 Stew. 344.

"Though a bond or note has a valid existence between the original parties, yet, if the assignment upon it be in fact a forgery, or be made by any one without authority; or under any circumstances, which will sustain the defense, that the assignment is not the act of the assignor, for the reason that no actual or sufficient assignment has been made, the maker, though justly indebted to the payee, may successfully resist a recovery by the fictitious assignee, and the debt continues to subsist in favor of the payee or other rightful holder." McCausland *v.* Drake, 3 Stew. 344, 352.

"But if the instrument has been executed for a valid consideration between the original parties, and the payee had voluntarily assigned the same, he has thereby transferred to the assignee, whatever right of action he had. It is immaterial to the original debtor, to whom he is required to make payment; the want of consideration, fraud, or illegality between the assignor and assignee, is a matter of perfect indifference to him. He ought not to be permitted to question the motives of others." McCausland *v.* Drake, 3 Stew. 344, 352.

§ 46. —— Recourse by Assignee to Assignor.

The assignee of a bond may sue his

assignor, if he has used due diligence to obtain payment from the obligor, without success. Ivey *v.* Sanderson, 6 Port. 420. See, also, Cavanaugh *v.* Tatum, 4 Stew. & P. 204; Roberts *v.* Kilpatrick, 5 Stew. & P. 96.

Prior to the passing of the statute of 1832 subjecting bonds payable in bank to the law merchant, it was not necessary, in order to charge the assignor, that a demand of payment should be made at the bank. Woodcock *v.* Campbell, 2 Port. 456.

§ 47. Bona Fide Purchasers.

§ 48. —— In General.

It is the settled doctrine of the supreme court, though contrary to the weight of authority elsewhere, that taking negotiable bonds as collateral security for a pre-existing debt, even though forbearance of indulgence be granted, is not a purchase for value; but, when it is taken in payment of such pre-existing debt, at its full value, the party becomes a purchaser for value, and is entitled to protection if not chargeable with notice. Reid *v.* Bank, 70 Ala. 199, citing Fenouille *v.* Hamilton, 35 Ala. 319; Bank *v.* Hall, 6 Ala. 639.

Where, under a statute, the state guaranties railroad bonds, which are diverted from the purpose for which the state's guaranty was made, one who, in the usual course of business, exchanges for such bonds the stock of another company, is a holder for value, without regard to the market value of the stock. Gilman *v.* New Orleans & S. R. Co., 72 Ala. 566.

Under Act Feb. 1, 1870, providing that, after the completion of the first twenty miles of railroad, its bond should be indorsed by the state, to be applied in the further construction of the road, if a subsequent holder of such bond seeks to enforce the state's liability as indorser, the original misappropriation of them being shown, the law casts on him the burden of proving that he acquired them in good faith, for value, and in the usual course of business. Gilman Sons & Co. *v.* New Orleans, etc., R. Co., 72 Ala. 566, cited on this point in note in 22 L. R. A., N. S., 719. See, also, Wallace *v.* Branch Bank, 1 Ala. 565; Ross *v.* Drinkard, 35 Ala. 434, 435.

S., a corporation, made a deed of property for consideration named of $25,000 to E., a corporation, which issued 300 bonds of $100 each, payable to bearer, reciting that they were secured by a trust deed of said property executed by E. These bonds were distributed among the stockholders of S., one of whom sold 60 of the same for $6,000 to complainant, who did not know the facts, or that his seller was such stockholder. The records showed clear title to the property to be in E. Held, that complainant was a bona fide holder of said bonds as against a creditor of S., who had caused said deed to be set aside as fraudulent. Lebeck *v.* Ft. Payne Bank, 22 So. 75, 115 Ala. 447. See Ft. Payne Bank *v.* Alabama Sanitarium, 103 Ala. 358, 15 So. 618; Spence *v.* Mobile, etc., R. Co., 79 Ala. 576.

§ 49. —— Actual Notice.

Bonds were issued by the M. & M. Ry. Co. under Act Feb. 25, 1870, purporting to be first mortgage bonds, and referring to the act which required that the first $1,500,000 of such bonds should be used only in purchase and exchange for the bonds of the M. & M. R. Co., to whose rights and property said M. & M. Ry. Co. had succeeded, but contained no reference to Act Aug. 5, 1868, under which said M. & M. R. Co. was incorporated by the consolidation of the A. & F. R. Co. and the M. & G. N. R. Co., nor to the charge thereby declared in favor of creditors of the original companies. Held, that a purchaser of the bonds of the M. & M. Ry. Co. was charged with notice of the incumbrance in favor of the creditors of said original companies, though a mortgage securing such debts was never recorded, or in fact never existed. Spence *v.* Mobile & M. Ry. Co., 79 Ala. 576.

§ 50. —— Constructive Notice, and Facts Putting on Inquiry.

Lines drawn across a bond raise the presumption that it has been satisfied, but such presumption may be rebutted by evidence, to be determined on by a jury. Pitcher *v.* Patrick, 1 Stew. & P. 478. See post, "Presumptions and Burden of Proof," § 74.

Negotiable bonds not due, with attached coupons past due and unpaid, do not thereby appear dishonored on their face; but the presence of such unpaid coupons is a material circumstance bearing on the question whether the purchaser acquired them in good faith, and without notice. Morton *v.* New Orleans, etc., R. Co., 79 Ala. 590, 592.

The dishonor of unpaid interest coupons does not charge a purchaser with notice of equities or defenses. State *v.* Cobb, 64 Ala. 127.

Where bonds refer on their face to the deed of trust securing them, and the deed expressly provides that the entire debt, principal and interest, shall become due and payable within ninety days after refusal to pay any semiannual coupon, a purchaser with knowledge of such demand and refusal is not an innocent purchaser without notice. Morton *v.* New Orleans, etc., R. Co., 79 Ala. 590.

§ 51. —— Title and Rights Acquired.

"A purchaser of negotiable bonds before due, for a valuable consideration, in good faith, and without what is equivalent to actual knowledge or notice of a defect of title, holds them by a title valid as against every other person. Even gross negligence at the time of purchase does not, alone, defeat the purchaser's title." Spence *v.* Mobile, etc., R. Co., 79 Ala. 576, 586.

"A purchaser may have had suspicion of a defect of title, or knowledge of circumstances which would excite such suspicion in the mind of a prudent man; or he may have disregarded notices of stolen bonds; and yet, if he had purchased for value in good faith, his title can not be impeached. * * * It must be shown that he did not purchase honestly." Spence *v.* Mobile, etc., R. Co., 79 Ala. 576, 586.

Railroad bonds, when indorsed by the state, as provided by Act Nov. 17, 1868, being negotiable, regular on their face, and reciting in the indorsement a compliance by the company with the conditions of the statute, an innocent holder for value is not affected by any fraud or mistake in their overissue. State *v.* Cobb, 64 Ala. 127, cited on this point in note in 36 L. R. A. 434.

The negotiable bonds of a corporation having been issued by authority, their transfer as collateral security for existing debts also being authorized, and some of them having been thus transferred to a commercial partnership, with whom the corporation had extensive dealings for a series of years, and who were stockholders in the corporation, the rights of said partnership as a holder in good faith are not affected by the fact that their debt against the corporation was not communicated to the other stockholders, and was not known to them, nor by the fact that the indebtedness did not appear by the books of the corporation, to which the stockholders had access, nor by the further fact that said partnership, as stockholders, received dividends while the debt to them was being contracted. Lehman *v.* Tallassee Mfg. Co., 64 Ala. 567.

§ 52. —— Defenses as against Bona Fide Purchasers in General.

Where bonds were issued by a county in payment of a subscription for railroad stock, the fact that unfulfilled promises were made by officers of the road, to citizens of the county, that the road would run through the county, to induce them to vote for the subscription, will not affect the right of innocent purchasers of the bonds for value to recover thereon. Carpenter *v.* Greene County, 130 Ala. 613, 29 So. 194. See the title COUNTIES. See ante, "Title and Rights Acquired," § 51.

§ 53. —— Purchaser of Accommodation Bonds.

The state-indorsed bonds of the N. O. & S. R. Co. were applied in violation of Sess. Acts 1869-70, pp. 149-157, authorizing such indorsement, in payment of the contractor for work done in building the road. Held, that the state was liable as accommodation indorser to a bona fide holder for value, who acquired the bonds in the usual course of business, without notice of their original misapplication. Morton *v.* New Orleans, etc., R. Co., 79 Ala. 590.

IV. PERFORMANCE OR BREACH OF CONDITION.

§ 54. Sufficiency of Performance of Condition.

The doctrine in relation to partial performance of mutual covenants, which go to a part only of the consideration on both sides, where the part unperformed can be compensated in damages (Boone *v.* Eyer, 1 H. Bl. 273, note a), has no application to the case of a penal bond for the payment of money on the performance of a condition precedent. Rives *v.* Baptiste, 25 Ala. 382.

§ 55. Excuses for Nonperformance.

If the condition of a bond is one imposed by law, a breach of it caused by the act of God will be excused, if, however, the condition is one written into the bond as the contract of the parties, it will not be excused, although the breach is caused by inevitable accident, storm, fire, flood, or the act of a stranger. The condition, if the result of contract, must be performed. Meriwether *v.* Lowndes County, 89 Ala. 362, 7 So. 198. See, also, Warren *v.* Wagner, 75 Ala. 188; Nave *v.* Berry, 22 Ala. 382. See post, "In General," § 58.

Where the condition of a penal bond is that the obligor shall restore or deliver a certain slave at a time specified, the death of the slave, or that he runs away and the obligor can not recover him by proper effort and diligence, is an excuse for his nonperformance. Falls *v.* Weissinger, 11 Ala. 801. See Burgess *v.* Sugg, 2 Stew. & P. 341; Perry *v.* Hewlett, 5 Port. 318; Givhan *v.* Dailey, 4 Ala. 336.

Where the bond of a contractor recites that the consideration paid by the county is both for the work of building a bridge and for the execution of the bond, and one of the undertakings of said bond is an obligation to keep the entire bridge in good repair for a stipulated period, the obligor can not avoid his liability to rebuild as to one span because the county furnished all the materials for this part of the bridge, and paid him the additional sum of $25 for superintending its erection. Meriwether *v.* Lowndes County, 89 Ala. 362, 7 So. 198.

§ 56. Discharge from Performance.

See ante, "Excuses for Nonperformance," § 55.

§ 57. Breach of Condition.

§ 58. —— In General.

A city made proposals for building a wall; providing, among other things that the walls was to last 10 years, and requiring bond, with security, for the faithful performance of the contract. J. W. undertook the work, and gave the bond, with surety, which recited most of the terms specified in the proposals, which were attached to the bond. The bond concluded with, "Now, if the said J. W. shall do accordingly all matters and things as stated in said specification alluded to," etc., then the bond to be void. Held that, the wall having been carried away by a freshet before the end of ten years, the principal and surety were liable for damages. Ready *v.* City of Tuskaloosa, 6 Ala. 327.

Where a bridge builder executes a bond conditioned that the bridge built shall be "kept in good repair," and shall "remain safe continuously for the period of five years, for the passage of travelers," etc., and said bridge is washed away by flood within less than five years, an action will lie on the bond for breach thereof, upon failure to rebuild. Meriwether *v.* Lowndes County, 89 Ala. 362, 7 So. 198. See, also, Warren *v.* Wagner, 75 Ala. 188; Nave *v.* Berry, 22 Ala. 382. See ante, "Excuses for Nonperformance," § 55.

§ 59. —— Bonds of Agents or Employees.

A cashier's bond, conditioned "safely to keep all moneys," etc., does not render the obligors responsible for money violently robbed from him while in the discharge of his duty. Huntsville Bank *v.* Hill, 1 Stew. 201.

§ 60. Payment.

A credit indorsed on a bond, which is legible, though an attempt seems to have been made to erase it, is prima facie evidence of payment pro tanto. Clark *v.* Simmons, 4 Port. 14.

A forwarded a bill of exchange to B with instructions to negotiate it, and, with the proceeds, discharge a bond held by C against A. B indorsed the bill, and took an assignment of the bond. Held, that the transaction operated as a discharge of the bond, and that B's remedy was upon the bill, if he should become liable as indorser. Cox *v.* Robinson, 2 Stew. & P. 91.

V. ACTIONS.

§ 61. Right of Action.

§ 62. —— Nature and Grounds in General.

In order to recover on a bond conditioned to abide the decree of equity on a foreclosure, it must appear that a decree of equity has been rendered on the precise point contained in the conditions. Barnes *v.* Peck, 1 Port. 187.

§ 63. —— Title to Sustain Action.

A obtained a judgment for the use of B, against C, and sued out a ca. sa., and died, after which C executed a prison-bounds bond, which was made payable to A, for the use of B. Held, that the executors of A could not maintain a suit on this bond, against C, for a breach of the condition. Tait *v.* Parkman, 15 Ala. 253.

An action of debt on a bond payable to the governor for the time being, and his successors in office, can not be maintained in the name of the obligee, as governor, after he has gone out of office, unless the suit is brought for the use of a third person, who may be responsible for the costs, and entitled to the recovery. Chaudron *v.* Fitzpatrick, 19 Ala. 649. See, also, Bagby *v.* Chandler, 8 Ala. 230; Lake *v.* Governor, 2 Stew. 395.

Section 2129 of the Code, which provides that "every action founded upon a promissory note, bond, or other contract, express or implied, for the payment of money, must be prosecuted in the name of the party really interested, whether he have the legal title or not," embraces a debt created by bond, which bond has been lost. Glassell *v.* Mason, 32 Ala. 719.

§ 64. —— Conditions Precedent.

Where the payment of money, secured by a penal bond, is made to depend on the performance of condition precedent, an action can not be maintained on the bond until the condition has been fully performed. Rives *v.* Baptiste, 25 Ala. 382. See, also, Bailey *v.* White, 3 Ala. 330; Jones *v.* Sommerville, 1 Port. 437.

There is no statute which requires the sheriff to return "forfeited" a bond taken in a suit in chancery, conditioned for the forthcoming of property if the decree requires it; hence the obligee may maintain an action thereon without showing such a return. Falls *v.* Weissinger, 11 Ala. 801.

The act of 1818 declares that all joint bonds shall have the same effect in law as if they were joint and several. Consequently, where a bond executed by a number of persons requires that a demand of performance shall be made in order to put them in default, it is enough to prove a demand of the obligor against whom suit is brought. Whitsett *v.* Womack, 8 Ala. 466.

Although the courts will not require the performance of every minute particular of a condition, unless its full and exact performance is part of the essence of the contract; yet, where the execution of a trust deed is a condition precedent to the payment of money secured by a penal bond, the obligor has the right to insist upon a complete execution of the trust before he can be held liable on his bond. Rives *v.* Baptiste, 25 Ala. 382.

On partial settlement between two assignees of a partner's share in an unsettled land company, the prior assignee, who held the control of the entire share, transferred to other lands valued at a specified sum, and took from him a bond conditioned as follows: "Now, I consent and agree to bind myself, my heirs," etc., "to refund to the said C. the said amount, with interest thereon, if my claim on said share of said B. shall be or is unfounded, and if I am not authorized to receive the same, and also to refund, with interest, any amount that may be overpaid in the settlement this day made." Held, that an action could not be maintained on this bond to recover the amount of an alleged overpayment until the fact of such overpayment had been ascertained on final settlement of the partnership affairs. Cowles *v.* Garrett, 30 Ala. 341.

Code 1886, § 1457, which provides that where a bridge is guarantied by the bond of the builder to stand for a stipulated period, and said bridge is washed away, the commissioners' court shall, upon the fact being made known to them by any freeholder of the county, notify the contractor to rebuild, and, in case of his refusal or neglect to do so in a reasonable time, shall order suit to be brought on such bond, does not make the giving of such information by a freeholder a condition precedent to the action of the court in giving notice to rebuild, or its authority to order suit brought, but it makes a duty, otherwise discretionary, mandatory on the court. Meriwether *v.* Lowndes County, 89 Ala. 362, 7 So. 198.

§ 65. Nature and Form of Remedy.

The action of debt is a proper remedy on a bond conditioned for the performance of covenants. Meakings *v.* Ochiltree, 5 Port. 395.

That a bond is good as a statutory bond, and enforceable in the method provided by the statute, does not of itself prevent its enforcement by a common-law action. Jaffe *v.* Fidelity & Deposit Co. (Ala.), 60 So. 966.

§ 66. Defenses.

The plea of non est factum is a good defense to an action on a bond where the principal had induced the defendant to sign it by representing to him that it was a mere recommendation of the principal's efficiency. Smith *v.* Kirkland, 81 Ala. 345, 1 So. 276.

"If the appellant was absolved from the obligation and condition of his bond by a rescission of the contract which it evidenced, his absolution formed matter of legal defence." Moore *v.* Dial, 3 Stew. 155, 157.

"It has been long settled in this state, by a line of decisions which seems to be supported by the weight of authority, that it is a good defense to an action on a bond that a defendant, who is a surety, intrusted the bond to the principal obligor as an escrow, with authority to deliver it only on the express condition that other named persons should join as sureties in its execution prior to such delivery, and that the instrument was delivered to the obligee in violation of this condition." Smith *v.* Kirkland, 81 Ala. 345, 1 So. 276, 277. See, also, Guild *v.* Thomas, 54 Ala. 414; Bibb *v.* Reid, 3 Ala. 88.

There are two established modifications of the above rule: (1) It does not apply to commercial paper which has come into the hands of a bona fide purchaser before maturity, who is without notice of the condition. Marks *v.* First Nat. Bank, 79 Ala. 550. (2) It does not apply where the surety, having knowledge or notice of the delivery of the bond, suffers the principal to act under it to the prejudice of the obligee, so as to waive the condition, and thus estop the surety from insisting on the defense. Wright *v.* Lang, 66 Ala. 389; Smith *v.* Kirkland, 81 Ala. 345, 1 So. 276, 277.

It is no defense to an action on a bond that the consideration was the hire of a slave for a year, who in two or three months thereafter was disabled from performing any labor, in the absence of an agreement that the full hire was not to be paid in such case. Outlaw *v.* Cook, Minor 257.

Where the obligation of a bond is absolved by a rescission of the contract of which it was evidence, an action on the bond may be defended at law. Moore *v.* Dial, 3 Stew. 155.

If a bond be paid by a third person at the request of the obligor, a suit can not be afterwards maintained upon it in the name of the obligee for the use of the person by whom such payment was made. Simmons *v.* Walker, 18 Ala. 664. See, also, Harrison *v.* Hicks, 1 Port. 423.

Want or Failure of Consideration.—By statute, want or failure of consideration is a good defense to an action on a bond. Giles *v.* Williams, 3 Ala. 316.

Nonperformance of Agreement as Part of Consideration.—It it not a good bar to an action on a bond that it was given in part of the price of land, which the plaintiff obligated himself to convey to the defendant by a certain day, which he did not do. Gilchrist *v.* Dandridge, Minor 165.

Estoppel.—Where a bond signed by sureties on condition that it shall not be delivered until others have also signed it is delivered in violation of the condition, failure of the sureties to repudiate their obligation on notice thereof estops them from relying on the condition in defense to an action thereon by the obligee, who relied on the supposed security of the bond. White Sewing-Mach. Co. *v.* Saxon, 121 Ala. 399, 25 So. 784. See ante, "Partial Execution, and Failure of Others to Sign," § 12.

§ 67. Parties.

A demurrer will lie, if all obligors on a bond are not made parties, unless a sufficient excuse is shown in the bill for the omission. Watts *v.* Gayle, 20 Ala. 817. See Moore *v.* Armstrong, 9 Port.

697, See post, "Declaration, Complaint, or Petition," § 69.

A bond to a number of obligees, conditioned to pay several and distinct judgments in favor of each, must be sued in the name of all of the obligees, or the survivors of them, upon the principle, that they in whom the legal interest is vested, must join in an action at law. Gayle *v.* Martin, 3 Ala. 593.

On a joint and several bond, an action lies against any one or more of the obligors, at the option of plaintiff. McKee *v.* Griffin, 60 Ala. 427. See Jones *v.* Pitcher, 3 Stew. & P. 135; Whitsett *v.* Womack, 8 Ala. 466; Henderson *v.* Hammond, 19 Ala. 340; Boswell *v.* Morton, 20 Ala. 235; Duramus *v.* Harrison, 26 Ala. 326; Rupert *v.* Elston, 35 Ala. 79; Ingersoll *v.* Robinson, 35 Ala. 392.

Although the obligees in a sealed bond may not be jointly entitled to the damages which may be recovered for its breach, a suit is properly brought in both their names, the bond being a joint bond. Gayle *v.* Martin, 3 Ala. 593; Miller *v.* Garrett, 35 Ala. 96.

Upon a bond executed to several, with condition to pay them such costs and damages as they might sustain by the wrongful suing out of an attachment, a joint action may be maintained, though the attachment was levied on the separate property of each, in which they have not a joint interest. Boyd *v.* Martin, 10 Ala. 700. See the title ATTACHMENT.

An action on an attachment bond, payable to several persons jointly, and conditioned for the payment to them of "all such damages as they may sustain from the wrongful or vexatious suing out of the attachment" can only be maintained by all the obligees jointly, though the alleged damage may have accrued to only one of them. Masterson *v.* Phinizy, 56 Ala. 336.

Where a bond is assigned to the executrix of the obligor and another, and the executrix assigns her interest therein to her coassignee, the latter may maintain a bill in equity on the bond against the executor and executrix of the obligor. Crawford *v.* Childress, 1 Ala. 482. See ante, "Assignment," § 40.

Death of Proper Plaintiff or Co-Obligee.—On the death of one of two joint obligees, the right of action is in the survivor; and on the latter's death only his representatives may sue, and those of the co-obligee should not be joined. Bebee *v.* Miller, Minor 364. See the title PARTIES.

If two obligees are both dead, the representatives of both can not join in a suit on the bond. Bebee *v.* Miller, Minor 364. See the title PARTIES.

Proper Defendants on Death of One Joint Obligor.—On the death of one of several joint obligors, the remedy for a breach necessarily becomes several, in the absence of a statute authorizing a joint action against the survivors, and the personal representative of the deceased; but, if the personal representative of the deceased is improperly joined as a defendant with the survivors, his name may be struck out by amendment, or a discontinuance entered as to him, without thereby discontinuing the action as against the others. Reed *v.* Summers, 79 Ala. 522. See, also, Jones *v.* Engelhardt, 78 Ala. 505; Whitaker *v.* Van Horn, 43 Ala. 255; Reynolds *v.* Simpkins, 67 Ala. 378.

Sureties Joining with Principal.—Sureties in a bond can not join with their principal in a bill to coerce payment of the bond from a third person, and, if they do so join, the bill will be dismissed. Whitaker *v.* Degraffenreid, 6 Ala. 303. See, also, Bowie *v.* Minter, 2 Ala. 406.

Bonds Payable to Governor as Chief Executive.—"Official bonds payable to the governor eo nomine, and his successors in office, are, in legal effect, obligations to the governor as the chief executive officer of the state, and may be sued and declared on without noticing the obligee's name, and that where a suit is brought in the obligee's name (describing him officially) who was superseded in office before its commencement, it will be regarded as an action by the governor, and the name of the individual will be regarded as surplusage." Bagby *v.* Chandler, 8 Ala. 230.

Insolvent Obligor.—In an action on a joint and several bond an insolvent obligor need not be made a party. Watts *v.* Gayle, 20 Ala. 817. See ante, "Title to Sustain Action," § 63, post, "Declaration, Complaint, or Petition," § 69.

§ 68. Pleading.

§ 69. —— Declaration, Complaint, or Petition.

In declaring on a bond with condition, the plaintiff may declare upon the penalty, or set out the condition and assign breaches, at his election. If he pursues the latter course, advantage may be taken of an insufficient assignment of breaches in the same manner as if they had been assigned in answer to a plea of performance. Anderson *v.* Dickson, 8 Ala. 733; Watts *v.* Sheppard, 2 Ala. 425.

Where an officer levied nine executions on the same property, and took nine bonds, it was held that he might bring an action of debt, and declare on all the bonds in one count. Sugg *v.* Burgess, 2 Stew. 509. See the title EXECUTION.

The complaint must state a good excuse for nonjoinder of some of several joint obligors. Watts *v.* Gayle, 20 Ala. 817.

In an action upon a penal bond, the plaintiff may declare on the bond without assigning breaches; and this is good, although a condition is shown on oyer. Herndon *v.* Forney, 4 Ala. 243.

In debt on a bond, a count on the penalty alone, not noticing the condition, is sufficient. Holley *v.* Acre, 23 Ala. 603.

Assignment of Breaches.—In the assignment of breaches, the plaintiff should not go beyond the defendant's contract, so as to make it uncertain, whether it has been broken; yet surplusage furnishes no ground of demurrer. Watts *v.* Sheppard, 2 Ala. 425.

In debt on bond, the breaches assigned in the declaration must show that the plaintiff has a cause of action. Garrett *v.* Logan, 19 Ala. 344; Watts *v.* Sheppard, 2 Ala. 425.

In an action against one of several obligors, it is sufficient to assign a breach as to him. Mayfield *v.* Allen, Minor 274.

If the declaration be substantially defective, in the assignment of breaches, the plaintiff can not strike them out after demurrer. Governor *v.* Wiley, 14 Ala. 172. See also, Watts *v.* Sheppard, 2 Ala. 425.

Where several breaches are assigned if the defendant demurs to the whole, if one be good, the declaration will not be held ill; the correct practice is, to demur to the breaches severally, or only to such as are defective. Watts *v.* Sheppard, 2 Ala. 425.

In assigning a breach of a bond, if the damages claimed to have been sustained exceed the penalty of the bond it is proper to assign the nonpayment of the penalty; but, if the damages do not exceed the penalty, then the breach will be for the nonpayment of the damages actually sustained. Hill *v.* Rushing, 4 Ala. 212.

In assigning breaches, it is sufficient to state the intention of the parties as it may be collected from the entire instrument, without using the precise terms in which the intention is expressed. Watts *v.* Sheppard, 2 Ala. 425.

Where a contract with a county for hiring convicts the hire money to be paid quarterly, and failure to pay any quarterly installment is made a breach of the bond securing the contract, a complaint for breach of the bond, if nonpayment of more than one installment is relied on as a breach, may include all breaches in a single count, but should assign each breach separately. Sloss Iron & Steel Co. *v.* Macon County, 111 Ala. 554, 20 So. 400.

The insufficiency of one of several breaches assigned in a complaint on a bond does not render the whole complaint insufficient, if other assignments are good. Watts *v.* Sheppard, 2 Ala. 425; Wilson *v.* Cantrell, 19 Ala. 642; Williamson *v.* Woolf, 37 Ala. 298; Flournoy *v.* Lyon, 70 Ala. 308; Coleman *v.* Pike County, 83 Ala. 326, 3 So. 755.

Whether the statute which authorizes the assignment of more than one breach allows the plaintiff to assign more breaches than there are distinct stipulations, or things to be done, or whether only one reach of **each stipulation,** etc., can be assigned, quære. Wade *v.* Killough, 5 Stew. & P. 450.

If the defendant does not, by his plea, tender an issue, the plaintiff may assign breaches in his replication. State *v.* Wiley, 14 Ala. 172.

Necessity.—It is not necessary to assign as a breach any fact which is admitted by the bond itself. Anderson *v.* Dickson, 8 Ala. 733.

Averments.—In an action on a bond, it is not necessary to aver that the bond was delivered. Spence *v.* Rutledge, 11 Ala. 590.

When a duty is to be performed to the obligee, or his assigns, upon the performance of a particular act, in a suit by the assignee, averring a demand by him of the duty, it is essential for him to aver that the obligor had notice of the assignment. Burt *v.* Henry, 10 Ala. 874, 875. See, also, Williams *v.* Harper, 1 Ala. 502. See ante, "Assignment," § 40.

In an action on a bond given to contest a claim of exemptions, assignments of breach in the complaint which did not aver that defendants failed to prosecute the contest to effect were demurrable. Kirby *v.* Forbes, 141 Ala. 294, 37 So. 411. See Pryor *v.* Beck, 21 Ala. 393.

A count averring a breach of the condition of a bond, without stating the condition, is demurrable, in failing to comply with the form in Civ. Code 1886, p. 791. Pike County *v.* Hanchey, 24 So. 751, 119 Ala. 36.

In proceedings on a penal bond, after performance of defendant's contract in part, it is sufficient to aver nonperformance of the residue. Watts *v.* Sheppard, 2 Ala. 425.

A complaint on a contractor's bond, setting out the bond in full, including the building contract, and averring that such contract was unperformed in specified particulars, from which the damages claimed resulted, and that settlement had been demanded of defendant and refused, sufficiently alleged a breach of the bond and stated a cause of action. Fidelity & Deposit Co. of Maryland *v.* Robertson, 34 So. 933, 136 Ala. 379.

A count, in a complaint on a written instrument under seal for the payment of money, alleging that defendant executed said instrument by having his name signed thereto and making his mark, did not necessarily show that there was no witness to the instrument, and hence was not demurrable on that ground. Penton *v.* Williams, 43 So. 211, 150 Ala. 153, citing Alabama Warehouse Co. *v.* Lewis, 56 Ala. 514; Bickley *v.* Keenan, 60 Ala. 293; Bates *v.* Harte, 124 Ala. 427, 430, 26 So. 898.

§ 70. —— Plea, Answer, or Affidavit of Defense.

The defendant may plead non est factum, and also a special plea that the signature and seal of one of the obligors have been canceled without his consent. Tindal *v.* Bright, Minor 103. See, post, "Issues, Proof, and Variance," § 72.

The plea of non est factum to an action on a bond, if not sworn to, is a nullity, and will be stricken from the files on motion. Garnett *v.* Roper, 10 Ala. 842.

A plea alleging non est factum affirms a fact in bar of the action, and if it is stated for the first time on appeal, it should not conclude to the country. Tindal *v.* Bright, Minor 103.

In an action on a cashier's bond conditioned "safety to keep all money," a plea, setting up as a defense a violent robbery of the money while defendant was in discharge of his duties, is defective, if it does not set out the place and circumstances of the robbery, so as to show that defendant was in the discharge of his duties as cashier. Planters', etc., Bank *v.* Hill, 1 Stew. 201.

A plea alleging that a bond was obtained by fraud, covin and misrepresentation is bad. Even in this state, where the consideration of a bond may be impeached, the facts which constitute the fraud must be stated. Giles *v.* Williams, 3 Ala. 316. See, also, Swift *v.* Fitzhugh, 9 Port. 39, 63; Mordecai *v.* Tankersly, 1 Ala. 100.

Where suit is brought against the principal and the sureties, each may sever and plead as many pleas as he may deem necessary. Williams *v.* Hinkle, 15 Ala. 713. See Johnson *v.* Wren, 3 Stew. 172; Stanley *v.* Hill, 9 Port. 368; Turner *v.* Brown, 9 Ala. 866, 867.

In an action on a bond, matter of defeasance contained therein need not be set out, but this must be taken advantage of by plea. Booth *v.* Comiegys, Minor 201, citing Mullins *v.* Cabiness, Minor 21.

The defendant may plead performance generally, when no specific breach is assigned. Tait *v.* Parkman, 15 Ala. 253.

The proper course to compel an assignment of breaches, is to plead performance, or such other plea as will show a continuance of the condition. Herndon *v.* Forney, 4 Ala. 243. See, also, Davis *v.* Dickson, 2 Stew. 370.

To a declaration in debt on a bond which sets out the condition and breach, nil debet is not a good plea. Reid *v.* Nash, 23 Ala. 733; Ansly *v.* Mock, 8 Ala. 444.

Where breaches are specifically assigned in the declaration, a general plea of performance is insufficient. Each breach should be answered, and the time, place, and manner of performance be set forth. Tait *v.* Parkman, 15 Ala. 253; Reid *v.* Nash, 23 Ala. 733. See, also, Marrow *v.* Weaver, 8 Ala. 288.

A plea alleging "that the said supposed writing obligatory, if it was signed by him, was signed in blank, and for a totally different object, and for a sum of money, if any at all was to be secured thereby, of a less amount, and to different purposes than the plaintiff alleged," is defective, as uncertain and argumentative. Manning *v.* Norwood, 1 Ala. 429.

Obligors executing a bond under seal can not impeach its consideration, except by special plea in an action founded on the bond, nor raise the question of its validity by an objection to the admission of the bond in evidence. Johnson *v.* Caffey, 59 Ala. 331.

A, holding a bond of B, placed it for collection in the hands of C, an attorney who was indebted to D. The attorney and D influenced B, in consideration of a surrender to him of his bond to A, and a promise from the attorney that he would satisfy A, to execute a bond to D in discharge of the bond to A. D brought suit on the last bond against B, who pleaded the above facts, and in addition alleged that the attorney had not paid the first bond, and that A had brought suit thereon against B. Held, that this was not a sufficient plea of failure of consideration. Craig *v.* Blow, 3 Stew. 448.

§ 71. —— Replication or Reply and Subsequent Pleadings.

In proceedings on a penal bond, if defendant puts in a plea which does not tender an issue, the plaintiff may assign breaches in his replication. Watts *v.* Sheppard, 2 Ala. 425. See ante, "Declaration, Complaint, or Petition," § 69.

Where the declaration on a penal bond contains a count on the penalty, and another setting out the condition and assigning breaches, a replication which assigns different breaches from those previously assigned will be supported, as it respects the count on the penalty. State *v.* Wiley, 14 Ala. 172.

In an action against a surety on a bond, where defendant pleads non est factum, a replication by plaintiff, averring that defendant did in fact sign the bond, but alleging that he signed it on the fraudulent representation of his principal obligor that it was a mere recommendation, and not a bond, constitutes a fatal departure from a declaration which declares on the instrument as a bond, and not as a mere recommendation. Smith *v.* Kirkland, 81 Ala. 345, 1 So. 276.

Debt on bond executed by defendant, payable to plaintiff as administrator of A, deceased. The defendant craved oyer of the condition which was set out, and pleaded several special pleas, each averring performance. The condition recited that defendant, said A, and two others had become securities for one B as receiver in a chancery suit; that B had made default, and plaintiff, as administrator of A, had paid a certain amount on account of said default, and to secure the same had taken from B his six promissory notes, which are described, with a mortgage on his real and personal estate. It then concludes, "Now, in the event the said B shall fail to pay said notes, and the mortgaged property prove insufficient to pay the same on a sale thereof, and the said C [plaintiff] be unable to collect said notes of said B at law, then shall I pay said C one-fourth of the final amount of loss he may sustain by reason of his paying up said default as aforesaid, then this obligation to be void," etc. The plaintiff replied the mortgage, with its objects and stipulations, and his sale of the property under a power contained in the mortgage, the proceeds to be applied to the aggregate sums mentioned in the notes; also, that he commenced suit against B to recover the aggregate amount of said notes, as he was authorized to do, under the terms and stipulations of the mortgage, and recovered judgment, on which an execution was regularly issued and returned "No property found," and that said notes remain unpaid, except to the extent of the money arising from said sale. Defendant craved oyer of the mortgage, and demurred to the replication. The mortgage recited all the facts which were recited in the condition of the bond, and provided that, in the event said B should fail to pay each of said notes at maturity, or within 90 days thereafter, then all of said notes should be forthwith due and payable, and plaintiff might forthwith commence suit at law or in chancery "for the recovery of the whole debt covered by said six notes." And, in the event of such default, the mortgage contained a power of sale, the proceeds to be applied to the payment of said debt and interest and the balance, if any, to be paid to said B. The notes, bond, and mortgage were all executed on the same day. It was held that the replication was good, as the mortgage was to be taken as part of the subject matter of the contract shown by the condition of the bond, and as part of the condition in effect. Rives *v.* Toulmin, 19 Ala. 288. See also, Bates *v.* Bank, 2 Ala. 451.

§ 72. —— Issues, Proof, and Variance.

A written instrument for the payment of money must be regarded, in a suit thereon, as the act of defendant, where its execution is not put in issue by a plea of non est factum. Penton *v.* Williams, 43 So. 211, 150 Ala. 153; Wimberly *v.* Dallas, 52 Ala. 196; Bickley *v.* Keenan & Co., 60 Ala. 293.

A defendant can not plead non est factum, except it be accompanied with an affidavit of its truth. This provision does not apply to a replication. Tindal *v.* Bright, Minor 103; Parks *v.* Greening, Minor 178.

In an action by a county for breach by defendant of its bond securing a contract made with the probate judge of the county in its behalf for the hiring of convicts, by nonpayment of quarterly installments of hire money, quarterly reports rendered by defendant to the county treasurer, and received by him, or which were rendered to the judge of probate or clerk of the circuit court, and were acted on by the county treasurer, are admissible under a general or special plea of payment. Sloss Iron & Steel Co. *v.* Macon County, 111 Ala. 554, 20 So. 400.

Code, § 2769, provides that every written contract, the foundation of the suit, purporting to be executed by the party sought to be charged, is evidence of the existence of the debt, or that the party understood to perform the duty for which it was given, and was made on sufficient consideration, but may be impeached by plea. By § 2770 such contract must be received in evidence without proof of execution, unless its execution be denied by plea. Held that, in an action on a bond, where it is set forth in the complaint as the foundation of the suit, and purports to have been executed by defendants, and neither its consideration nor execution is impeached by plea, it is admissible in evidence, though it was executed without statutory authority. Bryan *v.* Kelly, 85 Ala. 569, 5 So. 346, citing Johnson *v.* Caffey, 59 Ala. 331.

Mistake in Name of Party.—The mistake in the name of one of the obligees is in a most essential and vital part. It enters into the legal obligation of the contract, and it should not be corrected by the admission of parol evidence on the trial at law. Gayle *v.* Hudson, 10 Ala. 116, 131.

A bound executed by "Jas. W. Y." will be admitted in evidence under a declaration upon a bond alleged to have been executed by "James W. Y." Robbins *v.* State, 6 Ala. 839.

A bond in which Hudson and Jones are obligees can not be sued and recovered on, at law, in the name of Hudson and James, though plaintiffs allege and offer to prove that James, and not Jones, was intended to be an obligee, and that the insertion of the wrong name was a mere mistake. Gayle *v.* Hudson, 10 Ala. 116. See Paysant *v.* Ware, 1 Ala. 160.

A bond signed "Pilip T." will support a declaration upon a bond as signed "Philip T." Taylor *v.* Rogers, Minor 197.

Proof.—The execution of the bond need not be proved, unless the defendant make affidavit of the truth of his plea. Coleman v. Pike County, 83 Ala. 326, 3 So. 755.

Where plaintiff in an action against a city alleged a cause of action on a bond, it could not recover on proof of an unsealed instrument. Gutta Percha & Rubber Mfg. Co. v. City of Attalla (Ala.), 39 So. 719.

A declaration on a bond is not sustained by proof of a promissory note. Davis v. McWhorter, 26 So. 119, 122 Ala. 570.

At common law, an affidavit to a plea of non est factum was not necessary. Tindal v. Bright, Minor 103.

Oyer can not be craved of a bond which is not the foundation of the action. Tuskaloosa v. Lacy, 3 Ala. 618.

Variance.—Where the complaint is on a bond under seal, and the proof is of an unsealed promise to pay, the variance is fatal. Hughes v. Spratling, 57 So. 629, 3 Ala. App. 517, Breitling v. Marx, 123 Ala. 222, 26 So. 203; Burton v. Dangerfield, 141 Ala. 285, 291, 37 So. 350; New York Life Ins. Co. v. McPherson, 137 Ala. 116, 119, 33 So. 825.

Where one sues on a bond or bill single, proof of a deed of trust is a fatal variance, entitling defendants to a verdict. Union Fertilizer Co. v. Johnson, 43 So. 752, 150 Ala. 159, citing Phillips v. Americus Guano Co., 110 Ala. 521, 18 So. 104; Davis v. McWhorter, 122 Ala. 570, 26 So. 119.

Where a bond recites a contract to build a one-story dwelling house, and a complaint on the bond for breaches of said contract sets out a contract in terms to build a dwelling house, and there is nothing in it indicating that the house is to be other than a one-story house, there is no discrepancy between the contract indicated by the reference in the bond and the contract set out in the complaint as being that intended to be secured by the bond. Forst v. Leonard, 112 Ala. 296, 20 So. 587.

§ 73. Evidence.

§ 74. —— Presumptions and Burden of Proof.

When a bond is found in the possession of the grantee or obligee, the presumption is that it was delivered to him. Firemen's Ins. Co. v. McMillan, 29 Ala. 147. See, also, Houston v. Stanton, 11 Ala. 412; McMorris v. Crawford, 15 Ala. 271.

On a plea of non est factum, proof that the signature of the obligor was genuine raises the presumption that he executed the bond by sealing and delivering it. Manning v. Norwood, 1 Ala. 429.

"It is not necessary, in declaring upon a writing obligatory, to allege its delivery to the obligee; it will be inferred from his possession, that it was duly delivered, and if the reverse is true, it devolves upon the obligor to prove it, if it can avail him anything." Spence v. Rutledge, 11 Ala. 590, 592; Firemen's Ins. Co. v. McMillan, 29 Ala. 147.

Where, under a statute, the state guaranties railroad bonds, which are diverted from the purpose for which the state's guaranty was made, it will not be presumed that one to whom the bonds are assigned had notice of their diversion. Gilman v. New Orleans & S. R. Co., 72 Ala. 566.

If, at any time before a final trial, the note or bond on which the action has been brought, undergo any alteration, or receive any impression, indicating its destruction or satisfaction, it would appear to be but a necessary and reasonable requisition on the plaintiff that he should afford the explanation. If the act done was the result of a mistake or accident; or if any effect was designed by it different from its ordinary import, he alone must be presumed to know the circumstances, and to possess the means of explanation. Pitcher v. Patrick, 1 Stew. & P. 478, 481. See ante, "Constructive Notice, and Facts Putting on Inquiry," § 50.

§ 75. —— Admissibility.

A clerk or any other person before whom the obligor in a bond acknowledges it, and who has taken a copy, is competent, the original being lost, and the copy thus taken produced, to prove the execution of the bond. Rowland v. Day, 17 Ala. 681.

Where a bond is delivered by a co-obligor to another on the conditions that another co-obligor sign before it should be valid, evidence given by the co-obligor, to whom it was delivered, is admissible to show that the condition which had been imposed upon it by those who did sign had been released. Bibb *v.* Reid, 3 Ala. 88.

In an action upon a bond, if there is no election contest, proof of the judgment rendered on the contest was relevant, as showing that the contest had ended and that the costs were due. McWhirter *v.* Frazier, 129 Ala. 450, 29 So. 445.

In an action upon a bond, if there is no issue which imposes upon the plaintiff the onus of proving its genuineness, it should not be rejected as evidence because it has interlineations which he does not account for. Perhaps, if it had been offered as evidence without having been made the basis of an action, and the interlineations were such as to warrant the suspicion that they had been made after the bond was executed, or without authority, they should be accounted for. Whitsett *v.* Womack, 8 Ala. 466.

In an action by a county for breach by a company of its bond securing a contract made with its probate judge in its behalf for the hiring of convicts, by nonpayment of quarterly installments, where the contract provided for quarterly settlements, evidence that the probate judge made an abortive effort to obtain a conference with the company's president, to secure an adjustment of the accounts, is irrelevant. Sloss Iron & Steel Co. *v.* Macon County, 111 Ala. 554, 20 So. 400.

§ 76. —— Weight and Sufficiency.

The testimony of a person before whom the obligor acknowledged the execution of a lost bond, together with a production by him of a copy of the lost instrument, is sufficient to prove the execution and contents of the original bond. Rowland *v.* Day, 17 Ala. 681.

The execution of a bond by persons styling themselves "commissioners" of a county is not proof of the fact against third persons. Carter *v.* Garrett, 13 Ala. 728.

Proof that a bond was signed with reference to a building contract, and kept in possession of the principals until the subsequent reduction of the contract to writing, and the signing thereof, when both instruments were delivered together, is sufficient to support the averment in the complaint that at the time of the execution and delivery of such bond the principals entered into the contract, for, though a bond may be signed at one time, its execution does not occur until delivery. Forst *v.* Leonard, 22 So. 481, 116 Ala. 82.

§ 77. Damages and Amount of Recovery.

§ 78. —— In General.

In an action on a penal bond given to the state by a plank-road company in consideration of a loan, conditioned for the faithful application of the money, the measure of damages for the breach is the damages proved to have been actually sustained, and not the amount of the money loaned. Jemison *v.* State, 47 Ala. 390.

§ 79. —— Debt or Actual Damages, or Penalty.

In a suit upon a bond, interest by way of damages may be recovered beyond the penalty of the bond. Tyson *v.* Sanderson, 45 Ala. 364.

In actions upon penal bonds with collateral conditions, the plaintiff can never recover more damages than the penalty. Tyson *v.* Sanderson, 45 Ala. 364. See, also, Hill *v.* Rushing, 4 Ala. 212; Herndon *v.* Forney, 4 Ala. 243. See, also, note in 55 L. R. A. 387, 392.

Where, in an action against a surety on a trustee's bond, the uncontroverted evidence showed a breach of the bond, and that plaintiff had suffered damage in a sum greater than the amount of the bond, the court properly directed a verdict for the entire penalty. Ladd *v.* Smith (Ala.), 10 So. 836. See the title TRUSTS.

§ 80. —— Suggestion on Record of Additional Breaches.

After judgment, by default or on demurrer, for the plaintiff, he may suggest breaches on the roll. State *v.* Wiley, 14 Ala. 172. See ante, "Declaration, Complaint, or Petition," § 69.

§ 81. Trial.

§ 82. —— Questions for Jury.

In an action upon a covenant executed

by two obligors, with a credit indorsed signed by one of them for the plaintiff, the jury may presume that credit was properly entered, and allow it. Rivers *v.* Loving, 1 Stew. 395.

The delivery of a bond is a question of fact. Bibb *v.* Reid, 3 Ala. 88. See ante, "Necessity and Sufficiency," § 15.

§ 83. Judgment.

§ 84. —— Form as to Recovery of Damages or Penalty.

A judgment on an appeal bond may be amended nunc pro tunc to limit it to the penalty thereof. Sherry *v.* Priest, 57 Ala. 410. See McBarnett *v.* Breed, 6 Ala. 476; Witherington *v.* Brantley, 18 Ala. 197; McKeen *v.* Nelms, 9 Ala. 507, 510; Hill *v.* Rushing, 4 Ala. 212; Pryor *v.* Beck, 21 Ala. 393, 397.

The judgment in an action on a bond for the performance of covenants should be for the penalty, with nominal damages and costs. Garnett *v.* Yoe, 17 Ala. 74, cited on this point in note in 62 L. R. A. 437, 455.

In an action upon a penal bond, judgment may be entered either for the amount of the penalty, to be discharged by the sum assessed by the jury, or for the amount of such assessed sum. Moore *v.* Harton, 1 Port. 15, cited on this point in note in 62 L. R. A. 446, 456.

The surety is not bound beyond the penalty of the bond, and a judgment against him for a larger sum will be amended, at the costs of the plaintiff in error. Seamans *v.* White, 8 Ala. 656, cited on this point in note in 55 L. R. A. 390, 391.

Bondsmen.

See the titles BAIL; BONDS; PRINCIPAL AND SURETY; REPLEVIN.

Book Accounts.

See the title ACCOUNT, ACTION ON.

Book Debts.

See the title ACCOUNT, ACTION ON.

Books.

See the titles BANKS AND BANKING; CRIMINAL LAW; EVIDENCE; EXEMPTIONS; SCHOOLS AND SCHOOL DISTRICTS.

Books of Account.

See the titles ACCOUNT, ACTION ON; EVIDENCE; INSURANCE; PARTNERSHIP.

Borrowing.

See the titles BAILMENT; MONEY LENT; USURY.

Boss.

See the title MASTER AND SERVANT.

BOUNDARIES.

Cross References.

As to boundaries of Indian reservations, see the title INDIANS. As to ownership of trees on boundaries, see the title ADJOINING LANDOWNERS. As to the rights and liabilities of owners of land bounded by bodies or streams of water, see the titles NAVIGABLE WATERS; WATERS AND WATERCOURSES. As to the rights and liabilities of owners of land bounded by highways, see the titles FENCES; HIGHWAYS; PARTY WALLS.

I. DESCRIPTION.

§ 1. Relative Importance of Conflicting Elements.

§ 1 (1) In General.

Neither weight nor effect will be given a description in a deed in terms of quantity, except for the purpose of relieving some otherwise irremediable ambiguity in the more particular description, and, though a description by monuments, corners, and boundaries contains more than the amount specified by acres, the specific description will control. Busbee *v.* Thomas, 175 Ala. 423, 57 So. 587.

A deed conveying a lot on the side of an alley, which describes the depth of the lot so as to take in part of the alley, but further describes it as extending to a point on the alley and thence along the boundary line of the alley, does not convey any part of the alley. Barker *v.* Mobile Elect. Co., 173 Ala. 28, 55 So. 364.

Establishment of Original Line of Survey—What Should Receive First Attention.—In establishing an original line of survey, according to the field notes used in such survey, attention is given first to calls for natural or artificial monuments, and, if these are not to be found, to courses and distances, with the variation of the needle from the true meridian as indicated for the original survey on the field notes. Taylor *v.* Fomby, 22 So. 910, 116 Ala. 621.

§ 1 (2) Control of Natural Objects and Monuments over Other Elements in General.

Distances in a description will always yield to fixed boundaries clearly and certainly established. Page *v.* Whatley, 50 So. 116, 162 Ala. 473.

Where different parts of the description in a deed of patent conflict, those particulars which are most stable, and certain, and least liable to be mistaken, are to prevail. It has been the established rule of construction, that a description of boundaries by known and visible natural and artificial monuments or landmarks is generally to be preferred to a description by courses and distance and other measurements. Taylor *v.* Fomby, 116 Ala. 621, 22 So. 910, 912.

How Boundaries Are Determined.—Streets, which are well defined and designated by some natural or artificial monument, must govern course and distance in fixing the boundaries of lands; but streets which, in the infancy of a city or town, are only undefined portions of land dedicated to public use, themselves requiring to be located, would furnish very uncertain guides in arriving at the boundaries of other lands. Saltonstall *v.* Riley, 28 Ala. 164.

When Rule Does Not Apply.—The rule that, in the description of the boundaries of land conveyed, monuments, whether natural or artificial, dominate courses and distances, does not apply where, by giving monuments a controlling influence, absurd consequences would ensue, or where it is obvious that courses and distances furnish the most certain guides to the location and quantity of the land, in which case the latter must be followed. Barker *v.* Mobile Electric Co., 173 Ala. 28, 55 So. 364.

§ 1 (3) Control of Metes and Bounds or Courses and Distances over Other Elements.

Effect of Line Written Across a Plat.—Where the length of a line is written across a plat which accompanies a grant of land, it will not control the boundaries which are expressly declared in the grant. Hallett *v.* Doe, 7 Ala. 882. See, also, Magee *v.* Hallett, 22 Ala. 699, 720.

Title Acquired by Purchaser of Government Lands.—The purchaser of government lands acquires, by his patent, title to all of the land embraced within the boundary lines of the tract purchased, even though the survey be inaccurate, for the boundaries, when found, must control the notes and plat of the survey. Lewen *v.* Smith, 7 Port. 428.

Description of Premises Conveyed by Mortgage.—Where lands are incorrectly described by government numbers, but correctly by metes and bounds, the latter description controls. Chadwick *v.* Carson, 78 Ala. 116. See, also, Payne *v.* Crawford, 102 Ala. 397, 14 So. 854.

Description of Premises in Conveyance.—Where a conveyance describes the premises by clear and distinct metes and bounds, from which the boundaries can be readily ascertained, such description must prevail over any general words or description also added. Guilmartin *v.* Wood, 76 Ala. 204.

§ 1 (4) Control of Lines Marked or Surveyed over Other Elements.

Description by Metes and Bounds.—When a deed describes the land conveyed as "a piece of land about one hundred feet long or wide," further described by metes and bounds, and the land is at the date of conveyance fenced and known to the purchaser, the description by metes and bounds controls the statement as to quantity. Thompson *v.* Sheppard, 85 Ala. 611, 5 So. 334. See the title DEEDS.

When Due Allowances Are to Be Made for Variations.—In ascertaining the boundaries of land, where the lines establishing by the United States survey are obvious, they must be followed, though made on an assumed or wrong magnetic variation, and it is only when lost lines and corners are to be renewed that due allowance should be made for the variation of the magnetic needle from the true meridian. Taylor *v.* Fomby, 22 So. 910, 116 Ala. 621.

Discrepancy between Corners.—Where a navigable stream intervenes in running the lines of a section, the surveyor stops at that point, and does not continue across the river. The fraction thus made is complete, and its contents can be ascertained. Therefore, where there is a discrepancy between the corners of a section as established by the United States, and the lines as run and marked, the latter does not yield to the former. Lewen *v.* Smith, 7 Port. 428.

Sale by Metes and Bounds.—Where the land conveyed is described by the government surveys, and as containing so many acres more or less, it is a sale by metes and bounds; and, in the absence of fraud, the actual quantity, whether more or less than the estimation at the purchase, will not avail either party. Dozier *v.* Duffee, 1 Ala. 320.

§ 2. Courses and Distances.

It is well settled that, where a line is described as running towards one of the cardinal points, it must run directly in that course, unless it is controlled by some object. Hagen *v.* Campbell, 8 Port. 9.

"What is most material and most certain in a description, shall prevail over that which is less material and less certain. Thus, course and distance shall yield to natural and ascertained objects; as a river, a stream, a spring or a marked tree." Miller *v.* Cullum, 4 Ala. 576, 581.

§ 3. Location of Corners.

Mode of Ascertaining Lost Corner or Boundary.—In ascertaining the lost corner or boundary of a section, which must be presumed, in the absence of evidence to the contrary, to have been established and marked in the original survey, recourse may be had to the unobliterated marks and corners of that survey, the field notes and plat, and subsequent surveys made under their guidance, although such subsequent surveys are not proved to correspond, in every particular, with the original survey. If only a portion of one of the boundary lines, leading to the lost corner, has been obliterated, the remaining portion, whether straight or not as marked, must be considered as established; and the corner must be presumed, in the absence of evidence to the contrary, to be at the point where the marked line, if continued, would intersect the township line. But, if the lost corner is proved to have been at another point, the lost portion of the boundary must be ascertained by running a straight line from the point at which the marks disappear to that corner. Billingsley *v.* Bates, 30 Ala. 376.

Conclusiveness of Corners as to True Location.—2 U. S. Stat. 313, and 3 U. S. Stat. 366, relating to the survey of public lands of the United States, do not make the corners of subdivisions of fractional sections, as fixed by the United States surveyors, conclusive as to the true location of such corners, but such corners are to be placed equidistant from the section corners on the same line, so that, if the original United States surveyor has made a mistake in the location, the corner may be changed. Nolen *v.* Parmer, 24 Ala. 391.

Survey of Public Domain.—The United States, in providing for the survey of the public domain, established the rule that sections of lands should be held to contain the exact quantity returned by the surveyor general, so that the corners of sections fixed by such survey can not be removed. Walters *v.* Commons, 2 Port. 38.

What Purchaser Takes.—In the case of sections, the government has arranged their boundaries, marked their lines and corners, and declared the contents; and the purchaser of an entire section takes all within those limits, be it more or less than the quantity returned by the surveyor; but, in the purchase of a less quantity than a section (as between the several holders of a section), the contents of such several parts must be determined by reference to the entire section; and the purchaser of a half or quarter section is entitled to one-half or one-quarter of whatever the section contains. In such case, the half-mile posts or corners are to be placed equidistant between the corners of a section; for these half-mile posts are not definitely fixed by law, as in the case of section corners. Walters *v.* Commons, 2 Port. 38.

§ 4. Location of Lines.

Where the place of beginning a survey is fixed and certain, the line must be run from that point, according to the courses and distances, in order to ascertain the precise position of a tract of land. Miller *v.* Cullum, 4 Ala. 576, 582.

A plat or plan of survey may be referred to in a grant, and become part of it; showing the proper lines, and ascertaining the locality. Hagen *v.* Campbell, 8 Port. 9.

And where the distance marked out in a plat can not be included by allowing the lines to deviate, the grant which refers to the plat, must be construed to mean, that the lines shall be extended without a variation of course. Hagen *v.* Campbell, 8 Port. 9.

Marked and Established Boundaries.—Each section, or separate subdivision of a section, is independent of any other section in the township, and must be governed by its marked and established boundaries. Lewen *v.* Smith, 7 Port. 428.

§ 5. Designation, Quantity, and Location of Land.

Where a patent calls for a subdivision of a fractional quarter section, described as lying north of a certain creek and containing a specified number of acres, it embraces all the land in the subdivision north of the creek, though the actual number of acres exceeds the number specified in the patent. Stein *v.* Ashby, 24 Ala. 521.

Construction of Deed as to Clause Containing Statement of Quantity.—The land conveyed was described in a deed partly by its numbers and the government surveys and partly by metes and bounds. Then followed the words, "containing seven hundred and two acres, and the same being the settlement of lands at present occupied by said H.," the vendor. Held, that the reference to the grant was merely descriptive, and not controlling. Wright *v.* Wright, 34 Ala. 194.

Extent of Grant.—In 1767 the British government granted to private individuals a certain tract of tide lands in the district of Mobile, lying west of the Mobile river, and having the highwater mark of the river for its eastern boundary. The grant was confirmed by the Spanish government in 1807. The Spanish grant recited a shortage of acreage in the grant of 1767, and, as compensation for the error, was made to embrace the distance marked out in a plat (which was made part of the grant) as being from the river to the limits east of the land, and left unsurveyed in 1767, because it was then an impassible marsh. The plat showed the north and south boundary lines of the original tract extended without deviation of course. Held that, as the British grant already extended to high-water mark, the Spanish grant extended across the marsh lands to the channel of the Mobile river. Hagen *v.* Campbell, 8 Port. 9.

§ 6. Maps, Plats, and Field Notes.

Conveyance—When without Reference to Quantity.—A deed conveying "the south part of the east half of the northeast quarter of § 27, township 16, and range 12, containing forty 10-100 acres," is not a conveyance of the S. ½ of the half quarter section without reference to quantity, but of the number of acres mentioned of the S. ½ of that half quarter section. Lamar *v.* Minter, 13 Ala. 31.

§ 7. Waters and Watercourses.

§ 8. —— In General.

It is well settled, at common law, that the person whose land is bounded by a stream of water which changes its course gradually by alluvial formations, shall still hold by the same boundary including the accumulated soil. No other rule can be applied on just principles. Every proprietor, whose land is thus bounded, is subject to loss by the same means which may add to his territory; and as he is without remedy for his loss in this way, he can not be held accountable for his gain. Hagen *v.* Campbell, 8 Port. 9, 26.

"A grant of land bounded upon a fresh water stream or river, where the tide neither ebbs nor flows, extends ad filum aquæ; but a grant bounded upon a navigable river extends to the edge of the water only." Bullock *v.* Wilson, 2 Port. 436, 447.

Extent of Title to Land Bordering on Navigable Stream.—The title of an owner of land bordering on a navigable stream extends to low-water mark. Webb *v.* City of Demopolis, 95 Ala. 116, 13 So. 289, 21 L. R. A. 62. See the title NAVIGABLE WATERS.

A conveyance of land, one side of which is bounded by a public navigable river, passes all the land between high-water mark and the ordinary stage of water. Hess *v.* Cheney, 83 Ala. 251, 3 So. 791, cited on this point in note in 42 L. R. A. 504. See the title NAVIGABLE WATERS.

Riparian Rights On Navigable River.—When a person owns land on a navigable river, or an island in the river, his ownership extends to the margin of the water at ordinary stage, and embraces the land between high and low water mark. Williams *v.* Glover, 66 Ala. 189. See the title NAVIGABLE WATERS.

Right of Land Owners to Soil in Bed of Stream below Low-Water Mark.—Every watercourse which is suitable for the ordinary purposes of navigation, whether above or below tide water, is a public highway; and the owners of land bounded thereon have no right of soil to the bed of the stream below low-water mark. Bullock *v.* Wilson, 2 Port. 436. See the title NAVIGABLE WATERS; WATERS AND WATERCOURSES.

Extent of Title to Land on Margin of Navigable River—How Determined.—Whether the title of a proprietor of land on the margin of a navigable river extends to high-water mark, low-water mark, or the middle of the stream, is not a federal question, though he claim under a grant from the United States, but is to be determined by the laws of the state in which the land is situated. Webb *v.* City of Demopolis, 95 Ala. 116, 13 So. 289, 21 L. R. A. 62.

Conveyance by U. S. Patent.—A patent by the United States to land along a stream where the tide ebbs and flows conveys to the high-tide line along the shore. Mobile Transp. Co. *v.* City of Mobile, 30 So. 645, 128 Ala. 335, 64 L. R. A. 333.

§ 9. —— Construction of Language of Description.

The words "seventy acres of land, being and lying in the southwest corner of the southwest quarter of section 14, township 12, range 5, of land sold at L," are a good description in a deed, and include the land in an equal square, and a deed which professes to convey a moiety of a tract of land, but describes the part conveyed by metes and bounds, conveys only such part as is within the limits designated, although it may be less than a moiety. Lamar *v.* Minter, 13 Ala. 31, 37.

The term "northerly" in a grant, where there is no object to direct its inclination to the east or to the west, must be construed to mean north, and there being no object to control, it must be a due north line. Hagen *v.* Campbell, 8 Port. 9, 31.

Where the term "river," is used in a grant, as a boundary—high, or low, water mark must be intended—not a middle point. Hagen *v.* Campbell, 8 Port. 9.

"Where the land sold is described by definite boundaries, in regard to which there can be no mistake, if it be followed by a statement, as containing—number of acres, or other phrase of like import, it is to be deemed a mere matter of description, and not as a covenant warranting the quantity intended to be conveyed." Hess *v.* Cheney, 83 Ala. 251, 3 So. 791, 792.

Reservations in Grant of Lands Bounded by River.—In a grant of lands bounded by a river, the reservation of a road or right of way upon the bank does not prevent the fee in the land from vesting in the grantee, nor limit his riparian rights. Hagen *v.* Campbell, 8 Port. 9. See the title NAVIGABLE WATERS.

Extent of Grant.—A grant of land on the west side of the river Mobile, "terminated by the bank of said river on the east side," passed a title to the grantee to high-water mark only. Hagen *v.* Campbell, 8 Port. 9. See the title NAVIGABLE WATERS.

Definition of "Bank" of a River.—The "bank" of a river is that space of rising ground above low-water mark which is usually covered by high water, and the term, when used in a grant to designate a precise line, is vague and indefinite. Howard *v.* Ingersoll, 17 Ala. 780.

§ 10. —— Artificial Bodies of Water.

Construction of Boundary in Deed for Land, and Admissibility of Parol Evidence to Explain.—In an action to recover damages for the erection of a milldam, which overflowed plaintiff's lands, the words "down the east bank of said creek to the ford below the mill, thence with the center of the creek to the section line," are properly construed by the court to mean the top of the bank above the ford, and not the low-water line, when it is shown that the plaintiff's vendor, at the time of the sale and conveyance to him, also owned the adjacent lands on the opposite side of the creek, and had erected on them a mill, with a dam extending across the creek, which he continued to use after the sale and conveyance to the plaintiff, and until he sold them to the defendant. Jenkins *v.* Cooper, 50 Ala. 419, cited on this point in note in 42 L. R. A. 507.

§ 11. Roads, Ways, and Public Grounds.

§ 12. —— Public Ways.

§ 12 (1) In General.

Extent of Boundary of Land Bounded by Highway.—Where land sold is described as bounded by highway, the boundary is the middle of such highway. Columbus & W. Ry. Co. *v.* Witherow, 82 Ala. 190, 3 So. 23; Moore *v.* Johnson, 87 Ala. 220, 6 So. 50.

§ 12 (2) Effect of Location, Dedication, or Occupation.

Street Named as Boundary—Construction Placed Upon It.—Where a street is named in a deed as a boundary of the land conveyed, it will be construed, in the absence of evidence to the contrary, to mean the street as actually opened and in use. Southern Iron Works *v.* Central of Georgia Ry. Co., 31 So. 723, 131 Ala. 649.

§ 13. —— Railroad Rights of Way.

Construction of Language—Amount Conveyed.—A deed conveying all the land in a certain lot south of a "railway cut" conveys only the land south of the upper and outer edge of the cut. Newton *v.* Louisville & N. R. Co., 110 Ala. 474, 19 So. 19.

§ 15. Priority of Surveys.

Grants Overlapped in Description.—Where tracts of land conveyed separately and simultaneously to plaintiff and defendant by a common grantor overlapped in description, but defendant's grant was based on a prior survey, plaintiff's grant was subservient. Adams *v.* Wilson, 34 So. 831, 137 Ala. 632.

II. EVIDENCE, ASCERTAINMENT, AND ESTABLISHMENT.

§ 16. Nature and Form of Remedy.

Where, on a bill filed to settle and to establish a boundary line between two adjoining lots, it is averred that the respondent has at various times moved the line between the lots, and was encroaching upon the complainant's lands; that the true boundary line between such lots had become confused and uncertain, and had been moved at various times by the defendant, against the objection of the plaintiff, and as the result of all such acts the true boundary line has become confused, uncertain, and obliterated—it avers sufficient facts to confer jurisdiction upon a court in equity to establish the boundary line between said lots, and upon proof of such averments the complainant is entitled to the relief prayed for. Guice *v.* Barr, 30 So. 563, 130 Ala. 570.

Complainant can not maintain a bill in equity to establish disputed boundaries when such bill shows that he is in possession of all the land claimed. Ashurst *v.* McKenzie, 92 Ala. 484, 9 So. 262.

Disputed Boundaries—What Court Has Power.—A court of equity has power and jurisdiction to establish disputed boundaries between adjoining parcels of land; and this jurisdiction will be exercised when the obliteration or confusion of the boundary line has resulted from the acts of one of the owners of the adjoining property in fraud of the other's rights, or by a failure of such owner to discharge the obligation resting upon him to preserve the correct boundary line. Guice *v.* Barr, 30 So. 563, 130 Ala. 570.

Sufficiency of Allegations.—A bill to establish a boundary, alleging that defendant, being the owner of sections 20 and 21, conveyed section 20 to complainant by a deed merely describing the land as "all of section 20" in a certain township and range; that during the time the two sections belonged to defendant or those under whom she claimed title, the boundary line between the sections was destroyed; that such destruction was caused by the negligence of defendant, or those under whom she claimed; that the boundary was obliterated at the date on which defendant conveyed the land to complainant, who was ignorant thereof; that defendant remained the owner of section 21; that defendant did not at the date of the sale point out to complainant the boundary, and has not done so, though requested; and that complainant employed the county surveyor to locate the boundary, but was prohibited by defendant by threats of violence—states a cause of action within the jurisdiction of chancery to determine the boundary; the acts of defendant amounting to a fraud on complainant. Hays *v.* Bouchelle, 41 So. 518, 147 Ala. 212.

§ 17. Jurisdiction.

Where the line is marked only by monuments at its terminal points, the boundary running directly between them, the destruction of these monuments under like circumstances, and consequent confusion and dispute as to the location of the line, would present a case for equitable action in fixing and declaring the boundary. Ashurst *v.* McKenzie, 92 Ala. 484, 9 So. 262.

Chancery Jurisdiction of Disputed Boundaries.—Chancery has no jurisdiction to determine disputed boundaries where there is no confusion or obliteration thereof, but the sole question is a legal one as to which of certain existing monuments are the correct ones. Ashurst *v.* McKenzie, 92 Ala. 484, 9 So. 262.

The jurisdiction of chancery to establish disputed boundaries is not original or independent, and chancery will not undertake to settle obscured or confused boundaries, unless some equity is superinduced by the act of the parties or of those through whom they claim. Hays *v.* Bouchelle, 41 So. 518, 147 Ala. 212.

Pleading.—Where, in an action to recover a strip of land as a part of the governmental subdivision of a section, the issue involved the proper location of the boundary line between that subdivision and the adjacent subdivision which belonged to defendant, defendant must disclaim and suggest a dispute as to the boundary as provided by Code 1907, § 3843. Jeffreys *v.* Jeffreys (Ala.), 62 So. 797.

§ 18. Admissibility of Evidence.

§ 19. —— In General.

§ 19 (1) In General.

"In England, reputation, or the declarations of deceased persons, are not evidence, in questions of boundary, between individuals, though admissible in questions of public right; but in the United States a different rule has generally prevailed." Farmer's Heirs *v.* Mobile, 8 Ala. 279, 284.

Where the description in a conveyance of land is by meets and bounds, evidence of the situation and locality of the premises, and of their identity, according to the description in the conveyance, is admissible. But such evidence is not admissible to show a mistake in the description, or to alter or vary the boundary, or to substitute another and different boundary for the one expressed in the conveyance. Guilmartin *v.* Wood, 76 Ala. 204, 209.

Though a deed furnished the means for locating the boundaries of land, yet their actual location being an independent inquiry, a witness could testify to where they were. Middlebrooks *v.* Sanders (Ala.), 61 So. 898.

Acts of Possession and Ownership.—In an action involving a disputed boundary, it was not error to permit a party to show an instance in which her agent objected to the presence on the disputed strip of a person who had purchased from the opposite party, since it bore on the question of possession and control. Cooper *v.* Slaughter, 175 Ala. 211, 57 So. 477, 478.

Testimony of Witness as to Location of Corner.—Where there was no fixed and official establishment by monument of a corner, the testimony of a witness as to the location of the corner, based on his statements of the surrounding facts, which determined his location, was admissible. Lecroix *v.* Malone, 47 So. 725, 157 Ala. 434.

Proof of Boundary by General Reputation.—The boundaries of a public lot may be proved by general reputation. Therefore a deed for an adjoining lot, calling for the "king's bakehouse lot" as its northern boundary, is admissible to prove, as general reputation, that, at the date of the deed, the bakehouse lot had an ascertained boundary; and the conduct of the party claiming under such deed is also evidence of the general reputation, at the time, of the true boundary of the bakehouse lot. Whether such evidence would be admissible in the case of a private lot, quære. Farmer *v.* City of Mobile, 8 Ala. 279.

§ 19 (2) Reputation or Tradition.

"The territorial boundaries of public municipal jurisdictions, when they grow to be ancient, are unmarked by artificial monuments; and, where there is not of them higher evidence, may be proved by general reputation. Morgan *v.* Mobile, 49 Ala. 349." Tidwell *v.* State, 70 Ala. 33, 43.

Proof of Ancient Boundary.—Proof of general reputation is admissible to establish an ancient boundary to an incorporated city of which there is no recorded survey, and which is not marked by visible monuments. Morgan *v.* City of Mobile, 49 Ala. 349. See the title EVIDENCE.

Reputation is admissible to prove an ancient boundary. Shook *v.* Pate, 50 Ala. 91. See the title EVIDENCE.

§ 19 (3) Testimony of Surveyors and Their Assistants.

When Competent.—Testimony of a surveyor as to how and where he ran the lines called for in the description of the boundaries of a piece of land is competent. Bullock *v.* Wilson, 2 Port. 436.

Parol Evidence.—In trespass to try title, a surveyor may not only prove his survey, but may give parol evidence explanatory of it. Cundiff *v.* Orms, 7 Port. 58.

Landowner As Competent Witness.—On the issue of the true location of a boundary line, a landowner is a competent witness as to the particulars of a survey of the line, where he was present at the survey, and testifies from his own knowledge of the facts. Wheeler *v.* State, 21 So. 941, 114 Ala. 22.

§ 19 (4) Agreement, Acquiescence, and Practical Location by Parties.

In an action for trespass involving a disputed boundary line, where there was evidence of an agreement apparently binding the parties to appoint surveyors and abide by their survey, it was not error to charge that, if the jury believed that the defendant made an agreement with plaintiff to have the line ascertained by a survey, the jury might consider the agreement, in connection with the other evidence, to determine whether defendant's possession of the disputed strip had been adverse. Cooper *v.* Slaughter, 175 Ala. 211, 57 So. 477, 478.

Location of Division—Competent Evidence.—In ejectment to determine a disputed boundary line, it was competent for defendant to prove the location of a division fence, as bearing on the issue whether defendant had encroached on plaintiff's land. Ross *v.* Roy (Ala.), 39 So. 583.

§ 20. —— Documentary Evidence.

§ 20 (1) Maps and Plats.

Maps held properly admitted in boundary suit. Cooper *v.* Slaughter, 175 Ala. 211, 57 So. 477.

§ 20 (2) Formal Proceedings and Adjudications Other than Actions.

A commission for the examination of claims under Spanish grants made a special report on a grant which was void. An act of congress was passed confirming the report, and providing for the location and survey of lands to which the title was thereby confirmed. Neither the report nor the act ascertained the limits or boundaries. Held, that reference must be had either to the survey made under the act or to the patent consequent upon the survey, for the purpose of ascertaining the location of the land. Kennedy *v.* Jones, 11 Ala. 63.

Relevancy of Evidence.—Where, in ejectment, the real issue involved is as to the true boundary of the land conveyed in a deed from plaintiff to the defendant, which boundary is described as a public road, and the evidence shows that there existed at the time of the execution of the deed two roads, either of which might answer to the description contained in the deed, proceedings of the commissioners' court of the county wherein the land was situated to establish a public road answering to the description of the public road as described in the deed is admissible. Davis *v.* Blacksher Co., 30 So. 790, 131 Ala. 401.

§ 20 (3) Records of Surveys.

Relevancy of Evidence to Show Boundary.—In an action to recover damages for breaking and entering plaintiff's enclosure, and carrying away the rails of his fence, the true boundary between the parties being one of the controverted questions in the case, evidence of the "field notes of the survey of the section of land in which the fence in controversy was situated and of a survey made according to said field notes by a county surveyor of said county, and that the plaintiff had notice of the survey so made by the county surveyor," is relevant and admissible for the defendant, for "the purpose of showing his title, and the actual boundary of his land, and that said fence was upon his land." Bridges *v.* McClendon, 56 Ala. 327, 335; Dailey *v.* Fountain, 35 Ala. 26. See, also, Avary *v.* Searcy, 50 Ala. 54, 56.

County Boundary Lines.—"The boundary lines of countries are but seldom marked by natural objects, or artificial monuments, discernible by the naked eye. Often they are referred to the lines of the governmental survey of the public lands, and sometimes to places designated by names, which change, or become obsolete. There is no provision of law requiring any survey and marking of the boundaries, and a record of it as evidence of the fact. The boundary is, of consequence, subject to parol evidence; and if its location is matter of dispute, generally it must be left to a jury to say where is its true location." Miller *v.* Cullum, 4 Ala. 576; Tidwell *v.* State, 70 Ala. 33, 42.

Evidence Admissible to Determine Quantity Conveyed.—Where land conveyed is bounded on one side by a public navigable river, a survey extending only to the top of the bank is not admissible to determine the quantity conveyed, without connecting evidence as to the quantity embraced between the top of the bank and the ordinary stage of water. Hess *v.* Cheney, 83 Ala. 251, 3 So. 791.

Survey and Diagram, and Testimony of Surveyor.—A surveyor's diagram is not even prima facie evidence of the boundaries, as against "the opposite party," who has not received the notice required by Rev. Code, § 953, although the surveyor may give his opinion founded on the survey. Bridges *v.* McClendon, 56 Ala. 327.

Ex Parte Survey.—A survey of a disputed line, made by any other person than the county surveyor, is not competent evidence against a party who had no notice of it, and who did not participate in making it. Avary *v.* Searcy, 50 Ala. 54.

§ 21. Weight and Sufficiency of Evidence.

In General.—Evidence held to show that an alley was located on the land of an individual who held exclusive possession thereof as his own, so that the adjacent owner had no rights therein. Barker *v.* Mobile Elect. Co., 173 Ala. 28, 55 So. 364.

Evidence in ejectment involving a dispute as to boundaries, tried by the court without a jury, held, sufficient to support findings and a judgment for the defendant. Christopher *v.* Webb, 171 Ala. 638, 54 So. 627.

Proof of County Boundaries.—The effect of general reputation and unbroken user for sixty years, as evidence that a certain ridge of earth was the one referred to in a statute designating the boundary line of a county, can not be destroyed by a private unofficial map of a railway company made only four or five years before trial, and designating a different ridge as the county line. Tidwell *v.* State, 70 Ala. 33.

§ 22. Trial of Issues.

§ 23. —— Conduct in General.

Equitable Jurisdiction of Disputed Boundaries—How Effectuated.—The jurisdiction of courts of equity to establish disputed boundaries is effectuated through the appointment of commissioners, whose duty it is to go upon the lands, ascertain, fix, and mark the true boundary line, and report their action to the court; and therefore it would be impertinent and beyond the authority conferred upon such commissioners for them to include in their report any statement to the effect that they had found upon investigation that the respondent had encroached upon the complainant's lot, or that the respondent had obliterated the line. Guice *v.* Barr, 30 So. 563, 130 Ala. 570.

§ 24. —— Questions for Jury.

§ 24 (1) In General.

The location on the ground of boundaries described in the deed is a question of fact. Miller *v.* Cullum, 4 Ala. 576.

Identification of Property.—Where plaintiff in ejectment introduced an ancient deed as evidence of title, which the defendants attached for uncertainty of description, and a witness testified that he had lived in the neighborhood of the land practically all his life, that the original trustees under which the plaintiffs claimed were in possession of the tract before the war, and that he had seen a stake at the north west corner frequently prior to 1860, under the latitude allowed in the proof of ancient boundaries, it was for the jury to say whether or not this stake was a stake referred to in the deed. Busbee *v.* Thomas, 175 Ala. 423, 57 So. 587.

Boundaries Fixed by Grant.—When the boundary lines of a grant are fixed by the grant itself, the question as to what these lines are is purely one of law. Magee *v.* Hallett, 22 Ala. 699.

Construction and Operation of Conveyance—Question for Court or Jury.—Where the boundaries of land conveyed depend on extrinsic evidence, the jury should be allowed to pass on the parol testimony, and determine what facts were proved. Humes *v.* Bernstein, 72 Ala. 546. See, also, Vann *v.* Lunsford, 91 Ala. 576, 8 So. 719.

Lines Run by Certified Copies of Original Notes.—Where a line was run by certified copies of the original field notes, and by the calls for natural monuments indicated thereon, the location thereof was a fact to be determined by the jury from all the evidence. Taylor *v.* Fomby, 22 So. 910, 116 Ala. 621. See, also, Billingsley *v.* Bates, 30 Ala. 376, 381; Morgan *v.* Mobile, 49 Ala. 349, 350; Jenkins *v.* Cooper, 50 Ala. 419, 423; Tidwell *v.* State, 70 Ala. 33, 42.

§ 24 (2) Agreement, Recognition, or Acquiescence.

Implied Assent.—Whether one who stands by and sees a division line run between his land and the land of another, without making objection, thereby assents to it, is a question for the jury. Wheeler *v.* State, 109 Ala. 56, 19 So. 993.

§ 25. —— Instructions.

Agreement of Parties—Acquiesce.—A charge that, if the jury believed that a boundary line, the location of which was involved in an action, was in dispute, and that the adjoining owners caused it to be established and acquiesced in the line as established, the plaintiff would be deemed the owner of all lands up to such line, was a correct statement of the law; the word "deemed" being equivalent to "presumed" and the word "acquiesce" not necessarily meaning only momentary acquiescence. Cooper *v.* Slaughter, 175 Ala. 211, 57 So. 477, 478.

Affirmative Charge—Conflicting Evidence.—Where, in an action in the nature of ejectment involving a disputed boundary, possession was the only issue joined, and the evidence as to whether the land in question was in a section belonging to plaintiff or in another section belonging to defendants was in irreconcilable conflict, the general affirmative charge, with hypothesis, requested by plaintiff, was properly refused. Shiver *v.* Hardy, 39 So. 669, 145 Ala. 660.

§ 26. Agreements between Parties.

§ 26 (1) Validity in General.

Effect of Agreement between Landowners as to Division Line.—Where landowners agree to select men to run a division line, and that, having run the line from one of its terminal points to the other, the men should run and retrace it to the beginning point, the retracing forms a substantial part of the agreement, and can not be dispensed with, except by the consent of the owners. Wheeler *v.* State, 109 Ala. 56, 19 So. 993.

Necessity of Writing.—The common-law submission to arbitration of a disputed boundary need not be in writing, and may be made in writing by an agent having only parol authority. Cooper *v.* Slaughter, 175 Ala. 211, 57 So. 477.

Mutual Agreement — Consideration.—Contract held properly received in evidence, over objection that it was not mutual, and was without consideration. Cooper *v.* Slaughter, 175 Ala. 211, 57 So. 477.

§ 26 (2) Conclusiveness and Effect of Agreement.

Where adjoining owners agree on a certain dividing line, one of them going into possession of the lands under the agreement, and remaining in possession up to such line uninterrupted and exclusively, claiming to own them, for ten years, gets a title which can be devested only by a conveyance, or by adverse possession by another for the statutory period. Pittman *v.* Pittman, 27 So. 242, 124 Ala. 306.

§ 27. Estoppel in General.

Complainant, in a bill to enjoin the execution of a writ of possession, averred that, previous to his purchase of the lot in controversy, his grantor had called on defendant to point out his northern boundary line, which he did, and, on his representation that such line was fifty feet south of the center of a railroad track, purchased the lot, which lay between such northern boundary and the track; that subsequently, complainant, being about to purchase such lot, called on defendant to point out his northern boundary line, and he pointed out the same line. The railway company had not acquired title which was in defendant, to such fifty feet adjacent to its track, but it was open to acquisition by condemnation, and parties owning the land adjacent to the track regarded their lots as extending to within fifty feet of the center of the railway track, and defendant so regarded it in pointing out his north boundary line. Held not sufficient to estop defendant from claiming his title to such fifty feet. Formby *v.* Hood, 24 So. 359, 119 Ala. 231.

§ 28. Recognition and Acquiescence.

In General.—In an action to recover the penalty imposed by Code 1896, § 4137, for the willful cutting of trees on the land of another, it is competent for defendant to show that plaintiff recognized a surveyed boundary line between the parties, according to which the trees cut stood on defendant's land. Long *v.* Cummings, 156 Ala. 577, 47 So. 109.

Acts of Predecessors in Title.—In an action to recover the penalty imposed by Code 1896, § 4137, for the willful cutting of trees on the land of another, it is competent for defendant to show that plaintiff's predecessors in title recognized and accepted a certain surveyed boundary between the parties, according to which the trees cut stood on defendant's land. Long *v.* Cummings, 47 So. 109, 156 Ala. 577.

§ 29. Official Surveys.

§ 29 (1) In General.

Disputes — How Governed. — All disputes as to the boundaries of land are to be governed by the United States surveys, unless there is some statute to the contrary. Taylor *v.* Fomby, 22 So. 910, 116 Ala. 621.

§ 29 (2) Conclusiveness in General.

Where a sale of land is made according to the government surveys, and these are taken as the standard of quantity, both parties are bound by it, and neither can claim for loss or gain. Minge *v.* Smith, 1 Ala. 415.

When Erroneous Lines May or May Not Be Corrected.—The boundaries of sections of land, and their lines and corners, as fixed by the United States, can not be altered by any other survey; but the lines run to divide the sections into halves and quarters, if erroneous, may be corrected. Nolin *v.* Parmer, 21 Ala. 66. See, also, Walters *v.* Commons, 2 Port. 38.

Boundaries of Public Lands.—The corners and boundaries of sections, as marked and run by the United States surveyors in their original surveys, although not located with mathematical precision, are established by law as the proper corners and boundaries, and can not be altered or controlled by other surveys. Billingsley *v.* Bates, 30 Ala. 376.

§ 29 (3) Presumption as to Correctness and Regularity.

Surveys Accepted as Correct.—Where a survey has been made and returned by the surveyor, it shall be held to be mathematically true as to the lines run and marked, and the corners established, and contents returned. Lewen *v.* Smith, 7 Port. 428.

§ 30. Removal of Landmarks.

Rule at Common Law.—The removal of a landmark designating a corner or any other point of a boundary line is not punishable as a crime at common law. Robinson *v.* State (Ala.), 62 So. 303.

Offense under Statute.—The offense of removing a landmark under Code 1907, § 6393, punishing any person who willfully removes or defaces any monument or post designating a corner or any other point of a boundary line, is complete, where the removal of a landmark was intentionally done without lawful excuse or necessity, without regard to motive; the word "willfully" meaning intentional without lawful excuse or necessity. Robinson *v.* State (Ala.), 62 So. 303.

The removal by an owner of land of a post erected and used to designate a boundary line between him and the adjacent owner after the county surveyor had located the boundary line elsewhere is within Code 1907, § 6393, punishing any person willfully removing any monument designating a corner or other point of a boundary line, though the county surveyor advised the removal to avoid confusion. Robinson *v.* State (Ala.), 62 So. 303.

Code 1907, § 6393, punishing the willful removal of any monument erected or used to designate a corner or any other point of a boundary line, makes the offense of removing a boundary landmark punishable without reference to the ownership of the land. Robinson *v.* State (Ala.), 62 So. 303.

The object of Code 1907, § 6393, punishing one who willfully removes any monument designating any point of a boundary line, is to preserve landmarks as such, when erected or used in good faith to designate a boundary, and it is immaterial whether the landmark removed was correctly placed. Robinson *v.* State (Ala.), 62 So. 303.

Evidence.—Where, on a trial for removing a boundary line mark, the evidence showed that the post removed was used to designate a corner of a tract, that the affidavit alleged that the post was erected to designate the corner, while Code 1907, § 6393, punishes the removal of any post erected or used to designate any boundary landmark, was immaterial. Robinson *v.* State (Ala.), 62 So. 303.

Box Cars.

See the title MASTER AND SERVANT.

Boxing Matches.

See the title PRIZE FIGHTING.

Boycott.

See the titles CONSPIRACY; INJUNCTION.

Brake—Brake Beam.

See the titles MASTER AND SERVANT; RAILROADS.

Brakeman.

See the titles CARRIERS; MASTER AND SERVANT; RAILROADS.

Branch Banks.

See the title BANKS AND BANKING.

Branch Railroads.

See the title RAILROADS.

Breach.

See the titles BAIL; CONTRACTS; TRUSTS. And see the particular titles throughout this work; for instance, as to breach of agreement to arbitrate, see the title ARBITRATION AND AWARD; as to breach of condition of bonds or undertakings of various kinds, see the titles APPEAL AND ERROR; BONDS; EXECUTORS AND ADMINISTRATORS; GUARDIAN AND WARD; RECEIVERS; etc.; as to breach of promise of marriage, see the title BREACH OF MARRIAGE PROMISE; as to breach of warranties and covenants of various kinds, see the particular titles such as COVENANTS; DEEDS; INSURANCE; SALES; etc.

BREACH OF MARRIAGE PROMISE.

Cross References.

See, generally, the titles CONTRACTS; DAMAGES; MARRIAGE; SEDUCTION.

As to promise of marriage as element of offense of seduction, see the title SEDUCTION.

§ 1. Requisites and Validity of Contracts.

§ 2. —— Consideration and Mutuality.

A mutual contract to marry is requisite to sustain an action for breach of promise. Espy *v.* Jones, 37 Ala. 379.

§ 3. Construction of Contract.

See ante, "Requisites and Validity of Contracts," § 1.

Where the defendant, upon the day fixed for the marriage, wrote to the plaintiff's father, desiring him to inform her of the defendant's determination to postpone the marriage, at least for the present, her assent to the proposal can not be inferred from her silence, or from her omission to respond to the note. Kelly *v.* Renfro, 9 Ala. 325, 66 L. R. A. 799.

§ 4. Defenses.

It is a full defense, where the defendant has bona fide offered to marry the plaintiff, although the defendant's conduct previous to the offer, had been such as would justify the plaintiff in terminating the engagement, but she had not signified her intention to terminate it. Kelly *v.* Renfro, 9 Ala. 325.

If any man has been paying his addresses to one that he supposes a modest person, and afterwards discovers her to be loose and immodest, he is justified in breaking any promise of marriage he may have made to her; but, to entitle a defendant to a verdict on that ground, the jury must be satisfied that the plaintiff was a loose and immodest woman, and that he broke his promise on that account, and that he did not know her character at the time of the promise. Espy *v.* Jones, 37 Ala. 379.

§ 5. Pleading.

Sufficiency of Complaint.—Where the contract was to marry in a reasonable time, it is sufficient for the plaintiff to allege her readiness to marry the defendant, that a reasonable time had elapsed, the defendant's failure to marry her, and his continued neglect and refusal so to do. Clements *v.* Moore, 11 Ala. 35.

An allegation that the defendant, without reference to time, had married another woman previous to the institution of the suit, is equivalent to an averment that the plaintiff had offered to marry the defendant, and her proposal had been rejected; or rather, is a substitute for such averments. Clements *v.* Moore, 11 Ala. 35.

§ 6. Evidence.

§ 7. —— Character and Conduct of Parties.

The promise of the woman may be proved by evidence of her conduct and actions as well as by express words. Espy *v.* Jones, 37 Ala. 379.

§ 8. Damages.

§ 9. —— Aggravation of Damages.

Seduction before Marriage Promise.—If seduction can ever be allowed to aggravate the damages, it is only in those cases where the seduction follows the promise, and is effected by means of it. A seduction before the promise is not admissible for that purpose. Espy *v.* Jones, 37 Ala. 379, 26 L. R. A. 431; 4 L. R. A., N. S., 617.

§ 10. —— Mitigation of Damages.

Criminal Misconduct of Plaintiff.—If a man promises to marry a woman whom he supposes to be modest and chaste, and subsequently discovers that she is otherwise, he is justified in withdrawing from the engagement; but if the criminal misconduct of the plaintiff was not only known to the defendant when he made the promise, but had been encouraged and participated in by him, he will not be heard to urge such misconduct in mitigation of the damages. Espy *v.* Jones, 37 Ala. 379.

Subsequent Offer of Marriage.—An offer of marriage subsequent to the breach may be considered in mitigation of damages. Kelly *v.* Renfro, 9 Ala. 325, 41 L. R. A., N. S., 851.

§ 11. Trial.

§ 12. —— Instructions.

It is error to charge that, if there was a promise to marry, and breach of that promise by defendant, the jury must find for plaintiff, without regard to any testimony that had been introduced tending to justify the breach. Espy *v.* Jones, 37 Ala. 379.

BREACH OF THE PEACE.

Cross References.

See, generally, the titles AFFRAY; ASSAULT AND BATTERY; DISORDERLY CONDUCT; DISTURBANCE OF PUBLIC ASSEMBLAGE; DUELING; FORCIBLE ENTRY AND DETAINER; PRIZE FIGHTING; RIOT; UNLAWFUL ASSEMBLY; WEAPONS.

As to homicide committed in preserving the peace, see the title HOMICIDE. As to insults leading to breach of the peace as being libel, see the title LIBEL AND SLANDER. As to the carrying of shooting weapons or firearms as a breach of the peace, see the title WEAPONS. As to pointing weapon at another as being a breach of the peace, see the title WEAPONS.

§ 1. Nature and Elements of Offenses.

Sending a Threatening or Abusive Letter.—Within Code 1907, § 6218, making it an offense to send a threatening or abusive letter, which may tend to provoke a breach of the peace, a letter is "abusive" which is offensive, and charges the sendee with a degradation of character, or a moral obliquity; as is a letter calling the attention to an unpaid bill, stating that, if the sendee knew how contemptible he appeared in the matter, he would pay the bill at once, and that, if he did not pay it in a short time, the sender would have to proceed in some way to collect it, and concluding, "I know how worthless and contemptible you are, but this is news to you." Peters *v.* State, 51 So. 952, 166 Ala. 35.

Disorderly Language as Disturbance of Peace.—A conviction, under a statute making it unlawful for any person to disturb the peace of others by violent, offensive, or boisterous conduct or carriage, or by profane, obscene, or offensive language, can not be sustained upon the testimony of one witness, that her family lived in the same house with defendant's family, in an adjoining room, and that she heard the defendant in his own room quarreling with his wife, that he was not talking very loud, and she heard no cursing or swearing, but that the father of the witness was sick and the talking disturbed him. Ellis *v.* Pratt City, 113 Ala. 541, 21 So. 206, cited in note in 32 L. R. A., N. S., 508.

Threatening to Commit a Breach of the Peace.—Code, § 5162, et seq., authorizes a magistrate to issue a warrant for the arrest of one who has threatened or is about to commit an offense on the person or property of another, and provides that, if there is reason to fear the commission of such offense, defendant must give security to keep the peace. Held, not to make threatening a breach of the peace an offense, and that a warrant of arrest reciting that complaint had been made that the offense of threatening a breach of the peace had been committed, and charging a person named with the commission of such offense, was void on its face. Howard *v.* State, 25 So. 1000, 121 Ala. 21.

§ 2. Indictment, Information, or Complaint.

§ 3. —— Requisites and Sufficiency.

An indictment under Code 1907, § 6218, making it an offense to send a threatening or abusive letter, which "may tend" to provoke a breach of the peace, is sufficient in charging the sending of a threatening and abusive letter, which "tended" to provoke a breach of the peace. Peters *v.* State, 51 So. 952, 166 Ala. 35. See Johnson *v.* State, 152 Ala. 46, 48, 44 So. 670.

§ 4. —— Issues, Proof, and Variance.

A conviction under Code 1907, § 6218, of sending a threatening or abusive letter, may be had under an indictment charging the sending of it to C., on proof that it was sent to C. & Co., and that C. did business under the name of C. & Co., Peters *v.* State, 51 So. 952, 166 Ala. 35.

§ 5. Security to Keep the Peace.

§ 6. —— Grounds for Requiring.

In a proceeding under Code 1907, §§ and consequently that C. & Co. was C. 7520-7540, to keep the peace, all that the affidavit need show is that defendant has threatened or is about to commit an offense against the person or property of another; and an affidavit charging a threat to kill a specified person is sufficient to sustain a warrant. Cox *v.* State, 47 So. 1025, 157 Ala. 1.

§ 7. —— Review.

A probate judge has no jurisdiction, on habeas corpus or otherwise, to revise an order of a justice of the peace requiring a party to give security to keep the peace and directing his imprisonment until such security is given. An appeal to the circuit court is the only mode of revising the action of the justice. Ex parte Coburn, 38 Ala. 237; Tomlin *v.* State, 19 Ala. 9.

§ 8. —— Liabilities on Bonds.

The circuit court may render judgment for costs on the appeal bond against the securities of a party who has appealed from the order of a justice of the peace, requiring him to find sureties to keep the peace. Tomlin *v.* State, 19 Ala. 9.

Breach of Warranty of Covenant.

See references under BREACH.

Breaking.

See the titles BURGLARY; ESCAPE. As to right to break open door in making levy of execution or attachment, see the titles ATTACHMENT; EXECUTION.

BRIBERY.

Cross References.

As to bribery of voters or officers of election, see the title ELECTIONS. As to extortion under color of office, see the title EXTORTION. As to impeachment and removal from office for bribery, see the title OFFICERS, and titles of particular classes of officers.

§ 1. Nature and Elements of Offenses.

§ 1 (1) Nature and Elements in General.

To perfect the crime of bribery, there must be an acceptance of the promise, or gift, either express, or implied. Barefield *v.* State, 14 Ala. 603, 606.

A mere offer, which is rejected, does not constitute a promise or gift under the statute. Barefield *v.* State, 14 Ala. 603.

"An offer to bribe a judicial officer, is a high offense at the common law, and one that deserves severe punishment. It is an attempt to corrupt the fountain of justice, and to pervert the object and end of government. Such an offense was severely punished at the common law, and might well have been made a penitentiary crime. But we can not come to the conclusion, that the statute intended to punish by imprisonment in the penitentiary, the mere offer to bribe." Barefield *v.* State, 14 Ala. 603, 605. See post, "Sentence and Punishment," § 8.

§ 1 (2) Bribery of Jurors and Particular Classes of Officers.

A county solicitor is a "ministerial officer," within the meaning of the statute (Rev. Code, § 3564) fixing the punishment for the acceptance of a bribe by "any ministerial officer of any court." Diggs *v.* State, 49 Ala. 311.

Under Code 1876, § 4118, making it bribery to offer a juror "any gift, gratuity, or thing of value," defendant can be convicted for offering to give his labor to a juror "to chop cotton for a week." Caruthers *v.* State, 74 Ala. 406.

Under the statute denouncing an offer or promise made to a juror with intent "to bias the mind or influence the decision of the juror," the two alternative intents are not to be taken as the same thing. White *v.* State, 103 Ala. 72, 16 So. 63.

§ 2. Indictment or Information.

§ 3. —— Requisites and Sufficiency.

In an indictment for bribery, a general description of the offense is all that is requisite. Caruthers *v.* State, 74 Ala. 406.

An indictment for bribery was not demurrable in failing to allege the Christian name of the officer corruptly solicited, or that his name was to the grand jury unknown. Roden *v.* State, 5 Ala. App. 247,

59 So. 751, citing, Crittenden *v.* State, 134 Ala. 145, 32 So. 273; Knight *v.* State, 152 Ala. 56, 44 So. 585; Thompson *v.* State, 48 Ala. 165.

An indictment for offering to bribe a juror, which alleges that the juror at the time was employed with eleven others in the trial of a designated offense, need not allege that he had been summoned, sworn, or impaneled. Caruthers *v.* State, 74 Ala. 406.

§ 4. Evidence.

§ 5. —— Presumptions and Burden of Proof.

On an indictment for bribery, the burden is on the state to prove that the intent was to influence the juror. White *v.* State, 103 Ala. 72, 16 So. 63.

§ 6. —— Admissibility.

The bribe money, when properly identified, was admissible in evidence in a bribery case. Roden *v.* State, 5 Ala. App. 247, 59 So. 751.

In a trial for bribing a town marshal to permit defendant to unlawfully sell intoxicating liquors, a United States revenue license issued to defendant was admissible to show motive. Roden *v.* State, 5 Ala. App. 247, 59 So. 751.

In a trial for bribing a town marshal, the marshal's testimony that he turned the bribe money over to the city attorney was admissible to show the connection between his testimony and that of another witness, identifying the money subsequently introduced in evidence. Roden *v.* State, 5 Ala. App. 247, 59 So. 751.

To disprove corrupt intent, on the charge of bribery, defendant may show that he was drunk, and therewith any other facts going to show that he did not know what he was doing, but can not offer a witness to testify that he was so drunk as not to know what he was doing. White *v.* State, 103 Ala. 72, 16 So. 63, citing Chatham *v.* State, 92 Ala. 47, 9 So. 607; King *v.* State, 90 Ala. 612, 8 So. 856; Armor *v.* State, 63 Ala. 173.

Where, on trial for offering to bribe a juror, it appeared that the offer was in writing, signed "Carethers," while defendant's name was "Caruthers," it was proper to allow the writing to go to the jury, though it was not addressed to the juror who, it was alleged, was sought to be bribed. Caruthers *v.* State, 74 Ala. 406.

On indictment for offer to bribe a juror, where the defense is intoxication, the person to whom the offer is alleged to have been made, having known defendant many years, may testify that he thinks that defendant was talking with his usual intelligence; that that is his recollection. White *v.* State, 103 Ala. 72, 16 So. 63.

§ 7. —— Weight and Sufficiency.

An indictment of defendant for a certain crime, with the docket and entries, is competent, on an indictment for offer to bribe a juror, to show that the offer had relation to said case then pending. White *v.* State, 103 Ala. 72, 16 So. 63.

§ 8. Sentence and Punishment.

An offer to bribe a justice of the peace corruptly to decide a cause not then pending, but afterwards to be instituted before him, the bribe not being accepted or the suit instituted, though indictable at common law, is not punishable by confinement in the penitentiary, under the statute of Alabama. Barefield *v.* State, 14 Ala. 603. See ante, "Nature and Elements in General," § 1 (1).

BRIDGES.

§ 27 (4) —— Notice of Defects.
§ 27 (5) Instructions.
§ 27 (6) Verdict, Findings, and Judgment.

Cross References.

See, generally, the titles CANALS; COUNTIES; DRAINS; EMINENT DOMAIN; HIGHWAYS; MUNICIPAL CORPORATIONS; RAILROADS; STATUTES; TAXATION; TURNPIKES AND TOLLROADS.

As to injuries to passenger as result of defect in bridge on station premises, see the title CARRIERS. As to special or local laws for establishment and regulation of bridges, see the title STATUTES. As to authority of legislature to authorize the erection of bridges for public use, see the title CONSTITUTIONAL LAW. As to violation of rights of ferry owner by the erection of a toll bridge, see the title CONSTITUTIONAL LAW. As to constitutionality of law making it a misdemeanor for a contractor to neglect to repair a public bridge, see the title CONSTITUTIONAL LAW. As to rights in and use of bridges by street railroad companies, see the title STREET RAILROADS. As to power of state to tax bridge over navigable stream, see the title TAXATION. As to power of bridge company to contract in behalf of count, see the title COUNTIES. As to bridges over turnpikes, see the title TURNPIKES AND TOLLROADS. As to process to compel construction of bridges, see the title MANDAMUS. As to location of township road over approach to county bridge, see the title HIGHWAYS. As to easement over land under bridge, see the title EASEMENTS. As to delegation of power of eminent domain to bridge companies, see the title EMINENT DOMAIN. As to contracts for use of bridge for railroad purposes, see the title RAILROADS. As to construction and maintenance of bridge over drains, see the title DRAINS. As to construction and maintenance of bridges over canals, see the title CANALS. As to construction and maintenance of bridges as taking property without due process of law, see the title CONSTITUTIONAL LAW. As to condemnation of property for bridge as taking for public use, see the title EMINENT DOMAIN. As to collision of vessel with bridge, see the title SHIPPING. As to bridges at railroad crossings, see the title RAILROADS. As to measure of damages to vessel in collision with drawbridge, see the title NAVIGABLE WATERS. As to construction of statutes relating to bridges, see the title STATUTES. As to obstruction of navigation as the result of the negligent operation of a drawbridge, see the title NAVIGABLE WATERS. As to licensing of a bridge, the upper part of which is used by a railroad, see the titles LICENSES; RAILROADS. As to licensing of a toll bridge on a railroad's right of way, see the title RAILROADS. As to taxation of bridge used by trains engaged in interstate commerce, see the titles COMMERCE; TAXATION. As to authority of county commissioners to levy a special tax to build and repair bridges, see the title CONSTITUTIONAL LAW. As to liability of county for injuries resulting from a failure to keep roads and bridges in repair, see the titles COUNTIES; HIGHWAYS.

I. ESTABLISHMENT, CONSTRUCTION, AND MAINTENANCE.

§ 1. Right to Establish and Maintain in General.

"The laying off, regulating, and keeping in repair, roads, highways, bridges and ferries, for the public use and convenience of the citizens, is an exercise of the supreme authority of the state, coeval with the institution of civil society, and indispensable to the free exercise of social and commercial intercourse. It is a part of the eminent domain, and as such is treated by all writers on Public Law. Our legislature, in the exercise of this authority, have delegated to the Judge of the county court and commissioners of roads in each county in this state, the power to lay out public roads, to discontinue and alter the same, when found useless, so as to make them more useful (Aik. Dig. 358)—to establish ferries, by granting licenses to individuals under certain regulations (Aik. Dig. 363); and to erect free bridges, under the direction of the overseers, or to grant licenses for toll bridges to individuals, under certain regulations. If the county court could then, have authorized the erection of a bridge under the general road laws, it is not perceived that the legislature, who have invested the county court with this discretion, are prohibited from making the grant directly." Dyer *v.* Tuskaloosa Bridge Co., 2 Port. 296.

Establishing a Private Bridge.—Under the proviso to the first section of the act of 1839, relative to the establishment of toll bridges, etc., any person may establish a private bridge. Harrell *v.* Ellsworth, 17 Ala. 576.

Nature and Use of Bridge.—"But whether a bridge or a ferry, it must be a private one, that is to say, it must be limited to his own use. To this extent he may draw away the business and property of an established bridge, but no further. If he permits travelers, etc., to pass by his road and bridge, that would otherwise cross the established bridge, it is a violation of the law and of the rights of the proprietor of the established bridge, and he is responsible for it, because no such thing was intended. He must use his private bridge so as not to injure others. The legislature has not indicated an intention, however, to limit his own use of such private ferry or bridge, and we can not do so." Harrell *v.* Ellsworth, 17 Ala. 576, 584.

§ 2. Character of Bridge as Highway.

A public bridge is a part of the public road on which it is located. Pickens County *v.* Greene County, 171 Ala. 377, 54 So. 998.

When Bridge Becomes Part of Public Highway.—As soon as the free bridge or free causeway was finished and received by the commissioners court and opened for travel over them, they became a part of the public highways of the state, which passed at once under the care and supervision of the overseer of public roads of the counties in which they might lie. Rev. Code, 1341; Clay's Digest, p. 512, § 21. Barbour County *v.* Horn, 48 Ala. 566, 573.

§ 3. Constitutional and Statutory Provisions.

The fifth section of the act of 1839, which provides that no licensed toll bridge or ferry shall be established on the same water course, within two miles, by water, of any toll bridge or ferry already established, was intended to limit the power of the commissioners' court, and not to enlarge the privilege of wrongdoers to erect bridges without authority beyond the prescribed limits. Harrell *v.* Ellsworth, 17 Ala. 576.

Authority of Commissioners' Court to Establish Free Bridges.—"Code 1896, § 957, confers on commissioners' court original jurisdiction to establish, change, or discontinue bridges within the county, in conformity with the provisions of the Code, § 2498 invests it with authority to establish free bridges, without expressly confining them to public highways." Barks *v.* Jefferson County, 24 So. 505, 119 Ala. 600.

§ 4. Establishment by Public Authorities.

§ 5. —— Contribution to Expenses.

Section 3025 provides that whenever a bridge on the line between two counties is necessary, and the work is too great to be done by the overseers, the same must be built at the joint expense of such counties. Held, that the court of county commissioners of one county can not without the concurrence of the court of another county make the latter county liable for the expense of erecting a bridge on the line of the two counties, for a bridge becomes necessary within the meaning of this act only when it has been declared so by the concurring judgment of the commissioners' courts of both counties. Pickens County *v.* Greene County, 171 Ala. 377, 54 So. 998.

§ 6. —— Taxes and Assessments.

Power of County to Levy Special Tax.—Under the constitution 1875, art. 10, § 5, it is clear that no county could levy in any one year a greater rate of taxation on the value of property therein than one-half of one per centum, except to pay past debts and for public buildings and bridges; and that a county could not levy a special tax for any purpose other than those expressed in the proviso of said § 5, if such special tax together with the tax for general purposes exceeded one-half of one per cent. Birmingham Mineral R. Co. *v.* Tuscaloosa County, 137 Ala. 260, 34 So. 951, 952, citing Garland *v.* Board of Revenue, 87 Ala. 223, 227, 6 So. 402; Hare *v.* Kennerly, 83 Ala. 608, 3 So. 683; Keene *v.* Jefferson County, 135 Ala. 465, 33 So. 435.

Curative Act Validating an Increased Levy.—Act Feb. 21, 1899 (Acts 1898-99, p. 1212), authorized the county commissioners' court to levy a special bridge tax, not to exceed one-tenth of 1 per cent, under which such court in June, 1900, levied a tax of one-fourth of 1 per cent for county buildings and bridge purposes, after which Act Feb. 27, 1901 (Acts 1900-01, p. 1255), was passed, repealing the act of 1899 limiting the bridge tax rate, and Act March 1, 1901, was passed, being an act to ratify and confirm a levy of taxes by the commissioners' court of T. county for the purpose of building necessary public bridges, and paying interest on bridge bonds and other bonded indebtedness of the county, which attempted to validate such levy. Held, that the constitutional provision authorizing a special tax for bridge purposes was limited to levies for the payment of past debts for public buildings and bridges, and hence the curative act of March 1st, purporting to validate an increased levy to pay a contemplated future indebtedness, was void. Birmingham Mineral R. Co. *v.* Tuscaloosa County, 34 So. 951, 137 Ala. 260.

Using Tax Money to Improve Public Roads.—Pamph. Acts 1896-97, pp. 1228-1236, providing that no part of the county revenues levied for general purposes shall be used in building bridges, and requiring the county commissioners annually to levy a special tax not exceeding one-tenth of one per centum, to be used in building and repairing bridges, and authorizing the setting apart of a sum out of the taxes levied for general purposes to be applied to the improvement of public roads, does not violate Const., art. 11, § 5, providing that no county shall be authorized to levy a greater rate of taxation in any one year than one-half of 1 per cent. State *v.* Street, 23 So. 807, 117 Ala. 203.

Levy of Special Tax for Erection of Railroad Bridge.—Const., art. 11, § 5, declares that no county shall be authorized to levy a larger rate of taxation in any one year, on the value of the taxable property therein, than one-half of 1 per centum, except that they may be authorized to levy special taxes for the erection of necessary bridges. Held, that a railroad bridge to be used by a corporation distinct from the county does not come within the class of bridges mentioned, and the act is unconstitutional in so far as it authorizes the levy of a special tax for the erection of such bridge. Garland *v.* Board of Revenue, 87 Ala. 223, 6 So. 402.

§ 7. Bridge Companies.

§ 8. —— Franchises, Privileges, and Powers.

Authorizing Erection of Toll Bridges.—The legislature has the same right to authorize the erection of toll bridges which it has vested in the county courts. Dyer *v.* Tuskaloosa Bridge Co., 2 Port. 296, cited in Columbus *v.* Rodgers, 10 Ala. 37, 49; Ex parte Tate, 39 Ala. 254, 267; Alabama, etc., R. Co. *v.* Kenney, 39 Ala. 307, 311.

Who May Object to Breach of Condition—Individual.—Where the commissioners grant to a party a license to establish a toll bridge on a condition to be performed, and he is in possession of the privilege, his right to its enjoyment can not be called in question by an individual on the ground of his failure to perform the condition. Such a power belongs exclusively to the commissioners' court. Harrell *v.* Ellsworth, 17 Ala. 576.

Act Assigning Right to Build Toll Bridge.—Act March 6, 1848, assigning to Jacob Maberry the right to build a toll bridge formerly conferred by an act to the Centreville Bridge Company, gave to such Maberry the rights of such company, free from all liability to forfeiture for any previous act or omission of the company. State *v.* Centreville Bridge Co., 18 Ala. 678.

Power to Take Guaranty by Bond or Otherwise.—Under the authority to allow or license the establishment of toll bridges and toll causeways, the power is also given to take a guaranty by bond or otherwise, that the same shall continue safe for the passage of travelers and other persons for a stipulated time. Barbour County *v.* Horn, 48 Ala. 566, 572. Clay's Digest, p. 513, § 26.

§ 9. Construction.

§ 9 (1) Contracts—In General.

Bond Made Payable to Probate Judge.—If a bridge is built under a contract with the court of county commissioners, and a guaranty bond is executed by the contractor, pursuant to a requirement of the court the bond is not void because it was made payable to the "judge of the probate court and his successors in office." Barbour County *v.* Horn, 41 Ala. 114.

As to liability of county for injuries when no bond taken, see post, "Liability as between Contractor and County," § 22 (3).

§ 9 (2) —— Performance or Breach of Contract.

Evidence Showing Carelessness in Construction.—In an action to cancel county warrants for the cost of a bridge, evidence held to show that sand was removed from inside the casing for the principal pier of the bridge, and that it should have been removed in a workmanlike construction of the bridge. Converse Bridge Co. *v.* Geneva County, 168 Ala. 432, 53 So. 196.

Bound to Procure Solid Foundation for Pier.—Contractors who agreed to build a bridge in a workmanlike manner at a particular location were bound to procure a solid foundation for the principal pier, though they might thereby have been deprived of all profit or have sustained a loss, and even if the location of the bridge was selected by the company. Converse Bridge Co. *v.* Geneva County, 168 Ala. 432, 53 So. 196.

§ 9 (3) Actions.

Sufficiency of Evidence — Causes of Bridge Collapse.—In an action to cancel county warrants for the cost of a bridge, and to recover payments made, evidence held insufficient to show that the fall of the bridge was caused by cross-currents or by an unusual freshet, causing logs to strike against the principal pier. Converse Bridge Co. *v.* Geneva County, 168 Ala. 432, 53 So. 196.

In an action to cancel warrants for the cost of a bridge, and to recover payments thereon, evidence held insufficient to show that the principal pier rested on a part of a fallen pier, causing the new pier to lean upstream. Converse Bridge Co. *v.* Geneva County, 168 Ala. 432, 53 So. 196.

§ 10. Maintenance and Repair.

§ 10 (1) Counties.

As to the liability of a county for injuries from defective bridges, see post, "Care Required and Liability of Public Authorities in General," § 20.

Duty of County as to Public Roads or Bridges.—There is no general law of this state requiring counties of the state to keep the public roads, or bridges in the public roads, in safe repair, and this is not a duty incident to the authority granted in the charter of their corporation. Covington County *v.* Kinney, 45 Ala. 176; Sims *v.* Butler County, 49 Ala. 110, 114.

§ 10 (2) Contracts and Bonds.

Authority of County to Sue on Bond of Contractor.—The authority of a county to sue on the bond of a contractor, the condition of the bond being that a bridge built by him shall be kept in good repair for five years, and the authority to take all preliminary steps necessary thereto, is an implied incident of the contract, and of general statutory powers conferred on counties as bodies corporate in any court of record. Code, §§ 886, 1457; James *v.* Conecuh County, 79 Ala. 304; Meriwether *v.* Lowndes County, 89 Ala. 362, 7 So. 198, 199.

Action on Bond of Contractor in Name of County.—Under Code, § 1693, providing that when a bridge which has been erected by contract with county commissioners, and a bond taken from the builder conditioned to keep it in repair for a stipulated period, becomes unsafe, the commissioners shall, upon the facts being made known to them by a freeholder of the county, notify the builder to repair it, the commissioners may maintain an action on the bond in the name of the county without previous information by a freeholder. James *v.* Conecuh County, 79 Ala. 304.

Measure of Damages.—In an action on a bond given by a bridge contractor under Code, §§ 1692, 1693, conditioned to keep the bridge in repair for a stipulated period, the measure of damages is the reasonable cost of making necessary repairs during the period covered by the bond. James *v.* Conecuh County, 79 Ala. 304.

Condition of Bond Not Altered by Flood.—Where a contractor executes a bond conditioned that a bridge built by him shall be "kept in good repair," and shall "remain safe continuously for the period of five years, for the passage of travelers," etc., and said bridge is washed away by flood within less than five years, an action will lie on the bond if the contractor refuses to rebuild. Meriwether *v.* Lowndes County, 89 Ala. 362, 7 So. 198.

Act of God as an Excuse.—There is a long line of cases, both in England and this country, which settle the proposition that an unconditional express covenant to repair or keep in repair is equivalent to a covenant to rebuild, "and binds the covenantor to make good any injury which human power can remedy, even if caused by storm, flood, fire, inevitable accident, or the act of a stranger;" and that, while an act of God will excuse the nonperformance of a duty created by law, it will not excuse a duty created by contract to keep a bridge in repair. Meriwether *v.* Lowndes County, 89 Ala. 362, 7 So. 198, 199; Nave *v.* Berry, 22 Ala. 382; Warren *v.* Wagner, 75 Ala. 188.

Estoppel by Recitals in Bond to Avoid Liability.—Where the bond of a contractor recites that the consideration paid by the county is both for the work of building a bridge and for the execution of the bond, and one of the undertakings of the bond is an obligation to keep the entire bridge in good repair for a stipulated period, the obligor can not avoid his liability to rebuild a certain span because the county furnished all the materials for it, and paid him an additional sum of $25 for superintending its erection. Meriwether *v.* Lowndes County, 89 Ala. 362, 7 So. 198.

§ 10 (3) Judicial Supervision.

"Our decisions leave no room to doubt that the court of county commissioners, in respect to the establishment, change, or discontinuance of roads, bridges, causeways, and ferries within its county exercises for the people of the county a legislative, and hence a discretionary, power in which it is not to be guided alone by evidence produced according to legal rules, but as well by its own knowledge of geography of the county, the convenience and necessities of the people, and their ability to meet the expenditures involved. 'No other tribunal can intervene to revise or control its action.' Commissioners' Court *v.* Bowie, 34 Ala. 461; Commissioners' Court *v.* Moore, 53 Ala. 25; Askew *v.* Hale County, 54 Ala. 639; Barks *v.* Jefferson County, 119 Ala. 600, 24 So. 505." Pickens County *v.* Greene County, 171 Ala. 377, 54 So. 998, 999.

§ 11. Rebuilding after Destruction.

As to liability of contractor on bond where bridge is destroyed, see ante, "Contracts and Bonds," § 10 (2).

Authority of Commissioners' Court to Compel Rebuilding of Bridge—Notice.—Code Ala. 1886, § 1457, which provides that where a bridge is guaranteed by the bond of the bridge to stand for a stipulated period, and said bridge is washed away, the commissioner's court shall upon the fact being made known to them by any freeholder of the county, notify the contractor to rebuild, and, in case of his refusal or neglect to do so in a reasonable time, shall order suit to be brought on such bond, does not make the giving of such information by freeholder a condition precedent to the action of the court in giving notice to rebuild, or its authority to order suit brought, but it makes a duty, otherwise discretionary, mandatory on the court. Meriwether *v.* Lowndes County, 89 Ala. 362, 7 So. 198.

§ 12. Injuries to Bridges, Approaches, or Appliances.

Who May Destroy Worthless Bridge.—The worthless and decayed condition of a public bridge, erected by authority of law, or the peril attending its crossing, will not authorize its destruction or injury by one not suffering particular annoyance or injury. Owens *v.* State, 52 Ala. 400.

Indictment for Destroying Bridge—Sufficiency.—An indictment, under Rev. Code, § 3737, charging the willful destruction or injury, otherwise than by burning, of a designated public bridge erected by authority of law on a specified road, need not contain an averment of its ownership and value. Owens *v.* State, 52 Ala. 400.

§ 13. Offenses Incident to Construction and Maintenance.

Failure to Keep in Repair as Obstruction of Public Road.—Failure to keep in repair a public bridge on a public road by one charged with that duty is not an obstruction of the public road, within Rev. Code, § 1361, making such obstruction punishable as a misdemeanor. Malone *v.* State, 51 Ala. 55.

II. REGULATION AND USE FOR TRAVEL.

§ 14. Statutory and Municipal Regulations.

As to liability between contractor and municipality, see post, "Liability as between Contractor and County," § 22 (3).

Jurisdiction of Commissioners' Court.—A court called the commissioners' court of revenues and roads was established in 1821, and, among other things, its jurisdiction was made to comprehend all powers in relation to roads, bridges, highways, ferries, and causeways, which are at present, given to and exercised by the orphan's court. Toulmin's Laws of Ala., p. 200, §§ 28, 29, 30. The law of the Code restricts the powers of the commissioners' court to contracting for the building of toll bridges in which a guaranty is required and none others. Code, §§ 1189, 1191, 1196, 1197; the Revised Code, §§ 1381, 1393, 1389, 1390. Barbour County *v.* Horn, 48 Ala. 649.

§ 15. Licenses and Taxes.

Bridge on Railroad's Right of Way.—That a toll bridge is on the right of way of a railroad company does not prevent a license being required. Southern Ry. Co. *v.* Mitchell, 37 So. 85, 139 Ala. 629.

Bridge Resting in Two Counties.—The fact that a bridge is in two counties does not affect the amount of the tax. The state collects but one license tax and issues but one license, and it is not concerned whether the tax is paid in one county or the other. Southern R. Co. *v.* Mitchell, 139 Ala. 629, 37 So. 85.

License Tax on Toll Bridges by Statute.—Acts 1900-01, p. 2620, § 17, subd. 38, provides that each toll bridge not within two miles of a town or city of 2,000 inhabitants shall pay a license tax of $5, that if it is within two miles of a city of 2,000 inhabitants and less than 5,000 it shall pay $50, and if within two miles of a city of 5,000 or more, $75. Held, that a bridge having a city of more than 5,000 inhabitants within two miles of one end and a city of more than 2,000, but less than 5,000, within two miles of the other end, is liable to a tax of $75, and not only $50, on the theory that it is a bridge within two miles of a city of 2,000 inhabitants and less than 5,000. Southern R. Co. *v.* Mitchell, 37 So. 85, 139 Ala. 629.

§ 16. Mode and Purposes of Use.

Upper Part of Bridge Used by Railroad.—The fact that the upper portion of a bridge is used as a railroad bridge does not prevent a toll bridge license being required. Southern R. Co. *v.* Mitchell, 37 So. 85, 139 Ala. 629.

§ 17. Tolls.

Statutes Granting the Power to Prescribe and Receive Reasonable Tolls.—Act Feb. 11, 1893 (Loc. Laws 1892-93, p. 491), empowering a certain corporation to construct a bridge, and authorizing it to "take" reasonable tolls, did not grant the power to prescribe tolls, though the act was silent respecting the fixing of tolls and there was no express reservation of the power to the legislature. Tallassee Falls Mfg. Co. *v.* Commissioners' Court of Tallapoosa County, 48 So. 354, 158 Ala. 263.

Nor did Act Feb. 11, 1893 (Loc. Laws 1892-93, p. 491), § 2, empowering the corporation to establish all regulations deemed expedient for the management of traffic over the bridge, imply a grant of power to prescribe tolls. Tallassee Falls Mfg. Co. *v.* Commissioners' Court, 158 Ala. 263, 48 So. 354.

Act Aug. 6, 1907 (Loc. Laws 1907, p. 758), authorizing in § 1 the commissioners' court of Tallapoosa county to regulate and fix the rate of toll to be charged by the owner of a certain bridge, did not confer on the court the power to deprive the owner of the right to receive reasonable tolls. Tallassee Falls Mfg. Co. *v.* Commissioners' Court, 158 Ala. 263, 48 So. 354.

Use by Travelers of Private Bridge to Escape Payment of Toll.—Equity will restrain the owner of a private bridge from permitting travelers subject to the payment of toll at an established bridge to pass over his bridge in violation of the rights of the proprietor of the established bridge, and decree to the latter a pecuniary recompense for the losses thereby sustained. Harrell *v.* Ellsworth, 17 Ala. 576.

Indictment for Taking Illegal Toll—Sufficiency.—In an indictment against the keeper of a public bridge, for exacting illegal toll (Code, § 1199) there must be an averment that the bridge was licensed by the commissioners' court of the county, and the prescribed rates of toll must be specified. An averment that the bridge "was chartered by the commissioners' court" of the county, and that the defendant, "being employed as the keeper of said bridge, did demand and collect from B. F. P. larger toll than is authorized by said charter," is not sufficient. Lewis *v.* State, 41 Ala. 414.

§ 18. Liabilities for Injuries.

§ 19. —— Care Required of Bridge Companies and Proprietors.

Defective Bridge Constructed by Hotel Proprietor Used by Railroad.—One who, to give access to his hotel, constructs a bridge on the land of a railroad company, and turns it over to the company for its use, is not liable for personal injuries caused by a defect in the bridge due to the company's failure to repair it. Watson *v.* Oxanna Land Co., 92 Ala. 320, 8 So. 770.

§ 20. —— Care Required and Liability of Public Authorities in General.

As to presentation of claim for injuries caused by the falling of a bridge, as a condition precedent to an action against county, see the title COUNTIES. As to duty of county to maintain and repair bridges, see ante, "Counties," § 10 (1).

At Common Law.—Neither municipalities nor their officers are, at common law, liable for injuries to travelers resulting from failure to maintain or repair public bridges. Askew *v.* Hale County, 54 Ala. 639.

Exception — Public Bridge Built by Contract.—There is no statute in this state imposing a liability on counties because of injuries sustained by travelers from defects in a highway; nor because of injuries resulting from permitting a bridge to remain out of repair except in case of a public bridge built by contract and a failure of the commissioner's court to take from the contractor a bond or guaranty; or the expiration of the term of guaranty before the occurrence of the injury. Revised Code, § 1396; Askew *v.* Hale County, 54 Ala. 639, 643.

Liability of Counties.—Code Ala. 1886, § 1456, requiring that bridges erected by contract with the county commissioners, shall "continue safe for the passage of travelers and other persons;" that a person injured by a defect in such bridge may sue on the guaranty of the contractor; and if no guaranty is taken he may "sue and recover damages of the county," makes the liability of the county, when no guaranty is taken, in all respects, the same as the contractor's when the guaranty is given. Lee County *v.* Yarbrough, 85 Ala. 590, 5 So. 341; Askew *v.* Hale County, 54 Ala. 639.

Rev. Code, § 1396, which gives a right of action for injuries occasioned by a defect in a bridge, is applicable to a suit therefor brought against a county, though the bridge may have been built before the passage of such act, if the injury occurred thereafter. Barbour County *v.* Horn, 48 Ala. 649.

Discretion of Bridge Commissioners.—"When a bridge becomes decayed and unfit for use, the county commissioners may, by contract, erect a new bridge, and by a guaranty, secure the county against liability for a time; or they may undertake to repair the existing decayed bridge.

In repairing, they may adopt such mode as they deem advisable—by contract or otherwise; but whatever mode be adopted, the county is responsible for the manner in which the duty is performed." Greene County *v.* Eubanks, 80 Ala. 204, 207.

Liability through Neglect of Road Commissioners.—The authority which the court of county commissioners exercise over the subject of roads and bridges is governmental in its character, and the county would not, upon common-law principles, be liable for any injury which might result from the failure to exercise that authority in a manner the most conducive to the safety of the public. But the legislature has unquestionably the power to impose such liability; and we think they have done so, to the extent necessary to sustain the ruling of the court below. Smoot *v.* Wetumpka, 24 Ala. 112; City Council *v.* Gilmer, 33 Ala. 116; Dargan *v.* Mobile, 31 Ala. 469; Barbour County *v.* Brunson, 36 Ala. 362, 367.

Necessity for Erection by County.—An action does not lie against a county, to recover damages for injuries caused by the fall of a public bridge (Rev. Code, § 1396), unless the bridge was erected by contract with the court of county commissioners; the mere failure of said court to keep a public bridge in repair, after having intentionally omitted to place it in any road precinct, and having assumed jurisdiction and control over it, imposes no liability on the county. Sims *v.* Butler County, 49 Ala. 110.

In Alabama, a county is only liable for injuries occurring from an unsafe bridge, when it is a bridge erected by contract with the county commissioners before the adoption of the Code, or a toll bridge erected since under the provisions of the Code. A bridge erected by the citizens on a public road, and not under a contract with the commissioners' court, is not such a bridge as the county is bound to keep in repair under the Code. Covington County *v.* Kinney, 45 Ala. 176.

§ 21. —— Statutory Provisions as to Liabilities of Municipalities and Officers.

As to liability of public authorities in general, see ante, "Care Required and Liability of Public Authorities in General," § 20.

Application of § 1203 of Code.—Section 1203 of the Code, giving a remedy for injuries caused by defects in bridges, refers as well to free as to toll bridges. Barbour County *v.* Brunson, 36 Ala. 362.

Failure to Repair Bridges as Required by Act of Incorporation.—When the act incorporating the municipal authorities of a city makes it their duty to keep in repair the bridges and streets within the corporate limits, and in consideration thereof relieves them from other duties, an action on the case lies against them for a neglect of this duty, in favor of a person who is thereby injured. Smoot *v.* City of Wetumpka, 24 Ala. 112; Acts of Ala. 1839, p. 47, § 11.

§ 22. —— Duty and Ability to Repair.

As to duty to maintain and repair, in general, see ante, "Maintenance and Repair," § 10.

§ 22 (1) In General.

Duty to Repair Bridges Fixed by Statute.—The effect and operation of the statute Code, § 1692, are to devolve on the county the legal duty to keep such bridge in a safe condition, either when no guaranty has been taught or after the stipulated time has expired. Greene County *v.* Eubanks, 80 Ala. 204, 206.

§ 22 (2) Bridges Erected by Railroad Companies.

Bridge Connecting Station and Hotel—Used by Railroad.—A railroad company is liable for personal injuries sustained by a passenger by reason of a defect in a bridge erected near the tracks, on the company's station grounds, which it permits its passengers to use in going from the train to and from the hotel for meals, though the bridge may have been erected by the owner of the hotel, who also agreed with the company to keep it in repair. Watson *v.* Oxanna Land Co., 92 Ala. 320, 8 So. 770.

§ 22 (3) Liability as between Contractor and County.

Commencement and Duration of County's Liability.—"The liability of a county for damage, caused by a defect in a bridge erected by contract, commences on a failure to take a guaranty, or if taken, at the expiration of the time; and the length of time such liability shall continue is not fixed or limited by the statute." Greene County *v.* Eubanks, 80 Ala. 204, 207.

Liability of County Where No Bond Taken.—Code 1896, § 27, provides that personal representatives may recover for decedent's death caused by the wrongful act, omission, or negligence of any person or corporation. Id., § 2512, provides that, where a county fails to take a guaranty of the safety of a bridge from the builder, it shall be liable for injuries caused by defects therein. Held, that a county is liable in damages at the suit of the personal representatives for the death of one caused by the collapse of a bridge, a guaranty of the safety of which the county had not secured from the builder thereof. Shannon *v.* Jefferson County, 125 Ala. 384, 27 So. 977; Barks *v.* Jefferson County, 119 Ala. 600, 24 So. 505.

Code 1886, § 1456, requiring that bridges erected by contract with the county commissioners, shall "continue safe for the passage of travelers and other persons;" that a person injured by a defect in such bridge may sue on the guaranty of the contractor; and that, if no guaranty is taken, he may "sue and recover damages of the county"—makes the liability of the county, when no guaranty is taken, in all respects the same as the contractor's when the guaranty is given. Lee County *v.* Yarbrough, 85 Ala. 590, 5 So. 341.

Repairs as Constituting a New Bridge.—Under Code, § 1692, providing that counties shall be liable for injuries caused by a defective bridge, where they fail to require of the contractor a bond that it shall continue safe for passage for a stipulated time, or the stipulated period has expired, the county is liable for injuries so long as the bridge remains part of the established public highway, and can not avoid liability by claiming that, by repairs made under contract, a new bridge was virtually erected. Greene County *v.* Eubanks, 80 Ala. 204.

Liability of Contractor Where No Bond Given.—No action by a person injured through a defect in a bridge lies against the person who has contracted with the county to keep such bridge in repair, where no bond was required for the faithful performance of the contract. Williams *v.* Stillwell, 88 Ala. 332, 6 So. 914.

§ 23. —— Notice of Defects or Obstructions.

Character of Notice Required.—In order to recover damages for injuries sustained through the failure of a railroad company to keep a bridge in repair, it is not necessary that the company should have actual notice of the defect. South & N. A. R. Co. *v.* McLendon, 63 Ala. 266.

As to what constitutes negligence in failure to keep bridge in repair, see the title NEGLIGENCE.

§ 24. —— Proximate Cause of Injury.

Stepping in Hole Outside Usual Route of Travel.—Where a bridge maintained by a railroad company as an approach to a crossing is reasonably safe and convenient for the use of the traveling public, the company is not responsible for an injury sustained by the stepping of plaintiff's mule through a hole which is near one end of the bridge, and out of the usual route of travel. Patterson *v.* South & N. A. R. Co., 89 Ala. 318, 7 So. 437.

Injury to Stray Horse Not within the Statute.—An injury to a stray horse which has broken from an inclosure and is running at large is not within the statute giving persons injured an action for damages arising from defects in bridges. Lee County *v.* Yarbrough, 85 Ala. 590, 5 So. 341.

§ 25. —— Contributory Negligence of Person Injured.

That plaintiff was driving over the bridge at a rate of speed prohibited by ordinance does not preclude a recovery for injuries due to the defective condition of the bridge, where the rate of speed did not contribute to the injuries. Town of Cullman *v.* McMinn, 109 Ala. 614, 19 So. 981.

§ 26. —— Notice of Claim for Injury.

As to presentation of claim in suit brought against a county, see the title COUNTIES.

Presenting Claim as Condition Precedent.—A claim against a county for damages sustained from the falling of a public bridge must be presented to the commissioner's court, and disallowed in whole or in part, as required by Code, § 2903, before an action on it can be maintained against the county. Schroeder *v.* Colbert County, 66 Ala. 137.

Time within Which Claim Must Be Presented.—No action lies against a county for damages sustained by a fall from a defective bridge until the demand has been presented for allowance within twelve months after it accrued. Barbour County *v.* Horn, 41 Ala. 114.

§ 27. Actions for Injuries.

§ 27 (1) Pleading.

Sufficiency of Complaint—In General.—When an action is brought to recover damages for injuries caused by the fall of a bridge, it is not necessary to aver in the declaration that the bridge was broken without any fault on the part of plaintiff, nor that he could not pass the street of which the bridge formed a part without crossing the bridge. An averment that it was defendant's duty to keep the bridge in repair, and that the injury resulted from its unsafe and rotten condition, which rendered it incapable of sustaining the usual burdens which were accustomed to pass over it, is sufficient. Smoot *v.* City of Wetumpka, 24 Ala. 112.

Notice in Defects.—A complaint in an action against a municipality for injuries due to a defective bridge, not describing the defect, and merely alleging that the bridge was out of repair for a "long length of time," does not sufficiently show constructive notice on the part of the municipality of the existence of the defect. Town of Cullman *v.* McMinn, 109 Ala. 614, 19 So. 981.

Failure to Exercise Judicial Power Properly.—A count averring that the bridge was private property, not belonging to the corporation, and had become a public nuisance from its unsafe and rotten condition, and that said corporation, knowing this, failed to abate it, as they by law were authorized and required to do, whereby, etc., is bad on demurrer. The failure to exercise judicial power properly, in the absence of malice and corrupt intention, constitutes no ground of action. Smoot *v.* City of Wetumpka, 24 Ala. 112.

Nature of Bridge Should Be Shown.—In an action against a county for damages occasioned by a fall from an imperfect bridge, established under contract with the commissioners' court, made before the adoption of the Code, the declaration should show that the bridge was a toll bridge. Barbour County *v.* Horn, 48 Ala. 566.

Authority of Commissioners' Court Should Be Shown.—In an action against a county for damages, suffered as a result of a fall from an imperfect bridge, established under a contract with the commissioners' court, made before the adoption of the code, the declaration should show that the commissioners' court had authority to make the contract. Barbour County *v.* Horn, 48 Ala. 649, 664.

Special Liability of Counties Must Be Shown.—The liability imposed upon counties for injuries resulting from the defective or unsafe condition of bridges built for public use on the public highways is special and defined by statute, and the complaint in an action to recover for such injuries must set forth a statement of facts which show the existence of this special liability. Barbour County *v.* Horn, 48 Ala. 649.

Presenting Claim to Court of County Commissioners.—In an action against a county on a claim for damages sustained from the falling of a public bridge, the complaint is bad if it does not aver that the claim was presented to the court of county commissioners, itemized and verified by affidavit, as required by Code 1876, § 827. Schroeder *v.* Colbert County, 66 Ala. 137, citing Barbour County *v.* Horn, 41 Ala. 114.

Nature of Object Frightening Mule.—A complaint for personal injuries alleged that defendant, a railroad company, negligently permitted a bridge over its tracks to become out of repair, in that there was a hole in it and the planks were rotten, and that plaintiff's mule became frightened at it because of said defects and jumped over it, causing plaintiff to fall from the wagon. Held, that the complaint was demurrable for not showing that the object that frightened the mule was calculated to frighten a horse of ordinary gentleness. Northern Alabama Ry. Co. *v.* Sides, 26 So. 116, 122 Ala. 594.

§ 27 (2) Damages.

When Entitled to Compensatory Damages.—Under Code 1896, § 2512, providing that, where a county fails to take a guaranty from a bridge builder that a bridge is safe for travel, the county shall be liable for injuries caused thereby, and under Code, § 27, providing that a personal representative may maintain an action for the wrongful act, omission, or negligence of any corporation causing defendant's death, plaintiff, in an action for death caused by the collapse of a bridge, for which the county had taken no guaranty, is not entitled to compensatory damages. Shannon *v.* Jefferson County, 125 Ala. 384, 27 So. 977; Richmond, etc., R. Co. *v.* Freeman, 97 Ala. 289, 11 So. 800.

§ 27 (3) Questions for Jury.

§ 27 (4) —— Notice of Defects.

As to alleging notice of defects in complaint, see ante, "Pleading," § 27 (1).

§ 27 (5) Instructions.

As to hypothetical instruction as a ground for setting aside a verdict, see post, "Verdict, Findings, and Judgment," § 27 (6).

§ 27 (6) Verdict, Findings, and Judgment.

Verdict—Setting Aside for Hypothetical Instruction.—In an action for death caused by the collapse of a bridge, a guaranty of which the county had not secured, no evidence was introduced as to degree of negligence of defendant, or as to mitigating circumstances in its favor. An abstract instruction was given charging the jury that if they believed, from the evidence, that the negligence was so slight, or so characterized by mitigating circumstances, as to warrant nominal damages, they should impose such damages. Held, that, where it is not apparent on the record that the jury was misled by such instruction, a verdict of $1,000 will not be set aside upon the assumption that it was arrived at upon the hypothesis stated in such instruction. Shannon *v.* Jefferson County, 125 Ala. 384, 27 So. 977.

Briefs.

See the titles APPEAL AND ERROR; CRIMINAL LAW; EXCEPTIONS, BILL OF.

BROKERS.

Cross References.

See the titles CONTRACTS; CUSTOMS AND USAGES; EXCHANGES; FACTORS; FRAUDS, STATUTE OF; GAMING; INSURANCE; MASTER AND SERVANT; PAWNBROKERS; PRINCIPAL AND AGENT; VENDOR AND PURCHASER.

I. REGULATION AND CONDUCT OF BUSINESS IN GENERAL.

§ 1. Who Are Brokers.

A person engaged in selling on commission in a city merchandise by sample for his several principals, having an office where his samples are exhibited, is a local commercial broker, though he makes special arrangements in advance with those by whom he is employed, and is their sole representative in his city. Stratford *v.* Montgomery City Council, 110 Ala. 619, 20 So. 127.

Definitions.—The definition of a broker seems to be, that he is an agent employed to make contracts and bargains between other persons in matters of trade, commerce or navigation, for a compensation commonly called brokerage. Story on Agency, § 28. Stephens *v.* Bailey, 149 Ala. 256, 42 So. 740, 741.

Same—Real Estate Broker.—A "real estate broker," strictly speaking, is but a middleman whose office it is to bring the principals together for negotiation with each other, and trade upon such terms as may be mutually satisfactory. Handley *v.* Shaffer (Ala.), 59 So. 286.

Factor and Broker Distinguished.—The legal distinction between a broker and a factor is that the factor is intrusted with the property the subject of the agency; the broker is only employed to make a bargain in relation to it. 1 Parsons on Contract 78. Perkins *v.* State, 50 Ala. 154.

§ 2. Licenses and Taxes.

As to effect on brokers' contract for commission of his failure to take out license, see post, "Necessity of License," § 21.

A municipal license tax, imposed on all brokers selling merchandise by sample for nonresident principals exclusively, is unconstitutional, as a regulation of interstate commerce. Stratford *v.* City Council, 110 Ala. 619, 20 So. 127.

Slaves.—Act Feb. 7, 1856, § 1, so amends sub. 17, § 397, Code, as to exempt from license or tax the sale of slaves by brokers, etc., provided that affidavit is made that the slaves so sold or offered for sale are the property of a resident of the state, and that such resident has owned said slaves for more than one year preceding the offer for sale within the state. The second section provides that the act shall apply only to such slaves as may be sold by any broker, etc., on commission for citizens of the state, and which slaves have been owned in the state for more than one year preceding the sale, and shall not apply to any slaves owned by any broker, etc., or other person selling slaves on speculation. Held, that said act does not prohibit a broker or agent for the sale of slaves from selling one of his own slaves without a license. Brooks *v.* Pollard, 36 Ala. 573.

II. EMPLOYMENT AND AUTHORITY.

As to commission, see post, "Employment of Broker," § 20.

§ 3. Relation to Principal in General.

A company which is to receive a commission from a borrower for procuring a loan, and which makes out all the papers without knowing from whom the loan is to be obtained, and before submitting them to the lender, is the agent of the borrower in procuring the loan. Land Mortgage, Investment & Agency Co. of America *v.* Preston, 24 So. 707, 119 Ala. 290; Hamil *v.* American Freehold Land Mortg. Co. of London, 28 So. 558, 127 Ala. 90.

§ 4. Appointment or Employment.

"When a real estate broker asks and obtains from the owner the price of certain real estate, or the price at which the owner is willing to sell, this, without more, does not establish the relation of principal and agent between the owner and broker." Stephens *v.* Bailey, 149 Ala. 256, 42 So. 740, 741.

Sufficiency of Contract.—"A contract of employment of a broker need not state the employment in terms, but it is sufficient if it states it in substance and in effect. An agreement between the parties may show an employment of the agent. Birmingham Land, etc., Co. *v.* Thompson, 86 Ala. 146, 5 So. 473." Stephens *v.* Bailey, 149 Ala. 256, 42 So. 740, 741.

§ 5. Evidence of Agency.

See post, "Evidence," § 49.

§ 5 (1) Presumption and Burden of Proof.

"It is also stated, 'that the burden of proving the existence of the employment, is upon the person claiming compensation for his services; and whether or not, there was an employment of the broker who claims commissions, is a question for the jury in conflicting evidence.' 23 Am. & Eng. Ency. Law (2 Ed.) 911, 912, and authorities there cited." Stephens *v.* Bailey, 149 Ala. 256, 42 So. 740, 741.

§ 5 (2) Weight and Sufficiency.

Evidence considered and held not to show appointment of broker as agent to sell property. Webb *v.* Ward, 122 Ala. 355, 25 So. 48.

§ 6. Revocation of Agency.

See post, "Revocation of Authority," § 23.

Authority to sell land can not be revoked by a letter mailed to the brokers, but never received by them. Sayre *v.* Wilson, 86 Ala. 151, 5 So. 157.

"To be irrevocable, it seems now well settled that the power to sell property conferred upon a broker, must create an interest in the thing itself, or in the property which is the subject of the power"—and an interest in the proceeds of the sale does not constitute such an interest in the property. Cronin *v.* American Securities Co., 163 Ala. 533, 50 So. 915.

§ 7. Breach by Principal of Contract of Employment.

"The defendant, by directing the plaintiff not to proceed in reference to one of the services, altered and breached the contract. There was an implied term in the contract that the plaintiff should have an opportunity to perform both services, and, when his performance was prevented or dispensed with as to one, the contract was thereby set aside by the employer, and the plaintiff was relegated to a suit for damages for a breach of the contract, or one on a quantum meruit for services actually performed. 9 Cyc. 638, 639; 7 Ency. Law (2d Ed.) 150-152; Anvil Min. Co. *v.* Humble, 153 U. S. 552, 14 S. Ct. 876, 38 L. Ed. 814; The Eliza Lines, 199 U. S. 119, 128, 26 S. Ct. 8, 50 L. Ed. 115; Roehm *v.* Horst, 178 U. S. 1, 20 S. Ct. 780, 44 L. Ed. 953." Worthington *v.* McGarry, 149 Ala. 251, 42 So. 988, 990.

§ 8. Authority Conferred.

§ 9. —— In General.

A broker's general authority to invest his principal's money will not authorize him to also invest his own for his principal's account. Bradfield *v.* Patterson, 106 Ala. 397, 17 So. 536.

§ 10. —— Purchase or Sale of Real Property.

Where agents wrote the owner of a lot, submitting an offer of $1,500, less commissions, and the owner replied that he thought $1,700 a fair price, and that it would be acceptable to him, the agents were authorized to sell for $1,700 gross. Campbell *v.* Lombardo, 44 So. 862, 153 Ala. 489.

A contract with reference to the sale of lands may be constituted of an employment to sell land for another, and, not being for the sale of land, will not be offensive to the statute of frauds because not in writing. Ivy Coal & Coke Co. *v.*

Long, 36 So. 722, 139 Ala. 535, cited in note in 9 L. R. A., N. S., 934.

Necessity of Writing.—As to necessity of writing to brokers recovery of commission, see post, "Necessity of Contract in Writing," § 22.

No Power to Conclude Sale.—In the absence of a special agreement, the general authority of an agent for the sale of real property is only to find a purchaser willing to buy on the terms fixed by the owner, and he has no power to conclude a sale. Minto *v.* Moore, 55 So. 542, 1 Ala. App. 556; Davis *v.* Clausen, 2 Ala. App. 378, 57 So. 79.

Employment of Broker Does Not Give Him Exclusive Right to Sell.—As to effect on broker's commission of transaction in which broker has no part, see post, "Transactions Effected without Aid of Broker," § 25. As to effect on broker's commission of sale through other agent, see post, "Procuring Cause of Contract or Transaction," § 31. As to effect on broker's commission of owner's selling, see post, "Negotiations Direct with Principal," § 33.

There is a right in the owner to employ two or more brokers to sell a piece of property. Wefel *v.* Stillman, 151 Ala. 249, 44 So. 203, 211.

A landowner, by employing an agent to effect a sale thereof, does not thereby preclude himself from employing other agents to sell it, or from selling it himself, provided he acts in good faith. Smith *v.* Sharp, 50 So. 381, 162 Ala. 433; Crook *v.* Forst, 116 Ala. 395, 22 So. 540.

The owner of land placed in the hands of an agent for sale has a right to fix a net value on it and the terms of sale; and if the agent can not effect a sale, so that the owner may realize such net value, or upon the terms fixed, the owner may dispose of it at such price and on such terms. Crook *v.* Forst, 22 So. 540, 116 Ala. 395.

§ 11. Delegation of Authority.

As to effect on commission, see post, "Right to Compensation in General," § 19. As to right of assistant to commission, see post, "Persons Entitled," § 44.

The legal maxim, that an agent can not delegate his authority to a subagent, can be invoked only by the principal when sought to be charged by the act of the subagent. Harralson & Co. *v.* Stein, 50 Ala. 347; Ewell on Agency (Evan's Ed.), p. 53, note. The maxim in question, furthermore, does not prohibit the employment of subordinates, but rather of substitutes. Burns *v.* Campbell, 71 Ala. 271, 287.

III. DUTIES AND LIABILITIES TO PRINCIPAL.

§ 12. Nature of Broker's Obligation.

"Though much alike in some respects, there are some important distinctions between a broker's undertaking to negotiate or effect a sale and one merely to find a purchaser, although they are often dealt with by courts as being identical in nature and results. The failure to distinguish between these two differing classes of contracts, and the attempt to apply to one class all of the principals which regulate the other, have produced many of the inconsistencies and much of the confusion with which the reported cases on this subject seem to be bound. The distinction is clearly emphasized in the two cases of Montross *v.* Eddy, 94 Mich. 100, 53 N. W. 916, 34 Am. St. Rep. 323, and McDonald *v.* Maltz, 94 Mich. 172, 53 N. W. 1058, 34 Am. St. Rep. 331. See, also, Wiggins *v.* Wilson, 55 Fla. 346, 45 So. 1011, and Blodgett *v.* Suix City R. Co., 63 Iowa, 606, 19 N. W. 799." Handley *v.* Shaffer (Ala.), 59 So. 286, 291.

Duty to Disclose Facts in His Knowledge.—It is the general duty of the agent to disclose to his principal every fact that is within his knowledge, that is material to his principal's interest in respect to the transaction to which his agency relates, including the agent's own interest therein, and his relations with the adverse party. The duty to make such disclosures depends upon the nature and terms of the agency; i. e., whether the principal is entitled to the skill and judgment of the broker and reasonable endeavors to induce his customers to purchase on the terms specified, and therefore may rely upon their exercise in his behalf. Handley *v.* Shaffer (Ala.), 59 So. 286, 291.

§ 13. Skill and Care Required.

Brokers, in the discharge of their

agency, are bound only to the exercise of reasonable skill and diligence, and, so long as they are guilty of no bad faith, and exercise the same care and diligence that a prudent man would exercise in like business, they are entitled to reasonable compensation for their services. Edwards on Factors and Brokers, § 69; 1 Parsons on Contracts (6 Ed.) 100. Guesnard *v.* Louisville & N. R. Co., 76 Ala. 453, cited in note in 45 L. R. A. 35.

An agent employed to sell ordinarily owes to his principal the duty to use such skill and industry as may be requisite to accomplish the object of his employment, and with full fidelity to the just interests of his employer. Handley *v.* Shaffer (Ala.), 59 So. 286.

§ 14. Purchases and Sale on Margin.

As to right of broker to recover advances, see post, "Reimbursement of Advances, Expenses, or Losses," § 43.

At common law, a note and mortgage given to a broker in consideration of commissions earned in the purchase and sale of futures, and for advances made by him in carrying on such transactions, are valid, if he has no other interest in the transactions. Peet *v.* Hatcher, 112 Ala. 514, 21 So. 711, cited in note in 11 L. R. A., N. S., 578.

§ 15. Individual Interest of Broker.

As to duty of agent to disclose interest, see ante, "Nature of Broker's Obligation," § 12.

Plaintiff, being anxious to sell his interest in a certain firm, requested one B. to find him a purchaser. Nothing was said about compensation to B., nor was any authority given to him to sell. Thereafter B. brought a written proposition, which was accepted in writing by the seller. Held, that the fact that the purchase was for the joint benefit of the purchaser and B. did not render it invalid, there being no sufficient proof of agency on the part of B. Webb *v.* Ward, 25 So. 48, 122 Ala. 355.

It is bad faith in a broker to buy the property at less than the price fixed by the owner with a view of reselling to a prospective purchaser at a profit to himself. Alford *v.* Creagh (Ala.), 62 So. 254.

§ 16. Acting for Parties Adversely Interested.

As to duty to disclose, see ante, "Nature of Broker's Obligation," § 12. As to effect on broker's commission, see post, "Bad Faith, Fraud, or Misconduct of Broker," § 39; "Commissions from Both Parties," § 40.

A broker, acting in negotiations as the agent of the vendor, can not act for the purchaser in the same transaction, since that would put him between conflicting interests. Minto *v.* Moore, 55 So. 542, 1 Ala. App. 556.

The general rule is: "that a real estate broker or agent, who is negotiating a sale of property or otherwise acting in the usual line of his business, can not represent both parties to the transaction without their mutual knowledge and consent." Green *v.* Southern States Lumber Co., 141 Ala. 680, 37 So. 670, 672.

Custom of Stock Exchange.—A pledgee of stock, empowered to sell it on the stock exchange, employed a member of the exchange to effect the sale. Held, that the fact that the purchaser of the stock had employed the same member to purchase on the exchange, at a limited price, stock of the character offered by the pledgee, would not invalidate the sale, where such member, according to the rules of the exchange, procured a fellow member to make the bid, and where neither the pledgee nor the purchaser had any knowledge of each other's intentions, or of their instructions to such member. Terry *v.* Birmingham Nat. Bank, 99 Ala. 566, 13 So. 149.

§ 17. Fraud of Broker or His Agent.

Brokers, taking land received in exchange in their own name fraudulently, and a purchaser of a portion of the land from them with notice, held liable for the fair rental value of the portion sold. Dean *v.* Roberts (Ala.), 62 So. 44.

§ 18. Actions for Negligence or Wrongful Acts of Broker.

Where brokers fraudulently took a conveyance of land belonging to their principal in their own name, they are liable on the conveyance being set aside for the rental value of the property held by them under the conveyance, subject to a credit for taxes paid. Dean *v.* Roberts (Ala.), 62 So. 44.

IV. COMPENSATION AND LIEN.

§ 19. Right to Compensation in General.

Employing subordinate to make sale. See ante, "Delegation of Authority," § 11.

A contract to procure the purchase of a post office site by the government is not to be condemned because compensation is contingent on the success of the undertaking. Bush *v.* Russell (Ala.), 61 So. 373.

Where plaintiff acted for a third person in making a sale of the latter's property to defendant, whose promise was only to pay the price of the property sold, plaintiff could not recover from defendant commissions for making the sale, on the theory that such commissions were due for services rendered him, though it might be found that the price of the property was so fixed as to include the commissions, which were to be paid directly to plaintiff. Moses *v.* Beverly, 34 So. 825, 137 Ala. 473.

A broker employed to sell cotton at a certain commission may employ a subordinate to sell the cotton on a smaller commission, and recover from his principal the commission stipulated. Burns *v.* Campbell, 71 Ala. 271.

A broker may recover commissions upon procuring sales from a subagent, though the owner did not know that the purchaser was procured by the subagent. Alford *v.* Creagh (Ala.), 62 So. 254.

§ 20. Employment of Broker.

See ante, "Employment and Authority," II.

"In order to entitle a broker to recover compensation for his services, it is necessary that the person, from whom he claims, shall have employed him to render the services out of which his claim arises, or that there should have been such acceptance and ratification of his services by such person as will, in the eyes of the law, amount to the same thing as an original employment." Stephens *v.* Bailey, 149 Ala. 256, 42 So. 740.

The right of the real estate agent to compensation depends upon the fact of his employment by the seller to sell the designated property. No one, it would seem, on sound principal, has the legal right to charge another for services rendered, unless he has been employed by that other, by contract express or implied, that he would compensate him therefor. Stephens *v.* Bailey, 149 Ala. 256, 42 So. 740, 741.

Where an offer was in writing and was preceded by a verbal offer in practically the same terms which was substantially accepted by the broker by writing to the owner for the land numbers pursuant to the owner's promise at the time of the verbal offer, and the owner furnishes such numbers and renews his offer of employment in more favorable terms, an acceptance of such last offer will be implied, though the broker does not inform the owner thereof. Alford *v.* Creagh (Ala.), 62 So. 254.

§ 21. Necessity of License.

See ante, "Licenses and Taxes," § 2.

That plaintiff has not taken out a state license to engage in the real estate business, as required by the revenue laws, would not invalidate a contract by him to sell land on commissions. Alford *v.* Creagh (Ala.), 62 So. 254.

That a broker employed to sell land had not taken out a license did not invalidate his contract. Smith *v.* Sharp, 50 So. 381, 162 Ala. 433.

§ 22. Necessity of Contract in Writing.

As to necessity of writing to agents authority to sell, see ante, "Purchase or Sale of Real Property," § 10.

A contract of employment for the sale of realty on commissions need not be in writing under the statute of frauds. Alford *v.* Creagh (Ala.), 62 So. 254.

A contract for broker's commissions on the sale of land is not required by the statute of frauds to be in writing. Hutto *v.* Stough & Hornsby, 47 So. 1031, 157 Ala. 566.

In an action to recover commissions or compensation for the sale of land by a broker, that the contract with the broker was within the statute of frauds is no defense. Stephens *v.* Bailey & Howard, 42 So. 740, 149 Ala. 256.

The fact that a contract made with a proposed purchaser is voidable under the statute of frauds is no defense to an action by the brokers against the vendor for commissions, where the purchaser has not shown any intention to take advantage of the statute. Sayre *v.* Wilson, 86 Ala. 151, 5 So. 157.

§ 23. Revocation of Authority.

As to sufficiency of revocation of agency, see ante, "Revocation of Agency," § 6. As to what agencies irrevocable, see ante, "Revocation of Agency," § 6.

As a general principle, an authority to sell land may be revoked at any time before sale, and the owner will not thereby incur any obligation to the agent Cronin *v.* American Securities Co., 50 So. 915, 163 Ala. 533.

Where a real-estate agent's authority to sell lands upon certain terms is revoked, and the owner, in good faith, thereafter sells upon less favorable terms to one who had declined to purchase from the agent, such agent is not entitled to commissions. Bailey *v.* Smith, 103 Ala. 641, 15 So. 900, cited in note in 44 L. R. A. 347, 621.

Necessity for Notice of Revocation of Authority.—Where a broker, employed to find a purchaser, has begun negotiations, no revocation of his authority is possible, unless brought home to him by actual notice. Alexander *v.* Smith (Ala.), 61 So. 68.

Time of Revocation.—A principal can not defeat a broker's right to compensation for procuring a purchaser by revoking his authority pending negotiations with the customer. Handley *v.* Shaffer (Ala.), 59 So. 286.

An agreement by land brokers, at the owner's request that a certain lot might be withdrawn from market, made after they had effected a sale of it, and under the mistaken belief that the lot proposed to be withdrawn was a different one, would not prevent recovery of commissions for the sale. Sayre *v.* Wilson, 86 Ala. 151, 5 So. 157.

Promise to Pay Broker as if Sale Had Been Made.—Where an owner of land revoked an agent's authority to sell, and told the agent that he would be taken care of as if he had made the sale, and the owner then made a sale through his own efforts, the promise to the broker was without consideration. Cronin *v.* American Securities Co., 50 So. 915, 163 Ala. 533.

§ 24. Abandonment of Employment by Broker.

The owner of a lot, who had placed it in a broker's hands for sale, wrote him that she felt at liberty to withdraw "from the proposition under consideration" if she chose. The broker replied that upon receipt of her letter he had seen his client, but could not make the deal, and that it looked like the matter was closed, unless she would accept a lower offer. Held, that the broker's letter terminated the agency at the time of mailing, and he was not entitled to commissions on a sale of the lot negotiated by him next day. Jackson *v.* Parrish, 47 So. 1014, 157 Ala. 584; Haygood *v.* Parrish, 47 So. 1015, 158 Ala. 675.

§ 25. Transactions Effected without Aid of Broker.

As to right of broker to sell, or appoint other brokers, see ante, "Purchase or Sale of Real Property," § 10.

Where the owner of land agreed to pay plaintiff a commission for selling it to a corporation that plaintiff might promote for the purchase, and while plaintiff was endeavoring to bring the deal about the owner withdrew the offer and sold the land himself, he was not liable for commissions; plaintiff's efforts not having in any way tended to the consummation of the sale. Cronin *v.* American Securities Co., 50 So. 915, 163 Ala. 533.

§ 26. Sufficiency of Services of Broker.

See post, "Failure to Complete Contract or Transaction Negotiated," § 35.

§ 27. —— In General.

Where defendant agreed to pay $1,000 in consideration of plaintiff's services in procuring for defendant a conveyance of certain mineral land, defendant, having received the benefit of plaintiff's efforts in accordance with the contract, could not by the mere form in which the transaction was subsequently completed impair his obligation to pay. Lamar *v.* King, 53 So. 279, 168 Ala. 285.

To recover commissions for procuring the sale of realty, plaintiff must show that he was the cause of procuring a satisfactory purchaser within a reasonable time after he agreed to do so, who was able, ready, and willing to purchase on the terms fixed by his contract of employment. Alford *v.* Creagh (Ala.), 62 So. 254.

§ 28. —— Performance of Contract of Employment.

A broker employed to procure a purchaser without specification as to price is not entitled to compensation, unless the purchaser is accepted by the principal on his own terms. Handley *v.* Shaffer (Ala.), 59 So. 286.

Where, in an action for commissions on the sale of land, which accrued to a third person and was transferred to plaintiff, no proof was produced from which the value of any services rendered outside the special contract could have been found chargeable to defendant, it was not error to instruct that the performance of the contract was a prerequisite to the right to compensation. Ivy Coal & Coke Co. *v.* Long, 36 So. 722, 139 Ala. 535.

Selling on Credit.—Where a real estate broker was engaged to find a purchaser for land at a fixed price, and the contract said nothing as to the terms of sale, it was not necessary, to entitle him to commissions, that he should find a purchaser for cash; a purchaser who bought on terms satisfactory to the owner being sufficient. Alexander *v.* Smith (Ala.), 61 So. 68.

Where a real estate broker was employed to sell land at a fixed. price, but without terms of payment, the acceptance by the owner of a purchaser who did not pay cash estops him from denying that the terms offered were satisfactory. Alexander *v.* Smith (Ala.), 61 So. 68.

Necessity for Complying with Conditions.—While, as a general rule, a broker employed by an owner of real estate to sell it becomes entitled to reasonable compensation when through his services such real estate is sold, where the contract contains conditions the broker must comply therewith. Mabry *v.* Bailey, 5 Ala. App. 383, 59 So. 322.

Securing Options.—A contract of employment to obtain options on properties stated that the options should be at a price at which the party for whom they were purchased "may buy." Held, that the intent of the parties was that the option obtained should be at a price which was satisfactory to the purchaser, and, if shown to be so, the conditions of the contract were fully complied with. Worthington *v.* McGarry, 42 So. 988, 149 Ala. 251.

Where one party undertakes for a certain compensation to obtain options on certain properties for another party, it is not necessary that there should be an actual purchase of the properties under the options before the compensation is earned. Worthington *v.* McGarry, 149 Ala. 251, 42 So. 988.

Where a party under a contract is to secure for a second party options on certain properties, and the second party directs him not to proceed in reference to securing the option on one of the properties, this is a breach of the contract, for which the second party is liable for damages. Worthington *v.* McGarry, 42 So. 988, 149 Ala. 251.

Plaintiff and defendant entered into a contract whereby defendant agreed to pay plaintiff a certain sum if the plaintiff should secure for him certain options on ore lands and on the majority of the stock of a corporation. Plaintiff secured the options, except as to the stock in the corporation. Held, that plaintiff is not entitled to compensation under the contract for securing the ore option by alleging and proving that he was prevented in endeavoring to obtain the other by defendant. Worthington *v.* McGarry, 149 Ala. 251, 42 So. 988.

§ 29. —— Performance of Services within Time Specified.

A broker employed to sell is entitled to his compensation if he produces a person, able, ready, and willing to buy on the principal's terms, within the period allowed, or, if the time is not limited, before revocation of the agency. This assumes that the broker's negotiations have produced a result so complete that nothing remains to be done but acceptance by the principal. Handley *v.* Shaffer (Ala.), 59 So. 286.

Where one employs a broker to negotiate the purchase of property, the broker has a reasonable time within which to perform the service, and an understanding reached, after the making of an alleged contract of employment, that the broker was to get the deed by a certain day, did not make his right to commission depend upon the arrival of the deed by that day. Hanna *v.* Espalla, 42 So. 443, 148 Ala. 313.

To make an owner of land liable for a sale by an authorized agent after the time fixed for making the sale, or after a reasonable time if no time was fixed, the broker must show an express or implied extension of time, and such extension would be implied from the owner's subsequent acceptance of an actual purchaser procured in reliance on the contract. Alford *v.* Creagh (Ala.), 62 So. 254.

§ 30. —— Bringing Parties Together.

See post, "Ability and Willingness of Party Procured to Perform Contract," § 32; "Negotiations Direct with Principal." § 33; "Failure to Complete Contract or Transaction Negotiable," § 35.

A broker employed to sell land is entitled to his compensation if he brings the parties together, and a sale is consummated by the seller himself. Smith *v.* Sharp, 50 So. 381, 162 Ala. 433.

A broker employed to sell real estate earns his commissions when he procures a purchaser able and willing to conclude the bargain on the terms proposed or acceptable to the owner. Crook *v.* Forst, 22 So. 540, 116 Ala. 395; Sayre *v.* Wilson, 86 Ala. 151, 5 So. 157, 160; Birmingham Land, etc., Co. *v.* Thompson, 86 Ala. 146, 5 So. 473, 474; Hutto *v.* Stough, 157 Ala. 566, 47 So. 1031; Smith *v.* Sharp, 162 Ala. 433, 50 So. 381.

A broker employed to sell land for a commission is entitled to compensation when a sale is made by his principal to a purchaser procured by the broker, though all the negotiations were conducted by the principal with the purchaser, provided the broker is the efficient means of bringing the minds of the principal and purchaser together. Davis *v.* Clausen, 2 Ala. App. 378, 57 So. 79.

"The theory of the law is that, when the broker has brought the minds of the buyer and seller to an agreement upon the terms of sale, and the buyer is able, willing, and ready to buy, this is a constructive consummation of the sale, so far as the broker is concerned, because he has done all that he is required to do." Sayre *v.* Wilson, 86 Ala. 151, 5 So. 157, 161, cited in note in 44 L. R. A. 322, 606, 616, 617, 619, 620, 622.

§ 31. —— Procuring Cause of Contract or Transaction.

In determining whether a broker has earned a commission for procuring a purchaser, it is enough that the efforts of the broker, acting upon the purchaser, are the efficient cause of his offer to purchase, but they need not be the sole cause. Handley *v.* Shaffer (Ala.), 59 So. 286.

To earn commissions for finding a purchaser, a broker need not participate in the negotiations; it being enough that he is an efficient cause of the offer to purchase. Alexander *v.* Smith (Ala.), 61 So. 68.

Instructions Stating the Law Correctly.—In an action by a broker for commissions for procuring a purchaser for lands, instructions that to be the procuring cause of a sale it is not necessary that plaintiff should have conducted all the negotiations leading to the sale, it being sufficient if he set in motion the machinery by which the work was done, and that he need not be present at the meeting, held proper. Handley *v.* Shaffer (Ala.), 59 So. 286.

§ 32. —— Ability and Willingness of Party Procured to Perform Contract.

See ante, "Bringing Parties Together," § 30.

"If he has negotiated to sell the property to a minor, or a lunatic, or a feme covert, or other person who is legally incapacitated to bind himself to perform the terms required, the owner may refuse to accept the proffered purchaser, and incurs no obligation to pay commissions for the service of procuring such a buyer." Sayre *v.* Wilson, 86 Ala. 151, 5 So. 157, 161.

"If an unsatisfactory purchaser is found —one who is not able, or ready or willing to accept and perform the proffered terms—the owner may refuse to accept him, and is under no liability to pay the broker for his services." Sayre *v.* Wilson, 86 Ala. 151, 5 So. 157, 161.

"The sale of one of the lost owned by appellant is shown to have been contracted to be made to a married woman —one Mrs. Mayberry. The terms of the sale provided for a cash payment of one-half of the purchase money, and the remainder to be paid in twelve months. A feme covert, in this state, being at that time incapable of binding herself personally for the payment of the purchase money, the appellant could properly objected to Mrs. Mayberry as an unsatisfactory purchaser. But if he knew her status, and did not object for that reason, or declined to consummate the sale on other specified grounds, this objection must be construed to have been waived by him." Sayre *v.* Wilson, 86 Ala. 151, 5 So. 157, 161.

Acceptance by Principal Conclusive Evidence of.—In determining whether a broker has earned a commission for producing a purchaser, his principal's acceptance of the purchaser is conclusive that the purchaser was able, ready, and willing to buy. Handley *v.* Shaffer (Ala.), 59 So. 286.

Revoking Offer to Buy Conclusive of Unwillingness.—While a broker who finds a customer ready, able, and willing to purchase at the seller's price is entitled to commissions, yet if the prospective customer's order is revocable at pleasure, his revocation thereof is conclusive evidence that he is not willing to purchase, so that where plaintiff, who was authorized to take orders for the sale of flour for defendant mill, took two orders for a certain kind of flour which the prospective purchaser canceled when defendant explained to him the quality of the flour, plaintiff was not entitled to commissions, defendant not being at fault for truthfully stating the quality of the flour. Richardson *v.* Olathe Milling & Elevator Co., 52 So. 659, 167 Ala. 411.

§ 33. —— Negotiations Direct with Principal.

§ 33 (1) In General.

A landowner can not avail himself of the service of an agent who procured a purchase to effect a sale himself to such purchase, and thereby deprive the agent of his commission. Crook *v.* Forst, 116 Ala. 395, 22 So. 540, cited in note in 44 L. R. A. 613, 621, 15 L. R. A., N. S., 273, 274.

Where a real estate broker did everything necessary to earn the commission under his contract with a landowner to procure a purchaser, he can not be deprived of his commission because the landowner's sale of the property was without intending to defraud him of his compensation. Alexander *v.* Smith (Ala.), 61 So. 68.

Fair dealing between the parties should demand of the owner of land placed in the hands of a broker, that he disclose his intention to the agent, before concluding the sale to a purchaser procured by the broker. Crook *v.* Forst, 116 Ala. 395, 22 So. 540, 541, cited in note in 44 L. R. A. 338, 344, 348.

Where real estate brokers were interrupted in their negotiations for a sale of the property by the request of the landowner to hold the proposition for a few days, and during such few days, without terminating the agency, the owner continued the negotiations along the same line, and concluded the sale, the brokers are entitled to their commissions. Hutto *v.* Stough, 157 Ala. 566, 47 So. 1031, cited in note in 34 L. R. A., N. S., 1052.

Knowledge That Party Was Sent by Broker.—Where a real estate agent with whom property is listed to be sold merely procures another to look at the property with a view to buying it, and it does not appear that the owner knew or could have known that the agent had so shown the property to such other, the agent is not entitled to a commission, on a sale of the property by the owner to such other. Sharpley *v.* Lee Moody & Co., 44 So. 650, 152 Ala. 549.

Ordinarily, a broker's right to compensation for procuring a purchaser is unaffected because his principal did not know that the purchaser was procured by the broker, but special circumstances may require the broker to inform his principal that one with whom the latter is negotiating is a customer sent by the broker, if such information is necessary to enable the principal to protect himself against deception, imposition, or loss. Handley *v.* Shaffer (Ala.), 59 So. 286.

Same—Duty of Broker to Disclose That Fact.—Where a broker is employed to make a sale of property belonging to his principal, it is clearly his duty to disclose to his principal the fact that he has found a purchaser; and, if the broker is aware that the person with whom he is negotiating is about to approach or has approached his principal with a view of dealing with him independently, it would be the broker's duty to inform his principal that such person is the former's customer, in order that the principal may be able to protect his own as well as his brokers interests, by either declining to thus deal with the purchaser, or by so dealing as to make due allowance for the brokers commission. In such a case, the principal is not upon notice that anyone approaching him to buy may be a customer of his broker, and he is under no duty to find out. If, however, the principal has actual knowledge of the relation existing between the purchaser and the broker, he is bound to respect the rights of the latter. Handley *v.* Shaffer (Ala.), 59 So. 286.

Same—Duty of Principal to Make Inquiry.—Where a broker is employed, not to effect a sale of his principal's property, but merely to find a purchaser for it, the principal is upon notice that everyone who approaches him to buy the property may be a customer of his broker, and it is his duty, if in doubt upon the subject, to ascertain whether or not the purchaser is a customer of his broker and if so, to respect the rights of the latter. Handley *v.* Shaffer (Ala.), 59 So. 286.

§ 33 (2) Sale in Which Broker Has Been Instrumental, or to One Introduced or Procured by Broker, or with Whom Broker Has Negotiated.

"Both the broker and principal must act in good faith, and any attempt on the part of the principal to evade his liability by a mere device, when the sale was really procured in good faith by the broker, will not have the effect of depriving the broker of his commissions. Henderson *v.* Vincent, 84 Ala. 99, 4 So. 180; Crook *v.* Forst, 116 Ala. 395, 22 So. 540." Hutto *v.* Stough, 157 Ala. 566, 47 So. 1031, 1033, cited in note in 43 L. R. A. 606, 608.

Where real estate agents employed to sell land within a certain time, after the expiration of the time, at the request of the owner and on a promise by him that he will pay them a commission if a sale is effected, irrespective of the purchase price, and though the sale be made directly by him, write to a prospective purchaser, with whom they have been in correspondence, offering the land for a certain price, and the purchaser, as a result of the letter, purchases the land directly from the owner, the agents are entitled to their commissions. Holland *v.* Howard, 105 Ala. 538, 17 So. 35, cited in note in 44 L. R. A. 341.

§ 34. —— Contract or Transaction Negotiated Different from That Authorized.

§ 34 (1) In General.

Where a broker was authorized to sell real estate for not less than a specified price, one-third cash and the balance in one and two years, with interest at 6 per cent the purchaser to pay a proportionate amount of the taxes for the current year, and he sold the property under a contract requiring the seller to furnish an abstract of title at his cost, and authorizing the purchaser to pay the balance "on or before" one or two years, the contract was not a compliance with the broker's authority, and he was not entitled to commission thereon. Crosthwaite *v.* Lebus, 41 So. 853, 146 Ala. 525.

§ 34 (2) Contract or Sale by Owner on Different Terms or for Different Prices.

Where a broker, employed to procure a purchaser of real estate, handed to a third person a description of the property with the statement that it could be bought for a certain sum, and his act was the procuring cause of the subsequent sale made by the owner to the third person for a less sum, the broker was entitled to reasonable compensation for the services rendered. Davis *v.* Clausen, 2 Ala. App. 378, 57 So. 79.

Fraudulent Devices to Save Commission.—A landowner can not, merely to save the commissioners, agreed to be paid to his broker, effect a sale of the land placed in the hands of the latter, at a small reduction in the price at which the agent was authorized to find a purchaser, or make immaterial charges in the terms of the sale. Crook *v.* Forst, 116 Ala. 395, 22 So. 540.

"The owner of real estate can not avail himself of the services of an agent employed by him, who procured a purchaser, to effect the sale himself to such purchaser, and thereby deprive the agent of his commissions; nor can he, merely to save the commissions agreed to be paid to the agent, effect such sale at a small reduction of price," or by making immaterial changes; and it has been said that "fair dealing between the parties should demand of the dealer that he disclose his intention to the agent before concluding the sale." Crook *v.* Forst, 116 Ala. 395, 22 So. 540; Smith *v.* Sharp, 162 Ala. 433, 50 So. 381, 384, cited in note in 34 L. R. A., N. S., 1051, 1054.

Waiver of Right to Insist on Terms.—Where a broker introduces a prospective purchaser, and the seller undertakes to conduct the negotiations, and finally sells for less than the terms named in the contract of employment, he thereby waives his right to insist on the terms of the contract in that respect, and is liable at least for a reasonable commission. Smith *v.* Sharp, 50 So. 381, 162 Ala. 433.

§ 35. Failure to Complete Contract or Transaction Negotiated.

See ante, "Bringing Parties Together," § 30; "Contract or Transaction Negotiated Different from That Authorized," § 34.

§ 36. —— In General.

And if a purchaser able, ready, and willing to complete the sale is found by the broker, and the sale is not consummated owing to the principal's fault, he can not cut off the broker's right to commissions. Birmingham Land, etc., Co. *v.* Thompson, 86 Ala. 146, 5 So. 473; Sayre *v.* Wilson, 86 Ala. 151, 5 So. 157; Chambers *v.* Seay, 73 Ala. 372; Henderson *v.* Vincent, 84 Ala. 99, 4 So. 180, cited in note in 43 L. R. A. 593, 595.

A real estate agent, employed to effect a sale of land on specified terms, is entitled to his commission, where he procures a purchaser able, ready, and willing to buy on the terms specified, and the owner accepts him, though the sale may not thereafter be completed. Sharpley *v.* Lee Moody & Co., 44 So. 650, 152 Ala. 549.

Under a contract between a broker and the owner of land by which the former is to be paid a commission on obtaining a customer and effecting a contract of sale, the broker having presented T. as a purchaser, and the owner having accepted him and entered into an executory contract of sale with him the broker is entitled to commission, though the contract is not carried out; and it is immaterial that, after the contract is entered into, he aids the owner in his efforts to get T. to carry out the contract, or that he then says he is unable to get T. to comply therewith, or that T. and the owner modify the contract. Bingham *v.* Davidson, 37 So. 738, 141 Ala. 551.

§ 37. —— Defect in Principal's Title.

A land agent is not entitled to commissions or compensation "for procuring a purchaser of a plantation," when it is shown that the intended purchaser declined to complete the contract, without fault or negligence on the part of the principal, on account of a supposed defect of title. Blankenship *v.* Ryerson, 50 Ala. 426, cited in note in 43 L. R. A. 613.

The broker, or real estate agent, employed to effect the sale of land on specified terms, becomes entitled to his commissions, or agreed compensation, when he procures a person who is able, ready and willing to buy on the terms specified, and the vendor accepts him, although the purchaser afterwards declines to complete the contract on account of a defect in title. Birmingham Land, etc., Co. *v.* Thompson, 86 Ala. 146, 5 So. 473, and in Sayre *v.* Wilson, 86 Ala. 151, 5 So. 157; Stephens *v.* Bailey, 149 Ala. 256, 42 So. 740, 741, cited in note in 43 L. R. A. 593, 595.

When a proposed purchaser agrees to buy, and nothing is said about the title, he has a right to believe he will get a good title, and the inducement to buy is that the purchaser may acquire a good and indefeasible title, and if, after investigation, a defect in the title is discovered, the purchaser has a right to repudiate the contract without incurring any liability on account thereof, and the repudiation of such a contract by the purchaser will not excuse the principal from his obligation to pay the broker's commissions. Birmingham Land, etc., Co. *v.* Thompson, 86 Ala. 146, 5 So. 473; Flinn *v.* Barber, 64 Ala. 193; Cullum *v.* Branch of the Bank, 4 Ala. 21, 28, cited in 43 L. R. A. 609, cited in note in 43 L. R. A. 609.

Defect Curable.—A real estate broker induced one P. to enter into a contract for the purchase of certain land of defendant, nothing being said about the title. Afterwards P. discovered that there was a large amount of purchase money due on the land. Held, that the fact that P., who stated that he was able to complete the purchase, refused to do so, on account of a defect in the title, although the purchase money stipulated to be paid by him would have enabled defendant to clear off the incumbrance, could not defeat the right of the broker to recover his commission from defendant. Birmingham Land & Loan Co. *v.* Thompson, 86 Ala. 146, 5 So. 473, cited in notes in 44 L. R. A. 322, 597, 606. 616, 619, 3 L. R. A., N. S., 576, 577.

Broker's Commission to Be Paid Out of Purchase Money.—Plaintiff agreed to purchase land of defendant, and to make the first payment when a "good and sufficient warranty deed was tendered," and the other payments in installments thereafter, and defendant agreed to pay plaintiff a commission on each payment when made. Plaintiff formed a company to take the land under the contract, and it refused to accept a deed tendered by defendant, and, before chancery proceedings to clear the title had been consummated, notified defendant that it would not carry out the trade. Held, that plaintiff was not entitled to commissions for making the sale. Louisville & N. R. Co. *v.* Shepard, 28 So. 202, 126 Ala. 416.

§ 38. —— Default or Refusal of Principal.

In General.—See ante, "Sufficiency of Services of Broker," § 26.

As to principal's right to refuse where purchaser produced is not competent, etc., see ante, "Ability and Willingness of Party Procured to Perform Contract," § 32.

Where the employment of a broker is to procure a purchaser on specific terms, and he procures one able, ready, and willing to buy on such specified terms, he is entitled to compensation, though the sale is not made through the principal's fault. Handley *v.* Shaffer (Ala.), 59 So. 286.

If the seller refuses to deliver goods sold for him by a broker, or improperly prevents the consummation of the sale, he is liable to the broker for commissions. Richardson *v.* Olathe Milling & Elevator Co., 52 So. 659, 167 Ala. 411.

Where the broker has performed his contract by finding purchaser able and willing to buy on terms stated by principal, the fact that the sale is not consummated, by reason of the owner's fault, is no bar to the recovery of commissions. Chambers *v.* Seay, 73 Ala. 372; Henderson *v.* Vincent, 84 Ala. 99, 4 So. 180; Sayre *v.* Wilson, 86 Ala. 151, 5 So. 157, 161.

Capricious Refusal to Accept Purchaser.—A broker's right to compensation for producing a purchaser able, ready, and willing to buy on the principal's terms can not be defeated by the principal's capricious refusal to accept such purchaser. Handley *v.* Shaffer (Ala.), 59 So. 286.

Burden of Showing Principal's Refusal.—Without some evidence that the entire performance of the agreement to purchase was prevented by some act or neglect of the principal, the agent's right to a commission for procuring purchaser is not proved. Blankenship *v.* Ryerson, 50 Ala. 426, cited in note in 44 L. R. A. 602.

§ 39. Bad Faith, Fraud, or Misconduct of Broker.

See ante, "Acting for Parties Adversely Interested," § 16.

§ 39 (1) In General.

A real estate agent loses his right to commissions for selling realty if he is guilty of fraud or bad faith toward the owner. Alford *v.* Creagh (Ala.), 62 So. 254.

Where a broker is merely employed to bring his principal and a prospective purchaser together so that they may negotiate as they choose, no confidence being reposed in the broker, he need not further advise his principal than to enable the latter to protect himself against deception, imposition and loss, and no question of his good faith can be raised to defeat his compensation. Handley *v.* Shaffer (Ala.), 59 So. 286.

In a suit to cancel a conveyance taken by brokers fraudulently in their own name, on an exchange of land in behalf of their principal, the brokers have no claim to compensation on the conveyance being set aside for the fraud. Dean *v.* Roberts (Ala.), 62 So. 44.

In an action by a real estate broker to recover compensation for procuring a purchaser at a fixed price, it was not proof of the broker's unfaithfulness as matter of law to show that the purchaser understood the broker to intimate that the property might be secured at a less price. Alexander *v.* Smith (Ala.), 61 So. 68.

§ 39 (2) Sale for Inadequate Price or Price Less than Might Have Been Procured.

A real estate agent, employed to sell land, must act in good faith in his employer's interest, and hence must impose upon the purchaser the terms and conditions of sale fixed by the owner, and breaches his duty to the owner if he leads the purchaser to believe that the property can be bought for less than the price fixed. Alford *v.* Creagh (Ala.), 62 So. 254.

Defendant agreed to pay plaintiffs, real estate brokers, a certain commission for selling his property at a certain price. H., the purchaser, refused, in the first place, to pay the required price, but afterwards instructed an agent to buy and give the full price, if he could not get it for less. The agent bought the property for less of another broker, plaintiffs having omitted to inform defendant that H. would pay the full price. Held, that plaintiffs did not act in good faith by such omission, and were not entitled to a commission for effecting a sale. Henderson *v.* Vincent, 84 Ala. 99, 4 So. 180, cited in notes in 43 L. R. A. 593, 595, 606, 608, 15 L. R. A., N. S., 273, 45 L. R. A. 34, 25 L. R. A., N. S., 737, 44 L. R. A. 322, 323, 338, 344, 345, 595, 608, 616, 618, 620.

§ 39 (3) Representing Adverse Interest.

The rule prohibiting a real estate agent from recovering compensation for selling property, where he was agent of both buyer and seller, applies unless both parties know of his inconsistent relation and consent thereto. Green *v.* Southern States Lumber Co., 50 So. 917, 163 Ala. 511, cited in note in 24 L. R. A., N. S., 660.

§ 40. Commissions from Both Parties.

See ante, "Acting for Parties Adversely Interested," § 16.

§ 40 (1) In General.

Plaintiff was employed by defendant to find a purchaser for lands, and was also under an agreement with certain prospective purchasers by which he was to participate with them in the advantages of the purchase, if made. He induced these purchasers to inspect the lands, and, on their objecting to the price, which, unknown to them, included plaintiff's commissions from defendant, urged them to make the purchase, and finally induced them to agree to do so. Afterwards, when they discovered the dual character of plaintiff's agency, they refused to consummate the contract, and defendant refused to pay plaintiff commissions, whereupon he brought suit therefor. Held, that a charge that, if defendant employed plaintiff to find a purchaser at a price which would be satisfactory to defendant and the purchaser, defendant could not defeat the action by proof that plaintiff was also to be paid for services by the purchaser, was erroneous. Green *v.* Southern States Lumber Co., 37 So. 670, 141 Ala. 680, cited in note in 24 L. R. A., N. S., 660.

§ 40 (2) Knowledge of Double Employment.

A real estate broker who is negotiating a sale of property, or otherwise acting in the usual line of his business, can not represent both parties to the transaction without their mutual knowledge and consent; and, if he attempts to do so, he forfeits all right to any compensation or commissions from either. Green *v.* Southern States Lumber Co., 37 So. 670, 141 Ala. 680.

§ 41. Rate or Amount of Compensation.

§ 42. —— Contracts as to Compensation.

An agreement authorizing plaintiff to sell certain lands owned by defendant at a commission of fifty cents an acre, and further provided that, "if any trade be made within twelve months with parties brought to" defendant by plaintiff, defendant would protect plaintiff in his commission, by the latter provision contemplated any trade which might result from negotiations by defendant with a party brought to him by plaintiff, and not participated in by plaintiff, and made plaintiff for twelve months a "real estate broker" in the strictest sense; that is, a middleman, whose office is to bring the principals together, with the understanding that they are to negotiate with each other and trade upon mutually satisfactory terms. Shannon *v.* Lee (Ala.), 60 So. 99.

§ 43. Reimbursement of Advances, Expenses, or Losses.

The general rule is, that, even when such contracts are in fact wagers, if in them the broker or agent has no interest; if in any event he can not gain or lose; whether there is profit or loss, he is entitled to his commission only—the principal is bound to reimburse him for advances, if he subsequently executes his note or bill, or makes an express promise to pay them; or if, with full knowledge of the facts, without objection, he permits the transaction to proceed, if there be not a statute pronouncing the transaction illegal and void. Hawley *v.* Bibb, 69 Ala. 52, followed in Hubbard *v.* Sayre, 105 Ala. 440, 17 So. 17, cited in 11 L. R. A., N. S., 578.

Brokers fraudulently taking title to land in their own name held to have no right to a sum of money loaned, where it had realized an equal sum by a sale of a portion of the property to a bona fide purchaser. Dean *v.* Roberts (Ala.), 62 So. 44.

§ 44. Persons Entitled.

Where plaintiff was authorized by the owner of land to sell it, and agreed to share the commissions with defendant in case the latter found a purchaser, the contract was unilateral, binding on neither party until defendant found a purchaser. Wefel *v.* Stillman, 44 So. 203, 151 Ala. 249.

Plaintiff alleged that he was authorized to sell land by the owners thereof, and that he agreed to divide the commissions with defendant if the latter would find a purchaser; that defendant recovered of the owners the commission on sale of the land, but refused to pay plaintiff his share. Defendant alleged that during the negotiations for sale of the land plaintiff worked in opposition to defendant, and endeavored to make a sale to other parties, and that plaintiff was thereby estopped from claiming that he was jointly interested with defendant in selling the land. Held, that the plea was irrelevant and properly stricken; there being nothing in the case to indicate that plaintiff was not entitled to find a purchaser himself. Wefel *v.* Stillman, 151 Ala. 249, 44 So. 203.

A complaint alleged that plaintiff had been authorized to sell lands by the owners thereof, and that it was agreed between plaintiff and defendant that if the latter would find a purchaser plaintiff and defendant would divide the commissions, that the commissions recovered by defendant in a suit against the owners were earned under and pursuant to the agreement, and that defendant refused to pay plaintiff his share. Held, that the complaint did not aver with sufficient clearness defendant's employment by plaintiff, and his acceptance and performance of service under such employment, whereby commissions were earned and paid to him. Wefel *v.* Stillman, 151 Ala. 249, 44 So. 203.

Plaintiff alleged that he was authorized to sell land by the owners thereof, and agreed with defendant to divide the commissions with the latter if he would find a purchaser; that on sale of the land defendant recovered the entire commission in a suit against the owners and refused to pay plaintiff his share. Defendant alleged that plaintiff was not the party really interested in the action, because he had himself been paid by the owners, and had agreed to hold them harmless against claims for commissions made by any one claiming under plaintiff, and that plaintiff's action was for the purpose of recovering part of the commission paid defendant, in order that it might be repaid to the owners under plaintiff's contract of guaranty. Held, that defendant was not limited to proof of the facts alleged to sustain the plea. Wefel *v.* Stillman, 151 Ala. 249, 44 So. 203.

§ 45. Persons Liable.

The owner of real property wrote to a number of brokers, asking them to sell his property. A broker, who received one of these letters, and who, without having the sole sale of the property or listing it on his books, found a purchaser, and submitted the purchaser's offer of a sum to net the owner the sum fixed by him, which left a surplus as the broker's commission and cost of abstracts to be furnished to the purchaser's attorneys. Held that, though the broker may not have understood his relation to the owner, he was as a matter of law acting as the agent of the owner, and hence such purchaser was not liable to the agent for commissions on the acceptance of his offer. Minto *v.* Moore, 55 So. 542, 1 Ala. App. 556.

In a suit against two defendants for a broker's commission for procuring a purchaser for lands under a joint employment by defendants, it was error to refuse to instruct that the jury must find for defendants, if one of them alone employed plaintiff. Handley *v.* Shaffer (Ala.), 59 So. 286.

A husband may make for himself, so as to incur an individual liability, a contract with a broker to procure a purchaser for land belonging to his wife and her sister. Alford *v.* Creagh (Ala.), 62 So. 254.

Purchaser Does Not Impliedly Contract to Pay Brokers Commission.—Where plaintiff acted for a third person in making a sale of the latter's property, to defendant whose promise was only to pay the price of the property sold, no inference could be drawn that there was an express or implied agreement on defendants part to pay the plaintiff a definite sum as commission for making the sale. Moses *v.* Beverly, 137 Ala. 473, 34 So. 825.

Broker Procured by Guardian.—Where plaintiff's own evidence shows that, in employing him as a real estate broker to effect a sale of lands, defendant acted as guardian of the owner, and had no personal or private interest in the property, all of which was known to plaintiff, such evidence will not support a count in assumpsit charging defendant individually, since, where one person contracts avowedly in behalf of another, his act binds his principal only, unless he superadds his individual responsibility by special stipulation. Hudson *v.* Scott, 28 So. 91, 125 Ala. 172.

V. ACTIONS FOR COMPENSATION.

§ 46. Nature and Form of Action.

A broker can not recover commission from the purchase of land sold him, in an action on account stated, though it might be found from the evidence that the price of the property was fixed so as to include plaintiff's commission which was to be paid directly to plaintiff. Moses *v.* Beverly, 137 Ala. 473, 34 So. 825.

§ 47. Defenses.

See ante, "Necessity of Contract in Writing," § 22.

Defendant could not avoid liability for broker's services rendered in effecting a loan for her, to be secured by mortgage, on the ground that there was an agreement that the money was to be used in the erection of a sawmill for the purpose of converting timber into lumber, and that the mortgage contained a clause restraining her from cutting timber except for necessary and ordinary purposes or requirements of the farm, when in her written application for the loan she stated merely that the money was to be used "for the education of children and for general improvement." Loan Co. of Alabama *v.* Deans, 94 Ala. 377, 11 So. 17.

"In an action to recover commissions or compensations for the sale of land by a broker, the statute of frauds is not available as a defense. Sayre *v.* Wilson,

86 Ala. 151, 152, 5 So. 157." Stephens *v.* Bailey, 149 Ala. 256, 42 So. 740, 741.

§ 48. Pleading.

§ 48 (1) Declaration, Complaint, or Petition.

A complaint to recover a broker's commission, alleging employment to procure a purchaser, and that plaintiff "did obtain such purchaser, who subsequently did purchase said property," is insufficient, as authorizing recovery for procuring a purchaser before the employment began or some other person than defendants. Handley *v.* Shaffer (Ala.), 59 So. 286, 287.

In a suit for a broker's commissions for procuring a purchaser for land, it was not a good answer and plaintiff knowingly permitted the purchaser to negotiate with defendant without disclosing to defendant that the purchaser was procured through the broker's efforts, etc., where the pleas did not aver any facts imposing on the broker the duty to disclose to defendants the fact that the purchaser was the broker's customer, and where they did not aver defendant's ignorance of that fact. Handley *v.* Shaffer (Ala.), 59 So. 286.

Special counts in a complaint, based on a claim by plaintiff to commissions earned in negotiating a sale by a third person to defendant of certain turpentine rights, held sufficient as against demurrer. Moses *v.* Beverly, 34 So. 825, 137 Ala. 473.

Showing Employment. — A complaint to recover a broker's commission for procuring a purchaser for land is insufficient, where it does not connect the procurement with any contractual service to defendant, though it alleges the procurement of the purchaser ready, able, and willing to buy on terms agreed to by defendants, and that the lands were sold on such terms. Handley *v.* Shaffer (Ala.), 59 So. 286.

In an action by a real estate broker, the complaint alleged that defendant authorized plaintiff to sell defendant's property on specified terms, which were fully complied with by plaintiff, and that when reported to defendant he approved and accepted the offer of the purchaser, who was able and willing to pay for the property, but that defendant refused to consummate the sale. Held, that the complaint sufficiently showed an employment of plaintiff. Stephens *v.* Bailey, 149 Ala. 256, 42 So. 740.

In an action by a real estate broker, the complaint alleged that defendant employed plaintiff to obtain for him a purchaser for a certain piece of property, agreeing with plaintiff that he should be paid for his services all of the purchaser's price above a certain sum. Held sufficient in the averment of the employment of plaintiff. Stephens *v.* Bailey & Howard, 149 Ala. 256, 42 So. 740.

Necessity of Averring Performance.— A complaint for a broker's commission for procuring a purchaser for lands should aver performance of the contract of employment by plaintiff according to its terms. Handley *v.* Shaffer (Ala.), 59 So. 286.

Averring That Purchaser Is Ready, Able, and Willing.—In an action by real estate brokers to recover commissions, an averment that plaintiffs found purchasers at the prices fixed by defendant, and that he refused to consummate the sale, is fatally defective, on demurrer, in not alleging that such purchasers were able, ready, and willing to carry out the sale. Sayre *v.* Wilson, 86 Ala. 151, 5 So. 157, distinguished in Lunsford *v.* Bailey, 142 Ala. 193, 38 So. 362.

In an action by brokers on a contract whereby they agreed to procure for defendant a customer for her property at a specified price, the complaint alleging a compliance with the contract by plaintiffs was not demurrable for failing to allege that the customer was ready, able, and willing to pay for the property. Lunsford *v.* Bailey & Howard, 38 So. 362, 142 Ala. 319, cited in note in 29 L. R. A., N. S., 534.

Necessity for Showing Terms of Contract.—A complaint, in a real estate broker's action, which alleged that plaintiff was a real estate broker and as such engaged by defendant to sell for him certain real estate, that he found a purchaser ready, willing, and able to purchase it at a price defendant was willing to accept, that he brought the purchaser and defendant together, that the purchaser bought the real estate, but that defendant failed and refused to pay him for his services, and that the reasonable value thereof was due, was bad on demurrer, since it did not show the terms and conditions of the contract. Mabry *v.* Bailey, 5 Ala. App. 383, 59 So. 322.

Necessity of Showing the Owner's Right to Sell.—Where defendant did not base his refusal to carry out an agreement to purchase property upon any invalidity of the owner's title, it was not necessary for a broker, in suing for a commission for negotiating the purchase, to show that the title was clear. Hanna *v.* Espalla, 42 So. 443, 148 Ala. 313.

§ 48 (2) Issues, Proof, and Variance.

Counts in a complaint alleged that plaintiff acted for a third person in the sale to defendant of turpentine rights belonging to the third person; that the rights sold extended to the trees comprised in about 50,000 acres; that the consideration promised by defendant was a net price per acre to be paid to the third person, and commissions to be paid to plaintiff. The evidence showed that what was actually sold was the third person's turpentine rights then owned within a described territory, said to contain 50,000 acres, less 3,000 acres reserved, together with such turpentine rights within that territory as might be acquired by the third person within a fixed period. The rights so owned and sold, including subsequent acquisitions, did not extend to lands exceeding 35,000 acres. Held, a fatal variance between the allegations and proof. Moses *v.* Beverly, 34 So. 825, 137 Ala. 473.

In an action for commissions on the sale of land, that in stating the legal effect of the contract of employment no mention was made of a provision therein that the commissions were to be paid out of the first purchase money did not constitute a substantial variance. Smith *v.* Sharp, 50 So. 381, 162 Ala. 433.

§ 49. Evidence.

See ante, "Evidence of Agency," § 5.

§ 50. —— Admissibility.

§ 50 (1) In General.

A contract made through real estate agents by correspondence for the sale of certain lots specified the prices and terms of sale. Held, that evidence of a prior oral agreement that the sales should be made subject to defendant's approval, and that the deeds should contain certain conditions, is inadmissible in an action to recover commissions. Sayre *v.* Wilson, 86 Ala. 151, 5 So. 157.

In an action for commissions for procuring a purchaser for realty, who, pursuant to an agreement with the owner, afterwards canceled the contract to purchase, a question to the purchaser claimed to have been procured, whether his habit was to abandon his obligations without notice, was properly excluded. Green *v.* Southern States Lumber Co., 50 So. 917, 163 Ala. 511.

In an action for a real estate broker's commission for negotiating a purchase which defendant refused to consummate, evidence that before an agreement for purchase was reached plaintiff had submitted an offer to the owner as the purported agent of defendant was admissible to show the relationship of the parties and defendant's effort to purchase the property for plaintiff. Hanna *v.* Espalla, 42 So. 443, 148 Ala. 313.

In an action by a broker for compensation in procuring a purchaser; evidence of the length of time covered by the broker's correspondence with the landowner is properly admitted. Alexander *v.* Smith (Ala.), 61 So. 68.

Where defendant pleaded that plaintiff's commissions for the sale of roofing were not payable until the purchase price was paid, the court erred in refusing to permit defendant to prove such fact. Long-Lewis Hardware Co. *v.* Ewing (Ala.), 62 So. 341.

Oral Agreement as to Compensation.—Where the correspondence by which plaintiffs were employed as brokers to sell land does not cover the question of compensation, a prior oral agreement as to the commissions to be charged may be shown in an action to recover commissions. Sayre *v.* Wilson, 86 Ala. 151, 5 So. 157.

Evidence to Prove for Whom Broker Was Employed.—Defendant, sued for commissions for obtaining a purchaser for land belonging to C., on the theory that defendant, acting for himself, and not as agent for C., employed plaintiff, may not show that the purchaser brought his action to recover the amount he had paid on the purchase against C., and not against defendant; plaintiff not being shown to have had any knowledge of, or to have advised or consented to, such action of the purchaser, and so not being bound thereby. Agee *v.* Messer-Moore Ins. & Real Estate Co., 51 So. 829, 165 Ala. 291.

On the issue of a broker's fraud in representing both parties, defendant held entitled to show that he acted as agent for T. in other matters connected with the construction of certain houses for which he negotiated a sale of roofing from defendant to T., and for which he claimed commissions. Long-Lewis Hardware Co. *v.* Ewing (Ala.), 62 So. 341.

As tending to prove that defendant, acting for himself, and not as agent for C., employed plaintiff to obtain a purchaser for land belonging to C., a corporation, evidence that defendant had an option to purchase the stock of C. was competent. Agee *v.* Messer-Moore Ins., etc., Co., 165 Ala. 291, 51 So. 829.

On the question of defendant's liability for commissions for the obtaining by plaintiff of a purchaser for land belonging to C., on the theory that defendant, acting for himself, and not as agent of C., employed plaintiff, it is immaterial that defendant, acting for C., sold the land shortly afterwards to another party, and at a less price than that for which plaintiff had sold it; the purchaser obtained by plaintiff having refused to complete his purchase. Agee *v.* Messer-Moore Ins., etc., Co., 165 Ala. 291, 51 So. 829.

To Prove Time for Payment.—Where plaintiff claimed defendant contracted to pay him $1,000 for his services in inducing a conveyance of certain mineral land to defendant, payment to be made when defendant should sell the land to others, a deed of the land so purchased and of other lands owned by defendant by which he parted with his title thereto was admissible to show the happening of the event which fixed the time of payment. Lamar *v.* King, 168 Ala. 285, 53 So. 279.

Where plaintiff sued on a special contract for services in inducing a conveyance of certain land to defendant payable when it should be sold to prospective purchasers, it was competent for plaintiff to prove the deed passing title to the land to defendant and the execution of defendant's note for the purchase money. Lamar *v.* King, 53 So. 279, 168 Ala. 285.

Demand of Abstract of Title.—In an action for a broker's commission for negotiating a purchase which defendant refused to consummate, it was inadmissible to show that defendant had demanded an abstract of title from the owner, where the latter had not agreed to furnish one. Hanna *v.* Espalla, 148 Ala. 313, 42 So. 443.

When Right of Action for Compensation Has Been Transferred.—In an action on an account for commissions transferred to plaintiff, it was proper on cross-examination to question the assignor, who rendered the services, relative to the negotiations between the purchasers of the lands, the plaintiff, and himself, and as to the transaction as consummated. Ivy Coal & Coke Co. *v.* Long, 36 So. 722, 139 Ala. 535.

In an action on an account for commissions transferred to plaintiff, a witness for defendant may be questioned as to the interest the purchasers had in the land, and as to what induced defendant to make the sale; such questions being pertinent to matters introduced by plaintiff. Ivy Coal & Coke Co. *v.* Long, 36 So. 722, 139 Ala. 535.

Evidence of Revocation of Authority.—The testimony of one of two brokers, who were partners in the business, that the firm never received an alleged letter revoking their authority, was competent to show, in an action to recover commissions, that neither he nor his partner received it. Sayre *v.* Wilson, 86 Ala. 151, 5 So. 157.

Good Faith of Principal.—In an action by a real estate agent for commissions for the sale of land, the defense was that the authority to sell was conditional on defendant's being able to purchase a certain other lot. Held, that it was competent for defendant to show that he made reasonable effort to make such purchase, as such proof tended to show his good faith. Wilson *v.* Klein, 90 Ala. 518, 8 So. 130.

§ 50 (2) Evidence as to Procuring Cause of Contract or Transaction.

Where, in an action by a broker for compensation for procuring a purchaser, the evidence showed that the owner conducted negotiations with the purchaser, and the purchaser testified that the broker called his attention to the property before the purchase, but stated that he could not remember whether the broker was the first person who called his attention to the property, the testimony of third persons that they called the purchaser's attention to the property, and that, after the purchase, the purchaser told them that he had them to thank for the purchase, was admissible to aid in determining the procuring cause of the sale. Davis *v.* Clausen, 2 Ala. App. 378, 57 So. 79.

Evidence of Ability and Willingness of Party Procured to Perform.—In an action for a broker's commission for negotiating a purchase which defendant refused to consummate, a deed and receipt, purporting to have been signed and acknowledged by the owner, and proof of a tender, were admissible, without further proof, as tending to show that defendant could have obtained the property at his offer, had he desired to do so, where no objection was raised as to their form of genuineness. Hanna *v.* Espalla, 148 Ala. 313, 42 So. 443.

§ 50 (3) Letters, Documents, or Books.

Correspondence between defendant and the owner respecting defendant's authority and the nature of his dealings with the owner was admissible, not as declarations of third persons against plaintiff, but as tending to show the authority given defendant by the owner and what he did thereunder. Wefel *v.* Stillman, 44 So. 203, 151 Ala. 249.

§ 50 (4) Evidence as to Default or Refusal of Principal to Complete Contract.

Where, in an action for a broker's commission for negotiating a purchase which defendant refused to consummate, there was testimony for plaintiff that defendant had demanded the return of a writing executed September 10th, alleged to show a contract of employment, at the same time recognizing his obligation to pay plaintiff a commission, defendant should have been permitted to show that the paper he demanded referred to another transaction, and that at the same time plaintiff presented a statement for other commissions, not including the one sued on, and did not, prior to October 21st, make demand for the sum claimed. Hanna *v.* Espalla, 148 Ala. 313, 42 So. 443.

§ 50 (5) Evidence of Value of Services.

Where, in an action for a broker's commission for negotiating a purchase, it appeared that, if he had been employed, he was entitled to a fixed commission under a contract, evidence was inadmissible to show what was a reasonable commission for the service. Hanna *v.* Espalla, 148 Ala. 313, 42 So. 443.

Original Contract.—Where a broker introduces a prospective purchaser, and the seller undertakes to conduct the negotiations and finally sells the property for less than the terms named in the contract of employment, the original contract is admissible in an action by the broker as a basis for the ascertainment of reasonable compensation. Smith *v.* Sharp, 50 So. 381, 162 Ala. 433.

Customary Charges in Community.—In the absence of an agreement for commissions, established and customary charges for like services in the community are competent evidence, in an action by real estate agents to recover commissions, to prove what is a fair and reasonable charge. Sayre *v.* Wilson, 86 Ala. 151, 5 So. 157.

§ 51. Weight and Sufficiency.

Evidence in an action for commissions for procuring a sale of realty, held to show that the sale was not made in a reasonable time. Alford *v.* Creagh (Ala.), 62 So. 254.

Evidence, in an action for procuring a purchaser for realty, held to show that plaintiff's subagent was guilty of bad faith toward the owner so as to defeat a recovery of commissions by plaintiff for making a sale. Alford *v.* Creagh (Ala.), 62 So. 254.

§ 52. Trial.

§ 52 (1) Questions for Jury in General.

Evidence in an action for broker's commissions for the sale of land consummated by defendant himself, after plaintiff had introduced the purchaser, held to present a question for the jury whether plaintiff's agency was revoked before the sale. Hutto *v.* Stough & Hornsby, 47 So. 1031, 157 Ala. 566.

§ 52 (2) Questions for Jury as to Employment of Broker, Construction of Contract, or Ratification of Acts of Broker.

"Whether or not the plaintiffs, as real estate agents, were employed by defendant to sell his property, is a question of fact when the evidence is in conflict, proper for the determination of the jury." Stephens *v.* Bailey, 149 Ala. 256, 42 So. 740, 741.

In an action by a real estate broker to recover compensation for finding a purchaser for defendant's property, evidence considered, and held, that the question of plaintiff's employment was for the jury. Stephens *v.* Bailey, 42 So. 740, 149 Ala. 256.

§ 52 (3) Questions for Jury as to Sufficiency of Services of Broker.

In determining whether a broker has earned a commission for procuring a purchaser, what amounts to the "procurement" is a question of fact. Handley *v.* Shaffer (Ala.), 59 So. 286.

§ 52 (4) Instructions in General.

There being evidence that defendant only contracted with plaintiff in reference to a sale to a certain party, which sale fell through, defendant was entitled to a charge that plaintiff could not recover if the contract was so limited. Wefel *v.* Stillman, 44 So. 203, 151 Ala. 249.

Improper Instructions.—Where plaintiff claimed defendant agreed to pay him $1,000 for his services in procuring a conveyance to defendant of certain land when defendant should sell the land, while defendant claimed that the land was to be so sold as to net a profit of $1,000 each for plaintiff and defendant, and that plaintiff's right to recover depended on that contingency, an instruction referring to the evidence containing passages that defendant was working to make money out of the land and out of the others if he could, that he was not working for nothing, and, if he could not make money out of the particular tract in question, that tract would enable him to sell other lands in connection therewith, also that it made no difference whether defendant made anything out of the land in question because he might lose on that land and make something out of the additional land, was misleading and prejudicial. Lamar *v.* King, 53 So. 279, 168 Ala. 285.

Defendant's requested instruction, in an action for obtaining a purchaser for land, in which there was some evidence that B. was partner of defendant, and some that he was his agent, that defendant was not liable for any mistake of B., unless B. was his agent, or defendant ratified the mistake, was properly refused, as tending to mislead the jury to believe it was necessary to a recovery that B. was agent of defendant, and that if his partner, and jointly interested in the sale, this would not make defendant liable for B.'s acts. Agee *v.* Messer-Moore Ins., etc., Co., 165 Ala. 291, 51 So. 829.

Defendant's requested instruction, in an action for commissions for obtaining a purchaser for land, who, after making a payment, declined to consummate the purchase, assigning as a reason that the land did not all lie in one body, that unless defendant, or some one authorized by him, represented to the purchaser that the land lay in a body, or ratified such representation, if such was made, plaintiff could not recover, was properly refused; it not being necessary, as assumed, that plaintiff or some one authorized by him represented that the land so lay, etc., as there might be a recovery, though no such representation was made by any one. Agee *v.* Messer-Moore Ins., etc., Co., 51 So. 829, 165 Ala. 291.

In an action by a broker for commission for procuring a purchaser, a charge directing the jury's attention to the acts of defendant's wife as determinative of plaintiff's right to the commission held improper, as being misleading. Alexander *v.* Smith (Ala.), 61 So. 68.

VI. RIGHTS, POWERS, AND LIABILITIES TO THIRD PERSONS.

§ 53. Contracts in General.

When a broker is authorized by his

nonresident principal to buy cotton of a particular quality and at a specified price, and to draw on his principal for the purchase money, the bank to which he applies, and which advances to him in good faith the money to pay for the cotton, taking his draft on his principal, is not bound to inquire whether the price and the quality of the cotton conform to the terms of the order. These matters were submitted to the discretion of the broker, and persons dealing in good faith with him had a right to rely on his representations in reference to them. Whilden *v.* Merchants' & Planters' Nat. Bank, 64 Ala. 1, 38 Am. Rep. 1.

Repudiation or Ratification of Broker's Acts.—When a broker buys cotton for his principal on an order, and the principal receives it without objection as to the time within which the order was filled, he thereby acquiesces in and ratifies the purchase, so far as time was a material element, and can not afterwards raise any objection to the time within which it was made. Whilden *v.* Merchants' & Planters' Nat. Bank, 64 Ala. 1.

§ 54. Estoppel by Broker's Acts.

Where land was sold by a broker who made certain representations to induce defendant to purchase, which representations were known to the broker to be false, but were relied upon by defendant to his injury, plaintiff, by availing himself of the benefits of the transaction, is bound by the representations, whether the latter was his appointed agent or not. Williamson *v.* Tyson, 105 Ala. 644, 17 So. 336.

Brother.

See the title DESCENT AND DISTRIBUTION.

BUILDING AND LOAN ASSOCIATIONS.

Cross References.

See the titles ASSOCIATIONS; CORPORATIONS.

As to acts ultra vires of building and loan associations, see the title CORPORATIONS. As to rights and liabilities of building and loan association when organized under general corporation law, see the title CORPORATIONS. As to the right of a stockholder to sue the corporation of which he is a member, see the title CORPORATIONS. As to statements of agent or officer as binding on association, see the title PRINCIPAL AND AGENT. As to consideration of foreign laws to determine whether contracts are usurious, see the title EVIDENCE. As to exemptions, on foreclosure by building and loan association, see the title HOMESTEAD. As to validity of statute exempting building and loan associations from usury laws, when act not covered by title, see the title STATUTES. As to retroactive effect of such acts, see the title STATUTES. As to the power of the legislature to exempt "solvent credits" from taxation, see the title TAXATION. As to what law governs as to usury, see the title USURY. As to interest, see the title INTEREST.

§ 1. Incorporation and Organization.

Public Policy as to Formation of Building and Loan Associations under General Incorporation Laws.—The Code of 1867, § 1755, expressly authorized the formation and incorporation of building and loan associations, and as amended by the act of March 3, 1870, it extended not only to building and loan associations, but to an association for any lawful enterprise, not inconsistent with the constitution and laws of this State. Pamph. Acts, 1869-70, 308. The formation of corporations under general laws, rather than by special legislative enactment, has been for a number of years past a favorite public policy, as indicated by constitutional provision and legislative enactment. Cahall *v.* Citizens' Mut. Bldg. Ass'n, 61 Ala. 232, 242.

Declaration of Purpose of Incorporation—Sufficiency.—A declaration filed by persons desiring to form a building and loan association as follows: "The undersigned, being desirous of forming a building and loan association, make the following declaration: The general object for which said association is formed is the saving of funds from monthly payments of the members, to be advanced to those desiring to invest it, to the end that the profits arising from the business thus transacted shall, with the monthly payments, largely reduce the number of months required to make each share worth its par value"—sufficiently expresses the intention of the declarants; and the scheme of intended operation, so far as it is disclosed, is consistent with and adapted to the exercise of the powers expressly conferred by the statute relating to such associations, including the building of houses and the lending of money to its members, and such powers need not be defined in the declaration. Sheldon *v.* Birmingham, etc., Loan Ass'n, 121 Ala. 278, 25 So. 820.

§ 2. Name and Seal.

The use of the word "National," in the corporate name of a building and loan association, is not a violation of Rev. St. U. S., § 5243, prohibiting its use by banking corporations. Lomb *v.* Pioneer Savings & Loan Co., 106 Ala. 671, 17 So. 670.

§ 3. Membership.

§ 3 (1) Who Are Members.

Where plaintiff applied for membership in a foreign building and loan association, and received, as a member, 16 shares of stock in the company before a mortgage securing a loan made by the association was executed, such facts were sufficient to establish that he was a member of the association before receiving the loan. Beckley *v.* United States Savings & Loan Co., 40 So. 655, 147 Ala. 195.

Effect of Notice of Intention to Withdraw.—The by-laws of a building association allowed stockholders to withdraw their stock on giving the corporation sixty days' notice of their intention to do so. Held, that the mere giving notice of an intention to withdraw did not make the person giving it cease to be a stockholder. Decatur Bldg., etc., Co. *v.* Neal, 97 Ala. 717, 12 So. 780, cited in note in 35 L. R. A. 291.

§ 3 (2) Death of Member.

Under a provision in the charter of a building and loan association, enacted by the general assembly, that, in the event of the death of a stockholder, who had obtained an advance, his heirs or legal representatives were entitled to continue the relation of stockholders, the death of a member operates a dissolution of his membership, terminating his connection with the association; and upon his heirs or devisees, and not upon his personal representative, is conferred the privilege of succeeding to, or continuing the membership. And if such privilege is exercised by the heirs or devisees, they become members, not in a representative capacity, but in their own right; and they are subject individually to the duties and liabilities of membership. Montgomery, etc., Loan Ass'n *v.* Robinson, 69 Ala. 413.

Where the charter of such association further provides that, if the heirs or devisees were unable or unwilling to continue the membership of a deceased stockholder, who had obtained a loan or advance, the association is required to act as if default had occurred while the stockholder was living, and it also provides that a stockholder may redeem his property mortgaged to secure such loan or advance, by payment of such a sum of money as would, at the rate of premium at which the corporate funds were selling at the time of redemption, produce the same monthly interest as that which the stockholder had been paying on the advance, in no event being less than the net sum advanced—the association can not neglect or delay indefinitely the foreclosure of the mortgage, and thus suffer dues, interest and fines to accumulate, increasing the mortgage debt and burdening the equity of redemption; but it must proceed promptly to a foreclosure of the mortgage. Montgomery, etc., Loan Ass'n *v.* Robinson, 69 Ala. 413.

In such case, the liability of the mortgaged premises is the same amount that could have been demanded of the decedent, if, at the instant of his death, he had offered to redeem. Montgomery, etc., Loan Ass'n *v.* Robinson, 69 Ala. 413.

§ 4. Stock.

§ 5. —— Subscriptions and Issuance in General.

§ 5 (1) In General.

Where complainant became a stockholder in a building and loan association, with notice that a certain kind of stock was authorized by the by-laws, he can not, in equity, have his contract of subscription annulled because of the issuance of such stock. Johnson *v.* National Building & Loan Ass'n, 28 So. 2, 125 Ala. 465.

Stockholders, Not Borrowers, Exempt from Payment of Premiums and Interest.—In the absence of legislative prohibition it is within the legitimate scope of the business of a building and loan association to include among its stockholders a nonborrowing class paying stock subscriptions by installments and exempted from interest and premium charges to which borrowers are subject. Bell *v.* Southern Home Building & Loan Ass'n, 37 So. 237, 140 Ala. 371.

§ 5 (2) Fraud and Misrepresentation.

Duty to Return Stock.—Upon showing misrepresentations in securing subscription for shares, it was not necessary, in order to rescind a contract with a loan association and recover the amount paid thereunder, for the rescinding party to return the stock received, if the association would not have accepted the stock and returned the money, had it been tendered. Southern Loan, etc., Co. *v.* Gissendaner, 4 Ala. App. 523, 58 So. 737.

§ 6. —— Paid-Up Stock.

Right to Issue.—A building and loan association, in the absence of legislative prohibition, and in accordance with its by-laws, may issue paid-up stock, though its charter contains no express authority therefor. Johnson *v.* National Building & Loan Ass'n, 28 So. 2, 125 Ala. 465; Bell *v.* Southern Home Building & Loan Ass'n, 37 So. 237, 140 Ala. 371.

§ 7. —— Maturity of Shares.

§ 7 (1) In General.

Where a member of a building association has defaulted in his contract as a stockholder, the association is under no obligations to mature his stock. Motes *v.* People's Building & Loan Ass'n, 34 So. 344, 137 Ala. 369, cited in note in 43 L. R. A., N. S., 881.

Right to Change Maturity from Definite to Indefinite Time.—The contract of subscription to stock in a building and loan association, in addition to the usual payment of monthly installments, provided for the levying and collecting of extra assessments, and expressly stipulated that the stock should mature at a definite and fixed time. After having subscribed for stock in said association, a shareholder borrowed money from it, to secure the payment of which he gave a mortgage on real estate, and also transferred his stock in the association as collateral security. Subsequently, and before the expiration of the time for the maturity of the stock and of the loan, upon condition that the association would release him from all liability for the extra assessments provided for in the original subscription contract, the shareholder and borrower agreed that the period for the maturity of his stock should be changed from a definite and fixed term to an indefinite time, and that he would continue his monthly payments thereon until the profits appropriated thereto were sufficient to pay off the mortgage debt, when the same should be applied in discharge of said debt, and all liabilities between the parties canceled. Held, that the said subsequent agreement by which the original contract of subscription was altered was binding between the parties, and the fact that at the time of such alteration no particular assessments had been actually levied was immaterial. Pioneer Savings & Loan Co. *v.* Nonnemacher, 30 So. 79, 127 Ala. 521, cited in note in 43 L. R. A., N. S., 877, 884.

§ 7 (2) Power to Contract as to Time and Amount.

Representations of a building and loan association or its agents as to the time and the amount that would be required to mature its stock are merely expressions of opinion as to what will occur in the future, and are not fraudulent, though they be not verified. Bell *v.* Southern Home Building & Loan Ass'n, 37 So. 237, 140 Ala. 371.

A stockholder in a building association may not have his mortgage to it canceled on the ground that it agreed with him that a certain number of payments, which he thereafter made would mature his stock; Code 1896, §§ 1122-1137, under which it was incorporated, not authorizing it to make such a contract. Richter *v.* Southern Building & Loan Ass'n, 34 So. 562, 137 Ala. 521, cited in note in 15 L. R. A., N. S., 504.

§ 7 (3) Effect of By-Laws, Stock Certificates, and Contracts in General.

Where a borrowing member of a building and loan association had been a nonborrowing member over four years prior to the time of becoming a borrowing member, she was chargeable with knowledge of the by-laws entering into her borrowing contract showing that the length of time and the number of payments required to mature her stock were dependent on the exigencies of business. Bell *v.* Southern Home Building & Loan Ass'n, 37 So. 237, 140 Ala. 371.

§ 7 (4) Effect of Statements or Representations.

Estimate as to Maturity of Stock—Opinion or Guaranty.—An estimate made by a building and loan association as to the time when stock will mature can not be held to be a guaranty, but is merely the expression of an opinion. Ebersole *v.* Southern Building & Loan Ass'n, 41 So. 150, 147 Ala. 177.

A representation that building and loan association stock would be worth par in a certain time, though false was no ground for the avoidance of a contract of stock subscription, since the representation related to a matter equally open to both parties. Johnson *v.* National Building & Loan Ass'n, 28 So. 2, 125 Ala. 465. See, also, Lake *v.* Security Loan Ass'n, 72 Ala. 207.

§ 8. —— Withdrawal of Member and Redemption of Shares.

§ 8 (1) Notice.

Participating in Stockholders' Meeting after Notice.—Knowingly and intentionally participating as a stockholder in stockholders' meetings held six and ten months after giving notice of withdrawal constitutes a waiver of the right to withdraw under said notice. Decatur Bldg., etc., Co. *v.* Neal, 97 Ala. 717, 12 So. 780.

§ 8 (2) Amount to Be Recovered or Paid in General.

A by-law of such corporation, providing, that a shareholder, who has obtained a loan, may withdraw from the association and have his loan cancelled, by payment to the association of the amount of the loan, less the amount of money which he has paid in as monthly installments on the stock held by him, reserves to the shareholder a privilege which he may exercise or not, at his pleasure. If he elect to exercise it, he must comply with the terms thereby prescribed, which were voluntarily assumed by him, when he obtained the loan. Under this by-law, the shareholder is entitled to have his loan credited with the money which he has paid in as monthly installments on his stock, but not with money which he has paid for and on account of the premiums at which he bid in his loan. Security Loan Ass'n *v.* Lake, 69 Ala. 456, cited in note in 35 L. R. A. 289, 297.

§ 9. Dues, Fines, and Assessments.

§ 10. —— Dues or Payments on Stock.

A building association wrote the purchaser of a borrowing member's stock and lands mortgaged to secure the loan, in answer to an inquiry when the stock would mature, that it estimated its stock to mature in six or seven years, but required dues to be paid for only six years, interest and premium to be paid to maturity. Held, that there was no binding agreement by the association not to collect dues after the sixth year, there being no promise by it to that effect. Johnson *v.* Southern Building & Loan Ass'n, 26 So. 201, 121 Ala. 524.

A resolution of a building association to collect stock dues for a fixed period only does not apply to a borrowing member, who procured his stock before the adoption of the resolution, and whose mortgage requires him to pay until maturity of the stock. Johnson *v.* Southern Building & Loan Ass'n, 26 So. 201, 121 Ala. 524.

Liability for Membership Fee in Foreign Association.—Plaintiff, being a Minnesota corporation, and having its business domicile in that state, and defendant having constituted herself a stockholder, such act must be deemed to have been performed in Minnesota, and governed by the laws of that state; and her membership fee, together with an attorney's fee expressly provided for foreclosure of the mortgage, is collectible. Falls *v.* United States Sav., etc., Co., 97 Ala. 417, 13 So. 25. See, also, Farmers', etc., Loan Ass'n *v.* Kent, 30 So. 874, 131 Ala. 246.

§ 11. —— Assessments for Expenses or Losses.

Losses are to be assessed and deducted according to the by-laws, and, when not so assessed and deducted, a member is not chargeable therewith. Gwin *v.* National Bldg., etc., Ass'n, 121 Ala. 572, 25 So. 843, cited in note in 43 L. R. A., N. S., 877, 880.

§ 12. —— Forfeitures for Nonpayment.

Forfeitures for the nonpayment of premiums are a necessary means, for insurance, or building and loan companies, of protecting themselves from embarrassment, and delinquency can not be allowed except at the option of the companies. Southern Bldg., etc., Ass'n *v.* Anniston Loan, etc., Co., 101 Ala. 582, 15 So. 123, 127, cited in note in 43 L. R. A., N. S., 876, 880.

A shareholder of a building and loan association organized under Code, pt. 2, tit. 1, c. 4, pp. 378, 379, and authorized to make needful by-laws, and compel compliance by forfeiture, to secure a loan, executed to it a mortgage, and assigned to the association, as collateral security, his stock, and stipulated that upon default in payment of his installments, interest, premiums, or fines, the bond should become due, and authorized the association to forfeit his stock under the by-laws to that effect, which were made a part of his contract. Held, that, upon his failure to comply with the conditions of his contract in the payment of dues, the association might forfeit the amount paid on the stock without crediting his indebtedness therewith. Southern Bldg., etc., Ass'n *v.* Anniston Loan, etc., Co., 101 Ala. 582, 15 So. 123, cited in note in 29 L. R. A. 131.

§ 13. Officers and Agents.

Inducing Party to Sign Contract.—One dealing with the agent of a building and loan association could rely upon his statements as to what the association would do if she purchased the stock and could assume that the agent was acquainted with the terms of the contract with the association which he induced her to sign. Southern Loan, etc., Co. *v.* Gissendaner, 4 Ala. App. 523, 58 So. 737.

A loan association can not limit the authority of its agent to make representations as to the terms of a contract with the association if one contracting with it through the agent was induced not to read her application before she signed it by the agent's misrepresentations as to its purpose and meaning. Southern Loan, etc., Co. *v.* Gissendaner, 4 Ala. App. 523, 58 So. 737.

§ 14. Powers, Rights, and Liabilities of Associations in General.

The general incorporation laws in force in September, 1871, especially Act 1870, p. 308, authorized the formation of a corporation "to purchase, hold and convey real estate; to loan money thereon to the members of the association for building purposes," etc.; and the declaratory act of March 3, 1870, with reference to building and loan associations, did not abridge the capacity conferred on them, when incorporated under the general law, of taking, holding, disposing of or conveying, by lease or fee, real estate, so far as limited by its charter, or as its business might require. Cahall *v.* Citizens' Mut. Bldg. Ass'n, 61 Ala. 232.

§ 15. Loans.

§ 16. —— In General.

Association's Right to Say How Part of Loan Shall Be Expended.—Where a building association made a loan of $600 to a stockholder on condition that he would expend $300 in the improvement of his property, which he mortgaged to the association to secure the loan, the stockholder could not contend that such expenditure was for the benefit of the association, and that he could not be charged with that amount as a loan. Motes *v.* People's Building & Loan Ass'n, 34 So. 344, 137 Ala. 369.

§ 17. —— What Law Governs.

§ 17 (1) In General.

An application for membership by a citizen of this state in a foreign building and loan association having its place of business in another state was sent to its office there, where it was accepted, and stock issued. An application for a loan was made by the member at such office, and the note secured by mortgage was dated at the place where the office was. Dues of the association were payable and were paid by the mortgagor there. The note and mortgage were delivered at such place, and after their delivery the check drawn for the amount of the loan, after being mailed to the mortgagor and indorsed by him, was paid by the association to his indorsee, a bank in the place where the association's office was located. Held, that the contracts of subscription for stock and for the loan thereon were foreign contracts, and were to be governed by the laws of the state where made. Farmers' Savings & Building &

Loan Ass'n *v.* Kent, 30 So. 874, 131 Ala. 246.

§ 17 (2) As to Interest and Usury.

A statute of Minnesota, authorizing a corporation of its creation to contract for and recover more than 8 per cent for a loan, is obnoxious to the Alabama statute (Code 1886, § 1754); declaring usurious all contracts for the payment of more than 8 per cent interest on loans, and providing that they can not be enforced except as to the principal. Falls *v.* United States Sav., etc., Co., 97 Ala. 417, 13 So. 25.

The opinion of the court in this case declaring a contract made with a Minnesota Corporation, usurious; on the ground that the statute of Minnesota giving such corporation the right to charge excessive rates of interest had no binding force in Alabama, does not seem to have been followed by other decisions. But the rulings are now placed on the dual relation of stockholder and borrower and held not usurious. Falls *v.* United States Sav., etc., Co., 97 Ala. 417, 13 So. 25. Sec, as distinguishing this case, Pioneer, etc., Loan Co. *v.* Nonnemacher, 127 Ala. 521, 30 So. 79.

Where a loan made in Alabama by a Minnesota savings and loan association was governed by the law of Minnesota, the fact that a premium was charged for the loan did not render it usurious, as expressly provided by Gen. St. Minn. 1894, § 2794. Beckley *v.* United States Savings & Loan Co., 40 So. 655, 147 Ala. 195.

Contract Provisions as to Which Law Governs.—When a contract is not entered into with the intent and purpose of evading the usury laws, parties may contract for the payment of interest according to the law of either the place of making the contract or the place of its performance, without offending the usury laws of this state. Barrett *v.* Central, etc., Loan Ass'n, 130 Ala. 294, 30 So. 347; Pioneer, etc., Loan Co. *v.* Nonnemacher, 127 Ala. 521, 30 So. 79; United States Sav., etc., Co. *v.* Beckley, 137 Ala. 119, 33 So. 934, cited in note in 26 L. R. A., N. S., 1138.

Where the by-laws of a building and loan association provide that money due from members shall be paid at the home office, and that all contracts with the association shall be deemed to have been made there, a loan contract made between the association and a member residing in a state different from that in which the home office is located must be deemed one to be performed within the state of the home office, and must be governed by the law of that state in determining whether it is usurious or not. Allen *v.* Riddle, 37 So. 680, 141 Ala. 621; Pioneer Savings & Loan Co. *v.* Nonnemacher, 127 Ala. 521, 30 So. 79.

§ 18. —— Power to Make and Right to Receive.

Code, § 1943, subd. 5, authorizes building and loan associations to loan money to shareholders on real-estate security, subject to the terms and conditions prescribed by their by-laws; but such a loan is not ultra vires, although made in violation of the by-laws. Kelly *v.* Mobile Building & Loan Ass'n, 64 Ala. 501.

§ 19. —— Premiums.

Under Code 1886, § 1556, providing (subdivision 9) that a building association may loan its funds on such conditions as prescribed by its by-laws, and (subdivision 10) that it may lend to the highest bidder, such a company is not required to loan to the highest bidder, or call for bids, unless its by-laws so prescribe. Beyer *v.* National Building & Loan Ass'n, 31 So. 113, 131 Ala. 369.

A written bid filed with the association by a stockholder of a building and loan association for a loan is a sufficient bid therefor under the laws of Tennessee, it being unnecessary that the bid be made in person. Farmers' Savings & Loan Ass'n *v.* Kent, 30 So. 874, 131 Ala. 246.

§ 20. —— Usury.

§ 20 (1) Amenability to Usury Laws Generally.

Under Code 1886, § 1556, subd. 9, providing that building and loan associations may make loans to their shareholders on real-estate mortgage security on such terms as may be prescribed by their by-laws, an association organized under general laws is not restricted by the statute regulating interest, when issuing stock and lending money to its members, and hence an agreement by a member to pay more than the legal rate of interest, if made in accordance with the by-laws, is not usurious. National Building & Loan Ass'n *v.* Ballard, 27 So. 971, 126 Ala. 155.

§ 20 (2) Provisions of Charter.

Incorporation by Act of Assembly.—Where, by the act of the general assembly incorporating a building and loan association, authority was given to expose to sale, at each monthly meeting of the association, the amount paid into the treasury, at public outcry to the highest bidder among the members, each of whom was authorized, for each and every share of stock held by him to purchase an advance of two hundred dollars and no more; and the stockholder purchasing such loan or advance, was thereby required to allow the premium at which he bid in such advance or loan, to be deducted, and to give his note for the amount of such advance, and to pay, in addition to the monthly dues required from all members, one dollar and thirty-three and one-third cents per month for each share of stock, or at the rate of eight per cent per annum, on the whole amount, including the premium—such a transaction, having legislative sanction, is free from usury. Montgomery, etc., Loan Ass'n *v.* Robinson, 69 Ala. 413, cited in note in 18 L. R. A. 133.

§ 20 (3) Statutory Regulations.

The general assembly ordained the statute against usury, and its power to designate the transactions which shall be deemed offensive to, or which shall be excepted from the influence of the statute, can not be questioned. When that body lends express sanction to a particular transaction, that transaction is withdrawn, and excepted from the operation of the statute. Montgomery, etc., Loan Ass'n *v.* Robinson, 69 Ala. 413, cited in note in 26 L. R. A., N. S., 1135. See, also, Security Loan Ass'n *v.* Lake, 69 Ala. 456, cited on this point in 26 L. R. A., N. S., 1135.

§ 20 (4) Usurious Contracts and Transactions in General.

An agreement by a member to pay a building and loan association certain dues and assessments and a legal rate of interest on a loan is not usurious. Johnson *v.* National Building & Loan Ass'n, 28 So. 2, 125 Ala. 465, cited in note in 43 L. R. A., N. S., 880.

Lease Declared Mortgage.—A stipulation for the payment of monthly rent, in a contract between a building and loan association and one of its stockholders, for the lease of a house and lot which it had advanced the money to buy, taking the title in its own name, and binding itself to convey to him in fee on repayment of the money advanced and expended, held usurious, the contract having, at the suit of the stockholder, been declared to be a mortgage, and the monthly rent reserved being fifteen per cent of the amount advanced. Mobile Building & Loan Ass'n *v.* Robertson, 65 Ala. 382.

§ 20 (5) Effect of Member's Participation in Profits.

Where the borrower from a building and loan association is also a stockholder, and shares in the profits arising from the business of lending its money, he will not be heard to attack the mortgage for usury. Hayes *v.* Southern Home Building & Loan Ass'n, 26 So. 527, 124 Ala. 663.

As a Stockholder and Borrower Obligations Separate and Distinct.—A subscriber for stock in a foreign building and loan association pays his membership fee, and the subscription contract stipulates that, if the subscriber pays all his dues and assessments, the stock shall mature at a designated time. The day after so subscribing, he makes application to the association for a loan, which was subsequently obtained, to secure which he executes a note and a mortgage on real estate, and transfers to the association, as collateral security for the mortgage debt, his stock so subscribed for. The mortgage debt was made payable at the time fixed in the subscription contract for the maturity of the stock. The note and mortgage provided for the payment of five per cent interest and five per cent premium per annum, payable monthly, and were payable at the home office. The legal rate of interest in the state of the association's residence was ten per cent. Said subscriber and shareholder participated in the profits, and had an equal voice with the other shareholders in the management and control of the association. Held, there was a dual contractual relation of shareholder and borrower borne by said person to the association, and the respective duties and obligations as shareholder and borrower resting upon him are separate and distinct, and therefore it can not be said that such subscription and borrowing constituted but one single transaction, which took such form as a scheme or device to avoid the usury laws. Pioneer Savings & Loan Co. *v.* Nonnemacher, 30 So. 79, 127 Ala. 521.

§ 20 (6) Stipulations for Payments on Shares.

The by-laws of a building and loan association requiring members to pay certain dues and assessments, and, in addition, the legal rate of interest on loans, do not render such loans usurious, since the obligation to pay on stock is distinct from the obligation to pay interest. Farmers' Savings & Building & Loan Ass'n *v.* Kent, 30 So. 874, 131 Ala. 246, cited in note in 43 L. R. A., N. S., 880.

§ 20 (7) Premiums Considered as Usury in General.

Where the by-laws of a buiding and loan association prescribe that the amount of the premium bid for a loan shall be deducted from the loan, and that the borrower shall pay interest on the gross amount of the loan at the rate of eight per cent per annum, a loan so made is not usurious. Sheldon *v.* Birmingham Building & Loan Ass'n, 25 So. 820, 121 Ala. 278.

Under the laws of Tennessee the manner of payment of the premium bid by a member of a building and loan association for a loan—that is, whether the premium is deducted from the amount of the loan or is paid separately, the borrower receiving at the same time the full amount of the loan, or whether a separate obligation be given therefor—will not render the loan usurious. Farmers' Savings & Building & Loan Ass'n *v.* Kent, 30 So. 874, 131 Ala. 246.

§ 20 (8) Payment of Premium as Separate Obligation.

The obligation of a borrowing member of a building and loan association to pay premiums is separate from his obligation to pay interest on the loan when the contract and the by-laws of the association so provide, and no statute is thereby contravened. Bell *v.* Southern Home Building & Loan Ass'n, 37 So. 237, 140 Ala. 371; Interstate, etc., Loan Ass'n *v.* Brown, 128 Ala. 462, 29 So. 656; Barratt *v.* Central, etc., Loan Ass'n, 130 Ala. 294, 30 So. 347; Beyer *v.* National Bldg., etc., Ass'n, 131 Ala. 369, 31 So. 113; M·tes *v.* People's Bldg., etc., Ass'n, 137 Ala. 369, 34 So. 344, cited in note in 26 L. R. A., N. S., 1136, 43 L. R. A., N. S., 881.

Payments on Shares, Like Premiums, Considered Separate Obligation from Interest Due on Loans.—Payments for shares and interest due on loans are separate and distinct transactions, in the absence of special contractual provisions. Not to be combined to constitute usury; nor the payments on shares used to extinguish the loan. Sheldon *v.* Birmingham, etc., Loan Ass'n, 121 Ala. 278, 25 So. 820, citing Southern Bldg., etc., Ass'n *v.* Anniston Loan, etc., Co., 101 Ala. 582, 15 So. 123.

The court say: "The complainant bears a dual relation to the defendant company—that of a member or stockholder in said association, and that of a borrower from the same. His contract with the association as a stockholder and member is distinct from that as a borrower. As a member of the association, he agrees to pay certain dues and assessments, and become entitled to certain privileges and benefits, and as a borrowing member he obligates himself to pay the loan obtained, with interest and premiums. The contract of loan, as set out in the mortgage, being such as the association was authorized by law to make, is not usurious. Montgomery, etc., Loan Ass'n *v.* Robinson, 69 Ala. 413; Security Loan Ass'n *v.* Lake, 69 Ala. 456; Southern Bldg., etc., Ass'n *v.* Anniston Loan, etc., Co., 101 Ala. 582, 15 So. 123, 29 L. R. A. 120; Sheldon *v.* Birmingham, etc., Loan Ass'n, 121 Ala. 278, 25 So. 820; Hayes *v.* Southern, etc., Loan Ass'n, 124 Ala. 663, 26 So. 527." Johnson *v.* National Bldg., etc., Ass'n, 125 Ala. 465, 28 So. 2, 6. See, also, Interstate, etc., Loan

Ass'n *v.* Brown, 128 Ala. 462, 29 So. 656, cited in note in 18 L. R. A. 133.

§ 20 (9) Premiums Fixed by Competition in General.

Code 1886, § 1556, provides that a building and loan association, when it has funds on hand, may lend the same to the highest bidder therefor, on such terms as may be prescribed by the by-laws. The by-laws prescribed that none but members should be allowed to bid for a loan, and that the amount of premium bid should be deducted from the amount of the loan. The complainant, being a stockholder, bid an amount for a loan, which was deducted therefrom, and gave a note and mortgage for the gross amount of the loan, bearing interest at the rate of eight per cent per annum, which, thus calculated, was more than the legal rate. Held, that the transaction, being expressly authorized by the legislature, whether the premium be treated as interest or otherwise, was legal. Sheldon *v.* Birmingham Building & Loan Ass'n, 25 So. 820, 121 Ala. 278, cited in note in 26 L. R. A., N. S., 1135.

§ 20 (10) Premiums Fixed Arbitrarily and without Competitive Bidding.

A mortgage securing a loan was neither invalid nor usurious because the money was not put up to the highest bidder. Beckley *v.* United States Savings & Loan Co., 40 So. 655, 147 Ala. 195.

§ 20 (11) Premiums Payable by Installments.

A loan made by a building association is not rendered usurious because a monthly payment as premium is required in addition to the interest. Beyer *v.* National Building & Loan Ass'n, 31 So. 113, 131 Ala. 369, cited in note in 43 L. R. A., N. S., 880.

§ 20 (12) Pleading and Evidence.

The transferee of a borrower's stock in a building association, together with the lands mortgaged to it, can not plead usury; that being a defense personal to the debtor. Johnson *v.* Southern Bldg., etc., Ass'n, 121 Ala. 524, 26 So. 201.

A bill filed by a borrower from a building and loan association, seeking to have the foreclosure of a mortgage given by the complainant to the defendant enjoined upon the ground that there was usury in the transaction, which fails to set out the note which the mortgage was given to secure, and the certificate of stock subscribed for by the complainant, or the charter or the by-laws of the defendant association, or the substance of the same, is defective, and open to demurrer. Barrett *v.* Central Building & Loan Ass'n, 30 So. 347, 130 Ala. 294.

Bills Not Showing Usury.—Where complainant executed a mortgage to the defendant building and loan association, by which, in consideration of a loan of $1,500, she agreed to pay the defendant monthly $10.50 as dues on stock, and $10.50 as premium, and $7.50 as interest on the loan, such payments to continue until the maturity of the stock, which was to be credited with certain dividends, a bill in equity which alleged that the contract was usurious, and merely annexed the mortgage as an exhibit, without setting up the by-laws of the association or the plan on which such dividends were to be earned and declared, or any extraneous facts showing the contract was usurious in its inception, was not sufficient to constitute a cause of action, since the mortgage was not by its terms usurious. Tutwiler *v.* National Building & Loan Ass'n of Montgomery, 28 So. 654, 127 Ala. 103.

On a bill filed by a borrower from a building and loan association, seeking to have a mortgage contract declared usurious, and the foreclosure of the mortgage enjoined, and said contract, by its terms, does not purport to bind the mortgagor to pay more than the sum borrowed, with legal interest, and the by-laws or charter provisions of the association are not set out in the bill, and there are no extraneous facts averred in the bill as existing when the contract was made, rendering it usurious, and there is only a general statement on the part of the complainant that it was the intention and understanding of the parties to charge a usurious rate of interest, such bill is defective, and subject to demurrer; the statements as to the intention to charge usury being a mere conclusion or opinion of the pleader. Barrett *v.* Central Building & Loan Ass'n, 30 So. 347, 130 Ala. 294.

§ 21. —— Payment and Satisfaction.

§ 21 (1) In General.

The fact that a building association has gone out of business as such is no defense against the payment of a loan by a stockholder. Motes *v.* People's Building & Loan Ass'n, 34 So. 344, 137 Ala. 369.

§ 21 (2) Application of Dues or Payments on Stock in General.

Payments on Stock Not Applied on Loans.—A member of a building and loan association by becoming a borrower assumes an interest-bearing debt to the association separate from the debt created by his subscription for stock therein, and is not entitled to have payments made on account of stock treated as payments on the sum borrowed. Bell *v.* Southern Home Building & Loan Ass'n, 37 So. 237, 140 Ala. 371; Sheldon *v.* Birmingham, etc., Loan Ass'n, 121 Ala. 278, 25 So. 820, cited in note in 43 L. R. A., N. S., 880.

§ 21 (3) Provisions of Contract, Certificate, Charter, or By-Laws as to Applying Dues or Payments on Stock.

Provisions Indorsed on Certificate.—Where the shares of a member of a building and loan association were transferred to the association as part security for the loan, and the rules and terms of the transfer, indorsed on the stock, required payments thereon to be continued, and the borrower is entitled to have the withdrawal value of the stock applied in part payment of the loan, the relation of borrower and stockholder are separate, and payments made on stock transferred may not be applied upon the loan. Hayes *v.* Southern Home Building & Loan Ass'n, 26 So. 527, 124 Ala. 663, cited in note in 43 L. R. A., N. S., 884.

Action of Parties Held to Change Contract.—Where a mortgage to a building and loan association provides that monthly payments shall be applied to the payment of stock in the company, and not to the reduction of the mortgage debt, they will be so treated; but if, subsequent to the execution of the mortgage, they are applied by the mortgagee, with the assent of the mortgagor, to the mortgage debt, rather than the stock subscription, such application will be upheld as a modification of the original agreement by mutual assent. Capital City Ins. Co. *v.* Jones, 30 So. 674, 128 Ala. 361, cited in note in 43 L. R. A., N. S., 877.

§ 21 (4) Application of Value of Stock.

Applied in Part Payment of the Loan.—Whenever the stock has been fully paid up by the profits earned by the association, the holder of the stock can have its value applied in part payment of the loan. And it is this only that they have the right to have applied as a credit upon their mortgage debt. And this they can not demand and enforce should they make default for six months in the payment of their dues, for upon such forfeiture they would not be entitled to have the mortgage debt abated to the extent of the aggregate of the payments made by them on their stock subscription prior to their default. Gwin *v.* National Bldg., etc., Ass'n, 121 Ala. 572, 25 So. 843.

§ 21 (5) Amounts Payable.

Shareholder Not Entitled to Any Credit for Stock upon Forfeiture.—A shareholder of a building and loan association organized under Code pt. 2, tit. 1, c. 4, pp. 378, 379, and authorized to make needful by-laws, and compel compliance by forfeiture, to secure a loan, executed to it a mortgage, and assigned to the association, as collateral security, his stock, and stipulated that, upon default in payment of his installments, interest, premiums, or fines, the bond should become due, and authorized the association to forfeit his stock under the by-laws to that effect, which were made a part of his contract. Held that, upon his failure to comply with the conditions of his contract in the payment of dues, the association might forfeit the amount paid on the stock without crediting his indebtedness therewith. Southern Building & Loan Ass'n *v.* Anniston Loan & Trust Co., 101 Ala. 582, 15 So. 123, 29 L. R. A. 120, cited in note in 29 L. R. A. 177.

As to the forfeiture of stock for nonpayment of premiums and the stock not to apply in reduction of mortgage, the court say: "The policy of the law favored the forfeiture, the statute authorized it, the rules of the association and the contract of the parties provided for it, and the association declared it, in accordance with the terms of the contract and by-laws. We find thus erected, against our declaring this forfeiture unconscionable and inequitable, as we are asked to do in this bill, a barrier so high, we are unable to surmount it. The appellant is entitled to the full amount of its said loan, principal and interest, according to the terms of the contract, * * * without any abatement for the value of the stock forfeited; and if the same is not promptly paid, in redemption of its said mortgage by the complainant in the cross bill, or the complainant in the original bill—the complainant having submitted itself to the authority of the court to that end—it is entitled to a decree of foreclosure of its said mortgage, and to a sale of the real property therein described, for the payment of its said debt and interest." Southern Bldg., etc., Ass'n *v.* Anniston Loan, etc., Co., 101 Ala. 582, 15 So. 123, 128, 29 L. R. A. 120.

§ 22. —— Forfeitures for Nonpayment.

By Statute, Stock over a Year Old, Value to Be Credited to Loan.—Where a statute of force in a state wherein a foreign building and loan association is incorporated and has its domicile requires that, whenever such association shall declare any of its stock forfeited for noncompliance with its by-laws and regulations, the holder of said stock, if it is more than a year old, shall be allowed the withdrawal value of said stock, if a borrower from such building and loan association, after he has executed his mortgage upon said real estate, and assigned his stock as collateral security, and has carried his stock for more than a year, makes default in the payment of the installments upon his stock as required by the by-laws and regulations of the association, and ceases to pay the interest and premium upon the loan, upon the association declaring the stock forfeited such borrower must be given the withdrawal value of his stock at the time of such forfeiture, which he is entitled to have credited upon the mortgage debt. Pioneer Savings & Loan Co. *v.* Nonnemacher, 30 So. 79, 127 Ala. 521.

§ 23. Mortgages and Liens.

§ 24. —— In General.

§ 24 (1) Requisites and Validity of Mortgages.

A stockholder in a building and loan association has such an interest in upholding the mortgage as to disqualify him from conducting the separate examination and acknowledgment of a married woman secure to a mortgage of the homestead. Hayes *v.* Southern, etc., Loan Ass'n, 124 Ala. 663, 26 So. 527.

§ 24 (2) Construction and Operation.

Lease Construed a Mortgage.—A building and loan association, organized under Rev. Code, §§ 1755-1761, and having power to make loans to its stockholders, secured by mortgage on real estate, and also to purchase and lease property to them, advanced money to one of its stockholders, or at his instance, in the purchase of a house and lot, taking the title to itself, and leasing it to him at a stipulated annual rent payable monthly. The association covenanted to keep the premises insured, to the amount of the money advanced, and, in case of a loss, to apply the proceeds of the insurance to rebuilding or repairing for the benefit of the stockholder, who covenanted to pay taxes and repairs. The privilege was reserved to the stockholder to become entitled to a conveyance in fee, at any time during the continuance of the lease, on making payment of the money advanced; and on partial payments being made, not less than a specified sum, the insurance and rent should be proportionally reduced. Held, that the contract was, in legal effect, a mortgage, though the writing was, in form, a lease. Mobile Building & Loan Ass'n *v.* Robertson, 65 Ala. 382.

§ 24 (3) Assignments of Mortgage or Debt.

A building association, by a quitclaim deed, conveyed its interest in a mortgage held by it. The deed recited that a third party desired to withdraw his certificate, and that it should be applied as a partial payment on the debt of the mortgagor, and that a quitclaim deed be made to his wife. The granting clause recited that in consideration of a payment of a sum of money and of the cancellation of certain certificates the land was conveyed. The other certificate referred to was that of the mortgagor, which had been pledged by him as security for the mortgage. Held, that the granting clause showed that the certificate other than the one of the mortgagor was withdrawn in consideration for the deed, and was not to be applied on the mortgage as a payment. McMillan *v.* Craft, 33 So. 26, 135 Ala. 148.

§ 24 (4) Transfer of Property Mortgaged or of Equity of Redemption.

Where a mortgagor conveys different parcels of mortgaged property, to different persons, at different times, by warranty deeds containing no reference to the mortgage, retaining a portion himself, the part retained constitutes the primary fund which must be first sold to satisfy the mortgage, and, if insufficient, resort may then be had to that conveyed in the inverse order of alienation. Farmers' Sav., etc., Ass'n *v.* Kent, 117 Ala. 624, 23 So. 757.

§ 24 (5) Cancellation, Release, or Satisfaction.

Payments on Stock Are Not Applied as a Partial Satisfaction of Mortgage.—A borrowing member of a building association was to pay so much a month on her stock, which included premium, dues, and interest, which payments were to continue until, with the dividends, they equaled the par value of the stock. Under the by-laws of the association, whenever the stock was fully paid up, it could be applied in part payment of the loan, but, in case of six months' default in the payments, they were to be forfeited. Held, that the payments were not partial payments on the mortgage securing the loan, and hence the borrower could not compel the association to enter them as a partial satisfaction on the margin of the record of the mortgage as authorized by Code, § 1065. Gwin *v.* National Building & Loan Ass'n, 25 So. 843, 121 Ala. 572.

§ 25. —— Foreclosure.

§ 25 (1) Exercise of Power of Sale.

Where the value of parcels of property subject to a building and loan mortgage is greatly in excess of the amount due, which is disputed and uncertain, and can only be ascertained by an examination of the officers of the association who are proceeding to sell the whole for a small balance claimed to be due, equity will order an accounting, and enjoin the sale. Farmers' Savings & Building & Loan Ass'n *v.* Kent, 23 So. 757, 117 Ala. 624.

§ 25 (2) Right of Action and Defenses.

An allegation in a bill by a stockholder to enjoin a building association from foreclosing a mortgage executed by him to it that his "arrearities were caused by respondent's wrong," without any statement of fact to show in what the wrong consisted, amounts to no charge at all. Motes *v.* People's Building & Loan Ass'n, 34 So. 344, 137 Ala. 369.

Statements and Calculations as to Future Value of Stock as a Defense.—The fact that the officer of a building and loan association represented to one who took its stock that, after the payment of a certain number of installments, the stock would be worth a certain sum, is insufficient, though the representation proved untrue, to warrant an injunction restraining the sale of property mortgaged to secure a loan to such stockholder, it appearing that there was no willful misrepresentation or any representation of fact made. Lake *v.* Security Loan Ass'n, 72 Ala. 207.

Usury Only a Partial Defense.—"The plea of usury is very fully sustained. With us, however, usury is only a partial defense. It extends only to a denial of all interest, when the party contracting to receive usury is the complainant. The rule in chancery is different from that which prevails at common law. Dawson *v.* Burrus, 73 Ala. 111; Uhlfelder & Co. *v.* Carter, 64 Ala. 527." Falls *v.* United States Sav., etc., Co., 97 Ala. 417, 13 So. 25, 27.

§ 25 (3) Pleading.

An Averment of Payment, Manner of Payment, Sufficiency of Payment—and

a Demand for Accounting, Not Demurrable as Inconsistent and Repugnant.—Where, in a bill filed against a building and loan association to enjoin the foreclosure of a mortgage and to have the mortgage canceled, the relief prayed for is based upon averments therein showing that the mortgage debt has been fully paid, there is no repugnancy in an amendment thereof which contains alternative averments showing in detail how the mortgage indebtedness has been settled, the manner of securing the loan from defendant, his subscription for stock in the association, which it was stipulated should mature at a designated time, and then avers that complainant has paid all installments and assessments against his stock during said stipulated period, and that the value of his stock, which was held by defendant as collateral for the mortgage debt, was more than sufficient to pay off the mortgage indebtedness, and then prays for a statement of account between complainant and defendant, and for a decree over against the defendant for any balance that might be ascertained to be due complainant; and such bill, as so amended, is not subject to demurrer for inconsistency and repugnancy. Pioneer Savings & Loan Co. *v.* Nonnemacher, 30 So. 79, 127 Ala. 521.

§ 26. Actions by and against Associations.

§ 26 (1) Right of Action and Defenses.

Where a shareholder in a loan association asks for and is given a statement of his account on withdrawal, the bylaws providing for payment of the withdrawal value on thirty days' notice, which is given, and there are sufficient withdrawal funds to pay him, the undertaking to pay such value is unconditional, and the shareholder may recover it by action. National Guarantee Loan & Trust Co. *v.* Yeatman, 25 So. 1003, 121 Ala. 594.

Proceedings to Forfeit Charter.—Proceedings to forfeit charter of corporation will not lie for wrong to creditors and stockholders in the administration of its affairs, by the assumption of questionable rights, there being adequate remedy in action for damages, but there must have been ultra vires acts, willful and continued, and relating to some franchises granted. Johnson *v.* Southern Bldg., etc., Co., 132 Ala. 50, 31 So. 375.

Corporate Rights Should be Exhausted before Appeal to Courts.—Where, by reason of either intentional mismanagement or of merely improvident management, the nonborrowing membership of a building and loan association has become so disproportionate to the borrowing class as to decrease profits, and thereby postpone the maturing of stock beyond the expected period of maturity, a borrowing member not choosing to withdraw from the association in accordance with its by-laws must seek a remedy through the association's governing board or agents before resorting to the courts. Bell *v.* Southern Home Building & Loan Ass'n, 37 So. 237, 140 Ala. 371.

A stockholder can not maintain a suit against the corporation attacking the issuance of certain stock as being in excess of corporate authority until he has done all in his power within the corporation to redress the wrong complained of. Where there is no dispute as to the amount of a loan made by a building and loan association to a member, nor as to the payments made thereon by him, a bill for an accounting will not lie against the association. Johnson *v.* National Bldg., etc., Ass'n, 125 Ala. 465, 28 So. 2.

§ 26 (2) Pleading.

An information to forfeit charter of building and loan association, to show a violation of Code, § 1136, requiring it to set out in its by-laws a withdrawal value of all shares "on which all dues and charges for one year or more have been paid," should aver that there are such shares. State *v.* Southern Building & Loan Ass'n, 31 So. 375, 131 Ala. 50.

Allegations Not Showing Fraud.—In an action to annul the contract and for an accounting by a borrower from a building association, an allegation that defendant's agent stated that the monthly payments would mature the stock in six years, and the loan then be liquidated, does not show fraud, since the statements were of opinion as to what would occur in the future, and the agent is not alleged to have known them to be false, or to have told them with intent to deceive.

Beyer *v.* National Building & Loan Ass'n, 31 So. 113, 131 Ala. 369.

Inconsistent Allegations.—Where, in an action to annul the contract and for accounting by a borrower from a building association, the original bill sets up the contract, requiring specified monthly payments, each, for stock, premium, and interest, an allegation in the amended bill, inconsistent therewith, that all such payments should be credited on the bond, is demurrable. Beyer *v.* National Building & Loan Ass'n, 31 So. 113, 131 Ala. 369.

The averment that complainant was never a stockholder, and that a sale of a loan to her was not made at auction, is neutralized by averments that certain payments made by her were required of her under the by-laws, which are set out, and show that loans can only be made to the highest bidder, who must be a shareholder, and that she secured the loan with an alleged issuance to her of 82 shares of stock and can not be deemed an averment of noncompliance with a statute requiring the loan to be made to the highest bidder, who must be a stockholder. Sheldon *v.* Birmingham Building & Loan Ass'n, 25 So. 820, 121 Ala. 278.

§ 26 (3) Evidence.

A loan association certificate provided that any deficiency from losses, after application of profits thereto, "might" be charged to the shares. The by-laws, made a part of the contract, specifically stated how this should be done. Held, in an action by a shareholder for the amount due him, that proof of an attempt to charge such losses in a manner not provided by the by-laws was properly excluded. National Guarantee Loan & Trust Co. *v.* Yeatman, 25 So. 1003, 121 Ala. 594.

§ 26 (4) Judgment or Decree, and Damages.

Decree Based on Insufficient Allegations of Frauds—Set Aside.—An allegation, in a bill to rescind a building and loan contract and mortgage, that complainant was induced to become a member and borrow money on the faith of representations made in the association's prospectus, and by its agents, that its shares would mature in six years, which representations were known to be false, and made with intent to deceive complainant, was not a sufficient allegation of fraud, since it is not stated in what time the shares did mature, and they might have matured in less time than represented, and hence a decree based on such bill, though pro confesso, will be set aside. National Building & Loan Ass'n *v.* Ballard, 27 So. 971, 126 Ala. 155.

§ 27. Insolvency and Receivers.

Shares Pro Rata with Other Members.—Where a member of a building association, by reason of compliance with its by-laws, becomes entitled to withdraw before notice to him of its insolvency, and the amount of his withdrawal is evidenced by a certificate issued to him by the association before the appointment of a receiver, such member does not thereby become a creditor, but must share in the distribution of the assets pro rata with other members who had not signified an intention to withdraw. Walker *v.* Terry, 35 So. 466, 138 Ala. 428.

§ 28. Dissolution.

It is not enough for an information to forfeit charter of a building and loan association to allege adoption of a by-law contravening the Code, without stating any specific act under the by-law. Johnson *v.* Southern Building & Loan Ass'n, 31 So. 375, 132 Ala. 50.

§ 29. Foreign Associations.

§ 29 (1) Carrying on Business within State.

Prosecution of Suits Is Not Doing Business.—The prosecution of suits in the courts of this state is not the doing of business here, within the constitutional and statutory provision requiring foreign corporations to have a known place of business, and an authorized agent or agents thereat, before doing any business within the state. McCall *v.* American, etc., Mortg. Co., 99 Ala. 427, 12 So. 806. See, also, Eslava *v.* New York, etc., Loan Ass'n, 121 Ala. 480, 25 So. 1013.

Place of Security Not Necessarily Place of Transaction.—A bill which shows that the land subject to the mortgage is in the state, and that the mortgagor resides therein, is not demurrable as showing a transaction occurring in the state, since there is no law forbidding a foreign corporation to make loans in the course of business done in its home state on security of lands in Alabama. American Building, Loan & Tontine Savings Ass'n *v.* Haley, 31 So. 88, 132 Ala. 135.

Foreign Corporations, Subject to State Laws.—The fact that most of the provisions of the Code conferring powers upon building and loan associations are applicable only to those organized under the statutes of the state does not prohibit foreign associations from doing business in the state within their chartered powers, subject to the restrictions imposed by the laws of the state. Eslava *v.* New York National Building & Loan Ass'n, 25 So. 1013, 121 Ala. 480.

That an association derives its powers from another state is immaterial, since the right of foreign associations of this character to do business here upon compliance with the conditions prescribed by law is recognized. Interstate, etc., Loan Ass'n *v.* Brown, 128 Ala. 462, 29 So. 656, 658.

§ 29 (2) Designation of Agent and Place of Business.

Designation of Person and Place as Compliance with Statute.—Where a corporation had a place of business in Birmingham, Ala., and an agent at such place, it complied sufficiently with Const., art. 14, § 4, providing that no foreign corporation shall do business in Alabama unless it have at least one known place of business, and one authorized agent, and with Sess. Acts 1886-87, § 4, providing that no foreign corporation shall transact any business in Alabama before filing in the office of the secretary of state a sealed, written instrument designating at least one known place of business in Alabama, and an authorized agent. Falls *v.* United States Sav., etc., Co., 97 Ala. 417, 13 So. 25. See, also, Eslava *v.* New York, etc., Loan Ass'n, 121 Ala. 480, 25 So. 1013.

Effect of Failure to Designate Agent and Place of Business.—Under Code 1896, § 1316, providing that foreign corporations doing business in the state shall file with the secretary of state a statement in writing giving the name of an agent and a known place of business as a condition of their right to do business in the state, a bond and mortgage given to a foreign building and loan association doing business in the state without having complied with the statute are void. Hanchey *v.* Southern Home Building & Loan Ass'n, 37 So. 272, 140 Ala. 245.

§ 29 (3) Deposit of Securities and Obtaining License or Permit.

Failure to Pay License Does Not Vitiate Contracts.—The failure of a foreign building and loan association to comply with that provision of Act Feb. 7, 1893, requiring all building and loan associations, whether foreign or domestic, to pay a license fee for doing business in this state, does not vitiate contracts arising in such business. Eslava *v.* New York National Building & Loan Ass'n, 25 So. 1013, 121 Ala. 480.

§ 29 (4) Loans.

Loans Governed by Same Laws as Domestic Associations.—The lending of money by building and loan associations, organized under the general laws of this state, according to the building and loan plan, and on such terms as are prescribed by the by-laws of such association, and in accordance with the provisions of the statute relating thereto, is not restricted by the statute regulating the rate of interest generally, and such contracts are not void for usury. The fact that a building and loan association derives its power under the general statutes of another state does not affect or change the principle here announced, since foreign corporations of this character, upon compliance with the conditions prescribed by the laws of this state, have a right to enter into such contracts. Interstate Building & Loan Ass'n *v.* Brown, 29 So. 656, 128 Ala. 462.

§ 29 (5) Mortgages.

After a sale under the power in a trust deed made to a foreign building association, and a conveyance by the trustee to such association as purchaser, the legal title is vested in the association, though the trust deed might be invalid owing to the failure to deposit securities and pay a license tax as required by law, and this invalidity can not avail the grantor in ejectment by him against the association. Shahan *v.* Tethero, 21 So. 951, 114 Ala. 404.

Transaction Must Be in State.—Although a bill by a foreign building association to foreclose a mortgage on lands in the state fails to allege compliance with Code, § 1316, and the following sections, providing that a foreign corporation, before doing business in the state, must file a statement designating an agent and place of business in the state, it is not demurrable, unless it shows upon its face that the mortgage was executed, or the transaction giving rise to it occurred, in the state. American Building, Loan & Tontine Savings Ass'n *v.* Haley, 31 So. 88, 132 Ala. 135.

As to same ruling on ground of deposit of securities, see Eslava *v.* New York, etc., Loan Ass'n, 121 Ala. 480, 25 So. 1013.

§ 29 (6) Actions by or against Associations.

Right to Dismiss Action for Violation of Statute as to Place of Business and Agent.—Under Code 1896, § 1316, providing that foreign corporations doing business in the state shall file with the secretary of state a statement in writing giving the name of an agent and a known place of business as a condition of their right to do business in the state, it is error to dismiss for want of equity a bill to cancel a bond and mortgage given to a foreign building and loan association doing business in the state without having complied with the statute. Hanchey *v.* Southern Home Building & Loan Ass'n, 37 So. 272, 140 Ala. 245.

Building Contracts.

See the titles CONTRACTS; MECHANICS' LIENS.

Building Restrictions and Restrictive Agreements.

See the titles DEEDS; MUNICIPAL CORPORATIONS.

Buildings.

See the titles ARSON; BURGLARY; FIXTURES; MUNICIPAL CORPORATIONS. As to courthouses and courtrooms, see the title COURTS. As to insurance of buildings, etc., see the title INSURANCE. As to licenses and taxation with reference to buildings, for the use thereof, see the titles LICENSES; TAXATION. As to liens for constructions and repairs, see the title MECHANICS' LIENS. As to public buildings, see the titles COUNTIES; MUNICIPAL CORPORATIONS; SCHOOLS AND SCHOOL DISTRICTS; etc.

Bulk Stock Law.

See the title FRAUDULENT CONVEYANCES.

Burden of Proof.

See the titles CRIMINAL LAW; EVIDENCE. And see the particular titles throughout this work.

BURGLARY.

Cross References.

See the titles ARSON; CRIMINAL LAW; HUSBAND AND WIFE; LARCENY; MASTER AND SERVANT; PRINCIPAL AND AGENT; RAPE; ROBBERY; TENANCY IN COMMON.

I. OFFENSES AND RESPONSIBILITY THEREFOR.

§ 1. Nature and Elements of Offenses.

§ 2. —— In General.

The offense consists in violating the common security of the dwelling house in the night time, for the purpose of committing a felony. State *v.* McCall, 4 Ala. 643, 644.

Definition.—"'The word burglary' says Mr. Chitty, in an excellent and accurate treatise on criminal law, 'is a compound of the saxon term "burgh," a house, "laron," theft;' 3 Chitt. Cr. Law 1101." Anderson *v.* State, 48 Ala. 665, 666.

"The crime of burglary may be defined to be, the breaking and entering a dwelling house in the night time, with intent to commit a felony." State *v.* McCall, 4 Ala. 643, 644.

"Burglary is now defined to be the breaking and entering the house of another in the night time with intent to commit felony therein. Jacob Law. Dict., Burglary, 3 Inst., 63; 3 Chitt. Cr. Law, p. 1101; 4 Bla. Com. 224; 2 Russ. on Crs., p. 2, Metcalf's Ed. 1831." Anderson *v.* State, 48 Ala. 665, 666.

Character of House and Intent Most Important Elements.—The character of the house, and the intent with which it is broken and entered, make the offense of burglary. Crawford *v.* State, 44 Ala. 382, 384.

Burglary and Grand Larceny.—"Under our Code, burglary and grand larceny are distinct felonies of the same grade, subject to the same nature of punishment, and may be joined in the same indictment, but are not subject to the doctrine of merger. Johnson *v.* State, 29 Ala. 62; Hamilton *v.* State, 36 Ind. 286, 10 Am. Rep. 22; Oliver *v.* State, 37 Ala. 134; Whar. Amer. Crim. Law, vol. 1, § 564." Bell *v.* State, 48 Ala. 684, 694.

§ 3. —— Intent.

See post, "Intent," § 13; "Intent," § 23. As to instructions stating law as to intent, see post, "As to Intent," § 34 (2).

Necessity of Felonious Intent.—It is an essential element of the crime of burglary, that the breaking and entering should be accomplished with an intent to steal, or to commit some felony. Barber *v.* State, 78 Ala. 19.

"Intent to Steal."—The "intent to steal," as an element of burglary, is made the equivalent of an intent to commit a felony, though the value of the thing intended to be stolen may be less than twenty-five dollars, and its larceny a misdemeanor. Walker *v.* State, 63 Ala. 49, 50, cited in note in 34 L. R. A., N. S., 245.

To constitute the offense of larceny from a dwelling house, etc., under the statute to punish, "every person who shall enter any dwelling house," etc., and commit the crime of larceny therein, the entry must be made to commit a larceny. State *v.* Chambers, 6 Ala. 855.

Time of Intent.—The entry must appear to have been made with the immediate intent to commit a felony, as distinguished from the previous intent to procure admission to the dwelling house. 1 Leach's C. L. 452; East's P. C. 491. State *v.* McCall, 4 Ala. 643.

It is not essential to the crime of burglary that the intent to commit felony shall exist before the breaking. It must be concurrent with the breaking and entering, and may be formed at the moment of time the breaking occurs. Jackson *v.* State, 102 Ala. 167, 15 So. 344, 345.

Where a person entered a building and his entry is licensed, if he forms the intent to commit the felony after the licensed entry, the crime of burglary is not committed. Lowder *v.* State, 63 Ala. 143; Hild *v.* State, 67 Ala. 39, 40; Carter *v.* State, 68 Ala. 96, 98.

"The evidence of the intent shows it to have been felonious, notwithstanding the meat was put between the ceiling and weather-boarding of the building at a time when he went into it on the business of the mistress of the house, and was then intrusted with the key of the building for that purpose." Fisher *v.* State, 43 Ala. 17, 20.

Necessity for Consummation of Intent.—It is immaterial in a prosecution for burglary whether or not the felonious intent with which the defendant broke and entered the house be consummated. Anderson *v.* State, 48 Ala. 665.

Breaking into the house with intent to steal is the gravamen of the offense of burglary. It is not required that there shall be a theft committed. Wicks *v.* State, 44 Ala. 398, 400, cited in note in 34 L. R. A., N. S., 249.

§ 4. —— Character of Building.

See post, "Description of Building," § 14.

Statute Relating to Nature or Contents of Building Burglarized.—Code 1886, § 3786, making burglary to consist in breaking into and entering, with intent to steal or commit a felony, "a dwelling house, * * * or into any shop, * * * in which any goods, merchandise, or other valuable thing is kept for use, sale, or deposit," the two clauses of which are separated in the printed copy of the Code by a comma only, is governed by the original manuscript adopted by the legislature, in which a semicolon appears, and is a legislative adoption of the judicial construction of § 3695 of the prior Code, which was the same as the manuscript of § 3786, and which has been construed to contain two distinct clauses—one making it burglary to enter a dwelling house, and the other a burglary to enter a building in which goods are kept. Potter *v.* State, 92 Ala. 37, 9 So. 402, cited in note in 34 L. R. A., N. S., 248.

Dwelling House. — What constitutes buildings within curtilage, see post, "Situation of Building," § 5.

A two-storied house, of which the front room on the first floor was used as a storehouse, and the back room (which also contained a few boxes of goods, and communicated with the front by a door in the partition) as a sleeping room by the owner, while his clerks, who were unmarried men, and took their meals at an hotel, slept in the rooms on the second floor, is a dwelling house, both within the common-law definition of burglary, and under §§ 3308, 3309, Code. Ex parte Vincent, 26 Ala. 145, cited in Henry *v.* State, 39 Ala. 679, 681.

Same—Hotel.—"An hotel may or may not be a dwelling house, according to the facts as to its occupancy and habitation. So, each separate room in an hotel may be a dwelling house, within the provisions of our statute, according to such facts, though ordinarily a house is an entirety, each room being merely a constituent part of it. But it can not be said, as a matter of law, that every hotel is a dwelling house, or that any particular room in an hotel is a dwelling house, where the averment is, as here, a mere general description of, or rather, reference to the property as a certain hotel or a 'sample room' in a particular hotel. And, of course, such 'sample room' can not be affirmed, from its mere designation, to be 'a shop, store, warehouse, or other building, structure, or inclosure' in which goods, merchandise, or other valuable thing is kept for use, sale, or deposit." Thomas *v.* State, 97 Ala. 3, 12 So. 409, 410.

Building Other than Dwelling.—As to necessity of alleging and proving that warehouse contained property of value, see post, "Occupancy of Building," § 6.

Under Code, § 4417, declaring guilty of burglary any person who, with intent to commit a felony, breaks into a shop, store, warehouse, or other building, structure, or inclosure in which any goods or merchandise are kept for sale or deposit, provided such structure or inclosure, "other than a shop, store, warehouse or building, is specially constructed or made to keep such goods, merchandise," etc., it is not necessary for an indictment to allege, or for the evidence to show, that the building burglarized was "especially constructed or made to keep" goods or merchandise, where it was a permanent and substantial structure, and not a temporary one erected for a special purpose. Smith *v.* State, 37 So. 157, 140 Ala. 146.

Same—Warehouse—What Is.—A covered structure, used for storing cotton bales, one side and end of which are planked up, and the others left open, so that wagons can drive under to load and unload, which, together with two acres of land connected with it, is inclosed by a plank fence nine feet high, the gates of which are kept locked, constitutes a "warehouse," within the meaning of Rev. Code, § 3707, relating to larceny from a warehouse. Hagan *v.* State, 52 Ala. 373; Bennett *v.* State, 52 Ala. 370, 372.

Same—Railroad Car.—Code, § 3787, provides for the punishment, as burglary, of the breaking, and entering, etc., of a railroad car. Johnson *v.* State, 98 Ala. 57, 13 So. 503.

Same—Depot.—An indictment for burglary, charging that defendant broke into, etc., a railroad depot in which goods, wares, merchandise or clothing, things of value, were kept for use, sale, or deposit, was demurrable for not showing a breaking into a building or structure of the kind mentioned in the statute. Dickinson *v.* State, 41 So. 929, 148 Ala. 676.

§ 5. —— Situation of Building.

See post, "Description of Building," § 19 (1).

Buildings in Curtilage.—"For the purposes of the offense of burglary, it is said the term 'dwelling house' comprehends all buildings within the curtilage or inclosure, etc., 1 Hale's P. C. 358, 559; Hawk. P. C. Ch. 38, § 12; East's P. C. 492, 493, 501, 508." State *v.* McCall, 4 Ala. 643, 644.

Same—What Buildings Are within Curtilage.—Though it appeared that the smoke house entered was about forty yards from the owner's dwelling house, and not within the same inclosure, the jury might properly conclude that it was "within the curtilage" of such dwelling house, within the meaning of Code, § 3786. Wait *v.* State, 99 Ala. 164, 13 So. 584.

Breaking into a building, the front and door of which are in the yard of a dwelling house, although the rear is not within the yard, and the breaking was in that part of the building, is within the meaning of a statute defining burglary as breaking and entering "into a dwelling house or any building within the curtilage of a dwelling house," etc. Rev. Code, § 3695. Fisher *v.* State, 43 Ala. 17, cited in Washington *v.* State, 82 Ala. 31, 32, 2 So. 356.

Location of Railroad Car.—On a trial under Code, § 3787, for breaking into a railroad car "upon or connected with a railroad in this state," it is not necessary to prove that the car was "standing on" the tracks of the railroad company. Johnson *v.* State, 98 Ala. 57, 13 So. 503.

§ 6. —— Occupancy of Building.

There can be no conviction on an indictment for burglary in a dwelling house, unless it is proved that some one resided in the house. Fuller *v.* State, 48 Ala. 273.

The term "dwelling house," as used in § 3308 of the Code, has the same meaning as in the definition of burglary at common law; and the following § (3309) was intended to soften the rigor of the old statute (Clay's Dig., p. 472, § 4), by narrowing the meaning of the term, in requiring that there should be a white person in the house at the time the offense was committed, and that the building should be joined to and parcel of the dwelling house. Ex parte Vincent, 26 Ala. 145.

Cotton House.—To warrant a conviction, under Rev. Code, § 3695, for breaking into and entering a cotton house, it must be alleged and proved that property of value was in the house. Rowland *v.* State, 55 Ala. 210, cited in note in 34 L. R. A., N. S., 248, 249.

§ 7. —— Breaking and Entry.

§ 7 (1) What Constitutes Breaking.

"To constitute the offense of burglary, as charged in the indictment, there must have been evidence that the storehouse mentioned had been broken and entered by the accused with the intent to steal. There must have been a substantial and forcible irruption, connected with an entry. The degree of force may be very slight—it may consist in the mere unloosing or displacing of any fastening provided for the security of the house; still, there must be an actual or constructive breaking into the house." Green *v.* State, 68 Ala. 539, 541.

To constitute burglary, there must be a breaking, removing, or putting aside of something material, which constitutes a part of the dwelling house, and is relied on as a security against intrusion. If the entrance be effected through an opening previously there without forcible enlargement of it, this can not be a burglarious entry, unless it be effected through an open chimney. Carter *v.* State, 68 Ala. 96.

Chimney.—Getting into the chimney of a house with intent to steal is a sufficient breaking to constitute burglary, though the party does not enter any of the rooms in the house. Donohoo *v.* State, 36 Ala. 281.

As to sufficiency of entry through chimney, see post, "Breaking without Entry, Entry without Breaking, and Breaking after Entry," § 7 (3).

Sufficiency of Force to Constitute a Breaking.—The degree of force or violence which may be used in the breaking is not of importance on trial for burglary —it may be very slight. The lifting the latch of a door; the picking of a lock, or opening with a key; the removal of a pane of glass, and, indeed, the displacement or unloosing of any fastening, which the owner has provided as a security to the house, is a breaking—an actual breaking —within the meaning of the term as employed in the definition of burglary at common law, and as it is employed in the statute. Walker *v.* State, 63 Ala. 49, 50.

It does not require violent or mechanical force to constitute a burglarious entry. If any force be employed to remove or displace that which has been placed to close an opening in a dwelling house, or to protect the contents within, this is sufficient to constitute burglary. Carter *v.* State, 68 Ala. 96.

Breaking Through Outside Shell of Double Wall.—The fact that the prisoner went into the smoke-house, on the business of the mistress of the house, before the time the offense is charged to have been committed, and while there dropped the meat, afterwards taken, down between the ceiling and weather-boarding of the house, so that it could be taken out, by prizing up one of the weather-boards, will not change the character of the breaking and entering, so as to make the offense a mere larceny, instead of burglary. Fisher *v.* State, 43 Ala. 17.

Same—Opening Shutters—Window Being Unbroken.—Breaking open the shutters of a window, and protruding the hand within them, is not such an entry as will constitute the crime of burglary, the sash and glass not being broken. State *v.* McCall, 4 Ala. 643.

Breaking by Use of Fire.—A breaking, to constitute burglary, may be done by fire as well as by other means. The entrance and the intent being shown, the breaking is not lost in the consumption of the building. White *v.* State, 49 Ala. 344.

Size of Entrance Made.—To constitute burglary, any breaking that enables the prisoner to take the property out through the breach, with his hands, is a breaking sufficient, if the intent was felonious. Fisher *v.* State, 43 Ala. 17.

Same—Boring Hole Through Floor.—One who, intending to steal shelled corn, bores a hole through the floor of a corncrib from the outside, and thus draws the corn into a sack below, is guilty of burglary. Walker *v.* State, 63 Ala. 49, cited in Carter *v.* State, 68 Ala. 96, 98; Green *v.* State, 68 Ala. 539, 541; Miller *v.* State, 77 Ala. 41, 44.

Digging under Wall of Floorless Building.—Where a building made of logs rests on the ground, and is without a floor, an entrance effected by digging under the wall is such a breaking as constitutes burglary. Pressley *v.* State, 111 Ala. 34, 20 So. 647.

§ 7 (2) What Constitutes Entry.

"Any, the least entry, is sufficient by means of the hand, or foot, or even by an instrument with which it is intended to commit a felony. East's P. C. 490; Foster's C. L. 107; 1 Hawk. P. C. Ch. 38, § 7; 1 Hale's P. C. 555." State *v.* McCall, 4 Ala. 643, 645.

The entry must appear to have been made with the immediate intent to commit a felony, as distinguished from the previous intent to procure admission to the dwelling house. Where it appeared that a centre-bit had penetrated through the door, from chips found in the inside of the house, yet as the instrument had been introduced for the purpose of breaking, and not for the purpose of taking the property or committing any other felony, it was held the entry was incomplete. 1 Leach's C. L. 452; East's P. C. 491; State *v.* McCall, 4 Ala. 643, 645.

§ 7 (3) Breaking without Entry, Entry without Breaking, and Breaking after Entry.

Entry Through Previously Existing Opening.—A gin house no longer used for ginning cotton contained two rooms, a lint room and a gin room, and the occupant of the latter crawled through a hole in the partition, which hole was made for the purpose of allowing the cotton to pass from the gin into the lint room, into the former room, and stole seed cotton belonging to the occupant of said room. Held, that the offense of burglary had not been committed. Stone *v.* State, 63 Ala. 115.

One who abstracts corn from a crib by thrusting his arm through an opening between the chinks is not guilty of burglary, where he neither made nor enlarged the opening for that purpose. Miller *v.* State, 77 Ala. 41.

Same—Entering Through Open Window or Door.—Entering a house through an open door or window is not burglary. Pines *v.* State, 50 Ala. 153; Green *v.* State, 68 Ala. 539.

Entering a storehouse, through an open window, is not a burglarious entrance; nor is the person so entering guilty of burglary, because he removed the bar of the door while within, and opened it to let in his accomplice, if none of them in fact entered. Ray *v.* State, 66 Ala. 281.

Same—Entering by Chimney.—"By the common law, descending the chimney of a house is actual breaking; as much so in legal effect as would be the forcible breaking into a house by any other means. 3 Green. Ev., § 76. And such was recognized to be the law by this court in Donohoo *v.* State, 36 Ala. 281." Walker *v.* State, 52 Ala. 376, 377. See, also, Carter *v.* State, 68 Ala. 96.

Going down a chimney into a house used for storing cotton, with the intent to steal, and getting out through a window by breaking the inside fastening, is a sufficient "breaking into and entering" to constitute burglary as defined by Rev. Code, § 3695. Walker *v.* State, 52 Ala. 376.

Same—Same—Necessity of Actually Entering a Room.—Where a person enters the chimney of a storehouse at the top, intending to go down such chimney into the store to steal, he is guilty of burglary, though he does not in fact get through the chimney into the building where the goods are. Olds *v.* State, 97 Ala. 81, 12 So. 409; Donohoo *v.* State, 36 Ala. 281.

Breaking into Inner Compartment after Entry.—An entry into the second story of a mill by passing through the open door of the lower story, and then pushing aside a board loosely fastened over a hole in the upper floor, held to be a burglarious breaking and entering. Carter *v.* State, 68 Ala. 96.

Hiding in House and Breaking Out with Stolen Property.—Concealing oneself in a house, and breaking out, in the night, carrying away stolen goods, will not sustain a conviction under a statute punishing any one who breaks into and enters a house. Brown *v.* State, 55 Ala. 123, cited in Ray *v.* State, 66 Ala. 281, 282; Miller *v.* State, 77 Ala. 41, 44.

§ 8. Defenses.

§ 9. —— Consent of Owner or Occupant of Building.

Where the proof showed that the prisoner proposed to a servant a plan for robbing his employer's office by night; that the servant disclosed the plan to his employer, by whom it was communicated to the police; that the master, acting under the instructions of the police, furnished the servant with the keys of his office on the appointed night; that the servant and the prisoner went together to the office, where the servant opened the door with the key, and they both entered through the door, and were arrested in the house by the police—held, that there could be no conviction of burglary. Allen *v.* State, 40 Ala. 334.

§ 10. Persons Liable.

In this state, all who in any manner participate in the commission of a burglary are guilty, without regard to the former distinction of principal and accessories in such offense. Wicks *v.* State, 44 Ala. 398.

The testimony must show an actual participation in the commission of the alleged offense before a party can be convicted of aiding and abetting such offense. Wicks *v.* State, 44 Ala. 398, cited in Martin *v.* Tally, 102 Ala. 25, 15 So. 722.

Employees with Right to Enter Building.—A servant and office boy of an attorney at law, intrusted with the key of the front door of the office, and entering at night by using the key, with intent to steal, the attorney sleeping, according to custom, in an inner room, is guilty of burglary; but not so if the boy is in the habit of sleeping in the office, to the knowledge of his employer, and enters to go to bed, and, after entering, forms the design to steal. Lowder *v.* State, 63 Ala. 143, cited in Hild *v.* State, 67 Ala. 39, 40; Carter *v.* State, 68 Ala. 96, 98.

An employee left in charge of a house, and entering and stealing from a closed though unlocked room, which in his employment he had no right to enter, held guilty of burglary. Hild *v.* State, 67 Ala. 39.

Where defendant entered prosecutrix's pantry with intent to steal after the pantry had been locked, he was guilty of burglary, though he might have had a right of access to the pantry in the performance of his duties as a servant. Pointer *v.* State, 41 So. 929, 148 Ala. 676.

II. PROSECUTION AND PUNISHMENT.

§ 11. Indictment or Information.

§ 12. —— Requisites and Sufficiency in General.

An indictment charging that defendant "broke into and entered the storehouse of R. D. with intent to steal, where there was at the time of such breaking and entering into said storehouse goods, merchandise, or other valuable things was kept for use," etc., is sufficient, though ungrammatical. Pond *v.* State, 55 Ala. 196.

Joining Count Charging Larceny.—It is no objection to an indictment for burglary, that it also avers the consummation of a larceny in the building alleged to have been entered. Barber *v.* State, 78 Ala. 19; Wolf *v.* State, 49 Ala. 359; Bailey *v.* State, 116 Ala. 437, 22 So. 918.

A count in an indictment which charges defendant with the crime of burglary in the form prescribed by volume 2, Code 1886, p. 268, form 20, is not rendered defective by further charging that defendant, after having burglariously entered the house, feloniously took and carried away therefrom certain moneys and articles of merchandise. Walker *v.* State, 97 Ala. 85, 12 So. 83.

An indictment which charged defendant with breaking into the dwelling house of R. with intent to steal, and with feloniously taking away therefrom greenbacks, silver dollars, etc., without an averment of the ownership of the money, charges burglary only. Bowen *v.* State, 106 Ala. 178, 17 So. 335.

Same—Conviction on Either or Both Charges.—Under a count charging that the defendants "broke into and entered" a certain described building, mentioned in § 3695 of the Revised Code, "with the intent to steal," and "feloniously took and carried away" certain specified articles of personal property of a specified third person "of the value of more than one hundred dollars," there may be a conviction for either or both of the offenses charged (burglary or larceny). Bell *v.* State, 48 Ala. 684.

§ 13. —— Intent.

An averment of the existence of the intent to steal or to commit a felony, at the time they broke into and entered the building, is essential to make a count a good one for burglary. Oliver *v.* State, 17 Ala. 587; Ogletree *v.* State, 28 Ala. 693; Bell *v.* State, 48 Ala. 684, 694.

Charging in Language of Statute.—Burglary charged in the language of the statute is sufficiently charged. Mason *v.* State, 42 Ala. 543.

Effect of Failure to Charge Felonious Intent.—A count in an indictment alleging that the accused "broke into and entered" a building described, and "feloniously took and carried away" certain property, described, "of the value of more than $100," but containing no averment that the breaking and entry were "with intent to steal or to commit a felony therein," charges grand larceny only. Bell *v.* State, 48 Ala. 684.

An averment in an indictment for burglary under Rev. Code, § 3695, that the accused broke and entered, etc., "with intent to set fire to or burn the store" of a person named, without averring that he broke and entered "with intent willfully to set fire," etc., is bad on demurrer. Pairo *v.* State, 49 Ala. 25.

Same—Effect of Alleging Commission of Felony.—An indictment for burglary, though failing to allege a felonious intent, is good, if it allege that a felony was committed. Barber *v.* State, 78 Ala. 19.

"It has been allowed, in indictments for burglary, to charge what the defendants did steal, as a substitute for the averment of the intent to steal. But when this is done, there can be no conviction unless the actual stealing is proved; because, if the larceny, which includes the intent, was not committed, there is no allegation of burglary. 2 Bish. Crim. Law, § 152." Wolf *v.* State, 49 Ala. 359, 360.

Alternative Averments as to Intent.—Under Code 1886, § 4383, providing that when an offense may be committed by different means, or with different intents, these may be charged in the same count in the alternative, an indictment for burglary may allege, in a single count, that the act was committed with the intent to steal or rape. Dismukes *v.* State, 83 Ala. 287, 3 So. 671.

Alleging Consummation of Felonious Intent.—A count in an indictment, which alleges that the intent to steal with which the building was broken and entered, is not bad, because it also alleges that the intent was executed by a larceny of goods in the building. Murray *v.* State, 48 Ala. 675.

§ 14. —— Description of Building.

See ante, "Character of Building," § 4.

Where, in an indictmnet for burglary, the only description of the house, room, or inclosure broken into is "a sample room in the Arlington Hotel, a building in" a certain city, it is insufficient, since it does not show that such hotel or room was a dwelling house, or that such room was a shop, store, warehouse, or other structure, in which goods, merchandise, or other valuable thing was kept for use, sale, or deposit. Thomas *v.* State, 97 Ala. 3, 12 So. 409.

Dwelling House.—An indictment for burglary, which charges that the defendant broke into and entered "the dwell house" of a certain person, is fatally defective; the omission of the three letters "ing" from the word "dwelling" being a matter of substance. Parker *v.* State, 22 So. 791, 114 Ala. 690.

Situation of Building.—Under Cr. Code, § 3786, which provides that any person who, with intent to steal, or to commit a felony, breaks into and enters a dwelling house or any building "within the curtilage of a dwelling house," or into any building in which any "valuable thing is kept for use, sale, or deposit," shall be guilty of burglary, an indictment which charges that defendant broke into and entered a smoke house with intent to steal need not aver that such building was within the curtilage of a dwelling house. Pressley *v.* State, 111 Ala. 34, 20 So. 647.

Alleging House Was Made for Use It Is Put to.—An indictment for burglary of a chicken or hen house need not allege that the house was specially made to keep such goods, merchandise, or other valuable things. Lucas *v.* State, 39 So. 821, 144 Ala. 63, 3 L. R. A., N. S., 412.

An indictment which charges that the accused broke and entered a gin house, the property of W. R., in which was kept, for use, sale, or deposit, seed-cotton, a thing of value, etc., is sufficient, without an additional averment that the gin house was specially constructed for the use to which it was applied. Under the statute (Code, § 4343), only structures of a temporary character, erected for special purposes or occasions, require such additional descriptive averment. Stone *v.* State, 63 Ala. 115.

Alleging Nature of Building in Disjunctive.—Under Code 1907, § 6415, providing that a burglary may be committed in a store in which goods, wares, merchandise, or other valuable thing is kept, an indictment which describes the store as a place where goods, merchandise, "or" clothing, "or" things of value are kept is demurrable, as not describing the property mentioned as things of value, so as to enable the court to determine whether they were within the general terms of the statute. Hawkins *v.* State (Ala. App.), 62 So. 974.

It is no objection to an indictment for burglary, under the forms allowed by the Code, that the house broken into is alleged, in the disjunctive, to have been "a building within the curtilage of a dwelling house, or a shop, storehouse, warehouse, or other building of W. H." Ward *v.* State, 50 Ala. 120.

§ 15. —— Occupancy of Building.

See ante, "Occupancy of Building," § 6.

§ 16. —— Ownership or Possession of Building.

The Alabama statutes have not changed or abrogated the common law rule, that in indictments for burglary the ownership of the building entered must be precisely laid, and proved as averred. Beall *v.* State, 53 Ala. 460.

Ownership in Two or More Jointly.—Where the prosecutor, by consent of the owner of the freehold, erects on it a building, for their mutual convenience, which is in their joint use at the time of the burglary, the ownership is properly laid in them jointly. Webb *v.* State, 52 Ala. 422, cited in Matthews *v.* State, 55 Ala. 65, 71.

Same—Partnership.—Under Code 1876, § 4800, providing that when any property in relation to which an offense is committed belongs to several partners or owners it is sufficient to allege that the ownership is in one or more of them, an indictment for burglary from joint owners of a house need not lay ownership in more than one. White *v.* State, 72 Ala. 195.

Same—Same—Necessity of Alleging Names of Members of Firm.—An indictment under Rev. Code, § 3695, for breaking and entering a store or other building of a partnership in which goods, merchandise, or other valuable things were kept with intent to steal, is insufficient where it fails to aver the names of the persons comprising the firm. Davis *v.* State, 54 Ala. 88. See, also, Edmonds *v.* State, 87 Ala. 12, 6 So. 54.

Alleging Ownership in Tenant of Building.—An indictment for burglary properly lays the ownership of the building broken and entered in the person having, at the time of the burglary, the undisputed occupancy and possession thereof. Matthews *v.* State, 55 Ala. 65.

It is sufficient, in an indictment for burglary, to lay the ownership of the building broken into and entered, in the person in the possession and occupancy thereof. Peck *v.* State, 41 So. 759, 147 Ala. 100.

Same—Alleging Ownership in Lessee.—An indictment for burglarizing an hotel should lay the ownership of the hotel in the lessee in possession, and not in the owners of the fee. Thomas *v.* State, 97 Ala. 3, 12 So. 409.

Alleging Ownership in Estate of Decedent.—An indictment for burglary, describing the house in which the offense was committed as "the property of the estate of the late John Tate," does not contain any averment of ownership, and is fatally defective. Overruling, on this point, Murray *v.* State, 48 Ala. 675; Anderson *v.* State, 48 Ala. 665; Beall *v.* State, 53 Ala. 460.

An indictment for burglary, under the Alabama statute, for breaking and entering the pick-room of a gin house with intent to steal, is not bad on demurrer, because the gin house is described as "the property of the estate of Mrs. Lewis." This is a sufficient description of the house alleged to be broken and entered, though it should appear that Mrs. Lewis was dead, before the alleged time of the commision of the offense charged. Anderson *v.* State, 48 Ala. 665, overruled by Beall *v.* State, 53 Ala. 460.

Ownership of Railroad Car.—In an indictment under this statute, the ownership of the car broken into and entered is an indispensable averment. Graves *v.* State, 63 Ala. 134.

In an indictment under Code 1876, § 4344, making breaking and entering a railroad car burglary, the allegation of ownership should be of the real owner, though the car be in the possession of and used by another. Johnson *v.* State, 73 Ala. 483. See, also, Graves *v.* State, 63 Ala. 134.

Where a foreign railroad car was in use by the Southern Railway Company for the transportation of freight at the time it was broken open and goods stolen therefrom, the ownership of the car was properly laid in such railway company. Burrow *v.* State, 41 So. 987, 147 Ala. 114.

Averring Corporate Character of Owner.—An indictment charging that defendant, with intent to steal, broke into and entered a building, to wit, the depot of the Southern Railway Company, etc., the said depot being the property of the Southern Railway Company, a corporation, sufficiently averred corporate character. Peck *v.* State, 41 So. 759, 147 Ala. 100.

An indictment charging the breaking and entering the "store of the Perry Mason Shoe Company," but not alleging that the company was a corporation, nor, if it was a partnership, giving the names of the partners, is bad. Edmonds *v.* State, 87 Ala. 12, 6 So. 54.

Alleging Ownership of Wife's Property in Husband.—In an indictment for burglary of a smoke house used in connection with the dwelling occupied by a husband and wife, both being the property of the wife, the ownership may be laid in the husband where the smoke house is on the same premises as the dwelling, is subjected to the ordinary family uses, and the husband carries the key to, and owns and controls meat kept in, such house. Richardson *v.* State, 22 So. 558, 115 Ala. 113.

Alleging Ignorance of Christian Name by Grand Jury.—A count in an indictment for burglary laying the ownership of the house in "——— Martin, whose Christian name was to the grand jury unknown," will, after plea of not guilty, support a conviction, though the grand jury by reasonable diligence could have learned said Christian name. Jackson *v.* State, 102 Ala. 167, 15 So. 344, following Wells *v.* State, 88 Ala. 239, 7 So. 272.

§ 17. —— Description and Ownership of Property in Building or Stolen from Building.

Alleging Ownership of Partnership Property.—When it is necessary in an indictment to aver the ownership of property, it is sufficient to lay it in any one or more of several partners or owners. Williams *v.* State, 67 Ala. 183.

Alleging Ownership of Corporation's Property.—An indictment for burglary is sufficient if it avers ownership in a corporation by the corporate name. Bailey *v.* State, 22 So. 918, 116 Ala. 437.

An indictment for burglary from a corporation need not aver that it is either a foreign or a domestic corporation, or that it had power to acquire the property, or that the defendant was not a stockholder. Bailey *v.* State, 22 So. 918, 116 Ala. 437.

Averring Purpose for Which Goods Were Kept in Railroad Car.—An indictment under Code 1876, § 4344, for breaking and entering a railroad car with intent to steal, is bad if it does not aver that the goods in the car were kept for use, or on deposit, or for transportation as freight. Graves *v.* State, 63 Ala. 134.

Necessity of Averring That Property Was Kept in Store, etc.—Code, § 3695, provides that one breaking and entering any shop, store, warehouse, or other building, where goods, merchandise or other valuable thing is kept for use, sale, or deposit, with intent to steal, is guilty of burglary. Held, that an indictment charging accused with breaking and entering a shop, but omitting to state that any goods, merchandise, or other valuable thing was there kept for use, sale, or deposit, was insufficient. Crawford *v.* State, 44 Ala. 382, cited in note in 34 L. R. A., N. S., 248.

Value of Property in Building—When Necessary to Allege.—An indictment for burglary, under Rev. Code, § 3596, charging the entering a store, etc., "in which goods, wares, and merchandise, and other valuable things, were kept for use, sale, or deposit," held to be fatally defective, for not describing the valuable things, and averring the value. Neal *v.* State, 53 Ala. 465, cited in Davis *v.* State, 54 Ala. 88, 89; Henderson *v.* State, 70 Ala. 23, 24, cited in note in 34 L. R. A., N. S., 249.

An indictment charging the breaking and entry of a building in which "goods, merchandise, or other valuable thing" was kept for use is demurrable for not describing the other valuable thing so that the court might know it was valuable. Pickett *v.* State, 60 Ala. 77.

Same—Following Wording of Statute.—An indictment, under Rev. Code, § 3695, for "breaking into and entering any" "building in which goods, merchandise, or other valuable thing is kept," "with intent," etc., must specify the property or "valuable thing," the general description in the words of the statute being insufficient. Danner *v.* State, 54 Ala. 127, cited in note in 34 L. R. A., N. S., 249.

An indictment following the general language of Rev. Code, § 3695, for breaking and entering a shop, store, or other building in which goods, merchandise, or other valuable things were kept, with the intent to steal, without specifying the article or articles constituting the "other valuable things," or averring their value, is insufficient. Davis *v.* State, 54 Ala. 88, cited in note in 34 L. R. A., N. S., 249.

Same—Necessity of Alleging Value of Cotton in Cotton House.—An indictment for burglary (Rev. Code, § 3695), which charges the prisoner with breaking and entering a house, in which cotton was stored at the time, without an averment that it was a thing of value, is fatally defective. Norris *v.* State, 50 Ala. 126; Webb *v.* State, 52 Ala. 422; Robinson *v.* State, 52 Ala. 587, cited in note in 34 L. R. A., N. S., 248.

To warrant a conviction under Rev. Code, § 3695, for breaking into and entering a cotton house, it must be alleged that property of value was in the house. Rowland *v.* State, 55 Ala. 210.

Same—Sufficient Allegations of Value.—An indictment under Rev. Code, § 3695, for burglary, alleging that the building broken into contained certain specified articles, "things of value," which were there kept "for use, sale, or deposit," sufficiently alleges the value of the goods. Hurt *v.* State, 55 Ala. 214, cited in note in 34 L. R. A., N. S., 249; Williams *v.* State, 67 Ala. 183, cited in note in 34 L. R. A., N. S., 249; Kelly *v.* State, 72 Ala. 244, cited in note in 34 L. R. A., N. S., 249.

"The indictment is sufficient. It contains an averment of every fact essential to constitute the statutory offense of burglary. It was not necessary to aver the value of the corn kept in the crib. The averment that it was 'a valuable thing,' is sufficient. Norris *v.* State, 50 Ala. 126; Webb *v.* State, 52 Ala. 422." Matthews *v.* State, 55 Ala. 65, 70, cited in note in 34 L. R. A., N. S., 248, 249.

Same—When Not Necessary to Allege Value.—Under Code 1876, § 4343, punishing burglary in a house "in which any goods, merchandise, or other valuable thing is kept for use, sale, or deposit," an indictment charging the theft of specific goods need not allege value, but otherwise of anything but goods and merchandise. Henderson *v.* State, 70 Ala. 23, cited in Kelly *v.* State, 72 Ala. 244, 245; Hurst *v.* State, 79 Ala. 55, 59.

An indictment for burglary charging that accused broke into and entered a certain storehouse, "in which goods and merchandise were kept for use, sale, or deposit, with intent to steal," is not bad on demurrer because it fails to allege that "said goods and merchandise were of any value, or were valuable things." Wicks *v.* State, 44 Ala. 398.

An indictment charging the breaking and entry of a building in which "goods and merchandise" were kept for use, need not describe the goods and merchandise, or allege them to be of value, as the law presumes their value. Pickett *v.* State, 60 Ala. 77.

Same—Same—Necessity of Alleging Specific Value.—An indictment for the burglary of a store need not allege the specific value of the goods stolen. Kelly *v.* State, 72 Ala. 244.

Averment in an indictment for burglary that meal and flour, things of value, were there kept, is sufficient. The value in dollars and cents need not be stated. Matthews *v.* State, 55 Ala. 65, cited in note in 34 L. R. A., N. S., 249.

§ 18. —— Breaking and Entry.

An indictment for burglary must allege an entry. One which charges that the defendant "broke into the storehouse of M. D.," etc., "with the intent to steal," is fatally defective, because it does not aver an entrance. Pines *v.* State, 50 Ala. 153.

§ 19. —— Issues, Proof, and Variance.

§ 19 (1) Description of Building.

There was evidence that, in the building entered the owner had kept her cotton seed, meat, and other things; that there was a partition in the building, with a door in it; that the owner had no other smoke house; and that the breaking was done at the end where the meat was kept. Held, that there was evidence that the building entered was a "smoke house," as charged in the indictment. Wait *v.* State, 99 Ala. 164, 13 So. 584.

§ 19 (2) Ownership of Building.

Alleging Ownership in Tenant.—Under an indictment charging the breaking into and entering the store of M. with intent to steal, it is immaterial who owned the building, so long as M. occupied it as a store. Hale *v.* State, 26 So. 236, 122 Ala. 85.

Alleging Ownership of Wife's Property in Husband.—On a trial for the burglary of a dwelling house alleged to be the property of a certain man, proof that the legal title to the house was in the man's wife is not a fatal variance, when the man and wife occupied the house as their home. Young *v.* State, 100 Ala. 126, 14 So. 872.

There can be no conviction of burglary on a count laying the ownership of the house in a married woman, living in the house with her husband, who was the head of the family, since on these facts he will be presumed the owner. Jackson *v.* State, 102 Ala. 167, 15 So. 344.

Alleging Ownership in One of Two Joint Owners.—An indictment charging a conspiracy to commit a burglary with intent to steal the goods of S. is supported by proof that the goods belonged to S. and another, who was his dormant partner. Spradling *v.* State, 17 Ala. 440.

Ownership by Corporation.—Where the indictment for breaking and entering a railroad car alleges that the railroad company is a corporation, such allegation must be proved as laid. Johnson *v.* State, 73 Ala. 483.

When the car broken into was alleged to be the property of the B. Railroad Company, evidence that the stock of the B. Company was owned by the L. Company is incompetent to show any variance on the question of ownership. Johnson *v.* State, 98 Ala. 57, 13 So. 503.

Same—Alleging Ownership in Manager of Corporation.—Where an indictment for the burglary of a store lays the ownership of the premises in "W. H. B., business manager" of a private corporation, while the evidence shows that the store belongs to the corporation, the variance is not cured by the fact that the manager also used the store as a post office, with which the corporation had nothing to do; the presumption being, in conformity to the custom of the country, that he carried on the post office as licensee of the corporation, and not as its tenant. Aldridge *v.* State, 88 Ala. 113, 7 So. 48.

Same—Proof of Incorporation.—Where accused was charged with burglarizing a railroad car, the property of the Southern Railway Company, a corporation, etc., no proof of the incorporation of such company was required, as provided by Acts 1900-01, p. 2285, in the absence of a plea denying the existence of the corporation. Burrow *v.* State, 41 So. 987, 147 Ala. 114.

Same—When Corporate Name Has Been Changed.—The building burglarized was alleged to be the property of the T. C., I. & R. Co. The evidence showed that the company was originally incorporated as the T. C. & R. Co., but that afterwards, and before indictment, the charter was amended by changing the name to T. C., I. & R. Co. Held no variance. Brown *v.* State, 22 So. 458, 115 Ala. 74.

§ 19 (3) Value and Description of Property Stolen.

On the trial of an indictment under

Rev. Code, § 3695, for burglary in a house in which cotton was kept for use, strict correspondence between the allegations and proof as to the value of the cotton is not essential. If the thing on deposit is of any real pecuniary value, proof of such value will support the averment. Webb *v.* State, 52 Ala. 422.

Unnecessary Allegations as to Value.—Where an indictment for burglary unnecessarily alleges that there were goods of value in the house, the allegation must be proven. Gilmore *v.* State, 99 Ala. 154, 13 So. 536.

Where an indictment for burglary charged that defendant, with intent to steal, broke into and entered a store "in which goods, merchandise, or watches, things of value, were kept for use, sale, or deposit," etc., the words "things of value" were used as descriptive of the term "watches" only, and it being unnecessary to aver or prove that the goods and merchandise had value, it was immaterial that there was no evidence as to the value of a watch alleged to have been stolen, and found in defendant's possession, or as to the things kept in the store; it having been proved that goods were kept for sale in the store, as alleged. McCormick *v.* State, 37 So. 377, 141 Ala. 75, cited in note in 34 L. R. A., N. S., 249.

§ 20. Presumptions and Burden of Proof.

See post, "Intent," § 30 (2); "Effect of Possession of Property Stolen," § 31.

The possession, recently after a burglary, of goods which were stolen in the commission of the offense, throws upon the possessor the burden of explaining the possession. Neal *v.* State, 53 Ala. 465.

On indictment for burglary it is proper to charge that, if defendant, soon after the commission of the burglary, was found in possession of a part of the goods stolen, this would cast on him the burden of explaining his possession. Cooper *v.* State, 87 Ala. 135, 6 So. 303.

§ 21. Admissibility of Evidence.

§ 22. —— In General.

The defendant, a boy under fourteen years of age, sells two green hog hides shortly after a house is burglarized, from which two green hog hides were stolen, and, if Gasmus was the only person in the community in which the boy resided and where the burglary was committed who kept such articles for sale, it seems clear that the testimony that he was the only person in the neighborhood who skinned hogs was relevant and admissible. Key *v.* State, 4 Ala. App. 76, 58 So. 946, 948.

Other Burglaries.—Where a defendant is on trial for burglary, evidence of one or more burglaries, committed by the defendant, for which he is not on trial, is prima facie irrelevant, and when the record fails to show any ground for the admission of such evidence, the supreme court will not look at the record of another case, in the supreme court, between the same parties, to show that no error was committed, as was determined in regard to the same evidence in that case. Mason *v.* State, 42 Ala. 543.

§ 23. —— Intent.

See ante, "Intent," § 3; "Intent," § 13.

Evidence of a conversation between the accused and the person living in the house before the burglary, tending to show a belief that there was money in the house, is admissible. Gilmore *v.* State, 99 Ala. 154, 13 So. 536.

On a trial for burglary of a store, evidence as to the condition in which a safe therein was found the morning after it was entered is admissible; such condition being a material circumstance to show the intent with which the store had been broken into. Russell *v.* State (Ala.), 38 So. 291.

§ 24. —— Identity and Ownership of Property in Building or Stolen from Building.

A stamp book, which was like one taken from a burglarized store, and which was found in the woodshed of a codefendant to which a trial, followed by dogs, led, along which trail were found papers taken from the store, and which also led to a house where a witness testified the defendant and his codefendant left some stolen papers the night of the burglary, was admissible, even though the state's witness could not positively identify it, since the other facts and circumstances were sufficient to take to the jury the question whether it was the same book as the one stolen. Allen *v.* State, (Ala. App.), 62 So. 971.

On a prosecution for burglary, it was proper to permit a witness to testify that certain goods carried to the police headquarters were the goods found near the door of the burglarized store. Dupree *v.* State, 42 So. 1004, 148 Ala. 620.

On a trial for burglary of a storehouse, evidence that the owner of the premises showed to certain persons samples of goods taken therefrom, and that said persons afterwards found goods similar thereto on defendant's premises, was immaterial on the question of the identity of the goods found with those stolen. Crane *v.* State, 111 Ala. 45, 20 So. 590.

Identifying Coins.—A witness may be permitted to see coins found on defendant, for the purpose of identifying them as those stolen; it being, however, for the jury to say whether they were the ones taken. Russell *v.* State (Ala.), 38 So. 291.

On a trial for the burglary of a house, and the stealing therefrom of four $10 gold pieces, evidence that accused, when arrested, had on his person a $5 gold piece, and that about that time he handed ten silver dollars to a person with him, to hold, is admissible, in connection with evidence that he also handed a $10 gold piece with the silver, and had opportunities to change the pieces. Hicks *v.* State, 99 Ala. 169, 13 So. 357.

§ 25. —— Identity, Presence, and Acts of Accused.

In a burglary trial, evidence tending to show that defendant, when arrested, had on a shirt different from the one he wore the day before, and that the shirt found in defendant's house was the one worn by the man seen in the laundry burglarized the night before, was admissible to identify defendant as the person seen in the laundry, and to contradict his testimony tending to show that it was another person. Henderson *v.* State, 55 So. 437, 1 Ala. App. 154.

Acts in Connection with Confession.—Evidence is admissible, in a trial for burglary, to prove acts of the accused, performed in connection with confessions (which were ruled out) made to an officer who had him in custody, and who promised to release him if he would point out where he got the property found on him. Mountain *v.* State, 40 Ala. 344.

Connecting Two Persons as Accomplices.—As a circumstance tending to show that defendant and one indicted with him for the burglary were traveling and acting together as burglars, testimony that one of them paid the hotel bill of both is admissible. Russell *v.* State (Ala.), 38 So. 291.

On a prosecution for burglary, it was proper to permit the state to show that on the night of the crime defendant and others were together in a barroom, and were soon thereafter seen together in an eating house near the bar; the evidence of several witnesses tending to show that the burglary was committed, or planned and committed, by such persons. Dupree *v.* State, 42 So. 1004, 148 Ala. 620.

§ 26. —— Incriminating Circumstances in General.

Evidence that a certain actress played at the city the night of the burglary is made relevant by evidence that the persons whose safe was blown open sold all the tickets that night, and that defendant and one indicted with him had said that they bought the last tickets that night; these circumstances tending to show that these men were together, and they probably saw the safe in which the money was kept. Russell *v.* State (Ala.), 38 So. 291.

Tracks.—On the trial of defendant for burglary of a railroad car, it was not error to allow the state to show that tracks of a man were found on the ground near the car. Leonard *v.* State, 43 So. 214, 150 Ala. 89.

At a trial for burglary a witness was permitted, against defendant's objection, to testify that he had seen two pairs of men's shoes, "number nines," in an old uninhabited house about three-quarters of a mile from defendant's residence. Evidence previously given tended to identify goods found in this old house as having come from the burglarized storehouse, and a valise found in defendant's possession was shown to have contained goods of like kind. It also appeared that defendant and another who was suspected of being implicated in the burglary both wore a No. 9 shoe, and that on the morning after the burglary tracks of two men had been seen in the public road going to and coming from the burglarized storehouse. Held, that the evidence objected to was relevant. England *v.* State, 89 Ala. 76, 8 So. 146, cited in note in 12 L. R. A., N. S., 210.

Articles Found Near the Crime—Pictures.—Evidence of the finding near the safe in a store, the morning after it was broken into by burglars, of two pictures —the negatives of two men—which witnesses subsequently testified were the photographs of defendant and his codefendant, is admissible as a circumstance. Russell *v.* State (Ala.), 38 So. 291.

Same—Burglary Tools.—As tending to show the burglarious intent with which parties broke into a store, testimony that the next morning a chisel, hammer, and a drill, which was an attachment to a jimmy, were found near the safe, and that they were not there before, is admissible. Russell *v.* State (Ala.), 38 So. 291.

Flight—Leaving Family Behind.—Where defendant was charged with burglary of a railroad car and there was evidence tending to show his flight immediately after the discovery of the stolen goods, a part of which were found in the mine where defendant worked, it was competent to show that he was a married man and did not carry his family away with him, but sent for them after he had left the county. Leonard *v.* State, 150 Ala. 89, 43 So. 214.

Remarks as to Property Later Stolen.—Evidence that on the afternoon before the burglary, when the safe, of the persons who sold the tickets for the theater was robbed, defendant and his coindictee, while in the adjoining store, said to the proprietor that they had just bought the last tickets for the play, and that a nice bunch of money would be realized from the sale, is relevant, as tending to show that they were informing themselves as to the location and surroundings of the premises, and that the amount of money particularly attracted their notice. Russell *v.* State (Ala.), 38 So. 291.

Refusal to Allow Unconstitutional Search.—The refusal of a defendant charged with burglary to allow his house to be searched without a warrant for that purpose, being the assertion of a constitutional right, can not be construed into a criminative circumstance, and is therefore inadmissible in evidence against him. Murdock *v.* State, 68 Ala. 567.

§ 27. —— Possession by Accused of Property Stolen.

On a trial for the burglary of a storehouse, where the proprietors of the store have identified certain articles of merchandise found in defendant's possession as having been taken from the store, the articles themselves are admissible in evidence. Walker *v.* State, 97 Ala. 85, 12 So. 83, cited in note in 12 L. R. A., N. S., 211.

Where, in a prosecution for burglary, it was shown that defendant worked for prosecutrix, that flour and meat were stolen from prosecutrix's pantry to which defendant had access, the state was entitled to show that on the day following the night of the larceny defendant carried goods similar to those stolen to the house of a certain woman where the goods were found, and to show the relation existing between defendant and the woman. Pointer *v.* State, 41 So. 929, 148 Ala. 676.

In Connection with Other Evidence—Concealing Property.—In a prosecution for burglary, the fact that a watch stolen from the store burglarized was in defendant's possession in another state about six weeks thereafter was admissible, in connection with evidence that defendant, when found with the watch, had concealed it in his sleeve, and made contradictory statements, some of which were necessarily false, as to how he obtained possession thereof. McCormick *v.* State, 37 So. 377, 141 Ala. 75, cited in note in 12 L. R. A., N. S., 220.

Explaining Possession.—One found in possession of a watch alleged to have been taken from a shop by the breaking into an entering the same with intent to steal, may explain his possession, and this explanation may go to the jury, with the proof of possession. Crawford *v.*

State, 44 Ala. 45, cited in note in 12 L. R. A., N. S., 215.

It being proper in a criminal case to admit all evidence offered by defendant which may legitimately throw light on the question of who committed the offense, and the only testimony connecting defendant with the charge of entering a dwelling and taking a pistol therefrom being that of the owner's son that when he entered the house he found defendant there, defendant was entitled to show that said son owed L. certain money, that he promised L. to get his father's pistol and give it to him in payment of the debt, and that on the morning after the burglary he did give said pistol to said person. Mason *v.* State, 45 So. 472, 153 Ala. 46.

§ 28. —— Matters of Defense.

On an indictment for burglary, where it is shown that a valise, part of the stolen property, was found in defendant's house shortly afterwards, and there is evidence that defendant was in another state at the time of the burglary, evidence is competent to show that on his return, and as soon as he discovered the valise, he asked his wife, "Whose valise is that, and how came it here?" Henderson *v.* State, 70 Ala. 23, cited in Alabama, etc., R. Co. *v.* Hawk, 72 Ala. 112, 118, cited in note in 12 L. R. A., N. S., 219.

Recent Possession of Stolen Property, and Declarations Explanatory Thereof.—The possession of stolen goods, or other fruits of crime, recently after the commission of the offense, is prima facie guilty possession; yet, if the accused, when first found in the possession of such property, and before he has had an opportunity to fabricate evidence exculpatory of himself, gives a reasonable and probable account of the manner in which he acquired the possession, such evidence should always be allowed to go to the jury, as tending to rebut the presumption of guilt which might otherwise arise. "This principle has not always been observed in the past decisions of this court—notably in the case of Taylor *v.* State, 42 Ala. 529; and, perhaps, in Maynard *v.* State, 46 Ala. 85." Henderson *v.* State, 70 Ala. 23, cited in note in 12 L. R. A., N. S., 204.

§ 29. Weight and Sufficiency of Evidence.

§ 30. —— In General.

§ 30 (1) Proof of Corpus Delicti.

On a prosecution for burglary, the corpus delicti may be proved by circumstantial evidence. Dupree *v.* State, 42 So. 1004, 148 Ala. 620.

§ 30 (2) Intent.

To constitute the offense of larceny from a dwelling house, etc., under the statute, to punish "every person who shall enter any dwelling house," etc., and commit the crime of larceny therein, the entry must be made with the intent to commit a larceny, and, if made against the consent of the owner, it is conclusive of the intent; otherwise, if the entry is permissive. State *v.* Chambers, 6 Ala. 855.

§ 30 (3) Identity and Value of Stolen Property.

"There was evidence tending to prove the commission of the burglary alleged in the indictment during a night in May, 1911, and that when the fact was discovered on the following morning there was missing from the store of Anthony, which had been broken into, some cigars and and eighteen or twenty broken boxes of plug tobacco. There was also evidence tending to prove that late in the following night the appellant and one West, who was joined with him in the indictment, carried to the store of one Whatley and sold to him a lot of tobacco of the same kinds as that which was missed from Anthony's store, and which the next morning was found at Whatley's store by two policemen, who went there with a search warrant, and who delivered to Anthony some of the tobacco there found by them. Anthony testified that the tobacco which was brought back to him by the policemen was in boxes with his (Anthony's) name on them, and that he found at Whatley's store some cigars with his (Anthony's) name on them. Evidence of such circumstances afforded a basis for inference that the tobacco, in the sale of which to Whatley the appellant participated, was the same, or a part of the tobacco which had disappeared from Anthony's store." Cogbill *v.* State (Ala. App.), 62 So. 406.

In the trial of one charged with burglary in breaking and entering a corncrib, and taking corn therefrom, it is not error to charge the jury that they may conclude that the corn was of value if the proof shows that it was used for feeding purposes. Miller *v.* State, 77 Ala. 41.

§ 31. —— Effect of Possession of Property Stolen.

See ante, "Presumptions and Burden of Proof," § 20.

§ 31 (1) In General.

On a trial for burglary, it is not error to refuse a charge that proof of the recent and unexplained possession by the defendant of goods stolen from the store at the time of the burglary raised a presumption that the defendant stole the goods, but not that he had committed the burglary. Neal *v.* State, 53 Ala. 465, cited in note in 12 L. R. A., N. S., 219.

Sufficiency for Conviction.—The recent and unexplained possession by the defendant, of goods stolen from a house at the time it was burglariously entered, is evidence upon which the jury may convict of burglary. Neal *v.* State, 53 Ala. 465, 466.

Necessity of Proof of Corpus Delicti.—To make the possession of goods evidence against a person charged with stealing them, the larceny must be proved. Fuller *v.* State, 48 Ala. 273, cited in note in 12 L. R. A., N. S., 199.

To make the possession of goods evidence against a person charged with burglary, the burglary must be proved. Fuller *v.* State, 48 Ala. 273.

Sufficiency to Prove Corpus Delicti.—In the trial of one for burglary, evidence that two hides were stolen, and evidence tending to show that defendant had the two stolen hides in his possession shortly after the burglary, was sufficient, if believed, to establish the corpus delicti. Key *v.* State, 4 Ala. App. 76, 58 So. 946.

Possession of goods stolen from a house, a short time after the theft, is competent evidence of the theft, if this possession is not shown to be innocent, and if the theft was connected with a burglary, it is also competent evidence, so far as it goes, of the burglary also. Murray *v.* State, 48 Ala. 675, cited in note in 12 L. R. A., N. S., 209.

Possession Must Be of Goods Stolen Recently.—Possession of stolen goods by the accused, even though unexplained and exclusive, does not authorize the inference of his complicity in the burglary charged, unless it is also recent, or soon after the commission of the offense; and while the word recent, in this connection, is not capable of any exact definition, but varies, within a certain range, with the conditions of each particular case, and though there may be cases in which the court may, as matter of law, pronounce the possession recent; yet the question is usually one of fact for the determination of the jury, and a charge which ignores it, or withdraws it from their consideration, is erroneous. White *v.* State, 72 Ala. 195, cited in note in 12 L. R. A., N. S., 204.

Sufficiency of Possession by Two Persons of Property to Establish Confederacy.—Evidence that defendant and D. sat together in a car on a train coming from the city where the burglary had been committed the night before, and separated when arriving at a certain station, and that articles corresponding to those stolen were found on one of them, and burglar's tools were found on the other, is pertinent to show that they were confederates in committing the burglary. Russell *v.* State (Ala.), 38 So. 291, cited in note in 12 L. R. A., N. S., 220.

§ 31 (2) Effect of Possession Not Exclusive.

On prosecution of a man and wife for burglary, evidence that some of the stolen property was found thirteen months after the burglary in the possession of the wife, the husband being then in jail on another charge, was evidence to go to the jury; it further appearing that on a search of the house, just prior to the husband's arrest on such other charge, none of the stolen property was found. Randolph *v.* State, 100 Ala. 139, 14 So. 792.

§ 31 (3) Effect of Possession Accompanied by Other Evidence.

The rule that while the unexplained possession of recently stolen goods does not, as a matter of law, raise a presumption of guilt, yet, if the evidence beyond a reasonable doubt establishes a larceny accomplished by burglary, the unexplained recent possession by the defendant of the stolen goods is a fact from which the jury may conclude that the person in whose possession they were found committed the burglary. Key *v.* State, 4 Ala. App. 76, 58 So. 946.

"The recent possession of stolen goods, without an explanation of such possession, necessarily implies a connection with the felonious taking. And such taking must be referred to the deposit where the owner left his goods. If these were left in a house, and the house is found broken into and entered and the goods taken away, and the goods, or a portion of them, found with accused and concealed, this connects his possession with all the facts that reasonably lead back to the original taking. Then, if there was no other testimony in favor of the accused except the possession of the goods after the house had been found broken and entered, he might be convicted upon such testimony alone." Wicks *v.* State, 44 Ala. 398, 401.

§ 32. Trial.

§ 33. —— Questions for Jury.

Under an indictment for burglary, in breaking and entering a "cotton house" with intent to steal, the prisoner being identified as the guilty agent by his shoes, which fitted tracks found leading from the cotton house to a neighboring gin house, and thence to the house where he lived; and the evidence being conflicting as to whether any of the cotton found in the gin house was the stolen cotton of the prosecutor—a charge which instructs the jury, "that whether the cotton went to said gin house or not, was a question not necessary to be considered by them," is not an invasion of the province of the jury, nor otherwise objectionable. Walker *v.* State, 49 Ala. 398, 399.

§ 34. —— Instructions.

§ 34 (1) In General.

On a trial for burglary, an instruction that the jury may consider the fact that defendant voluntarily tried his feet in tracks said to be his, as a circumstance in his favor, is properly refused, as defendant can not make evidence for himself. Potter *v.* State, 92 Ala. 37, 9 So. 402.

Where there is evidence that defendant had a defective foot, and that tracks made by the burglar showed a similar deformity, an instruction that the jury could not find defendant guilty from this fact alone is properly refused, as it singles out one criminating circumstance, thus tending to mislead and confuse the jury, and necessitating an explanatory charge. Cooper *v.* State, 88 Ala. 107, 7 So. 47.

As to Degree of Proof.—In a prosecution for burglary, defendant's request to charge the jury that, "unless the evidence against the prisoner should be such as to exclude, to a moral certainty, every hypothesis but that of his guilt of the offense imputed to him, they must find him not guilty," should be given. Riley *v.* State, 88 Ala. 193, 7 So. 149.

Defendant's requested charge on a prosecution for burglary that, no matter how strong the circumstances, if they can be reconciled with the theory that another than defendant committed the crime, he should be acquitted, is properly refused, as ignoring the reasonableness of the other theory suggested, and the fact that his coindictee might be found to have actually committed the offense, while he was so connected with him therein as to be equally guilty. Russell *v.* State (Ala.), 38 So. 291.

Argumentative Instructions.—On a trial for burglary, a requested charge, that "the jury may look to the fact that the defendant worked with Mr. Black [the owner of the house entered] after this alleged offense, to see whether or not this shows guilty conscience on his part, and, if they think it tends to show innocence on his part, then they ought to consider such evidence, and give the defendant the benefit of all proper inferences," is properly refused, as being merely argumentative. Riley *v.* State, 88 Ala. 188, 7 So. 104.

As to Possession of Burglar's Tools.—On trial of one indicted under Code 1886, § 3788, providing that "any person who has in his possession any implement or instrument designed and intended to aid in the commission of burglary or larceny in this state, or elsewhere," is guilty of a misdemeanor, it is proper to refuse to charge that, in order to convict, it must appear that the implements found in defendant's possession "were designed and intended to aid in the commission of burglary or larceny in this state," as the place where the implements are intended to be used is not a constituent part of the offense. Davis *v.* State, 87 Ala. 10, 6 So. 266.

§ 34 (2) As to Intent.

A charge that the intent to steal must have existed "before, and not after," accused entered the house, is properly refused. Jackson *v.* State, 102 Ala. 167, 15 So. 344.

In a prosecution for breaking and entering a dwelling with intent to commit rape, a charge to the effect that if the defendant broke into and entered the house with intent to gratify his passion upon the person of a female, "either by force or by surprise, and against her consent," he was guilty as charged, was erroneous, as authorizing a conviction without proof of force. McNair *v.* State, 53 Ala. 453.

§ 34 (3) As to Possession of Stolen Property.

A requested charge, "While the law is that the recent possession of stolen goods, if unexplained, may justify a conviction, yet if defendant has explained his possession * * * to the reasonable satisfaction of the jury, and if, upon a fair consideration of all the evidence, the jury have a reasonable doubt, growing out of any part of the evidence, as to defendant's guilt, the jury must acquit him," not only correctly states the law in respect of possession and explanation thereof, but does not authorize acquittal on a reasonable doubt resting on a part of the evidence, only, requested. Hale *v.* State, 26 So. 236, 122 Ala. 85.

On a prosecution for burglary, an instruction "that, if the jury believe the evidence, they must find the defendant guilty," is improper when the only evidence of guilt is a presumption founded wholly on the possession by accused of goods stolen from the burglarized building. Crawford *v.* State, 44 Ala. 45, cited in White *v.* State, 72 Ala. 195, 200; Amos *v.* State, 73 Ala. 498, 502; Dodson *v.* State, 86 Ala. 60, 5 So. 485.

A requested charge, on a trial under an indictment charging the breaking into and entering a store with intent to steal, that, even if defendant was found in possession of the stolen goods, yet if the jury had a reasonable doubt as to whether he stole them, or as to whether he broke and entered with the intent to steal, they should acquit, is erroneous, as requiring an acquittal of burglary on a reasonable doubt of the actual stealing. Hale *v.* State, 26 So. 236, 122 Ala. 85.

Instructions Calculated to Obscure Effect of Other Evidence.—Where, in a prosecution for burglary, a watch taken from the store burglarized was found in defendant's possession, and he attempted to conceal it, and made inconsistent statements concerning it, requested instructions calculated to unduly obscure and avoid the effect of such concealment and defendant's inconsistent statements were properly refused. McCormick *v.* State, 37 So. 377, 141 Ala. 75.

A requested charge as to the effect of mere possession of stolen goods, without other evidence of guilt, is improper, where there is other evidence tending to prove defendant's guilt. Hicks *v.* State, 99 Ala. 169, 13 So. 375, cited in note in 12 L. R. A., N. S., 210.

Confusing and Misleading Instructions.—Evidence of unexplained possession of stolen property soon after a burglary is admissible and it is error to charge that, while such possession is prima facie evidence of larceny, yet, even if defendant had the stolen money, he could not be convicted, unless the evidence convinced the jury, "to the exclusion of every reasonable hypothesis other than that the defendant broke and entered the dwelling house with the intent to steal," as such charge is confusing and misleading. Dodson *v.* State, 86 Ala. 60, 5 So. 485, cited in note in 12 L. R. A., N. S., 200.

§ 34 (4) As to Explanation of Possession.

Upon an indictment for breaking into a dwelling and stealing goods, the evidence showed that the premises had been broken into, and certain goods removed, which were afterwards found in the defendant's possession; that the defendant, after his arrest, made contradictory statements as to the means by which he acquired the goods, and on the trial he testified that he bought them from a man whom he did not know, nor did he know where such person got them. The defendant thereupon asked the court to charge: "If the jury believe all the evidence in the case, they must acquit the defendant." Held, that such charge was properly refused. Ross *v.* State, 82 Ala. 65, 2 So. 139, cited in note in 12 L. R. A., N. S., 204.

§ 35. —— Verdict.

Though the several counts in an indictment for burglary charge the ownership of the premises burglarized and the things stolen in different persons, yet, where they manifestly relate to a single burglary, a general verdict is sufficient. Towns *v.* State, 111 Ala. 1, 20 So. 598.

A verdict finding the accused "guilty of burglary" is sufficient as a general verdict, and is not vitiated by the addition of the words, "and we find that the offense was committed since the 1st day of June, 1866, by agreement of counsel," the reason of this addition being that a new penal code went into operation on that day. Mountain *v.* State, 40 Ala. 344.

§ 36. Sentence and Punishment.

Where there is a conviction of both burglary and grand larceny, charged in the same count, but one punishment should be awarded. Bell *v.* State, 48 Ala. 684.

Burial.

See the titles CEMETERIES; DEAD BODIES. As to liability of estates for burial expenses, see the title EXECUTORS AND ADMINISTRATORS.

Burying Grounds.

See the title CEMETERIES. See also, the title PERPETUITIES.

Business.

As to business hours, see the title BILLS AND NOTES. As to power of infants and married women to carry on business, see the titles HUSBAND AND WIFE; INFANTS. As to restraining injuries to or interference with business, see the title INJUNCTION.

Buyer and Seller.

See the titles SALES; VENDOR AND PURCHASER.

By-Laws.

See the titles BANKS AND BANKING; CORPORATIONS; and similar titles. See, also, the title MUNICIPAL CORPORATIONS.

By-Standers.

See the titles JURY; NEW TRIAL.

Calendar.

See the titles CRIMINAL LAW; JUSTICES OF THE PEACE. As to hearing of civil cases on appeals or writs of error, see the title APPEAL AND ERROR.

Calls.

See the title BOUNDARIES. As to calls on unpaid stock subscriptions, see the title CORPORATIONS.

CANCELLATION OF INSTRUMENTS.

Cross References.

See the titles ALTERATION OF INSTRUMENTS; BILLS AND NOTES; BONDS; CONTRACTS; DEEDS; EQUITY; FRAUD; FRAUDULENT CONVEYANCES; MORTGAGES; PARTIES; REFORMATION OF INSTRUMENTS; WILLS.

I. RIGHT OF ACTION AND DEFENSES.

§ 1. Right to Cancellation.

§ 2. —— In General.

Chancery has not the power arbitrarily to annul or rescind contracts to administer justice, but is bound by rules and precedents. Sadler *v.* Robinson, 2 Stew. 520.

"When the remedy for recovery of damages at law is inadequate, equity may decree the cancellation of a contract, at the issuance of a party who has substantially complied with it, for its nonperformance by the other party, and where the parties can be placed substantially in statu quo." Ferris *v.* Hoagland, 121 Ala. 240, 25 So. 834, 836.

Where county warrants are issued for the cost of building a bridge, the contractors guaranteeing to build it in a workmanlike manner, where the bridge collapsed a year after its building on account of unworkmanlike manner of its construction, the county may maintain a suit in equity to cancel the warrant and recover the money paid on the contract. Converse Bridge Co. *v.* Geneva County, 53 So. 196, 168 Ala. 432.

Cancellation and Refusal to Enforce.—"There is a marked distinction between rescinding a contract and refusing to enforce one, and it is well settled, that a court of equity may refuse to rescind a contract, when it would not specially enforce it. Beck *v.* Simmons, 7 Ala. 71; Seymour *v.* Lelancy, 3 Cow. 530, 15 Am. Dec. 270; Jackson *v.* Ashton, 11 Pet. 248, 9 L. Ed. 698." Parks *v.* Brooks, 16 Ala. 529, 540.

Cancellation of Deed Including Land by Mistake in Transfer.—After the death of the vendor, leaving infant heirs, the purchaser may come into equity, to have his deed reformed and canceled, as to a tract of land to which the vendor had no title, and which was included in the deed by mistake. Williams *v.* Mitchell, 30 Ala. 299, 310.

Cancellation by Fraud.—Equity has jurisdiction to cancel a contract procured by fraud. Andrews *v.* Frierson, 33 So. 6, 134 Ala. 626.

Same—Misrepresentation.—A misrepresentation by the vendor, in regard to a material fact, which operated as an inducement to the purchaser, upon which the purchaser had a right to rely, and by which he was actually deceived and injured, is a fraud, and confers upon the purchaser the right to avoid the contract, whether executed or executory. Foster *v.* Gressett, 29 Ala. 393, 397.

"Where the vendor of land represented to a person who afterwards became the purchaser, that an open unmarked line would so run as to include a field of forty acres of rich bottom land on an adjoining tract, worth more than the residue of the land proposed to be sold; this representation of the vendor, which was an inducement to the purchase, was false, and he was so informed before he made it: Held, that this was such a misrepresentation of a material fact, as would authorize a court of chancery to rescind the contract. Camp *v.* Camp, 2 Ala. 632, 638; Elliott *v.* Boaz, 9 Ala. 772, 779.

"While a court of equity will rescind a contract procured by a misrepresentation by the vendor of land relating to the subject matter of the contract, and constituting an inducement to the purchaser, upon which he had a right to rely, and did rely, and by which he was actually deceived and injured, the representation must be the affirmation of a fact, in contradistinction of a mere expression of opinion." Lockwood *v.* Fitts, 90 Ala. 150, 7 So. 467.

Undue Influence.—Where one claiming as devisee seeks to recover the land from one in possession under a deed from testator subsequent to the will, a bill alleging that the deed was procured by undue influence, and praying that it be canceled on that ground, presents grounds for equitable relief. Letohatchie Baptist Church *v.* Bullock, 32 So. 58, 133 Ala. 548.

Mistake or Fraud as Necessary Grounds.—A bill which averred that a deed was executed in order to get the tenant of the grantor to vacate the property, and that the grantee promised to destroy the deed within a year, but had not done so, and asking its cancellation, but which did not allege any mistake of fact or fraudulent intent on the part of the grantee, was properly dismissed. Stacey *v.* Walter, 28 So. 89, 125 Ala. 291.

Residence of Defendant in Another State.—A court of equity will not rescind a contract where the vendor, although unable to make title, is perfectly solvent, and has been guilty of no fraud, on the ground that he is a resident of another state, when it is shown that he was such at the time of the contract, and has so continued ever since. Parks *v.* Brooks, 16 Ala. 529, cited in Magee *v.* McMillan, 30 Ala. 421.

Mortgage for Loan of Confederate State Bonds.—A mortgage will not be cancelled, nor declared void, because its consideration was a loan of Confederate

States bonds. Micou *v.* Ashurst, 55 Ala. 607.

§ 3. —— Invalidity of Instrument.

Equity has general jurisdiction to cancel void instruments affecting title to realty which do not appear on their face to be void. Smith *v.* Roney (Ala.), 62 So. 753.

Equity will not take jurisdiction to cancel a deed merely on the ground that it is uncertain. Hawthorne *v.* Jenkins (Ala.), 62 So. 505.

That respondent, by intentionally deceiving complainant by promises not intended to be kept, induced him to execute a deed which he thought to be a mortgage, pursuant to respondent's intention to defraud complainant, and that respondent afterwards mortgaged the land for a pre-existing debt to correspondent, who purchased under foreclosure, that correspondent demands possession, and that complainant offers to do equity by paying any charge upon the land, the lifting of which may be necessary to the relief prayed, entitles complainant to a cancellation of the several instruments. Gewin *v.* Shields, 52 So. 887, 167 Ala. 593.

§ 4. —— Unconscionableness, Improvidence, or Hardship.

In the absence of equities, the courts will not relieve a party from the hardships of an improvident contract. Sheldon *v.* Birmingham Building & Loan Ass'n, 25 So. 820, 121 Ala. 278.

§ 5. —— Performance or Discharge of Obligation.

Where a bill to cancel a mortgage made by complainant's intestate avers full payment of the mortgage, and offering to do equity by payment of what may be found due on the mortgage, and by submission to such decree as the court may render, the averments will authorize relief as against the mortgage. Hartley *v.* Matthews, 96 Ala. 224, 11 So. 452.

§ 6. —— Executed Contracts.

Bill to Set Aside Executed Contract. —See post, "In General," § 32 (1).

A contract, even though executed, may be canceled for fraud. Foster *v.* Gressett, 29 Ala. 393; Baker *v.* Maxwell, 99 Ala. 558, 14 So. 468.

A bill to rescind a contract whereby plaintiffs conveyed to defendant certain land in consideration of the transfer to them of certain chattel and real-estate mortgages, on the ground of fraudulent representations of defendant as to the title of the mortgagors to the mortgaged land, and the existence at the time of the mortgaged chattels, is not bad because it shows that the contract is wholly executed. Baker *v.* Maxwell, 99 Ala. 558, 14 So. 468.

§ 7. —— Injury Sustained or Anticipated.

A contract can not be avoided for fraudulent representations unless damage is shown. Bomar *v.* Rosser, 31 So. 430, 131 Ala. 215.

§ 8. Adequate Remedy at Law.

§ 9. —— In General.

"The test is, not that he has a remedy at law, but whether or not the remedy will be adequate and complete, or that he will not be subjected to vexatious litigation at a distance of time. Merritt *v.* Ehram, 116 Ala. 278, 22 So. 514." Southern States, etc., Ins. Co. *v.* Wheatley, 173 Ala. 101, 55 So. 620, 621.

It is the office of chancery to interpose, to cancel an instrument, when the law is unintentionally harsh, by the application of general principles to particular cases; or where the law forums, by reason of their rules of procedure, are so restricted in the dispensation of justice as not to embrace within their reach particular cases, because of the complexity of facts or the peculiarity of the remedy. Sadler *v.* Robinson, 2 Stew. 520, 523.

As a rule equity will refuse to entertain bills to cancel instruments affecting title to realty, where complainant is not in possession of the land, since complainant in such case has an adequate legal remedy. Smith *v.* Roney (Ala.), 62 So. 753.

A wife, whose husband sells land for which she has paid in part, and whose claim is a lien on the land, is not entitled to have the sale canceled, without showing that she can not obtain full relief out of its proceeds. Shelby *v.* Tardy, 84 Ala. 327, 4 So. 276.

The fact that a grantee, when he obtained the deed, did not intend to carry out the obligation therein expressed, of caring for the grantor during life, and of making improvements on the land, which was the consideration for the deed, is not ground for canceling the deed, since the grantor has an adequate remedy upon the obligation. Gardner *v.* Knight, 27 So. 298, 124 Ala. 273.

A deed conveying land in consideration of an agreement to support the grantor can not be canceled for breach of the undertaking, the remedy being by an action on the undertaking. Gardner *v.* Knight, 27 So. 298, 124 Ala. 273.

In Cases of Fraud.—Equity has jurisdiction to relieve against a conveyance obtained by fraud, though the complainant may have a concurrent remedy at law. Waddell *v.* Lanier, 62 Ala. 347; Smith *v.* Cockrell, 66 Ala. 64, 74, cited in note in 5 L. R. A., N. S., 1050.

§ 10. —— Void Instruments.

Instruments, though void, will be canceled in proper cases if they cast a cloud upon title to land. Gewin *v.* Shields, 52 So. 887, 167 Ala. 593.

Equity will afford specific relief, such as a court of law can not give, against an instrument which was executed on Sunday, but purporting on its face to have been executed on Saturday, notwithstanding the instrument may also be void at law. Smith *v.* Pearson, 24 Ala. 355.

Where a bill to set aside a deed alleges facts which, if true, show the deed to be absolutely void, as that the grantor was insane at the time, thereby showing that complainants have a complete and adequate remedy at law, it should be dismissed. Boddie *v.* Bush, 33 So. 826, 136 Ala. 560.

§ 11. —— Defense to Action on Instrument.

When the vendor of land fraudulently induces the vendee to purchase, by showing him lands of a superior quality, which are purchased, and afterwards lands of inferior quality are conveyed, the vendee can not make a defence at law, when sued for the purchase money. His relief is in equity, which can render complete justice to each party, by rescinding the contract, or allowing compensation. Calloway *v.* McElroy, 3 Ala. 406.

F., claiming money due him from plaintiff under a contract, drew an order on plaintiff for a portion of the amount, in favor of defendant. Defendant sued plaintiff and also instituted attachment against F. for the same sum, and garnished plaintiff as debtor to F. Plaintiff filed a bill averring that the alleged indebtedness was under a fraudulent contract for services as auctioneer rendered to plaintiff by F., procured by defendant's false representations that F.'s commissions were no higher than charged by other auctioneers, and that his services were more valuable, and alleging that defendant had a secret agreement with F. to share commissions under the contract. Plaintiff prayed a decree canceling the contract, enjoining the suits at law, and directing payment only of the reasonable value of the services. Held, that it was error to dismiss on the ground that there was adequate remedy at law, as F. never having brought suit on the contract, no judgment could be rendered in the actions brought by defendant which would be a defense to an action brought by F. Andrews *v.* Frierson, 33 So. 6, 134 Ala. 626.

Where Deed Is Fraudulently Altered.—The deed under which plaintiff claims in an ejectment suit will not be canceled on the ground that it and the record thereof have been fraudulently altered. Wilson *v.* Miller, 39 So. 178, 143 Ala. 264.

Where There Is Danger of Losing Evidence to Establish the Defense.—One induced by fraud to make a purchase, giving notes and a mortgage in part payment, has not an adequate remedy at law, though the notes and mortgage are nonnegotiable, as action thereon may be delayed until evidence to establish his defense is not available, and hence he may maintain a bill for cancellation. Merritt *v.* Ehrman, 22 So. 514, 116 Ala. 278, cited in note in 5 L. R. A., N. S., 1038.

When Right to Defend at Law Lost.—Where the mortgagee took the mortgaged property by writ of seizure after payment of the mortgage debt, and brought detinue to recover it, the mortgagor could have shown payment of the debt to defeat recovery, and, if judgment went against her in the detinue action, could have appealed. Where she did not set up such defense in the detinue action, but permitted judgment to go against her, she can not afterwards sue to compel the surrender and cancellation of the mortgage on the ground that the debt has been paid. Hardeman *v.* Donaghey, 170 Ala. 362, 54 So. 172.

§ 12. —— Recovery of Consideration or of Property Conveyed.

"The deed being absolutely void at law, no necessity exists for invoking the exercise of the jurisdiction of a court of equity to have it declared void. As the law affords a plain and adequate remedy for a recovery of the possession of the lands, the bill is without equity. Daniel *v.* Stewart, 55 Ala. 278; Tyson *v.* Brown, 64 Ala. 244; Peeples *v.* Burns, 77 Ala. 290; Smith *v.* Cockrell, 66 Ala. 64; Arnett *v.* Bailey, 60 Ala. 435; Lehman, etc., Co. *v.* Shook, 69 Ala. 486; Curry *v.* Peebles, 83 Ala. 225, 3 So. 622; Armstrong *v.* Conner, 86 Ala. 350, 5 So. 451; Williams *v.* Lawrence, 123 Ala. 588, 26 So. 647; Brown *v.* Hunter, 121 Ala. 210, 25 So. 924." Wilkinson *v.* Wilkinson, 129 Ala. 279, 30 So. 578, 579.

Where a contract was made by which plaintiff gave defendant a half interest in a lot allowed him to control the rents and profits, and provided that it should not be sold within ten years without his consent, and the contract is attacked on the ground of plaintiff's mental incapacity, the remedy at law, by recovery of possession of the lot, is inadequate, and a bill to cancel the contract may be maintained. Luffboro *v.* Foster, 92 Ala. 477, 9 So. 281.

Where the grantor in a deed which was procured by fraud delivered possession to the grantee, he can not regain possession, so as to maintain an action in equity to cancel the deed, by contracting with the tenants of such grantee to lease the premises to them. Treadwell *v.* Torbert, 32 So. 126, 133 Ala. 504.

Where There Is a Legal Remedy by Which to Regain Possession.—One claiming as devisee who seeks to recover the land from one in possession under a deed from testator subsequent to the will which deed the devisee claims is void because the grantor lacked mental capacity, and because it attempts to convey the homestead without his wife joining, has a plain and adequate remedy at law, and hence can not maintain a bill in equity to set the deed aside. Letohatchie Baptist Church *v.* Bullock, 32 So. 58, 133 Ala. 548.

On a bill filed for the purpose of having a certain conveyance declared void and canceled upon the ground that the grantor therein is non compos mentis, and incapable of contracting, where it appears that the complainant was out of possession of the property at the time of the institution of the suit, there exists no necessity for invoking the jurisdiction of a court of equity, and such bill is without equity; the law affording a plain and adequate remedy for the recovery and possession of the land. Wilkinson *v.* Wilkinson, 30 So. 578, 129 Ala. 279.

Where Ejectment Proper Action.—A purchaser, at a sheriff's sale of execution, of lands fraudulently conveyed by the judgment debtor, has a plain and adequate remedy at law by action of ejectment, and that he can not come into chancery, before acquiring possession at law, to obtain cancellation of the fraudulent conveyance, as a cloud on his title. Smith *v.* Cockrell, 66 Ala. 64; Grigg *v.* Swindal, 67 Ala. 187; Pettus *v.* Glover, 68 Ala. 417.

A bill will not lie to cancel a deed made by an alleged insane person, where he is not in possession of the land at the time it is filed, there being an adequate remedy by ejectment. Galloway *v.* McLain, 31 So. 603, 131 Ala. 280.

Where the grantor in a deed which was procured by duress or other fraud is not in possession of the land, and can bring ejectment, he can not maintain an action in equity to cancel the deed or remove cloud from his title. Treadwell *v.* Torbert, 32 So. 126, 133 Ala. 504.

Where Detinue Proper Action.—Where the mortgagee of chattels converted the mortgaged property after the debt was paid, and the legal title had revested in the mortgagor, pursuant to statute, the mortgagor could have recovered the property in detinue. He can not sue in equity to compel the surrender of the mortgage and its cancellation; the legal remedy being adequate. Hardeman *v.* Donaghey, 170 Ala. 362, 54 So. 172.

§ 13. —— Recovery of Damages.

Equity will not cancel a deed whereby land was conveyed to a manufacturing company in consideration of its agreement to establish its works thereon and operate them for a stated time, and of the incidental benefits expected to accrue therefrom to the grantor, because of the company's failure to operate the works for the stipulated time; the remedy being an action at law for breach of the agreement. Piedmont Land & Improvement Co. *v.* Piedmont Foundry & Machine Co., 96 Ala. 389, 11 So. 332.

When Action Will Lie on Covenants of Warranty.—A grantee under a contract for the sale of land, which was induced by fraudulent representations by the vendor, is entitled to maintain a suit in equity to compel a rescission of the contract, though he may also sue at law on the covenants of warranty contained in the deed. Perry *v.* Boyd, 28 So. 711, 126 Ala. 162.

Where a purchaser of real estate enters into possession under a conveyance with covenants of warranty, though the grantor has no title, if he has committed no fraud, and is not insolvent, and there is no other independent equity, the grantee is protected by the grantor's covenants of warranty and a rescission of the contract will not be decreed. Fields *v.* Clayton, 23 So. 530, 117 Ala. 538.

A purchaser of land under a deed with covenants of warranty, who has taken and continues in possession under such purchase and conveyance, can not, in the absence of fraud in the sale or the insolvency of his vendor, in defense of a bill filed by the vendor to enforce his lien for the purchase money, maintain a cross bill for the rescission of the sale, on the ground that his vendor was without title, notwithstanding the fact that the title to such land was at the time of such sale in the United States, and that the vendee had since such sale and conveyance entered the land as a homestead. Vice *v.* Littlejohn, 22 So. 488, 116 Ala. 276.

Same—Deceit.—The jurisdiction of equity to rescind a contract, for fraud, is not taken away because the purchaser may also have a remedy at law for deceit, or on his covenants of warranty. Cullum *v.* Bank, 4 Ala. 21; Baptiste *v.* Peters, 51 Ala. 158, 160; Southern States Fire, etc., Ins. Co. *v.* Wheatley, 173 Ala. 101, 55 So. 620; Fay, etc., Co. *v.* Independent Lumber Co. (Ala.), 59 So. 470.

A court of equity will rescind a contract for the sale of land, at the suit of a purchaser who contracted for a good title, and who has abandoned the possession on discovering that his vendor had no title, although the proof shows only a mistake on the part of the vendor, in his assertions of title, without fraudulent misrepresentations, and although the purchaser might have a remedy, by action at law, for deceit, or on his covenants of warranty. Baptiste *v.* Peters, 51 Ala. 158, cited in Porter *v.* Collins, 90 Ala. 510, 8 So. 80; Perry *v.* Boyd, 126 Ala. 168, 28 So. 711.

Where Trover or Trespass Proper.—Where the mortgagee of chattels converted the mortgaged property after the debt was paid and the legal title had revested in the mortgagor pursuant to statute, the mortgagor could have recovered damages for taking of the property in trover or trespass, but he can not sue in equity to compel the surrender of the mortgage and its cancellation, as his legal remedy is adequate. Hardeman *v.* Donaghey, 170 Ala. 362, 54 So. 172.

§ 14. —— Insolvency of Defendant.

The bill to cancel a mining lease for breaches, and for an accounting as for rents, by alleging that defendant is insolvent and unable to work the property as contemplated by the contract, shows that any remedy at law would be neither adequate nor complete. Peerless Coal Co. *v.* Lamar (Ala.), 60 So. 837.

N. sold to G. land, giving a title bond for a portion and a deed for the balance. The purchaser gave three notes, the first two due absolutely, and the last on condition of full title. N. transferred all the notes, became insolvent, and left the state, without being able to make title to one quarter section of land. Held, that the payment by G. in good faith of the note first due, and of the conditional one, with notice of the transfer of the second note, will not entitle him to be relieved in equity against the payment of such second note. Graham *v.* Nesmith, 18 Ala. 763.

A purchaser of land had stipulated for a good title, on payment of the purchase money. The title was in heirs who were nonresidents. The parties to a bond indemnifying such purchaser against a mortgage on the land were also nonresidents. One of the vendors was shown to be insolvent, and the other did not show his ability to respond in damages. The vendors had no title. Held, that a court of chancery would afford relief by rescission. Griggs *v.* Woodruff, 14 Ala. 9.

Where a vendor has died insolvent, the vendee may file a bill against his representative to rescind the sale and for a return of the purchase money, for the fraudulent representation of the vendor that he had title when he had none, without surrendering possession of the premises. Greenlee *v.* Gaines, 13 Ala. 198.

"If there be fraud or failure of title, and the vendor is insolvent, equity will interpose and grant what relief it can, whether the purchaser have a deed and is in possession or not. Younge *v.* Harris, 2 Ala. 108; McLemore *v.* Mabson, 20 Ala. 137; Walton *v.* Bonham, 24 Ala. 513; Kelly *v.* Allen, 34 Ala. 663." Parker *v.* Parker, 93 Ala. 80, 9 So. 426, 427.

Insolvency as Prerequisite to Cancellation for Breach of Warranty.—Equity has no jurisdiction to decree rescission of a contract for the sale of land on the ground of breach of warranty, where it is not shown that the vendor was insolvent. Parker *v.* Parker, 93 Ala. 80, 9 So. 426.

§ 15. Ratification.

See post, "Limitations and Laches," § 29.

Knowledge.—As to necessity of alleging knowledge in answer, see post, "Plea or Answer," § 33.

A confirmation of an invalid contract, to be operative as such, must be made with full knowledge of all the facts, the ignorance of which rendered the previous contract void, and with the intent that such act should confirm it. Johnson *v.* Johnson, 5 Ala. 90.

Where it does not appear that complainants had knowledge of the fraud at the time they transferred the mortgagees to such third person, or at any time before the bill was filed, the bill is not bad on the ground that it shows that the fraud had been condoned and the transaction ratified, or that complainants were guilty of laches. Baker *v.* Maxwell, 99 Ala. 558, 14 So. 468.

Plaintiff, who had conveyed defendant land in consideration of defendant's transfer to him of certain mortgages, is not deprived of his right to compel a reconveyance, for defendant's fraudulent representations as to the title of the mortgagors, by the fact that he assigned the mortgages for value to a third person, if he had no knowledge of the fraud at the time of the assignment, and if he afterwards took an assignment back from such third person. Baker *v.* Maxwell, 99 Ala. 558, 14 So. 468.

Same—Effect of Discovery of Second Ground for Cancellation after Contract Ratified as to First.—Submission to one fraudulent misrepresentation does not bind the party to submit to all he afterwards discovers; and if, upon afterwards discovering more, he brings his bill to rescind, his first submission will not bind him even as to the misrepresentations already submitted to. Pierce *v.* Wilson, 34 Ala. 596.

Ratification Induced by Undue Influence.—A court of equity will not rescind a contract on account of the vendor's fraud, when it is shown that the purchaser, after becoming fully apprised of the fraud, ratified and confirmed the contract; but this principle does not apply where the purchaser, being a weak and feeble old man, and having unlimited confidence in the vendor, is induced, by professions of friendship and promises of indulgence on the part of the latter, to execute a mortgage to secure the payment of the purchase money, and afterwards to release the equity of redemption. Thompson *v.* Lee, 31 Ala. 292.

How Contract May Be Ratified.—But the right to a rescission of the contract on the ground of fraud may be lost, either by an affirmance of the contract after the discovery of the fraud, or by the failure to manifest the election to disaffirm it within a reasonable time after the discovery of the fraud. Foster *v.* Gressett, 29 Ala. 393.

Same—Exercising Rights of Ownership over Property.—Equity will not rescind a contract at the instance of the purchaser, when it appears that his bill was not filed within a reasonable time after his discovery of the alleged fraud; that he sold a portion of the property after the discovery, thus depriving himself of the power to place the defendant in statu quo; and did sundry other acts under the authority of the rights conferred on him by the contract. Betts *v.* Gunn, 31 Ala. 219, cited in Stephenson *v.* Allison, 123 Ala. 439, 26 So. 290.

Where a party to a contract with a full knowledge of fraudulent circumstances invalidating it, enters into new stipulations regarding it, a court of equity will not afterwards rescind the contract at his instance. Sadler *v.* Robinson, 2 Stew. 520, cited in Thompson *v.* Lee, 31 Ala. 304.

A party will not be permitted to rescind and cancel a contract, if he fails to promptly disaffirm same after a discovery of the fraud. He can not deal with the property acquired under the sale as his own after discovering the fraud and afterwards rescind. Stephenson *v.* Allison, 123 Ala. 439, 26 So. 290; Dill *v.* Camp, 22 Ala. 249; Barnett *v.* Stanton, 2 Ala. 181; Graybill *v.* Drennen, 150 Ala. 227, 43 So. 568, 570; Garrett *v.* Lynch, 45 Ala. 204.

In a suit to rescind an exchange of lands and to cancel the conveyance of complainant on the ground of fraudulent representations as to the value and location of lots conveyed by defendant, the testimony showed that the exchange was made in March, and that in April complainant discovered that the lots were not as valuable as represented, nor situated where he had been led to suppose them to be. There was a mortgage on the lots, which complainant assumed in consideration of six additional lots. In May he began to negotiate with defendant for the exchange of other lands, and in July he wrote to defendant's agent, stating that he wished to exchange the lots included in the second agreement, as well as those in the first exchange, for renting property, so that he might be able to meet the interest due on the mortgage in September. In August he notified defendant that he would not execute the second agreement, and offered to rescind the exchange already consummated. Held, that he had waived his right to rescind by continuing to treat the property as his own after discovery of the alleged frauds. Lockwood *v.* Fitts, 90 Ala. 150, 7 So. 467.

Same—Treating Contract as in Force.—"Mr. Pomeroy says: 'All these considerations as to the nature of misrepresentation require great punctuality and promptness of action by the deceived party upon his discovery of the fraud. * * * If, after discovering the untruth of the representations, he conducts himself with reference to the transaction as though it was still subsisting and binding, he thereby waives all benefit of and relief from the misrepresentations." 2 Pom. Eq. Jur., § 897." Lockwood *v.* Fitts, 90 Ala. 150, 7 So. 467, 468; Howle *v.* North Birmingham Land Co., 95 Ala. 389, 11 So. 15, 16.

Same—Delay.—Long acquiescence in a contract that might have been rescinded is ratification. Sheffield, etc., Coal Co. *v.* Neill, 87 Ala. 158, 6 So. 1, 2.

"Undue and unnecessary delay in exercising the power of rescission is regarded as evidence of an election to treat the sale as valid, but is dependent for its weight upon existing circumstances." Orendorff *v.* Tallman, 90 Ala. 441, 7 So. 821, 822.

Same—Receiving Benefit under Contract.—One who, after the discovery of the fraud by which he was induced to enter into a contract, treats the contract as in force, and receives benefits therefrom, can not thereafter disaffirm it. Stephenson *v.* Allison, 123 Ala. 439, 26 So. 290.

§ 16. Estoppel or Waiver.

See post, "Limitations and Laches," § 29.

"The right to rescind may be waived by the party in whom it resides, whether he be the one originally injured, or his successor in interest; and such waiver may be implied from conduct inconsistent with an intention to exercise it, including acquiescence in the transaction for an unreasonable length of time. Howle *v.* North Birmingham Land Co., 95 Ala. 389, 11 So. 15; Lockwood *v.* Fitts, 90 Ala. 150, 7 So. 467." Walling *v.* Thomas, 133 Ala. 426, 31 So. 982, 983.

Defendant, who had employed complainant's son, after the termination of the employment, accused the son of having embezzled funds from defendant, and he stated to one who acted as the son's adviser that, if a settlement was not made, the son would be prosecuted, whereupon such person and the son visited complainant and stated that the prosecution would be commenced unless she made a conveyance of certain real estate which was done and which defendant accepted. Held, that complainant was not estopped in an action to cancel the conveyance from setting up the truth of the transaction and obtaining relief in equity. Martin *v.* Evans, 50 So. 997, 163 Ala. 657.

Defendant, deriving his title to land from an entry at the land office, sold it to plaintiff's testator. Defendant's entry was afterwards vacated for fraud, and the vendee dying, the land was sold by his executor, under an order of the probate court, and bid off by him. Held, that the executor was not precluded, by becoming the purchaser at such sale, when all the vendee's right and interest in the land had been extinguished prior thereto by the cancellation of the entry, from having the contract rescinded in equity. Bryant *v.* Boothe, 30 Ala. 311.

Waiver by Accepting Bond Indemnifying against Fraud.—A party to a contract waives his right to rescind it for fraud by which he was induced to enter into it, by accepting a bond from the other party as indemnity for any loss which he may sustain through the alleged fraud. Griggs *v.* Woodruff, 14 Ala. 9.

Accepting Conveyance after Discovery of Defect in Title.—A party entitled to rescind a contract for the purchase of lands, because of failure of title as to part, waives that right by accepting a conveyance of the residue without objection. Harrison *v.* Deramus, 33 Ala. 463.

§ 17. Conditions Precedent.

§ 18. —— In General.

One in possession of land need not first test his title in an action at law before suing to cancel an instrument as a cloud. Gewin *v.* Shields, 52 So. 887, 167 Ala. 593.

Restoration of Possession to Real Property.—The purchaser of land, who has entered under the contract, can not rescind the contract without giving up possession of the land. Duncan *v.* Jeter, 5 Ala. 604; Parks *v.* Brooks, 16 Ala. 529.

Where the vendee, on discovering that a portion (one-fourth) of the land purchased, including the dwelling house and improvements, was public land, voluntarily entered it before his notes for the purchase money were due, and then insisted on a rescission of the contract, but did not offer to restore the land. Held, that the purchaser was not entitled to a rescission of the contract. Gallagher *v.* Witherington, 29 Ala. 420.

When Restoration Unnecessary.—Where a vendee retains possession of the land, a court of equity will not rescind the contract, unless these be some special ground for its interposition—such as the vendor's inability to make title, coupled with his insolvency, or fraud in the sale. Parks *v.* Brooks, 16 Ala. 529.

Same—Retention of Possession Necessary to Purchaser's Indemnity.—In a case free from fraud, equity will not rescind a conveyance on account of a want, or defect of title, but will leave the purchaser to his remedy at law, if he has not abandoned or restored possession, unless its retention is necessary to his reimbursement or indemnity. Thompson *v.* Sheppard, 85 Ala. 611, 5 So. 334.

Where a vendee of land, who has paid a part of the purchase, and has been put in possession of the land, and has made improvements thereon more valuable than the use, seeks to have the sale rescinded in equity for fraud, he need not first abandon the possession, but may retain it as a lien for reimbursement, accounting for rents. Bailey *v.* Jordan, 32 Ala. 50.

Same—Insolvency.—If a vendee of land wishes to rescind the contract of sale he must abandon the possession, unless some circumstance, such as the insolvency of the vendor, or other sufficient cause authorizes the retention of possession for his indemnity. Duncan *v.* Jeter, 5 Ala. 604; Clemens *v.* Loggins, 1 Ala. 622; Griggs *v.* Woodruff, 14 Ala. 9.

If a vendor is insolvent, the vendee, who proposes to rescind the contract, is not bound to abandon the possession before he can file a bill to enforce a rescission. Elliott *v.* Boaz, 9 Ala. 772.

Same—Purchase Induced by Fraud.—When a purchaser of land seeks a rescission of the contract in equity, on the ground of mistake, want of title, or defect of title, he is required first to abandon the possession of the land, unless its retention is necessary for his reimbursement or indemnity; but, where fraud is the ground of his application, a different rule prevails. Garner, etc., Co. *v.* Leverett, 32 Ala. 410.

It is not a prerequisite to the maintenance of a bill by a purchaser of real estate to compel a rescission of the contract for fraud that a deed of reconveyance should have been tendered or possession of the property restored or abandoned to the vendor. Perry *v.* Boyd, 28 So. 711, 126 Ala. 162.

Where a purchaser of land seeks equity to rescind the contract of purchase on the ground of fraud, it is not necessary that he should first abandon the possession of the land. Garner *v.* Leverett, 32 Ala. 410.

"The authorities all agree, that if a purchaser has been induced by fraudulent means to enter into a contract, and expends money, or pays it as purchase money, he may apply to a court of equity for a rescission and relief, without yielding up the possession. Edwards *v.* McLeary, 1 Cooper's Sel. Cases, 308; 2 Swanston, 303. But in the case of Duncan *v.* Jeter, 5 Ala. 604." Parks *v.* Brooks, 16 Ala. 529, 539.

Averment That Restoration of Possession Will Cause Injury to Plaintiff.—Where a vendee of land seeks by his bill a rescission of the contract, and an account for purchase money paid, and improvements, an averment that, in the event of a rescission of the contract, he will lose a considerable portion of the purchase money and of the amount due for improvements, if he is compelled to abandon all recourse upon such interest in the land as the vendor has, and to trust to the personal responsibility and solvency of the vendor, shows a sufficient excuse for the retention of possession. Read *v.* Walker, 18 Ala. 323.

§ 19. —— Performance by Plaintiff.

If the vendee of land wishes to rescind the contract of sale, he must pay, or offer to pay the purchase money, according to his contract. Duncan *v.* Jeter, 5 Ala. 604; Clemens *v.* Loggins, 1 Ala. 622.

When Tender of Performance Unnecessary.—When the vendor is unable to make title, a tender of the purchase money, and demand of title, is not essential to the vendee's right to maintain an action to rescind the contract. Griggs *v.* Woodruff, 14 Ala. 9.

Where the vendor has no title, and can not procure or cause one to be made, the law does not impose on the vendee the useless ceremony of preparing and tendering a deed, before he can apply to a court of equity for a rescission of the contract, since he would not be bound, under such circumstances, to accept the deed, although the vendor should be willing to execute it. Read *v.* Walker, 18 Ala. 323.

§ 20. —— Notice and Demand.

See post, "Limitations and Laches," § 29.

To maintain a bill to cancel a mortgage, given to secure the payment of a sum for the privilege of selling a patent right in a given territory, on the ground that plaintiff was induced to execute it by false and fraudulent representations of defendants, plaintiff must show a demand for a cancellation of the contract and defendants' refusal. Stephenson *v.* Allison, 26 So. 290, 123 Ala. 439.

"Where the purpose of the seller is to rescind, he should give an explicit notice to that effect, or do some positive act of equivalent import, which will put the opposite party on his guard, or else manifest his intention to rescind by filing his bill. It has been held in many cases that a vendor of land can not put an end to a contract of sale, without a formal and reasonable notice that, unless the purchaser shall fulfill it, and vendor will not hold himself bound. Falls *v.* Carpenter, 1 Dev. & B. Eq. 237. It has accordingly been decided that 'a notice that nonperformance by a certain day would be regarded as equivalent to a refusal to fulfill the contract is not tantamount to a notice that the contract would then be considered as rescinded.' Johnson *v.* Evans, 50 Amer. Dec. 678, note. We may safely say, in the absence of suit brought, or of a formal notice, that no word or act will operate as notice of such intention which is not positive in its character and unambiguous in meaning, as showing a clear purpose to put an end to the contract, unless the opposite party shall comply with his part of the agreement in a reasonable time. Bryant *v.* Isburgh, 74 Amer. Dec. 659, note." Sheffield, etc., Coal Co. *v.* Neill, 87 Ala. 158, 6 So. 1, 2.

When Offer to Rescind Not Necessary.—"An offer to rescind the contract by the vendee will be dispensed with, if the vendor by his answer shows the offer, if it had been made, would not have been acceded to. Elliott *v.* Boaz, 9 Ala. 772." Griggs *v.* Woodruff, 14 Ala. 9, 19.

Where the vendor of lands, in answer to a bill by the vendee for a rescission, insists that the sale was fair and bona fide, and an offer made to him to rescind would have been unavailing, the bill should not be dismissed because it is not proved that an offer was in fact made before it was filed. Elliott *v.* Boaz, 9 Ala. 772.

Where the vendor of land, who induced the purchaser to buy by fraudulent representations, removed from the state with all his property before the fraud was discovered, and after he had collected about one-half of the price, and had transferred a note for the balance to a nonresident, who recovered judgment thereon, and the vendee died a few months after the purchase, and before the fraud was discovered, and one of his heirs was a minor when a bill for rescission was filed by the heirs, there was no necessity of an offer to rescind prior to the filing of the bill. Foster *v.* Gressett, 29 Ala. 393.

Delay in Offer to Rescind.—Prompt action is required in all cases, where a party is invested with an option to rescind, where there has been or is likely to be a rapid fluctuation in the market price value of the property. Gilmer *v.* Morris, 80 Ala. 78. "He will not be permitted," it has been said, "to lie by and watch for the rise or fall in the value of the property, and then act according to his interest in the matter." The just reason, given by Chief Justice Ruffin, supra, is "because a favorable change ought not to profit him who would not run the risk of an unfavorable one." Sheffield, etc., Coal Co. *v.* Neill, 87 Ala. 158, 6 So. 1, 2.

An offer to rescind, six months after complainants learned of the vendor's want of title, is made within a reasonable time when it appears that complainants were strangers, and citizens of another state, and that yellow fever was prevalent where the vendors lived during the time between the discovery and the offer. Orendorff *v.* Tallman, 90 Ala. 441, 7 So. 821.

§ 21. —— Restoration of Former Status of Parties.

"The complainant is not entitled to a rescission of the contract described in the bill, because there is no offer on his part to place the defendant in statu quo." Betts *v.* Gunn, 31 Ala. 219, 221.

When Relief at Law Is Sought.—While equity, in decreeing rescission of a conveyance for duress, may require the grantor seeking relief to restore the consideration as a consideration precedent, yet a court of law has no such power, and the grantor seeking relief at law must voluntarily put the other party in statu quo, which includes a restoration of the payment made by the grantee to protect the title and made as provided in the contract of sale. Royal *v.* Goss, 45 So. 231, 154 Ala. 117.

§ 22. —— Restoration of Consideration or Benefit.

§ 22 (1) In General.

"The party who would disaffirm a fraudulent contract must return whatever he has received from it. This is on a plain and just principle. He can not hold on such part of the contract as may be desirable on his part, and avoid the residue, but must rescind in toto, if at all." Stephenson *v.* Allison, 123 Ala. 439, 26 So. 290, 292.

Before the successors in interest of the signer of a chattel mortgage can bring an action for the recovery of the property on the ground of the incapacity of the mortgagor at the time it was executed, they must disaffirm the contract and tender the amount of the consideration. Snead *v.* Scott (Ala.), 62 So. 36.

The principal, seeking to set aside the agent's purchase at the mortgage sale, will be required, at least, to refund the purchase money paid, with interest, moneys expended in repairs and permanent improvements, taxes, and other lawful charges, with interest thereon; while the agent will be required to account for rents and profits, or, if in possession, for use and occupation, as of the value of the property when he took possession, not estimating the increased value by reason of his improvements. Adams *v.* Sayre, 76 Ala. 509.

When a material fact is misrepresented, and the other party relies and acts upon it, a court of equity will, at the suit of the latter, rescind the contract; and, when a purchaser is entitled to a rescission of the contract by reason of material misrepresentations of the seller upon which the purchaser relied, the purchase money, if paid, must be refunded, and, if not paid, its collection will be enjoined without regard to the solvency of the vendor. Lanier *v.* Hill, 25 Ala. 554; Kelly *v.* Allen, 34 Ala. 663; Baptiste *v.* Peters, 51 Ala. 158; Perry *v.* Boyd, 126 Ala. 162, 28 So. 711, 712; New England Mortg., etc., Co. *v.* Powell, 97 Ala. 483, 12 So. 55, 57.

When Restoration of Consideration Unnecessary.—"We have recently considered the question, whether it is indispensable to the maintenance of a bill for the rescission of a contract on the ground of fraud, that there should have been an antecedent restoration, of what the complainant had received under the contract; and we regard that question as settled in the negative. Garner, etc., Co. *v.* Leverett, 32 Ala. 410; Bailey *v.* Jordan, 32 Ala. 50. See, also, Abbott *v.* Allen, 2 Johns. Ch. 519, 7 Am. Dec. 554; Parham *v.* Randolph, 4 How. (Miss.) 435, 35 Am. Dec. 403; Edwards *v.* M'Leay, Coop. 308; S. C., 2 Swanst. 302." Martin *v.* Martin, 35 Ala. 560, 566.

Where a bill to avoid a conveyance shows that the use of the land during defendant's possession has been of greater value than the consideration paid, an offer to return the consideration is unnecessary. Walling *v.* Thomas, 31 So. 982, 133 Ala. 426.

"Equity will not assist one to repudiate a contract and retain its benefits. Hence a bill for rescission must ordinarily offer to do equity, by restoring the party called on to rescind such consideration as he has paid, with interest or other compensation for its use. But exception to this rule occurs where the defendant has been fully reimbursed of his expenditures by what he has received under the contract. Highby *v.* Whittaker, 8 Ohio, 198; Wilson *v.* Moriarty, 77 Cal. 596, 20 Pac. 134; 18 Enc. Pl. & Prac. 834." Walling *v.* Thomas, 133 Ala. 426, 31 So. 982, 983.

Offer to Refund Consideration Made in Bill.—See post, "Offer to Restore Consideration or Benefits," § 32 (4).

While one who, owing to the undue influence of others, is led to execute a contract to his prejudice, must disaffirm the transaction at the earliest moment after discovery of the fraud, and offer to return whatever he has received he may make the offer to return in a bill filed by him to set aside the contract, his failure to do so prior to the bill being only material as affecting the question of costs. McLeod *v.* McLeod, 34 So. 228, 137 Ala. 267.

§ 22 (2) Consideration for Deed or Mortgage.

A complainant who seeks to have a cloud removed from his title to his homestead, by having a mortgage executed by him annulled as to the homestead, must offer to repay the amount he has received on such mortgage, with lawful interest, before he can receive the aid of a court of equity. Grider *v.* American Freehold Land Mortg. Co., 99 Ala. 281, 12 So. 775.

Equity will decree the cancellation of a mortgage acknowledged by one incompetent to take acknowledgments only on condition that mortgagee return any unpaid portion of the money borrowed, or its equivalent, with legal interest. Hayes *v.* Southern Home Building & Loan Ass'n, 26 So. 527, 124 Ala. 663.

A mortgage given to a foreign corporation for a loan will not, at the instance of the mortgagor, be canceled as a cloud on his title because the corporation, when it took the mortgage, had not complied with the requirements prescribed by statute as conditions precedent to its right to do business in the state, without the mortgagor returning the amount due on the mortgage, with lawful interest. George *v.* New England Mortgage Security Co., 109 Ala. 548, 20 So. 331.

Where Mortgage Was Given to Secure Pre-Existing Debt.—The rule that in order to rescind an invalid mortgage the mortgagor must return the money obtained does not apply where the mortgage was given to secure a pre-existing indebtedness. Jenkins *v.* Jonas Schwab Co., 35 So. 649, 138 Ala. 664.

§ 22 (3) Contracts of Sale of Land.

Where a mortgagor seeks to set aside a purchase under a mortgage, by his agent, of property which was in the agent's control, with power to rent and sell it, he will be required to do equity by paying the amount paid for the property. Adams *v.* Sayre, 76 Ala. 509.

Where the proceeds of land sold under a void order of probate are applied by the administrator in part to the debts of the estate, and the balance given to the guardian, and by him used for minor heirs of the intestate, they, never having tendered back the price, can not assert title to the land. Robertson *v.* Bradford, 73 Ala. 116; Ellis *v.* Ellis, 84 Ala. 348, 4 So. 868.

Repaying Money Advanced by Purchaser to Pay Mortgage.—Where a purchaser in a deed procured by duress from the grantor paid a mortgage assumed as a part of the consideration, the grantor as a condition precedent to avoiding the deed must repay the amount within a reasonable time after the removal of the duress, or the deed will be binding. Royal *v.* Goss, 154 Ala. 117, 45 So. 231.

Offering to Set-Off the Consideration Received.—Offer by a grantor, seeking to cancel a deed of homestead because of imperfect execution, to set-off against the price received, which he should return, a claim against the grantee for timber cut on the land, in the absence of agreement for such set-off, or of intervening equity requiring it, is not a sufficient offer to do equity to entitle him to the relief sought. Loxley *v.* Douglas, 25 So. 998, 121 Ala. 575.

§ 23. Persons Entitled to Cancellation.

§ 24. —— In General.

See post, "Parties," § 30.

The heir of the grantee of land is a proper party plaintiff to cancel a conveyance to his ancestor from a fraudulent grantor. Foster *v.* Gressett, 29 Ala. 393.

Party Out of Possession.—A court of equity will entertain a bill filed to have a deed cancelled, the execution of which is shown by proper averments to have been procured by fraud and undue influence, notwithstanding the fact, that the complainant is out of possession. Shipman *v.* Furniss, 69 Ala. 555.

A wife joined with her husband in conveying her separate estate by trust deed to secure his debt, and afterwards, under a settlement of the debt and the asserted liability of the land, executed with him an absolute deed, reciting the agreement of settlement, and conveying to the creditor a portion of the land, the evidence of the debt being given up and the trust deed canceled. Held, that she could maintain a bill against the creditor and a purchaser from him to have the absolute deed canceled, though she was not in possession of the land. Ryall *v.* Prince, 71 Ala. 66, following Boyleston *v.* Farrior, 64 Ala. 564. Cited in Bergan *v.* Jeffries, 80 Ala. 349; Bone *v.* Lansden, 85 Ala. 562, 6 So. 611.

§ 25. Persons as to Whom Instruments May Be Cancelled.

§ 26. —— In General.

See post, "Parties," § 30.

Where a note has been given by the vendee of real estate for the purchase money, equity will interpose against recovery thereon even in the hands of an assignee, if the equitable defense would have been available against the payee. Smith *v.* Pettus, 1 Stew. & P. 107.

Defendant, who had employed complainant's son, after the termination of the employment accused the son of having embezzled funds from defendant, and he stated to one who acted as the son's adviser that if a settlement was not made the son would be prosecuted, whereupon such person and the son visited complainant, and stated that the prosecution would be commenced unless she should make a conveyance of certain real estate, which was done, and which defendant accepted. Held, that defendant was the beneficiary of the wrong perpetrated on complainant, and was responsible for the acts of the son and his adviser, though they did not act as his agents, and cancellation could be had as against him. Martin *v.* Evans, 50 So. 997, 163 Ala. 657.

§ 27. —— Bona Fide Purchasers.

A married woman can not avoid a mortgage or conveyance executed by her of her separate estate, on the ground of fraud and false representations on the part of her husband, of which the mortgagee was ignorant and innocent. Vancleave *v.* Wilson, 73 Ala. 387; Pacific Guano Co. *v.* Anglin, 82 Ala. 492, 1 So. 852.

A note, for which a wife furnished the consideration, was made, without her knowledge, payable to her husband as well as herself, as was also a mortgage whereby it was secured. She indorsed note in blank, and delivered it to her husband, that he might use the proceeds in business with his brother. The husband indorsed the note, and delivered it and the mortgage to defendant, to whom he was indebted as a partner in another business, in which the wife had informed defendant that her property should not be used. Defendant knew that the husband was without funds with which to pay value for the note. Defendant transferred the note and mortgage as collateral to innocent purchasers, who executed the power in the mortgage by selling the premises to defendant. Held, that the transfer of the note to defendant, his assignment, and the sale would be annulled, and the wife would be decreed to be the sole owner of the note and mortgage; defendant not being an innocent purchaser, and the rights of his assignees not being involved. Lockwood *v.* Tate, 96 Ala. 353, 11 So. 406.

II. PROCEEDINGS AND RELIEF.

§ 28. Form of Remedy.

While the facts which will authorize the cancellation of an instrument will often afford ground for another action at law, that remedy lies only in equity. Gewin *v.* Shields, 52 So. 887, 167 Ala. 593.

§ 29. Limitations and Laches.

See ante, "Ratification," § 15; "Estoppel and Waiver," § 16; "Notice and Demand," § 20.

Necessity of Negativing Laches in Bill.—See post, "Excuse for Laches," § 32 (2).

§ 29 (1) Laches in General.

Where a bill by a grantor to cancel deed avers that he is in possession, and avers nothing to show that he ever surrendered possession under the deed, or recognized the grantee's title, he can not be charged with laches. Treadwell *v.* Torbert, 25 So. 216, 122 Ala. 297.

"Staleness or laches is founded upon acquiescence in the assertion of adverse rights, and unreasonable delay on complainant's part in not asserting her own, to the prejudice of the adverse party. Pom. Eq. Jur., § 419; 12 Am. & Eng. Enc. Law 533; 3 Brick. Dig., p. 366, § 463." Treadwell *v.* Torbert, 122 Ala. 297, 25 So. 216, 217.

Proceedings for the cancellation of an instrument must be begun promptly on discovering the ground of invalidity, and failure to proceed within a reasonable time bars the action. Smith *v.* Robertson, 23 Ala. 312.

When Time Begins to Run.—Notwithstanding a fraud may have been committed, the bar, from lapse of time will be effectual, unless a suit is prosecuted within a reasonable time after the discovery of the fraud; and it is not true, in equity, that time does not commence running until after the discovery of the fraud. Johnson *v.* Johnson, 5 Ala. 90.

What Is "Reasonable Time."—"What will be considered a reasonable time for moving to disaffirm may depend on the situation and condition of the parties, and the circumstances of the particular case. Orendorff *v.* Tallman, 90 Ala. 441, 7 So.

821; 18 Enc. Pl. & Prac. 826." Walling *v.* Thomas, 133 Ala. 426, 31 So. 982, 983.

"The right to rescission may be lost by failure to manifest an election to disaffirm the contract within a reasonable time. What constitutes a reasonable time must be determined from the circumstances of the case. Foster *v.* Gressett, 29 Ala. 393." Orendorff *v.* Tallman, 90 Ala. 441, 7 So. 821, 822.

Action by Heir after Discovery of Fraud.—A deed made two years before the death of a grantor will not be set aside for undue influence in an action commenced six years thereafter by her heirs, who had at all times been aware of her mental condition, when it appears that the parties can not be placed in statu quo. Dent *v.* Long, 90 Ala. 172, 7 So. 640.

Where the purchaser of land died eight months after his purchase, without having discovered the fraud of his vendor, and his heirs, one of whom was a minor up to the filing of a bill to rescind, filed such bill within one year after discovery of the fraud and within 4 years from the date of the purchase, the remedy was not barred by laches. Foster *v.* Gressett, 29 Ala. 393.

Intervening Rights.—"Though a party has the right to determine whether or not he will rescind a contract, so long as he has made no election, if, while considering, the position of the other party is materially affected or changed, or innocent third persons have acquired intervening rights in consequence of his unreasonable and unexplained delay, he will be precluded from exercising his right to rescind. Clough *v.* Railway Co., L. R. 7 Exch. 26." Dent *v.* Long, 90 Ala. 172, 7 So. 640, 642.

Necessity for Prompt Action.—The right to rescind a contract because of fraud or fraudulent representations must be asserted promptly. Dean *v.* Oliver, 131 Ala. 634, 30 So. 865.

A party who seeks to rescind a sale of lands on account of fraud, defect of title, or want of authority in the vendor to sell, must be diligent and prompt, diligent to discover the fraud, etc., and prompt to avail himself of the discovery, when made. If he retains the possession and enjoyment of the lands, with notice of the facts giving him a right to rescind, that right will be lost, unless he can show some good excuse for his delay. Garrett *v.* Lynch, 45 Ala. 204; 2 Pom. Eq. Jur., § 897; Howle *v.* North Birmingham Land Co., 95 Ala. 389, 11 So. 15, 16.

"No proposition is better settled than, 'if the party defrauded would disaffirm the contract, he must do so at the earliest practical moment after discovery of the cheat. That is the time to make his election, and it must be done promptly and unreservedly. He must not hesitate; nor can he be allowed to deal with the subject matter of the contract and afterwards rescind. The election is with him. He may affirm or disaffirm the contract, but he can not do both; and if he concludes to abide by it, as upon the whole advantageous, he shall not afterwards be permitted to question its validity.'" Stephenson *v.* Allison, 123 Ala. 439, 26 So. 290, 292; McLeod *v.* McLeod, 137 Ala. 267, 34 So. 228, 229.

Same—Awaiting Termination of Litigation Concerning Subject Matter.—A client is not entitled to cancellation of a conveyance to his attorney, even if it was obtained without the latter disclosing information, if the client did not act promply, but awaited termination of litigation affecting the property. Dawson *v.* Copeland, 173 Ala. 267, 55 So. 600.

Instances Where Laches Held Fatal.—An administrator purchased of one of the distributees, shortly after he came of age, all his interest in his father's estate, the administrator having rendered no inventory of the estate or stated an account, and the purchase was made at a grossly inadequate price. Held, that after the lapse of eleven years from the making of such contract equity would not lend its aid to rescind it and compel the administrator to account to the distributee, who had, when the contract was made or soon afterwards, knowledge of circumstances sufficient to put him on inquiry, and six years afterwards had actual notice of the fraud. Johnson *v.* Johnson, 5 Ala. 90.

A bill for the rescission of a contract of purchase, on the ground of the vendor's false representations, was filed thirteen or fourteen years after the discovery of the fraud, and, although it alleged that the complainant abandoned the land on the discovery of the fraud, it showed no act on his part which would have precluded him from enforcing the specific execution of the contract, if a favorable fluctuation of the price of the land had made it his interest to do so, and the laches was held fatal to the relief, on demurrer for the want of equity. Askew *v.* Hooper, 28 Ala. 634, cited in Harrison *v.* Deramus, 33 Ala. 463.

Complainant sold a lot of land to defendant at auction, the terms being one-fourth cash, the balance on time, with mortgage security; but complainant's managing agent, without authority, took from defendant a draft for the first payment, and notes and mortgage for the deferred payments, and executed a deed for the lot, to be delivered when the draft was paid. Shortly afterwards, the deed was by mistake recorded, but complainant retained it. The draft was never paid, and complainant continued to hold it, as well as the notes and mortgage. No notice of rescission was ever served on defendant, but a quitclaim deed was demanded of him. This bill to rescind was brought two years and seven months after the deed was recorded, the lot having in the meantime increased considerably in value. Held, that the delay was fatal to the relief asked. Sheffield Land, Iron & Coal Co. *v.* Neill, 87 Ala. 158, 6 So. 1.

A vendee was guilty of laches, and not entitled to the cancellation of a contract for the sale of land on the ground of the vendor's fraud, where, after discovering such fraud, he made a payment on the contract, and waited more than two years, and till after the filing of a bill to enforce the vendor's lien, before disaffirming the contract. Howle *v.* North Birmingham Land Co., 95 Ala. 389, 11 So. 15.

In a suit by a mortgagor to set aside a conveyance of his equity of redemption to the mortgagee on the ground of fraud, complainant was barred by laches where he failed to file his bill for more than seven years after the execution of the conveyance, and more than six years after he was informed that defendant repudiated the agreement and refused to permit him to redeem as he had promised. Goree *v.* Clements, 94 Ala. 337, 10 So. 906.

Complainant deeded land to defendant's intestate in November, 1895, and filed a bill to cancel the same in January, 1899, alleging that the sole consideration was the vendee's promise to convey certain other land to him, and that he did not intend at the time to do so, and had never done so. It did not appear that complainant had ever requested a deed from the vendee up to the time of his death, over two years later, or that he ever made known to the vendee's administrator his claim against the estate until November, 1898, when the land was sold to pay the vendee's debts. The complaint did not show when complainant first ascertained that his vendee did not intend to execute the deed as promised. Held not to show that complainant had acted with reasonable diligence. Dean *v.* Oliver, 30 So. 865, 131 Ala. 634.

A party who seeks the rescission of a contract, on the ground of fraud, must move within a reasonable time after the discovery of the fraud. What is a reasonable time must depend on the circumstances of each particular case. Here, a rescission was refused, because the infant, after attaining his majority, and with knowledge of the fraud, accepted from his guardian a deed for the land, remained in possession more than seven years after the sale, and more than five years after the discovery of the fraud, and showed no excuse for his delay. Kern *v.* Burnham, 28 Ala. 428.

§ 29 (2) Accrual of Cause of Action.

Plaintiffs, W. and the heirs of one F., sued in 1888 to set aside a conveyance. The complaint alleged that W. and F., his brother, purchased in 1843 some land of H., who transferred to them the receiver's certificate of entry; that in 1845 a patent was issued to them by the United States; that F. and H. lived on the land until F. died, in 1845; that H., in 1863, sold the land to defendant; that plaintiffs were ignorant that either W., who lived some distance from the land, or F., had interest therein, until the patent was accidently discovered by them in 1887; that, after the death of F., W. asked H. for his papers; that he gave him one, saying nothing about the patent, or the transaction with F. in 1843; and that defendant knew of the fraud. Held that, under Code 1886, § 2630, which provides that in actions for relief against fraud which are barred by the statute of limitations the cause of action accrues only from the discovery by the party aggrieved of the fraud, this answer to the statute of limitations was available at law, and, in the absence of averments showing the necessity of equitable relief, the bill must be dismissed. Tillison *v.* Ewing, 87 Ala. 350, 6 So. 276.

§ 29 (3) Excuse for Delay.

See post, "Excuse for Laches," § 32 (2).

Where complainants in a suit to avoid a conveyance, as obtained from their ancestress by undue influence, aver that they have continuously asserted their rights, and postponed proceeding, relying on promises made by defendant, a delay for nearly three years after the death of their ancestress before beginning legal proceedings is not such laches as preclude their prosecution of the action. Walling *v.* Thomas, 31 So. 982, 133 Ala. 426.

To a bill to set aside, as a mistake, a provision in a marriage settlement for the "natural heirs" of the wife, they must be defendants; and, as they can not be ascertained until her death, it is no laches to delay the bill until her death. Shackelford *v.* Bullock, 34 Ala. 418.

A bill to set aside a deed alleged that S., the grantor, conveyed the property to a daughter of his second wife by her first marriage, in 1868—the deed reciting that a former deed, made in 1858, being lost during the war, he executed this one in lieu thereof; that the latter deed was recorded; that he, after the war, and before making the deed of 1868, erected buildings thereon, and resided there until the death of his wife, in 1876, with his stepdaughter, who was treated as one of the family. There was no special averment of acts of ownership by S. after the deed was made. S. resided with his son, in Mississippi, from 1876 until his death in 1882. Complainants alleged undue influence on the part of the stepdaughter, and their ignorance of any fraud in the matter until 1887, one year before suit brought. No concealment of the grantee's interest in the property was alleged. Held, that there was no such excuse shown for the delay in prosecution of the suit as to bar the running of the statute. Scruggs *v.* Decatur Mineral & Land Co., 86 Ala. 173, 5 So. 440.

§ 29 (4) Statutory Limitations.

The statute of limitations is not applicable in equitable cases, but a court of equity will often adopt a period similar to that prescribed for analogous cases at law. Askew *v.* Hooper, 28 Ala. 634.

A bill in equity to set aside a deed to land, where there has been acquiescence in an adverse possession for ten years before suit, is barred, under Code 1886, § 3419, unless there are excusable circumstances taking the case out of the operation of the statute. Scruggs *v.* Decatur Mineral & Land Co., 86 Ala. 173, 5 So. 440.

§ 30. Parties.

See ante, "Persons Entitled to Cancellation," § 23; "Persons as to Whom Instruments May Be Cancelled," § 25.

§ 30 (1) In General.

The distributee and assignee are the only proper parties plaintiff and defendant, respectively, to a bill seeking to set aside, on the ground that it was fraudulently procured, an assignment by a distributee of his distributive interest in the decedent's estate. Marsh *v.* Richardson, 49 Ala. 430.

§ 30 (2) Parties Plaintiff.

A father (since deceased) and mother having conveyed the fee of land to a daughter, reserving a life estate, one who took a deed from the daughter, alone after she and her mother had conveyed the land by a deed of trust, can, without joining the mother, maintain a bill to set aside the deed of trust as fraudulently procured only so far as the remainder is affected. Gandy *v.* Fortner, 24 So. 425, 119 Ala. 303.

If one of several joint makers of a note, given for the purchase money of land, promises a third person that he will pay it if the latter purchases it, and the latter takes the note on the faith of that promise, the promisor may, notwithstanding his promise, join with the other makers of the note in a bill for the rescission of the contract of sale, but he will not be entitled to any relief against the holder, who purchased on the faith of his promise. Lanier *v.* Hill, 25 Ala. 554.

§ 30 (3) Parties Defendant.

A bill was filed by a corporation for the purpose of annulling a certain resolution adopted by its board of directors, and for cancellation of certain deeds conveying corporate lands, made pursuant to such resolution, and for an accounting with the defendant as trustee. It was further averred that the defendant, after having received in accordance with the resolution alleged to have been fraudulently passed by its board of directors deeds of conveyance to certain lots owned by the complainant, sold and conveyed said lots to different persons for value and without notice. Held, that such vendees of the defendant were necessary parties to the bill, since the cancellation of the deed, as prayed, from the complainant to the defendant, would materially affect the vendee's title to the land. Mobile Land Imp. Co. *v.* Gass, 29 So. 920, 129 Ala. 214.

Heirs of Vendor.—The heirs at law of the vendor are not necessary parties defendant to a bill, filed by the purchaser against his administrator, for a cancellation of the deed, as to a tract of land to which the vendor had no title, and which was included in the deed by mistake. Williams *v.* Mitchell, 30 Ala. 299.

Vendor's Mortgagee. — The vendor's mortgagee is not a proper party defendant to a suit to rescind a contract of sale, as he is not concerned in the transactions between the vendor and vendee; the land being always subject to his claim. Orendorff *v.* Tallman, 90 Ala. 441, 7 So. 821.

Joinder of Parties Defendant. — A mortgage was given by a partnership to the sureties on an administrator's bond, as security for a loan made by the administrator to the firm, and also for the benefit of the heirs. A bill to foreclose said mortgage, in which the heirs were complainants, and the administrator and his sureties, the firm, the attaching creditors of the firm, and the sheriff were respondents, alleged that the creditors, proceeding separately, attached the mortgaged property; that part thereof was sold by the sheriff, and the proceeds appropriated by them; and that the sheriff sold a mortgaged lot and gave a conveyance thereof. The bill prayed for foreclosure, that the administrator account, and that the administration be removed into the chancery court, and that the sheriff's deed be canceled. Held, that there was no misjoinder of parties defendant. Smith *v.* Smith, 106 Ala. 298, 17 So. 680.

Where a bill to rescind a contract for the purchase of stock and for the surrender of notes given therefor by complainant, on the ground of fraud inducing the purchase, avers that on discovery of the fraud, and before the certificate of stock was received, complainant offered to rescind the contract, and that the defendant declined, and also refused to deliver to him his notes, and that the notes were discounted and the proceeds placed to the credit of defendant, but does not join as defendant the bank holding the notes, the bill shows equity, and can be maintained, whether the holder be a bona fide holder or not. Southern States Fire & Casualty Ins. Co. *v.* Whatley, 173 Ala. 101, 55 So. 620.

§ 31. Pleading.

§ 32. —— Bill, Complaint, or Petition.

§ 32 (1) In General.

Under a bill which specifically asks the cancellation of a mortgage because given to secure a debt founded on an alleged illegal consideration, the complainant can not have a decree establishing the mortgage, and allowing him to redeem; nor can the bill be framed with a double aspect, asking either a cancellation or redemption. Micou *v.* Ashurst, 55 Ala. 607.

A complaint for specific performance alleged that the ancestor of plaintiffs and defendants executed a deed to one of plaintiffs and another to defendants; that the latter deed covered also personal property; that to avoid litigation it was agreed by all the heirs, that the property should be sold and divided equally between all of the heirs, and the agreement was made an exhibit to the bill; that, to carry out the agreement as to the sale and distribution, all the heirs executed a deed to defendants, conveying all property left by their ancestor and included in the two deeds; that the grantees in the deed have wholly failed to perform their contract, and are converting the property to their own use, and cancellation and specific performance are prayed for. Held, that the bill could not be sustained as for the cancellation for want of facts, and it could not be amended, so as to make it one for cancellation, without working an entire change in the cause of action. O'Briant *v.* O'Briant, 49 So. 317, 160 Ala. 457.

Showing Privity.—The bill, in terms and effect alleging the relation of landlord and tenant exists between the parties, shows such a privity between them as to authorize a bill to cancel the lease for breaches, and for an accounting as for rents. Peerless Coal Co. *v.* Lamar (Ala.), 60 So. 837.

Alleging Residence of Parties by Inference.—In an action to set aside a conveyance by a married woman, on the ground that her husband had not joined in the deed, an averment that the husband was of sound mind and resided with his wife, and did not give his consent to the conveyance, "as required by the statute of Alabama," in effect avers that the wife resided in Alabama, and is good as against a general demurrer. Bell *v.* Burkhalter (Ala.), 57 So. 460.

Averring Interest of Vendor.—In an action to set aside as fraudulent a deed of lands, the habendum clause of which reads, "to have and to hold what interest and title I may and do have by reason of my survivorship of my late wife, to whom said lands belonged," the bill must show what interest the vendor had, and its value, and deny the adequacy or payment of the consideration. Moorer *v.* Moorer, 87 Ala. 545, 6 So. 289.

Showing Possession in Complainant.—A bill to cancel a conveyance by an alleged insane person, averring that complainant "never delivered possession * * * to either of the grantees, * * * either at the time of execution of said deeds or at any time thereafter," does not show that complainant had possession when it was filed, and should be dismissed. Galloway *v.* McLain, 31 So. 603, 131 Ala. 280.

Description of Land Involved.—Where a bill is filed in equity to annul the sale of land and to cancel the conveyance thereof for fraud, a description of the land involved in the suit is sufficient if it furnishes data from which the identity of the land may be fixed with certainty by evidence aliunde. Pinkston *v.* Boykin, 30 So. 398, 130 Ala. 483.

Averring Facts Constituting Frauds.—"Before cancellation can be decreed for fraud practiced in the procurement of complainant's deed, the bill must aver facts from which fraud is the legal result; the rule being that averments of conclusions are insufficient to raise an issue of fraud. Mountain *v.* Whitman, 103 Ala. 630, 16 So. 15; Little *v.* Sterne, 125 Ala. 609, 27 So. 972; Warren *v.* Hunt, 114 Ala. 506, 21 So. 939." Pratt Land, etc., Co. *v.* McClain, 135 Ala. 452, 33 So. 185, 186.

Averring Name of Defendant's Agent Who Committed the Fraud.—Where a bill to set aside a conveyance of land for fraud alleged that the fraud was practiced through defendant's agent, and that it was by reason of the fraud so practiced that plaintiff was deceived, the name of the person who was alleged to have acted as defendant's agent should be averred, and this notwithstanding the fact that, as such person was defendant's agent, he would be presumed to know his name and identity. Pinkston *v.* Boykin, 30 So. 398, 130 Ala. 483.

Repugnancy.—In an action to cancel a mortgage, and enjoin a foreclosure of same, the bill alleged that the complainant received $1,000 of defendant corporation, which sum was still unpaid, and gave his note for $1,200, secured by the mortgage; that if the mortgage was an Alabama transaction it was void, because defendant, being a foreign corporation, did not have a known place of business in the state as required by the constitution, and if it was a New York transaction, the papers having been delivered there, it was void for usury; and that complainant was not indebted to defendant in any sum, but complainant offered, if he was mistaken in this, to pay defendant whatever sum the court adjudged to be due —held, that the court properly overruled a demurrer assigning repugnancy, in that the bill averred that the mortgage was void under the laws of New York, and also under the laws of Alabama, and at the same time stated facts showing that the mortgage was legal in the latter state, and offered to submit to its jurisdiction; since the real repugnancy was the allegation that the mortgage was made in two different states, and this point was not properly presented by the demurrer. New England Mortg., etc., Co. *v.* Powell, 97 Ala. 483, 12 So. 55.

Contradictory Averments. — When a bill to cancel a deed contains averments that the consideration for the conveyance was an agreement to support the grantor and to make improvements on the land, and the deed, as set out in the bill, contains similar recitals, a further averment in the bill that the grantee took advantage of grantor's infirmities, and procured the execution of the deed without consideration, is contradictory, and affords no ground for relief. Gardner *v.* Knight, 27 So. 298, 124 Ala. 273.

Same—When One Averment Erroneous.—In an action to cancel a mortgage, and the deed made on foreclosure thereof, the bill alleged that the debt had been paid before foreclosure, that the property had been bought in by the mortgagee, and that the mortgagors had no power to execute the mortgage. Held, that the bill was not bad on demurrer as being based on antagonistic rights, when the averment that the mortgagors had no power to execute the mortgage was erroneous. Dickerson *v.* Winslow, 97 Ala. 491, 11 So. 918.

Duplicity.—A mortgagor's bill averring full payment, and yet offering to pay any balance found due on account, and asking for a cancellation, or for an account and redemption, is not bad for duplicity. Fields *v.* Helms, 70 Ala. 460.

Executed Contract.—See ante, "Executed Contracts," § 6.

A bill was filed by a corporation for the purpose of annulling a certain resolution adopted by its board of directors, and for the cancellation of certain deeds conveying corporate land, made pursuant to said resolution, and for an accounting with the defendant as trustee. It was averred that the defendant, after having received, in accordance with the resolution alleged to have been fraudulently passed by its board of directors, deeds of conveyance to certain lots owned by the complainant, sold and conveyed said lots to different persons for value and without notice. Held that, it nowhere appearing in the bill that any consideration was paid by the defendant for the lots in question or that any benefits resulted to the complainant, as the bill sought to annul an illegal and unauthorized contract of the board of directors whereby the corporation had been deprived of its property to the injury of its stockholders, it was not subject to demurrer on the ground that it showed an executed contract between the company and defendant. Mobile Land Imp. Co. *v.* Gass, 29 So. 920, 129 Ala. 214.

To Set Aside Deed to Insolvent Estate. —Where a deed of a decedent's estate by an heir to decedent's administrator recited that the estate had been judicially declared insolvent, a bill for relief from that deed and another executed by the administrator to a third person must negative the recital and affirm the solvency of the estate. Boddie *v.* Ward, 44 So. 105, 151 Ala. 198; Boddie *v.* Colburn, 44 So. 108, 151 Ala. 669.

§ 32 (2) Excuse for Laches.

See ante, "Ratification," § 15; "Estoppel and Waiver," § 16; "Limitations and Laches," § 29.

Where a bill avers that a deed was obtained from complainants' decedent, while her mind was unsound, at one-fourth the value of the land, and by influence of one in whom she reposed confidence, and thereafter she continued to decline into a state of insanity until her death, such allegations show a right in the grantor to have the sale avoided, and rebut all presumption that acquiescence caused her failure to assert such right. Walling *v.* Thomas, 31 So. 982, 133 Ala. 426.

Necessity of Negativing Laches in Complaint. — Laches, being defensive matter, need not be negatived by complainant. Pratt Land, etc., Co. *v.* McClain, 135 Ala. 452, 33 So. 185.

§ 32 (3) Setting Out, and Description of Instrument.

A bill in equity for the cancellation of a deed is not bad on demurrer because it alleges that the deed was executed to complainant, it being apparent that defendant was intended; especially where a copy of the deed was attached as a part of the bill, whereby the error was cured. Piedmont Land & Improvement Co. *v.* Piedmont Foundry & Machine Co., 96 Ala. 389, 11 So. 332.

§ 32 (4) Offer to Restore Consideration or Benefits.

See ante, "Restoration of Consideration or Benefit," § 22.

Necessity for Offer.—In a suit by a mortgagee who has purchased the mortgaged premises under a power of sale in the mortgage, to compel the mortgagor to elect whether he will affirm or disaffirm the sale, a cross bill asking cancellation of the mortgage contract on the ground of usury, which does not offer to repay the principal of the loan and legal interest, should be dismissed for failure of defendant to offer to do equity. American Freehold Land Mortg. Co. *v.* Sewell, 92 Ala. 163, 9 So. 143, 13 L. R. A. 299.

A bill to have an absolute deed declared a mortgage, and canceled as a cloud on complainants' title, was filed by complainants as heirs of their deceased mother, and not as devisees, and alleged that complainants' mother owned the land during coverture as her statutory separate estate; that during her coverture she and her husband conveyed the land to defendant by absolute warranty deed, but that said deed was only a mortgage security for the husband's debt; and that defendant acquired and maintained possession of the land for several years, and received the rents and profits. The husband survived his wife. Held that, as the husband, under Code 1886, § 2353, became entitled to the use of his wife's real estate for life, upon her death intestate, the conveyance, if a mortgage, was a valid mortgage of his interest; and as the bill neither alleged payment nor offered to pay and redeem, it was without equity. Bone *v.* Lansden, 85 Ala. 562, 6 So. 611.

Same—When Not Necessary.—Where the bill avers that complainants have not, nor ever had, possession of the land, it need not allege that they have abandoned or restored it to defendants. Orendorff *v.* Tallman, 90 Ala. 441, 7 So. 821.

Sufficiency of Offer.—In a bill to rescind a contract, an offer to credit the defendant with the amount received under the contract, or perform and abide by the decree, etc., is a sufficient offer to do equity. Martin *v.* Martin, 35 Ala. 560, cited in Rogers *v.* Torbut, 58 Ala. 523.

In an action to cancel a mortgage on the ground that the mortgagee was a foreign corporation, and took the same without being entitled to do business in the state, plaintiff stated in his bill that, "if said interest notes, past due, are held valid, in any event, complainant hereby offers, and is able and willing and ready, to pay the same." Held, that the bill was bad on demurrer, as it did not offer to repay all plaintiff had received on the mortgage. Ross *v.* New England Mortg., etc., Co., 101 Ala. 362, 13 So. 564.

Same—Necessity for Offering to Pay Interest.—A bill for the cancellation of a deed for fraud, which offers to refund the consideration to the grantees or to such of them as the court may deem entitled thereto, or to allow the same to be credited upon plaintiff's distributive share of the estate as widow, without paying or tendering the money into court or saying anything of interest, is a sufficient offer of restoration, since interest may be considered as a mere incident to the principal sum and covered by the offer to refund. Wilks *v.* Wilks (Ala.), 57 So. 776.

Same—Conditional Offer.—Where a bill filed to vacate a sale of land for fraud averred that defendant had received rents and profits more than sufficient to repay him the amount paid in the purchase, but that, if not, plaintiff offered to pay any sum which should finally appear to be due and owing the defendant, and to perform such other things as the court may determine, fully submitting himself to the equity of the court was a sufficient offer on plaintiff's part to do equity. Pinkston *v.* Boykin, 30 So. 398, 130 Ala. 483.

In an action to cancel a mortgage, and enjoin a foreclosure of same, the bill alleged that the complainant received $1,000 of defendant corporation, which sum was still unpaid, and gave his note for $1,200, secured by the mortgage; that if the mortgage was an Alabama transaction it was void, because defendant, being a foreign corporation, did not have a known place of business in the state, as required by the constitution, and if it was a New York transaction, the papers having been delivered there, it was void for usury; and that complainant was not indebted to defendant in any sum; but complainant offered, if he was mistaken in this, to pay defendant whatever sum the court adjudged to be due. Held, that the offer to pay, though not unequivocal, was sufficient to bring the case under the rule that he who asks equity must do equity. New England Mortg., etc., Co. *v.* Powell, 97 Ala. 483, 12 So. 55.

Same—Offer to Bring Consideration into Court.—The bill averred that plaintiff, immediately on learning of the pretended sale, tendered back the money paid and notes given on its account, repudiated it, and notified M. and the purchaser that it would not comply with it. Held, that the bill need not offer to bring the money and notes into court, as this need only be done before final relief granted. Miller *v.* Louisville & N. R. Co., 83 Ala. 274, 4 So. 842.

Asking Court to Ascertain Amount Due.—A bill which alleges that a bond and mortgage is ultra vires, and asks its cancellation, does not treat it as valid, so as to be repugnant, because asking that the amount of money necessary for complainant to restore be ascertained. Southern Building & Loan Ass'n *v.* Casa Grande Livery Stable Co., 24 So. 886, 119 Ala. 175.

§ 32 (5) Averment of Ground of Cancellation in General.

A bill to rescind a sale of land at the instance of the vendee, which avers that the sale was induced by misrepresentations on the part of the vendor, and that these were made either fraudulently or mistakenly, is not sufficient to justify relief on the ground of mistake. Porter *v.* Collins, 90 Ala. 510, 8 So. 80.

The averment that complainant relied upon the assurances of defendant to complete the belt road as he agreed to do at the time he sold the land will not supply a failure to set forth the facts necessary to constitute an assurance or promise to complete the road. Birmingham Warehouse & Elevator Co. *v.* Elyton Land Co., 93 Ala. 549, 9 So. 235.

Showing Ground for Equitable Relief.—A bill to cancel a contract of sale for fraud, relying upon extrinsic evidence to establish the fraud and negativing an adequate remedy at law, states a case for equitable relief. J. A. Fay & Egan Co. *v.* Independent Lumber Co. (Ala.), 59 So. 470.

Where a vendee of land, who has paid the purchase money, and, by the terms of the bond, has a present right to the title, files his bill to rescind the contract, and for an account of the purchase money paid, etc., the general charge that the defendant has no title to the land, that it is incumbered with the dower of the wife of A., one of the previous owners, and that it will be impossible for the defendant to procure a title for many years to come, makes out at least a prima facie case of equitable cognizance, and is sufficient to require the defendant to answer. Read *v.* Walker, 18 Ala. 323, cited in Magee *v.* McMillan, 30 Ala. 421; Kelly *v.* Allen, 34 Ala. 663.

§ 32 (6) Fraud in General.

A bill to rescind a contract of sale of land, which avers that defendants, by false representations that they had a sufficient title, induced plaintiffs to enter into the contract, when in fact the title was in another, of which plaintiffs were ignorant, is sufficient, without alleging the facts to show want of title in defendants. Orendorff *v.* Tallman, 90 Ala. 441, 7 So. 821.

A bill to cancel a conveyance of land for fraud, alleging that the defendant, by fraudulent devices, trickery, and affirmative misrepresentation of facts through his agent, misled and deceived complainant as to the value of the land, which was done with intent to defraud complainant, and that it did deceive and defraud, which deceit and fraud led him to make the sale and convey the land to the defendant for less than one-half its value, and that the bill was filed immediately on discovering the fraud, and contained no allegation showing that complainant was wanting in diligence in not sooner discovering the fraud, was not demurrable for want of equity. Pinkston *v.* Boykin, 30 So. 398, 130 Ala. 483.

Where a bill to rescind a contract whereby complainants conveyed to defendant certain land in consideration of the transfer to them of certain mortgages held by defendant alleges particular concealments and misrepresentations by defendant as to the property nominally covered by the mortgages, and as to the title of the mortgagor to lands conveyed by one of them, and that complainants were induced thereby to convey the land to defendant and take the mortgages in payment, it is sufficient to entitle complainants to relief, so far as relief depends on the fraud of defendant. Baker *v.* Maxwell, 99 Ala. 558, 14 So. 468.

A bill to rescind a contract whereby plaintiffs conveyed to defendant certain land in consideration of the transfer to them of certain chattel and real-estate mortgages, on the ground of fraudulent representations of defendant as to the title of the mortgagors to the mortgaged land and the existence at the time of the mortgaged chattels, need not negative the solvency of such mortgagors, nor aver that the debts secured by the mortgages were not enforceable aside therefrom. Baker *v.* Maxwell, 99 Ala. 558, 14 So. 468.

Allegations of Fraud Must Be Direct and Positive.—He who seeks the rescission of a contract on the ground of fraud, or undue influence must show his right to relief by distinct and pointed allegations clearly proved. Bailey *v.* Litten, 52 Ala. 282; Smith *v.* Collins, 41 So. 825, 148 Ala. 672; Abel *v.* Collins, 41 So. 826, 148 Ala. 673.

Where fraud is alleged as a ground to annul and vacate a sale of land, the material averment showing the fraud should be made directly and positively, and not be left to be deduced by inference from the averments of the bill. Pinkston *v.* Boykin, 30 So. 398, 130 Ala. 483.

In a bill, seeking to set aside a deed for fraud, it is not necessary to charge the fraud in totidem verbis. If the bill states, with directness and precision, facts and circumstances, constituting fraud, it is sufficient. Kennedy *v.* Kennedy, 2 Ala. 571, cited in Love *v.* Graham, 25 Ala. 192; Chambers *v.* Cook, 42 Ala. 175.

Where, in a suit to cancel a contract for the purchase of land upon the ground of fraud, the complaint alleges that defendant's president pointed out two lots as suitable for a warehouse and elevator corporation, saying: "We are building our belt railway right down * * * street, so that, you see, we will pass that ground 500 feet on its east side;" and, "We are at work on it now; the engineers are out there now at work at it;" whereupon plaintiff was induced to purchase the lots; and alleges a failure to build the road—a failure to aver that the representations were false and fraudulently made, with intent to deceive, or an equivalent averment, is a fatal defect. Birmingham Warehouse & Elevator Co. *v.* Elyton Land Co., 93 Ala. 549, 9 So. 235.

Fraudulent Representations as to Mutual Facts.—Where the fraudulent representations alleged were of material facts conducive to the transaction, such bill is not defective on the ground that the representations were not such as complainants had a right to rely on, because, by the exercise of diligence, they could have ascertained their falsity. Baker *v.* Maxwell, 99 Ala. 558, 14 So. 468.

Alleging Fraud in General Terms.—An allegation of fraud in general terms, without stating the facts constituting it, is insufficient, and a demurrer to the bill is not a confession of the fraud. Penny *v.* Jackson, 85 Ala. 67, 4 So. 720.

Alleging Belief That There Was Fraud.—A bill to cancel a deed executed by complainant and her husband alleged that complainant was coerced by her husband, and that complainant believed the grantee had heard of the overbearing conduct of her husband, and complainant believed the the grantee had used influence over the husband in order to secure the conveyance. Held to charge immaterial matter, complainant's belief not being issuable. Pratt Land & Improvement Co. *v.* McClain, 33 So. 185, 135 Ala. 452.

Showing Reliance on Representations.—A bill in equity, seeking to rescind a contract for fraud, alleged that the purchaser was a stranger to the lands bought; that the vendor represented his title to be good, when it was not; and that, "by this fraudulent representation, and his deed purporting to convey said lands to complainant, with warranty of title against all other persons, he induced complainant to pay him $1,500 for said lands, and to give his note for $1,500 more." Held, that the allegation sufficiently showed that the purchaser, in making the contract, relied on his vendor's misrepresentations, and was thereby misled. Bailey *v.* Jordan, 32 Ala. 50, cited in Orendorff *v.* Tallman, 90 Ala. 441, 7 So. 821.

§ 32 (7) Incapacity, Duress, and Undue Influence.

The bill in a suit to cancel notes and a mortgage on the ground that they were given under duress alleged that complainants were conducting a laundry business, which necessitated the use of horses and wagons, and which were kept at the livery barn of defendant, who claimed to hold them for a debt for the board of the horses; that complainants tendered $25 in full payment of the debt, but defendant demanded the payment of a larger sum as a condition for his surrendering the property; that defendant knew that complainants' business would be ruined unless they could obtain the use of their horses and wagons; that complainants, in order to secure possession of such property, executed the notes and mortgage in question as demanded by defendant; that they had no legal remedy whereby they could secure such possession in time to prevent the ruin of their business; that they were indebted to defendant in a small sum, which they tendered to him; that defendant was insolvent, and was in possession of the notes and mortgage; that complainants had no remedy except in equity to secure the cancellation of the notes and mortgage. Held, that the bill was good on demurrer for insufficiency of its allegations to show duress. Glass *v.* Haygood, 31 So. 973, 133 Ala. 489.

Stating Facts Constituting Influence.—An averment that decedent, at a time when he was "very feeble both in mind and body, was persuaded and induced, through some undue and improper influence unknown to complainants, to execute" a certain deed, is entirely insufficient, in that it does not state the facts constituting such influence. Jackson *v.* Rowell, 87 Ala. 685, 6 So. 95, 4 L. R. A. 637.

Alleging Results of Influence.—A complaint alleged that by reason of undue influence on the part of defendants complainant was induced to execute a release of his interest in the estate of a deceased son for an inadequate sum. Held, that the complaint was not demurrable on the ground that the averments as to undue influence were not sufficiently specific, it being necessary only to allege the result, rather than the particular acts. McLeod *v.* McLeod, 34 So. 228, 137 Ala. 267.

Alleging Mode of Exerting Influence.—Where a bill to cancel a deed on the ground that it was procured by undue influence alleges the persons who exerted such influence, it is sufficient, and need not allege the mode in which such influence was exerted. Letohatchie Baptist Church *v.* Bullock, 32 So. 58, 133 Ala. 548.

§ 33. —— Plea or Answer.

In a suit to set aside a sale of corporate stocks and bonds for misrepresentation as to the corporation's mines and business, a plea that after complainants became the owners of the stock, and were directors of and in control of the corporation, they sold the bonds to D. & Co., in consideration of certain indebtedness due from the corporation to D. & Co., and that thereafter complainants purchased the bonds with full knowledge of all the facts concerning the issuance thereof, was fatally defective for failure to charge complainants with knowledge or notice as to the condition of the corporation's mines or business. Graybill *v.* Drennen, 150 Ala. 227, 43 So. 568.

A bill to set aside a sale of land and a mortgage alleged that the judgment under which the sale was made was assigned to defendant as security for money advanced to the judgment creditor at the request of complainant, to satisfy the judgment; that the mortgage was executed to defendant to secure the same debt and an additional sum, defendant agreeing to receive it instead of the judgment;

and that the judgment was thereby satisfied. The judgment was afterwards revived by consent of complainant, and an execution issued, and land sold thereunder. Defendant pleaded the revival of the judgment in bar. Held insufficient, as not covering all the equities of the case, since, if the mortgage and judgment were to secure the same debt, both could not be enforced except to satisfy such debt, and proof that the judgment was not satisfied would not necessarily defeat complainant's right to relief. Lyon *v.* Dees, 84 Ala. 595, 4 So. 407.

Where the bill charges that a false and fraudulent representation was made by defendant as to his ability to convey the fee simple in a certain lot to plaintiff, in exchange for other lots which he had received from plaintiff, and the answer asserts an ability to comply with the representations, this put defendant on proof of his ability as asserted. Wellborn *v.* Tiller, 10 Ala. 305.

Necessity for Averring That Plaintiff Did Not Rely upon Misrepresentations.—In a suit to cancel a sale of certain bonds and stock of a corporation for false representations concerning their value, a plea alleging that complainants before the purchase had an examination made of the property and business of the corporation by an expert, and were informed of the condition of the property before entering into the contract of purchase, was fatally defective for failure to aver that complainants did not act on the representations, or that they did act on the result of the investigation. Graybill *v.* Drennen, 43 So. 568, 150 Ala. 227.

When Necessary to Allege Plaintiff's Knowledge of Fraud.—See ante, "Ratification," § 15.

In a suit to set aside a sale of corporate stock and bonds for fraud, a plea alleging that complainants immediately after the purchase assumed control of the corporation, and managed and operated its mines and business for twelve months before offering to rescind the contract, was fatally defective for failure to charge that complainants discovered the fraud, or were negligent in not doing so, during the time they were in possession of the property. Graybill *v.* Drennen, 150 Ala. 227, 43 So. 568.

In a suit to set aside a sale of corporate stock and bonds for fraud, a plea charging a ratification of the sale on complainant's part, but pretermitting any notice or knowledge of the falsity of the facts complained of in the bill at the time of the alleged ratification, was fatally defective. Graybill *v.* Drennen, 150 Ala. 227, 43 So. 568.

§ 34. —— Amended and Supplemental Pleadings.

A bill can not pray to have a mortgage set aside and cancelled, as inoperative and void, or in the alternative, for an account and redemption under it; and if the original bill pays the former relief only, an amendment asking the other, in the alternative, can not be allowed. Tatum Bros. *v.* Walker, 77 Ala. 563.

A bill by a married woman to cancel two mortgages, as having been made in evasion of the statute prohibiting the mortgaging of the statutory separate estate of a married woman, should be amended, before or at the final hearing, to conform to proof showing the validity of one of the mortgages because the mortgagee had no notice of the attempted evasion; and, where such amendment is not made, the bill should be dismissed, without prejudice to complainant's right to relief against the other mortgagees. Allen *v.* McCullough, 99 Ala. 612, 12 So. 810.

Motion to Dismiss Supplying Amendment.—A bill by the owner of a vineyard to cancel an agreement with another to cultivate it, and gather the crop, because the latter has not performed on his part, will, on motion to dismiss, be regarded as amended so as to allege that the nonperformance was without the owner's fault and that there was a substantial compliance by the latter, or a waiver thereof. Ferris *v.* Hoagland, 25 So. 834, 121 Ala. 240.

Striking Out Name of Party.—Where a wife is joined as a defendant with her husband and the mortgagees, in a bill filed by her testamentary trustee which seeks to set aside and cancel the mortgage of her property, executed by her and her husband to secure a recited indebtedness, her name may be stricken out by amendment, and joined as co-

complainant with the trustee. Tatum Bros. *v.* Walker, 7 Ala. 563.

§ 35. —— Issues, Proof, and Variance.

"Relief can not be granted on facts developed in evidence but not alleged, any more than upon facts alleged and not proved. Park *v.* Lide, 90 Ala. 246, 7 So. 805, and cases cited." Porter *v.* Collins, 90 Ala. 510, 8 So. 80, 81.

A bill to rescind a sale of land on the ground of the vendor's misrepresentations as to the proximity of the property to a certain town is not sustained by proof that, after the transaction had been fully closed, the vendor casually remarked that he understood the land was within a mile and a quarter of the town in question, when, in fact, it was four miles away. Porter *v.* Collins, 90 Ala. 510, 8 So. 80.

On the maturity of a mortgage, the mortgagors executed to the mortgagee a deed, absolute in form, the expressed consideration being the debt secured and an individual debt of one of the mortgagors. On a bill to declare the deed a mortgage, and allow a redemption, there was no pretense but that the conveyance was intended to be in satisfaction of the mortgage and individual debt, but they claimed that they were to be allowed two years in which to redeem. Held that, the bill not having asked for relief on the grounds of inadequacy of price, and the proofs not showing any gross inadequacy, the deed should not be set aside as oppressive. Peagler *v.* Stabler, 91 Ala. 308, 9 So. 157.

Fatal Variances.—In a suit to set aside an absolute conveyance of an equity of redemption by a mortgagor to the mortgagee, which is intended as a mortgage, there is a fatal variance where the bill alleges that defendant promised a "reasonable and convenient time in which to pay the debt," and complainant testifies that he was to pay it when able. Goree *v.* Clements, 94 Ala. 337, 10 So. 906.

Proof of Mistake Will Not Support Allegation of Fraud.—A bill was filed to obtain the rescission of a contract on the ground of fraud, but the evidence showed only an honest mistake. Held, that the variance between the allegations and the proof was fatal. Williams *v.* Sturdevant, 27 Ala. 598.

On a bill filed by a vendee for the rescission of a contract, alleging a fraudulent misrepresentation of a material fact by the vendor, if the evidence shows an honest mistake only, the intent being immaterial, the variance between the allegrata and probata is not fatal, and relief will be granted on proof of the mistake. Lanier *v.* Hill, 25 Ala. 554.

When Variance Not Material.—A bill for the rescission of a contract of sale alleged that the vendor sold and conveyed to two of the complainants, while the deed, which was made an exhibit to the bill, conveyed the lands to one of the complainants only. Held to be no material variance, as the defendant could not have been taken by surprise. Lanier *v.* Hill, 25 Ala. 554.

When Not Necessary to Prove Plaintiff's Interest in Property.—Where, in an action to require a mortgage to be surrendered and canceled, defendant claims solely through plaintiff under the mortgage, plaintiff's interest in the property stands admitted, and need not be proved. Sheats *v.* Scott, 32 So. 573, 133 Ala. 642.

When Fraud Ground of Relief Sought.—Where the remedy is predicated in the bill on the ground of fraud and the proof of fraud fails, the bill will be dismissed. Pierce *v.* Brassfield, 9 Ala. 573.

In suits for the rescission of contracts on account of fraud, that rule as in suits for specific performance is not applied with the same strictness which exacts a correspondence between the allegations and proof of the terms of the contract. Lanier *v.* Hill, 25 Ala. 554; Pierce *v.* Wilson, 34 Ala. 596, 607.

§ 36. Evidence.

§ 37. —— Presumptions and Burden of Proof.

In actions to avoid a deed on the ground of inadequacy of consideration and undue influence arising from the relation of the parties, the burden is on the grantee to prove that it is equitable in every respect. Burke *v.* Taylor, 94 Ala. 530, 10 So. 129.

The burden of proving that a mortgage executed by a wife was given as security for her husband's debt is on the wife, seeking to cancel the mortgage on that ground. Gafford *v.* Speaker, 125 Ala. 498, 27 So. 1003.

The burden of proving a grantor's mental incompetency is on those who assail the conveyance. Chancellor *v.* Donnell, 95 Ala. 342, 10 So. 910.

§ 38. —— Admissibility.

Though an attempted mortgage is void as a conveyance, yet it may be looked to for the purpose of ascertaining other terms of the contract, in order that the entire controversy involved in the proceedings for its cancellation may be settled. Hayes *v.* Southern Home Building & Loan Ass'n, 26 So. 527, 124 Ala. 663.

§ 39. —— Weight and Sufficiency.

In a suit to cancel a written contract on the ground of fraud and duress, evidence examined, and held insufficient to sustain a decree for complainants. Sellers, Bullard & Co. *v.* Grace, 43 So. 716, 150 Ala. 181.

In a suit to cancel a timber contract, defendant's evidence held to show that defendant's representative did not deceive complainant when the contract was made, nor tell him defendant would not deed him the land unless he conveyed the timber. McCaskill *v.* Scotch Lumber Co., 44 So. 405, 152 Ala. 349.

In an action to cancel a mortgage, and a deed given on foreclosure thereof, on the ground that the mortgage was given by complainant, a married woman, as security for her husband's debt, and was therefore void, it appeared from the recitals in the mortgage that the debt secured was complainant's own debt, and two witnesses testified positively, and three in corroboration, to the same effect; and it was proven that, after the sale under the mortgage, complainant had occupied the premises for sixteen months as tenant to the vendee at that sale, paying him rent during that time. Held that, in the face of this evidence, the testimony of complainant and her husband contra is not sufficient to justify a court of equity in granting the relief prayed. Gafford *v.* Speaker, 125 Ala. 498, 27 So. 1003.

In a suit by a mortgagor to set aside a conveyance of his equity of redemption to the mortgagee on the ground of fraud, complainant testified that when the mortgage became due defendant promised that if he would make a deed to the property he would allow him a reasonable time to repay the debt, and would permit him to collect and hold the rents for the current year. The mortgage debt was $560, and complainant testified that the property was worth $1,200. The bill alleged a long friendship between the parties, and an agreement on the part of the defendant to extend the mortgage debt when due, which agreement was denied by defendant. It was not alleged that defendant made any false representations as to the legal effect of the deed. Held, that the evidence failed to show fraud or undue advantage. Goree *v.* Clements, 94 Ala. 337, 10 So. 906.

Degree of Proof of Fraud.—In order to support a decree rescinding or canceling a lease for fraud, the evidence must amount to more than a mere probability of the truth of the charge of fraud or a mere preponderance of the evidence that such charges are true. Smith *v.* Collins, 41 So. 825, 148 Ala. 672; Abel *v.* Collins, 41 So. 826, 148 Ala. 673.

§ 40. Trial or Hearing.

§ 41. —— Conduct in General.

Code 1907, § 3374, as amended by Laws 1909 (Sp. Sess.), p. 14, provides that a conveyance which is acknowledged and recorded may be received in evidence without further proof, and where it is lost or destroyed the court may receive a certified copy of the record in place of the original, unless the party against whom the copy is offered shall file an affidavit that the conveyance is a forgery. In an action for the cancellation of a conveyance and its record on the ground that the signature of the grantor was a forgery, and that the certificate of the acknowledgment was false, in which the complainant set out a certified copy of the conveyance, and the defendants denied the allegations of the bill, the complainant filed an affidavit that the conveyance was a forgery. Held that, as the question of title under the conveyance was not in issue, and the defendants were not actors asserting rights under the conveyance, they were not bound after the filing of the affidavit to offer a certified copy of the conveyance, since that would result in shifting upon the defendants the burden of proof, which, under the issues, was upon the complainants. Freeman *v.* Blount, 172 Ala. 655, 55 So. 293.

§ 42. Relief Awarded.

§ 43. —— In General.

Upon a bill to rescind a contract for the sale of land, upon the allegation that the vendor fraudulently represented that a portion of the tract included in the bond for title was contiguous to the residue, when in truth it was remote from it, and did not adjoin the other lands, the vendee is not entitled to relief by way of compensation, although the vendor admits there was a mistake, and a portion of the land sold omitted out of the bond for title, and another portion not sold inserted. Pierce *v.* Brassfield, 9 Ala. 573, cited in Williams *v.* Mitchell, 30 Ala. 299; Block *v.* Stone, 33 Ala. 329.

§ 44. —— Cancellation, Surrender, or Reconveyance.

Where an absolute deed expressed upon its face a money consideration, and was shown by extrinsic proof to have been executed on a promise by the grantee to the grantor that he would hold or dispose of the property conveyed for the use of the heirs of the grantor, which promise he refused to perform, it was held that the measure of the relief to which the heirs were entitled in equity was the cancellation of the deed, and that this result could not be avoided by the grantor's offering to pay the consideration expressed in it. Kennedy *v.* Kennedy, 2 Ala. 571.

§ 45. —— Alternative, Additional, or Incidental Equitable Relief.

Where the heirs of the vendee seek to rescind the contract under circumstances entitling them to retain possession of the property, up to the final decree, they should have a fair allowance for any improvements made by them, which are absolutely necessary to render the possession of the land beneficial and profitable, such as necessary fencing and all indispensable buildings on a plantation; and they should be charged, not only with rents, but also with any deterioration of the value of the land which accrued by their injurious or injudicious cultivation of it. Foster *v.* Gressett, 29 Ala. 393, cited in Bryant *v.* Boothe, 30 Ala. 311; Scott *v.* Greggs, 49 Ala. 191.

Complainant sold his land in Alabama to defendant for a cash payment and an interest in certain lands in Florida. Complainant knew nothing of the Florida lands, and relied on defendant's representations as to its quality and value, which representations were untrue. Held that, as defendant had made extensive improvements on the Alabama land before receiving notice of a claim for rescission, and the parties therefore could not be placed in statu quo, entire rescission was forbidden, but that complainant was entitled, under a prayer for general relief, to have the contract rescinded as to the Florida lands, and to a vendor's lien on the Alabama land to the amount of the estimated value of the Florida lands. Bullock *v.* Tuttle, 90 Ala. 435, 8 So. 69.

Enjoining Collection of Purchase Money.—When the vendee makes out a case which entitles him to a rescission of the contract, the collection of the purchase money will be enjoined, without regard to the solvency of the vendor; and the same rule obtains against an assignee of the vendor, unless the notes were mercantile, and passed in the course of trade to a bona fide holder. Lanier *v.* Hill, 25 Ala. 554.

Same—Canceling Notes for Purchase Money.—In rescinding a contract, at the instance of purchasers, on account of a common mistake of fact, a court of equity will order the negotiable notes given for the purchase money to be canceled, though there is a complete defense at law. Scruggs *v.* Driver, 31 Ala. 274.

Abatement of the Purchase Money.—Where the jurisdiction of equity has attached, on a bill filed by a purchaser, for the purpose of reforming and partially canceling his deed, the court may also, as incidental to this ground of relief, allow an abatement of the purchase money, on account of the vendor's misrepresentations respecting the location of the boundary lines. Williams *v.* Mitchell, 30 Ala. 299.

Recovery of Purchase Money Paid.—On bill filed for the rescission of a contract on the ground of mistake, and the cancellation of the outstanding notes given for purchase money, the jurisdiction of equity having once attached, the court will go on and do complete justice between the parties, although there is an adequate remedy at law to recover a portion of the purchase money already paid. Scruggs *v.* Driver, 31 Ala. 274.

Same—Giving Lien for Repayment of Purchase Money.—On the rescission of a contract, in favor of the vendee, the chancellor rendered a decree declaring a lien on the land for the repayment of the purchase money, and ordering it to be sold by the register if the money was not repaid by a specified day. Held, that the chancellor was authorized to enforce its payment in the mode adopted in his decree. Foster *v.* Gressett, 29 Ala. 393, cited in Bailey *v.* Jordan, 32 Ala. 50; Scott *v.* Greggs, 49 Ala. 191.

In rescinding a contract for the sale of lands at the instance of the purchaser, the court may decree a lien on the land in his favor for the purchase money paid; but in such case, the land being the homestead exemption of the vendor, which is not liable for his contract debts, the lien in favor of the purchaser is subordinate to the claim of the vendor's heirs for the rent while the purchaser was in possession. McWilliams *v.* Jenkins, 72 Ala. 480.

Giving Equitable Offset.—Where the bill prays the rescission of a contract, or the canceling or reforming of an instrument, and an account of matters growing out of the contract, and prays for other and further relief, the court may, denying the relief specially prayed, establish an equitable offset in favor of the plaintiff. Betts *v.* Gunn, 31 Ala. 219, cited in Bell *v.* Thompson, 34 Ala. 633; McDonnell *v.* Finch, 131 Ala. 85, 31 So. 594.

§ 46. —— Recovery of Consideration or of Damages.

Where a purchaser files a bill in equity for the reformation or rescission of a contract on the ground of fraud, but fails to establish his case on either point, the court has no jurisdiction to render a pecuniary judgment in his favor, for moneys advanced and paid out by him under the contract, or for damages resulting from the defendant's fraudulent representations and breach of warranty of title. Betts *v.* Gunn, 31 Ala. 219, cited in Bell *v.* Thompson, 34 Ala. 633.

§ 47. —— Relief to Defendant.

On setting aside an absolute deed on the suggestion of fraud, where the grantee has in good faith made expenditures on the property embraced by it, he is entitled to reimbursement of the same with interest. Kennedy *v.* Kennedy, 2 Ala. 571, cited in McKinley *v.* Irvine, 13 Ala. 681.

In a suit to set aside a note and mortgage, given to secure an attorney's fee which the complainant claimed was contingent, the court can not decree that the attorney shall be entitled to one-half the fee secured by the mortgage. Birmingham Lot Co. *v.* Taylor (Ala.), 62 So. 521.

Where a purchaser of land from a broker, who fraudulently took title in his own name, was notified of the principal's claim before purchase, on title being declared to be in the principal the purchaser can not recover for improvements made on the land purchased. Dean *v.* Roberts (Ala.), 62 So. 44.

Upon a bill in equity brought by the purchaser of land for the rescission of a contract, the plaintiff is not entitled to a deduction from the amount of rents and profits received by him during his possession of the land, for his counsel fees in the suit for rescission. Garner *v.* Leverett, 32 Ala. 410.

§ 48. Judgment or Decree and Enforcement Thereof.

Where, pending a suit to cancel a conveyance to defendant, he died, and the suit was revived against his heirs and against his administrator and widow, and the heirs and administrator allowed decrees pro confesso to be taken, the widow having had no estate in the lands, under Code 1907, § 3754, and there being no allegations to show that she had a dower interest, and the decrees pro confesso, under section 3163, admitting all allegations of the bill and dispensing with proof, a decree for complainant would be entered. Martin *v.* Evans, 50 So. 997, 163 Ala. 657.

§ 49. Costs.

Where defendant offered all the relief which the court decreed, and the complainant refused to accept it, it was held that the chancellor did not err in imposing upon the complainant the entire costs of the suit. Gallagher *v.* Witherington, 29 Ala. 420.

Candidates.

See the title ELECTIONS.

Capita.

As to taking per capita, see the titles DESCENT AND DISTRIBUTION; WILLS. As to per capita tax, see the title TAXATION.

Capital—Capital Stock.

As to corporate capital in general, see the titles BANKS AND BANKING; CORPORATIONS; RAILROADS; etc. As to taxation of capital stock, see the title TAXATION.

Capital Punishment.

See the titles ARSON; CRIMINAL LAW; HOMICIDE; RAPE.

Capitation Tax.

See the title TAXATION.

Care—Carelessness.

See the titles CARRIERS; MASTER AND SERVANT; NEGLIGENCE; RAILROADS; SHIPPING.

Carnal Knowledge.

See the titles ADULTERY; DISORDERLY HOUSE; INCEST; LEWDNESS; RAPE; SEDUCTION.

CARRIERS.

III. Carriage of Live Stock.

Cross References.

See the titles COMMERCE; CORPORATIONS; FERRIES; MASTER AND SERVANT; SHIPPING; TELEGRAPHS AND TELEPHONES.

As to the nature of an action against a carrier by passenger for breach of duty, see the title ACTION. As to the nature of an action against a common carrier for a breach of contract of shipment of goods or live stock either by failure to deliver or failure to deliver within a specified time, see the title ACTION. As to the construction, regulation, and operation of railroads in general, see the title RAILROADS. As to the construction, regulation, and operation of street railroads in general, see the title STREET RAILROADS. As to the duty of railroad companies to furnish accommodations and facilities at stations, see the title RAILROADS.

I. CONTROL AND REGULATION OF COMMON CARRIER.

(A) IN GENERAL.

§ 1. Who Are Common Carriers.

As to carriers of passengers, see post, "Who Are Carriers," § 149.

"A common carrier is one who undertakes for hire or reward, to transport the goods of such as choose to employ him from place to place." Babcock *v.* Herbert, 3 Ala. 392, 396; Central R., etc., Co. *v.* Lampley, 76 Ala. 357, 364.

Flatboat—Necessity for Readiness to Carry Goods of Public.—If the owners of a flatboat hold themselves out to the public generally as ready and willing to carry any cotton that may be shipped on their boat, they are liable as common carriers; but, if they only propose to carry the cotton of particular persons, they can not be held liable as common carriers to a third person, with whom the master of the boat, in violation of their instructions, makes a contract for freight. Steele *v.* McTyer, 31 Ala. 667.

Right to Compensation as Affecting Liability.—It is not necessary, to constitute one a common carrier, that a stipulation should be entered into as to the amount of freight to be paid. But, unless a right to compensation exists, the common-law liability of a common carrier is not created, though there may be the responsibility of a mandatary incurred. Knox *v.* Rives, 14 Ala. 249; Central Railroad & Banking Co. *v.* Lampley, 76 Ala. 357, 364.

The delivery of freight to a carrier, and its acceptance, and transportation thereof according to directions, without payment or promise of reward, make the carrier liable only for damages caused by its gross negligence. Louisville & N. R. Co. *v.* Gerson, 102 Ala. 409, 14 So. 873.

"**Hackmen, cartmen, and wagoners,** engaged in the carriage of goods or persons for hire, by the common law are regarded as common carriers, and the power lies in the legislature, in the absence of constitutional restraint or limitation to regulate, to prescribe the rules according to which their business may be conducted. Munn *v.* Illinois, 94 U. S. 113. The power may be, and is often, delegated to municipal corporations, to be exercised for the promotion of the public convenience. When the power has been delegated in terms of the charter employed in the amended charter, the validity of ordinances prescribing the times, places, and manner in which the employment is to be pursued has been uniformly sustained." Lindsey *v.* Anniston, 104 Ala. 257, 16 So. 545, 546.

Custom of Steamboat to Carry Cash Letters.—The owners of a steamboat are responsible as common carriers for the loss of a cash letter delivered to the clerk, if the jury find that it is the general custom of steamboats to carry such letters, although they are delivered to the clerk and carried without charge. Garey *v.* Meagher, 33 Ala. 630. But see ante, catchline, "Right to Compensation as Affecting Liability."

Although ordinarily a steamboat may not be compelled to take charge of a letter containing cash, yet, if the general usage of boats in a particular trade to take charge of such letters is shown. the delivery of such letter to a particular boat will be governed by this common usage. Hosea *v.* McCrory, 12 Ala. 349.

In an action against the owners of a steamboat to recover the value of a sealed package of money delivered by plaintiff to the clerk of such boat for transportation, the proof was that, although it was the uniform custom of steamboats to carry cash letters. no charge was made for such service, unless a receipt was demanded by the shipper, when a charge of one-fourth of 1 per cent was made upon the amount of the bills. Held, that it was not improper for the court to leave to the jury the question of fact, whether cash letters belonged to that class or character of goods which the boat undertook to carry for hire. Knox *v.* Rives, 14 Ala. 249.

A public ferryman who has given bond as required by law, is a common carrier. Babcock *v.* Herbert, 3 Ala. 392, cited in note in 68 L. R. A. 154. See, generally, the title FERRIES.

Express Companies.—Express companies are "common carriers." Southern Express Co. *v.* Ramey, 51 So. 314, 164 Ala. 206.

In this state, express companies are subject to all the common-law liabilities of common carriers. Southern Exp. Co. *v.* Hess, 53 Ala. 19.

Express companies who are engaged, not only in the transportation of small parcels, packages, and articles of value, properly so called, but also in the carriage of goods, wares, and merchandise, and the great staples and products of the country, are common carriers, and subject to the liabilities imposed by law upon such carriers. Southern Exp. Co. *v.* Crook, 44 Ala. 468.

Railroad Companies.—"It is now too well settled in this state to admit of question that railroad companies are common carriers, and, as such, that they are amenable to the liabilities imposed by the law applicable to common carriers, as the same is administered in this state. Selma, etc., R. Co. *v.* Butts, 43 Ala. 385." Southwestern R. Co. *v.* Webb, 48 Ala. 585. See, to the same effect, Selma, etc., R. Co. *v.* Butts, 43 Ala. 385; Mobile, etc., R. Co. *v.* Hopkins, 41 Ala. 486; Mobile, etc., R. Co. *v.* Prewitt, 46 Ala. 63, 67.

Custom of Railroad to Deliver Cars on Spur Track.—A railroad, which serves business houses located along a spur track by delivering to them cars of freight and cars to be freighted and shipped, is a common carrier with respect to the use it makes of the track, and is, as such, bound to treat the houses along the track without discrimination, and can not discontinue its service as to one and continue it as to others. W. C. Agee & Co. *v.* Louisville & N. R. Co., 37 So. 680, 142 Ala. 344, cited in notes in 12 L. R. A., N. S., 508, 41 L. R. A., N. S., 680.

§ 2. Licenses and Taxes.

City License Tax on Railroad.—A railroad company's liability to pay a license tax required of a company running cars through the city, for transporting freight or passengers to or from it, is not affected by its not having an agent or office in the city. Nashville, C. & St. L. Ry. Co. *v.* Alabama City, 32 So. 731, 134 Ala. 414.

Municipal Taxes on Express Companies.—The authority of a city under its charter to collect specific taxes on express companies doing business therein is not taken away as to the Southern Express Company by the provision of an act in relation to said company declaring "nor shall any municipal corporation levy any percentage tax upon the receipts of said company." City Council of Montgomery *v.* Shoemaker, 51 Ala. 114.

Effect of Act 1892-93 on Right of City to Levy License Tax.—Act 1892-93, providing that express companies shall pay a privilege tax to the state, and that no company which has paid such tax shall be liable to pay any other tax in the state precludes a city from levying a license tax on an express company. Douglass *v.* City of Anniston, 104 Ala. 291, 16 So. 133.

As Act 1892-93, providing for a state privilege tax on express companies, furnishes a remedy for its violation, the fact that an express company is in default thereunder will not authorize a city to levy a license tax on such company. Douglass *v.* Anniston, 104 Ala. 291, 16 So. 133.

§ 3. Charges.

Classification of Goods.—A shipment of box car loads of pieces of hickory, 30 inches in length and running from 10 to 30 inches in diameter and either in their natural round state as cut from the trunk of trees or split in sections is not a shipment of logs within Acts Sp. Sess. 1907, p. 112, fixing rates on logs, especially where the shipper denominated the shipment as a specified number of cords. Monogram Hardwood Co. *v.* Louisville, etc., R. Co., 6 Ala. App. 629, 60 So. 949.

Blocks of wood from 6 to 15 inches in diameter and 38 to 42 inches long, sawed from round logs in their natural state, are not classified as "logs and box materials" by the 110 commodities act (Laws 1907, p. 209); and a contract for their transportation, which describes them as cordwood, at the rate fixed for cordwood, is binding on the shipper and carrier; and the mere fact that the consignee or subsequent buyer may manufacture the blocks into barrel heads does not justify the carrier in reclassifying them as logs and box material, and demanding a higher rate as a condition precedent to a delivery. Southern Ry. Co. *v.* Lowe, 170 Ala. 598, 54 So. 51.

Rate on Local Freight—Time of Basis Freight.—The rate on freight "carried over the whole line of its road," which furnishes the basis for the additional 50 per cent allowed by Acts 1873, p. 62, for the transportation of "local freight," is the rate charged on freight taken on at one terminus and discharged at the other, and not the rate for freight brought from or carried to a point beyond the termini of the road. The basis rate is the rate prevailing at the time of shipment. Mobile & M. Ry. Co. *v.* Steiner, 61 Ala. 559.

Power of Municipality to Fix Rate for Hire of Hacks.—An ordinance fixing a rate for hire of hacks, etc., and imposing fine or imprisonment for refusal to pay such rate, was within the legislative authority of a municipality authorized to regulate such conveyances. Bray *v.* State, 37 So. 250, 140 Ala. 172.

§ 4. Preferences and Discriminations.

As to interstate commerce, see post, "Preferences and Discriminations," § 11.

Rebate—Aid of Industrial Enterprises under Code 1886.—Under Code 1886, § 1161, which prohibits railroad companies from making any departure from their published freight rates except to aid in the development of industrial enterprises in the state, an agreement to allow a rebate on coal shipped to a miller, and used by him in manufacturing corn into meal, is valid. Louisville & N. R. Co. *v.* Fulgham, 91 Ala. 555, 8 So. 803, cited in note in 6 L. R. A., N. S., 227.

Compression of Cotton by Plant of Railroad's Selection.—A carrier made no distinction in rate between compressed and uncompressed cotton, but included in its rate the cost of compression, and uncompressed cotton in a designated district was compressed at a distant place at the carrier's expense at a plant in which it was interested. A plant existed in the designated district, but the carrier declined to pay the cost of compression there, though such cost was not greater than that paid at the other plant. It accorded to both places the same privilege as to rebilling and through rating. Held, that the carrier was not guilty of discrimination, in violation of Act Feb. 23, 1907 (Laws 1907, pp. 123, 129) §§ 17, 32. Railroad Commission of Alabama *v.* Central of Georgia Ry. Co., 49 So. 237, 159 Ala. 550.

"The question of differential rates on compressed and uncompressed cotton, in the territory affected, is not a factor in the case. The commission's order itself eliminates that consideration, for a reason therein given. Hence, it necessarily follows that the discrimination complained against is wholly predicated upon the practice of the carrier in selecting the plant at which compression of cotton shipped over its lines shall be, at its cost and expense, compressed. As indicated, the compression is a service of no concern to the producer. It simply enables the carrier to put two bales of compressed cotton in a space one uncompressed bale would occupy. The carrier pays the cost and expense of a process resulting in such benefit peculiarly and only to it. Naturally, those concerned with the Union Springs Compress and the people of that community are interested in the patronage of that plant. Any defection of business of that character therefrom affects the enterprise and the business activity of Union Springs. But, natural and certainly righteous as their stated interests are, that alone can not avail to condemn the described practice of this carrier. Such a practice is in no sense a discrimination or a favoritism violative of the enactments in question. The practice is only an exercise by the carrier of its clear right to economize its shipping facilities at its own expense, just as it has the right to locate its shops wherever it sees fit, or to buy its equipment in any market, and this without violating any law of which we know, and without the breach of any duty to any interest or community." Railroad Comm. *v.* Central, etc., R. Co., 159 Ala. 550, 49 So. 237, 238.

Agreement to Hold Train for Shipment of Stock.—Under Code 1907, § 5540, making a common carrier, directly or indirectly giving any undue or unreasonable preference or advantage to any person, guilty of unlawful discrimination, punishable by fine, construed with Act Feb. 4, 1887, c. 104, §§ 3, 6, 24 Stat. 380 (U. S. Comp. St. 1901, pp. 3155, 3156), and Act Feb. 19, 1903, c. 708, 32 Stat. 847 (U. S. Comp. St. Supp. 1911, p. 1309), forbidding common carriers subject to the act to make any undue or unreasonable preference, a common carrier's agreement, in advance of issuing its bill of lading, to hold a certain train at a certain time and place for the shipment of live stock is an unreasonable preference and void. Louisville, etc., R. Co. *v.* Jones, 6 Ala. App. 617, 60 So. 945.

Under Code 1907, § 5540, declaring a carrier giving any undue or unreasonable preference or advantage to any person, guilty of unlawful discrimination, construed with Act Feb. 4, 1887, c. 104, §§ 3, 6, 24 Stat. 380 (U. S. Comp. St. 1901, pp. 3155, 3156), and Act Feb. 19, 1903, c. 708, 32 Stat. 847 (U. S. Comp. St. Supp. 1911, p. 1309), declaring it unlawful for a common carrier, subject thereto, to give any undue or unreasonable preference, a shipper can not recover damages for a breach of a carrier's special contract to hold a certain train, at a certain time and place, for his convenience in the shipment of live stock. Louisville, etc., R. Co. *v.* Jones, 6 Ala. App. 617, 60 So. 945.

§ 5. Proceedings to Enforce or to Prevent Enforcement of Regulations.

The courts may compel carriers to perform a positive duty imposed by law, and may restrain acts in excess of the powers granted. Horton *v.* Southern Ry. Co., 173 Ala. 231, 55 So. 531.

Remedy for Excessive Charges.—Mandamus is not the proper remedy for excessive charges by a railway company; that under Code, § 1698, allowing double damages, etc., being adequate. State *v.* Mobile & M. Ry. Co., 59 Ala. 321.

Sufficiency of Petition for Mandamus.—In a petition for a mandamus to compel a railway company to accept lawful freight rates, without discrimination, an allegation that the relator tendered "bales of lint cotton" to the company, without specifying any number, is fatally indefinite in being insufficient to enable the court, upon awarding the writ, to command the company to do a specific act or thing. State *v.* Mobile & M. Ry. Co., 59 Ala. 321.

§ 6. Damages for Violations of Regulations.

Recovery for Excess Charges.—Code, § 3460, provides that any railroad which shall exact more than the rate specified in any bill of lading, or shall make any overcharge, shall be liable for double the damages sustained, unless the service as to which the extortion was committed was performed at rates previously approved by the railroad commissioners, when only actual damages may be recovered. Held that, where bills of lading for coal shipped specified a rate of 50 cents per ton, and defendant exacted 70 cents per ton, and contended, in an action to recover the excess, that the 50-cent rate was a mistake, and that the 70-cent rate had been authorized by the railroad commissioners, and had been posted in all freight depots, but failed to prove that such rate had been so allowed or posted in the place to which the coal was shipped, plaintiff was entitled to recover under the statute. Southern Ry. Co. *v.* Anniston Foundry & Machine Co., 33 So. 274, 135 Ala. 315.

§ 7. Penalties for Violations of Regulations.

Penalty for Excessive Charge.—Under Act of April 19, 1873, providing a penalty for excessive charges on freight by railroad companies, the rate which furnishes the basis for such penalty is that charged on freight taken at one terminus of the road and discharged at the other, and not the rate for freight brought from or carried to a point beyond either terminus. Lotspeich *v.* Central Railroad & Banking Co., 73 Ala. 306. See post, "Rates of Freight," § 118.

§ 8. Offenses by Persons Dealing with Carriers.

Riding of Freight Cars—Evidence.—Evidence held to sustain a conviction of riding on a freight car without authority from the conductor of the train or permission of the engineer, and with the intention of being transported free. Gains *v.* State, 43 So. 137, 149 Ala. 29.

(B) INTERSTATE AND INTERNATIONAL TRANSPORTATION.

See, generally, the titles COMMERCE; CONSTITUTIONAL LAW; MASTER AND SERVANT.

§ 9. Statutory Provisions.

Application to Shipment over Lines without the State.—Code, § 1159, providing that carriers exacting exorbitant charges for freight are guilty of extortion, and liable for double the damages sustained, does not apply to shipments over lines without the state. Mobile & O. R. Co. *v.* Dismukes, 94 Ala. 131, 10 So. 289, 17 L. R. A. 113.

§ 10. Charges in General.

Parties to an interstate shipment are presumed to contract with reference to the acts of congress on that subject, and such contracts can not be construed with reference to any other law. Southern Ry. Co. *v.* Harrison, 24 So. 552, 119 Ala. 539, overruling Mobile & O. R. Co. *v.* Dismukes, 94 Ala. 131, 10 So. 289, 17 L. R. A. 113. See notes in 63 L. R. A. 525, 14 L. R. A., N. S., 401.

It is not in the contemplation of the interstate commerce law that persons dealing with common carriers should be held to know their published schedules of rates. Mobile & O. R. Co. *v.* Dismukes, 94 Ala. 131, 10 So. 289, 17 L. R. A. 113, overruling Mobile, etc., R. Co. *v.* Dismukes, 94 Ala. 131, 10 So. 289, 17 L. R. A. 113. See notes in 63 L. R. A. 525, 14 L. R. A., N. S., 401.

§ 11. Preferences and Discriminations.

See, also, ante, "Preferences and Discriminations," § 4.

A privilege granted to a shipper by a carrier to prevent freight being carried over a competing line is unjustifiable, and will not relieve the carrier from being amenable to the interstate commerce act. Central of Georgia R. Co. *v.* Patterson, 6 Ala. App. 494, 60 So. 465.

Free Storage for Indefinite Period.—A contract which gives a shipper the right to remove his goods after their arrival at his convenience is a special contract, whereby the carrier agrees to furnish to the shipper free storage for his goods for an indefinite period, dependent on the shipper's convenience, and is discriminatory in violation of the Interstate Commerce Act Feb. 4, 1887, c. 104, §§ 3,

6, 24 Stat. 380 (U. S. Comp. St. 1901, pp. 3155, 3156), and Elkins Act Feb. 19, 1903, c. 708, 32 Stat. 847 (U. S. Comp. St. Supp. 1911, p. 1309), prohibiting unreasonable preferences, since storage is an incident of transportation, so that the granting of a special storage privilege as a part of the service covered by the rate charged for carriage is a preference. Central, etc., R. Co. *v.* Patterson, 6 Ala. App. 494, 60 So. 465.

§ 12. Contracts in Violation of Regulations.

Contract for Rate in Violation of Statute.—Under Interstate Commerce Act, § 6, requiring interstate carriers to post their tariffs, and prohibiting them from charging rates other than those published, a contract for the transportation of an interstate shipment at less than the published rate approved by the interstate commerce commission is invalid; and the carrier may collect the rate as published, regardless of that fixed by the bill of lading. Southern Ry. Co. *v.* Harrison, 24 So. 552, 119 Ala. 539, 43 L. R. A. 385, overruling Mobile & O. R. Co. *v.* Dismukes, 94 Ala. 131, 10 So. 289. See notes in 65 L. R. A. 525, 14 L. R. A., N. S., 401.

Effect of Partial Invalidity on Right to Recover for Injury to Goods.—A bill of lading of an interstate shipment, which contains clauses repugnant to the Interstate Commerce Act (Act Feb. 4, 1887, c. 104, 24 Stat. 386 [U. S. Comp. St. 1901, p. 3169]) § 20, as amended by Act June 29, 1906, c. 3591, § 7, 34 Stat. 593 (U. S. Comp. St. Supp. 1909, p. 1163), is not thereby entirely vitiated, but the holder thereof may recover for a failure to safely transport the goods. Central of Georgia Ry. Co. *v.* Sims, 53 So. 826, 169 Ala. 295.

II. CARRIAGE OF GOODS.

(A) DELIVERY TO CARRIER.

§ 13. Duty of Carrier to Receive and Transport Goods.

A common carrier is in general bound to transport all goods that are properly offered for that purpose. Atlantic Coast Line R. Co. *v.* Rice, 52 So. 918, 169 Ala. 265, cited in note in 39 L. R. A., N. S., 641.

"A common carrier is bound to transport all freight and passengers which offer, within the line of his usual business, and an unreasonable failure or refusal is a breach of the duty imposed by the nature and character of his employment. 2 Redf. Rail. 219, § 182." Evans *v.* Memphis, etc., R. Co., 56 Ala. 246, 252.

Duty to Accept as Affected by Condition of Goods.—A carrier has the right to inspect proffered shipments and to refuse them when not in fit condition for transportation, and, where ordinary observation would discover their unfitness, it is the duty of the carrier to refuse the shipment in order that the shipper may put it into a fit condition for transportation. Atlantic, etc., R. Co. *v.* Rice, 52 So. 918, 169 Ala. 265, cited in note in 39 L. R. A., N. S., 641.

§ 14. Duty to Furnish Shipping Facilities or Means of Transportation.

"Upon a tender of goods to a common carrier for shipment, the carrier is bound, by reason of its general relation to the public, to make all reasonable efforts to furnish facilities for their transportation." Central, etc., R. Co. *v.* Sigma Lumber Co., 170 Ala. 627, 54 So. 205, 206.

§ 15. Acts Constituting Delivery to and Acceptance by Carrier.

Deposit of Goods—Notice.—To render a common carrier liable for the loss of goods, there must have been an actual delivery of the goods to him, or a constructive delivery, with notice to him of an intention thereby to place them in his care and custody. Merely placing them in such a position that he could easily have taken them, but without calling his attention to them, is not sufficient. O'Bannon *v.* Southern Exp. Co., 51 Ala. 481.

In an action against a railroad company for failure to deliver cotton received by it for transportation, etc., it is not liable for cotton stolen or lost after a deposit on a platform at a station house, unless it be shown that the railroad company or its agents had notice of the deposit, and received the cotton for transportation as a common carrier. Southwestern R. Co. *v.* Webb, 48 Ala. 585.

Custom or Usage as to Delivery of Freight.—The rules observed by shippers in their general transactions with the depot agent of a railroad company touching the delivery of freight for shipment, if continuous or general, though not universal, may grow into a usage, authorizing others to treat it as the proper rule, and as an element of the contract of shipment, although the usage may be in conflict with regulations established and promulgated by the company's superintendent, known to the shippers, and no notice of it is traced to the superintendent. Montgomery, etc., R. Co. *v.* Kolb, 73 Ala. 396, cited in note in 32 L. R. A., N. S., 314.

A deposit of cotton in a street along the side of the platform of a railroad depot, or in the railroad cotton yard, for shipment, in pursuance of a custom or usage adopted or sanctioned by the depot agent, may amount to a delivery to the railroad company, although no receipt is given by the agent to the shipper, and such usage or custom is contrary to the established regulations of the company, known to the shipper, and no notice thereof is traced to the superintendent or managing agent of the company. Montgomery & E. Ry. Co. *v.* Kolb, 73 Ala. 396, cited in note in 32 L. R. A., N. S., 314.

Goods Received for Shipment to Fictitious Firm and Embezzled by Agent.—The agent of an express company at S. induced a bank at J., by fraud, to send money to a fictitious firm at S., and the express company received and receipted for the package at J., and shipped it to S., where the agent embezzled it. Held, that the money sent was constructively in the possession of the express company, and could be recovered from it by the bank. Jasper Trust Co. *v.* Kansas City M. & B. R. Co., 99 Ala. 416, 14 So. 546, cited in note in 37 L. R. A. 180.

Question for Jury.—In an action against a carrier for failure to deliver goods intrusted to him, whether there was an actual delivery to him for transportation is a question of fact to be determined by the jury, under appropriate charges by the court. Southwestern R. Co. *v.* Webb, 48 Ala. 585.

Evidence — Weight. — Defendant carrier's rules provided that cotton should not be allowed to remain on the shipping platform over night without written directions for its shipment given by the owner to defendant. Held that, on the question whether plaintiff's cotton was delivered to defendant for shipment on a certain day or the day following, the fact that the cotton was placed on the shipping platform on the first day, and plaintiff's testimony that he then gave defendant's agents verbal shipping directions, is not a preponderance of evidence, over the testimony of two of defendant's agents that they received no shipping directions until the second day, and that the cotton was placed on the platform without consent. Louisville & N. R. Co. *v.* Echols, 97 Ala. 556, 12 So. 304.

§ 16. Delivery to Carrier as Condition Precedent to Liability.

"In all actions against common carriers of goods the first step in the plaintiff's proof is to show delivery of the goods to the carrier. He makes out no case until that is done." Capehart *v.* Granite Mills, 97 Ala. 353, 12 So. 44, 47.

§ 17. Actions for Refusal to Receive or Transport Goods.

Nature of Remedy.—Damages from breach of a carrier's express contract to furnish cars at a specified time are recoverable in an action on the contract; but, in the absence of an express contract, the proposing shipper has no action save for a breach of the carrier's general common-law duty to furnish cars within a reasonable time. Central of Georgia Ry. Co. *v.* Sigma Lumber Co., 170 Ala. 627, 54 So. 205.

(B) BILLS OF LADING, SHIPPING RECEIPTS, AND SPECIAL CONTRACTS.

§ 18. What Law Governs.

Where a shipper contracted in New York with a carrier to ship goods and deliver them at Birmingham, Ala., the contract, so far as delivery was involved, was to be wholly performed in Alabama, and the carrier's liability for failure to deliver depended upon the law of that state. Southern Express Co. *v.* Gibbs, 46 So. 465, 155 Ala. 303.

§ 19. Authority of Agents and Employees.

Power to Bind Company to Deliver Goods at Certain Rate.—Plaintiffs, desiring to trade certain goods for others owned by persons at a distance, plaintiffs to pay charges on both shipments, asked the freight clerk of defendant express company what the charges would be. The clerk informed them that the charges on the goods plaintiffs were to receive would be not more than a certain sum. This shipment was necessarily made over two lines of express, one of which had no connection or contract with defendant. The clerk had authority to give rates generally, but it was not his duty to give rates on unconnecting lines, whose charges were unknown to him. Held, that his general authority empowered him to bind the company to deliver the goods at a certain rate, even in the case of a mistake on his part, which inflicted loss on the company. Southern Exp. Co. *v.* Boullemet, 100 Ala. 275, 13 So. 941. But see post, "Rates of Freight," § 118.

Usage.—The delivery of a letter containing cash to the clerk of a steamboat is a delivery to the master, for the purpose of charging him; and it is not necessary to show a special authority to the clerk to receive such letters, when a general usage of boats in the trade is to receive them. Hosea *v.* McCrory, 12 Ala. 349.

Ratification.—Though an agent has no authority to make a contract for delivery of freight at a certain point, the carrier, having undertaken to carry it out, is liable for loss from negligent performance amounting to breach of contract. Nashville, C. & St. L. R. Co. *v.* Smith, 31 So. 481, 132 Ala. 434, cited in note in 31 L. R. A., N. S., 36.

Question for Jury.—Whether or not a bill of lading was signed by a certain person as agent for the carrier is a question of fact for the jury. Tishomingo Sav. Inst. *v.* Johnson, Nesbitt & Co., 40 So. 503, 146 Ala. 691.

Admissibility of Evidence to Show Ratification.—In an action against a railroad company for failure to deliver goods shipped, the receipt issued was signed by "R. B. S., R. R. Agent, per J. R. B." B. testified, on behalf of plaintiff, that he was appointed subagent by S.; that the president and superintendent of the road knew that he was acting as such agent, and made no objection; that the officers of the road frequently gave him directions about the business, and that freight had been delivered on at least two occasions on the production of his receipts, which were similar in form to the one given to plaintiff. Held, that the evidence was admissible as tending to prove a ratification of the agency. Alabama & T. R. R. Co. *v.* Kidd, 29 Ala. 221.

§ 20. Validity of Bill of Lading or Receipt.

"A bill of lading, regular on its face and issued by a carrier or its authorized agent, is a certificate that the person to whom it is issued is the shipper of the property or the goods therein described, that they really existed, and are subject to the order and direction of the shipper, unless the bill of lading furnishes notice that such is not the fact." Jasper Trust Co. *v.* Kansas, etc., R. Co., 99 Ala. 416, 14 So. 546.

"**A bill of lading stands for and represents the goods** therein receipted for during their transit, and until they are completely delivered to the person entitled to them, but no longer." American Nat. Bank *v.* Henderson, 123 Ala. 612, 26 So. 498; Allen, etc., Co. *v.* Maury & Co., 66 Ala. 10; Veitch *v.* Atkins Grocery, etc., Co., 5 Ala. App. 444, 59 So. 746, 750; Wayland *v.* Mosely, 5 Ala. 430.

§ 21. Construction and Operation of Bill of Lading.

§ 21½. In General.

A bill of lading is of a dual character and effect; one is that of a receipt, and the other, that of a contract. Alabama Great Southern R. Co. *v.* Norris, 52 So. 891, 167 Ala. 311; McTyer *v.* Steele, 26 Ala. 487; Cox *v.* Peterson, 30 Ala. 608.

Evidence as to Performed Parol Agreement.—Where the shipper is impliedly bound on the face of the bill of lading to pay the freight of goods, it may be shown by parol evidence that the carrier received them under an agreement with a third person to pay the freight, if such person has in fact paid it. Wayland *v.* Mosely, 5 Ala. 430.

Direction to "Notify."—A direction in a bill of lading to "notify" a named person shows that he is not intended as the consignee. Atlantic Coast Line R. Co. *v.* Dahlberg Brokerage Co., 170 Ala. 617, 54 So. 168.

Misstatement of Quantity.—Where a carrier's agent, on receiving a shipment of cotton, did not weigh it, but issued a bill of lading on a certificate of a compress company, which delivered the cotton in a sealed car, and the bill stated, "contents and condition of contents of packages unknown," though the cotton weighed less than the weight given in the bill, whereby the consignee, who purchased from the consignor, was deceived, to his injury, the carrier was not liable to the consignee, either under general principles or under Code 1896, § 4223, making a carrier liable for loss resulting from the issuance of a bill of lading when no property has been received. Alabama Great Southern R. Co. *v.* Commonwealth Cotton Mfg. Co., 42 So. 406, 146 Ala. 388, cited in note in 34 L. R. A., N. S., 1180.

"While the carrier may bind himself as to the quantity receipted for by express stipulation, and while there may be cases in which the carrier is liable because of fraud or intentional misstatement, or of such gross overvaluation as to be evidence of fraud, yet in a case like this, where the goods were stated to be 50 bales of cotton and 50 bales were delivered, where the bill of lading contained the saving clause as in this case, the carrier was not responsible for the deficiency in weight. As stated by Lord Mansfield: 'If the master qualifies his acknowledgment by the words "Contents unknown," he acknowledges nothing.' Hutchinson on Carriers (2d Ed.), § 125a; Porter on Bills of Lading, pp. 38, 39, 40, 43." Alabama, etc., R. Co. *v.* Commonwealth Cotton Mfg. Co., 146 Ala. 388, 42 So. 406, 408.

"The general principle is, in so far a bill of lading is a receipt, it is 'only prima facie evidence that the carrier has received the goods, or that it has received the quantity named; and, like all mere receipts, they may be shown to have been given by mistake or not to speak the truth.' Hutchinson on Carriers (2d Ed.), § 122. The practice among carriers or their agents of signing bills of lading before the actual receipt of the goods has given rise to a considerable amount of litigation; and, while there are a few cases to the contrary, it is fully settled now, by the great weight of authority, that such bills of lading, whether in the hands of the original party or of an assignee, do not create any liability against the carrier. The theory of these cases is that the agent of the carrier has no authority to give a bill of lading until the goods are received for transportation, and the party who takes such a bill of lading has full knowledge of the want of authority. Hutchinson on Carriers (2d Ed.), § 123." Alabama, etc., R. Co. *v.* Commonwealth Cotton Mfg. Co., 146 Ala. 388, 42 So. 406.

Issuance by Intermediate Carrier before Receipt of Goods.—Shippers represented to an intermediate carrier, to whom a consignment was about to be delivered from the initial carrier, that they had sold the goods to an out of town purchaser, who wished to obtain a bill of lading before leaving for his home. To accommodate him and the shippers, and expecting soon to obtain possession of the goods, the intermediate carrier issued a bill of lading for them. Held, that the bill of lading was not fraudulent, within Code 1896, § 4223 (Code 1886, § 1179), making a carrier liable for all damages resulting from the issuance by it of a bill of lading for goods not in its possession. Thompson *v.* Alabama Midland R. Co., 24 So. 931, 122 Ala. 378.

§ 22. —— As a Receipt.

A bill of lading is an acknowledgment of the receipt of the property by the carrier. Williams *v.* Louisville & N. R. Co. (Ala.), 58 So. 315.

In an action against a transportation company for failure to deliver certain cotton, it appeared that the bill of lading was issued by one H., who was engaged in the transfer business and was accustomed to transfer cotton to the river landing for shipment by defendant's boats; that H. was authorized by defendant to issue bills of lading for it, but that there was an express agreement that defendant should not be responsible for the cotton till it was actually delivered at the river, which agreement was known to the shippers. There was no proof of actual delivery of the cotton to defendant, except the identification of the bill of lading by H., and there was evidence to the contrary. Held, that an instruction that the issuance by H., under defendant's authority, of the bill of lading was prima facie evidence of delivery to defendant, was erroneous. Capehart *v.* Granite Mills, 97 Ala. 353, 12 So. 44.

Parol Evidence.—So far as a bill of lading acknowledges the receipt of goods, and states their condition, it may be contradicted by parol evidence, but in other respects is to be treated as other written contracts. Wayland *v.* Mosely, 5 Ala. 430.

§ 23. —— As a Contract.

A bill of lading is a contract, the language of which is subject to the rules of construction which govern other contracts. Logan *v.* Mobile Trade Co., 46 Ala. 514; Alabama Great Southern R. Co. *v.* Norris, 167 Ala. 311, 52 So. 891, 892.

Construed Against Carrier.—"In construing a bill of lading, given by the carrier for the safe transportation and delivery of goods, shipped by a consignor, the contract will be construed most strongly against the carrier, and favorably to the consignor, in case of doubt in any matter of construction. Alabama, etc., R. Co. *v.* Thomas, 89 Ala. 234, 7 So. 762, 763.

A bill of lading is a contract to safely carry and deliver. Williams *v.* Louisville & N. R. Co. (Ala.), 58 So. 315.

A bill of lading for a shipment of goods by a boat bound from S. to M. provided for the payment of a certain amount to N., and for the privilege of reshipping at M. or A., and that "it is understood and agreed that the above goods are to be sent through at the above rates, if any boats are going through to W." Held to impose an obligation to send the goods to W., either from A. or M. Logan *v.* The Mobile Trade Co., 46 Ala. 514, cited in note in 31 L. R. A., N. S., 43.

Failure of Shipper to Sign.—"It is true the bill of lading is issued by the carrier, and is merely signed by the agent alone, but in the absence of fraud, if it is accepted by the shipper or his agent, it becomes binding on him as he is assumed to have read it, or, if he does not read it, it is his own fault, and, if he can not read, he should ask that it be read to him. Western Railway *v.* Harwell, 91 Ala. 340, 8 So. 649; Jones *v.* Cincinnati, etc., R. Co., 89 Ala. 376, 8 So. 61; Alabama, etc., R. Co. *v.* Little, 71 Ala. 611; Steele *v.* Townsend, 37 Ala. 247." Williams *v.* Louisville, etc., R. Co. (Ala.), 58 So. 315, 318.

Parol Evidence.—A bill of lading may partake of the character of both a receipt and a contract, and in the latter quality can not be contradicted or varied by parol evidence. McTyer *v.* Steele, 26 Ala. 487; Cox *v.* Peterson, 30 Ala. 608; Wayland *v.* Mosely, 5 Ala. 430; Williams *v.* Louisville, etc., R. Co. (Ala.), 58 So. 315, 318; Louisville, etc., R. Co. *v.* Fulgham, 91 Ala. 555, 8 So. 803; Tallassee Falls Mfg. Co. *v.* Western R. Co., 117 Ala. 520, 23 So. 139.

Where a bill of lading expressly provided that the carrier would not be liable as a common carrier after the arrival of the goods at their destination, and the bill was free from ambiguity, evidence that a custom existed allowing plaintiff more than a reasonable time in which to remove freight was properly excluded, since evidence of a local, particular usage was not admissible to change the written contract; such usage being in existence at the time of the execution of the contract, and expressly stipulated against. Tallassee Falls Mfg. Co. *v.* Western Ry. of Alabama, 29 So. 203, 128 Ala. 167.

"Although a bill of lading is issued by the carrier, it may of course be shown that this was not the contract of shipment, but that the shipment was under another and different contract, whether oral or in writing." Elliott on Railroads, § 1415, et seq. Alabama, etc., R. Co. *v.* Norris, 167 Ala. 311, 52 So. 891, 892.

§ 24. Negotiability and Transfer of Bill of Lading.

§ 25. —— Negotiability and Assignability.

A bill of lading is not a negotiable instrument. Moore *v.* Robinson, 62 Ala. 537; Voss *v.* Robertson, 46 Ala. 483.

The statute, Code 1886, § 1179, relating to the issuance of false bills of lading enacted to prevent frauds, sometimes perpetrated through spurious bills of lading, was not intended to make them negotiable instruments, like bills of exchange. Jasper Trust Co. *v.* Kansas, etc., R. Co., 99 Ala. 416, 14 So. 546.

§ 26. —— Rights of Transferee as against Carrier.

Where a bill of lading was sent to a bank as security for an attached draft, a delivery of the goods by the carrier to another than the bank was a conversion, entitling the bank to maintain trover against the carrier. Tishomingo Sav. Inst. *v.* Johnson, Nesbitt & Co., 40 So. 503, 146 Ala. 691.

Recovery of Advances on False Bill of Lading.—A bona fide purchaser of a false bill of lading from the person to whom it was issued by a railroad company's agent may hold the company liable to the extent of advances made on it, under Code 1886, § 1179, which provides that any carrier which issues a bill of lading, as if property had been received, shall be liable to any person injured thereby. Jasper Trust Co. *v.* Kansas City, M. & B. R. Co., 99 Ala. 416, 14 So. 546.

The agent of an express company, who was also agent of a railroad company, issued fictitious bills of lading, as shipped by a fictitious firm, and induced a bank to discount a draft, accompanied by the bill of lading, drawn on the supposed consignee. The proceeds of the draft, which was shipped by the bank to the fictitious firm through the express company, were embezzled by the agent. Held, that the bank could recover from the express company the money so shipped without first surrendering to the company the bill of lading. Southern Exp. Co. *v.* Bank of Tupelo, 108 Ala. 517, 18 So. 664.

False Bill of Lading Issued to Fictitious Firm.—Where a railroad company's agent issued a bill of lading to a fictitious firm for goods never received, and indorsed it to a bank with the name of such firm, the bank was put on inquiry concerning the indorsing firm, and could not recover from the railroad company for advances on the bill, under Code 1886, § 1179. Jasper Trust Co. *v.* Kansas City, M. & B. R. Co., 99 Ala. 416, 14 So. 546.

§ 27. —— Rights and Liabilities of Transferee as to Persons Other than Carrier.

Where an agent purchased cotton for his principals, and sent the bill of lading, with draft on the principals attached, to a bank, which credited the proceeds of the draft to the seller of the cotton and held the bill of lading as security, the bank obtained title to the cotton. Tishomingo Sav. Inst. *v.* Johnson, Nesbitt & Co., 40 So. 503, 146 Ala. 691.

The indorsement and delivery of a bill of lading on the discount of a draft drawn by the consignor of the goods represented by the bill of lading, for the purchase price of such goods, operate to pass to the transferee a special title to the goods, as against the consignor and his creditors, defeasible only on acceptance and payment of the draft by the consignee. American Nat. Bank *v.* Henderson, 26 So. 498, 123 Ala. 612.

Nature of Title Acquired.—Assignments of bills of lading are not governed by the commercial law, but the transferee simply acquires the title of the transferror to the goods described thereby. J C. Haas & Co. *v.* Citizens' Bank, 39 So. 129, 144 Ala. 562, 1 L. R. A., N. S., 242; First Nat. Bank *v.* Wilkesbarre Lace Mfg. Co., 162 Ala. 309, 50 So. 153; Commercial Bank *v.* Hurt, 99 Ala. 130, 12 So. 568; Jasper Trust Co. *v.* Kansas, etc., R. Co., 99 Ala. 416, 14 So. 546; Cosmos Cotton Co. *v.* First Nat. Bank, 171 Ala. 392, 54 So. 621, 622. See notes in 18 L. R. A., N. S., 1221, 1222, 32 L. R. A., N. S., 1173, 1174.

An unconditional transferee of a bill of lading gets title only to the thing shipped, and not to what the consignor should have shipped. Cosmos Cotton Co. *v.* First Nat. Bank, 171 Ala. 392, 54 So. 621.

The transferee of a bill of lading attached to a draft for the purchase money takes a special property only, defeasible by acceptance and payment of the draft. Cosmos Cotton Co. *v.* First Nat. Bank, 171 Ala. 392, 54 So. 621.

The indorsement of a draft for the price of cotton sold, with the bill of lading attached, by the seller, who was the payee, to plaintiff bank for discount, did not vest the legal title to the cotton for the sale of which the draft was drawn in the bank, nor constitute the bank the seller of the cotton. Bank *v.* Jones Cotton Co., 156 Ala. 525, 46 So. 971, cited in note in 18 L. R. A., N. S., 1222.

Depositee as Agent.—Where the seller of goods ships them in the name of the buyer and attaches the bill of lading to a draft on the buyer for the price and deposits the draft with a bank for collection, the bank and its correspondent become his agents with full power of disposition over the goods, since the delivery of the bill of lading is a symbolic delivery of the goods for all the purposes incident to the collection of the draft and delivery of the bill of lading to the buyer. Veitch *v.* Atkins Grocery, etc., Co., 5 Ala. App. 444, 59 So. 746.

Title as Against True Owner.—Where a bill of lading for a car load of apples was obtained from a carrier by a person having no right to the apples, the transfer of such bill of lading to a bank was ineffective to pass title as against the true owner. Merchants' Nat. Bank *v.* Bales, 41 So. 516, 148 Ala. 279. See, to the same effect Moore *v.* Randolph, 52 Ala. 530, 537; Jasper Trust Co. *v.* Kansas, etc., R. Co., 99 Ala. 416, 421, 14 So. 546; Commercial Bank *v.* Hurt, 99 Ala. 130, 12 So. 568.

The bill of lading on a shipment of cotton is not negotiable, so as to entitle a transferee from a person in possession to hold the cotton as against the true owner. Voss *v.* Robertson, 46 Ala. 483.

Rights against Person to Whom Goods Wrongfully Delivered.—Where a bill of lading was sent to a bank as security for an attached draft, a delivery of the goods by the carrier to another than the bank was a conversion, entitling the bank to maintain detinue against the party to whom the wrongful delivery was made. Tishomingo Sav. Inst. *v.* Johnson, Nesbitt & Co., 40 So. 503, 146 Ala. 691.

Liability of Transferee.—Where a bank discounted a draft with a bill of lading attached before maturity, in the ordinary course of business, the drawee and acceptor could not, when sued on the draft, plead failure or want of consideration. Bank *v.* Jones Cotton Co., 156 Ala. 525, 46 So. 971, cited in note in 18 L. R. A., N. S., 1222.

A seller of cotton, pursuant to instructions from the buyer, shipped it to the buyer under a bill of lading, in which he was named as shipper and a bank as consignee, the bill stating that the buyer should be notified, and the seller drew a draft on the buyer, payable to the bank, and the bill of lading was attached to the draft, which was deposited by the seller. The buyer paid the draft, and subsequently it was ascertained that there was a deficiency of several pounds. Held, that the bank was not liable to the buyer. First Nat. Bank *v.* Wilkesbarre Lace Mfg. Co., 162 Ala. 309, 50 So. 153, cited in note in 32 L. R. A., N. S., 1173.

A payee bank which in the ordinary course of business cashed a draft with blank indorsed bill of lading attached or placed the proceeds thereof to the credit of the consignors-drawers, and which forwarded the same for collection, did not become liable to the drawee-consignee upon payment of the draft for a breach of the contract of sale arising from a shortage in weight or deterioration in quality of the cotton covered by the bill of lading. Cosmos Cotton Co. *v.* First Nat. Bank, 171 Ala. 392, 54 So. 621.

Liability of Transferree Who Becomes Absolute Owner of Goods.—Where a seller consigned the goods in his own name, having the bill of lading made out to himself, and assigned the bill, accompanied by a draft on the buyer to a bank to which the draft was made payable, and which paid the seller for the goods, the bank became the absolute owner of the goods and of the debt due from the buyer, and on constructively delivering the goods to the buyer by an assignment of the bill of lading and the acceptance and payment of the draft by the buyer became liable to him to the same extent as the seller would have been, but for the assignment, for any shortage in the goods.

J. C. Haas & Co. v. Citizens' Bank, 39 So. 129, 144 Ala. 562, 1 L. R. A., N. S., 242, distinguished in Cosmos Cotton Co. v. First Nat. Bank, 171 Ala. 392, 54 So. 621, 32 L. R. A., N. S., 1173. See notes in 18 L. R. A., N. S., 1221, 1222; 32 L. R. A., N. S., 1173, 1174.

§ 28. Receipt for Goods.

Where the consignor retains the carrier's receipt for goods as the only contract of carriage, it can not be shown by parol that the goods were sent C. O. D. Smith v. Southern Exp. Co., 104 Ala. 387, 16 So. 62.

Where diamonds in an unmarked package are delivered by a servant of the sender to an express company, with a note directing them to be sent C. O. D., and the package is given to the servant, who fails to show it to the sender, the company is not liable for failure to collect on delivery, as the sender is charged with notice of the contents of the receipt. Smith v. Southern Exp. Co., 104 Ala. 387, 16 So. 62.

§ 29. Contracts for Transportation of Goods.

§ 30. —— Requisites and Validity.

Necessity for Writing.—A contract of shipment need not be in writing. Alabama Great Southern R. Co. v. Norris, 52 So. 891, 167 Ala. 311; McNeill v. Atlantic, etc., R. Co., 161 Ala. 319, 49 So. 797.

Failure of a common carrier to give receipts for merchandise delivered to him, as required by Code, § 2139, does not affect his liability relative to such goods. Montgomery & E. Ry. Co. v. Kolb, 73 Ala. 396.

Contract for Indemnity against Liability on Bill of Lading Issued before Receipt of Goods.—Code, §§ 4219, 4223, prohibit a common carrier from issuing bills of lading in advance of the actual receipt of the goods, under penalty of liability in damages to any person injured thereby. Plaintiff railroad company declared on an agreement with defendant warehousemen whereby, in consideration of plaintiff's issuing bills of lading on defendant's warehouse receipts without requiring the actual delivery of the goods, defendants would make good any shortage in the goods, or indemnify plaintiff for any liability so incurred. Held, the contract was void, as illegal, notwithstanding defendants' part of it was not violative of the statute. Jemison v. Birmingham & A. R. Co., 28 So. 51, 125 Ala. 378.

Admissibility of Freight Bill to Prove Contract.— In an action by the shipper to recover damages for injuries to certain goods which defendant, as a common carrier, undertook to transport down the Coosa river from Rome to Greensport, and part of which were loaded on a lighter attached to the side of the steamer, and which was sunk by striking a snag, plaintiff offered to read a receipted freight bill, the items appearing under the headline, "Freight per steamer Georgia to Greensport;" the contention being that defendant violated the contract by using the lighter. Held, that the freight bill was not admissible to prove the contract, it not being a bill of lading. Coosa River Steamboat Co. v. Barclay, 30 Ala. 120.

Effect of Classification of Goods under Contract.—A carrier, classifying goods received for shipment with knowledge of their character, and collecting the freight under such classification, can not avoid the contract, or its liability for failure to ship according to the contract, on the ground that the goods did not belong to the class named. St. Louis & S. F. R. Co. v. Cash Grain Co., 50 So. 81, 161 Ala. 332.

§ 31. —— Performance or Breach.

Special Contract.—Upon tender of goods to a carrier for shipment, it is bound to make all reasonable efforts to furnish facilities for their transportation; but, where it enlarges its liability by an unconditional express promise to move the goods at a certain time, such contract must be strictly performed, and unavoidable accident or even impossibility preventing compliance will be no defense unless it is so stipulated in the contract. Central of Georgia Ry. Co. v. Sigma Lumber Co., 170 Ala. 627, 54 So. 205.

If the carrier expressly promised to receive and remove the lumber by its next train, it would be its duty to do so. Central, etc., R. Co. v. Sigma Lumber Co., 170 Ala. 627, 54 So. 205.

§ 32. Contracts for Means of Transportation.

§ 33. —— Requisites and Validity.

The contract of a carrier to furnish a person with a certain number of cars, at a certain price per car, for shipment of freight, is not unilateral or without consideration, where it imposes on such person the obligation to load the cars and have weekly inspection and shipments. Baxley *v.* Tallassee & M. R. Co., 29 So. 451, 128 Ala. 183, cited in note in 13 L. R. A., N. S., 164.

§ 34. —— Performance or Breach.

A carrier is not relieved from liability for breach of its contract to furnish cars, though at the date of and during the time covered by the contract it did not have or own any cars. Baxley *v.* Tallassee & M. R. Co., 29 So. 451, 128 Ala. 183.

§ 35. Actions for Breach of Contract.

As to waiver of tort and suit on contract, see the title ACTIONS.

§ 35 (1) Pleading.

Petition.—A complaint, alleging that defendant, a common carrier, promised and agreed with plaintiff for a reward to receive and transport some staves from a designated place, that plaintiff was notified by defendant to have the staves prepared for loading, and that defendant wrongfully refused to accept and transport the staves when tendered, to plaintiff's damage, was not demurrable for failing to allege that plaintiff promised and agreed to ship the staves and pay the freight thereon; the word "agreed" being defined as "brought into harmony, united in opinion, settled by consent," and the allegation that plaintiff was notified by defendant to have the staves prepared for loading showing at least that plaintiff was to accept the contract by acting, and not by written acceptance. Mott *v.* Jackson, 172 Ala. 448, 55 So. 528.

Issues.—In an action for breach of contract by a carrier to furnish cars for shipment of timber, the damages sought being the profits which but for such breach plaintiff would have made on his contract to furnish the timber to W., the question whether plaintiff had to turn over his contract with W. to certain persons to pay them what he owed them is not within the issues, there being interposed only the plea of general issue and special pleas that the contract sued on was indefinite and unilateral. Baxley *v.* Tallassee & M. R. Co., 29 So. 451, 128 Ala. 183, cited in note in 53 L. R. A. 86, 89.

Variance.—Where, in an action against a carrier on a bill of lading, the complaint alleged the bill of lading in the form prescribed by the Code, the fact that the bill introduced in evidence contained special limitations of the carrier's common-law liability did not constitute a variance. Louisville & N. R. Co. *v.* Landers, 33 So. 482, 135 Ala. 504; Nashville, C. & St. L. Ry. *v.* Cody, 34 So. 1003, 137 Ala. 597, overruling N. C. & St. L. R. Co. *v.* Parker, 123 Ala. 683, 27 So. 323.

§ 35 (2) Evidence.

Admissibility—Ordinance to Show Reasonable Charge.—Plaintiff, suing a transfer company for breach of its duty under its contract to carry, for $2.50 paid it, the coffined body of plaintiff's small child from one station to another, may introduce an ordinance fixing the price of 25 cents for drayage of a trunk between such stations, as affording a basis for arriving at the fair and reasonable charge for carrying the body; it having been taken in the ordinary mode of transporting baggage on a dray mingled with trunks. Birmingham Transfer, etc., Co. *v.* Still (Ala.), 61 So. 611.

Sufficiency of Evidence as to Nature of Service.—That a transfer company contracted for $2.50 to carry the coffined body of a small child six or seven blocks from one station to another, and that the charge for carrying a trunk between them was 25 cents, is sufficient evidence that the parties contemplated a different service than that given carriage of the body on a dray mingled with trunks, the negroes in charge sitting on them. Birmingham Transfer, etc., Co. *v.* Still (Ala.), 61 So. 611.

§ 35 (3) Damages.

A carrier is liable for breach of its contract to give notice of the arrival of goods to the consignee, embodied in the contract by Code 1907, § 5604, to the extent of any damages which naturally and proximately result therefrom. Greek-American Produce Co. *v.* Illinois Cent. R. Co., 4 Ala. App. 377, 58 So. 994.

Where defendant carrier, at the time it contracted to furnish plaintiff cars for shipment of timber, had notice of the existence of the contract of W. to purchase the timber from plaintiff, or knew that such contract was in contemplation, and before default in supplying the cars had notice that it had been made, and that the timber was to be delivered to W. in performance of plaintiff's contract with W., the measure of damages for failure to furnish the cars is the profit which, but for such failure, plaintiff would have made out of his contract with W. Baxley *v.* Tallassee & M. R. Co., 29 So. 451, 128 Ala. 183, cited in note in 53 L. R. A. 86, 88, 89.

Exemplary Damages.—Plaintiff, suing a transfer company for breach of its duty under its contract, for $2.50 paid it, to take the coffined body of his child between stations, may, as a basis for arriving at the fair and reasonable charge for the service rendered, carriage of the body on a dray mingled with trunks, introduce an ordinance fixing the charge for carrying trunks at 25 cents. Birmingham Transfer, etc., Co. *v.* Still (Ala.), 61 So. 611.

(C) CUSTODY AND CONTROL OF GOODS.

§ 36. Rights of Carrier.

Since a common carrier is not absolved from liability to the owner of the goods by the torts of third persons, the carrier can sue for the wrong, a recovery by him being a bar to a subsequent action by the owner for the same injury. Steamboat Farmer *v.* McCraw, 26 Ala. 189.

A carrier when it receives goods, and is in possession of them as a common carrier, has a special property in them which will support an action in detinue or trover or trespass against any one who wrongfully dispossesses it. Walker *v.* Louisville, etc., R. Co., 111 Ala. 233, 20 So. 358.

Condition Precedent to Recovery of Possession of Goods from Consignee.—A common carrier, after delivery of the goods to the consignee, without demanding payment of the price due the consignor, in whom the title to the goods was to remain until payment, can not recover possession of the goods, which he was induced to deliver to the consignee by the fraud of the latter, without paying to the consignee the amount of the freight paid by him on the delivery of the goods to him. Walker *v.* Louisville & N. R. Co., 111 Ala. 233, 20 So. 358.

Carrier as Trespasser.—Where a shipper loaded wood on railroad cars, and the railroad company was not a party to the taking, it did not become a trespasser, though subsequently notified by the owners of the wood not to ship it. Nashville, C. & St. L. Ry. *v.* Walley, 41 So. 134, 147 Ala. 697.

§ 37. Stoppage in Transitu.

"Notwithstanding property is * * * vested in the consignee, by delivery to a carrier, there yet remains with the consignor, the right of resuming it again, under some circumstances, before it actually gets into the possession of the consignee. This is called the right of stoppage in transitu, and, when exerted, revests the property in the consignor as much as if he had never parted with the possession. This right was originally adopted in courts of equity; and being founded upon principles of equity and natural justice, is now established in courts of law. It is exercised when goods have been sold and not paid for, by reason of credit being given or otherwise, and the vendee, to whom they have been consigned, becomes insolvent—and, as its designation indicates, exists only during the transit of goods, and ceases when they come into the possession of the buyer." Jones *v.* Sims, 6 Port. 138, 161. See, generally, the title SALES.

§ 38. Actions by or against Carriers in Respect to Goods.

§ 38 (1) Title to Maintain Action against Carrier.

Persons Having Beneficial Interest.—Although the consignee is, prima facie, the proper person to bring suit against a common carrier for loss of property intrusted to his care, yet one who has a beneficial interest in the performance of the contract, or a special property or interest in the subject matter of the agreement, may support an action in his own name. Southern Exp. Co. *v.* Caperton, 44 Ala. 101, cited in note in 36 L. R. A., N. S., 69.

Buyer—Where Goods Consigned to Agent of Seller.—A contract for sale of coal which contemplates delivery by the seller to a carrier f. o. b. for the buyer, and which provides that the carrier's track scales weight at the seller's mines shall govern settlements, does not give the buyer a right of action for a loss of part of a shipment consigned by the seller to its agent, and under Code 1907, § 2490, providing that, where suits are brought in the name of the person having the legal right for the use of another the beneficiary must be considered as the sole party, the agent may not maintain an action for the use of the buyer, though there was a delivery to the buyer of the bills of lading without indorsement. Zimmern's Coal Co. *v.* Louisville, etc., R. Co., 6 Ala. App. 475, 60 So. 598.

"The mere delivery of the bills of lading, without indorsement, did not operate as a transfer to the electric company of the title to the subject of the shipment, or to vest it with the rights of action of the consignor or the consignee. Louisville, etc., R. Co. *v.* Barkhouse, 100 Ala. 543, 13 So. 534; Byrd *v.* Beall, 150 Ala. 122, 127, 43 So. 749. One's consignment of goods to his own agent can not be regarded as a fulfillment of his contract to deliver such goods to another at the place of the shipment, or as having the effect of making the carrier liable to the holder of such an executory contract for loss or injury to the goods while in course of transportation. So long as the coal remained the property of the consignor, and at its risk, any right of action for loss of part of the shipment accrued to it. The evidence did not show that this right of action has in any way passed to the electric company. We are not of opinion that the evidence showed that it had such ownership or interest in the coal while it was in transit as to entitle it to maintain an action for loss of part of the coal during that time." Zimmern's Coal Co. *v.* Louisville, etc., R. Co., 6 Ala. App. 475, 60 So. 598, 600.

The right of a purchaser of property, to whose agent, as consignee, it is shipped, to sue the carrier for nondelivery, is not affected by the fact that another paid the seller for the property and took an order for the amount on the purchaser. Louisville, etc., R. Co. *v.* Allgood, 113 Ala. 163, 20 So. 986.

§ 38 (2) Right of Consignor to Sue Carrier.

The shipper's present ownership of his claim against a carrier for loss of freight is an essential element of the cause of action. Northern Alabama Ry. Co. *v.* Feldman, 1 Ala. App. 334, 56 So. 16.

A consignor may maintain an action for damage from a failure of a carrier to deliver goods within a reasonable time though they are consigned to another, the presumption that the consignee has title being merely prima facie. Southern R. Co. *v.* Proctor, 3 Ala. App. 413, 57 So. 513.

In assumpsit by the shipper against a common carrier for nondelivery of goods, the bill of lading, reciting that the carrier received of the consignors goods to be delivered to the consignee, who is to pay the freight, is only prima facie evidence that the legal title by the shipment vested in the consignee, and the presumption may be rebutted by extrinsic evidence. Jones *v.* Sims, 6 Port. 138, cited in note in 26 L. R. A., N. S., 438.

Goods Shipped under Contract Providing for Delivery.—When goods are shipped under a contract by which the shipper is to deliver them to the consignee, the shipper may maintain suit against the carrier for their loss or injury. Gulf Compress Co. *v.* Jones Cotton Co., 172 Ala. 645, 55 So. 206.

Goods Shipped at Risk of Consignor.—If the consignee is not in fact the owner of the goods—if he is the mere agent or factor of the consignor—and, in the course of transportation, the goods are at the risk of the consignor, the right of action resides in him. Hutch. Carr., § 720. Louisville, etc., R. Co. *v.* Allgood, 113 Ala. 163, 20 So. 986, 988, cited in note in 36 L. R. A., N. S., 69, 72.

Plaintiff, cotton company, delivered cotton to a compress company and subsequently delivered the warehouse receipts of that company to a railway company and received in exchange bills of lading. The cotton company shipped the cotton over the railway line to a purchaser under a contract requiring that the cotton should be delivered in good condition to the purchaser's mills "landed," and drafts for the purchase price with bills of lading attached were drawn by the cotton company on the purchaser and honored before the cotton was delivered at its destination. Held, that "landed" meant that the cotton company was responsible for the entire shipment of cotton and for damages to it until delivered at the point of destination, and therefore the right of recovery for damages to the cotton resulting from exposure to the weather while in the possession of the compress company was in the cotton company, although it had not been called on to repay any of the purchase price. Southern Ry. Co. *v.* Jones Cotton Co., 52 So. 899, 167 Ala. 575, cited in note in 36 L. R. A., N. S., 69, 72.

Sale and Return—Failure of Carrier to Deliver.—Where plaintiff shipped goods to a customer to be tested by him, and purchased if satisfactory, and defendant railroad did not deliver the goods to the customer, the title remained in plaintiff, so as to entitle it to maintain trover. Louisville & N. R. Co. *v.* Kauffman & Co., 37 So. 659, 141 Ala. 671.

Where Consignee Agent of Consignor.—Where the consignee is a mere agent of the consignor without any other interest, a right of action against the carrier for failure to deliver or for loss or injury to the freight while in transit is in the consignor alone. Zimmern's Coal Co. *v.* Louisville, etc., R. Co., 6 Ala. App. 475, 60 So. 598.

Goods Injured after Arrival When Shipped under Contract to Deliver F. O. B. at Destination.—Where the seller contracts to deliver goods "f. o. b." at the place to which they are to be shipped, and pays the freight to such place, on the arrival of the boat by which the goods are transported at such place the carrier ceases to be the agent of the seller, and becomes the agent of the purchaser, and the seller can not maintain an action against the carrier for injuries to the goods after such arrival, and before they were unloaded. Capehart *v.* Furman Farm Imp. Co., 103 Ala. 671, 16 So. 627.

§ 38 (3) Right of Consignee to Sue Carrier.

"The general rule is that prima facie a bill of lading operates a transfer to the consignee of the title to the goods shipped; and, in the absence of evidence removing the presumption, an action against the carrier for failure to deliver, or for the loss or injury to the goods while in his possession, will lie only at the suit of the consignee. Robinson *v.* Pogue, 86 Ala. 257, 5 So. 685; Capehart *v.* Furman Farm Imp. Co., 103 Ala. 671, 16 So. 627; Louisville, etc., R. Co. *v.* Allgood, 113 Ala. 163, 20 So. 986, cited in note in 36 L. R. A., N. S., 69, 72; Southern Exp. Co. *v.* Caperton, 44 Ala. 101; Southern R. Co. *v.* Jones Cotton Co., 167 Ala. 575, 52 So. 899.

One who has bought property agreeing to pay therefor when sales are made by the consignees, to whom he has it shipped, who are to pay the freight at the point of destination, remitting to him the proceeds less the freight, is the general owner, and entitled to sue the carrier for failure to deliver. Louisville & N. R. Co. *v.* Allgood, 20 So. 986, 113 Ala. 163, cited in note in 36 L. R. A., N. S., 69, 72.

The consignee of corn delivered to a railroad company for transportation, having bought and paid the freight on it, is the proper party to sue for its nondelivery. South & N. A. R. Co. *v.* Wood, 72 Ala. 451.

Effect of Interest of Third Persons in Goods.—The consignee of goods may maintain an action against a common carrier for their loss, although another person was the owner of them, or was jointly interested in them with him. Southern Exp. Co. *v.* Armstead, 50 Ala. 350, cited in note in 36 L. R. A., N. S., 69, 70.

Where a shipment containing household goods, some of which belonged to a husband and wife, some to the husband, and others to the wife, were all consigned to the husband at the point of destination, he had capacity to sue for injuries to the entire shipment, though he was not the absolute owner of all the property. Walter *v.* Alabama Great Southern R. Co., 39 So. 87, 142 Ala. 474, cited in note in 36 L. R. A., N. S., 69.

Suit for Benefit of Real Owner.--An action against a common carrier, for failure to deliver goods intrusted to it, is properly brought in the name of the consignees alone, notwithstanding they are prosecuting the suit for the benefit of another whom they hold liable for the value of the goods. Mobile & G. R. Co. *v.* Williams, 54 Ala. 168, cited in note in 36 L. R. A., N. S., 70.

Question for Jury.—When a quantity of corn is delivered to a railroad company for transportation, the consignee having bought it and paid the freight on it, he is the proper party to sue for its nondelivery, and not the consignor from whom he bought it; but the evidence as to these facts being conflicting, the question is properly submitted to the decision of the jury. South, etc., R. Co. *v.* Wood, 72 Ala. 451.

Where the evidence is conflicting as to whether property to be transported by a carrier was to be delivered to the vendors or the vendee, the fact that the bill of lading was deposited in the postoffice attached to a draft drawn on the vendee for the purchase money does not, in the absence of evidence that the bill was properly indorsed, raise a conclusive presumption that the title has passed to the vendee, but the question of ownership is for the jury. Alabama, etc., R. Co. *v.* Mount Vernon Co., 84 Ala. 173, 4 So. 356. See notes in 2 L. R. A., N. S., 1079, 39 L. R. A., N. S., 310, 311. And see the title SALES.

Effect of Disclaimer by Consignee.—Though a bill of lading vests the legal title to the goods in the consignee, if the latter disclaims an interest in them, and never accepted the consignment, it will be presumed that the legal title revested in the consignor, so that an action for loss of the goods can not be maintained in the name of the consignee for the benefit of a third person who claims that the goods were shipped to the consignee as factor for such third person. Ezell *v.* English, 6 Port. 311, cited in note in 36 L. R. A., N. S., 69, 72.

(D) TRANSPORTATION AND DELIVERY BY CARRIER.

§ 39. Duties as to Transportation in General.

Adequacy and Sufficiency of Vehicles Furnished.—In the respect to the adequacy of carriage, a railroad company meets its duty and obligation when it furnishes such as is most in use, and is approved by persons skilled and experienced in the business, as necessary and proper for safe transportation, having in view the kind and nature of the freight; and the omission of any part or appliance, permanent or usual in the construction or preparation of a car, and which is necessary and proper to its adequacy for the general uses and purposes of railroad transportation, is prima facie negligence; but to charge the company with negligence because of the omission of some peculiar adventitious and temporary preparation, the necessity or propriety must be shown by extraneous evidence. East Tennessee, etc., R. Co. *v.* Johnston, 75 Ala. 596.

Duty of Railroad Company in Assigning Cars in Making Up Train.—While, in making up a train, large discretion must be allowed a railroad company in assigning cars to different positions, it is, nevertheless, the duty of the company, having regard to the nature and character to all kinds and classes of freight received by it for transportation, to assign a car loaded with freight of a particular nature such position, so far as may be consistent with the safety and interests of other shippers, as will cause the least exposure to danger. East Tennessee, etc., R. Co. *v.* Johnston, 75 Ala. 596.

§ 40. To Whom Delivery May Be Made.

The carrier may be justified in delivering to the true owner although he has given a bill of lading to a third person as shipper. Young *v.* East Alabama R. Co., 80 Ala. 100, cited in notes in 38 L. R. A., 364, 12 L. R. A., N. S., 259.

§ 41. Presentation of Bill of Lading or Shipping Receipt.

A carrier delivers goods at its peril to one without a bill of lading. Atlantic Coast Line R. Co. *v.* Dahlberg Brokerage Co., 170 Ala. 617, 54 So. 168.

The delivery of a shipment of lumber to the wrong person, without the production or assignment of the bill of lading renders the carrier liable as for conversion. Mobile, J. & K. C. R. Co. *v.* Bay Shore Lumber Co., 51 So. 956, 165 Ala. 610.

When the vendor and shipper of goods takes the bill of lading in his own name, he thereby retains the title in himself, and the carrier can not rightfully deliver the goods to any other person, except on his order, or transfer of the bill of lading. Young *v.* East Alabama R. Co., 80 Ala. 100, cited in notes in 38 L. R. A. 362, 364, 12 L. R. A., N. S., 259.

Delivery to Holder of Unindorsed Bill of Lading.—Possession of a bill of lading by one other than the consignee, without indorsement, does not justify the delivery of the consignment to such person. Louisville & N. R. Co. *v.* Barkhouse, 100 Ala. 543, 13 So. 534, cited in notes in 37 L. R. A. 178, 38 L. R. A. 363.

Effect of Custom.—A custom on the part of a carrier or of carriers generally at a particular place to deliver goods to one other than the consignee, who merely holds the bill of lading without any indorsement, does not justify such delivery. Louisville & N. R. Co. *v.* Barkhouse, 100 Ala. 543, 13 So. 534, cited in notes in 37 L. R. A. 178, 38 L. R. A. 363.

Delivery to Buyer Who Rejected Draft with Bill of Lading Attached.—A carrier can not justify delivery of freight to a buyer who had rejected the consignor-consignee's draft with bill of lading attached, on the ground that the buyer had a contract with the consignor's principal for delivery of similar goods. Atlantic, etc., R. Co. *v.* Dahlberg Brokerage Co., 170 Ala. 617, 54 So. 168.

Ratification of Delivery—Sufficiency of Evidence.—Where a proposed buyer of goods rejected the consignor-consignee's draft with bill of lading attached, that after the carrier delivered the goods to the buyer the draft was again presented is not conclusive evidence of the consignor's ratification of the delivery. Atlantic, etc., R. Co. *v.* Dahlberg Brokerage Co., 170 Ala. 617, 54 So. 168.

§ 42. Place of Delivery.

Duty of Railroad Company.—The general rule that the undertaking of a common carrier to transport goods to a particular destination includes the obligation of safe delivery to the consignee or his agent does not apply to railroad companies. A universal custom relieves them from the duty of personal delivery to the consignee. South & North Alabama R. Co. *v.* Wood, 66 Ala. 167, cited in note in 40 L. R. A., N. S., 774.

Delivery on Siding.—A carrier and shipper could contract that property, destined to a station which had no regular agent or depot, when delivered on the siding, should be considered delivered to the consignee and afterwards held at his risk. Southern Ry. Co. *v.* Barclay, 1 Ala. App. 348, 56 So. 26.

When a consignee of goods is fully advised at the time of shipment that the railroad company has no depot or agent at the place of destination, the exigencies of its business not requiring such, the liability of the company as common carrier terminates with the safe delivery of the car containing the goods on a side track at such place, and no liability as warehouseman will be assumed. South & North Alabama R. Co. *v.* Wood, 66 Ala. 167, cited in note in 40 L. R. A., N. S., 774.

Delivery to Independent Warehouseman.—Where a railroad company gives a receipt for freight to be delivered to its agent at the terminus of the road, and the agent there deposits it in a warehouse not belonging to the company, evidence of its custom to deposit freight in that warehouse is admissible in behalf of the company in an action against it by the shipper for the loss of the shipment, since, if the custom existed and was properly proved, it might relieve the company from liability for the loss of the goods in the hands of its agent. Alabama & T. R. R. Co. *v.* Kidd, 29 Ala. 221.

Gratuitous Promise to Deliver Car at Another Place.—In the absence of a custom authorizing the agent of a railroad company, at the request of the consignee, after the car has reached its destination, to undertake to deliver it at another place, or to another person than the consignee, such an undertaking is nothing more than a personal accommodation on the part of the agent, and can not render his principal liable. Melbourne *v.* Louisville & N. R. Co., 88 Ala. 443, 6 So. 762.

Duty of Express Company.—Where an express company deposited goods on the platform of the railroad depot at the place of destination, without delivering them to the consignee, or placing them in the custody of any person, held, that this was gross negligence, and rendered the company liable as a common carrier for their loss, although the company's agent, to whom they were tendered by the consignor's messenger for shipment, at first declined to receive them because the company had no agent at the place of destination, and was not allowed to use the depot of the railroad company, and although the shipping agent, in signing the receipt, added the words "owner's risk," but without the knowledge or consent of the consignor, and although the consignee, when he ordered the goods to be forwarded by the express company, knew that the company had no agent at the place of destination, and he had lately received goods forwarded by it under receipts containing the same added words. Southern Exp. Co. *v.* Armstead, 50 Ala. 350, cited in notes in 14 L. R. A., N. S., 393, 34 L. R. A. 138.

Where it is the custom for consignees to call for packages at the carrier's office on being notified of their arrival, the carrier is not bound to make a personal delivery, in order to be relieved of liability for the loss of a package by theft from the carrier's warehouse after notice to the consignee, and an opportunity for him to obtain the package. Southern Exp. Co. *v.* Holland, 109 Ala. 362, 19 So. 66, cited in notes in 33 L. R. A. 67, 14 L. R. A., N. S., 394.

Sufficiency of Delivery of Carrier by Water.—A steamboat carrier, having goods consigned to a consignee at a landing where there had been a warehouse keeper who usually received and took care of goods landed there, can not avoid liability by proving a delivery of goods at the usual place on the river bank, without any protection or guard, when the landing had in the meantime been broken up by an inundation, and the washing away of the buildings and the removal of the persons which constituted it a landing. Stone *v.* Rice, 58 Ala. 95.

Under a written contract by which the owners of a steamboat bound themselves, as common carriers, to deliver certain goods at a specified point, the loss of the goods by fire after having been deposited in a warehouse at the highest point to which, on account of the low stage of the water, the boat could ascend the river, does not excuse the defendant's failure to deliver the goods at the special place. Cox *v.* Peterson, 30 Ala. 608.

Usage and Custom of Carriers by Water.—While a carrier on a river may avoid liability for nondelivery of goods to the consignee by proof that the goods were delivered at the landing to which they were consigned, in accordance with the custom of the community in receiving goods destined to that point, yet such a custom could not be upheld as reasonable which would justify a steamboat carrier in putting off goods consigned to such a landing at the usual place on the river bank, without any protection, when the landing had been broken up by an inundation and the washing away of the buildings, and the persons in charge had removed. Stone *v.* Rice, 58 Ala. 95.

In an action against the owners of a steamboat, as common carriers, for failing to deliver goods at the place specified in their bill of lading, evidence of a custom among the steamboat men to ascend the river as high as the stage of the water in it permitted, and then to land their cargo and deposit the goods in warehouses, is not admissible for the defendants. Cox *v.* Peterson, 30 Ala. 608.

Waiver or Consent.—The unqualified refusal of a consignee to receive goods tendered it by the carrier is a waiver of the right to insist on a delivery at the usual place of delivery. Central of Georgia Ry. Co. *v.* Montmollen, 39 So. 820, 145 Ala. 468.

Where a bill of lading contains a stipulation that the goods shall be delivered "into a warehouse or to assigns" at a certain landing, the warehouseman at the landing is the consignee; and, if he consents that the goods be landed at a point less than 10 feet above the surface of the water, the consignor can not recover for damages to the goods by a flood on the ground that defendant violated Code, §§ 896, 897, making carriers liable in double the value of the goods damaged by flood, if they are landed at a point less than 10 feet perpendicular above the surface of the water. Winston *v.* Cox, 38 Ala. 268.

§ 43. Notice to Consignee.

See, also, post, "Termination of Liability," § 65.

General Rule.—By the weight of authority, no obligation rests on a railroad company to give special notice to the consignee of the arrival of goods. South & N. A. R. Co. *v.* Wood, 66 Ala. 167.

What Law Governs.—Where the delivery of an interstate shipment was made in Alabama, the shipment was governed by the laws of Alabama as to the subject of delivery and sufficiency of notice of delivery. Greek-American Produce Co. *v.* Illinois Cent. R. Co., 4 Ala. App. 377, 58 So. 994.

Validity of Statute Requiring Notice.—Code 1907, § 5604, requiring railroad companies to give notice by mail or otherwise to the consignee of the arrival of shipments, is not unconstitutional or unreasonable. Greek-American Produce Co. *v.* Illinois Cent. R. Co., 4 Ala. App. 377, 58 So. 994.

When Notice Required under Code, § 1180.—Notice to the consignee of the arrival of the goods at their destination is not necessary before the reasonable time begins to run after which the carrier's liability as such terminates, and its liability as a warehouseman begins, unless the place of destination is a town of 2,000 inhabitants, having a daily mail, in which case such notice is required by Code, § 1180. Columbus & W. Ry. Co. *v.* Ludden, 89 Ala. 612, 7 So. 471.

Nature of Requirement to Give Notice.—Code 1896, § 4224, providing that the relation of common carrier continues in towns and cities of 2,000 population or more and having a daily mail unless within 24 hours after arrival of freight notice is given the consignee formally or through mail, did not lay upon the carrier a duty to notify the consignee, but merely determined the time of termination of the strict liability of the carrier. Central, etc., R. Co. *v.* Burton, 165 Ala. 425, 51 So. 643, cited in note in 25 L. R. A., N. S., 939.

To Whom Notice to Be Given.—Where goods are consigned to the shipper's order, with instructions to notify a third person of their arrival, notice thereof to such third person is sufficient to relieve the carrier of its liability as a carrier, and create the liability of warehouseman. Collins *v.* Alabama, etc., R. Co., 104 Ala. 390, 16 So. 140; Southern R. Co. *v.* Adams Mach. Co., 165 Ala. 436, 51 So. 779. See notes in 8 L. R. A., N. S., 242; 18 L. R. A., N. S., 429.

Under Code 1907, § 5604, requiring railway companies to give notice by mail or otherwise to the consignee of the arrival of shipments, one to whom freight was consigned was entitled to notice of arrival, though in fact the agent for the real owner. Greek-American Produce Co. *v.* Illinois Cent. R. Co., 4 Ala. App. 377, 58 So. 994.

Where a shipper told a railroad agent that certain persons were his agents to receive and remove the goods, and that on arrival the railroad agent might notify a third person, who would notify the shipper's agents, such third person was the shipper's agent to receive notice, regardless of the fact that the railroad agent also undertook to notify the agents who were to remove the goods, but did not do so. Hearn *v.* Louisville, etc., R. Co., 6 Ala. App. 483, 60 So. 600.

Effect of Custom to Give Notice.—A custom of a carrier at the destination of goods to give notice of their arrival did not have the effect of imposing the positive duty to give such notice, but merely affected the time of termination of the liability of the carrier as such. Central, etc., R. Co. *v.* Burton, 165 Ala. 425, 51 So. 643, cited in note in 25 L. R. A., N. S., 939.

Manner of Notice.—If a consignee had

actual notice of the arrival of freight and its readiness for delivery, and did not demand it in a reasonable time thereafter, the manner of notice is immaterial. Southern R. Co. *v.* Adams Mach. Co., 165 Ala. 436, 51 So. 779.

Code 1896, § 4224, provides that a common carrier, if the destination of freight is a city or town having 2,000 or more inhabitants and a daily mail, is not relieved from responsibility as a carrier by a deposit or storage of freight, unless within 24 hours after its arrival notice is given, the consignee personally or through the mail. Compliance with the statute is not shown where one alleged notice was mailed "within a day or two" after arrival of the goods, and another notice was mailed 18 days after and only two days before the goods were burned. Southern R. Co. *v.* Adams Mach. Co., 165 Ala. 436, 51 So. 779.

Where a carrier complies with Code, 1896, § 4224, requiring notice of the arrival of freight to be mailed to a consignee within 24 hours to terminate liability as a common carrier, the mailing of the notice, postage paid, is notice to the consignee, but, where it does not comply therewith, the fact that notice is mailed is only rebuttable evidence of its receipt. Southern R. Co. *v.* Adams Mach. Co., 165 Ala. 436, 51 So. 779.

§ 44. Duties of Carrier in Making Delivery.

Failure of a delivering carrier to have a waybill for the freight shipped furnished no ground for such carrier's refusal to deliver the goods to the owner and consignee after arrival on demand. Bowdon *v.* Atlantic Coast Line Ry. Co., 41 So. 294, 148 Ala. 29.

Manner of "Track Delivery."—Code 1907, § 5604, providing that railroad companies shall deliver freight at their depots or warehouses, or, in case of "track delivery," shall place loaded cars at an accessible place for unloading within 24 hours after arrival, by the words "track delivery," means tracks maintained by the railroad companies at an accessible place for unloading, for the purpose of delivering freight in carload lots. Greek-American Produce Co. *v.* Illinois Cent. R. Co., 4 Ala. App. 377, 58 So. 994.

Duty to Unload.—A car load of bricks was consigned to plaintiff at "Cloverfield Sta." There was no station agent or side track there, and no one was upon the ground to receive the bricks. After waiting a few minutes, during which the locomotive whistle was repeatedly sounded, the car was carried to a station a mile beyond, and left upon a side track. Held that, since the loaded car could not be left upon the track, it was the duty of the company to unload and leave the bricks upon the ground, and, the freight having been prepaid, plaintiff was entitled to recover their value. Louisville & N. R. Co. *v.* Gilmer, 89 Ala. 534, 7 So. 654.

§ 45. Duties of Consignee or Owner as to Delivery.

Rule Requiring Consignee to Receive Freight within Certain Time.—A rule requiring a consignee to receive the freight within 48 hours after notice of its arrival is not unreasonable. Gulf City Const. Co. *v.* Louisville & N. R. Co., 25 So. 579, 121 Ala. 621.

Computation of the reasonable time in which a consignee may apply for and remove freight begins when it is at the place and ready for delivery in the usual manner. Southern R. Co. *v.* Adams Mach. Co., 165 Ala. 436, 51 So. 779, cited in note in 25 L. R. A., N. S., 938.

Period Held to Exceed Reasonable Time.—Eighteen days between the mailing of notice of the arrival of goods at their destination and their destruction by fire is more than a reasonable time for their removal by the consignee. Southern R. Co. *v.* Adams Mach. Co., 165 Ala. 436, 51 So. 779, cited in note in 25 L. R. A., N. S., 938.

§ 46. Acts Constituting Delivery.

Delivery by Expressman.—An expressman who agrees to carry a trunk to a depot, to be taken there at once, for a train leaving the next morning, is not liable for its loss; he having delivered it at the depot at the place set apart for such baggage, and called the attention of the baggage agent thereto, and told him to whom it belonged, and on what train it was going. Anniston Transfer Co. *v.* Gurley, 107 Ala. 600, 18 So. 209, cited in note in 21 L. R. A., N. S., 190.

Delivery on Track.—When a consignee of goods is fully advised at the time of shipment that the railroad company has no depot or agent at the place of destination—the exigencies of its business not requiring such—the liability of the company as common carrier terminates with the safe delivery of the car containing the goods on a side track at such place, and no liability as warehouseman will be assumed. South & N. A. R. Co. *v.* Wood, 66 Ala. 167. See, to same effect, Alabama, etc., R. Co. *v.* Kidd, 35 Ala. 209; Southern R. Co. *v.* Barclay, 1 Ala. App. 348, 56 So. 26. See note in 40 L. R. A., N. S., 774.

Where a contract of affreightment is entered into by a railroad company for transportation to a certain point and delivery to the consignees, its liability ceases when it has transported the car to such point, and given the consignees an opportunity to receive and carry away the goods; and it is not bound to deliver the car to another road for more convenient delivery, unless it is shown that it is the custom or usage to do so. Melbourne *v.* Louisville & N. R. Co., 88 Ala. 443, 6 So. 762, cited in note in 31 L. R. A., N. S., 44, 89, 98.

§ 47. Failure or Refusal of Consignee to Receive Goods.

"A failure by the carrier to deliver goods within a reasonable time does not establish a conversion, but is a mere breach of contract; and the consignee can not refuse to accept the goods on the ground of the delay and recover their full value, unless the delay destroyed the value of the goods entirely or caused what is equivalent to a total loss." Central, etc., R. Co. *v.* Montmollen, 145 Ala. 468, 39 So. 820.

Excuse for Refusal to Accept.—Where, in an action against a carrier for failure to deliver goods, the carrier proved an offer to deliver the same personally to the consignee, who refused to accept, the consignee must, in order to recover, prove that the goods were in a damaged condition, or that some of the articles were lost, and that he sustained damages in consequence of the delay in making the attempted delivery. Central of Georgia Ry. Co. *v.* Montmollen, 39 So. 820, 145 Ala. 468, cited in note in 25 L. R. A., N. S. 843.

Right of Seller and Carrier on Refusal of Consignee to Receive Goods.—Where a buyer, to whom goods are consigned, wrongfully refuses to receive them on their arrival within a reasonable time, the seller is authorized to rescind the sale, and the carrier is not guilty of conversion in complying with the seller's orders to ship the goods back to him. Stafsky *v.* Southern Ry. Co., 39 So. 132, 143 Ala. 272, cited in note in 30 L. R. A., N. S., 1072.

Where a carrier tenders goods to the consignee, and the latter denies ownership or obligation to receive the same, and the carrier, in reliance on such denial, returns the goods to the shipper on the latter's order, the consignee is estopped to sue the carrier for conversion. Stafsky *v.* Southern Ry. Co., 39 So. 132, 143 Ala. 272, cited in note in 30 L. R. A., N. S., 1072.

§ 48. Delivery of Goods Shipped C. O. D.

Where a shipper sent a package, by her servant, to an express company, with instructions to be carried C. O. D., but the company gave a receipt which was not in the form of a receipt for package sent C. O. D., and the shipper knew it was not, the receipt operates as a refusal to send the package C. O. D.; and, if the shipper accepts and retains the receipt, it is conclusive, and she can not recover of the company for a delivery without collection. Smith *v.* Southern Exp. Co., 104 Ala. 387, 16 So. 62.

Where diamonds in an unmarked package are delivered by a servant of the sender to an express company, with a note directing them to be sent C. O. D., and the package is given to the servant, who fails to show it to the sender, the company is not liable for failure to collect on delivery, as the sender is charged with notice of the contents of the receipt. Smith *v.* Southern Exp. Co., 104 Ala. 387, 16 So. 62.

§ 49. Liability for Failure or Refusal to Deliver.

Goods Lost after Failing to Deliver on Demand.—Where goods were received at their destination several days before a fire which destroyed them, the carrier, who, on demand of the consignee, refused to deliver them without a sufficient excuse, was liable for their loss. Louisville & N. R. Co. *v.* McGuire, 79 Ala. 395, cited in notes in 8 L. R. A., N. S., 237, 241, 17 L. R. A., 693.

Excuses for Failure to Deliver.—Under a written contract, by which the owners of a steamboat bound themselves, as common carriers, to deliver certain goods at a specified point, the loss of the goods by fire, after having been deposited in a warehouse at the highest point to which, on account of the low stage of the water, the boat could ascend the river, does not excuse the defendant's failure to deliver the goods at the specified place. Cox *v.* Peterson, 30 Ala. 608.

Goods were received at their destination several days before a fire which destroyed them, and the consignee, who had several times requested the delivery of the goods, was refused by the carrier because they were piled beneath other goods. In an action for the value of the goods destroyed, held, that the excuse for nondelivery was insufficient to relieve the carrier from liability. Louisville & N. R. Co. *v.* McGuire, 79 Ala. 395, cited in notes in 17 L. R. A. 693, 8 L. R. A., N. S., 237.

The acceptance of a portion by the consignee, at a place different from that specified in the contract, though admissible in the mitigation of damages, does not discharge the common carrier from liability for the residue. Cox *v.* Peterson, 30 Ala. 608.

Conversion—Necessity for Demand and Refusal.—Where possession of certain freight for transportation was legitimately obtained by a railroad, there must have been a demand therefor by the consignee and a refusal by the road to deliver the same in order to show conversion, unless there was proof of a dealing with the property by the road otherwise. Louisville & N. R. Co. *v.* Britton, 39 So. 585, 145 Ala. 654.

Necessity for Showing Issuance of Bill of Lading.—Plaintiff, to recover of a carrier for failure to deliver goods need not show that a bill of lading was issued, if the delivery of the goods for shipment is shown. Alabama Midland Ry. Co. *v.* Darby, 24 So. 713, 119 Ala. 531.

Estoppel of Carrier.—Where one, without title to goods, delivers them to a carrier, on whom he afterwards gives plaintiff an order for them, and the carrier accepts the order, and receives the charges for freight, in an action of detinue against the carrier for refusal to deliver the goods the carrier is estopped to show that the goods belonged to a third person. Young *v.* East Alabama R. Co., 80 Ala. 100.

§ 50. Liability for Misdelivery.

An express company, which delivered a package to a person other than the consignee, without requiring any proof that he was connected with the consignee, except letters produced by him addressed to the consignee, was liable for wrong delivery, although the person receiving the package was the one who actually ordered its contents from the shipper, where the agent of the express company had no knowledge of the order. Southern Exp. Co. *v.* Ruth & Son, 5 Ala. App. 644, 59 So. 538.

Evidence of a custom or usage is never admissible to justify the act of a carrier in delivering goods to persons other than the consignee or to whom the consignee has not authorized the delivery. Mobile, J. & K. C. R. Co. *v.* Bay Shore Lumber Co., 51 So. 956, 165 Ala. 610.

Misdelivery by Independent Warehouse.—A carrier, on arrival of goods at destination, placed them in the warehouse of a third person, who by mistake delivered them to a person not authorized to receive them. Held, that the carrier was liable to the owner. Alabama & T. R. Co. *v.* Kidd, 35 Ala. 209, cited in note in 37 L. R. A. 177.

Evidence, Insufficient to Show Goods Received by Persons as Agent of Consignees.—In an action to recover the value of bricks, as upon failure of the carrier to deliver them according to the contract of shipment, it appeared that the bricks were left by the company at a station beyond the place of destination designated in the contract of shipment. Held, the fact that certain tenants of the consignee and owner asked at the station if plaintiff's bricks had come, and unloaded them and placed them on the ground, is not sufficient, in the absence of other proof of authority, to show that they received them as plaintiff's agents. Louisville & N. R. Co. *v.* Gilmer, 89 Ala. 534, 7 So. 654.

§ 51. Actions for Failure to Deliver or Misdelivery.

§ 51 (1) Conditions Precedent.

The owner of property shipped to agents of his may sue the carrier for nondelivery, though he had not paid or offered to pay the freight, and the carrier had not claimed, demanded, or looked to him for payment thereof. Louisville & N. R. Co. *v.* Allgood, 20 So. 986, 113 Ala. 163.

§ 51 (2) Form of Action.

Trover is the proper remedy in case of delivery of property by a common carrier through mistake to a person not entitled thereto. Louisville, etc., R. Co. *v.* Barkhouse, 100 Ala. 543, 13 So. 534.

Case of trover may be brought against a carrier for not delivering goods, but trover can not be sustained without proof of conversion. Bullard *v.* Young, 3 Stew. 46.

Trover will lie against a common carrier for a misdelivery, or an appropriation of the property to its or his own use, or for any act or dominion of ownership antagonistic to, and inconsistent with plaintiff's claim or right; but not for goods lost by accident or stolen, or for nondelivery, unless there be a refusal to deliver while the carrier is in possession, nor for any act or omission which amounts to negligence merely, and not to an actual wrong. Central Railroad & Banking Co. *v.* Lampley, 76 Ala. 357, cited in note in 5 L. R. A., N. S., 459.

A. undertook to carry certain flour for B. to a certain place, and, having deposited it by the way, a part of the flour was taken by mistake by C. B. refusing to receive the residue, C. received it, and paid for the whole. This was a conversion by A. sufficient to support trover by B. Bullard *v.* Young, 3 Stew. 46.

If a consignee is ready and willing to pay the freight due on having the goods delivered to him, and the carrier refuses to deliver them, unless he will pay more than is due, the consignee may maintain detinue for the goods, or trover for their conversion, without making a formal tender, or paving the money into court. Long *v.* Mobile & M. R. Co., 51 Ala. 512.

§ 51 (3) Pleading.

Complaint in Code Form.—In an action against a carrier to recover for its failure to deliver goods shipped by plaintiff, a complaint in the form prescribed by the Revised Code is sufficient whether the cause of action be ex contractu or ex delicto. Southern Exp. Co. *v.* Crook, 44 Ala. 468.

Averment of Ownership.—In an action against a common carrier for a failure to deliver freight, a count in the declaration employing no other averment of ownership in the plaintiff than the word "claims" is not sufficient on demurrer. Montgomery & W. P. R. Co. *v.* Edmonds, 41 Ala. 667.

Averring Defendant to Be Common Carrier.—In order to recover against a common carrier, as such, for failure to deliver in safety property, transported under a contract, express or implied, the complaint must aver that defendant is a common carrier. Louisville & N. R. Co. *v.* Gerson, 102 Ala. 409, 14 So. 873. See to the same effect Knox *v.* Rives, etc., Co., 14 Ala. 249, 257; Haynie *v.* Waring & Co., 29 Ala. 263, 265; Central R., etc., Co. *v.* Lampley, 76 Ala. 357, 364; Montgomery, etc., R. Co. *v.* Kolb, 73 Ala. 396; Melbourne *v.* Louisville, etc., R. Co., 88 Ala. 443, 449, 6 So. 762; Louisville, etc., R. Co. *v.* Gerson, 102 Ala. 409, 14 So. 873, 874.

Sufficiency of Plea.—A plea by a carrier, sued for the nondelivery of goods, which alleges that before it ascertained that the same was intended for plaintiff, the plaintiff had left the United States, preventing the carrier from delivering the goods to him, and the carrier did not receive instructions from him to deliver the goods to any other person, was demurrable because it contained no matter of avoidance of the fulfillment of the carrier's contract, and failed to show an attempt by notice through the mails or otherwise to effect a delivery. Broadwood *v.* Southern Express Co., 41 So. 769, 148 Ala. 17.

In an action against a railroad company for misdelivery of goods, where the complaint alleges that they were deliverable to the order of plaintiffs, who delivered the bills of lading to defendant with the agreement that the goods were to be delivered to another on his payment for the same, but does not allege that such agreement was part of the original contract with defendant, or that the goods were marked to indicate that the price was to be collected, a plea that the agreement was with defendant's agent, who was acting beyond his authority, and as plaintiffs', and not defendant's agent, is good, since in such case his failure to collect before delivery could not bind defendant. Cox *v.* Columbus & W. Ry. Co., 91 Ala. 392, 8 So. 824, cited in note in 38 L. R. A. 365.

A carrier defended an action for failure to deliver one case of goods included in a shipment by setting up in a special plea in the terms of a special contract under which the shipment was made, avoiding liability unless claim for the loss or damages was made promptly after arrival, and if delayed more than 30 days after the delivery of the property, or after a due time for delivery, no liability would be imposed on the carrier. The shipment, minus the case, was delivered February 27th, and claim was made May 16th. Held, that the plea was defective, since, the action being for a failure to deliver, the plea should have alleged that no claim was made within 30 days after due time for delivery. Louisville, etc., R. Co. *v.* Price, 159 Ala. 213, 48 So. 814, cited in note in 31 L. R. A., N. S., 1183.

Matters Provable under General Issue.—A carrier, when sued for failure to deliver goods, may, to relieve itself of the breach set up in the complaint and denied by the general issue, prove, without a special plea, an attempted delivery. Central of Georgia Ry. Co. *v.* Montmollen, 39 So. 820, 145 Ala. 468.

In detinue against a carrier for freight, brought by the consignee, if when the consignee demanded the freight he had no bill of lading and refused to pay the invoice price of the freight or show his ownership, it was a defense and could be shown under the general issue. Louisville & N. R. Co. *v.* McCool, 52 So. 656, 167 Ala. 644.

Variance.—In an action against a carrier for failing to deliver freight to plaintiff, who was both consignor and consignee, there was no material variance between allegation that plaintiff drew a draft on a proposed purchaser of the goods with bill of lading attached and proof that the draft was drawn in the name of plaintiff's principal. Atlantic, etc., R. Co. *v.* Dahlberg Brokerage Co., 170 Ala. 617, 54 So. 168.

§ 51 (4) Evidence.

Burden of Proof—Delivery to True Owner.—To justify a delivery of freight without the consignor's order, the carrier must prove that the person to whom delivery was made was the true owner entitled to immediate possession. Atlantic, etc., R. Co. *v.* Dahlberg Brokerage Co., 170 Ala. 617, 54 So. 168.

Evidence to Show Title.—In an action against a railroad for the conversion of plaintiff's goods, a sales bill reciting purchase by plaintiff of the goods from a shoe company, in connection with evidence that it was paid, showed title in plaintiff and his right to immediate possession of the goods, in the absence of contrary evidence. Louisville & N. R. Co. *v.* Britton, 39 So. 585, 145 Ala. 654.

In an action against a railroad for the conversion of a case of slippers, a sales bill reciting a purchase by plaintiff of the goods from a shoe company was properly admitted in evidence, though it was not shown by whom it was made out, where the evidence tended to show that it was received by plaintiff from the shoe company and that he had paid it; it being a matter of no importance as to the particular individual making out the bill. Louisville & N. R. Co. *v.* Britton, 39 So. 585, 145 Ala. 654.

Unindorsed Bill of Lading.—In an action against a transportation company for failure to deliver certain cotton, it appeared that on the back of the bill of lading was written the name of the firm to whom it was issued, "per P. C., Atty.," who was a member of the firm. There was no evidence that P. C., or any other member of the firm, made the indorsement. Held, that the admission of such bill of lading in evidence on behalf of plaintiff as indorsee was erroneous, since there was no proof of indorsement. Capehart *v.* Granite Mills, 97 Ala. 353, 12 So. 44.

Amount of Charges Paid.—In an action for failure to deliver a case of goods included in a shipment which was delivered, evidence of what freight charges consignor had paid on the case is admissible. Louisville, etc., R. Co. *v.* Price, 48 So. 814, 159 Ala. 213.

Evidence to Show Nondelivery at Destination.—In an action against a carrier for failure to deliver freight, evidence that the consignees had never received the freight was admissible, as tending to show that it had never been delivered at the station, as the contract of shipment provided. Alabama Midland Ry. Co. *v.* Thompson, 32 So. 672, 134 Ala. 232.

Evidence of Custom to Demand Receipt Before Delivery of Goods.—Evidence of a party's mode of dealing is admissible against him, when relevant to any fact to be ascertained by the jury; and it may be shown, in a suit against a railroad company for failing to deliver goods shipped, for which it produces in evidence the receipt of the consignee, that its course of dealing was to demand and receive payment of freight and a receipt for the goods before their delivery. Mobile & G. R. Co. *v.* Williams, 54 Ala. 168.

Evidence of Conversion.—In an action against a carrier for the conversion of plaintiff's goods, evidence was admissible to show that the carrier's claim agent showed witness that plaintiff's goods were in the box addressed to plaintiff, which the agent said belonged to plaintiff and offered to sell to witness. Louisville, etc., R. Co. *v.* Britton, 149 Ala. 552, 43 So. 108.

Though a carrier may lawfully withhold goods until the bill of lading is produced, if it bases its refusal to deliver on that ground, its general and unqualified refusal to deliver is evidence of a conversion. Louisville, etc., R. Co. *v.* Britton, 149 Ala. 552, 43 So. 108.

Unprejudicial Evidence.—In an action against a transportation company for failure to deliver cotton at the place designated in the bill of lading, where there is no claim that the cotton was delivered to any one at that place, evidence as to what transportation lines carried cotton to such place, and the efforts plaintiff made to find the cotton in question, is not prejudicial to defendant. Capehart *v.* Granite Mills, 97 Ala. 353, 12 So. 44.

Sufficiency.—In an action by a shipper against a carrier for the conversion of a car load of lumber by delivering it to a wrong person, the defense that defendant was justified in making the delivery, because the invoice delivered by plaintiff to the person receiving the lumber described the car containing it in connection with another car rightfully delivered to such person, is not sustained, where the evidence shows that the invoice described the lumber in the car actually sold to such person, and did not describe the lumber in suit. Mobile, J. & K. C. R. Co. *v.* Bay Shore Lumber Co., 51 So. 956, 165 Ala. 610.

§ 51 (5) Damages.

In an action against a carrier for goods lost in transportation, or not delivered, the measure of damages is the value of the goods at the place of destination, and the interest thereon, deducting the unpaid cost of transportation. Capehart *v.* Granite Mills, 97 Ala. 353, 12 So. 44; Echols *v.* Louisville & N. R. Co., 90 Ala. 366, 7 So. 655. See, also, South, etc., R. Co. *v.* Wood, 72 Ala. 451; Southern R. Co. *v.* Moody, 151 Ala. 374, 44 So. 94, 95; Alabama, etc., R. Co. *v.* Little, 71 Ala. 611.

Evidence of Value at Place of Shipment.—Though the measure of damages in an action against a common carrier for failure to deliver cotton which it has undertaken to transport is the value of the cotton at the point of destination, with interest from the time it should have been delivered, less freight charges, yet evidence of the value at the point of shipment is relevant to the inquiry as to value at the point of delivery; and the carrier can not complain that the proof of value is confined to the place of shipment, as the presumption is that the value there is less than at the point of destination. Echols *v.* Louisville & N. R. Co., 90 Ala. 366, 7 So. 655; South, etc., R. Co. *v.* Wood, 72 Ala. 451.

Damages Where Delivery Refused.—Where, in an action against a carrier for failure to deliver goods, the carrier proved delivery, which was not accepted, it was error to include in the judgment for the consignee the full value of the goods; the recovery being limited to the damages sustained in consequence of the goods being in a damaged condition and by delay in making the attempted delivery. Central of Georgia Ry. Co. *v.* Montmollen, 39 So. 820, 145 Ala. 468.

§ 51 (6) Trial and Judgment.

Instruction Abstractly Correct.—In an action for nondelivery of goods, an instruction that defendant, in the absence of a contract to the contrary, is bound to carry and deliver the goods in a reasonable time, regardless of any unexpected or extraordinary pressure of business, is abstractly correct, and is not ground for reversal, though the record on appeal fails to show any evidence as to a pressure of business. Louisville & N. R. Co. *v.* Touart, 97 Ala. 514, 11 So. 756.

Directing Verdict.—In an action against a carrier for failure to deliver three bales of a shipment of cotton, the general affirmative charge in favor of plaintiffs was properly given where there was no evidence to rebut plaintiffs' positive evidence to the effect that the bales were never delivered. Southern R. Co. *v.* Cortner, 3 Ala. App. 400, 58 So. 84.

Questions for Jury—Proper Place for Delivery.—Where a shipment is billed to a point which is not on a railroad, but near it, what is the proper place of delivery by the carrier is a question for the jury, where the evidence is conflicting. Louisville & N. R. Co. *v.* Bernheim, 21 So. 405, 113 Ala. 489.

Unreasonableness of Refusal to Delivey without Bill of Lading.—In an action against a railroad for the conversion of plaintiff's goods, a refusal on demand to deliver the goods without the bill of lading therefor was a qualified one, the reasonableness whereof was a question for the jury. Louisville & N. R. Co. *v.* Britton, 39 So. 585, 145 Ala. 654.

Nondelivery.—There was evidence that goods shipped to New York over defendant railroad arrived there within two weeks, and were properly stored there for three years, ready for delivery, and that the consignee did not appear to receive them; that the connecting carrier unsucessfully tried to find the consignee; and that finally the property was sold for charges. There was, on the other hand, evidence that the goods did not reach New York within six weeks, that defendant's agent was unable to trace them five months after their shipment, and that repeated inquiries were made for the goods at the connecting carrier's depots in New York within two months after the shipment. Defendant had agreed to deliver the goods in New York. Held, that the question of nondelivery was for the jury. Alabama G. S. R. Co. *v.* Eichofer, 100 Ala. 224, 14 So. 56.

Payment of Freight.—In an action against a carrier for the conversion of plaintiff's goods, held, under the evidence, a question for the jury whether plaintiff paid the freight. Louisville etc., R. Co. *v.* Britton, 149 Ala. 552, 43 So. 108.

Time for Delivery.—A carrier defended an action for failure to deliver one case of goods included in a shipment by setting up in special plea the terms of a special contract under which the shipment was made, avoiding liability unless claim for the loss or damages was made promptly after arrival, and if delayed more than 30 days after the delivery of the property, or after a due time for delivery, no liability would be imposed on the carrier. The shipment, minus the case, was delivered February 27, and claim was made May 16. Held, that in the absence of any agreement the court could not say as a matter of law from February 27 to May 16 a due time for delivery had elapsed. Louisville, etc., R. Co. *v.* Price, 159 Ala. 213, 48 So. 814, cited in note in 31 L. R. A., N. S., 1183.

Neither could the court say as a matter of law that, because part of the freight had been delivered on February 27, a reasonable time had elapsed for the case not delivered. Louisville, etc., R. Co. *v.* Price, 159 Ala. 213, 48 So. 814, cited in note in 31 L. R. A., N. S., 1183.

(E) DELAY IN TRANSPORTATION OR DELIVERY.

§ 52. Liability of Carrier for Delay.

"Although the delivery of goods be

delayed for an unreasonable time, the carrier can not be charged for the conversion of the goods, unless demand has been made and refused while the goods are in its possession. Its only liability is for damages caused by the deterioration in value of the goods themselves during the time of delay. 2 Hutchinson on Carriers (3d Ed.), p. 717, § 651; 6 Cyc. 442, 444, 449." Southern R. Co. *v.* Moody, 169 Ala. 292, 53 So. 1016.

§ 53. Demurrage, and Liability of Consignee or Owner for Delay.

Right to Charge Demurrage.—A railroad company may legally charge storage or demurrage for its cars used and occupied by consignees beyond a reasonable time after the contract of transportation has been fulfilled. Southern R. Co. *v.* Lockwood Mfg. Co., 142 Ala. 322, 37 So. 667, 669.

Lien for Demurrage.—The placing by a carrier of a car on the team track, to be unloaded by the consignee, is not such an absolute delivery to him of the lumber therein as to cut off any future right of lien thereon of the carrier for demurrage charges because of the consignee not unloading in the time limit therefor. Southern Ry. Co. *v.* Lockwood Mfg. Co., 37 So. 667, 142 Ala. 322, 68 L. R. A. 227.

Voluntary Payment—Recovery Back.—A consignee, having received notice of arrival of the goods, and knowing that, if left in the cars after a certain time, demurrage charges would accrue, did not tender the freight charges due nor demand the goods until some time thereafter, when it paid the demurrage charges to the railroad company, knowing that such payment was subject to the action of a certain association, to which the money belonged, to refund. Held, that the payment was voluntary, and could not be recovered back, though the notice of arrival stated excessive freight charges. Gulf City Const. Co. *v.* Louisville & N. R. Co., 25 So. 579, 121 Ala. 621.

Unauthorized Statement of Agent as to Return of Charges.—A consignee of freight paid demurrage charges for car service, knowing that they could not be refunded by the railroad company without the consent of an association to which the money belonged, the railroad company's agent stating that the consignee would have no trouble in getting the charges back. Held, that such statement was not binding on the association, the agent not being shown to have had authority to make it. Gulf City Const. Co. *v.* Louisville & N. R. Co., 25 So. 579, 121 Ala. 621.

§ 54. Actions for Delay.

§ 55. —— Pleading.

Complaint—Allegation as to Special Damages.—A complaint in an action against a carrier for delay in the delivery of a car load of stoves, which alleged that there was no market for the stoves at the point of destination, that plaintiff owned teams and hired drivers in peddling stoves, that during the delay in the delivery the teams and drivers were unemployed, resulting in loss to plaintiff, that the carrier, "or its agent, or its agent at" point of destination, knew that there was no market for the stoves, except as above set forth, and that plaintiff was sustaining the expense specially claimed and made necessary by the delay of the carrier, but which failed to allege that any notice was given to the carrier at the time of the making of the contract for shipment of the special circumstances on which plaintiff's claim for damages was based, was insufficient to authorize the recovery of such damages. Pilcher *v.* Central of Georgia Ry. Co., 46 So. 765, 155 Ala. 316.

Plea.—A plea, in an action against a carrier for failure to deliver freight within a reasonable time, which does not show that the cars referred to therein contained the freight, or that the shipper was responsible for the matters set up, and which does not show that the matters alleged might not have had reference to a different shipment, is bad. St. Louis & S. F. R. Co. *v.* Cash Grain Co., 50 So. 81, 161 Ala. 332.

In an action against a carrier for damages from delay in delivering fruit shipped, a plea attempting to set up contributory negligence of the consignee in failing to call for it for four days after arrival, but averring no duty of the consignee to do so, nor any notice of the arrival, nor any facts that would relieve the carrier from giving such notice, was bad. Western Ry. of Alabama *v.* Hart, 49 So. 371, 160 Ala. 599.

A plea which averred the failure of the consignee to present the bill of lading and call for the fruit within a reasonable time as the proximate cause of the damage, and that the bill required notice of arrival of the fruit, but did not aver that notice of its arrival was given, was bad, since the failure to present the bill of lading and call for the fruit might have been due to the want of notice. Western Railway *v.* Hart, 160 Ala. 599, 49 So. 371.

Variance.—An averment that plaintiff contracted with a railway company for the transportation of the corpse of his infant is not supported by proof that he furnished the money to another, who acted as his agent in purchasing the tickets, where neither the agency nor the fact that the agent was using plaintiff's money is disclosed to the company. Lucas *v.* Southern Ry. Co., 25 So. 219, 122 Ala. 529.

§ 56. —— Evidence.

Evidence That Charges Resulted from Delay.—Where the complaint, in an action against a carrier for unreasonable delay in the delivery of lumber to be furnished by plaintiff to a third person under a contract requiring delivery to a vessel under a charter party stipulating for demurrage, alleged that plaintiff had a contract to deliver lumber to a vessel within her lay days, and by which he was required to pay demurrage incurred in furnishing the cargo, plaintiff was properly permitted to testify that he had such a contract to show that demurrage charges proximately resulted from the carrier's delay in delivery. Southern R. Co. *v.* Lewis, 165 Ala. 451, 51 So. 863.

Knowledge of Special Circumstances.—Where, in an action against a carrier for delay in delivering lumber to a vessel, rendering plaintiff liable to demurrage charges, the issue was whether the carrier had notice of the charter party making plaintiff liable for demurrage charges, evidence that all charter parties made provision therefor was competent to show the carrier's knowledge. Southern R. Co. *v.* Lewis, 165 Ala. 451, 51 So. 863.

Evidence of Delay.—In view of Code 1896, § 4224, providing that a common carrier, if the place of destination of freight is a city of a certain size, etc., is not relieved from liability as a common carrier by reason of a storage of freight, unless within 24 hours after the arrival thereof notice is given the consignee, the fact that a railroad failed to give the consignee of cotton notice of its arrival until a certain date, in an action against the road for delay in delivering the cotton, was some evidence that the delivery was delayed until at or close to that date. Southern R. Co. *v.* Cofer, 43 So. 102, 149 Ala. 565, cited in note in 34 L. R. A., N. S., 638.

Where bills of lading for cotton bound the railroad only to transport with as reasonable dispatch as its general business would permit, evidence, in an action against the road by the shipper for delay in delivering the goods, that a subsequent shipment reached the same destination prior to the first shipment, was competent in respect to delay on defendant's part, and in refutation of its plea that an unprecedented amount of freight prevented it from hauling the cotton more expeditiously. Southern R. Co. *v.* Cofer, 149 Ala. 565, 43 So. 102.

Consent to Delay.—A delay probably injurious being shown, it is admissible to show that, before starting, the plaintiff consented to a delay, if necessary. Johnson *v.* Lightsey, 34 Ala. 169.

§ 57. —— Damages.

§ 57 (1) Elements and Measure of Damages in General.

Natural and Proximate Consequences.—The damages recoverable from a carrier for delay in delivering goods received for transportation are such as are the natural and proximate results of its acts and such as reasonably might have been expected to be within the contemplation of the parties at the time of entering into the contract. Pilcher *v.* Central, etc., R. Co., 155 Ala. 316, 46 So. 765. See, to same effect, Southern R. Co. *v.* Moody, 151 Ala. 374, 44 So. 94.

Damages Resulting from Act of Plaintiff.—Where a corpse arrived an hour before the time appointed for the funeral, and plaintiff, the widow of deceased, of her own accord postponed the funeral until the following day, she is not entitled to damages for mental anguish because of delay, though before the arrival of the corpse some of the friends of the family had departed. Alabama City, G. & A. Ry. Co. *v.* Brady, 49 So. 351, 160 Ala. 615.

Where the funeral was voluntarily postponed by plaintiff, the carrier causing delay in the arrival of the corpse is not liable for the expense of re-embalming the body, necessitated by postponement of the funeral. Alabama, etc., R. Co. *v.* Brady, 160 Ala. 615, 49 So. 351, cited in note in 38 L. R. A., N. S., 433.

Expenses Incurred.—A shipper, suing a carrier for delay in the transportation and delivery of a shipment, can not recover the expenses incurred by him on a trip to the point of destination to look after the shipment. Southern R. Co. *v.* Coleman, 153 Ala. 266, 44 So. 837, cited in note in 30 L. R. A., N. S., 483, following Southern R. Co. *v.* Webb, 143 Ala. 304, 315, 39 So. 262.

A carrier who used due and reasonable diligence in delivering a shipment is not liable to the consignee for expenses incurred by him in going to the station prepared to receive it before its arrival. Thompson *v.* Alabama Midland R. Co., 24 So. 931, 122 Ala. 378.

Interest.—Where the period a public ginnery was stopped in consequence of the failure of a carrier to promptly transport and deliver a part of the machinery thereof was so short that the ginnery had no rental value, interest on its value for that period is the proper measure of damages, if claimed. Southern R. Co. *v.* Coleman, 153 Ala. 266, 44 So. 837, cited in note in 30 L. R. A., N. S., 483.

Exemplary Damages.—Proof that the agent of a carrier at the destination of a shipment did not locate the car in which the same was is proof of simple negligence only, and does not authorize exemplary damages for delay in the delivery of the shipment. Southern R. Co. *v.* Coleman, 153 Ala. 266, 44 So. 837, cited in note in 30 L. R. A., N. S., 483.

Nominal Damages—Speculative Profits.—An owner of a public ginnery delivered a part of the machinery to a carrier for transportation to a designated point, to be repaired by the consignee. The carrier delayed the delivery of the machinery. The owner testified that 75 cents was a fair profit for ginning a bale of cotton, but he could only estimate the number of bales that went to his gin during the days his plant was shut down in consequence of the delay. The 75 cents profit depended on contingencies. Held, that the owner was entitled to nominal damages only; the estimate of what he might have earned by operating the gin, had the shipment been promptly delivered, being speculative. Southern R. Co. *v.* Coleman, 153 Ala. 266, 44 So. 837, cited in note in 30 L. R. A., N. S., 483.

Measure of Damages.—The measure of damages for delay in delivering goods received by a carrier for transportation is the difference between the market value of the goods at the time of delivery and at the time when by reasonable diligence they should have been delivered, together with incidental damages naturally flowing from the delay, and special damages where the shipper informed the carrier when the contract of shipment was made of special circumstances requiring expedition in the shipment. Pilcher *v.* Central, etc., R. Co., 155 Ala. 316, 46 So. 765.

In an action against a common carrier, where the complaint alleged a breach of the contract to deliver certain goods, and the proof showed only unresonable delay in delivery, the court erred in rendering judgment for the total value of the property. Southern Ry. Co. *v.* Moody, 44 So. 94, 151 Ala. 374, cited in note in 42 L. R. A., N. S., 783.

Computation According to Provision in Contract.—Where bills of lading provided that the amount of any damage for which any carrier should become liable should be computed at the value of the cotton shipped at the time and place of shipment, it was error, in an action by the shipper for delay in delivering the cotton, to charge that the damages should be estimated according to the price of the cotton at the place of delivery.

Southern Ry. Co. *v.* Cofer, 43 So. 102, 149 Ala. 565.

§ 57 (2) Special Damage Dependent on Knowledge of Circumstances.

A carrier is not liable for special damages for delay unless it knows at the time of the making of the contract of the special circumstances requiring prompt shipment. Southern R. Co. *v.* Lewis, 165 Ala. 451, 51 So. 863.

Where the carrier has notice that delay in the delivery will result in an unusual loss there may be a recovery therefor. Pilcher *v.* Central, etc., R. Co., 155 Ala. 316, 46 So. 765.

Where a carrier undertaking to deliver lumber to a vessel knew at the time of the making of the contract that the adverse party would be compelled to pay demurrage charges if the cargo was delayed, but delayed delivery for an unreasonable time and thereby forced the adverse party to become liable for demurrage, the carrier was liable for the amount of the demurrage. Southern R. Co. *v.* Lewis, 165 Ala. 451, 51 So. 863.

Notice after Contract Made.—A notice to a carrier by a shipper of the expense and loss which the shipper will sustain by delay in the delivery of the goods, given subsequent to the execution of the contract of shipment, does not change the contract or the obligation thereon, and does not authorize a recovery of special damages resulting from the delay. Pilcher *v.* Central, etc., R. Co., 155 Ala. 316, 46 So. 765.

Notice after Arrival of Goods—Failure to Make Delivery.—Where notice is given of circumstances which will occasion special damages after the contract to carry has been performed and after the goods have arrived for delivery, it is liable for such special damages where it negligently fails to make such delivery. Southern R. Co. *v.* Lewis, 165 Ala. 451, 51 So. 863.

That a carrier did not know when contracting for the transportation of lumber that demurrage would accrue by reason of a delay did not relieve it from liability for demurrage charges, where, after the arrival of the lumber at destination, it undertook to deliver the lumber to a vessel with knowledge that a delay in delivery would incur liability for demurrage. Southern R. Co. *v.* Lewis, 165 Ala. 451, 51 So. 863.

§ 58. —— Trial.

Question for Jury.—Whether an electric railroad company used due diligence in clearing its track of a wreck, so as to transport a corpse with promptness, is a question for the jury. Alabama City, G. & A. Ry. Co. *v.* Brady, 49 So. 351, 160 Ala. 615, cited in note in 38 L. R. A., N. S., 433.

(F) LOSS OF OR INJURY TO GOODS.

§ 59. Care Required of Carrier in General.

The railroad companies of this state are common carriers, and they are liable to the strictest accountability for all losses occasioned by their neglect to discharge the duties attached by law, to the trust of common carriers. Selma, etc., R. Co. *v.* Butts, 43 Ala. 385.

§ 60. Nature of Liability as Common Carrier.

In the absence of a special contract, a carrier's obligation is to transport the goods to destination, assuming liability for loss occasioned, except by an act of God, the public enemy, or the fault of the owner or his agent. Barron *v.* Mobile & O. R. Co., 2 Ala. App. 555, 56 So. 862; Louisville, etc., R. Co. *v.* McGuire & Co., 79 Ala. 395; South, etc., R. Co. *v.* Wood, 66 Ala. 167; Alabama, etc., R. Co. *v.* Quarles, 145 Ala. 436, 40 So. 120; Mobile, etc., R. Co. *v.* Hopkins, 41 Ala. 486, 499; Louisville, etc., R. Co. *v.* Bernheim, 113 Ala. 489, 21 So. 405, 407; Alabama, etc., R. Co. *v.* Little, 71 Ala. 611; Louisville, etc., R. Co. *v.* Sherrod, 84 Ala. 178, 4 So. 29; Alabama, etc., R. Co. *v.* Thomas, 89 Ala. 234, 7 So. 762.

The exceptions other than those legally possible of creation by special contract, to the exacting common-law liability of a common carrier of goods, are the acts of God and of the public enemy, where no negligence of omission or commission concurred therewith. Atlantic Coast Line R. Co. *v.* Rice, 52 So. 918, 169 Ala. 265.

At common law, a common carrier is absolutely liable for the safety of goods intrusted to it for transportation, and is responsible for any loss or injury to the goods not caused by the act of God, the public enemy, or fault of the complaining party. Southern R. Co. *v.* Levy, 39 So. 95, 144 Ala. 614; Louisville & N. R. Co. *v.* Cowherd, 120 Ala. 51, 23 So. 793; Louisville & N. R. Co. *v.* Brewer (Ala.), 62 So. 698; Jones *v.* Pitcher & Co., 3 Stew. & P. 135; Morton *v.* Louisville, etc., R. Co., 128 Ala. 537, 557, 29 So. 602; Alabama, etc., R. Co. *v.* Little, 71 Ala. 611; South, etc., R. Co. *v.* Henlein, 52 Ala. 606; Steele *v.* Townsend, 37 Ala. 247, 254.

Carriers by Water.—The common-law rule fixing the liability of carriers extends as well to carriers by water as to carriers by land. Jones *v.* Pitcher, 3 Stew. & P. 135.

Effect of Custom.—In an action against the owners of a steamboat to recover the value of a cargo of cotton, evidence of a custom to carry torchlights at night on board steamboats can not be received to affect the liability of the owners for a loss by fire caused by the negligent use of such lights. Hibler *v.* McCartney, 31 Ala. 501.

Accidental Loss by Fire.—A common carrier, receiving goods for transportation, is an insurer, except against the act of God or the public enemy, or the wrong or negligence of the party complaining; and is liable for the accidental loss of the goods by fire. Louisville, etc., R. Co. *v.* McGuire & Co., 79 Ala. 395.

Loss by Robbery.—The owners of a steamboat are liable as common carriers for a loss of goods by robbery. Boon *v.* The Belfast, 40 Ala. 184.

Robbery is no defense to a common carrier by water on an inland river for the loss of goods; and this principle was not changed by the act of congress which declared robbery on any river where the tide ebbs and flows to be piracy, which would be a good defense for the lost goods. The Belfast *v.* Boon, 41 Ala. 50.

§ 61. What Law Governs.

Under the laws, railroad companies are common carriers, and subject to all the liabilities of such carriers; and where suit is brought against a railroad company for failure to deliver freight received for transportation, under a contract made and to be performed wholly in another state, it will be presumed, in the absence of proof to the contrary, that the common law, as to common carriers, prevailed in the state where such contract was entered into and was to be performed. Southwestern R. Co. *v.* Webb, 48 Ala. 585.

§ 62. Condition of Goods.

Where a carrier accepts goods improperly packed, their condition being open to ordinary observation, the duty attaches of using due care for their safe carriage, and the carrier is subject to all the liabilities ordinarily attaching to an ordinary shipment of the same character. Atlantic Coast Line R. Co. *v.* Rice, 52 So. 918, 169 Ala. 265.

§ 63. Nature and Validity of Contract for Transportation.

"A carrier is liable at common law by reason of the hire." Ladd *v.* Chotard, Minor 366.

To make a carrier subject to the stringent liability imposed by the common law on common carriers, there must be privity of contract, express or implied, between him and the person who employs him, and a right on his part to compensation for his services. Central R., etc., Co. *v.* Lampley, 76 Ala. 357.

A contract, imposing upon a carrier the exclusive duty of safe-keeping, may be implied by usage, or by a particular course of dealing between the parties; but the implication that the carrier assumes the duty of immediate transportation, and hence the responsibility of an insurer, without knowing to what place and to whom goods are to be shipped, must be clear. Central of Georgia Ry. Co. *v.* Sigma Lumber Co., 170 Ala. 627, 54 So. 205.

Contract as Affected by Post-Office Laws.—Where the proof shows the delivery of a letter or package containing money, to be carried between two places, at each of which is a post office, a recovery may be had on a count charging the defendant as a bailee to deliver the money on request, even if the contract to carry is conceded to be invalid, as opposed to the post-office laws. Hosea *v.* McCrory, 12 Ala. 349.

§ 64. Commencement of Liability.

A carrier's liability for goods as a carrier begins when they are delivered to it ready for immediate transportation. Central of Georgia Ry. Co. *v.* Sigma Lumber Co., 170 Ala. 627, 54 So. 205.

Necessity for Delivery.—H., a warehouseman, who was also cotton agent for defendant railroad company, issued bills of lading for defendant for the shipment of certain cotton still in his warehouse, and for which warehouse receipts were still outstanding, and delivered the bills to plaintiff's agent, who knew when he received them that the cotton was still in the warehouse, and that the warehouse receipts had not been surrendered. H. had no authority to issue bills of lading for cotton, as agent for carrier, until the cotton had been loaded on the cars, of which fact plaintiff's agent also had knowledge, and the cotton covered by the bills was burned while still in the warehouse, the night after the bills were issued. Held, that the carrier was not liable therefor, under the rule that delivery, actual or constructive, is necessary to impose responsibility or liability on the carrier. Loveman & Co. *v.* Alabama, etc., R. Co., 175 Ala. 316, 57 So. 817.

Goods Loaded on Car.—Though there was a course of dealing between a carrier and a lumber company, whereby the carrier received for shipment from plaintiff's mill, where the carrier had no office or agent, lumber placed upon cars on the side track, and the carrier at the lumber company's request placed cars upon the side track to be loaded by the lumber company for transportation, and the lumber company notified the carrier's conductor on its train going east to have its next train going west stop and get the lumber, which it failed to do and the goods were destroyed by fire, the carrier was not, as matter of law, bound to take away the cars of lumber on its next train, in the absence of an express contract to that effect. Central of Georgia Ry. Co. *v.* Sigma Lumber Co., 170 Ala. 627, 54 So. 205. See post, "Proximate Cause of Loss or Injury," § 72.

§ 65. Termination of Liability.

In the absence of statutory regulations, the liability of a common carrier continues, after the goods have reached their destination, until the consignee has had a reasonable time to remove them; and after that time he is liable only as a warehouseman, or bailee for hire. Louisville, etc., R. Co. *v.* McGuire & Co., 79 Ala. 395; Southern Exp. Co. *v.* Holland, 109 Ala. 362, 19 So. 66.

In absence of statute, a railroad company's liability as a carrier of freight terminates after a reasonable time has elapsed for the removal of the freight by the consignee after arrival at destination. Greek-American Produce Co. *v.* Illinois Cent. R. Co., 4 Ala. App. 377, 58 So. 994; Southern Exp. Co. *v.* Holland, 109 Ala. 362, 19 So. 66. See, also, Alabama, etc., R. Co. *v.* Kidd, 35 Ala. 209, 218.

Delivery of Goods.—A carrier's liability for injuries to goods can not survive a delivery and acceptance prior to the damage. Barclay *v.* Southern Ry. Co., 6 Ala. App. 502, 60 So. 479.

Where the shipper of a carload of household goods took charge of them when they were switched onto a siding at a station which had no depot or agent, and commenced unloading them, locking the car for the night to finish the next day, there was a complete delivery of the car to him, so that the carrier was not liable for damage to the goods from rain the night after he began unloading. Southern R. Co. *v.* Barclay, 1 Ala. App. 348, 56 So. 26, cited in note in 40 L. R. A., N. S., 774.

Duty to Remove Goods within Reasonable Time.—It is as much a part of the contract that the owner or consignee shall be ready at the place of destination to receive the goods when they arrive, or within a reasonable time thereafter, as that the carrier shall transport and deliver them. Alabama & T. R. R. Co. *v.* Kidd, 35 Ala. 209, cited in 17 L. R. A. 693.

Necessity for Notice.—When no notice was given to plaintiff by a carrier until long after the arrival of his goods, and on the same day that he received the notice, he went to get them, the liability of defendant as a common carrier had not ceased. Alabama Midland Ry. Co. *v.* Darby, 24 So. 713, 119 Ala. 531.

Code, § 4224, providing that a common

carrier can be relieved from its liability as a carrier on the arrival of freight in a "city or town having two thousand inhabitants" only by giving a certain notice, makes no distinction between incorporated and unincorporated cities and towns; and incorporation need not be shown, to take advantage of the statute. Louisville & N. R. Co. *v.* Johnson, 33 So. 661, 135 Ala. 232.

Under Code 1896, § 4224, providing that the relation of common carrier continues in towns or cities of 2,000 population or more and having a daily mail, unless within 24 hours after the arrival of freight notice thereof is given the consignee formally or through the mail, and Code 1907, § 6137, containing the same provision, except that with reference to the population, where the conditions prescribed do not exist, there is no primary duty on defendant to give notice of the arrival of the goods, to terminate the strict liability of a carrier, unless a proper custom to the contrary then prevailed at the destination. Central of Georgia Ry. Co. *v.* Burton, 51 So. 643, 165 Ala. 425.

Failure to Receive after Notice.—Where plaintiff, on a certain day, expected a package by express at a place where it was customary for consignees to call for packages upon notice of their arrival, and plaintiff, in the evening of the same day, and in time to receive the same, was notified of the arrival of said package, but directed the express company to retain the package until the next day, and it was stolen that night without fault on the part of the company, the company is not liable for its loss. Southern Exp. Co. *v.* Holland, 109 Ala. 362, 19 So. 66, cited in notes in 33 L. R. A. 67, 14 L. R. A., N. S., 394.

Distance of Consignee from Destination as Affecting Reasonable Time.—The fact that the consignee lives 28 miles from the place to which the goods are consigned will not be considered in determining what is a reasonable time after the arrival of the goods within which he should have called for them. Columbus & W. Ry. Co. *v.* Ludden, 89 Ala. 612, 7 So. 471, cited in note in 8 L. R. A., N. S., 242.

Time Held Insufficient.—In the absence of statute or custom, from the arrival of goods at destination on Friday at 3 p. m. to Monday at 1:45 a. m. was not a reasonable time for their removal by the consignee so as to terminate the liability of the carrier as such. Central, etc., R. Co. *v.* Burton, 165 Ala. 425, 51 So. 643, cited in note in 25 L. R. A., N. S., 939.

Time to Remove Goods Held Sufficient.—Plaintiff received 437 bales of cotton, which had been shipped over defendant's road. Plaintiff immediately began to haul the cotton in wagons to its factory, which was six miles distant. The station platform would only hold about 100 bales, and the rest were allowed to remain in the cars until room was made for them on the platform. Six days after its arrival 103 bales on the platform and 25 bales in a car were destroyed by fire. Held, that such six days was a reasonable time within which the cotton might have been removed, as a matter of law, and hence the liability of the defendant as a common carrier had ceased, under the bill of lading, providing that liability as a carrier ceased on the arrival of the goods at their destination. Tallassee Falls Mfg. Co. *v.* Western Ry. of Alabama, 29 So. 203, 128 Ala. 167, cited in note in 8 L. R. A., N. S., 242.

Termination of Liability by Stoppage En Route.—Where a carload of lumber was shipped under a waybill providing for stoppage en route at a planing mill, and delivery to the planing mill company, that the lumber might be planed and then reshipped to destination, and the lumber was destroyed by fire while at the planing mill, it was then in the possession of plaintiff, or his agent, the planing mill company, so that defendant's liability was terminated for the time being, and it was not liable for destruction of the lumber without its fault. Barron *v.* Mobile, etc., R. Co., 2 Ala. App. 555, 56 So. 862.

§ 66. Acts or Omissions Constituting Negligence by Carrier in General.

When a carrier undertakes to transport perishable goods in cars having appliances for ventilation, it assumes the duty to make all the appliances available for the safe transportation of the goods, in the absence of anything in the contract to the contrary. Western Ry. of Alabama *v.* Hart, 49 So. 371, 160 Ala. 599.

§ 67. Deviation or Delay.

See post, "Proximate Cause of Loss or Injury," § 72.

§ 68. Mode or Means of Transportation.

A carrier must provide safe and suitable cars for transporting goods, and can not avoid liability for not doing so by using another's cars, the latter being its agents; but, if the consignor undertakes to furnish the cars used in transportation, the carrier is not liable for a loss resulting from their defective condition. Central, etc., R. Co. *v.* Chicago Varnish Co., 169 Ala. 287, 53 So. 832.

Agreement of Carrier to Keep Consignor's Cars in Repair.—Where the freight was shipped in cars leased by the carrier from the consignor under an agreement by which the carrier was to keep the cars in repair at the consignor's cost, the carrier was liable for loss of freight caused by defects therein. Central, etc., R. Co. *v.* Chicago Varnish Co., 169 Ala. 287, 53 So. 832.

§ 69. Negligence of Agents or Servants.

Carriers are responsible, by reason of the duties imposed by law upon them as carriers, for the negligence of their servants in and about the carriage of freight, including its receipt for future carriage, and where the servant is acting within his authority, the carrier is responsible, though the wrong or damage be done inadvertently and with the purpose to accomplish its business in an unlawful manner. St. Louis & S. F. R. Co. *v.* Cavender, 170 Ala. 601, 54 So. 54.

Where the owner of cotton delivers to a railway company the warehouse receipts of a compress company, and the railway company accepts them and issues bills of lading thereon to the owner, and the cotton is injured by exposure to the weather after delivery to the compress company, both the railway company and the compress company are liable for the loss, the railway company because it occurred while in the hands of its agent, the compress company, and the compress company being liable as a bailee for the owner, and its liability to the owner could not be defeated by its accepting the cotton in bailment from the railway company. Southern Ry. Co. *v.* Jones Cotton Co., 52 So. 899, 167 Ala. 575.

A railway company had an arrangement with a compress company, by which on delivery to the railway company by the owner of cotton of the compress company's warehouse receipts the railway company issued bills of lading for the shipment of the cotton. Plaintiff cotton company, after contracting for the sale and delivery of cotton which it had delivered to the compress company, delivered the warehouse receipts of the compress company to the railway company and bills of lading were issued by the railway company thereon. Held, that the railway company recognized the compress company as its agent to keep the cotton, pending its loading into the cars, and became responsible for the compress company's negligence therein. Southern R. Co. *v.* Jones Cotton Co., 167 Ala. 575, 52 So. 899.

§ 70. Act of God, Vis Major, or Inevitable Accident.

Proximate Cause.—The inevitable accidents, which constitute a legal excuse for the carrier, must be the immediate, not the remote, cause of the loss, and must be beyond the prevention or control of human prudence. Jones *v.* Pitcher, 3 Stew. & P. 135; Sprowl *v.* Kellar, 4 Stew. & P. 382.

Acts of God, or inevitable accidents, which constitute a legal excuse for the loss of or damage to goods by the sinking or destruction of a steamboat or other vessel, must appear to be the immediate and legal cause of the loss or damage. Sprowl *v.* Kellar, 4 Stew. & P. 382.

A severe tropical storm of extraordinary intensity, which forced waters up out of a bay and flooded railroad yards, constituted an act of God, which relieves the railway company from liability for damage to freight, if no negligence of the company contributed to the injury. Louisville, etc., R. Co. *v.* McKenzie, 5 Ala. App. 605, 59 So. 345.

The sudden and unprecedented overflow of a river is such an act of God as will relieve a railroad company from liability for damage to freight, caused thereby, if, after knowledge of the danger, they did not unnecessarily expose it, but made all effort to save it. Smith *v.* Western Ry. of Alabama, 91 Ala. 455, 8 So. 754, 11 L. R. A. 619, cited in notes in 29 L. R. A., N. S., 671, 672, 39 L. R. A., N. S., 646.

Concurrent Negligence of Carrier.—See post, "Proximate Cause of Loss or Injury," § 72.

§ 71. Contributory Negligence of Owner.

Where the proximate cause of loss of goods was the negligence of the shipper in marking or packing, the carrier is not responsible. Broadwood *v.* Southern Express Co., 41 So. 769, 148 Ala. 17.

Negligence of Consignor Imputed to Consignee.—In an action by a consignee against a common carrier for damages to goods which were improperly loaded by the consignor, the negligence of the consignor is imputed to the consignee. McCarthy *v.* Louisville & N. R. Co., 102 Ala. 193, 14 So. 370, cited in notes in 29 L. R. A., N. S., 665, 1215.

Notice to Carrier of Improper Loading.—A carrier is liable for injury to goods shipped, though they were improperly loaded by the consignor, if the improper loading was apparent to the ordinary observation of the carrier's servants. McCarthy *v.* Louisville & N. R. Co., 102 Ala. 193, 14 So. 370, cited in notes in 29 L. R. A., N. S., 665, 29 L. R. A., N. S., 1215.

Effect of Want of Evidence to Remove Presumption Against Carrier.—In an action against a common carrier for injury to goods shipped, plaintiff is entitled to judgment, though the improper loading of the goods contributed to the injury, if there is no evidence to remove the presumption of negligence on the part of the carrier. McCarthy *v.* Louisville & N. R. Co., 102 Ala. 193, 14 So. 370, cited in notes in 29 L. R. A., N. S., 665, 1215.

§ 72. Proximate Cause of Loss or Injury.

Where goods are injured or destroyed by providential causes while in the possession of a carrier in default, the carrier is liable, since its default is an operative cause concurrent with the act of God. Central of Georgia Ry. Co. *v.* Sigma Lumber Co., 170 Ala. 627, 54 So. 205.

The failure of a carrier to move a car load of lumber, after being made ready for shipment and notice thereof, renders it liable for the loss of the lumber by its subsequent destruction in the burning of adjacent property without the carrier's fault. Green *v.* Louisville & N. R. Co., 59 So. 937, 163 Ala. 138.

A consignment of flour was delivered to a carrier for shipment. It was retained four days before being forwarded. Upon the day of its arrival at its destination, at 1 o'clock p. m., notice of its arrival was sent to the consignee. On the morning of the next day, at 1 o'clock, a cyclone damaged the goods. Held, that the carrier was liable for the damage, since its negligence, resulting in the delay at the place of shipment, continued to be an active cause until the consignee had a reasonable time after their arrival within which to remove the goods. Alabama Great Southern R. Co. *v.* J. A. Elliott & Son, 43 So. 738, 150 Ala. 381, 9 L. R. A., N. S., 1264, cited in note in 31 L. R. A., N. S., 1133.

Where a carrier retained in its possession cotton received for transportation for a period of 11 days, without forwarding the same, and on the eleventh day the cotton was destroyed by a cyclone which practically destroyed the town from which the cotton was to be shipped, the carrier was guilty of negligence in failing to transport the cotton within a reasonable time, and was therefore precluded from claiming that the cotton was destroyed by an act of God in defense of an action for loss thereof. Alabama Great Southern R. Co. *v.* Quarles & Couturie, 40 So. 120, 145 Ala. 436, 5 L. R. A., N. S., 867, cited in note in 31 L. R. A., N. S., 1133.

In an action against steamboat owners for the loss of goods, it appeared that on the voyage a storm arose which caused the boat to lay to, and, while thus laying to, it took in water, and was in a sinking condition. Held, that the storm, in order to constitute a legal excuse for the loss as being an act of God or an inevitable accident, must have been the immediate, not the remote, cause of the loss, and if the loss was caused by the sinking of the boat, and that could have been prevented by prudence and skill on the part of the officers of the boat, the owners were liable. Sprowl *v.* Kellar, 4 Stew. & P. 382.

Plaintiff delivered leather to defendant

at G. for shipment to P., without giving any directions as to the route. Defendant's usual route was by way of C., where connection was made with its main line north. The leather was delivered on Saturday, after the defendant's train to C. had left, and defendant had no train for C. on Sunday. Defendant operated a short line from G. to A., where it connected with the line of another company, by which the leather might have been forwarded at 4:30 p. m. on the day it was received; but it was retained for shipment by way of C., and was burned that night. Held, that defendant was negligent in failing to ship by way of A. Louisville & N. R. Co. *v.* Gidley, 24 So. 753, 119 Ala. 523.

§ 73. Actions for Loss or Injury.

§ 74. —— Nature and Form.

"A common carrier may be sued, for breach of the contract to carry and deliver safely, or in case for neglect of the duty resting on him, or, sometimes, in trover for a conversion." Whilden & Sons *v.* Merchants', etc., Nat. Bank, 64 Ala. 1, 27.

Trover will lie against a common carrier for a misdelivery, or an appropriation of the property to its or his own use, or for any act or dominion of ownership antagonistic to and inconsistent with plaintiff's claim or right; but not for goods lost by accident or stolen, or for nondelivery, unless there be a refusal to deliver while the carrier is in possession; nor for any act or omission which amounts to negligence merely, and not to an actual wrong. Central Railroad & Banking Co. *v.* Lampley, 76 Ala. 357, cited in 5 L. R. A., N. S., 459.

§ 75. —— Rights of Action.

An action may be maintained against a carrier for loss of goods without proof of demand at the place of destination, when the evidence shows that the goods never reached the destination. Louisville & N. R. Co. *v.* Meyer, 78 Ala. 597.

§ 76. —— Defenses.

Waiver of Defense.—Where failure to deliver goods on demand of the consignee is not placed on the ground of a lien for charges, a carrier can not plead such lien in defense of a subsequent action for loss of the goods. Louisville & N. R. Co. *v.* McGuire, 79 Ala. 395.

§ 77. —— Pleading.

Allegation That Defendant Is Common Carrier.—A complaint against a railroad for the loss of a box, alleging that the box was delivered to defendant "to be carried by it as a common carrier of freight," sufficiently alleges that the box was delivered to defendant as a common carrier. Kansas City, M. & B. R. Co. *v.* Spann, 40 So. 83, 145 Ala. 679.

In an action by a consignee to recover for cotton lost by defendants as carriers, an allegation that defendants, "before and at the time of shipment, were the owners and proprietors of the boat, and copartners in freighting, and which boat had been usually employed in conveying and transporting cotton for hire," sufficiently alleged that the owners were common carriers. Jones *v.* Pitcher, 3 Stew. & P. 135.

In an action by a consignee to recover for cotton lost by defendants as carriers, an allegation that defendants, "before and at the time of shipment, were the owners and proprietors of the boat, and copartners in freighting, and which boat had been usually employed in conveying and transporting cotton for hire," sufficiently alleged that the owners were common carriers. Jones *v.* Pitcher, 3 Stew. & P. 135.

Undertaking to Carry.—In a declaration against a common carrier for negligence, it must be alleged that he accepted or undertook to carry the goods, or no judgment can be rendered thereon. Sommerville *v.* Merrill, 1 Port. 107.

Delivery.—In a declaration against a carrier for the loss of goods, it is necessary to aver a delivery of the goods to him, and the omission to make such an averment would be fatal on general demurrer. Jordan *v.* Hazard, 10 Ala. 221.

Breach of Duty Sufficiently Charged.—A count of the complaint, alleging that the goods mentioned therein were received by defendant railroad company to be carried between certain points, "which the defendant did not safely and securely and within a reasonable time carry and deliver the said goods for plaintiff, and the said goods were lost," sufficiently charged breach of duty to carry safely within a reasonable time, so as to state a cause of action, even though it did not clearly show that the negligence resulted in the loss of the goods. Northern Alabama R. Co. *v.* Feldman, 1 Ala. App. 334, 56 So. 16.

Plea.—The plea of defendants sued for injuring a piano while moving it in the line of their business under a contract from one house to another that plaintiff was guilty of contributory negligence, by consenting to an insufficient number of men attempting to move or load it on defendants' wagon, is bad, because not alleging plaintiff's knowledge of the necessary number of men to properly move it. Smiley Son & Co. *v.* Keith, 3 Ala. App. 354, 57 So. 127.

Variance.—The complaint being framed in conformity to Code 1876, p. 703, form No. 13, providing a form of complaint in actions against common carriers for failure to deliver goods intrusted to them to be delivered for a reward, and containing no count charging liability as warehouseman, the evidence showed that some of the goods were delivered in a damaged condition, and the rest not at all. It appeared that the undelivered goods were, when destroyed, in defendant's custody as warehouseman, and failed to show that they were of any value. Held a fatal variance. Alabama G. S. R. Co. *v.* Grabfelder, 83 Ala. 200, 3 So. 432; Kennedy Bros. *v.* Mobile, etc., R. Co., 74 Ala. 430. See note in 17 L. R. A. 693.

Under a complaint in the form prescribed for the nondelivery of goods by a carrier (Code, p. 703, Form No. 13), a recovery can not be had on proof that they were delivered in a damaged condition. South, etc., R. Co. *v.* Wilson, 78 Ala. 587.

§ 78. —— Presumptions and Burden of Proof.

Prima Facie Case.—In an action against a carrier as such for loss of goods, a prima facie case is established by proof that the carrier received the goods for transportation and failed to deliver them safely. Southern Ry. Co. *v.* Levy, 39 So. 95, 144 Ala. 614; Barron *v.* Mobile, etc., R. Co., 2 Ala. App. 555, 56 So. 862; South, etc., R. Co. *v.* Henlein, 52 Ala. 606, 612.

Burden of Proof—Ownership of Claim.—The carrier's plea of the general issue, in an action for loss of freight, cast upon the shipper the burden of proving his present ownership of his claim for loss of his freight. Northern Alabama R. Co. *v.* Feldman, 1 Ala. App. 334, 56 So. 16.

Loss Occurring without Fault of Carrier.—In an action against a carrier for failure to deliver goods, where the delivery of the goods to the carrier, and the failure of the carrier to deliver them at their destination is shown, the burden of proof is on the carrier that the loss occurred without its fault. Moulton *v.* Louisville & N. R. Co., 29 So. 602, 128 Ala. 537; Barron *v.* Mobile, etc., R. Co., 2 Ala. App. 555, 56 So. 862; Steele *v.* Townsend, 37 Ala. 247; South, etc., R. Co. *v.* Henlein, 52 Ala. 606, 612. See to same effect Louisville, etc., R. Co. *v.* Cowherd, 120 Ala. 51, 23 So. 793, 795; Alabama, etc., R. Co. *v.* Quarles, 145 Ala. 436, 40 So. 120, 121.

The burden is on a carrier in order to escape liability for loss or damage of a consignment received by it to trace the loss or damage to negligence of the shipper, or one or more of the exceptions with which its negligence did not occur. Atlantic Coast Line R. Co. *v.* Rice, 52 So. 918, 169 Ala. 265.

Termination of Liability before Injury.—Where the plaintiff in an action against a carrier for injuries to goods delivered to him for transportation has shown such delivery and the injury, the burden is upon the defendant to prove that his liability had terminated before the injury occurred. South & N. A. R. Co. *v.* Wood, 66 Ala. 167.

Delivery to Carrier of Goods in Damaged Condition.—In an action for damages for injuries to goods while in charge of the defendant as a common carrier, the burden is on him to show as a defense that, when delivered to him, the goods were in a damaged condition. Montgomery & W. P. R. Co. *v.* Moore, 51 Ala. 394.

Burden of Proof as to Nondelivery of Part of Freight Shipped to a Flag Station.—Where, in an action against a railroad company, as a common carrier, to recover damages for the failure to deliver a quantity of corn received by it for transportation to a designated point on the road, at which there was neither depot nor agent, it was shown that the corn was received by the company and transported in good condition to the place of destination, and the car in which it was shipped was placed on a sidetrack for the consignee, where it remained for several days, with no one in charge of, or protecting it, and that when the corn was taken from the car and measured, there was a deficiency in quantity, held, that the burden of proof was on the plaintiff to show that the loss occurred between the time when the corn was received by the company, and the time when the car containing it was left on the sidetrack, that being, under the facts of this case, a delivery, and not on the defendant to show that the loss occurred after the car was placed on the sidetrack. South, etc., R. Co. *v.* Wood, 71 Ala. 215.

Burden of Proof Where Railroad Sued as Voluntary Bailee.—Under a count seeking recovery against a railroad company as a voluntary bailee of goods which were destroyed before delivery to the consignee, the burden of proof was on the plaintiff to show that the negligence averred. Frederick *v.* Louisville & N. R. Co., 31 So. 968, 133 Ala. 486, cited in note in 22 L. R. A., N. S., 977.

When Question Immaterial.—Where, in an action by a shipper against a carrier for damage to goods, the defense was that the goods reached destination in good condition, it was immaterial whether the burden of proving that the goods were in good condition when they were received by the carrier was placed on plaintiff or defendant. St. Louis & S. F. R. Co. *v.* Musgrove, 45 So. 229, 153 Ala. 274.

§ 79. —— Admissibility of Evidence.

Relevancy.—In an action against a railroad company to recover the value of cotton received for transportation, and destroyed by fire while on board of the cars, the value of the car burnt has no relevancy to the question at issue. Montgomery & W. P. R. Co. *v.* Edmonds, 41 Ala. 667.

As to Care Exercised.—In an action against a railroad company to recover the value of cotton lost by the company while being transported over its road, defendant can not introduce evidence of the caution and skill of the conductor of the train who had charge of the cotton while in transit, if plaintiff did not attempt to predicate its claim to damages on proof of the want of skill of the conductor. Montgomery & W. P. R. Co. *v.* Edmonds, 41 Ala. 667.

In an action against a railroad company, as a common carrier, to recover the value of cotton lost by fire while being transported over its road, it was not error to refuse to permit the question to be answered, whether everything was done which could be done to save the cotton from being burned. Montgomery & W. P. R. Co. *v.* Edmonds, 41 Ala. 667, cited in note in 39 L. R. A., N. S., 644.

Evidence to Show Negligence or the Contrary.—In an action against a common carrier for injuries to goods shipped by sea, the fact that similar articles shipped in the same way were usually in a damaged and broken condition on their arrival, or that they usually arrived uninjured, may be shown by either party, as tending to show negligence, or the contrary. Steele *v.* Townsend, 37 Ala. 247.

Where defendant's drayman, sent for plaintiff's trunks, negligently came into collision with a railroad train on his journey with the trunks to the depot, resulting in the trunks becoming broken and the contents lost or injured, evidence that the drayman was drunk when he called for the trunks was admissible. Kates Transfer, etc., Co. *v.* Klassen, 6 Ala. App. 301, 59 So. 355.

Evidence of Value.—In an action against a carrier for the loss of a manuscript, constituting a school text-book, dealing with a subject on which there was no text-book, it was proper to permit plaintiff to testify as to the time spent in the preparation of the manuscript and what he considered it worth. Southern Express Co. *v.* Owens, 41 So. 752, 146 Ala. 412, 8 L. R. A., N. S., 369.

Extent of Damage.—In an action against a carrier for injuries to plaintiff's trunks and contents, testimony of plaintiff, in answer to a question as to the amount of damage, that some of the articles contained in the trunks were torn and some full of grease and dirt and unfit for use, was admissible as descriptive of the extent of the damage and was not objectionable as an invasion of the jury's province in undertaking to give the amount of damage with reference to pecuniary loss. Kates Transfer, etc., Co. *v.* Klassen, 6 Ala. App. 301, 59 So. 355.

Evidence to Show Quantity.—In an action against a railroad company to recover the value of 23 bales of cotton received by the company as a common carrier, and destroyed while in its possession, it is competent for the plaintiff to prove the weight of the 25 bales which were delivered to the company, and of 2 of the bales which were not lost, in order to enable the jury to ascertain the weight of the 23 bales which were destroyed. Montgomery & W. P. R. Co. *v.* Edmonds, 41 Ala. 667.

In an action against a railroad company as a common carrier, for the failure to deliver a quantity of corn received for transportation, the quantity received being a material question, the person who delivered it for the plaintiff having testified to the quantity, as ascertained from the number of barrels and the quantity of shelled corn measured out of one barrel, he may state, as a fact corroborating his measurement and calculation, that he afterwards filled the same barrel with corn out of the same crib, and again measured it out, with the same result as before. South, etc., R. Co. *v.* Wood, 66 Ala. 167.

Custom to Deliver without Requiring Production of Bill of Lading.—Where, in an action against a carrier for loss of goods destroyed in the delivering carrier's depot, defendant claimed that the goods had been destroyed by fire after the expiration of a reasonable time within which the consignee should have removed them, and after defendant had refused to deliver when delivery was first demanded because no waybill had been received from the initial carrier, it was competent for plaintiff to show that the delivering station was a prepay station, and that it was the custom of defendant's agent to deliver freight at such station to the owner or consignee without requiring the production of a bill of lading. Bowdon *v.* Atlantic Coast Line Ry. Co., 41 So. 294, 148 Ala. 29.

Refusal to Deliver Goods after Arrival.—For the purpose of showing that goods when injured, were in the possession of defendant as carrier and not as warehouseman, evidence that the failure of defendant's agent to deliver the goods on the morning of their arrival, before they were injured, to those plaintiff sent for them, was wrongful, is material. Louisville & N. R. Co. *v.* Dunlap, 41 So. 826, 148 Ala. 23.

In an action against a common carrier for goods alleged to have been received by it from a connecting carrier, but never delivered at their destination, the declaration of defendant's agent that the goods were burned in a car at that destination, made to plaintiff several days after the fire, is not admissible against defendant. Louisville, etc., R. Co. *v.* Carl, 91 Ala. 271, 9 So. 334.

Bill of Lading—Proof of Execution.—A bill of lading not declared upon is not evidence in an action to recover for goods lost by a carrier, without proof of its execution. Peck *v.* Dinsmore, 4 Port. 212.

Parol Proof to Show Shipper as Agent of Plaintiff.—Where, in an action to recover for goods lost by a carrier, plaintiff produces a bill of lading, such production is an admission that the undertaking of the carrier is in writing, and parol proof that the goods were shipped by the shipper named therein as the agent of plaintiff is inadmissible. Peck *v.* Dinsmore, 4 Port. 212.

Admission Implied from Resting Defense on Specific Ground.—When a carrier refuses to pay damages demanded for injury to goods on the ground that they were carried at "owner's risk," the jury may infer a waiver of other grounds of defense, and an admission that the goods were damaged while in possession of the carrier. South & N. A. R. Co. *v.* Wilson, 78 Ala. 587.

§ 80. —— Sufficiency of Evidence.

Degree of Proof Required.—A requested instruction in an action against a carrier for injury to goods that the burden of proof is on plaintiff to show that defendant failed to use due care exacts too high a measure of proof, the burden being not to show or prove facts certainly or absolutely, but only to the reasonable satisfaction of the jury. Smiley Son & Co. *v.* Keith, 3 Ala. App. 354, 57 So. 127.

A charge requiring a carrier to "satisfy" the jury that a loss of goods could not have been prevented by the exercise of due care requires too high a degree of proof, and is therefore erroneous. Louisville & N. R. Co. *v.* Gidley, 24 So. 753, 119 Ala. 523.

Identity of Goods.—In an action against a railroad company to recover for nine bales of cotton, the average weight, class, and value of which was shown by the evidence, a charge directing the jury that it was not necessary to identify the cotton by marks or brands, or by a certain number of pounds, if they were satisfied "in regard to the nine particular bales of cotton," and were able to say the nine bales sued for were the property of the plaintiffs, was not error. Montgomery & E. Ry. Co. *v.* Kolb, 73 Ala. 396.

Sufficiency—Loss in Transit.—In an action against the last of several connecting carriers for failure to deliver one barrel of molasses of a car load shipped to plaintiff, he did not show what number of barrels was shipped, or that their condition was different on arriving at their destination. The evidence showed that the empty barrel was dry, and that no head for it was found in the car. Held, that no loss in transit was shown, and plaintiff is not entitled to recover. Cooper *v.* Georgia Pac. Ry. Co., 92 Ala. 329, 9 So. 159, cited in note in 31 L. R. A., N. S., 102, 105.

Undertaking to Carry.—In an action against a carrier for the loss of goods, evidence that the goods were shipped in the name of a person as the agent of plaintiff, and were the property of plaintiff, is not sufficient to establish an undertaking to carry. Peck *v.* Dinsmore, 4 Port. 212.

Loss Caused by Act of God.—In an action against a railway company for damage to a shipment, evidence held to show that the loss was caused by an act of God, consisting in an unusual storm, and without the carrier's fault. Louisville, etc., R. Co. *v.* McKenzie, 5 Ala. App. 605, 59 So. 345.

Damage to Goods Prior to Delivery by Carrier.—In an action against a carrier for damages to goods, evidence held insufficient to warrant a finding that the goods were damaged prior to the carrier's delivery to a drayman at destination. St. Louis & S. F. R. Co. *v.* Musgrove, 45 So. 229, 153 Ala. 274.

Agreement to Pay Damages.—In an action against a carrier for injury to a shipment, evidence held insufficient to show an agreement by the carrier's agent to pay the damages. Louisville, etc., R. Co. *v.* McKenzie, 5 Ala. App. 605, 59 So. 345.

Evidence Insufficient to Sustain Recovery.—Evidence in an action against a carrier for loss of freight by fire held insufficient to sustain a recovery on the first count of the complaint based on its common-law liability as an insurer under its contract. Southern Ry. Co. *v.* W. T. Adams Mach. Co., 51 So. 779, 165 Ala. 436.

§ 81. —— Damages.

Reasonable Market Value.—The true measure of damages for the loss of goods is their reasonable market value, and not the price for which they were sold, and that a suit is on a bill of lading for a breach of contract to deliver can make no difference, in the absence of special damages arising from the alleged breach. Southern Ry. Co. *v.* T. A. Hatter & Son, 51 So. 723, 165 Ala. 423.

Goods Having No Market Value.—Where certain photographs belonging to plaintiff and other articles having no market value were lost and damaged by the negligence of a carrier, plaintiff for that reason was not barred of the right to recover damages therefor, but was entitled to recover the value of the goods to her. Kates Transfer, etc., Co. *v.* Klassen, 6 Ala. App. 301, 59 So. 355.

Amount of Recovery as Affected by Part Payment by Buyer.—By the terms of a sale of machinery, $400 of the price was to be paid on delivery, and of this the buyers had paid $100, and the seller had it consigned to its own order, and drew on the buyers. bill of lading attached, for $300. Held, that the seller under these conditions could sue the carrier in case of its loss for its full value, and recovery could not be reduced by the amount paid on account for which it was bound to account to the buyers. Southern Ry. Co. *v.* W. T. Adams Mach. Co., 51 So. 779, 165 Ala. 436.

Expense — Proximate Cause. — Where plaintiff notified a transfer company that she desired her baggage taken to the station in time for a particular train, and defendant contracted to perform such service, but, by reason of the negligence of its driver in coming into collision with a railroad train, plaintiff's trunks became broken and the contents lost and damaged, requiring that plaintiff postpone her journey a day and a night used in regaining her baggage, the expense of such delay constituted a proximate consequence of defendant's breach of contract, for which plaintiff was entitled to recover special damages. Kates Transfer, etc., Co. *v.* Klassen, 6 Ala. App. 301, 59 So. 355.

§ 82. —— Questions for Jury.

Negligence.—In an action against a carrier for loss of goods by fire after arrival at destination, evidence that there was no fire left in the depot where the goods were, and that the place was fastened up, sufficiently negatived its negligence so as to require the jury's determination of that issue. Central of Georgia Ry. Co. *v.* Burton, 51 So. 643, 165 Ala. 425.

Negligence in Attempting to Extinguish Fire.—Plaintiff was the consignee of a car of wagons, which was destroyed by fire while in transit over the defendant road. The fire in the car was discovered a little after midnight, when the train was between stations, about four miles from B., a station with a large water tank, and which the train had just left. The wagons were properly packed in the car without any inflammable material, and the car door sealed, with the usual car seals. On discovering smoke issuing from the car, the train was stopped, but no flame was discovered until the conductor opened the door of the car. A small hole was cut through the roof of the car, through which a few pails of water were poured, but, the hole being so small, some of the water was lost. On the conductor's orders, the train was cut, and the burning car taken four miles, to W., a station where there was no water tank or appliances for extinguishing fires. Held, in an action for failure to deliver the wagons, that the evidence, though not conflicting, was such that different minds might reasonably draw different inferences therefrom in regard to defendant's diligence in attempting to extinguish the fire, and hence it was error for the court to give a general charge in favor of the defendant. Moulton *v.* Louisville & N. R. Co., 29 So. 602, 128 Ala. 537.

Possession of Goods.—In an action against a railway company for its failure to deliver goods shipped, in which the evidence is conflicting as to whether they were ever received for shipment, and whether freight was ever paid on them, an instruction, given by the court of its own motion, that, "if the jury believe from the evidence that defendant received pay on the freight for the goods in question, that was sufficient evidence that the defendant had the goods at that time in possession," is erroneous, as invading the province of the jury. Mobile & G. R. Co. *v.* Williams, 52 Ala. 278.

Inquiry as to Arrival of Goods.—An agent for a shipper of goods, making inquiry over the telephone as to the arrival of goods, directed what other persons should say while he stood at their elbow, and an operator at a telephone connection repeated the inquiry to the carrier's agent. Held, that the reliability and accuracy of the means of communication was for the jury in an action for loss of the goods, and that it was for them to say, also, whether the message which finally reached defendant fairly apprised it of the fact that plaintiff was inquiring for the particular goods in question. Southern R. Co. *v.* Adams Mach. Co., 165 Ala. 436, 51 So. 779.

Reasonable Time for Removal of Goods.—In an action for loss of freight, computation of the reasonable time in which the consignee might have applied for and removed it was a question for the jury. Southern R. Co. *v.* Adams Mach. Co., 165 Ala. 436, 51 So. 779, cited in note in 25 L. R. A., N. S., 938.

§ 83. —— Instructions.

Charge Excluding Issue.—In an action for loss of freight destroyed by fire at its destination, a charge as to defendant's common-law liability as an insurer, which pretermitted all inquiry whether the goods were ready for delivery, was properly refused. Southern R. Co. *v.* W. T. Adams Mach. Co., 51 So. 779, 165 Ala. 436.

Instruction Not Based on Issues.—In an action against a railroad company, the complaint being framed in substantial conformity to Code Ala. 1876, p. 703, Form No. 13, providing a form of complaint in actions against common carriers for failure to deliver goods intrusted to them to be delivered for a reward, and containing no count charging liability as a warehouseman, it is error to instruct the jury as to defendant's duties and liabilities as a warehouseman. Alabama, etc., R. Co. *v.* Grabfelder, 83 Ala. 200, 3 So. 432.

(G) CARRIER AS WAREHOUSEMAN.

§ 84. Change in Nature of Liability of Carrier in General.

At common law, after the carrier's liability as carrier had terminated, he was liable only as warehouseman. Louisville, etc., R. Co. *v.* Brewer (Ala.), 62 So. 698.

§ 85. Goods Awaiting Transportation.

A common carrier is responsible as such only when freight is delivered to and accepted by it for immediate transportation in the usual course of business, so that where a common carrier receives goods, and something remains to be done before they can be transported, as where they are delivered to the carrier without instructions as to their destination, or to await orders or until charges for transportation are paid, the responsibility of a carrier is not that of an insurer, but that of a warehouseman, who is held only to ordinary care for their safety. St. Louis & S. F. R. Co. *v.* Cavender, 170 Ala. 601, 54 So. 54.

§ 86. Goods Awaiting Delivery.

Reasonable Time after Arrival.—The liability of a common carrier is not necessarily terminated by the arrival of the goods at destination, but such liability ceases and that of a warehouseman begins only after the owner or consignee has had a reasonable time after the arrival at destination to remove the goods. Bowdon *v.* Atlantic Coast Line Ry. Co., 41 So. 294, 148 Ala. 29; Alabama, etc., R. Co. *v.* Kidd, 35 Ala. 209; Mobile, etc., R. Co. *v.* Prewitt, 46 Ala. 63, 67; Collins *v.* Alabama, etc., R. Co., 104 Ala. 390, 16 So. 140; Louisville, etc., R. Co. *v.* McGuire & Co., 79 Ala. 395; Columbus, etc., R. Co. *v.* Ludden, 89 Ala. 612, 7 So. 471; Southern Exp. Co. *v.* Holland, 109 Ala. 362, 19 So. 66; Kennedy Bros. *v.* Mobile, etc., R. Co., 74 Ala. 430; Louisville, etc., R. Co. *v.* Oden, 80 Ala. 38. See notes in 16 L. R. A., N. S., 935; 17 L. R. A. 693; 18 L. R. A., N. S., 428.

The liability of a carrier, as such, does not end, and its liability as a warehouseman begins, until a reasonable time after the goods have reached their destination, and have been deposited in the carrier's depot or warehouse, or otherwise made ready for delivery to the consignee. Columbus & W. Ry. Co. *v.* Ludden, 89 Ala. 612, 7 So. 471.

Where a piano, which could have been removed from the carrier's depot in about an hour, was shipped over a continuous line of railroad, and the distance from the place of shipment to the destination is such that the property might reasonably have been expected to arrive on the day of the shipment or the next day, and it is allowed to remain three days after its arrival, the carrier will be held liable only as a warehouseman. Columbus & W. Ry. Co. *v.* Ludden, 89 Ala. 612, 7 So. 471, cited in note in 17 L. R. A. 693.

What Is Reasonable Time.—What is a reasonable time for a consignee to accept a shipment, where not regulated by statute depends upon the circumstances of each case, such as the proximity of the consignee to the point of delivery and his knowledge of the arrival of the shipment. Central, etc., R. Co. *v.* Merrill & Co., 153 Ala. 277, 45 So. 628, cited in notes in 16 L. R. A., N. S., 935, 18 L. R. A., N. S., 428.

A shipment was ready for delivery by a railroad company to the consignee at about noon March 27, and was burned that night after 10 o'clock. It did not appear where the consignee resided or was engaged in business, or that he knew of its arrival or readiness for delivery. Held that, the daylight within that period being only seven hours, it was not a reasonable time within which the company's liability should be changed from that of a carrier to that of a warehouseman. Central, etc., R. Co. *v.* Merrill & Co., 153 Ala. 277, 45 So. 628, cited in notes in 16 L. R. A., N. S., 935, 18 L. R. A., N. S., 428.

Where Goods to Be Delivered to Agent of Carrier.—If the carrier undertake to deliver to his own agent, instead of the owner, he becomes liable as warehouseman after the arrival of the goods. Alabama & T. R. R. Co. *v.* Kidd, 35 Ala. 209; Mobile, etc., R. Co. *v.* Prewitt, 46 Ala. 63. See note in 17 L. R. A. 693.

Time after Notice under Statute.—Under Code 1907, § 5604, requiring a common carrier within 24 hours after arrival of freight to notify the consignee, and § 5613, giving the consignee 48 hours, computing from 7 a. m. of the day following the notice of the arrival, within which to remove the freight, a carrier, who within the 24 hours notified the shipper's agent to receive notice, after the time for removal, held the goods as a warehouseman, and was not liable for their loss by fire. Hearn *v.* Louisville, etc., R. Co., 6 Ala. App. 483, 60 So. 600.

Where goods are shipped to a city, and the railroad company, within twenty-four hours after their arrival, gives notice by mail to the consignee, and places them in its depot, its liability as common carrier ceases and that of warehouseman begins, under Code, § 1180, which provides that, if the destination of freight is a city having 2,000 inhabitants or more, and a daily mail, the carrier is relieved of responsibility as such by deposit of freight in a depot or warehouse, when, within twenty-four hours after its arrival, notice is given to the consignee personally or through the mails. Collins *v.* Alabama G. S. R. Co., 104 Ala. 390, 16 So. 140; Southern Ry. Co. *v.* Lockwood Mfg. Co., 142 Ala. 322, 37 So. 667. See notes in 8 L. R. A., N. S., 242, 18 L. R. A., N. S., 429.

Failure or Refusal to Remove Goods.—Where the consignees fail to remove goods for more than three days after notice of arrival and request to remove, the railroad company is only liable as warehouseman. Anniston & A. R. Co. *v.* Ledbetter, 92 Ala. 326, 9 So. 73, cited in notes in 17 L. R. A. 696, 8 L. R. A., N. S., 242.

Where defendant refused to deliver goods carried by it unless the consignee would accept all, which he refused to do, on account of damage to some of them, and two weeks later the goods were destroyed by the burning of the depot, the action for the value thereof should have been against defendant as a warehouseman, and not as a carrier. Frederick *v.* Louisville & N. R. Co., 31 So. 968, 133 Ala. 486.

If a railroad company safely transmits goods to their destination, and informs the consignee of their arrival, and affords him a reasonable opportunity for their removal, its liability as a common carrier ceases; and if they are then left in its possession it becomes liable only as a warehouseman. Kennedy *v.* Mobile & G. R. Co., 74 Ala. 430, cited in note in 17 L. R. A. 693.

Termination of Liability as Warehouseman.—A carrier's liability as a warehouseman for injury to goods can not survive delivery and acceptance prior to the damage. Barclay *v.* Southern Ry. Co., 6 Ala. App. 502, 60 So. 479.

Question of Law.—As to what is a reasonable time after the lapse of which liability as a carrier ends, and that of a warehouseman begins, is a question of law for the court. Columbus & W. Ry. Co. *v.* Ludden, 89 Ala. 612, 7 So. 471. See, to the same effect, Tallassee Falls Mfg. Co. *v.* Western Railway, 128 Ala. 167, 29 So. 203, 205.

§ 87. Duties of Carrier as Warehouseman.

The responsibility of a railroad company keeping goods in its depot after the termination of the transit is that of a warehouseman for hire, and it is therefore bound to exercise ordinary diligence. Southern Ry. Co. *v.* Aldredge & Shelton, 38 So. 805, 142 Ala. 368; Collins *v.* Alabama, etc., R. Co., 104 Ala. 390, 16 So. 140, 141; Mobile, etc., R. Co. *v.* Prewitt, 46 Ala. 63, 68.

A charge requiring a carrier to keep a sufficient watch to preserve goods stored in its depot from loss by fire imposes too great a burden on the carrier, where it was only liable for the exercise of reasonable care and diligence. Louisville & N. R. Co. *v.* Gidley, 24 So. 753, 119 Ala. 523.

If the owner of goods consigned to the owner, care of the railroad company is not ready or present to receive them on their arrival at the point of destination, the goods may be properly deposited in the warehouse of the company, whose liability as common carrier then ceases; and its responsibility is that of warehouseman for hire, without reference to the fact whether actual storage is charged or not. Mobile & G. R. Co. *v.* Prewitt, 46 Ala. 63, cited in note in 17 L. R. A. 693.

Delivery to Independent Warehouseman.—Where a common carrier has no warehouse at the point of destination, it may relieve itself of further liability, after its duties as a carrier are at an end, by delivering the goods to a responsible warehouseman for the owner or consignee. Louisville, etc., R. Co. *v.* Brewer (Ala.), 62 So. 698.

Responsibility for Act of Warehouseman Where Carrier Undertakes to Deliver to Own Agent.—If the carrier undertake to deliver to his own agent, instead of the owner, he becomes liable as warehouseman after the arrival of the goods; and a warehouseman with whom they store it is his, and not the owner's, agent, and the carrier is liable if the goods are thence delivered to an unauthorized person. Alabama & T. R. R. Co. *v.* Kidd, 35 Ala. 209, cited in note in 17 L. R. A. 693.

§ 88. Acts or Omissions Constituting Negligence.

Giving Incorrect Information as to Goods.—A carrier's responsibility as a warehouseman having attached, it is still liable for giving incorrect information misleading the consignee so as to prevent removal before the goods are lost, though the loss is not imputable to any other or different negligence. Southern Ry. Co. *v.* W. T. Adams Mach. Co., 51 So. 779, 165 Ala. 436.

Storing Powder in Warehouse.—Whether the storing by a railway company, in its warehouse in a city, of 1,200 pounds of powder is a nuisance depends on locality and circumstances, and the burden of proving negligence in storing the same, whereby a shipper's goods were injured, is on him who alleges it. Collins *v.* Alabama G. S. R. Co., 104 Ala. 390, 16 So. 140.

§ 89. Actions Involving Liability as Warehouseman.

Burden of Proof as to Negligence.—Where a railroad company failed to deliver on demand goods intrusted to it, which it was liable to keep as a warehouseman for hire, or did not account for such failure, prima facie negligence would be imputed to it, and the burden was on it to prove that the loss was occasioned without any want of ordinary care on its part. Southern Ry. Co. *v.* Aldredge & Shelton, 38 So. 805, 142 Ala. 368, cited in note in 22 L. R. A., N. S., 977.

Admissibility of Evidence.—Where, in an action against a carrier for loss of goods stored, it appeared that when plaintiffs called for the goods they could not carry them all, and requested defendant's agent to allow those not carried to remain in the warehouse until they could call for them, which was assented to, evidence as to how far plaintiff lived from the depot was inadmissible. Southern Ry. Co. *v.* Aldredge & Shelton, 38 So. 805, 142 Ala. 368.

It was error for the court to refuse to charge that the fact that plaintiff lived twenty-seven miles from the depot should not be considered by them for any purpose. Southern Ry. Co. *v.* Aldredge & Shelton, 38 So. 805, 142 Ala. 368.

Question for Jury—Want of Ordinary Care.—Where a carrier's agent testified that the depot in which the goods sued for were kept was a safe place, and that it was kept locked at night, and also in the day, whenever defendant's employees were not present, which was all the evidence on that subject, in an action for failure to deliver the goods whether or not there was a want of ordinary care was for the jury. Southern Ry. Co. *v.* Aldredge & Shelton, 38 So. 805, 142 Ala. 368.

Instructions.—Where, in an action against a carrier for loss of goods stored, there was no evidence that A. received the goods from the carrier's agent, but the evidence was clear that the goods never went out of the possession of defendant's agent until they were lost, a requested instruction that if defendant received the goods from the carrier's agent, and asked him to allow them to remain until he could send back for them, and when he sent back for them they were not there, such facts did not establish defendant's negligence, was properly refused. Southern Ry. Co. *v.* Aldredge & Shelton, 38 So. 805, 142 Ala. 368.

Where, in an action against a carrier for loss of goods stored, the court charged that the burden was on plaintiff to prove to a reasonable certainty that the goods were lost on account of defendant's negligence, and if the evidence as to negligence was so equally balanced that the jury were not convinced to a reasonable certainty that the goods were lost on account of negligence, and if the goods were kept in defendant's depot with reasonable care, plaintiff could not recover, such instructions cured error in refusing to charge that if the jury were reasonably satisfied that the defendant kept the goods in its depot with reasonable care, and that some one stayed in the depot in the day, and kept it locked at night, plaintiff could not recover. Southern Ry. Co. *v.* Aldredge & Shelton, 38 So. 805, 142 Ala. 368.

In a suit for damages for loss of goods, if there are two counts in the complaint, the one on a contract of common carriers, and the other on a contract of a warehouseman without hire, a charge asked by the defendant under the latter count that the company is only responsible for losses and injuries occasioned by gross negligence, is proper, and should be given. Mobile, etc., R. Co. *v.* Prewitt, 46 Ala. 63.

Instructions as to Degree of Proof.—In an action against a carrier for loss of goods stored, a requested instruction that, if the jury were not satisfied to a reasonable certainty whether the goods were left with defendant at defendant's risk or at plaintiff's risk, the jury could not find a verdict for plaintiff, was properly refused, as requiring too high a degree of proof. Southern Ry. Co. *v.* Aldredge & Shelton, 38 So. 805, 142 Ala. 368, cited in note in 22 L. R. A., N. S., 977.

(H) LIMITATION OF LIABILITY.

As to limitation of liability in contract for transportation of live stock, see post, "Limitation of Liability," § 138.

§ 90. Nature of Right to Limit Liability.

A carrier may, by special contract, limit his common-law liability. South & N. A. R. Co. *v.* Henlein, 52 Ala. 606; Grey *v.* Mobile Trade Co., 55 Ala. 387. See notes in 14 L. R. A. 435, 17 L. R. A. 340.

"This responsibility, being founded on the most salutary grounds of public policy, was originally considered as beyond the reach of the carrier himself, and as beyond the reach of limitation by special contract with the shipper. But we consider it as now well settled, that, while the carrier can not limit his liability by any general notice, he may legally contract for exemption from that extraordinary responsibility imposed by the common law, by which he becomes an insurer. Steele *v.* Townsend, 37 Ala. 247. To this extent he may go, in the limitation of his liability, but not further. Public policy forbids that he should be allowed to contract for exemption from liability for damage occasioned by the negligence, willful default, or tort, of himself or his servants." Mobile, etc., R. Co. *v.* Hopkins, 41 Ala. 486, 499; Mobile, etc., R. Co. *v.* Jarboe, 41 Ala. 644, 647.

§ 91. Liabilities Subject to Limitation.

§ 92. —— In General.

A carrier, within the limits of public policy and consideration of right and justice, may, by a special contract, limit its liability as an insurer of goods carried. Barron *v.* Mobile & O. R. Co., 2 Ala. App. 555, 56 So. 862; Alabama Great Southern R. Co. *v.* Little, 71 Ala. 611; Steele *v.* Townsend, 37 Ala. 247; Central R., etc., Co. *v.* Smitha, 85 Ala. 47, 4 So. 708; Atlantic, etc., R. Co. *v.* Dothan Mule Co., 161 Ala. 341, 49 So. 882; Southern Exp. Co. *v.* Owens, 146 Ala. 412, 41 So. 752, 753.

While a carrier may contract against some of its common-law liabilities, it can not by special contract relieve itself of all such liabilities, nor of the results of its own negligence. Nashville, C. & St. L. Ry. *v.* Hinds, 5 Ala. App. 596, 59 So. 670.

A common carrier may, by special contract, limit his liability as to every cause of injury excepting that arising from his own or his servants' negligence. South

& N. A. R. Co. *v.* Henlein, 52 Ala. 606, cited in note in 17 L. R. A. 340.

A provision in a bill of lading limiting the carrier's liability to damages resulting only from negligence of itself or its agents is reasonable and binding. Louisville & N. R. Co. *v.* Landers, 33 So. 482, 135 Ala. 504.

Act of God.—A common carrier can limit its liability against loss occasioned by an act of God, where there is no concurring or intervening negligence on its part. Louisville & N. R. Co. *v.* McKenzie, 5 Ala. App. 605, 59 So. 345.

A carrier of freight is not precluded from asserting release of liability for damage to a shipment through an act of God by accepting and retaining the freight charges paid. Louisville, etc., R. Co. *v.* McKenzie, 5 Ala. App. 605, 59 So. 345. See, to the same effect, Alabama, etc., R. Co. *v.* Elliott & Son, 150 Ala. 381, 43 So. 738, 9 L. R. A., N. S., 1264; Alabama, etc., R. Co. *v.* Quarles, 145 Ala. 436, 40 So. 120, 5 L. R. A., N. S., 867; Smith *v.* Western Railway, 91 Ala. 455, 8 So. 754, 11 L. R. A. 619; Alabama, etc., R. Co. *v.* Thomas, 89 Ala. 234, 7 So. 762; Columbus, etc., R. Co. *v.* Bridges, 86 Ala. 448, 5 So. 864; Louisville, etc., R. Co. *v.* McGuire & Co., 79 Ala. 395; Coosa River Steamboat Co. *v.* Barclay, 30 Ala. 120; Jones *v.* Pitcher & Co., 3 Stew. & P. 135; Alabama, etc., R. Co. *v.* Little, 71 Ala. 611.

Loss by Fire or Other Casualty.—A stipulation in a bill of lading exempting the carrier from loss or damage by fire or other casualty while in transit, or in depots or places of transshipment, is valid, except as against losses sustained resulting from negligence of the carrier or its servants. Louisville & N. R. Co. *v.* Oden, 80 Ala. 38, cited in note in 8 L. R. A., N. S., 236.

A stipulation in a bill of lading that the carrier will not be "liable for damages (either from fire or other cause) as common carriers for any article after it has been transported to its place of destination, and been placed in the depot of the company," is valid; and, upon the storage of the goods in the depot at their destination, the carrier's responsibility thereafter is that of the warehouseman. Western Ry. Co. *v.* Little, 86 Ala. 159, 5 So. 563, cited in note in 17 L. R. A. 693.

Termination of Liability as Common Carrier on Arrival at Destination.—A stipulation in a bill of lading that a carrier shall be liable only as a warehouseman after the arrival of the freight at its destination, and that the consignee shall take it away as soon as it is ready for delivery, without providing for notice to the consignee when it is so ready, is unreasonable and void. Louisville & N. R. Co. *v.* Oden, 80 Ala. 38.

Notice as to Arrival of Goods.—What notice a shipper or consignee should have as to the arrival of goods at destination is a matter as to which parties to the bill of lading may contract at their pleasure. Southern Ry. Co. *v.* W. T. Adams Mach. Co., 51 So. 779, 165 Ala. 436.

§ 93. —— Negligence or Misconduct.

Although the liability of a common carrier may be reasonably limited by special contract, public policy will not permit common carriers, even by special contract, to be exempted from damages for losses occasioned by the negligence or misfeasance of themselves or their servants. Southern Exp. Co. *v.* Crook, 44 Ala. 468; Southern R. Co. *v.* Jones, 132 Ala. 437, 31 So. 501; Alabama, etc., R. Co. *v.* Thomas, 83 Ala. 343, 3 So. 802; S. C., 89 Ala. 234, 7 So. 762; Atlantic, etc., R. Co. *v.* Dothan Mule Co., 161 Ala. 341, 49 So. 882; Southern Exp. Co. *v.* Caperton, 44 Ala. 101; Southern Exp. Co. *v.* Owens, 146 Ala. 412, 41 So. 752; Alabama, etc., R. Co. *v.* Little, 71 Ala. 611. See notes in 14 L. R. A. 435; 19 L. R. A., N. S., 1012.

A common carrier can not contract against liability for loss resulting from its negligence. South & N. A. R. Co. *v.* Henlein, 56 Ala. 368; Nashville, etc., Railway *v.* Hinds, 5 Ala. App. 596, 59 So. 670.

Though common carriers may limit their common-law liability by special contracts, they can not thus protect themselves against the consequences of their own negligence. Steele *v.* Townsend, 37 Ala. 247.

A carrier can not limit its liability for loss or damage to an interstate shipment from negligence of its own or any connecting line. Robertson *v.* Southern Ry. Co., 4 Ala. App. 385, 59 So. 232.

A bill of lading provided that "no carrier shall be liable for loss or damage not accruing on its portion of the route, nor after said property is ready for delivery to the consignee." Held that, the stipulation being intended to qualify or limit the common-law liability and therefore to be strictly construed against the carrier and in favor of the shipper, the term "carrier" should be taken as referring, not merely to the transportative capacity of the company, but to the contracting entity in its dual capacity of common carrier and warehouseman and the stipulation so construed, being one undertaking to contract against liability for loss, however negligently it might be inflicted, was void. Central, etc., R. Co. *v.* Merrill & Co., 153 Ala. 277, 45 So. 628.

§ 94. Mode or Form of Limitation.

§ 95. —— In General.

Custom or Usage.—Parol evidence is inadmissible to show that, by a custom existing on a particular river, flat-boatmen were not responsible for a loss caused by dangers of the river, although the bill of lading contained no such exception. Boon & Co. *v.* Steamboat Belfast, 40 Ala. 184, 188, overruling Steele *v.* McTyer, 31 Ala. 667, 677.

§ 96. —— Notice.

General notices, in relation to the liabilities of common carriers, are of no avail unless reduced to the form of a special stipulation, and signed by the party sending the goods, or be so brought home to his knowledge as to show his assent thereto, and be also just and reasonable. Southern Exp. Co. *v.* Crook, 44 Ala. 468. See, to the same effect, Steele *v.* Townsend, 37 Ala. 247.

§ 97. —— Bill of Lading or Shipping Receipt.

Although a common carrier can not limit his common-law liability by any general notice, he may do so by special contract with the shipper; and a bill of lading given by the carrier, and accepted by the shipper, is a special contract, within the meaning of this rule. Steele *v.* Townsend, 37 Ala. 247; Alabama, etc., R. Co. *v.* Little, 71 Ala. 611, 614.

A common carrier, by inserting the words, "not accountable for rust or breakage," in a bill of lading delivered to a shipper, limits his common-law liability. Steele *v.* Townsend, 37 Ala. 247.

Limitation as to Amount of Liability.—A common carrier can not limit his liability for the loss of goods by a stipulation in a printed receipt that he will not be liable beyond a specified sum, where the receipt appears to be such as is generally used without reference to the nature or value of the goods received. Southern Exp. Co. *v.* Armstead, 50 Ala. 350. See post, "Limitation of Amount of Liability," § 101.

§ 98. Consideration.

Reduced rates given for the transportation of freight is a sufficient consideration to support a special contract exempting the carrier from liability for loss or damage by fire not caused by the carrier's negligence. Mouton *v.* Louisville & N. R. Co., 29 So. 602, 128 Ala. 537.

A stipulation fixing the carrier's liability in case of total loss in consideration of a reduced rate of transportation, there being no imposition or undue advantage taken, will be upheld, although the goods may have been destroyed through the carelessness of the carrier's servants. Louisville & N. R. Co. *v.* Sherrod, 84 Ala. 178, 4 So. 29; apparently overruled in Southern Express Co. *v.* Owens, 146 Ala. 412, 41 So. 752. See notes in 14 L. R. A. 433, 1 L. R. A., N. S., 986.

§ 99. Assent of Consignor or Owner.

A bill of lading given by a common carrier, on the delivery of goods to him for transportation, and accepted by the shipper or consignor with knowledge of its contents, or with the opportunity of acquiring knowledge thereof, if he is reasonably prudent, limiting the extraordinary liability of the carrier, is deemed and regarded as a special contract. Alabama, etc., R. Co. *v.* Little, 71 Ala. 611; Steele *v.* Townsend, 37 Ala. 247; Mouton *v.* Louisville, etc., R. Co., 128 Ala. 537, 29 So. 602, 604.

Acceptance of Bill by Shipping Goods.—In an action by the consignee against a carrier for failure to deliver goods, the bill of lading, which was made out by the consignors on their own special blank, but was not signed by the consignors or consignee, and only by the carrier's agent, was properly admitted in evidence, as the consignors, by shipping the goods under the bill, accepted the same, and were bound thereby, though they had not signed it. Mouton *v.* Louisville & N. R. Co., 29 So. 602, 128 Ala. 537.

Failure to Read.—A contract signed by a shipper of live stock, which releases the carrier and its connecting lines from liability for any damage not caused by their negligence, binds the shipper, in the absence of fraud or misrepresentation, whether he read it or not. Western Ry. Co. *v.* Harwell, 91 Ala. 340, 8 So. 649.

Acceptance of Bill by Person Unable to Read.—Where a bill of lading, containing a clause limiting the liability of each connecting road to loss or injury suffered while the goods are on its line, is accepted by the shipper, there is a legitimate limitation of liability, which is binding on each of the contracting parties, even though the shipper was unable to read, and did not know that the limiting clause was in the bill of lading. Jones *v.* Cincinnati, S. & M. Ry. Co., 89 Ala. 376, 8 So. 61, distinguishing Louisville & N. R. Co. *v.* Meyer, 78 Ala. 597. See note in 31 L. R. A., N. S., 11, 66, 70, 76, 77.

Bill of Lading Subsequently Given.—Where a carrier receives freight for shipment to a point beyond its line, accepting payment for the entire route, and the bill of lading is not delivered at that time, but is forwarded by mail to the place of destination, the shipper is not bound by a stipulation therein limiting the carrier's liability to losses occurring on its own line. Louisville & N. R. Co. *v.* Meyer, 78 Ala. 597, cited in note in 31 L. R. A., N. S., 11, 66, 70, 77.

Power of Consignor to Bind Consignee.—In an action against a carrier by the consignee for failure to deliver goods, the bill of lading, which contained a stipulation exempting the carrier from liability for loss or damage to the goods by fire, and which was made out by the consignors on one of their own special blanks, was properly received in evidence, as the consignors were necessarily the agents of the consignee for the shipment, and could bind the consignee by the bill of lading without express authority. Mouton *v.* Louisville & N. R. Co., 29 So. 602, 128 Ala. 537, cited in note in 36 L. R. A., N. S., 71.

§ 100. Operation and Effect of Limitation in General.

§ 100 (1) In General.

Strict Construction Against Carrier.—Contracts creating special limitation on the liability of the carrier for his own defaults are to be strictly construed against the carrier, and the same rule applies as to a release against accrued damages. St. Louis & S. F. R. Co. *v.* Cavender, 170 Ala. 601, 54 So. 54; Steele *v.* Townsend, 37 Ala. 247, 255; Louisville, etc., R. Co. *v.* Meyer, 78 Ala. 597, 600; Louisville, etc., R. Co. *v.* Touart, 97 Ala. 514, 11 So. 756, 757; Alabama, etc., R. Co. *v.* Thomas, 89 Ala. 234, 7 So. 762; Central, etc., R. Co. *v.* Merrill & Co., 153 Ala. 277, 45 So. 628, 629. See, to the same effect, Southern R. Co. *v.* Webb, 143 Ala. 304, 39 So. 262, 265.

A bill of lading provided that "no carrier shall be liable for loss or damage not accruing on its portion of the route, nor after said property is ready for delivery to the consignee." Held, that, the stipulation being intended to qualify or limit the common-law liability and therefore to be strictly construed against the carrier and in favor of the shipper, the term "carrier" should be taken as referring, not merely to the transportative capacity of the company, but to the contracting entity in its dual capacity of common carrier and warehouseman. Central, etc., R. Co. *v.* Merrill & Co., 153 Ala. 277, 45 So. 628.

Time of Termination of Liability.—Notwithstanding a bill of lading provided that the railroad company would not be liable as a common carrier after the freight had reached its destination, public policy so modified the contract as to give the consignee a reasonable time within which to remove the goods after arrival before such liability ceased. Tallassee Falls Mfg. Co. *v.* Western Ry. of Alabama, 29 So. 203, 128 Ala. 167. See note in 18 L. R. A., N. S., 428.

Exemption for Liability Against Robbery.—A mere depredator is not a robber, within a bill of lading exempting a carrier from liability for injury to the shipment caused by "robbery." Louisville & N. R. Co. *v.* Dunlap, 41 So. 826, 148 Ala. 23.

"Dangers of the River."—An owner of a steamboat, when sued for the loss of goods by fire, may show by parol that the exceptive words "dangers of the river," in the bill of lading, by custom and usage include dangers by fire. Hibler *v.* McCartney, 31 Ala. 501; McClure *v.* Cox, 32 Ala. 617; Sampson *v.* Gazzam, 6 Port. 123; Ezell *v.* Miller, 6 Port. 307.

The owners of a steamboat are liable as common carriers for a loss of goods by robbery, and parol evidence is inadmissible to show a custom exempting the owners of boats engaged in navigating the river from liability for loss caused by the forcible and illegal seizure of a boat by a body of armed men without the fault of the officers or crew, where the only exception specified in the bill of lading is "dangers of the river." Boon *v.* The Belfast, 40 Ala. 184, limiting Sampson *v.* Gazzam, 6 Port. 123, and overruling Steele *v.* McTyer, 31 Ala. 667.

Effect.—The acceptance of a bill of lading, stipulating that no carrier or party in possession of property should be liable for loss or damage by causes beyond its control or by floods or fire, relieved the carrier from an insurer's liability, with familiar exceptions, and limited liability to loss or damage by negligence of the carrier. Central of Georgia Ry. Co. *v.* Burton, 51 So. 643, 165 Ala. 425.

§ 100 (2) Loss Caused by Negligence or Wrongful Act of Carrier.

A carrier is liable for damage to goods carried "at owner's risk" if caused by his negligence. South & N. A. R. Co. *v.* Wilson, 78 Ala. 587.

A provision in a bill of lading restricting the carrier's liability will not be construed as protecting him from the consequences of his own negligence. Grey *v.* Mobile Trade Co., 55 Ala. 387.

In an action against a carrier for injury to goods by breakage, it appeared that the carrier by contract stipulated for exemption from liability for breakage. Held, that the exemption did not extend to such injury, when caused by his own negligence. Steele *v.* Townsend, 37 Ala. 247.

A carrier by boat, who has received goods under a contract exempting it from liability for loss by fire, is liable to the shipper for loss by fire caused by the carrier's negligence and by its failure to have on the boat proper appliances for extinguishing fire. Grey *v.* Mobile Trade Co., 55 Ala. 387.

A common carrier may not limit its liability for losses caused by its own negligence, and is liable for its negligence in delivering goods to a stranger, notwithstanding a special agreement exempting it from liability for a loss arising from any cause whatever, unless shown to have occurred through the fraud or gross negligence of its agents or servants. Southern Exp. Co. *v.* Crook, 44 Ala. 468, cited in note in 37 L. R. A. 177.

Knowledge of Owner of Act of Negligence.—Notwithstanding the owner of goods transported by a railroad company assumes the risk of loss by fire, the railroad company is responsible for loss resulting from the negligence of its servants, although occasioned by fire; and a notification to the owner that the goods would be carried on an uncovered car would not relieve the company from liability, if the putting the goods on such car was negligence. Montgomery & W. P. R. Co. *v.* Edmonds, 41 Ala. 667.

Showing Due Care and Diligence.—A bill of lading exempting a carrier from liability for loss by fire relieves it from its common-law liability, but imposes on it the burden of showing that it used due care and diligence to prevent the accident which caused the loss. Louisville & N. R. Co. *v.* Gidley, 24 So. 753, 119 Ala. 523.

In determining the degree of diligence required of a common carrier, regard must be had to the nature of the goods, and the perils attending the particular mode of transportation employed. Where a cargo of cotton, or other article highly inflammable or ignitible, is transported on a steamboat on an inland river, under a bill of lading which excepts "dangers of the river and fire," the carrier, to excuse himself for a loss by fire within the exception, must show that he employed that degree of diligence which very careful and prudent men take of their own affairs. Grey *v.* Mobile Trade Co., 55 Ala. 387.

§ 101. Limitation of Amount of Liability.

As to consideration, see ante, "Consideration," § 98.

§ 101 (1) In General.

Statutory Provision.—The Commodity Act (Gen. Acts 1907, p. 209), and Gen. Acts Sp. Sess. 1907, p. 125, fixing rates to be charged by railroads, did not operate to validate provisions of bills of lading exempting carriers from liability for loss of goods, except as to the amount stipulated in such bills. Alabama Great Southern R. Co. *v.* McCleskey, 49 So. 433, 160 Ala. 630.

Validity of Stipulation.—A stipulation in a bill of lading that in the event of loss or damage to goods the carrier will only be responsible for their value at the place and time of shipment is reasonable and valid. Louisville & N. R. Co. *v.* Oden, 80 Ala. 38; Southern R. Co. *v.* Cofer, 149 Ala. 565, 43 So. 102.

"It will be observed that no exemption from liability on account of negligence is involved in this stipulation, but the sole effect of it is to fix the place at which the price of the cotton shall be ascertained in respect to the admeasurement of damages. It has been held that such stipulations in bills of lading are reasonable and enforceable. This being true, the general rule which fixes the value of the goods at the place of delivery at the time at which they should have been delivered as the one for the admeasurement of damages was varied by the contract of the parties; and the court erred in the oral charge to the jury requiring the damages to be estimated with respect to the price of cotton at Selma, instead of Randolph, and in permitting evidence of the value of cotton at Selma." Southern R. Co. *v.* Cofer, 149 Ala. 565, 43 So. 102, 103.

Reasonableness of Valuation.—It is now well settled that a common carrier may, by special contract, limit or qualify his liability as an insurer, or his common-law liability, that is, his liability for losses occurring by unavoidable accidents, not within the exception of "the act of God, or of the public enemy, or the fault of the party complaining," not only touching the risks or accidents for which he is answerable, but also as to the amount of damages for which he will be liable in the event of loss or injury, when the purpose appears to secure a reasonable and just proportion between his liability and his compensation. Alabama, etc., R. Co. *v.* Little, 71 Ala. 611; Atlantic, etc., R. Co. *v.* Dothan Mule Co., 161 Ala. 341, 49 So. 882. See notes in 14 L. R. A. 435, 31 L. R. A., N. S., 311.

Construction.—Defendant carried a bale of cotton under a contract limiting its liability to a certain sum if the value of the "package" was not stated at the time of shipment. Held, that the failure of the shipper to state the value of the bale did not relieve the carrier from liability for its failure to deliver, as a bale of cotton was not a package, within the contract. Southern Exp. Co. *v.* Crook, 44 Ala. 468, cited in note in 37 L. R. A. 177.

§ 101 (2) Limitation of Amount Where Value Is Not Disclosed.

See, also, post, "Loss Caused by Negligence or Wrongful Act of Carrier," § 101 (3).

Where the printed receipt issued by a carrier on receiving bales of cotton for shipment contained conditions limiting the carrier's liability to a certain sum, unless the value of each "package" should be named, but it did not appear that the attention of the shipper was called to the condition, or that the value of the cotton was required to be given, the limitation did not apply to relieve the carrier from liability for a loss to the full value of the cotton. Southern Exp. Co. *v.* Crook, 44 Ala. 468, cited in note in 37 L. R. A. 177.

If the size or appearance of a package fairly indicates that its value is greater than the sum so named, the carrier will be presumed to waive the necessity of stating a value, unless the attention of the shipper is called to the conditions, and the value of the package is required to be given. Southern Exp. Co. *v.* Crook, 44 Ala. 468.

§ 101 (3) Loss Caused by Negligence or Wrongful Act of Carrier.

"It is conceived to be settled in Alabama on principles of public policy that a common carrier can not contract at all for immunity from liability for the loss of or injury to property resulting from his own or his servant's negligence. It is conceived to be settled in this state also that, in consideration of reduced freight charges and the like, the shipper and the carrier may contract that, in case of loss or injury, whether resulting from negligence or other cause, the value of the property at the time and place of shipment, not exceeding an expressed sum, shall be the measure of recovery. And it has also been declared by this court that under such contract recovery will be limited to the sum so expressed, unless the real value of the property is greatly disproportionate thereto—so much greater than the stipulated maximum of value and liability as to render the contract unreasonable, and therefore not binding on the shipper. We have no doubt of the correctness of the first proposition. Of the soundness of the second the writer has always had the gravest doubts. Indeed, if it were an open question, he should adopt the views expressed in the dissenting opinion of Manning, J., in South, etc., R. Co. *v.* Henlein, 52 Ala. 606, 616. He does not see how this proposition can logically stand with the first stated above. But, conceding it to be settled, the limitation upon it embraced in the third proposition shears it to a large extent of its evil tendencies and possibilities, and brings the law back toward the salutary and true doctrine that common carriers can not stipulate, under any circumstances, against liability for the consequences of their own negligence." Southern R. Co. *v.* Jones, 132 Ala. 437, 31 So. 501, 502.

Arbitrary or Disproportionate Valuation.—Where the loss resulted from the negligence of defendant's servants, the measure of damages is the market value of the goods, though the bill of lading contains an arbitrary limitation of defendant's liability to the amount of $5 per 100 pounds. Georgia Pac. Ry. Co. *v.* Hughart, 90 Ala. 36, 8 So. 62, cited in notes in 14 L. R. A. 434, 435, 1 L. R. A., N. S., 987, 31 L. R. A., N. S., 311.

It is violative of public policy for a carrier, as a paid bailee, to limit the extent of its liability for the negligence of itself or its agents or servants by an agreed valuation upon consideration of reduced charges for carriage of goods, when such agreed valuation is disproportionate to the real value of the goods, though the contents of the package or its real value be not disclosed to the carrier. Southern Express Co. *v.* Gibbs, 46 So. 465, 155 Ala. 303, cited in note in 19 L. R. A., N. S., 1007.

A carrier can not limit its liability for negligence by an agreed valuation o. the goods, on consideration of reduced charges, when the agreed valuation is greatly less than the real value and the contents or its value are not disclosed. Southern Express Co. *v.* Owens, 41 So. 752, 146 Ala. 412, 8 L. R. A., N. S., 369, apparently overruling Louisville, etc., R. Co. *v.* Sherrod, 84 Ala. 178, 4 So. 29. See notes in 14 L. R. A. 434, 1 L. R. A., N. S., 986, 987.

Value of Goods Held Recoverable.—A stipulation in a bill of lading that, "in consideration of rates inserted, it is agreed that in case of loss or damage the same shall be adjusted at a valuation of twenty dollars per barrel," does not relieve the railroad company from paying the full value of the goods where the loss was caused by its own negligence. Alabama Great Southern R. Co. *v.* Little, 71 Ala. 611, cited in notes in 14 L. R. A. 435, 31 L. R. A., N. S., 311.

A carrier, when sued for nondelivery of goods intrusted to it for transportation, claimed that at the time of the shipment the value as given by the shipper was stated at a specified sum. No fraud or deceit was practiced on the carrier by the shipper. The failure of the carrier to deliver the goods resulted from its own negligence. Held, that the consignee was entitled to recover the value of the goods, though exceeding the valuation fixed by the shipper. Broadwood *v.* Southern Express Co., 41 So. 769, 148 Ala. 17.

§ 102. Requirement of Notice of Loss.

A stipulation in a bill of lading, limiting the time within which claims for damages shall be presented, is valid, provided the time fixed is reasonable. Nashville, etc., Railway *v.* Long & Son, 163 Ala. 165, 50 So. 130; Atlantic, etc., R. Co. *v.* Ward, 4 Ala. App. 374, 58 So. 677.

Manner of Presenting Claim.—Under a provision of a contract of shipment requiring the presentation of claims for damages within a specified time, the commencement of an action within that time is a sufficient presentation of the claim. Southern Express Co. *v.* Ruth & Son, 5 Ala. App. 644, 59 So. 538.

Time Held Unreasonable.—A stipulation in a receipt given by a common carrier, that he should not be liable for loss of a package, unless a claim for the loss was made within 30 days from the date of the receipt, is unreasonable, tending to fraud, and inoperative. Southern Exp. Co. *v.* Caperton, 44 Ala. 101; Southern Exp. Co. *v.* Bank, 108 Ala. 517, 18 So. 664; Southern Exp. Co. *v.* Owens, 146 Ala. 412, 41 So. 752, 8 L. R. A., N. S., 369; Louisville, etc., R. Co. *v.* Price, 159 Ala. 213, 48 So. 814. See notes in 17 L. R. A., N. S., 630, 31 L. R. A., N. S., 1181.

A stipulation, in a bill of lading for the shipment of money by an express company, that the company shall in no event be liable for any loss unless a claim therefor is made in writing within 32 days from the date of the shipment contract, is void, as being unreasonable. Southern Exp. Co. *v.* Bank of Tupelo, 108 Ala. 517, 18 So. 664, cited in note in 31 L. R. A., N. S., 1183.

A stipulation, in a bill of lading for the carriage of freight from Alabama for delivery at St. Louis, that claims for damage must be made to the agent at the point of delivery promptly after the arrival of the property, and if delayed more than 30 days after the delivery, or in due time for the delivery, no carrier shall be liable, is invalid, because unreasonable. Nashville, etc., Railway *v.* Long & Son, 163 Ala. 165, 50 So. 130.

Time Held Reasonable.—A stipulation in a shipping contract that any claim for loss or damage shall be presented in writing within four months after delivery, or reasonable time for delivery, is reasonable and valid. Atlantic Coast Line R. Co. *v.* Ward, 4 Ala. App. 374, 58 So. 677.

A stipulation, in a contract with a carrier for the transportation and delivery of goods, that it and every other carrier to whom the same may be delivered for transportation shall not be liable for any loss unless the claim therefor shall be presented in writing within 90 days after the date of the receipt, with receipt attached, is reasonable. Broadwood *v.* Southern Express Co., 41 So. 769, 148 Ala. 17, cited in note in 31 L. R. A., N. S., 1183.

Action for Wrong Delivery—Effect of § 4297, Code 1907.—It is not a defense to an action against an express company for wrong delivery of a package that the claim for damages was not presented within 90 days, as required by the contract of shipment, in view of Code 1907, § 4297, providing that stipulations in a contract, forfeiting a right of action thereon for failure to present a claim, are void, but that stipulations requiring a party to give information peculiarly within his knowledge to the other party are valid. Southern Exp. Co. *v.* Ruth & Son, 5 Ala. App. 644, 59 So. 538.

§ 103. Limitation of Liability as Ground of Defense.

§ 104. —— Pleading.

Plea.—In an action against a carrier for failure to deliver leather received for shipment, defendant pleaded that plaintiff accepted a bill of lading exempting defendant from liability for loss by fire occurring while the goods were in the depot, awaiting transit; that said leather was received and kept by defendant in its depot, with due care, for shipment; and that before any train passed, or should have passed, in the direction which it should have been shipped, the depot and goods were burned, without defendant's fault or negligence. Held, that the plea was not demurrable for failure to allege the direction in which the leather was to have been shipped, or that it was contracted to be shipped in any particular direction, or that by the use of reasonable care it might have been shipped before the breaking out of the fire. Louisville & N. R. Co. *v.* Gidley, 24 So. 753, 119 Ala. 523.

Plea Held Insufficient.—In an action for damage to fruit from delay in delivery, when shipped under a contract limiting the carrier's liability for loss from decay caused by the weather and arising during the ordinary time and method of transportation, a plea alleging the limitation and that the damage was caused by decay or changes in weather was bad for failure to negative the carrier's negligence as the proximate cause of the decay. Western Ry. of Alabama *v.* Hart, 49 So. 371, 160 Ala. 599.

Replication.—In an action against a carrier for loss of property, defendant pleaded a clause in the contract providing that no carrier or party in possession of the goods should be responsible for loss by fire, and set up that the property was destroyed by fire occurring in its depot without fault on its part. The replication averred that the town where the loss occurred had over 2,000 population having a daily mail service, and that he was not notified of the arrival of the property within 24 hours, as required by law. Code, § 4224, requires notice in such a city within 24 hours, in order that a company may be relieved from its liability as a carrier by the storage of the goods in a warehouse. Held, that the replication was demurrable as neither denial nor confession and avoidance of the plea. Louisville & N. R. Co. *v.* Johnson, 33 So. 661, 135 Ala. 232.

Variance.—Where an action against a carrier was brought for breach of its common-law liability, the fact that the evidence showed a special contract materially varying the common-law liability constituted no variance. Louisville, etc., R. Co. *v.* Landers, 135 Ala. 504, 33 So. 482, 484; Nashville, etc., Railway *v.* Cody, 137 Ala. 597, 34 So. 1003, 1004, overruling Nashville, etc., R. Co. *v.* Parker, 123 Ala. 683, 27 So. 323.

§ 105. —— Presumptions and Burden of Proof.

The doctrine that a carrier may restrict his liability by a special contract does not extend to changing the rules as to the burden of proof of negligence. Grey *v.* Mobile Trade Co., 55 Ala. 387.

Loss Caused by Excepted Peril.—Where goods are received in good condition, and found to be damaged when delivered, the burden of proof is upon the carrier to show that the damage arose from some excepted peril. Montgomery & W. P. R. Co. *v.* Moore, 51 Ala. 394; Grey *v.* Mobile Trade Co., 55 Ala. 387; South, etc., R. Co. *v.* Henlein, 52 Ala. 606; Alabama, etc., R. Co. *v.* Little, 71 Ala. 611; Central, etc., R. Co. *v.* Burton, 165 Ala. 425, 51 So. 643; East Tennessee, etc., R. Co. *v.* Johnston, 75 Ala. 596, 597; Louisville, etc., R. Co. *v.* Shepherd (Ala.), 61 So. 14, 16. See note in 29 L. R. A., N. S., 665.

Defendant, in an action for injury to goods while in its possession as carrier, has the burden of showing its exemption from liability, under the provision of the bill of lading that it should not be liable for injury by robbery, riots, and strikes. Louisville & N. R. Co. *v.* Dunlap, 41 So. 826, 148 Ala. 23.

Want of Negligence by Carrier.—Where a carrier accepted goods for transportation under a limited liability contract, the burden was on it, in an action for injuries to the goods, to establish, not only that the cause of the loss was within the limitation, but that the loss and the cause thereof were without negligence on its part. Southern Ry. Co. *v.* Levy, 39 So. 95, 144 Ala. 614; South, etc., R. Co. *v.* Henlein, 52 Ala. 606; Central, etc., R. Co. *v.* Burton, 165 Ala. 425, 51 So. 643; Louisville, etc., R. Co. *v.* Shepherd (Ala.), 61 So. 14, 16.

"The true interpretation of the rule is stated in Steele *v.* Townsend, 37 Ala. 247. 'The correct view is, that the loss is not brought within the exception, unless it appears to have occurred without negligence on the part of the carrier; and as it is for the carrier to bring himself within the exception, he must make at least a prima facie case, showing that the injury was not caused by his neglect;' and we may add, if the evidence is in equipoise, the case is not brought within the exception." Louisville, etc., R. Co. *v.* Oden, 80 Ala. 38, 43.

When loss or damage to goods occurs while they are in the custody of the carrier, though carried at "owner's risk," the carrier must make at least a prima facie showing that it was not caused by his negligence. South, etc., R. Co. *v.* Wilson, 78 Ala. 587.

In an action against a carrier to recover for the loss of goods received under a contract exempting it from all liability except negligence, the burden of proving that the loss was caused without negligence is on the carrier. Louisville & N. R. Co. *v.* Cowherd, 23 So. 793, 120 Ala. 51, cited in note in 29 L. R. A., N. S., 663.

Where a bill of lading contained an express stipulation that the carrier was "not accountable for rust or breakage," held, that proof of injury to the goods by breakage made a prima facie case of negligence of the carrier, and that the onus was upon him to show due care, unless the nature of the goods furnished evidence of itself that due care and vigilance could not have prevented the injury. Steele *v.* Townsend, 37 Ala. 247.

§ 106. —— Sufficiency of Evidence.

In a bill of lading given by a railroad company, an exception or stipulation in the words "taken at owner's risk" does not change the character of the employment, but only exempts the company from its liability as insurer, and the company, when sued for a failure to deliver the goods, was not relieved from the onus of making at least a prima facie showing that the loss was not caused by its neglect; and the showing that the transaction occurred during the war, and that the railroad was frequently used by the military authorities, and there was a great want of safety and certainty in the transportation of freight, did not make out such prima facie case. Mobile & O. R. Co. *v.* Jarboe, 41 Ala. 644.

A common carrier, which relies on a special contract exempting it from liability for the destruction by fire of goods delivered to it for transportation, must show, not only that the goods were so destroyed, but also that such destruction was not caused by any fault on its part; and the owner of the goods is entitled to recover where he shows that they were delivered to the carrier 16 and 40 hours before their destruction by a fire in its warehouse, and the carrier fails to show either that it could not have forwarded them by the use of reasonable diligence before the fire, or that it used reasonable care to guard against the fire. Louisville & N. R. Co. *v.* Touart, 97 Ala. 514, 11 So. 756.

§ 107. —— Questions for Jury.

Reasonableness of Limitation.—It is a question for the determination of the court whether a carrier's special contract with a shipper, restricting the carrier's liability in other respects than protecting the carrier against its liability for its own or its servant's negligence, is reasonable. South & N. A. R. Co. *v.* Henlein, 52 Ala. 606.

(I) CONNECTING CARRIERS.

§ 108. Duties in General.

A railroad company can not be compelled to give a bill of lading making it responsible for freight beyond its line. Lotspeich *v.* Central Railroad & Banking Co., 73 Ala. 306, cited in note in 31 L. R. A., N. S., 3, 8, 31.

§ 109. Special Contracts for Through Transportation.

A common carrier receiving goods to carry, marked to a destination beyond its line, is bound, under an implied contract, to carry and deliver at the place named, unless it liability be limited by special agreement. Mobile & G. R. Co. *v.* Copeland, 63 Ala. 219, cited in note in 31 L. R. A., N. S., 5.

An initial carrier which has undertaken to transport cotton from one point to another over connecting lines, without expressly limiting its liability, is regarded as contracting for the safe delivery at the point of destination. Alabama G. S. R. Co. *v.* Mt. Vernon Co., 84 Ala. 173, 4 So. 356, cited in note in 31 L. R. A., N. S., 5, 90.

An undertaking by a carrier to send a shipment beyond the port of destination, at the rates fixed, "if any boats are going through," imposes liability on such carrier for a loss when such shipment was sent through, whether by its own boats or by those of another carrier. Logan *v.* Mobile Trade Co., 46 Ala. 514, cited in note in 31 L. R. A., N. S., 43.

§ 110. Delivery to Succeeding Carrier.

"Where a railroad or other common carrier receives goods consigned beyond the terminus of its own road, with the agreement to deliver to a connecting line, the contract of shipment imposes not only the duty to transport safely over its own road, but to safely deliver to the next connecting carrier. The duty assumed, in other words, is both to safely carry and to safely deliver. Wells *v.* Thomas, 72 Amer. Dec. 228, note pp. 236, 237; Alabama, etc., R. Co. *v.* Thomas, 83 Ala. 343, 3 So. 802. In such case the liability of the first road or carrier does not necessarily terminate with the arrival of the goods at its own terminal depot, although its responsibility as carrier may terminate there, if there is no further duty of carriage, in order to make the connection with the other road over which the goods are to be transported. If there be any duty to carry the goods over an intermediate short line, connecting its own terminal depot with the other connecting road, in order to complete the act of delivery, its liability on the intermediate line obviously is that of a carrier, and not of a forwarder, especially if this line be a part of its own road." Alabama, etc., R. Co. *v.* Thomas, 89 Ala. 234, 7 So. 762, 763, cited in 19 L. R. A., N. S., 1012.

Where an initial carrier places a loaded car on the side track of a connecting carrier, without notice to the latter, and without any mark of the name and address of the consignee, or any waybill or shipping directions, the connecting carrier is only a bailee of the car, and its stringent liability as common carrier does not attach until such waybill or directions are given, or until it is informed to what place the car is to be forwarded, and to whom delivered. Mt. Vernon Co. *v.* Alabama G. S. R. Co., 92 Ala. 296, 8 So. 687.

Defendant had received a car loaded with cotton upon its side track, preparatory to shipment over its line, from the E. A. Ry. Co., which made the contract for transportation with the owner. The two companies had made arrangements for shipping goods over each other's lines, and defendant's agent had reported the car to the car accountant; but there was no evidence of any shipping directions from the E. A. Ry. Co. Held that, though it was customary for defendant to receive such company's cars on its side track for transportation, yet it will not be presumed that the former assumed the responsibility of a carrier before knowing to whom and where to ship the cotton. Alabama G. S. R. Co. *v.* Mount Vernon Co., 84 Ala. 173, 4 So. 356.

Evidence that it was customary for the initial carrier, having no side track, to place loaded cars on the side track of the connecting carrier, and for the latter, when commencing the transportation over its road, to take the car from that point, without requiring a further delivery, falls short of showing a custom by which merely placing loaded cars on the side track devolved on the connecting carrier the duty of immediate transportation, or constituted a complete delivery, before a waybill or other shipping directions were furnished; and is insufficient to charge the connecting carrier with liability as a common carrier for the destruction of goods in a car while on the side track, and before receiving any directions as to their shipment. Mt. Vernon Co. *v.* Alabama G. S. R. Co., 92 Ala. 296, 8 So. 687.

Obeying Instructions of Shippers.—"The carrier, in undertaking to forward goods beyond the terminus of its own route, is bound to obey all reasonable instructions of the shipper or consignor not in conflict with the terms of the contract of shipment, and if he disregard such instructions, and the goods be lost by reason of this act of negligence, he will be liable for their value, although the loss may occur in the possession of another carrier or person. Johnson *v.* Transportation Co., 88 Amer. Dec. 416. If, in forwarding, shipments are made in a manner prohibited by the sender, the carrier so forwarding is liable as an insurer for the safe delivery of the articles so sent." Alabama, etc., R. Co. *v.* Thomas, 89 Ala. 234, 7 So. 762, cited in note in 19 L. R. A., N. S., 1012.

Notice of Instructions to Consignee as to Transshipping.—A railroad company first receiving goods, which takes charge of them to be carried over its own road and to be forwarded to a person beyond its own means of transportation, the goods being directed to a particular consignee, at the place where the goods are first to be delivered and transshipped, must deliver the goods to such consignee with notice of the instructions of the consignor to have them forwarded to the place of their ultimate destination. This notice should be given in a reasonable time after the arrival of the goods at the point of reshipment, and by some agent and servant of the company particularly charged with the performance of this duty. Selma & M. R. Co. *v.* Butts, 43 Ala. 385, cited in note in 31 L. R. A., N. S., 88.

Carrier Acting as Forwarder.—"In so far as the carrier acts as a mere forwarder, assuming as agent of the consignor to have the goods forwarded by a connecting line, he is liable only as bailee for the exercise of ordinary care, or such care as persons of ordinary prudence exercise in reference to their own property under like circumstances. Railroad Co. *v.* Schumacker, 96 Amer. Dec. 510; Hooper *v.* Wells, 85 Amer. Dec. 211; Story, Bailm. § 444." Alabama, etc., R. Co. *v.* Thomas, 89 Ala. 234, 7 So. 762, cited in note in 19 L. R. A., N. S., 1012.

§ 111. Delay in Transportation or Delivery.

Delay Resulting from Failure to Give Notice to Succeeding Carrier.—If a railroad company, outside of its regular contract, and without an additional consideration, undertakes to deliver a car on the line of another road, and it is the custom in such cases to notify the other road of the delivery of the car, its destination, and name of the consignee, and it fails to give such notice, the company is liable for delay in transportation resulting from failure to give the notice. Melbourne *v.* Louisville & N. R. Co., 88 Ala. 443, 6 So. 762, cited in note in 31 L. R. A., N. S., 44, 89, 98.

§ 112. Loss of or Injury to Goods.

§ 112 (1) Liability in General.

Where parts of a continuous line of transportation are owned by different carriers, between whom no connection exists, in the absence of a special contract each is liable only for injuries occurring on his portion of the line. Montgomery & W. P. Ry. Co. *v.* Moore, 51 Ala. 394, cited in note in 31 L. R. A., N. S., 8, 94, 97; Ellsworth *v.* Tartt, 26 Ala. 733; Lotspeich *v.* Central R., etc., Co., 73 Ala. 306.

Before the enactment of Act June 29, 1906, c. 3591, § 7, 34 Stat. 595 (U. S. Comp. St. Supp. 1909, p. 1166), and Code Ala. 1907, § 5546, in effect making the initial carrier responsible for any loss or injury caused by any carrier to which the property is delivered, or over whose line it passes, each of several connecting carriers was responsible only for loss occurring on its own line. Central of Georgia Ry. Co. *v.* Chicago Varnish Co., 53 So. 832, 169 Ala. 287, cited in note in 31 L. R. A., N. S., 62, 69, 70, 71, 108.

What Law Governs.—The liability of the several connecting carriers with respect to loss of freight en route are to be determined by the law as it was when the contract of shipment was made. Central of Georgia Ry. Co. *v.* Chicago Varnish Co., 53 So. 832, 169 Ala. 287, cited in note in 31 L. R. A., N. S., 62, 69, 70, 71, 108.

§ 112 (2) Effect of Agreements between Connecting Lines and Joint Liability.

Defendant was the only express company in B., and received goods from another company, with which it had a mileage agreement, in either of two ways, one of which, being longer than the other, was of benefit to defendant, and for this purpose it sent labels to its customers directing goods to be expressed the longer way, and to plaintiff, a large patron, it gave a letter addressed to the other company directing the shipments to him over the longer route. A consignor delivered goods to the other company consigned to plaintiff which he never received, and he sued defendant for the loss. Held not to show any partnership between the two companies so as to charge defendant with the loss, in the absence of a showing that the goods were delivered to it. Southern Exp. Co. *v.* Saks, 160 Ala. 621, 49 So. 392, cited in note in 31 L. R. A., N. S., 49, 94, 97, 105.

Held, also, that facts did not show that defendant had made the other company its agent so as to render defendant liable, in the absence of evidence that it had received the goods. Southern Exp. Co. *v.* Saks, 160 Ala. 621, 49 So. 392, cited in note in 31 L. R. A., N. S., 49, 94, 97, 105.

Evidence Held to Show Agency.—When two carriers connect at a point from which the one is accustomed to receive, for the purpose of completing transportation, goods carried by the other and destined to points on its line—the goods in question being thus received—and the only evidence of their relation to each other is that they do not pro rate freight, the one carrier will be held to be the agent of the other carrier, and of the consignor and consignee, for the transportation of the goods to their destination. Southern Exp. Co. *v.* Hess, 53 Ala. 19, cited in note in 31 L. R. A., N. S., 106, 107.

§ 112 (3) Liability of Initial Carrier.

Liability under Bill of Lading for Delivery Beyond Route.—Where a common carrier gives a bill of lading for goods to be delivered beyond its route, and does not by express agreement limit its liability to loss or injury suffered on its own line, it thereby binds itself for the safe delivery of the goods at destination, and is liable for injuries to the goods, whether on its own line or that of a connecting carrier. Southern Ry. Co. *v.* Levy, 39 So. 95, 144 Ala. 614; Mobile, etc., R. Co. *v.* Copeland, 63 Ala. 219, 222; Jones *v.* Cincinnati, etc., R. Co., 89 Ala. 376, 8 So. 61, 62. See note in 31 L. R. A., N. S., 5, 66, 77.

Liability after Termination of Connecting Carriers Liability.—The Carmack amendment, providing that the initial carrier receiving an interstate shipment shall be liable to the lawful holder of the bill of lading for any loss caused by a connecting carrier, does not make the initial carrier liable, where the connecting carrier's liability as a carrier has ceased. Louisville, etc., R. Co. *v.* Brewer (Ala.), 62 So. 698.

An initial carrier is responsible alone for loss of goods by it as such. Gulf Compress Co. *v.* Jones Cotton Co., 47 So. 251, 157 Ala. 32.

§ 112 (4) Liability of Intermediate or Last Carrier.

See, also, ante, "Special Contracts for Through Transportation," § 109.

In the absence of special contract or the existence of a relation of partnership or agency between an initial and a connecting carrier, a connecting carrier is liable only for loss or damage occurring on its own line. Southern Exp. Co. *v.* Saks, 160 Ala. 621, 49 So. 392; Montgomery, etc., R. Co. *v.* Moore, 51 Ala. 394; Ellsworth *v.* Tartt, 26 Ala. 733; Kansas, etc., R. Co. *v.* Foster, 134 Ala. 244, 32 So. 773. See note in 31 L. R. A., N. S., 49, 94, 97, 105.

When parts of a continuous line or route of transportation are owned by different carriers, between whom no connection is shown to exist, each carrier is liable, in the absence of a special contract, only for losses and injuries occurring on his own particular portion of the route. Montgomery & W. P. R. Co. *v.* Moore, 51 Ala. 394, cited in note in 31 L. R. A., N. S., 8, 94, 97.

When a carrier receiving goods for carriage to their destination makes arrangements with another carrier to transport them over its line, and deliver them to the next succeeding carrier, such intermediate carrier's liability begins with the receipt of the goods, and ends with their delivery to the next carrier. Alabama G. S. R. Co. *v.* Mount Vernon Co., 84 Ala. 173, 4 So. 356.

Failure to Get Waybill as Affecting Duty to Safely Transport.—That a carrier, receiving goods from a connecting line, failed to get a waybill or other information as to whom the goods were consigned, whether through its own negligence or not would not relieve it from the duty to safely transport the goods, where the owner did not prevent it from obtaining the waybill or information. Western Ry. of Alabama *v.* Hart, 49 So. 371, 160 Ala. 599.

Duty of Connecting Carrier as to Informing Itself Whether Car Properly Loaded.—Where goods are improperly loaded in a closed car, which comes from the initial carrier to a connecting carrier with its doors closed, the improper loading is not "apparent" to the connecting carrier, nor need it open the car to see whether the loading was properly done. McCarthy *v.* Louisville & N. R. Co., 102 Ala. 193, 14 So. 370.

Contributory Negligence of Shipper as Defense.—In an action against a connecting carrier for injuries to goods, contributory negligence of the shipper in loading the goods on the car of the initial carrier was no defense. Walter *v.* Alabama Great Southern R. Co., 39 So. 87, 142 Ala. 474.

§ 113. Carrier as Forwarder or Warehouseman.

Effect on Liability of Initial Carrier.—An initial carrier is not liable as a carrier for an interstate shipment over lines of connecting carriers, where the goods were held at their destination by the last carrier as a warehouseman, after a reasonable time for their removal had elapsed subsequent to the mailing of the notice of their arrival, in accordance with the requirements of Code 1907, § 6137. Louisville, etc., R. Co. *v.* Brewer (Ala.), 62 So. 698.

§ 114. Limitation of Liability.

§ 114 (1) Power to Limit Liability to Carrier's Own Line.

Liabilities Imposed by Interstate Commerce Act.—A carrier may not by contract limit the liabilities imposed on it by Interstate Commerce Act (Act Feb. 4, 1887, c. 104, 24 Stat. 386 [U. S. Comp. St. 1901, p. 3169]) § 20, as amended by Act June 29, 1906, c. 3591, § 7, 34 Stat. 593 (U. S. Comp. St. Supp. 1909, p. 1163), making the initial carrier of an interstate shipment liable for any loss or injury thereto caused by any connecting carrier, because of the rate charged for the transportation. Central of Georgia Ry. Co. *v.* Sims, 53 So. 826, 169 Ala. 295, cited in note in 31 L. R. A., N. S., 28, 70, 71.

§ 114 (2) Requisites and Validity of Contract.

Consideration.—A limitation of liability of an initial carrier for injuries to a shipment of lumber to those occurring on its line requires no other consideration than the shipment itself. McNeill *v.* Atlantic Coast Line R. Co., 49 So. 797, 161 Ala. 319.

Assent.—Where a shipper of goods over the lines of connecting carriers does not receive a bill of lading from the initial carrier limiting its common-law liability contemporaneously with the delivery of the goods to such carrier, the carrier assumes a common-law liability. Southern Ry. Co. *v.* Levy, 39 So. 95, 144 Ala. 614, cited in note in 31 L. R. A., N. S., 5, 66, 77.

Defendant's railroad line connected at P. with a line of steamers for Liverpool. Plaintiff's agent, desiring to ship 100 bales of cotton for plaintiff, applied to defendant railroad company for a rate for such amount to be shipped on a specified date by a specified steamer. Defendant, before answering, ascertained whether the steamship company would accept the cotton for that steamer, and, being informed that it would, named the rate, and agreed by telegraph to ship the cotton on that date by the steamer named. Defendant company transported the cotton to the dock, and tendered the same to the steamship company, but the master refused it, under an alleged custom authorizing him to say what freight he would take or refuse on any particular trip, and the cotton was thereafter shipped on a different vessel, to plaintiff's damage. Held, that defendant railroad company was liable for breach of contract, notwithstanding the issuance of a bill of lading, providing that it should only be liable for damages occurring to freight while on its own line, and that its liability as a common carrier ceased on tendering the freight to its connecting carrier, etc. Louisville, etc., R. Co. *v.* Williams, 5 Ala. App. 615, 56 So. 865.

"The fact that appellee, before the Saltmarsh reached Pensacola, made a special arrangement with appellant for the shipment of the cotton by that steamer on her return to Liverpool in June, and the fact that the booking agent in Montgomery did not make the contract on behalf of appellant until he had received special authorization so to do from the foreign freight agent of appellant in Louisville, Ky., and that the foreign freight agent in Louisville made a special arrangement with the general agents of the Saltmarsh in New York for the shipment to be made on that particular trip, preclude us from holding that the mere reception of an unread bill of lading, issued in accordance with custom, by appellant upon the delivery of the cotton at Pensacola was intended by any of the parties to in any way alter the contract which had previously been made. Appellee had no contract with the Saltmarsh for the shipment of the cotton. Appellant did have a valid contract with that steamer for its shipment, and, having failed to require the Saltmarsh to carry out its contract with it, appellant is not only legally but morally responsible to appellee for the damages resulting to him from the breach of the contract." Louisville, etc., R. Co. *v.* Williams, 5 Ala. App. 615, 56 So. 865, 867.

§ 114 (3) Operation and Effect of Limitation.

Where plaintiff shipped household goods over a route consisting of several connecting carriers, under a bill of lading limiting the liability of each to negligence occurring on its own line, the discharging or delivering carrier was only liable for injuries to the property occurring on its line, or while the goods were in its possession. Walter *v.* Alabama Great Southern R. Co., 39 So. 87, 142 Ala. 474, cited in note in 31 L. R. A., N. S., 8, 94.

Discharge of Duty of Initial Carrier.—Where a bill of lading limited the carrier's liability to its own line, and required delivery to another carrier on the route to destination, if the destination was not on the initial carrier's own line, such carrier's duty might be discharged by delivery to the connecting carrier designated in the bill, or, if none be designated and there were several, by a delivery to a proper connecting carrier on the route "in the usual and customary way." Southern Ry. Co. *v.* Goldstein Bros., 41 So. 173, 146 Ala. 386, cited in note in 31 L. R. A., N. S., 78.

§ 114 (4) Right of Subsequent Carrier to Benefit of Limitation by First Carrier.

Where the shipper of a carload of mules signs a special contract, which purports on its face to be made with the initial carrier "and its connecting lines," releasing the carriers from liability for any damage not caused by their negligence, and providing that its terms shall inure to the benefit of connecting lines unless they stipulate otherwise, a connecting carrier which receives and transports the mules in the same car, under this contract, is entitled to the benefit of its exemptions, notwithstanding no rate for the entire distance is fixed by it. Western Railway *v.* Harwell, 91 Ala. 340, 8 So. 649, cited in note in 18 L. R. A., N. S., 91.

§ 115. —— Pleading.

Complaint—Form Prescribed by Statute.—A complaint against a common carrier, alleging that plaintiff claimed of defendant $1,000 for loss and injury to goods delivered to a connecting carrier, operating with defendant a through route to destination; that defendant did not deliver the goods to plaintiff, who was consignee, in good and proper condition, or in the condition they were in when received by it; and that such goods, when delivered to plaintiff, were badly broken, injured, and damaged, and a large part thereof wholly unfit for use, etc.—was substantially in the form prescribed by Code 1896, p. 946, No. 15, and was not, therefore, demurrable. Walter *v.* Alabama Great Southern R. Co., 39 So. 87, 142 Ala. 474.

Pleas.—Two counts in a complaint charged the failure to deliver a car load of lumber shipped over the carrier's line, and another count charged failure to deliver within a reasonable time. Defendant in a special plea alleged that the lumber was shipped to a place not on its line, that it was agreed between the parties that defendant's liability should cease on delivery of the lumber to a connecting carrier, which it did to a carrier specified, and that the shipment sustained no damages while in possession of defendant. Held, that the plea was not demurrable for failure to show that the connecting carrier carried the lumber to its destination, or that defendant was notified of the delivery of the lumber to the connecting carrier or of its arrival, as no duties of that kind were specified in the contract alleged. McNeill *v.* Atlantic, etc., R. Co., 161 Ala. 319, 49 So. 797, cited in note in 31 L. R. A., N. S., 67, 75.

Where, in an action against the delivering carrier for injuries to goods, defendant specially pleaded that the goods were delivered to a transportation company in B. for transportation to M., and that the receiving carrier issued its bill of lading for goods, stipulating for exemption from liability for fire, and that the property was damaged or destroyed by fire through no fault or negligence on defendant's part, such plea was not demurrable for failure to allege the receipt of the bill of lading by the shipper prior to, or contemporaneous with, the receipt of the goods by the carrier; such contemporaneous delivery of the bill of lading being presumed, in the absence of an allegation to the contrary in a replication to the plea. Southern Ry. Co. *v.* Levy, 39 So. 95, 144 Ala. 614, cited in note in 31 L. R. A., N. S., 5, 66, 77.

Same—Setting Out Contract.—A carrier was charged in one count in the complaint with a failure to deliver a car load of lumber shipped by plaintiff, and in another count was charged with a failure to deliver within a reasonable time. Defendant alleged that the shipment was to a point not on its line, and that it was agreed in a contract of shipment that defendant's liability should cease when it delivered the lumber to the connecting carrier, and that it so delivered the lumber to the connecting carrier. Held, that defendant's plea was not demurrable for failure to attach as an exhibit or set out the specific contract of shipment alleged, as the contract was not alleged to be in writing, and it was not necessary for the contract to be in writing. McNeill *v.* Atlantic, etc., R. Co., 49 So. 797, 161 Ala. 319, cited in note in 31 L. R. A., N. S., 67, 75.

Double Plea.—Where, in an action against a carrier for injuries to goods, one of defendant's pleas raised an issue of contributory negligence, and also denied that the goods were damaged while in defendant's possession, and that it was only liable under the bill of lading for injuries occurring while the goods were in its possession, defendant was bound to sustain the truth of both such defenses. Walter *v.* Alabama Great Southern R. Co., 39 So. 87, 142 Ala. 474.

Replication—Waiver of Stipulation.—In an action against a terminal carrier for loss of goods, the carrier pleaded the failure of the consignee to give notice of damage within 90 days, as stipulated in the contract of carriage. A replication alleged that within 90 days after the date of the shipment the consignee called at the office of defendant and made inquiry for the goods, and was advised that the goods had not arrived; that he thereupon telegraphed to the shipper requesting that the initial carrier trace them; that the shipper, with the sanction of the agent of the initial carrier and within 90 days after the date of the shipment, wrote to the initial carrier's office of the nondelivery of the goods and inclosed a copy of the receipt; and that within 90 days after the shipment the initial carrier was advised of the nondelivery of the goods, whereupon it began an investigation for the recovery thereof and waived the provision in the contract requiring a claim for the goods to be made in writing. Held, that the replication did not show a waiver of the stipulation by the terminal carrier. Broadwood *v.* Southern Express Co., 41 So. 769, 148 Ala. 17, cited in note in 31 L. R. A., N. S., 1183.

Matters Provable under General Issue.—In an action against a connecting carrier for delay, defendant was entitled to prove, under a plea of general issue, that whatever delay there was, was caused by the initial carrier, with which the contract of shipment was made; and that there was no delay in transportation or delivery on defendant's part. Central, etc., R. Co. *v.* Strickland-Metcalf Grocery Co., 4 Ala. App. 372, 5[illegible] So. 678.

Variance.—Where the complaint, in an action against an intermediate carrier, alleges that it contracted to carry goods to their destination, and the proof shows that the initial carrier contracted to carry them there, and made arrangements with the intermediate carrier to carry them to the end of its line only, there is a fatal variance. Alabama G. S. R. Co. *v.* Mt. Vernon Co., 84 Ala. 173, 4 So. 356.

§ 116. —— Evidence.

See, also, post, "Evidence," § 145.

§ 116 (1) Presumptions and Burden of Proof.

Under the presumption that a fact, continuous in its nature, continues to exist until the contrary is shown, it is presumed, as against a connecting carrier, that the goods were received in the same order as when received by the initial carrier; but such presumption does not affect the liability of the latter, and when loss is shown the burden is upon the initial carriers, or any subsequent carrier shown to have had possession of the goods, to prove that they were not lost while in its possession, if they are sued for such loss. Central of Georgia Ry. Co. *v.* Chicago Varnish Co, 53 So. 832, 169 Ala. 287.

Suit against Initial Carrier—Delivery to Connecting Line.—In an action for failure to deliver goods at their destination on a connecting line, for which goods defendant railroad company issued a bill of lading, limiting its liability to damages occurring while the goods were under its control, it is proper to refuse to direct a verdict for defendant where the evidence fails to show that the goods were delivered safely to the connecting line. Georgia Pac. Ry. Co. *v.* Hughart, 90 Ala. 36, 8 So. 62; Louisville, etc., R. Co. *v.* Jones, 100 Ala. 263, 14 So. 114.

Condition of Goods on Delivery to Connecting Line.—Where goods are delivered to a carrier for transportation to a point beyond its own line under a through bill of lading, which stipulates against liability for injury beyond its own line, and the goods are in a damaged condition when delivered by the connecting carrier to the consignee, the presumption is that the receiving carrier delivered them to the connecting carrier in good condition, and the presumption must be overcome before the consignor can recover for such damage from the receiving carrier. Louisville & N. R. Co. *v.* Jones, 100 Ala. 263, 14 So. 114, cited in note in 31 L. R. A., N. S., 110.

Action against Last Carrier—Damage to Goods.—Where there is a partial delivery of a consignment by the last carrier, and that carrier is sued, the presumption of receipt by it of the goods in the same condition as when delivered to the initial carrier exists and casts on the defendant the burden of exculpating itself by showing that the loss or damage did not occur while the goods were in its custody. Southern Exp. Co. *v.* Saks, 160 Ala. 621, 49 So. 392; Southern Exp. Co. *v.* Hess, 53 Ala. 19; Montgomery, etc., R. Co. *v.* Culver, 75 Ala. 587; Cooper *v.* Georgia Pac. R. Co., 92 Ala. 329, 9 So. 159; Louisville, etc., R. Co. *v.* Jones, 100 Ala. 263, 14 So. 114. See note in 31 L. R. A., N. S., 49, 94, 97, 105.

Where the contract of the last of a line of connecting express companies, which has made only a partial delivery of goods, is such that it is liable only for losses occurring on its own, and not on connecting lines, and there is any evidence of the delivery of the goods to it, and that the loss could have occurred while they were in its custody, it must account for the loss. Southern Exp. Co. *v.* Hess, 53 Ala. 19.

Where, in a suit against a connecting carrier for injuries to goods, there was evidence that the defendant was the discharging or delivering carrier, and that the goods were received in a damaged condition, though delivered for shipment in good condition, the burden was on the defendant to show that the goods were not injured while in its possession, but were delivered in the same condition they were received from its connecting carrier, though the shipment was made under a contract limiting the liability of each carrier to injuries occurring on its own line. Walter *v.* Alabama Great Southern R. Co., 39 So. 87, 142 Ala. 474, cited in note in 31 L. R. A., N. S., 894.

Receipt of Goods.—In an action against the last carrier for loss of or damage to goods, the burden of proof is on the plaintiff to establish the receipt of the goods by the defendant, unless some relation of agency or partnership or some special contract affects the status. Southern Exp. Co. *v.* Saks, 160 Ala. 621, 49 So. 392, cited in note in 31 L. R. A., N. S., 49, 94, 97, 105.

§ 116 (2) Admissibility of Evidence.

Bill of Lading Given by Initial Carrier.—Where one of two connecting carriers has delivered to the other, at the point of connection, goods to be delivered at a point on the latter's line, the bill of lading given the consignor by the first company is admissible in evidence, as against the second company, for the purpose of showing the goods delivered, their condition at the time of delivery, and the terms of the shipment. Southern Exp. Co. *v.* Hess, 53 Ala. 19, cited in note in 31 L. R. A., N. S., 106, 107.

§ 117. —— Trial.

Instructions.—Where a connecting carrier was only liable for injuries to goods occurring on its own line, a requested instruction that plaintiff was entitled to recover, unless defendant delivered the goods to another connecting carrier and ceased from that time to exercise all jurisdiction and control over the goods before delivery of the same plaintiff, was properly refused, as pretermitting any inquiry as to whether the injury to the goods occurred on defendant's line, or while in defendant's possession as a carrier. Walter *v.* Alabama Great Southern R. Co., 39 So. 87, 142 Ala. 474.

(J) CHARGES AND LIENS.

§ 118. Rates of Freight.

Contract for Special Rate to Industrial Enterprise.—Where a consignee knew that defendant was giving special freight rates of 50 cents per ton on coal to other industrial enterprises in a town to which plaintiff contracted for the shipment of coal at such rate with defendant's agent, the fact that plaintiff also knew that the general tariff rate on coal for such haul was 70 cents per ton did not justify the defendant in charging the 70-cent rate of coal shipped under plaintiff's contracts. Southern Ry. Co. *v.* Anniston Foundry & Machine Co., 33 So. 274, 135 Ala. 315.

Recovery of Excess Due in Case of Underpayment—Interstate Shipment.—Under the interstate commerce law, providing for the publication of freight rates, the mistakes of the agents of those engaged in interstate commerce will not preclude the carrier from collecting the excess due in case of underpayment, or the shipper or consignee from collecting an overpayment. Louisville, etc., R. Co. *v.* McMullan, 5 Ala. App. 662, 59 So 683.

The rule that, where a creditor, with full knowledge of the facts, accepts less than the amount due from his debtor, he is thereafter precluded from collecting the excess, did not preclude the carrier from collecting a balance due it. Louisville, etc., R. Co. *v.* McMullan, 5 Ala. App. 662, 59 So. 683.

Rate for Local Freight.—The court adheres to its decision in Harrell *v.* Mobile, etc., R. Co., 59 Ala. 321, 325 that the second section of the act of April 19th, 1873, which provides that railroad companies "may for the transportation of local freight, demand and receive not exceeding fifty per cent more than the rate charged for the transportation of the same description of freight, over the whole line of its road," does not authorize the addition of fifty per cent, on the charge over the whole road, irrespective of the distance the freight may be carried, but only an additional fifty per cent more per mile, for the distance local freight is carried, than the per mile rate charged on goods carried over the whole line. Mobile, etc., R. Co. *v.* Steiner, etc., Co., 61 Ala. 559.

The rate on freight carried over the whole line of a railroad company, which furnishes the basis for the additional fifty per cent allowed by the act of the general assembly, approved April 19, 1873, for the transportation of "local freight," is the rate charged on freight taken on at one terminus, and discharged at the other; and not the rate for freight brought from, or carried to a point beyond either terminus of the road. Mobile, etc., R. Co. *v.* Steiner, etc., Co., 61 Ala. 559, reaffirmed on this point. Lotspeich *v.* Central R., etc., Co., 73 Ala. 306.

§ 119. Charges for Storage.

A consignee must remove goods within a reasonable time, or he becomes liable for storage, and the carrier becomes merely a warehouseman. Central of Georgia Ry. Co. *v.* Patterson, 6 Ala. App. 494, 60 So. 465. See, to the same effect, Gulf City Constr. Co. *v.* Louisville, etc., R. Co., 121 Ala. 621, 25 So. 579; Southern R. Co. *v.* Lockwood Mfg. Co., 142 Ala. 322, 37 So. 667, 669.

Charges for car service where goods are left in the car by the consignee after a reasonable time subsequent to their arrival, of which the consignee has notice, are legal. Gulf City Const. Co. *v.* Louisville & N. R. Co., 25 So. 579, 121 Ala. 621.

Evidence as to Reasonable Charge.—On the issue of charges which may properly be made by a railroad for storing freight in its depot, testimony as to the reasonable charges for storing property of the kind in question in warehouses in the town where the depot is located is competent, even conceding that a railroad is entitled to charge a higher storage rate than is customary with other warehousemen. Central of Georgia Ry. Co. *v.* Turner, 39 So. 30, 143 Ala. 142.

§ 120. Rebates.

Where a carrier verbally agrees to allow a rebate, and afterwards gives a bill of lading which contains no such provision, the promised rebate can not be recovered, as parol evidence is not admissible to vary the terms of the bill; but this rule does not apply where the carrier posts for public inspection at his office an order allowing authorized special rates for certain classes of freight, and directing the freight to be paid for at regular tariff rates, and in such a case the shipper may recover the overcharge. Louisville & N. R. Co. *v.* Fulgham, 91 Ala. 555, 8 So. 803.

§ 121. Rights of Connecting Carriers.

The last of several connecting carriers may pay the charges due to the previous carriers, and have a lien for, and collect from, the consignee, not only his own compensation, but also the amount so paid. Converse Bridge *v.* Collins, 119 Ala. 534, 24 So. 561, 562.

The waybill showing a through billing at a certain price, which was paid by the last carrier, it could not recover of the consignee for its own charges. Converse Bridge Co. *v.* Collins, 24 So. 561, 119 Ala. 534.

A carrier presented to a preceding carrier a bill of lading marked in one place "Prepaid," and in another "Collect." The freight had been prepaid, but the waybill did not show it. Held, that the last carrier was charged with knowledge putting it on inquiry which would have led to notice of prepayment; and hence, on receiving the shipment, it was not justified in paying preceding charges. Converse Bridge Co. *v.* Collins, 24 So. 561, 119 Ala. 534.

§ 122. Persons Liable for Charges.

Evidence—Performed Agreement of Third Person to Pay Freight.—Where the shipper is impliedly bound on the face of the bill of lading to pay the freight of goods, it may be shown by parol evidence that the carrier received them under an agreement with a third person to pay the freight, if such person has in fact paid it. Wayland *v.* Mosely, 5 Ala. 430.

§ 123. Actions for Charges.

Waiver of Proof of Publication of Rates.—Where, on the trial of an action against a consignee to recover the difference between a published rate and that actually charged by mistake, the cause was so conducted by the defense as to indicate that, if evidence of the posting of the rates, as required by the interstate commerce law, necessary or pertinent, it was waived, the failure to show such posting would not prejudice the plaintiff's case. Louisville, etc., R. Co. *v.* McMullan, 5 Ala. App. 662, 59 So. 683.

In an action against a consignee for the balance of a freight rate underpaid, publication of the rates, as required by the interstate commerce law, held not necessary to be shown. Louisville & N. R. Co. *v.* McMullan, 5 Ala. App. 662, 59 So. 683.

Recoupment of Damages for Injuries.—The owner of live stock transported by a railway when sued for the freight charges may recoup damages sustained by reason of injuries to the stock through the railroad's neglect. South & N. A. R. Co. *v.* Henlein, 56 Ala. 368.

§ 124. Lien for Charges.

A common carrier has a lien on the goods transported by him, for the freight due the whole route, may retain the goods till the freight is paid. Long *v.* Mobile & M. R. Co., 51 Ala. 512; Southern R. Co. *v.* Lockwood Mfg. Co., 142 Ala. 322, 37 So. 667, 669; Crass *v.* Memphis, etc., R. Co., 96 Ala. 447, 11 So. 480, 481.

Lien for Paid Customs Duties.—The government's lien on goods for duties is preserved in favor of a common carrier that has paid them. Guesnard *v.* Louisville & N. R. Co., 76 Ala. 453.

Nature of Lien.—A common carrier is entitled to a lien for freight upon the goods carried, and the right to retain possession of them until his reasonable charges are paid, this lien existing independently of any remedy given by statute for its enforcement, and may be enforced by a court of chancery. Crass *v.* Memphis, etc., R. Co., 96 Ala. 447, 11 So. 480, 481.

Waiver. — Where failure to deliver goods on demand of the consignee is not placed on the ground of a lien for charges, a carrier can not plead such lien in defense of a subsequent action for loss of the goods. Louisville & N. R. Co. *v.* McGuire, 79 Ala. 395.

Enforcement.—Code, § 1182, though affording an adequate remedy at law for the enforcement of a carrier's lien, by allowing a sale to pay charges, does not, in the absence of express provision, take away any previous equitable remedy. Crass *v.* Memphis & C. R. Co., 96 Ala. 447, 11 So. 480.

When goods are delivered by a common carrier at their place of destination, and are not taken out of his custody by the consignee within 60 days, if they are not of a perishable character (or 90 days, if not perishable), they may be advertised and sold by him, for nonpayment of freight and charges, "after 30 days' notice" (Rev. Code, §§ 1884-85); and he is not required to wait until the expiration of the 60 or 90 days, as the case may be, before advertising the sale. Western R. Co. *v.* Rembert, 50 Ala. 25.

Liability for Sale in Bad Faith.—In selling freight for charges, a carrier is bound to use reasonable diligence to ascertain the character of the packages from the external indications, and to communicate his knowledge to bidders; and if he fails to do so, and sells valuable freight to a favorite having superior knowledge, at a nominal price, he and the purchaser are liable to an action of damages by the injured party. Nathan *v.* Shivers, 71 Ala. 117.

An agent of a common carrier is not only held to good faith in making a sale under the statute of packages held for freight, but also to reasonable diligence in ascertaining and giving notice of the contents of the packages. Reasonable diligence in such case requires that the agent must examine all external indicia and marks on or about the packages, and all other sources of information, reasonably within his reach; but he is neither required nor authorized to break or open the packages for the purpose of ascertaining their contents. Nathan Bros. *v.* Shivers, 71 Ala. 117.

Whether the agent knew, or could have learned, or had just grounds for believing what were the contents of the packages, and whether he acted in good faith in giving the notice prescribed by statute, and in making the sale, are questions for the jury, under appropriate instructions from the court. Nathan Bros. *v.* Shivers, 71 Ala. 117.

(K) DISCRIMINATION AND OVERCHARGE.

§ 125. Excessive Charges.

Effect of Mistake by Carrier's Agent.—The fact that a freight rate specified by the carrier's agent in a bill of lading was fixed by the agent by mistake did not authorize the carrier to exact from the consignee an increased rate. Southern Ry. Co. *v.* Anniston Foundry & Machine Co., 33 So. 274, 135 Ala. 315. But see Louisville, etc., R. Co. *v.* McMullan, 5 Ala. App. 662, 59 So. 683.

Mistake of Agent—Interstate Shipment.—Under the interstate commerce law, providing for the publication of freight rates, the mistakes of the agents of those engaged in interstate commerce will not preclude the carrier from collecting the excess due in case of underpayment, or the shipper or consignee from collecting an overpayment. Louisville, etc., R. Co. *v.* McMullan, 5 Ala. App. 662, 59 So. 683.

§ 126. Actions for Excess of Charges Paid.

§ 126 (1) Nature of Action.

An action against a carrier by a consignee for overcharge in freight which he was required to pay in order to obtain the freight was in the nature of action for money had and received. Southwestern Alabama Ry. Co. *v.* W. C. Maddox & Son, 41 So. 9, 146 Ala. 539.

§ 126 (2) Right of Action.

Where a carrier of freight, bound by the classification and rates made in the contract of shipment, changed the classification and demanded a higher rate as a condition precedent to delivery, the shipper, paying the excess, may recover it back. Southern Ry. Co. *v.* Lowe, 170 Ala. 598, 54 So. 51.

Payments Held Not to Be Voluntary.—Where a carrier withheld goods from the consignee and refused to deliver them without the payment of excessive freight, the payment could not be regarded as voluntary. Southwestern Alabama Ry. Co. *v.* W. C. Maddox & Son, 41 So. 9, 146 Ala. 539.

Where a consignee paid an excess of freight charged over the rate specified in the bill of lading under protest, such additional payment was not voluntary, so as to preclude him from maintaining an action to recover the same. Southern Ry. Co. *v.* Anniston Foundry & Machine Co., 33 So. 274, 135 Ala. 315.

If a shipper pays rates established in violation of law by the carrier, rather than forego his services, such payment is not voluntary, in the legal sense, and the shipper may maintain his action for money had and received to recover back the illegal charge. Mobile & M. Ry. Co. *v.* Steiner, 61 Ala. 559.

§ 126 (3) Pleading.

Sufficiency of Complaint.—A count of a complaint in an action to recover for a freight overcharge alleged that defendant was a common carrier, and undertook to haul logs at a fixed price, but, instead of charging plaintiff the stipulated freight rate, defendant extorted an excessive rate, and refused to haul or deliver the logs unless plaintiff would pay such sum; that plaintiff offered to pay the reasonable charge, and demanded that the logs should be hauled for such freight charges, which defendant refused to do, and the plaintiff was compelled to pay such extortionate and illegal rate to an amount stated, in order to have the freight moved, and that plaintiff paid such charge under protest, reserving a right to recover back the overcharge and paid to defendant a sum named which was more than the proper and contracted charges or rate; that defendant extorted from plaintiff the sum named, which defendant refuses to pay back to plaintiff. Held to state a good cause of action. Fairford Lumber Co. *v.* Tombigbee Valley R. Co., 51 So. 770, 165 Ala. 275.

§ 126 (4) Evidence.

Opinion of Railroad Commission.—Where, in an action against a carrier for alleged overcharges, there were two counts in the complaint for charges collected after the rendition of an opinion of the railroad commission, which by Code 1896, § 3496, is prima facie evidence of charges made subsequent to the determination, such opinion was admissible, though the complaint also contained demands for overcharges prior to the determination of the commission. Anniston Mfg. Co. *v.* Southern Ry. Co., 40 So. 965, 145 Ala. 351.

Evidence of Efforts to Collect Overcharges.—In an action against a terminal carrier by a consignee to recover overcharges on freight, the bill of lading issued by the initial carrier, which showed the proper freight rate, having been introduced in evidence, it was proper to permit the treasure of the shipper to detail his efforts to collect the overcharges and to admit correspondence between the witness and defendant's agents in regard to the overcharges, as the defendant was the agent of the carrier issuing the bill. Southwestern Alabama Ry. Co. *v.* W. C. Maddox & Son, 41 So. 9, 146 Ala. 539.

Incompetent Evidence as to Reasonable Charge.—In an action against a carrier for alleged overcharges, a question as to what was considered among railroad men as a reasonable rate, which question was not limited to the rate between the points in issue, was properly disallowed. Anniston Mfg. Co. *v.* Southern Ry. Co., 40 So. 965, 145 Ala. 351.

In an action against a carrier for alleged overcharges, evidence as to the rate charged by another carrier for hauling similar material between different points was irrelevant. Anniston Mfg. Co. *v.* Southern Ry. Co., 40 So. 965, 145 Ala. 351.

In an action against a carrier for alleged overcharges, it was not error for the court to refuse to permit plaintiff to prove what rates defendant charged in another state. Anniston Mfg. Co. *v.* Southern Ry. Co., 40 So. 965, 145 Ala. 351.

Sufficiency.—Where, in an action to recover excessive freight charges paid and a statutory penalty, the only evidence for the reasonableness of freight charges for shipping compressed cotton was that the charges paid by the shipper on a shorter route for uncompressed were 50 per cent less, it being common knowledge that compressing reduces the bulk about one-half, such evidence is not sufficient to go to the jury. Lotspeich *v.* Central Railroad & Banking Co., 73 Ala. 306.

III. CARRIAGE OF LIVE STOCK.

§ 127. Nature of Carrier's Duties and Liabilities in General.

A carrier accepting live stock for transportation, with issuing a bill of lading, thereby assumes, as to such shipment, the common-law liabilities of a common carrier. Northern Alabama Ry. Co. *v.* Bidgood, 5 Ala. App. 658, 59 So. 680.

In the absence of contract limiting the liability, a carrier is an insurer against such loss or damage to live animals received for shipment, as do not arise from acts of God or the public enemy, nor from the nature or propensities of animals, against which due care could not provide. Atlantic Coast Line R. Co. *v.* Rice, 52 So. 918, 169 Ala. 265.

§ 128. Duty to Receive for Transportation.

Facilities for Receiving Stock.—A railroad company holding itself out as a carrier of live stock is under legal obligation to provide proper facilities, such as stock yards, for receiving live stock offered to it for shipment. St. Louis & S. F. R. Co. *v.* Cavender, 170 Ala. 601, 54 So. 54.

§ 129. Duties in Respect to Transportation.

§ 130. —— Mode or Means of Transportation.

Transportation.—Under the rule adopted in this state, when not modified by special contract, a common carrier, undertaking to transport cattle, assumes the full obligations to furnish safe and suitable vehicles, and an adequate road, and to exercise due care and foresight to guard against loss or injury from external sources. East Tennessee, etc., R. Co. *v.* Johnston, 75 Ala. 596.

Omission to "Bed" Car.—When the liability of the railroad company is not modified by contract, and it undertakes the transportation of cattle under the common-law liability for safe delivery, it can not be affirmed, as matter of law, that the failure to "bed" a car for the transportation of cattle with straw or other material, is negligence per se; but if it is shown that such a course is usual and customary, and is such a precaution as a prudent, competent, and faithful man, experienced in the business, would take, the company will be responsible for any injury caused by its omission in this regard. East Tennessee, etc., R. Co. *v.* Johnston, 75 Ala. 596, cited in note in 23 L. R. A., N. S., 278, 279.

Duty of Carrier as to Assigning Cars in Making Up Train.—Although a railroad company may have, consistently with its duty to other shippers, placed a car loaded with cattle at a greater distance from the engine, yet, if the injury suffered was not caused by the proximity of the cattle to the engine, the company is not liable therefor, in the absence of negligence on its part causing the loss. East Tennessee, etc., R. Co. *v.* Johnston, 75 Ala. 596, 598. See, also, ante, "Duties as to Transportation in General," § 39.

§ 131. —— Food, Water, and Rest.

Where a carrier was aware that no one representing the shipper was traveling with certain stock as required by the shipping contract, it was the carrier's duty to feed, water, and exercise necessary care for them. Louisville & N. R. Co. *v.* Smitha, 40 So. 117, 145 Ala. 686.

Under Act Cong. June 29, 1906, a carrier can not by any contract with the shipper, relieve itself of the prescribed duty of feeding and watering animals, if their owner or custodian fails to do so and its failure to perform the duty imposed upon it by the statute is negligence per se. Southern Ry. Co. *v.* Proctor, 3 Ala. App. 413, 57 So. 513.

In an action for injuries to cattle delivered to a carrier for shipment caused by an unreasonable delay in delivery, the plaintiff may show that the cattle were injured by being deprived of food and water for a long time. Southern R. Co. *v.* Proctor, 3 Ala. App. 413, 57 So. 513.

Right of Carrier to Unload and Feed against Protest of Shipper.—A carrier transporting horses under a special contract that they shall be unloaded for the purpose of feeding by the shipper, has the right to unload and feed the horses, even against the shipper's protest, where, unless so unloaded and fed, the horses would have been kept in the cars unfed for a longer period than allowed by law. Nashville, C. & St. L. Ry. Co. *v.* Parker, 27 So. 323, 123 Ala. 683.

§ 132. Duties in Respect to Delivery.

Where a consignor directed the agent of a railway company in writing to ship hogs to consignees named, and a bill of lading was furnished to the consignor, naming the persons designated by the consignor as consignees, and there was no change in the contract, but the hogs were not delivered to the consignees, but to third parties, the carrier is liable for their value. Southern Ry. Co. *v.* Webb, 41 So. 420, 148 Ala. 661, cited in note in 31 L. R. A., N. S., 310.

Plaintiff having directed defendant's agent as to the consignees of certain hogs, a contract of affreightment was executed naming such persons as consignees. Plaintiff directed his servant to drive the hogs to the place of shipment and put them into the car, which had been previously ordered, and such servant, without any authority, directed the words "Union Stockyards" to be written on the waybill in pencil under the names of the consignees, whereupon the hogs were delivered to the stockyards company. Held, that defendant was not authorized to make such delivery, and that the same constituted a conversion of the hogs. Southern Ry. Co. *v.* Webb, 39 So. 262, 143 Ala. 304.

Failure of a shipper to accompany his hogs and unload them on arrival at destination, as provided by the contract of affreightment, did not relieve the carrier from liability for misdelivery. Southern Ry. Co. *v.* Webb, 39 So. 262, 143 Ala. 304.

Effect of Right to Lien on Liability for Misdelivery.—Where a carrier instead of delivering certain hogs to the consignees, delivered them to a stockyards company, and thereby converted them, it was immaterial to the carrier's liability that it was entitled to retain the hogs until the freight was paid. Southern Ry. Co. *v.* Webb, 39 So. 262, 143 Ala. 304.

Recovery of Freight Charges in Absence of Evidence of Payment.—In an action against a railroad company for failure to deliver certain live stock alleged to have been received by defendant as carrier, plaintiff could not recover freight charges, in the absence of any evidence that such charges had been paid. Johnson *v.* Alabama, etc., R. Co., 140 Ala. 412, 37 So. 226.

§ 133. Delay in Transportation or Delivery.

Liability for Effect on Propensities of Animals.—A carrier is liable for all injury done to live stock in transportation that is referable to negligent delay in transporting them, through the effect of such delay upon the physical condition, or latent vicious propensities, of the animals, whereby they are reduced in weight, and injure each other. Richmond & D. R. Co. *v.* Trousdale, 99 Ala. 389, 13 So. 23.

§ 134. Loss or Injury.

§ 135. —— Liability in General.

A carrier assumes the same responsibility for the safe carriage and delivery of animals as in the carriage of other property, except injuries resulting from the nature, habits, propensities, viciousness, or other inherent qualities of the animals. Louisville & N. R. Co. *v.* Smitha, 40 So. 117, 145 Ala. 686, cited in note in 18 L. R. A., N. S., 91.

Conversion by Third Person.—Under a bill of lading for shipment of live stock, providing that the shipper should load, unload, feed, and water the stock while in transit, and that any expense incurred by the carrier in feeding, watering, etc., should be assessed against the stock, where the carrier employed a third person to unload, etc., it was its duty to see that the third person performed his duty; and it was liable for a conversion of two of the animals by the third person. Nashville, etc., Railway *v.* Hinds, 5 Ala. App. 596, 59 So. 670.

Live Stock Awaiting Delivery.—Responsibility of a carrier as regards injury to a shipment of horses is not terminated by arrival at destination of the car containing them, or by the placing of it on the side track there, but continues till delivery, actual or constructive, of the car to the consignee, or till they have a reasonable time, after knowledge or notice of arrival, to call for and receive the horses. Alabama, etc., R. Co. *v.* Gewin & Son, 5 Ala. App. 584, 59 So. 553.

§ 136. —— Inherent Qualities, Propensities, or Defects.

A carrier undertaking the transportation of live animals, in the absence of a special contract, is chargeable on its common-law liability for their safe delivery, but is not responsible for loss or injuries resulting from their nature or propensities. South & N. A. R. Co. *v.* Henlein, 52 Ala. 606; East Tennessee, etc., R. Co. *v.* Johnston, 75 Ala. 596; Louisville, etc., R. Co. *v.* Smitha, 145 Ala. 686, 40 So. 117; Central R., etc., Co. *v.* Smitha, 85 Ala. 47, 4 So. 708; Western Railway *v.* Harwell, 91 Ala. 340, 8 So. 649; Atlantic, etc., R. Co. *v.* Rice, 169 Ala. 265, 52 So. 918, 919. See note in 18 L. R. A., N. S., 91.

Effect on Propensities Caused by Delay.—See ante, "Delay in Transportation or Delivery," § 133.

Disease Developing after Delivery.—In an action against a carrier for damages to a dog in transportation, an instruction to find for defendant if the consignee receipted for the dog in good condition, and after such receipt the dog developed disease from which it died, is properly refused, since such request did not include as a necessary element of defendant's nonliability that the disease did not originate from injury received in the transportation. Southern Exp. Co. *v.* Ashford, 28 So. 732, 126 Ala. 591.

§ 137. —— Contributory Negligence of Owner.

That a shipper of dogs delivered them to a carrier in a crate which was insufficient, so that a dog escaped, was not negligence exonerating the carrier; the defense of contributory negligence not being available in such case. Atlantic Coast Line R. Co. *v.* Rice, 52 So. 918, 169 Ala. 265.

Proximate Cause of Injury.—The plaintiff shipped a stallion in a freight car of the defendant, and to insure ventilation left the side door open, nailing some strips of board across the opening. The slats were kicked off, and the stallion escaped uninjured, and, after wandering some distance, strayed upon the track at another point, and was killed by defendant's train. Held, that the plaintiff's negligence resulting in the liberation of the animal was not the proximate cause of the injury, and would not preclude a recovery. Louisville & N. R. Co. *v.* Kelsey, 89 Ala. 287, 7 So. 648.

§ 138. Limitation of Liability.

See, also, ante, "Limitation of Liability," II, (H).

§ 138 (1) Power to Limit Liability in General.

Where a carrier of live stock is entitled to limit its common-law liability by a contract of affreightment, it can not exempt itself by contract from the negligence of its servants. Louisville & N. R. Co. *v.* Smitha, 40 So. 117, 145 Ala. 686, cited in note in 18 L. R. A., N. S., 91; Atlantic, etc., R. Co. *v.* Dothan Mule Co., 161 Ala. 341, 49 So. 882.

Special contracts made by common carriers with shippers of cattle, restricting and avoiding their liability for the unusual risks peculiar to the transportation of such freight, are maintained and upheld by the courts, when the limitations are just and reasonable, and do not exempt the carriers from liability from any loss or injury caused by their own act or negligence. East Tennessee, etc., R. Co. *v.* Johnston, 75 Ala. 596.

Though shippers of live stock agree to release the carrier from liability for all loss or damage to such stock which is not the result of the willful negligence of its agents, the carrier is liable for damages arising from its own or its servants' negligence. Louisville & N. R. Co. *v.* Grant, 99 Ala. 325, 13 So. 599.

Exemption from Liability for Negligence Less than Gross.—An exception imposed by carriers of cattle relieving them from all liability for negligence less than gross is invalid. East Tennessee, V. & G. R. Co. *v.* Johnston, 75 Ala. 596. See, to the same effect, Alabama, etc., R. Co. *v.* Thomas, 83 Ala. 343, 3 So. 802. See note in 19 L. R. A., N. S., 1012.

§ 138 (2) Power to Limit Extent of Liability.

See, also, post, "Operation and Effect of Limitation of Amount of Liability," § 138 (6).

Where the bill of lading issued by a railroad company on receipt of a horse for transportation contains a stipulation that, in consideration of reduced rates, liability of the carrier shall be limited to the value of the horse expressed therein, such stipulation is void as against public policy in case the value so stated is greatly below the true value, whether the carrier is informed of the true value or not. Southern Ry. Co. *v.* Jones, 31 So. 501, 132 Ala. 437.

Injuries Resulting from Negligence.—While a carrier of live stock may by special contract with a shipper qualify its common-law liability, both as to risk of accident and as to the amount of damages, if the limitation is made to secure a reasonable and just proportion between liability and compensation, it can not contract for immunity from liability for the loss of, or injury to, property resulting from its own or its servant's negligence. Atlantic, etc., R. Co. *v.* Dothan Mule Co., 161 Ala. 341, 49 So. 882.

Limitations of Amount Held Valid.—A stipulation in a contract for the shipment of a car load of mules that, in consideration of a reduced rate of freight, the carrier shall in no case be liable for more than $100 for a mule, is valid. Western Ry. Co. *v.* Harwell, 91 Ala. 340, 8 So. 649; S. C., 97 Ala. 341, 11 So. 781.

A common carrier and the owner of live stock made a special contract, wherein it was agreed that, in consideration of reduced rates and a free pass to the owner, the latter should attend the stock and care for it, at his own expense, in case of accidents, and that the value at the time and place of shipment, not to exceed $50 per head for ordinary beef cattle, should be the measure of recovery for any loss for which the carrier might be liable. Held, that the contract was reasonable and valid; and that the carrier, if not wanting in the diligence required of him, was not liable for losses occasioned by the owner's inattention to the duties undertaken by him. South & N. A. R. Co. *v.* Henlein, 52 Ala. 606, cited in note in 14 L. R. A. 434.

Where stock is received by a common carrier for transportation, it may stipulate in consideration of reduced rates, and a free passage to the owner of the stock or his agent, that, upon damage to the stock for which the carrier would be liable, the value at the place and date of shipment shall govern in the settlement, in which the amount claimed shall not exceed $150 for a horse or mule, $50 for cattle, and $25 for other animals. South & N. A. R. Co. *v.* Henlein, 56 Ala. 368.

§ 138 (3) Power to Impose Conditions with Regard to Giving Notice of Loss.

A stipulation of a shipping contract that, as a condition precedent to recovery of damages for loss or injury, the shipper must give notice before removing the live stock, and before mingling them with other stock, and that such notice must be served within one day after delivery at destination, being unreasonable and contrary to law, was void. Nashville, etc., Railway *v.* Hinds (Ala. App.), 60 So. 409.

§ 138 (4) Power to Impose Duties on Shipper as to Care of Stock.

A carrier of live stock may make a special contract with the shipper, whereby the latter assumes the duty of guarding the stock against such risks as might be incurred by a lack of proper bedding in the car. Louisville, etc., R. Co. *v.* Shepherd (Ala. App.), 61 So. 14.

There is nothing unreasonable in the provision of a special contract made by a railroad company for the transportation of cattle, by which the owner assumes the duty of loading, transferring and unloading the cattle; and for any injury caused by overloading or other improper loading, the company, if without fault or negligence on its part, is not liable. East Tennessee, etc., R. Co. *v.* Johnston, 75 Ala. 596, 597, cited in note in 23 L. R. A., N. S., 278, 279.

§ 138 (5) Operation and Effect of Limitations in General.

The execution and delivery to the carrier, after the animal shipped was dead, of a paper called "Limited Liability Live Stock Contract," which does not purport to be a release of damages, does not affect the shipper's right to recover for the loss. Southern Express Co. *v.* Ramey, 51 So. 314, 164 Ala. 206.

Release in Transportation Contract of

Accrued Damages Resulting from Carrier's Negligence.—A contract for the transportation of live stock provided that, in consideration of a reduced rate, the shipper released all causes of action for any damages that had accrued to him by any prior written or verbal contract concerning the stock. Held, that an action to recover for injuries to stock sustained while in the carrier's stock pens awaiting transportation arrangements, and one the day before the execution of the contract set out, being based on the carrier's negligence in the performance of duties imposed upon it by law, and without regard to the will or contract of the carrier, was not affected by the release contained in the subsequent freight contract. St. Louis & S. F. R. Co. *v.* Cavender, 170 Ala. 601, 54 So. 54.

§ 138 (6) Operation and Effect of Limitation of Amount of Liability.

Where Goods Misdelivered.—A provision in a contract for shipment of hogs that, should damage occur for which the carrier might be liable, the value at the place and date of shipment should govern the settlement, in which the amount claimed should not exceed $5 for each hog, had no application to a chain for damages for misdelivery, and did not prevent plaintiff from recovering damages, consisting of a fall in the market price at the place of destination. Southern Ry. Co. *v.* Webb. 39 So. 262, 143 Ala. 304, cited in note in 31 L. R. A., N. S., 310.

Stallion Killed by Defendant's Train after Escape from Car.—Plaintiff shipped a stallion in a freight car of defendant's, and to insure ventilation left the side door open, nailing some strips of board across the opening. The slats were kicked off, and the stallion escaped uninjured, and, after wandering some distance, strayed upon the track at another point, and was killed by defendant's train. Held, that the measure of damages is the value of the horse, and is not limited by the terms of the shipping contract, which stipulated that, for any injuries resulting from a failure of the company to perform its conditions, "the amount claimed should not exceed for a stallion or jack, $200." Louisville & N. R. Co. *v.* Kelsey, 89 Ala. 287, 7 So. 648.

§ 138 (7) Operation and Effect of Stipulations Requiring Shipper to Load, Unload, and Care for Stock.

Where defendant agreed, in consideration of being released from all liability except for fraud and gross negligence, to transport horses at a reduced rate, the shipper to have free passage on the train with the horses, and to care for them through the route, it is not liable for injury to the horses caused by want of proper care on the route, though it allowed the shipper to ride on its passenger train. Central Railroad & Banking Co. *v.* Smitha, 85 Ala. 47, 4 So. 708, cited in note in 18 L. R. A., N. S., 91.

A shipper, having assumed, by special contract, the duty of proper storage of his cattle, and having accepted and loaded the car without objection, and with knowledge that it was not bedded, can not hold the company liable for negligence because of a failure to bed the car, or because of the insufficiency of the bedding. In such case, by his contract he virtually agrees that, in respect of the particular transaction, the carrier is not to be regarded as in the exercise of his public employment, but as a private person, who incurs no responsibility beyond that of an ordinary bailee or hire, and answerable, only for misconduct or negligence. East Tennessee, etc., R. Co. *v.* Johnston, 75 Ala. 596, 597, cited in note in 23 L. R. A., N. S., 278, 279.

Where a shipper of cattle contracts with a railroad company for the use of a car for the transportation of cattle, having reference to the cars in use on the defendant's road, in the absence of any stipulation for any particular kind of car, the extent of the company's obligation is to furnish a safe, serviceable and adequate car, adapted to the use intended; and the shipper retaining control and charge of the cattle, and assuming the risk and responsibility of loading, his understanding of the contract may be inferred from the fact that he had provided material for bedding the car; and the company will not be held liable for any loss or injury arising from his fault or neglect in this regard. East Tennessee, etc., R. Co. *v.* Johnston, 75 Ala. 596, cited in note in 23 L. R. A., N. S., 278, 279.

Interstate Shipments.—Under Act Cong. June 29, 1906, c. 3594, 34 Stat. 607 (U. S. Comp. St. Supp. 1909, p. 1178), which prohibits the confining of animals in cars for more than 28 consecutive hours without unloading them in a humane manner into properly equipped pens for rest, water, and food, at the costs of the shipper, or on his default by the carrier, with a right to a lien for food furnished, where a shipment of cattle is interstate, the carrier can not by any contract with the shipper relieve itself from the duty of feeding and watering the animals in a proper case. And a failure of the shipper in an interstate shipment to perform the duty imposed upon it is negligence per se. Southern R. Co. *v.* Proctor, 3 Ala. App. 413, 57 So. 513.

Failure to Give Shipper Opportunity to Comply with Contract.—A railroad company, which, without giving the shipper an opportunity to attend to the loading, puts cattle carried over its own line in cars furnished by another company, hauls them over a connecting track, and then delivers to it, is liable, in tort for breach of duty growing out of the contract of shipment, for injuries in transit over the second line, caused by negligence at the time of the transfer in not supplying bedding and partitions, and in overcrowding, though the contract of shipment limits the carrier's liability to "gross or wanton negligence," and to that of a forwarding agent only in delivering to the next line, and provides that the shipper is to load and unload and care for the cattle. Alabama G. S. R. Co. *v.* Thomas, 89 Ala. 294, 7 So. 762, cited in notes in 19 L. R. A., N. S., 1012, 23 L. R. A., N. S., 279, 31 L. R. A., N. S., 80, 84.

A carrier is not relieved from liability for damages to a shipment of cattle from want of proper care by a stipulation of the shipping contract that the shipper will load and unload the cattle and care for them while awaiting shipment or delivery at feeding or transfer points en route, or when unloaded for any purpose, and will pay the carrier for any expense incurred in caring for the stock, where it does not appear that the shipper or his agent were permitted to or did accompany the cattle, or were notified where, when, and how the cattle would be stopped for feed and water. Nashville, etc., Railway *v.* Hinds (Ala. App.), 60 So. 409.

Effect on Duty to Provide Proper Means for Unloading and Waiver of Provision.—A contract for shipment of live stock, providing that the shipper should load and unload the stock at his risk, would not exempt the carrier from liability for failure to prepare proper chutes for unloading the stock, especially where it waived the provision by unloading the stock itself and without insisting upon its performance by the shipper. Atlantic, etc., R. Co. *v.* Dothan Mule Co., 161 Ala. 341, 49 So. 882.

Failure of Shipper to Comply with Contract Not Contributing to Injury.—Where a contract for the shipment of live stock required the shipper or his agent to ride on the freight train on which the animals were being transported, the shipper's failure so to do was no defense to the carrier's liability for injuries to the stock, unless such failure contributed thereto. Louisville & N. R. Co. *v.* Smitha, 40 So. 117, 145 Ala. 686.

§ 138 (8) Operation and Effect of Stipulation for Notice of Claim for Damages.

Effect of Statute on Failure to Give Notice.—Under an express provision of Code 1907, a shipper's failure to give notice in writing of a claim for loss or injury to live stock before removing it or intermingling it with other live stock, does not defeat his action therefor. Northern Alabama Ry. Co. *v.* Bidgood, 5 Ala. App. 658, 59 So. 680.

Injuries Not Discovered before Removal—Notice Given on Discovery.—Where a bill of lading for a shipment of cattle provides that the shipper, as a prerequisite to any right to recover for injury to the cattle, shall, before removal of the cattle from the place of delivery, and before their mingling with other cattle, give written notice of any damages, the requirement is complied with where the shipper does not discover injuries, and could not have done so, before removal, but he gives notice thereof within a reasonably short time after discovery of the injury. Louisville & N. R. Co. *v.* Landers, 33 So. 482, 135 Ala. 504.

That an owner to whom a bill of lading has been issued gives written notice of injury to certain cattle before their removal does not preclude him from the right of giving additional notice of other injuries within a reasonable time after their discovery. Louisville & N. R. Co. *v.* Landers, 33 So. 482, 135 Ala. 504.

Where the contract stipulates that the shipper must notify the company's agent in writing of a claim for injury before removing the animals from the place of delivery, the shipper has a reasonable time after the removal, in case the injury is not then discovered by ordinary diligence, in which to give the notice; and where he removes the animals December 29th, and notifies the agent January 4th, it is a question for the jury whether the notice was given in a reasonable time. Western Railway *v.* Harwell, 91 Ala. 340, 8 So. 649, affirmed in Western R. Co. *v.* Harwell, 97 Ala. 341, 11 So. 781.

Application to Claim for Misdelivery.—A provision in a contract of affreightment that it should be a condition precedent to the right of the shipper to recover damage for loss or injury to the live stock that he give notice in writing of his claim to the agent of the carrier actually delivering the stock to him, whether at destination or at any intermediate point where the same may be actually delivered, before the stock is removed from the place of destination and before the stock is intermingled with other stock, has no application to a claim for damages for misdelivery. Southern Ry. Co. *v.* Webb, 39 So. 262, 143 Ala. 304.

Injuries for Recovery Not Included in Notice.—Where, under a bill of lading requiring written notice of injury before removal, the only notice given the carrier as to the death of cattle was for certain cattle that had died before removal, the shipper could not recover for cattle that died after the removal. Louisville & N. R. Co. *v.* Landers, 33 So. 482, 135 Ala. 504.

§ 138 (9) Waiver of Notice or of Defects Therein.

Where defendant carrier denied any right of plaintiff to look to it for damages for injury to plaintiff's cattle complained of, because plaintiff had no contract with defendant, such denial was inconsistent with an intention on defendant's part to recognize any contractual liability to plaintiff if the stipulation for notice was complied with, and was therefore a waiver of plaintiff's compliance with such stipulation. Louisville, etc., R. Co. *v.* Shepherd (Ala. App.), 61 So. 14.

§ 139. Connecting Carriers.

§ 139 (1) In General.

When a railroad company, as a common carrier, receives cattle for transportation over its road, to be delivered at its terminus to the next connecting road, and hence by other connecting roads to the place of destination in other state, the duty of the receiving road is limited to the safe transportation of the cattle over its own road, and their proper delivery at the terminus of its road to the next connecting road. Alabama, etc., R. Co. *v.* Thomas, 83 Ala. 343, 3 So. 802, cited in notes in 19 L. R. A., N. S., 1012, 23 L. R. A., N. S., 279, 31 L. R. A., N. S., 80, 84.

§ 139 (2) Delay in Transportation or Delivery.

Duty on Refusal of Connecting Carrier to Receive.—Where a connecting carrier, over whose line a shipment of live stock was routed, refused to accept the same, it was the duty of the initial carrier to notify the consignor of such fact, and obtain further shipping directions, unless the property was of such a perishable nature that the delay would be calculated to injure or destroy it. Louisville & N. R. Co. *v.* Duncan & Orr, 34 So. 988, 137 Ala. 446; Southern R. Co. *v.* Wallace, 175 Ala. 72, 56 So. 714. See notes in 19 L. R. A., N. S., 1012, 31 L. R. A., N. S., 87.

Section of Circuitous Route after Refusal of Connecting Carrier to Receive.—Where a connecting carrier, over whose line a shipment was routed, refused to receive and transport the same, in the absence of notice of such refusal to the consignor, the initial carrier was liable for the exercise of ordinary care and prudence in selecting another carrier to transport the consignment, and was liable for injuries to the consignment caused by delay resulting from the selection of a carrier having a circuitous route, which might have been avoided. Louisville & N. R. Co. *v.* Duncan & Orr, 34 So. 988, 137 Ala. 446, cited in notes in 19 L. R. A., N. S., 1012, 31 L. R. A., N. S., 87.

§ 139 (3) Validity of Contract Limiting Liability.

A railroad company receiving cattle for transportation as a common carrier can not limit its liability to injuries caused by "gross or wanton negligence," or to that of a mere agent of the consignor in the matter of delivering the cattle to the next connecting road; such stipulations being contrary to public policy. Alabama G. S. R. Co. *v.* Thomas, 83 Ala. 343, 3 So. 802, cited in note in 31 L. R. A., N. S., 56.

§ 139 (4) Operation and Effect of Limitation.

Right of Subsequent Carrier to Benefit by Limitation of First Carrier.—Where the shipper of a car load of mules signed a contract purporting to be made with the receiving carrier "and its connecting lines," releasing the carriers from liability for any damage not caused by their negligence, and providing that its terms shall inure to the benefit of connecting lines, unless they stipulate otherwise, a connecting carrier, which receives and transports the mules in the same car under this contract, is entitled to the benefit of its exemptions, notwithstanding no rate for the entire distance is fixed by it. Western Ry. Co. *v.* Harwell, 91 Ala. 340, 8 So. 649; S. C., 97 Ala. 341, 11 So. 781.

Plea—Ratification and Acceptance.—In an action against a connecting carrier for an injury to stock while in its possession, a plea that the waybill showed that the mules were shipped "at a release rate, which was a reduced rate of freight," is not equivalent to an allegation that defendant accepted and ratified a contract made by the original carrier releasing it and connecting carriers at their option from liability for damages not caused by negligence. Western Ry. Co. *v.* Harwell, 97 Ala. 341, 11 So. 781.

Act of Agent at Connecting Point as Relieving Shipper from Duty Imposed by Bill.—An agent at a station at which cattle are to be turned over by one railroad company to another, who has authority to keep them in the original cars, or to transfer to others, acts in the scope of his employment in telling the shipper that there will be no change, and thereby relieves him of the duty imposed by the bill of lading of preparing and loading the cars. Alabama G. S. R. Co. *v.* Thomas, 89 Ala. 294, 7 So. 762, cited in notes in 19 L. R. A., N. S., 1012; 23 L. R. A., N. S., 279; 31 L. R. A., N. S., 80, 84.

§ 140. Actions against Carriers of Live Stock.

§ 141. —— Nature and Form.

As to action being in tort or on the contract, see the title CONTRACTS.

Where, upon the carrier's inability to ship the stock to destination because of quarantine, they were shipped back to the original shipping point and tendered to the shipper, when he declined to receive them and directed the carrier to do whatever it saw fit, and the stock were sold and the money held for the shipper, he could not recover as for a conversion of the stock at the original shipping point. Southern R. Co. *v.* Wallace, 175 Ala. 72, 56 So. 714.

§ 142. —— Rights of Action.

Stock Returned to Shipping Point Because of Quarantine Regulations.—If the shipper directed that cattle be returned to the original shipping point from an intermediate point upon the carrier's inability to forward them to destination because of quarantine, he could not recover from the carrier for their conversion at such intermediate point. Southern Ry. Co. *v.* Wallace, 175 Ala. 72, 56 So. 714.

Who May Sue.—Where plaintiff's agent, without disclosing his agency, shipped her horse over defendant's road under a contract in which such agent was named as both consignor and consignee, and the horse, while being so carried, was injured by defendant's negligence, plaintiff, as owner, may recover the damages for such injury. Southern R. Co. *v.* Jones, 132 Ala. 437, 31 So. 501, 502.

§ 143. —— Defenses.

Failure to Deliver Caused by Act of Shipper.—If a shipper contracted for the transportation of cattle and a horse in one car, and the shipment of the cattle was prevented by legal quarantine, and the shipper refused to permit the horse to be shipped separately, he could not recover against the carrier for failure to deliver the horse at destination. Southern R. Co. *v.* Wallace, 175 Ala. 72, 56 So. 714.

Receipt—Failure to Examine at Time of Delivery.—In an action against a carrier for damages to a dog in transportation, that the consignee removed the dog at its destination in the agent's absence and receipted for it in good condition is not a conclusive defense against recovery, where the consignee had not examined the dog at the time of giving such receipt. Southern Exp. Co. *v.* Ashford, 28 So. 732, 126 Ala. 591.

§ 144. —— Pleading.

§ 144 (1) Complaint.

Code From—Negligence as Implied.—Where a complaint against a carrier was in the form prescribed by Code, p. 946, negligence of the carrier is a legal implication where negligence is essential to fix liability, though the words of the form do not expressly aver negligence. Nashville, C. & St. L. Ry. Co. *v.* Parker, 27 So. 323, 123 Ala. 683.

Complaint Substantially Following Statute.—Under Code 1907, § 5382, form 15, which provides the form of complaint on a bill of lading of a common carrier as follows: "The plaintiff claims of the defendant —— dollars for the failure to deliver certain goods," etc.—a complaint which charges "that the defendant failed to deliver cattle" intrusted to it for carriage by the consignor, "within a reasonable time and that by reason of such delay the plaintiff was damaged," substantially follows the statutory charge of breach of duty, and is sufficient. Southern R. Co. *v.* Proctor, 3 Ala. App. 413, 57 So. 513.

Averment as to Assumption of Duties as Common Carrier.—A complaint which alleges that the plaintiff "delivered to the defendant as a common carrier" a carload of cattle "to be shipped * * * for hire" sufficiently charges that the defendant, as a common carrier, assumed the duties of that relation to the plaintiff as a person interested in the stock shipped. Southern R. Co. *v.* Proctor, 3 Ala. App. 413, 57 So. 513.

A complaint which claims damages for injuries to a carload of cattle "shipped by the defendant as a common carrier for hire for the plaintiff" sufficiently charges that the defendant as a common carrier undertook for hire the carriage of the property for the plaintiff as a person interested in the goods shipped. Southern R. Co. *v.* Proctor, 3 Ala. App. 413, 57 So. 513.

Alternative Averments.—Where the complaint in an action against a carrier for injuries to live stock charged alternatively that it was either the duty of defendant, the initial carrier, to transport the stock to destination on its own lines, or to deliver the stock at some unidentified point to a connecting carrier having a direct route from the junction point to destination, and that the loss resulted from defendant's failure to perform the carriage itself, or from its failure to forward the consignment by a connecting carrier having a direct route, such alternative averments did not constitute a statement of either cause of action, and the complaint was demurrable. Louisville & N. R. Co. *v.* Duncan & Orr, 34 So. 988, 137 Ala. 446.

Alternative Averment Held Good.—A complaint in an action against a carrier of live stock for alleged injuries to plaintiff's live stock, which alleges in the alternative that defendant or its servant or agent received the live stock without averring that such servant or agent in receiving the live stock was acting for the defendant within the scope of his employment, is good on demurrer. St. Louis, etc., R. Co. *v.* Cavender, 170 Ala. 601, 54 So. 54.

Necessity for Alleging Defensive Matter.—Where the complaint, in an action for delay in transporting live stock, bases the right of recovery upon the defendant's breach of a contract to transport the stock on a certain train, the fact that such contract was not made, or was subsequently modified or merged into another contract, was defensive matter, the absence of which, from the complaint, did not render it demurrable on that ground. Louisville & N. R. Co. *v.* Jones, 6 Ala. App. 617, 60 So. 945.

Effect of Averment of Further and Cumulative Negligence.—Where a complaint in an action to recover for injuries sustained to live stock has stated a cause of action for negligence of the carrier in caring for the live stock after it had received them preparatory to transportation, the nature of the pleading is not affected by the fact that the pleader adds an averment of further and cumulative negligence also affecting the safe receipt and keeping of the animals for shipment by alleging that an agent of defendant operating a train negligently blew the whistle of his engine as a proximate consequence of which plaintiff's live stock were greatly scattered and damaged. St. Louis, etc., R. Co. *v.* Cavender, 170 Ala. 601, 54 So. 54.

In an action against a carrier, where the complaint stated a good cause of action for damages for the carrier's negligence in caring for live stock while held by it, pending the arrangement for its transportation, the addition as a part of one of the good counts of an averment of negligence also affecting the safe receipt and keeping of the live stock for shipment by alleging that a servant of the defendant operating a train negligently blew the whistle of his engine, as a proximate consequence of which the live stock was frightened and damaged, without alleging that the engineer was engaged in defendant's business when he blew the whistle, is good as against a demurrer to the entire count, in view of the statute which requires pleadings to be as brief as is consistent with clearness. St. Louis, etc., R. Co. *v.* Cavender, 170 Ala. 601, 54 So. 54.

§ 144 (2) Plea.

Averment as to Terms of Special Contract.—In an action against a carrier for injuries to a horse while in transit, a plea alleging that the horse was shipped under a special contract, but tendering the mere naked conclusion of the pleader as to the construction of the contract without referring to its substance or indicating what terms of the contract relieved the defendant from liability, and giving no facts to enable the court to determine the validity of the contract or the correctness of the pleader's construction of it, was insufficient. Nashville, etc., R. Co. *v.* Parker, 123 Ala. 683, 27 So. 323.

Plea as to Undertaking by Shipper to Provide Bedding.—In an action for injuries to live stock en route, a plea, after alleging that the animals were shipped under a special contract, made in consideration of a reduced rate, by which plaintiff agreed, at his own expense, to provide such bedding or other suitable appliances in the car as would enable the animals to stand securely on their feet, and that plaintiff failed to provide such bedding, and the animals were injured by reason thereof, was not defective as amounting to a guaranty by the shipper that the animals would stand securely while in the car, without reference to violent shocks or rough usage to which they might be exposed by the negligent handling of the train. Louisville, etc., R. Co. *v.* Shepherd (Ala. App.), 61 So. 14.

Averment as to Failure to Give Notice.—Where a contract for the transportation of 28 mules provided that, as a condition precedent to the owner's right to recover any damages for loss or injury thereto, the owner or person in charge should give notice in writing of his claim to some officer of the delivering road or its nearest station agent, before the stock was removed from destination or place of delivery and before it was mingled with other stock, pleas in an action for the carrier's failure to deliver one of the mules, alleging that neither the owner nor the person in charge of the stock on his behalf gave any notice in writing of the loss of the mule before removal of the remainder from the place of destination, and that neither defendant nor its agent at destination counted the mules, and did not know the number that were in the car, nor that one was alleged to have been missing, stated a valid defense to the action. Central of Georgia Ry. Co. *v.* Henderson, 44 So. 542, 152 Ala. 203.

Failure to Allege That Carrier's Negligence Did Not Contribute to Injury.—A plea that plaintiff's cattle were injured by reason of being weak, or overloading, suffocation, heat, fright, or viciousness, within a provision of the shipping contract releasing the carrier from liability for injuries so caused, was fatally defective for failure to further allege that defendant's negligence in transporting the cattle did not contribute to the injury. Louisville, etc., R. Co. *v.* Shepherd (Ala. App.), 61 So. 14.

In an action against a carrier for injuries to animals en route, a plea that under a special contract plaintiff agreed to furnish suitable bedding to enable the animals to stand securely, and that they were injured by plaintiff's failure to do so, was fatally defective for failing to further allege that defendant's own negligence did not contribute to the result. Louisville, etc., R. Co. *v.* Shepherd (Ala. App.), 61 So. 14.

§ 144 (3) Replication.

In an action for injuries to stock in transit, the plea alleged failure to comply with the requirement in the shipping contract of notice to the carrier of the claim, and the replication averred that within the time allowed by the contract plaintiff's agent made a claim upon the defendant, and that defendant denied any liability, on the ground that plaintiff's remedy was against the initial carrier. Held, that the replication was good against a demurrer, on the ground that it did not show that the notice was given to, and the denial of liability was made by, an agent authorized by the terms of the shipping contract to bind defendant. Louisville, etc., R. Co. *v.* Shepherd (Ala. App.), 61 So. 14.

§ 144 (4) Issues, Proof, and Variance.

Complaint in Code Form—Proof of Special Contract.—Where, in an action against a carrier for breach of a contract for the transportation of hogs, plaintiff's first count in his complaint was in the Code form, he was entitled to recover thereon, though the evidence showed that the shipment was made under bills of lading containing special stipulations. Southern Ry. Co. *v.* Webb, 39 So. 262, 143 Ala. 304, following Louisville, etc., R. Co. *v.* Landers, 135 Ala. 504, 33 So. 482, which overrules Nashville, etc., R. Co. *v.* Parker, 123 Ala. 683, 27 So. 323.

Where the complaint claims damages of a carrier for injuries to cattle transported over its road under a written contract, which bound defendant to deliver safely at the terminus of its road to the next connecting company, while the proof shows that the cattle, having been safely carried to the terminus of defendant's road, and there delivered to the next connecting road, were then put into unfit cars, in violation of the promise of defendant's depot agent that the cars should not be changed, and were afterwards injured before reaching their destination, even if defendant is liable for the promise of its agent, there is a fatal variance between allegations and proof. Alabama G. S. R. Co. *v.* Thomas, 83 Ala. 343, 3 So. 802.

Failure to Give Food, Water, etc., Substantially Shown.—Where a complaint against a carrier for damages to a dog in transportation avers the injury was occasioned by failure to give him proper attention in the matter of food, water, and exercise, defendant's liability is established by proof of failure to give an adequate supply of such things, though it may have given some of them. Southern Exp. Co. *v.* Ashford, 28 So. 732, 126 Ala. 591.

§ 145. —— Evidence.

§ 145 (1) Presumptions and Burden of Proof.

§ 145 (1a) In General.

Presumption of Authority of Agent.—Station agents are presumed to have power to make contracts for the transportation of freight and to do whatever is necessary to forward it, and where an agent at a station on a railroad holding itself out as a carrier of live stock receives into the carrier's stock yards cattle delivered there for future shipment he must be taken, prima facie at least, as acting within the scope of his duty. St. Louis, etc., R. Co. *v.* Cavender, 170 Ala. 601, 54 So. 54.

Prima Facie Case.—In an action against a carrier for loss of an animal in transit, plaintiff establishes a prima facie case by proof of delivery of the animal to defendant and its failure to redeliver the same, and the burden is then on defendant to rebut the presumption of negligence from the fact of loss. Southern Express Co. *v.* Ramey, 51 So. 314, 164 Ala. 206.

Evidence in an action against an express company for the death of an animal in transit held to place on defendant the burden of rebutting the presumption that the loss was the result of its negligence. Southern Express Co. *v.* Ramey, 51 So. 314, 164 Ala. 206.

Burden of Showing Want of Negligence.—Where plaintiff has shown injury to live stock while in the custody of a carrier, the burden is on the carrier to show that it did not result from any negligence on the part of its servants or agents, or that it was within one of the specified exceptions to the contract of affreightment. Louisville & N. R. Co. *v.* Smitha, 40 So. 117, 145 Ala. 686; Alabama, etc., R. Co. *v.* Gewin & Son, 5 Ala. App. 584, 59 So. 553.

Where a contract by the shipper of a car load of mules provides that the railroad company shall not be liable for any damage not resulting from its own negligence, the burden of proof, in an action for injury to the mules, remains on the company to show that the injury did not result from its negligence, and it is proper to refuse to charge that if defendant has shown that its car, track, and equipments were adequate, and that there was no negligence on its part, the fact that it does not appear how the injury occurred is not sufficient to fix liability on defendant, but that the burden of proof is on plaintiff to show that the injury resulted from defendant's act. Western Ry. Co. *v.* Harwell, 91 Ala. 340, 8 So. 649, cited in note in 17 L. R. A. 340.

Showing Injuries Not to Have Occurred While in Possession of Carrier.—Where, in an action for injury to a shipment of stock, the uncontradicted evidence showed the relation of shipper and common carrier, the burden was on the carrier to prove that the stock were not injured while in its custody. Nashville, etc., Railway *v.* Hinds (Ala. App.), 60 So. 409.

Showing That Delay Did Not Cause Injuries.—Where there is unreasonable delay on the part of a carrier in transporting live stock, and the stock, when delivered, is found to be in an unsound condition, the burden is on the carrier to show that such unsound condition is not due to the unreasonable delay. Richmond & D. R. Co. *v.* Trousdale, 99 Ala. 389, 13 So. 23. See to same effect Louisville & N. R. Co. *v.* Smitha, 40 So. 117, 145 Ala. 686.

Showing Injury after Delivery to Second Carrier.—In an action against the second of two connecting carriers for nondelivery of stock shipped, the burden is on plaintiff to show that the injury occurred after the animals came into the possession of defendant. Western Ry. Co. *v.* Harwell, 97 Ala. 341, 11 So. 781.

§ 145 (1b) Limitation of Liability.

Presumption of Assent to Contract.—A recital in a contract, framed as a limitation of the liability of a carrier of live stock, that the rate is a reduced rate is prima facie evidence of that fact, and the shipper having executed the contract, in the absence of fraud or mistake alleged, is presumed to have known and consented to its terms. St. Louis, etc., R. Co. *v.* Cavender, 170 Ala. 601, 54 So. 54.

Showing Injuries to Be within Exemption Clause.—Injury to a horse while in the custody of defendant as a carrier being shown, it has the burden of showing that it happened without its fault, or under such circumstances that by a valid provision of the contract of shipment it was exempt from liability. Alabama, etc., R. Co. *v.* Gewin & Son, 5 Ala. App. 584, 59 So. 553; Louisville, etc., R. Co. *v.* Smitha, 145 Ala. 686, 40 So. 117.

Showing Car to Be Unsafe Where Contract Recites Examination.—Where a contract by the shipper of a car load of mules recites that the shipper has examined the car, and found it safe and suitable, the burden is on him, in an action for damages, to show that it was unsafe. Western Ry. Co. *v.* Harwell, 91 Ala. 340, 8 So. 649, cited in notes in 17 L. R. A., N. S., 1035, 36 L. R. A., N. S., 412.

Notice as Condition Precedent.—In an action against a terminal carrier for injuries to cattle, burden was on defendant to establish a plea setting up, as a condition of plaintiff's right to recover, his duty to give notice, in writing, of his claim to some officer of defendant, or its nearest station agent, before the stock was removed, and alleging a failure to comply therewith, on which defendant had joined issue by a replication alleging waiver. Louisville, etc., R. Co. *v.* Shepherd (Ala. App.), 61 So. 14.

Ratification of Contract by Connecting Carrier.—Where the shipper of a car load of mules signed a contract purporting to be made with the receiving carrier "and its connecting lines," releasing the carriers from liability for any damage not caused by their negligence, and providing that its terms shall inure to the benefit of all connecting lines, the mere fact that the connecting carrier received and forwarded the mules raises no presumption that it did so under the terms of such contract, and to avail as a defense to an action for injury to the mules a ratification of the contract must be shown. Western Ry. Co. *v.* Harwell, 97 Ala. 341, 11 So. 781.

§ 145 (2) Admissibility of Evidence in General.

Place of Injury.—In an action against a carrier for injuries to a horse in transit, evidence that a bill was presented at the terminus of the journey for feeding the horse at an intermediate station, where it was unloaded for the purpose, was admissible as tending to show where the injury occurred. Nashville, C. & St. L. Ry. Co. *v.* Parker, 27 So. 323, 123 Ala. 683.

Condition of Cattle on Delivery.—In an action against a carrier for failure to deliver cattle within a reasonable time, testimony that they were properly fed and watered before shipment, and were then in good condition, and that ordinarily cattle so shipped would be ready for the market as soon as they had been fed and watered after delivery from the car, together with evidence as to the actual condition of the cattle upon their delivery to the consignees, and as to how long they were kept before they were in condition to be put on the market, was proper. Southern R. Co. *v.* Proctor, 3 Ala. App. 413, 57 So. 513.

Consent of Shipper to Unload Horse.—In an action against a carrier for injuries to a horse while in transit, caused by the horse being unloaded for feeding, where plaintiff testified that such unloading was without his consent, evidence that plaintiff paid the bill for feeding the horse was competent as tending to show that the horse was in fact unloaded with plaintiff's consent. Nashville, C. & St. L. Ry. Co. *v.* Parker, 27 So. 323, 123 Ala. 683.

Custom to Bed Cars.—When a special contract is entered into between a railroad company and the owner of cattle, for the transportation of cattle, and is silent as to the kind of car to be furnished, and as to any special preparation of the car, and, while providing that the shipper shall retain control and charge of the cattle, and assume the risk and responsibility of loading, it is also silent as to what special duties were undertaken by him in these particulars, evidence of a usage or custom, by which it is to bed the car, known to him, and upon which he had acted in making previous shipments, is admissible for the purpose of interpreting and explaining the intention, meaning and understanding of the parties in making the special contract. East Tennessee, etc., R. Co. *v.* Johnston, 75 Ala. 596, 597, cited in note in 18 L. R. A., N. S., 90.

Opinion as to Time of Inquiry.—The opinion that the wound on a horse's head was inflicted 8 or 10 hours before the arrival of the train at G. was relevant on the issue of its infliction when defendant's liability as a carrier had not terminated; there being evidence that such liability continued up to 8 hours before such arrival. Alabama, etc., R. Co. *v.* Gewin & Son, 5 Ala. App. 584, 59 So. 553.

Value of Animal Killed to Show Reasonableness of Limitation.—Evidence of the value of an animal killed during shipment was relevant to show whether the limitation of liability by the shipment contract was grossly unreasonable, or greatly less than the real value. Nashville, etc., Railway *v.* Hinds (Ala. App.), 60 So. 409.

Apparent Good Condition on Delivery to Connecting Carrier.—In an action against a terminal carrier for injuries to live stock, evidence that it had been defendant's general practice not to receive a car of cattle from a connecting carrier without making an objection if any of the cattle were injured, and that the car in question was accepted without objection, was competent to show that the cattle, when received, had not sustained apparent injuries. Louisville, etc., R. Co. *v.* Shepherd (Ala. App.), 61 So. 14.

§ 145 (3) Weight and Sufficiency of Evidence in General.

Number of Mules Received for Shipment.—A carrier's receipt for 28 mules together with the testimony of a witness that his firm operated a stockyard and received the 28 mules to be shipped to plaintiff, and that all of them were delivered to defendant, was sufficient to show that defendant received that number for transportation. Central of Georgia Ry. Co. *v.* Henderson, 44 So. 542, 152 Ala. 203.

Express Company Shown to Be Common Carrier.—That an express company received a dog for transportation for a reward, which was the regular charge for transporting such freight, and that the company was provided with offices and managers along its line, who attended to its freights, is sufficient to show that it was a common carrier, though no witness stated that it was. Southern Exp. Co. *v.* Ashford, 28 So. 732, 126 Ala. 591.

Ratification of Contract by Connecting Carrier.—The contract made between a shipper of a car load of mules and the receiving carrier for transportation from C. to M. and from M. to O. by connecting lines released the carriers from liability for any damage not caused by their negligence, and provided that its terms should inure to the benefit of connecting lines, unless stipulated otherwise. On arriving at O., one of the animals was found to be injured. The evidence showed that defendant received the mules at M., and forwarded them to O. in the same car in which they were shipped from C., and under the same waybill; that the waybill showed that O. was the destination of the car; that the shipment was at owner's risk, and at a reduced rate of freight. Defendant's agent testified that the freight charged was the established release rate when stock was shipped at owner's risk. Defendant's printed tariff in force at the time showed that the release rate was much lower than that charged when stock was shipped at carrier's risk. There was no evidence that plaintiff made any contract with defendant other than the one made by the receiving carrier. Held, that defendant accepted the terms of the contract made by the receiving carrier, and was entitled to the benefit thereof. Western Ry. Co. *v.* Harwell, 97 Ala. 341, 11 So. 781.

§ 146. —— Damages.

The measure of damages for injuries to cattle shipped by railroad, resulting in death, is the market value of the cattle at the place of destination, less the expense of transportation, although such place is beyond the terminus of the company's road, and it was not liable for injury occurring beyond its terminus. East Tennessee, etc., R. Co. *v.* Johnston, 75 Ala. 596, 598, cited in note in 18 L. R. A., N. S., 90.

Expenses.—Where defendant railroad company misdelivered certain hogs to a stockyards company, instead of the consignee, plaintiff was entitled to recover a sum which he was required to pay the stockyards company for feeding the hogs before he could regain possession thereof. Southern Ry. Co. *v.* Webb, 39 So. 262, 143 Ala. 304.

Expense Not Proximate Cause of Carriers Default—Trip.—Plaintiff was not entitled to recover expense incurred by him on a trip to the place of destination of the hogs in order to recover them; such expense not being the proximate or natural consequence of the carrier's breach of contract. Southern Ry. Co. *v.* Webb. 39 So. 262, 143 Ala. 304.

§ 147. —— Trial.

§ 147 (1) Questions for Jury in General.

§ 147 (2) —— Care of Stock Awaiting Transportation or Delivery.

Cattle Awaiting Transportation—Failure of Plaintiff to Load Promptly.—In an action for damages to live stock received by a defendant into its stock pens for transportation, where the plaintiff under the contract of affreightment was to load the cattle upon the cars, and under which the defendant was not to be liable by reason of the stock being wild and unruly, or in consequence of fright, it was shown that on the afternoon of the day on which the cattle were received by defendant it furnished a car for loading, but that the plaintiff failed to load them that day and that, after the plaintiff failed to load, the cattle on that same day broke from the pens and inflicted upon themselves or each other the injuries for which the plaintiff sought recovery. Held that, on these facts. the plaintiff was not as a matter of law negligent. St. Louis & S. F. R. Co. *v.* Cavender, 170 Ala. 601, 54 So. 54.

§ 147 (3) —— Delay in Transportation.

Unreasonable Delay.—Where, in an action for injuries to stock, whether a delay in transportation was reasonable was a question of mixed law and fact for the jury, it was proper for the court to refuse to charge that the animals were not confined in the cars an unreasonable time. Louisville & N. R. Co. *v.* Smitha, 40 So. 117, 145 Ala. 686.

§ 147 (4) —— Limitation of Liability.

Whether Injury Attributable to Lack of Bedding.—Where, in an action against a carrier for injuries to cattle in transit from a failure to promptly deliver, the court instructed that the defendant was not liable for any damages to the cattle attributable to a lack of proper bedding, it made it a question for the jury whether the injury was attributable in whole or in part to the lack of bedding, and gave the defendant the full benefit of a stipulation in the shipping contract against liability on that ground. Southern R. Co. *v.* Proctor, 3 Ala. App. 413, 57 So. 513.

Estimation of Damages.—In an action for injuries to a shipment of cattle from failure to deliver within a reasonable time, evidence as to the amount of damage to the cattle held sufficient to go to the jury for the estimation of damages under a stipulation of the shipping contract that value at the place and date of shipment would govern in the event of damage for which the carrier might be liable. Southern R. Co. *v.* Proctor, 3 Ala. App. 413, 57 So. 513.

Compliance with Stipulation as to Notice.—Where, in an action for damages sustained from the failure of a carrier to deliver promptly cattle shipped, there was evidence tending to support a replication to the defendant's plea that the plaintiff had not complied with a stipulation in the contract of shipment as to the giving of notice of injuries, the jury were entitled to determine the question. Southern R. Co. *v.* Proctor, 3 Ala. App. 413, 57 So. 513.

Where the contract stipulates that the shipper must notify the company's agent in writing of a claim for injury before removing the animals from the place of delivery, the shipper has a reasonable time after the removal, in case the injury is not then discovered by ordinary diligence, in which to give the notice; and where he removes the animals December 29th, and notifies the agent January 4th, it is a question for the jury whether the notice was given in a reasonable time. Western R. Co. *v.* Harwell, 97 Ala. 341, 11 So. 781, affirming 91 Ala. 340, 8 So. 649, cited in note in 7 L. R. A., N. S., 1043.

§ 147 (5) —— Liability of Connecting Carrier.

Negligence of Terminal Carrier as Causing Injury.—In an action against a railroad for injuries to horses, it appeared that it was the last of three connecting lines, and plaintiffs averred that such injury was caused by defendant's negligence. Defendant receipted for the stock as in "good order and condition," and there was other evidence that the horses were unhurt when received by defendant, and were injured when they reached their destination. Held, that whether or not the horses were injured by defendant's negligence was for the jury. Louisville & N. R. Co. *v.* Grant, 99 Ala. 325, 13 So. 599.

Effect of Testimony as Showing Delivery in Good Condition to Second Carrier.—In an action by a shipper against the delivering carrier for damages to live stock, defendant requested a charge that the mere fact that a certain witness testified that the animals sued for did not show damage when they were unloaded by the initial carrier did not prove that they were in good condition when delivered to defendant. Held properly refused, because whether or not such testimony of the witness proved such fact was a question for the jury, and not for the court. Central, etc., R. Co. *v.* Dothan Mule Co., 159 Ala. 225, 49 So. 243, cited in note in 31 L. R. A., N. S., 103.

§ 147 (6) Instructions.

§ 147 (7) —— Delay in Transportation.

Misleading Instruction.—Where a car of stock was in transit more than a day longer than it should have been if running on schedule time, a request to charge that defendant was not bound to transport the stock on its fast train was properly refused as misleading. Louisville & N. R. Co. *v.* Smitha, 40 So. 117, 145 Ala. 686.

Charge Disregarding Evidence of Delay.—Where there was evidence justifying a finding of unreasonable delay in transportation of stock, an instruction that, if the stock were brought over defendant's line without any unnecessary jar or rough handling, defendant was not liable for injuries they received, was properly refused. Louisville & N. R. Co. *v.* Smitha, 40 So. 117, 145 Ala. 686.

Charge Denying Recovery for Delay.—Where, in an action against a carrier for injuries to certain stock, delay in delivery might have been the cause of damage to them, which delay was the result of defendant's negligence, a request to charge that plaintiff could not recover for delay in delivery was properly refused. Louisville & N. R. Co. *v.* Smitha, 40 So. 117, 145 Ala. 686.

§ 147 (8) —— Care of Stock by Carrier.

Where a complaint against a carrier for damages to a dog in transportation avers the injury was occasioned by failure to give him proper food and water, an instruction postulating that plaintiff must show defendant's failure to give the dog food, water, and exercise is properly refused. Southern Exp. Co. *v.* Ashford, 28 So. 732, 126 Ala. 591.

Charge as to Duty of Guarding Against Fever.—In an action against a carrier for injuries to live stock, an instruction that the carrier owed no duty to guard the animals against fever was properly refused, as exempting the carrier from liability, though the fever resulted from its negligence. Louisville & N. R. Co. *v.* Smitha, 40 So. 117, 145 Ala. 686.

Injuries Occurring While Horse Reloaded.—In an action against a carrier for injuries to a horse while in transit, an instruction that, if the injury occurred by the horse slipping on the bridge while being reloaded after unloading for feeding, the verdict should be for defendant, was erroneous, as ignoring the propriety of unloading the horse at the time, and the good order of the facilities for reloading, and whether due care was observed by defendant's servants. Nashville, C. & St. L. Ry. Co. *v.* Parker, 27 So. 323, 123 Ala. 683.

Misleading and Argumentative Instruction.—Where, in an action for injury to a shipment of live stock, a witness testified that he helped in the loading, and called the attention of defendant's agents to cracks in the car, and that the agent instructed him to load notwithstanding, the court properly refused to instruct that plaintiff could not recover if the injuries were due to bedding having been lost through cracks in the car, and plaintiff's agent knew of such cracks when he loaded the stock, and knew or had reasonable grounds to believe that the bedding would be thus lost and the cattle thereby injured; such instruction being not only improper and misleading in view of this evidence, but being erroneous, in that it gave undue prominence to evidence, and was argumentative. Nashville, etc., Railway *v.* Hinds (Ala. App.), 60 So. 409.

Injuries Occurring at Destination.—The requested charge, in an action for injury to one of a shipment of horses, to find for defendant carrier, if it delivered the stock on its side track at 2:30 a. m. in good condition, and thereafter did not touch the car, and the injury occurred 8 or 10 hours before 1:30 p. m. of the same day, was bad, as requiring a verdict for it, though the jury found from the evidence that the injury occurred before defendant's liability as a carrier terminated, and that there was no explanation of how the injury was inflicted. Alabama, etc., R. Co. *v.* Gewin & Son, 5 Ala. App. 584, 59 So. 553.

The requested charge of defendant, in an action against a carrier for injury to one of a shipment of horses, to find for defendant if the animal was injured after G., one of the consignees, first saw it, is bad, as ignoring the proposition that the carrier's liability was not terminated as soon as one of the consignees saw the animals after their arrival at destination, before they had a reasonable time, after knowledge or notice of their arrival, to call for and take charge of them. Alabama, etc., R. Co. *v.* Gewin & Son, 5 Ala. App. 584, 59 So. 553.

There being evidence that the animal was injured while defendant as carrier was still liable for it, the general affirmative charge was properly denied it, in the absence of uncontradicted evidence of how the injury was inflicted. Alabama, etc., R. Co. *v.* Gewin & Son, 5 Ala. App. 584, 59 So. 553.

§ 147 (9) —— Limitation of Liability.

Power to Waiver Stipulation.—In an action against a terminal carrier for injuries to cattle, a request to charge that only an officer of defendant, or the nearest station agent to the stock yards where the cattle were unloaded, had authority to waive the provisions for notice of injury, requiring that notice, in writing, shall be given to some officer of the delivering carrier, or its nearest station agent, before the stock is removed, was properly refused as involving the untenable proposition that the existence of such a contract deprived the carrier of the right, by the act of any duly authorized representative other than those specified, to waive the requirement as to notice of loss or injury. Louisville, etc., R. Co. *v.* Shepherd (Ala. App.), 61 So. 14.

Injuries Inflicted by Other Animals.—A requested charge for a verdict, if it be found the injury to one of a shipment of horses was inflicted by some of the others, without negligence of the carrier, was bad; the contract of shipment exempting it only in case of injury through any of the animals "being vicious, wild, unruly, or weak." Alabama, etc., R. Co. *v.* Gewin & Son, 5 Ala. App. 584, 59 So. 553.

A carrier's requested charge for a verdict if it be found the injury to one horse occurred from viciousness of any of the others was bad; the stipulation of the contract of shipment, pleaded as a defense, relieving the carrier from liability for an injury, so occurring, only in case of its happening "without fault or negligence" on its part. Alabama, etc., R. Co. *v.* Gewin & Son, 5 Ala. App. 584, 59 So. 553.

§ 147 (10) —— Liability of Connecting Carriers.

In an action by a shipper of live stock to recover damages from the delivering carrier for injury to the live stock delivered by the carrier to the shipper, an instruction declared that "where the carriage of freight is to be over several connecting carriers, as was the case here, it seems that if the consignee, the consignee bringing the suit in this case, shows to the jury that the animals were in good condition when delivered to the initial carrier, and that they were not in good condition when delivered by the discharging carrier, and the suit is against the discharging carrier, then these facts alone, without any more, put the burden on the defendant, the discharging carrier, to show to the reasonable satisfaction of the jury that the harm and injury did not come to the animals while they were in the keep of the discharging carrier, and that is the law in this case." Held, that this was a clear and explicit statement of the law in relation thereto, and that the instruction was by no means abstract, and was clearly applicable to the case. Central, etc., R. Co. *v.* Dothan Mule Co., 159 Ala. 225, 49 So. 243, cited in note in 31 L. R. A., N. S., 103.

Improper Assumption of Facts.—Where defendant was a party, as connecting carrier, to a contract of shipment of horses consigned to plaintiff at A., on defendant's road, and defendant there delivered the car to the S. Railroad, authorized by plaintiffs to there receive it, under a separate contract for its carriage to G., an instruction, in an action for injury to one of the horses, discovered on arrival at G., that the law presumes the injury was received while the animal was in the possession of the S. company, improperly assumes that the S. company was the delivering company under the contract to which defendant was a party. Alabama, etc., R. Co. *v.* Gewin & Son, 5 Ala. App. 584, 59 So. 553.

IV. CARRIAGE OF PASSENGERS.

(A) RELATION BETWEEN CARRIER AND PASSENGER.

§ 148. Nature of the Relation.

The relation of carrier and passenger is contractual, and requires the carrier merely to carry the passenger between the agreed points; the law raising the duty to care for the passenger's comfort and safety while the relation continues. Waldrop *v.* Nashville, etc., Railway (Ala.), 62 So. 769.

"The relationship of carrier and passenger is dependent upon the existence of a contract of carriage, express or implied, between the carrier and passenger, made by themselves or their respective agents." Louisville, etc., R. Co. *v.* Glasgow (Ala.), 60 So. 103, 105.

"It may be declared as a general rule that the relations of carrier and passenger are founded in contract, either expressed or implied, made upon a valuable, but not necessarily a pecuniary, consideration, 'and when such relations bring one of the parties into contract with a material agency which the contract requires the other party to supply, the law exacts of him who supplies that agency the duty of exercising care in its selection, maintenance in repair, and operation.' 2 Amer. & Eng. Enc. Law., p. 739." North Birmingham St. R. Co. *v.* Liddicoat, 99 Ala. 545, 13 So. 18, 19.

§ 149. Who Are Carriers.

"A comon carrier of passengers is one who is engaged in a public calling, which imposes upon him the duty to serve all without discrimination. 6 Cyc. 533." Birmingham R., etc., Co. *v.* Adams, 146 Ala. 267, 40 So. 385.

Elevator in Store.—A merchant who operates an elevator in his store for the transportation of his customers sustains the relation of carrier to a customer who is directed by him to take the elevator, and is consequently bound to exercise the highest degree of care for the customer's safety while the latter is actually aboard or is entering the elevator. Morgan *v.* Saks, 38 So. 848, 143 Ala. 139, cited in note in 2 L. R. A., N. S., 745, 756, 758.

§ 150. Duty to Receive and Transport Passengers.

The public character of the business of a common carrier of passengers imposes on such carrier the duty of receiving and carrying without discrimination in vehicles, in use by it for public carriage, all persons fit to be carried, who may properly present themselves for transportation, so long as there are accommodations for passengers in such vehicle. Birmingham R., etc., Co. *v.* Anderson, 3 Ala. App. 674, 57 So. 103.

Action for Refusal to Furnish Transportation—Complaint.—A complaint in an action against a common carrier of passengers for damages for refusal to accept plaintiff as such a passenger, alleging that plaintiff on a certain date applied to the servants or agent of the carrier in charge of one of the cars for transportation thereon, but such servant, acting within the scope of his employment, wrongfully and without legal excuse refused to permit plaintiff to become a passenger on the car or to be transported thereon, and that her intention and desire to become a passenger and be transported was known to the servant, is not sufficient to show such a relation between the plaintiff and the carrier as to put the latter under the duty of accepting plaintiff as a passenger. Birmingham R., etc., Co. *v.* Anderson, 3 Ala. App. 674, 57 So. 103.

§ 151. Who Are Passengers.

§ 152. —— In General.

To constitute one a passenger, it is not necessary that the carrier should be a common carrier, nor that the train or car should be used or adapted primarily for carrying passengers, and one may be a passenger, though he pay nothing for his carriage; the only essential being that he is accepted as a passenger for transportation by the carrier. Lawrence *v.* Kaul Lumber Co., 171 Ala. 300, 55 So. 111.

"The word 'passenger,' ex vi termini, means 'one who travels in some public conveyance by virtue of a contract, express or implied, with the carrier, on the payment of fare or that which is accepted as an equivalent therefor.'" Birmingham R., etc., Co. *v.* Adams, 146 Ala. 267, 40 So. 385, 386.

"A passenger may be defined to be one who undertakes, with the consent of the carrier, to travel in a conveyance furnished by the latter, otherwise than in the service of the carrier as such. Shearman & Red. on Neg., § 488. The relation of carrier and passenger is dependent upon the existence of a contract of carriage, express or implied, between the carrier and passenger, made by themselves or their respective agents; and this relation begins when a person puts himself in the care of the carrier or directly within its control, with the bona fide intention of becoming a passenger, and is accepted as such by the carrier. There is, however, seldom any formal act of delivery of the passenger's person into the care of the carrier, or of acceptance by the carrier of one who presents himself for transportation; hence, the existence of the relation is generally to be implied from the attendant circumstances. But it is undoubtedly the rule that these circumstances must be such as will warrant the implication that one has offered himself to be carried and the offer has been accepted by the carrier. And this, of course, necessarily involves the existence of the fact that the person must signify his intention to take passage either by words or conduct, and those in charge of the car must assent by words or conduct to his becoming a passenger. North Birmingham St. R. Co. *v.* Liddicoat, 99 Ala. 545, 13 So. 18." Alabama, etc., R. Co. *v.* Bates, 149 Ala. 487, 43 So. 98, 99.

§ 153. —— Payment of Fare.

Child Accompanying Mother.—A small child, riding on a street car in company with his mother, who pays a fare for herself, is a passenger, although no fare is paid for such child, where there is a general custom on the part of the street railway not to charge fare for the carriage of small children. Ball *v.* Mobile Light & R. Co., 39 So. 584, 146 Ala. 309.

Person Boarding Train in Good Faith.—A person boarding a train in good faith believing that her ticket was good is a passenger, and the carrier requiring her to disembark owes her a duty as such. Central of Georgia Ry. Co. *v.* Bagley, 173 Ala. 611, 55 So. 894.

Presumption as to Intention of Paying Fare.—Ordinarily, where a person boards a train with money sufficient to pay his fare, it will be presumed that he intends to pay his fare until his fare is demanded, unless his conduct should be such as to show that he was trying to evade a demand being made on him, by secreting himself or otherwise; but, if he fails to pay after demand and opportunity to pay, the presumption ceases. Broyles *v.* Central, etc., R. Co., 166 Ala. 616, 52 So. 81.

Effect of Fraud.—Where intestate at the time of his injury had obtained permission to ride on a local freight train by falsely representing to the conductor that he was riding on an employee's pass, he was a trespasser, and not a passenger, as to whom the carrier was only liable for willful or wanton injury. Neyman *v.* Alabama Great Southern R. Co., 172 Ala. 606, 55 So. 509.

Where plaintiff, with her mother, enters a train, and on demand for fare the mother gives a pass, issued for others, which the conductor takes, a fraud is practiced on the carrier, and the plaintiff is a trespasser on the train, even though she did not know about the pass, and hence she could not recover for injuries resulting from simple negligence. Broyles *v.* Central, etc., R. Co., 166 Ala. 616, 52 So. 81.

§ 154. —— Employees of Carrier.

See, generally, the title MASTER AND SERVANT.

A section hand, injured while riding back and forth to work on a car, without charge, pursuant to a rule of the company, is not a passenger, but is in the exercise of a mere privilege connected with his employment. Birmingham Ry., Light & Power Co. *v.* Sawyer, 47 So. 67, 156 Ala. 199, cited in note in 37 L. R. A., N. S., 250.

§ 155. —— Employees of Others Carried under Contract with Carrier.

Mail agents, postal clerks, and express messengers are passengers on the train on which they ride while working, and while they can not rely upon the contract between the carrier and the government to impose a liability on the carrier in their favor, they may rely upon the legal duty of one undertaking to perform even a gratuitous service to exercise the care which the nature of the undertaking requires. Southern Ry. Co. *v.* Harrington, 53 So. 57, 166 Ala. 630.

§ 156. —— Conveyances and Places Not Proper for Passengers.

Person Outside of Vestibule.—Where a train of street railway cars was so crowded inside the cars as not to admit of others entering, but it continued to stop at each stopping place, and others were allowed to get on, a person who got on the car and stood outside the vestibule was a passenger, though he had not been seen by the conductor, and though his fare had not been collected. Birmingham Ry., Light & Power Co. *v.* Bynum, 36 So. 736, 139 Ala. 389, cited in note in 17 L. R. A., N. S., 160.

Person on Freight Train.—If a railroad company permits a passenger to ride upon a freight train, it is liable to him for negligently injuring him, although not required to transport the passenger on such train, and not a common carrier of passengers as to that means of transportation. Birmingham R., etc., Co. *v.* Adams, 146 Ala. 267, 40 So. 385, 386.

§ 157. —— Invitation or Acquiescence of Carrier's Employees.

An invitation from an employee not connected with the running of a train on which a person was invited to ride would not create the relation of passenger. Thompson *v.* Nashville, C. & St. L. Ry., 49 So. 340, 160 Ala. 590; Broslin *v.* Kansas, etc., R. Co., 114 Ala. 398, 21 So. 475; Holmes *v.* Birmingham, etc., R. Co., 140 Ala. 208, 37 So. 338. See note in 37 L. R. A., N. S., 425.

Where a carrier is not a common carrier of passengers, and has not expressly contracted to carry in the particular case, if the presence of a person entering on its train and taking passage is without the knowledge and consent of any one in charge of the train, he is but a trespasser; if on invitation, or with the knowledge and acquiescence of an agent, not authorized nor shared in by his principal, he is a licensee; but if on the invitation, express or implied, of the carrier, its manager, or any authorized agent, he is a passenger. Lawrence *v.* Kaul Lumber Co., 171 Ala. 300, 55 So. 111.

Where a person, not an employee of the railroad company, rides, with the acquiescence of the superintendent, on a car which he knows is for the use of the company's employees only, and not for passengers, he does so under a mere license, and the company is responsible for injuries sustained by him, or his death, only when caused by its wanton or intentional wrong. McCauley *v.* Tennessee Coal, Iron & Railroad Co., 93 Ala. 356, 9 So. 611, cited in note in 37 L. R. A., N. S., 427.

Permission Secured by Fraud.—See ante, "Payment of Fare," § 153.

§ 158. —— Pleading.

§ 158 (1) Complaint.

"It was necessary to aver a contract, either express or implied, to constitute the relation of passenger and carrier, since a tort by the carrier can not be committed upon a passenger as such, unless such relation is shown to exist. 5 Am. & Eng. Ency. Law (2d Ed.) 486; Hutchinson on Carriers, § 554; Western Union Tel. Co. *v.* Krichbaum, 132 Ala. 535, 31 So. 607." Southern R. Co. *v.* Bunnell, 138 Ala. 247, 36 So. 380, 382.

Duty Sufficiently Shown.—A complaint alleging that plaintiff, while a passenger upon defendant's railway, was injured, etc., was not defective for failure to show that defendant owed any duty to plaintiff; the existence of the duty being inferable from the allegation of the relation of carrier and passenger. Birmingham Ry., Light & Power Co. *v.* Adams, 40 So. 385, 146 Ala. 267.

Averment as to Relation of Carrier and Passenger Held Sufficient.—A complaint alleging that plaintiff, while a passenger upon defendant's railway, was injured, etc., was sufficient to show that the relation of carrier and passenger existed at the time of the injury, although there was no direct allegation that defendant was a common carrier. Birmingham Ry., Light & Power Co. *v.* Adams, 40 So. 385, 146 Ala. 267.

Failure to Show Relation of Carrier and Passenger.—In an action against a railroad company for injuries to plaintiff by the giving way of a handle on the car which plaintiff took hold of while entering it, a complaint, which fails to allege that it was at a station provided for passengers, or at a place where it was usual or customary to receive passengers, or that plaintiff was invited or knowingly permitted to attempt to board the car, or that he was in any way accepted as a passenger, fails to show any relation existing between the parties devolving on defendant the duty towards plaintiff of maintaining its car in repair. North Birmingham Ry. Co. *v.* Liddicoat, 99 Ala. 545, 13 So. 18, cited in 38 L. R. A. 789.

An allegation of the complaint, in an action against a street railway company for an assault, that it was committed "while plaintiff was engaged in or about becoming a passenger on said car," did not show that plaintiff was a passenger. Birmingham Ry. & Electric Co. *v.* Mason, 34 So. 207, 137 Ala. 342.

In an action for the death of a person in attempting to board an electric car, the count not averring that the decedent was attempting to board the train at a station provided for passengers, or at a place where it was usual or customary to receive passengers or that he was invited or knowingly permitted to board the car by an authorized servant of the company, or that he was in any manner accepted as a passenger, is demurrable as failing to show the relation of carrier and passenger. Smith *v.* Birmingham Ry., Light & Power Co., 41 So. 307, 147 Ala. 702.

Negativing Status of Trespasser.—While plaintiff, suing for injury sustained upon the track or premises of a railroad company and relying upon simple negligence, must show that he is not a trespasser, an averment that he had gone to the carrier's premises to take passage upon its train, then due or about due, is sufficient. Louisville & N. R. Co. *v.* Glasgow (Ala.), 60 So. 103.

§ 158 (2) Plea.

Allegation As to Presence of Passenger on Train without Right.—Where a complaint for causing the death of a passenger does not charge that the defendant was a common carrier, but only that it operated a train on a railway, and that decedent was being carried by defendant as a passenger, pleas alleging that the deceased voluntarily, without invitation, and without compensation to the defendant, boarded the car on which he was riding show a complete defense to counts of the complaint, based on simple negligence. Lawrence *v.* Kaul Lumber Co., 171 Ala. 300, 55 So. 111.

In pleas alleging that decedent, without invitation from defendant, boarded the car on which he was riding, the word "invitation" is a term of considerable breadth, including not only express invitation, but the invitation that may be implied from custom, usage, or conduct on the part of the carrier, or of its servants, if notorious or actually known to the carrier or its alter ego. Lawrence *v.* Kaul Lumber Co., 171 Ala. 300, 55 So. 111.

§ 158 (3) Issues, Proof and Variance.

Matters to Be Proved.—In an action against a carrier for injuries to a passenger, the allegation that plaintiff was a passenger on defendant's car at the time he was injured is a material allegation, and must be proved. Birmingham Ry., Light & Power Co. *v.* Sawyer, 47 So. 67, 156 Ala. 199.

Variance—Relation.—Where the complaint alleged the relation of carrier and passenger, the relation as alleged was a material averment; and, where the proof conclusively showed the relation of master and servant, it was error to refuse a general affirmative charge for defendant. Birmingham Ry., Light & Power Co. *v.* Stanfield, 50 So. 51, 161 Ala. 488.

§ 159. —— Evidence.

Burden of Showing Plaintiff to Be Passenger.—One suing a carrier for injuries received while a passenger must establish the fact that he was a passenger at the time, though during the trial there is no suggestion of a denial of that fact. Birmingham R., etc., Co. *v.* McCurdy, 172 Ala. 488, 55 So. 616.

In an action for injuries alleged to have occurred while plaintiff was boarding one of defendant's cars as a passenger, while the car was standing at a regular stopping place for the reception of passengers, the burden was on plaintiff to prove that he was a passenger. Alabama City, G. & A. Ry. Co. *v.* Bates, 43 So. 98, 149 Ala. 487.

Admissibility.—Where a carrier claimed that plaintiff, suing for injuries, was not a passenger because she was riding on a pass issued to another, a question to plaintiff as a witness, whether it was customary for her to ride on a pass, is properly excluded, since it did not cover the issue. Broyles *v.* Central, etc., R. Co., 166 Ala. 616, 52 So. 81.

Where a carrier claimed that an injured passenger was a trespasser because riding on a pass issued to another given to the conductor by plaintiff's mother, who was sitting beside her, it is proper to ask the conductor whether he knew that the plaintiff and her mother were known by him to be the persons to whom the pass was issued, since, if they were not, they would be trespassers, and not passengers. Broyles *v.* Central, etc., R. Co., 166 Ala. 616, 52 So. 81.

Custom Not to Charge Fare for Children.—On the issue of whether a small child, riding on a street car in company with his parent, but for whom no fare was paid, was a passenger, evidence of a general custom on the part of the street railway not to charge fare for the carriage of small children is competent. Ball *v.* Mobile Light & R. Co., 146 Ala. 309, 39 So. 584.

Sufficiency. — Testimony that "there were about seven or eight passengers on the car, and [plaintiff] was one of the passengers," raises a question for the jury on the issue of whether plaintiff was a passenger or not. Ball *v.* Mobile Light & R. Co., 146 Ala. 309, 39 So. 584.

Evidence Held to Show Plaintiff Passenger.—In an action against a carrier for injuries to a street car passenger, evidence held to justify a finding that plaintiff was a passenger at the time, in view of the fact that there is no presumption that she was wrongfully on the car. Birmingham R., etc., Co. *v.* McCurdy, 172 Ala. 488, 55 So. 616.

§ 160. Commencement and Termination of Relation.

§ 160 (1) In General.

"This relation [of the carrier passenger] begins when a person puts himself in the care of the carrier, or directly within its control, with the bona fide intention of becoming a passenger, and is accepted as such by the carrier. There is, however, seldom any formal act of delivery of the passenger's person into the care of the carrier,' or of acceptance by the carrier of one who presents himself for transportation; hence the existence of the relationship is generally to be implied from the attendant circumstances. But it is undoubtedly the rule that these circumstances must be such as to warrant the implication that one has offered himself to be carried, and the offer has been accepted by the carrier. And this, of course, necessarily involves the existence of the fact that the person must signify his intention to take passage, either by words or by conduct, and those in charge of the car must assent by words or conduct to his becoming a passenger." Alabama, etc., R. Co. *v.* Bates, 149 Ala. 487, 490, 43 So. 98; S. C., 155 Ala. 347, 46 So. 776; Louisville, etc., R. Co. *v.* Glasgow (Ala.), 60 So. 103, 105.

§ 160 (2) Going to or Awaiting Train.

The relation of carrier and passenger begins when the contract of carriage having been made, or the passenger having been accepted as such by the carrier, he has come upon the carrier's premises or has entered any means of conveyance provided by the carrier. North Birmingham St. R. Co. *v.* Liddicoat, 99 Ala. 545, 13 So. 18, 19.

Where a railroad company habitually received and set down passengers at a platform at a flag station, prospective passengers waiting there for a train then due are not trespassers, regardless of whether the railroad company intended it as a waiting place. Louisville & N. R. Co. *v.* Glasgow (Ala.), 60 So. 103. See, to the same effect, North Birmingham St. R. Co. *v.* Liddicoat, 99 Ala. 545, 13 So. 18, 19.

Person Attempting to Board Train at Proper Place.—One attempting to board a train at a regular station with intent to become a passenger is a passenger. Birmingham & A. R. Co. *v.* Norris, 4 Ala. App. 363, 59 So. 66.

A complaint, aside from its express averment that plaintiff and her children were defendant's passengers, and that it was its duty to carry them on its car from G. to B., shows such relation by the allegations that defendant was a common carrier of passengers by means of an electric car running from G. to B.; that plaintiff, with her children with her, was at G., at the proper place used by defendant for receiving passengers on the car, for the purpose of boarding said car and being carried thereon as defendant's passengers from G. to B.; that the car stopped at said place for the purpose of receiving passengers, but that she did not board it by reason of the servant in charge of the car negligently failing to allow her a reasonable time or opportunity to do so. Birmingham Ry., Light & Power Co. *v.* Wise, 42 So. 821, 149 Ala. 492.

Person Waiting in Station to Buy Ticket by Invitation.—Where a person went to a station at 11 o'clock in the evening to purchase a ticket and board a train which left at four in the morning, and was told by the agent to wait until he could sell him a ticket, the right to remain in the station did not depend upon whether he went there a reasonable time before the train left, since there was an invitation to remain for the purpose of buying a ticket. Louisville, etc., R. Co. *v.* Kay (Ala.), 62 So. 1014.

Person Entering Car Prematurely.—Plaintiff had a pass on defendant's construction train to T., and, when the engine started to the water tank, boarded a flat car in front of the engine, and was injured. Held, that if, before the train went to T., it was necessary for the engine to go to the tank for water, and plaintiff knew, or should have known, that the train was going to the tank, and would return to the station, he could not recover as a passenger unless the conductor told him to board the train. Brown *v.* Scarboro, 97 Ala. 316. 12 So. 289, cited in note in 33 L. R. A., N. S., 584.

It was error to charge that if plaintiff had a pass which authorized him to go to T. on that train, and he believed that when the train started it was going to T., and got aboard after a statement, "All out for Troy," and was not ordered off, he was rightfully on the train, whether it was going to the tank or not. Brown *v.* Scarboro, 97 Ala. 316, 12 So. 289.

It was also error to charge that if plaintiff was not rightfully on the train, and those in charge of it saw he was on it, it was their duty to tell him that the train was going to the tank. Brown *v.* Scarboro, 97 Ala. 316, 12 So. 289.

§ 160 (3) Reaching Destination and Leaving Train or Carrier's Premises.

The relation of passenger and carrier continues to exist only until the passenger has had reasonable time and opportunity to alight from a train, and to leave the carrier's premises in the ordinary manner. Alabama City, G. & A. Ry. Co. *v.* Cox, 173 Ala. 629, 55 So. 909; Alabama, etc., R. Co. *v.* Godfrey, 156 Ala. 202, 47 So. 185; Southern R. Co. *v.* Burnett, 6 Ala. App. 568, 60 So. 472, 473. See note in 41 L. R. A., N. S., 745.

A carrier's obligation to a passenger continues until he has a reasonable opportunity to leave the station, but not after the passenger has left the station and is on the way to his hotel; and where the hack in which a passenger was when assaulted by a trainman was standing in a public street, over which the railroad did not have dominion, and the passenger had been accepted as such by the hack company, his relation of passenger with the railroad company had terminated, so that it was not liable for the assault. Southern R. Co. *v.* Burnett, 6 Ala. App. 568, 60 So. 472.

Steam Railroads.—The relation of carrier and passenger does not terminate, in case of steam railroads, at the moment the passenger alights at the station, but continues until he has had a reasonable opportunity to leave the carrier's premises in a proper manner and by the usual way. Waldrop *v.* Nashville, etc., Railway (Ala.), 62 So. 769; Southern R. Co. *v.* Burnett, 6 Ala. App. 568, 60 So. 472, 473.

Street Railways.—The relation of a street car passenger does not end when he leaves the car, but continues until he has reasonable opportunity to leave the carrier's roadway, after the car reaches the place to which he is entitled to be carried. Melton *v.* Birmingham Ry., Light & Power Co., 45 So. 151, 153 Ala. 95, 16 L. R. A., N. S., 467; Montgomery St. Railway *v.* Mason, 133 Ala. 508, 32 So. 261; Waldrop *v.* Nashville, etc., Railway (Ala.), 62 So. 769, 770. See note in 20 L. R. A, N. S., 1019.

Passenger Carried Beyond Destination—Gratuitous Acts of Carrier's Servants.—Where the passenger has been carried beyond his destination through no wrong or negligence of the carrier, and is safely landed at some other station, the carrier is not liable for injuries he may sustain in attempting to return to the proper station unless they attempted to transport him back and he was negligently injured, and as no duty rests on the defendant to get him back to the station the act of the carrier's servants in advising or directing him as to his return would be gratuitous acts for which the company would not be liable. Birmingham R., etc., Co. *v.* Seaborn, 168 Ala. 658, 53 So. 241.

§ 160 (4) Changing Cars or Leaving Train Temporarily.

As to rule of street railway company refusing a second fare when passenger changes from one car to another of same train, see post, "Rules of Carrier," § 161.

Where a passenger train has stopped at a station, passengers, during the stop, may walk out of the car in which they are seated onto the station platform, or over the car platforms into another car, without losing their right to protection as passengers. Central of Georgia Ry. Co. *v.* Storrs, 53 So. 746, 169 Ala. 361.

A passenger who is injured by falling into a hole in a platform erected near the tracks of the railroad company, and used by passengers going to and from an hotel for meals, is not precluded from recovering for the injury by the fact that he left the train, and went to the hotel to keep a private business appointment. Watson *v.* Oxanna Land Co., 92 Ala. 320, 8 So. 770.

§ 161. Rules of Carrier.

See, also, post, "Rules of Carrier," § 167.

A common carrier of passengers may establish reasonable rules and regulations in regard to the times and places of receiving passengers. Birmingham Ry., Light & Power Co. *v.* Anderson, 3 Ala. App. 674, 57 So. 103; Pullman Co. *v.* Krauss, 145 Ala. 395, 40 So. 398, 4 L. R. A., N. S., 103; North Birmingham St. R. Co. *v.* Liddicoat, 99 Ala. 545, 13 So. 18.

Rule Requiring Ticket for Freight Train.—To entitle a railroad company to enforce a published rule requiring passengers to obtain tickets as a condition precedent to the right to ride on one of its freight trains, the company must afford passengers reasonable facilities for purchasing tickets, and for that purpose must keep its ticket office open for a reasonable time before the departure of the train. Evans *v.* Memphis & C. R. Co., 56 Ala. 246, cited in note in 20 L. R. A. 486, 24 L. R. A., N. S., 760, 29 L. R. A., N. S., 300.

Rule of Street Railway Prohibiting Passengers from Passing from One Car to Another.—The rule of a street railway company operating motors and trailers as part of the same train with a conductor on each car, requiring each conductor to collect and register fares from all the passengers on his car, and prohibiting a passenger, who had paid fare on one of the cars of the train, from passing to the other without again paying his fare on that car, was reasonable and enforceable. Birmingham R., etc., Co. *v.* McDonough, 153 Ala. 122, 44 So. 960, 13 L. R. A., N. S., 445; Birmingham R., etc., Co. *v.* Stallings, 154 Ala. 527, 45 So. 650.

(B) FARES, TICKETS, AND SPECIAL CONTRACTS.

§ 162. Acts and Statements of Agents or Employees.

Representations as to Route.—An agent, in an office maintained by a carrier for the purpose, among others, of giving information to intending passengers in reference to routes of travel, was acting within the scope of his authority in representing that a designated route was the best and quickest. Southern Ry. Co. *v.* Nowlin, 47 So. 180, 156 Ala. 222, cited in notes in 24 L. R. A., N. S., 1181, 31 L. R. A., N. S., 231.

Effect of Giving Wrong Ticket.—When a passenger calls for a particular ticket and pays the fare demanded by the ticket agent, he is entitled to the ticket for which he paid, and if the agent by mistake gives him a wrong ticket, the carrier by whose agent the ticket is sold is bound by the real contract between the parties. Pullman Co. *v.* Riley, 5 Ala. App. 561, 59 So. 761.

Knowledge of Mistake by Passenger.—Where a passenger knows or has reason to believe that the ticket handed him by the carrier's agent is not the ticket for which he called, he can not thereafter complain that he received an improper ticket. Pullman Co. *v.* Riley, 5 Ala. App. 561, 59 So. 761.

(C) PERFORMANCE OF CONTRACT OR TRANSPORTATION.

§ 163. Duties as to Transportation in General.

See, also, post, "Care Required and Liability of Carrier in General," § 176.

"Common carriers owe the duty to passengers to carry them safely, to conserve by every reasonable means their convenience, comfort and peace throughout the journey, and protect them from insult and personal violence, whether from another passenger, or stranger, or an employee or servant of the carrier. Birmingham R., etc., Co. *v.* Baird, 130 Ala. 334, 30 So. 456, 54 L. R. A. 752." Birmingham R., etc., Co. *v.* Mason, 137 Ala. 342, 34 So. 207.

§ 164. Performance of Special Contract.

Where defendant contracted to carry plaintiff and companions in an automobile from one place to another and return, and the automobile broke down, and defendant could perform his contract only by sending another automobile for plaintiff and his companions, defendant was under obligation to send out another automobile. Taxicab Co. *v.* Grant, 3 Ala. App. 393, 57 So. 141.

Where a defendant contracted to carry plaintiff and his companions in an automobile from one place to another, and the automobile broke down, and defendant failed within a reasonable time after being informed of the accident to carry plaintiff and his companions, the act of plaintiff in leaving the automobile and walking back was not a waiver of performance. Taxicab Co. *v.* Grant, 3 Ala. App. 393, 57 So. 141.

§ 165. Route, Time, and Means of Transportation.

Within proper limits, carriers may make schedules, create routes, and prescribe transfer points at which passengers, traveling beyond, must change cars. Central, etc., R. Co. *v.* Ashley, 159 Ala. 145, 48 So. 981, 984.

Publicity as to Regulations Concerning Schedule, etc.—"A primary duty rests upon the carrier of passengers to give publicity to its regulations, whether of schedule, including places whereat its train will stop for the discharge or reception of passengers, or of routing on its roadway, embracing points of change to another line of its roadway or that of another company, to the end that an ordinarily prudent and intelligent traveler may be informed of the facts essentially necessary for him to accomplish his journey. The reason for such duty inheres in the nature of the service afforded by such agencies, in connection with the power possessed by carriers to formulate and enforce such reasonable regulations as the conduct of the business requires." Central, etc., R. Co. *v.* Ashley, 159 Ala. 145, 48 So. 981, 984.

Misdirection of Passenger.—A carrier, which, on inquiry by an intending passenger, negligently failed to inform her as to the best and quickest route of travel, is liable for any injury proximately resulting, though the passenger did not purchase her ticket until the next day after receiving the information, where she purchased it in reliance thereon, and though she had the opportunity of consulting the official railroad guide as to routes, from which the carrier got its information. Southern Ry. Co. *v.* Nowlin, 47 So. 180, 156 Ala. 222, cited in notes in 24 L. R. A., N. S., 1181, 31 L. R. A., N. S., 231.

§ 166. Receiving and Taking up Passengers.

See, also, ante, "Rules of Carrier," § 161.

Duty to Maintain Waiting Rooms.—The common law does not impose upon a railroad company the duty of establishing and maintaining a comfortable waiting room at stations for persons intending to become passengers on its trains; and no such duty exists unless imposed by the charter of the company, or by a statutory regulation, or by some other legislative authorization conferring the power upon a railroad commission to impose such duty. Page *v.* Louisville, etc., R. Co., 129 Ala. 232, 29 So. 676.

While the statute confers authority on a railroad commission to require railroads to maintain, at stations along their lines, sufficient waiting rooms, suitably heated, etc., for the comfort of passengers (Code, § 3451), where, in an action brought to recover damages against a railroad company resulting from a failure to maintain a suitable waiting room at a station along its road, the complaint contains no averments that the requirement above referred to was ever made by the railroad commission with reference to the particular station, no duty is shown to exist from the defendant to the plaintiff under such statute, and no cause of action is stated thereunder. Page *v.* Louisville & N. R. Co., 29 So. 676, 129 Ala. 232, cited in note in 9 L. R. A., N. S., 375, 391.

A passenger may rely on a direction of trainmen as to the proper car to be taken, and is not chargeable with contributory negligence for following that direction, although a mistake resulting therefrom might have been avoided by making other inquiries or taking other steps of that nature. Robertson *v.* Louisville & N. R. Co., 37 So. 831, 142 Ala. 216.

In an action against a railroad company because a gateman at a union depot negligently misdirected plaintiff to a train of another road, based on the theory that the gateman was defendant's agent only, and not a joint agent of defendant and others, proof that the gateman was defendant's servant, that while so acting he misdirected plaintiff, and that thereby plaintiff suffered injury, authorizes a recovery irrespective of the theory of joint agency. Louisville & N. R. Co. *v.* Cannon, 48 So. 64, 158 Ala. 453.

Same—Aggravating Circumstances.—A passenger who sustains damages by reason of having been directed by the carrier's employees to take the wrong car is entitled to recover, whether or not the act of the employees was negligent, inadvertent, willful, knowing, or malicious; but willfulness, malice, or other aggravating circumstances may be shown, as bearing on the amount of recovery. Robertson *v.* Louisville & N. R. Co., 37 So. 831, 142 Ala. 216.

Failure of Train to Stop—Proximate Cause of Injuries.—Plaintiff purchased a railroad ticket, and was informed by the agent that a certain train would stop at the station and take him to his destination. The train passed without stopping, and, upon being informed by the agent that no other train would pass until the afternoon,. plaintiff walked to his destination. Held that, plaintiff being in the same position after the train had passed as he was before he purchased the ticket, the injuries resulting from his walk were not a natural sequence of the failure of the carrier to stop the train, and he could not recover damages therefor. Malcomb *v.* Louisville & N. R. Co., 46 So. 768, 155 Ala. 337. But see Southern R. Co. *v.* Nowlin, 156 Ala. 222, 47 So. 180. See, also, ante, "Route, Time and Means of Transportation," § 165.

§ 167. Rules of Carrier.

See, also, ante, "Rules of Carrier," § 161.

A carrier of passengers has a common-law right to make reasonable rules for the conduct of its business. Birmingham Ry., Light & Power Co. *v.* McDonough, 44 So. 960, 153 Ala. 122, 13 L. R. A., N. S., 445.

Manner of Enforcing Rule.—A carrier is responsible for an unjust application of a reasonable rule, or for enforcing it with undue severity. Birmingham R., etc., Co. *v.* McDonough, 153 Ala. 122, 44 So. 960, 13 L. R. A., N. S., 445.

Rule Requiring Separation of White and Colored Passengers.—A rule of a street railroad requiring colored passengers to sit in the front end of its cars, and white passengers in the rear end, is reasonable. Bowie *v.* Birmingham Railway & Electric Co., 27 So. 1016, 125 Ala. 397, 50 L. R. A. 632.

Rule Forbidding Standing on Platform.—A regulation of a railroad company, forbidding passengers to stand on the platform while the car is in motion, is reasonable and proper; and a passenger who violates the rule with knowledge of it does so at his peril. McCauley *v.* Tennessee, etc., R. Co., 93 Ala. 356, 9 So. 611, following Alabama, etc., R. Co. *v.* Hawk, 72 Ala. 112.

Rule as to Travelling on Freight Train.—A railroad company may make a rule permitting passengers to travel on a particular freight train only, between certain stations on its line. South & N. A. R. Co. *v.* Huffman, 76 Ala. 492.

Question of Law.—When the existence of a rule of a carrier requiring white and colored passengers to occupy different parts of the same car is established by the evidence, and its violation is shown, the reasonableness of the rule is purely a question of law for the court, and not a mixed question of law and fact. Bowie *v.* Birmingham R., etc., Co., 125 Ala. 397, 27 So. 1016.

§ 168. Changes and Transfers to Connecting Lines.

Duty to Advise Passengers as to Regulations Concerning Transfers.—Carriers can within proper limits make schedules, create routes, and prescribe transfer points at which passengers traveling beyond must change cars, but owe the duty to advise passengers by reasonable means of such regulations. Central of Georgia Ry. Co. *v.* Ashley, 48 So. 981, 159 Ala. 145, cited in note in 39 L. R. A., N. S., 663.

A street railway conductor's failure to issue a serviceable transfer, when bound to do so, makes the company liable for injuries suffered by a passenger in consequence. Birmingham Ry., Light & Power Co. *v.* Turner, 45 So. 671, 154 Ala. 542.

Passenger Changing to Wrong Car—Direction of Employees.—A passenger who bought a ticket to her destination, but left the proper car at an intermediate station, where she got on the wrong car, and was consequently left at that station, and exposed to inconveniences and hardships, could recover from the railroad, or not, according as to whether her action was or was not directed by railroad employees on the train on which she was riding. Robertson *v.* Louisville & N. R. Co., 37 So. 831, 142 Ala. 216, cited in notes in 2 L. R. A., N. S., 111, 24 L. R. A., N. S., 1181.

§ 169. Carrying to and Stopping at Destination.

The duty of a railroad company as a common carrier of passengers is not performed until it delivers its passenger at the station to which he has paid his fare. Birmingham Ry., Light & Power Co. *v.* Seaborn, 53 So. 241, 168 Ala. 658.

"'Passengers are entitled to be carried to their destination, and carriers have no right to put them off the train before reaching it.' Louisville, etc., R. Co. *v.* Quinn, 146 Ala. 330, 39 So. 756." Alabama, etc., R. Co. *v.* Cox, 173 Ala. 629, 55 So. 909, 911.

Duties of Steam and Street Railways Compared.—There is but one difference between the contract of a railroad company to carry a passenger to a particular station on its line and that of a street car company to do so, and that difference is that the former is always an express contract, while the latter is usually an implied one. The railroad company bases its charges for carrying on mileage, hence must know in advance the passenger's destination, so as to collect the proper fare. This done, the person is a passenger by express agreement to the station to which he has paid mileage. On the other hand, the street car company usually charges a flat fare, which the passenger pays, often without ever informing the conductor of the destination which he has in mind; yet he is nevertheless a passenger to such destination, by implied agreement, resulting from custom, provided that destination is a station at which the car he is on makes regular stops, or will stop upon request, and he makes seasonable request. Birmingham R., etc., Co. *v.* Arnold (Ala. App.), 60 So. 988, 989.

Notice to Conductor of Stopping Place of Passenger.—The taking up by a conductor of a ticket to a flag station is sufficient notice to him that the passenger desires to get off at that station, and it is the duty of the conductor to take up the tickets within a reasonable time after leaving a station. Louisville & N. R. Co. *v.* Seale, 49 So. 323, 160 Ala. 584; Alabama, etc., R. Co. *v.* Cox, 173 Ala. 629, 55 So. 909.

Duty of Street Car to Stop upon Signal of Passenger.—Where the relation of carrier and passenger exists between a street railway company and one who takes passage on its cars, there is an implied duty, resulting from custom, to stop the vehicle upon the signal of the passenger at any regular stopping place, and allow the passenger to alight. Birmingham R., etc., Co. *v.* Arnold (Ala. App.), 60 So. 988.

Passenger on Wrong Train—Ejection before Destination Reached.—A passenger by mistake entered a train which was not allowed to carry passengers beyond a station ten miles short of his destination, and he was so informed by the conductor on presenting his ticket. Plaintiff declined to leave the train, though offered an opportunity, but traveled to the station ten miles short of his destination, where he was ejected by the conductor. Held, that plaintiff could recover if he was induced to enter the train by having it pointed out as his train by the agent who sold him his ticket. South & N. A. R. Co. *v.* Huffman, 76 Ala. 492.

Notifying Passenger of Arrival at Destination.—In Pullman Co. *v.* Lutz, 154 Ala. 517, 45 So. 675, the supreme court, after discussing the duties of sleeping car companies as to notifying passengers of arrival at their destination, said that it does not mean to intimate, in what was said in respect to the duty imposed by law on sleeping car companies, that the common carrier is thereby relieved of its duty to likewise notify passengers of arrival at their destination. Pullman Co. *v.* Lutz, 154 Ala. 517, 45 So. 675.

Carrying Passenger beyond Destination.—"'Common carriers are liable in damages to passengers who are carried beyond their destination without fault on the part of the passenger, whether resulting from the negligence of the carrier or a breach of his contract.' North Alabama Tract. Co. *v.* Daniel, 158 Ala. 414, 48 So. 50." Alabama, etc., R. Co. *v.* Cox, 173 Ala. 629, 55 So. 909, 912.

When a train runs past the station and stops, it is the conductor's duty to cause it to be returned, in order that plaintiff may depart at the station; and, if that duty is not waived by the plaintiff, and is not performed, plaintiff is entitled to an action. Louisville, etc., R. Co. *v.* Dancy, 97 Ala. 338, 11 So. 796, 797.

If in such case the conductor offers to return, or manifests to plaintiff a purpose to do so, and plaintiff would not wait for the brakes to be put in condition that he might do so; or if she otherwise waited such return and voluntarily left the train—no action will lie. Louisville, etc., R. Co. *v.* Dancy, 97 Ala. 338, 11 So. 796, 797.

If in such case the conductor does not offer to return, or manifest to plaintiff a purpose to do so; and if plaintiff leaves the train, as the best thing she could do, after the conductor has had reasonable opportunity to make known to her a purpose on his part to return, if he had such a purpose—then she is entitled to an action. Louisville, etc., R. Co. *v.* Dancy, 97 Ala. 338, 11 So. 796.

Passenger Carried beyond Destination —Notice of Violation of Rules.—Plaintiff applied to defendant's ticket agent for a ticket to go on the limited train to a certain point. The ticket was refused, because the limited train did not stop at that point. Plaintiff then applied to the conductor, who told her to get on the limited train without a ticket, and that he would let her off at her destination; but she was carried to the station beyond her destination. It appeared that there was another daily train which stopped at plaintiff's station. Held, that plaintiff had sufficient notice that any agreement the conductor might make to put her off at the place she named would be a violation of the rules of the company, and no recovery can be had of the company because of the conductor's failure to keep his agreement. Alabama G. S. R. Co. *v.* Carmichael, 90 Ala. 19, 8 So. 87, 9 L. R. A. 388.

Passenger Carried beyond Destination Not a Regular Stopping Place.—In an action against a railroad company, plaintiff alleged a failure and refusal to stop the train at her destination, and that she was put off, with her baggage, against her protest and objection, half a mile further on. The evidence showed without contradiction that the train operators made every effort to stop the train, and it was not done owing to imperfect communication with the engineer, it not being a regular stopping place. It also appeared that plaintiff left the train without any protest or objection. Held, that the affirmative charge requested by defendant should have been given. Louisville & N. R. Co. *v.* Dancy, 97 Ala. 338, 11 So. 796, cited in note in 17 L. R. A., N. S., 1227, 1228, 1230.

§ 170. Discharging and Setting Down Passengers.

It is the duty of a carrier of passengers

to stop its train long enough for passengers to get off at their stopping places; such length of time may in cases depend upon peculiar circumstances, but in general it is such as passengers using reasonable diligence require. Louisville, etc., R. Co. *v.* Cornelius (Ala.), 62 So. 710; Alabama Mid. R. Co. *v.* Johnson, 123 Ala. 197, 26 So. 160, 161; Montgomery, etc., R. Co. *v.* Stewart, 91 Ala. 421, 8 So. 708; Birmingham Union R. Co. *v.* Smith, 90 Ala. 60, 8 So. 86.

It is the duty of a railroad, as a common carrier of passengers, to safely deliver them at the station to which they have paid fare, and such duty includes the announcement of the arrival of the train, and a reasonable opportunity to leave the cars at a place safe and convenient for alighting. Central, etc., R. Co. *v.* Carlisle, 2 Ala. App. 514, 56 So. 737.

Duty of Street Railways.—"Our decisions hold that the duty of a street railway carrier is not performed when it lands its passenger at a time and at a place of such unknown environment to him that, in his first effort to depart after alighting, he walks into unknown danger. Montgomery St. Railway *v.* Mason, 133 Ala. 508, 32 So. 261." Waldrop *v.* Nashville, etc., Railway (Ala.), 62 So. 769, 770.

It was wantonly negligent for a motorman to run his car at a high rate of speed on entering a station and passing another car on an adjoining track, which had stopped or was stopping to discharge passengers. Birmingham Ry., Light & Power Co. *v.* Landrum, 45 So. 198, 153 Ala. 192, cited in note in 21 L. R. A., N. S., 888.

Custom of Stopping at Particular Place.—Where trains of defendant railroad company were accustomed to stop at a platform, though it was neither constructed nor owned by the company, there is an implied contract that passengers may stop there. Louisville & N. R. Co. *v.* Johnston, 79 Ala. 436.

Notice of Arrival at Destination.—The duty imposed on a sleeping car company to notify its patrons of arrival at destination does not relieve the carrier of the same duty. Pullman Co. *v.* Lutz, 45 So. 675, 154 Ala. 517.

Promise to Inform Passenger of Arrival.—Where, in an action against a carrier for carrying plaintiff beyond her destination, the evidence tended to show that the conductor had promised to inform her when the train arrived at her destination, and that she had relied on this promise, a charge that, if this was true, plaintiff was not obliged to listen for or depend on the call of the station by the brakeman, is correct. Louisville & N. R. Co. *v.* Quick, 28 So. 14, 125 Ala. 553.

§ 171. Actions Arising Out of Breach of Contract.

§ 172. —— Pleading.

§ 172 (1) Complaint.

Action for Failure to Establish and Maintain Depot.—In order to maintain an action against a railroad company under the statute for damages resulting from a failure to establish and maintain a depot sufficient for the accommodation of passengers in a given town (Code, p. 974; Acts 1896-97, p. 956), it is necessary that the complaint should aver that the defendant's road was being operated through the corporate limits of the particular town, and that said town had more than 1,000 inhabitants. Page *v.* Louisville & N. R. Co., 29 So. 676, 129 Ala. 232.

Action for Refusal to Stamp Return Ticket.—A court in a complaint against a railroad company alleging the purchase by plaintiff of a round-trip ticket from defendant, providing that the holder shall be identified before a certain designated agent of the company before presenting the same for return passage, and that such ticket shall be void unless stamped by such agent, and alleging that plaintiff presented herself for identification as required, but that said agent refused to stamp the ticket, and that, when she presented the same for passage, she was ejected from the train, states a cause of action for the refusal to stamp the ticket. McGhee *v.* Reynolds, 23 So. 68, 117 Ala. 413.

Allegations as to Placing Passenger Wrongfully in Smoking Car.—A count in a complaint for injuries received from accommodation furnished, which alleged that plaintiff boarded defendant's train, which contained at least one first-class car, and paid first-class fare; that he was blind, and so constituted physically that the inhaling of tobacco smoke in large quantities would make him sick, and defendant's servant wrongfully and negligently caused plaintiff to remain in a smoker, where the air was so laden with smoke that as a proximate consequence thereof plaintiff was made sick—was not insufficient because failing to allege that plaintiff was placed in the car against his protest or objection; those allegations not being necessary in an action for simple negligence. Louisville & N. R. Co. *v.* Weathers, 50 So. 268, 163 Ala. 48.

Likewise a count embracing the above count, with additional averments that defendant's servant, acting within the line of his authority as such, being informed that to inhale tobacco smoke would make plaintiff sick, nevertheless wrongfully and wantonly, or wrongfully and intentionally, caused plaintiff, against his protest, to be or remain in a car where there was a large quantity of tobacco smoke, known as a "second-class" or "smoker," and thereby the servant so acting wrongfully, wantonly, and vexatiously caused plaintiff to suffer the said injuries and damages, was sufficient. Louisville, etc., R. Co. *v.* Weathers, 163 Ala. 48, 50 So. 268.

Allegations as to Causing Plaintiff to Alight at Wrong Place.—A complaint against a street railway company for failing to set plaintiff down at her proper destination at night, alleging that the relation of passenger and carrier existed between the parties and that it was defendant's duty to set plaintiff down at a particular street, but that it negligently failed to do so, stated a cause of action. Birmingham R., etc., Co. *v.* McDaniel, 6 Ala. App. 322, 59 So. 334.

Plaintiff alleged that on a specified day she was a passenger on one of defendant's cars for the common carriage of passengers for hire, that defendant's conductor in charge of the car willfully, etc., directed plaintiff to alight in the night time at a place that was not her destination but which was strange to her; that he knew that if plaintiff was put off in the night time in a strange place she would suffer mental distress, inconvenience, and annoyance, but, notwithstanding such knowledge, consciously, willfully, wantonly, etc., caused her to alight at a different place than her destination to her great damage, etc. Held, that such count was fatally defective for failure to allege facts showing the plaintiff's right to be carried to the place styled her "place of destination," and also for failure to show that the conductor's act in setting her down at the place he did was wrongful. Birmingham R., etc., Co. *v.* McDaniel, 6 Ala. App. 322, 59 So. 334.

In an action by a passenger for being compelled to debark short of his desired destination, counts in the complaint, failing to aver with certainty that such destination was one of the scheduled or customary stopping places of the train for the taking on and discharge of passengers, was fatally defective. Cook *v.* Southern Ry. Co., 45 So. 156, 153 Ala. 118.

Allegations as to Carrying Passenger Beyond Destination.—A complaint, alleging that plaintiff's signals to stop near his home were ignored, that the car proceeded to the terminal, that plaintiff stayed on the car to go home on the return trip, that at a car shed between the terminal and plaintiff's destination the conductor told plaintiff that he would have to sleep in the shed or walk, that when the car began to back into the shed plaintiff got off, whereupon the car was immediately run on toward plaintiff's home, that plaintiff unsuccessfully tried to reboard the car, that both the motorman and conductor taunted him with having to sleep in the shed or walk, that he had to walk home, and that he was and had been sick, etc., was not demurrable as not specifying what act plaintiff relied on, or whether it was a servant of defendant who taunted plaintiff, etc. North Alabama Traction Co. *v.* Daniel, 48 So. 50, 158 Ala. 414.

A complaint in an action against a street car company for carrying a passenger beyond her destination, which averred that plaintiff was a passenger on one of defendant's street cars, known as the Boyles line, to Canal Station, and paid the fare charged for carrying plaintiff to that station, and that defendant contracted to carry her there, is sufficient, for the relation of passenger and carrier obligated the street car company to stop at the station named and allow plaintiff a reasonable opportunity to alight; and though it is necessary for plaintiff to prove that, in addition to payment of the fare mentioned, Canal Station was a regular stopping place at which the car she was on would stop upon the request of a passenger, and that she made such request, those facts are matters of evidence which need not be averred. Birmingham R., etc., Co. *v.* Arnold (Ala. App.), 60 So. 988.

The averment of the complaint of a passenger for being carried beyond his destination that his mother, also a passenger with him, when paying the fares to the conductor, told him plaintiff desired to get off at a certain point, which is on said line, and a regular stop for cars thereon, and that the conductor agreed to put plaintiff off there, shows a duty of the conductor to afford him an opportunity to get off there. Birmingham R., etc., Co. *v.* Elmit, 6 Ala. App. 657, 60 So. 982.

A complaint, in a passenger's action for damages for carrying her beyond her destination, averring that defendant "negligently failed or refused to stop said train * * * a sufficient length of time for the plaintiff to alight while the train was not in motion" was not objectionable as requiring too long a stop by defendant and not alleging that plaintiff did not have a reasonable time in which to alight. Louisville, etc., R. Co. *v.* Cornelius (Ala.), 62 So. 710.

Allegations as to Carrying Passenger Beyond Destination Held Insufficient.—The complaint of a passenger, alleging that her destination was a certain point on the carrier's line, and that the conductor negligently failed to stop the car, as it was his duty to do, at such point long enough for her to alight, whereby she was carried past it, is insufficient in not stating facts showing a duty to stop there, or that it was a regular or customary stopping place, or that he agreed or consented to stop. Birmingham R., etc., Co. *v.* Elmit (Ala. App.), 60 So. 981, followed in Birmingham R., etc., Co. *v.* Elmit, 6 Ala. App. 657, 60 So. 982.

The complaint of a passenger, alleging that the conductor willfully failed to stop the car at the point stated to have been plaintiff's destination, like one for negligence, is insufficient; it stating no facts showing a duty to stop there. Birmingham R., etc., Co. *v.* Elmit (Ala. App.), 60 So. 981, followed in Birmingham R., etc., Co. *v.* Elmit, 6 Ala. App. 657, 60 So. 982.

Necessity for Pleading Special Damages.—Special damages not the necessary result of a breach of a contract to carry a passenger are not recoverable unless specially pleaded. Louisville, etc., R. Co. *v.* Sanders (Ala. App.), 61 So. 482.

Complaint Held Sufficient.—In an action for damages in being set down at a wrong station, the amended complaint, held to show the relation of passenger and carrier, the duty violated, and to state a substantial cause of action. Southern Ry. Co. *v.* Melton, 47 So. 1008, 158 Ala. 404.

§ 172 (2) Plea.

A plea in an action for breach of contract to carry plaintiff and companions in an automobile from one place to another and return, which alleges that, after the breaking down of the automobile, plaintiff left the disabled car, and could not be found when defendant reached the car with another automobile, but which fails to aver that plaintiff was at fault in leaving the broken-down car before another car came, or that defendant exercised proper care in sending relief after notice, is bad on demurrer. Taxicab Co. *v.* Grant, 3 Ala. App. 393, 57 So. 141.

A plea which fails to show that any negligence of plaintiff proximately contributed to the breaking down of the car, and which shows that the results were attributable to the act of defendant, is bad on demurrer. Taxicab Co. *v.* Grant, 3 Ala. App. 393, 57 So. 141.

§ 172 (3) Issues, Proof and Variance.

Matters to Be Proved.—In an action for damages against a carrier for breach of its duty to permit a passenger to remain on the train until the regular stopping place for the train to which he had a ticket was reached, it must be proved that, under the schedule and rules, such station was a stopping place for such train, and that plaintiff was wrongfully deprived of the right to remain on the train. Louisville, etc., R. Co. *v.* Thomason, 6 Ala. App. 365, 60 So. 506. See to same effect, Birmingham R., etc., Co. *v.* Arnold (Ala. App.), 60 So. 988.

The allegations of a complaint, in an action against a railroad company because its gateman at a union depot negligently misdirected plaintiff as to a train of another railroad, that plaintiff purchased a ticket over the latter road from defendant is descriptive of the wrong imputed to defendant, and must be proved, though the pleader might have confined his averment to the allegation that he had purchased a ticket omitting the allegation that it was purchased from and sold by defendant. Louisville, etc., R. Co. *v.* Cannon, 158 Ala. 453, 48 So. 64.

Immaterial Allegations.—In an action by a passenger against a carrier for damages from failure to notify her where to change cars, an allegation that the motive power used was steam was immaterial, and need not be proved. Central of Georgia Ry. Co. *v.* Ashley, 48 So. 981, 159 Ala. 145.

Variance—Passenger Put Off the Train.—An allegation in an action for damages sustained by a passenger in being set down at a station other than her destination, that she was "put off the train," when read in connection with the allegation that the conductor told her that it was her station and that in reliance thereon she got off, meant no more than she got off the train in response to the conductor's invitation; and there was no material variance in that respect between the allegation and the proof. Southern R. Co. *v.* Melton, 158 Ala. 404, 47 So. 1008, 1009.

Where, in an action against a carrier, the wrong complained of was causing plaintiff to get off the train, and it was proved that plaintiff was a passenger entitled to be carried to a certain station, and was wrongfully put off before reaching such station, there was no fatal variance. Louisville & N. R. Co. *v.* Quinn, 39 So. 756, 146 Ala. 330.

Purchase of Ticket.—There is no variance between the allegation that a ticket was purchased from defendant carrier, its agent or servant, and proof that the ticket was purchased from another company as an initial carrier, but was recognized as valid by defendant as a connecting carrier. Alabama City, G. & A. Ry. Co. *v.* Brady, 49 So. 351, 160 Ala. 615.

Variance Held Fatal.—Where the complaint, in an action against a railroad company for the conductor's refusal to stop its train at the proper station, alleges that he "willfully refused" to stop, and carried her several hundred yards beyond, "without her consent and against her protest," and the evidence shows that the conductor only neglected to stop, and that plaintiff consented to alight at the further place without objection or protest, there is a fatal variance. Louisville & N. R. Co. *v.* Johnston, 79 Ala. 436.

A complaint, in an action against a railroad company because its gateman at a union depot misdirected plaintiff as to a train of another railroad, that plaintiff purchased a ticket over the latter road from defendant, and that defendant sold him the ticket, is descriptive of the wrong imputed to defendant, and must be proved, and is not supported by proof that the ticket agent at the depot sold tickets for all the roads entering it. Louisville & N. R. Co. *v.* Cannon, 48 So. 64, 158 Ala. 453.

§ 173. —— Evidence.

Irrelevant Evidence.—In an action by a passenger against a carrier for requiring plaintiff to get off the train before reaching the station called for by plaintiff's ticket, evidence that after plaintiff left the train the engine went to a water tank near such station was not admissible for the purpose of showing whether or not it was dangerous for the train to go to such station. Louisville & N. R. Co. *v.* Quinn, 39 So. 756, 146 Ala. 330.

Declaration of Agent in Reference to Past Transaction.—In an action against a carrier for having to change cars when an agent had represented that a change of cars was unnecessary, a timetable given plaintiff's husband afterward by the agent was not admissible in evidence, since it was not res gestæ and stood on the same footing as a declaration of an agent in reference to a past transaction. Louisville, etc., R. Co. *v.* Thomason, 6 Ala. App. 365, 60 So. 506.

Custom of Mother to Meet Daughter at Destination.—In an action against a street railway for negligently carrying plaintiff beyond her destination, where damages were sought on the ground that plaintiff was not met by her mother with a lantern as soon as she might otherwise have been, a question seeking to elicit evidence tending to show that the conductor knew that plaintiff's mother habitually met her with a lantern is proper. Birmingham R., etc., Co. *v.* Arnold (Ala. App.), 60 So. 988.

Similar Transactions.—In an action by a passenger for being carried beyond her destination, testimony of a witness that this was the first time he had ever seen a passenger carried by a flag station is inadmissible. Louisville & N. R. Co. *v.* Seale, 49 So. 323, 160 Ala. 584.

Evidence to Show Wilful Misdirection.—In an action by a passenger for damages resulting from having taken the wrong car in pursuance to a direction of the railroad's flagman, the fact that plaintiff was a witness in another case involving misconduct on the part of the flagman was not competent as tending to show that he willfully directed her to the wrong car. Robertson *v.* Louisville & N. R. Co., 37 So. 831, 142 Ala. 216.

Condition of Plaintiff after Leaving Train.—In an action by a passenger for being carried beyond her destination, it was proper to allow a witness to answer the question as to what became of plaintiff immediately after she came to witness' house, as the answer had a bearing on the condition of plaintiff. Louisville, etc., R. Co. *v.* Seale, 160 Ala. 584, 49 So. 323.

Where a passenger is carried beyond his destination, in an action for damages therefor, the fact that plaintiff was sick when she left the train, though unknown to the conductor, and the rough condition of the track back to the station over which plaintiff walked, are admissible in evidence to show the relation between subsequent aggravation of her sickness and defendant's wrongful act. East Tennessee, V. & G. R. Co. *v.* Lockhart, 79 Ala. 315, cited in note in 17 L. R. A., N. S., 1226, 1227, 1228, 1230.

Knowledge of Passenger's Presence on Train and Destination.—In an action by a passenger for being carried beyond her destination, evidence as to what the rules of the company are as to where passengers get on and off the train is admissible, as bearing upon the questions whether employees knew that plaintiff had boarded the train and whether she had had an opportunity to inform the employees of her destination; and evidence as to what was the custom and usage of defendant about trains leaving the station at which plaintiff boarded the train was also admissible for the same reasons. Louisville, etc., R. Co. *v.* Seale, 160 Ala. 584, 49 So. 323.

Aggravating Circumstances.—In an action against a carrier for taking a passenger past his destination, evidence of conversations between plaintiff and the conductor and motorman of the car, tending to show aggravation of the wrong and bearing on the issue of plaintiff's right to recover punitive damages, was admissible. North Alabama Tract. Co. *v.* Daniel, 3 Ala. App. 428, 57 So. 120.

Sufficiency of Evidence to Prove Custom.—Evidence of a witness who had traveled on a train about once a month for more than a year was not sufficient to prove custom on the part of the trainmen in calling stations or announcing change of cars. Southern Ry. Co. *v.* Wooley, 48 So. 369, 158 Ala. 447.

§ 174. —— Damages.

§ 174 (1) Elements and Measure of Damages in General.

The measure of damages for carrying a passenger beyond his station is compensation merely for the actual loss sustained, in the absence of some element of gross disregard of his rights, or of facts showing insult or abuse; but the carrier is responsible for the discomfort, expenses, and charges proximately resulting from the breach of contract. Central of Georgia Ry. Co. *v.* Morgan, 49 So. 865, 161 Ala. 483, cited in note in 41 L. R. A., N. S., 745.

Plaintiff purchased a ticket to S. from the station agent of defendant, and by his direction entered a departing train which did not stop at S., and was compelled to get off at a station three miles from S. Held, that plaintiff was entitled to the actual damages sustained from the mistake of the agent. Alabama G. S. R.

Co. *v.* Heddleston, 82 Ala. 218, 3 So. 53, cited in notes in 2 L. R. A., N. S., 507, 24 L. R. A., N. S., 1179.

The plaintiff, who was a young girl about eight years of age, being carried about one mile beyond her destination, and put off at a place with which she was not familiar, would naturally be frightened by her condition and surroundings, and attempt to walk rapidly along the track back to the station; and for damages resulting from these natural consequences of the defendant's wrongful act, a recovery may be had. East Tennessee, etc., R. Co. *v.* Lockhart, 79 Ala. 315, cited in note in 7 L. R. A., N. S., 1183.

In an action against a street railway for damages for carrying plaintiff, a passenger, beyond her destination, where the complaint counted on one single contract, although it appeared that plaintiff was carried beyond her destination going out, and that on the return trip of the car the conductor failed to stop at her stopping place, a recovery may be had for damages for being carried by the station on her return trip. Birmingham R., etc., Co. *v.* Arnold (Ala. App.), 60 So. 988.

Physical Suffering and Inconvenience.—A passenger who was not informed of the stopping place nearest his destination, and who was carried by, so that he was compelled to walk four miles instead of one, may recover for the added fatigue, annoyance, and inconvenience. Louisville, etc., R. Co. *v.* Sanders (Ala. App.), 61 So. 482. See, also, Louisville, etc., R. Co. *v.* Quick, 125 Ala. 553, 28 So. 14.

Special Damages.—Damages for blistered feet from not being informed of a train's stopping place nearest his destination, as a result of which a passenger had a longer walk to his destination, are not a necessary result of the carrier's negligence, but are in their nature special damages. Louisville, etc., R. Co. *v.* Sanders (Ala. App.), 61 So. 482.

Trouble and Inconvenience in Returning to Destination.—A passenger who is carried beyond his destination may recover from the carrier damages for his trouble and inconvenience in getting back to his destination. East Tennessee, V. & G. R. Co. *v.* Lockhart, 79 Ala. 315, cited in note in 17 L. R. A., N. S., 1226, 1227, 1228, 1230.

Anxiety and Physical Injuries Suffered after Return to Destination.—In an action against a carrier for carrying plaintiff beyond her destination, the anxiety and physical injury caused by her exposure to rain and cold after being returned to her destination are not proper elements of damage. Louisville & N. R. Co. *v.* Quick, 28 So. 14, 125 Ala. 553, cited in note in 17 L. R. A., N. S., 1028.

§ 174 (2) Nominal or Substantial Damages.

Evidence Justifying Only Nominal Damages.—Where, in an action against a carrier for failure to stop at a passenger's destination, he alleged that in consequence of such breach of duty he suffered great physical and mental pain and was put to great trouble and expense, and, having a large amount of money on his person, was put in great fear, etc., but the evidence showed that after leaving the train he walked directly to his home and was only compelled to walk about a mile further than he would have walked had he alighted at his destination, and there was no evidence that he suffered mental or physical pain, or that he had a large amount of money as alleged, or was compelled to go through a lonely country, etc., he was, at most, entitled to recover only nominal damages. Blackburn *v.* Alabama Great Southern R. Co., 39 So. 345, 143 Ala. 346, cited in note in 17 L. R. A., N. S., 1231. See Louisville, etc., R. Co. *v.* Dancy, 97 Ala. 338, 11 So. 796.

§ 174 (3) Mental Suffering.

Where plaintiff is carried beyond her destination by no fault of her own, but by failure of the carrier's agent to perform his duty, the company is liable in damages for whatever vexation, anxiety, and physical injury she may have suffered in consequence of such wrongful act in returning to the point of destination. Louisville & N. R. Co. *v.* Quick, 28 So. 14, 125 Ala. 553, cited in note in 17 L. R. A., N. S., 1228. See, to same effect, Louisville, etc., R. Co. *v.* Dancy, 97 Ala. 338, 11 So. 796.

§ 174 (4) Exemplary Damages.

Willfulness or Gross Negligence.—Punitive damages may be recovered of a carrier by a passenger, where through willfulness or gross negligence of the conductor the passenger was carried by the place at which, when paying her fare, she told the conductor she wanted to get off. Birmingham Ry., Light & Power Co. *v.* Nolan, 32 So. 715, 134 Ala. 329, cited in note in 17 L. R. A., N. S., 1231.

In an action by a passenger to recover damages for injuries, the evidence showed that plaintiff purchased a ticket to a certain point on defendant's road, but that it carried her two to four hundred yards beyond the station, and on request refused to move the train back to the station; that she got off the train in a heavy rain storm, with a young baby in her arms, and got thoroughly wet before reaching the station house, and in consequence became sick. Held sufficient to warrant the giving of exemplary damages. Alabama G. S. R. Co. *v.* Sellers, 93 Ala. 9, 9 So. 375, cited in note in 17 L. R. A., N. S., 1231. See, also, Louisville, etc., R. Co. *v.* Dancy, 97 Ala. 338, 11 So. 796, 797.

Where, in an action for leaving plaintiff, a passenger, at a station short of her destination, there was evidence justifying an inference that defendant's flagman was guilty of wantonness in directing plaintiff to remove to the wrong car, an instruction that punitive damages could not be claimed was properly refused. Southern Ry. Co. *v.* Wooley, 48 So. 369, 158 Ala. 447.

Unintentional Error — Negligence. — Where plaintiff, having been compelled to debark from defendant's train short of his desired destination, suffered no other injury than an expenditure of 50 cents for a hack, and the conductor's act in compelling such debarkation was not attended with any element of aggravation, but was due to a mere unintentional error of judgment, plaintiff could not recover punitive damages. Cook *v.* Southern Ry. Co., 45 So. 156, 153 Ala. 118.

One is not entitled to punitive damages because he had to change cars when told by the ticket seller that no change was necessary, where the change to the accommodation train only caused a loss of twelve minutes in reaching the destination; the representation of the agent arising only from negligence or ignorance of the schedule and not from willfulness. Louisville, etc., R. Co. *v.* Thomason, 6 Ala. App. 365, 60 So. 506.

In an action against a railroad company for damages for failure to stop and take up passengers at a flag station, it was error to charge that an award of punitive damages might be made if the engineer could, by the exercise of ordinary care and diligence, have seen the signal to stop and understood it. St. Louis, etc., R. Co. *v.* Garner (Ala.), 51 So. 273.

§ 174 (5) Excessive Damages.

Misinformation as to Route.—A verdict for $1,500 for failure by a carrier to inform a passenger as to the best and quickest route as not excessive, where as a result of the misdirection the route taken was slower and less desirable than another route, and she was compelled to make four or five stops and as many changes of cars, in one or two instances traveling on a freight train to make connections, and was two days in making the trip, and compelled to stand for a long time, and was greatly shaken, and, being in poor health, which was communicated to the carrier, was made worse by the trip and put to expense for medicine and medical attention. Southern Ry. Co. *v.* Nowlin, 47 So. 180, 156 Ala. 222.

Placing Passenger in Improper Car.—Where plaintiff, who was blind, was placed in the smoking car of his train by defendant's servants, over his protest that he held first-class ticket and was entitled to ride in the first-class coach, and that tobacco smoke always made him sick, and was actually made sick by the smoke, a verdict for $700, while large, is not so excessive as to require the interference by the supreme court, especially where the trial court has refused a new trial on such ground. Louisville, etc., R. Co. *v.* Weathers, 163 Ala. 48, 50 So. 268.

Carrying Passenger Beyond Destination.—A passenger with a ticket boarded a train which did not stop at his station. The conductor refused to stop the train or to slow down to enable the passenger to alight, but he was carried to the next station, where he alighted. He lost several hours there, and was exposed to the cold in the nighttime, and suffered from a cold in the head thereafter. The evidence was conflicting on the issue as to what occurred between the passenger and the conductor and between the passenger and the station agent at the station where he alighted. Held, that a verdict of $500, reduced by the court to $250, was not excessive. Central, etc., R. Co. *v.* Morgan, 161 Ala. 483, 49 So. 865, cited in note in 41 L. R. A., N. S., 745.

Plaintiff, a street car passenger, signaled defendant's servants to stop the car on which he was riding at a point near his home, but the car was not stopped there or at the next street crossing, a point equally near plaintiff's home, but plaintiff was taken to the end of the line and then compelled to walk back. There was also evidence indicating an aggravation of the wrong by mistreatment on the part of defendant's employees. Held, that a verdict awarding plaintiff $1,000 damages was not excessive. North Alabama Tract. Co. *v.* Daniel, 3 Ala. App. 428, 57 So. 120, cited in note in 41 L. R. A., N. S., 746.

Failure to Notify of Place to Change Cars.—Where a passenger, as a result of the carrier's failure to notify her where to change cars, was deflected in her journey and compelled to bear added travel and sojourn in hotels, resulting in annoyance, illness, anxiety, and some expense, a recovery of $500 was not excessive. Central of Georgia Ry. Co. *v.* Ashley, 48 So. 981, 159 Ala. 145.

Verdict Held Excessive.—$1,750 damages was excessive recovery for a street car company's failure to permit him to alight at his destination, and for indignities inflicted by employees, though he had to walk half a mile, and had been sick, and was made nervous, and was insulted by the employees, where he suffered no serious or permanent injuries and had habitually taunted the motorman on former trips. North Alabama Traction Co. *v.* Daniel, 48 So. 50, 158 Ala. 414, cited in note in 41 L. R. A., N. S., 746.

A verdict of $150 to a man of thirty-two, in robust health, who did not lose any part of his wages thereby, who, because of defendant's failure to inform him of the stopping place nearest his destination, was obliged to walk four miles instead of one to his place of work, carrying a bag of tools on a warm day, and was thereby fatigued, annoyed, and inconvenienced, was excessive. Louisville, etc., R. Co. *v.* Sanders (Ala. App.), 61 So. 482.

§ 175. —— Trial.

§ 175 (1) Questions for Jury.

Sufficiency of Time for Taking up Tickets.—Evidence in an action by a passenger for being carried by her destination held to make the question whether the conductor had had a reasonable time after leaving the station in which to take up tickets a question for the jury. Louisville, etc., R. Co. *v.* Seale, 160 Ala. 584, 49 So. 323.

Authority of Agent of One Company to Sell Ticket for Another Company.—Where a railroad ticket sold by the agent of one company was recognized as valid for passage to some extent over the road of another company, the authority of the agent to sell the ticket is a question for the jury. Alabama City, G. & A. Ry. Co. *v.* Brady, 49 So. 351, 160 Ala. 615.

Negligence.—Plaintiff, a passenger, on giving her ticket to the conductor, told him that she desired to alight at A. and that she was not acquainted with the stations along the road. Thereafter defendant's flagman asked plaintiff where she was going, told her that the car she was on did not go to A., and directed her at a junction to go into another car, which proved to be the wrong car, and plaintiff was compelled to leave the train and await another; the right car having left. Held, that whether defendant was negligent was for the jury. Southern Ry. Co. *v.* Wooley, 48 So. 369, 158 Ala. 447.

Gross Negligence.—In an action against a street railway company for damages for carrying a passenger beyond her station, evidence held to present a question for the jury whether the conductor was guilty of such gross negligence in failing to stop that punitive damages might be awarded. Birmingham Ry., Light &

Power Co. *v.* Arnold (Ala. App.), 60 So. 988; Birmingham R., etc., Co. *v.* Nolan, 134 Ala. 329, 32 So. 715, 716.

Wantonness.—Plaintiff, a passenger, on giving her ticket to the conductor, told him that she desired to alight at A. and that she was not acquainted with the stations along the road. Thereafter defendant's flagman asked plaintiff where she was going, told her that the car she was on did not go to A., and directed her at a junction to go into another car, which proved to be the wrong car, and plaintiff was compelled to leave the train and await another; the right car having left. Held, that if the flagman knew that the car occupied by plaintiff was the proper car to convey her to her destination, and that the other was the wrong car, and realized that his action would probably result in inconvenience and injury to plaintiff, wantonness might be fairly attributed to him, a purpose to injure not being an ingredient of wantonness, and the question of wantonness was for the jury. Southern R. Co. *v.* Wooley, 158 Ala. 447, 48 So. 369.

§ 175 (2) Instructions.

Carrying Passenger Beyond Destination.—In an action by a passenger to recover damages for injuries by being carried beyond her station, where the complaint alleged that plaintiff was "compelled to get off" the train, it was proper to refuse a charge that there could be no recovery unless force was used by the conductor in getting her off. Alabama G. S. R. Co. *v.* Sellers, 93 Ala. 9, 9 So. 375.

In an action against a carrier for failure to discharge plaintiff at his destination, instructions that, if plaintiff left the car at the barn and started to walk home, he then ceased to be a passenger, and defendant owed him no further duty, and that plaintiff ceased to be a passenger when he got on the sidewalk, whether he left the car voluntarily or not, were properly refused; it being immaterial to the question whether defendant committed a breach of duty in failing to discharge plaintiff at his destination, and in wrongfully putting him off at another place. North Alabama Tract. Co. *v.* Daniel, 3 Ala. App. 428, 57 So. 120.

In an action for injuries to a street car passenger for failure and refusal of defendant's servants to stop the car to allow plaintiff to get off at his destination and wrongfully allowing him to alight at a different and distant place, an instruction that defendant could not take advantage of its own wrong by inducing a passenger by misrepresentations to alight, and then declare a severance of his relations with him as a passenger in order to avoid liability, did not constitute reversible error. North Alabama Tract. Co. *v.* Daniel, 3 Ala. App. 428, 57 So. 120.

A charge, in a passenger's action for damages for being carried beyond her station, that the jury must find that defendant negligently failed to stop long enough for plaintiff to get off in safety, though not as comprehensive as it might have been, was not erroneous. Louisville, etc., R. Co. *v.* Cornelius (Ala.), 62 So. 710.

In an action against a carrier for carrying a passenger past her destination, the court properly refused to charge that if plaintiff, after being carried past her station, got off the train voluntarily, and was not put off by defendant's agents or servants, or some of them, the jury must bring in a verdict for defendant. Louisville, etc., R. Co. *v.* Seale, 160 Ala. 584, 49 So. 323.

Claim for Refusal to Back Train to Stopping Place—Efforts to Stop Train.—Where the claim for damages is for refusing to move a train back to the stopping place, obliging plaintiff to alight in a rain, and not for running beyond, it is proper to refuse to charge that, in determining whether defendant was negligent, the jury may take into consideration the character of the train, and the efforts made to stop it at the proper place in the first instance. Alabama G. S. R. Co. *v.* Sellers, 93 Ala. 9, 9 So. 375.

Charge on Directing Passenger to Wrong Car.—In an action against a railroad for damages sustained by a passenger by reason of having gotten onto the wrong car, the complaint alleged that defendant's "conductor or flagman" directed plaintiff to the wrong car. Plaintiff's evidence showed that both the conductor and flagman separately and at different times gave plaintiff the direction complained of. Defendant's flagman testified that he gave plaintiff no such direction, and had nothing to do therewith. The conductor was not examined, and hence plaintiff's testimony as to what he told her was uncontroverted. Held, that a charge that plaintiff could not recover unless defendant's "conductor and flagman" told plaintiff to get on the wrong car was erroneous and prejudicial. Robertson *v.* Louisville & N. R. Co., 37 So. 831, 142 Ala. 216.

(D) PERSONAL INJURIES.

§ 176. Care Required and Liability of Carrier in General.

As to instructions, see post, "Degree of Care Required in General," § 211 (2).

§ 176 (1) Care Required in General.

See, also, post, "Number and Efficiency of Employees," § 179 (5).

A carrier must exercise the highest degree of care in the carriage of passengers. Louisville & N. R. Co. *v.* Dilburn (Ala.), 59 So. 438; Louisville, etc., R. Co. *v.* Mulder, 149 Ala. 676, 42 So. 742; Birmingham R., etc., Co. *v.* Sawyer, 156 Ala. 199, 47 So. 67; Montgomery, etc., R. Co. *v.* Mallette, 92 Ala. 209, 9 So. 363; Alabama, etc., R. Co. *v.* Hill, 93 Ala. 514, 9 So. 722; Richmond, etc., R. Co. *v.* Greenwood, 99 Ala. 501, 14 So. 495, 500.

It is a carrier's duty to use a very high degree of care to safely transport its passengers, doing all that human care, vigilance, and foresight can reasonably do, in view of the character and mode of conveyance adopted, consistent with the practical operation of its cars. Southern Ry. Co. *v.* Cunningham, 44 So. 658, 152 Ala. 147.

A carrier's obligation is to carry his passenger safely and properly and to treat him respectfully. Culberson *v.* Empire Coal Co., 47 So. 237, 156 Ala. 416.

A carrier owes the duty to a passenger to provide a safe place for him to ride, to see that he is treated with respect by its servants, and not to expose him to unnecessary peril. Carleton *v.* Central of Georgia Ry. Co., 46 So. 495, 155 Ala. 326.

Highest Degree of Care Used by Persons in That Business.—The relationship between a carrier and passenger calls for the exercise by the carrier of the highest degree of care, skill, and diligence known to persons engaged in that business. Alabama, etc., R. Co. *v.* Robinson (Ala.), 62 So. 813; Louisville, etc., R. Co. *v.* Glasgow (Ala.), 60 So. 103.

There is no error in a charge that "the law requires the highest degree of care and diligence and skill, by those engaged in the carriage of passengers by railroads, known to careful, diligent, and skillful persons engaged in such business." Montgomery & E. Ry. Co. *v.* Mallette, 92 Ala. 209, 9 So. 363.

In an action for injuries to a passenger while in a Pullman car, caused by a table handled by a porter falling on her hand, a charge that the railroad company owed to its passengers the duty to exercise the highest degree of care, skill, and diligence known to skillful and diligent persons in like business was not erroneous. Louisville & N. R. Co. *v.* Church, 46 So. 457, 155 Ala. 329.

"Highest Degree of Care" Defined.—Though carriers of passengers are bound in respect to their duty to carry safely to exercise the highest degree of care, skill, and diligence, and are liable for the slightest degree of negligence proximately resulting in injury, the term "highest degree of care" is a relative one and means the highest degree required by law in any case where human safety is at stake, and the highest degree known to usage and practice of very careful, skillful, and diligent persons engaged in the same business by similar means of agencies, but does not mean that every "possible or conceivable" act of care precaution which might increase or even assure the safety of a passenger must be taken, only such as are practicable under the circumstances, viz, reasonably consistent with the practicable operation of the carrier's business, being required. Birmingham R., etc., Co. *v.* Barrett (Ala.), 60 So. 262.

"Strict Diligence."—An instruction that the law requires "strict diligence" on the part of the carriers of passengers is proper. Alabama G. S. R. Co. *v.* Hill, 93 Ala. 514, 9 So. 722.

Duty as to Safety Not Absolute.—The

law does not impose on carriers the duty of absolutely warranting the safety of passengers, and for casualties against which human sagacity can not provide, nor the utmost prudence prevent, a carrier is not liable. Irwin *v.* Louisville & N. R. Co., 50 So. 62, 161 Ala. 489. See, also, Culberson *v.* Empire Coal Co., 156 Ala. 416, 47 So. 237.

Not Highest Degree of Care Known to Human Skill.—An instruction that it was the duty of defendant carrier to exercise the highest degree of care known to human skill and foresight in the carriage of passengers, and it was liable for the slightest degree of negligence, was erroneous as requiring too high a degree of care. Birmingham R., etc., Co. *v.* Barrett, 4 Ala. App. 347, 53 So. 760; S. C., 60 So. 262.

Duty to Protect from Violence and Insults.—A carrier must carry passengers safely, and conserve by every reasonable means their safety throughout the journey, and protect them from insult or personal violence. Alabama City, G. & A. Ry. Co. *v.* Sampley, 53 So. 142, 169 Ala. 372, cited in note in 32 L. R. A., N. S., 1208.

A carrier is obliged to protect its passengers from violence and insults, from whatever source, and, though it is not an insurer of its passenger's safety against every possible danger, it is bound to use all such reasonable precautions as human judgment is capable of to make the passenger's journey safe and comfortable. Culberson *v.* Empire Coal Co., 156 Ala. 416, 47 So. 237. See, to same effect, Birmingham R., etc., Co. *v.* Glenn (Ala.), 60 So. 111.

Duration of Duty.—The duty of a carrier to protect its passengers is not confined to the carrier's vehicle but extends during the entire continuance of the relation. Nashville, etc., Railway *v.* Crosby (Ala.), 62 So. 889.

Duty as Affected by Nature of Vehicle Used.—A carrier of passengers is bound to exercise the highest degree of care to avoid injury to those whom he undertakes to carry as passengers, and for injuries resulting from a failure of duty in this regard the carrier is liable; and this rule applies without regard to the vehicle used for conveyance. Southern Ry. Co. *v.* Crowder, 30 So. 592, 130 Ala. 256. See, also, post, "Liability as to Passengers on Freight or Mixed Trains," § 176 (4).

§ 176 (2) Liability of Street Railroad Companies.

"It can not be doubted that street railway companies, as common carriers of passengers for hire, are under the duty of exercising the highest degree of diligence and care in conserving the safety of their passengers, and are responsible for the slightest neglect." Montgomery St. Railway *v.* Mason, 133 Ala. 508, 32 So. 261.

The court instructed that, if the car was suddenly jerked forward when plaintiff was alighting, she could recover, unless guilty of negligence proximately contributing to her injury. On objection the court modified the charge, to the effect that the defendant did not owe plaintiff the absolute duty to deliver her safely; that they were not insurers—absolute insurers—of the safety of passengers; but that they owed to the passenger the highest degree of care in delivering him safely. Held that, as modified, the instruction was correct. Birmingham Ry., Light & Power Co. *v.* King, 42 So. 612, 149 Ala. 504.

There is no error in giving a charge that it is the duty of a street car company as a common carrier of passengers to use such care, skill, and diligence toward passengers as a careful and prudent person engaged in that business would exercise. Alabama City, G. & A. Ry. Co. *v.* Bates, 46 So. 776, 155 Ala. 347.

§ 176 (3) Liability as to Passenger in Station.

The degree of care required of a carrier in protecting its passengers varies according to time and place; a high degree of care being required while the passenger is on the carrier's vehicle, and only ordinary care while the passenger is waiting at the carrier's station. Nashville, etc., Railway *v.* Crosby (Ala.), 62 So. 889.

§ 176 (4) Liability as to Passengers on Freight or Mixed Trains.

A railway company, admitting a passenger

into a caboose attached to a freight train, incurs the same liability for his safety as though he had taken passage on a regular passenger train. Southern R. Co. *v.* Burgess, 143 Ala. 364, 42 So. 35.

"It is neither expected nor required that a passenger upon a freight train shall be provided with all the comforts and conveniences which are usually afforded passengers on a regular passenger train; but there is, on that account, no diminution in the obligation of those in charge of the freight train to convey its passengers with becoming and all necessary care, and to deliver them safely at or conveniently near their respective places of destination. It is the duty of a railroad company engaged in the transportation of passengers, whether by freight or passengers trains, to so run and manage its trains, and to so handle its passengers, that no one shall be injured by its own negligence. Nothing ruled in the case of Southern R. Co. *v.* Crowder, 130 Ala. 256, 30 So. 592, is contrary to the doctrine above stated, but that case supports it." Southern R. Co. *v.* Burgess. 143 Ala. 364, 42 So. 35, 36.

Persons taking passage on a mixed train by permission of the common carrier assume no risks from the lack of proper care on the part of the carrier; nor does the fact that such train is composed mainly of freight cars lessen the degree of care resting upon the carrier, which requires of it all care available for the passenger's safety consistent with the practical operation of said train. Southern Ry. Co. *v.* Crowder, 30 So. 592, 130 Ala. 256.

An instruction, in an action for injuries to a passenger on a freight train, that a carrier owes to its passengers the duty to exercise the highest degree of diligence known to diligent persons engaged in like business, does not require too high a degree of care in the carriage of passengers on freight trains. Southern R. Co. *v.* Burgess, 143 Ala. 364, 42 So. 35.

Waiver of Precautions Inconsistent with Ordinary Use of Train.—When a passenger chooses to be transported on a train, not adapted to passenger service, such as a freight or a logging train, while he does not waive the carrier's duty of due care with respect to his safety, he does waive all precaution, whether in equipment or operation, which are inconsistent with the ordinary use and conduct of such a train, and assumes the risk of injury from accident incident to such train when equipped and operated in the usual way. Lawrence *v.* Kaul Lumber Co., 55 So. 111, 171 Ala. 300.

§ 176 (5) Care Required as to Passengers Riding in Places Not Designed for Them.

The fact that a passenger on a street car assumes a dangerous position does not alter his character as a passenger, or alter the degree of care that the carrier owes to him. Birmingham Ry., Light & Power Co. *v.* Bynum, 36 So. 736, 139 Ala. 389.

§ 176 (6) Care as to Passengers Who Do Not Pay Fare.

See ante, "Payment of Fare," § 153.

§ 176 (7) Liability of Carrier Not a Common Carrier of Passengers.

A carrier which is not a common carrier of passengers is liable to a passenger for injury proximately caused by its simple negligence. Lawrence *v.* Kaul Lumber Co., 171 Ala. 300, 55 So. 111.

§ 177. Care as to Persons under Disability.

A carrier, knowingly accepting as a passenger a person physically unable to take care of herself, must render to her such special assistance as her condition requires, so that she may be safely transported. Williams *v.* Louisville & N. R. Co., 43 So. 576, 150 Ala. 324, 10 L. R. A., N. S., 413.

Intoxicated Passenger.—The fact that a passenger has by intoxication voluntarily deprived himself of the ability to exercise ordinary care does not furnish any excuse for the conductor to force him from a place of safety in the train to one where it will require extraordinary care to avoid injury, and when the intoxication is apparent to the conductor it calls for extra precaution on his part. Central of Georgia Ry. Co. *v.* Carleton, 51 So. 27, 163 Ala. 62.

Care Required after Destination Reached.—Where an intoxicated passenger so demeans himself as to justify his ejection, and on reaching his destination in the nighttime leaves the train, and his body is found on the track under such circumstances as to show injury by another train which passed during the night, the railroad company is not liable, it being under no obligation to guard the passenger through the night. Nash *v.* Southern Ry. Co., 33 So. 932, 136 Ala. 177, cited in note in 8 L. R. A., N. S., 298.

§ 178. Persons to Whom Carrier Is Liable.

See, also, ante, "Who Are Passengers," § 151.

Assault on Person Not a Passenger.—A carrier is not liable for an assault committed by its servant or agent on a person not a passenger, and having no relation with the carrier, nor in any way encroaching on its rights, unless committed by its authority and under its direction. Birmingham Ry. & Electric Co. *v.* Mason, 34 So. 207, 137 Ala. 342.

Passenger Acting as Brakeman.—A railroad is not liable for injuries to a passenger while acting as brakeman, under the orders of the conductor, whom he was under no obligation to obey, and by whom he was not employed for that purpose. Georgia Pac. Ry. Co. *v.* Propst, 83 Ala. 518, 3 So. 764.

Trespasser.—A carrier owes only the duty not to injure wantonly a trespasser on its cars. Broyles *v.* Central, etc., R. Co., 166 Ala. 616, 52 So. 81.

One going on a passenger train to collect a debt from a passenger is a trespasser, so that the railroad company is only bound not to wantonly or willfully injure him, or to negligently do so after discovering his peril. McElvane *v.* Central of Georgia Ry. Co., 54 So. 489, 170 Ala. 525, cited in note in 37 L. R. A., N. S., 419.

Where intestate at the time of his injury had obtained permission to ride on a local freight train by falsely representing to the conductor that he was riding on an employer's pass, he was a trespasser, and not a passenger, as to whom the carrier was only liable for willful or wanton injury. Neyman *v.* Alabama Great Southern R. Co., 172 Ala. 606, 55 So. 509.

But for injuries to a licensee or trespasser a carrier which is not a common carrier of passengers is liable only for wanton negligence, or willful wrong, including its failure to exercise due care to avert injury after the danger is apparent. Lawrence *v.* Kaul Lumber Co., 171 Ala. 300, 55 So. 111.

§ 179. Acts or Omissions of Carrier's Employees.

§ 179 (1) Who Are Employees.

Employee Not Connected with the Carriage of Passengers.—The protection which a carrier owes to its passengers does not make it liable for an injury inflicted by one to whom it had not intrusted the performance of any duty connected with the carriage or protection of the passengers, unless the carrier or an employee charged with such a duty could reasonably have anticipated that a passenger would be subjected to injury, or was at fault in some respect in failing to prevent it. Alabama, etc., R. Co. *v.* Pouncey (Ala. App.), 61 So. 601.

Employee under Contract Not to Drink Whiskey While in Carrier's "Employ."—In an action against a railroad company for personal injuries to a passenger, the evidence showed that the engineer through whose negligence the accident occurred was under contract not to go into a saloon, or drink whiskey, while in defendant's "employ." Held, that he was in such employ during the interval from his arrival at a terminus of the road on one day until his departure therefrom on the next day. Kansas City, M. & B. R. Co. *v.* Phillips, 13 So. 65, 98 Ala. 159.

§ 179 (2) For What Acts of Employee Carrier Liable in General.

A common carrier is liable to any one sustaining the relation of passenger to it for an injury resulting from any act of its servants or employees, whether willful and malicious or not, and even though such act is not done in the course or within the scope of the servant's or agent's employment; the rule that the master is not liable for injury resulting from the willful and malicious acts of his agent, not done within the scope of his employment, not being applicable when the injury is inflicted upon a passenger by the carrier's agent or servant. Birmingham Ry. & Electric Co. *v.* Baird, 30 So.

456, 130 Ala. 334, 54 L. R. A. 752, cited in note in 40 L. R. A., N. S., 1007, 1051, 1056, 1068, 1073, 1077, 1083. But see post, catchline, "Accidental Act Not Incidental to Employment."

Where a carrier intrusts to its servants the performance of its duty to carry a passenger safely and properly, and to treat him respectfully, it is responsible for the manner in which the servants execute the trust. Culberson *v.* Empire Coal Co., 156 Ala. 416, 47 So. 237, cited in note in 40 L. R. A., N. S., 1076.

Liability Based on Breach of Absolute Duty.—When a passenger is disturbed by a servant of a carrier engaged in some service, the carrier's liability is bottomed not on the theory of negligence but rather upon the breach of an absolute duty. Nashville, etc., Railway *v.* Crosby (Ala.), 62 So. 889.

Negligence. — Though the obligation of a carrier is not that of an insurer, it must exercise the highest degree of care, and is bound to protect its passengers from the negligence of its employees. Louisville & N. R. Co. *v.* Mulder, 42 So. 742, 149 Ala. 676.

In an action for injuries to a passenger, a charge that, unless the jury believe from the evidence that defendant's servant or agent was guilty of negligence, they must find for defendant, was proper. Sweet *v.* Birmingham Ry. & Electric Co., 39 So. 767, 145 Ala. 667.

Requesting Passenger to Go on Platform.—The act of the conductor in requesting a passenger to go on the platform of a coach because of the crowded condition of the coach is an act done in managing the train. Central of Georgia Ry. Co. *v.* Brown, 51 So. 565, 165 Ala. 493, cited in note in 29 L. R. A., N. S., 326.

Granting Permission to Passenger to Leave Train Temporarily.—A conductor is the representative of the carrier in charge of a train, and controls the operation thereof, and he acts within the scope of his power if, while stopping at a place at which it is not customary to receive passengers, he grants a permission to a passenger to temporarily leave the train. Birmingham R., etc., Co. *v.* Jung, 161 Ala. 461, 49 So. 434, cited in notes in 22 L. R. A., N. S., 758, 30 L. R. A., N. S., 271.

Failure to Prevent Trespasser from Leaving Moving Train.—Since a passenger train conductor did not have the right to prevent a trespasser boarding the train at a station from alighting therefrom while it was moving two miles an hour in leaving the station, his failure to prevent him from alighting was not negligence, making the company liable for injuries sustained in alighting. McElvane *v.* Central of Georgia Ry. Co., 54 So. 489, 170 Ala. 525.

Accidental Act Not Incidental to Employment.—As a passenger was about to enter the car, one of the carrier's employees, in warding a blow aimed at him in sport by another employee, accidentally backed against the passenger, and pushed him from the station platform. Held, that the carrier was not liable, the employees' acts not being incidental to their employment. Goodloe *v.* Memphis & C. R. Co., 107 Ala. 233, 18 So. 166, 29 L. R. A. 729, cited in notes in 3 L. R. A., N. S., 605, 23 L. R. A., N. S., 1059, 40 L. R. A., N. S., 1007, 1008, 1049, 1072.

"What these parties did to cause plaintiff's injury was not in the line of their respective engagements, or that of either of them, to their employer; it was not fairly incidental to their employment; it was not done in pursuance of an express or implied authority from the master to do it; it was the result of the conduct of these employees who, in the commission of the injurious act, however innocently done, had stepped aside from the purposes of the agency committed to them, and inflicted an independent wrong on the plaintiff; and they, if anybody, and not the defendant company, are liable for it." Goodloe *v.* Memphis, etc., R. Co., 107 Ala. 233, 18 So. 166, 167. But see, Birmingham R., etc., Co. *v.* Baird, 130 Ala. 334, 30 So. 456, 54 L. R. A. 752. See notes in 3 L. R. A., N. S., 605, 23 L. R. A., N. S., 1059, 40 L. R. A., N. S., 1007, 1008, 1049, 1072.

Individual Suggestions of Station Agent.—In the absence of a showing to the contrary, it is not within the scope of a station agent's authority to suggest to or invite passengers leaving trains at the station to go to any particular hotel not owned by the carrier, or to follow any particular route in reaching such hotel, unless such route has otherwise received the sanction of the carrier, though it may be within his authority to inform passengers alighting from trains of a safe way of egress from the depot or approaches reasonably near thereto. Alabama Great Southern R. Co. *v.* Godfrey, 47 So. 185, 156 Ala. 202.

A statement of a station agent, made to a passenger alighting from a train at night, in going into the depot to deposit his grip, that a hotel man was there with a light, and that if the passenger would hurry he could catch up with him, amounted only to the agent's individual suggestion, for which the carrier was not responsible, unless the route taken to the hotel was within depot grounds or approaches thereto or was a passageway which the carrier had otherwise expressly or impliedly invited the public to use as a means of ingress or egress to or from its depot and platforms. Alabama, etc., R. Co. *v.* Godfrey, 156 Ala. 202, 47 So. 185.

§ 179 (3) Assault or Personal Violence.

A carrier is bound to protect its passengers from willful and malicious injury by its servants acting within the scope of their employment. Southern Ry. Co. *v.* Wideman, 24 So. 764, 119 Ala. 565, Southern R. Co. *v.* Hanby (Ala.), 62 So. 871; Lampkin *v.* Louisville, etc., R. Co., 106 Ala. 287, 17 So. 448.

A carrier must not only protect its passenger against violence and insults of co-passengers, but a fortiori against the violence and insults of its own servants; and if this duty to the passenger is not performed, and a passenger is assaulted and insulted through the negligence or willful misconduct of the carrier's servants the carrier is liable. Culberson *v.* Empire Coal Co., 156 Ala. 416, 47 So. 237, 40 L. R. A., N. S., 1076.

Where a conductor strikes a passenger, the company is liable, unless it is done in self-defense, or to save himself from bodily harm. Birmingham Ry., Light & Power Co. *v.* Mullen, 35 So. 701, 138 Ala. 614, cited in notes in 32 L. R. A., N. S., 1202, 33 L. R. A., N. S., 280, 40 L. R. A., N. S., 1008, 1051, 1078, 1084.

If the conductor of a train assaults a passenger otherwise than under a necessity to defend himself or a passenger from battery, or in rightfully ejecting the passenger, who, by his conduct to other passengers or otherwise, has forfeited his right to carriage, the carrier is liable. Birmingham R., etc., Co. *v.* Baird, 130 Ala. 334, 30 So. 456, 54 L. R. A. 752, cited in note in 40 L. R. A., N. S., 1007.

Duration of Duty.—A carrier must carry passengers safely and conserve by every reasonable means their safety throughout the journey and protect them from insult or personal violence from its employees, and such duty continues until the passenger is safely landed at his destination. Alabama, etc., R. Co. *v.* Sampley, 169 Ala. 372, 53 So. 142, cited in notes in 32 L. R. A., N. S., 1203, 40 L. R. A., N. S., 1008, 1051, 1060, 1061, 1071.

Presenting Pistol at Passenger.—Where a motorman while in charge of a car assaulted a passenger by pointing a pistol at him, and compelling him to leave the car, and the motorman did not thereby undertake to defend another passenger, or eject the passenger because of his conduct towards other passengers, the carrier was liable, unless the motorman acted in self-defense. Birmingham R., etc., Co. *v.* Tate (Ala. App.), 61 So. 32.

A street railway company, whose conductor assaulted a passenger by presenting a pistol at him at close range, was civilly liable unless the conductor was free from fault in bringing on the difficulty resulting in the use of the pistol and unless it reasonably appeared to him that it was necessary for him to present the pistol to protect his own person from a battery at the hands of the passenger, and hence the court did not err in charging that the assault could not be justified so as to relieve the company from liability unless the conductor was free from fault in bringing on the difficulty and unless it appeared to him reasonably and not merely fancifully that it was reasonably necessary to assault the passenger in order to protect himself or the person of another passenger, and unless the means adopted were in kind and degree no more than was reasonably necessary for such protection. Birmingham R., etc., Co. *v.* Coleman (Ala.), 61 So. 890.

Liability for Assault Continued after Passenger Has Left Car.—Where a conductor attacked a passenger before he alighted from the car and continued the assault after the passenger had left the car, the carrier was liable not only for the initial assault but for the consequences following therefrom in natural sequence and as a part of one continuous transaction. Alabama, etc., R. Co. *v.* Sampley, 169 Ala. 372, 53 So. 142, cited in notes in 32 L. R. A., N. S., 1203, 40 L. R. A., N. S., 1008, 1051, 1060, 1067, 1071.

Aiding Illegal Search.—Where the servants of a carrier participated in an illegal search of a passenger, the carrier is liable for the assault and battery, though the servant believed the seach to be legal. Nashville, etc., Railway *v.* Crosby (Ala.), 62 So. 889.

Where the peace officer did not request the servant of defendant to assist him in searching plaintiff, the acts of the servant in participating in the illegal arrest and search can not be excused upon the theory that an officer may require assistance even in making an illegal arrest. Nashville, etc., Railway *v.* Crosby (Ala.), 62 So. 889.

Excuses—Wrongful Act of Passenger.—A carrier is not liable for injuries inflicted on a passenger by a servant of the carrier for another passenger, where the injury was the result of the wrongful act or misconduct of the passenger injured; and a carrier is not liable for an assault made upon a passenger in self-defense. Culberson *v.* Empire Coal Co., 156 Ala. 416, 47 So. 237; Birmingham R., etc., Co. *v.* Baird, 130 Ala. 334, 30 So. 456, 461. See note in 40 L. R. A., N. S., 1076.

Abusing Language as Justification.—Abusive language or opprobrious epithets alone are insufficient to justify the commission of an assault by a conductor on a passenger. Birmingham Ry., Light & Power Co. *v.* Mullen, 35 So. 701, 138 Ala. 614; Birmingham R., etc., Co. *v.* Baird, 130 Ala. 334, 30 So. 456, 54 L. R. A. 752. See notes in 32 L. R. A., N. S., 1202, 40 L. R. A., N. S., 1007, 1008, 1051, 1078, 1084, 33 L. R. A., N. S., 280.

Assault Committed in Retaliation or for Revenge.—No conductor can assault a passenger in retaliation for an assault committed upon him, or for abusive words, or in revenge or punishment under any circumstances, without rendering the carrier liable for damages. Birmingham Ry. & Electric Co. *v.* Baird, 30 So. 456, 130 Ala. 334, 54 L. R. A. 752, cited in note in 40 L. R. A., N. S., 1007, 1051, 1056, 1068, 1073, 1077, 1083. See, also, Southern R. Co. *v.* Hanby (Ala.), 62 So. 871.

Belief of Justification as Excuse.—The fact that a conductor who assaulted a passenger honestly and mistakenly supposed that he was justified would not exempt the company from liability, where such was not the case. Birmingham Ry., Light & Power Co. *v.* Mullen, 35 So. 701, 138 Ala. 614, cited in notes in 32 L. R. A., N. S., 1002, 40 L. R. A., N. S., 1008, 1051, 1078, 1084, 33 L. R. A., N. S., 280.

§ 179 (4) Abusive and Insulting Language.

The contract of carriage of female passengers implies that the carrier will protect them against obscenity, immodest conduct, or wanton approach. Birmingham R., etc., Co. *v.* Parker, 161 Ala. 248, 50 So. 55, cited in notes in 32 L. R. A., N. S., 1202, 40 L. R. A., N. S., 1008, 1053, 1057.

The carrier's duty to protect female passengers from indecent assaults by its servants should not be frittered away by nice questions as to whether the servants were acting within the scope of their authority. Birmingham R., etc., Co. *v.* Parker, 161 Ala. 248, 50 So. 55, cited in notes in 32 L. R. A., N. S., 1202, 40 L. R. A., N. S., 1008, 1053, 1057.

While it is not every epithet which is abusive or insulting to a person to whom it is addressed that will constitute an actionable injury, when spoken in the presence and hearing of a female passenger, yet the speaking of language which, by common consent among civilized people, is regarded as vulgar, coarse, immodest, and offensive to ordinary female sensibilities or disrespective to the female presence, will not be tolerated by the carrier's servants or others, and if indulged in, in the presence and hearing of a female passenger, it is actionable. Birmingham R., etc., Co. *v.* Glenn (Ala.), 60 So. 111.

§ 179 (5) Number and Efficiency of Servants.

In an action for personal injuries received while alighting from defendant's dummy train, it was error to charge that defendant was liable for injuries resulting from the failure of defendant's agents "to take all such precautions to avoid the injury as would be suggested by the highest degree of care, skill, and diligence, by men of extraordinary care, skill, and diligence in carrying passengers by dummy line railways," as it required too high a standard of qualification for employment on railroads. Gadsden & A. U. Ry. Co. *v.* Causler, 97 Ala. 235, 12 So. 439.

§ 180. Acts of Fellow Passengers or Other Third Persons.

§ 180 (1) Duty to Protect Passenger from Acts of Fellow Passengers.

A carrier owes to its passengers the duty of protecting them from violence and insults of other passengers, so far as it can be done in the exercise of a high degree of care, and is liable for its own or its servant's neglect in this particular, when by exercising proper care the violence might have been foreseen and prevented. Montgomery Tract. Co. *v.* Whatley, 152 Ala. 101, 44 So. 538; Birmingham R., etc., Co. *v.* Baird, 130 Ala. 334, 30 So. 456, 54 L. R. A. 752. See notes in 32 L. R. A., N. S., 1206, 37 L. R. A., N. S., 727, 40 L. R. A., N. S., 1007.

Where the conductor and other servants on a train could have prevented injuries to a passenger from assault committed by other passengers, by interfering to protect him, and knowingly or willfully failed to do so after knowing of the threatened danger to the passenger assaulted, their failure to interfere was a breach of duty to the passenger assaulted for which the carrier would be answerable. Culberson *v.* Empire Coal Co., 47 So. 237, 156 Ala. 416, cited in note in 32 L. R. A., N. S., 1206.

Duration of Duty.—A carrier must carry passengers safely and conserve by every reasonable means their safety throughout the journey and protect them from insult or personal violence from other passengers or strangers, and such duty continues until the passenger is safely landed at his destination. Alabama City, G. & A. Ry. Co. *v.* Sampley, 53 So. 142, 169 Ala. 372, cited in notes in 32 L. R. A., N. S., 1203, 40 L. R. A., N. S., 1008, 1051, 1060, 1067, 1071.

Anticipating Misconduct.—It is the duty of a common carrier to protect its passengers against violence, whether from its servants or strangers, but the carrier's liability to protect from the misconduct of others arises only when the wrong is actually foreseen in time to prevent the misconduct or is of such nature and is perpetrated under such circumstances that it might be anticipated. Nashville, etc., Railway *v.* Crosby (Ala.), 62 So. 889; Southern R. Co. *v.* Hanby (Ala.), 62 So. 871; Batton *v.* South, etc., R. Co., 77 Ala. 591. See note in 55 L. R. A. 717.

Use of Profane and Insulting Language.—It is the duty of a carrier's employees to prevent, as far as possible, use by passengers of profane and insulting language in the presence of a female passenger. Southern R. Co. *v.* Lee, 167 Ala. 268, 52 So. 648; Batton *v.* South, etc., R. Co., 77 Ala. 591. See, to the same effect, Birmingham R., etc., Co. *v.* Glenn (Ala.), 60 So. 111. See also, note in 55 L. R. A. 717.

Though a rule of a railroad or a state law prohibited colored passengers from riding in the same coach with white passengers, this did not justify the carrier's employees in permitting other passengers to use profane and indecent language in their effort to compel a colored servant accompanying a white passenger to leave the coach. Southern R. Co. *v.* Lee, 167 Ala. 268, 52 So. 648.

Failure to Require Drunken Fellow Passenger to Be Seated.—If an intoxicated street car passenger weighing about 225 pounds was unable to stand, and his condition was known to the conductor, the conductor was negligent toward other passengers in permitting him to walk up and down the aisle while the car was in motion. Montgomery Tract. Co. *v.* Whatley, 152 Ala. 101, 44 So. 538, cited in notes in 32 L. R. A., N. S., 1206, 37 L. R. A., N. S., 727.

A carrier's servant may eject a drunken and disorderly passenger, when necessary to protect other passengers against his insults or violence; but, if injury to another passenger could have been avoided by requiring the drunken passenger to be and remain seated, the carrier can not avoid liability for the injury by the servant's failure to perform that duty. Montgomery Tract. Co. *v.* Whatley, 152 Ala. 101, 44 So. 538, cited in notes in 32 L. R. A., N. S., 1206, 37 L. R. A., N. S., 727.

Death Occurring during Difficulty between Employees and Fellow Passenger.—Where a negro passenger on a street car shot into the car, on leaving it after a difficulty with the conductor, the conductor's act in leaving the car to preserve his own safety would rather tend to draw the fire away from the car, and was not negligence which would support an action for the death of a passenger. Gooch *v.* Birmingham R., etc., Co. (Ala.), 58 So. 196.

Where, after a difficulty with the conductor of a street car, a negro passenger, who had left the car, commenced to shoot into it, when the motorman threw his controller lever at him, the act of the motorman was such a violation of his duty to the passengers as would render the company liable for the death of one who was shot. Gooch *v.* Birmingham R., etc., Co. (Ala.), 58 So. 196.

§ 180 (2) Acts of Third Persons in General.

Common carriers owe the duty to passengers not only to carry them safely and expeditiously between the termini of the route expressed in the contract, but also to conserve, by every reasonable means, their convenience, comfort, and peace throughout the journey, and protect them from insult, indignities, and personal violence; and in the discharge of this duty it is immaterial whence the disturbance of the passenger's peace, comfort, or personal safety is threatened,—whether from another passenger, a stranger, or from an employee or servant of the common carrier. Birmingham Ry. & Electric Co. *v.* Baird, 30 So. 456, 130 Ala. 334, 54 L. R. A. 752; cited in 40 L. R. A., N. S., 1007, 1051, 1058, 1068, 1073, 1077, 1083.

Under the rule that a carrier is bound to protect a female passenger from avoidable insult and discomfort, from indignities and personal violence, it is immaterial whence the disturbance of the passenger's peace and comfort and personal security or safety comes or is threatened, whether from another passenger, from a trespasser or stranger, or from another servant of the carrier or from the particular servant to whom the duty of protection peculiarly rests. Birmingham R., etc., Co. *v.* Glenn (Ala.), 60 So. 111.

Injury Not Reasonably Anticipated.—Where neither the carrier nor its agents know of danger to a passenger, and could not reasonably anticipate or provide against injury, the carrier is not liable for an injury suffered at the hands of a stranger, though it is bound to protect its passengers from all dangers which are known, or by the exercise of a high degree of care ought to be known, whether occasioned by its own servants or strangers. Irwin *v.* Louisville & N. R. Co., 50 So. 62, 161 Ala. 489. See, also, Batton *v.* South, etc., R. Co., 77 Ala. 591; Nashville, etc., Railway *v.* Crosby (Ala.), 62 So. 889, 892. See note in 55 L. R. A. 717.

A railroad company is not liable at the suit of a female passenger for insulting and disorderly conduct by intruders into the station room where plaintiff was awaiting the arrival of her train, it not appearing that the company had notice of any facts which would justify their expectation of such conduct. Batton *v.* South & N. A. R. Co., 77 Ala. 591, cited in note in 55 L. R. A. 717.

Concurring Negligence of Carrier and Stranger.—See post, "Negligence of Third Persons Contributing to Injury," § 199 (4).

Want of Negligence of Carrier—Interference of Stranger with Appliances.—A railroad company is not liable for injuries to a passenger if there was no negligence in the operation or equipment of the train alleged to have produced the accident, and the accident was caused by latent and undiscoverable defects, or the interference of a stranger with its appliances. Western Ry. of Alabama *v.* Walker, 22 So. 182, 113 Ala. 267.

Action of Officers of the Law.—Where a known officer of the law invested with general authority arrests or searches a passenger, the carrier's servants are not bound to inquire whether he is acting officially and with lawful authority. Nashville, etc., Railway *v.* Crosby (Ala.), 62 So. 889.

Where a known officer of the law in the apparent exercise of his official authority disturbs the peace and personal security of a passenger, it is not the duty of the carrier's servants to intervene unless the officer's conduct is known to be illegal. Nashville, etc., Railway *v.* Crosby (Ala.), 62 So. 889.

§ 181. Act of God, Vis Major, or Inevitable Accident.

A railroad company is not liable for injuries to a passenger if there was no negligence in the operation or equipment of the train alleged to have produced the accident, and the accident was caused by latent and undiscoverable defects, or the interference of a stranger with its appliances. Western Ry. of Alabama *v.* Walker, 22 So. 182, 113 Ala. 267.

§ 182. Condition and Use of Premises.

As to care of persons accompanying passenger, see post, "Care as to Persons Accompanying Passengers," § 198.

§ 182 (1) In General.

Right to Use Depot.—A railroad company which built the station house and waiting room at a certain station can not arbitrarily deny the use thereof to a particular passenger, even though it was not legally required to maintain a waiting room at that particular station by Code 1907, § 5489, requiring the maintenance of depots at stations having a certain population. Waldrop *v.* Nashville, etc., Railway (Ala.), 62 So. 769.

Duty as to Care of Passenger at Destination—Ejection from Waiting Room.—In the absence of special circumstances, a carrier performs its whole duty by conveying the passenger to his destination, and need not care for the passenger while he makes preparation to further continue his journey. Waldrop *v.* Nashville, etc., Railway (Ala.), 62 So. 769.

If a railroad passenger's condition upon reaching the depot at his destination is such that to at once leave the waiting room would endanger his health or safety, he can not be summarily ejected from the depot, but must be given an opportunity to further safely continue his journey or obtain assistance. Waldrop *v.* Nashville, etc., Railway (Ala.), 62 So. 769.

It appeared that when defendant's train, on which plaintiff was a passenger, reached the station of her destination the weather was very cold and a heavy rain was falling, which condition continued for several hours, and that plaintiff, on alighting, entered the waiting room, which defendant had opened for the protection of passengers, and sent for a conveyance to take her and her children from the depot, and that, though the conveyance would have arrived in a few minutes, defendant's employees did not permit plaintiff to remain in the waiting room until the conveyance arrived, and, knowing the conditions of the weather, caused plaintiff to leave the waiting room, resulting in her becoming cold and wet and sick. Held, that the facts stated made defendant liable for injuries resulting from plaintiff's expulsion. Waldrop *v.* Nashville, etc., Railway (Ala.), 62 So. 769.

Duty as to Providing Privy Accommodations.—See the title RAILROADS.

§ 182 (2) Duty with Regard to Means of Entrance to and Exit from Premises.

One going to a railroad station with a good faith intention to take passage must be provided with a safe way of ingress and egress to and from the cars, and with a safe waiting place. Waldrop *v.* Nashville, etc., Railway (Ala.), 62 So. 769; North Birmingham St. R. Co. *v.* Liddicoat, 99 Ala. 545, 13 So. 18, 19.

A railroad company owes the persons having business with it the duty of keeping in safe condition all portions of its depot, platforms, and approaches thereto, to which the public will naturally resort, and all portions of its station grounds reasonably near to the platforms, where passengers will naturally go. Alabama, etc., R. Co. *v.* Godfrey, 156 Ala. 202, 47 So. 185.

Platform on Depot Grounds Used as Passageway to Hotel.—A railroad company is liable for personal injuries sustained by a passenger by reason of a defect in a platform erected near the tracks, on the company's station grounds, which it permits its passengers to use in going from the train to and from the hotel for meals, though the platform may have been erected by the owner of the hotel, who also agreed with the company to keep it in repair. Watson *v.* Oxanna Land Co., 92 Ala. 320, 8 So. 770; Watson *v.* East Tennessee, V. & G. R. Co., 92 Ala. 320, 8 So. 770.

A passenger sued to recover of a railroad company for personal injuries occasioned by his stepping into a hole in a bridge, which was constructed on the company's right of way, and connected its depot platform with an hotel. The bridge had been constructed by the hotel proprietor, and turned over to the company for the use of passengers in going to and from the hotel for meals. It was several inches lower than the depot platform, and was not connected with the ticket office, except through another room. The company had never repaired or exercised any control over it, and it had not been used by the company for any purpose within three years prior to the accident. Held, that passengers could not be presumed to know in regard to the ownership or control of such a structure, and that the company was liable. East Tennessee, V. & G. R. Co. *v.* Watson, 94 Ala. 634, 10 So. 228, cited in note in 23 L. R. A., N. S., 634.

Passageway to Hotel Not in Proximity to Depot Grounds.—A carrier is under no obligation to maintain a safe passageway for its passengers to and from any particular hotel, unless under exceptional circumstances, such as eating houses where trains are stopped for passengers to get meals, or hotels in which the carrier is interested, or situated within or adjoining depots or depot grounds; and a carrier, furnishing safe and sufficient egress from its depot grounds, complies with its obligation to its passengers. Alabama, etc., R. Co. *v.* Godfrey, 156 Ala. 202, 47 So. 185.

Use of Tracks as Approaches.—Where a railroad furnished open, free, and safe exit from its depot to a highway, mere acquiescence by it in the use of its track by passengers at a place 235 yards from the depot, while the passengers were going to a hotel in which it had no interest, did not make it liable to such passengers beyond its liability to mere licensees. Alabama, etc., R. Co. *v.* Godfrey, 156 Ala. 202, 47 So. 185.

A culvert on a main line of a railroad 235 yards from a depot is not an approach to the depot platform or a portion of the station grounds reasonably near to the platform, where passengers will be likely to go, within the rule requiring a railroad to keep in safe condition all portions of its depot platforms and approaches thereto and all portions of its station grounds reasonably near thereto, where passengers will naturally go. Alabama, etc., R. Co. *v.* Godfrey, 156 Ala. 202, 47 So. 185.

§ 182 (3) Duty to Keep Premises Lighted.

Where a railroad company has erected an office and platform, at a station, for the transaction of business with the public, they should be safe, and adapted for that purpose, and should, for the safety of passengers, be lighted a proper time before the arrival and departure of trains. Alabama G. S. R. Co. *v.* Arnold, 84 Ala. 159, 4 So. 359, cited in notes in 1 L. R. A., N. S., 851, 33 L. R. A., N. S., 861.

Where the alleged cause of injury was a failure to light a station, an instruction to find for defendant is properly refused where the evidence fails to show that, in the construction and maintenance of its ticket office, platform, approaches, and lights, it conformed to what was customary at similar stations of well-regulated roads. Alabama G. S. R. Co. *v.* Arnold, 84 Ala. 159, 4 So. 359, cited in notes in 1 L. R. A., N. S., 851, 33 L. R. A., N. S., 861.

§ 183. Taking Up Passengers.

§ 183 (1) Starting Car Prematurely or Allowing Passenger Insufficient Time to Board Car.

Duty of Operatives of Steam Railroad.—A conductor of a steam railroad train must hold the train, stopping at a regular station for passengers to board it, a reasonably sufficient time to permit passengers to board it, but his duty then ceases unless he knows, or ought to know, from the facts that the movement of the train will probably result in some injury to a passenger then in the act of boarding the train. Birmingham, etc., R. Co. *v.* Norris, 4 Ala. App. 363, 59 So. 66.

If a passenger was induced to attempt to board defendant's train by its immediate invitation, it was under the duty of holding it until she could do so safely, notwithstanding the train may have stopped sufficiently long for her to accomplish that end, and this though she may have been attempting to get on without the knowledge of the conductor of person in charge thereof. Alabama Midland Ry. Co. *v.* Horn, 31 So. 481, 132 Ala. 407.

Where a passenger was assisted to the platform of a train by the conductor, but before or immediately after she entered the door the train was violently struck by cars, injuring her, and the conductor knew, or should have known, of her position on the coach, the law imposed on the conductor the duty of holding the train for a sufficiently reasonable time to permit the passenger to reach her seat in safety, and his failure to do so was actionable negligence. Birmingham, etc., R. Co. *v.* Norris, 4 Ala. App. 363, 59 So. 66.

Duty of Operatives of Street Car.—It is not the duty of operatives of a street car to keep the car stationary until a passenger has seated himself, and a passenger injured while in the act of taking a seat, in consequence of the starting of the car, can not recover unless the car was recklessly started. Birmingham Ry. Light & Power Co. *v.* Hawkins, 44 So. 983, 153 Ala. 86.

The motorman has not done his full duty by ascertaining before he starts the car that no one is in the act of getting on the "platform or steps;" but if a passenger is getting on the car, though simply having hold of the handles thereof, it is his duty not to start. Birmingham Ry., Light & Power Co. *v.* Lee, 45 So. 292, 153 Ala. 79.

§ 183 (2) Duty as to Persons Attempting to Board Car at Improper Time and Place.

Where the death of a person attempting to board a street car was caused by the jerking of the car, the street car company is liable only if the attempt was made at a regular stopping place, or a place where it was the habit of the company to take on or discharge passengers. Smith *v.* Birmingham Ry., Light & Power Co., 41 So. 307, 147 Ala. 702.

In an action for death of a person attempting to board a street car, an instruction basing the street car company's liability on the negligence of the conductor and motorman was not erroneous because it ignored the presence of the street flagman and the train dispatcher on the car at the time of the accident, where the evidence did not show that these persons had any duties with reference to the discharge of passengers or that they saw the decedent in time to save him. Smith *v.* Birmingham Ry., Light & Power Co., 41 So. 307, 147 Ala. 702.

In an action for death of a person attempting to board a west-bound street car at the intersection of the car line with a railroad, an instruction that if, after the motor car had crossed the west railroad track, the decedent was standing at a place near a pole between the west railroad track and the main-line track, then the conductor did not have to look out for him when the car stopped, if it did not stop west of the transfer track, was not error. Smith *v.* Birmingham Ry., Light & Power Co., 41 So. 307, 147 Ala. 702.

Train Stopping for Passengers at Other than Usual Place.—Where a train stops at a station for the purpose of taking and setting down passengers, and intending passengers are notified to get aboard, a starting of the train before all have had a reasonable time to get in the cars is negligence, although the train had not stopped at its usual stopping place at the station. Alabama G. S. R. Co. *v.* Siniard, 26 So. 689, 123 Ala. 557.

§ 183 (3) Slowing Up to Receive Passenger and Then Suddenly Increasing Speed.

In an action against a railroad company for injuries sustained by a passenger while attempting to board a moving train, defendant is liable where it appears that the train, instead of coming to a full stop at the station, as it should have done, merely slacked its speed to the rate of about two miles per hour; that while the train was moving at such rate the conductor cried, "All aboard!" whereupon plaintiff attempted to board the train; and that, while plaintiff was in such position that any sudden and unexpected acceleration of speed involved great peril to him, the conductor, with full knowledge of plaintiff's position, caused the train to suddenly start forward, whereby plaintiff was injured—though plaintiff may have been guilty of contributory negligence in attempting to board the moving train. Montgomery & E. Ry. Co. *v.* Stewart, 91 Ala. 421, 8 So. 708, cited in note in 21 L. R. A. 356.

§ 183 (4) Taking Up Passengers Who Have Temporarily Left Train.

Where a car stops at a place where it is customary for persons to take passage, it is the carrier's duty to use due care to determine, before moving the cars, that no person is in the act of boarding the same; and if the place is not one where it is customary to receive passengers, but the car has stopped, and a passenger receives permission of the conductor to temporarily leave the car, it is the duty of defendant's servants to exercise due care to know before moving the car that the passenger is not in the act of re-entering the car, or in a position which would be rendered perilous by moving the car; but, if the place where a car is stopped is not the place where passengers are received, there is no breach of duty to one who is attempting to get aboard, if the car is started while he is in a perilous position, unless the servants of the carrier know that by such movement his position is rendered perilous. Birmingham Ry., Light & Power Co. *v.* Jung, 49 So. 434, 161 Ala. 461, cited in notes in 22 L. R. A., N. S., 758, 30 L. R. A., N. S., 271.

§ 184. Sufficiency and Safety of Means of Transportation.

§ 185. —— In General.

"'Skill' and 'care,' in and about the carrying of a passenger on a railway, are not confined to the mere competency and watchfulness of the officers in charge of the train. Nor are these qualifications the only factors which enter into the inquiry whether or not the carrier conducted itself negligently or unskillfully in the particular service. The track, locomotive machinery, or the rolling stock may be unskillfully or negligently constructed, or may be negligently permitted to remain out of repair. If a railway corporation, in either of the conditions named, carry a passenger and he suffers injury from defective structure, or failure to make proper repairs, this is negligence or unskillful conduct on the part of the corporation, and gives a right of action. * * * Lest we be misunderstood, we will repeat here what we have heretofore said. Railroads are not required to adopt every new invention. It is sufficient if they conform to such machinery and appliances as are in ordinary use by well-regulated railroad companies." Louisville, etc., R. Co. *v.* Allen, 78 Ala. 494; Propst *v.* Georgia Pac. R. Co., 83 Ala. 518, 3 So. 764; Louisville, etc., R. Co. *v.* Jones, 83 Ala. 376, 3 So. 902, 904.

§ 186. —— Railroad Locomotives and Cars.

A carrier of passengers must provide cars and appliances of the most approved type in general use by others engaged in a similar occupation, and exercise a high degree of care to maintain and keep them in suitable repair and efficient for their intended purpose. Irwin *v.* Louisville, etc., R. Co., 161 Ala. 489, 50 So. 62.

Carriers of passengers must provide vehicles as safe as skill and foresight can reasonably make them, and the various appliances with which they are equipped must be kept in a safe and suitable condition; and if a passenger is injured, owing to any defect or unsafe condition of the vehicles, carriages, or cars, or of the appliances, the carrier is liable. Irwin *v.* Louisville, etc., R. Co., 161 Ala. 489, 50 So. 62.

Warming Coaches—Mail Cars.—A railroad company must warm its coaches for safety and comfort of passengers, and its duty extends to mail cars in which postal clerks ride, in the absence of contract exempting them from doing so. Southern Ry. Co. *v.* Harrington, 52 So. 57, 166 Ala. 630, cited in note in 26 L. R. A., N. S., 1059.

Proximate Cause of Injury.—See post, "Proximate Cause of Injury," § 199.

§ 187. —— Railroad Tracks and Roadbeds.

"Skill and care, such as a railroad company should exercise in carrying passengers, are not confined to mere competency and watchfulness of the employees in charge of the train, but include the track and roadbed, for the proper quality and condition of which the company is responsible. Louisville, etc., R. Co. *v.* Jones, 83 Ala. 376, 3 So. 902; Birmingham Union R. Co. *v.* Alexander, 93 Ala. 133, 9 So. 525; Birmingham *v.* Starr, 112 Ala. 98, 20 So. 424." Louisville, etc., R. Co. *v.* Sandlin, 125 Ala. 585, 28 So. 40, 42.

§ 188. —— Elevators.

The act of the proprietor of a store in leaving the door of the passenger elevator shaft open, and thus leaving the shaft without obstruction to prevent customers from walking into it while the elevator is on another floor, is negligence, with respect to such customers. Morgan *v.* Saks, 38 So. 848, 143 Ala. 139, cited in note in 2 L. R. A., N. S., 745, 756, 758.

§ 189. Management of Conveyances.

§ 190. —— In General.

§ 190 (1) In General.

Duty as to Signals.—It is negligence for a railroad company to furnish the station master and the conductor similar uniforms, and to give them similar signals, with different meanings whereby an engineer starts his train on a signal intended for another purpose causing a collision in which a passenger is injured. Kansas City, M. & B. R. Co. *v.* Sanders, 98 Ala. 293, 13 So. 57.

Manner of Enforcing Rule as to Separation of White and Colored Passengers.—While a carrier may make and enforce regulations providing different cars for white and colored passengers, a conductor, in requiring the white passengers to leave the car provided for colored passengers, was bound to do so in a reasonable manner and at such a time and under such circumstances as would not expose the passenger to increased danger. Carleton *v.* Central of Georgia Ry. Co., 46 So. 495, 155 Ala. 326.

A conductor is not justified in ordering or compelling a white passenger in the negro coach to go into another coach while the train is running at a dangerous rate of speed. Central of Georgia Ry. Co. *v.* Carleton, 51 So. 27, 163 Ala. 62.

Use of Drop Doors Over Car Steps When Train at Station.—In absence of special circumstances, the drop doors over the steps of a vestibuled train need not be kept down when the train is standing at a station for passengers, during which time trainmen must pass on and off the train; and that passengers at stations were habitually resorting to the rear platform without acquiescence of the carrier, shown by keeping the drop door down at stations, though known by the carrier, did not impose on it the duty of foregoing the ordinary use of the appliance. Clanton *v.* Southern Ry. Co., 51 So. 616, 165 Ala. 485, cited in note in 35 L. R. A., N. S., 592.

§ 190 (2) Duty to Notify Passengers of Danger.

"In Whart. Neg., § 649, it is said: 'When danger approaches, it is the duty of the officers of the road to notify passengers, so that they can take steps to avoid it; and failure to give such notice is negligence." Montgomery St. Railway *v.* Mason, 133 Ala. 508, 32 So. 261, 266.

Where Danger Obvious.—"If there be any danger in standing near an open sidedoor of a car, when the train is starting or in motion, it is not an unreasonable presumption that persons of ordinary prudence are aware of it;" and when a person, so standing, is thrown from the car by the shock attendant on its coupling with the train, and thereby injured, he can not complain that he was not notified of his danger, nor warned of the coming shock. Thompson *v.* Duncan, 76 Ala. 334.

§ 190 (3) Duty to Avoid Misleading Passengers as to Movements of Train.

A carrier, charged with negligence in causing a passenger to go out on the steps of the car where the sudden stopping of the train would throw him off, may be liable, though the train is stopped in the usual manner. Southern Ry. Co. *v.* Roebuck, 31 So. 611, 132 Ala. 412.

Where a street car, having failed to stop at a crossing in compliance with a passenger's request, slows up beyond such crossing to such an extent as to imply an invitation to him to alight, it is the duty of the operatives not to cause the car to jerk suddenly so as to endanger his safety. Birmingham Railway &

Electric Co. *v.* James, 25 So 847, 121 Ala. 120.

§ 190 (4) Effect of Provisions of Statutes or Ordinances.

Ordinance Requiring Street Car to Stop at Railroad Crossing.—The violation by a street car driver of a city ordinance providing that street cars shall come to a complete stop before going onto railroad crossings is negligence. Selma Street & Suburban Ry. Co. *v.* Owen, 31 So. 598, 132 Ala. 420.

Failure to Ring Bell or Blow Whistle.—Failure to ring the bell or blow the whistle before leaving a station, as required by Code 1907, § 5473, is negligence per se. McElvane *v.* Central of Georgia Ry. Co., 54 So. 489, 170 Ala. 525. See, generally, the title RAILROADS.

The statutory provisions requiring the engineer, or other person in charge of a moving train of cars, to blow the whistle, or ring the bell, on approaching a depot or stopping place (Code, §§ 1699, 1700), are intended for the protection of the travelling public, or persons not on the train; and passengers on the train are not, ordinarily, included in the letter or spirit of the statute, and can not complain of its violation, when suing for damages on account of personal injuries, to which the failure to ring the bell could have had no tendency to contribute; though cases may occur, possibly, in which passengers, or other persons permissively on the train, are entitled to have such signals given, as a warning to hasten their departure. Alabama, etc., R. Co. *v.* Hawk, 72 Ala. 112.

A passenger who was injured by falling from the platform of a car while the train was in motion can not complain of the company's failure to comply with Code 1876, § 1697, requiring that a signal be given when a train is approaching a stopping place. Alabama Great Southern R. Co. *v.* Hawk, 72 Ala. 112.

Proximate Cause of Injury.—See post, "Proximate Cause of Injury," § 199.

§ 191. —— Overloading or Crowding.

It was a carrier's duty to provide a passenger with a seat and with a reasonably safe place in which to ride. Alabama Great Southern R. Co. *v.* Gilbert, 6 Ala. App. 372, 60 So. 542.

Where a commercial railroad company overcrowds its train, it must exercise a care proportioned to the increased risk caused by such overcrowding. Alabama, etc., R. Co. *v.* Gilbert, 6 Ala. App. 372, 60 So. 542.

§ 192. —— Rate of Speed.

With respect to the safety of passengers, a rate of speed may be dangerous and negligent per se. St. Louis & S. F. R. Co. *v.* Savage, 50 So. 113, 163 Ala. 55.

"There is natural tendency to haste when late, and, while it is generally stated that no mere rate of speed constitutes per se negligence, this rule is in most cases formulated for the purpose of cases in which persons or animals are injured by coming on the track. East Tennessee, etc., R. Co. *v.* Deaver, 79 Ala. 216. 'Railway companies being engaged in the business of conveying passengers and property, and that business being regarded of the highest importance, the speed of trains may be regulated with that end in view.' 3 Elliott on Railroads, § 1204. 'There may, however, be peculiar circumstances involved in the particular case which might justify the conclusion that there was negligence in running at a high rate of speed.' 4 Elliott on Railroads, § 1589. Certainly with respect to the safety of passengers carried upon the train it can not be denied that a rate of speed may be excessive, dangerous, and negligent." St Louis, etc., R. Co. *v.* Savage, 163 Ala. 55, 50 So. 113, 114.

§ 193. —— Sudden Jerks and Jolts.

Carriers must use a very high degree of care to avoid injuring passengers through sudden jerks, jars, or lurches of the cars. Birmingham Ry., Light & Power Co. *v.* Yates, 53 So. 915, 169 Ala. 381.

"It is not every increase in the speed of a car, or starting of same, whether with or without a jerk, that amounts to negligence. Mobile, etc., R. Co. *v.* Bell, 153 Ala. 90, 45 So. 56. The complainant, in order to charge a breach of duty, should aver that the starting, increase of speed, or jerk was negligently made or caused by the servants of the defendant, else the act of omission should be such as to amount to negligence from the facts disclosed in the complaint." Birmingham R., etc., Co. *v.* Parker, 156 Ala. 251, 47 So. 138.

§ 194. —— Collision.

It is negligence for a street car driver to drive his car onto a railroad crossing without first stopping and looking and listening for trains. Selma Street & Suburban Ry. Co. *v.* Owen, 31 So. 598, 132 Ala. 420.

§ 195. —— Derailment of Railroad Cars.

Evidence that plaintiff was injured by the derailment of a car on which he was a passenger entitles him to recover, unless defendant reasonably satisfies the jury that the derailment was not due to negligence, and could not have been prevented by the exercise of the highest degree of care, skill, and diligence on the part of the carrier. Montgomery & E. Ry. Co. *v.* Mailette, 92 Ala. 209, 9 So. 363.

§ 196. Protection of Passengers from Incidental Dangers.

Ordinarily a railroad company is not required to anticipate that a missile will be thrown through a car window by a stranger and injure a passenger, and is not required to see that the blind is closed or lowered to prevent it, the glass and blinds being intended only to admit and exclude light and air for the comfort and pleasure of passengers; and, in the absence of any showing that such an assault or injury could have been reasonably anticipated, the carrier can not be held liable for the injury. Irwin *v.* Louisville & N. R. Co., 50 So. 62, 161 Ala. 489.

§ 197. Setting Down Passengers.

§ 197 (1) In General.

Duty as to Stopping Street Car without Signal from Passenger.—In an action against a street railway company for injuries, where the plaintiff testified that his place of business was in the middle of the block below the crossing where he attempted to get off, and that the motorman saw him arise from his seat, and go to the door to get off at the crossing, and it was shown by the motorman that plaintiff was in the habit of riding to the middle of the block before getting off, it was not error to refuse to instruct that if the car came to a stop, and plaintiff got up to leave, and was seen by the motorman, it was not necessary for plaintiff to ring the bell, even though such was the rule with passengers. McDonald *v.* Montgomery St. Ry., 110 Ala. 161, 20 So. 317.

§ 197 (2) Starting Train before Passenger Has Alighted or While He Is Alighting

It was a railway conductor's duty to stop his train at a passenger's destination long enough to enable the passenger to alight. Dilburn *v.* Louisville & N. R. Co., 47 So. 210, 156 Ala. 228; Alabama Mid. R. Co. *v.* Johnson, 123 Ala. 197, 26 So. 160; Birmingham Union R. Co. *v.* Smith, 90 Ala. 60, 8 So. 86; Southern R. Co. *v.* Burgess, 143 Ala. 364, 42 So. 35; Alabama, etc., R. Co. *v.* Cox, 173 Ala. 629, 55 So. 909, 912.

Where a carrier's train has reached a passenger's destination, the carrier must exercise the highest degree of practicable care to afford the passenger sufficient time and opportunity to alight and if the usual sufficient time be not given, and the passenger is compelled to go on to the next station, or if a sudden start is made while he is in the act of alighting and injury occurs, the carrier is liable. Louisville, etc., R. Co. *v.* Dilburn (Ala.), 59 So. 438.

Trains Drawn by Dummy Engines.—The duty of a railroad, operating cars by dummy engines without fixed stopping places, to a passenger alighting from its cars, is not discharged by merely stopping a reasonable time for such passenger to alight; but it is the duty of the conductor, before giving the signal to start, to see that no passenger is in the act of alighting, or in a position which would be rendered dangerous by putting the car in motion. Highland Ave. & Belt R. Co. *v.* Burt, 92 Ala. 291, 9 So. 410, 13 L. R. A. 95, cited in note in 11 L. R. A., N. S., 140; Sweet *v.* Birmingham R., etc., Co., 136 Ala. 166, 33 So. 886.

The passenger does not assume the risk of injury from jerks or jars negligently permitted or occasioned while he is preparing to alight, or is in the act of alighting. Southern R. Co. *v.* Morgan (Ala.), 59 So. 432.

Immaterial Whether or Not Movement of Train Violent.—Where a passenger on a freight train was warranted in assuming that the place where the caboose stopped was the place at which she was expected to alight, it was the duty of the carrier to stop the train long enough for her to alight in safety, or to warn her of the danger resulting from the further movement of the train in time to avert injury, and it was immaterial whether the movement of the train producing injury was an incident to the ordinary operation of such trains, or was unnecessarily violent. Southern Ry. Co. *v.* Burgess, 42 So. 35, 143 Ala. 364.

Passenger Alighting after Lapse of Reasonable Time.—A carrier's servants are bound to presume that there may be persons in the cars desiring to alight, and, unless they know there are not, they have no right to start the trains until they have waited long enough to allow such passengers to alight, nor, even after waiting a reasonable time, are they entitled to start the trains without using reasonable care to ascertain if there are passengers in the act of alighting, but, if reasonable time has been given, the carrier's servants are not required "to know" that all persons intending to stop at the station have alighted in safety. Louisville, etc., R. Co. *v.* Dilburn (Ala.), 59 So. 438.

"When the train of an ordinary railroad is brought to a standstill at the proper and usual place for receiving passengers and for permitting passengers to alight, and remains stationary for a reasonably sufficient time for this purpose, the duty of the trainmen in this regard has been performed; but, while the performance of this duty may relieve the trainmen from the further duty of seeing and knowing that the passengers are on or off as the case may be, even this would not excuse from culpability if those in charge of the train in fact saw or knew that its movement would probably imperil the passenger in the act of getting off or on the train, and in disregard of the peril caused the train to move, and thereby inflict the injury." Highland Ave., etc., R. Co. *v.* Burt, 92 Ala. 291, 9 So. 410, 13 L. R. A. 95; Sweet *v.* Birmingham R., etc., Co., 136 Ala. 166, 33 So. 886; Birmingham, etc., R. Co. *v.* Norris, 4 Ala. App. 363, 59 So. 66, 68.

A carrier, having offered a reasonable opportunity for passengers to alight and being without knowledge or reason to know of the perilous position of a passenger then attempting to alight, is entitled to act upon the presumption that passengers will exercise due care to avoid perilous positions. Central of Georgia Ry. Co. *v.* McNab, 43 So. 222, 150 Ala. 332.

A very old, infirm woman was injured in alighting from defendant's train on which she had been a passenger. The train stopped the usual length of time, which appeared to be a reasonable length of time for passengers to alight. The servants of the carrier had notice of the passenger's enfeebled condition, and though she claimed that the entrance of other passengers delayed her exit until the train had started, it appeared that these passengers were not directed or authorized to enter. Held, that the railroad company was not guilty of negligence in starting the train before the passenger alighted. Nashville, etc., Railway *v.* Casey, 1 Ala. App. 344, 56 So. 28.

§ 197 (3) Starting Street Car before Passenger Has Alighted or While He Is Alighting.

A car being at a regular stopping place for letting off passengers, and having stopped, it was the carrier's duty, through its agents operating the car, failure to discharge which would be negligence, to inform itself whether a passenger was in the act of leaving the car, and so in a position which would be rendered perilous by putting the car in motion. Birmingham R., etc., Co. *v.* Mayo (Ala.), 61 So. 289. See, to the same effect, Birmingham R., etc., Co. *v.* McGinty, 158 Ala. 410, 48 So. 491.

It is the duty of the conductor of an electric car, when his car has stopped to allow passengers to alight, to see that no passenger is in a position which would render it dangerous to start the car, before giving the signal to start, although the car is running on schedule time, and stops only at regular stations. Birmingham Railway & Electric Co. *v.* Wildman, 24 So. 548, 119 Ala. 547, cited in note in 11 L. R. A., N. S., 140.

It is the duty of the driver of a horse car, when signaled to stop, to ascertain who and how many of his passengers intend to alight at that place, to wait a sufficient length of time to enable them to alight in safety by the exercise of reasonable diligence, and, in any event, to see and know that no passenger is in the act of alighting, or is otherwise in a position which would be rendered perilous by the motion of the car, when he again puts the car in motion, and if he fail in any of these respects, and injury results, his employer is liable. Birmingham Union Ry. Co. *v.* Smith, 90 Ala. 60, 8 So. 86, cited in notes in 4 L. R. A., N. S., 141, 11 L. R. A., N. S., 140.

Duty to Know Position of Passenger after Car Has Stopped Reasonable Time.—It was an electric railway company's duty to hold a car at a stopping place sufficient time to allow passengers to alight, and not to start it while a passenger was alighting; but it would have been a defense to an action for injury to him that the car had stopped a sufficient time, and that those in charge did not know that he was alighting. Birmingham Ry., Light & Power Co. *v.* McGinty, 48 So. 491, 158 Ala. 410. See, to the same effect, Armstrong *v.* Montgomery St. R. Co., 123 Ala. 233, 26 So. 349; Sweet *v.* Birmingham R., etc., Co, 136 Ala. 166, 33 So. 886; Birmingham R, etc., Co. *v.* Moore, 148 Ala. 115, 42 So. 1024.

Sudden Movement as Negligence Dependent on Circumstances—Any starting or stopping of a street car with a sudden or unusual jerk or movement while a passenger is alighting, whether at a stopping place or not and whether known to defendant's servants or not, is not per se actionable negligence; whether it is so or not depending on the circumstances of time and place or on the knowledge of the carrier's responsible agents that they may injure an exposed passenger. Birmingham R., etc., Co. *v.* Barrett (Ala.), 60 So. 262.

A charge, exonerating a carrier from liability for injuries to an alighting passenger if the jury find that the crew of the car did not know that she intended to alight before reaching the usual stopping place, is properly refused. Birmingham Ry., Light & Power Co. *v.* Girod, 51 So. 242, 164 Ala. 10.

§ 197 (4) Duty to Provide Safe Place and Means for Alighting.

A street railway company is required to exercise the highest degree of care in selecting a place at which to stop its cars to allow passengers to alight. Mobile Light & R. Co. *v.* Walsh, 40 So. 560, 146 Ala. 295; Montgomery St. Railway *v.* Mason, 133 Ala. 508, 32 So. 261. See notes in 16 L. R. A., N. S., 467, 469, 32 L. R. A., N. S., 884.

Plaintiff became a passenger on defendant's street railway on a dark night, and on alighting from the car at his destination tripped on taking his first step over a pile of lumber left at the place by defendant the day previous while repairing a bridge. Held, that the defendant was liable in failing to provide a reasonably safe place for the landing of its passengers. Montgomery St. Ry. *v.* Mason, 32 So. 261, 133 Ala. 508, cited in note in 32 L. R. A., N. S., 884.

Right of Passenger to Assume That Place Is Safe.—It is the duty of persons operating a street car to know that the place at which the car is stopped to allow a passenger to alight is reasonably safe, and the passenger has a right to assume that it is safe, unless it is obviously dangerous. Mobile Light & R. Co. *v.* Walsh, 40 So. 559, 146 Ala. 290; Alabama, etc., R. Co. *v.* Cox, 173 Ala. 629, 55 So. 909, 912. See notes in 16 L. R. A., N. S., 467, 469, 32 L. R. A., N. S., 884.

Stopping Train over Trestle after Calling Station.—Where the conductor on a railroad train calls the name of a station, and the engineer, before reaching there, though without the conductor's knowledge, stops the train over a trestle, to take on water, the company is liable for injuries sustained by a passenger in getting off the train, if he was not notified, and the surroundings did not show, that he was not at the station. Richmond & D. R. Co. *v.* Smith, 92 Ala. 237, 9 So. 223, cited in note in 2 L. R. A., N. S., 115.

§ 197 (5) Duty to Warn Passenger of Dangers.

See, also, post, "Passenger Set Down beyond Station, Platform, or Other Landing Place," § 197 (8).

If there is a dangerous place at the landing, it is the duty of the conductor to warn those about stepping out. And he must give notice to all if any danger in alighting is probable, and this doctrine applies to street railway companies. Montgomery St. Railway *v.* Mason, 133 Ala. 508, 32 So. 261; Birmingham R., etc., Co. *v.* Seaborn, 168 Ala. 658, 53 So. 241.

§ 197 (6) Duty to Assist Passenger in Alighting.

Duty as to Assisting Passengers.—It is not the duty of a railroad to assist passengers to alight from its cars except where it has accepted as a passenger one who is unable, through disability, to care for himself, and such disability is known at the time of the acceptance, or where a passenger is too sick or disabled to safely alight without aid. Central, etc., R. Co. *v.* Carlisle, 2 Ala. App. 514, 56 So. 737.

The fact that a husband was carrying a baby did not render him unable to assist his wife in alighting from the train, so as to make it the duty of the carrier's servants to assist her. Central, etc., R. Co. *v.* Carlisle, 2 Ala. App. 514, 56 So. 737.

Where a woman passenger is accompanied by her husband apparently capable of assisting her, the duty of the carrier to give her assistance is suspended, and no recovery can be had for its nonexercise. Central, etc., R. Co. *v.* Carlisle, 2 Ala. App. 514, 56 So. 737.

Though a female passenger was carrying a valise, a parasol, and a fan when she attempted to alight from the carrier's vehicle, her condition was not one of such obvious infirmity or disability that she was entitled to the assistance of the carrier's servants. Central, etc., R. Co. *v.* Carlisle, 2 Ala. App. 514, 56 So. 737.

Nonconformity to Rule Requiring Assistance to Lady Passengers.—Even though a railway's rules require conductors to assist lady passengers in alighting, nonconformity to the rule would impose no liability on the carrier unless known to and relied upon by a passenger to hurt her, such duty being wholly gratuitous. Central, etc., R. Co. *v.* Carlisle, 2 Ala. App. 514, 56 So. 737.

Degree of Care Necessary in Rendering Assistance.—Where a railroad company offers to assist a passenger to alight from its cars, it is bound to exercise due care in rendering such assistance. Central, etc., R. Co *v.* Carlisle, 2 Ala. App. 514, 56 So. 737.

§ 197 (7) Injuries Received after Alighting and While Leaving Train or Station.

"As a general rule, it may be said that the relation of carrier and passenger does not cease with the arrival of the train at the passenger's destination, but continues until the passenger has had reasonable time and opportunity to safely alight from the train at the place provided by the carrier for the discharge of passengers, and to leave the carrier's premises in the customary manner." Alabama, etc., R. Co. *v.* Cox, 173 Ala. 629, 55 So. 909, 911.

§ 197 (8) Passenger Set Down beyond Station, Platform, or Other Landing Place.

Where a passenger is wrongfully or negligently carried past his destination it is the duty of those in charge of the train to either back it to the station or to notify the passenger how and when to alight, warn him of any dangers incident to alighting at that point, and give him such assistance or instructions as may be necessary to assure his safe return, and if, without the fault of the passenger, he is injured in making his way back to the station the company is liable. Birmingham Ry., Light & Power Co. *v.* Seaborn, 53 So. 241, 168 Ala. 658, cited in note in 41 L. R. A., N. S., 745.

In an action for personal injuries to a passenger carried beyond her station, received while attempting to walk back to the station, it is immaterial whether the carrier's conductor knew that the passenger did not know of a safe route from the point where she alighted back to the station, or that the trainmen had reason to believe that the passenger would encounter danger. Alabama City, G. & A. Ry. Co. *v.* Cox, 55 So. 909, 173 Ala. 629, cited in note in 41 L. R. A., N. S., 745.

Where a street car passenger on a dark night signaled the conductor to let her off at a regular stopping place, and the conductor understood, but failed to let her off there. and let her off beyond, where the track was very rough, and while attempting to cross the track fell and was injured, the company was negligent, entitling her to recover, unless she was guilty of contributory negligence in crossing the track, or unless she assumed the risk. Melton *v.* Birmingham Ry., Light & Power Co., 45 So. 151, 153 Ala. 95, cited in notes in 32 L. R. A., N. S., 885, 37 L. R. A., N. S., 266.

§ 198. Care as to Persons Accompanying Passengers.

Where one assists a passenger, with the knowledge of the agent of the carrier, whose duty it is to assist passengers on or off the trains, it is presumed that such assistance is rendered with the carrier's approval, so that it must exercise the same degree of care toward such person as toward a passenger. McElvane *v.* Central of Georgia Ry. Co., 54 So. 489, 170 Ala. 525.

"It is undoubtedly the law that 'a carrier owes a duty to persons who come upon a train accompanying passengers, with the intention of getting off before the train starts or for the purpose of meeting passengers who are about to alight. And especially is there such a duty when the passenger requires assistance which the servants of the carrier do not undertake to render. But if the servants of the carrier have no notice or knowledge of the intention of one thus coming on board to get off before the starting of the train, they owe him no additional duty as to affording him an opportunity to safely alight.' 6 Cyc., p. 615." Southern R. Co. *v.* Patterson, 148 Ala. 77, 41 So. 964.

Giving Reasonable Time to Alight.—Where one boards a train solely for the purpose of assisting an old lady, nearly blind, at her request, to take passage on it, before doing so having approached the conductor, and told him of her condition and need of assistance, and been requested by him to render such assistance, so that the conductor is bound to know of his intention to alight before the train starts, it is the duty of the conductor to give him a reasonable time to alight before starting the train; and not having done so, and such person having in consequence been injured in alighting, without any contributory negligence, after the starting of the train, the carrier is liable therefor. Southern Ry. Co. *v.* Patterson, 41 So. 964, 148 Ala. 77, cited in note in 22 L. R. A., N. S., 911.

Alighting from Moving Train.—One who entered a railway train as an escort for a woman, to find her a seat, and who was injured in the endeavor to leave the train while it was under way, with some papers in his hand, held without remedy. Central R. & Banking Co. *v.* Letcher, 69 Ala. 106, cited in notes in 21 L. R. A. 354, 3 L. R. A., N. S., 433.

Condition and Use of Carrier's Premises.—All the property of a railroad company, including its depots and adjacent yards and grounds, is its private property, on which no one is invited, or can claim a right to enter, except those persons who have business with the railroad; which class embraces, not only passengers, but protectors and friends attendant on their departure, or awaiting their arrival. To the class of persons thus having business, the railroad company is under obligation to keep in safe condition all parts of its platforms, with the approaches thereto, to which the public do, or would naturally resort, and all portions of the station grounds reasonably near to the platform, where passengers would be likely to go, and to provide safe waiting-rooms, and to keep the depot and platform well lighted at night. Montgomery, etc., R. Co. *v.* Thompson, 77 Ala. 448.

§ 199. Proximate Cause of Injury.

§ 199 (1) Condition and Use of Carrier's Premises.

Failure to Have Premises Lighted.—Where, in an action for injuries caused by the alleged failure of a railroad company to have its depot premises properly lighted, there is evidence tending to show that the fall and injury of plaintiff immediately followed his leaving the ticket office to take the train, it can not be affirmed on the evidence, as matter of law, that the absence of a light was not the proximate cause. Alabama G. S. R. Co. *v.* Arnold, 80 Ala. 600, 2 So. 337, cited in note in 7 L. R. A., N. S., 1179.

§ 199 (2) Sufficiency and Safety of Means of Transportation.

Defective Bell Rope.—In an action against a railroad company for injuries to a passenger, where it appeared that the accident occurred to a freight train having one passenger car attached, the fact that the bell rope from the engine did not reach to the passenger car at the end of the train would not, of itself, entitle plaintiff to a recovery, unless such neglect was the cause of the injury. Mobile & M. R. Co. *v.* Ashcraft, 48 Ala. 15.

Car Negligently Loaded — Injury Caused by Derailment.—A witness who boarded a freight train with deceased testified that one of the flat cars was loaded with sewer pipe, held on by standards, one of which was lost during the trip; and one of the pipes fell off, and that, when witness told the conductor he ought to stop, the latter refused, whereupon witness said he would not ride behind a car in that condition, and jumped off. Subsequently a derailment occurred, in which deceased, who was sitting on a box car behind the flat car, was killed. Held, insufficient to show that his death was due to the willful and wanton misconduct of the conductor. Beyer *v.* Louisville, etc., R. Co., 114 Ala. 424, 21 So. 952.

§ 199 (3) Management of Conveyances.

Failure to Ring Bell or Blow Whistle.—Negligence by a railroad company in starting a passenger train from the station without ringing the bell or blowing the whistle, in violation of Code 1907, § 5473, was not the proximate cause of injuries to a trespasser injured by being jerked off the train by its sudden starting while he was preparing to get off. McElvane *v.* Central of Georgia Ry. Co., 54 So. 489, 170 Ala. 525.

Defendant's negligence, causing imminent danger of a car colliding with that on which plaintiff was a passenger, or an appearance of such danger, was the proximate cause of her injury, whether she jumped off, or was pushed off by a companion, or another passenger jumped off onto her after she had got off. Birmingham Ry. & Electric Co. *v.* Butler, 33 So. 33, 135 Ala. 388.

§ 199 (4) Negligence of Third Person Contributing to Injury.

Anticipating Conduct of Stranger.—A carrier is not liable for injuries to a passenger arising from the misconduct of third persons unless the wrongful conduct is actually foreseen in time to prevent the injury or is of such nature and is perpetrated under such circumstances that it might have been anticipated. Nashville, etc., Railway *v.* Crosby (Ala.), 62 So. 889.

Concurring Negligence of Carrier and Stranger.—If a passenger's injury is the result of the concurring negligence of a stranger and the carrier, the latter is liable. Irwin *v.* Louisville & N. R. Co., 50 So. 62, 161 Ala. 489.

§ 200. Companies or Persons Liable.

Effect of Transfer of Franchise with Legislative Consent.—Where a street-railway company transfers its property and franchises, without legislative consent, to another company, it is still liable for injuries to a passenger; and such passenger, having sued the original company, need not show that the railroad was actually operated by such company at the time of the injury. Ricketts *v.* Birmingham St. Ry. Co., 85 Ala. 600, 5 So. 353.

Several Proprietors of Different Portions of Stage Line.—Where several proprietors of different portions of a stage line, by agreement among themselves, appoint a common agent at each end of the route to receive the fare and give through tickets, this does not of itself constitute them partners as to passengers who purchase through tickets, so as to render each proprietor liable for losses occurring on any portion of the line. Ellsworth *v.* Tartt, 26 Ala. 733.

§ 201. Actions for Injuries.

§ 202. —— Nature and Form.

Where a passenger is injured through the negligence of a carrier, he may sue upon the contract, alleging the negligent acts of defendants as a breach of the contract, or proceed in tort, making the negligence the ground of his right of recovery; and if he sues for the tort he must show that he stands in the relation of a passenger of the carrier, to establish his right to recover for its negligence. Malcomb *v.* Louisville & N. R. Co., 46 So. 768, 155 Ala. 337.

§ 203. —— Conditions Precedent.

Notice of Accident.—A passenger injured by a carrier need not notify it of the accident before bringing an action for damages. Birmingham Ry. & Electric Co. *v.* Wildman, 24 So. 548, 119 Ala. 547.

§ 204. —— Pleading.

§ 204 (1) Declaration, Complaint, or Petition in General.

Imminency of Collision.—A complaint in an action for damages against a street railway company which averred that the car on which plaintiff was a passenger was "about to collide with" a locomotive sufficiently alleged that a collision was imminent. Selma Street & Suburban Ry. Co. *v.* Owen, 31 So. 598, 132 Ala. 420.

A complaint for personal injury, alleging that defendant's agent negligently caused another car "to appear to be in imminent danger" of colliding with the car on which plaintiff was a passenger, whereupon she jumped, is defective in not showing that the appearance was such as to convince a reasonable person of the imminence of the danger. Birmingham Ry. & Electric Co. *v.* Butler, 33 So. 33, 135 Ala. 388.

Manner in Which Plaintiff Injured.—A complaint alleging that plaintiff, while a passenger upon defendant's railway, was injured, and that his injuries were proximately caused by the negligence of defendant's servants, was not demurrable on the ground that it did not specify with sufficient particularity the manner in which plaintiff was injured. Birmingham Ry., Light & Power Co. *v.* Adams, 40 So. 385, 146 Ala. 267.

The complaint, in an action against a railroad company for injuries received by one waiting at its flag station to take passage, need not set up the instrumentality of the injury or the manner in which it was received. Louisville, etc., R. Co. *v.* Glasgow (Ala.), 60 So. 103.

Manner of Injury Sufficiently Shown.—A complaint, in an action against a railway company for the death of a passenger, which alleges that decedent was violently thrown from a train, sufficiently shows the manner of the infliction of the injuries. Kansas City, M. & B. R. Co. *v.* Matthews, 39 So. 207, 142 Ala. 208.

Place of Injury.—The allegation in a complaint that plaintiff was injured while on a car of defendant, which operated its cars in the city of Birmingham, was a sufficient allegation as to the place where the injury occurred. Birmingham R., etc., Co. *v.* Moore, 148 Ala. 115, 42 So. 1024.

§ 204 (2) Allegations as to Relation of Carrier and Passenger.

Necessity of Showing Relation.—A count, in a complaint against a carrier for injuries, which charges simple negligence and fails to show that plaintiff was rightfully in the car, is insufficient, since, if plaintiff were a trespasser, defendant owed only the duty not to wantonly injure. Broyles *v.* Central, etc., R. Co., 166 Ala. 616, 52 So. 81.

Averment Showing Defendant to Be Public Carrier.—An averment that defendant was operating street cars as a common carrier of passenger for reward is an averment that defendant was a public carrier of passengers. Birmingham R., etc., Co. *v.* Selhorst, 165 Ala. 475, 51 So. 568.

Relation Sufficiently Shown.—In an action by a passenger for an assault by the conductor, a general averment in the complaint that plaintiff was a passenger at the time of the assault, is sufficient, and it need not allege that the passenger was at the time on the car of the carrier. Alabama City, G. & A. Ry. Co. *v.* Sampley, 53 So. 142, 169 Ala. 372.

Where a complaint alleged that plaintiff was a passenger on defendant's car when she received the injury complained of, the duty of the defendant toward her was thus shown, and the averment of a failure to perform this duty was sufficient. Birmingham R., etc., Co. *v.* Moore, 148 Ala. 115, 42 So. 1024.

In an action by a passenger against a carrier for an assault committed upon him by other passengers, the complaint alleged that defendant was a corporation operating a railroad and engaged in carrying passengers for hire and that plaintiff was a passenger on one of defendant's cars. Held, that the complaint sufficiently averred that the plaintiff was a passenger and that defendant was a carrier of passengers for hire. Culberson *v.* Empire Coal Co., 156 Ala. 416, 47 So. 237.

A complaint in an action against a carrier which alleges that plaintiff was at a station to be carried as a passenger; that she was weak and hardly able to walk; that the train, on reaching the station, stopped to take on passengers; and that the carrier, through its servants, accepted her as a passenger and transported her to her destination, and received her fare, and through its servants proceeded to assist her to board the train, but performed the service negligently, causing injury to her —shows, as against a demurrer, that plaintiff at the time of the injuries had been accepted as a passenger, that the servants knew of her physical condition, and that they acted within the scope of their authority, and states a cause of action. Williams *v.* Louisville & N. R. Co., 43 So. 576, 150 Ala. 324, 10 L. R. A., N. S., 413.

Complaint Insufficient to Show Relation.—A count in a complaint against a railway company for personal injuries claimed to have been received in a collision of cars on one of which plaintiff was at the time alleged that while plaintiff was on such car "at the request or invitation of defendant, its agents, or employees, in violation of its duty to plaintiff, the defendant, its agents or employees, propelled said car wantonly, willfully, or intentionally," etc. Held, that it did not allege facts showing that plaintiff was a passenger, nor that the car was a passenger car, nor that the agent or employee who invited or requested him to go on the car was acting within the scope of his employment, and was therefore demurrable. Thompson *v.* Nashville, C. & St. L. Ry., 49 So. 340, 160 Ala. 590, cited in note in 37 L. R. A., N. S., 425.

§ 204 (3) Allegations as to Negligence in General.

Charging Negligence in General Terms.—In an action for injuries to a passenger, it is sufficient to charge negligence in general terms. Birmingham R., etc., Co. *v.* Wright, 153 Ala. 99, 44 So. 1037; Birmingham R., etc., Co. *v.* Hunnicutt, 3 Ala. App. 448, 57 So. 262. See, to the same effect, Birmingham R., etc., Co. *v.* Haggard, 155 Ala. 343, 46 So. 519.

A complaint in an action for injuries to a passenger which avers the negligence of the carrier in such general language as to amount to hardly more than a statement of a mere conclusion is good as against a demurrer. Birmingham R., etc., Co. *v.* McCurdy, 172 Ala. 488, 55 So. 616.

Injuries Caused by Negligent Conduct of Business.—A complaint averring that plaintiff's intestate was a passenger on one of defendant's street cars, and that defendant then and there so negligently conducted said business that by reason of such negligence plaintiff's intestate received personal injuries, which caused his death, sufficiently alleges the negligence of defendant. Armstrong *v.* Montgomery St. Ry. Co., 26 So. 349, 123 Ala. 233.

A count in a complaint, alleging that defendant was a common carrier, and that it so negligently conducted its business that by reason of such negligence plaintiff's intestate who was a passenger on one of defendant's trains, received personal injuries which caused his death, stated a cause of action for simple negligence. Louisville, etc., R. Co. *v.* Perkins, 152 Ala. 133, 44 So. 602.

A complaint for injuries to a passenger, which alleges the existence of the relation of carrier and passenger just before and at the time of the injuries, and which states that the carrier, failing in its duty to carry the passenger safely, so negligently conducted its business that by reason of such negligence the passenger received as a proximate result thereof personal injuries, states a cause of action for simple negligence, and is good as against a demurrer. Birmingham R., etc., Co. *v.* Wright, 153 Ala. 99, 44 So. 1037.

Complaints Held to Charge Simple Negligence.—A count, after stating plaintiff's relation as a passenger, and the duty of defendant's servant not to increase the speed of the car after being advised that plaintiff desired to alight, alleged that defendant's motorman, well knowing that plaintiff was seeking to alight, and that a sudden jerk would probably throw plaintiff from the car, with wanton, willful, and reckless negligence suddenly increased the speed of the car, and, as a proximate consequence thereof, plaintiff was thrown from the car and injured. Held, that such count did not present a charge of willful injury, but tendered an issue of negligence only. Birmingham Ry., Light & Power Co. *v.* Glover, 38 So. 836, 142 Ala. 492.

A complaint for injuries to a street car passenger, which alleges that it was the duty of the company to carry plaintiff safely, and "that, failing in this duty, and with a reckless disregard for the safety of plaintiff, and knowing that the probable consequences thereof would be to inflict injury on plaintiff," the employees in charge of the car, acting within the scope of their duties, willfully, wantonly, or intentionally ran the car while the passenger was in the act of alighting, so that he was injured, only charges simple negligence, and is good as against a demurrer raising the question of a joinder of corporate negligence with negligence of employees; the word "this" referring only to the duty of the company, and the conjoined sentence beginning with the words "with a reckless disregard" referring to the circumstances under which the company, as distinguished from the employees failed to perform its duty. Birmingham R., etc., Co. *v.* Wright, 153 Ala. 99, 44 So. 1037.

A count, in a complaint against a carrier for injuries, alleging that the wreck was caused by the gross or reckless negligence of defendant, and that said gross and reckless negligence consisted in allowing rotten, unsound, and insecure crossties to remain under the rails of said road, etc., charges only simple negligence, and hence a failure to aver that plaintiff was rightfully on the train makes the count demurrable. Broyles *v.* Central, etc., R. Co., 166 Ala. 616, 52 So. 81.

A complaint which alleges that the plaintiff, while under the influence of liquor, boarded an open car and rode on the train, and that the road was new and rough, and that running the train at a fast rate of speed would cause it to jolt, and to endanger those on the open car, and that these facts were well known to the engineer, but, with full knowledge of them, he willfully and wantonly ran the engine at the high rate of speed, etc., states a cause of action for negligence only, and not for willful or wanton injury, because it fails to show that at the time of the injury the engineer was conscious that his act would probably result in injury; the expression "with full knowledge of said facts" only showing that he knew the elements of the dangerous situation. Alabama Cent. R. Co. *v.* Humphries, 53 So. 1013, 169 Ala. 369.

§ 204 (4) Wanton or Willful Injury.

See, also, post, "Wanton or Willful Acts," § 204 (7).

Inconsistency and Repugnancy.—A complaint in an action for injuries to a passenger by the derailment of a train alleged the defective condition of the ties, knowledge on the part of defendant of such condition of the ties, and that, notwithstanding, the cars were propelled along the track at a great rate of speed, recklessly, wantonly, and intentionally, and as a proximate consequence thereof the coach in which plaintiff was riding was derailed and plaintiff injured. Held, that the facts stated were insufficient to predicate a charge of willful and wanton misconduct, and rendered the complaint demurrable for inconsistency and repugnancy. St. Louis & S. F. R. Co. *v.* Pearce, 49 So. 247, 159 Ala. 141.

Allegations Held Insufficient to Show Liability to Trespasser.—The complaint in an action for injuries to plaintiff, who had boarded a train to see a passenger on business, that while plaintiff was alighting, and the train was moving at not more than two or three miles an hour, it made a violent start, and while within a few hundred feet of the depot began running at the unlawful speed of not less than 15 miles an hour, by reason of which plaintiff was thrown from the step, and that the resulting injuries were the direct result of the engineer in beginning to run the train at an unlawful speed, did not allege such negligence as would make the company liable for injuries to plaintiff, a trespasser; it not showing that the engineer knew that plaintiff was alighting when he increased the speed of the train. McElvane *v.* Central of Georgia Ry. Co., 54 So. 489, 170 Ala. 525.

§ 204 (5) Acts of Employees, Fellow Passengers and Other Third Persons.

§ 204 (5a) Negligent Acts of Employees.

Allegation as to Acts Being within Scope of Duties.—Where, in an action for injuries to a passenger, the relation of passenger and carrier is averred, it was not essential that the negligence imputed to defendant's servants should be alleged to have been the result of acts within the scope of their duties. Birmingham Ry., Light & Power Co. *v.* Harden, 47 So. 327, 156 Ala. 244.

Scope of Authority Sufficiently Alleged.—A complaint alleging that defendant's servant, acting within the line of his duty, wantonly caused plaintiff's minor son to fall from the car, sufficiently averred that the servant was acting within the scope of his authority. Birmingham Ry., Light & Power Co. *v.* Chastain, 48 So. 85, 158 Ala. 421.

Showing Relation of Master and Servant—Consciousness of Danger and Wantonness.—A count, alleging wanton injury to a passenger by the sudden movement of a street car, should aver that employee or employees in charge of the car, who caused the sudden movement or jerk of the car, or whose negligence is relied on for recovery, were the servant or servants of the defendant; that they were conscious of the danger and wantonly inflicted the injury. Birmingham R., etc., Co. *v.* Barrett, 4 Ala. App. 347, 58 So. 760.

Name of Negligent Employee.—It is not necessary to allege the name of the carrier's employee whose negligence caused the injury. Armstrong *v.* Montgomery St. Ry. Co., 26 So. 349, 123 Ala. 233; Birmingham R., etc., Co. *v.* Goldstein (Ala.), 61 So. 281; Kansas, etc., R. Co. *v.* Matthews, 142 Ala. 298, 39 So. 207.

In an action against a carrier for injuries to a street car passenger, the complaint alleged that the injury was wantonly or willfully inflicted by the agents or servants of the defendant who were in charge of the car and while acting within the scope of their authority. Held, that this averment was not insufficient for failure to give the names of the agents or servants, or failure to state definitely whether it was the motorman or conductor who caused the injury, as such matters are best known to defendant, and the passenger is not presumed to have knowledge upon that point. Birmingham R., etc., Co. *v.* Goldstein (Ala.), 61 So. 281.

Complaint Held to Charge Negligence to Conductor Alone.—A complaint against an electric railway company for injury to a passenger, alleging that the defendant, "by its servants or agents, the conductor who was in charge of said train, acting within the general line of his employment," ordered him from a safe place in the forward car to the rear car, and that while attempting to comply with the order and standing on the rear platform of the first car, he was thrown to the ground by a sudden jerking of the train, negligently caused "by the servants in charge of" the train, is not susceptible of a construction charging negligence to any one excepting the conductor. Birmingham R., etc., Co. *v.* Yates, 169 Ala. 381, 53 So. 915.

Complaint Not Objectionable as Insufficient Attempt to Particularize Negligence.—Under Code 1896, § 3441, requiring operators of trains to stop 100 feet before crossing another railroad and not to proceed until they know that the way is clear, a complaint in an action by a street car passenger for injuries in a collision at a railroad crossing, alleging that the operatives of the car negligently ran the same on the railroad crossing without first knowing that the track was clear, and that by reason of such negligence plaintiff was injured, etc., was not objectionable as an insufficient attempt to particularize defendant's negligence. Montgomery St. Ry. Co. *v.* Lewis, 41 So. 736, 148 Ala. 134.

Acts of Servant Causing Violent Jolt.—Allegations of complaint, in a railroad passenger's action for personal injuries, that defendant's agents, acting within the scope of their employment as such, wantonly or intentionally caused plaintiff to suffer the injuries described by wantonly or intentionally causing the car to knowing that it would likely cause some become suddenly or violently jolted, passengers to suffer personal injury, sufficiently alleged negligence. Western Railway *v.* Foshee (Ala.), 62 So. 500.

Act of Servant Causing Passenger to Be Thrown from Train.—A complaint against a street railway company, alleging that a passenger was thrown very violently to the ground through the negligence of the company's servants and agents in carrying him as a passenger, though general in its averments of negligence, conforms to the rule permitting in such cases a nonspecific allegation of the negligence relied on. Birmingham R., Light & Power Co. *v.* Haggard, 46 So. 519, 155 Ala. 343.

A complaint, in an action against a railway company for the negligent death of a passenger, which shows that decedent was a passenger, and that as such passenger he was, through the negligence of the company's servants, thrown from the train and killed, is sufficient, without alleging who the negligent servants were, or their duties in the operation of the train, or that the injury resulted from the company's negligence. Kansas City, M. & B. R. Co. *v.* Matthews, 39 So. 207, 142 Ala. 298.

A complaint against an electric railway company for injury to a passenger which alleged the relation of carrier and passenger, that the conductor ordered plaintiff from a safe place on a car, and that while plaintiff was attempting to comply with the order and standing on the rear platform, the conductor negligently increased the speed of the train and caused the same to make a sudden and severe jerk or motion, directly causing plaintiff to be thrown to the ground and injured, sufficiently showed a breach of duty by the company and injury therefrom. Birmingham R., etc., Co. *v.* Yates, 169 Ala. 381, 53 So. 915.

A complaint in an action against a carrier, which alleges that decedent was a passenger, that the conductor, while acting within the scope of his authority, ordered decedent to leave a coach and go into another while the train was in motion, that decedent, while attempting to comply with the order, was thrown from the train and killed, and that his death was proximately caused by the negligence of the carrier's servant, states a cause of action. Central, etc., R. Co. *v.* Carleton, 163 Ala. 62, 51 So. 27.

Complaints Held Sufficient.—A complaint in an action against a carrier, which alleges that decedent was a passenger, and that his death was proximately caused by the negligence of the trainmen in and about the carriage of decedent as a passenger, or which alleges wanton, willful, and intentional misconduct of the trainmen, states a cause of action as against a demurrer. Central, etc., R. Co. *v.* Carleton, 163 Ala. 62, 51 So. 27.

By the first count of a complaint plaintiff claimed damages, in that defendant was, on a certain date, a common carrier of passengers, and that plaintiff was a passenger on one of its cars, and, when approaching a certain point in the street, plaintiff was thrown with great violence against one of the seats, and one or more persons were thrown against her with great force, greatly injuring her side and one of her ribs, and alleged other damages, and in closing averred that her injuries were proximately caused by the negligence of defendant's servants or agents, or some of them, in charge or control of the car, in the negligent manner in which they ran or operated the same. Count 2 adopted and made a part thereof all of the first count down to the closing averment, and added an averment that her injuries were proximately caused by the negligence of the motorman, who had control of the car on which she was riding, in the negligent manner in which he operated the same. Held, that the counts were not subject to demurrer on the ground that they were vague, uncertain, and indefinite, and that it did not appear with sufficient certainty what duty defendant owed plaintiff, or wherein or how defendant violated any duty owed her. Birmingham Ry., Light & Power Co. *v.* Oden, 51 So. 240, 164 Ala. 1.

§ 204 (5b) Wanton or Willful Acts.

A count of a complaint, alleging that defendant's servant "wantonly and recklessly or intentionally" injured plaintiff, will be held a charge of wantonness and intentional injury. Birmingham Ry., Light & Power Co. *v.* Lee, 45 So. 292, 153 Ala. 79.

The count of a complaint for injury to plaintiff at a certain time and place while a passenger on defendant's car, alleging that its servant or agent in charge or control thereof, acting within the line and scope of his authority as such, wantonly or intentionally caused plaintiff to be injured, is not subject to demurrer for uncertainty and indefiniteness. Birmingham R., etc., Co. *v.* Fisher, 173 Ala. 623, 55 So. 995.

A count, alleging that while plaintiff was a passenger on defendant's car its servants or agents, within the scope of their employment, wantonly or willfully inflicted upon him the wounds and injuries set out, and that such wounds and injuries were the proximate consequences of the wantonness or willfulness of "defendant, its servants or agents, as aforesaid," sufficiently showed that the wantonness and willfulness complained of was that of defendant's servants or agents, and not that of defendant itself; the word "aforesaid" limiting the general averment immediately preceding, and referring back to the preceding particular averments. Birmingham R., etc., Co. *v.* Taylor, 6 Ala. App. 661, 60 So. 979.

The count of a complaint alleging that while plaintiff, a passenger on defendant's car, was engaged in or about alighting from it, defendant's servant in charge of the car having knowledge and notice that plaintiff was so engaged, and that to cause him to fall to the ground would be highly dangerous to him, nevertheless, with said knowledge or notice, defendant, through said servant, wantonly or intentionally caused plaintiff to fall or be thrown to the ground, sufficiently charges wanton or intentional misconduct, even if not expressly averring knowledge of the danger, the averment of wantonness or intention being made as to causing the fall—an act so naturally and apparently dangerous to plaintiff as to charge the perpetrator with the knowledge of the danger. Birmingham R., etc., Co. *v.* Lindsey, 140 Ala. 312, 37 So. 289.

A complaint, in an action for injuries to a passenger while attempting to board a street car, which alleges that the injuries complained of were proximately caused by the wantonness of the conductor in charge of the car while acting within the scope of his employment, in that he, knowing that the passenger was in the act of boarding the car, and knowing that to cause the car to start forward would likely injure the passenger, wantonly caused the car to start forward and wantonly inflict the injuries complained of, sufficiently charges wantonness. Birmingham R., etc., Co. *v.* Selhorst, 165 Ala. 475, 51 So. 568.

The averment of the complaint that defendant's servant, in charge of its car, while acting in the line and scope of his authority as such servant, wantonly or intentionally prevented plaintiff from boarding said car as aforesaid, and thereby wantonly or intentionally caused plaintiff to suffer said injuries, it being theretofore alleged that said servant failed to allow plaintiff a reasonable time or opportunity to board said car, is sufficient as against a demurrer that it does not show that the injury was wantonly or intentionally inflicted. Birmingham Ry., Light & Power Co. *v.* Wise, 42 So. 821, 149 Ala. 492.

§ 204 (5c) Assaults or Abusive Language.

Averring Acts within Scope of Authority.—A complaint which alleges that plaintiff was a passenger on a train of defendant, that defendant's train servant used towards plaintiff abusive or insulting language, and as a proximate consequence thereof plaintiff was greatly humiliated, is demurrable for failure to show that the servant was acting within the scope of his authority. Alabama, etc., R. Co. *v.* Pouncey (Ala.), 61 So. 601. But see Birmingham R., etc., Co. *v.* Mason, 137 Ala. 342, 34 So. 207.

A count in the complaint in an action against a carrier for an assault committed by one of its servants having alleged that plaintiff was at the time a passenger on defendant's car, it was not necessary to aver that it was committed within the scope of the servant's duty. Birmingham Ry. & Electric Co. *v.* Mason, 34 So. 207, 137 Ala. 342.

Assault Sufficiently Charged.—An allegation in the complaint in a passenger's action for assault that the conductor wantonly assaulted plaintiff by grasping her by the arm and shoulders was equivalent to an allegation that he wantonly grasped her by the arm and shoulder, and sufficiently charged wanton assault. Birmingham R., etc., Co. *v.* Parker, 161 Ala. 248, 50 So. 55.

A complaint which alleges that "——, who was a brakeman or flagman on defendant's train, and an employee of defendant," insulted and threatened plaintiff, who had paid full fare for a first-class ticket, and was traveling on defendant's train, and "did assault and beat plaintiff by striking him over the head," etc., when plaintiff was getting off the train at his destination, sufficiently charges that the acts complained of were committed while plaintiff was a passenger, by a brakeman in the employ of defendant, while in the discharge of his duty as brakeman. Lampkin *v.* Louisville & N. R. Co., 106 Ala. 287, 17 So. 448, cited in note in 40 L. R. A., N. S., 1007, 1051, 1053, 1072.

Matters Alleged in Aggravation.—An allegation in the complaint in a passenger's action that the conductor wantonly assaulted plaintiff by grasping her by the arm and shoulder, by winking and smiling at her, did not mean that the conductor grasped plaintiff by winking and smiling at her, and only charged one assault; the smiling and winking only being alleged in aggravation. Birmingham R., etc., Co. *v.* Parker, 161 Ala. 248, 50 So. 55.

Assault Made in Self-Defense.—See post, "Pleading Matters of Defense," § 204 (10).

§ 204 (5d) Acts of Fellow Passengers and Third Persons.

Necessity and Sufficiency of Averments as to Anticipation of Wrong.—The complaint in an action against a carrier for damages to a passenger by an illegal search must state facts sufficient to show that the carrier's servants should have intervened to protect the passenger, to wit, a knowledge of the intended wrong, or reasonable grounds to anticipate it, in time to interfere with the execution. Nashville, etc., Railway *v.* Crosby (Ala.), 62 So. 889.

Where, in an action by a passenger against a carrier for assault committed upon him by other passengers, the complaint alleged that the conductor or other servants of the carrier knew of the impending danger to the plaintiff, and knowingly failed or refused to interfere to protect him, an allegation that "such negligence on the part of the servants of the defendant resulted in the injuries to plaintiffs" sufficiently averred that the servants could have prevented the injury complained of. Culberson *v.* Empire Coal Co., 156 Ala. 416, 47 So. 237.

Where a complaint against a carrier charged an assault and battery on plaintiff, while a passenger of defendant, by a stranger, and that all of the wrongs and injuries to plaintiff were known to defendant, or would have been known by it by the exercise of reasonable care and diligence, and that defendant negligently permitted plaintiff to be assaulted, beaten, bruised, and otherwise ill-treated, without protecting him, etc., it did not sufficiently allege that the carrier knew, or from the attendant circumstances should have known, of the threatened injury to plaintiff in time to have prevented it, and was therefore demurrable. Southern R. Co. *v.* Hanby (Ala.), 62 So. 871.

§ 204 (6) Taking Up Passengers.

A complaint, in an action for injuries to a passenger while attempting to board a street car, which alleges that the injuries were caused proximately by the car men while acting within the scope of their employment, because of the negligent manner in which they operated the car, sufficiently sets out the negligence relied on. Birmingham R., etc., Co. *v.* Selhorst, 165 Ala. 475, 51 So. 568.

Jerk While Passenger Boarding Car.—A complaint, in a passenger's injury action, which alleges that as he was in the act of boarding the street car, and was on one of its steps, the car men negligently caused the car to jerk or lurch, causing the passenger to be thrown to the ground, is sufficient, though it does not aver that the car had come to a stop when the passenger attempted to board it, since the complaint implied notice to the car men of the passenger's position. Birmingham R., etc., Co. *v.* Selhorst, 165 Ala. 475, 51 So. 568.

Failing to Give Passenger Sufficient Time to Resume Seat.—In an action against a carrier for injuries to a passenger, resulting from the negligence of defendant in failing to give plaintiff sufficient time to resume his place in the cars after he had alighted on the train stopping at a siding, an amended complaint held to sufficiently allege defendant's negligence. Birmingham Ry., Light & Power Co. *v.* Jung, 49 So. 434, 161 Ala. 461, cited in 22 L. R. A., N. S., 758, 36 L. R. A., N. S., 271.

Allegation Not Showing Attempt to Board Car at Proper Place.—The allegation that plaintiff attempted to board the car a short distance south of where defendant's line crossed another railroad does not, by reason of the statutory requirements that trains shall be brought to a full stop before crossing the tracks of an intersecting line, raise the inference that the car was at rest, as it is not averred that the train was on a north-bound trip, or that it was within a hundred feet of the crossing, the distance at which trains are obliged to stop. North Birmingham Ry. Co. *v.* Liddicoat, 99 Ala. 545, 13 So. 18, cited in note in 38 L. R. A. 789.

§ 204 (7) Management of Conveyances.

A general allegation of the complaint that the passenger's injuries were proximately caused by the negligent manner in which the defendant operated the train upon which he was riding was sufficient as an allegation of negligence. Alabama, etc., R. Co. *v.* Gilbert, 6 Ala. App. 372, 60 So. 542; Birmingham R., etc., Co. *v.* Glover, 142 Ala. 492, 38 So. 836.

In an action for injuries to plaintiff's wife, a complaint, after alleging that she was a passenger on defendant's train, averring that the injuries were proximately caused by defendant's negligence in the manner in which it ran or operated a certain street car, sufficiently charged actionable negligence. Birmingham R., etc., Co. *v.* Barrett, 4 Ala. App. 347, 58 So. 760; Birmingham R., etc., Co. *v.* Harris, 165 Ala. 482, 51 So. 607; Birmingham R., etc., Co. *v.* Selhorst, 165 Ala. 475, 51 So. 568; Birmingham R., etc., Co. *v.* Oden, 164 Ala. 1, 51 So. 240; Birmingham R., etc., Co. *v.* Jordan, 170 Ala. 530, 54 So. 280; Central, etc., R. Co. *v.* Carleton, 163 Ala. 62, 51 So. 27; Armstrong *v.* Montgomery St. R. Co., 123 Ala. 233, 26 So. 349.

Averment as to Negligent Operation Causing Fall.—Counts of a complaint charging simple negligence of defendant, a common carrier, to the injury of plaintiff, a passenger on one of its cars, by alleging that it so negligently conducted itself in and about carrying her thereon that at a certain time and place she was thrown or caused to fall, are sufficient. Birmingham R., etc., Co. *v.* Fisher, 173 Ala. 623, 55 So. 995.

A complaint for injury to a passenger on a train states defendant's negligence with sufficient certainty and definiteness by averments that defendant negligently failed to safely carry her, but so negligently and unskillfully conducted itself in that regard that she was thrown to the floor. Southern R. Co. *v.* Crowder, 33 So. 335, 135 Ala. 417.

The complaint alleged that while plaintiff was a passenger the car upon which he was riding was suddenly and violently jarred or jolted, so that as a proximate consequence thereof plaintiff was thrown or caused to fall and was injured, and that defendant was guilty of negligence in carrying plaintiff as a passenger, and as a proximate consequence of such negligence the car on which plaintiff was riding was suddenly and violently jolted. Held, that the complaint sufficiently alleged negligence. Western Railway *v.* Foshee (Ala.), 62 So. 500.

"This case may be differentiated from Birmingham R., etc., Co. *v.* Weathers, 164 Ala. 23, 51 So. 303, on the consideration that in that case there was no effort to aver, generally or otherwise, a negligence antedating the alleged sudden jerk in the line of causation, nor was it averred that the sudden jerk was negligently caused. The complaint in that case was rested upon the bare fact that plaintiff was injured by an insolated, unrelated jerk, which was without characterization, except that it was alleged to have been sudden. This was held insufficient. Here, as we have seen, there is an averment of negligence which operated through a sudden and violent jar or jolt to plaintiff's injury." Western Railway *v.* Foshee (Ala.), 62 So. 500, 502.

Same—Petition Held Insufficient.—A complaint alleging that, while plaintiff was a passenger on defendant's car, "said car started or jerked, or the speed thereof was suddenly increased, and as a proximate consequence thereof plaintiff was thrown or caused to fall or struck on or against said car or some hard substance therein, and was made sick and sore; * * * that he was thrown or caused to fall or be struck as aforesaid, and to suffer said injuries and damage by reason and as the consequence of the negligence of defendant in or about carrying plaintiff as defendant's passenger," is insufficient to state a cause of action, as it does not allege that defendant or its agents were guilty of negligence. Birmingham Ry., Light & Power Co. *v.* Weathers, 51 So. 303, 164 Ala. 23, distinguished in Western Railway *v.* Foshee (Ala.), 62 So. 500.

Passenger Thrown Off Train.—A complaint for injuries to a street car passenger, alleging the relation of the parties, and then charging that defendant was negligent, in that, while the car on which plaintiff was riding was crowded, plaintiff and others were obliged to stand on the running board and the car was negligently run at such a high rate of speed that it swayed, rocked, or lunged, so that plaintiff was thrown or knocked off and injured, stated a cause of action and was not demurrable. Birmingham R., etc., Co. *v.* Hunnicutt, 3 Ala. App. 448, 57 So. 262.

Confinement in Toilet Room.—A complaint alleging that, while plaintiff was a passenger on defendant's road, as a proximate consequence of defendant's negligence she was confined for a considerable time in a toilet room owning to the door becoming fastened or obstructed, as a consequence of which she became sick, her health and physical stamina were greatly impaired, she suffered great mental and physical pain and anguish, was made uncomfortable, annoyed, and chagrined, that the attention of many people was called to the fact that she was so confined, and she suffered great inconvenience, annoyance, and was compelled to be separated from two of her small children for a long time, sufficiently charged a breach of defendant's duty to safely carry her as a passenger as it had contracted to do. Alabama, etc., R. Co. *v.* Robinson (Ala.), 62 So. 813.

Jolting Car.—Where a complaint alleged that while plaintiff was a passenger a portion of the train which had been detached from plaintiff's car ran back with great force against such car, and injured plaintiff, etc., and that plaintiff's injuries proximately resulted from defendant's negligence in the operation of the train, it was not demurrable in that the facts constituting negligence were insufficiently stated. Kansas City, M. & B. R. Co. *v.* Butler, 38 So. 1024, 143 Ala. 262.

Causing Persons or Objects to Fall on or Injure Passenger.—A complaint for injury to an electric railway passenger, alleging a severe shock, concussion, or explosion on the car, causing another person to fall against plaintiff, resulting in stated injuries, as a proximate cause of defendant's negligence in carrying her, sufficiently pleads negligence. Birmingham Ry., Light & Power Co. *v.* Jordan, 54 So. 280, 170 Ala. 530.

A complaint alleging that in the car in which plaintiff was riding, on the wall over the seat given him, defendant railroad company had negligently hung, placed, or affixed a bottle containing a fluid, and that the bottle was broken or exploded, and the contents negligently spilled on plaintiff's clothes and person, alleges with sufficient certainty the negligence of defendant. Alabama G. S. R. Co. *v.* Collier, 112 Ala. 681, 14 So. 327.

A complaint in an action for injuries

to a passenger, which alleges that while plaintiff was a passenger, and was being carried by defendant as such on a train, her hand was caught in the car on the train between a table on the train and the wall of the car, and was injured, and that the injuries were occasioned as a proximate consequence of the negligence of defendant in and about carrying plaintiff as a passenger, sufficiently sets out, as against a demurrer, the negligence of defendant. Louisville & N. R. Co. *v.* Church, 46 So. 457, 155 Ala. 329, cited in note in 29 L. R. A., N. S., 810.

§ 204 (8) Setting Down Passengers.

General —Averments.—A complaint, alleging that while a passenger was in the act of alighting from a street car it started forward with a sudden, violent jerk, throwing her to the floor and injuring her, and that her injuries were proximately caused by the negligence of defendant in the negligent manner in which it ran or operated the car, was sufficient as against demurrer. Birmingham R., etc., Co. *v.* Gonzales (Ala.), 61 So. 80, distinguishing Birmingham R., etc., Co. *v.* Parker, 156 Ala. 251, 47 So. 138, and Birmingham R., etc, Co. *v.* Weathers, 164 Ala. 23, 51 So. 303.

A complaint in an action for injuries to a street car passenger while alighting, which alleges that the injuries resulted as the proximate consequence of the negligence of the carrier or its servants in charge of the operation of the car, sufficiently charges the liability of the carrier as against a general demurrer. Birmingham R., etc., Co. *v.* McCurdy, 172 Ala. 488, 55 So. 616.

A complaint in an action against a carrier for injuries to a passenger, which alleges that the carrier so negligently conducted itself that, while the passenger was alighting from the train, the train was jolted and the passenger caused to fall and be injured, charges negligence, under Code 1896, § 3285, requiring pleadings to present the facts in an intelligible form, and providing that no objection can be allowed for defect of form. Southern Ry. Co. *v.* Burgess, 42 So. 35, 143 Ala. 364.

A complaint by an electric car passenger for injuries, alleging that plaintiff claims of defendant $5,000 as damages, for that on a specified date plaintiff was a passenger on defendant's electric car, and while in an effort to alight was thrown down and injured, etc., and that all her injuries and damages were proximately caused by reason of the negligence of one or more of its servants, acting within the scope and line of their employment, and in the control, management, and operation of such car, on which plaintiff was at the time a passenger, was not demurrable for failure to sufficiently allege the negligence to which the injury was ascribed. Birmingham Ry., Light & Power Co. *v.* Harris, 51 So. 607, 165 Ala. 482.

General Averments Not Overcome by Particular Allegations.—Plaintiff's complaint charged that his wife took passage on defendant's car and paid fare thereon; that when she reached her destination the car was stopped, but just before she arose from her seat it moved forward with a jerk, and she was thrown violently against a seat and injured; and that the injury proximately resulted from the negligent way in which defendant conducted itself in and about carrying her to her destination. The second count was the same, except that it alleged that the injuries were due to the negligent way in which defendant handled the car on which plaintiff's wife was riding. Held, that neither count was demurrable on the ground that the general averment of negligence was overcome by the particular facts charged. Birmingham R., etc., Co. *v.* Wilcox (Ala.), 61 So. 908.

A count for injury while attempting to alight from a car, averring the surroundings, and that the motorman negligently started the car, throwing the passenger, but not ascribing the negligence to the detailed circumstances in another count does not predicate the negligence on them, and so is not insufficient because they do not show negligence. Selma St., etc., R. Co. *v.* Campbell, 158 Ala. 438, 48 So. 378.

Under a complaint for injury to a passenger, describing how she was injured, alleging negligence generally, she can show any actionable negligence as a carrier. Birmingham Ry., Light & Power Co. *v.* Jordan, 54 So. 280, 170 Ala. 530, distinguishing Birmingham R., etc., Co. *v.* Weathers, 164 Ala. 23, 51 So. 303.

Allegation as to Increasing Speed at Time of Alighting.—A count alleging that plaintiff informed defendant's conductor of his desire to alight at a certain point; that it then became the duty of defendant's servant, after slackening the speed of the car, not to increase the speed until plaintiff had alighted, or had a reasonable opportunity to do so, but that, notwithstanding such duty, defendant's servant negligently, suddenly, and greatly increased the speed of the car before plaintiff had alighted or had a reasonable opportunity to alight, in consequence of which negligence plaintiff's body was thrown from the car, etc., though faulty in assuming, instead of alleging, that defendant's servant slackened the speed on being informed that plaintiff desired to alight, was nevertheless good as against a demurrer on the ground that it failed to allege increase of speed at the time plaintiff was in the act of alighting. Birmingham Ry. Light & Power Co. *v.* Glover, 38 So. 836, 142 Ala. 492.

Necessity for Averring Knowledge of Plaintiff's Position.—A complaint alleging wanton negligence against defendant's servants or some of them in suddenly starting a street car, knowing that plaintiff was disembarking, is insufficient in not averring that all of the servants knew of the plaintiff's position, or that those who started the car knew of it. Birmingham Ry., Light & Power Co. *v.* Bennett, 39 So. 565, 144 Ala. 369.

Allegation as to Injuries Received While Returning to Station.—A complaint for injuries to a passenger carried beyond her station, and required to alight and walk back to the station, need not allege that her eyesight was defective, or that she could not see at night, or that her affliction was apparent to the conductor, in order to state a cause of action. Alabama, etc., R. Co. *v.* Cox, 173 Ala. 629, 55 So. 909.

Averment of Failure to Provide Safe Place to Alight.—In an action against a street railway company for injuries received by a passenger on alighting from a car, a complaint alleging the failure of the defendant to provide a safe place for alighting is not demurrable in not averring what constitutes a safe place, nor in giving a minute description of the place where the stop was made and of the alleged injuries. Montgomery St. Ry. *v.* Mason, 32 So. 261, 133 Ala. 508.

Allegations as to Injuries Received on Leaving Premises.—A complaint in an action for injuries to a passenger which alleges that he alighted at a depot in the night time, that while passing from the depot along a much-traveled pathway he fell into a ditch and was injured, that the pathway was on the carrier's premises, and was habitually used with its knowledge and acquiescence by its passengers in leaving its depot and trains, at and before the time of the injury by the invitation of the carrier, and that the carrier negligently allowed the pathway to remain unsafe, makes a case of a passenger leaving a train by a route which he, as well as passengers in general, was invited by the carrier to use, and states a cause of action as against a demurrer. Alabama Great Southern R. Co. *v.* Godfrey, 47 So. 185, 156 Ala. 202.

Petitions Held Sufficient.—The complaint, alleging that when defendant's train, on which plaintiff was a passenger, approached her destination, blew for the station, and began to slow down, a trainman announced the station, and she in obedience went to the car platform, and by the time she had reached it the train had arrived at the depot and had slowed down to almost a standstill, and that immediately after she had reached the platform, preparatory to alighting, the servants in charge of the train caused it to suddenly and without warning start violently forward, thereby hurling her to the ground, inflicting certain injuries, states a cause of action, without showing contributory negligence. Southern Ry. Co. *v.* Hundley, 44 So. 195, 151 Ala. 378.

A complaint claimed specified damages against an electric railway company on allegations that, while plaintiff passenger was alighting at his destination, the car started or jerked, or the speed thereof was suddenly increased, proximately causing him to fall, resulting in specified injuries; that he was thrown or caused to fall through and as a proximate consequence of defendant's negligence in and about carrying him as its passenger. Held, that the complaint was not demurrable as being vague, uncertain, and indefinite, as not showing any duty or any violation of any duty. Birmingham Ry., Light & Power Co. *v.* McGinty, 48 So. 491, 158 Ala. 410.

A complaint in an action for personal injuries to passenger, causing death, alleging that "deceased gave the usual signal to stop the car, whereupon the motorman * * * slowed up and stopped, or so nearly so as to render it reasonably safe for deceased to proceed to alight, whereupon deceased proceeded to alight, placing himself in a standing position on the platform or running board alongside the car for that purpose, * * * whereupon the motorman, negligently failing to look and see whether deceased was in a place of danger, * * * started the car with a sudden motion, * * * thereby throwing deceased violently from said car," is not objectionable, in that it does not show whether he was injured by reason of attempting to get off the car after it had stopped, or while it was moving, and that it does not show that the motorman was informed of his desire to get off the car. Armstrong *v.* Montgomery St. Ry. Co., 26 So. 349, 123 Ala. 233.

In an action against a carrier for injuries to a passenger, the complaint alleged that plaintiff notified the conductor of her intention to alight at a certain street intersection, that the car came to a full stop, and before plaintiff had time to alight the car suddenly started, and as a direct and proximate result thereof plaintiff was thrown to the ground and injured in certain respects, and it was alleged that the damage was caused by defendant's negligence in so starting the car. Demurrers were interposed on the ground that the complaint joined an action of trespass with one in case, on the ground that the cause of action was improperly set forth and that the averments of the complaint were not alleged as facts, and on the ground that the averments were vague, uncertain, and indefinite, and that no facts were alleged putting defendant on notice as to what negligence was relied on by plaintiff. Held, that the demurrers were properly overruled. Birmingham Ry., Light & Power Co. *v.* Moore, 43 So. 841, 151 Ala. 327.

A complaint alleged that defendant was a common carrier, operating an electric line, and that on a certain date plaintiff was a passenger in said cars; that on reaching a station the car stopped, and while plaintiff was alighting the car moved, throwing the plaintiff on the ground and severely injuring her; that said injuries were proximately caused by negligence of defendant's employees, in charge of the car, in the management thereof. Count 2 charged the negligence to the motorman in the operation of the car, and count 3 charged the negligence to the conductor. Held, that the complaint was sufficient, and not subject to demurrers as vague and uncertain, and not stating facts showing the defendant's employees negligent, or how they were negligent, or that they were negligent in the line of their employment. Birmingham Ry., Light & Power Co. *v.* King, 42 So. 612, 149 Ala. 504.

A complaint in an action against a street railway company for injuries received by a passenger while alighting from a car, in consequence of the sudden starting of the car, which alleged that the car stopped at the intersection of designated streets, which was plaintiff's point of destination; that she attempted to alight there; that before she had fully got off the car was put in motion, and as a proximate consequence thereof she was thrown to the ground; that the starting of the car caused the injuries complained of; and that the car was negligently operated—states a cause of action as against the objections that it fails to sufficiently state defendant's negligence, that it fails to allege that defendant put the car in motion while she was alighting, that it fails to allege that the car stopped for the purpose of allowing passengers to alight, that it fails to show that the place where the car stopped was a regular stopping place for passengers to alight, and that it fails to show that defendant's servants had notice of her attempt to alight. Birmingham Ry.,

Light & Power Co. *v.* Handy (Ala.), 39 So. 917.

Petitions Held Insufficient.—A count in a petition averred that plaintiff was a passenger, etc., and "was waiting to alight, or engaged in or about alighting therefrom," and "said car was started or jerked, or the speed suddenly increased, and as a proximate consequence plaintiff was thrown," is demurrable, in that its allegations of negligence were insufficient, since it is not every increase in the speed of a car or starting of same, whether with or without a jerk, that amounts to negligence. Birmingham Ry., Light & Power Co. *v.* Parker, 47 So. 138, 156 Ala. 251.

The count, in an action against a carrier for injury to a passenger from the starting of the car while he was attempting to alight from it, averring that the motorman in charge willfully, wantonly, and negligently started the car back, and that the conductor and other employees of defendant knew it was necessary for plaintiff to get off at the corner of B. and S. streets, but not averring that they knew he had to get off at the particular point at said crossing, or that this was the place of making transfers, and that this was so known to the servant starting the car, and not averring consciousness by the motorman of plaintiff's peril, or that the car was started at a point where its starting was known to the motorman as being dangerous, or that the motorman knew plaintiff was preparing to alight or in the act of alighting when he started the car, or that people customarily transferred at that particular point, does not charge wanton or willful misconduct. Selma St., etc., R. Co. *v.* Campbell, 158 Ala. 438, 48 So. 378.

§ 204 (9) Averments as to Proximate Cause.

So far as pleading proximate cause in an action for injury to a passenger, it is enough that the facts averred lead, with requisite certainty, to the conclusion that the injury proximately resulted from the negligence charged. Birmingham R., etc., Co. *v.* Fisher, 173 Ala. 623, 55 So. 995.

Where, in an action for injuries to a passenger, each count of the complaint alleged facts sufficient to show prima facie negligence under the doctrine res ipsa loquitur, they were not demurrable. Western Railway *v.* McGraw (Ala.), 62 So. 772.

Failure to Allege Specific Act of Negligence.—In an action for injuries to a passenger, a count alleging facts sufficient to establish a prima facie case of negligence under the doctrine res ipsa loquitur was not defective for failure to allege a particular or a specific act of negligence. Western Railway *v.* McGraw (Ala.), 62 So. 772.

Casual Connection Sufficiently Shown.—A complaint, in an action against a railway company for the death of a passenger, which alleges that he was, through the carelessness of the company's servants, thrown from the train and so injured as to cause his death, sufficiently shows the negligence of the company and the infliction of decedent's injuries, and that the injuries resulted from the company's negligence, as against a demurrer on the grounds that it does not show the casual connection between decedent's death and the company's negligence, that it does not show the injuries sustained by decedent, and that it does not show wherein the company or its agents were negligent. Kansas City, M. & B. R. Co. *v.* Matthews, 39 So. 207, 142 Ala. 298.

Allegation Not Showing Negligence to Be Proximate Cause of Injury.—In an action against a street railroad for injuries to a passenger, a complaint which charges the negligence to the act of the conductor in signaling the motorman to go ahead while the plaintiff was on the side board or step preparatory to alighting, and avers the act of the motorman in starting the car with a sudden jerk as being the proximate cause of the injury, but does not aver that the start was negligently made, is bad and subject to demurrer because the negligence averred was not the proximate cause of the injury. Mobile Light & R. Co. *v.* Bell, 45 So. 56, 153 Ala. 90.

Proximate Cause Averred to Be Consequential Instead of Intentional Result of Conduct.—A complaint in an action for injuries to a street car passenger, which ascribes the injury to the company's negligently running the car while the passenger was in the act of alighting, avers the proximate cause to be the consequential, as distinguished from the intentional, result of the misconduct charged, and states a cause of action in case, as against a demurrer. Birmingham R., etc., Co. *v.* Wright, 153 Ala. 99, 44 So. 1037.

§ 204 (10) Pleading Matters of Defense.

Matter Available in Support of Contributory Negligence.—That a passenger carried beyond her station pursued a dangerous way back to the station, when a safe way was obvious and open to her selection, was available only in support of the defense of contributory negligence, and she need not negative it in her pleadings. Alabama, etc., R. Co. *v.* Cox, 173 Ala. 629, 55 So. 909.

Safe Way Available in Return to Station.—The complaint, in an action by a passenger for personal injuries received while returning to a station beyond which he had been negligently carried, need not negative the fact that there was an open, obvious, and safe way which the passenger could have traveled back to the station, since that fact was available in defense. Alabama, etc., R. Co. *v.* Cox, 173 Ala. 629, 55 So. 909.

Assault Made in Self-Defense.—The fact that an assault committed on a passenger was committed in self-defense, and was brought on by the misconduct of the person assaulted, is defensive matter, and it is not necessary that the complaint in an action against the carrier for the assault should allege that the assault was not committed in self-defense, or that it was unlawfully made, but it is sufficient if it avers an assault. Culberson *v.* Empire Coal Co., 156 Ala. 416, 47 So. 237.

§ 204 (11) Plea or Answer.

Striking Out Averments.—In an action for personal injuries to passenger, a plea that the car was equipped with bell and cord attached so that passengers could notify the motorman when they wished the car stopped should be stricken out, in the absence of an averment that the passenger did not pull the cord or ring the bell. Armstrong *v.* Montgomery St. Ry. Co., 26 So. 349, 123 Ala. 233.

Fact Which Must Be Specially Pleaded.—Where a carrier carrying a passenger beyond her station, and requiring her to alight and walk back to the station, believed that the injury sustained by the passenger while walking back to the station was proximately caused by her defective eyesight, and not by the negligence of the trainmen, it must by special plea allege such facts, in the absence of any allegation in the complaint as to defective eyesight. Alabama, etc., R. Co. *v.* Cox, 173 Ala. 629, 55 So. 909.

Failure to Negative Negligence Concurring with Act of Third Person.—In an action against a carrier for injuries to a passenger by derailment, pleas, alleging generally that derailment was caused by a third person, but which did not negative that defendant's negligence may have concurred with that of the third person in causing the injury, were insufficient. Western Railway *v.* McGraw (Ala.), 62 So. 772.

§ 205. —— Issues, Proof, and Variance.

§ 205 (1) Issues Raised by and Evidence Admissible under Pleadings.

Acts of Servants as Embraced in Allegation of Carrier's Negligence.—In an action for injuries to a passenger, an allegation of negligence on the part of the carrier is sufficient to embrace the negligence of the carrier's servants. Birmingham Ry., Light & Power Co. *v.* Moore, 42 So. 1024, 148 Ala. 115.

A complaint in an action for injury to a passenger, thrown from the platform of a coach by the lurch of the train, which alleges negligence generally as to the manner in which the carrier conducted its business as such, is broad enough to cover negligence of the conductor in requiring the passenger to leave the coach and stand on the platform. Central etc., R. Co. *v.* Brown, 165 Ala. 493, 51 So. 565, cited in note in 29 L. R. A., N. S., 326.

The charge of negligence, in a complaint alleging that plaintiff's injuries were caused by defendant's negligent conduct of its business while carrying her as a passenger, being general, proof of any actionable negligence of defendant or any of its employees in such respect is sufficient. Mobile, etc., R. Co. *v.* Barber, 2 Ala. App. 507, 56 So. 858.

Condition of Track as Embraced in Allegation of Negligent Performance.—Where the complaint only charges defendant railway company with negligently performing its duty to a passenger, whereby the car in which he was ran off the track and he was injured, evidence is admissible of defects in the track that may have caused the accident. Richmond & D. R. Co. *v.* Vance, 93 Ala. 144, 9 So. 574.

Evidence Admissible under Allegation of Assault by Conductor and Others.—Where, in an action by a passenger for an assault, the complaint alleged that the conductor assaulted the passenger and also permitted other persons to assault him, evidence that while the passenger and the conductor were fighting some person ran from the car and struck the passenger, and that the conductor did not undertake to prevent such person striking the passenger, was responsive to the issue, and was properly admitted, though the passenger subsequently failed to prove that the conductor knew or had reason to anticipate that such person was about to assault the passenger, thereby not showing the carrier's responsibility for such assault. Alabama City, G. & A. Ry. Co. *v.* Sampley, 53 So. 142, 169 Ala. 372, cited in note in 32 L. R. A., N. S., 1208, 40 L. R. A., N. S., 1008, 1051, 1060, 1067, 1070.

Allegation as to Injuries Sustained While Boarding Train.—An averment in a complaint in an action for injuries to a passenger while boarding a train that "plaintiff was engaged in or about boarding" the train, when injured, covers every reasonably necessary act of plaintiff in going up the steps of the car, walking across the platform, entering the door, and going down the aisle to the nearest unoccupied seat, and taking a seat. Birmingham, etc., R. Co. *v.* Norris, 4 Ala. App. 363, 59 So. 66.

Allegation as to Injury Sustained While Engaged in Alighting.—Where a complaint for injuries to a passenger alleged that she was engaged "in or about alighting" from the car, the words "in or about" were sufficiently broad in their signification to cover the entire passage from the car from beginning to end. Birmingham R., etc., Co. *v.* Glenn (Ala.), 60 So. 111.

Where a complaint alleged that plaintiff, a passenger, was thrown down and injured while engaged in alighting, the terms "engaged in alighting" includes all the acts transpiring from the moment the passenger arises for that purpose until he gets clear of the car, provided there is no interruption of his passage. Birmingham R., etc., Co. *v.* Glenn (Ala.), 60 So. 111.

"Operating the Train" as Referring to Failure to Furnish Safe Place in Which to Ride.—In a passenger's action for injuries from being thrown from the platform of a fast moving train, the words "operated the train" in a count of the complaint stating that the injuries were caused by the negligent manner in which defendant operated the train, meant "controlled the movement and speed of the train" in view of its crowded condition, and has no reference to defendant's failure to perform its duty to furnish plaintiff with a reasonably safe place in which to ride. Alabama, etc., R. Co. *v.* Gilbert, 6 Ala. App. 372, 60 So. 542.

Allegation as to Condition of Roadbed.—Under counts alleging negligence in failing to have the roadbed in proper condition at or near the place where the passenger car in which plaintiff was riding was derailed, for failing to have the track in proper condition, and in that the track was so constructed that when the train ran on it the rails spread, evidence that, at the embankment where the wreck occurred, water was allowed to stand in the ditch beside the road, and in the pits from which earth for the embankment was taken, is admissible, in connection with evidence that the cross-ties on the embankment were decayed so that the spikes holding down the rails and braces would work out; that there was a curve at that point, and the embankment was of clay, which seeped water; and that the ties would spring up and down, and water would work out at the ends of the ties. Louisville & N. R. Co. *v.* Sandlin, 28 So. 40, 125 Ala. 585.

Negligence in Employment of Engineer as Negligence in Carrying Passenger.—Under an allegation that defendant railroad company negligently "conducted itself in and about the carrying" of a passenger, evidence of negligence in employing the engineer or in retaining him is admissible. Kansas City, M. & B. R. Co. *v.* Sanders, 98 Ala. 293, 13 So. 57.

§ 205 (2) Matters Admissible under General Denial.

In a passenger's action for injuries alleged to have been caused by the negligence and wantonness of the railroad company's servants or agents, it could be shown under the general issue that such injuries were due to unavoidable accident. Carlisle *v.* Central, etc., R. Co. (Ala.), 62 So. 759.

§ 205 (3) Matters to Be Proved.

Relation of Carrier and Passenger and Negligence That of Employees.—In an action against a street railway company for injury to passenger, by pleading, besides the general issue, contributory negligence, and by answering interrogatories filed under express authority of Code 1896, § 1850 et seq., the company did not waive the necessity for plaintiff supporting by proof averments that the car on which plaintiff was a passenger when injured was operated by the company and that the negligence imputed was that of its employees; the interrogatories and answers not being in evidence. Birmingham Ry., Light & Power Co. *v.* Haggard, 46 So. 519, 155 Ala. 343.

Attempt to Leave Train at Improper Time, Place, etc.—To entitle a carrier, sued for injuries to a passenger while alighting from a freight train, to a verdict on a plea that the passenger negligently attempted to leave the car in an improper manner and at an improper time and place, and as a proximate result thereof was injured, it must be shown that the passenger attempted to leave the train in an improper manner and at an improper time and place. Southern Ry. Co. *v.* Burgess, 42 So. 35, 143 Ala. 364.

§ 205 (4) Variance between Allegations and Proof.

Variance Affecting Only Amount of Recovery.—In an action for injuries to a passenger by a carrier's failure to stop the train at her destination, a variance between the complaint and the evidence as to when plaintiff told the conductor of her infirm condition affected only the amount of the recovery and not the right of action, and therefore did not justify the giving of a general charge for defendant. Louisville & N. R. Co. *v.* Seale, 55 So. 237, 172 Ala. 480.

Failure to Prove Matters Affecting Gravity of Negligence.—In a female passenger's action against a railroad for damages through defendant's employees permitting other passengers to use offensive language, in an effort to compel plaintiff's colored servant to leave the car, an allegation that plaintiff's condition was so feeble as to be open to ordinary observation only affected the gravity of defendant's negligence, and failure to prove the same was not fatal to the action. Southern Ry. Co. *v.* Lee, 52 So. 648, 167 Ala. 268.

Place of Injury.—A complaint against a street railway company alleged that a passenger was injured while alighting "at" C., which appears to have been a shed station, and not a town or city. The evidence showed that the accident occurred about two car lengths from the station. Held, that there was no variance. Birmingham Ry., Light & Power Co. *v.* McGinty, 48 So. 491, 158 Ala. 410.

In an action against a street railway company for injury to an alighting passenger, there was no fatal variance between averment that the accident occurred "at or near the intersection of Eleventh Avenue and Twenty-Fourth Street South," in Birmingham, Ala., and proof that the accident occurred at Fourteenth Street; it appearing that the cause of action stated in the complaint was identical with the one presented by the evidence. Birmingham R., etc., Co. *v.* Lide (Ala.), 58 So. 990.

Where, in an action for injuries to a passenger, the venue of the offense was placed "at East Lake," and the evidence showed that it was "at the loop at East Lake," and that the station designated at East Lake was at another point, there was no material variance. Birmingham R., etc., Co. *v.* Glenn (Ala.), 60 So. 111.

Failure to Furnish Safe Place.—A complaint in an action for injuries to a passenger thrown from the platform of the coach by a lurch of the train, which alleges the duty of the carrier to furnish sufficient coaches for the passengers, and that it failed to furnish to the passenger a safe place in which to travel, and that in consequence thereof the passenger was in an unsafe place, is supported by evidence that the conductor required the passenger to surrender a safe place inside the coach and to occupy an unsafe place on the platform because of the crowded condition of the coach; for it was necessary for the passenger to go on the platform, and he went there under the pressure of that necessity and in obedience to the request of the conductor, the platform was for the time the place furnished him. Central, etc., R. Co. *v.* Brown, 165 Ala. 493, 51 So. 565; cited in note in 29 L. R. A., N. S., 326.

Collision as Caused by Servants of One or Both Trains.—The complaint, charging in one place the injury to plaintiff, occasioned by collision of two trains, as resulting from the negligence of those in charge of the train on which he was a passenger, and in another place charging negligence of those in charge of both trains, permits a recovery on proof of negligence in the handling of the one train, so that a charge that, unless there was negligence of the servants in charge of both trains, which caused the injury, plaintiff could not recover, is properly refused. Central of Georgia Ry. Co. *v.* Geopp, 45 So. 65, 153 Ala. 108.

Immaterial Variance as to Which Employee Used Profane Language.—Where a complaint alleged that profane language was used in plaintiff's presence by the conductor of a trailer on which plaintiff was riding, while the evidence showed that the language was used by the conductor of the motor car, to which the trailer was attached, the variance was immaterial. Birmingham R., etc., Co. *v.* Glenn (Ala.), 60 So. 111.

Failure to Prevent Illegal Search.—In an action against a carrier for damages for the failure of its servants to protect plaintiff from an illegal search, proof that when the officer told defendant's servant that plaintiff was accused of stealing a watch he said, "Search her in the freight room," does not constitute a variance, not being necessarily a direction to make the search so as to become a participant therein, but only the designation of a suitable place. Nashville, etc., Railway *v.* Crosby (Ala.), 62 So. 889.

Variance as to Particular Servant Causing Jerk.—An electric railway passenger, suing for injury on the theory that the conductor was negligent in causing a sudden jerk or jar of the car, or its negligently high speed, could not recover if the speed or jar was caused by the motorman without any signal or co-operation by the conductor. Birmingham Ry., Light & Power Co. *v.* Yates, 53 So. 915, 169 Ala. 381.

Willful Acts.—While, in an action against a street-railway company for injuries which the complainant alleges were due to the willful acts of defendant's servants, proof of simple negligence is not sufficient, where the evidence is open to the interpretation that the servants' acts were willful, the question is for the jury, and an instruction that there was a fatal variance between allegations and proof is properly refused. Highland Ave. & B. R. Co. *v.* Winn, 93 Ala. 306, 9 So. 509, cited in notes in 21 L. R. A. 361, 38 L. R. A. 790.

Allegations as to Negligent Carrying—Injury Caused by Defects in Track.—In an action against a railroad company for personal injuries causing death, the complaint in the first count ascribed the accident to a loose wheel, and in the second alleged that defendant "did not use due and proper skill in and about the carrying of deceased, but so negligently and unskillfully conducted itself in that behalf, and in conducting, managing, and directing the coach and the engine by which deceased was carried, that she was cast, with violence," etc. Held, that if the accident was caused by a sunken joint in the track; plaintiff would not be prevented by his pleadings from a recovery. Louisville & N. R. Co. *v.* Jones, 83 Ala. 376, 3 So. 902, cited in note in 13 L. R. A., N. S., 606.

Variance as to Destination of Passenger.—Any variance between a complaint for injury to a passenger while alighting at C., averring that he was a passenger on the train and paid his fare to C., and proof that he was a passenger and paid his fare to L., a station one mile beyond C., is immaterial; the passenger, after paying the conductor his fare, being told by him that the train did not stop at L., and he then having proposed to get off at C., to which the conductor assented. Southern Ry. Co. *v.* Lollar, 33 So. 32, 135 Ala. 375.

Variance as to Being Thrown from Train Held Immaterial.—There is no variance between a complaint, in an action against a railway company for the negligent death of a passenger, which alleges that he was violently thrown from a train and fatally injured, and the proof that he voluntarily stepped from a moving train onto a station platform, lost his footing and fell, and received the fatal injury. Kansas City, M. & B. R. Co. *v.* Matthews, 39 So. 207, 142 Ala. 298.

Fatal Variance as to Time, Place and Cause of Injury.—A complaint, in an action for injuries sustained in alighting from a train, alleged that plaintiff was thrown from the train when it started to move off at the station, and that he was thrown by the moving off of the t.ain. The evidence showed that the place where plaintiff fell from the train was 300 yards from the station, and that the train had attained a speed of at least 15 miles an hour. Plaintiff testified that after the train was some distance from the station he fell off, but that how he came to do so he did not know. Held, that there was a fatal variance between the complaint and the evidence as to the time, place and cause of the injury. Central of Georgia Ry. Co. *v.* McNab, 43 So. 222, 150 Ala. 332.

Variance as to Place of Stopping.—Where an ordinance prohibits trains of street cars from stopping on the east side of a street when moving westward, or on the west side when moving eastward, and in an action against the street car company for negligence the complaint alleges that the negligence was the failure of the train to stop a sufficient length of time on the west side of the street to enable plaintiff to alight, and the evidence shows a failure to stop a train going west on the east side, there is a fatal variance. North Birmingham St. R. Co. *v.* Calderwood, 89 Ala. 247, 7 So. 360.

Time of Jerk Throwing Passenger.—The complaint for injury to a passenger by being thrown from the platform of a car at a station which was her destination being based on a sudden jerk before the train came to a standstill, she can not recover on evidence that the train came to a stop a reasonable time for her to alight before the jerk. Southern Ry. Co. *v.* Hundley, 44 So. 195, 151 Ala. 378.

Where the complaint in an action for injury to a passenger alleges that immediately after she reached the platform of the car, preparatory to alighting, the car was started violently, without warning, throwing her off, she can not recover on evidence that the jerk of the car, throwing her off, came as she was stepping to the ground. Southern R. Co. *v.* Hundley, 151 Ala. 378, 44 So. 195.

Variance as to Passenger Being Compelled to Leave Train.—A complaint for injuries charged that plaintiff was "compelled and forced" to alight from defendant's car while in motion, and that the injuries were received by reason of defendant's agent's negligence in so "forcing and compelling." Held, that the allegations were not sustained by evidence that the conductor approached plaintiff in the car, and said, "We have got no time; hurry up;" and repeated that several times while plaintiff was getting out. South & N. A. R. Co. *v.* Schaufler, 75 Ala. 136, cited in note in 21 L. R. A. 362.

Variance as to Manner in Which Passenger Thrown Off.—Where a count in a declaration alleges that plaintiff, was attempting to board an electric street car, was thrown between the cars, and the evidence shows that after stepping on the platform of the car he was thrown under the car, it constitutes a variance. Birmingham Ry. & Electric Co. *v.* Brannon, 31 So. 523, 132 Ala. 431.

In an action against a street-railway company for killing plaintiff's intestate, all the witnesses fixed the place of the accident midway between two streets. Two witnesses for plaintiff testified that the train stopped at said place, when said witnesses and deceased, with his arms full of bundles, boarded the cars, and that the train started up with a jerk, which caused one of said witnesses to be thrown backward, striking deceased, who was then on the bottom step, and throwing him to the ground. Two witnesses for defendant and the train employees testified that the train was moving at from four to seven miles an hour when deceased attempted to board it, and that the train did not stop between said streets; and one of said witnesses testified that no one was with deceased at the time he attempted to board the train. A city ordinance prohibited trains from stopping between said streets. The trainmen testified that the trucks which passed over deceased were thrown from the track. Held that, as a count in the complaint alleged that deceased was upon the platform of said train, and was thrown off before he had time to enter, there was a variance between said count and the evidence. Birmingham Railway & Electric Co. *v.* Clay, 108 Ala. 233, 19 So. 309.

Allegation of Negligence—Evidence Showing Willful Injury.—Plaintiff's intestate, a man over 80 years of age, was a passenger on one of defendant's trains, with a ticket to G. He did not alight at a junction point, but was found next morning some distance therefrom in a frozen condition, from the effects of which he died. A witness saw two white men in the uniform of defendant railroad company come onto the rear platform of the rear car of the train on which deceased was riding and push him, while the train was running, from the platform at a point near where he was found, where the ground was rough and uneven. Held to establish a cause of action for willful injury, and therefore insufficient to sustain a count for negligence. Louisville, etc., R. Co. *v.* Perkins, 152 Ala. 133, 44 So. 602.

§ 206. —— Presumptions and Burden of Proof.

§ 206 (1) In General.

Res Ipsa Loquitur.—Where a passenger is injured by the breaking down or overturning of a car by derailment, collision or sudden jolt of the train, or from some cause within the car, or by obstruction on or near the track, a prima facie presumption will arise that the accident has been due to the negligence of the carrier, but not so where the accident causing the injury is to the passenger and not to the vehicle, or where the injury is caused while the passenger is alighting from the vehicle by stepping on an object improperly left on the platform, etc., in which case the injury will not be sufficient to charge the carrier with negligence. Western Railway *v.* McGraw (Ala.), 62 So. 772. See, also, Georgia Pac. R. Co. *v.* Love, 91 Ala. 432, 8 So. 714.

Where an injury to a passenger is such as to give rise to the presumption of negligence under the doctrine res ipsa loquitur, the burden is on the carrier to exonerate itself from liability by showing that the accident was inevitable, or that it could not have been avoided by the exercise of the utmost care reasonably consistent with the prosecution of his business. Western Railway *v.* McGraw (Ala.), 62 So. 772.

Burden of Proof as to Showing Negligence.—A passenger can not recover against a railroad company for negligent damage, unless he offers some evidence of the negligence alleged. Louisville & N. R. Co. *v.* Cornelius, 6 Ala. App. 386, 60 So. 740. See ante, catchline, "Res Ipsa Loquitur."

"Proof of mere injury, without more, does not raise a presumption of negligence, sufficient to impose on the company the burden to prove due care on its part. In order to recover, it is incumbent on plaintiff to show an accident from which the injury resulted, or circumstances of such character as to impute negligence. Birmingham Union R. Co. *v.* Hale, 90 Ala. 8, 8 So. 142." McDonald *v.* Montgomery St. Railway, 110 Ala. 161, 20 So. 317, 320, cited in note in 13 L. R. A., N. S., 602.

Where a passenger suffers injury, the law, in the absence of explanation by the carrier, presumes that it was the result of the carrier's fault, and it has the burden of overcoming the presumption. Birmingham Ry., Light & Power Co. *v.* McCurdy, 172 Ala. 488, 55 So. 616, following Louisville, etc., R. Co. *v.* Jones, 83 Ala. 376, 3 So. 902, which is limited in Georgia Pac. R. Co. *v.* Love, 91 Ala. 432, 8 So. 714. See ante, catchline, "Res Ipsa Loquitur."

Proximate Cause.—A railroad passenger, claimed to have been damaged by the company's negligence, must offer some evidence that the negligence shown resulted in his injury. Louisville, etc., R. Co. *v.* Cornelius, 6 Ala. App. 386, 60 So. 740.

§ 206 (2) Authority of Servant.

The law presumes that a porter, employed and assigned by the Pullman Company to control the interior of a sleeping car, in which a passenger was riding, exercised such control with the assent of the railroad company. Louisville & N. R. Co. *v.* Church, 46 So. 457, 155 Ala. 329, cited in note in 23 L. R. A., N. S., 1059.

§ 206 (3) Where Injury Is Caused by Sudden Jerks or by Suddenly or Prematurely Starting Car.

Whether or not evidence of a jerk of a car, whereby a passenger was injured, will sustain a charge of negligence depends on the violence of the jerk, the situation of the passenger at the time, and the carrier's duty to know that situation. Birmingham R., etc., Co. *v.* Mayo (Ala.), 61 So. 289.

Sudden Jerk While Passenger Alighting.—Testimony that, while plaintiff was in the act of alighting from defendant's street car, the driver suddenly started the car with a jerk, which caused her to fall, whereby she was injured, established a prima facie case of negligence in the management of the car, and throws the burden of disproof on defendant. Birmingham Union Ry. Co. *v.* Hale, 90 Ala. 8, 8 So. 142, cited in notes in 7 L. R. A., N. S., 1078, 13 L. R. A., N. S., 602, 611, 23 L. R. A., N. S., 891.

Bumping Caboose So as to Throw Down Passenger.—Where a passenger is injured, while riding in the caboose of a freight train, by the engine and rest of the train, which had been severed from the caboose, coming back against it with such force as to throw the passenger down, the law presumes, in the absence of all explanation, that the injury was caused by the company's negligence, and casts upon it the burden of overturning the presumption or showing that diligence and careful observance of duty could not have prevented the injury. Georgia Pac. Ry. Co. *v.* Love, 91 Ala. 432, 8 So. 714.

§ 206 (4) Where Injuries Are Caused by Collision, Derailment, or Breaking of Machinery, etc., and Defects Therein.

Where a passenger is injured by the breaking down or overturning of a car by derailment, collision or sudden jolt of the train, or from some cause within the car, or by obstruction on or near the tract, a prima facie presumption will arise that the accident has been due to the negligence of the carrier. Western Railway *v.* McGraw (Ala.), 62 So. 772; Birmingham Union R. Co. *v.* Hale, 90 Ala. 8, 8 So. 142; Montgomery, etc., R. Co. *v.* Mallette, 92 Ala. 209, 9 So. 363; Birmingham R., etc., Co. *v.* Moore, 148 Ala. 115, 42 So. 1024. This rule, however, applies as to passengers and not employees. Louisville, etc., R. Co. *v.* Godwin (Ala.), 62 So. 768.

Accident to Train.—Mere proof that an accident occurring to a train caused injury to a passenger establishes a prima facie presumption that the accident was due to the carrier's negligence. Louisville, etc., R. Co. *v.* Godwin (Ala.), 62 So. 786; Central, etc., R. Co. *v.* Geopp, 153 Ala. 108, 45 So. 65. See note in 29 L. R. A., N. S., 812.

Collision.—Where a passenger on defendant's street car was injured by the car colliding with another, and there is no evidence explanatory of the collision, the negligence of defendant is presumed. Birmingham Ry., Light & Power Co. *v.* Moore, 42 So. 1024, 148 Ala. 115; Birmingham R., etc., Co. *v.* Sawyer, 156 Ala. 199, 47 So. 67. See notes in 13 L. R. A., N. S., 604, 29 L. R. A., N. S., 812.

Where a passenger has shown that his injury was the result of a collision or other accident to the train a prima facie case is made. Central of Georgia Ry. Co. *v.* Geopp, 45 So. 65, 153 Ala. 108, cited in note in 29 L. R. A., N. S., 812.

Derailment.—In an action against a railroad company for personal injuries sustained by reason of the derailment of the car in which plaintiff was a passenger, the burden is on defendant to show that the derailment was not due to its negligence. Alabama G. S. R. Co. *v.* Hill, 93 Ala. 514, 9 So. 722.

If, in an action to recover for personal injuries resulting from the derailment of defendant's car, the evidence of negligence aside from the derailment is equally balanced, the derailment sufficiently shows negligence entitling plaintiff to recover. Montgomery & E. Ry. Co. *v.* Mallette, 92 Ala. 209, 9 So. 363, cited in note in 13 L. R. A., N. S., 606.

Wreck.—Plaintiff having shown an injury caused by the wreck of defendant's train while he was a passenger thereon, or at least having offered evidence which made it necessary to consider his injury under such circumstances as one hypothesis of the case, that hypothesis proven cast upon the defendant the burden of reasonably satisfying the jury that the wreck was not due to its negligence. St. Louis & S. F. R. Co. *v.* Savage, 50 So. 113, 163 Ala. 55, cited in note in 29 L. R. A., N. S., 810.

§ 206 (5) Injury Resulting from Unavoidable Cause.

The rule that proof that a passenger is injured casts on the carrier the burden of proving its freedom from negligence does not apply, where the passenger's evidence shows that his injury resulted probably from some unavoidable cause and some cause outside the ordinary control of the carrier; the burden being on the passenger to reasonably satisfy the jury that his injury is justly attributable to the carrier's negligence. Central, etc., R. Co. *v.* Brown, 165 Ala. 493, 51 So. 565, cited in note in 29 L. R. A., N. S., 814.

§ 206 (6) Where Acts Committed by Third Persons.

Burden of Proving Knowledge of Illegality of Search.—In an action by a passenger for damages for the failure of a carrier's servants to protect her from an illegal search, the passenger has the burden of proving knowledge on the part of the servants that the search which was by an officer was illegal. Nashville, etc., Railway *v.* Crosby (Ala.), 62 So. 889.

§ 206 (7) Injuries Sustained While Riding in Dangerous Place.

Presence on Platform Due to Overcrowding or Negligence of Carrier.—In a passenger's action for injuries from being thrown from the platform of a fast moving train, the burden was on plaintiff to show that his presence on the platform was due to an overcrowded condition on the train. Alabama, etc., R. Co. *v.* Gilbert, 6 Ala. App. 372, 60 So. 542.

Where a passenger was injured by being thrown from the platform by a lurch of the train no more violent than the lurching of trains commonly incident to their rapid movement when operated with due care, he must prove that his presence on the platform while the train was in motion was due to the carrier's negligence. Central, etc., R. Co. *v.* Brown, 165 Ala. 493, 51 So. 565, cited in note in 29 L. R. A., N. S., 814.

§ 207. —— Admissibility of Evidence.

§ 207 (1) In General.

Materiality and Relevancy.—In an action against a railway company for the death of a passenger, killed while alighting from a train, plaintiff could not show whether decedent was "disabled in the War." Dilburn *v.* Louisville, etc., R. Co., 156 Ala. 228, 47 So. 210.

In an action for damages by illness occurring on three days in January, defendant could not show that plaintiff brought another suit against it to recover for illness occurring thereafter in February. Southern R. Co. *v.* Harrington, 166 Ala. 630, 52 So. 57.

In an action for injuries to a passenger while attempting to board a street car, the refusal to let him testify that his boy knew he had fallen was not erroneous. Birmingham Ry., Light & Power Co. *v.* Selhorst, 51 So. 568, 165 Ala. 475.

In an action for injuries to a passenger on a street car, it was proper to refuse to permit the motorman to answer a question as to whether he remembered whether he "had on another white lady," as if he had answered it in the affirmative it would have corroborated the plaintiff, and if he had answered in the negative the answer would have amounted to nothing, and there was no duty on plaintiff's part to introduce such white woman as a witness. Birmingham Ry., Light & Power Co. *v.* Moore, 43 So. 841, 151 Ala. 327.

In an action by a railroad postal clerk against a railroad company for damages resulting from illness caused by failure to heat the mail car in which plaintiff worked, evidence that plaintiff was a "chronic kicker" was properly excluded. Southern R. Co. *v.* Harrington, 166 Ala. 630, 52 So. 57.

§ 207 (2) Relation of Carrier and Passenger.

Where the issue was whether persons riding on a train were trespassers because riding on a pass which was issued to others, the conductor of the train may properly testify as to what a passenger must have to entitle him to ride. Broyles *v.* Central, etc., R. Co., 166 Ala. 616, 52 So. 81.

Where a carrier claimed that one injured while riding on a train was a trespasser because riding on a pass not issued to her, the conductor may be properly questioned as to whether he agreed to let plaintiff ride without paying her fare or showing some other right to ride in the train, and whether he had any right to permit plaintiff to ride without paying her fare or being provided with a pass, since it was competent to show that the conductor did not knowingly permit plaintiff to ride on a pass not issued to her. Broyles *v.* Central, etc., R. Co., 166 Ala. 616, 52 So. 81.

Where the issue was whether one injured while riding on a train was a trespasser, because riding on a pass issued to another, the conductor may testify whether he was under duty to compel passengers to identify themselves as the persons named in the passes. Broyles *v.* Central, etc., R. Co., 166 Ala. 616, 52 So. 81.

Where a carrier claims that one injured while riding on a train was a trespasser, because riding on a pass not issued to her, which pass was given to the conductor by her mother, who was traveling with her, testimony of the conductor that the mother stated that she was giving the pass for her daughter as well as herself, in tones loud enough for her daughter to hear, is not subject to a general objection that it was incompetent, immaterial, and irrelevant. Broyles *v.* Central, etc., R. Co., 166 Ala. 616, 52 So. 81.

§ 207 (3) Notice to Carrier of Matters Calling for Exercise of Care.

Under a complaint ascribing plaintiff's injuries to the wanton negligence of defendant's employees in charge of a street car on which plaintiff was a passenger, and alleging that such negligence consisted in their causing a car to cross a railroad crossing without stopping, knowing that a train was approaching and that there would probably be a collision, etc., evidence that the street car was at the time crowded with passengers, and "that there were many people on the car," was admissible as supporting the alleged probability and defendant's appreciation that passengers would be injured by the collision. Birmingham Ry., Light & Power Co. *v.* Rutledge, 39 So. 338, 142 Ala. 195.

§ 207 (4) Acts or Omissions, and Competency of Carrier's Employees.

Manner and Tone of Voice Accompanying Abusive Language.—A passenger suing for the abusive and insulting language of an employee of the carrier may show the manner and tone of voice accompanying the language. Alabama, etc., R. Co. *v.* Pouncey (Ala.), 61 So. 601.

Matters Leading Up to Assault—Purpose of Admission.—Abusive or insulting language by a street car conductor towards a passenger can not be justified; the passenger being entitled at least to nominal damages, and evidence that the abuse or insult was brought about by the misconduct of the passenger being competent only in mitigation of damages. Birmingham R., etc., Co. *v.* Coleman (Ala.), 61 So. 890.

Where, in an action by a passenger for an assault by the conductor, the evidence showed that the assault followed a wrangle concerning the failure of the passenger and his companions to leave the car at their destination, it was proper to show the facts whether their failure to leave the car was due to their carelessness or to the conductor's failure to announce the station as shedding light on the contentions of the parties and to mitigate the damages, though neither reason for failing to get off would be conclusive on the right to recover. Alabama City, G. & A. Ry. Co. *v.* Sampley, 53 So. 142, 169 Ala. 372, cited in notes in 32 L. R. A., N. S., 1203, 40 L. R. A., N. S., 1008, 1051, 1060, 1067, 1076.

§ 207 (5) Condition of Vehicles and Appliances.

Evidence to Show Unheated Condition of Mail Car.—In an action by a railroad postal clerk against a railroad company for damages for illness caused by defendant's failure to heat its mail car, plaintiff could show that the car was wet and damp as tending to show that it would be uncomfortable Southern R. Co. *v.* Harrington, 166 Ala. 630, 52 So. 57.

In an action by a railroad postal clerk for damages caused by illness from failure to heat the mail car in which he worked, evidence as to the temperature of the express car in the same train was not relevant, where it appeared that the express and mail cars were heated differently in some respects, though each contained steam pipes from the engine, and the evidence showed that the mail car was cold while the express car was comfortable. Southern R. Co. *v.* Harrington, 166 Ala. 630, 52 So. 57.

Complaint of Condition of Car.—In an action by a railroad postal clerk for damages caused by illness resulting from a railroad company's failure to heat a mail car, plaintiff could show that he complained to defendant of the unheated condition of the car to show actual notice. Southern R. Co. *v.* Harrington, 166 Ala. 630, 52 So. 57.

Insufficiency of Car Bell Rope—Knowledge of Conductor.—In an action by a passenger for personal injuries from the cars running off the track, evidence is admissible to prove the insufficiency of the car bell rope, and that the conductor's attention had been called to the fact of its having been hit by sacks thrown by other servants of the company. Mobile & M. R. Co. *v.* Ashcraft, 49 Ala. 305.

Uncovered Space between Cars.—On an issue whether the space between passenger cars on a train was negligently left uncovered, evidence as to whether any cars had been constructed within the last five years with platforms like those on the car in question was admissible. Central of Georgia Ry. Co. *v.* Storrs, 53 So. 746, 169 Ala. 361.

§ 207 (6) Condition of Track or Roadbed.

In an action against a railway company for injuries caused by the derailment of a car, where the evidence tends to show that the derailment was caused by the breaking of a rail, which gave way because of the defective condition of the cross-ties under it, and of the rail itself, evidence of the defective condition of other rails and cross-ties near by is admissible. Alabama G. S. R. Co. *v.* Hill, 93 Ala. 514, 9 So 722.

§ 207 (7) Taking Up and Setting Down Passengers.

Familiarity with Place Where Passenger Alighted.—In an action against a railway company for the death of a passenger, killed while alighting from a train at his station, plaintiff could show how long decedent had lived near the station, as tending to show whether he was familiar with the place where he attempted to alight and whether he was negligent in attempting to alight. Dilburn *v.* Louisville, etc., R. Co., 156 Ala. 228, 47 So. 210.

Length of Time Train Stopped.—In an action for injuries sustained in alighting from a train, testimony of another passenger as to what he had time to do immediately upon his getting off the train and before regaining the same, which was then moving off, was competent on the issue as to how long the train stopped. Central, etc., R. Co. *v.* McNab, 150 Ala. 332, 43 So. 222.

Where, in an action for injuries sustained in alighting from a train, it was alleged that defendant failed to allow plaintiff a reasonable time in which to alight from the train after reaching the station, evidence of the length of time the train stopped was competent. Central, etc., R. Co. *v.* McNab, 150 Ala. 332, 43 So. 222.

In an action for injuries sustained in alighting from a train, evidence, on the issue as to how long a train stopped, of the details of a conversation held by witness with another passenger, who alighted and returned to the train, was inadmissible. Central, etc., R. Co. *v.* McNab, 150 Ala. 332, 43 So. 222.

Speed of Car Striking Alighting Passenger.—In an action against a street railway company for injury to an alighting passenger, injured while crossing a track, that the car which struck him was running from six to ten miles an hour and ran two or three car lengths after striking him may be considered on the question of the company's negligence. Birmingham Ry., Light & Power Co. *v.* Landrum, 45 So. 198, 153 Ala. 192.

Duty of Motorman as to Allowing Passengers to Board before Starting.—On the issue of willfulness or wantonness in the injury to plaintiff by the starting of defendant's street car, the evidence tending to show that plaintiff was in the act of boarding the car, that the motorman saw or could with diligence have seen him in such attempt when the car was started, and that the motorman was notified of plaintiff's physical infirmity and his consequent slowness of gait, and was requested by plaintiff's son not to start the car till plaintiff got on, testimony of the motorman that it was the motorman's duty to see that every one was ready to get on the car got on before he started was admissible. Birmingham Ry., Light & Power Co. *v.* Lee, 45 So. 292, 153 Ala. 79.

Results of Being Put Off at Wrong Place.—In an action against a carrier for failure to stop at a flag station for plaintiff to alight, evidence as to the condition of the ground between the place where plaintiff alighted and her home to which she was compelled to walk was admissible to show probable result of having to get off where she did and walk to her home. Louisville & N. R. Co. *v.* Seale, 55 So. 237, 172 Ala. 480.

Alighting of Other Passenger at Same Time.—Where, in an action for injuries to a passenger, defendant's witness had stated that E., another passenger, got off the car at the same place where plaintiff did, and about the same time, and, having testified that the car was stationary when E. alighted, afterwards testified that it was moving, defendant was entitled to ask the witness further whether E. got off the car before or after plaintiff fell. Birmingham R., etc., Co. *v.* Barrett (Ala.), 60 So. 262.

Speed in Approaching Crossing Where Negligence Based on Jerk and Sudden Stop.—Where, in an action against a street railway company, the negligence alleged was in starting the car with a jerk as plaintiff was getting on, and then suddenly stopping, it was error to permit the conductor to be asked on cross-examination how fast they ran when approaching the crossing. Birmingham Ry. & Electric Co. *v.* Ellard, 33 So. 276, 135 Ala. 433.

Evidence to Show Regular Stopping Place.—In an action for the death of a person attempting to board a street car, evidence that the place where he attempted to board the car was one where people were passing and repassing generally was not relevant to the issue whether it was one of the stopping places of the company's cars. Smith *v.* Birmingham Ry., Light & Power Co., 41 So. 307, 147 Ala. 702.

§ 207 (8) Management of Conveyances.

Evidence to Show Sudden Jerk.—Where, in an action against a railway company for injuries received by a passenger in consequence of the sudden jerking of the train, the evidence showed that there were only two persons in the car, that both of them were thrown down and one of them injured, and a witness testified that there was no unusual jerk, it was not error to overrule an objection to the question asked the witness as to whether he would consider a movement of a car such as to throw all the passengers down and injure one of them a usual movement thereof. Southern Ry. Co. *v.* Branyon, 39 So. 675, 145 Ala. 66.

Cause of Passenger Being Thrown Off Car.—Where another passenger of a street car was thrown against plaintiff as the car, which was crowded, was running at a high rate of speed, and plaintiff was thrown from the car and injured, evidence as to the apparent condition of the passenger who struck plaintiff—whether drunk or sober—at the time of the accident, was admissible. Birmingham R., etc., Co. *v.* Hunnicutt, 3 Ala. App. 448, 57 So. 262.

Evidence to Show Unusual Speed.—In an action for injuries to a passenger in a wreck evidence that defendant's train was behind time was admissible to show that it was being operated at an unusual and immoderate rate of speed. St. Louis, etc., R. Co. *v.* Savage, 163 Ala. 55, 50 So. 113.

In an action for injuries to a passenger in a wreck, plaintiff claimed that the train was running at a dangerous speed, and defendant asked the engineer if he could have stopped at a public crossing. Held, that the evidence called for involved facts and purposes foreign to the issue. St. Louis, etc., R. Co. *v.* Savage, 163 Ala. 55, 50 So. 113.

Car Too Heavily Loaded.—In an action for injury, the question, "How long, how wide, and how thick is a sack of guano?" is relevant and admissible, where the answer tends to show that a car containing the fertilizer was too heavily loaded, which was one of the grounds of negligence imputed to defendant. Kansas City, M. & B. R. Co. *v.* Smith, 90 Ala. 25, 8 So. 43.

§ 207 (9) Other Accidents or Similar Transactions.

Frequency of Uncoupling of Similar Couplings.—In an action against a street railway company for injuries sustained by a passenger owing to cars becoming uncoupled because of defective couplings, it appearing that the couplings used were the same as those used at a time when a witness was employed by defendant, it was proper to permit him to be asked how often in his experience couplings had become uncoupled or broken loose. Birmingham Ry., Light & Power Co. *v.* Bynum, 36 So. 736, 139 Ala. 389.

Frequency of Accidents.—In an action by a passenger against a railroad company for injuries caused by the derailment of its train, evidence that the train on which the accident occurred, and of which witness was a conductor, had run off the track seven or eight times within a month before the accident, was admissible. Mobile & M. R. Co. *v.* Ashcraft, 48 Ala. 15.

In such action, it is competent for the plaintiff to prove that, about two weeks before the accident by which he was injured, the defendant's cars had run off the track twice during one trip. There is no better evidence of negligence than the frequency of accidents. Mobile, etc., R. Co. *v.* Ashcraft, 49 Ala. 305.

Habit of Alighting in Middle of Block.—In an action against a street-railway company for injuries, where the plaintiff testified that his place of business was in the middle of the block below the crossing where he attempted to get off, and that the motorman saw him arise from his seat, and go to the door to get off at the crossing, it was competent to show by the motorman that the plaintiff was in the habit of riding to the middle of the block before getting off, and had several times requested the motorman to slow down, and let him off there. McDonald *v.* Montgomery St. Ry., 110 Ala. 161, 20 So. 317.

Showing That Passengers Alight at Similar Places without Injury.—In an action by a passenger for injuries sustained while alighting from a street car, which it was alleged was stopped at a dangerous place, evidence that there were a great number of other places in the city just as dangerous, and at which passengers were constantly alighting without injury, was not admissible. Mobile Light & R. Co. *v.* Walsh, 40 So. 560, 146 Ala. 295.

"The cases decided by this court and relied upon by appellant as supporting his contention on this point do not go further than to hold that testimony that other persons alighting from defendant's cars at the place where the injury occurred, if conditions were shown to be the same as when the accident to plaintiff happened, was admissible. East Tennessee, etc., R. Co. *v.* Thompson, 94 Ala. 636, 10 So. 280; Birmingham Union R. Co. *v.* Alaxander, 93 Ala. 133, 9 So. 525; Birmingham *v.* Starr, 112 Ala. 98, 20 So. 424; Davis *v.* Common Council, 137 Ala. 206, 33 So. 863. We are unwilling to extend the rule declared in those cases to the length we are here asked to go. Indeed, we think they have gone to the full limit—much further than the courts in other states have gone." Mobile, etc., R. Co. *v.* Walsh, 146 Ala. 295, 40 So. 560, 564.

Circumstances Surrounding Alighting of Passenger at Different Place.—Where, in an action for injuries sustained in alighting from a train, it appeared that plaintiff was a car length from the platform where another witness alighted, evidence as to the manner in which witness alighted, and that the porter of the train helped and lifted her off while the train was in motion, was inadmissible. Central, etc., R. Co. *v.* McNab, 150 Ala. 332, 43 So. 222.

Crowded Condition of Platform at Different Place.—Where, in an action for injuries sustained in alighting from a train, it appeared that plaintiff was a car length from the platform where other witnesses alighted, evidence as to the condition of the platform as to being crowded where such witnesses alighted was inadmissible. Central, etc., R. Co. *v.* McNab, 150 Ala. 332, 43 So. 222.

§ 207 (10) Custom or Course of Business.

Immaterial Custom.—In an action against a railway company for the death of a passenger, killed while alighting from a train at his destination, plaintiff could not show how long the train customarily stopped, since, if it stopped sufficiently long to enable plaintiff in his known condition to alight, any custom was immaterial. Dilburn *v.* Louisville, etc., R. Co., 156 Ala. 228, 47 So. 210.

Custom Not Known to Passenger or Conformed with.—In an action for injuries to a passenger in running to her destination after having been carried past it, evidence of the custom as to what was done with passengers carried beyond their destination was not admissible, especially where there was no evidence that the passenger was informed of the custom or that the carrier offered to conform therewith. Birmingham Ry., Light & Power Co. *v.* Seaborn, 53 So. 241, 168 Ala. 658.

Applicability of Custom as to Time.—In an action against a street-railway company for injuries, where a witness had been allowed to testify as to a public rule to ring the bell to stop the car at crossings, the error was cured by showing subsequently that such was the rule at the time plaintiff was injured. McDonald *v.* Montgomery St. Ry., 110 Ala. 161, 20 So. 317.

Custom of Stopping at Particular Place.—Where, in an action for injuries to a passenger, she alleged that her car stopped at a place where it was customary to stop to let off passengers, and that as she was attempting to alight the car suddenly started, whereby she was injured, it was proper to permit a witness to testify that cars usually stopped there to let off passengers. Birmingham Ry., Light & Power Co. *v.* Taylor, 44 So. 580, 152 Ala. 105.

In an action against a street railroad for negligently causing the death of a passenger, evidence that the place where the injury occurred was one which had, by the custom of the railroad, become a stopping place for receiving and discharging passengers, was competent. Birmingham Ry., Light & Power Co. *v.* Enslen, 144 Ala. 343, 39 So. 74.

Duties of Postal Clerk.—In an action by a railroad postal clerk for damages caused by illness due to working in an unheated car, plaintiff could testify as to his duties as postal clerk in the car and how long he was compelled to remain therein. Southern R. Co. *v.* Harrington, 166 Ala. 630, 52 So. 57.

§ 208. —— Sufficiency of Evidence.

Degree of Proof Required.—In order to recover damages from a railroad company for injuries causing the death of a passenger, the right need not be established beyond all doubt, a preponderance of evidence being sufficient. Louisville & N. R. Co. *v.* Jones, 83 Ala. 376, 3 So. 902.

As to Relation of Passenger and Carrier—Negligent Taking Up of Passenger.—Plaintiff, shortly before a train on which he intended to take passage was due to leave a station, went into a saloon, where he met the conductor, who asked him if he was going on it. Plaintiff replied that he was, and the conductor said, "All right!" and left the place. Plaintiff remained until the train was pulling out, when he ran and tried to board it while it was running at the rate of from one to three miles an hour, but fell and was injured. He testified that, when he undertook to take hold of the railing of the car, the train gave a jerk and threw him back; the jerk being caused by putting on more steam. Held insufficient to prove actionable negligence on the part of the railroad company, because of the failure to show that plaintiff was a passenger, or to prove that the jerk was anything more than was necessary in the movement of the train. Southern Ry. Co. *v.* Johnson, 144 Ala. 361, 39 So. 376.

In an action for injuries to a street car passenger in a collision between the car and the railroad train at a crossing, evidence held sufficient to warrant a finding that the operatives of the street car were guilty of a violation of Code 1896, § 3441, requiring the operatives of a car to come to a full stop at a railroad crossing. Montgomery St. Ry. Co. *v.* Lewis, 41 So. 736, 148 Ala. 134.

In an action against a railroad for injuries to a passenger caused by a sudden stop of the train, a verdict for plaintiff held against the weight of the evidence. Southern Ry. Co. *v.* Hill (Ala.), 39 So. 987.

As to Negligence in Taking Up Passenger.—Proof that a passenger was injured by the sudden and untimely starting of a train which she was attempting to board is sufficient to entitle her to recover, without showing that each person in charge of the train was negligent. Alabama G. S. R. Co. *v.* Siniard, 26 So. 689, 123 Ala. 557, cited in note in 13 L. R. A., N. S., 612.

Same—Evidence Insufficient.—In an action against a street-railway company for killing plaintiff's intestate, all the witnesses fixed the place of the accident midway between two streets. Two witnesses for plaintiff testified that the train stopped at said place, when said witnesses and deceased, with his arms full of bundles, boarded the cars, and that the train started up with a jerk, which caused one of said witnesses to be thrown backward, striking deceased, who was then on the bottom step, and throwing him to the ground. Two witnesses for defendant and the train employees testified that the train was moving at from four to seven miles an hour when deceased attempted to board it, and that the train did not stop between said streets; and one of said witnesses testified that no one was with deceased at the time he attempted to board the train. A city ordinance prohibited trains from stopping between said streets. The trainmen testified that the trucks which passed over deceased were thrown from the track. Held, that the preponderance of the evidence was so greatly in defendant's favor as to require a new trial after verdict for plaintiff. Birmingham Electric Ry. Co. *v.* Clay, 108 Ala. 233, 19 So. 309.

Evidence Insufficient to Show Steps Defective.—In an action against a carrier for injuries received by a passenger who fell while alighting from a train, evidence held insufficient to show that the steps of the train were defective. Central, etc., R. Co. *v.* Carlisle, 2 Ala. App. 514, 56 So. 737.

Negligence in Setting Down Passenger.—Evidence held to sustain recovery against a railway company on the theory of negligent injury to passenger while alighting. Central of Georgia Ry. Co. *v.* Johnson, 2 Ala. App. 501, 56 So. 756.

Knowledge of Intention to Search Passenger or Illegality Thereof.—In an action against a carrier for damages for an illegal search of plaintiff, a passenger, evidence held insufficient to show that defendant's servants knew plaintiff was about to be assaulted or searched by the woman who claimed to have lost a watch and caused the search. Nashville, etc., Railway *v.* Crosby (Ala.), 62 So. 889.

In an action by a passenger for damages from an illegal search, evidence held insufficient to show that defendant's servants knew of the illegality. Nashville, etc., Railway *v.* Crosby (Ala.), 62 So. 889.

As to Use of Pathway on Invitation of Carrier.—Evidence held to show that passengers using a pathway across a railroad right of way did not use it on the invitation of the company, and the persons using it could not recover for injuries sustained in consequence of the defective condition of the pathway. Alabama Great Southern R. Co. *v.* Godfrey, 47 So. 185, 156 Ala. 202.

As to Rule of Carrier.—In an action against a railroad company by a woman who was injured while alighting from a train, evidence held insufficient to show a rule requiring conductors to physically assist lady passengers in alighting. Central, etc., R. Co. *v.* Carlisle, 2 Ala. App. 514, 56 So. 737.

§ 209. —— Damages.

§ 209 (1) Elements and Measure of Damage.

Where a railroad company, in an action by the administrator of a passenger killed in an accident, contests only the amount of damages under a writ of inquiry, the jury may consider any alleged negligence of defendant's employees which tended to cause the accident. Kansas City, M. & B. R. Co. *v.* Sanders, 98 Ala. 293, 13 So. 57.

An engineer, in the nighttime, started for the next station on the signal of the station master, whom he supposed was the conductor, as they both wore similar uniforms. At the next station there was no night operator, and the engineer, discovering his mistake, commenced to back the train without placing any lights at the rear end, and a collision occurred, in which a passenger was killed. Held, that the jury, in assessing damages on a writ of inquiry, could consider the negligence of having no night operator, and having the conductor and station master dressed alike, in determining the degree of the fault of the railroad company, though such negligence was not the immediate cause of the injury. Kansas City, M. & B. R. Co. *v.* Sanders, 98 Ala. 293, 13 So. 57.

Pendency of Other Actions Arising Out of Same Collision.—On a writ of inquiry to determine the amount of damages for causing the death of a railroad passenger in a collision, it is not error to refuse to instruct that the pendency of other actions by other passengers injured by the same collision might be considered. Kansas City, M. & B. R. Co. *v.* Sanders, 98 Ala. 293, 13 So. 57.

§ 209 (2) Elements of Damage for Assault or Insulting Language by Employee or Fellow Passengers.

Damages for mental suffering, independent of other injury, may be recovered for shock to a female passenger by profane and insulting language used in her presence by the carrier's employee. Birmingham Ry., Light & Power Co. *v.* Glenn (Ala.), 60 So. 111.

Fxemplary Damages.—Where a street car conductor unlawfully and without justification assaults a passenger, at the same time humiliating him by abusive and insulting language, the jury in its discretion may award exemplary damages. Birmingham R., etc., Co. *v.* Coleman (Ala.), 61 So. 890.

Mitigation of Damages.—The fault of the passenger short of producing a necessity to strike in self-defense will neither justify the conductor in striking nor relieve the carrier from liability for his act. Possibly such fault could be considered in mitigation of damages. Alabama, etc., R. Co. *v.* Sampley, 4 Ala. App. 464, 58 So. 974; S. C., 169 Ala. 372, 53 So. 142; Birmingham R., etc., Co. *v.* Coleman (Ala.), 61 So. 890, 892.

§ 209 (3) Exemplary Damages.

As to punitive damages in case of assault of passenger by servant, see ante, "Elements of Damage for Assault or Insulting Language by Employee or Fellow Passengers," § 209 (2).

Gross Negligence.—Punitive damages may be recovered for gross negligence on the part of carrier in an action against it by a passenger for injuries, but for a less degree of negligence actual damages alone should be assessed. Mobile & M. R. Co. *v.* Ashcraft, 48 Ala. 15.

"The rule settled in this state is that exemplary damages may be awarded in an action against a railroad company for personal injuries received, when the negligence is of such character and degree as to evince a grossly careless disregard of the safety of the public, or, what is of equivalent import, recklessness, wantonness or willfulness. South, etc., R. Co. *v.* McLendon, 63 Ala. 266." Richmond, etc., R. Co. *v.* Vance, 93 Ala. 144, 9 So. 574, 576.

In an action for personal injuries, sustained by reason of the derailment of defendant's railway car, owing to the breaking of a rail, evidence that the cross-ties near the place of derailment were "unsound," "decayed," "rotten," and the rails old and defective ones, and that they were from time to time replaced by other old rails, warrants the finding of such gross negligence on defendant's part as will authorize an award of exemplary damages. Alabama G. S. R. Co. *v.* Hill, 93 Ala. 514, 9 So. 722, following 90 Ala. 71, 8 So. 90, 9 L. R. A. 442.

Not Necessary to Be "Entire Want of Care."—An instruction which limits the authority to impose exemplary damages on a carrier of passengers for injuries sustained by reason of derailment of a car to cases in which there is an "entire want of care" on the part of defendant in the maintenance of its track is properly refused. Alabama G. S. R. Co. *v.* Hill, 93 Ala. 514, 9 So. 722.

Wanton or Willful Conduct of Servant.—In a passenger's action for injuries, if there is evidence from which the jury can fairly infer that the act of defendant's servants or agents was wanton or willful, an instruction withdrawing the question of punitive damages is properly denied. Birmingham R., etc., Co. *v.* Taylor, 6 Ala. App. 661, 60 So. 979.

Consciousness of Probable Consequence of Discoverable Defect.—The fact that the track where an accident occurred was therefore defective, and that defendant's officers and servants might have known it, does not render defendant liable for punitive damages, unless there was a probable consciousness on their part that such an accident would be the probable consequence of such defects. Richmond & D. R. Co. *v.* Vance, 93 Ala. 144, 9 So. 574.

Accident Due to Concurrence of Latent Defect with Known One.—Punitive damages are not allowable where the accident was due to the concurrence of a latent defect, not discoverable, with a known defect, and where it could not have occurred without such latent defect. Richmond & D. R. Co. *v.* Vance, 93 Ala. 144, 9 So. 574.

Proportioning Punitive Damages to Actual Damages.—In an action against a railroad company by a passenger for injuries, punitive damages awarded should bear proportion to the actual damages sustained. Mobile & M. R. Co. *v.* Ashcraft, 48 Ala. 15.

Violation of Statute as to Stopping at Railroad Crossing.—Where the statute required an engineer to stop for a railroad crossing, but nevertheless, though knowing the location of the crossing, and that trains could not be stopped, after coming in sight of each other, unless they had obeyed the statute, he ran upon the crossing without slackening his speed of 30 miles an hour, and a collision ensued, his employer may be made liable for punitive damages by one injured in the collision. Richmond & D. R. Co. *v.* Greenwood, 99 Ala. 501, 14 So. 495.

Running Train When Overcrowded at Usual Rate of Speed.—It is not wanton negligence for a conductor to run an overcrowded passenger train at the usual, proper, and customary speed of a train which is not overcrowded, and hence exemplary damages are not recoverable for injury to a passenger from being thrown from the platform of an overcrowded train run at the ordinarily proper speed. Alabama, etc., R. Co. *v.* Gilbert, 6 Ala. App. 372, 60 So. 542.

Carrying Passenger beyond Destination.—Where a railroad passenger, when he had been carried 1½ miles beyond his station, told the flagman the circumstances, and asked him if he could not stop the train and let him off, and was told that that could not be done, and he was carried on to a large city several miles further on, the passenger was not entitled to punitive damages for being carried beyond his station, there being no element of aggravation or insult. Louisville, etc., R. Co. *v.* Cornelius, 6 Ala. App. 386, 60 So. 740.

Questions for Jury.—See post, "Exemplary Damages," § 210 (17).

§ 209 (4) Excessive Damages.

In an action by a passenger against a common carrier to recover damages for an assault made by the conductor upon one of the defendant's cars, where there is evidence tending to show that the plaintiff, who is disabled at the time of the assault, was badly beaten by the conductor, a verdict and judgment fixing the plaintiff's damages at $2,500 can not be said to be excessive. Birmingham Ry. & Electric Co. *v.* Baird, 30 So. 456, 130 Ala. 334, 54 L. R. A. 752, cited in note in 40 L. R. A., N. S., 1007, 1051, 1056, 1068, 1073, 1077, 1085.

In an action against a railroad company by a passenger to recover damages for personal injuries, where it is shown that by reason of the acts complained of the plaintiff sustained serious hurts, that the bone in her hip joint was fractured, which would result in permanent injury to plaintiff and in the impairment of her general health, and materially affect the use of her leg, causing it to stiffen and shorten, the assessment of $15,000 damages by the jury can not be said to be excessive. Southern R. Co. *v.* Crowder, 130 Ala. 256, 30 So. 592.

§ 210. —— Questions for Jury.

§ 210 (1) In General.

Where the evidence in the action showed causal negligence on the part of the company's trainmen, the company was not entitled to an affirmative charge. Kansas City, M. & B. R. Co. *v.* Matthews, 39 So. 207, 142 Ala. 298.

§ 210 (2) Existence of Relation of Carrier and Passenger.

"Whether or not a person is a passenger is generally a question for the jury, and always so when different inferences may be drawn from the testimony. Brown *v.* Scarboro, 97 Ala. 316, 12 So. 289; North Birmingham St. R. Co. *v.* Liddicoat, 99 Ala. 545, 13 So. 18.

Person Going to Flag Station to Take Train.—While the relation as carrier and passenger is dependent upon the existence of contract of carriage, such contract may be either expressed or implied, and proof that a person entered a common carrier's vehicle or premises with the intention of becoming a passenger raises an implication of that relation; hence, proof that plaintiff went to a flag station on the road of defendant company for the bona fide purpose of taking a train, then about due, makes it a question for the jury whether he become a passenger. Louisville, etc., R. Co. *v.* Glasgow (Ala.), 60 So. 103, 104.

Person Boarding Conveyance.—Where there is testimony tending to show that plaintiff was, when injured, attempting to board one of appellant's cars with the bona fide intention of riding thereon, upon paying the customary fare; while, on the other hand, there is testimony tending to show that his attempt to board the train at the time and place mentioned was prompted by a mere boyish propensity—in common parlance, to "steal a ride," as he had done or attempted to do on other occasions—the question is one for the jury under proper instructions from the court. North Birmingham St. R. Co. *v.* Liddicoat, 99 Ala. 545, 13 So. 18, 20.

The fact that plaintiff presented himself on the platform of a street car, and was approaching the entrance of the car, or had put his hands upon the handholds and raised his foot with the purpose of entering, all of which the conductor knew, did not, as a matter of law, make him a passenger, since, while there may be an implied acceptance by the company of a person as a passenger, the mere knowledge by the conductor that plaintiff intended to board the train with intent to take passage is not of itself an acceptance as a matter of law. Alabama City, G. & A. Ry. Co. *v.* Bates, 46 So. 776, 155 Ala. 347.

§ 210 (3) Acts or Omissions of Carrier's Employees.

Mental Distress as Resulting from Offensive Language.—Whether plaintiff, a female passenger, suffered mental distress in consequence of alleged offensive language used by defendant's conductor, was an inferential fact, to be gathered by the jury from the nature of the language used and the circumstances of the case, direct proof being neither required nor permissible. Birmingham R., etc., Co. *v.* Glenn (Ala.), 60 So. 111.

Whether Person Using Violence in Assisting Passenger to Alight Is Auditor.—Evidence, in a passenger's action for injury, that the person who assisted a passenger from a train with alleged violence was the carrier's auditor, held sufficient to go to the jury. Mobile & O. R. Co. *v.* Barber, 2 Ala. App. 507, 56 So. 858.

§ 210 (4) Number and Efficiency of Employees.

Whether the operation by a street-railroad company of its cars without a conductor constitutes negligence is a question for the jury. Armstrong *v.* Montgomery St. Ry. Co., 26 So. 349, 123 Ala. 233.

§ 210 (5) Acts of Fellow Passengers or Other Third Persons.

Consent to Illegal Search.—Where plaintiff, a woman, who was illegally searched on the premises of the defendant railroad company after she had begun a journey, went with an officer of the law first to the freight room and then to the waiting room where she was searched, her failure to object or protest is not, as a matter of law, a consent to the search; the question being one for the jury. Nashville, etc., Railway *v.* Crosby (Ala.), 62 So. 889.

§ 210 (6) Starting or Moving Car While Passenger Is Boarding Same.

Wantonness.—If defendant motorman saw plaintiff alighting and started the car with a jerk, whereby she was injured, the question whether the starting of the car was for the jury. Birmingham Ry., Light & Power Co. *v.* Moore, 50 So. 115, 163 Ala. 43.

Where, in an action for injuries to a passenger while attempting to board a street car, there was evidence authorizing the inference that he was in a perilous position when the car was started, and the conductor admitted that he gave the signals for the car to start, and that he saw the passenger before he did so, and that the car was started from his signals, and there was evidence that the passenger was in the act of boarding the car, and was not securely on the platform when the car started, the question of wanton conduct of the conductor was for the jury, though he claimed that the passenger was on the platform when he signaled the car to start. Birmingham Ry., Light & Power Co. *v.* Selhorst, 51 So. 568, 165 Ala. 475.

§ 210 (7) Railroad Locomotives and Cars.

Negligence in Having Door Fastenings in Safe Condition.—In a passenger's action for injuries and discomfort caused by confinement in a toilet room, where she testified that she made every effort to unfasten the door to the room, and there was evidence that the porter after entering the room through a window prized off either the lock or the receiver, there was sufficient evidence to make a question for the jury as to defendant's negligence in failing to have the fastenings to the door in a safe and proper condition. Alabama, etc., R. Co. *v.* Robinson (Ala.), 62 So. 813.

Negligence in Not Keeping Space between Cars Covered.—In an action for injury to a passenger by getting his foot caught between the bumpers of two passenger cars, as he was crossing from one car to another while the train was stopping at a station, and claimed to have been caused by some improper action of the air brake, or because the space was not covered, the carrier's negligence held for the jury. Central of Georgia Ry. Co. *v.* Storrs, 53 So. 746, 169 Ala. 361.

Slipping Caused by Defect in Steps.—In a passenger's action for injuries caused by slipping on the steps of a car, evidence held insufficient to present a question for the jury as to whether the slipping was caused by a defect in the steps. Carlisle *v.* Central, etc., R. Co. (Ala.), 62 So. 759.

§ 210 (8) Tracks and Equipment of Street Railroads.

The question of the carrier's negligence in failing to provide a safer coupling was one for the jury. Birmingham Ry., Light & Power Co. *v.* Bynum, 36 So. 736, 139 Ala. 389.

§ 210 (9) Management of Conveyances in General.

Negligence in Closing Door on Passenger's Hand.—In an action against a carrier to recover for injuries to plaintiff's hand by closing a car door on it, it is a question for the jury whether the conductor, in closing the door before seeing that plaintiff had cleared it, was exercising due care. Louisville & N. R. Co. *v.* Mulder, 42 So. 742, 149 Ala. 676.

Anticipating Injury from Intoxicated Passenger.—In an action against a carrier for personal injury to a passenger caused by an intoxicated passenger falling, whether the conductor in the exercise of the care required by law could have foreseen that the intoxicated passenger might do injury to some other passenger, held, under the evidence, a question for the jury. Montgomery Traction Co. *v.* Whatley, 44 So. 538, 152 Ala. 101.

Negligence in Not Lighting Vestibule or Not Keeping Drop Door Down.—Where a passenger left the vestibuled coach she had boarded and went on the rear platform while the train was standing at the station at night, for the sole purpose of standing there, because the coach was hot and uncomfortable, and was injured by falling down the steps, because the drop door was raised, and because of the absence of a light, the court could not declare as a matter of law that the carrier was negligent in failing to have the drop door down, or in failing to have the drop door down or in the failing to maintain a light in the vestibule. Clanton *v.* Southern Ry. Co., 51 So. 616, 165 Ala. 485, cited in note in 35 L. R. A., N. S., 592.

§ 210 (10) Causing Passenger to Fall from Car.

Negligence in Jerking Car.—Whether an electric railway conductor was negligent toward a passenger who was thrown from the car by a jerking thereof, held, under the evidence, a jury question. Birmingham Ry., Light & Power Co. *v.* Yates, 53 So. 915, 169 Ala. 381.

Whether a carrier failed to furnish proper accommodation for a passenger inside, and made it necessary for him to stand on the platform, from which he was thrown by a lurch of the train, held, under the evidence, for the jury. Central of Georgia Ry. Co. *v.* Brown, 51 So. 565, 165 Ala. 493.

Pushing Passenger from One Coach to Another While Train in Motion.—In an action for the death of plaintiff's intestate by falling from a train while in rapid motion as he was being pushed from the car provided for colored passengers into that intended for white passengers by a conductor, whether intestate was killed by breach of duty on the part of such conductor held for the jury. Carleton *v.* Central of Georgia Ry. Co., 46 So. 495, 155 Ala. 326.

Speed of Overcrowded Train.—Where, in a passenger's action for injuries from being thrown from the platform of a fast moving train, the evidence was conflicting on whether the train was overcrowded and he rode on the platform from necessity, the question whether defendant was negligent in running its train at 30 or 35 miles per hour was for the jury, though such was the proper speed for ordinary passenger trains. Alabama, etc., R. Co. *v.* Gilbert, 6 Ala. App. 372, 60 So. 542.

§ 210 (11) Sudden Lurches, Jerks, or Jolts.

See, also, ante, "Causing Passenger to Fall from Car," § 210 (10).

Knowledge by Passenger of Jerks in Operating Freight Train.—It is a matter of common knowledge that jerks and jars ordinarily attend the handling and running of freight trains, and more than that of regular passenger trains, so that it is error to submit to the jury whether one who became a passenger on a freight train had such knowledge. Southern Ry. Co. *v.* Crowder, 33 So. 335, 135 Ala. 417.

Jerk Throwing Passenger from Seat.—Evidence that a street car was stopped with unusual suddenness and a jerk, and that by the sudden stopping of the car plaintiff was thrown from his seat and injured, raises a question for the jury on the issue of negligence in the manner of stopping the car. Ball *v.* Mobile Light & R. Co., 39 So. 584, 146 Ala. 309, cited in note in 34 L. R. A., N. S., 227.

§ 210 (12) Setting Down Passengers in General.

Where the evidence in an action for injuries to a passenger while attempting to alight from a street car was in conflict as to whether the employees in control of the car were negligent, but there was evidence tending to show their negligence, the question was for the jury. Birmingham Ry., Light & Power Co. *v.* Pritchett, 49 So. 782, 161 Ala. 480.

Injury Caused by Closing of Gates Operated by Motorman—Wantonness.—Where it appeared from some of the evidence that the plaintiff was injured as the result of the closing of two entrance gates, blocking, when closed, the passage from the platform, over the step, to the ground, which gates were operated by means of a lever operated by the motorman from his position on the car, that it did not appear from the testimony that the closing (if so) of the gates on this occasion was otherwise caused than by the means and by the servant indicated; that the motorman testified, on cross-examination, that from his place he "could see a passenger in the act of getting off" the car; that the cars "are all arranged so the motorman can look back through the car and then look into the mirror and see what is going on along the gate side of the car, and at the place for passengers to get off," it was held, that if, as some of the testimony tended to show, the gates were closed while plaintiff was in the act of alighting from the step flush with the outer edge of which the lower lines of the gates were constructed, it was open to the jury to find from the testimony that the motorman operated the lever, and that he could have seen and did see the plaintiff then so situated with reference to the gates as that, if they were then closed, the plaintiff would be struck by one or both of them. And, that if these conclusions were entertained by the jury, it was then further open to them to find that the act of closing the gates under those circumstances, was so colored as to bring the event within the aggravated wrong charged in the complaint. Birmingham R., etc., Co. *v.* Fisher, 173 Ala. 623, 55 So. 995, 996.

§ 210 (13) Starting or Moving Car While Passenger Is Alighting.

In an action for the death of a railway passenger, killed while alighting from a train after it had stopped at his destination and was moving again, held, under the evidence, questions for the jury whether sufficient time was given him in which to alight, and whether there was a negligent jerk of the train. Dilburn *v.* Louisville & N. R. Co., 47 So. 210, 156 Ala. 228.

In an action for injury to an alighting passenger, held, under the evidence, a jury question whether the conductor saw that the passenger was about to alight and might have prevented it, or prevented the starting of the car while he was alighting. Birmingham Ry., Light & Power Co. *v.* McGinty, 48 So. 491, 158 Ala. 410.

Plaintiff was injured while alighting from a train, drawn by a dummy which ran along certain streets, stopping at crossings for passengers. There was evidence that, as it approached a certain street, a signal from a person taking passage having been given, the train was brought nearly to a stop, and that thereupon plaintiff with her left hand holding a bundle, and her right the hand railing, descended the steps of the car platform about the time the other passenger got aboard, and as she reached the bottom step, and was about to step from the train, its speed was quickened with a jerk, whereby she was thrown to the ground. Plaintiff testified that the dummy stopped regularly at the crossing. Held, that the question of negligence was for the jury. Sweet *v.* Birmingham Ry. & Electric Co., 33 So. 886, 136 Ala. 166.

§ 210 (14) Setting Down Passenger at Improper Time or Place.

Where the undisputed evidence showed that a carrier stopped its train beyond a station, and that a passenger destined for that station alighted at night to walk back to the station, that she was aged and feeble, and that she was injured while attempting to walk back to the station, and the evidence was conflicting as to whether the train stopped at the station for the reception or discharge of passengers, the liability of the carrier was for the jury. Alabama City, G. & A. Ry. Co. *v.* Cox, 55 So. 909, 173 Ala. 629.

Negligence in Ascertaining Destination of Passenger.—In an action against a carrier for carrying plaintiff beyond a flag station, her destination, whether the carrier's conductor was negligent in not ascertaining that there was a passenger for that station, was for the jury. Louisville & N. R. Co. *v.* Seale, 55 So. 237, 172 Ala. 480.

Implied Invitation to Alight.—In an action against a street railroad company for injuries to a passenger who fell while alighting from a car, evidence held to require submission to the jury of the question whether the stopping of the car at a point where the passenger alighted constituted an implied invitation to alight at that place. Mobile Light & R. Co. *v.* Walsh, 40 So. 559, 146 Ala. 290.

§ 210 (15) Providing Safe Place or Means for Alighting from Cars.

Whether a carrier is negligent in placing a footstool on uneven ground, resulting in injury to a passenger, is a question for the jury. Atlanta & B. Air Line Ry. *v.* Wheeler, 46 So. 262, 154 Ala. 530.

§ 210 (16) Proximate Cause of Injury.

In an action against a street railway company for injury to an alighting passenger claimed to have been caused by sudden starting of the car, whether the injury was caused proximately by the company's negligence or by her own contributory negligence, held, under the evidence, jury questions. Birmingham R., etc., Co. *v.* Lide (Ala.), 58 So. 990.

§ 210 (17) Exemplary Damages.

Evidence of willfulness and wantonness in the injury to a passenger while alighting from an electric car, with consequent right to impose punitive damages, held sufficient to go to the jury. Birmingham Ry., Light & Power Co. *v.* Fisher, 55 So. 995, 173 Ala. 623.

Compelling Passenger to Ride in Improper Place and without Comforts.—Where, according to her evidence, a woman accompanied by two small children without an escort, who was sick and unable to walk, and whose condition was made known to the conductor, was placed by him, against her protest and objection, in the baggage car, where she wes required to ride on a wooden chair or stool without the comforts provided for passengers in a regular passenger coach, the question of punitive damages was for the jury, since, if the conductor against her protest adopted a course of conduct likely to result in inconvenience and injury to her, wantonness might be inferred. Nashville, etc., Railway *v.* Blackmon (Ala.), 61 So. 468.

Injury from Collision Caused by Failure to Stop at Crossing.—Where, besides plaintiff, other passengers on the train have testified that its speed near the railroad crossing where the collision occurred was thirty to forty miles an hour, that it was not stopped, nor even slowed, at the stop post, and the trainmen on the colliding train have sworn that, when they were at the crossing, the engines were in full view of one another, and the train carrying plaintiff was one hundred and fifty feet away, the question of punitive damages against plaintiff's carrier is properly submitted. Richmond & D. R. Co. *v.* Greenwood, 99 Ala. 501, 14 So. 495.

Injuries from Collision Caused by Backing Train without Signal Lights.—In an action against a railroad company for personal injuries, it appeared that, on the night of the injury, plaintiff was a passenger on defendant's train; that, while the train was waiting at a certain station for the arrival of a train from which it was to receive a sleeper, the station master signaled the engineer to "pull out," and make room for the incoming train; that the station master wore a uniform similar to the conductor's, carried a similar lantern, and used a signal similar to that given by the conductor when about to leave the station; that the engineer, thinking the station master was his conductor, left the station without him, or the extra sleeper, and did not discover his mistake until he reached the next station; that, there being no night operator at such station, the engineer, without placing a light on the rear car, attempted to back his train to the last station to get the conductor and extra sleeper; that while on the way the train collided with a freight train, whereby plaintiff was injured. Held, that the question of punitive damages was for the jury. Kansas City, M. & B. R. Co. *v.* Phillips, 98 Ala. 159, 13 So. 65.

Putting Passenger Off at Wrong Station.—Where, in an action by a passenger for being put off at the wrong station, plaintiff testified that she gave the conductor a ticket to a certain station, and he, a short time afterwards, informed her that she had reached her destination, and put her off at the wrong station in the night, with her small children, the question of exemplary damages is properly sumitted, though the conductor denied plaintiff's evidence as to telling her she had reached her station. Alabama, etc., R. Co. *v.* Arrington, 1 Ala. App. 385, 56 So. 78.

Sudden Jerk While Passenger Alighting—Language Showing Animus of Servant.—Where, in an action for injuries to a female passenger as she was endeavoring to alight, by the sudden jerking of the car, plaintiff's husband testified that he remonstrated with the conductor about jerking the car, and the later replied: "G—— d—— you, I am running this car," the proof was sufficient to justify submitting to the jury the issue of punitive damages. Birmingham R., etc., Co. *v.* Glenn (Ala.), 60 So. 111.

Passenger Injured by Operation of Swinging Gates.—Where there was evidence that plaintiff, his mother, and several other small children wece on their feet to alight from a street car, the mother having reached the back of the car, the children the rear platform, and plaintiff the steps, when the swinging gates were closed, catching plaintiff's hands, and that, after moving a car length and one-half or two lenghts, the car was stopped, the gates thrown suddenly open, and plaintiff thrown to the ground, the question of wantonness was for the jury, although the motorman, who was looking after the passengers while the conductor ate his breakfast, testified that he looked back before starting the car and saw no one attemping to alight; and hence the withdrawal of the question of punitive damages was properly denied. Birmingham R., etc., Co. *v.* Taylor, 6 Ala. App. 661, 60 So. 979.

§ 211. —— Instructions.

§ 211 (1) Existence of Relation of Carrier and Passenger.

In an action for injuries to plaintiff while boarding defendant's train as a passenger, an instruction defining a passenger as "one who is boarding a car, or who is attempting to board a car, or at the station of a company operating a car, for the purpose of being carried on the cars from one point to another," was erroneous, as was a statement therein that "he becomes a passenger when, with the intention of boarding a train, he attempts to board for the purpose of riding." Alabama City, G. & A. Ry. Co. *v.* Bates, 149 Ala. 487, 43 So. 98.

§ 211 (2) Degree of Care Required in General.

See, also, ante, "Care Required and Liability of Carrier in General," § 176.

An instruction, in an action for injuries to a passenger on a freight train, that a carrier owes to its passengers the duty to exercise the highest degree of diligence known to "very" diligent persons engaged in like business, is not objectionable as requiring a standard of extraordinary care because of the use of the word "very." Southern Ry. Co. *v.* Burgess, 143 Ala. 364, 42 So. 35.

§ 211 (3) Acts of Carrier's Employees, Fellow Passengers, or Third Persons.

As to charge on burden of proving plea of justification, see post, "Presumptions and Burden of Proof," § 211 (11).

Assault Continued after Passenger Has Left Train.—Where the evidence was conflicting whether defendant's conductor assaulted plaintiff while on the car, knocked him off, and then followed and continued to beat him, or whether the assault commenced after plaintiff had ceased to be a passenger, an instruction that if the conductor assaulted plaintiff while on the car, or on the steps of the car, and thereafter followed and assaulted him, defendant was liable, unless such assault was in self-defense, was not error. Alabama, etc., R. Co. *v.* Sampley, 4 Ala. App. 464, 58 So. 974.

Force Permissible to Keep Passenger out of Wrong Part of Car.—In an action against a carrier for damages for assault and battery committed by its conductor upon a passenger, the court charged that, "even though it be the duty of the conductor to keep [plaintiff] out of that part of the car for white people, yet it was the duty of the conductor not to use any more force than was necessary for that purpose, and, if no force was necessary, then it was the duty of the conductor not to use any force to injure plaintiff." Held, that the giving of such charge was not reversible error, even if it be conceded that it is argumentative and abstract. Birmingham Ry. & Electric Co. *v.* Mason, 39 So. 590, 144 Ala. 387.

Self-Defense.—Where, in an action by a passenger for an assault by the conductor, the carrier sought to show that the assault was in necessary defense of the conductor's person, a charge that if the passenger first struck the conductor, and the conductor only struck the passenger to protect himself from assault, the jury should find for the carrier, was proper. Alabama City, G. & A. Ry. Co. *v.* Sampley, 53 So. 142, 169 Ala. 372.

Charge as to Liability of Railroad Company for Negligence of Pullman Car Porter.—Where, in an action for injuries to a passenger while in a Pullman car, caused by the negligence of a porter of the car, there was nothing to show that the porter was not the servant of the railroad company, and he might have been the servant of the railroad company, or employed and controlled jointly by it and the Pullman Company, the refusal to charge that the jury could not find that the railroad company's agents were guilty of any negligence proximately causing the injuries was proper. Louisville & N. R. Co. *v.* Church, 155 Ala. 329, 46 So. 457.

In an action for injuries to a passenger, caused by a table handled by a porter of a Pullman car falling on her hand, a charge that if the jury believed that the table fell because of an unforeseen accident, and one that could not have been anticipated by reasonable care and foresight on the part of the railroad company or the Pullman Company, the jury must find for the railroad company, was misleading, as leading the jury to believe that they could not find for plaintiff unless the accident was foreseen or anticipated by the railroad company or the Pullman Company, regardless of the acts or omissions of their servants. Louisville, etc., R. Co. *v.* Church, 155 Ala. 329, 46 So. 457.

As to Which Employees Owe Due Care.—A charge requiring a verdict for defendant on proof of due care of its trainmen is properly denied where the accident may have been caused by the negligence of other of its employees. Montgomery & E. Ry. Co. *v.* Mallette, 92 Ala. 209, 9 So. 363.

§ 211 (4) Starting or Moving Car While Passenger Is Boarding Same.

In an action against a street car company for injuries sustained while boarding a car, a charge that negligence is the failure to do what a reasonable and prudent person would have done under the circumstances or the situation, or doing that which a prudent person under existing circumstances would not have done, was not erroneous when applied to a carrier of passengers. Alabama City, G. & A. Ry. Co. *v.* Bates, 155 Ala. 347, 46 So. 776.

In an action for injury to a passenger while entering a car, an instruction that it was not necessary to keep the car stationary until she reached the inside of the car was properly refused, as tending to mislead, where there was testimony that the car was started improperly. Birmingham R., Light & Power Co. *v.* Hawkins, 153 Ala. 86, 44 So. 983.

Reasonable Time to Obtain Seat—Sudden Movement of Coach.—Where, in an action for injuries to a passenger while boarding a train, the evidence showed that the conductor assisted plaintiff to the platform of the coach, and plaintiff testified that she got to the door as quickly as she could to get a seat, but could not get through, that, when she got to the door, the coach gave a jerk, causing injury, and the carrier's evidence tended to show that there was no unusual movement of the train, a charge that if plaintiff was in the act of boarding the train as a passenger and the conductor assisted her on the platform of the coach, and there left her, and, before plaintiff had time to enter the coach and procure a seat, the coach was struck by cars, causing a sudden jerk of the coach and injury to plaintiff, the carrier was liable, properly submitted the issues whether plaintiff had a reasonable time within which to obtain a seat, and whether there was a sudden movement of the coach. Birmingham, etc., R. Co. *v.* Norris, 4 Ala. App. 363, 59 So. 66.

Knowledge by Crew of Attempt to Board Car.—The crew of a street car, or some of them, being chargeable with the duty of knowing before starting that no one was in the act of boarding or attempting to board the car, defendant street railway company is not entitled to a charge that, if plaintiff attempted to board its car after it had started and without the knowledge of the crew, he could not recover, as their failure to know that he was in the act of getting on might be negligence. Birmingham Ry., Light & Power Co. *v.* Lee, 153 Ala. 79, 45 So. 292.

In an action against a carrier for injuries received while plaintiff was attempting to board a car, there was evidence that plaintiff tried to catch the first car, and was injured by the last car catching his leg. Held, that a request to charge that plaintiff can not recover unless the jury are satisfied that, when the train was signaled to go forward, plaintiff was in the act of boarding the car and was injured by the train starting while he was in that position, was properly refused as disregarding the inference from the evidence that the car was in motion when plaintiff undertook to board it, and as disregarding the duty resting on the conductor to know before causing the train to be started that plaintiff was not in the act of getting aboard thereof, provided that permission had been granted to plaintiff to leave the car temporarily, as claimed by him. Birmingham Ry., Light & Power Co. *v.* Jung, 161 Ala. 461, 49 So. 434, cited in note to 22 L. R. A., N. S., 758, 30 L. R. A., N. S., 271.

§ 211 (5) Causing Passenger to Fall from Train.

Charge as to Necessity for Riding on Running Board.—Where each count of the complaint alleged that plaintiff was compelled to ride on the running board of defendant's street car because of its overcrowded condition, and that plaintiff was thrown therefrom and injured, he was bound to prove such allegation as alleged, and hence the court should have charged at defendant's request that, before the jury could find for plaintiff, they must be reasonably satisfied that plaintiff was compelled, on account of the overcrowded condition of the car, to ride on the running board. Birmingham R., etc., Co. *v.* Hunnicutt, 3 Ala. App. 448, 57 So. 262.

§ 211 (6) Collision or Derailment.

Charge as to Duty of Stopping at Railroad Crossing.—In an action for injuries to a street car passenger by collision with a railroad train at a crossing, an instruction that there was no duty on the part of the operatives of the car to come to a full stop before the crossing the railroad, unless they knew or had reasonable cause to know that a train was approaching, was properly refused, as contravening Code 1896, § 3441, expressly imposing such duty. Montgomery St. Ry. Co. *v.* Lewis, 148 Ala. 134, 41 So. 736.

An instruction that it was the duty of the operator in charge of the train to have brought the same to a full stop before attempting to cross the street car tracks, and that the operatives of the street car were entitled to assume that the train would be so stopped unless the facts and circumstances were such as to indicate that the train would not be stopped, was properly refused as misleading, and as ignoring the duty imposed on the operators of the street car to stop by Code 1896, § 3441. Montgomery St. Ry. Co. *v.* Lewis, 148 Ala. 134, 41 So. 736.

Charge Ignoring Fact That Negligence of Flagman May Have Caused Collision.—In an action against a railway company for injury to a passenger, an instruction that if defendant was not negligent in operating the trains, and the collision was caused by the parting of one of the trains through no defect in the appliances thereof, and those in charge of such train promptly and properly used all means known to skillful trainmen to prevent the accident, the jury must find for defendant, was properly refused, as tending to mislead the jury, where they could have found that the collision was caused by the negligence of the company's fireman or flagman, who was sent forward to flag the train upon which plaintiff was a passenger, in not giving the signal at a sufficient distance between the train. Southern Ry. Co. *v.* Cunningham, 152 Ala. 147, 44 So. 658.

§ 211 (7) Setting Down Passengers in General.

Carrying Passenger Beyond Destination.—In an action for injury to a passenger by failure to stop for her to alight, an instruction that if plaintiff refused to go to the station beyond when the conductor offered to take her to that station, and the conductor did offer so to do, and, after refusing, plaintiff told the conductor to let her off where she was, and the train was then stopped and she voluntarily got off, she could not recover, was properly refused, as implying an obligation on plaintiff to go to the next station. Louisville & N. R. Co. *v.* Seale, 172 Ala. 480, 55 So. 237.

§ 211 (8) Starting or Moving Car While Passenger Is Alighting.

Assumption of Fact.—A charge assuming that plaintiff alighted from the car may be taken by the jury as an intimation that he was not thrown from the car, as claimed by him, and is therefore bad. Birmingham R., etc., Co. *v.* Lindsey, 140 Ala. 312, 37 So. 289.

Charge on Effect of Evidence.—In an action for death of a passenger, claimed to have been caused by a sudden jerk of a street car while he was alighting, a passenger testified for the company that, to the best of his recollection, the car stopped at the crossing. All of the company's testimony was not introduced to show that the car so stopped. Held, that a charge that some of the testimony offered by the company tended to show that the car stopped at the crossing was not erroneous. Birmingham Railway & Electric Co. *v.* James, 121 Ala. 120, 25 So. 847.

In an action for death of a passenger, claimed to have been caused by a sudden jerk of the car while he was alighting therefrom, a witness testified that the car slowed up almost to a standstill, it being hard to tell whether it was going or standing still. The court charged that some witnesses testified that the car so nearly stopped that its motion was almost imperceptible, but subsequently withdrew the statement, saying merely that some of the testimony tended to show that the car slowed up. Held not error. Birmingham Railway & Electric Co. *v.* James, 121 Ala. 120, 25 So. 847.

Invading Province of Jury.—In an action for injuries to a passenger, instructions stating in effect that defendant was guilty of negligence if it slowed up its train to receive a passenger, and after so slowing up moved off more rapidly without seeing that plaintiff, who was wishing to get off, was not in a position of peril, were bad, in that they took from the jury the question of defendant's negligence. Sweet *v.* Birmingham Ry. & Electric Co., 39 So. 767, 145 Ala. 667, cited in notes in 22 L. R. A., N. S., 744, 30 L. R. A., N. S., 277.

Acting on Misleading Movement of Train.—In an action for injuries to a passenger, a charge that plaintiff was entitled to recover if defendant negligently moved the train more rapidly after slowing down at the station at which plaintiff wished to alight, provided plaintiff acted on the slower motion of the train and attempted to get off, and such clower motion was such as to make plaintiff believe that it was safe to act upon it, and the injury was occasioned by the increased speed, was bad, in that it hypothesized defendant's negligence on plaintiff's belief under the circumstances, and not on the belief of a reasonably prudent person. Sweet *v.* Birmingham Ry. & Electric Co., 39 So. 767, 145 Ala. 667, cited in note in 22 L. R. A., N. S., 744, 30 L. R. A., N. S., 277.

Duty to Know Passenger's Position.—There being evidence that a street car passenger was injured, while alighting, by a sudden increase in the speed of the car, it was proper to refuse to charge that it was not the conductor's duty to know of the passenger's position of peril at the time the speed of the car was increased. Birmingham Ry., Light & Power Co. *v.* Girod, 51 So. 242, 164 Ala. 10.

§ 211 (9) Providing Safe Place or Means for Alighting.

Charge as to Invitation to Alight.—In an action against a street railroad company for injuries to a passenger, alleged to have been caused by negligence in stopping the car at a place where it was dangerous to alight, a requested instruction that plaintiff, having alleged that defendant negligently invited her to alight at the place of injury, could not recover without proving that defendant "did issue such invitation," was misleading because of the quoted words. Mobile Light & R. Co. *v.* Walsh, 40 So. 560, 146 Ala. 295.

In an action against a street railroad company for injuries to a passenger who fell while attempting to alight, an instruction that, when a car is stopped at or near the place where the passenger gives the signal for it to stop, this may be taken as an invitation to alight, was not objectionable as withdrawing from the jury the question whether or not stopping the car at the place where plaintiff was injured constituted an invitation to alight there. Mobile Light & R. Co. *v.* Walsh, 40 So. 560, 146 Ala. 295.

Alighting from Moving Train.—In an action for injury to one alighting from a street car and struck by a passing car while attempting to cross tracks behind the car from which he alighted, an instruction that, if he alighted before the car reached his station and while it was in motion, he could not recover, was properly refused, since under it he could not recover, though he alighted just before the car stopped and while it was moving very slowly. Birmingham Ry., Light & Power Co. *v.* Landrum, 45 So. 198, 153 Ala. 192.

Misleading Charge as to Loss of Right to Complain of Violation of Custom.—In an action for injury to one alighting from one street car and struck by another while attempting to cross tracks behind the car from which he alighted, an instruction that if plaintiff alighted before his car reached the regular stopping place, and if a custom to give warning signals when passing a standing car and to reduce speed or stop opposite the standing car existed when plaintiff was hurt and was for the benefit altogether of passengers alighting from the standing car, and if plaintiff alighted at such point to escape paying fare, then he was not entitled to complain of any violation of such custom, was properly refused, as being involved and misleading. Birmingham R., etc., Co. *v.* Landrum, 153 Ala. 192, 45 So. 198.

Duty as to Stopping Passing Cars.—In an action against a street railway company for injury to an alighting passenger, struck by a passing car while crossing tracks behind and east of the car from which he alighted, an instruction that, if he was injured while crossing the track at a point east of the regular stopping place, the company owed him no duty to cause the car which struck him to be stopped opposite the car from which he alighted while it was standing at the stopping place, was properly refused, as not showing how far east of the stopping place the plaintiff was when injured. Birmingham R., etc., Co. *v.* Landrum, 153 Ala. 192, 45 So. 198.

In an action against a street railway company for injury to a passenger, struck by a passing freight car while passing behind the car from which he alighted, an instruction that, if the passenger car was moving when the freight car passed it, it was not the company's duty to have reduced the speed of the freight car or to have stopped it opposite the passenger car, was properly refused, for not distinguishing between a rapid or slow movement of the passenger car, since a passenger may alight from a slowly moving car, and since a passenger car within a very short distance of a station is likely to be discharging passengers, and it would be culpable neligence for another car, operated by the same company upon the same highway, to pass it at a full or very rapid speed. Birmingham R., etc., Co. *v.* Landrum, 153 Ala. 192' 45 So. 198.

Duty as to Signals from Passing Car.—In an action against a street railway company for injury to an alighting passenger, struck by a passing car while attempting to cross a track, an instruction that the motorman on such car was not bound to give signals, except when passing or about to pass another car, was properly refused, as tending to mislead the jury, where the evidence showed that plaintiff was injured at a station where the car from which he alighted stopped, or so near the station as not to have relieved the motorman of the duty of giving signals of the approach of the car that injured plaintiff. Birmingham R., etc., Co. *v.* Landrum, 153 Ala. 192, 45 So. 198.

§ 211 (10) Proximate Cause of Injury.

See, also, post, "Presumptions and Burden of Proof," § 211 (11).

The hypotheses to a recovery in instructions in an action for injury to a passenger must include the condition that the negligence or wrong charged in the complaint afforded the proximate cause of the injury. Birmingham Ry., Light & Power Co. *v.* Fisher, 55 So. 995, 173 Ala. 623.

Charges Held Proper.—An instruction that if a passenger was injured in the manner and form alleged in her complaint as a proximate consequence of defendant's negligence as alleged, and she was not guilty of contributory negligence, she was entitled to recover, was proper. Birmingham R., etc., Co. *v.* Barrett (Ala.), 60 So. 262.

A charge that it was the duty of defendant carrier to use the highest care, and if it did not use such care, and as a result plaintiff received his injuries, he should have verdict, predicates recovery on a result produced solely by defendant's fault. Southern Ry. Co. *v.* Roebuck, 31 So. 611, 132 Ala. 412.

Failure to Hypothesize That Act Was Proximate Cause of Injury.—In an action for injuries to an alighting passenger from the starting of the car, an instruction that plaintiff would be entitled to recover if the car was negligently started was erroneous, for failing to hypothesize that the starting of the car was the proximate cause of the injury. Birmingham Ry., Light & Power Co. *v.* Moore, 50 So. 115, 163 Ala. 43.

§ 211 (11) Presumptions and Burden of Proof.

Proving Plea of Justification of Assault.—In a passenger's action against a street car company for an assault by its conductor, it was proper to charge that the burden of proving its plea of justification was on the company. Birmingham R., etc., Co. *v.* Coleman (Ala.), 61 So. 890.

Proving Injuries as Proximate Cause of Sickness.—Where, the complaint alleged other injuries than one claimed to have caused appendicitis, it was not error to refuse to charge that the burden of proof is on the plaintiff to show that the injuries alleged were the proximate cause of the appendicitis. Birmingham Ry., Light & Power Co. *v.* Moore, 50 So. 1024, 148 Ala. 115.

Misleading Charge as to Measure of Proof.—Instructions requested by defendant that the burden was on plaintiff to prove that she was injured by the carelessness of the driver of a street car, and if the testimony left the jury in uncertainty as to whether she was so injured, the jury must find for defendant; and that the burden of proving that the car was not stopped a reasonable time to allow plaintiff to alight therefrom was on plaintiff—were misleading as to the measure of proof, and properly refused. Birmingham Union Ry. Co. *v.* Hale, 90 Ala. 8, 8 So. 142, cited in notes in 7 L. R. A., N. S., 1078, 13 L. R. A., N. S., 602, 611, 23 L. R. A., N. S., 891.

§ 211 (12) Conformity to Pleadings and Issues.

Charges Properly Submitting Issues.—In an action against a street-railway company for injuries alleged to be due to the negligence of defendant, where the pleas were "not guilty" and "contributory negligence," it was proper to charge that the plaintiff could not recover unless his injuries were occasioned solely by negligence of the defendant. McDonald *v.* Montgomery St. Ry., 110 Ala. 161, 20 So. 317.

The complaint having averred that the car was standing still when plaintiff attempted to board it, and charged negligence in the starting of it with a sudden jerk while he was so attempting, and there having been no plea of contributory negligence, but only the general issue, requested instructions that plaintiff does not sue for damages from attempting to board a moving car, and if it was moving when he attempted to board it there can be no recovery in the action, should be given. Alabama, etc., R. Co. *v.* Bullard, 157 Ala. 618, 47 So. 578, cited in note in 30 L. R. A., N. S., 277.

Charge Held Erroneous.—The instruction, in an action counting on negligence in starting up a car while plaintiff was attempting to board it when it was standing still, that if plaintiff attempted to board it when it was dangerous to do so because of its rapid speed, and because of this plaintiff fell and was injured, then, if the injury was so caused by defendant's negligence, verdict should be for plaintiff, is erroneous, as, under the facts hypothesized, plaintiff's negligence, and not that of defendant, certainly not that counted on, caused the injury. Alabama City, G. & A. Ry. Co. *v.* Bullard, 47 So. 578, 157 Ala. 618, cited in note in 30 L. R. A., N. S., 277.

Charges Properly Refused.—Where, in an action against a street railway company, negligence was charged in one count in starting the car with a jerk, and in another with suddenly stopping, an instruction that if the jury "believe from the evidence that by the starting of the car the plaintiff was not jerked, slung, or thrown one way, and by the stopping of the car she was not jerked, slung, or thrown the other way, the verdict must be for the defendant," was properly refused. Birmingham Ry. & Electric Co. *v.* Ellard, 33 So. 276, 135 Ala. 433.

Where, in an action against a railway company for injuries to a passenger, the evidence showed a direct wrong on the part of the conductor, instructions predicating a recovery on his negligence were properly refused. Louisville & N. R. Co. *v.* Quinn, 39 So. 617, 145 Ala. 657.

Where a count in the complaint in an action against a carrier of passengers for personal injuries caused by derailment of a car alleges that defendant was negligent in running its train at too great speed, and also in maintaining a defective track at the place of derailment, a request to find for defendant on such count, because there is no evidence of negligence as to the speed of the train, is properly refused. Alabama G. S. R. Co. *v.* Hill, 93 Ala. 514, 9 So. 722.

In an action for personal injuries sustained while leaving a horse car, plaintiff's evidence tended to show that the car was standing still when she attempted to get off, and was started with a jerk as she was stepping to the ground, while the evidence of defendant showed that plaintiff was entirely free from the car before it was again started. Held, that defendants' requests for instructions which based its right to a verdict upon the assumption "that the moment plaintiff started to get off was simultaneous with the starting of the car," and that the car was in motion when she attempted to get off, were properly refused. Birmingham Union Ry. Co. *v.* Smith, 90 Ala. 60, 8 So. 86.

Where the complaint alleged that while plaintiff was a passenger he was assaulted by the conductor of the train, and the evidence tended to show that he was assaulted, and was knocked off the train by the conductor, who jumped off and continued the assault, and there was no evidence that the assault was necessary in self-defense, plaintiff could recover, if the jury found that he was actually assaulted while on the train, although they found that he was not knocked off by the conductor; and hence instructions to find for defendant, unless plaintiff had sustained the burden of proving that he was knocked off the train by the conductor, were properly denied. Alabama, etc., R. Co. *v.* Sampley, 4 Ala. App. 464, 58 So. 974.

(E) CONTRIBUTORY NEGLIGENCE OF PERSON INJURED.

§ 212. Application of the Doctrine to Carriers in General.

Where a passenger, by his own negligence or want of ordinary care and prudence, has so far contributed to injuries received by him that, but for such contributory negligence on his part, the injury would not have happened, he can not recover therefor. South & N. A. R. Co. *v.* Schaufler, 75 Ala. 136, cited in note in 21 L. R. A., 362.

In an action for injuries to a passenger, a charge that, if plaintiff was guilty of negligence which contributed approximately in the slightest degree to her injury, the jury must find for defendant, was proper. Sweet *v.* Birmingham Ry. & Electric Co., 39 So. 767, 145 Ala. 667.

§ 213. Awaiting and Seeking Transportation.

Standing Near Track.—A person at or near a station awaiting his train is not guilty of contributory negligence in standing near the track, unless he gets so close as to be struck by an ordinary train; and hence, in an action for injuries received by one while waiting at a railroad company's flag station, pleas, not showing that plaintiff was so near the track as to be in danger of an ordinary train, are insufficient. Louisville, etc., R. Co. *v.* Glasgow (Ala.), 60 So. 103. See post, "Pleading," § 226.

One killed by being struck by a projection from a passing freight train, while standing on the platform at a railroad station, waiting for a train, was not guilty of negligence in being on the platform, unless he knew that the train or projection would extend over same while passing, and he had a right to rely on the safety of the platform as against passing trains. Metcalf *v.* St. Louis & S. F. R. Co., 47 So. 158, 156 Ala. 240.

Walking in Front of Engine.—Plaintiff wishing to reach a train, between which and himself another train was standing on a downgrade, walked along some thirty feet past the engine of the latter, and, turning, stepped on the track in front of it. He did not look back nor listen, and was struck by it and injured. Neither the bell nor whistle was sounded, and there was no evidence that the engineer saw his perilous position in time to warn him, or knew he would attempt to cross. Held, he was guilty of contributory negligence, and could not recover. East Tennessee, V. & G. Ry. Co. *v.* Kornegay, 92 Ala. 228, 9 So. 557.

Falling over Lumber.—Where a passenger, in passing from the station to a train, fell over lumber obstructing the platform in part, which he knew was on the platform, but had forgotten at the time he fell, he was guilty of contributory negligence. Wood *v.* Richmond & D. R. Co., 100 Ala. 660, 13 So. 552.

§ 214. Entering Conveyance.

§ 214 (1) In General.

See post, "In General," § 230 (1).

Failure to Call for Light or Assistance.—Where a passenger has purchased a ticket, intending to take passage on the expected train, and remains in the office until the approach of the train is announced, and when he does what all other persons, in like circumstances, had done for years, without accident or injury, he can not be deemed prima facie guilty of a want of ordinary care, if he fails to call for a light or assistance in taking the train, although familiar with the situation. Alabama G. S. R. Co. *v.* Arnold, 80 Ala. 600, 2 So. 337.

§ 214 (2) At Place Other than Station or Platform.

In an action for the death of a person attempting to board a street car, where there was no evidence to show wanton or intentional misconduct of the street car employees, or to show that they knew decedent was in peril, an instruction that, if decedent attempted to board defendant's car at a place where they did not usually or frequently stop to take on or let off passengers, the jury must find for the defendant, was not error. Smith *v.* Birmingham Ry., Light & Power Co., 41 So. 307, 147 Ala. 702.

The carrier may, by proper notice, prohibit the receiving or discharging of passengers at other places than the stations provided by it, and persons attempting, uninvited, to board its trains at such other places, in the absence of wanton or willful negligence on the part of the carrier, act at their own peril until they have entered its carriage, or are accepted as passengers. North Birmingham St. Ry. Co. *v.* Liddicoat, 99 Ala. 545, 13 So. 18.

"If a carrier is in the habit of receiving or discharging passengers at a place other than a regular station, or persons are invited or directed by its authorized servants to board or alight from its cars at such other places, they have the right to presume that it is safe to board or quit the train at such place, unless the risk in doing so is so obvious that a man of ordinary care and prudence would not, under like circumstances, make the attempt. * * * It is immaterial for what purpose its cars are stopped at such place, other than a regular station, whether in consequence of a duty enjoined on it by law, as when approaching the track of an intersecting road, or arising from convenience or necessity in the usual mode of operating its trains. If the public are in the habit of entering or quitting its cars at such place, without objection from its agents or servants, such persons are entitled to the protection of all the duties imposed upon the carrier in receiving and discharging passengers at its regular stations, except in so far as it may be relieved therefrom by obvious risks, incident to the nature and condition of such place of customary use. The customary use of such place for receiving and discharging passengers may become so generally known and well established as to impose upon the carrier the duty of maintaining such place in as safe and convenient condition as a regular station, and to authorize a passenger, without notifying the conductor or other servant of the carrier of his desire or intention to board the train, to presume that a reasonable opportunity will be afforded him for that purpose, and that it is safe to do so. A passenger attempting to board a train at such place, and under such circumstances, is as much justified in the assumption that the carrier's cars are in a safe condition as he would be were he attempting to board them at a regular station; for the duty of the carrier to so maintain them attaches in all cases and under all circumstances where the relation of carrier and passenger exists, either by express contract or implication of law." North Birmingham St. R. Co. *v.* Liddicoat, 99 Ala. 545, 13 So. 18, 19.

§ 214 (3) Boarding Moving Car.

See post, "Boarding Moving Conveyance," § 230 (3).

Where a person attempts to board a car in the nighttime, when the train is running from four to six miles an hour, and when he is incumbered by a bundle, he is guilty of negligence. Smith *v.* Birmingham Ry., Light & Power Co., 41 So. 307, 147 Ala. 702, cited in note in 30 L. R. A., N. S., 275.

In an action for personal injuries sustained in striking against a high platform while boarding a train, evidence that plaintiff stood near by for two minutes while the train was waiting; that the conductor gave the signal, "All aboard," before the train started; that when plaintiff attempted to board the train it was moving several miles per hour; that he knew of the dangerous proximity of the platform, but did not "have the matter in his mind at the time;" and that the conductor had often warned him not to board a moving train—shows that plaintiff was negligent. McLaren *v.* Alabama Midland Ry. Co., 100 Ala. 506, 14 So. 405, cited in note in 22 L. R. A., N. S., 759.

§ 215. In Transit.

§ 216. —— Dangerous Position.

§ 216 (1) Standing in Car.

See post, "Pleading," § 226; "Conduct While in Transit in General," § 230 (4)

§ 216 (2) Riding on Platform.

See post, "Disobedience of Rules of Carrier," § 219; "Proximate Cause of Injury," § 223; "Presumptions and Burden of Proof," § 227; "Riding on Platform," § 230 (5).

"'It is negligence, except under special circumstances, for a passenger to stand upon the platform of a car of a rapidly moving commercial railroad train. The inevitable lurching and jerking of a train so propelled makes the danger obvious to the ordinary understanding, and the negligence self-evident.' Clanton *v.* Southern R. Co., 165 Ala. 485, 51 So. 616, 27 L. R. A., N. S., 253; Central, etc., R. Co. *v.* Brown, 165 Ala. 493, 51 So. 565. * * * Necessity alone can warrant the assumption by a passenger of a position upon the platform of a rapidly moving commercial train. Mere considerations of personal comfort or choice can not justify or excuse such action." Alabama, etc., R. Co. *v.* Gilbert, 6 Ala. App. 372, 60 So. 542, 544; Watkins *v.* Birmingham R., etc., Co., 120 Ala. 147, 24 So. 392, 43 L. R. A. 297.

In an action for injuries received by a passenger who was thrown from a moving car by a sudden jerk, the passenger can not recover if he was standing on the platform when there was room for him to sit or stand in the car, and the negligence of the motorman would not have caused the injury if the passenger had been inside. McDonald *v.* Montgomery St. Railway, 110 Ala. 161, 20 So. 317. See notes in 38 L. R. A. 787, 13 L. R. A., N. S., 602, 29 L. R. A., N. S., 325.

That an electric railway passenger unnecessarily and negligently left a place of safety on a car and walked to the rear platform while the car was moving so rapidly as to make his position highly and obviously dangerous to one of ordinary prudence, and when it was manifest that he would probably fall from the car, and that as a proximate consequence of such attempt plaintiff fell from the car and was injured, shows a good defense to his claim for such injury. Birmingham Ry., Light & Power Co. *v.* Yates, 53 So. 915, 169 Ala. 381.

When Passenger Goes upon Platform to Alight.—A passenger going upon the platform of a moving train for the purpose of getting off after the train is stopped, and remaining there only long enough to ascertain that the train would not stop longer, is not riding on the platform, within the meaning of the regulation which prohibits his riding there. Central Railroad & Banking Co. *v.* Miles, 88 Ala. 256, 6 So. 696, cited in note in 4 L. R. A., N. S., 141.

"**When a train is over crowded,** a passenger who can not obtain the accommodations to which he is entitled may refuse to ride upon that train, and the train crew, if he elects to ride upon that train and to stand upon a platform of a car, have a right to presume that, in assuming the extra hazardous position upon the train, he will so far as he reasonably can, protect himself from being thrown from the train by a 'lurch or jerk no more violent than the lurching or jerking of trains known to be a necessary incident to their rapid movement when operated with due care.' American Railroad Law (Baldwin) 311." Alabama, etc., R. Co. *v.* Gilbert, 6 Ala. App. 372, 60 So. 542, 545.

§ 216 (3) Limb or Other Part of Person Protruding from Car.

For a passenger on a steam railway to protrude his arm beyond the outer edge of the window is negligence per se which will defeat a recovery for any injury to which it proximately contributed. Georgia Pac. Ry. Co. *v.* Underwood, 90 Ala. 49, 8 So. 116, cited in note in 16 L. R. A. 92.

§ 216 (4) Riding in Car Not Intended for Passengers.

A passenger killed in a derailment while riding on top of a box car, instead of in the caboose, which remained on the track—no one therein being injured—was negligent. Beyer *v.* Louisville & N. R. Co., 21 So. 952, 114 Ala. 424.

§ 217. —— Changing Position.

See ante, "Riding on Platform," § 216 (2).

Falling Through Drop Door.—Where a passenger, knowing the purpose of drop doors on the platform of a vestibuled train and of the reasonable use of the same while the train was at a station, left the coach she had boarded and went upon the platform for the sole purpose of standing there while the train was at the station, and she was injured by falling down the steps, because the drop floor was raised, and because of the absence of a light, she was negligent, precluding a recovery. Clanton *v.* Southern Ry. Co., 51 So. 616, 165 Ala. 485.

She assumed the risk of injury, though the carrier knew that passengers habitually resorted to the platform, where the carrier did not acquiesce therein by keeping the drop door down at stations. Clanton *v.* Southern R. Co., 165 Ala. 485, 51 So. 616, cited in note in 37 L. R. A., N. S., 518.

Going to Engine for Water.—There being no water in defendant's coach, plaintiff went to the engine to get some, and in attempting to pass from the tender to the platform of the coach he grasped the brake, which was loose, just as the engineer put on the air brakes. The suddenness of the jerk and the turning of the brake caused him to fall between the engine and the coach. Plaintiff knew that, there being no steps on the engine, he would have to pass over the iron railing to the coach. Held, that his extreme negligence contributing to his injury was a complete defense. McDaniel *v.* Highland Ave. & B. R. Co., 90 Ala. 64, 8 So. 41, cited in note in 34 L. R. A. 721.

Passing from One Street Car to Another.—As the running board of an open street car, and the steps of a closed car, are not intended as a means of passing from one car to another, where a passenger is injured by attempting to pass by such means, his contributory negligence will defeat a recovery for the injury, even if the trainmen were negligent in suddenly increasing the speed of the train. Hill *v.* Birmingham Union Ry. Co., 100 Ala. 447, 14 So. 201.

Where a passenger is directed by an agent of the carrier, acting in the line of his duty, to pass from one car to another while the train is in motion, and the danger in doing so is not obvious, he is not negligent in attempting to obey, and where injury results the carrier is liable. Central of Georgia Ry. Co. *v.* Carleton, 51 So. 27, 163 Ala. 62, cited in note in 37 L. R. A., N. S., 519.

§ 218. Leaving Conveyance.

See post, "Pleading," § 226.

§ 218 (1) In General.

"It is undoubtedly the duty of carriers to stop their trains at stations long enough for passengers to alight in safety, and it is the correlative duty of the passengers to exercise due care and due diligence in quitting the train. Birmingham Union R. Co. *v.* Smith, 90 Ala. 60, 8 So. 86; Alabama Mid. R. Co. *v.* Johnson, 123 Ala. 197, 26 So. 160." Southern R. Co. *v.* Burgess, 143 Ala. 364, 42 So. 35, 38.

Duty of Passenger to Inquire as to Safety of Place.—A plea assuming that it was the duty of a passenger to inquire of a street railway company or its agent as to whether the place of stopping is a reasonably safe place for him to alight was properly overruled. Montgomery St. Ry. *v.* Mason, 32 So. 261, 133 Ala. 508.

Alighting Backwards.—Evidence that, in alighting from a train, a passenger attempted to step from the car platform backwards, warrants a charge that he can not recover, if the injury resulted from his attempting to leave the car in a negligent manner. Watkins *v.* Birmingham

Railway & Electric Co., 24 So. 392, 120 Ala. 147, 43 L. R. A. 297.

§ 218 (2) Preparing to Leave Conveyance before It Stops.

See post, "Proximate Cause of Injury," § 223; "Preparing to Leave Conveyance before It Stops," § 230 (7).

A street car passenger is not negligent in arising when the car is slowing down for a station and going on the platform preparatory to alighting when the car stops. Birmingham Ry., Light & Power Co. *v.* Barrett (Ala.), 60 So. 262.

§ 218 (3) Alighting at Place Other Than Station or Platform.

See post, "Alighting from Moving Train or Car in General," § 218 (4).

Alighting between Stations in General.—Where a passenger was injured in attempting to alight from a car in motion between stations, he can not recover. Tannehill *v.* Birmingham Ry., Light & Power Co. (Ala.), 58 So. 198.

Where Passenger Carried Past Destination.—Where a carrier, taking a passenger beyond his destination, stops the train and lets him off he may assume that the place selected is reasonably safe for the purpose. Birmingham Ry., Light & Power Co. *v.* Anderson, 50 So. 1021, 163 Ala. 517.

Where a street car is run past the place at which a passenger has signaled his desire to alight, and stopped at an unusual and dangerous place, and the passenger in alighting there does no more than an ordinarily prudent person would have done under the circumstances, he is not guilty of contributory negligence. Mobile Light & R. Co. *v.* Walsh, 40 So. 560, 146 Ala. 295.

Implied Invitation to Alight—Calling Station.—"When the name of the station is called, and soon thereafter the train is brought to a standstill, a passenger may reasonably conclude that it has stopped at the station, and endeavor to get off, unless the circumstances and indications are such as to render manifest that the train has not reached the proper and usual landing place." Smith *v.* Georgia Pac. R. Co., 88 Ala. 538, 7 So. 119, 121.

"A railroad company, being a carrier of passengers, is under obligation to use reasonable care to transport them safely. This general duty includes the specific duty not to expose them to unnecessary danger, and not intentionally or negligently mislead them by causing them to reasonably suppose that their point of destination has been reached, and that they may safely alight, when the train is in an improper place. Calling out the name of the station is customary and proper, so that passengers may be informed that the train is approaching the station of their destination, and prepare to get off when it arrives at the platform. The mere announcement of the name of the station is not an invitation to alight, but, when followed by full stoppage of the train soon thereafter, is ordinarily notification that it has arrived at the usual place of landing passengers. Whether the stoppage of the train, after such announcement and before it arrives at the platform, is negligence, depends upon the attendant circumstances." Smith *v.* Georgia Pac. R. Co., 88 Ala. 538, 7 So. 119, 120. See notes in 2 L. R. A., N. S., 116; 15 L. R. A. 348.

In an action for personal injuries there was evidence that plaintiff was in the habit of leaving defendant's dummy train, on which he was riding, at a certain street crossing; that those in charge of the train knew this; that the train passed the crossing without stopping, but when approaching the next crossing it came to a full stop; that nothing was said that the train was to back to plaintiff's usual stopping place; that plaintiff had previously left the train where it stopped; and that, after plaintiff had got off, and was reaching back for his crutches, the train, without warning, backed, and knocked him down. Held, that it was proper to charge that plaintiff was not negligent in getting off, if he believed he had an implied invitation to do so, and the train was stopped for that purpose. Gadsden & A. U. Ry. Co. *v.* Causler, 97 Ala. 235, 12 So. 439, cited in note in 37 L. R. A., N. S., 265, 266.

Where the conductor on a railroad train calls the name of a station, and the engineer, before reaching there, though without the conductor's knowledge, stops the train over a trestle, and a passenger steps off and is injured, the fact that the night was dark, that the conductor himself did not at first know that he had not reached the station, and that he could not see the trestle without the aid of his lantern, is sufficient to show that a passenger was not negligent in attempting to alight. Richmond & D. R. Co. *v.* Smith, 92 Ala. 237, 9 So. 223, cited in note in 2 L. R. A., N. S., 115.

Implied Invitation—Obvious Danger.—As defendant's train was approaching a station, its name was called, and the train was stopped very soon thereafter, to take the side track for the passage of another train. When it stopped, plaintiff, whose destination it was, went out of the rear door of the car, and was descending with one foot on the first step of the car, and the other about touching the ground, when the train moved to go forward to the depot, which caused him to fall. The place of the stoppage was in a cut, about 200 yards from the depot building. It was about 1 o'clock p. m. All the surroundings indicated that the spot at which he attempted to leave the train was not the proper place for alighting. Held, that defendant was not liable for the injuries caused by the fall. Smith *v.* Georgia Pac. Ry. Co., 88 Ala. 538, 7 So. 119, 7 L. R. A. 323.

§ 218 (4) Alighting from Moving Train or Car in General.

See post, "Alighting from Moving Conveyance," § 230 (8).

In General.—"As a general rule, alighting from a moving car is not necessarily negligence per se. There may be exceptional circumstances attending the attempt thus to alight, such as the great speed of the train, the age or infirmity of the passenger, or his being incumbered with bundles or children, or other facts, which render the attempt so obviously dangerous that the court may, where the testimony is undisputed, declare as matter of law that the passenger's conduct was reckless and negligent. Hunter *v.* Louisville, etc., R. Co., 150 Ala. 594, 43 So. 802, 9 L. R. A., N. S., 848; Watkins *v.* Birmingham R., etc., Co., 120 Ala. 147, 24 So. 392, 43 L. R. A. 297; Kansas, etc., R. Co. *v.* Matthews, 142 Ala. 298, 39 So. 207; Sweet *v.* Birmingham R., etc., Co., 136 Ala. 166, 33 So. 886; Nellis, St. R. R. Accident Law, p. 190. * * * Of course, a person might be guilty of negligence per se in stepping off a moving car in an opposite direction from which it was going, when he would not be if stepping in the direction it was going, and when going at the same rate of speed. But it can not be said to be negligence as matter of law to step off a slowly moving car, even if the party steps in an opposite direction from which it was going." Birmingham R., etc., Co. *v.* Dickerson, 154 Ala. 523, 45 So. 659, 660; Birmingham R., etc., Co. *v.* James, 121 Ala. 120, 25 So. 847. The same may be said as to holding onto the rail. If the train is moving slowly, and the station platform is on a level with the car, it might be wise to hold onto the rail until the passenger had adapted his gait to the speed of the train. Dilburn *v.* Louisville, etc., R. Co., 156 Ala. 228, 47 So. 210, 213. See note in 38 L. R. A. 787, 789, 30 L. R. A., N. S., 270, 277, 22 L. R. A., N. S., 742, 744.

"In Ricketts *v.* Birmingham St. R. Co, 85 Ala. 600, 5 So. 353, we said, and generally very correctly, that stepping from a moving car without necessity, when injury is caused thereby, which could have been avoided by remaining on the car—by the exercise of ordinary diligence—is negligence, which will defeat a recovery because of prior negligence of the agents or servants of the company. Central R., etc., Co. *v.* Letcher, 69 Ala. 106; Thompson *v.* Duncan, 76 Ala. 334. 'When a passenger leaves a moving car, he incurs more or less danger because he is affected by its momentum. * * * As in boarding, so in alighting, the passenger assumes the risk of all injuries, caused by the ordinary momentum of the cars. Unless informed by signals or otherwise, the driver and conductor are not bound to know that a passenger expects to leave the car or wishes to have it stopped.' Booth, St. Ry. Law, § 337." McDonald *v.* Montgomery St. Railway, 110 Ala. 161, 20 So. 317, 322.

Care Required.—A passenger alighting from a moving train was not guilty of contributory negligence unless the risk was such as a man of ordinary care and prudence would not have undertaken under the circumstances. Louisville, etc., R. Co. *v.* Dilburn (Ala.), 59 So. 438.

A passenger is guilty of contributory negligence in attempting to get off a moving car at a time when a reasonably prudent person similarly situated would not attempt to alight. Sweet *v.* Birmingham Ry. & Electric Co., 39 So. 767, 145 Ala. 667.

Implied Invitation to Alight.—The slowing up of a train for a station is not an invitation to the passenger to alight while the train is in operation or moving, or for the passenger to place himself in a position of peril. Sweet *v.* Birmingham Ry. & Electric Co., 39 So. 767, 145 Ala. 667.

Instances Where Passenger Held Negligent.—Where a passenger, who had stood upon the car steps two or three minutes before attempting to alight and was by the passing objects enabled to determine the speed of the train, and who was incumbered with baggage, attempted to alight while the train was running from six to ten miles an hour, he was guilty of contributory negligence as a matter of law. Hunter *v.* Louisville, etc., R. Co., 150 Ala. 594, 43 So. 802.

In an action by a passenger against a street-railroad company for personal injuries, the court properly directed a verdict for defendant, where plaintiff was injured in attempting to get off a car while it was crossing a public street, in violation of the rules of the company; none of the employees of the company having done anything to cause her to take the step. Calderwood *v.* North Birmingham St. Ry. Co., 96 Ala. 318, 11 So. 66.

Stepping unnecessarily from a moving street car, with a keg of lead in hand, when danger and injury would have been avoided by remaining on the car, is negligence which will defeat recovery because of prior negligence of the servants of the car company. Ricketts *v.* Birmingham St. Ry. Co., 85 Ala. 600, 5 So. 353.

Where a street car passenger stepped off a car while it was going at a high rate of speed, with his face toward the rear of the car, he was guilty of contributory negligence. Birmingham Ry., Light & Power Co. *v.* Glover, 142 Ala. 492, 38 So. 836.

As defendant's train was approaching a station, the name of the station was called, and the train was stopped soon afterwards at a crossing with another railroad. When it stopped, plaintiff, whose destination was the station called, went out of the rear door of the car, and, though the train was by this time again in motion, jumped from the car, and fell on a platform about 10 feet below the crossing. It was at night, and there were no lights, no depot building, or any other landmark, where the train stopped, to indicate a station. Plaintiff was acquainted with the location, and knew of the crossing. Held, that defendant was not liable for the injuries caused by the fall. East Tennessee, V. & G. R. Co. *v.* Holmes, 97 Ala. 332, 12 So. 286, following Smith *v.* Georgia Pac. Ry. Co., 88 Ala. 538, 7 So. 119. See note in 21 L. R. A. 360.

A passenger, incumbered with hand baggage, who alighted from a train moving six miles an hour, on a dark night, before it had reached the platform of the station where he was to get off, and with which he was familiar, and with no reason to believe the train would not stop as usual, was negligent. South & North Alabama R. Co. *v.* Schaufler, 75 Ala. 136, cited in 31 L. R. A. 362.

§ 218 (5) Alighting from Moving Car on Failure to Stop at Station.

See post, "Alighting from Moving Conveyance," § 230 (8).

§ 218 (6) Alighting from Moving Car on Failure to Stop for Sufficient Time.

See post, "Alighting from Moving Conveyance," § 230 (8).

A passenger who attempts to step from a car while it is in motion can not recover for injuries in consequence thereof, even though he had reached his destination, and the train had not stopped for a reasonable lenght of time to allow him to alight. Louisville & N. R. Co. *v.* Lee, 97 Ala. 325, 12 So. 48. See note in 21 L. R. A. 365, 22 L. R. A., N. S., 746.

Where an old and infirm woman was unable to alight from a train during the time it stopped, she was guilty of contributory negligence in attempting, with the aid of her son, to alight after the train had started. Nashville, C. & St. L. Ry. *v.* Casey, 1 Ala. App. 344, 56 So. 28.

Where decedent, an infirm man, over

sixty-five years of age, and incumbered with bundles, attempted to alight from a moving train at his destination after the train had started and against the protest of a flagman, who testified that he requested decedent not to step off until the train could be stopped, defendant was entitled to an instruction that, if he stepped from the car while it was in motion and against the protest of a flagman, acting within the scope of his employment, who offered to stop the train to let decedent get off, but notwithstanding this he stepped off, he assumed all the risk of alighting safely, and defendant was not liable. Louisville, etc., R. Co. *v.* Dilburn (Ala.), 59 So. 438.

§ 218 (7) Defective or Unlighted Platform.

While the servants of a street railroad company are charged with the duty of knowing whether a place at which a car is stopped to allow passengers to alight is reasonably safe, the passenger is charged with no such duty, and is not negligent in alighting at such place, unless the danger is obvious. Mobile Light & R. Co. *v.* Walsh, 146 Ala. 295, 40 So. 560.

In an action by a passenger against the railroad company for injuries caused by a hole in a platform erected near the tracks, and used by passengers going to and from an hotel for meals, plaintiff testified that there were no lights except from the hotel and car windows, and that he did not see the hole until he stepped into it, though he might have done so had he looked for it. The testimony of defendant's witnesses was vague. They testified that plaintiff might have seen the hole had he "looked carefully." Held, that plaintiff was not negligent. Watson *v.* Oxanna Land Co., 92 Ala. 320, 8 So. 770.

§ 218 (8) Leaving Premises by Improper Course.

In an action against a railroad company to recover for personal injuries, it appeared that plaintiff arrived at defendant's Union Depot on one of its trains, and, desiring to find a certain building, made inquiry of a stranger, who pointed in the direction of the steep bank of a river, about fifty yards from the depot, and at the further end of the platform. The platform was well lighted, extending from the depot to the river, but a house intervened between where plaintiff went and the lights on the platform. Plaintiff fell down the bluff in the dark. Held, that plaintiff was guilty of contributory negligence. Montgomery & E. Ry. Co. *v.* Thompson, 77 Ala. 448.

§ 218 (9) Crossing Other Tracks.

See post, "Crossing Tracks after Alighting from Car," § 230 (10).

Passing Around Car—Failure to Look and Listen.—A carrier owes a duty to passengers alighting at a regular station that while making their egress they be not struck by other cars, and, though a passenger must exercise care for his safety, he may assume that the tracks between the alighting place and the station will be kept safe while he is crossing; and hence the mere fact that he fails to look and listen for approaching cars before attempting to cross will not as a matter of law constitute contributory negligence, preventing a recovery if he is struck by such a car. Birmingham Ry., Light & Power Co. *v.* Landrum, 153 Ala. 192, 45 So. 198, cited in note in 21 L. R. A., N. S., 888.

But see Birmingham R., etc., Co. *v.* Oldham, 141 Ala. 195, 37 So. 452, where it was held that where plaintiff, upon alighting from a street car at a street crossing, passed around behind it, and upon a parallel track, without looking to see whether there was a car approaching thereon, and was struck and injured by a car going in the opposite direction, the question of his contributory negligence is not affected by the fact that the rules of the company required the car to stop on meeting another, which had stopped to take on or discharge passengers, and also to sound the bell at crossings, which was not done; it not appearing that such rules were customarily observed.

Crawling between Freight Cars.—A man, on getting off a passenger train at a small station, attempted to crawl between two cars of a long freight train standing on a side track, and was killed by the starting of the train without proper signals. Held, that his administratrix could not recover of the company for the killing. Memphis & C. R. Co. *v.* Copeland, 61 Ala. 376.

§ 219. Disobedience of Rules of Carrier.

See ante, "Rules of Carrier," § 167.

Reasonableness.—A rule of a street-car company that passengers must not leave its cars while they are in motion is a reasonable one. Armstrong *v.* Montgomery St. Ry. Co., 123 Ala. 233, 26 So. 349.

Knowledge of Passenger.—A passenger can not be charged with negligence in violating a rule of the carrier, unless he knew the rule. Armstrong *v.* Montgomery St. Ry. Co., 123 Ala. 233, 26 So. 349; Birmingham R., etc., Co. *v.* Girod, 164 Ala. 10, 51 So. 242.

Standing on Platform.—A regulation of a railroad company forbidding passengers to stand on the platform while the car is in motion is reasonable and proper, and a passenger who violates the rule with knowledge of it does so at his peril. McCauley *v.* Tennessee Coal, Iron & Railroad Co., 93 Ala. 356, 9 So. 611, following Alabama G. S. R. Co. *v.* Hawk, 72 Ala. 112, cited in note in 21 L. R. A., N. S., 721.

§ 220. Acts by Permission or Direction of Carrier's Employees.

See post, "Acts by Permission or Direction of Carrier's Employees," § 230 (11).

A passenger on a street car has a right to rely upon the assurance of safety implied from an invitation to alight from the car at a point where it was stopped after the passenger had signified his desire to alight. Mobile Light & R. Co. *v.* Walsh, 146 Ala. 295, 40 So. 560.

Defendant's train, instead of coming to a full stop at a station, as it should have done, merely slackened its speed to the rate of two miles an hour, and the conductor cried, "All aboard," whereupon plaintiff attempted to board the train. While plaintiff was in such a position that a sudden and unexpected increase of speed would place him in great danger, the conductor, with full knowledge of plaintiff's position, caused the train to suddenly start forward, whereby plaintiff was injured. Held, that plaintiff could recover for his injuries, though his negligence contributed to the accident, since the actions of defendant invited him into the danger. Montgomery & E. Ry. Co. *v.* Stewart, 91 Ala. 421, 8 So. 708, cited in note in 21 L. R. A. 356.

Obvious Danger.—Where, an adult passenger leaves a moving train, under the advice or direction of the conductor, he can not recover for injuries received as a result where such advice or direction is so opposed to common prudence as to make it an obvious act of recklessness or folly. South & N. A. R. Co. *v.* Schaufler, 75 Ala. 136, cited in note in 21 L. R. A. 362.

Whether or not it is negligence in a passenger to step off a moving train at the invitation of the conductor depends upon the further inquiry as to whether or not the train was going at such speed as to render the attempt obviously hazardous. Highland Ave., etc., R. Co. *v.* Winn, 93 Ala. 306, 9 So. 509, cited in note in 38 L. R. A. 790.

§ 221. Negligence as to Incidental Dangers.

Remaining in Unheated Car.—A passenger can not recover foı illness caused by failure to heat the coach, if his contributory negligence proximately caused the injury, and the passenger's failure to protect himself from unnecessary cold or provide sufficient clothing may or may not be contributory negligence according to the circumstances. Southern Ry. Co. *v.* Harrington, 166 Ala. 630, 52 So. 57, cited in note in 26 L. R. A., N. S., 1059. See post, "Pleading," § 226.

Since a postal clerk is required by act of congress to remain in the mail car while on duty, he is not prima facie guilty of contributory negligence precluding recovery for illness by remaining in the car knowing that it is so insufficiently heated as to be uncomfortable. Southern R. Co. *v.* Harrington, 166 Ala. 630, 52 So. 57, cited in note in 26 L. R. A., N. S., 1059.

§ 222. Acts in Emergencies.

See post, "Proximate Cause of Injury," § 223; "Acts in Emergencies," § 230 (12).

Apparent Danger.—"As said by Chief Justice Black in Railroad Co. *v.* Aspell, 23 Pa. 147, 62 Am. Dec. 323: 'If, therefore, a person should leap from the car under the influence of a well-grounded fear that a fatal collision is about to take place, his claim against the company for the injury he may suffer will be as good as if the same mischief had been done by the apprehended collision itself.' This doctrine is fully recognized in this state. Central, etc., R. Co. *v.* Forshee, 125 Ala. 199, 27 So. 1006; 1 Shear. & R. Neg., § 84; 7 Am. & Eng. Enc. Law, pp. 399, 400." Selma St., etc., R. Co. *v.* Owen, 132 Ala. 420, 31 So. 598, 601.

Where a passenger was injured while attempting to leave a moving street car which apparently was about to collide with a locomotive, the fact that the danger was only apparent did not make her action in leaving the car amount to contributory negligence. Selma Street & Suburban Ry. Co. *v.* Owen, 132 Ala. 420, 31 So. 598.

A complaint in an action for injuries alleged that, just as defendant's street car on which plaintiff was a passenger went onto a railroad crossing, the driver turned to plaintiff and exclaimed. "The train is right on us!" whereupon plaintiff looked and saw an engine coming at a high rate of speed, and, it appearing that a collision was imminent, she attempted to jump off, and was injured by falling. There was in fact no collision. Held, that the complaint made a sufficient case of apparent necessity for plaintiff to leave the moving car. Selma Street & Suburban Ry. Co. *v.* Owen, 132 Ala. 420, 31 So. 598.

A passenger who was injured by jumping from a moving street car which was about to be run over by a locomotive was under no duty to notify the driver that she wished to alight. Selma Street & Suburban Ry. Co. *v.* Owen, 132 Ala. 420, 31 So. 598.

Care Required of Passenger.—In an action for injuries received by a passenger while attempting to leave a moving street car which apparently was about to collide with a locomotive, the refusal to give an instruction that if plaintiff acted contrary to the way an ordinarily prudent person would have acted, and this conduct contributed to the injury, she could not recover, was error, where the subject of such instruction was not covered by any other instruction in the case. Selma Street & Suburban Ry. Co. *v.* Owen, 132 Ala. 420, 31 So. 598, cited in note in 30 L. R. A., N. S., 275.

§ 223. Proximate Cause of Injury.

See post, "Questions for Jury," § 230.

Riding on Platform.—In an action for injuries to a passenger, some witnesses testified that, when the street car had slowed up nearly to a standstill, the passenger attempted to alight, and by a sudden jerk of the car was thrown down. Other witnesses testified that the passenger was thrown from the platform after the car had started, and while it was going six or eight miles an hour. It was admitted that the passenger was negligently riding on the steps or platform in violation of the rules. Held, that a charge that such negligence, alone, would not defeat a recovery, unless it proximately contributed to the injury, was proper. Birmingham Railway & Electric Co. *v.* James, 121 Ala. 120, 25 So. 847.

Where a train, which was slowing up as it neared a street crossing, suddenly, with a jerk, increased its speed, so as to throw off a passenger attempting to alight at such street, who had gone on the platform steps preparatory to alighting, the passenger's want of ordinary care in standing on such steps does not bar his recovery, if it did not contribute to the accident. Watkins *v.* Birmingham Railway & Electric Co., 24 So. 392, 120 Ala. 147, 43 L. R. A. 297.

Where a person who has been riding on the platform of a railroad car, in violation of the company's rule, is injured by the backing of the car after he has gotten off, there is no such causal connection between his violation of such rule and the injury suffered as will preclude him from bringing an action against the railroad company for negligence. Gadsden & A. U. Ry. Co. *v.* Causler, 97 Ala. 235, 12 So. 439, following Western Railway *v.* Mutch, 97 Ala. 194, 11 So. 894, cited in note in 37 L. R. A., N. S., 265, 266.

Acts in Emergency.—Where the negligence of a street car driver in driving onto a railroad crossing without stopping to look for trains seemed about to result in a collision, and a passenger, in endeavoring to escape from the car, was injured by a fall, the driver's negligence was the proximate cause of the injury. Selma Street & Suburban Ry. Co. *v.* Owen, 31 So. 598, 132 Ala. 420.

§ 224. Willful Injury by Carrier's Employees.

See post, "Willful Injury by Carrier's Employees," § 230 (13).

In a passenger's action for injuries, contributory negligence and assumption of risk were not defenses to the counts which alleged that the injuries were due to the wantonness of the company's servants or agents. Carlisle *v.* Central, etc., R. Co. (Ala.), 62 So. 759; Birmingham R., etc., Co. *v.* Jung, 161 Ala. 461, 49 So. 434, 436.

§ 225. Contributory Negligence as Ground of Defense.

§ 226. —— Pleading.

Necessity of Pleading—Unheated Car—Insufficient Clothing.—In an action by a railroad mail clerk for damages by illness because of a railroad company's failure to heat the mail car in which plaintiff worked, defendant could not rely on plaintiff's contributory negligence in wearing insufficient clothing unless it was pleaded. Southern Ry. Co. *v.* Harrington, 52 So. 57, 166 Ala. 630.

Necessity of Denying Negligence.—An electric railway company's plea of contributory negligence to a passenger's complaint for injury was not bad for failing to deny the negligence charged by him. Birmingham Ry., Light & Power Co. *v.* Yates, 53 So. 915, 169 Ala. 381.

Sufficiency of Plea—In General.—In an action for injuries to a passenger while attempting to board a street car, a plea of contributory negligence, which fails to set out the constituents of the contributory negligence, is insufficient. Birmingham R., etc., Co. *v.* Selhorst, 165 Ala. 475, 51 So. 568.

Same—Awaiting Transportation—Standing Near Track.—Where a complaint against a railroad company alleged that plaintiff's intestate went to a regular station for receiving and discharging passengers, and while standing on the platform, waiting for a train, he was struck by a projection from a passing freight train, knocked under the train, and killed, a plea that he was guilty of negligence contributing proximately to his injury, in that he negligently took a position too near to the passing train, is no answer to the complaint, as it does not negative the fact that he was standing on the platform, where defendant's servants were accustomed to receive and discharge passengers, or charge him with knowledge of the projection. Metcalf *v.* St. Louis, etc., R. Co., 156 Ala. 240, 47 So. 158.

Same—Negligence in Boarding Car.—A plea setting up contributory negligence, for that "plaintiff negligently boarded or negligently attempted to board said car," is demurrable as too general, because not setting out the manner in which he boarded or attempted to board it. Birmingham Ry., Light & Power Co. *v* Lee, 45 So. 292, 153 Ala. 79.

Same—Standing in Car.—In a street car passenger's action for injuries, alleged to have been caused by a violent jerk as she was preparing to alight, pleas, alleging that while she was going from her seat to the door of the car, the car was in motion, that it was her duty to exercise reasonable care to support herself, but that she negligently failed to exercise such care, and that while standing in the aisle, or on the platform, while the car was in motion, she negligently failed to support and maintain herself in a standing position, were insufficient, since they were susceptible of the construction that she failed to make use of the external supports afforded, but failed to show facts, such as age or physical infirmity, requiring such precautions. Birmingham R., etc., Co. *v.* Gonzalez (Ala.), 61 So. 80.

Same—Riding on Platform—Rules—Notice.—A plea of contributory negligence of a passenger, injured in alighting from an electric car, which alleges that she was guilty of negligence proximately contributing to her injuries, in that she rode on the platform in violation of a rule published in the car in such a way that she could have seen it, is insufficient as failing to show notice of the rule and causal connection between its violation and the injury. Birmingham Ry., Light & Power Co. *v.* Girod, 51 So. 242, 164 Ala. 10.

Same—Negligence in Alighting.—In an

action against a street railway company for injuries received by a passenger on alighting from a car, a plea attempting to set up contributory negligence by alleging that when the car stopped the lights from the car shone for ten or twelve feet on either side of the track, and that the plaintiff could have seen the alleged lumber and debris before he stepped thereon by the exercise of ordinary and reasonable care, is defective in not alleging that the plaintiff failed to exercise ordinary and reasonable care, or that he saw the lumber. Montgomery St. Ry. *v.* Mason, 32 So. 261, 133 Ala. 508.

A plea, in an action against a railway company for the death of a passenger, which alleges that decedent was guilty of contributory negligence, in that he alighted from a moving train in the nighttime without requesting the train to stop, is bad, because requiring the jury to find that decedent was guilty of contributory negligence in alighting while the train was in the slightest motion, though the motion was such as to involve the risk a man of ordinary prudence would take under the circumstances. Kansas City, M. & B. R. Co. *v.* Matthews, 39 So. 297, 142 Ala. 298.

The plea, in an action for injury to a passenger from the sudden starting of the train while she was on the car platform, preparatory to alighting, alleging that in the nighttime plaintiff had gone on the steps of the car while it was going too rapidly for a woman to attempt to alight, that she had nothing in her hand, and could easily have held the railing of the car, and, had she done so, the sudden starting of the car without warning would not have thrown her off, is good. Southern Ry. Co. *v.* Hundley, 44 So. 195, 151 Ala. 378, cited in note in 21 L. R. A., N. S., 721.

In an action for injuries to a passenger while alighting from one of defendant's cars, defendant pleaded that plaintiff was herself guilty of contributory negligence in that she negligently attempted to alight from the car while it was moving at a rate of speed exceeding five miles per hour, with her hands incumbered with bundles, and that she was injured in such attempt, and would not have been injured had she used one of her hands as any reasonably prudent person would have done, and also in that she negligently attempted to alight without using her hands as she might have done and thereby avoided the injury, and as any reasonably prudent person would have done, and in negligently attempting to alight from the car while it was moving. Held, that both of such pleas disclosed facts to which the law attached the conclusion that plaintiff was guilty of negligence proximately contributory to her injury, and were not demurrable. Birmingham R., etc., Co. *v.* Mindler, 3 Ala. App. 444, 57 So. 113.

It not being necessarily negligence for a passenger to alight from a moving car, even by stepping in the opposite direction to the movement of the car, a plea of contributory negligence in so doing, which does not show the speed of the car, is insufficient. Birmingham Ry., Light & Power Co. *v.* Dickerson, 45 So. 659, 154 Ala. 523, cited in note in 30 L. R. A., N. S., 271, 272.

Same Willful Injury.—Where a count in a complaint in an action for injuries to a passenger charged simple negligence, it was error to sustain demurrers to pleas setting up contributory negligence as an answer to the count, on the ground that the pleas were interposed to a count for willfulness or wantonness. Birmingham R., etc., Co. *v.* Wright, 153 Ala. 99, 44 So. 1037.

Issues Provable.—Where a complaint claimed that plaintiff's intestate was killed by being struck by a projection from a passing freight train while he was standing on a platform, waiting for a passenger train, contributory negligence in attempting to get onto the freight train was provable under the plea of the general issue. Metcalf *v.* St. Louis, etc., R. Co., 156 Ala. 240, 47 So. 158.

In an action against a railroad company for personal injuries resulting from stepping from a passenger coach onto a defective footstool, where the defendant averred that plaintiff negligently stepped on the stool after discovering its condition, evidence that plaintiff did not discover the condition of the stool in time to avoid stepping on it was relevant on the issue of contributory negligence. Atlanta & B. Air Line Ry. *v.* Wheeler, 46 So. 262, 154 Ala. 530.

§ 227. —— Presumptions and Burden of Proof.

Riding on Platform.—That a street car passenger was riding on the platform when injured in a collision raises a presumption of contributory negligence, so as to require him to show in an action for resulting injuries that his position there did not contribute to his injury. Alabama City, G. & A. Ry. Co. *v.* Ventress, 54 So. 652, 171 Ala. 285.

Knowledge of Ordinance—Place of Stopping.—A passenger on a street car which was moving to the west pulled the bell rope, and then attempted to alight on the east side of the street, where the car by ordinance was prohibited from stopping. In an action to recover for personal injuries, held, that plaintiff was presumed to know the ordinance prohibiting cars from stopping until they crossed the street. North Birmingham St. R. Co. *v.* Calderwood, 89 Ala. 247, 7 So. 360.

§ 228. —— Admissibility of Evidence.

Declarations Made by Persons Leaping from Car to Avoid Injury.—The plaintiff having received his injuries by leaping from the car, while others who remained inside were not hurt, it is proper for him to prove that others besides himself did the same, and also their declarations at the time of their reason for so doing, to show the reasonableness of his conduct and to avoid the charge of contributory negligence. Mobile, etc., R. Co. *v.* Ashcraft, 48 Ala. 15.

Decedent's Knowledge of Surroundings.—Evidence as to the surroundings at the place of the injury and decedent's familiarity or lack of it therewith held admissible. Louisville & N. R. Co. *v.* Dilburn (Ala.), 59 So. 438.

Circumstances—Knowledge of Servants—Wanton Negligence.—Actual knowledge by a carrier's servants of the peril of a passenger, sufficient to render the carrier guilty of wanton negligence, so as to excuse contributory negligence, may be proved by circumstances from which such knowledge is a legitimate inference. Birmingham Ry., Light & Power Co. *v.* Jung, 49 So. 434, 161 Ala. 461.

§ 229. —— Sufficiency of Evidence.

Alighting between Stations—Assumption of Risk.—In an action for injury to a street car passenger, a plea that she assumed the risk by voluntarily and knowingly alighting between stations, appreciating the danger of doing so, was unsupported, where the evidence showed that the passenger, with the conductor's assistance, alighted from the car before she knew she was beyond her destination, or between that station and the next one. Melton *v.* Birmingham Ry., Light & Power Co., 45 So. 151, 153 Ala. 95.

§ 230. —— Questions for Jury.

§ 230 (1) In General.

Placing Hand in Door Jamb.—In an action against a carrier to recover for injuries to plaintiff's hand by having the car door shut on it by the conductor, it is a question for the jury whether plaintiff, in placing his hand on the door jamb, was guilty of contributory negligence. Louisville, etc., R. Co. *v.* Mulder, 149 Ala. 676, 42 So. 742.

Carrying Past Destination—Failure to Notify Conductor.—In an action against a carrier for carrying plaintiff beyond a flag station, her destination, whether plaintiff was negligent in not informing the conductor or flagman that she wished to get off there was for the jury. Louisville & N. R. Co. *v.* Seale, 55 So. 237, 172 Ala. 480.

§ 230 (2) Entering Conveyance in General.

See ante, "Entering Conveyance," § 214.

Failure to Grasp Handholds.—A party who gets onto the step of a street car before grasping the handholds on the body of the car and the platform, or either of them, and though, after being on the step, he catches the rear platform handhold with the hand furthest from it, having to reach across his body to do so—his right hand being incapacitated by reason of packages he is carrying—is not negligent, as a matter of law, in such attempt to board the car. Birmingham Ry. & Electric Co. *v.* Brannon, 31 So. 523, 132 Ala. 431, cited in note in 30 L. R .A., N. S., 275, 277.

§ 230 (3) Boarding Moving Conveyance.

See ante, "Boarding Moving Car,"

§ 214 (3); post, "Alighting from Moving Conveyance," § 230 (8).

"It can not be affirmed as a universal proposition of law that it is negligence per se for a person to attempt to board a moving train. The age and physical condition of the person making the attempt, the rate of speed of the train, the nature of the car and of the place, and all the attendant facts and circumstances enter into the question; and while any one of these facts might possibly be sufficient to justify the conclusion of negligence as matter of law, ordinarily it is a question for the jury, the test being whether a person of ordinary care and prudence would, under similar circumstances have made the attempt. Montgomery, etc., R. Co. *v.* Stewart, 91 Ala. 421, 8 So. 708." North Birmingham St. R. Co. *v.* Liddicoat, 99 Ala. 545, 13 So. 18, 20; Birmingham R., etc., Co. *v.* Jung, 161 Ala. 461, 49 So. 434, cited in note in 22 L. R. A., N. S., 758, 30 L. R. A., N. S., 971.

It is not necessarily negligent to attempt to mount a slowly moving street car. Birmingham Ry., Light & Power Co. *v.* Lee, 45 So. 292, 153 Ala. 79; Birmingham Electric Ry. Co. *v.* Clay, 108 Ala. 233, 19 So. 309; Birmingham R., etc., Co. *v.* Brannon, 132 Ala. 431, 31 So. 523, cited in note in 30 L. R. A., N. S., 275, 277. See note in 30 L. R. A., N. S., 227, 271, 275.

§ 230 (4) Conduct While in Transit in General.

See, ante, "In Transit," § 215.

Failing to Take Seat.—Where an injury to a street car passenger was alleged to have resulted from defendant's negligence in starting the car with a sudden and unusual jerk, plaintiff was not guilty of contributory negligence as a matter of law in failing to take her seat before the car started, though she had time to do so and there were vacant seats. Cutcliff *v.* Birmingham Ry., Light & Power Co., 41 So. 873, 148 Ala. 108.

Riding on Engine—Willful Injury.—Where plaintiff left his place on the car where it was customary for persons having passes to ride, and, at the request of the fireman, stepped on the engine, and was at work cleaning the headlight when the injury was received, it was for the jury to say whether plaintiff's negligence proximately contributed to his injury, and whether, if it did, his negligence was overcome by the wanton negligence of defendant's servants; and a charge which ignores the inquiry whether plaintiff's contributory negligence was overcome was properly refused. Brown *v.* Scarboro, 97 Ala. 316, 12 So. 289.

§ 230 (5) Riding on Platform.

See ante, "Riding on Platform," § 216 (2).

Plaintiff was riding on the front platform of a street car, and, while passing around a curve, was thrown from the car. He testified that the rear platform was crowded, and he had to get on the front; that he had to stay there because the car seemed full. There was evidence for defendant that there was ample room to stand inside the car. Held, that an instruction was proper which authorized the jury to find plaintiff free from negligence in riding on the front platform if there was a reasonable necessity, real or apparent, for his doing so. Highland Ave. & B. R. Co. *v.* Donovan, 94 Ala. 299, 10 So. 139, cited in note in 12 L. R. A., N. S., 831, 833, 24 L. R. A. 710.

Whether a passenger, injured by being thrown from the platform by a lurch of the train, was negligent in being on the platform, held under the evidence for the jury. Central of Georgia Ry. Co. *v.* Brown, 51 So. 565, 165 Ala. 493.

A passenger, whose hand was injured by having the car door shut on it, is not as a matter of law guilty of contributory negligence in disobeying a notice forbidding passengers to stand on the platform, where the train was not in motion and he was in the act of entering the car after being stopped on the platform by the conductor. Louisville, etc., R. Co. *v.* Mulder, 149 Ala. 676, 42 So. 742.

Where a passenger on a street car, which was so crowded that he could not enter the car proper, stood on a projection outside of the vestibule, and was injured owing to a car in the rear of that on which he was being carried riding up onto the rear of such car owing to the breaking of a defective coupling, the question whether plaintiff was guilty of contributory negligence which proximately contributed to his injury was one for the jury. Birmingham Ry., Light & Power Co. *v.* Bynum, 36 So. 736, 139 Ala. 389.

A charge that a passenger, riding on the platform of an electric car without supporting herself with either hand, is guilty of contributory negligence, is properly refused. Birmingham R., etc., Co. *v.* Girod, 164 Ala. 10, 51 So. 242.

§ 230 (6) Leaving Conveyance in General.

See ante, "Leaving Conveyance," § 218.

In an action against a street railroad company for injuries to a passenger who fell while alighting, evidence held to require submission to the jury of the question whether the passenger was guilty of contributory negligence. Mobile Light & R. Co. *v.* Walsh, 40 So. 559, 146 Ala. 290.

Stepping on Defective Footstool.—In an action against a railroad company for personal injuries received in stepping from a passenger coach onto a defective footstool, the question whether plaintiff was negligent in stepping on the stool as she did, and whether it was the proximate cause of the injury was for the jury. Atlanta & B. Air Line Ry. *v.* Wheeler, 46 So. 262, 154 Ala. 530.

Alighting Backwards.—A passenger, alighting from a car which had stopped, is not negligent as a matter of law because she attempts to alight with her back in the direction in which the car was going; she having the right to assume that the car would remain stationary until she had alighted. Birmingham Ry., Light & Power Co. *v.* Handy (Ala.), 39 So. 917.

§ 230 (7) Preparing to Leave Conveyance before It Stops.

See ante, "Preparing to Leave Conveyance before It Stops," § 218 (2).

It is not negligent in law for a passenger to take, with ordinary care, a position on the steps of a car preparatory to alight, nor for him to attempt to alight from a train moving so slowly, that it would not appear dangerous to do so, to a man of ordinary prudence. The question of negligence vel non should be submitted to the jury. Birmingham R., etc., Co. *v.* James, 121 Ala. 120, 25 So. 847, 851; Watkins *v.* Birmingham R., etc., Co., 120 Ala. 147, 24 So. 392, cited in note in 21 L. R. A., N. S., 716.

Whether a passenger was guilty of negligence in going upon the running board of the car preparatory to alighting, while it was in motion, was a question for the jury. Armstrong *v.* Montgomery St. Ry. Co., 26 So. 349, 123 Ala. 233, cited in note in 10 L. R. A., N. S., 356.

For a passenger to leave a car and take a position on the platform steps preparatory to alighting while the car is still in motion, is not negligence per se; a trainman, just after announcing the near approach to H., having called, "All out for H." Southern Ry. Co. *v.* Roebuck, 31 So. 611, 132 Ala. 412, cited in note in 21 L. R. A., N. S., 719.

Ordinarily, it is not as a matter of law, contributory negligence for a passenger, when the street car is slowing up to allow him to alight, to go upon the platform or steps before the car has actually stopped. Birmingham Railway & Electric Co. *v.* James, 25 So. 847, 121 Ala. 120.

Where a street car slows up to allow a passenger to alight, and he is injured by a sudden jerk thereof, his attempting to alight before the car actually stops can not be held contributory negligence, as matter of law, but it is for the jury to determine, though the passenger carried a small bundle under one arm (which, however, was not shown to have incumbered him), whether he was negligent or not. Birmingham Railway & Electric Co. *v.* James, 25 So. 847, 121 Ala. 120.

In an action for injury to a passenger, from the sudden starting of the train while she was on the car platform preparatory to alighting, the plea alleged that in the night time plaintiff had gone on the steps of the car while it was going too rapidly for a woman to attempt to alight, that she had nothing in her hand and could easily have held the railing of the car, and had she done so the sudden starting of the car without warning would not have thrown her off. Held, that the question of contributory negligence was for the jury. Southern Ry. Co. *v.* Hundley, 44 So. 195, 151 Ala. 378, cited in note in 21 L. R. A., N. S., 721.

Plaintiff was injured while alighting

from a train, drawn by a dummy which ran along certain streets, stopping at crossings for passengers. There was evidence that, as it approached a certain street, a signal from a person taking passage having been given, the train was brought nearly to a stop, and that thereupon plaintiff, with her left hand holding a bundle and her right the hand railing, descended to the steps of the car platform about the time the other passenger got aboard, and as she reached the bottom step, and was about to step from the train, its speed was quickened with a jerk, whereby she was thrown to the ground. Plaintiff testified that the dummy stopped regularly at the crossing. Held, that the question of plaintiff's contributory negligence was for the jury. Sweet *v.* Birmingham Ry. & Electric Co., 33 So. 886, 136 Ala. 166.

§ 230 (8) Alighting from Moving Conveyance.

See ante, "Alighting from Moving Train or Car in General," § 218 (4).

Whether the plaintiff, under the evidence, was guilty of contributory negligence in alighting from a moving car, is a question for the jury, and not one of law for the court. Birmingham R., etc., Co. *v.* James, 121 Ala. 120, 25 So. 847; Watkins *v.* Birmingham R., etc., Co., 120 Ala. 147, 24 So. 392, 34 L. R. A. 297; Birmingham R., etc., Co. *v.* Willis, 143 Ala. 220, 38 So. 1016; Birmingham R., etc., Co. *v.* Harden, 156 Ala. 244, 47 So. 327; Louisville, etc., R. Co. *v.* Dilburn (Ala.), 59 So. 438; Ricketts *v.* Birmingham St. R. Co., 85 Ala. 600, 5 So. 353; Hunter *v.* Louisville, etc., R. Co., 150 Ala. 594, 43 So. 802, 9 L. R. A., N. S., 848. See note in 30 L. R. A., N. S., 273.

"While there are some cases which hold that the act of a passenger in voluntarily leaving a car while it is in motion constitutes contributory negligence, the better doctrine, and that sustained by the great weight of authority, is that such conduct on the part of the passenger is not negligence per se. There may be, it is true, exceptional circumstances attending the attempt thus to alight, such as the great speed of the train, the age or infirmity of the passenger, or his being incumbered with bundles or children, or other facts which render the attempt so obviously dangerous that the court may, where the testimony is undisputed, declare as a matter of law that the passenger's conduct was reckless and negligent. But ordinarily it is for the jury to say whether he acted as a reasonably cautious and prudent man would act under like circumstances." Watkins *v.* Birmingham R., etc., Co., 120 Ala. 147, 24 So. 392, 394; Southern R. Co. *v.* Morgan, 171 Ala. 294, 54 So. 626; Birmingham R., etc., Co. *v.* Girod, 164 Ala. 10, 51 So. 242, 245; Montgomery, etc., R. Co. *v.* Stewart, 91 Ala. 421, 8 So. 708; Central R., etc., Co. *v.* Miles, 88 Ala. 256, 6 So. 696; Highland Ave., etc., R. Co. *v.* Burt, 92 Ala. 291, 9 So. 410, 13 L. R. A. 95; Birmingham R., etc., Co. *v.* Lee, 153 Ala. 79, 45 So. 292, 293. See note in 21 L. R. A., N. S., 716.

In an action against a street railway company for injury to an alighting passenger, an instruction to find for defendant if plaintiff alighted while the car was in motion held erroneous. Birmingham Ry., Light & Power Co. *v.* Lide (Ala.), 58 So. 990.

In an action for personal injuries to a passenger, it appeared that when the train stopped at the station, which the conductor knew to be plaintiff's destination, the latter promptly left his seat, for the purpose of getting off; but the train started before he reached the door, and was in motion when he reached the platform, where he was told by a porter that the train would not stop longer. He knew there was a bell rope, to signal the engineer to stop the train; but he did not pull the rope, as the train was moving so slowly that he thought there was no danger, and, accordingly, descended the steps, holding to the side rail with his left hand, and, stepping off in the direction the train was moving, sustained the injuries complained of. The speed of the train at the time was variously stated at from 2½ or 3 to 4 or 5 miles an hour. Held, that the question of plaintiff's negligence was for the jury. Central Railroad & Banking Co. *v.* Miles, 88 Ala. 256, 6 So. 696.

In an action for the death of a railroad passenger killed while alighting from a train after it had stopped at his destination and was moving again, held, under the evidence, a question for the jury whether he proceeded with ordinary prudence to reach the step or was in the act of stepping, and whether it was contributory negligence for him to attempt to alight while the cars were moving. Dilburn *v.* Louisville & N. R. Co., 47 So. 210, 156 Ala. 228, cited in note in 22 L. R. A., N. S., 742.

Where the complaint, in an action for injuries to a passenger in alighting from a car, predicated a recovery on a jerk, resulting in the throwing of plaintiff to the ground, charges pretermitting consideration of this issue, and assuming that as matter of law it is negligence to alight from a moving car, were properly refused. Birmingham R., etc., Co. *v.* Harden, 156 Ala. 244, 47 So. 327.

It is not negligence in all cases, as a matter of law, for a passenger to step off a moving car at right angles therewith, since the speed of the car must materially influence the determination of the question. Birmingham R., etc., Co. *v.* Harden, 156 Ala. 244, 47 So. 327, cited in note in 30 L. R. A., N. S., 271.

A passenger, incumbered with small bundles, who steps from an electric car in the dark, while it is slowing up to stop and is barely moving, is not guilty of contributory negligence as a matter of law. Birmingham R., etc., Co. *v.* Girod, 164 Ala. 10, 51 So. 242.

Whether a passenger, attempting to alight from a train when in motion after he has been cautioned against making the attempt, was negligent, was for the jury. Kansas City, M. & B. R. Co. *v.* Matthews, 39 So. 207, 142 Ala. 298, cited in note in 22 L. R. A., N. S., 743.

Whether a passenger was negligent in attempting to alight on his left foot from a train moving to his left at a rate of one or two miles an hour was for the jury. Kansas City, M. & B. R. Co. *v.* Matthews, 39 So. 207, 142 Ala. 298.

Whether a person familiar with a depot was negligent in alighting from a train in the nighttime, in a dark place, when the train had just started from the depot and was moving at the rate of one or two miles an hour, was for the jury. Kansas City, M. & B. R. Co. *v.* Matthews, 39 So. 207, 142 Ala. 298, cited in note in 30 L. R. A., N. S., 271, 272.

§ 230 (9) Alighting from Conveyance at Place Other than Station or Platform.

See ante, "Alighting at Place Other Than Station or Platform," § 218 (3).

Whether a passenger alighting from a freight train at a place other than the place where passengers usually alight from passenger trains acted with due diligence was for the jury. Southern Ry. Co. *v.* Burgess, 42 So. 35, 143 Ala. 364.

A passenger on a freight train was injured while alighting. The point where the caboose stopped was not the usual place for passengers to alight from passenger trains. The evidence showed that the carrier was in the habit of allowing passengers to alight from freight trains where the caboose was not usually carried to the platform for passengers to alight from passenger trains. Held, that whether the passenger was justified in assuming that the place where the caboose stopped was the place where the carrier expected that she would alight was for the jury. Southern R. Co. *v.* Burgess, 143 Ala. 364, 42 So. 35.

If the conductor of the street car was not in his place on the car, and the train stopped anywhere on the street in apparent response to the pulling of the bell cord by plaintiff, and she, believing reasonably that the stop was made for the purpose of allowing her to alight, was injured in attempting to do so, the question of contributory negligence is one of fact for the jury. North Birmingham St. R. Co. *v.* Calderwood, 89 Ala. 247, 7 So. 360.

§ 230 (10) Crossing Tracks after Alighting from Car.

See ante, "Crossing Other Tracks," § 218 (9).

In an action against a street railway company for injury to an alighting passenger injured while crossing a track, whether he was guilty of contributory negligence held, under the evidence, a question for the jury. Birmingham Ry., Light & Power Co. *v.* Landrum, 45 So. 198, 153 Ala. 192.

§ 230 (11) Acts by Permission or Direction of Carrier's Employees.

See ante, "Acts by Permission or Direction of Carrier's Employees," § 220.

It seems to be settled by the authorities, that if the act advised to be done is one, in the doing in which the danger would not be apparent to a person of reasonable prudence, and the passenger acts under the influence of such advice, given by the conductor or manager in the line of his ordinary duties, it becomes the province of the jury to say how far the plaintiff's negligence may be excused. South, etc., R. Co. *v.* Schaufler, 75 Ala. 136.

Whether a customer in a store, who was directed by the proprietor to take the elevator, and, in response to such direction, walked rapidly in a dim light to the open door of the elevator shaft, and, without stopping to see that the elevator was not in place, stepped into the shaft, and fell, was guilty of contributory negligence, was a question for the jury; and it was immaterial that he might have ascended to the floor which he wished to reach by a stairway. Morgan *v.* Saks, 38 So. 848, 143 Ala. 139, cited in note in 2 L. R. A., N. S., 745, 756, 758.

§ 230 (12) Acts in Emergencies.

See ante, "Acts in Emergencies," § 222.

A woman may be justified in attempting to alight from a dummy street railroad train in motion, where she is in fear of being pushed off by the conductor, and the question in such a case is for the jury. Highland Ave., etc., R. Co. *v.* Winn, 93 Ala. 306, 9 So. 509, cited in note in 21 L. R. A. 361.

§ 230 (13) Willful Injury by Carrier's Employees.

See ante, "Willful Injury by Carrier's Employees," § 224; "Conduct While in Transit in General," § 230 (4).

Evidence in an action against a carrier for injuries to a passenger held sufficient to make the question of the wanton conduct of defendant's servants excusing contributory negligence, one for the jury. Birmingham R., etc., Co. *v.* Jung, 161 Ala. 461, 49 So. 434.

§ 230 (14) Proximate Cause of Injury.

See ante, "Proximate Cause of Injury," § 223.

In an action against a street railway company for injury to an alighting passenger claimed to have been caused by sudden starting of the car, whether the injury was caused proximately by the company's negligence or by her own contributory negligence held, under the evidence, jury questions. Birmingham R., etc., Co. *v.* Lide (Ala.), 58 So. 990.

§ 231. —— Instructions.

§ 231 (1) In General.

In a passenger's action for injuries, instructions held properly refused, because they did not hypothesize such a state of facts and circumstances as would authorize the legal conclusion that plaintiff was contributorily negligent. Southern R. Co. *v.* Morgan (Ala.), 59 So. 432.

§ 231 (2) Awaiting and Seeking Transportation.

In an action for personal injuries received by a passenger while waiting at a flag station, held that, under the evidence, defendant was not entitled to the general charge on the theory of contributory negligence. Louisville & N. R. Co. *v.* Glasgow (Ala.), 60 So. 103.

§ 231 (3) Conduct in Transit.

Riding on Platform.—In a street car passenger's action for injuries in a collision with a railroad train at a crossing, a requested charge that if the jury believed that plaintiff was negligent in riding on the street car platform and his negligence contributed to his injury, they must find for defendant, unless the injury was wanton, willful, or intentional, was properly refused as misleading; it being open to the construction that the jury must find for defendant if plaintiff's conduct contributed even remotely, to the injuries. Alabama City, G. & A. Ry. Co. *v.* Ventress, 54 So. 652, 171 Ala. 285.

§ 231 (4) Leaving Conveyance in General.

In an action against a railroad company for personal injuries resulting from stepping from a passenger coach onto a defective footstool, an instruction which pretermits plaintiff's discovery or knowledge of the way the stool was adjusted in time to stop was properly refused, where there was evidence that she had no such knowledge. Atlanta, etc., Railway *v.* Wheeler, 154 Ala. 530, 46 So. 262.

In an action for injuries to a passenger while alighting from a car through an alleged negligent jerk thereof, an instruction that, if plaintiff got off the car at a place where it was not usual to discharge passengers, it was not negligence for defendant's servants to cause the car to suddenly jerk, was properly refused, since, if not otherwise bad, it hypothesized the departure of plaintiff from the car, whereas, if so, the jerk of the car could not be negligent under such circumstances. Birmingham Ry., Light & Power Co. *v.* Harden, 47 So. 327, 156 Ala. 244.

§ 231 (5) Alighting from Moving Conveyance.

In passenger's action for injuries, instruction held properly refused, because by the use of the word "thereupon" for "therefrom" it predicated contributory negligence on the passenger's going on the platform or steps while the car was in motion, instead of on his stepping from the car while in motion. Southern R. Co. *v.* Morgan (Ala.), 59 So. 432.

In an action against a street car company, where the plaintiff claimed that she was injured by the starting of the car while she was attempting to alight, and the company denied that negligence, and claimed that plaintiff attempted to alight from the car while it was in motion, instructions that if she attempted to alight from the car while in motion between stations, she assumed the risk and could not recover, and that, while it was not negligence, as a matter of law, for a passenger to alight from a slowly moving street car, yet, if her alighting was the proximate cause of the injury, she can not recover, are correct, merely presents defendant's theory, and not the issue of contributory negligence. Tannehill *v.* Birmingham R., etc., Co. (Ala.), 58 So. 198.

In an action against a street railway company for injury to an alighting passenger, an instruction to find for the company if plaintiff alighted while the car was in motion was erroneous as preventing recovery if the car was in motion at all, however slight, when plaintiff alighted, and perhaps even though the motion began after she began to alight. Birmingham R., etc., Co. *v.* Lide (Ala.), 58 So. 990.

In a passenger's action for injuries, an instruction that, if plaintiff attempted to get off the train while in motion, after being warned not to do so, the jury should find for defendant was properly refused, since it did not require a finding that the passenger's act in this respect was a proximately contributing cause of his injury. Southern R. Co. *v.* Morgan (Ala.), 59 So. 432.

Where a passenger was killed while alighting after the train had started to leave his destination, requests to charge with reference to his contributory negligence, failing to hypothesize knowledge on his part that he had arrived at his destination, or that the train had stopped there, or that he was notified of the train's arrival, or failing to require that such negligence, if any, was the proximate cause of his death, etc., were properly refused. Louisville, etc., R. Co. *v.* Dilburn (Ala.), 59 So. 438.

Instruction that, if a passenger stepped from the train while in motion and was injured, he could not recover was properly refused, where the evidence would have justified a finding that he involuntarily stepped from the car. Southern R. Co. *v.* Morgan (Ala.), 59 So. 432.

An instruction, in an action against a railway company for the death of a passenger attempting to alight in the nighttime from a slowly moving train just starting after stopping at a depot, that no one has a right to leap from a moving train in the nighttime because he is carried beyond his destination, is properly refused, as abstract and argumentative. Kansas City, M. & B. R. Co. *v.* Matthews, 39 So. 207, 142 Ala. 298.

§ 231 (6) Acts in Emergencies.

In an action for injuries to a passenger attempting to board a passenger train, an instruction that "one brought into sudden danger by the wrong of another is not expected to act with coolness and deliberation as moved a reasonable man under ordinary circumstances" was erroneous for attempting to predicate, as a matter of law, lack of coolness and deliberation upon merely "sudden danger," however slight that danger might have been. Alabama City, G. & A. Ry. Co. *v.* Bates, 43 So. 98, 149 Ala. 487.

§ 231 (7) Proximate Cause of Injury.

See ante, "Conduct in Transit," § 231 (3); "Alighting from Moving Conveyance," § 231 (5).

In an action against a railroad company for personal injuries, an instruction to find for defendant if plaintiff was negligent in the slightest degree in any way set up in any of the defendant's pleas, which contributed to any of her alleged injuries, was properly refused for failure to postulate that plaintiff's negligence proximately contributed to her injury. Atlanta, etc., Railway *v.* Wheeler, 154 Ala. 530, 46 So. 262.

A requested instruction, in an action against a railway company for the death of a passenger, that, if in attempting to alight from the train he failed to do what a prudent man would have done, he was guilty of contributory negligence barring a recovery, is properly refused for failure to hypothesize that his negligence contributed to his injury. Kansas City, M. & B. R. Co. *v.* Matthews, 39 So. 207, 142 Ala. 298.

In an action for injuries to a passenger, claimed to have been caused by a sudden jerk of the car, throwing him off, a charge that, if the injury resulted from the passenger's riding on the platform, he could not recover, was properly refused, as it did not hypothesize such riding as the proximate cause. Birmingham Railway & Electric Co. *v.* James, 25 So. 847, 121 Ala. 120.

§ 231 (8) Conformity to Pleadings and Issues.

In an action for personal injuries, where there is some evidence of contributory negligence, it is proper to refuse to charge that if plaintiff was injured while a passenger on defendant's railroad, caused by the negligence and want of care of defendant's employees having control of the cars, defendant would be liable though the jury may be satisfied that the negligence was not gross, but slight, in its character, as the charge ignores the question of plaintiff's negligence. Thompson *v.* Duncan, 76 Ala. 334.

In an action for personal injuries, where there is some evidence of contributory negligence, it is proper to refuse to charge that if plaintiff was a passenger on defendant's railroad car, and was injured by an accident occurring while such passenger, and if such accident could have been avoided by the use of very great care and diligence by those in charge of the movement of the car, then defendant would be liable, as the charge ignores the question of contributory negligence. Thompson *v.* Duncan, 76 Ala. 334.

(F) EJECTION OF PASSENGERS AND INTRUDERS.

§ 232. Liability of Carrier for Acts of Employees.

Scope of Employment—Brakeman.—Where it is a brakeman's duty to put off persons not entitled to ride on the train, it being for him to determine who is not entitled to ride, his acts in putting persons off the train, whether rightfully or wrongfully, are within the scope of his employment. Southern Ry. Co. *v.* Wideman, 24 So. 764, 119 Ala. 565.

The fact that a brakeman had no instruction from the conductor to beat plaintiff does not free the company from liability for the willful injury inflicted by the brakeman in the attempted discharge of his duty of ejecting plaintiff from the train. Alabama G. S. R. Co. *v.* Frazier, 93 Ala. 45, 9 So. 303.

§ 233. Failure to Procure Ticket or Pay Fare.

§ 234. —— In General.

Refusal to Pay Fare.—Where a passenger on a railroad train refuses with profane and obscene language to pay his fare, it is the right and duty of the conductor to eject him at a reasonably safe time and place. Louisville & N. R. Co. *v.* Johnson, 92 Ala. 204, 9 So. 269, cited in notes in 26 L. R. A. 130, 15 L. R. A., N. S., 961.

Mislaid Ticket.—Where a passenger does not request additional time to search for his ticket which he has mislaid, the conductor may expel him at once, without giving him additional time. Louisville & N. R. Co. *v.* Mason, 4 Ala. App. 353, 58 So. 963.

It is the duty of a passenger of a train to surrender his ticket when called upon by the conductor, but he is entitled to reasonable time within which to produce it before being expelled, and, if he has lost or mislaid it and requests additional time to enable him to find it, the conductor should not expel him before giving him reasonable time to search for it, but, if he does not make such request, the conductor may expel him when he fails to produce the ticket within a reasonable time. Louisville, etc., R. Co. *v.* Mason, 4 Ala. App. 353, 58 So. 963.

§ 235. —— Defective or Invalid Tickets.

§ 235 (1) Failure to Comply with Conditions of Ticket.

Where a railroad ticket, conditioned that the same shall be void unless signed, dated, and stamped by a certain designated agent of the company, is presented for passage, showing a noncompliance with such condition, the conductor may, in default of payment of fare, expel the passenger in a proper manner. McGhee *v.* Reynolds, 23 So. 68, 117 Ala. 413.

A carrier issuing a round trip ticket which must be validated to be good for the return trip need not carry the passenger on the return ticket which has not been validated, and, where she refuses to pay fare, she may be ejected. Central of Georgia Ry. Co. *v.* Bagley, 55 So. 894, 173 Ala. 611.

Continuous Passage—Amount of Fare—Reasonableness of Rule.—A regulation of a railroad whereby a passenger who has forfeited a ticket providing for a continuous passage, but who has been carried almost to his destination before the mistake is discovered, is required to pay fare not only for the remaining distance, but for that which has already been traveled since the forfeiture of the ticket, is a reasonable regulation; and the passenger can not recover on being ejected for refusal to pay such fare. Manning *v.* Louisville & N. R. Co., 95 Ala. 392, 11 So. 8, 16 L. R. A. 55, cited in note in 31 L. R. A., N. S., 995, 16 L. R. A. 53.

§ 235 (2) Time Limit of Ticket Expired.

Plaintiff purchased a railroad ticket limited to the date indorsed thereon; and, though he did not read the indorsement, he knew that the company was selling such tickets, and his attention had been called to similar indorsements. On the conductor's refusal to accept said ticket, because it was out of date, plaintiff declined to pay fare, permitted himself to be led to the platform and gently ejected, after which he re-entered the car, and paid the fare to his destination. Held, that plaintiff had no cause of action against the company. McGhee *v.* Drisdale, 111 Ala. 597, 20 So. 391.

Connecting Trains—Where Passenger Accepted on First Train.—Plaintiff purchased a return ticket limited to expire May 20, 1900, and on that day presented himself for return passage at defendant's station in time to take a train scheduled to leave before midnight. The train was delayed, and did not leave until the next day. Plaintiff was accepted as a passenger by the conductor, and when it left the station his ticket was punched to a junction point, where plaintiff was required to change cars. On account of the delay, the connecting train had left the junction when plaintiff arrived, and the conductor of the next train refused to accept plaintiff's ticket, and ejected him, on the ground that the ticket had expired. Held, that the limit on the ticket fixed the latest time for commmencing, and not for completing the return journey, and that, as plaintiff was entitled to rely on defendant's train schedule, defendant was liable for such ejection. Morningstar *v.* Louisville & N. R. Co., 33 So. 156, 135 Ala. 251.

§ 235 (3) Effect of Mistake of Employee Issuing Ticket.

Plaintiff purchased a ticket over defendant's road to H., a station ten miles beyond B. S., and entered a freight train which was not authorized to carry passengers beyond B. S. He testified that the ticket agent directed him to take it. He was informed by the conductor, after starting, that he could not be carried beyond B. S., but he declined to leave the train, as the conductor offered him an opportunity to do, and declared that he would go on. He surrendered his ticket, which the conductor canceled, and rode to B. S., where he was required by the conductor to leave the train. Held, that defendant was not liable, unless the ticket agent gave the direction testified to by plaintiff. South & N. A. R. Co. *v.* Huffman, 76 Ala. 492.

§ 235 (4) Effect of Collateral Agreement with Ticket Agent.

Permit to Ride on Freight.—A passenger bought a ticket, and requested the ticket agent to procure him a permit to ride on a freight train, which the agent promised to do, and give the permit to the conductor. The agent procured the permit, but neglected to give it to the conductor, in consequence of which plaintiff was ejected from the train. Held, that plaintiff could recover of the carrier. Louisville & N. R. Co. *v.* Hine, 25 So. 857, 121 Ala. 234.

Plaintiff obtained a ticket of defendant's agent, who promised to procure plaintiff a permit to ride on a freight train, and to give it to the conductor, but the agent neglected to do so. In an action for plaintiff's ejection, held, that defendant's rule prohibiting passengers from riding without permits, and plaintiff's knowledge of the rule, were no defense. Louisville & N. R. Co. *v.* Hine, 25 So. 857, 121 Ala. 234.

§ 235 (5) Persons on Wrong Train or Carried Past Destination.

See ante, "Carrying to and Stopping at Destination," § 169; post, "Manner of Ejection in General," § 243.

§ 235 (6) Conclusiveness of Ticket as between Passenger and Conductor.

As to the right of a conductor to eject a passenger who is found riding on a train, on a ticket void on its face, it is proper to say, and we may announce, without elaboration, as the proper conclusion sustained by the great weight of authority, that the ticket is the sole and conclusive evidence of the conductor of a passenger's right, as such, to be on the train; that the conductor has the right to rely upon the express language of the contract as expressed in the ticket, and when it is void on its face, in default of payment of fare he may deny the right of the passenger to ride on such ticket, and expel him in a proper manner from the train. 4 Elliott, R. R., § 1594; Mechem's Hutch. Carr., § 580j; Manning *v.* Louisville, etc., R. Co., 95 Ala. 392, 11 So. 8; Alabama, etc., R. Co. *v.* Carmichael, 90 Ala. 19, 8 So. 87; South, etc., R. Co. *v.* Huffman, 76 Ala. 492; McGhee *v.* Reynolds, 117 Ala. 413, 23 So. 68, 71.

§ 236. —— Extra Fares or Charges.

Changing Cars.—Where a carrier has a rule which requires the collection of fares on each car of the train by the separate conductors on said cars, and that passengers changing cars must pay a second fare, a passenger, after taking passage on one car and paying his fare, is not authorized to take another car and refuse to pay a second fare when demanded, after being informed of the rule, although insufficient accommodations are provided on the first car. Birmingham Ry., Light & Power Co. *v.* Yielding, 46 So. 747, 155 Ala. 359.

Higher Rate for Cash Fare—Reasonableness.—A regulation of a street railway company requiring a higher rate where cash is paid the conductor than is charged for a ticket is not reasonable, and furnishes no justification for ejection of a passenger tendering only the price of a ticket, where he is taken on at a place where tickets are not for sale, though they are for sale at a station 1,000 feet away. Kennedy *v.* Birmingham Ry., Light & Power Co., 35 So. 108, 138 Ala. 225, cited in note in 24 L. R. A., N. S., 758.

"All the cases agree that carriers of passengers may require persons to purchase tickets before taking passage on their cars, and to this end may adopt a rule or regulation establishing a higher rate to be paid the conductor than the rate charged for a ticket. But to justify a discrimination in the rates, the carrier must provide the proper facility and accommodation for so purchasing the ticket. If the carrier fails to give the passenger a convenient and accessible place and an opportunity to buy his ticket before entering the car, the regulation is unreasonable and void, and is no defense to an action brought by the passenger for his ejection by the conductor after he has paid the ticket rate. 25 Am. & Eng. Ency. Law (1st Ed.) 1104-5; Redfield on Railways, 104, 105, and note; Elliott on Railroads, § 200." Kennedy *v.* Birmingham R., etc., Co., 138 Ala. 225, 35 So. 108, 109.

§ 237. —— Tender or Payment of Fare to Avoid Ejection.

Where a passenger's ticket was a proper one, but the conductor claimed otherwise and threatened to put him off the train, the passenger was not under any legal duty to pay fare to prevent his ejection. McGhee & Fink *v.* Cashin (Ala.), 40 So. 63.

The fact that, while plaintiff was being wrongfully ejected on the ground that she had not paid her fare, another passenger offered to pay the fare and plaintiff would not permit it, did not preclude plaintiff from recovering for all injuries and damages suffered after her refusal to permit such payment. Birmingham Ry., Light & Power Co. *v.* Lee, 45 So. 164, 153 Ala. 386, cited in note in 31 L. R. A., N. S., 996, 34 L. R. A., N. S., 282, 284.

§ 238. Disobedience of Carrier's Rules.

See ante, "Rules of Carrier," § 167; post, "Plea or Answer," § 253 (2).

Going from One Car to Another—Extra Fare—Notice of Rule.—Where a passenger goes from one street car to another after paying his fare, he may be ejected from the second car for refusing to again pay a fare, though when he entered the second car he did not know of the rule of the company requiring such payment; it being sufficient if he is informed of such rule and given an opportunity to pay the fare before being ejected. Birmingham Ry., Light & Power Co. *v.* Stallings, 45 So. 650, 154 Ala. 527.

Where, after plaintiff had paid his fare on a motor car, and gone to the trailer, and refused the demand of the conductor of the trailer for a second fare, he was informed of the carrier's rule that passengers must pay fare on the car on which they ride, and that he might return to the motor before he was ejected, a plea alleging such matters was not objectionable for failure to aver that plaintiff had knowledge of the rule before he boarded the car from which he was ejected. Birmingham Ry., Light & Power Co. *v.* McDonough, 44 So. 960, 153 Ala. 122, 13 L. R. A., N. S., 445.

§ 239. Disorderly Conduct.

Under Code 1896, § 3457, providing that conductors of trains may eject passengers when disorderly, or when using profane, vulgar, or obscene language, it was immaterial to the right of a conductor to eject a passenger for using obscene language whether his conduct was in fact offensive to other passengers. Nashville, C. & St. L. Ry. *v.* Moore, 41 So. 984, 148 Ala. 63.

"From the evidence in this record, the conduct of deceased was such, as for which the conductor would have been justified in ejecting him from the train at a proper place and under suitable conditions, having reasonable regard to the safety of his life and limb. Johnson *v.* Louisville, etc., R. Co., 104 Ala. 241, 16 So. 75; Louisville, etc., R. Co. *v.* Johnson, 108 Ala. 62, 19 So. 51, 31 L. R. A. 372." Nash *v.* Southern R. Co., 136 Ala. 177, 33 So. 932, 933.

§ 240. Intruders and Trespassers.

See post, "Manner of Ejection in General," § 243.

§ 241. Acts Constituting Ejection.

Coercion Through Fear.—Evidence in an action against a railway company for wrongfully ejecting a passenger, showing that the conductor told the passenger that it was dangerous for her with her infant children to go on the train to a station, may be sufficient to show that she was coerced by the conductor to leave the train, for coercion may result from fear. Louisville & N. R. Co. *v.* Quinn, 39 So. 616, 145 Ala. 657.

§ 242. Place of Ejection.

A conductor who requires a passenger to disembark from the train because of the insufficiency of her ticket and her refusal to pay the fare must know of the perils of the place where he requires the passenger to disembark. Central of Georgia Ry. Co. *v.* Bagley, 55 So. 894, 173 Ala. 611.

§ 243. Manner of Ejection in General.

"It is uniformly held that the right of the carrier to expel trespassers from its trains must be exercised with due regard for the safety, the life, and health of the person removed, and this, whether he be a bare trespasser, or was mislead into his wrongful position." Waldrop *v.* Nashville, etc., Railway (Ala.), 62 So. 769, 771.

Ejection While Train in Motion.—Where a passenger is on a wrong train by mistake, the company is liable if its conductor forcibly ejects him while the train is in motion. Louisville & N. R. Co. *v.* Whitman, 79 Ala. 328, cited in note in 40 L. R. A., N. S., 1007, 1051.

§ 244. Use of Force, and Resistance.

Excessive Force.—Though a carrier has the lawful right to eject a passenger, it is answerable in damages for any unnecessary force or violence inflicted upon him by its agent acting within the scope of their authority. Birmingham R., Light & Power Co. *v.* Yielding, 46 So. 747, 155 Ala. 359.

Code 1896, § 3457, invests conductors of passenger trains with the powers of police officers, and authorizes them to eject passengers who are disorderly or use profane, vulgar, or obscene language, using only such force as may be necessary to accomplish the removal. Held, that pleas attempting to justify the ejection of a passenger, which set up disorderly conduct on his part, but which did not aver that the conductor used only such force as was necessary to accomplish his removal, were bad. Moore *v.* Nashville, C. & St. L. Ry., 34 So. 617, 137 Ala. 495.

§ 245. Negligence in Ejecting Person under Disability.

Intoxicated Person.—A conductor of a train, ejecting an intoxicated person, must see that, considering the degree of intoxication, he is exposed to no unnecessary peril. Johnson *v.* Louisville & N. R. Co., 104 Ala. 241, 16 So. 75.

In an action for the death of plaintiff's intestate, it appeared that that deceased was a passenger on one of defendant's night trains; that he was very drunk, refused to pay his fare, and was thereupon ejected; that it was very dark and rainy, and that he was put off in a cut in the road, from which there was no way to escape except up or down the track, along the sides of which was room for a person to walk; that the track was ballasted with mixed stone, and rough; that at the south end were cattle guards which could be passed only by walking on the track; and that at this point deceased was struck by a train following close after the one from which he was ejected. Held, that defendant, in ejecting deceased in such a place was chargeable with negligence. Louisville & N. R. Co. *v.* Johnson, 108 Ala. 62, 19 So. 51.

The company is not liable for the death of a passenger rightfully ejected, when run over by another train after he was ejected, though he was intoxicated, where his intoxication was not sufficient to destroy consciousness, and the place where he was put off, with which he was familiar, was dangerous only to persons unnecessarily going on the track. Louisville & N. R. Co. *v.* Johnson, 92 Ala. 204, 9 So. 269, cited in note in 19 L. R. A. 328.

Aged Female Passenger.—A carrier in ejecting an aged female passenger must consider her safety, and not eject her at a dangerous place. Central of Georgia Ry. Co. *v.* Bagley, 55 So. 894, 173 Ala. 611.

§ 246. Readmission after Ejection.

Plaintiff was wrongfully ejected from defendant's train, but was invited by the conductor to re-enter the train, which the passenger refused to do until the train was backed to where he was standing. Held, that plaintiff could not recover his damage resulting from delay in his journey. Louisville & N. R. Co. *v.* Hine, 25 So. 857, 121 Ala. 234.

§ 247. Proximate Cause of Injury.

See post, "Contributory Act or Negligence of Person Ejected," § 248.

Selling Ticket to Place Quarantined.—The wrong committed by a ticket agent in giving a ticket to Y. only to a passenger buying a ticket to I., the agent knowing that yellow fever was prevalent near Y., and the danger and inconvenience of going about there, is the proximate cause of the passenger's suffering on account thereof; he being put off at Y., and not having money to buy a ticket to his destination. Kansas City, M. & B. R. Co. *v.* Foster, 32 So. 773, 134 Ala. 244.

§ 248. Contributory Act or Negligence of Person Ejected.

See ante, "Negligence in Ejecting Person under Disability," § 245; post, "Questions for Jury," § 256.

As to contributory negligence in general, see ante, "Contributory Negligence of Person Injured," IV, E.

Failure to Examine Ticket—Proximate Cause.—In an action against a railroad company for personal injury caused by wrongfully and violently ejecting plaintiff for a train, in which it appeared that plaintiff had asked for a ticket to his desired destination and been given one to the intermediate point at which he was ejected, negligence of plaintiff in not looking at his ticket when he purchased it, and in failing to purchase a ticket from the place where he was ejected to his destination, was too remote to constitute a defense. Southern Ry. Co. *v.* Bunnell, 36 So. 380, 138 Ala. 247, cited in note in 43 L. R. A., N. S., 586.

Place of Alighting.—A passenger, in good faith believing that her ticket was good, on being required to leave the train because of her failure to present a good ticket or pay fare, could assume that the place selected by the conductor for her to alight with the baggage carried by her, was safe. Central of Georgia Ry. Co. *v.* Bagley, 55 So. 894, 173 Ala. 611.

Walking on Track.—In an action against a railroad company by a passenger to recover damages for being wrongfully ejected from defendant's train, where the evidence shows that after the plaintiff was ejected he could not reach his destination on foot without having to wade a creek, except by traveling over defendant's track, the fact that he did walk along the defendant's track and cross its trestle over the creek in question does not make the plaintiff a trespasser; and a charge which assumes that the plaintiff was a trespasser is properly refused. Southern Ry. Co. *v.* Lynn, 29 So. 573, 128 Ala. 297, followed in Southern R. Co. *v.* Lynn, 129 Ala. 660, 30 So. 908. See note in 12 L. R. A., N. S., 359.

§ 249. Companies and Persons Liable.

§ 250. —— Connecting Carriers.

The ticket agent of one carrier is the agent of a connecting carrier, so as to make the latter liable for his act in giving a passenger a ticket to Y. only, when buying a ticket to I., both points being on latter company's road, but I. being more distant, so that the passenger was put off at Y.; the latter company having recognized tickets sold to points on its line by the former company, and received from it its proportional part of the price of such tickets, and having received said passenger's ticket for transportation to Y. Kansas City, M. & B. R. Co. *v.* Foster, 32 So. 773, 134 Ala. 244, cited in note in 31 L. R. A., N. S., 8.

§ 251. Actions for Wrongful Ejection.

§ 252. —— Nature and Form.

If a passenger holding a ticket is ejected from a train, his action against the carrier may be either in tort or on the contract. Louisville, etc., R. Co. *v.* Hine, 121 Ala. 234, 25 So. 857.

Where plaintiff was ejected from defendant's street car, while a passenger thereon, because the transfer tendered by him to defendant's conductor had been so negligently issued by the conductor of one of defendant's other cars as to be worthless, the fact that plaintiff might have sued for a breach of the contract of carriage did not deprive him of the right to sue in case for the negligence. Montgomery Traction Co. *v.* Fitzpatrick, 43 So. 136, 149 Ala. 511, 9 L. R. A., N. S., 851.

§ 253. —— Pleading.

§ 253 (1) Declaration, Complaint, or Petition.

In General.—In an action against a railroad company by a passenger for the alleged wrongful ejection from one of the defendant's trains, a complaint is sufficient and states a good cause of action which avers that the defendant was operating a railroad upon which passenger trains were run; that the plaintiff purchased from the defendant, for a reward, a ticket which entitled him to be carried as a passenger on one of the defendant's trains; and that after having purchased said ticket he boarded the train, to be carried to a station on the defendant's road, and, although the plaintiff tendered to the conductor on said train the ticket so purchased, the said conductor, in breach of the duty owing the plaintiff as a passenger, wrongfully and forcibly ejected him from the train. McGhee *v.* Cashin, 30 So. 367, 130 Ala. 561.

In an action against a carrier for wrongful ejection of plaintiff from its car, a count alleging that defendant's agent, acting within the scope of his authority, so negligently conducted himself in and about the carriage of plaintiff as defendant's passenger that as a proximate consequence thereof plaintiff was ejected from said train, was not subject to demurrer for failure to show the facts wherein defendant's servants negligently conducted themselves, and wherein plaintiff's ejectment was wrongful. Birmingham R., etc., Co. *v.* Yielding, 155 Ala. 359, 46 So. 747.

Where, in an action against a carrier for ejecting plaintiff from its car, a count alleged that as a proximate consequence of the ejection the plaintiff was wrenched and made sick and sore, the allegations of damages were sufficient as against demurrer. Birmingham R., etc., Co. *v.* Yielding, 155 Ala. 359, 46 So. 747.

A complaint in an action for injuries to a passenger, which alleges that defendant was a carrier, and that on the date named plaintiff was a passenger, and that a servant while acting as conductor or motorman assaulted plaintiff by pointing a pistol at him and compelling him to leave the car, states a cause of action as against a demurrer on the grounds that it does not appear that the assault was wrongful, and that there was not sufficient causal connection between the wrong and injuries and the assault. Birmingham R., etc., Co. *v.* Tate (Ala.), 61 So. 32.

Ejection from Station.—A complaint for damages caused by being forcibly ejected from a railroad station, which alleges that the plaintiff was in the station on the invitation of the agent to wait until he bought his ticket, is sufficient, even though it does not allege that it was a reasonable time before his train was due. Louisville, etc., R. Co. *v.* Kay (Ala.), 62 So. 1014.

Defective or Invalid Ticket.—In an action against a railroad company, a count of the complaint averred that plaintiff purchased a round-trip ticket from the defendant, which provided that, before it was good for return passage, the holder had to be identified as the original purchaser before the defendant's station agent at the place to which the plaintiff was going, who would, at that time, sign, date, and stamp the ticket as said agent; that plaintiff was carried as a passenger from the place of the purchase of the ticket to her point of destination, and, wishing to return, she presented the ticket to the defendant's said agent for his official stamp and signature, and offered to prove her identity as the contract on the ticket required her to do, in order to use the ticket for the return passage; but that, nowithstanding it was the said station agent's duty to sign, date, and stamp the said ticket, he refused to do so, and, by reason of said ticket not being so dated, stamped, and signed, the plaintiff was ejected from defendant's train while attempting to return to the place from which she started by the use of such ticket. Held, that said count stated a good cause of action for the alleged refusal of the defendant's agent to stamp, date, and sign the plaintiff's return-trip ticket, so as to make it available for her passage, but that it did not set forth a cause of action for the plaintiff's ejection from the train. McGhee *v.* Reynolds, 129 Ala. 540, 29 So. 961.

A complaint in an action against a railroad company alleged that plaintiff paid for a ticket to a certain station, but that the ticket agent of defendant wrongfully and negligently failed to give him a ticket to that station, but gave him one to an intermediate station, and that upon arriving at such intermediate station the conductor unlawfully and wrongfully and forcibly ejected plaintiff from the train, injuring him. It was further alleged that the injuries were by reason of the failure and negligence of the defendant's ticket agent to furnish to plaintiff the ticket for which he had applied, and in furnishing a ticket to an intermediate point, and by reason of the failure of defendant to convey the plaintiff safely to his destination. Held, that the paragraph contained two causes of action. Southern R. Co. *v.* Bunnell, 138 Ala. 247, 36 So. 380.

Defective or Invalid Transfer.—A complaint alleging that, owing to the negligence of one of defendant's conductors in issuing a worthless transfer, plaintiff, a passenger, was ejected from another of defendant's cars by the conductor thereof on tendering to the latter such transfer, sufficiently designated the conductor, without naming him. Montgomery Traction

Co. *v.* Fitzpatrick, 43 So. 136, 149 Ala. 511, 9 L. R. A., N. S., 851. See note in 24 L. R. A., N. S., 1180, 34 L. R. A., N. S., 282.

A complaint against a street railway company, averring that plaintiff was ejected from a car through a conductor's negligence in incorrectly punching a transfer given plaintiff to show his right to ride on the car from which he was ejected, sufficiently avers the negligence charged. Birmingham R. Light & Power Co. *v.* Turner, 154 Ala. 542, 45 So. 671.

Excessive Force.—In such a case, a count of the complaint containing the allegations as above set out, relating to the purchase of the ticket and the conditions contained therein, and the efforts to have same signed, dated, and stamped, and the refusal of the defendant's station agent to sign, date, and stamp said ticket, and his statement that the ticket was all right, and she could use it for return passage, then averred that after being so instructed by defendant's agent she boarded one of the defendant's trains as a passenger, and without any knowledge that she had no right to ride on said train by the use of said ticket, and while on said train, without any resistance on her part, she was rudely and forcibly ejected by defendant's conductor from said train, and "that said force and violence upon the part of said conductor was unnecessary to eject her from said train; that she had offered no resistance to his demands for her to leave the train, but had only besought him to allow her to remain; * * * that, notwithstanding all this, the said conductor wantonly, willfully, or intentionally forcibly ejected the plaintiff as aforesaid," causing the injuries complained of. Held, that said count states a cause of action in trespass, and claims a recovery for damages for the alleged excessive force used by the conductor in ejecting plaintiff from the train; and that, therefore, all of the averments in said count as to plaintiff presenting the ticket to the defendant's station agent, and the latter's statement and conduct in that connection, are foreign to the trespass sued on, and should, upon defendant's motion, have been stricken from said count. McGhee *v.* Reynolds, 129 Ala. 540, 29 So. 961.

Ejection from Moving Train.—A complaint in an action against a carrier, charging the wrongful ejection of plaintiff's intestate from a moving train and averring his consequent injury and death, states a good cause of action for the wrongful ejection of the intestate, and, as it does not charge the defendant with inflicting the injury, it is not necessary to aver a consciousness of the result of the wrongful ejection. Louisville & N. R. Co. *v.* Perkins, 144 Ala. 325, 39 So. 305, cited in note in 40 L. R. A., N. S., 1008, 1050.

Place of Ejection.—A complaint in an action for injuries to a passenger which alleges that the conductor negligently required the passenger to leave the train at a place highly dangerous for her to do so on his refusal to accept her ticket, and which sets forth the facts as to the dangers of the place for an old and infirm person to disembark, states a cause of action as against a demurrer. Central, etc., R. Co. *v.* Bagley, 173 Ala. 611, 55 So. 894.

Amendment of Complaint.—A complaint in an action against a street railway by a passenger, alleging that plaintiff was wrongfully ejected from defendant's street car by defendant's conductor, motorman, etc., was properly amended by adding a count alleging that, while a passenger on one of defendant's cars, plaintiff applied to defendant's conductor for a transfer to another car, and was given a transfer so negligently torn off that it could not be used, and that by reason thereof the conductor of the other car ejected plaintiff therefrom. The complaint as amended was not demurrable, since plaintiff, while not entitled to recover on the ground of a wrongful ejection, had a right of action for the breach of the contract to carry, or for defendant's negligence in not issuing a proper transfer. Montgomery Tract. Co. *v.* Fitzpatrick, 149 Ala. 511, 43 So. 136.

§ 253 (2) Plea or Answer.

Conductor as Police Officer.—A plea setting up in substance merely that the conductor at the time he was ejecting the passenger was acting as a police officer of the state was insufficient. Moore *v.* Nashville, C. & St. L. Ry., 34 So. 617, 137 Ala. 495.

Violation of Rules.—Where a violation of a carrier's rule is relied on as a defense to an action for ejection of a passenger, the rule must be brought forward by special plea. Birmingham R., etc., Co. *v.* McDonough, 153 Ala. 122, 44 So. 960, 13 L. R. A., N. S., 445. See ante, "Disobedience of Carrier's Rules," § 238.

In an action for ejection of a street car passenger from a trailer for his refusal to pay fare on it after he had paid fare on the motor, a plea alleging a rule prohibiting passengers from riding on different cars of the same train without paying fare on each car was not objectionable for failure to show that reasonable accommodations were furnished plaintiff on the car on which he paid his fare; the carrier's failure to do so, if any, being matter for replication. Birmingham R., etc., Co. *v.* McDonough, 153 Ala. 122, 44 So. 960, 13 L. R. A., N. S., 445.

In an action against a carrier for wrongful ejection of a passenger, a plea attempting to justify the ejection by alleging that plaintiff changed cars during the journey and refused to pay a second fare after changing was insufficient on demurrer, where it failed to show a rule of defendant requiring collection of a second fare in such cases. Birmingham R., etc., Co. *v.* Yielding, 155 Ala. 359, 46 So. 747.

Plaintiff alleged that defendant railway company was accustomed to carry pasengers on a certain freight train; that he purchased a ticket to ride thereon, and was assured by the ticket agent that he could ride thereon; and that he was wrongfully ejected by the conductor. Defendant pleaded that the coach on which plaintiff attempted to ride was being transported in connection with a freight train, but not for the transportation of passengers; that defendant's rules prohibited the carrying of passengers on such train; that the conductor had no knowledge of the alleged statements of the ticket agent; and that the ticket was unlimited, and could be used on any passenger train. Held, that such pleas did not deny the allegations of the complaint, nor were they good as pleas in confession and avoidance, and a demurrer thereto was properly sustained. Nashville, C. & St. L. Ry. Co. *v.* Bates, 133 Ala. 447, 32 So. 589.

In an action against a railroad company by a passenger to recover damages for the plaintiff's alleged wrongful ejection from a train of the defendant, where the complaint alleges that the plaintiff offered the conductor an "unlimited ticket," which plaintiff had bought from the defendant's agent, and that the conductor refused to receive said ticket, and then wrongfully and rudely ejected plaintiff, pleas of the defendant which aver that, at the time the ticket was purchased by the plaintiff and presented to the conductor, the defendant had a rule that such ticket should be good for a continuous passage, beginning on the day of sale, which rule was known to plaintiff, and, further, that notice of such rule was indorsed upon said ticket, but which did not negative the disuse or waiver of the rule by the defendant in the sale of the ticket alleged in the complaint to have been unlimited, present an insufficient answer to the complaint, and are subject to demurrer for failing to negative such disuse or waiver. Louisville & N. R. Co. *v.* Bizzell, 131 Ala. 429, 30 So. 777.

Tender of Worn Currency.—In an action against a street railroad company for ejection of a passenger, defendant's plea alleged that plaintiff tendered to the conductor a coin, as a fare, so worn that the conductor could not tell whether it had originally been a coin of the United States government or not, and that, when the conductor declined to receive the coin, plaintiff declined to pay his fare with any other money, and was ejected. Held that, irrespective of whether the plea was a good defense, it put in issue the condition of the coin. Mobile St. Ry. Co. *v.* Waters, 135 Ala. 227, 33 So. 42, cited in note in 35 L. R. A., N. S., 1031.

§ 253 (3) Replication.

Misplaced Ticket—Reasonable Time.—In an action by a passenger for his expulsion from a railroad train, the defendant's plea, averred that, when the conductor demanded of him his ticket or fare, plaintiff "refused" and "willfully failed" to present or tender any ticket or fare, and the conductor thereupon ejected him, and plaintiff's replication alleged that, when the conductor demanded his ticket or fare, he had misplaced his ticket in his clothing, and the conductor ejected him without giving him a reasonable time within which to produce the ticket. Held that, as the replication was in the nature of a confession and avoidance, it was insufficient, for, while the word "fail" at times is synonymous with "refuse," the word "refuse" here means to decline to accept, or reject, and the words "willfully fail" mean an intentional neglect, and so it does not show that plaintiff attempted to produce his ticket or notified the conductor that he had one, and requested reasonable time within which to search for his ticket, which was necessary before he could complain of his ejectment (citing 7 Words and Phrases, p. 631, and 8 Words and Phrases, p. 7468). Louisville, etc., R. Co. *v.* Mason, 4 Ala. App. 353, 58 So. 963.

§ 253 (4) Issues, Proof, and Variance.

See post, "Admissibility in General," § 254 (2).

Issues—Boisterous Conduct of Third Person.—In an action against a railroad company by a passenger to recover damages for being wrongfully ejected from the defendant's train where the only pleas interposed were that of the general issue, and a special plea setting up that the plaintiff was ejected on account of his boisterous conduct on the train, evidence relating to the boisterous conduct of other persons than the plaintiff, or showing that there was a subsequent difficulty between the conductor who ejected the plaintiff and the plaintiff, is wholly irrelevant and immaterial. Southern Ry. Co. *v.* Lynn, 128 Ala. 297, 29 So. 573, followed in Southern R. Co. *v.* Lynn, 129 Ala. 660, 30 So. 908.

Same—Conduct of Flagman Acting for Conductor.—A complaint in an action against a railroad company alleged that defendant's conductor wrongfully compelled the plaintiff, who had taken passage and paid his fare on one of defendant's trains, to leave the train at an intermediate station, and that in doing so the conductor was abusive, using language which was derogatory to his character for honesty, and which imported a charge that he was attempting to proceed on his journey without paying his fare. The evidence was that the conductor, after an altercation with the plaintiff as to whether the latter had paid his fare, determined upon putting him off, and directed the flagman to look after him. The flagman, in the presence of the conductor, and as part of the said altercation, told the plaintiff that he would have to pay his fare or they would put him off. The flagman testified that he was in the habit of helping the conductor take up tickets, and that he was authorized by the conductor to put off passengers when they would not pay their fare. Held that, as this evidence tended to show that the flagman was acting for the conductor, and in execution of the latter's orders, it was admissible in support of the allegation that the conductor himself had wrongfully compelled the plaintiff to leave the train; and although nothing was claimed on account of the abusive language of the flagman, and damages therefore could not be imposed on account of it, it was nevertheless admissible as a part of the res gestæ attending the ejection of the plaintiff. Alabama G. S. R. Co. *v.* Tapia, 94 Ala. 226, 10 So. 236.

Same—Receipt for Fare.—In an action against a railroad company by a passenger to recover damages for being wrongfully ejected from defendant's train, where the only pleas interposed were the general issue and a special plea setting up that the defendant was ejected on account of boisterous conduct, and the evidence showed that the plaintiff had paid his fare, and that in order for the plaintiff to reach his destination it was necessary for him to change cars from the mainline to the branch line, all question as to the duty of plaintiff, after having paid his fare from the place where he boarded the defendant's train on the main line to his destination to the conductor of the train on the main line, to obtain a check or other evidence of such payment from the conductor, is foreign to the issues pres nted in the pleadings, and evidence in reference thereto is inadmissible; and written charges requested by the defendant predicated upon the theory that it was plaintiff's duty to have gotten such check, or other evidence of payment, are properly refused. Such facts, to be available as a defense, should be presented under a proper plea. Southern Ry. Co. *v.* Lynn, 128 Ala. 297, 29 So. 573, followed in Southern R. Co. *v.* Lynn, 129 Ala. 660, 30 So. 908.

Same—Person under Disability.—The negligence of the conductor in leaving plaintiff on the platform after ejecting him from the car, knowing that he was so drunk as to be unable to take care of himself, not being counted on in the complaint, could not be made the basis of a recovery. Moore *v.* Nashville, C. & St. L. Ry., 137 Ala. 495, 34 So. 617, cited in note in 16 L. R. A., N. S., 197.

Where, in an action for injuries to a passenger required to disembark because her ticket was defective and because she refused a fare, the issues were the negligence of the carrier in requiring her to disembark at a dangerous place, and whether she was guilty of contributory negligence, the testimony that the passenger was old and infirm, that she was required to leave the train in the early morning before good daylight, that she carried a suit case, and that the conductor who saw her offered no assistance, that she left the car from the rear platform, and that the distance from the steps of the platform to the ground was between three and four feet, etc., was competent under the issues. Central, etc., R. Co. *v.* Bagley, 173 Ala. 611, 55 So. 894.

Same—Special Damages.—An averment of special damages in an action against a railroad company for wrongfully ejecting the plaintiff from one of its trains, in that it was necessary for him to telegraph his family and business associates of his whereabouts, does not apprise the defendant that plaintiff will attempt to prove that he had to send a telegraph to his brother to request him to attend to a matter of urgent business, which plaintiff's enforced delay prevented him from attending to in person. Alabama G. S. R. Co. *v.* Tapia, 94 Ala. 226, 10 So. 236.

Proof—Liability of Receivers.—In an action against receivers of a railroad company by a passenger to recover damages for the alleged wrongful ejection of the plaintiff from a train, where it is averred in the complaint that the defendants, as receivers, were operating a railroad upon which the said train was run, and that the plaintiff was ejected from the train by employees or agents of the defendants as such receivers, and the general issue and special pleas of contributory negligence are pleaded, in order for the plaintiff to recover he must prove the averments of the complaint that the defendants were receivers of and operated said road and had control thereof, and that the persons who ejected the plaintiff were in the employment of the defendants as such receivers. The plea of the general issue put these material averments in issue, and the fact that a special plea of contributory negligence was filed did not waive the necessity for proof which the plea of the general issue cast on the plaintiff. McGhee *v.* Cashin, 30 So. 367, 130 Ala. 561.

Same—When Servants Act Jointly.—Where plaintiff, a passenger on an electric car, alleged and proved that the ejection from the car was committed jointly by the conductor and motorman, it was not error to charge the jury to find for defendant if they believed from the evidence that the mortorman did not aid or assist in ejecting her. Bowie *v.* Birmingham Railway & Electric Co., 27 So. 1016, 125 Ala. 397, 50 L. R. A. 632.

Same — Misdirection and Ejection. — Plaintiff sued for damages for his wrongful and forcible ejection from a train which he had entered by misdirection of a station agent of the defendant. Held, that plaintiff could recover damages for the misdirection, although the proof did not sustain the allegation of forcible ejection. Alabama G. S. R. Co. *v.* Heddleston, 82 Ala. 218, 3 So. 53.

Variance—Moving Train.—Where a passenger sued a carrier for wrongful ejection from a train, and alleged that at the time the train was in motion, that allegation was mere aggravation of damages, not one material to the cause of action; and proof that the train was not in motion does not constitute material variance. Louisville, etc., R. Co. *v.* Penick (Ala.), 62 So. 965.

§ 254. —— Evidence.

§ 254 (1) Presumptions and Burden of Proof.

Improperly Punched Transfer.—In an action against a street railway company for ejecting a passenger who presented an improperly punched transfer, the burden was on him to show that the conductor on the first car was bound to issue a transfer to him to the car from which he was ejected. Birmingham Ry., Light & Power Co. *v.* Turner, 45 So. 671, 154 Ala. 542.

Failure to Show Ticket.—In an action by a passenger who was ejected from a railroad train, though he had a ticket, where the company defended on the ground that he failed to produce his ticket, the burden of proving that he intended to produce his ticket, and that he so notified the conductor, is on the plaintiff. Louisville, etc., R. Co. *v.* Mason, 4 Ala. App. 353, 58 So. 963.

§ 254 (2) Admissibility in General.

See ante, "Issues, Proof, and Variance," § 253 (4).

In General.—In an action against a railroad company for wrongfully ejecting plaintiff from the train before he reached the station for which he supposed he had purchased a ticket, evidence that plaintiff tried to get the conductor to lend him money to buy a ticket, and that plaintiff had only a few cents, was improperly admitted. Southern Ry. Co. *v.* Bunnell, 36 So. 380, 138 Ala. 247.

In an action against a railroad for wrongfully ejecting plaintiff from a car, testimony that on entering the car plaintiff went to his son, who was sitting down, and asked him to lend him fifteen cents; that cursing or profane language was used by others who were on the outside of the car; that after receiving the injuries plaintiff requested a witness to take care of him—was irrelevant. Moore *v.* Nashville, C. & St. L. Ry., 34 So. 617, 137 Ala. 495.

In an action against a railroad company for wrongfully ejecting plaintiff from its train before he reached the station for which he had attempted to purchase a ticket, defendant's conductor testified that the ticket he took up on one trip he usually took back on his next trip and sent them to another city. The ticket on which plaintiff rode was introduced in evidence by defendant. Held, that evidence that the conductor made no effort to obtain the return of the ticket which plaintiff used was outside the issues. Southern Ry. Co. *v.* Bunnell, 36 So. 380, 138 Ala. 247.

In an action against a street railroad for ejection of a passenger on the ground that fare tendered was not legal tender, an objection to a question to plaintiff as to where he got money to pay his fare after he was put off should have been sustained. Mobile St. Ry. Co. *v.* Watters, 33 So. 42, 135 Ala. 227, cited in note in 35 L. R. A., N. S., 1031.

Profane and Abusive Language.—"On the former appeal in this case it was ruled that evidence of the conductor's profane and abusive language to the plaintiff was relevant, and we see no reason now to depart from that ruling. The issues in this respect are the same as they were then. McGhee *v.* Cashin, 130 Ala. 561, 30 So. 367." S. C., 40 So. 63, 64.

Defective or Invalid Ticket.—In an action against a carrier for the ejection of a passenger by a conductor, who erroneously claimed that his ticket was not a proper one, there was no error in the admission of testimony of the plaintiff as to his exhibiting the ticket to other persons on the day he was ejected and after he had left the train. McGhee & Fink *v.* Cashin (Ala.), 40 So. 63.

Testimony of persons to whom the ticket was exhibited, descriptive of the same, when taken in connection with other evidence tending to identify it as the same ticket offered by plaintiff, was not erroneous. McGhee & Fink *v.* Cashin (Ala.), 40 So. 63.

It was competent for plaintiff to show where the ticket had been since the day he was ejected; the identity of the ticket being unquestioned. McGhee & Fink *v.* Cashin (Ala.), 40 So. 63.

Where a conductor erroneously claimed that plaintiff's ticket was not a proper one, and ejected him from the train, but plaintiff, after the ejection, got upon the train and paid the cash fare to a point beyond the one to which his ticket read, it was proper to sustain an objection to a question to plaintiff as to how he happened to buy a ticket to the place to which the ticket in question read, instead of the place to which he paid a cash fare. McGhee & Fink *v.* Cashin (Ala.), 40 So. 63.

In an action against a railway company for wrongfully ejecting plaintiff from its train before he had reached the station for which he had attempted to purchase a ticket, defendant's ticket agent at the station at which plaintiff purchased the ticket gave evidence tending to show that two tickets were called for to the point to which plaintiff desired to go, and that he made a mistake in issuing only one to that point. Held that evidence that he had made such mistakes before was inadmissible. Southern Ry. Co. *v.* Bunnell, 36 So. 380, 138 Ala. 247.

Character and Condition of Place.—Evidence is admissible to show the character and condition of the place where deceased was killed, the state of the weather, and the kind of night. Louisville, etc., R. Co. *v.* Johnson, 108 Ala. 62, 19 So. 51.

Res Gestæ.—Where one has purchased a ticket and takes passage upon a train operated upon a railroad, and the ticket on its face entitles him to be carried on the train on which he is riding, and he offers such ticket to the conductor, such person does not lose his character as a passenger by being ejected from the train by the conductor; nor is the conductor authorized, after such ejection to disregard any duty he owed such person as a passenger had he not been ejected; and abusive and insulting language used by a conductor towards such person while he was re-entering the train after his ejection for the purpose of continuing his journey constitutes part of the res gestæ of the ejection, and is admissible in evidence in an action to recover damages for being ejected from the train. McGhee *v.* Cashin, 130 Ala. 561, 30 So. 367.

On plaintiff's testimony, an assault on him by a brakeman in ejecting him from a train was willful and wanton, and without justification or palliation. According to defendant's evidence, it was committed under a reasonable apprehension of an immediate deadly attack by plaintiff on the conductor or brakeman. Held that, on the issues of fact thus presented, all that occurred and was said between plaintiff and the conductor and brakeman, and the language, manner, and conduct of the parties during the conversation just before and leading up to the assault, was competent as part of the res gestæ. Alabama G. S. R. Co. *v.* Frazier, 93 Ala. 45, 9 So. 303.

Cr. Code 1896, § 4345, providing that on the trial of the person for an assault, an assault and battery, or an affray, he may give in evidence any opprobrious words or abusive language used by the person assaulted at or near the time of the assault in extenuation or justification, has no application to an action for ejection of a passenger because of his alleged misconduct. Nashville, etc., Railway *v.* Moore, 148 Ala. 63, 41 So. 984.

§ 254 (3) Weight and Sufficiency.

In an action against a carrier for the wrongful ejection of a passenger, evidence considered, and held, that the trial judge should have granted defendant's motion for a new trial, on the ground that the verdict was contrary to the great weight of the evidence. Louisville & N. R. Co. *v.* Perkins, 144 Ala. 325, 39 So. 305.

§ 255. —— Damages.

See post, "Damages," § 257 (4).

As to place and sleeping cars, see post, "Actions for Injuries to or Ejection of Passenger," § 277.

§ 255 (1) Elements in General.

The measure of damages of a passenger, who, buying a ticket to one point, is given one to a less distant point, where he is ejected, is not confined to the mere cost of transportation between the two points. Kansas City, M. & B. R. Co. *v.* Foster, 134 Ala. 244, 32 So. 773.

Plaintiff, who was wrongfully ejected from defendant's freight train, was entitled to recover all damages proximately resulting from the wrong, including the expense and inconvenience to which he was put, and for humiliation and indignity suffered by him. Louisville & N. R. Co. *v.* Hine, 121 Ala. 234, 25 So. 857, cited in note in 12 L. R. A., N. S., 185.

Special Damages.—See ante, "Issues, Proof, and Variance," § 253 (4).

One wrongfully ejected from a street car may recover damages arising from his weak physical condition, drawn to the conductor's attention, and other damages proximately resulting from the wrong, including the expense and inconvenience to which he was put, and humiliation and indignity suffered. Birmingham R., etc., Co. *v.* Turner, 154 Ala. 542, 45 So. 671.

§ 255 (2) Fear, Humiliation, and Mental Suffering.

In an action against a carrier for wrongful ejection of a passenger, actual damages prayed for in the complaint include damages for wounded feelings and mental suffering. McGhee & Fink *v.* Cashin (Ala.), 40 So. 63.

Plaintiff, who was wrongfully ejected from defendant's train, can not recover damages for humiliation resulting from his being "guyed" about being put off, by persons who were not present when he was ejected, as such damages are too remote. Louisville & N. R. Co. *v.* Hine, 121 Ala. 234, 25 So. 857.

§ 255 (3) Aggravation, Mitigation and Reduction of Loss.

In an action against a railroad company, by a passenger, who, having purchased a ticket to travel on a freight train, by mistake entered a train which was not allowed to carry passengers beyond a station ten miles short of his destination, and, being so informed by the conductor upon presentation of his ticket, declined to leave the train, as he was offered an opportunity to do, and travelled to the station ten miles short of his destination, where he was required by the conductor to leave the train; a recovery can not be had for vindictive damages, if the conductor, in requiring him to leave the train, did not use any actual force to eject him, nor speak to him in a rude, rough, or angry manner. South, etc., R. Co. *v.* Huffman, 76 Ala. 492.

§ 255 (4) Exemplary Damages.

See ante, "Aggravation, Mitigation, and Reduction of Loss," § 255 (3).

Where the wrongful ejection of a passenger is accompanied by willfulness, exemplary damages may be awarded. Birmingham Ry., Light & Power Co. *v.* Lee, 153 Ala. 386, 45 So. 164.

Although plaintiff got on a train knowing that no passengers were allowed on it, and though it was the duty of the brakeman to put him off, still, if the latter, in the discharge of that duty, willfully assaulted and beat plaintiff, merely because he declined to get off while it was running at a rate of speed rendering the attempt hazardous, the company would be liable for punitive damages. Alabama G. S. R. Co. *v.* Frazier, 93 Ala. 45, 9 So. 303.

The use of abusive language in ejecting a prospective passenger from a station tends to show such circumstances of aggravation as to warrant the submission to the jury of the question of punitive damages. Louisville, etc., R. Co. *v.* Kay (Ala.), 62 So. 1014.

§ 255 (5) Inadequate or Excessive Damages.

Two hundred eighty-seven dollars was not an excessive recovery against a street railway company for wrongfully ejecting a passenger weakened by typhoid fever and compelled to walk home. Birmingham R., etc., Co. *v.* Turner, 154 Ala. 542, 45 So. 671.

§ 256. —— Questions for Jury.

See post, "Invading Province of Jury," § 257 (3).

Contributory Negligence.—Whether an aged female passenger, on being ejected from a train, was guilty of contributory negligence in disembarking at a place designated by the carrier's employees, is for the jury. Central, etc., R. Co. *v.* Bagley, 173 Ala. 611, 55 So. 894.

Awaiting Transportation—Reasonable Time.—Where the evidence is conflicting as to what was a reasonable time before a train was due to go to the station for the purpose of boarding it, the question of whether plaintiff went there more than a reasonable time before the train was due was for the jury. Louisville, etc., R. Co. *v.* Kay (Ala.), 62 So. 1014.

Safety of Place.—Whether a carrier justified in ejecting a passenger ejected her at a dangerous place, resulting in injuries to her, is for the jury. Central, etc., R. Co. *v.* Bagley, 173 Ala. 611, 55 So. 894.

Safe Place—Drunkenness—Knowledge.—The question whether the place was a proper one to eject a passenger, having reasonable regard for his safety, how drunk deceased was, and whether the conductor knew of his condition, are for the jury. Louisville, etc., R. Co. v. Johnson, 108 Ala. 62, 19 So. 51.

Question for Court—Rule.—The reasonableness of a given rule adopted by a carrier of passengers is, in an action for ejection, a question for the court. Birmingham Ry., Light & Power Co. v. McDonough, 153 Ala. 122, 44 So. 960, 13 L. R. A., N. S., 445.

§ 257. —— Instructions.

§ 257 (1) In General.

In an action for ejection of a passenger, a request to charge that the conductor of a railroad train is a police officer, whose duty it is to keep order on the train and to eject all persons who use obscene or abusive language in the presence and hearing of passengers, was misleading because of its omission of the qualification that the conductor may use only such force as may be necessary to accomplish the removal, as provided by Code 1896, § 3457. Nashville, etc., Railway v. Moore, 148 Ala. 63, 41 So. 984.

An instruction that if, at the time of plaintiff's alleged injury, he was a passenger on defendant's train on which M. was conductor; that plaintiff was disorderly in that he used profane and vulgar language, which made it necessary for the conductor to eject him, and plaintiff was injured because of his resistance, he could not recover—was properly refused as pretermitting all inquiry as to the degree of force, employed to overcome the resistance, and as asserting as a fact that plaintiff's act rendered it necessary for the conductor to eject him, and that his resistance was the cause of the injury. Nashville, etc., Railway v. Moore, 148 Ala. 63, 41 So. 984.

A charge, in an action for injuries to a passenger required to disembark from the train because of the insufficiency of her ticket and her refusal to pay fare, that, if the jury were not reasonably satisfied that the conductor knew of the passenger's infirmity and the peril attending her leaving the train at the time and place, the carrier was not liable for injuries sustained in alighting, was properly refused because misleading. Central of Georgia Ry. Co. v. Bagley, 173 Ala. 611, 55 So. 894.

In an action against a carrier for the wrongful ejection of a passenger, an instruction requiring the jury to find for defendant, unless the conductor threw the passenger off the train, was properly refused; there being no evidence that the ejection was by the conductor alone. Louisville & N. R. Co. v. Perkins, 144 Ala. 325, 39 So. 305.

§ 257 (2) Applicability to Pleadings and Issues.

Where, in an action against a street railroad for ejection of a passenger from a street car, the allegations of the plea put in issue whether the conductor, owing to the condition of the coin offered as fare, could determine it legal tender, and the conductor testified that he could not tell the coin from a piece of tin, it was error to instruct that, if the coin tendered were legal tender, plaintiff could recover, as ignoring the plea of defendant. Mobile St. Ry. Co. v. Watters, 135 Ala. 227, 33 So. 42, cited in note in 35 L. R. A., N. S., 1031.

§ 257 (3) Invading Province of Jury.

In an action against a railroad company by a passenger to recover damages for the alleged wrongful ejection of the plaintiff from one of the defendant's trains, where it is averred in the complaint, and the evidence introduced on the part of the plaintiff tends to show, that he offered the conductor of the defendant's train, upon which the plaintiff was riding, a ticket which was unlimited, and which the plaintiff had bought from the defendant's agent, and that the conductor refused to receive said ticket and ejected the plaintiff, but the evidence for the defendant tended to show that the ticket offered by the plaintiff was indorsed, "Good for continuous passage beginning on the day of sale," and that the ticket so indorsed was presented by the plaintiff some months after sale, this conflict in the evidence makes a question for the determination of the jury; and therefore a charge is properly refused, as being invasive of the province of the jury, which instructs them that "there is nothing whatever on the ticket limiting the time within which it might be used, nor is there anything on it to show the purchaser that it was in his discretion to use the ticket when he was disposed to do so." Louisville & N. R. Co. *v.* Bizzell, 131 Ala. 429, 30 So. 777.

Punitive damages are not recoverable as a matter of right, but their imposition is discretionary with the jury. Therefore a charge is properly refused, as being erroneous, which instructs the jury that the plaintiff, in an action against a railroad company for his wrongful ejection as a passenger, would, under given circumstances, be entitled to recover punitive damages. Louisville & N. R. Co. *v.* Bizzell, 131 Ala. 429, 30 So. 777.

In an action against a street railroad for ejection of a passenger, the defense was that the coin tendered as fare was so worn that the conductor could not determine it legal tender. The conductor, as a witness, while denying that the dime exhibited in evidence was the same that offered for plaintiff's fare, testified that the coin so exhibited was a good, visibly lettered dime. Held, that the court was justified in charging on the assumption that the dime introduced was of legal-tender quality. Mobile St. Ry. Co. *v.* Watters, 135 Ala. 227, 33 So. 42, cited in 35 L. R. A., N. S., 1031.

§ 257 (4) Damages.

In an action for ejecting a passenger from a train, a requested charge that the jury could not award any damages for abusive language of the conductor held properly refused under the evidence. Louisville, etc., R. Co. *v.* Penick (Ala.), 62 So. 965.

In an action for wrongful ejection of a passenger, an instruction that in assessing damages the jury were authorized, in their best judgment, to award a fair and reasonable compensation for any physical pain or mental suffering that they might believe plaintiff to have suffered, and also as a punishment to defendant, if they believed such damages should be awarded, was not improper. Birmingham Ry., Light & Power Co. *v.* Lee, 153 Ala. 386, 45 So. 164.

Where there was testimony that the conductor in ejecting a passenger told her she was "too damned slow," and that if they killed her they would pay for her, a requested charge that the jury could not award any damages for abusive language used by the conductor was properly refused. Louisville, etc., R. Co. *v.* Penick (Ala.), 62 So. 965.

In the absence of evidence that a carrier exercised diligence or care in employing a brakeman who threw a passenger off a train, an instruction that, if the carrier believed the brakeman a fit person, they might consider that fact in mitigation of damages, is abstract. Southern Ry. Co. *v.* Wideman, 119 Ala. 565, 24 So. 764.

(G) PASSENGERS' EFFECTS.

As to liability of palace and sleeping car companies, see post, "Duties and Liabilities as to Passenger's Effects," § 274.

§ 258. Rules of Carrier.

See post, "Mode and Form of Limitation in General," § 267 (2).

§ 259. Articles Constituting Personal Baggage.

A passenger can recover for loss, through the carrier's negligence, of opera glasses, a glass and brass compass, razor and strap and accoutrements, and nasal syringe, with accompaniments, together with the satchel containing such articles. Cooney *v.* Pullman Palace-Car Co., 25 So. 712, 121 Ala. 368, 53 L. R. A. 690.

§ 260. Transportation and Delivery to Passenger.

A delivery of baggage by a railroad company at the end of its route to the owner or to his agent terminates the liability of the company. Mobile & O. R. Co. *v.* Hopkins, 41 Ala. 486.

§ 261. Delay in Transportation or Delivery.

See post, "Notice to Carrier of Nature or Value of Goods," § 264; "Damages," § 269 (4).

§ 262. Loss or Injury.

§ 263. —— Baggage in General.

"While the transportation of baggage, as such, is incidental to the carriage of the owner as a passenger, and while the railroad companies are only responsible to passengers for injuries sustained from some negligence or wrong, they are liable for the safe delivery of their baggage in the same manner and to the same extent as carriers of merchandise. 2 Roer on R. Rds. 991." Montgomery, etc., R. Co. *v.* Culver, 75 Ala. 587, 591.

Defendant carrier, being liable for loss of baggage as an insurer, was liable for the value of plaintiff's trunk, which was lost or stolen while in its possession for carriage. Southern R. Co. *v.* Foster (Ala.), 60 So. 993.

§ 264. —— Notice to Carrier of Nature, or Value of Goods.

See post, "Connecting Carriers," § 268.

Where a carrier's baggageman, when requested to check plaintiff's baggage, was informed that plaintiff was a salesman, and that the baggage consisted of his samples, and the baggageman thereupon accepted and checked it as baggage, the carrier could not successfully resist an action for damages for delay in transportation, on the ground that the samples did not constitute such articles as it was required to accept and transport as baggage. St. Louis & S. F. R. Co. *v.* Lilly, 1 Ala. App. 320, 55 So. 937.

When Agent Obtains Knowledge Outside Scope of Employment.—A carrier whose agent sells a ticket to a passenger, and checks his valise, is not bound by the knowledge of the agent that the valise contains only merchandise; such knowledge not coming to the agent in the transaction of the carrier's business, but in the purchase of personal wearing apparel. Central of Georgia Ry. Co. *v.* Joseph, 28 So. 35, 125 Ala. 313, cited in note in 10 L. R. A., N. S., 1121.

§ 265. —— Contributory Negligence of Passenger.

See post, "Contributory Negligence," § 274 (4).

§ 266. Carrier as Warehouseman.

Failure of a passenger to call for his baggage within a reasonable time after arrival, though terminating the carrier's absolute liability therefor as an insurer, does not absolve it from liability as a warehouseman or bailee for the loss of the baggage through the negligence of its station agent. Central of Georgia Ry. Co. *v.* Jones, 43 So. 575, 150 Ala. 379, 9 L. R. A., N. S., 1240, cited in note in 38 L. R. A., N. S., 385, 387.

§ 267. Limitation of Liability.

§ 267 (1) Power to Limit Liability.

Willful Default or Tort of Servants.—A railroad company can not limit its responsibility for a passenger's baggage to a specified sum, and thus exempt itself from all liability for the willful default or tort of its servants, although such stipulation be made by special contract. Mobile & O. R. Co. *v.* Hopkins, 41 Ala. 486.

The issue of a "free ticket" by a railroad company to a passenger containing the following writing, "The person accepting this free ticket, in consideration thereof, assumes all risk of accident, and expressly agrees that the company shall not be liable, under any circumstances, whether of the negligence of their agents or otherwise, for any injury to the person or property," does not exempt the company from liability for the loss of baggage of the passenger occasioned by the willful default or tort of a servant of the company. Mobile & O. R. Co. *v.* Hopkins, 41 Ala. 486. See note in 14 L. R. A. 435, 23 L. R. A. 750, 19 L. R. A., N. S., 1008, 37 L. R. A., N. S., 236, 244.

§ 267 (2) Mode and Form of Limitation in General.

Rule of Carrier—Notice of Rule.—Plaintiff was a passenger for E. in a second-class car, with his dog. The conductor told him, under the company's rules, dogs must go in the baggage car. Plaintiff delivered the dog to the baggage master, and told him to put it off at E., and that he would not pay him any money for the dog. On arriving at E., the baggage master refused to deliver the dog without the payment of twenty-five cents, which plaintiff refused to give, and the dog was carried further on, and lost by the negligence of the baggage master. Plaintiff afterwards, and before learning of the loss of the dog, offered to pay what was due on it. Held, that plaintiff could recover for the dog from the company, though it had a rule providing only for the payment of a fee to the baggage master, and relieving itself of all liability; plaintiff not being informed of the rule, and having no knowledge of it. Kansas City, M. & B. R. Co. *v.* Higdon, 94 Ala. 286, 10 So. 282, 14 L. R. A. 515. See note in 740 L. R. A. 508, 39 L. R. A., N. S., 637.

§ 268. Connecting Carriers.

See post, "Evidence," § 269 (3).

Liability of Intermediate Carrier.—An arrangement, express or implied, between different connecting railroad companies, authorizing the companies operating the terminal roads to issue to passengers through tickets, and through checks for baggage, each being entitled only to the fare for transportation over its own line, does not render one of them liable for loss or damage to baggage sustained on the road of the other; nor does it impose on the intermediate company absotute liability for safe delivery, but merely the duty to receive from the company issuing the tickets and checks, to safely carry over its own road, and to deliver to the other connecting company. Montgomery, etc., R. Co. *v.* Culver, 75 Ala. 587.

Notice to Initial Carrier.—Where an initial carrier was authorized to and did sell a through ticket over other connecting roads, notice to the agent of the initial carrier of the contents of one of plaintiff's trunks was notice to the other connecting carriers. Southern R. Co. *v.* Foster (Ala.), 60 So. 993.

Where plaintiff bought a through ticket over connecting roads from the agent of the initial carrier and informed the initial carrier's baggage agent that one of her trunks contained merchandise, the trunk having been accepted as baggage with such notice, plaintiff was entitled to recover for the loss thereof from the connecting carrier, though it was not personal baggage. Southern R. Co. *v.* Foster (Ala.), 60 So. 993.

Larceny by Servant of Initial Carrier.—The placing of baggage by a railroad company in charge of the baggage master of a connecting steamboat line, to be delivered at the boat (if such baggage master was authorized by agreement between the railroad company and the steamboat company to receive upon the trains or at the depot of the railroad company the baggage of through passengers), would not discharge them from liability on account of the larceny of the baggage by one of the railroad company's servants, by reason of which it was not delivered at the boat, unless the baggage master was the agent of the passenger. Mobile & O. R. Co. *v.* Hopkins, 41 Ala. 486.

§ 269. Actions.

§ 269 (1) Rights of Action.

Husband—Parent of Infant.—In Richardson *v.* Louisville, etc., R. Co., 85 Ala. 559, 5 So. 308, 2 L. R. A. 716, cited in note in 1 L. R. A., N. S., 354, the father was permitted to maintain an action for the loss of the baggage of his wife and infant child, who were traveling together. But the decision was upon the ground that the title to the wife's and child's wearing apparel was in the father. The age of the infant, or whether the infant's fare was paid, does not appear. Apparently the only question involved was as to who could maintain the action.

§ 269 (2) Pleading.

Complaint — Sufficiency. — A count in an action against a carrier for its negligence in putting off plaintiff's trunk before its destination alleged that plaintiff's trunk was put off the car to which he transferred, but did not allege that the trunk was transferred to that car with the knowledge or consent of the defendant, nor that plaintiff had in any way acquired the right to have his trunk carried on that car. Held, that the count was bad on demurrer, for failure to show that the act complained of was a breach of defendant's duty. Birmingham R., etc., Co. *v.* Grant, 2 Ala. App. 552, 56 So. 769.

Same—Description of Baggage.—In an action by a passenger against a common carrier for damages for failure to deliver baggage, a description of the baggage in the complaint as "one trunk," containing designated articles of jewelry and merchandise, and "clothing and personal wearing apparel," is, on demurrer, sufficiently certain. Montgomery, etc., R. Co. *v.* Culver, 75 Ala. 587.

Variance.—When, in an action by a passenger against a corporation operating an intermediate line of railroad, for damages for the failure to deliver baggage, the contract is alleged to have been made with the defendant for the transportation of the baggage to a designated point, which is situate on the last connecting line to be there delivered to the plaintiff, and the proof shows that the contract was made with the company operating the first connecting line, and is an agreement on the part of the defendant for the transportation and delivery of the baggage, not to the plaintiff at the point of the destination, but to the company operating the last connecting line, there is a variance between the allegations and proof which is fatal to the right of recovery. Montgomery, etc., R. Co. *v.* Culver, 75 Ala. 587.

§ 269 (3) Evidence.

Presumptions and Burden of Proof.—If the carrier is both the receiving and delivering carrier, or liable for the safe delivery of baggage at the point of destination, proof that it was in good condition when received and in damaged condition when delivered, casts on him the burden of showing that the damage was occasioned by some cause exempting from absolute liability for safe delivery. Montgomery, etc., R. Co. *v.* Culver, 75 Ala. 587.

Same—Loss after Receipt.—Proof of the loss of plaintiff's trunk after its receipt by defendant for transportation under a through contract cast the burden on defendant to acquit itself of negligence. Southern R. Co. *v.* Foster (Ala.), 60 So. 993.

Same—Loss after Arrival.—In an action against a carrier for loss of a passenger's baggage, proof of the loss of the baggage after arrival raised a presumption that the carrier's agent was negligent. Central of Georgia Ry. Co. *v.* Jones, 150 Ala. 379, 43 So. 575, 9 L. R. A., N. S., 1240, cited in note in 38 L. R. A., N. S., 385, 387.

Connecting Carriers—Presumption as to Initial Carrier.—Where the contract of the receiving company is not for delivery beyond the terminus of its line, but merely to the connecting company, liability in case of nondelivery at the point of destination, or total loss, is prima facie on the receiving company, and on it is cast the burden of showing delivery to the connecting company; but this presumption does not arise in case of a delivery by the connecting company in bad order. South, etc., R. Co. *v.* Wood, 71 Ala. 215, explained and modified. Montgomery, etc., R. Co. *v.* Culver, 75 Ala. 587.

Same—Presumption against Delivering Company.—As against the delivering or discharging company the presumption prevails, in the absence of evidence, that the baggage continued in the same condition as when delivered to the receiving company and on it is cast the burden, in case of delivery in a damaged condition, of showing the condition of the baggage when received by it. Montgomery, etc., R. Co. *v.* Culver, 75 Ala. 587, 588.

Hence, in an action by a passenger, having a through ticket and a through check for his baggage over three connecting lines of railroad, operated by separate and independent companies, against the intermediate company for damages for failure to deliver his baggage, which had been received by it in good order from the first company and which was in a damaged condition when delivered by the last company at the point of destination, no special contract or arrangement between the companies being shown, a charge instructing the jury, that if the trunk was delivered to and received by defendant in good order, and when it was delivered to the plaintiff at the point of destination, it was badly broken and its contents taken out, it devolved on the defendant to show that it was delivered in good condition to the delivering company, and if it failed to show this, the plaintiff was entitled to recover is erroneous. Montgomery, etc., R. Co. *v.* Culver, 75 Ala. 587.

Same—Intermediate Carrier—Burden of Proof.—Where baggage, for the transportation of which over three connecting railroads, operated by separate and independent companies, through checks have been issued by one of the terminal roads, is shown to have been in good condition when delivered to the intermediate road, but damaged when delivered at the destination, it does not devolve on the intermediate road, in the absence of any special contract or arrangement between the companies, to show that it was in good condition when delivered to the last terminal road. Montgomery & E. Ry. Co. *v.* Culver, 75 Ala. 587, cited in note in 31 L. R. A., N. S., 102, 104, 109.

Admissibility—Contents—Oath.—In an action against a railroad company by a passenger to recover for the loss of baggage, plaintiff may prove the contents and value of his trunk by his own oath. Douglass *v.* Montgomery & W. P. R. Co., 37 Ala. 638, cited in note in 37 L. R. A., N. S., 589.

Same—Deviation.—In an action for loss of plaintiff's baggage, the fact that it was not carried on the same train with plaintiff and without her knowledge or default was deviated, while in transit by an intermediate carrier and did not follow the routing of plaintiff's ticket, was immaterial. Southern Ry. Co. *v.* Foster (Ala.), 60 So. 993.

§ 269 (4) Damages.

See post, "Actions for Loss of or Injury to Passenger's Effects," § 278.

Salesman's Samples—Delay.—In an action against a carrier for delay of the samples of a salesman traveling on commission, he could not recover profits lost, because he was unable to make sales during the delay; such profits being speculative and contingent, and incapable of being proved with the certainty required to constitute recoverable damages. St. Louis, etc., R. Co. *v.* Lilly, 1 Ala. App. 320, 55 So. 937.

Where a salesman traveling on commission was unable to do anything during the carrier's delay in transporting his samples, shipped as baggage, he was not limited to recovery of nominal damages, but was entitled to recover his actual reasonable expenses incurred during the delay, and compensation for the time lost, to be arrived at by proof of his reasonable wage per day, taking into consideration his experience as a salesman and his fitness for such employment. St. Louis, etc., R. Co. *v.* Lilly, 1 Ala. App. 320, 55 So. 937.

§ 269 (5) Questions for Jury.

Authority of Agent.—In an action against a railroad company to recover the value of certain baggage, on evidence that the baggage was delivered by the railroad company to the baggage master of a connecting steamboat line to be delivered to the boat, the question whether such baggage master was the agent of the railroad company or the agent of the passenger is a question for the jury. Mobile & O. R. Co. *v.* Hopkins, 41 Ala. 486.

(H) PALACE CARS AND SLEEPING CARS.

§ 270. Duties and Liabilities Incident to Ownership and Control in General.

A sleeping car company is a public service corporation and is liable in damages for breach of its duties to a member of the public which it is bound to serve. Pullman Co. *v.* Riley, 5 Ala. App. 561, 59 So. 761.

§ 271. Duty to Receive Passengers.

The right of a person to a berth or passage on a sleeping car is not unlimited, but is subject to such reasonable regulations as the sleeping car company may prescribe. Pullman Co. *v.* Krauss, 40 So. 398, 145 Ala. 395, 4 L. R. A., N. S., 103.

Excluding Insane and Diseased Persons.—A rule of a sleeping car company excluding from its cars insane persons and persons afflicted with contagious or infectious diseases is reasonable. Pullman Co. *v.* Krauss, 40 So. 398, 145 Ala. 395, 4 L. R. A., N. S., 103.

A sleeping car company is not bound to admit persons as passengers on its cars who are afflicted with a contagious or infectious disease, so that there would be a probability of other passengers contracting the same. Pullman Co. *v.* Krauss, 40 So. 398, 145 Ala. 395, 4 L. R. A., N. S., 103, cited in note in 26 L. R. A., N. S., 171.

§ 272. Contracts for Accommodations.

A sleeping car ticket is little more than a symbol, and when the ticket is not correct by reason of the mistake of the selling agent, the sleeping car company is bound by the contract in fact made. Pullman Co. *v.* Riley, 5 Ala. App. 561, 59 So. 761.

A sleeping car company having sold space in a particular sleeper to a passenger entitled to buy the same, the passenger acquires a special property right in that sleeper. Pullman Co. *v.* Riley, 5 Ala. App. 561, 59 So. 761.

Where a passenger's sleeping car ticket did not evidence the real contract, the company could not shield itself from liability for nonperformance by a regulation precluding its conductors from making inquiries as to the real contract, or from carrying it out. Pullman Co. *v.* Riley, 5 Ala. App. 561, 59 So. 761.

Where plaintiff purchased Pullman accommodations between two points good to leave on a particular train, she was not necessarily entitled to accommodations the entire distance in a through sleeper. Pullman Co. *v.* Riley, 5 Ala. App. 561, 59 So. 761.

Where plaintiff was entitled to Pullman accommodations on a particular train, but was required at an intervening point to leave that train and accept accommodations on the second section thereof, there was a breach of contract. Pullman Co. *v.* Riley, 5 Ala. App. 561, 59 So. 761.

A sleeping car passenger held not entitled to recover damages because for a part of the trip she was required to accept accommodations in a car and train different from that in which certain of her relatives had accommodations. Pullman Co. *v.* Riley, 5 Ala. App. 561, 59 So 761.

A sleeping car passenger held not entitled to recover damages for breach of contract because the car in which she was placed was attached to a second section of the train which arrived at destination at the same time the first section did. Pullman Co. *v.* Riley, 5 Ala. App. 561, 59 So. 761.

Rescission of Contract—Return of Purchase Money.—Where, after a sleeping car company had contracted to furnish plaintiff a berth in a sleeping car, it elected to rescind the contract because it alleged plaintiff was afflicted with a contagious disease, it was bound as a condition to such rescission to offer to return the purchase price of the ticket. Pullman Co. *v.* Krauss, 40 So. 398, 145 Ala. 395, 4 L. R. A., N. S., 103, cited in 5 L. R. A., N. S., 1015.

§ 273. Duties and Liabilities as to Person of Passenger.

Treatment from Servants.—A sleeping car company owes a duty to passengers occupying accommodations furnished by it to see that its servants treat such passengers with the due consideration and that they be not subjected to insult by them. Pullman Co. *v.* Riley, 5 Ala. App. 561, 59 So. 761.

Notification of Arrival.—Though a sleeping car company is neither a common carrier nor an innkeeper, it is a public servant as distinctly as either, and owes a duty to its patrons to notify them of arrival at destination. Pullman Co. *v.* Lutz, 45 So. 675, 154 Ala. 517.

§ 274. Duties and Liabilities as to Passenger's Effects.

As to liability of carriers in general, see ante, "Passenger's Effects," IV, G.

§ 274 (1) In General.

Nature of Liability.—Sleeping car companies are not liable, as common carriers of goods and innkeepers, for the property of their passengers. Pullman Palace-Car Co. *v.* Adams, 24 So. 921, 120 Ala. 581, 45 L. R. A. 767.

Care Required.—A passenger on a sleeping car left his satchel with an employee, who placed it in the car where it could be easily seen. From the time the passenger got on until the train reached a certain point no one boarded or left the car, but at that point several persons left the car carrying satchels. Several employees were on watch all night, but none knew of the loss of the passenger's satchel until he got up, though one of them was familiar with its appearance and was present when the other passengers got off. Held, that the company had not exercised reasonable care, and was liable. Cooney *v.* Pullman Palace-Car Co., 25 So. 712, 121 Ala. 368, 53 L. R. A. 690.

For What Property Liable—Pistol.—A passenger can not recover for the loss, through a carrier's negligence, of a pistol carried in his satchel. Cooney *v.* Pullman Palace-Car Co., 25 So. 712, 121 Ala. 368, 53 L. R. A. 690.

Same—Diamond Ring in Pocketbook.—A sleeping car company is not liable for negligently permitting a theft of a valuable diamond ring in the pocketbook of a sleeping passenger, who had refrained from wearing the ring because the setting had become loose, it being at the time no part of his personal attire. Pullman Palace-Car Co. *v.* Adams, 24 So. 921, 120 Ala. 581, 45 L. R. A. 767.

Same—Mileage Book.—A passenger who is a general traveling agent for a commercial house can recover for loss, through the carrier's negligence, of mileage tickets carried by him in his satchel; such tickets being usually carried by those doing much traveling. Cooney *v.* Pullman Palace-Car Co., 25 So. 712, 121 Ala. 368, 53 L. R. A. 690.

Notice to Carrier.—A sleeping car company is liable for negligently permitting thieves to steal a passenger's property while he was sleeping, though he did not notify the company that he had the property. Pullman Palace-Car Co. *v.* Adams, 24 So. 921, 120 Ala. 581, 45 L. R. A. 767.

§ 274 (2) Duty to Guard Property.

It is incumbent on sleeping car companies to secure efficient employees, to protect property of passengers from thieves. Pullman Palace-Car Co. *v.* Adams, 24 So. 921, 120 Ala. 581, 45 L. R. A. 767.

It is error to charge that plaintiff can not recover for property stolen in a sleeping car if the property was stolen while the porter was awake, as the porter might have been guilty of negligence other than that of sleeping. Pullman Palace-Car Co. *v.* Adams, 24 So. 921, 120 Ala. 581, 45 L. R. A. 767.

A sleeping car company may be liable for failing to keep a watch, whereby a passenger's property was stolen, though it was stolen after the passenger's companion had left the berth, and while he was walking up and down the aisle. Pullman Palace-Car Co. *v.* Adams, 24 So. 921, 120 Ala. 581, 45 L. R. A. 767.

§ 274 (3) Liability for Acts or Omissions of Employees or Fellow Passengers.

A sleeping car company is liable for property stolen from a passenger while asleep, in the nighttime, by a fellow passenger, where it did not keep a continuous and active watch to secure the safety of the property. Pullman Palace-Car Co. *v.* Adams, 24 So. 921, 120 Ala. 581, 45 L. R. A. 767.

§ 274 (4) Contributory Negligence.

Place of Leaving Articles.—The failure of a passenger in a sleeping car to put his pocketbook in the safest place in his berth does not preclude a recovery from the sleeping car company for negligently permitting a theft thereof, as it is bound to take reasonable care to prevent the theft of property placed in any part of a berth. Pullman Palace-Car Co. *v.* Adams, 24 So. 921, 120 Ala. 581, 45 L. R. A. 767.

A companion of one sleeping in the berth of a sleeping car, whose pocketbook was stolen, was not negligent, where he left the berth, and walked up and down the aisle of the car, without watching for thieves. Pullman Palace-Car Co. *v.* Adams, 24 So. 921, 120 Ala. 581, 45 L. R. A. 767.

The act of a passenger on a sleeping car, in putting a ring, that he was accustomed to wear, in his pocketbook while he slept, is not contributory negligence, precluding a recovery against the sleeping-car company for negligently permitting the theft thereof. Pullman Palace-Car Co. *v.* Adams, 24 So. 921, 120 Ala. 581, 45 L. R. A. 767.

The negligence of one's companion in a sleeping car berth will not preclude a recovery of the sleeping car company for negligence permitting a theft of property. Pullman Palace-Car Co. *v.* Adams, 120 Ala. 581, 24 So. 921, cited in note in 9 L. R. A., N. S., 409.

§ 275. Companies and Persons Liable.

Liability of Railroad Companies.—A railway company can not escape liability for injuries inflicted on a passenger on the ground that they were sustained in a sleeping car, owned by another company and which furnished its own agents, notwithstanding the passenger paid an additional fare to the sleeping car company for the privilege of riding in one of its cars, where it appears that the sleeping car was part of the company's train. Louisville & N. R. Co. *v.* Church, 46 So. 457, 155 Ala. 329.

A passenger, having a ticket for transportation and a Pullman car ticket, was injured while in a Pullman car by a table handled by a porter of the car falling on her hand. Held, that the railroad company was liable for any neglect of duty by the porter causing the injuries. Louisville, etc., R. Co. *v.* Church, 155 Ala. 329, 46 So. 457, cited in note in 23 L. R. A., N. S., 1059.

§ 276. Actions for Breach of Contract.

Complaint—Sufficiency.—In an action for breach of a sleeping car company's contract to furnish accommodations in a particular car between certain places, an allegation that plaintiff was required to leave the car by defendant's servant in charge held to sufficiently charge that such servant acted in the line of his employment. Pullman Co. *v.* Riley, 5 Ala. App. 561, 59 So. 761.

Where, in an action for breach of a sleeping car company's contract to furnish plaintiff accommodations in a particular car between certain points, a count of the complaint alleged that defendant was operating a through sleeping car for the carriage of passengers between such points, but other averments showed that no one was entitled to such accommodations except holders of a certain form of ticket over a specified railroad who also had bought and paid for sleeping car accommodations on such car, such count did not charge that the sleeping car company was a common carrier of passengers, but only that those rightfully occupying the car under contracts with defendant were entitled to occupy and enjoy the comforts thereof as passengers on the particular train of the railroad specified. Pullman Co. *v.* Riley, 5 Ala. App. 561, 59 So. 761.

Variance.—Where plaintiff charged breach of contract in that she was not permitted to occupy Pullman accommodations in a particular sleeper, but the proof showed that she was only entitled to Pullman accommodations on a particular train, the variance was fatal. Pullman Co. *v.* Riley, 5 Ala. App. 561, 59 So. 761.

Damages—Where Passenger Rejected.—In an action against a carrier for breach of a contract to furnish plaintiff sleeping car space, it was error for the court to refuse to charge that, if plaintiff had a contagious or infectious disease at the time he presented himself for passage on defendant's cars, he could recover only the sum paid for the sleeping car space, with interest thereon up to date. Pullman Co. *v.* Krauss, 40 So. 398, 145 Ala. 395, 4 L. R. A., N. S., 103.

Where, in an action against a sleeping car company for breach of contract to furnish plaintiff a berth, plaintiff, if entitled to recover, was at least entitled to the amount paid for his ticket, which constituted substantial damages, instructions that if the jury believed the evidence, or if plaintiff had a contagious or infectious disease at the time he presented himself for passage on defendant's car, the jury could assess no more than nominal damages in his favoı, were properly refused. Pullman Co. *v.* Krauss, 40 So. 398, 145 Ala. 395, 4 L. R. A., N. S., 103, cited in note in 5 L. R. A., N. S., 1015.

Question for Court—Reasonableness of Rules.—Whether a rule promulgated by a sleeping car company that persons known to be afflicted with any contagious or infectious disease or to be insane would not be permitted in the cars of the company was reasonable was a question for the court. Pullman Co. *v.* Krauss, 40 So. 398, 145 Ala. 395, 4 L. R. A., N. S., 103.

§ 277. Actions for Injuries to or Ejection of Passenger.

Failure to Notify — Ejection — Exemplary Damages — Excessiveness.—Where the servants of a sleeping car company failed to notify plaintiff of arrival at her destination, and the time, place, and manner in which plaintiff was put off the train thereafter were attended with circumstances of aggıavation, the court properly permitted her to recover exemplary damages. Pullman Co. *v.* Lutz, 45 So. 675, 154 Ala. 517.

Where a sleeping car company failed to notify a passenger of arrival at her destination, and the time, place, and manner in which she was subsequently ejected from the train was attended with circumstances of aggravation sufficient to entitle her to exemplary damages, she also having suffered mental anguish from fright because of her surroundings when ejected, a verdict allowing her $1,000 compensatory and $500 punitive damages was not excessive. Pullman Co. *v.* Lutz, 154 Ala. 517, 45 So. 675.

§ 278. Actions for Loss of or Injury to Passenger's Effects.

Complaint—Sufficiency. — A complaint by a passenger suing to recover property stolen in a sleeping car sufficiently shows that the sleeping car company was negligent by alleging that it failed to secure efficient employees to protect his property, without alleging that the company failed to have a watchman, or that its watchman failed to exercise proper care to protect plaintiff's property. Pullman Palace-Car Co. *v.* Adams, 24 So. 921, 120 Ala. 281, 45 L. R. A. 767.

Instructions.—In an action against a sleeping car company for property stolen in the car, it is improper to charge that the company was not negligent after reaching a certain station, though such is the fact, and to ignore evidence of negligence before the station was reached. Pullman Palace-Car Co. *v.* Adams, 24 So. 921, 120 Ala. 581, 45 L. R. A. 767.

Plaintiff and his companion were in the berth of a sleeping car, over which was suspended a hammock, in which was the companion's coat and plaintiff's vest. The companion testified that he got up in the night and took his coat, leaving plaintiff's vest. Plaintiff testified that, when he awoke, his vest was on the berth, on the outer edge of the cover, and that a pocketbook which was in his vest pocket was missing. Held, in an action against the sleeping-car company, that there was no evidence on which to predicate an instruction to find for the company if plaintiff's companion was so handling the vest as to cause the pocket-book to fall on the floor. Pullman Palace-Car Co. *v.* Adams, 24 So. 921, 120 Ala. 581, 45 L. R. A. 767.

It is error to charge that plaintiff can not recover if he was guilty of contributory negligence, without hypothesizing that the loss of the property sued for was caused by such contributory negligence. Pullman Palace-Car Co. *v.* Adams, 24 So. 921, 120 Ala. 581, 45 L. R. A. 767.

Damages — Value — Market Value.—A passenger is entitled to recover the value as testified to by him of baggage lost through the carrier's negligence, though such articles have no market value. Cooney *v.* Pullman Palace-Car Co., 25 So. 712, 121 Ala. 368, 53 L. R. A. 690.

Carrying Arms.

See the title WEAPONS.

Carrying on Business.

See the titles CORPORATIONS; LICENSES.

Cars—Car Service.

See the titles CARRIERS; COMMERCE; MASTER AND SERVANT; RAILROADS.

Car Shortage.

See the title CARRIERS.

Case.

See the titles ACTION; ACTION ON THE CASE.

Case Agreed.

See the titles APPEAL AND ERROR; SUBMISSION OF CONTROVERSY; TRIAL.

Case Certified.

See the titles APPEAL AND ERROR; CRIMINAL LAW.

Case Made.

See the titles APPEAL AND ERROR; SUBMISSION OF CONTROVERSY.

Case on Appeal.

See the titles APPEAL AND ERROR; CRIMINAL LAW.

Case Stated.

See ante, CASE AGREED.

Case Submitted.

See the title SUBMISSION OF CONTROVERSY.

Cashiers.

See the title BANKS AND BANKING.

Casualty.

See the particular titles throughout this work, as, for instance, in the case of death or personal injuries, see such titles as CARRIERS; DEATH; RAILROADS; etc.; in case of injury to property, see such titles as CARRIERS; FIRE; NEGLIGENCE; SHIPPING; etc.

Casualty Insurance.

See the title INSURANCE.

Casus Fortuitus.

See the particular titles throughout this work wherein the question would arise, such as, CONTINUANCE; CONTRACTS; CARRIERS; EXECUTION; HOMICIDE; MASTER AND SERVANT. Generally, as to inevitable accident, see the titles CARRIERS; MASTER AND SERVANT; NEGLIGENCE.

Catching Bargains.

See the titles ASSIGNMENTS; DESCENT AND DISTRIBUTION; FRAUD.

Cattle.

See the titles ANIMALS; CARRIERS; LARCENY; SALES. As to injury of animals on or near track, see the title RAILROADS.

Cattle Guard.

See the title RAILROADS. See also, the title MASTER AND SERVANT.

Causa Mortis.

See the title GIFTS.

Causa Proxima Non Remota Spectatur.

See the titles DAMAGES; NEGLIGENCE.

Cause.

As to cause of action, see the title ACTION. As to cause of death, see the titles DEATH; HOMICIDE; INSURANCE. As to challenge for cause, see the title JURY. As to probable cause, see the titles CARRIERS; COST; FALSE IMPRISONMENT; MALICIOUS PROSECUTION; MASTER AND SERVANT; NEGLIGENCE; RAILROADS; STREET RAILROADS.

Cause of Action.

See the title ACTION, and references there found.

Caution.

As to cautioning accused before receiving confession, see the title CRIMINAL LAW. As to cautioning witness, see the title WITNESSES. As to cautioning servant, see the title MASTER AND SERVANT.

Caveat.

See the titles PUBLIC LANDS; WILLS.

Caveat Emptor.

As to the application of the rule of caveat emptor to purchases at sales, see the particular titles throughout this work wherein such sales are involved, such as EXECUTORS AND ADMINISTRATORS; INFANTS; JUDGMENT; JUDICIAL SALES; MECHANICS' LIENS; MORTGAGES; PUBLIC LANDS; SALES; TAXATION; VENDOR AND PURCHASER.

Lightning Source UK Ltd.
Milton Keynes UK
UKHW010937261118
332983UK00012B/1345/P